# STALIN

# STALIN

## VOLUME I

### PARADOXES OF POWER,

### 1878–1928

## STEPHEN KOTKIN

PENGUIN PRESS

NEW YORK | 2014

PENGUIN PRESS
Published by the Penguin Group
Penguin Group (USA) LLC
375 Hudson Street
New York, New York 10014

USA • Canada • UK • Ireland • Australia
New Zealand • India • South Africa • China

penguin.com
A Penguin Random House Company

First published by Penguin Press, a member of Penguin Group (USA) LLC, 2014

Photograph credits appear on pages 913–14.

ISBN: 978-1-59420-379-4

Printed in the United States of America
1   3   5   7   9   10   8   6   4   2

*Book design by Marysarah Quinn*
*Maps by Jeffrey L.Ward*

*for John Birkelund*
   *businessman, benefactor, fellow historian*

Those that understand him smiled
at one another and shook their
heads. But, for mine own part, it
was Greek to me.

Shakespeare, *Julius Caesar* (1599)

# CONTENTS

PREFACE AND ACKNOWLEDGMENTS  xi


## PART I

## DOUBLE-HEADED EAGLE

CHAPTER 1 | An Imperial Son  11

CHAPTER 2 | Lado's Disciple  29

CHAPTER 3 | Tsarism's Most Dangerous Enemy  56

CHAPTER 4 | Constitutional Autocracy  88


## PART II

## DURNOVÓ'S REVOLUTIONARY WAR

CHAPTER 5 | Stupidity or Treason?  139

CHAPTER 6 | Kalmyk Savior  174

CHAPTER 7 | 1918: Dada and Lenin  227

CHAPTER 8 | Class War and a Party-State 289

CHAPTER 9 | Voyages of Discovery 342

**PART III**

# COLLISION

CHAPTER 10 | Dictator 422

CHAPTER 11 | "Remove Stalin" 472

CHAPTER 12 | Faithful Pupil 530

CHAPTER 13 | Triumphant Debacle 593

CHAPTER 14 | A Trip to Siberia 661

**CODA**

# IF STALIN HAD DIED

NOTES 741

BIBLIOGRAPHY 863

INDEX 915

# PREFACE AND ACKNOWLEDGMENTS

*Stalin*, in three volumes, tells the story of Russia's power in the world and Stalin's power in Russia, recast as the Soviet Union. In some ways the book builds toward a history of the world from Stalin's office (at least that is what it has felt like to write it). Previously, I authored a case study of the Stalin epoch from a street-level perspective, in the form of a total history of a single industrial town. The office perspective, inevitably, is less granular in examination of the wider society—the little tactics of the habitat—but the regime, too, constituted a kind of society. Moreover, my earlier book was concerned with power, where it comes from and in what ways and with what consequences it is exercised, and so is this one. The story emanates from Stalin's office but not from his point of view. As we observe him seeking to wield the levers of power across Eurasia and beyond, we need to keep in mind that others before him had grasped the Russian wheel of state, and that the Soviet Union was located in the same difficult geography and buffeted by the same great-power neighbors as imperial Russia, although geopolitically, the USSR was even more challenged because some former tsarist territories broke off into hostile independent states. At the same time, the Soviet state had a more modern and ideologically infused authoritarian institutional makeup than its tsarist predecessor, and it had a leader in Stalin who stands out in his uncanny fusion of zealous Marxist convictions and great-power sensibilities, of sociopathic tendencies and exceptional diligence and resolve. Establishing the timing and causes of the emergence of that personage, discernible by 1928, constitutes one task. Another entails addressing the role of a single individual, even Stalin, in the gigantic sweep of history.

Whereas studies of grand strategy tend to privilege large-scale structures and sometimes fail to take sufficient account of contingency or events, biographies tend to privilege individual will and sometimes fail to account for the larger forces at play. Of course, a marriage of biography and history can enhance both.

This book aims to show in detail how individuals, great and small, are both enabled and constrained by the relative standing of their state vis-à-vis others, the nature of domestic institutions, the grip of ideas, the historical conjuncture (war or peace; depression or boom), and the actions or inactions of others. Even dictators like Stalin face a circumscribed menu of options. Accident in history is rife; unintended consequences and perverse outcomes are the rule. Reordered historical landscapes are mostly not initiated by those who manage to master them, briefly or enduringly, but the figures who rise to the fore do so precisely because of an aptitude for seizing opportunities. Field Marshal Count Helmuth von Moltke the Elder (1800–91), chief of the Prussian and then German general staff for thirty-one years, rightly conceived of strategy as a "system of expedients" or improvisation, that is, an ability to turn unexpected developments created by others or by happenstance to one's advantage. We shall observe Stalin extracting more from situations, time and again, than they seemed to promise, demonstrating cunning and resourcefulness. But Stalin's rule also reveals how, on extremely rare occasions, a single individual's decisions can radically transform an entire country's political and socioeconomic structures, with global repercussions.

This is a work of both synthesis and original research over many years in many historical archives and libraries in Russia as well as the most important related repositories in the United States. Research in Russia is richly rewarding, but it can also be Gogol-esque: some archives are entirely "closed" to researchers yet materials from them circulate all the same; access is suddenly denied for materials that the same researcher previously consulted or that can be read in scanned files that researchers share. Often it is more efficient to work on archival materials outside the archives. This book is also based upon exhaustive study of scans as well as microfilms of archival material and published primary source documents, which for the Stalin era have proliferated almost beyond a single individual's capacity to work through them. Finally, the book draws upon an immense international scholarly literature. It is hard to imagine what Part I of this volume would look like without its reliance on the scrupulous work of Aleksandr Ostrovskii concerning the young Stalin, for example, or Part III without Valentin Sakharov's trenchant challenge to the conventional wisdom on Vladimir Lenin's so-called Testament. It was Francesco Benvenuti who presciently demonstrated the political weakness of Trotsky already during the Russian civil war, findings that I amplify in chapter 8; it was Jeremy Smith who finally untangled the knot of the Georgian affair in the early 1920s involving Stalin and Lenin, which readers will find integrated with my own discoveries in chapter 11. Myriad other scholars deserve to be singled out; they are, like those above, recognized in the endnotes. (Most of the scholars I cite base their arguments on archival or other primary source documents, and often I have consulted the original documents myself, either before or after reading their works.) As for our protagonist, he offers little help in getting to the bottom of his character and decision making.

*Stalin* originated with my literary agent, Andrew Wylie, whose vision is justly legendary. My editor at Penguin Press, Scott Moyers, painstakingly went through the entire manuscript with a brilliantly deft touch, and taught me a great deal about books. Simon Winder, my editor in the UK, posed penetrating questions and made splendid suggestions. Colleagues—too numerous to thank by name—generously offered incisive criticisms, which vastly improved the text. My research and writing have been buoyed by an array of remarkable institutions as well, from Princeton University, where I have been privileged to teach since 1989 and been granted countless sabbaticals, to the New York Public Library, whose treasures I have been mining for multiple decades and where I benefited extraordinarily from a year at its Cullman Center for Scholars and Writers under Jean Strouse. I have been the very fortunate recipient of foundation grants, including those from the American Council of Learned Societies, the National Endowment for the Humanities, and the John Simon Guggenheim Memorial Foundation. Perhaps the place from which I have drawn the greatest support has been the Hoover Institution, at Stanford University, where I started out as a visiting graduate student from the University of California at Berkeley, eventually becoming a visiting faculty participant in Paul Gregory's annual Soviet archives workshop, a National Fellow, and now an affiliated Research Fellow. Hoover's comprehensive archives and rare-book library, now skillfully directed by Eric Wakin, remain unmatched anywhere outside Moscow for study of the Russian-Soviet twentieth century.

# RUSSIAN EURASIA C. 1913

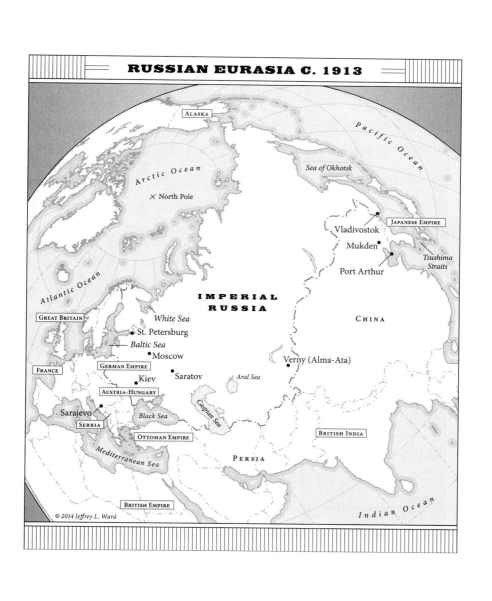

ALASKA

*Pacific Ocean*

*Arctic Ocean*

*Sea of Okhotsk*

✕ North Pole

Vladivostok

JAPANESE EMPIRE

Mukden

*Atlantic Ocean*

Port Arthur

*Tsushima Straits*

**IMPERIAL RUSSIA**

CHINA

GREAT BRITAIN

*White Sea*

• St. Petersburg

— *Baltic Sea*

• Moscow

Verny (Alma-Ata)

FRANCE

GERMAN EMPIRE

• Kiev     • Saratov     *Aral Sea*

AUSTRIA-HUNGARY

Sarajevo

SERBIA

*Black Sea*

*Caspian Sea*

BRITISH INDIA

OTTOMAN EMPIRE

*Mediterranean Sea*

PERSIA

BRITISH EMPIRE

*Indian Ocean*

© 2014 Jeffrey L. Ward

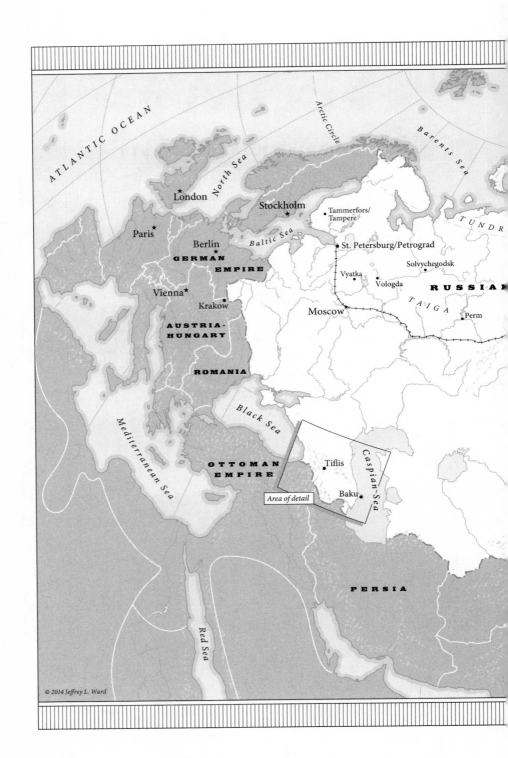

ATLANTIC OCEAN

Arctic Circle

Barents Sea

North Sea

London ★

Stockholm ★

Tammerfors/
Tampere

TUNDR

Paris ★

Baltic Sea

St. Petersburg/Petrograd ●

Berlin ★

Vyatka ●

Solvychegodsk ●

RUSSIAN

GERMAN

EMPIRE

Vologda ●

Vienna ★

TAIGA

Perm ●

Krakow ●

Moscow ●

AUSTRIA-
HUNGARY

ROMANIA

Black Sea

Mediterranean Sea

Caspian Sea

OTTOMAN
EMPIRE

Tiflis ●

Baku ●

Area of detail

PERSIA

Red Sea

© 2014 Jeffrey L. Ward

# STALIN'S AMBIT, PRE-1917

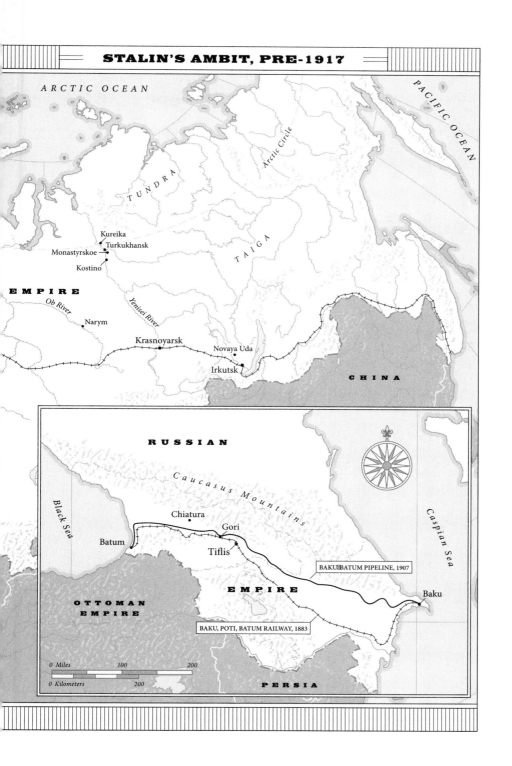

ARCTIC OCEAN

PACIFIC OCEAN

Arctic Circle

T U N D R A

T A I G A

Kureika
Turkukhansk
Monastyrskoe
Kostino

EMPIRE

Ob River

Yenisei River

Narym

Krasnoyarsk

Novaya Uda

Irkutsk

CHINA

RUSSIAN

Caucasus Mountains

Black Sea

Chiatura
Gori
Batum
Tiflis

Caspian Sea

BAKU–BATUM PIPELINE, 1907

Baku

OTTOMAN
EMPIRE

EMPIRE

BAKU, POTI, BATUM RAILWAY, 1883

0 Miles        100        200

0 Kilometers           200

PERSIA

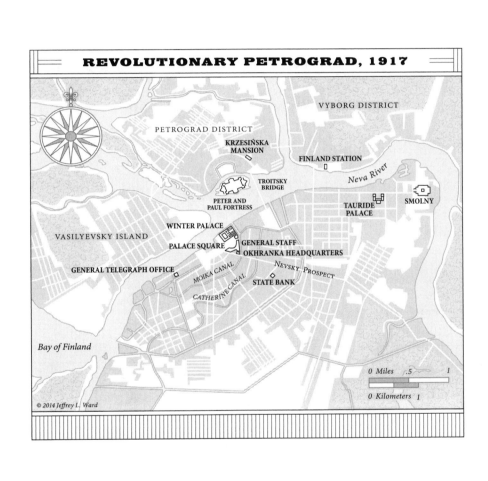

# REVOLUTIONARY PETROGRAD, 1917

VYBORG DISTRICT

PETROGRAD DISTRICT

KRZESIŃSKA MANSION

FINLAND STATION

TROITSKY BRIDGE

*Neva River*

PETER AND PAUL FORTRESS

TAURIDE PALACE

SMOLNY

WINTER PALACE

VASILYEVSKY ISLAND

PALACE SQUARE

GENERAL STAFF

OKHRANKA HEADQUARTERS

GENERAL TELEGRAPH OFFICE

MOIKA CANAL

NEVSKY PROSPECT

CATHERINE CANAL

STATE BANK

*Bay of Finland*

0 Miles .5 1

0 Kilometers 1

© 2014 Jeffrey L. Ward

## CIVIL WAR: HEARTLAND, 1919

FINLAND

YUDENICH

St. Petersburg/Petrograd

RSFSR

ANCIENT MUSCOVY HEARTLAND

Moscow

Tula

Oryol

Omsk

KOLCHAK

Don River

Volga River

DENIKIN

Tsaritsyn

Black Sea

Caspian Sea

0 Miles 200 400

0 Kilometers 400

© 2014 Jeffrey L. Ward

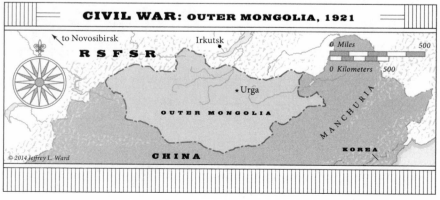

## CIVIL WAR: OUTER MONGOLIA, 1921

to Novosibirsk

Irkutsk

RSFSR

Urga

0 Miles 500

0 Kilometers 500

OUTER MONGOLIA

MANCHURIA

CHINA

KOREA

© 2014 Jeffrey L. Ward

# CIVIL WAR: SOVIET–POLISH WAR, 1920

FINLAND

St. Petersburg/Petrograd

ESTONIA

*Baltic Sea*

LATVIA

LITHUANIA

**GAI'S
CAVALRY ARMY**

Moscow

*NORTHERN AXIS*

Smolensk

EAST
PRUSSIA

Minsk

Danzig

Tula

*POLISH CORRIDOR*

*Pripet Marshes*

WESTERN FRONT
HEADQUARTERS

**R S F S R**

Toruń

Brest-Litovsk

Warsaw

Lublin

Równe/Rivne

*Volga River*

**POLAND**

SOUTHWESTERN FRONT
HEADQUARTERS

Lwów/Lviv/Lvov

*SOUTHERN AXIS*

Kiev

Kharkov

**BUDYONNY'S
FIRST CAVALRY ARMY**

HUNGARY

Tsaritsyn

ROMANIA

0 Miles    200

0 Kilometers    200

*CRIMEA*

**BARON WRANGEL
WHITE ARMY**

*Black Sea*

© 2014 Jeffrey L. Ward

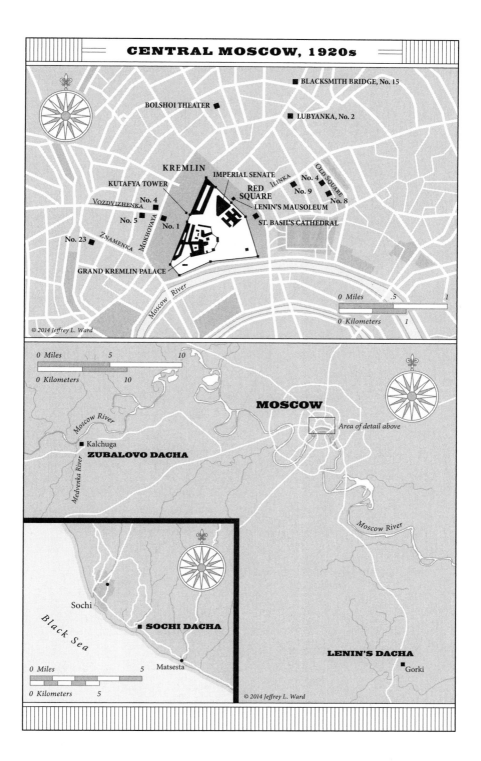

# CENTRAL MOSCOW, 1920s

BLACKSMITH BRIDGE, No. 15

BOLSHOI THEATER

LUBYANKA, No. 2

KREMLIN

IMPERIAL SENATE

KUTAFYA TOWER

RED SQUARE

ILINKA

OLD SQUARE

No. 4

No. 9

No. 8

VOZDVIZHENKA No. 4

LENIN'S MAUSOLEUM

No. 5

MOKHOVAYA

No. 1

ST. BASIL'S CATHEDRAL

No. 23

ZNAMENKA

GRAND KREMLIN PALACE

Moscow River

0 Miles .5 1

0 Kilometers 1

© 2014 Jeffrey L. Ward

0 Miles 5 10

0 Kilometers 10

MOSCOW

Area of detail above

Moscow River

Kalchuga

ZUBALOVO DACHA

Medvenka River

Moscow River

Sochi

SOCHI DACHA

Black Sea

LENIN'S DACHA

Gorki

Matsesta

0 Miles 5

0 Kilometers 5

© 2014 Jeffrey L. Ward

# DOUBLE-HEADED EAGLE

In all his stature he towers over Europe and Asia, over the
past and the future. This is the most famous and at the
same time the most unknown person in the world.

Henri Barbusse, *Stalin* (1935)

RUSSIA'S DOUBLE-HEADED EAGLE NESTED across a greater expanse than
that of any other state, before or since. The realm came to encompass not just
the palaces of St. Petersburg and the golden domes of Moscow, but Polish and
Yiddish-speaking Wilno and Warsaw, the German-founded Baltic ports of Riga
and Reval, the Persian and Turkic-language oases of Bukhara and Samarkand
(site of Tamerlane's tomb), and the Ainu people of Sakhalin Island near the
Pacific Ocean. "Russia" encompassed the cataracts and Cossack settlements of
wildly fertile Ukraine and the swamps and trappers of Siberia. It acquired borders on the Arctic and Danube, the Mongolian plateau, and Germany. The Caucasus barrier, too, was breached and folded in, bringing Russia onto the Black
and Caspian seas, and giving it borders with Iran and the Ottoman empire.
Imperial Russia came to resemble a religious kaleidoscope with a plenitude
of Orthodox churches, mosques, synagogues, Old Believer prayer houses, Catholic cathedrals, Armenian Apostolic churches, Buddhist temples, and shaman
totems. The empire's vast territory served as a merchant's paradise, epitomized
by the slave markets on the steppes and, later, the crossroad fairs in the Volga
valley. Whereas the Ottoman empire stretched over parts of three continents
(Europe, Asia, and Africa), some observers in the early twentieth century imagined that the two-continent Russian imperium was neither Europe nor Asia but
a third entity unto itself: Eurasia. Be that as it may, what the Venetian ambassador
to the Sublime Porte (Agosto Nani) had once said of the Ottoman realm—"more

a world than a state"—applied no less to Russia. Upon that world, Stalin's rule would visit immense upheaval, hope, and grief.

Stalin's origins, in the Caucasus market and artisan town of Gori, were exceedingly modest—his father was a cobbler, his mother, a washerwoman and seamstress—but in 1894 he entered an Eastern Orthodox theological seminary in Tiflis, the grandest city of the Caucasus, where he studied to become a priest. If in that same year a subject of the Russian empire had fallen asleep and awoken thirty years later, he or she would have been confronted by multiple shocks. By 1924 something called a telephone enabled near instantaneous communication over vast distances. Vehicles moved without horses. Humans flew in the sky. X-rays could see inside people. A new physics had dreamed up invisible electrons inside atoms, as well as the atom's disintegration in radioactivity, and one theory stipulated that space and time were interrelated and curved. Women, some of whom were scientists, flaunted newfangled haircuts and clothes, called fashions. Novels read like streams of dreamlike consciousness, and many celebrated paintings depicted only shapes and colors.[1] As a result of what was called the Great War (1914–18), the almighty German kaiser had been deposed and Russia's two big neighboring nemeses, the Ottoman and Austro-Hungarian empires, had disappeared. Russia itself was mostly intact, but it was ruled by a person of notably humble origins who also hailed from the imperial borderlands.[2] To our imaginary thirty-year Rip Van Winkle in 1924, this circumstance—a plebeian and a Georgian having assumed the mantle of the tsars—could well have been the greatest shock of all.

Stalin's ascension to the top from an imperial periphery was uncommon but not unique. Napoleone di Buonaparte had been born the second of eight children in 1769 on Corsica, a Mediterranean island annexed only the year before by France; that annexation (from the Republic of Genoa) allowed this young man of modest privilege to attend French military schools. Napoléon (in the French spelling) never lost his Corsican accent, yet he rose to become not only a French general but, by age thirty-five, hereditary emperor of France. The plebeian Adolf Hitler was born entirely outside the country he would dominate: he hailed from the Habsburg borderlands, which had been left out of the 1871 German unification. In 1913, at age twenty-four, he relocated from Austria-Hungary to Munich, just in time, it turned out, to enlist in the imperial German army for the Great War. In 1923, Hitler was convicted of high treason for what came to be known as the Munich Beer Hall Putsch, but a German nationalist judge, ignoring the applicable law, refrained from deporting the non-German citizen. Two years later, Hitler surrendered his Austrian citizenship and became stateless. Only in 1932 did he acquire German citizenship, when he was naturalized on a pretext (nominally, appointed as a "land surveyor" in Braunschweig, a Nazi party electoral stronghold). The next year Hitler was named chancellor of Germany, on his way to becoming dictator. By the standards of a Hitler or a Napoleon, Stalin grew up as an unambiguous subject of his empire, Russia, which had annexed most of Georgia fully seventy-seven years before his birth. Still, his leap from the lowly periphery was improbable.

Stalin's dictatorial regime presents daunting challenges of explanation. His power of life and death over every single person across eleven time zones—more than 200 million people at prewar peak—far exceeded anything wielded by tsarist Russia's greatest autocrats. Such power cannot be discovered in the biography of the young Soso Jughashvili. Stalin's dictatorship, as we shall see, was a product of immense structural forces: the evolution of Russia's autocratic political system; the Russian empire's conquest of the Caucasus; the tsarist regime's recourse to a secret police and entanglement in terrorism; the European castle-in-the-air project of socialism; the underground conspiratorial nature of Bolshevism (a mirror image of repressive tsarism); the failure of the Russian extreme right to coalesce into a fascism despite all the ingredients; global great-power rivalries, and a shattering world war. Without all of this, Stalin could never have gotten anywhere near power. Added to these large-scale structural factors were contingencies such as the abdication of Tsar Nicholas II during wartime, the conniving miscalculations of Alexander Kerensky (the last head of the Provisional Government that replaced the tsar in 1917), the actions and especially inactions of Bolshevism's many competitors on the left, Lenin's many strokes and his early death in January 1924, and the vanity and ineptitude of Stalin's Bolshevik rivals.

Consider further that the young Jughashvili could have died from smallpox, as did so many of his neighbors, or been carried off by the other fatal diseases that were endemic in the slums of Batum and Baku, where he agitated for socialist revolution. Competent police work could have had him sentenced to forced labor (*katorga*) in a silver mine, where many a revolutionary met an early death. Jughashvili could have been hanged by the authorities in 1906–7 as part of the extrajudicial executions in the crackdown following the 1905 revolution (more than 1,100 were hanged in 1905–6).[3] Alternatively, Jughashvili could have been murdered by the innumerable comrades he cuckolded. If Stalin had died in childhood or youth, that would not have stopped a world war, revolution, chaos, and likely some form of authoritarianism redux in post-Romanov Russia. And yet the determination of this young man of humble origins to make something of himself, his cunning, his honing of organizational talents would help transform the entire structural landscape of the early Bolshevik revolution from 1917. Stalin brutally, artfully, indefatigably built a personal dictatorship within the Bolshevik dictatorship. Then he launched and saw through a bloody socialist remaking of the entire former empire, presided over a victory in the greatest war in human history, and took the Soviet Union to the epicenter of global affairs. More than for any other historical figure, even Gandhi or Churchill, a biography of Stalin, as we shall see, eventually comes to approximate a history of the world.

WORLD HISTORY IS DRIVEN BY GEOPOLITICS. Among the great powers, the British empire, more than any other state, shaped the world in modern times. Between 1688 and 1815, the French fought the British for global supremacy. Despite France's greater land mass and population, Britain emerged the winner, mostly thanks to a superior, lean, fiscal-military state.[4] By the final defeat of Napoleon, which was achieved in a coalition, the British were the world's dominant power. Their ascendancy, moreover, coincided with China's decline under the Qing dynasty, rendering British power—political, military, industrial, cultural, and fiscal—genuinely global. The felicitous phrase "the sun never sets" that was used to describe the extent of the empire's holdings originated in connection with the earlier empire of Spain, but the saying was applied, and stuck, to the British. In the 1870s, however, two ruptures occurred in the British-dominated world: Prince Otto von Bismarck's unification of Germany, realized on the battlefield by Helmuth von Moltke the Elder, which, in lightning fashion, led to the appearance of a surpassing new power on the European continent; and the Meiji restoration in Japan, which imparted tremendous drive to a new power in East Asia. All of a sudden, imperial Russia faced the world's most dynamic new power on its restive western border, and Asia's most dynamic on its underpopulated eastern border. Russia had entered a new world. This was the world into which Stalin was born.

Even the package of attributes that we call modernity was a result not of some inherent sociological process, a move out of tradition, but of a vicious geopolitical competition in which a state had to match the other great powers in modern steel production, modern militaries, and a modern, mass-based political system, or be crushed and potentially colonized.[5] These were challenges that confronted conservative establishments especially. Everyone knows that Karl Marx, the radical German journalist and philosopher, loomed over imperial Russia like over no other place. But for most of Stalin's lifetime, it was another German—and a conservative—who loomed over the Russian empire: Otto von Bismarck. A country squire from a Protestant Junker family in eastern Branden-burg who had attended the University of Göttingen, joined a *Burschenschaften* (fraternity), and was known as a solid drinker and devotee of the female of the species, Bismarck had held no administrative posts as late as 1862, although he had been ambassador to Russia and to France. But in fewer than ten years, he had risen to become the Iron Chancellor and, using Prussia as his base, forged a mighty new country. Prussia, the proverbial "army in search of a nation," had found one. At the same time, the rightist German chancellor showed rulers everywhere how to uphold modern state power by cultivating a broader political base, developing heavy industry, introducing social welfare, and juggling alli-ances with and against an array of other ambitious great powers.

Bismarck the statesman was one for the ages. He craftily upended his legions of opponents, both outside and inside the German principalities, and instigated three swift, decisive, yet limited wars to crush Denmark, then Austria, then France, but he kept the state of Austria-Hungary on the Danube for the sake of the balance of power. He created pretexts to attack when in a commanding posi-tion or baited the other countries into launching the wars after he had isolated them diplomatically. He made sure to have alternatives, and played these alterna-tives off against each other. That said, Bismarck had had no master plan for Ger-man unity—his enterprise was an improvisation, driven partly by domestic political considerations (to tame the liberals in Prussia's parliament). But he had constantly worked circumstances and luck to supreme advantage, breaking through structural limitations, creating new realities on the ground. "Politics is less a science than an art," Bismarck would say. "It is not a subject that can be taught. One must have the talent for it. Even the best advice is of no avail if improperly carried out."[6] He further spoke of politics in terms of cards, dice, and other games of chance. "One can be as shrewd as the shrewdest in this world and still at any moment go like a child into the dark," Bismarck had remarked on the victory in the war he instigated in 1864 against Denmark.[7] This he complained was "a thankless job. . . . One has to reckon with a series of probabilities and improbabilities and base one's plans upon this reckoning." Bismarck did not invoke virtue, but only power and interests. Later this style of rule would become known as realpolitik, a term coined by August von Rochau (1810-73), a German National Liberal disappointed in the failure to break through to a constitution in 1848. In its origins, realpolitik signified effective practical politics to realize idealistic aims. Bismarck's style was more akin to the term raison d'état: calculating, amoral reason of state. Instead of principles, there were objectives; instead of morality, means.[8] Bismarck was widely hated until he proved brilliantly successful, then lionized beyond reason for having smashed France, made a vassal out of Austria, and united Germany.

Bismarck went on to form the Triple Alliance with Austria-Hungary and Italy (1882) and sign a secret "reinsurance treaty" with Russia (1888), extracting neutrality in the event of a conflict, thereby obviating a possible two-front war against France and Russia and accentuating the new Germany's mastery of the continent. His gifts were those of the inner sanctum. He did not possess a strong voice or self-confidence in speaking, and did not spend much time amid the public. Moreover, he was not the ruler: he served at the pleasure of the king (and then kaiser), Wilhelm I. In that all-important relationship, Bismarck showed psychological skill and tenacity, ceaselessly, efficaciously manipulating Wilhelm I, threatening his resignation, pulling all manner of histrionics. Wilhelm I, for his part, proved to be a diligent, considerate, and intelligent monarch, with the smarts to defer to Bismarck on policy and to attend to the myriad feathers his Iron Chancellor ruffled.[9] Bismarck strategized to make himself indispensable partly by making everything as complex as possible, so that he alone knew how things worked (this became known as his combinations). He had so many balls up in the air at all times that he could never stop scrambling to prevent any from dropping, even as he was tossing up still more. It must also be kept in mind that Bismarck enjoyed the benefit of the world's then-best land army (and perhaps second-best navy).

Other would-be statesmen across Europe went to school with Bismarck's example of "politics as art."[10] To be sure, from the perspective of London, which had well-established rule of law, Bismarck appeared as a menace. But from the perspective of St. Petersburg, where the challenges were finding a bulwark against leftist extremism, he looked like salvation. From any vantage point, his aggrandizement of Prussia via a German unification—without the support of a mass movement, with no significant previous experience of government, and against an array of formidable interests—ranks among the greatest diplomatic achievements by any leader in the last two centuries.[11] Moreover, paying indirect homage to a ruler he had vanquished, France's Napoleon III, Bismarck introduced universal manhood suffrage, banking conservatives' political fortunes on the peasants' German nationalism to afford dominance of parliament. "If Mephistopheles climbed up the pulpit and read the Gospel, could anyone be inspired by this prayer?" huffed a newspaper of Germany's outflanked liberals. What is more, Bismarck goaded Germany's conservatives to agree to broad social welfare legislation, outflanking the socialists, too. What made Bismarck's unification feat still more momentous was the added circumstance that the newly unified Germany soon underwent a phenomenal economic surge. Seemingly overnight the country vaulted past the world's number one power, Great Britain, in key modern industries such as steel and chemicals. As Britain became consumed with its (relative) "decline," the new Bismarckian Reich pushed to realign the world order. Germany was "like a great boiler," one Russian observed, "developing surplus steam at extreme speed, for which an outlet is required."[12] As we shall see, Russia's establishment—or, at least, its more able elements—became obsessed with Bismarck. Not one but two Germans, Bismarck and Marx, constituted imperial Russia's other double-headed eagle.

STALIN SEEMS WELL KNOWN TO US. An older image—that his father beat him; the Orthodox seminary oppressed him; he developed a "Lenin complex" to surpass his mentor, then studied up on Ivan the Terrible, all of which led to the slaughter of millions—has long been unconvincing, even in its sophisticated versions that combine analyses of Russian political culture and personality.[13] Humiliation does often serve as the wellspring of savagery, but it is not clear that Stalin suffered the predominantly traumatic childhood usually attributed to him. Despite a malformed body and many illnesses, he exhibited a vigorous intellect, a thirst for self-improvement, and a knack for leadership. True, he had a mischievous streak. "Little Soso was very naughty," recalled his companion Grigory Elisabedashvili. "He loved his catapult and homemade bow. Once, a herdsman was bringing his animals home when Soso jumped out and catapulted one in the head. The ox went crazy, the herd stampeded and the herdsman chased Soso, who disappeared."[14] But cousins who knew the young Stalin were able to keep in touch until his death.[15] Many of his schoolteachers also survived to compose memoirs.[16] Moreover, even if his childhood had been entirely miserable, as many have one-sidedly portrayed it, such a circumstance would explain little of the later Stalin. Nor can we find much help in Lev Trotsky's dismissal of Stalin as a mere product of the bureaucracy, a "*komitetchik* (committeeman) par excellence"—that is, a supposedly lesser being than either a real proletarian or a real intellectual (aka Trotsky).[17] Stalin's father and mother were both born serfs and they never got any formal education, but he emerged from a family of strivers, including his much maligned father. And Stalin's hometown, Gori, usually derided as a backwater, afforded an important measure of educational opportunity.

A newer image of the young Stalin, calling upon a wide array of recently available source materials (including reminiscences solicited and shaped in the 1930s by Lavrenti Beria), has recaptured the capable student and the talent. These memoirs, though, have also been used to depict an implausibly swashbuckling figure, a ladies' man and macho bandit of the colorful Orientalist variety.[18] This makes for gripping reading. It also contains several valuable revelations. Still, the new image, too, falls short of being persuasive. The young Stalin had a penis, and he used it. But Stalin was not some special Lothario. Both Marx and Engels fathered illegitimate children—Marx by his housekeeper, a paternity Engels protectively claimed—yet, obviously, that is not the reason Marx entered history.[19] A young Saddam Hussein wrote poetry, too, but the Iraqi was a bona fide assassin decades before becoming dictator in Baghdad. The young Stalin was a poet but no assassin. Nor was he some kind of Mafia don of the Caucasus, however much Beria might have thought such an image flattering of Stalin.[20] The young Stalin did attract small groups of followers at different times, but nothing permanent. Indeed, the overriding fact of Stalin's underground revolutionary activity is that he never consolidated a political base in the Caucasus. Stalin did not bring with him to the capital the equivalent of Saddam Hussein's "Tikriti network."[21] Examined soberly, the young Stalin had decidedly mixed success in mounting illegal printing presses, fomenting strikes, and plotting financial expropriations. His behind-the-scenes role in a spectacular 1907 daylight robbery in Tiflis—a fact established by Miklós Kun and beautifully rendered by Simon Sebag Montefiore—does show that the young Stalin would do just about anything for the cause.[22] But the robbery was not an end in itself. There *was* a cause: socialism and social justice, alongside the project of his own advancement. Nothing—not the teenage girls, the violence, the camaraderie—diverted him from what became his life mission.

This book will avoid speculative leaps or what is known as filling in the gaps in the record of Stalin's life.[23] It will seek to navigate with care among the vivid yet dubious stories. The future Stalin's past of underground revolutionary activities in the Caucasus is bedeviled by regime lies, rivals' slander, and missing documents.[24] Still, we can say for sure that the assertions he was *especially* treacherous in betraying comrades are comical in the context of what went on in Social Democrat ranks. Stalin was imperious (as imperious as Lenin and Trotsky) and prickly (as prickly as Lenin and Trotsky). He remembered perceived slights, something of a cliché in the blood-feud Caucasus culture but also common among narcissists (another word for many a professional revolutionary). True, more than most, the young Stalin perpetually antagonized colleagues by asserting claims to leadership whatever his formal assignments and achievements; then, invariably, he viewed himself as the wronged party. Stalin was often gregarious but also moody and aloof, which made him seem suspicious. And he generally gravitated toward people like himself: parvenu intelligentsia of humble background. (He "surrounded himself exclusively with people who respected him unconditionally and gave in to him on every issue," one foe later wrote.)[25] The wild revolutionary years of 1905–8 notwithstanding, the young Stalin was really mostly a pundit for small-print-run publications. But they were illegal and he was constantly on the run, tailed by the police as he scurried between Tiflis, Batum, Chiatura, Baku, and elsewhere in the Caucasus; Tammerfors (Russian Finland), London, Stockholm, Berlin, Vienna, and elsewhere in Europe; Vologda in European Russia's north and Turukhansk in Eastern Siberia.[26] Though the future Stalin was unusual in never seeking to emigrate, his early life—which between 1901 and 1917 included a total of some seven years in Siberian exile and prison, as well as short stints abroad—was more or less typical for the revolutionary underground. Especially from 1908 onward, he lived a life of penury, begging everyone for money, nursing resentments, and spending most of his time, like other prisoners and exiles, bored out of his mind.

The man who would become Stalin was a product of both the Russian imperial garrisons in Georgia, for which his father moved to Gori to make shoes, and the imperial administrators and churchmen, whose Russification measures gave him an education, but also, unwittingly, amplified the late-nineteenth-century Georgian national awakening that greatly affected him, too.[27] Later, Stalin's young son would confide in his older sister that their father, in his youth, had been a Georgian—and it was true. "Be full of blossom, Oh lovely land, Rejoice, Iverians' country, And you, Oh Georgian, by studying Bring joy to your motherland," a seventeen-year-old Jughashvili wrote in one of his precocious Georgian romantic poems ("Morning").[28] He published only in the Georgian language for the first twenty-nine years of his life. "He spoke exceptionally pure Georgian," recalled someone who met him in 1900. "His diction was clear, and his conversation betrayed a lively sense of humor."[29] To be sure, Stalin proved to be something of a bad Georgian, at least by stereotype: not honorable to a fault, not uncompromisingly loyal to friends and family, not mindful of old debts.[30] At the same time, Georgia was a diverse land and the future Stalin picked up colloquial Armenian. He also dabbled in Esperanto (the constructed internationalist language), studied but never mastered German (the native tongue of the left), and tackled Plato in Greek. Above all, he became fluent in the imperial language: Russian. The result was a young man who delighted in the aphorisms of the Georgian national poet Shota Rustaveli ("A close friend turned out to be an enemy more dangerous than a foe")[31] but also in the ineffable, melancholy works of Anton Chekhov, whose *Cherry Orchard* (1903) depicted a speculator's axes chopping down a minor nobleman's trees (the estate and mansion had been sold off to a vulgar bourgeois). Stalin immersed himself in both imperial Russian and Georgian history, too.

What differentiated the young Stalin in the Russian Bolshevik revolutionary milieu beyond his Georgian origins was his tremendous dedication to self-improvement. He devoured books, which, as a Marxist, he did so in order to change the world. Perhaps nothing stands out more than his intense political sectarianism (even in a culture where up to one third of the religiously Eastern Orthodox were schismatics). His youthful years involved becoming a Marxist of Leninist persuasion and battling not just tsarism but the factions of other revolutionaries.[32] Ultimately, though, the most important factor in shaping Stalin and his later rule, as we shall examine in detail, entailed something he encountered only partly as a youth: namely, the inner workings, imperatives, and failures of the imperial Russian state and autocracy. The immensity of that history reduces Stalin's early life to proper perspective. But it also sets the stage for grasping the immensity of his subsequent impact.

## CHAPTER 1

# AN IMPERIAL SON

My parents were uneducated people, but they treated me
not so badly.

Stalin, December 1931,
interview with Emil Ludwig, German journalist[1]

OVER THE MORE THAN FOUR CENTURIES from the time of Ivan the Terrible,
Russia expanded an average of fifty square miles *per day*. The state came to fill a
vast pocket bounded by two oceans and three seas: the Pacific and the Arctic; the
Baltic, the Black, and the Caspian. Russia would come to have a greater length of
coastline than any other state, and Russian fleets would be anchored at Kronstadt, Sevastopol, and (eventually) Vladivostok.[2] Its forests linked Russia to
Europe, and its steppe grasslands, 4,000 miles wide, connected Russia to Asia and
afforded a kind of "new world" to discover.

That said, the Russian empire defied nearly every possible prerequisite: its
continental climate was severe, and its huge open frontiers (borderless steppes,
countourless forests) were expensive to defend or govern.[3] Beyond that, much of
the empire was situated extremely far to the north. (Canadian agriculture was
generally on a line with Kiev, far below the farms surrounding Moscow or St.
Petersburg.) And although land was plentiful, there never seemed to be enough
bodies to work it. Incrementally, the autocracy had bound the peasantry in place
through a series of measures known as serfdom. Peasant mobility was never fully
eliminated—serfs could try to run away, and if they survived, were usually welcomed elsewhere as scarce labor—but serfdom remained coercively entrenched
until its emancipation, beginning in 1861.[4]

Russia's outward march, which overcame substantial resistance, transformed
its ethnic and religious makeup. As late as 1719, Russia was perhaps 70 percent
ethnic Great Russian (and more than 85 percent total Slav), but by the end of the
following century Russians made up just 44 percent (Slavs around 73 percent); in
other words, a majority of the population (56 percent) was other than Great

Russian. Among the other Slavs, Little Russians (or Ukrainians) stood at 18 percent, Poles at 6 percent, and White Russians (or Belorussians) at 5 percent. There were smaller numbers of Lithuanians, Latvians, Estonians, Finns, Germans, Georgians, Armenians, Tatars, Qalmyqs, and Siberian indigenes. In 1719, Russia had no Jews, but thanks to the late-eighteenth-century swallowing up of Poland, Jews would come to compose around 4 percent of the empire. They were legally confined (with exceptions) to the annexed territories in which they already lived—that is, old Poland-Lithuania and parts of western Ukraine, lands that constituted the Pale of Settlement.[5] They were forbidden from owning land, rendering them more urban and more professional than the rest of Russia's population. But for all the historical attention focused on Russia's 5 million Jews, it was Russia's Muslims, present going back to ancient Muscovy, who constituted the empire's second largest religious grouping after Eastern Orthodox Christians. Imperial Russia's Muslims had one of the realm's highest birthrates, and would come to exceed 18 million people, more than 10 percent of the population. Many of Russia's Muslims spoke a dialect of Persian, but most spoke Turkic languages, giving Russia several million more Turkic speakers than the "Turkish" Ottoman empire.

Russia's territorial aggrandizement had often come at Ottoman expense, as in the conquest of the Caucasus. These formidable mountain redoubts, wedged between the Black and Caspian seas, were higher than the Alps, but on either side of the chain, adjacent to the seashores, could be found narrow, easily passable lowlands—paths to conquest. In the western parts of the Caucasus, Turkic long served as a lingua franca, reflecting Ottoman rule; in the eastern parts, it was Persian, reflecting Iranian rule. Troops loyal to the Russian tsar had first reached the Caspian Sea in 1556—for a time, Ivan the Terrible took a Caucasus Turkic princess as a wife—but the Russian empire did not manage to seize Baku, the main Caspian settlement, from the Persian shah until 1722.[6] And it was not until the 1860s or so that generals in the Russian service managed to claim the entire uplands. In other words, the Russian advance into the Caucasus proceeded vertically, in essence a giant flanking maneuver around and then up the mountains that consumed more than 150 years and uncounted lives.[7] In Dagestan ("the mountainous land"), a territory that resembled British India's tribal northwest frontier, Russian counterinsurgency troops butchered entire indigenous villages to force them to give up suspected insurgents; the insurgents, for their part, directed vendettas against the indigenous Muslims, too, accused of cooperating with Russia. Also devastating were the axes of Slav peasant settlers, who moved into the steep yet fertile valleys and, to grow crops, removed the forest cover critical to the rebels. To top everything off, in the final drive to conquest in the 1860s and 70s, perhaps four hundred thousand of half a million highlander Circassians were driven or fled across the Ottoman border.[8] These deportations and massacres, accompanied by Slavic peasant homesteading, facilitated Russia's assimilation of the Caucasus, which is how the future Stalin would be born a subject of Russia.

All the ad hoc empire building—and there is no other kind—resulted in a jumble of contradictions. The so-called Old Believers, Eastern Orthodox Christians who refused to recognize the reformed Orthodox Church or the Russian state and had been banished or fled to the "remote" Caucasus, found they could survive only by supplying services to "the Antichrist," that is, to the Russian imperial army. Even so, the empire's Cossack shock troops, once free and wild frontiersmen who had become paladins of autocracy, remained chronically undersupplied and had to turn to the very mountaineers they were trying to subjugate in order to purchase weaponry. In turn, the antiempire mountaineers, with their picturesque cherkeskas—long woolen coats sporting rifle cartridges slotted across the chest—were recruited into the Retinue of the Tsar in St. Petersburg.[9] Perhaps the greatest contradiction lay in the circumstance that the Russian empire had been implanted in the Caucasus largely by invitation: Georgia's Christian rulers were battling both the Muslim Ottomans and the Muslim Safavids and invited Christian Russia's protection. That "protection," in practice, was effected by opportunistic imperial agents close to the scene, and soon took the form of annexations, in 1801 and 1810.[10] Russia terminated the Georgian Bagrationi dynasty and replaced the patriarch of the formerly independent Georgian Orthodox Church with a Russian Orthodox Church metropolitan (called an exarch). And yet, in another contradiction, the local "Russian" administration overflowed with Georgians, who were favored as fellow Christians. Thanks to Russian rule, Georgian elites obtained powerful new instruments for imposing their will over the lower orders, and over the many other peoples in the Caucasus. Such is empire: a series of bargains empowering the ambitious.

Within the Russian empire, Georgia was its own imperial project.[11] Of the 8.5 million inhabitants of the Caucasus enumerated in the late nineteenth century, about a third were Muslim, while one half were Eastern Orthodox, but of the latter only 1.35 million were ethnic Georgians (by language). This minority came to rule more than ever thanks to Russia. Of course, far from everything under Russian suzerainty was to Georgian liking. In 1840, imperial authorities in St. Petersburg decreed Russian as the sole language for official business in the Caucasus. This followed Russia's suppression (in 1832) of a conspiracy to restore the Georgian monarchy (some Georgian nobles had planned to invite local Russian officials to a ball and murder them). Most of the conspirators were exiled elsewhere within the Russian empire, but soon they were allowed to return and resume careers in Russian state service: the empire needed them. A majority of Georgian elites would become and remain largely Russophile.[12] At the same time, new infrastructure helped overcome barriers to tighter Russian incorporation. Between 1811 and 1864, a key military road was cut southward from the lowland settlement of Vladikavkaz ("rule the Caucasus") up through the high mountain pass—above seemingly bottomless chasms—on to Tiflis, the capital. Before the century was out, the Transcaucasus Railway would link the Black and Caspian seas. Above all, career opportunities induced many Georgians to master the Russian language, the greatest element of imperial infrastructure. Georgians memorized and retold stories about Georgia's heroic resistance to Russian conquest, but if they could, they also married into elite Russian families, indulged in Russian operas, and hankered after the peacock fan of imperial uniforms, titles, and medals along with the commodious state apartments, travel allowances, and cash "gifts."[13] What worked for elites became available on a lesser scale to the lower orders, who took advantage of the opportunities to go to new Russian-language schools in the Caucasus sponsored by the Russian Orthodox Church. Here, then, was the imperial scaffolding—conquest via Georgian collusion, Russification via the Orthodox Church—on which the future Stalin would climb.[14]

## SMALL-TOWN IDYLL

The future Stalin's hometown of Gori ("hill"), nestled in the rolling uplands of the Eastern Georgian valley of the Mtkvari River (Kura River, in Russian), had for centuries served as a caravan stop at the junction of three roads: one westward to the Black Sea, one eastward to the Caspian, and one northward through the Tskhinvali Pass to the steppe grasslands.[15] Gori, in other words, was no boondocks. In the heart of town, atop its highest hill, stood the yellow crenellated walls of a thirteenth-century fortress. Additional ruins, the gardens of grandees from when Gori had been the capital of the Georgian state of Kartli in the seventeenth century, could be found outside town. Also not far away were the famed mineral waters of Borzhomi, where Alexander II's brother, viceroy of the Caucasus, had erected a summer residence. In Gori proper, directly below the ancient fortress ruin, lay the Old Town. A second district, the Central Quarter, boasted numerous Armenian and Georgian churches, while a third, housing the barracks of the imperial garrison, was christened the Russian Quarter.[16] In 1871, this crossroads became a junction of the Russian empire railway that opened between Tiflis, the Caucasus capital, and Poti, a Black Sea port (conquered from the Ottomans in 1828). In the 1870s, Gori's narrow, crooked, filthy streets were home to perhaps 7,000 inhabitants, of whom a slight majority was Armenian, the rest being Georgian, with a few hundred Russians as well as some Abkhaz and Ossetians, who had migrated from nearby tribal villages. Gori merchants traded with Iran, the Ottoman empire, and Europe. Thanks to its strong merchant presence, as well as to the Orthodox Church, Gori had four schools, including a solid two-story church school founded by church authorities in 1818, not long after Georgia's incorporation into the Russian empire.[17] The upshot was that whereas in Tiflis one in fifteen inhabitants attended school—versus one in thirty for the entire Caucasus—in Gori one in ten inhabitants were in school.[18] For boys born on that "hill," doors could open to the future.

The future Stalin's father, Besarion Jughashvili (1850–1909), known as Vissarion in Russian and Beso for short, did not hail from Gori. His paternal grandfather (Zaza), a serf once arrested for his part in a peasant uprising, may have lived in a tribal Ossetian village; Beso's father, Vano, also a serf, tended vines in a village called Didi Lilo ("Greater Lilo"), population under 500, where Beso was born. Vano would carry his grapes to nearby Tiflis, about ten miles away, but he died before the age of fifty. Soon thereafter, bandits killed Vano's son Giorgi, an innkeeper, and Beso quit Didi Lilo to seek work in Tiflis, where he learned the shoemaker's trade at an Armenian-owned shop. Beso spoke some Armenian, Azeri Turkish, and Russian, though it is unclear whether he could write in his native Georgian. Around 1870, when he was twenty, he relocated to Gori, evidently at the invitation of another Armenian entrepreneur, Baramyants (Russified as Iosif Baramov). The latter owned a shoe workshop that had been commissioned to supply the imperial garrison in Gori.[19] The Russian empire was one far-flung garrison. By 1870, all of Siberia was secured by just 18,000 troops, but Kharkov, Odessa, and Kiev garrisoned 193,000 soldiers; Warsaw, another

126,000. At a time when British India counted 60,000 troops and 1,000 police, the Caucasus had 128,000 imperial soldiers. That made for a lot of feet needing boots. Baramyants hired a number of master artisans, including Beso, who seems to have enjoyed success and evidently was ambitious. Aided financially by "Prince" Yakobi "Yakov" Egnatashvili, a Gori wine grower, *dukhan* (pub) owner, and wrestling champion, Beso soon opened his own cobbler shop, becoming a self-standing artisan.[20]

Beso dispatched a matchmaker to win the hand of Ketevan "Keke" Geladze, said to be a slender, chestnut-haired teenage beauty with big eyes.[21] She, too, was both the offspring of serfs and a striver. Her surname was common in southern Ossetia, leading to speculation that she also had Ossetian blood, but like Beso's, her native tongue was Georgian. Keke's father, a bricklayer and serf who gardened for a wealthy Armenian and lived in a village outside Gori, married another serf, but he seems to have passed away before (or right after) Keke was born. Unusually, Keke's mother made sure the girl learned to read and write; at the time, very few Georgian females were literate. But Keke's mother, too, died, and the girl was raised by her mother's brother, also a serf. Serfdom in Georgia was extraordinary even by crazy-quilt imperial Russian standards: the leading Georgian nobles could own minor nobles as well as priests, while priests could own minor nobles. Partly that was because the tsarist state showed considerable deference to the expansive Georgian nobility, which accounted for 5.6 percent of Georgia's population, versus 1.4 percent for nobles in the empire as a whole. Serfdom's abolition in the Caucasus began three years later than in the rest of the Russian empire, in October 1864. That was about when Keke's family relocated from the village to Gori. "What a happy journey it was!" she reminisced to an interviewer late in life. "Gori was festively decorated, crowds of people swelled like the sea."[22] The Geladzes were free, but they faced the challenge of making a new life.

Keke's wedding to Beso, in May 1874 in Gori's Cathedral of the Assumption, took place in the grand Georgian style, with a boisterous, ostentatious procession through the town.[23] Yakov Egnatashvili, Beso's benefactor, served as one of Beso's best men. Father Kristopore Charkviani, another family friend, was said to have sung so beautifully at the ceremony that Prince Yakov tipped the priest the princely sum of 10 rubles. Beso, like most Georgians—literate or illiterate—could quote from Shota Rustaveli's twelfth-century *The Knight in the Panther's Skin,* an epic about three chivalrous friends who rescue a damsel from being forced into a marriage. Beso liked to wear a long Circassian blackcoat, cinched with a leather belt, over baggy trousers, which he tucked into leather boots—an epigone of Caucasus manhood. True, he was known to drink some of his shoe-maker earnings; then again, as per local custom, his customers often paid him with homemade wine. For all his typical faults, though, Keke viewed the artisan as a step up. "He was considered a very popular young man among my friends and they were all dreaming of marrying him," she recalled to the interviewer. "My friends nearly burst with jealousy. Beso was an enviable groom, a true Geor-gian knight, with beautiful mustaches, very well dressed—and with the special sophistication of the town dweller." Beso, she added, could be "unusual, peculiar, and morose," but also "clever and proud." "Among my friends," Keke concluded, "I became the desired and beautiful girl."[24]

In December 1878, four years into the marriage, when Keke was around twenty and Beso twenty-eight, the couple had a son, Ioseb—the future Stalin.[25] Ioseb was actually Beso and Keke's third son, which by Georgian and Eastern Orthodox tradition was viewed as a special gift of God. But their prior children had not survived. Beso and Keke's firstborn, Mikheil, had died in early 1876, age two months; their second (Giorgi) had died in June 1877, after about half a year.[26] Ioseb, whose diminutive in Georgian was "Soso" (or "Soselo"), grew up an only child, learning later of his brothers' ghosts. The three-person family rented a small timber-and-brick, single-room house from an Ossetian artisan. It was located in Gori's Russian Quarter, near the barracks of the imperial troops whose footwear Beso made. A mere ninety square feet, the structure had a table and four stools, a plank bed, a samovar, a trunk, and a kerosene lamp. Clothes and other belongings were placed on open shelves. There was a cellar, however, reached by winding stairs, and it was here that Beso kept his tools and opened his workshop, and Keke made a nursery for Soso.[27] Stalin's life, in other words, began in a basement.

The humble circumstances notwithstanding, the Jughashvili family story had the makings of a small-town idyll: the artisan, the beauty, and the (surviving) boy. Keke is said to have never let him out of her sight.[28] From around the age of two, Soso suffered the litany of childhood diseases (measles, scarlet fever), and Keke, fearful of losing yet another child, went to church frequently to pray. She also pro-duced insufficient milk, so Soso had to suck the breasts of their neighbors: Mrs. Egnatashvili as well as neighbor Masho Abramidze-Tsikhitatrishvili. Still, he grew, and was full of life. "He was a stubborn little boy," recalled Masho. "When his mother called him and he didn't feel like responding, he didn't stop playing."[29]

## GEOPOLITICAL RUPTURE,
## SURROGATE FAMILY SUCCOR

Running the streets of his Georgian hill town, little Soso was oblivious to the wider world, but in the same decade he was born, Germany had ostentatiously proclaimed the founding of the Second German Reich—the first had been the loose Holy Roman Empire—in the Hall of Mirrors at Versailles, where the great French Sun King Louis XIV had once received the many little German princes. Their geopolitical rupture of German unification and its follow-on rapid industrialization radically altered Russia's geopolitical space. Less ostentatiously, but almost as consequentially, in Japan in 1868, a group of rebels overthrew the Tokugawa Shogunate in Edo (Tokyo) and, as a way to legitimize their rebellion, nominally "restored" the dormant emperor, who took the name Meiji (enlightened rule). The process was by no means smooth, as major regions rebelled. But by 1872–73, nearly every important member of Japan's new leadership had traveled in an embassy to Europe and America, seeing firsthand not only the marvels of the advanced world, but also seeing that the advanced world was not a monolith. Japan's new leaders decided to take full advantage, adapting elements of each country separately: the centralized educational system of France appealed to them more than the looser American one, but instead of the French army, they eventually chose the German system of professional officers and a general staff, while opting for a British-style navy. "Knowledge," proclaimed the Meiji emperor, "shall be sought throughout the world, and thereby shall be strengthened the foundation of the imperial polity." This proclamation encapsulated the secret of great power ascendancy for the ages. To be sure, the new schools and other foreign imports were often resisted; it would take state power to force the transformation. Moreover, Japan's follow-on industrialization did not match Germany's. That said, Japan's economy took off, too, and dramatically transformed the balance of power in Asia, as a new power rose on Russia's other flank.

Also in the same decade the future Stalin was born, the United States of America had become the world's largest integrated national economy. The United States had only recently descended into a civil war, which claimed 1 million casualties, including 600,000 dead out of a population of 32 million, while also introducing ironclad ships, overhead balloon reconnaissance, trench warfare, and long-range rifles. (The war cut off the German journalist Karl Marx's freelance income from a *New York Tribune* no longer as interested in European affairs.) Contrary to Confederate hopes, however, the North's mills were not dependent on the South's supplies of raw cotton (growers in Egypt and India could make up the shortfalls). Some British statesmen, including William Gladstone, had cheered on the South, hoping for a diminution in U.S. power, but the British government never recognized the Confederacy's independence. Had an independent agrarian nation been victorious and consolidated in the U.S. South—one of the largest slave systems in the modern world—the British would have been doomed in the twentieth century, and the entire course of world events would have been radically altered. In 1860, the value of Southern slaves was three times the amount invested in manufacturing or railroads, representing more capital than any other American asset except land, but instead of the slave-based, cotton-growing South, the industrial North triumphed. Between 1870 and 1900, the reunited U.S. economy industrialized and tripled in size (with assistance from mass immigration from non-English-speaking, non-Protestant societies), producing a spectacular surge that eclipsed even the booms in Germany and Japan as the U.S. share of global output soared to nearly 30 percent. This American economic colossus, despite American colonial wars in the Philippines and Cuba, remained as yet mostly apart from world politics. Still, U.S. power had begun to loom over the world system, and would prove decisive in it.

These immense geopolitical facts that accompanied Stalin's birth and early life—a unified industrial Germany, a consolidated industrial Japan, an American power greater than any other in world history—would shake the tsarist regime to its core and, one day, confront Stalin, too. Of course, young Soso Jughashvili could have no inkling of the geopolitical processes that were shaping his world. Meanwhile, in 1880s Gori, in a sign of middling success, the proud new father Beso Jughashvili took on two artisan apprentices. One of them remembered always seeing butter on the Jughashvili table, though the family appears to have lived modestly, eating mostly *lobbio* and *lavash* (red beans and flatbread) as well as potatoes and *badrijani nigvzit* (eggplants stuffed with spiced walnut paste).[30] Another apprentice, Vano Khutsishvili, a mere one year younger than Soso, became like a foster brother for a time.[31] Music filled the home—Keke would serenade Soso with the polyphonous harmonies of Georgian folk songs. Beso, like most Georgian men, could play traditional instruments such as the double-reed *duduk* (which he had played at their wedding). At the same time, Beso seems to have been something of a brooder. Few firsthand descriptions of him survive. One recalled him as "a thin man, taller than average. He had a long face and a long nose and neck. He wore a moustache and beard, and his hair was jet-black." Later, various other men would be put forward as Stalin's "real" father. But two witnesses have pegged Soso as Beso's spitting image.[32]

Whatever Beso's role as a father, and the original promise of his union with Keke, the marriage disintegrated. Most biographers, following Keke's version, usually attribute the breakdown to Beso's alcoholism and inner demons, asserting either that Beso was a natural drunkard or that he took to the bottle from grief after the early death of his firstborn son and never stopped.[33] This may be true, although after that early tragedy, and particularly after the birth of Soso, Beso's workshop seems to have operated for a time. To be sure, the traditional Georgian-style shoes that he made may have had trouble competing with newer European styles.[34] That said, Keke, still young and pretty, may have been a cause of the trouble by flirting with married men: Yakov Egnatashvili, the Gori pub owner and wrestling champion; Damian Davrishevi, the Gori police officer; Kristopore Charkviani, the Gori priest—all of whom would be rumored as the future Stalin's real father. Whether Keke was flirtatious, let alone promiscuous, is unclear. She had been ambitious in marrying Beso the artisan, and she may have moved on to more prestigious men. Perhaps they targeted *her*.[35] Reliable evidence about the possible liaisons of the future Stalin's mother is lacking. Still, gossip about Keke's promiscuity circulated in Gori. Beso took to calling his son "Keke's little bastard," and once he appears to have tried to strangle his wife while denouncing her as a "whore."[36] (A common-enough epithet.) Beso is also thought to have vandalized the pub owned by Egnatashvili and to have attacked the police chief Davrishevi, who, in turn, may have ordered Beso to leave Gori. Around 1884, Beso did depart for Tiflis, hiring himself on at the Armenian-owned Adelkhanov Tannery.

Whoever was at fault, the result was a broken home.[37] By 1883, Keke and little Soso began a vagabond existence, moving house at least nine times over the next decade. And that was not the young boy's only misfortune. The same year his father left, little Soso contracted smallpox during an epidemic that ravaged many a Gori household. Three of their neighbor Egnatashvili's six children perished. Keke appealed to a female faith healer. Soso survived the fevers. But his face was permanently scarred, and he got tagged with the moniker "Poxy" (Chopura). Probably around this time (1884), age six, Soso's left elbow and shoulder began to develop abnormally, reducing the use of his left arm. Various causes have been put forward: a sleighing or wrestling accident; an accidental collision with a horse-drawn phaeton, which was followed by blood poisoning from an infected wound.[38] Soso was indeed struck near Gori's Roman Catholic cathedral by a rare (for Gori) phaeton, perhaps because he and other boys, in a game of chicken, would try to grab the axles.[39] Still, his withering limb may have had a genetic cause. Be that as it may, the elbow worsened over time. Keke, though, proved ever resourceful. To support the two of them, she cleaned and repaired other people's clothes and took care of their living quarters, including for the Egnatashvilis, where Soso often ate dinner. In 1886, she and Soso moved into the upper story of the home of Father Charkviani, one of Beso's former boon drinking companions. The move was likely necessitated by poverty but also seems to have been calculated: Keke implored Charkviani to get Soso into the Gori church school for fall 1886, when he would be already nearly eight. Failing that, she begged the priest to allow his own teenage sons to include Soso in the Russian lessons they gave to their younger sister, on whom the young Stalin may have developed his first crush.

Keke's scheming worked, thanks also to Soso's own ambitions. Biographers have often singled out the future Stalin for leading a "street gang" in Gori, as if street running was somehow distinctive for male youths, in the Caucasus or elsewhere.[40] Rather, what stood out were his bookworm and autodidact tendencies, which propelled him forward. In September 1888, nearing the age of ten, he joined some 150 boys, almost all of whom were seven or eight, in the parish school's mandatory preparatory program for Georgian boys. It was a two-year course, but his bootstrapped Russian proved good enough to vault him through in a single year. In fall 1889, he began the main four-year school curriculum, where his studiousness as well as his sweet alto singing voice were prized—a source of pride for the boy. And finally, at least for part of the day, he was out of his mother's grasp. On January 6, 1890, however, during the Feast of the Epiphany—celebrated in the Orthodox church as Jesus' baptism in the river Jordan—a runaway phaeton in Gori lurched into the onlookers where the church-school choir stood. Struck a second time! "Soso wanted to run across the street, but did not make it in time," recalled Simon Goglichidze, the Gori school choirmaster. "The Phaeton hit him, its connecting pole striking him in the cheek."[41] Soso lost consciousness and was carried home. How close the future Stalin, then eleven, came to death we will never know.[42] The driver was jailed for a month. "Fortunately," concluded Goglichidze, "the wheels only ran over the boy's legs," rather than his head.[43] But the accident permanently inhibited the future Stalin's gait, leading to a second derogatory nickname—"Crimped" (Geza).

Beso, it seems, arrived and took his injured son to Tiflis for medical treatment; Keke seems to have accompanied them, moving to the capital while Soso recuperated.[44] This may be the event that gave rise to the story, much repeated, that Beso "kidnapped" his son because the cobbler was hell-bent against his boy attending school.[45] The truth is murky. Beso appears to have voiced a *desire* to snatch Soso out of school, perhaps the year before, in 1889, and he may have been talked out of it (or forced to return the boy quickly). But the "kidnapping" might simply refer to the circumstance in 1890, once Soso had recovered, when Beso kept him in Tiflis, apprenticing him at the Adelkhanov Tannery. That huge enterprise was built in 1875, when Beso was living in Gori, by the Moscow-born Armenian magnate Grigory Adelkhanov, who had moved to Tiflis and become head of the city's Armenian-dominated credit association in the 1870s. Adelkhanov's plant was equipped with machines and from 1885 could turn out 50,000 pairs of footwear annually as well as 100,000 felt cloaks for the imperial troops. Its yearly revenue exceeded 1 million rubles, a colossal local sum in those days.[46] Beso and son lodged in a cheap room in an old section of Tiflis (Havlabar) and walked to work together across the metal bridge over the Mtkvari River, past the medieval Metekhi church high on the rocky cliffs, which the Russian empire had rebuilt as a prison.[47] Like Soso, many of the Adelkhanov laborers were underage, usually the children of adult workers who were expected to add to their fathers' wages, a practice common at Tiflis factories.[48] In other words, Beso's desire for his son to follow in his footsteps and learn his trade, however selfish, was the norm.[49]

Thanks to his father, the future leader of the world proletariat had an early brush with factory life, which was nasty. Adelkhanov's enterprise had a medical station, a benefit no other leather-working plant in Tiflis offered, but workdays were long, wages low, and job security precarious. The same mechanization that undercut independent artisans like Beso rendered elements of the factory's own workforce redundant over time. Adelkhanov's adult cobblers, moreover, were a rough lot, preying on the youngsters. As an apprentice, Soso may have served only as elder workers' fetcher, not even learning to make shoes. He was certainly subjected to the sickening stench of putrid raw leather in the dank basement, immeasurably worse than the cellar in which his mother had tried (and failed) to nurse him. Had Soso Jughashvili remained a proletarian in training at Adelkhanov, or run away and become a street urchin, there would likely have been no future Stalin. Instead—as every biographer has observed—Keke pressed her well-cultivated church connections to help her retrieve her beloved boy. Much like Klara Hitler, a pious Catholic who would dream that her son Adolf would rise to become a pastor, so Keke Geladze believed her boy Soso was destined for the Orthodox priesthood, a path that the abolition of serfdom had opened up for children of his modest background.[50] The boy would owe his return to the upward path of disciplined study and self-improvement to his determined mother.

Keke brooked no compromise. She rejected the Tiflis church authorities' proposed solution that Soso be allowed to sing in their Tiflis church-school choir while remaining with his father. She accepted nothing less than Soso's return to Gori for the start of the next school year in September 1890.[51] Her triumph over her husband in a deeply patriarchal society was supported by family friends, who took the woman's side, and by the boy himself: In the parental tug-of-war between becoming a priest (school) or a cobbler, Soso preferred school and, therefore, his mother. Unlike Beso, Keke was always ready to do whatever it took to make sure he had clothes on his back and his bills were paid. Ioseb "Soso" Iremashvili, who met the future Stalin by wrestling him on the parish school playground, recalled that his friend "was devoted to only one person—his mother."[52] And Keke, in turn, was devoted to him. Still, we should not idealize her. She was also domineering. "Stalin's severity came from his mother," recalled another Gori chum who later served as a lower-level member of the dictator's bodyguard detail (in charge of wine and foodstuffs). "His mother, Ekaterina Geladze, was a very severe woman, and in general a difficult person."[53] Beso, for his part, seems to have followed his wife and son back to Gori. If so, this was not the first time he had implored Keke for reconciliation. But the 1890 episode of Soso's recuperation and factory apprenticeship in Tiflis marked the final break in their marriage.[54] Beso refused to support the family financially (for what that was worth), and back at the Gori school, Soso was expelled for his family's failure to pay the 25-ruble tuition. "Uncle Yakov" Egnatashvili evidently stepped in and cleared the debt.

Uncle Yakov became Soso's valued surrogate father.[55] Much has been made over the young Stalin's infatuation with a celebrated novel, *The Patricide* (1882), by Aleksandre Qazbegi (1848–93), who was the scion of a princely Georgian family (whose grandfather had taken part in Georgia's annexation by Russia and obtained a mountain fief for it). The Russian imperial authorities targeted by Qazbegi's novel banned it, enhancing its considerable allure. In the story, a peasant boy, Iago, and a beautiful girl, Nunu, fall in love, despite family disapproval, but a Georgian official collaborating with the Russian empire rapes Nunu and imprisons Iago on trumped-up charges. Iago's best friend, Koba, a brave, laconic mountaineer (*mokheve*), swears an oath of revenge—"I'll make their mothers weep!"—and organizes a daring prison break for Iago. The Georgian official's men, however, kill Iago. Nunu dies from sorrow. But Koba vows revenge, hunts down and executes the arrogant official—"It is I, Koba!"—enforcing rough justice. Koba is the novel's only surviving character, outliving his enemies and his friends.[56] Among the young Stalin's several dozen early pseudonyms—including, briefly, Besoshvili (son of Beso)—Koba was the one that stuck. "He called himself 'Koba' and would not have us call him by any other name," recalled the childhood friend Ioseb Iremashvili. "His face would shine with pride and pleasure when we called him 'Koba.'"[57] This was the boy about him, one friend recalled, "We, his friends, would often see Soso . . . pushing his left shoulder slightly forward, his right arm slightly bent, holding a cigarette in his hand, hurrying through the streets among the crowds." The avenger Koba (meaning the indomitable, in Turkish) was certainly more flattering than Crimped or Poxy. But it is worth underscoring that Soso Jughashvili's surrogate father, Yakov Egnatashvili, also went by the nickname Koba, a kind of diminutive for his Georgian given name Yakobi.

Too much has been made of Beso's failings, and not enough of Yakov "Koba" Egnatashvili's support. Too much has also been made of the violence in Soso Jughashvili's early life. Beso beat his son out of anger, humiliation, or for no reason; the doting Keke beat the boy, too. (Beso struck Keke, and Keke sometimes thrashed Beso for being a drunkard.)[58] Of course, a sizable chunk of humanity was beaten by one or both parents. Nor did Gori suffer some especially violent Oriental culture. Sure, the annual commemoration of Great and Holy Monday (Easter week), recalling the 1634 expulsion of the Muslim Persians, entailed a nighttime all-Gori fistfight. The town divided into teams by ethnicity, reaching a thousand or more pugilists, and the brawl was refereed by drunken priests. Children launched the fisticuffs, before the adults joined, and Soso could not fail to take part.[59] But such festive violence—madcap bare fists, followed by sloppy embraces—was typical of the Russian empire, from Ukrainian market towns to Siberian villages. Gori did not stand out in the least. Moreover, other violent activities attributed to the young Stalin are scarcely unheard of in boys. Wrestling tournaments were celebrated in Gori, and among schoolmates on the playground, the lanky, sinewy Soso was said to fight hard, albeit dirty, displaying significant strength despite his withered left arm. Some say he would not shrink from bouts with the strongest opponents and, on occasion, got beaten silly. But Soso was evidently trying to follow in the footsteps of his celebrated surrogate father—the Egnatashvili clan members, led by their patriarch, were Gori's wrestling champions. "Little Stalin boxed and wrestled with a certain success," recalled Iosif "Soso" Davrishevi, the policeman's son.[60]

Beso's trajectory, by contrast, was further downward. He appears to have left the Adelkhanov Tannery not long after he failed to reinstall his son there. He tried his luck repairing shoes at a stall in the Armenian bazaar in Tiflis, but that seems not to have panned out. Thereafter, nothing is reliably known of how he survived; some sources indicate that eventually Beso became a vagrant, though there are also indications he kept plying his trade, perhaps in a clothing repair shop.[61] Later, the future Stalin would make light of his own "proletarian" origins resulting from his father's downward social mobility. "My father was not born a worker, he had a workshop, with apprentices, he was an exploiter," Stalin would tell his Red Army commanders in March 1938. "We lived none too badly. I was 10 when he went up in smoke [*razorilsia*] and became a proletarian. I would not say he entered the proletariat with joy. The whole time he cursed that he was unfortunate to enter the proletariat. But the circumstance that he was unlucky, that he went up in smoke, is made an achievement [*zasluga*] of mine. I assure you, this is a funny thing (laughter)."[62] In point of fact, Beso had never gotten off the rolls of his village commune in Didi Lilo and, therefore, he remained a member of the peasant estate—a juridical status that Beso passed on to his son (as recorded on Stalin's tsarist internal passports right through 1917). But although the future Soviet leader was a peasant de jure, and the son of a worker de facto, he himself, thanks to the support of Keke and "Uncle" Yakov, was rising up, into the demi-intelligentsia.

## FAITH IN GOD

Back at school for the 1890-91 academic year, Soso was compelled to repeat the grade because of the phaeton accident, but he threw himself into his studies with ever greater determination. He was said never to have shown up late to classes, and to have spent his spare time behind books—subsequent reminiscences that ring true.[63] "He was a very capable boy, always coming first in his class," one former schoolmate recalled, adding "he was [also] first in all games and recreation." Some classmates also recalled Soso as defiant when the Georgian boys were banished to the dunce corner for speaking their native tongue; some recalled he was not afraid, on other students' behalf, to approach the teachers, who wore imposing state uniforms (tunics with gold buttons). If Soso did speak to the teachers on behalf of other boys, that was likely because he had been picked by the Russian-language teacher—christened the "gendarme"—to serve as class monitor, an enforcer of discipline. Whatever role he may have played as an intermediary, all the teachers, including the Georgian ones, appreciated Soso's diligence and eagerness to be called upon.[64] He sang Russian and Georgian folk songs, along with Tchaikovsky songs; studied Church Slavonic and Greek; and was chosen to read out the liturgy and sing the hymns at church. The school awarded him David's Book of Psalms with the inscription: "To Iosif Jughashvili . . . for excellent progress, behavior and excellent recitation of the Psalter."[65] One schoolmate rhapsodized about Soso and other choirboys "wearing their surplices, kneeling, faces raised, singing Vespers with angelic voices while the other boys prostrated themselves filled with an ecstasy not of this world."[66]

There was a prosaic side as well: To make ends meet, Keke cleaned the school (for 10 rubles a month). She may also have worked as a domestic at the home of the schoolmaster, though at some point she became a regular seamstress for a local "fancy" clothes shop and, finally, settled them into an apartment (on Gori's Cathedral Street).[67] But soon, for exemplary academic performance, Soso's tuition was waived and on top of that he began receiving a monthly stipend of 3 rubles, later raised to 3.50 and then 7. This is perhaps the best evidence that the child from the broken home stood out as one of Gori's best pupils.[68] Graduating in spring 1894, at the advanced age of fifteen and a half, he could have gone on to the Gori Teachers Seminary, a further step up. An even better option presented itself: Choirmaster Simon Goglichidze was moving to the Tsar Alexander Teacher Training School in Tiflis and said he could bring his star Gori pupil along on a coveted fully funded state scholarship. That was no small matter for an indigent family. But instead, Soso sat the entrance examinations for the Theological Seminary in Tiflis, to become a priest. He excelled on the exams nearly across the board—Bible studies, Church Slavonic, Russian, catechism, Greek, geography, penmanship (though not in arithmetic)—and gained admission. It was a dream come true. The Tiflis seminary—alongside that city's secular gymnasia (elite high schools) for the boys and girls of the prosperous—represented the highest rung of the educational ladder in the Caucasus, where the Russian imperial administration refused to countenance a university. The seminary's six-year course of study (usually from age fourteen) led, at a minimum, to life as a parish priest or a village teacher in rural Georgia, but for those still more ambitious, the seminary could provide a stepping-stone to a university elsewhere in the empire.

In biography generally, the trope of the traumatic childhood—an outgrowth of the spread of Freudianism—came to play an outsized role.[69] It is too pat, even for those *with* genuinely traumatic childhoods. The future Stalin's childhood was certainly not easy: illnesses and accidents, forced house moving, straitened circumstances, a broken-down father, a loving but severe mother rumored to be a whore. But in adulthood, even as the dictator indulged roiling resentments that would seal the fate of most of his revolutionary colleagues, he would voice no special anger at his parents or his early life experiences. The future Kremlin leader experienced nothing of the bloody intrigues of the court childhoods of Ivan the Terrible or Peter the Great (to both of whom he would often be compared). Ivan's father died from a boil when the boy was three; his mother was assassinated when he was seven. The orphaned Tsar Ivan the Terrible was reduced (by his regents) to begging for his food, and he witnessed the elites' murderous struggle for power in his name, coming to fear his own pending bloody demise. The young Ivan took to tearing off birds' wings and throwing cats and dogs off buildings. Peter the Great's father died when he was four. Thereafter, the boy's life was under threat by the warring court factions that were connected to his father's two widows. After Peter was made tsar at age ten, the losing faction rebelled, and the young Peter witnessed relatives of his mother and friends being thrown onto upraised pikes. To be sure, some analysts have exaggerated the horrors of Ivan's and Peter's childhoods, offering pseudopsychological explanations for their often cruel reigns. Still, the most that could be claimed about the young Jughashvili was that he might have seen his father once come after his mother with a knife.

Next to what Ivan and Peter had gone through, what were the future Stalin's childhood tribulations? Consider further the early life of Sergei Kostrikov, known later under the revolutionary name Kirov, who would become Stalin's closest friend. Born in 1886 in a small town in Vyatka province, central Russia, Kirov would be considered as among the most popular of Stalinist party leaders. But his childhood was difficult: four of Kirov's seven siblings died in infancy, his father was a drunkard who abandoned the family, and his mother died of TB

when the boy was just seven. Kirov grew up in an orphanage.[70] A similar fate
befell another key member of Stalin's inner circle, Grigol "Sergo" Orjonikidze,
whose mother died when he was an infant, and whose father died when he was
ten. By contrast, the young Stalin had his doting mother and a variety of important mentors, as the strikingly numerous memoirs from that time indicate. Keke's
extended family lived close by, including her brother Gio and his children (Keke's
other brother, Sandala, would be killed by the tsarist police). And Beso's family
(his sister's children) remained a presence even after Beso lost the custody showdown in 1890.[71] Family was the glue of Georgian society, and Soso Jughashvili had
not only his own extended kin, but the surrogate kin provided by the Egnatashvilis (as well as the Davrishevis). Smalltown Gori took care of its own, forming a
tight-knit community.

In addition to his extended family and Gori schooling (a ticket upward), the
future Stalin's childhood had one more vital redeeming aspect: faith in God. His
destitute family had to find the means for the Orthodox seminary's hefty annual
tuition (40 rubles) and room and board (100 rubles), as well as for his surplice
school uniform. The sixteen-year-old Jughashvili petitioned for a scholarship and
was granted a partial one: free room and board.[72] For tuition, Keke appealed to
Soso's surrogate father, Koba Egnatashvili. Big Koba had the means to send his
two surviving natural sons to a gymnasium in Moscow, and he came through for
little Koba (Soso), too. But if the well-heeled Egnatashvili, or others, had ceased
to support Soso, or if the Russian rector at the seminary withdrew the partial
state scholarship, Jughashvili's studies would have been jeopardized. He had taken
a big risk by declining the full state scholarship at the secular teacher training
school arranged by Choirmaster Goglichidze. The reason must have been that
not only Keke but her son, too, was devout. "In his first years of study," allowed a
Soviet-era publication of reminiscences, "Stalin was very much a believer, going
to all the services, singing in the church choir. . . . He not only observed all religious rites but always reminded us to observe them."[73] Studying among the
monks at the seminary, the future Stalin may have thought to become a monk
himself. But changes in the Russian empire and in the wider world opened up a
very different path.[74]

## CHAPTER 2

# LADO'S DISCIPLE

Others live off our labor; they drink our blood; our
oppression quenches their thirst with the tears of our
wives, children, and kin.

Leaflets, in Georgian and Armenian,
distributed by Iosif Jughashvili, 1902[1]

TIFLIS EXUDED A HAUNTING, magical beauty. Founded in a gorge in the fifth
century, the residence of Georgian kings from the sixth, Tiflis—its Persian name,
also employed in Russian—was centuries older than ancient Kiev, let alone
upstart Moscow or St. Petersburg. In Georgian the city was called Tblisi ("warm
place"), perhaps for its fabled hot springs. ("I must not omit to mention," enthused
one nineteenth-century visitor, "that the baths of the city cannot be surpassed
even by those of Constantinople.")[2] Back when Russia annexed eastern Georgia,
in 1801, Tiflis had about 20,000 inhabitants, fully three quarters of them Armenian. By century's end, Tiflis had mushroomed to 160,000, with a plurality of
Armenians (38 percent), followed by Russians and Georgians, and a smattering
of Persians and Turks.[3] The city's Armenian, Georgian, and Persian neighborhoods ascended up the hills, their houses terraced in, with multilevel balconies
perched one above the other in a style reminiscent of the Ottoman Balkans or
Salonika. By contrast, the flat Russian quarter stood out for its wide boulevards
where one could find the imposing Viceroy's Palace, Opera House, Classical
Gymnasium No. 1, Russian Orthodox cathedral, and the private homes of Russian functionaries (*chinovniki*) and of the Armenian *haute bourgeoisie*. Imperial
Russia's 1860s Great Reforms had introduced municipal governing bodies with
restricted franchise elections, and wealthy Armenians came to compose the
vast majority of those eligible to vote in Tiflis' municipal elections, allowing
Armenian merchants to control the city duma. But they had no hold on the
imperial executive administration, which was run by appointed Russians, ethnic

Germans, and Poles, often relying on Georgian nobles, who enriched themselves through state office.[4] Still, the Georgians—no more than a quarter of the urban population—were to an extent upstaged in their own capital.

The urban distribution of power was glaring. On the wide tree-lined Golovin Prospect, named for a Russian general, the shops carried signs in French, German, Persian, and Armenian as well as Russian. Wares on offer included fashions from Paris and silks from Bukhara, useful for marking status, as well as carpets from nearby Iran (Tabriz), which helped distinguish interior spaces. By contrast, over at the city's labyrinthine Armenian and Persian bazaars, underneath the ruins of a Persian fortress, "everyone washes, shaves, gets a haircut, dresses and undresses as if at home in their bedroom," explained a Russian-language guide to the warrens of silversmiths and cooking stalls serving kebabs and inexpensive wines.[5] Tatar (Azeri) mullahs could be seen in their green and white turbans, while Persians went about in caftans and black-fur caps, their hair and fingernails dyed red.[6] One observer described a typical square (Maidan), near where Soso Jughashvili had briefly resided with his father in 1890, as "a porridge of people and beasts, sheepskin caps and shaved heads, fezzes and peaked caps," adding that "all shout, bang, laugh, swear, jostle, sing, work, and shake in various tongues and voices."[7] But beyond the Oriental riot of its streets—which made the guidebook writers ooh and aah—the years of the 1870s through 1900 saw a crucial transformation of society by the railroad and other industrialization, as well as a Georgian national awakening facilitated by an expanding periodical press and the connections from modern transportation. By 1900, Tiflis had acquired a small but significant intelligentsia and a growing industrial-worker class.[8]

It was in this modernizing urban milieu that Jughashvili—who was back in Tiflis as of 1894—entered the seminary and came of age, becoming not a priest but a Marxist and revolutionary.[9] Imported to Georgia in the 1880s, Marxism seemed to offer a world of certainties. But Jughashvili did not discover Marxism on his own. A headstrong twentysomething militant, Vladimir "Lado" Ketskhoveli (b. 1876) would serve as the revolutionary mentor for the future Stalin, who in looking back would call himself a disciple of Lado.[10] Lado was the fifth of six children born to a priest from a village just outside Gori. Three years Jughashvili's senior at the Gori church school and then at the Tiflis Theological Seminary, Lado acquired tremendous authority among the seminarians. Under Lado's influence, the young Jughashvili, already an energetic autodidact, found a lifelong calling in being an agitator and a teacher, helping the dark masses see the light about social injustice and a purported all-purpose remedy.

## GEORGIAN CULTURAL NATIONALIST

Compared with small-town Gori, the Caucasus capital offered a grand drama of incipient modernity, but Iosif Jughashvili did not see much of the city, at least not initially. His immediate world, the theological seminary, was dubbed the Stone Sack—a four-story bastion of neoclassical façade. If the main classical gymnasium stood at the pinnacle of the local educational hierarchy, the seminary—more accessible to poor youth—was not far behind. The building, at the southern end of Golovin Prospect on Yerevan Square, had been purchased by the Orthodox Church from a sugar magnate (Constantine Zubalashvili) to serve as the new home of the seminary in 1873. For the hundreds of students who lived on the top floor in an open-style dormitory, their daily regime generally lasted from 7:00 a.m. until 10:00 p.m. Ringing bells summoned them to morning prayers, followed by tea (breakfast), classes until 2:00 p.m., a midday main meal at 3:00, then a mere hour or so outside the walls, roll call at 5:00, evening prayers, tea (a light supper) at 8:00, homework, and lights out. "Day and night we were worked within barrack walls and felt like prisoners," recalled another Gori "Soso," Ioseb Iremashvili, who like the young Stalin was attending the seminary by way of the Gori church school.[11] Occasional leaves were granted to return to one's native village or town, but otherwise Sundays alone afforded some free time—but only after Orthodox Church services, which meant standing for three to four hours on stone tiles. Trips to the theater and other blasphemies were proscribed. Some seminarians, however, dared to escape to town after nightly roll call, despite the random night dormitory checks to ferret out reading of illicit materials by candlelight or onanism.

The regimentation for the teenage seminarians accustomed to indulgent families and the free play of the streets had to be frustrating, but the seminary also offered endless opportunity for passionate discussions with fellow students about the meaning of existence and their own futures, as well as the discovery of books and learning. Emphasis fell on sacred texts, of course, and on Church Slavonic and Russian imperial history. Ioseb "Soso" Jughashvili, now known in Russified form as Iosif, was in his element, and he performed well. He became the school choir's lead tenor, a high-profile achievement, given how much time the boys spent in church and preparing for church. He also developed into a voracious reader who started keeping a notebook of thoughts and ideas. In the classroom, he earned mostly grades of 4 (B), while achieving 5s (A's) in ecclesiastical singing, and earned 5 rubles for occasional singing in the Opera House. In the beginning years his only 3s (C's) came in final composition and Greek. He received the top mark (5) in conduct. As a freshman, Jughashvili placed eighth in a group of twenty-nine, and as a sophomore he rose to fifth. But in his third year, 1896-97, his rank slipped to sixteenth (of twenty-four), and by the fifth year he stood twentieth (of twenty-three), having failed scripture.[12] Because classroom seating was determined by academic results, his desk kept being moved farther from the teachers. Even the choir he loved so much ceased to hold his interest, partly because of recurrent lung problems (chronic pneumonia).[13] But the main cause of his declining interest and performance stemmed from a culture clash brought on by modernizing forces and political reactions.

In 1879, the year after Jughashvili had been born, two Georgian noblemen writers, Prince Ilya Chavchavadze (b. 1837) and Prince Akaki Tsereteli (b. 1840), had founded the Society for the Spread of Literacy Among Georgians. Georgians comprised many different groups—Kakhetis, Kartlians, Imeretians, Mingrelians—with a shared language, and Chavchavadze and Tsereteli hoped to spark an integrated Georgian cultural rebirth through schools, libraries, and bookshops. Their conservative populist cultural program intended no disloyalty to the empire.[14] But in the Russian empire, administratively, there was no "Georgia," just the two provinces (*gubernias*) of Tiflis and Kutaisi, and such was the hardline stance of the imperial authorities that the censors forbade any publication of the term "Georgia" (Gruziya) in Russian. Partly because many censors did not know the Georgian language—which was written neither in Cyrillic nor Latin letters—the censors proved more lenient with Georgian publications, which opened a lot of space for Georgian periodicals. But at the Tiflis seminary, to compel Russification, Georgian language instruction had been abolished in favor of Russian in 1872. (Orthodox services in Georgia were conducted in Church Slavonic and thus were largely unintelligible to the faithful, as they were even in the predominantly ethnic Russian provinces of the empire.) From 1875, the seminary in the Georgian capital ceased teaching Georgian history. Of the seminary's two dozen teachers, all of whom were formally appointed by the Russian viceroy, a few were Georgian but most were Russian monks, and the latter had been expressly assigned to Georgia because of their strong Russian nationalist views.

(Several would later join radical-right movements.) In addition, the seminary employed two full-time inspectors to keep the students under "constant and unremitting supervision"—even in the seminarians' free time—while recruiting snitches for extra eyes and ears.[15]

Expulsions for "unreliability" became commonplace, defeating the educational purpose of the seminary. In response to the heavy-handedness, Tiflis seminarians—many of them the sons of Orthodox priests—had begun (in the 1870s) to produce illegal newsletters and form secret discussion "circles." In 1884, a member of one such Tiflis seminary circle, Silibistro "Silva" Jibladze (who had led a revolt back in his junior seminary), struck the Russian rector in the face for denigrating Georgian as "dogspeak." As the boys well knew, the kingdom of Georgia had converted to the Christian faith half a millennium before the Russians did, and more than a century before the Romans. Jibladze was sentenced to three years in a punishment battalion. Then, in 1886, to empirewide notoriety, a different expelled student assassinated the Tiflis seminary rector using a traditional Caucasus dagger (*kinjal*).[16] More than sixty seminarians were expelled. "Some go so far as to excuse the assassin," reported the exarch of Georgia to the Holy Synod in St. Petersburg. "All in their hearts approve."[17] By the 1890s, the seminary students were staging strikes. In a boycott of classes in November 1893, they demanded better food (especially during Lent), an end to the brutal surveillance regime, a department of Georgian language, and the right to sing hymns in Georgian.[18] The Russifying ecclesiastics responded by expelling eighty-seven students—including the strike's seventeen-year-old leader, Lado Ketskhoveli—and shutting the doors in December 1893.[19] The seminary reopened in fall 1894 with two first-year classes, the 1893 and the 1894 admissions, the latter being Iosif Jughashvili's.

When the future Stalin started at the seminary, the harsh disciplinary mechanisms remained, but in a concession, courses in Georgian literature and history were reinstituted. In summer 1895, after his first year, Jughashvili, then sixteen and a half, took his own Georgian-language verses in person to the publishing nobleman Ilya Chavchavadze, without seminary permission. The editor of Chavchavadze's newspaper *Iveria* (a term for Eastern Georgia) published five of Jughashvili's poems, under the widely used Georgian nickname for Ioseb/Iosif: Soselo.[20] The verses, among other themes, depict the contrast between violence (in nature and man) and gentleness (in birds and music), as well as a wandering poet who is poisoned by his own people. Another poem served as a contribution to the fiftieth jubilee of the Georgian nobleman Prince Rapiel Eristavi, the young Stalin's favorite poet.[21] Eristavi's verses, the dictator would later say, were "beautiful, emotional, and musical," adding that the prince was rightly called the nightingale of Georgia—a role to which Jughashvili himself might have aspired. An affectionate sixth Jughashvili poem, "Old Ninika," published in 1896 in *Kvali* (*The Furrow*), the journal of another Tsereteli, Giorgi (b. 1842), featured a heroic sage narrating "the past to his children's children." In a word, Jughashvili, too, was swept up in the emotional wave of the fin-de-siècle Georgian awakening.

The spirit of the times that affected the young Jughashvili was well captured in the poem "Suliko" (1895), or "Little Soul," about lost love and lost national spirit. Written by Akaki Tsereteli, the cofounder of the Georgian Society, "Suliko" was set to music and became a popular anthem:

> In vain I sought my loved one's grave;
> Despair plunged me in deepest woe.
> Overwhelmed with bursting sobs I cried:
> "Where are you, my Suliko?"

> In solitude upon a thornbush
> A rose in loveliness did grow;
> With downcast eyes I softly asked:
> "Isn't that you, Oh Suliko?"

> The flower trembled in assent
> As low it bent its lovely head;
> Upon its blushing cheek there shone
> Tears that the morning skies had shed.[22]

As dictator, Stalin would sing "Suliko" often, in Georgian and Russian translation (in which form it would become a sentimental staple on Soviet radio). But in 1895–96, he had to conceal his own Georgian-language poetry publishing triumph from the Russifying seminary authorities.

Nationalism, of course, marked the age. Adolf Hitler, who had been born in 1889 near Brannau am Inn, in Austria-Hungary, was influenced by the shimmer of Bismarck's German Reich almost from birth. Hitler's father, Alois, a passionate

German nationalist of Austrian citizenship, worked as a customs official in the border towns on the Austrian side; his mother, Klara, her husband's third wife, was devoted to Adolf, one of only two of their five children to survive. Hitler moved with his family across the border, at age three, to Passau, Germany, where he learned to speak German in the lower Bavarian dialect. In 1894, the family moved back to Austria (near Linz), but Hitler, despite having been born and spending most of his formative years in the Habsburg empire, never acquired the distinctive Austrian version of German language. He would develop a disdain for polyglot Austria-Hungary and, with his Austrian-German speaking friends, sing the German anthem "Deutschland über Alles"; the boys greeted each other with the German "Heil" rather than the Austrian "Servus." Hitler attended church, sang in the choir, and, under his mother's influence, spoke about becoming a Catholic priest, but mostly he grew up imagining himself becoming an artist. An elder brother's death at age sixteen from measles (in 1900) appears to have severely affected Hitler, making him more moody, withdrawn, indolent. His father, who wanted the boy to follow in his footsteps as a customs official, sent him against his wishes to technical school in Linz, where Hitler clashed with his teachers. After his father's sudden death (January 1903), Hitler's performance in school suffered and his mother allowed him to transfer. Hitler would graduate (barely) and in 1905 move to Vienna, where he would fail to get into art school and lead a bohemian existence, jobless, selling watercolors and running through his small inheritance. The German nationalism, however, would stick. By contrast, the future Stalin would exchange his nationalism, that of the small nation of Georgia, for grander horizons.

## STUDENT POLITICS

"If he was pleased about something," recalled a onetime close classmate, Peti Kapanadze, of Jughashvili, he "would snap his fingers, yell loudly, and jump around on one leg."[23] In the fall of his third year (1896), when his grades would start to decline, Jughashvili joined a clandestine student "circle" led by the upperclassman Seid Devdariani. Their conspiracy may have been aided partly by chance: along with others of weak health, Jughashvili had been placed outside the main dormitory in separate living quarters, where he evidently met Devdariani.[24]

Their group had perhaps ten members, several from Gori, and they read non-religious literature such as belles lettres and natural science—books not even banned by the Russian authorities but banned at the seminary, whose curriculum excluded Tolstoy, Lermontov, Chekhov, Gogol, and even works of the messianic Dostoyevsky.[25] The boys obtained the secular books from the so-called Cheap Library run by Chavchavadze's Georgian Literacy Society, or from a Georgian-owned secondhand bookshop. Jughashvili also acquired such books from a stall back in Gori operated by a member of Chavchavadze's society. (The future Stalin, recalled the bookseller, "joked a lot, telling funny tales of seminary life.")[26] As at almost every school across the Russian empire, student conspirators smuggled in the works to be read surreptitiously at night, concealing them during the day. In November 1896, the seminary inspector confiscated from Jughashvili a translation of Victor Hugo's *Toilers of the Sea,* having already found him with Hugo's *Ninety-Three* (about the counterrevolution in France). Jughashvili also read Zola, Balzac, and Thackeray in Russian translation, and countless works by Georgian authors. In March 1897, he was caught yet again with contraband literature: a translation of a work by a French Darwinist that contradicted Orthodox theology.[27]

The monks at the seminary, unlike most Russian Orthodox priests, led a celibate existence, forswore meat, and prayed constantly, struggling to avoid the temptations of this world. But no matter their personal sacrifices, dedication, or academic degrees, to the Georgian students, they came across as "despots, capricious egotists who had in mind only their own prospects," especially rising to bishop (a status in the Orthodox tradition linked to the apostles). Jughashvili, for his part, might well have lost his interest in holy matters as a matter of course, but the seminary's policies and the monks' behavior accelerated his disenchantment, while also affording him a certain determination in resistance. He appears to have been singled out by a newly promoted seminary inspector, Priestmonk Dmitry, who was derided by the students as the "Black Blob" (*chernoe piatno*). The rotund, dark-robed Dmitry had been the seminary's teacher of holy scripture (1896) before becoming an inspector (1898). Even though he was a Georgian nobleman whose secular name was David Abashidze (1867–1943), he showed himself to be even more Georgia phobic than the chauvinist ethnic Russian monks. When Abashidze confronted Jughashvili over possession of forbidden books, the latter denounced the seminary surveillance regime, called him a

Black Blob, and got five hours in a dark "isolation cell."[28] Later in life, during his dictatorship, Stalin would vividly recall the seminary's "spying, penetrating into the soul, humiliation." "At 9:00 am, the bell for tea," he explained, "we go into the dining hall, and then return to our rooms, and it turns out that during that interval someone has searched and turned over all our storage trunks."[29]

The estrangement process was gradual, and never total, but the seminary that Jughashvili had worked so hard to get into was alienating him. The illicit reading circle to which he belonged had not been revolutionary in intent, at first. And yet rather than accommodate and moderate student curiosity, for what was after all the best belles lettres and modern science, the theologians responded with interdiction and persecution, as if they had something to fear. In other words, it was less the circle than the seminary itself that was fomenting radicalism, albeit unwittingly. Trotsky, in his biography of Stalin, would colorfully write that Russia's seminaries were "notorious for the horrifying savagery of their customs, medieval pedagogy, and the law of the fist."[30] True enough, but too pat. Many, perhaps most, graduates of Russian Orthodox seminaries became priests. And while it was true that almost all the leading lights of Georgia's Social Democrats emerged from the Tiflis seminary—like the many radical members of the Jewish Labor Federation (Bund) produced at the famed Rabbinical School and Teachers' Seminary in Wilno—that was partly because such places provided an education and strong dose of self-discipline.[31] Seminarians populated the ranks of imperial Russia's scientists (such as the physiologist Ivan Pavlov, of dog reflex fame), and the sons and grandsons of priests also became scientists (such as Dimitri Mendeleev, who invented the periodic table). Orthodox churchmen gave the entire Russian empire most of its intelligentsia through both their offspring and their teaching. Churchmen imparted values that endured their sons' or students' secularization: namely, hard work, dignified poverty, devotion to others, and above all, a sense of moral superiority.[32]

Jughashvili's discovery of inconsistencies in the Bible, his poring over a translation of Ernest Renan's atheistic *Life of Jesus,* and his abandonment of the priesthood did not automatically mean he would become a revolutionary. Revolution was not a default position. Another major step was required. In his case, he spent the 1897 summer vacation in the home village of his close friend Mikheil "Mikho" Davitashvili, "where he got to know the life of the peasants."[33] In Georgia, as in the rest of the Russian empire, the flawed serf emancipation had done little for the peasants, who found themselves trapped between land "redemption" payments to their former masters and newly uninhibited bandits who descended from mountain redoubts to exact tribute.[34] The emancipation did "liberate" the children of the nobility, who, without serfs to manage, quit their estates for the cities and, alongside peasant youth, took up the peasantry's cause.[35] Jughashvili's Georgian awakening evolved toward recognition of Georgian landlord oppression of Georgian peasants: the boy who had perhaps wanted to become a monk now "wished to become a village scribe" or elder.[36] But his sense of violated social justice linked up with what appears to be his ambition for leadership. In the illegal circle at the seminary, Jughashvili and the elder Devdariani were boon companions but also competitors for top position.[37] In May 1898, when Devdariani graduated and left for the Russian empire's Dorpat (Yurev) University in the Baltic region, Jughashvili got his wish, taking over the circle and driving it in a more practical (political) direction.[38]

Iosif Iremashvili—the other Gori "Soso" at the seminary—recalled that "as a child and youth he [Jughashvili] was a good friend so long as one submitted to his imperious will."[39] And yet it was right around this time that the "imperious" Jughashvili acquired a transformative mentor—Lado Ketskhoveli. Lado, after his expulsion for leading the student strike in 1893, had spent the summer reporting for Chavchavadze's newspaper *Iveria* on postemancipation peasant burdens in his native Gori district; after that, as per regulations, Lado was permitted to enroll in a different seminary, which he did (Kiev) in September 1894. In 1896, however, Lado was expelled from Kiev, too, arrested for possession of "criminal" literature, and deported to his native village under police surveillance. In fall 1897, Lado returned to Tiflis, joined a group of Georgian Marxists, and went to work in a printer's shop to learn typesetting so he could produce revolutionary leaflets.[40] He also reestablished contact with the Tiflis seminarians. Ketskhoveli was a recognized authority among them: his photograph hung on the wall of the seminarian Jughashvili's room (along with photos of Mikho Davitashvili and Peti Kapanadze).[41] Even though the Cheap Library of Chavchavadze's Georgian Literacy Society might have had a few Marxist texts, including perhaps one by Marx himself (*A Critique of Political Economy,* part of the *Das Kapital* trilogy), book-wise Tiflis was a far cry from Warsaw.[42] Lado, beginning in 1898, served as the main source of the young Stalin's transition from the typical social-justice orientation known as Populism to Marxism.[43]

## MARXISM AND RUSSIA

Karl Marx (1818–83), born to a well-off middle-class family in Prussia, was by no means the first modern socialist. "Socialism" (the neologism) dates from the 1830s and appeared around the same time as "liberalism," "conservatism," "feminism," and many other "isms" in the wake of the French Revolution that began in 1789 and the concurrent spread of markets. One of the first avowed socialists was a cotton baron, Robert Owen (1771–1858), who wanted to create a model community for his employees by paying higher wages, reducing hours, building schools and company housing, and correcting vice and drunkenness—a father-like approach toward "his" workers. Other early socialists, especially French ones, dreamed of an entirely new society, not just ameliorating social conditions. The nobleman Count Henri de Saint-Simon (1760–1825) and his followers called for social engineers under public, not private, property, to perfect society, making it fraternal, rational, and just, in an updated version of Plato's *Republic*. Charles Fourier (1772–1837) introduced a further twist, arguing that labor was the center of existence and should be uplifting, not dehumanizing; to that end, Fourier, too, imagined a centrally regulated society.[44] Not all radicals embraced centralized authority, however: Pierre-Joseph Proudhon (1809–65) attacked the banking system, claiming that big bankers refused to grant credit to small property owners or the poor, and advocated for society to be organized instead on the basis of cooperation (mutualism) so that the state would become unnecessary. He called his smaller-scale and cooperative approach anarchism. But Marx, along with his close collaborator Friedrich Engels (1820–95), a British factory owner, argued that socialism was not a choice but "the necessary outcome" of a larger historical struggle governed by scientific laws, so that, like it or not, the-then current epoch was doomed.

Many adherents of conservatism, too, denounced the evils of markets, but what made Marx stand out among the foes of the new economic order was his full-throated celebration of the power of capitalism and modern industry. Adam Smith's Scottish Enlightenment tome, *Wealth of Nations* (1776), had put forth influential arguments about competition, specialization (the division of labor), and the power of self-interest to increase social betterment. But in *The Communist Manifesto* (1848), a crisply written pamphlet, the-then twenty-nine-year-old Marx waxed lyrical about how "steam and machinery revolutionized industrial production" and how "the need of a constantly expanding market for its products chases the bourgeoisie over the whole surface of the globe."[45] These breakthroughs to "giant modern industry" and globalism, described by Marx in 1848 as accomplished facts, remained decades away, even in Britain, despite the industrial transformation there during Marx's German childhood. But Marx anticipated them. When explicitly looking into the future, Marx, unlike Smith, stipulated that global capitalism would lose its dynamism. In 1867, he published the first volume of what would become the trilogy called *Das Kapital,* responding to the classical British political economist David Ricardo as well as Smith. Marx posited that all value was created by human labor, and that the owners of the means of production confiscated the "surplus value" of laborers. In other words, "capital" was someone else's appropriated labor. The proprietors, Marx argued, invested their ill-gotten surplus value (capital) in labor-saving machinery, thereby advancing production and overall wealth, but also reducing wages or eliminating jobs; while the laborers, according to Marx, became locked in immiseration, capital tended to become concentrated in fewer and fewer hands, inhibiting further development. In the interest of further economic and social progress, Marx called for abolition of private property, the market, profit, and money.

Marx's revision of French socialist thought (Fourier, Saint-Simon) and British political economy (Ricardo, Smith) rested on what the German idealist philosopher Georg Wilhelm Friedrich Hegel had called the dialectic: that is, on a supposedly in-built logic of contradictions whereby forms clashed with their opposites, so that historical progress was achieved through negation and transcendence (*Aufhebung*). Thus, capitalism, because of its inherent contradictions, would give way, dialectically, to socialism. More broadly, Marx argued that history proceeded in stages—feudalism, capitalism, socialism, and communism (when everything would be plentiful)—and that the decisive motor was classes, such as the proletariat, who would push aside capitalism, just as the bourgeoisie had supposedly pushed aside feudalism and feudal lords. The proletariat in Marx became the bearer of Hegel's universal Reason, a supposed "universal class because its sufferings are universal"—in other words, not because it worked in factories per se, but because the proletariat was a victim, a victim turned redeemer.

Marx intended his analysis of society to serve as the leading edge in efforts to change it. In 1864, he joined with a diverse group of influential leftists in London, including anarchists, to establish a transnational body for uniting the workers and radicals of the world called the International Workingmen's Association

(1864–76). By the 1870s, critics on the left had attacked Marx's vision for the organization—to "centralize all instruments of production in the hands of the State, i.e., of the proletariat organized as the ruling class"—as authoritarian, provoking recriminations and splits. After Marx's death in 1883 in London (where he was buried), various socialist and labor parties founded a "Second International" in Paris (1889). In place of the "bourgeois-republican" "Marseillaise" of the 1789 French Revolution, the Second International adopted "L'Internationale"— the first stanza of which begins "Arise, ye wretched of the earth"—as the socialist anthem. The Second International also adopted the red flag, which had appeared in France as a stark contrast to the white flag of the Bourbon dynasty and of the counterrevolutionaries who wanted to restore the monarchy after its overthrow. Despite the French song and symbolism, however, German Social Democrats— devotees of the deceased Marx—came to dominate the Second International. Subjects of the Russian empire, many of them in European exile, would become the chief rivals to the Germans in the Second International.

In imperial Russia, the *idea* of socialism had taken hold nearly a half century before a proletariat had appeared and owed its phenomenal spread to the introspection of a self-described intelligentsia. The latter—literally, the intelligence of the realm—were educated yet frustrated individuals who initially came from the gentry, but over time also emerged from commoners granted access to high schools and universities. Russia's intelligentsia absorbed the same German idealist philosophy that Marx had, only without the heavy materialism that came from British political economy. Organized in small circles (Russian *kruzhok,* German *Kreis*), Russian socialists defended the dignity of all by generalizing from a sense of their own violated dignity. Alexander Herzen and Mikhail Bakunin, two mid-nineteenth-century sons of great privilege who knew each other, led the way. Each believed that in Russia the peasantry could serve as the basis for socialism because of the institution of the commune.[46] Communes furnished a collective buffer against frosts, droughts, and other challenges through periodic redistribution among households of land allotments (in separated strips) as well as other means.[47] Many peasants did not live under the commune, especially in the east (Siberia) as well as the west and south (Ukraine), where there had been no serfdom. But in the central regions of the Russian empire, the commune's powers were strengthened by the 1860s serf emancipation.[48] Because peasants in communes held no private property as individuals—either before or after emancipation—thinkers such as Herzen and Bakunin imagined the empire's peasants to be inherently socialist and therefore, they argued, in Russia socialism could appear essentially *before* capitalism. Armed with just such thinking in the aftermath of the 1860s serf emancipation, self-described Populists (*narodniki*), descended upon Russia's villages to lift peasants out of backwardness.

The Populists were in a hurry: capitalism had begun to spread and the Populists feared that the freed serfs were being turned into wage slaves, with the exploitative bourgeoisie taking the place of serf owners. At the same time, the much idealized egalitarianism of village life was thought to be under threat by the appearance of the kulak, or rich peasant.[49] But even poor peasants met the outside would-be tutors with hostility. After Populism's tactic of agitation failed to foster mass peasant uprising, some turned to political terror to spark mass uprising in cities (which would also fail). Other radicals, however, shifted their hopes from peasants to the incipient proletariat, thanks to the growing influence of Marx in Russia. Georgi Plekhanov (b. 1857), the father of Marxism in Russia, attacked the Populist argument that Russia could obviate capitalism because it possessed some supposed indigenous tendency (the peasant commune) toward socialism. Plekhanov went into European exile in 1880 (for what would turn out to be thirty-seven years), but his works in the 1880s—*Socialism and Political Struggle* (1883) and *Our Differences* (1885)—filtered back into Russia and made the case that historical stages could not be skipped: Only capitalism made socialism possible, and therefore Russia, too, would have to have a "bourgeois revolution" first, before a socialist revolution, even if the proletariat had to help the bourgeoisie achieve the bourgeois revolution.[50] This was what Marx had said. Late in life, though, Marx did seem to admit that England's experience, from which he had generalized, might not be universal; that the bourgeoisie might not be uniquely progressive (in historical terms); and that Russia might be able to avoid the full-blown capitalist stage.[51] This apparent heresy had emerged from Marx's reliance on the Russian economist Nikolai F. Danielson, who served as his confidant and supplied him with books on Russia. Still, the late Marx's quasi-Populist views on Russia were not widely known (they would not appear in Russian until December 1924). Plekhanov's Marxist critique of Populism held intellectual sway.

Danielson himself fed this dominance by collaborating on a Russian translation of *Das Kapital,* Marx's three-volume magnum opus, which appeared in the 1890s and attracted a fair audience of readers—including the future Stalin. In 1896, with publication of the third volume, the hesitant Russian censor finally recognized it as a "scientific" work, meaning it could circulate in libraries and be offered for sale.[52] By this time, Marxist political economy had appeared as an academic subject at some Russian universities, and even the turn-of-the-century director of one of the empire's largest textile plants in Moscow collected a vast trove of Marxiana.[53] Russia was then a country of 1 million proletarians and more than 80 million peasants. But Marxism displaced Populism as "the answer."

Marxism had spread to the Russian-controlled Caucasus as well, also beginning in the 1880s. It came partly from the leftist movements in Europe, via Russia, but also from the ferment in Russian Poland, whose influence reached Georgia through Poles sent into exile in the Caucasus or Georgians who studied in tsarist Poland. Georgian Marxism was also spurred by generational revolt. Noe Jordania emerged as the Plekhanov of the Caucasus. He had been born in 1869 into a noble family of western Georgia, attended the Tiflis Theological Seminary, and along with others like Silva Jibladze, the Tiflis seminarian who had slapped the Russian rector's face in 1884, established the Third Group (Mesame Dasi) in 1892. They aimed to contrast their avowedly Marxist association with the conservative Populism of Ilya Chavchavadze (First Group) and the national (classical) liberalism of Giorgi Tsereteli (Second Group). Traveling in Europe, Jordania had come to know Karl Kautsky, the Prague-born leading German Social Democrat, as well as Plekhanov. In 1898, at the invitation of Giorgi Tsereteli, Jordania took over the editorship of the periodical *Kvali*.[54] Under him, *Kvali* became the Russian empire's first legal Marxist periodical, stressing self-government, development, and Georgian cultural autonomy within Russian borders (reminiscent of the Austrian Social Democrats in the multinational Habsburg realm). Before long, Marxist literature—including 100 mimeographed copies of *The Communist Manifesto* translated from Russian into Georgian—would be smuggled into Tiflis and bolster the widening circles of young Caucasus radicals such as Jughashvili.[55]

Tiflis became their organizing laboratory. The city of petty traders, porters, and artisans, surrounded by a restive countryside, had 9,000 registered craftsmen, mostly in one- and two-person artels. Around 95 percent of its "factories" were workshops with fewer than ten laborers. But the big railroad depots and workshops (which had opened in 1883), together with several industrial tobacco plants and the Adelkhanov Tannery, did assemble a proletariat of at least 3,000 (up to 12,500 in the province as a whole). Tiflis railway workers had walked off the job in 1887 and 1889, and in mid-December 1898 they did so again, for five days—a major strike that Lado Ketskhoveli and other workers organized. Jughash-vili was in the seminary during that Monday-to-Saturday workweek job action.[56] But thanks to Ketskhoveli, Jughashvili's seminary student circle—which he had just come to control by May 1898—broadened to include half a dozen or so pro-letarians at the Tiflis railway depot and workshops. They usually met on Sun-days, in Tiflis' Nakhalovka (Nadzaladevi) neighborhood, which was bereft of sidewalks, streetlights, sewers, or running water.[57] Jughashvili lectured workers on "the mechanics of the capitalist system," and "the need to engage in political struggle to improve the workers' position."[58] Through Lado, he met the firebrand Silva Jibladze, who seems to have played a role in teaching Jughashvili how to agitate among the workers and in assigning him new "circles."[59] Jibladze may also have been the person to introduce Jughashvili to Noe Jordania.

Sometime in 1898, Jughashvili went to call upon Jordania at *Kvali*, just as Jughashvili had once approached the aristocrat Chavchavadze at the periodical *Iveria* (which then published his poetry). Gentle and professorial, the aristocrat Jordania, who projected little of a radical countenance, later recalled that his brash young visitor told him, "I have decided to quit the seminary to propagate your ideas among the workers." Jordania claims he quizzed the young Jughashvili on politics and society, then advised him to return to the seminary and to study Marxism more. The condescending advice was not well received. "I'll think about it," the future Stalin is said to have replied.[60] In August 1898, Jughashvili did join the Third Group of Georgian Marxists, following in Lado Ketskhoveli's footsteps.

The Third Group, technically, was not a political party, which were illegal in tsarist Russia, but in March 1898, in a private log house in the outskirts of Minsk, a small town in the empire's Pale of Settlement, a founding "congress" of the Marxist-inspired, German copycat Russian Social Democratic Workers' Party (RSDRP)—the future ruling party of the Soviet Union—took place. This was the second attempt (a previous effort to found the party, in Kiev, had failed). The Jewish Labor Bund (or Federation), which had been established five months ear-lier, provided logistical support for the Minsk gathering. There were a mere nine attendees, and just one actual worker (leading some present to object to their prospective party's name ["Workers'"].* The year 1898 happened to mark the

---

*Boris Eidelman (the main organizer), Stepan Radchenko, Aaron Kramer, Aleksandr Vannovsky, Abram Mutnik, Kazimir Petrusevich, Pavel Tuchapsky, Natan Vigdorchik, and Shmuel Kats (the sole worker).

fiftieth anniversary of Marx and Engels's *Communist Manifesto,* and the delegates, during the three-day gathering, approved their own manifesto, a withering denunciation of "the bourgeoisie," which they decided needed to be redrafted in order to be circulated, a task given to Pyotr Struve (b. 1870), the son of the Perm governor and an imperial law school graduate.[61] ("The autocracy created in the soul, thoughts, and habits of educated Russians a psychology and tradition of state apostasy," Struve later explained.)[62] The tsarist political police knew nothing of the Minsk congress, but the attendees were already on watch lists and soon most were arrested.[63] Vladimir Ulyanov, better known as Lenin, learned of the 1898 Minsk congress while off in Eastern Siberia serving a three-year term of internal exile, following fifteen months in prison, for disseminating revolutionary leaflets and plotting to assassinate the tsar. Minsk would turn out to be the only prerevolutionary RSDRP congress held on Russian empire territory.[64] But soon, in European exile, a group of socialist exiles that included Plekhanov, his two satellites Pinchas Borutsch (aka Pavel Axelrod) and Vera Zasulich as well as the upstarts Julius "Yuly" Tsederbaum (aka Martov) and Lenin, published a Russian-language newspaper, initially out of Stuttgart in December 1900. Aiming to unite Russia's revolutionaries around a Marxist program, it was called *Iskra* (*Spark*), as in "from a spark a fire will ignite."[65]

## AGITATOR, TEACHER

The future Stalin (like Lenin) would date his "party membership" from 1898. Back at the seminary, in fall and winter 1898–99, his infractions accumulated: arriving late at morning prayers; violating discipline at liturgy (evidently leaving early, complaining of leg pain while standing so long); arriving three days late from a leave in Gori; failing to greet a teacher (the former Inspector Murakhovsky); laughing in church; denouncing a search; leaving Vespers. Jughashvili received reprimands and had to do time in the seminary's solitary-confinement cell. On January 18, 1899, he was forbidden to leave the premises for the city proper for one month, evidently in connection with a discovery of a large cache of forbidden books. (Another student caught was expelled.)[66] More consequentially, following the Easter break, Jughashvili failed to sit his year-end exams. A May 29, 1899, entry in a Georgian exarchate official organ noted of Jughashvili: "dismissed [*uvolniaetsia*] from seminary for failure to appear at the examination for unknown reason."[67] This dismissal, with its enigmatic phrase "unknown reason," has been the subject of varying interpretations, including Stalin's own (subsequent) boast that he was "kicked out of an Orthodox theological seminary for Marxist propaganda."[68] But on more than one occasion, before he became ruler, he would state that he had suddenly been assessed a fee and could not pay it, and that going into his final year he faced the loss of his partial state financial support. Each time, however, he neglected to specify why he lost his state scholarship.[69] There also seems to be no extant indication that he appealed for financial help to Egnatashvili or another benefactor. And no such failure to pay was recorded in the formal expulsion resolution. Still, his straitened circumstances were well known (many times Jughashvili had implored the rector for financial assistance), and it could be that the disciplinarians, led by Inspector Abashidze, contrived to rid themselves of Jughashvili by exploiting his poverty.[70]

Four years after Jughashvili's 1899 expulsion, Abashidze would be promoted—ordained a bishop, a clear stamp of approval for his work.[71] In fact, the seminary's Russification policies had failed. Already in 1897–98, the Caucasus authorities seem to have concluded that the Tiflis seminary was harming Russia's interests and should be closed (according to the memoirs of one teacher). Rather than closing it right away, however, the ecclesiastics decided to institute a purge of the ethnic Georgian students.[72] The seminary forwarded lists of transgressing students to the gendarmerie.[73] In September 1899, forty to forty-five seminarians were forced out "at their own request." Soon, Georgian students would disappear from the seminary entirely. (The seminary would be altogether shuttered in 1907.)[74] Jughashvili could have been expelled as part of the large group in fall 1899. But Abashidze's vendetta may explain why Jughashvili's expulsion was done individually instead. Even so, we are left with the curiosity that no reason was given for Jughashvili's failure to sit his exams, and that he apparently did not petition to resit them. One possible clue: the year Jughashvili left the seminary he may have fathered a baby girl—Praskovya "Pasha" Georgievna Mikhailovskaya, who, in her adulthood, resembled him strongly.[75] Jughashvili's student circle was renting a hovel in Tiflis at the foot of holy Mount Mtatsminda for conspiratorial meetings, but the young men could also have used it for trysts.[76] Later, Stalin would place a letter he received about the paternity in his archive. If such circumstantial evidence can be accepted, that might explain why Jughashvili faced the loss of his state scholarship and did not appeal to resit his exams or to have his state funding reinstated.[77]

But biographers have noted further curiosities. Upon dismissal, Jughashvili owed the state more than 600 rubles—a fantastic sum—for failing to enter the priesthood or otherwise serve the Orthodox Church (or at least become a school-teacher). The rectorate wrote him a letter suggesting he become a teacher at a lower-level church school, but he did not take up the offer; yet the seminary does not appear to have employed the secular authorities to force him to make good his financial obligation.[78] And then this: in October 1899, without having paid the money he owed, Jughashvili requested and received an official seminary document testifying to his completion of four years of study (since his fifth remained incomplete). The expellee was assigned an overall "excellent" (5) for conduct.[79] These curiosities, in which, ordinarily, payment of a bribe would be suspected, may or may not be meaningful. When all is said and done, the future Stalin may have just outgrown the seminary, being two years older than his cohort and already deeply involved in Lado's revolutionary activities. Jughashvili was not going to join the priesthood, and a seminary recommendation to continue his studies at university seemed unlikely. The expulsion, Jughashvili supposedly confided to one schoolmate, was a "blow," but if so, he did not fight to stay.[80]

Jughashvili remained a book person, and more and more imagined himself in the role of teacher. He spent the summer of 1899 not in Gori but, again, in the village of Tsromi, with his buddy Mikho Davitashvili, a priest's son. They were visited by Lado Ketskhoveli. The police searched the Davitashvili's household but, it seems, the family had been forewarned, and the search turned up nothing. Still, Mikho was among the large group who did not continue at the seminary in September 1899 "at his own request."[81] Jughashvili would add many of the newly expelled boys from the seminary to the self-study circle he led.[82] He also continued to meet with and give lectures to workers. Then, in December 1899, not long after he had obtained his official seminary four-year study document—which he may have sought for employment purposes—Jughashvili landed a paying job at the Tiflis Meteorological Observatory, a state agency. It was a stroke of luck, but also linked to his association with the Ketskhovelis: Vano Ketskhoveli, Lado's younger brother, worked at the observatory and Jughashvili had already moved in with Vano in October 1899; a bit later, conveniently, one of the six employees left.[83] Jughashvili got paid relatively good money: 20–25 rubles per month (at a time when the average wage in the Caucasus was 14–24 rubles for skilled labor, and 10–13 for unskilled).[84] Besides shoveling snow in winter and sweeping dust in summer, he recorded temperatures and barometric pressures hourly. The future Stalin also spent a great deal of time reading and he became a dedicated agitator. When he had the night shift, during the day he could read up on Marxism or lecture groups of workers, which became his absolute passion.

Further inspiration came from questioning the socialist establishment. In solidarity with Lado Ketskhoveli, who sometimes hid overnight at the observatory, Jughashvili looked askance at Jordania's *Kvali*. As a legal publication, *Kvali* had to pass censorship and show restraint, offering a "diluted Marxism" that was anathema to younger radicals. *Kvali*'s feuilletons, Ketskhoveli and Jughashvili argued, "did nothing" for actual workers. Lado dreamed about starting his own illegal periodical and recruiting more young propagandists like Jughashvili.[85] Jordania and his supporters opposed an illicit periodical, fearing it would cast a shadow over their legal one. When Jughashvili wrote a critique of *Kvali*'s seeming docility and inaction, Jordania and the editors refused to publish it. Word got back to Jibladze and Jordania that Jughashvili was agitating against *Kvali* behind their backs.[86] But whatever the bad personal blood, a genuine difference in tactics was at stake: the future Stalin, in sync with Lado, insisted that the Marxist movement shift from educational work to direct action. Lado showed the way by organizing a strike of the city's horse-drawn tram drivers for January 1, 1900. The drivers, for their thirteen-hour workday, earned 90 kopecks, part of which was taken back in dubious workplace "fines." Their walkout briefly brought the capital to a halt, and forced a wage increase. *That was power.* There were risks, however, as Jordania and Jibladze had noted. One of the tram workers informed on Lado and in mid-January 1900 he barely escaped the Tiflis gendarmes, fleeing to Baku.[87] That same month, Jughashvili was arrested—for the first time. He had just turned twenty-one, legal age, a few weeks before.

The nominal charge was that his father, Beso, owed back taxes in Didi Lilo, the village Beso had left more than three decades earlier without, however, formally exiting the village rolls. Jughashvili was incarcerated in the Metekhi Prison fortress—the one on the cliff that he had walked past at age eleven on his way to work with his father at the Adelkhanov Tannery. Mikho Davitashvili and other friends seem to have assembled the money and paid off Beso's outstanding village debt, so Jughashvili was released. Keke arrived from Gori and, for a time, insisted on staying with him in his room at the observatory—this had to be embarrassing. She "lived in permanent anxiety over her son," recalled a neighbor and distant relative (Maria Kitiashvili). "I remember well how she would come over to our place and cry about her dear Soso—Where is he now, did the gendarmes arrest him?"[88] Soon, Keke herself would be monitored by the police and occasionally summoned for questioning. It remains unclear why the gendarmes did not arrest Beso, who was living in Tiflis (Iosif received handmade boots from his father on occasion).[89] Nor is it clear why Jughashvili was not arrested for his own debt to the state from the seminary scholarship. Police incompetence cannot be ruled out. But the arrest for Beso's debt does seem like a pretext, a warning to a young radical or perhaps a maneuver to mark him: Jughashvili was photographed for the police archive. He returned to his job at the observatory, but also continued his illegal political lectures and remained under surveillance. "According to agent information, Jughashvili is a Social Democrat and conducts meetings with workers," the police noted. "Surveillance has established that he behaves in a highly cautious manner, always looking back while walking."[90]

## UNDERGROUND

Amid the cock fighting, banditry, and prostitution (political and sexual) in the Caucasus, illegal socialist agitation hardly stood out, at least initially. As late as 1900, the overwhelming preponderance of Tiflis inhabitants under police surveillance were Armenians, who were watched for fear they maintained links to their coethnics across the border in the Ottoman empire. But just a few years later, most of the police dossiers on "political" suspects were of Georgians and Social Democrats—238 of them, including Jughashvili's.[91] On March 21, 1901, the police raided the Tiflis Observatory premises. Although Jughashvili was absent when the search of his and other employees' possessions took place, he may have been observing from not far away, been spotted and had his person searched, too.[92] If so, the police did not arrest him, perhaps because they wanted to keep him under further surveillance, to uncover others. Be that as it may, the future Stalin's meteorological career was over. He went underground, permanently.

Jughashvili now had no means of support, other than being paid for some private tutoring and sponging off colleagues, girlfriends, and the proletarians he sought to lead. He threw himself into conspiratorial activities, like establishing safe houses and opening illegal presses to help strikes and May Day marches. May Day had been established as a holiday by socialists around the world in order to commemorate the Haymarket riots in Chicago in 1886, when police had fired on strikers who sought an eight-hour workday. In Tiflis, May Day marches with red flags had been initiated in 1898 by railway workers. Held outside the city proper, the first three marches drew 25 people (1898), 75 (1899), then 400 (1900). For May Day 1901, Jughashvili was involved in plans for a bold, risky march right down Golovin Prospect, in the heart of Tiflis. He agitated among the city's largest concentration of workers, the Tiflis Main Railway Shops. The tsarist police made preemptive arrests and arrayed mounted Cossacks with sabers and long whips, but at least 2,000 workers and onlookers defied them, chanting "Down with autocracy!" After a forty-five-minute melee involving hand-to-hand combat, the streets of the Caucasus capital were soaked with blood.[93]

Russian Social Democrats were exiled for revolutionary activity by the tsarist police to the Caucasus—where, of course, they helped foment revolutionary activity—and Jughashvili met Mikhail Kalinin, among others.[94] But the twenty-six-year-old militant Ketskhoveli remained a key link to the imperial Russian Social Democrats and a role model for Jughashvili. Underground in Baku, Lado did start up a Georgian-language competitor to *Kvali,* christened *Brdzola* (the *Struggle*), a rowdy broadsheet that began appearing in September 1901. Referring to the bloody 1901 May Day clash in Tiflis, an (unsigned) essay in *Brdzola* (November-December 1901) defiantly rationalized that "the sacrifices we make today in street demonstration will be compensated a hundredfold," adding that "every militant who falls in the struggle or is torn from our ranks [by arrest] rouses hundreds of new fighters."[95] The illegal printing press, which Ketskhoveli established along with Avel Yenukidze, Leonid Krasin, and other Social Democrats in Baku, was hidden in the city's Muslim quarter and code-named "Nina"—Russian for Nino (the female patron saint of Georgia). It also published reprints of the recently founded Russian-language Marxist émigré newspaper *Iskra,* original copies of which were smuggled from Central Europe to Baku via Tabriz (Iran) on horseback.[96] Nina very soon became the largest underground Social Democrat printing press in the entire Russian empire, and would confound the tsarist police (from 1901 to 1907).[97] It was through the Nina printing press, as well as Lado's *Brdzola,* that the young Jughashvili became acquainted with the ideas of Lenin, who wrote many of the blistering (unsigned) editorials in the thirteen issues of *Iskra* that had appeared by the end of 1901.[98]

Ketskhoveli, obviating Jordania, afforded Jughashvili direct access to the pulse of Russian Social Democracy, helping him become an informed Marxist and militant street agitator. The latter persona was grafted onto Jughashvili's already deep-set autodidact disposition and his heartfelt vocation to enlighten the masses. From personal experience, however, Jughashvili would lament that workers often did not appreciate the importance of studying and self-improvement. During a meeting on November 11, 1901, of the newly formed Tiflis Committee of the Russian Social Democratic Workers' Party, he championed not the worker members but the demi-intelligentsia members—that is, types like himself and Lado. He argued that inviting workers to join the party was incompatible with "conspiracy" and would expose members to arrest. Lenin had propagated this vision in the pages of *Iskra*. He also wrote a wide-ranging pamphlet *What Is to Be Done?* (March 1902), a self-defense against a slashing attack (in September 1901) by other Marxists in the *Iskra* group. Lenin's advocacy for an intelligentsia-centric party would soon come to divide the *Iskra* group.[99] At the November 1901 Tiflis Committee meeting, meanwhile, a majority of Caucasus Social Democrats voted to admit workers to the party, against Jughashvili's Lenin-like urgings.[100] At the same time, the Tiflis Committee decided to send Jughashvili to agitate among workers in the Black Sea port of Batum.[101]

Batum was a high-profile assignment. Just twelve miles from the Ottoman border, the port had been seized from the Ottomans with the rest of Islamic Adjara (Ajaria) in the 1877–78 war and, after being joined to Russia's Transcaucasus Railway, became the terminal for exporting Russia's Caspian Sea oil. The world's longest pipeline from Baku to Batum was under construction (it would open in 1907) and its sponsors—the Swedish Nobel brothers of dynamite fame, the French Rothschild brothers of banking fame, and the Armenian magnate Alexander Mantashyan (b. 1842), known in Russified form as Mantashov—endeavored to break U.S. Standard Oil's near-monopoly in supplying kerosene to Europe.[102] Jughashvili, too, sought to ride the oil boom, for leftist purposes. (Soon *Iskra,* along with other Russian Marxist literature, began arriving there by boat from Marseilles.) The port city already had "Sunday Schools" for workers, established by Nikoloz "Karlo" Chkheidze (b. 1864), one of the founders of the Third Group, and Isidor Ramishvili (b. 1859), both close comrades of Noe Jordania.

The younger Jughashvili immersed himself in the workers' milieu, where he "spoke without an orator's refinement," a hostile fellow Georgian later recalled. "His words were imbued with power, determination. He spoke with sarcasm, irony, hammering away with crude severities," but then "apologized, explaining that he was speaking the language of the proletariat who were not taught subtle manners or aristocratic eloquence."[103] Jughashvili's worker pose became real when an acquaintance got him hired at the Rothschild oil company. There, on

February 25, 1902, amid slackening customer demand, 389 workers (of around 900) were let go with just two weeks' notice, provoking a total walkout two days later.[104] Mass arrests ensued. Secretly, the Caucasus military chief confided to the local governors that Social Democrat "propaganda" was finding "receptive soil" because of the workers' dreadful living and laboring conditions.[105] Moreover, the policy of deporting protesting workers to their native villages was only magnifying the rebellious waves in the Georgian countryside.[106] On March 9, a crowd carrying cobblestones sought to free comrades at the transit prison awaiting deportation. "Brothers, don't be afraid," one imprisoned worker shouted, "they can't shoot, for God's sake free us." The police opened fire, killing at least fourteen.[107]

The "Batum massacre" reverberated around the Russian empire, but for Jughashvili—who had distributed incendiary leaflets—it brought arrest on April 5, 1901. A police report characterized him as "of no specific occupation and unknown residence," but "a teacher of the workers."[108] Whether Jughashvili had any influence on worker militancy is unclear. But he was charged with "incitement to disorder and insubordination against higher authority."[109] Batum also set in motion the profound bad blood that would haunt Jughashvili in Caucasus Social Democrat circles. To replace him there, the Tiflis Committee sent David "Mokheve" Khartishvili. Back in Tiflis, Mokheve had argued that only workers ought to be full members of the Tiflis Committee, denying such status to intelligentsia (like Jughashvili). Once in Batum, Mokheve accused the imprisoned Jughashvili of having deliberately provoked the police massacre.[110] While Jughashvili was in prison, however, his Batum loyalists resisted Mokheve's authority. A police report—drawn from informants—observed that "Jughashvili's despotism has enraged many people and the organization has split."[111] It was during this imprisonment that Jughashvili began regularly using the pseudonym Koba, "avenger of injustice."[112] Members of the Tiflis Committee got angry at him. They would likely have been even angrier had they known that while wallowing for a year in the Batum remand prison in 1902–3, the future Stalin twice begged the Caucasus governor-general for release, citing "a worsening, choking cough and the helpless position of my elderly mother, abandoned by her husband twelve years ago and seeing me as her sole support in life."[113] (Keke also petitioned the governor-general for her son in January 1903.) Such groveling, if it were to become known, could have tainted a revolutionary's reputation. A prison doctor examined Jughashvili, but the gendarmerie opposed clemency.[114] Fifteen months after his arrest, in July 1903, Koba Jughashvili was sentenced by administrative fiat to three years' exile in the Mongol-speaking Buryat lands of Eastern Siberia.

Outside the bars of his cattle car, in November 1903, the future Stalin likely saw real winter for the first time—snow-blanketed earth, completely iced rivers. As a Georgian in Siberia, Koba the avenger nearly froze to death on his first escape attempt. But already by January 1904 he had managed to elude the village police chief, make it forty miles to the railhead, and arrive illegally all the way back in Tiflis.[115] He would tell three different stories about his escape, including one about hitching a ride with a deliveryman whom he plied with vodka. In fact, the future Stalin appears to have used a real or forged gendarmerie identity card—a trick that compounded the suspicions about his quick escape. (Was he a police collaborator?)[116] During his absence from Tiflis, there had been a congress to unify the South Caucasus Social Democrats and create a "union committee" of nine members; Jughashvili would be added to it.[117] Even so, his former Batum committee shunned him. He was associated with the police bloodbath and political split there, and after his quick return, he was distrusted as a possible agent provocateur.[118] Wanted by the police, he roamed: back to Gori (where he got new false papers), then Batum and Tiflis. His sometime landlady and mistress in the Batum underground, Natasha Kirtava-Sikharulidze, then twenty-two, had refused to accompany him to Tiflis; he cursed her.[119] Police surveillance in the Caucasus capital was intense and Jughashvili changed residences at least eight times in a month. He met up again with Lev Rozenfeld, better known as Kamenev, who helped him find a hideaway. One safe-house apartment belonged to Sergei Alliluyev, a skilled machinist who had been sent to Tiflis, hired on at the railway workshops, and married. The family home of the Alliluyevs (Stalin's future second father-in-law) in the Tiflis outskirts became a Social Democrat meeting center, providing refuge for agitators who, for a time, escaped arrest and deportation.[120]

Kamenev would also give Jughashvili a copy of the Russian translation of Machiavelli's *The Prince* (1869), although Russia's revolutionaries hardly needed the Italian political theorist.[121] Sergei Nechayev (1847–82), the son of a serf and the founder of the secret society the People's Retaliation, had observed in 1871, "Everything that allows the triumph of the revolution is moral, and everything that stands in its way is immoral."[122]

SUCH WERE THE LADO-INSPIRED early revolutionary years (1898–1903) in the life of the future dictator—a vocation as an agitator and teacher of the workers; a bloody confrontational May Day strategy in Tiflis; an illegal Marxist press as a rival to a legal one; accusations of provoking a police massacre and splitting the party in Batum; a long, rough prison stint in western Georgia; privately groveling before the Caucasus governor-general; a brief, freezing Siberian exile; suspicions of police collaboration; a life on the run. Almost in the blink of an eye, a pious boy from Gori, Jughashvili had gone from smuggling Victor Hugo into the Tiflis seminary to becoming a participant—albeit a completely obscure one—in a global socialist movement. That was largely thanks not to some Caucasus outlaw culture, but to tsarist Russia's profound injustices and repression. Open confrontation with the regime had been willfully pursued by young hotheads who imagined they were plumbing the depths of the autocracy's intransigence. Soon, however, this combative, risky approach would be adopted even by those Marxist socialists who had long resisted it, men such as Jordania and Jibladze of *Kvali*. The tsarist political system and conditions in the empire promoted militancy. In the Caucasus, as in the empire as a whole, leftists essentially leaped the stage of agitating for trade unionism—which remained illegal in Russia far later than in Western Europe—and went straight to violent overthrow of the abusive order.[123]

Even officialdom showed awareness (in internal correspondence) of the strong impetus to revolt: the factory regime was beyond brutal; landowners and their enforcers treated postemancipation peasants as chattel; any attempt to alleviate such conditions was treated as treason.[124] "First one becomes convinced that existing conditions are wrong and unjust," Stalin would later explain, persuasively. "Then one resolves to do the best one can to remedy them. Under the tsar's regime, any attempt genuinely to help the people put one outside the pale of the law; one found oneself hunted and hounded as a revolutionist."[125] If living under tsarism made him, like many other young people, a street-fighting revolutionary, Jughashvili also styled himself an enlightener—so far, almost exclusively in oral form—as well as an outsider and an underdog, an up-and-comer who bucked not only the tsarist police but also the uncomprehending revolutionary establishment under Jordania.[126] In seeking to lead protesting workers, Jughashvili had mixed success. Still, he did prove adept at cultivating a tight-knit group of young men like himself. "Koba distinguished himself from all other Bolsheviks," one hostile Georgian émigré recalled, "by his unquestionably greater energy, indefatigable capacity for hard work, unconquerable lust for power, and above all his enormous, particularistic organizational talent" aimed at forging "disciples through whom he could . . . hold the whole organization in his grasp."[127]

Before Jughashvili was launched on his own, however, Lado Ketskhoveli exemplified for him the daring professional revolutionary—battling injustice, living underground off his wits, defying tsarist police.[128] Leonid Krasin judged Lado an organizational genius. Sergei Alliluyev would deem Lado the most magnetic personality of the Caucasus socialist movement. But in spring 1902, *Brdzola* had ceased publication after just four issues, following extensive arrests of the Baku Social Democrats. (Its rival *Kvali* would soon be shuttered as well.) In September 1902, Ketskhoveli himself had been arrested and incarcerated in Tiflis' Metekhi Prison fortress. Distraught over the arrests of his comrades, Lado may have precipitated his own arrest by giving his real name during a police search of someone else's apartment. Standing by the extralarge cell embrasures and shouting out to fellow inmates and passersby, Lado, "a rebel [*buntar*]," "feared and hated" by the prison administration, appears to have baited the prison guards daily. A note he tried to smuggle out of Metekhi may have gotten Avel Yenukidze arrested. In August 1903, when Lado refused to stand down from the window, a prison guard, after a warning, shot and killed Lado, age twenty-seven, through the outside window of his locked cell.[129] The story would be told that Lado had been defiantly shouting "Down with the autocracy!" He seems to have been willing, perhaps even eager, to die for the cause.

Later, Stalin would not erase Lado's independent revolutionary exploits or existence, even as almost everyone else connected to the dictator at one time or another would be airbrushed.[130] (Lado's birth house would be included in newsreels featuring Soviet Georgia.)[131] The earliness of Lado's martyrdom certainly helped in this regard. But that circumstance highlights the fact that Iosif Jughashvili himself could have suffered the same fate as his first mentor: early death in a tsarist prison.

## CHAPTER 3

# TSARISM'S MOST
# DANGEROUS ENEMY

The Russian empire is everywhere in ferment. Unrest and apprehension prevail in all classes. This applies equally to labor, students, the nobility, including the highest Court society, industrialists, merchants, shopkeepers, and, last but not least, the peasants . . . The only proven method of dealing with this situation, which is often proposed abroad, is the granting of a constitution; if this were done here, the consequences would almost certainly be revolution.

Austro-Hungarian attaché in St. Petersburg,
memo to Vienna, 1902[1]

RUSSIAN EURASIA—104 NATIONALITIES SPEAKING 146 languages, as enumerated in the 1897 census—was the world's most spectacular kaleidoscope, but in truth, empire everywhere presented a crazy patchwork.[2] The key to empire in Russia, too, was not the multinationalism per se but the political system. The onset of Russia's modern state administration is usually attributed to Peter I, or Peter the Great (r. 1682–1725), even though major changes attributed to him often had roots in his father's and even his grandfather's reign.[3] Peter is also credited with Westernization, even though he distrusted the West and used it as a means to an end: namely, the source of technical skills.[4] Peter, whose mother was a (distant) Tatar descendant, did render Russia even more European culturally. Institutionally, he regularized a state administration on the Swedish model. And he introduced a Table of Ranks, a ladder of incentives to enhance competition for honor and privilege and to open state service to new men. By detaching status from birthright—or to put it another way, by making birthright a reward conferred by the state—Peter extended the governing authority's capacity. But he undercut all his own state building by involving himself in everything. As one foreign ambassador observed, Peter "finds daily, more and more, that in the whole realm not one of his blood relatives and boyars can be found to whom he can entrust an important office. He is therefore forced to take over the heavy burden of the realm himself, and to put his hand to a new and different government, pushing back the boyars (whom he calls disloyal dogs)."[5] In 1722, Peter unilaterally upgraded himself to "Emperor" (Imperator), a claim of parity with the (nonreigning) Holy Roman emperor. (He opted for "Emperor of All the Russias" rather than a proposed "Emperor of the East.") Above all, Peter built up his own persona, partly via court hazing rituals—dildo debauches, mock weddings—which accentuated the centrality of and access to the autocrat's person.[6] The drive for a strong state became conflated with an intense personalism.

Peter's method of state building also reinforced the circumstance whereby Russia's elites remained joined at the hip to the autocratic power. Russia never developed a fully fledged aristocracy with its own corporate institutions that would, eventually, decapitate the absolutism (although, finally, in 1730 some nobles in Russia did try).[7] True, Russia's gentry accumulated as much wealth as their counterparts in Austria or even England. And unlike in Austria or England, the Russian gentry also produced cultural figures of world distinction—Lermontov, Tolstoy, Turgenev, Glinka, Tchaikovsky, Rachmaninov, Skryabin, Mussorgsky. Further, Russia's gentry was an open estate: even bastards (such as Alexander Herzen) could attain noble status. But a still greater difference was that England's aristocracy acquired political experience as a ruling class in a constitutional monarchy. Russia's serf owners were all-powerful on their estates, but, ultimately, they lived under the autocrat's sufferance. Elite status in Russia was predicated on rendering service in exchange for rewards—which could be withdrawn.[8] In addition to *serving the sovereign* by employment in the state, Russian nobles had to work constantly just to maintain their standing in the hierarchy. True, most of Russia's privileged families managed to survive through the centuries under the autocrats. Still, not all Russia's elite clans did survive, and the difference between prosperous endurance versus exile or imprisonment could seem arbitrary.[9] Russia's high and mighty needed still higher-placed patrons to protect their property holdings and, sometimes, their very persons.

Multitudes of observers, including Karl Marx, asserted that "modern Russia is but a metamorphosis of Muscovy."[10] They were wrong: the post-Petrine Russian state and its capital, St. Petersburg, more closely resembled European absolutism than ancient Muscovy. But that circumstance was obscured. Russia's "soulless" pushers of paper, "brainless" bootlickers, and "craven" collectors of state decorations took an immortal drubbing in belles lettres, nowhere better than in Nikolai Gogol's *Inspector General*. Court circles too mocked Russia's parvenu "Your Excellencies." Aside from these memoirs and Gogol's sublime pen, which continue to beguile historians, we can find other important voices. Prince Boris A. Vasilchikov, for example, an aristocrat elected to the local governing council (*zemstvo*) near his estate, and later the governor of Pskov, had shared the contempt for imperial officialdom before he got inside. "During my two years' service as a minister I gained a very high opinion of the qualities of Petersburg officialdom," he wrote. "The level of personnel of the Petersburg chancelleries and ministries was extremely high as regards knowledge, experience and fulfillment of official duties . . . besides this, I was struck by their immense capacity for hard work."[11] To be sure, Vasilchikov also observed that few imperial Russian functionaries possessed broad horizons and many officials who did have vision remained averse to risk, unwilling to venture their views against opinions expressed above them.[12] Sycophancy could reach breathtaking heights. And officials relied upon school ties, blood and marriage relations, cliques, all of which could cover for mistakes and incompetence. Nonetheless, the authority of all-important patrons and protectors often stemmed from accomplishments, not just connections. Facts cannot compete with great stories from Gogol but they can be stubborn: imperial Russia developed a formidable fiscal-military state that proved capable of mobilizing impressive resources, certainly compared with its rivals the Ottoman or Habsburg empires.[13]

As late as the 1790s, when Prussia—with 1 percent of Russia's size in land—had 14,000 officials, the tsarist empire had only 16,000 and just a single university, which was then a mere few decades old, but over the course of the 1800s, Russian officialdom grew seven times more rapidly than the population, and by 1900 had reached 385,000, leaping some 300,000 only since 1850. True, although many of Russia's maligned provincial governors developed great administrative experience and skill, the low-prestige provincial apparatuses under them continued to suffer an extreme dearth of competent and honest clerks.[14] And some territories were woefully undergoverned: in the Ferghana valley, for example, the most populous district of tsarist Turkestan, Russia posted just 58 administrators and a mere 2 translators for at least 2 million inhabitants.[15] Overall, in 1900, while imperial Germany had 12.6 officials per 1,000 people, imperial Russia still had fewer than 4, a proportion reflecting Russia's huge population—130 million versus Germany's 50 million.[16] The Russian state was top heavy and spread thin.[17] Most of the provincial empire was left to be governed by local society, whose scope of governance, however, was restricted by imperial laws and whose degree of organization varied widely.[18] Some provinces, such as Nizhny Novgorod, did remarkably well.[19] Others, such as Tomsk, were mired in disabling corruption. Incompetence flourished most at the very top of the system. Many a deputy undertook machinations to depose his superior, which reinforced the inclination to hire mediocrities into the upper ranks, at least as top deputies, nowhere more so than in the tsars' appointments of ministers.[20] But despite the absence of a civil service examination in Russia—such as the one that guided recruitment of officialdom in imperial Germany and Japan—administrative needs did slowly begin to dictate hiring on the basis of university education and expertise.[21] Russia's functionaries (*chinovniki*) began to be recruited from all social ranks, and countless thousands of plebeians became nobles because of their state service, a path upward that would be tightened but never closed.

At the same time, unlike the absolutism in Prussia, Austria, Britain, or France, Russia's autocracy endured deep into modern times. Prussia's Frederick the Great (r. 1772–86) had called himself "the first servant of the state," thereby marking the state's separate existence from the sovereign. Russia's tsars would hand out a Siberian silver mine's worth of medals to state officials but, jealous of their autocratic prerogatives, they hesitated to recognize a state independent of themselves. The "autocratic principle" held even through the gravest crises. In 1855, when Alexander II succeeded his father, a dying Nicholas I had said to his son, "I want to take with me all the unpleasantness and the troubles and pass on to you an orderly, calm and happy Russia."[22] But Nicholas I had embroiled the empire in a costly Crimean War (1853–56), seeking to take advantage of a contracting Ottoman empire. Britain led a European concert against St. Petersburg, and Alexander II, at a loss of 450,000 imperial Russian subjects, found himself forced to accept defeat just before the conflict tipped into a world war.[23] After the debacle—Russia's first lost war in 145 years—Alexander II was constrained to countenance a series of Great Reforms, including a belated serf emancipation. ("It is better that this come from above than from below," the tsar warned the unconvinced nobles, who were scarcely mollified by the huge redemption payments the state collected on their behalf from peasants.)[24] But the tsar's own autocratic prerogatives remained sacrosanct. Alexander II permitted an unprecedented degree of domestic freedom in the universities, the press, the courts, but as soon as Russian subjects exercised that civil freedom, he pushed back.[25] The Tsar-Liberator—as he came to be known—refused a constitution, because, as his interior minister noted, Alexander II "was genuinely convinced that it would harm Russia and would lead to its dissolution."[26] But the tsar would not even let state law be applied to state officials, lest that diminish the autocrat's dispensation.[27] On the contrary, the granting of some local self-rule, some independence to the judiciary, and some autonomy to universities, alongside the freeing of the serfs, made a reassertion of autocratic power seem all the more urgent to Alexander II. Thus, the Great Reform moment to establish a parliament when it might have stuck—in the 1860s, and again in the 1880s—was fatally missed.[28]

Russia lacked not only a parliament but even a coordinated government, so as not to infringe on the autocrat's prerogatives. To be sure, Alexander II had approved a Council of Ministers to coordinate government affairs, but the effort (1857) was stillborn. In practice, the tsar shrank from relinquishing the power of having individual ministers obviate the collective body and report to him directly, and privately; the ministers colluded in the government reform's sabotage, not wanting to forgo the influence gained via private access to the autocrat.[29] Meetings of the Council, like any imperial audiences, mostly involved efforts to divine the "autocratic will," to avoid the catastrophe of being on the wrong side of decisions. Only the most skillful could manage, every now and then, to implant an idea as the tsar's own.[30] Courtiers and "unofficial" advisers, meanwhile, continued to make policy, even for the ministries, and the Russian government's operation remained uncoordinated and secretive—from officialdom. Tsarism suffered a debilitation it could not overcome: the imperatives of autocracy undermined the state. Of the resulting political regime, wags called it fairly simple: autocracy, tempered by occasional assassination. Open season had commenced in 1866, with the first of six attempts on Alexander II. He was finally blown to bits in 1881. Alexander III survived several close calls, including one in the company of his son Nicholas, the future tsar. In 1887, after a failed plot on Alexander III, Alexander Ulyanov, a member of the underground People's Will—and the elder brother of the-then seventeen-year-old Vladimir Ulyanov (the future Lenin)—refused an offer of clemency and was hanged. The inflexible autocracy had many enemies, including Iosif Jughashvili. But its most dangerous enemy was itself.

## MODERNITY AS GEOPOLITICAL
## IMPERATIVE

By the turn of the century, at least 100 political murders had been notched in imperial Russia. After that the pace picked up, as terrorist-assassins pursued what they called disorganization—provoking the police to make arrests and shed blood, which, in twisted terrorist logic, would galvanize society to revolt. The next royal family member hit was Moscow's governor, Grand Duke Sergei, a younger son of Alexander II (and an uncle of Nicholas II), who was decapitated by a bomb right inside the Kremlin in 1905. Until that year, politics in Russia was essentially illegal: political parties and trade unions were banned; censorship meant that few options for political discourse existed, other than tossing a "pomegranate" at an official's carriage and watching the body parts fly. (Grand Duke Sergei's fingers were found on a nearby rooftop.)[31] In response, the tsarist authorities had reorganized the political police, creating a formidable new body, the *Okhrannoe otdelenie*, which the terrorists promptly dubbed the *okhranka*—meaning, pejoratively, "the little security agency." Of course, not only Russia but also the European dynasties (Bourbon France, Habsburg Austria) had invented the practice of "policing," that is, using the institution of the police to help direct society; by comparison with its European peers, Russia's political police were not *especially* nefarious.[32] The *okhranka* intercepted mail via secret "black cabinets"—modeled on France's *cabinets noires*—where operatives steamed open letters, read invisible ink, and cracked revolutionaries' codes (such as they were).[33] Inevitably, Russia's police chiefs discovered their mail was perlustrated, too, and some tsarist officials took to sending letters to third parties that obsequiously flattered their bosses.[34] Even working along with Russia's regular Department of Police and Special Corps of Gendarmes, the shadowy *okhranka* never attained the societal coverage of its better-endowed French counterpart.[35] But the *okhranka*'s mystique enhanced its reach.

Many *okhranka* operatives were highly educated, forming a kind of "police intelligentsia," compiling libraries of revolutionary works in order to discredit the revolutionaries' ideas.[36] Operatives incorporated the latest international tradecraft, using E. R. Henry's book on fingerprinting from the London police and file methods from the German police.[37] Terror fighting proved sullying, however: the *okhranka* often felt constrained to allow terrorists to complete their assassinations so the police could track terror networks as fully as possible.[38] Worse, many *okhranka* infiltrators carried out the political murders themselves, to prove their bona fides and remain in a position to continue surveillance. Tsarist police assassinating other tsarist officials was a nasty business that exacerbated the internal divisions of rivalrous police cabals. The upshot was that senior *okhranka* operatives themselves were placed under surveillance, though fewer of them turned rogue than were murdered by their own turncoat agents.[39] The *okhranka* also suffered the disdain of Tsar Nicholas II, who almost never deigned to meet his *okhranka* chief.[40] And yet, though almost entirely without connections at court, the *okhranka* was the only part of the state genuinely moored in society. Moreover, despite the police agency's entanglement with the terrorists it was supposed to fight, and its alienation from the regime it was supposed to protect, the *okhranka* scored success after success.[41] It cast effective clouds over genuine revolutionaries by falsely naming them as police agents, and supported those revolutionary elements whose ascendancy would hurt the terrorist organizations. Stalin would be dogged his entire life, and beyond, by rumors that he was an undercover police agent (accusations his many enemies failed to prove).[42] Lev Trotsky, too, came under suspicion of police collaboration.[43] As one former *okhranka* chief boasted, "the revolutionaries . . . fell to suspecting each other, so that in the end no conspirator could trust another."[44]

Adroitly sowing discord among naturally fractious revolutionaries and stage-managing terrorists, however, could never redress the tsarist order's most profound vulnerability. The autocracy's core problem was not that it fell under political assault, or that authoritarianism was ipso facto incompatible with modernity, but that Russia's autocracy was deliberately archaic. Tsarism choked on the very modernity that it desperately needed and, to an extent, pursued in order to compete as a great power.[45]

What we designate modernity was not something natural or automatic. It involved a set of difficult-to-attain attributes—mass production, mass culture, mass politics—that the greatest powers mastered. Those states, in turn, forced other countries to attain modernity as well, or suffer the consequences, including defeat in war and possible colonial conquest. Colonies, from the point of view of the colonizers, were not just geopolitical assets (in most cases), but in the words of one historian, also "a form of conspicuous consumption on a national scale"—markers of geopolitical status, or the lack thereof, which drove an aggressiveness in state-to-state rivalries, as those on the receiving end could attest.[46]

Modernity, in other words, was not a sociological process—moving from "traditional" to "modern" society—but a geopolitical process: a matter of acquiring what it took to join the great powers, or fall victim to them.[47]

Consider the invention of systems to manufacture steel (1850s), a strong and elastic form of iron that revolutionized weapons and made possible a global economy by transforming shipping. Steel took off thanks in part to the invention of the electric motor (1880s), which made possible mass production: the standardization of core aspects of products, the subdivision of work on assembly lines, the replacement of manual labor by machinery, the reorganization of flow among shops.[48] These new production processes boosted world steel production from half a million tons in 1870 to twenty-eight million by 1900. But the United States accounted for ten million; Germany, eight; and Britain, five; a small number of countries had almost all the steel. To this picture one could add the manufacture of crucial industrial chemicals: synthetic fertilizers for boosting agricultural yields, chlorine bleach to make cotton, and explosives (Alfred Nobel's nitroglycerine dynamite, 1866) for mining, railroad construction, and assassinations. As some countries succeeded at modern industry, the world became divided between advantaged industrializers (Western Europe, North America, Japan) and disadvantaged raw material suppliers (Africa, South America, much of Asia).

Competitive modern attributes also included finance and credit facilities, stable currencies, and stock companies.[49] But in many ways, the new world economy rested upon peasants in the tropics who supplied the primary products (raw materials) necessary for industrial countries and, in turn, consumed many of the goods produced from their raw materials. Commercialization spurred specialization away from subsistence—in China, for example, vast acreage of subsistence agriculture had been converted to cotton to feed the English cotton mills—with the result that the spread of markets made possible huge increases in production. But that spread also undercut diverse crop raising (to minimize subsistence shortfalls) and reciprocal social networks (to enhance survival), meaning markets undercut the traditional methods for coping with cyclical drought, which was chronic. El Niño airflows (the recurrent warming of the Pacific Ocean) export heat and humidity to parts of the world, creating an unstable climate for farming: torrential rains, floods, landslides, and wildfires, as well as severe droughts. The upshot was three waves of famine and disease (1876–79, 1889–91, 1896–1900) that killed between 30 and 60 million people in China,

Brazil, and India. In India alone, 15 million people died of famine, equal to half the population of England at the time. Not since the fourteenth-century Black Death or the sixteenth-century disease destruction of New World natives had there been such annihilation. Had such mass death occurred in Europe—the equivalent of thirty Irish famines—it would be regarded as a central episode of world history. Besides the effects of commercialization and weather, additional factors came into play: The collapse of a U.S. railroad bubble, for example, led to an abrupt decline in demand for key tropical products. Above all, colonial rulers compounded the market and climate uncertainties with inept and racist rule.[50] Only in Ethiopia in 1889 was absolute scarcity an issue; these were not "natural" famines but man-made ones, the consequences of a world subjected to great power domination.

Modernity's power could be woefully mismanaged. While India was experiencing mass starvation, between 1870–1900, grain exports to Britain were increased, from 3 million to 10 million, supplying one-fifth of British wheat consumption. "Famine," admitted one British official in 1907, after thirty-five years of service, "is now more frequent than formerly and more severe."[51] But the British themselves were responsible. They had built the fourth largest railroad network in India to take advantage of their colony, but this technology that could have brought relief instead took food away. The British viceroy in India, Lord Lytton, opposed on principle local officials' efforts to stock grain or interfere with market prices. He demanded that the emaciated and the dying work for food because, he insisted, food relief would encourage shirking from work (not to mention cost public funds). When starving women attempted to steal from gardens, they were subjected to branding, and sometimes had their noses cut off or were killed. Rural mobs assaulted landowners and pillaged grain stores. British officials observed the desperation and reported it back home. "One madman dug up and devoured part of a cholera victim, while another killed his son and ate part of the boy," one report from India noted. The Qing rulers in China had resisted building railroads, fearing their use in colonialist penetration, so the capacity in China for famine relief was limited. Huge peasant revolts broke out—the Canudos war in Brazil, the Boxer rebellion in China (where posters noted: "No rain comes from Heaven. The Earth is parched and dry."). But the peasants could not, at that time, overthrow formal or informal imperialism.

Markets and a world economy made possible previously unimaginable prosperity, but most of the world had a difficult time appreciating the benefits. To be sure, the new world economy was not all encompassing. Many pockets of territory lived outside the opportunities and the pressures. Still, the world economy could feel like a force of nature. Electricity spurred soaring demand for copper (wires), drawing Montana, Chile, and southern Africa into the world economy, a chance for newfound prosperity, but also for subjecting their populations to wild price swings on world commodities markets. The consequences were huge. Beyond the waves of famine, the collapse of one bank in Austria in 1873 could trigger a depression that spread as far as the United States, causing mass unemployment, while in the 1880s and 1890s, Africa was devastated by recessions outside the continent—and then swallowed up in an imperial scramble by the modernity-wielding Europeans.[52]

Imperial Russia faced the modernity challenge with considerable success. It became the world's fourth or fifth largest industrial power, thanks to textiles, and Europe's top agricultural producer, an achievement of Russia's sheer size. But here was the rub: Russia's per capita GDP stood at just 20 percent of Britain's and 40 percent of Germany's.[53] St. Petersburg had the world's most opulent court, but by the time the future Stalin was born, Russia's average lifespan at birth was a mere thirty years, higher than in British India (twenty-three), but no better than in China, and well below Britain (fifty-two), Germany (forty-nine) and Japan (fifty-one). Literacy under Tsar Nicholas II hovered near 30 percent, lower than in Britain in the eighteenth century. The Russian establishment knew these comparisons intimately because they visited Europe often, and they evaluated their country not alongside third-rate powers—what we would call developing countries—but alongside the first-rank. Even if Russian elites had been more modest in their ambitions, however, their country could have expected little respite in the early twentieth century, given the unification and rapid industrialization of Germany and the consolidation and industrialization of Japan. When a great power suddenly knocks at your country's door, with advanced military technology, officers who are literate and capable, motivated soldiers, and well-run state institutions and engineering schools back home, you cannot cry "unfair." Russia's socioeconomic and political advance had to be, and was, measured relative to that of its most advanced rivals.[54]

Even contemporary revolutionaries recognized Russia's dilemmas. Nikolai Danielson, the lead translator of Marx's *Das Kapital* into Russian, worried that his preferred path for Russia of an unhurried, organic evolution to socialism via the peasant commune (a small-scale, decentralized economic organization)

could not survive the pressures of the international system, while Russia's bourgeoisie was not up to the challenge either. "On the one hand, emulating England's
slow-paced, 300-year process of economic development might leave Russia vulnerable to colonial domination by one or another of the world's great powers,"
Danielson wrote in a preface to the 1890s Russian edition of *Das Kapital*. "On the
other, a headlong, Darwinian introduction of 'western-style' free markets and
privatization might produce a corrupt bourgeois elite and a destitute majority—
without any increase in productivity rates." Russia seemed to face a frightful
choice between colonization by European countries or new depths of inequality
and poverty.[55]

For the tsarist regime, the stakes were high and so were the costs. Even after
conceding the Great Reforms, Russia's rulers continued to feel increasing fiscal
limits to their international aspirations. The Crimean War had clobbered state
finances, but the revenge victory in the Russo-Ottoman War (1877–78) cost Russia still more treasure. Between 1858 and 1880, Russia's budget deficit soared
from 1.7 to 4.6 billion rubles, which required huge foreign borrowing—from
Russia's geopolitical rivals, the European great powers.[56] Corruption meant that
substantial sums of state money went unaccounted for. (Treatment of state revenue as private income was perhaps most outlandish in the Caucasus, a sinkhole
of imperial finance.)[57] True, Russia escaped the fate of the Ottomans, who
became a financial and geopolitical client of Europe, or of the Qing (1636–1911),
who doubled the size of China, in parallel to Russia's expansion, only to go flat
broke and be subjected to a series of profoundly unequal international treaties,
including at the hands of Russia.[58] By the early 1900s, Russia's state budget tended
to be in surplus, thanks to taxes on sugar, kerosene, matches, tobacco, imported
goods, and above all, vodka. (The Russian empire's per capita alcohol consumption was lower than elsewhere in Europe but the state ran a monopoly on sales.)[59]
At the same time, however, Russia's army budget eclipsed state expenditure on
education by a factor of ten. And even then, the war ministry incessantly complained of insufficient resources.[60]

Competitive great-power pressures did help drive an expansion of Russia's
higher education system in order to produce state functionaries, engineers, and
doctors.[61] But the autocracy came to dread the very students it desperately
needed. When the autocracy tried to strangle moves for university autonomy,
students went on strike, which led to campus lockdowns.[62] Of those arrested in
the Russian empire between 1900 and 1905, the vast majority were under thirty

years of age.[63] Similarly, industrialization had taken off from the 1890s, giving Russia many of the modern factories critical to international power, yet industrial workers were striking, too, for an eight-hour workday and humane living conditions, leading to lockdowns. Rather than permit legal organizations and try to co-opt the workers—as was initially tried by a talented Moscow *okhranka* chief—the autocracy fell back upon repressing the workers whom the state's own vital industrialization was creating.[64] In the countryside, whose harvest remained the state's preeminent economic determinant, Russian grain exports fed large swaths of Europe while domestic food consumption grew, despite comparatively lower Russian yields on sown land.[65] But in spring 1902, in the fertile Poltava and Kharkov provinces of the south, peasants burst into mass rebellion, looting and burning gentry estates, demanding land-rent reductions as well as free access to forests and waterways, thereby prompting the novelist Lev Tolstoy to address petitions to the tsar.[66] The next year in western Georgia's Kutaisi province, among the forty square miles of vineyards and tea leaves of Guria, peasants were provoked by inept tsarist repression, and rebelled. The province lacked even a single industrial enterprise, and the uprising threw the Social Democrats for a loop. But after the peasants gathered, drew up demands, elected leaders, and took mutual oaths to loyalty, Georgian Social Democrats sought to lead them. Rents paid to landowners were reduced, freedom of speech was allowed, and the police were replaced by a new "red" militia in an autonomous "Gurian Republic."[67]

Imperial Russia had more than 100 million rural inhabitants living under extremely diverse conditions. Every country undergoing the modernization compelled by the international system was torn by social tensions. But Russia's tensions were magnified by the autocratic system's refusal to incorporate the masses into the political system, even by authoritarian means. And many would-be revolutionaries who had abandoned peasant-oriented Populism for worker-centric Marxism faced a rethinking.

## CRUSHING DEFEAT IN ASIA

For Russia, the inherent geopolitical imperative of achieving the attributes of modernity was rendered still costlier because of its geography. Great Britain's attempted containment of Russia failed: the Crimean War defeat on Russian soil had helped provoke a spasm of Russian conquest into Central Asia (1860s–80s) on top of a seizure of the Amur River basin from China (1860). But those land grabs had deepened Russia's challenge of having sprawling geography and a difficult neighborhood. The Russian empire—unlike the world's other great continental power—was not safely nestled between the two great oceans and two harmless neighbors in Canada and Mexico. Russia simultaneously abutted Europe, the Near East, and the Far East. Such a circumstance should have argued for caution in foreign policy. But Russia had tended to be expansionist precisely in the name of vulnerability: even as forces loyal to the tsar had seized territory, they imagined they were preempting attacks. And once Russia had forcibly acquired a region, its officials invariably insisted they had to acquire the next one over, too, in order to be able to defend their original gains. A sense of destiny and insecurity combined in a heady mix.

Russia had reached the Pacific in the seventeenth century but never developed its vast Asian territories. Dreams of trade with the Far East went unrealized, owing to the lack of reliable, cost-effective transport.[68] But then Russia built the Trans-Siberian Railway (1891–1903) linking the imperial capital with the Pacific.[69] (The United States had completed its transcontinental railroad in 1869.) Military and strategic considerations dominated Russia's railroad project as military circles clamored for a railroad not out of fear of Japan but of China. (Opponents of the railroad favored a naval buildup.)[70] But some officials put forward visions of force marching Siberia's economic development (in 1890, all of Siberia had 687 industrial enterprises, most of them artisanal and nearly 90 percent of them in food-processing and livestock).[71] The Trans-Siberian proved to be the most expensive peaceful undertaking in modern history up to that time, involving colossal waste, unmechanized exertion, and press-ganged peasant and convict labor, all of which paralleled construction of the contemporaneous Panama Canal (and presaged Stalin's pharaonic Five-Year Plans).[72] Russia's engineers had been dispatched on study trips to the United States and Canada in the 1880s, but back home they employed none of the lessons on the need for stronger rails and sturdy ballast.[73] Still, against domestic opposition and long odds, the line had been built, thanks to the willpower and clever manipulations of Finance Minister Sergei Witte.

Witte had been born in 1849 in Tiflis to a Swedish-Lutheran family (on his father's side) that had converted to Orthodoxy and served the Russian state in midlevel positions on the empire's southern frontier. His mother's family had higher status. Witte completed gymnasium in Kishinev and university in Odessa, where he began his long career by managing the Odessa railroads, making them profitable. In 1892, in the aftermath of the famine of 1891, he became finance minister in St. Petersburg. Just forty-three years old, with low imperial rank initially, widely dismissed as some kind of "merchant" (*kupets*), and with Ukrainian-accented Russian, Witte nonetheless became the dominant figure in turn-of-the-century imperial Russian politics, forcing even foreign policy into the purview of his finance ministry.[74]

Witte did not have the entire field to himself, of course. Just in terms of the executive branch of the state, he had to reckon with the ministry of internal affairs, the umbrella for the *okhranka*, as well as the regular police. In many ways, Russian governance, and even Russian politics, pivoted on the two great ministries, internal affairs and finance, and the rivalry between them. Both finance and internal affairs connived to expand at the central level, and to extend their writ into locales.[75] On the occasion of their joint one hundredth jubilee in 1902, each published a history of itself. Internal affairs told a story of imposing and maintaining domestic order, especially in rural Russia; finance, of the productive exploitation of Russia's natural and human resources, whence revenues could be collected.[76] Despite being overwhelmingly a peasant country, Russia had no separate agricultural ministry per se, though it did have an evolving, relatively small-scale (until 1905–6) ministry that was responsible for land, most of which belonged to the state or the imperial household.[77] A ministry of communications (railways) as well as one of commerce and industry existed as satellites of the powerful finance ministry. By the early 1900s, the budgetary resources commanded by the finance ministry exceeded by several times those available to internal affairs and its police.[78] The finance ministry was the great bureaucratic empire within the Russian empire.[79]

Witte also had to contend with the court. He came from a merely middling family background, was ill mannered, and had married a Jewish woman, all of which raised hackles in court society. But the physically imposing Witte, who had a massive head and torso, on short legs, imposed order on imperial budgets, filling state coffers by introducing the alcohol monopoly.[80] Also, he vastly broadened a recent finance ministry practice of vigorously pushing industrialization, and he did so by attracting foreign capital, playing off the French and Germans. Witte saw foreign debt as a way to help spur the accumulation of native capital. He also cherished the state machinery. Above all, Witte emphasized the geopolitical imperative of industrializing. "No matter how great the results so far, in relation to the needs of the country and in comparison with foreign countries our industry is still very backward," he wrote in a memorandum in 1900, urging

Nicholas II to maintain protective tariffs. Witte added that "even the military preparedness of a country is determined not only by the perfection of its military machine but by the degree of its industrial development." Without energetic actions, he warned, "the slow growth of our industries will endanger the fulfill-ment of the great political tasks of the monarchy." Russia's rivals would seize the upper hand abroad and achieve economic and possibly "triumphant political penetration" of Russia itself.[81] Like Stalin would, Witte lopsidedly prioritized heavy and large-scale industry at the expense of light industry and the welfare of the overwhelmingly rural population. Witte's ministry put out deliberately inflated consumption statistics to cover up the burdens imposed.[82] As it hap-pened, Witte also scribbled his orders in pencil directly on the memoranda of subordinates ("Discuss this again") ("Write a summary abstract"), and worked late into the evenings, both viewed as distinguishing traits of the future Soviet dictator. Witte further anticipated Stalin by a habit of pacing his office while others in attendance had to sit.

Witte imagined himself a Russian Bismarck, drawing inspiration from the Iron Chancellor's use of the state to promote economic development as well as his foreign policy realism. Witte also championed, at least rhetorically, what he called Bismarck's "social monarchy"—that is, a conservative program of social welfare to preempt socialism.[83] Witte possessed immense administrative abilities as well as the profound self-regard required of a top politician.[84] Besides being awarded the Order of St. Anne, first class—a tsarist precursor of the Order of Lenin—he received more than ninety state awards from foreign governments (unthinkable in the Soviet context). In turn, using finance ministry funds, he bestowed medals, state apartments, country homes, travel allowances, and "bonuses" on his minions, allies, clans at court, and journalists (for favorable coverage). From the finance ministry's offices on the Moika Canal, Witte enjoyed a grand vista onto the Winter Palace and Palace Square, but he also assiduously frequented the salons in the nobles' palaces lining the Fontanka Canal. In the autocracy, for a minister to become a genuinely independent actor was near impossible. Witte depended utterly on the tsar's confidence (*doverie*). Witte understood that another key to power entailed remaining well informed amid a deliberate non-sharing of information inside the government.[85] This required a broad informal network coursing through all the top layers of society. ("As a minister," wrote Witte's successor at the finance ministry, "one had no option but to play a role in Court and in Petersburg society if one was to defend the interests of one's department and maintain one's position.")[86] In other words, in tsarist government relentless intrigues were not personal but structural, and Witte was a master: he developed close links to dubious types in the *okhranka,* whom he employed for a variety of purposes, but his underlings in the finance ministry, too, had been tasked with overhearing and recording conversations of rivals, which Witte would edit and send to the tsar. After a decade of high-profile power at the top of the Russian state, which elicited endless attacks against Witte by rivals and societal critics of his harsh taxation policies, Nicholas II would finally lose confidence in him in 1903, shunting him to a largely ceremonial post (Witte "fell upward," contemporaries said). But his historic run at the finance ministry lasted a decade, making him one of Stalin's most important forerunners.

Witte emulated not just Bismarck but also his British contemporary in Africa, the diamond magnate Cecil Rhodes (1853–1902), and looked upon the Far East as his personal imperial space.[87] In order to shorten the route from St. Petersburg to the terminal point at Vladivostok ("rule the east"), Witte constructed a southerly branch of the Trans-Siberian right through the Chinese territory of Manchuria. Under the slogan of "peaceful penetration," he and other Russian officials imagined they were preempting Russia's rival imperialists (Britain, Germany, France) from carving up China the way they had the African continent.[88] Other Russian officials, while insisting that each forcible conquest had to be followed by another, in order to be able to defend the original gains, competed to gain the tsar's favor, one-upping Witte's supposedly measured push into China. The war ministry seized, then leased, Port Arthur (Lushun), a deep warm-water entrepôt on China's Liaodong Peninsula, which jutted ever so strategically into the Yellow Sea. But Russia's overall increasingly forward position in East Asia, in which Witte was complicit, ran smack up against not the European powers that so transfixed St. Petersburg elites, but an aggressive, imperialist Japan.[89]

Japan was in no way a power on the order of the world leader, Great Britain. Living standards in Japan were perhaps only one fifth of Britain's, and Japan, like Russia, remained an agriculture-dominated economy.[90] Japan's real wages, measured against rice prices, had probably been only one third of Britain's in the 1830s, and would still be only one third in the early twentieth century. Still, that meant that during Britain's leap, real wages in Japan had improved at the same rate as real wages improved in the leading power.[91] Although Japan was still exporting primary products or raw materials (raw silk) to Europe, within Asia, Japan exported consumer goods. Indeed, Japan's rapidly increasing trade had shifted predominantly to within East Asia, where it gained widespread admiration or envy for discovering what looked like a shortcut to Western-style modernity.[92] Japan was also rapidly building up a navy, just like Germany. (The conservative modernizer Bismarck was in his day the most popular foreign figure in Japan, too.)[93] Moreover, as an ally of Britain, rather than be subjected to informal imperialism, Japan led a shift in East Asia toward free trade, the ideology of the strong. Japan had defeated China in a war over the Korean Peninsula (1894–95) and seized Taiwan. Already in the 1890s, Russia's general staff began to draft contingency planning for possible hostilities with Japan, following the shock of Japan's crushing defeat of China. But partly for wont of military intelligence on Japan, although mostly because of racial prejudice, Russian ruling circles belittled the "Asiatics" as easily conquerable.[94] Whereas the Japanese general staff had estimated no better than a fifty-fifty chance of prevailing, perhaps hedging their bets, Russian ruling circles were certain they would win if it came to war.[95] The British naval attaché similarly reported widespread feeling in Tokyo that Japan would "crumple up."[96] Of all people, Nicholas II should have known better. As tsarevich, he had seen Japan with his own eyes, during an unprecedented (for a Russian royal) grand tour of the Orient (1890–91), where the sword of a Japanese assassin nearly killed the future tsar, and left a permanent scar on his forehead. (A cousin in Nicholas's party parried a second saber blow with a cane.) But as tsar, facing possible war, Nicholas dismissed the Japanese as "macaques," an Asian species of short-tailed monkey.[97]

Russo-Japanese negotiators had tried to find a modus vivendi through a division of spoils, exchanging recognition of a Russian sphere in Manchuria for recognition of a Japanese sphere in Korea, but each side's "patriots" kept arguing that they absolutely had to have *both* Manchuria and Korea to protect either one. Japan, which felt its weakness in the face of a combination of European powers encroaching in East Asia, would likely have compromised if Russia had been willing to do so as well, but it remained unclear what Russia actually would settle for. A clique of courtier intriguers, led by Alexander Bezobrazov, exacerbated Japan's suspicions with a scheme to penetrate Korea while enriching themselves via a forestry concession. Bezobrazov held no ministerial position, yet Nicholas, as an assertion of "autocratic prerogative," afforded the courtier frequent access, cynically using Bezobrazov to keep his own ministers, Witte included, off balance. Nicholas II's changeable and poorly communicated views, and his failure to keep his own government informed, let alone seek its members' expertise, rendered Russia's Far Eastern policy that much more opaque and incoherent.[98] Japanese ruling circles decided, before negotiations for a deal with Russia had been exhausted, and after prolonged internal debate and disagreement, to launch an all-out preventative war. In February 1904, Japan severed diplomatic relations and attacked Russian vessels at anchor at Port Arthur, a quick strike against the slow-moving Russian giant to demonstrate its underestimated prowess, before possibly seeking third-party mediation.[99] Russia's Pacific fleet fell to the Japanese, who also managed to land infantry on the Korean Peninsula to march on Russian positions in Manchuria. The shock was profound. "It is no longer possible to live this way," editorialized even the archconservative Russian paper *New Times* on January 1, 1905. That same day, Vladimir Lenin called the autocracy's immense military structure "a beautiful apple rotten at the core."[100] Russia dispatched its Baltic fleet halfway around the world, 18,000 nautical miles. Seven and a half months later, upon reaching the theater of hostilities in May 1905, eight modern battleships, built by St. Petersburg's skilled workers, were promptly sunk in the Tsushima Strait with the colors flying.[101]

The Russian state had subordinated everything to military priorities and needs, and the Romanovs had tied their image and legitimacy to Russia's international standing, so the Tsushima shock was devastating.[102] On land, too, the Japanese achieved startling victories over Russia, including the Battle of Mukden, then the largest military engagement in world history (624,000 combined forces), where Russia enjoyed a numerical advantage.[103] The stinging Mukden defeat came on the anniversary of Nicholas II's coronation.[104]

This debacle in the very arena that justified the autocracy's existence—great power status—not only exposed tsarism's political failings but threatened political collapse. Strikes had erupted at the military factories producing the weaponry for the war, so that by January 8, 1905, Russia's wartime capital was bereft of electricity and information (newspapers). On Sunday, January 9, 1905, seven days after a besieged Port Arthur fell to Japanese forces, thousands of striking workers and their families assembled at six points in the working-class neighborhoods, beyond the Narva and Nevsky gates, to march on the Winter Palace in order to present a petition to the "tsar-father" for the improvement of workers' lives, protection of their rights, and dignity by means of the convocation of a Constituent Assembly.[105] They were led by a conservative priest, carried Orthodox icons and crosses, and sang religious hymns and "God Save the Tsar" as church bells tolled. Nicholas II had repaired to his main residence, the Alexander

Palace in Tsarskoe Selo, outside the city, and had no intention of meeting the petitioners. The haphazard authorities on hand in the capital decided to seal off the city center with troops. The priest's group got only as far as the Narva Gate in the southwest, where imperial troops met them with gunfire when they sought to proceed farther. Amid dozens of bodies, the priest exclaimed, "There is no God anymore, there is no Tsar!" Shooting also halted unarmed marching men, women, and children at the Trinity Bridge, the Alexander Gardens, and elsewhere. Panic ensued and some petitioners trampled others to death. Around 200 people were killed across the capital that day, and another 800 were wounded—workers, wives, children, bystanders.[106] St. Petersburg's "Bloody Sunday" provoked far greater strikes, the looting of liquor and firearm shops, and all around fury.

Nicholas II's image as father of the people would never be the same. ("All classes condemn the authorities and most particularly the Emperor," observed the U.S. consul in Odessa. "The present ruler has lost absolutely the affection of the Russian people.")[107] In February 1905, the tsar vaguely promised an elected "consultative" Duma or assembly, which sent alarms through conservative ranks, while failing to quell the unrest. The next month, all universities were (again) locked down.[108] Strikers closed down the empire's railway system, forcing government officials to travel by riverboat to meet with the tsar in his suburban palace. In June 1905, sailors seized control of the battleship *Potemkin,* part of the Black Sea fleet—which was all Russia had left after the loss of its Pacific and Baltic fleets—and bombarded Odessa before seeking asylum in Romania. "The chaos was all-encompassing," one police insider wrote, adding that political police work "ground to a halt."[109] Strike waves swept Russian Poland, the Baltics, and the Caucasus, where "the whole administrative apparatus fell into confusion," recalled Jordania, the leader of Georgia's Marxists. "A de facto freedom of assembly, strike and demonstration was established."[110] The governor of Kutaisi province of the Caucasus went over to the revolutionaries. In Kazan and Poltava provinces, the governors had nervous breakdowns. Others lost their heads. "You risk your life, you wear out your nerves maintaining order so that people can live like human beings, and what do you encounter everywhere?" complained Governor Ivan Blok of Samara. "Hate-filled glances as if you were some kind of monster, a drinker of human blood." Moments later Blok was decapitated by a bomb. Placed in a traditional open casket, his twisted body was stuffed into his dress uniform, a ball of batting substituted for his missing head.[111]

The homefront had imploded. On the war's two sides, some 2.5 million men had been mobilized, with each side suffering between 40,000 and 70,000 killed. (Around 20,000 Chinese civilians also died.) In fact, because Japan could not replace its losses, its big victories like Mukden may have actually edged Tokyo closer to defeat.[112] But if Nicholas II was tempted to continue the war to reverse his military setbacks, he had no such opportunity. The failure of the Japanese to have sabotaged the Trans-Siberian—one of the critical transport modes for the enemy's troops and matériel—remains mysterious.[113] But the peasants were refusing to pay taxes and would destroy or damage more than 2,000 manor houses. Already by March 1905, the interior ministry had concluded that owing to uprisings, military call-ups had become impossible in thirty-two of the fifty provinces of European Russia.[114] European credits, on which the Russian state relied for cash flow, dried up, threatening a default.[115] On August 23, 1905 [September 5, in the West], Russia and Japan signed a peace treaty in Portsmouth, New Hampshire, brokered by U.S. President Theodore Roosevelt. Invited to intercede by Japan, Roosevelt proved eager to curb Tokyo's might in the Pacific (a harbinger of the future). Russia was well represented by Witte, who regained his lost luster and made the best of a bad situation.[116] Russia had to acknowledge defeat, but was absolved of paying war indemnities, while the only Russian territory relinquished was half of remote Sakhalin Island (a penal colony). Still, the defeat reverberated internationally (far more than the Ethiopian victory over Italy in 1896). Russia became the first major European power to be defeated in a symmetric battle by an Asian country—and in front of the world press corps. In a typical contemporary assessment, one observer called news of the victory "of a non-white people over a white people" nothing less than "the most important event which has happened, or is likely to happen, in our lifetime."[117]

## LEFTIST FACTIONALISM

Japan's military attaché in Stockholm was spreading bushels of money to tsarism's array of political opponents in European exile, but he expressed considerable frustration. "All of the so-called opposition parties are secret societies, where no one can distinguish opponents of the regime from Russian agents," the attaché reported to superiors, adding that the revolutionaries—or provocateurs?—all went by false names. In any case, his work, which *okhranka* mail interception exposed, proved utterly superfluous.[118] Russia's revolutionaries got far more assistance from the autocracy itself. While Russia's army, the empire's main forces of order, had been removed beyond its borders—for a war with Japan on the territories of China and Korea—Russia's revolutionaries were kept out of the battle. Even married peasants more than forty years old were targets of military recruiters, but subjects without permanent residence and with a criminal record were free to pursue rebellion at home.

The twenty-seven-year-old future Stalin, as described in a tsarist police report (May 1, 1904):

> Jughashvili, Iosif Vissarionovich: [legal status of] peasant from the village of Didi-Lido, Tiflis county, Tiflis province; born 1881 of Orthodox faith, attended Gori church school and Tiflis theological seminary; not married. Father, Vissarion, whereabouts unknown. Mother, Yeketerina, resident of the town of Gori, Tiflis province . . . Description: height, 2 arshins, 4.5 vershki [about 5' 5"], average build; gives the appearance of an ordinary person.[119]

Although his date of birth (1878) and height (5'6") were wrongly recorded, this deceptively "ordinary person," precisely because of his political activities, was exempt from military service—and as a result could position himself to be right in the thick of the 1905 uprising. The Georgian branch of the Russian Social Democratic Workers' Party assigned him to Chiatura, a hellhole in western Georgia where hundreds of small companies employed a combined 3,700 miners and sorters to extract and haul manganese ore.

Witte's father, the midlevel tsarist official, had opened Chiatura's manganese deposits around the middle of the nineteenth century.[120] By 1905, thanks to Sergei Witte's integration of Russia into the new world economy, the artisanal, privately held mines had come to account for no less than 50 percent of global manganese output. Tall piles of the excavated ore dominated the "skyline," waiting to be washed, mostly by women and children, before being exported for use in the production of German and British steel. With wages averaging a meager 40 to 80 kopecks per day, rations doused in manganese dust, and "housing" under the open sky (in winter workers slept in the mines), Chiatura was, in the words of one observer, "real penal labor (*katorga*)"—but the laborers had not been convicted of anything.[121] Even by tsarist Russia standards, the injustices in Chiatura stood not. When the workers rebelled, however, the regime summoned imperial troops as well as right-wing vigilantes, who called themselves Holy Brigades but were christened Black Hundreds. In response to the physical attacks, Jughashvili helped transform Social Democratic agitation "circles" into red combat brigades called Red Hundreds.[122] By December 1905, the worker Red Hundreds, assisted by young radical thugs, seized control of Chiatura and thus of half of global manganese output.

Only the previous year, Jughashvili had been calling for an autonomous Georgian Social Democratic Workers' Party separate from the All-Russia (imperial) Social Democrats—a vestige, perhaps, of his Russification battles at the seminary and in Georgia more broadly. But Social Democrats in Georgia rejected a struggle for national independence, reasoning that even if they somehow managed to break away, liberty for Georgia would never stick without liberty for Russia. Georgian comrades condemned Jughashvili as a "Georgian Bundist" and forced him to recant publicly. The future Stalin wrote out a *Credo* (February 1904) of his beliefs, evidently repudiating the idea of a separate Georgian party; seventy copies were distributed within Social Democratic Party circles.[123] Other than youthful romantic poetry, and two unsigned editorials in Lado's *Brdzola* that were later attributed to Stalin, the *Credo* was one of his first-ever publications (subsequent party historians assembling his writings never found it). This mea culpa was followed by an extended essay—which essentially launched his punditry career—in Georgian, dated September-October 1904, and titled "How Social Democracy Understands the National Question." Jughashvili targeted a recently formed party of Social Federalists whose Paris-based periodical demanded Georgian autonomy in both the Russian empire and in the socialist movement. He strongly repudiated the idea of separate "national" leftist parties, and resorted to sarcasm about Georgian nationalism.[124] In April 1905, a pamphlet addressed to the Batum proletariat noted that "Russian social democracy is responsible not only to the Russian proletariat but to all peoples of Russia, groaning under the yoke of the barbarian autocracy—it is responsible to all of humankind, to all of modern civilization."[125] Russia, not Georgia. The Credo episode had been a turning point.

In Chiatura, meanwhile, organizing mass direct action, Jughashvili was in his radical element—he helped transform nearly every mine into a battleground of Social Democratic Party factions, importing loyalists from his previous underground activity, especially Batum. Some observers marveled at his clique's intense loyalty. All the same, the Chiatura workers elected as their leader not Jughashvili but a tall, thin, charismatic Georgian youth named Noe Ramishvili (b. 1881). Ramishvili won over the mine workers partly by touting the superior role that his "Menshevik" faction of Caucasus Social Democrats accorded to rank-and-file workers in the party.[126] Jughashvili, who adhered to the Bolshevik faction of Caucasus Social Democrats, cursed his rivals as "worker-lovers."[127] From Chiatura, he wrote reports to the Bolshevik faction leader Vladimir Lenin, in European exile, about the life-and-death struggle—not against the tsarist regime, but against Menshevism.[128]

Bolshevik-Menshevik factionalism had broken out two years earlier, in July 1903, in a club room in London at the Russian Social Democratic Workers' Party's Second Congress (the first one since the founding effort, attended by nine people in Minsk in 1898). Beyond the reach of the tsarist police, the delegates adopted a charter and program ("The dictatorship of the proletariat is the prerequisite of the social revolution"), but two strong personalities, Lenin and Martov, clashed over party structure. The row started over a proposal by Lenin to reduce the editorial board of the periodical *Iskra* from six to three (Plekhanov, Lenin, Martov), a sensible proposition that nonetheless exploded in the hall (the minutes record "threatening shouts" and cries of "shame"). But the differences went deeper. All Russian Social Democrats viewed capitalism as an evil to be transcended, but Marxism held that history was supposed to proceed in stages and most of Russia's Marxists, following the elder statesman Plekhanov, held to the proposition that socialist revolution could triumph only after a "bourgeois revolution" had first taken place and accelerated Russia's capitalist development. In that view, Russia's workers were supposed to help Russia's weak bourgeoisie bring about constitutionalism, so that, decades hence, the workers could then transcend capitalism and advance to socialism. But what if the workers proved *unable* to take up this role? Martov captured the nub, writing that the "reconciliation of revolutionary-democratic with socialist tasks"—that is, the bourgeois revolution with the socialist revolution—"is the riddle which the fate of Russian society has posed to Russian social democracy."[129]

The question of workers' role in the historical process had already split the German Social Democrats. In Germany, it seemed that proletarians were not developing revolutionary but merely trade union consciousness (and capitalism was not breaking down)—a position stated plainly by Eduard Bernstein, who concluded that socialists ought to embrace amelioration and evolution, achieving socialism via capitalism, not organizing capitalism's annihilation. Karl Kautsky, a rival to Bernstein, branded him a Marxist "revisionist," and insisted that social-ism and then communism would still be reached via revolution. Tsarist condi-tions, meanwhile, did not allow a Bernstein "revisionist" approach in Russia, even had Lenin been so inclined—and he was not—because trade unionism and constitutionalism remained illegal. Lenin admired Kautsky, but went further, arguing for a conspiratorial approach because imperial Russia was different from Germany in the severity of the restrictions on freedom. In *What Is to Be Done?* (1902), Lenin foresaw revolution if "a few professionals, as highly trained and experienced as the imperial security police, were allowed to organize it."[130] His stance was denounced as un-Marxist—indeed, as Blanquist, after the French-man Louis Auguste Blanqui (1805–81), who had dismissed the efficacy of popu-lar movements in favor of revolution by a small group via a temporary dictatorship using force.[131] In some ways, however, Lenin was just reacting to the intense worker militancy in the Russian empire, such as the May Day march in Kharkov in 1900—about which he had written—and the violent clashes the next year between workers and police in Obukhov. True, Lenin did at times seem to be saying, like Bernstein, that workers, left to their own devices, would develop only trade union consciousness. But this made Lenin more, not less, radical. Most fundamentally, Lenin sought a party of *professional* revolutionaries to overcome the well-organized tsarist state, whose hyperrepressiveness militated against ordinary organizational work.[132] Lenin, however, could not convince the others: at the 1903 Congress, even though there were only four genuine workers out of fifty-one delegates, Martov's vision—a party organization more capacious than just "professional" revolutionaries—won the vote in a slim majority (28 to 23). Lenin refused to accept the result and announced the formation of a faction, which he called Bolsheviks (majoritarians) because he had won a majority on other, secondary questions. Martov's majority, incredibly, allowed itself to become known as Mensheviks (minoritarians).

Charges, countercharges—and misunderstandings—related to the split in summer 1903 would reverberate for the better part of a century. The *okhranka* could scarcely believe its good fortune: the Social Democrats had turned on each other! It was no longer enough for Social Democrat revolutionaries merely to struggle to evade arrest, while competing against rivals on the left like Socialist Revolutionaries (SRs), now they also had to battle the "other faction" in their own party at every party committee throughout the empire and abroad, even when they had a hard time articulating Bolshevik-Menshevik differences.[133] Of course, sectarianism among revolutionaries was as common as cuckolding. Still, Lenin's schismatism angered his heretofore close friend Martov, as well as Martov's allies, because they had just conspired with Lenin to curb the power of the Jewish Bund inside Russian Social Democratic ranks (only five Bundist delegates had been allowed to attend the 1903 Social Democratic Congress, despite the large Jewish proletariat).[134] And then—betrayal. Martov and his faction rejected various offers of mediation. Lenin's doctrinal position unmistakably involved a bid for power in the movement, but the split had begun as, and remained, at least partly personal. The internal polemics became mutually vicious—accusations of lies, treachery.

Once word of the split became widely known, Lenin was roundly denounced. In 1904, Rosa Luxemburg, the Polish-born revolutionary who would not meet Lenin for three more years, condemned his vision of organization as "military ultra-centralism." Trotsky, who sided with Martov, compared Lenin to the Jesuitical Catholic Abbé Emmanuel Joseph Sieyes—suspicious toward other people, fanatically attached to the idea, inclined to be dictator while claiming to put down supposedly ubiquitous sedition. Plekhanov would soon call Lenin a Blanquist. Lenin, for his part, worked diligently from his base in Geneva to recruit the strategically important, populous Caucasus branch of the Russian Social Democratic Workers' Party to his side, writing of the "reptilian vileness" of the party's Central Committee (his opponents). He might well have succeeded: after all, many members of Lenin's faction were exiled from European Russia to the Caucasus, where they spread Bolshevik influence. The future Stalin—who missed the 1903 London congress (he was in a tsarist remand prison)—got to know Lev Kamenev, an adherent of Lenin's faction, in Tiflis in 1904. But in January 1905, the leader of Georgian Marxists, Noe Jordania, returned to Georgia from European exile and steered the vast majority of Caucasus Marxists away from Lenin to Menshevism. Jughashvili had already clashed with Jordania as early as November 1901 by championing a narrower intelligentsia-centric party. Now he bucked Jordania again, remaining in the Bolshevik faction. For Jughashvili, therefore, the divide was partly personal, too. Doctrinally, the Leninist position of favoring professional revolutionaries over workers also suited Jughashvili's temperament and self-image.

Inevitably, Lenin's alleged personal influence came to be cited as the explanation for Jughashvili's early loyalties: the future Stalin is said to have long admired the Bolshevik leader from afar. But if he felt any hero worship for Lenin from a distance, their first encounter blunted it.[135] The two met in December 1905 at the Third Congress of the Russian Social Democratic Workers' Party in Tammerfors, in Russian-ruled Finland, where Jughashvili was one of the three delegates of the Bolshevik faction of the Caucasus.[136] Lenin had returned from Swiss exile to Russia only in November 1905, having chosen to sit out most of the revolutionary events of that year. Just shy of thirty-six, he was nearly a decade older than Jughashvili.[137] (The "patriarch" of all delegates, Mikho Tskhakaya from the Caucasus, was thirty-nine.) But Jughashvili observed at the Party Congress how provincial delegates, himself among them, attacked the elder Lenin's policy proposals and how the Bolshevik leader *backed down,* rationalizing that he was an émigré out of touch. "I expected to see the mountain eagle of our party, a great man, not only politically but physically, for I had formed for myself a picture of Lenin as a giant, as a stately, representative figure of a man," Stalin would recall. "What was my disappointment when I saw the most ordinary individual, below average height, distinguished from ordinary mortals by, literally, nothing."[138] (Stalin's writings between 1906 and 1913 would contain a mere two citations of Lenin.) Eventually, of course, Lenin would become Stalin's indispensable mentor, but it would take time for the Georgian—and most everyone else on the left—to appreciate Lenin's history-bending force of will. In any case, even as Russia's would-be Social Democratic revolutionaries were fighting tooth and nail among themselves over the nature of the coming revolution (bourgeois or socialist) and over party structure (inclusive or "professional"), tsarist political authority had already fallen into headlong disintegration, making revolution imminent.

## DISINTEGRATION AND RESCUE

While Jughashvili was organizing Red Hundreds in Chiatura, on October 8, 1905—following the signing of the Russo-Japanese peace treaty—a general strike shut down St. Petersburg. Within five days, more than 1 million workers had walked out empirewide, paralyzing the telegraph and rail systems. Troops could neither be brought home from the war—more than 1 million Russian soldiers were still in the Far Eastern theater, after the cessation of hostilities—nor deployed for internal police duty. Around October 13, a St. Petersburg soviet (or council) was established as a strike-coordinating committee; it would last some fifty days, and for two weeks of that period be headed by Lev Trotsky, a prolific writer and prominent Social Democrat who recently had returned from exile.[139] Warnings of a crackdown were announced on October 14, and the next day the authorities shuttered the capital's prestigious university for the year. Establishment figures, including members of the extended Romanov family, urged Nicholas II to make political concessions to close the breach between regime and society. In all of Europe, only the Ottoman empire, the Principality of Montenegro, and the Russian empire still lacked a parliament. Told to countenance changes that infringed on the autocratic principle and established a coordinated government, the tsar wrote to his mother, the Danish-born dowager empress, "Ministers, like chicken-hearts, assemble and discuss how to achieve unity of all ministers instead of acting decisively."[140] Fresh from Portsmouth, New Hampshire, the newly ascendant, proautocratic Sergei Witte moved to seize the moment, suggesting to the tsar that he had two choices to save the autocracy: grant a constitution, civil liberties, and above all, a coordinated ministerial government, or find someone who could implement a crackdown.[141] On October 15, Nicholas II asked his most trusted courtier, the hard-line Dmitry Trepov, Witte's archrival, whether Trepov—recently named governor-general of the capital—could restore order short of a civilian massacre. The latter replied on October 16 that "sedition has attained a level at which it is doubtful whether bloodshed could be avoided."[142]

The tsar wavered. He commissioned a draft manifesto for a merely consultative Duma.[143] Apparently, he also turned to his uncle, Grand Duke Nicholas, to assume dictatorial powers under a military dictatorship, to which the latter replied that the army had been depleted by the ongoing war in the Far East, and that if the tsar did not consent to Witte's program of political concessions, the grand duke would shoot himself.[144] Reluctantly, on October 17, crossing himself, Nicholas II signed the Manifesto on the Improvement of State Order, published the next day, "imposing"—in autocratic parlance—civil liberties as well as a bicameral legislature. No longer "consultative," as originally proposed back in February, the State Duma would be a lower house of "people's representatives" to be elected, albeit by a narrow suffrage—narrower than absolutist Spain had granted in 1680 for its towns in the New World—but with the right to issue laws. The franchise was granted to male citizens over twenty-five years of age, excluding soldiers and officers, but elections proceeded through four electoral colleges, and extra weight was given to communal, as opposed to individual, peasants.[145] At the same time, Russia's State Council—heretofore a largely ceremonial advisory body of appointed elites, as depicted in Ilya Repin's 1903 wall-sized oil painting—would become an upper house. The plan was that the upper house would serve as a conservative brake on the Duma. Half the new State Council's members would continue to be appointed by the tsar from among former ministers, governors-general, ambassadors—that is, "venerable old men, white haired or bald, with wrinkled skin and often bent with age, wearing uniforms and adorned with all of their decorations," as one insider described them. The other half was to be elected by designated bodies: the Orthodox Church, provincial assemblies, the stock exchange, the Academy of Sciences. By comparison, the United States would pass the Seventeenth Amendment providing for the direct election of senators in 1911; the entire British House of Lords was filled by hereditary peers.[146]

Far less dramatically, but no less consequentially, the tsar also conceded—for the first time—a unified government with a prime minister. Sergei Kryzhanovsky, who as deputy interior minister was tasked with outlining the need for and structure of a cabinet, assailed the "fragmentation" and fratricide of Russia's ministries. He warned that the convocation of a Duma would—like France's calling of the Estates General in 1789—provide a potent forum. The government had to be strong and united to manage the legislature, or else there could be French-style consequences for the monarchy. But ministers wanted strong government not solely because of a perceived need to manage the legislature. The model that Witte had in mind was Prussia's, which afforded the minister-president the authority—used to great effect by Bismarck—to control all contact between individual ministers and the monarch.[147]

A strong cabinet coordinated by a prime minister might seem an obvious necessity in any modern state, but globally it had arisen relatively recently. In Great Britain, the prime ministership owed its largely unplanned origins to the circumstance that King George I (r. 1714–27), of the Brunswick House of Hanover (a German state), could not speak English (he spent at least half the year in Hanover), so responsibility for chairing cabinet sessions fell to a newly created post of *prime* or first minister, a circumstance that would become institutionalized. Prussia acquired a prime minister equivalent—minister-president—and a cabinet of ministers in stages from 1849 through 1852 in an improvisation to deal with the surprise advent of a legislature in 1848.[148] (Russia's stillborn cabinet government of 1857 had not even included a prime minister.) But whereas the British prime minister post was awarded to the majority leader in the House of Commons, meaning he owed his status not to royal whim but to elected parliamentary majorities, Prussia's minister-president was appointed or removed by the monarch alone, without consideration of parliamentary (electoral) majorities.

Russia followed not the British example—a genuinely parliamentary system—but the Prussian one. True, the Duma could summon ministers for a report, but the tsar retained absolute power over ministers' appointment or dismissal, as well as an absolute veto over legislation, the right to dismiss the Duma and announce new elections, and the right to declare martial law. In addition, the ministers of foreign affairs, war, the navy, and the court fell outside the prime minister's portfolio. These circumstances allowed Nicholas II, not without Witte's connivance, to delude himself into thinking the concessions had not contravened his coronation oath to uphold autocracy. But he had: the work of Russia's then fourteen ministers—with the enumerated exceptions—would be coordinated by someone other than the tsar.[149]

That person turned out to be Witte, whom Nicholas II chose as Russia's first-ever prime minister.

Nicholas II had asked Witte to draft the October Manifesto, but knowing the tsar all too well and probably desirous of maintaining some distance from the document, Witte had passed the drafting task to an associate who happened to be staying at his home.[150] Still, Witte edited the drafts and was universally seen as the prime mover.[151] And yet, although at the pinnacle of power, Witte found himself suspended in the air, fully supported by no one—not by the stunned establishment, who were mostly proponents of unbridled autocracy and who, additionally, disliked Witte for his pedigree, gruffness, and Jewish wife; not by the narrow stratum of constitutionalists, who were still waiting for the promised constitution to be drafted and enacted; not by the elected representatives to the Petersburg Soviet, who in many cases expected the Duma would be a "bourgeois" sham; not by the striking workers and students, whose general strike had ebbed but who still desired social justice; and not by the rebellious peasantry, who freely interpreted the October Manifesto as a promise of pending land redistribution, which sparked new agrarian disturbances.[152] Witte was not even fully supported by Nicholas II, who promoted him yet still found him insolent. Nonetheless, by sheer force of personality, especially his drive to be informed, Witte proved able to impose coordination on much of the government, even in foreign policy and military affairs, whose ministers technically did not even report to the prime minister.[153]

Whatever Witte's impressive abilities, however, the introduction of a prime minister, alongside the promise of the still-to-come Duma, did not restore public order. On the contrary, opposition became more violent after the proclamation of the October Manifesto. The tsarist autocracy was saved—literally—by a tough conservative official who had once been fired for abusing his police power in connection with sexual indiscretions. Pyotr Durnovó (b. 1845), the scion of ancient nobility and a naval academy graduate, had been at sea during the 1860s Great Reforms. He then forsook the navy and became a longtime director of police (1884–93). After one of the "black cabinets" that he oversaw intercepted a love letter to the Brazilian chargé d'affaires from Durnovó's own mistress, he had the police break into the diplomat's apartment to steal the rest of her correspondence. The woman complained about the theft to her diplomat paramour, who at a court ball raised the matter with Tsar Alexander III. The latter is said to have remarked to his interior minister, "Get rid of this swine within twenty-four hours."[154] Durnovó retreated abroad, dismissed from state service, seemingly forever. Yet in 1895, after Alexander III's surprise death from illness at age forty-nine, Durnovó managed to resume his career, rising to deputy interior minister. On October 23, 1905, Witte named him acting interior minister, against the vociferous objections of liberals, and the hesitancy of Tsar Nicholas II.[155] Within three days, the Baltic sailors mutinied. By October 28, Durnovó had crushed their chaotic mutiny, ordering hundreds of executions. He contemplated an empirewide crackdown, but Witte (initially) insisted that Durnovó act within the parameters of the October Manifesto—after all, it had been signed by the tsar. Soon, however, Durnovó began to implement harsher measures, which, of course, greatly pleased the signatory of the October Manifesto, as well as much of state officialdom, once the measures appeared to be successful. "Everyone started to work, the machinery went into high gear" recalled one top *okhranka* official. "Arrests began."[156] Indeed, between the tsar's promise of a constitution (October 1905) and the promulgation six months later of the Fundamental Laws—Nicholas II refused to allow it to be called a constitution—Durnovó's police arrested many tens of thousands (by some estimates, up to 70,000).[157] Durnovó also sacked numerous governors and, more important, goaded the rest to seize back all public spaces.

Durnovó showed *initiative*. In mid-November 1905, when a new strike shut down the postal and telegraph system, he broke it by organizing citizen replacements. On December 3—the day after the Petersburg Soviet called for workers to withdraw their savings from state banks—he arrested around 260 deputies to the Soviet, half the membership, including Chairman Trotsky. Many officials warned this would provoke a repeat of the October 1905 general strike, but Durnovó countered that a show of force would shift the political dynamic. On December 7, 1905, an uprising broke out in Moscow, and Durnovó's critics looked prescient. But he went to Nicholas II at Tsarskoe Selo to report and seek instructions— without Prime Minister Witte, his (nominal) superior, whom Durnovó no longer bothered to consult even though by now Witte had come around to a hard-line approach. Durnovó did not even appear at the meetings of the government (Council of Ministers), or explain his absences therefrom.[158] The tsar, predictably, was keen to encourage the pre-1905 practice whereby ministers like Durnovó reported directly and privately to him. Nicholas II wrote to his mother, the dowager empress, "Durnovó—the interior minister—acts superbly."[159] Now, confronted by an uprising in Russia's ancient capital, Durnovó ordered it crushed: some 424 people were killed and 2,000 wounded.[160] Crackdowns took place all around the empire as well. "I earnestly request, in this and similar cases, that you order the use of armed force without the slightest leniency and that insurgents be annihilated and their homes burned," Durnovó bluntly instructed officials in Kiev province. "Under the present circumstances, the restoration of the authority of the Government is possible only by these means."[161] In Georgia, imperial troops bloodily recaptured the manganese mining settlement of Chiatura, removing the political base of Jughashvili and his Bolshevik followers. Imperial forces and Black Hundreds also routed the Georgian Menshevik peasant-citadel of the Gurian Republic. Crushed, the world's first-ever peasant republic led by Marxists, as one scholar wrote, would find echoes "in the fields, hills, and jungles of Asia."[162] For now, however, by the end of 1907, mass peasant uprisings had been snuffed out across the empire.[163] It was a stunning achievement.

RUSSIA'S AUTOCRACY had undergone a near-death experience. Altogether, an army of nearly 300,000, a size close to the land force that had battled the Japanese, was needed to suppress domestic unrest.[164] Such a vast mobilization for repression and regime survival would have been impossible had Russia's foes on its western flank, Germany and Austria-Hungary, decided to take what would have been easy advantage of the situation. Not even an actual attack from the West, merely a mobilization, would have paralyzed and likely doomed the tsarist regime.[165] Equally critical, the Russian forces of domestic repression were the same peasants in uniform who had been mutinying when—and because—the tsarist regime had appeared weak, and who now, when the regime showed its teeth again, resumed enforcing state order against rebellious workers, students, and fellow peasants.[166] Durnovó rallied them. This is one of those moments in the play of large-scale historical structures when personality proved decisive: a lesser interior minister could not have managed. When "the regime had tottered on the brink of an abyss," Vladimir Gurko, his deputy rightly concluded, it "was saved by . . . Durnovó, who adopted an almost independent policy and by merciless persecution of the revolutionary elements re-established a certain degree of order in the country."[167]

But this was also a moment when a statesman's talent, rather than shortcomings, proved detrimental to his country. Durnovó's rescue of Russia's autocracy—when it should have fallen—would end up having the perverse consequence of preparing the country for a far worse crash during a far worse war, which would serve as a template for a radical new order. Of course, it is impossible to know what would have transpired had Durnovó's exceptional resoluteness and police skill not saved tsarism in 1905–6. Still, one wonders whether the history of one sixth of the earth, and beyond, would have been as catastrophic, and would have seen the appearance of Stalin's inordinately violent dictatorship. Be that as it may, the respite Durnovó furnished to Russia would prove short-lived, frenetic, and full of rampant insecurities. "Long before the World War," recalled one contemporary, "all politically conscious people lived as on a volcano."[168]

## CHAPTER 4

# CONSTITUTIONAL AUTOCRACY

We are tired of everything. We are loyal people and cannot
go against the Government, but neither can we support
the current Government. We are forced to step to the side
and be silent. This is the tragedy of Russian life.

> A. I. Savenko, political rightist and anti-Semite,
> private letter intercepted by the *okhranka*, 1914[1]

Looking at that low and small head, you had the feeling that
if you pricked it, the whole of Karl Marx's *Capital* would
come hissing out of it like gas from a container. Marxism
was his element, there he was invincible. No power on earth
could dislodge him from a position once taken, and he
could find an appropriate Marx formula for every
phenomenon."

> A former fellow tsarist political prisoner speaking about
> the young Stalin in Baku prison, 1908[2]

RUSSIA'S STATE HAD ARISEN out of military exigencies, in an extraordinarily
challenging geopolitical environment, but also out of ideals, above all the autocratic ideal, yet Russia's long-enduring autocracy was anything but stable. Nearly
half the Romanovs, following Peter the Great, left their thrones involuntarily, as a
result of coups or assassinations. Peter himself had his eldest son and heir killed
for disobedience (thirteen of Peter's fifteen children by two wives predeceased
him). Peter was succeeded by his second wife, a peasant girl from the Baltic coast,
who took the name Catherine I, and then by his grandson, Peter II. In 1730, when
Peter II died from smallpox on the day of his wedding, the Romanov male line
expired. The throne passed to Peter II's relations, first to his father's cousin Anna
(r. 1730–40), and then, in a palace coup, to his half aunt Elizabeth (r. 1741–61).

Neither produced a male heir. The Romanov House avoided perishing altogether only thanks to the marriage of one of Peter the Great's two surviving daughters to the Duke of Holstein-Gottorp. This made the Romanovs a Russian-German family. Karl Peter Ulrich, the first Holstein-Gottorp-Romanov—who became Peter III—was an imbecile. He wore a Prussian military uniform to Russian state functions and lasted six months before being deposed in a putsch by his wife, a minor German princess named Sophie Auguste Frederike von Anhalt-Zerbst, who assumed the throne as Catherine II (or the Great). She fancied herself an enlightened despot, and made high culture a partner in the autocracy (something Stalin would emulate, ruling as he would from Catherine's imperial Senate in Moscow). The German Catherine was a Romanov only by marriage, but Russia's ruling family continued to emphasize its links, via the female line, back to Peter and to employ the Russian surname only. In 1796, Catherine was succeeded by her son Paul, who was assassinated in 1801; then came Paul's son Alexander I (r. 1801–25); Alexander's brother Nicholas I (r. 1825–55); Alexander II, who died in agony in 1881, his legs shattered by a terrorist's bomb; Alexander III, who became heir following the sudden death of his elder brother and who, in power, succumbed to kidney disease (nephritis) at age forty-nine in 1894; and finally, Nicholas II.[3]

Except for Alexander III, who married a Danish princess—his deceased elder brother's fiancée—all the "Romanov" descendants of the German Catherine took German-born wives. Such intermarriage transformed almost all of Europe's royalty into relations. Nicholas II's German spouse—Alix Victoria Helena Louise Beatrice, Princess of Hesse-Darmstadt—was the favorite granddaughter of Queen Victoria of England. Born in 1872, the year after German unification, Alix first met the tsarevich "Nicky" when she was eleven and he fifteen, during the wedding of her sister, Ella, to Nicholas's uncle. They met again six years later and fell madly in love. Tsar Alexander III and his wife, Empress Consort Maria Fyodorovna, initially opposed their son Nicholas's marriage to the shy, melancholic Alix, despite the fact that she was their goddaughter. Russia's monarchs preferred the daughter of the pretender to the French throne, to solidify Russia's new alliance with France. Queen Victoria, for her part, had favored Alix for the Prince of Wales of the United Kingdom, but she, too, came around. Kaiser Wilhelm II of Germany supported the Alix-Nicky match from the get-go, hoping to strengthen German-Russian bonds. Alix's arrival in Russia, however, proved ill starred, coinciding with the early death of Emperor Alexander III. "She has come to us behind a coffin," the crowd noted in their first glimpse of her, at the state funeral. "She brings misfortune with her."[4] The new empress consort dutifully converted to Orthodoxy (from Lutheranism) and took the name Alexandra. Her honeymoon with Nicholas II consisted of twice-daily Orthodox services and visits by notables to convey condolences about her father-in-law's untimely passing. She gave birth to four daughters in succession, which also set everyone on edge, because an imperial succession law passed in 1797 under Paul I (r. 1796–1801), the son of Catherine the Great, forbade another female to occupy the throne. Finally, in August 1904, in the tenth year of marriage, Alexandra produced a long-awaited male heir. Nicholas II named the boy for his favorite early Romanov ruler, Alexei, Peter the Great's father, harkening back to the Moscow days before the building of St. Petersburg.

Possessing an heir, finally, Nicholas II reveled in Interior Minister Pyotr Durnovó's tenacious crackdown a little more than a year later, but the tsar had not retracted the October Manifesto. And so, on April 27, 1906, the newly created State Duma opened in the Winter Palace with the monarch's (terse) address from the throne, in emulation of British custom. Nicholas II uncannily resembled his cousin King George V. But facing all the standing dignitaries, domestic and foreign, as well as the commoner-elected representatives, who had gathered in St. George's Hall, the tsar, raised on a dais, spoke a mere 200 words, which were followed by a tomblike silence.[5] Russia had become something that had never before existed: a constitutional autocracy, in which the word "constitution" was forbidden.[6] It was a liberal-illiberal muddle. The Duma met in the Tauride Palace, which had been given by the autocrat Catherine the Great to her court favorite, Prince Potëmkin, in 1783, for his conquest of Crimea; it had been repossessed from his family after his death, and used, most recently, to warehouse props of the imperial theater. The Tauride's interior winter garden was converted into a nearly 500-seat chamber, christened the White Hall. Despite the exclusion from the Duma of the small central Asian "protectorates" of Khiva and Bukhara as well as the Grand Duchy of Finland (which had its own legislature), many of the Russian delegates experienced shock at the stunning diversity of the empire's representatives, as if elites in the capital had been living somewhere other than imperial Russia. Inside the White Hall, under a gigantic portrait of Nicholas II, the principal advocates for constitutionalism, the Constitutional Democrats (Cadets)—a group led by Moscow University history professor Paul Miliukov—constituted the *opposition*.[7] Who, if anyone, supported the new constitutional autocracy remained unclear.

Prime Minister Sergei Witte, who had done more than anyone to urge the

Duma on the tsar, at its successful launch handed in his resignation, exhausted, infirm, and scorned.[8] Witte earned no special dispensation from the fact that he had been the lead locomotive behind Russia's spectacular industrial surge from the 1890s, or had helped bridge the chasm of 1905 between regime and society. Nicholas II found Witte devious and unprincipled ("Never have I seen such a chameleon of a man.").[9] The tsar immediately and everlastingly regretted the political concessions that Witte had helped wring. With Witte's fall, Durnovó, too, was obliged to step down, his historic service as interior minister having also lasted a mere six months, although Nicholas II allowed Durnovó to continue receiving his salary of 18,000 rubles per annum and awarded him a staggering cash gift of 200,000 rubles. (Witte received the Order of St. Alexander Nevsky, with diamonds.)[10] Durnovó yielded his portfolio to the Saratov province governor, Pyotr Stolypin, who in July 1906 managed to add the post of prime minister, thereby replacing both Durnovó and Witte.[11]

Tall, with blue eyes and a black beard, a figure of immense charm and sensitive to form—so unlike the abrasive Witte—Stolypin was a discovery. He had been born in 1862 in Dresden (where his mother was visiting relatives abroad) to an ancient Russian noble family. His father, who was related to the renowned writer Mikhail Lermontov, owned a Stradivarius that he himself played, and had served as adjutant to Alexander II and as commandant of Moscow's Grand Kremlin Palace; Stolypin's well-educated mother was the daughter of the general who had commanded the Russian infantry during the Crimean War and rose to viceroy of tsarist Poland. The boy grew up on his wealthy family's estates in tsarist Lithuania, territories of the bygone Polish-Lithuanian Commonwealth, and graduated in natural sciences (not law) from St. Petersburg Imperial University. (Dimitri Mendeleev, of the periodic table, was one of Stolypin's teachers.) Like Stalin, Stolypin suffered a withered arm, from a mysterious teenage malady; he wrote by using his good left hand to guide his right. The deformity precluded following his father and mother's relatives into a military career.[12] But in 1902, at age forty, Stolypin became governor of Grodno, in the Polish-Lithuanian western borderlands, encompassing his own properties. He was the youngest person in the Russian empire to hold a governorship. In 1903, he had been transferred to governor of Saratov, in central Russia's Volga valley, whose villages, unlike those in the western borderlands, had communes that periodically redistributed strips of land among peasants (the "repartitional" commune). Saratov also became known for political turbulence. The tsar had had occasion to tour the province, and Stolypin toiled indefatigably to ensure he would be surrounded by admiring subjects. During the brutal 1905–6 crackdown, Stolypin proved to be imperial Russia's most energetic governor, as well as an executive of courage and vision, willing to explain to assembled crowds his rationale for upholding the law and, if that failed, personally leading troops in repression. Stolypin's performance impressed the courtiers; Nicholas II telegrammed congratulations for "exemplary efficiency."

When Nicholas II had summoned him to his Alexander Palace residence in Tsarskoe Selo, just outside St. Petersburg, to inform him of his elevation to the premiership in the capital, Stolypin protested that he was unfit for such a high post and did not know the capital's elites. The tsar, tears in his eyes, grateful, perhaps, for the professed modesty and deference, grasped Stolypin's hand with both of his.[13] This handclasp has been seen, even more in retrospect than in prospect, as a historic opportunity that might have saved imperial Russia. Stolypin certainly stands out as one of the most commanding officials ever to hold a position of power in Russia: self-confident in a milieu of toadying, an accomplished orator as well as manager, a rare state official with a longer-term perspective. "If the state does not retaliate against evil deeds," Stolypin stated upon his appointment, "then the very meaning of the state is lost."[14] The provincial proved himself adept at gaining the tsar's confidence, and he quickly came to overshadow the entire establishment in St. Petersburg.[15] But the tasks before him were daunting. The critical keys to unlocking modernity included not just steel output and mass production, which Russia more or less did manage to attain, but also the successful incorporation of the masses into political systems, that is, mass politics.

Stolypin was determined to take full advantage of the new lease on life afforded to the regime by Durnovó's bravura crackdown, within the new situation created by Witte's successful urging on Nicholas II of the October Manifesto quasi-constitutionalism. During Stolypin's premiership (1906–1911), he endeavored, in his way, to reinvent the Russian political system. But Russia's conservative political establishment, furious at the constitutional autocracy, opposed outright Stolypin's efforts to conjure into being a polity on their behalf. The left, for different reasons—they were sobered by the defeat of the 1905 uprising and Stolypin's repression—would fall into despair as well. To be sure, our leftist protagonist Iosif "Koba" Jughashvili would perpetrate his most infamous revolutionary exploits under Stolypin. But whether those incendiary activities amounted to much remains questionable. By contrast, the aims and frustrations of Stolypin's reform programs, like those of Witte before him, tell us a great deal about the future Stalin's regime. At the time, viewing the world through a canonical Marxist prism, the future Stalin comprehended next to nothing of what Stolypin went through at the time. Stalin never met the tsarist prime minister, but to a very great extent he would later walk in his shoes.

## RUSSIA'S (SECOND) WOULD-BE BISMARCK

Two attributes seemed to define imperial Russia. First, its agriculture fed both Germany and England via exports but remained far from efficient: Russia had the lowest harvest yields in Europe (below Serbia, considered merely a "little brother"); its per-acre grain yields remained less than half those of France or even Austria-Hungary.[16] This made the peasants seem like an urgent problem that had to be addressed. Second, Russian political life had become riotous, self-defeating, insane. Many in the elite, not least Nicholas II, had expected the initial 1906 elections to yield a conservative peasant-monarchist Duma. Instead, the Constitutional Democrats enjoyed electoral success, which surprised even the Cadets. Once empowered by the ballot box, Russia's classical liberals showed no intention of cooperating with the autocracy, and Nicholas II had no intention of compromising with them.[17] Moreover, although the socialist parties had boycotted the First Duma elections, they changed their stance and got dozens of deputies elected to the Second Duma (thanks partly to peasant ballots). The *okhranka*, naturally, kept the deputies under surveillance, using informants and listening in on telephone conversations.[18] But the political police had no answer to the political intransigence on all sides. The latter, moreover, was greatly facilitated by the Duma's abysmal legislative procedures. No mechanisms existed to distinguish major from minor matters, so all were taken up as legislation rather than via mundane government regulations. Also, incredibly, the Duma lacked any fixed timetable for the progression of legislation; populous commissions of deputies would handle bills before they could be brought to the floor, and some commissions would deliberate on a single bill for eighteen months. When the bills did finally move to the next stage, they would be debated in the full Duma again without time limits.[19] In such procedural minutiae can institutions founder, especially when opposing political forces prove beyond reconciliation.

From the point of view of the Constitutional Democrats, the problem was that

Russia's constitutional revolution had not removed the autocracy. And indeed, Nicholas II used his prerogative to dismiss the Duma's first convocation after a mere seventy-three days. The autocrat was able, thanks to Article 87 of the Fundamental Laws, to issue laws by fiat during legislative recess. (Such laws were in theory supposed to be confirmed when the legislature resumed, but they remained in force while debate proceeded.)[20] The Second Duma in 1907, which served even more as a platform of antigovernment speechifying, was tolerated for fewer than ninety days. Then, on June 3, 1907, Stolypin unilaterally narrowed Duma suffrage still further by having Nicholas II employ Article 87 to alter the electoral provisions, a step that the Fundamental Laws expressly forbade.[21] "Coup d'état!" screamed the Constitutional Democrats, one of Stolypin's two main targets in the maneuver (the other target were those further to the left). It *was* a coup. But from Stolypin's point of view, the Cadets were hardly angels: in 1905–7, they colluded in antistate terrorism, condemning it publicly but covertly encouraging it, in order to weaken the autocracy. Many humble tsarist officials were killed in that collusion.[22] But whereas the intriguers at court egged on Nicholas II to terminate the Duma "experiment," Stolypin was trying to work with the legislature in order to root Russia's suspended-in-the-air government in some kind of political base that was compatible with the autocracy. "We want not professors, but men with roots in the country, the local gentry, and such like," Stolypin told the professor Bernard Pares, the founder of Russian studies in Britain, in May 1908.[23]

Stolypin was correct that passing legislation necessitated more than some "mystical union" between tsar and people. He imagined himself, like his very short-lived predecessor, Sergei Witte, as a Russian Bismarck. "I am in no way in favor of an absolutist government," the Iron Chancellor had told the German Reichstag. "I consider parliamentary *cooperation*—if properly practiced— necessary and useful, as much as I consider parliamentary *rule* harmful and impossible."[24] Russia's prime minister, too, accepted a parliament but not parliamentarism (a government controlled by parliament), and the Russian Duma, like the German Reichstag, was a representative institution that expressly strove not to be representative. To be sure, the German franchise had been much more inclusive: all German males over twenty-five had the right to vote. Moreover, thanks to its June 3, 1907, origins, imperial Russia's Third Duma would be relentlessly shadowed by predictions of new coups, a source of instability. But in Stolypin's calculation, all this was a necessary price to pay for acquiring the legal wherewithal to modernize the country.

In Saratov, Stolypin had observed the same injustices the radical young Stalin had observed in the Caucasus: workers suffering frequent trauma and long hours for low pay, nobles owning enormous tracts of land while peasants in rags worked tiny plots. As prime minister, Stolypin embarked on far-reaching social reforms. German industrial workers, thanks to the second plank of Bismarck's strategy (stealing the thunder of the left), had come to enjoy sickness, accident, and old-age insurance as well as access to subsidized canteens; Stolypin, at a minimum, wanted to introduce workmen's social insurance.[25] Most prominently, though, he wanted to encourage peasants to abandon the repartitional commune and consolidate farm land into more productice units.

Russian elites tended to view peasant society as backward and alien, and shared a determination to transform it.[26] (In fact, an observer could have looked at the Russian government *as a distinct society* alienated from the empire at large, especially from peasant society—the vast majority of the population.)[27] This elite view took on a predominantly economic inflection as the Russian establishment came to believe the peasants were becoming increasingly impoverished; a few officials, like Witte, back in his days as finance minister, had blamed "the poor condition of our peasantry" as the main brake on the Russian state's industrialization and geopolitical aggrandizement.[28] Stolypin went further, treating the peasantry as a regime-defining *political* problem. Such an analysis was not unique to Russia. In Prussia, reformers in the 1820s, seeking to counter the influence of the French Revolution, had argued that peasant property owners were the only reliable defenders of law and order and the state.[29] This was precisely Stolypin's view as well. Instead of blaming outside "revolutionary agitators" for rural disturbances, Stolypin pinpointed low rural living standards, and further noted that much of the peasant unrest in 1905–6 had been communally organized.[30] On the basis of his experience in the communeless western borderlands, moreover, he concluded that a prosperous individualist village was a peaceful village. Thus, his agrarian reforms, enabled by a November 9, 1906, decree, aimed to drive agricultural productivity *and* remove the basis for peasant unrest by creating an independent property-owning class among the peasants, who, once furnished with state credits and access to technology, would strike out on their own. In other words, Stolypin sought to transform both the physical rural landscape, overcoming the separated communal strips of land with consolidated farms, and the psychology of the rural inhabitant.[31]

Globally, the period of Stolypin's premiership was one of heightened striving to enlarge the capacities of the state. From the French Third Republic to the Russian empire, states of all types pursued ambitious projects such as the building of canals, roads, and railroads to integrate their territories and markets. They also promoted the settlement of new lands via subsidizing homesteading, draining marshes, damming rivers, and irrigating fields. Such statist transformationalism—building infrastructure, managing populations and resources—was often tested first in overseas possessions (colonies), then reapplied back home; sometimes it was developed first at home, then taken abroad, or to what were designated as imperial peripheries. Rule-of-law states when governing abroad often implemented many of the social engineering practices characteristic of non-rule-of-law states, but at home liberal orders differed from authoritarian ones in what practices were deemed acceptable or possible.[32] What stands out in all cases of state-led social engineering, though, was how the would-be "technocrats" rarely perceived the benefits, let alone the necessity, of converting subjects (domestic or imperial) into citizens. Technocrats generally saw "politics" as a hindrance to efficient administration. In that regard, Stolypin's idea of incorporating peasants—at least the "strong and the sober" among the peasantry—into the sociopolitical order on equal terms with other subjects was radical. To be sure, he intended property ownership to impart a stake more than a formal voice. Still, one adviser to the prime minister called him a "new phenomenon" on the Russian scene for seeking political support in parts of the wider populace.[33]

The reform proved to be a flexibly designed experiment, amalgamating years of prior discussion and effort, and allowing for adjustments along the way.[34] But both the political boost from newly created loyal yeoman and the full economic takeoff that Stolypin envisioned proved elusive. Of course, in any political system, major reforms are always fraught because institutions are more complex than perceived. Russia's peasant communes, in practice, were actually more flexible institutions than their critics understood.[35] But the commune's division of land into separated strips required coordination with others in the village, and rendered impossible the sale, lease, mortgage, or legal transfer of land by individuals, while inhibiting investment in lands that might be taken away. Communes did shield peasants from catastrophe in hard times, although that, too, depended on permanently pooling resources, inducing communes to resist any loss of members. With the reform, the formal consent of the commune was no longer required for exit. Exits were still complicated by red tape (court backlogs), as well as social tensions, but a substantial minority, perhaps 20 percent of European

Russia's 13 million peasant households, would manage to leave the commune during the reform. These new small private landowners, however, generally did not escape commune-style strip farming.[36] (A single holding could sometimes be divided into forty or fifty strips.) A shortage of land surveyors, among other factors, meant that many peasants who had privatized could not always consolidate.[37] Often, the most individually oriented peasants just decamped for Siberia, as the reform's enhancement of secure property rights significantly spurred migration in search of new land, but that reduced productivity at the farms they left.[38] The land question's complexity could be stupefying. But where privatized or even non-privatized farms *were* consolidated—the key aim of Stolypin's economic reforms—productivity rose significantly.[39]

In the end, however, Stolypin's economic and other reforms came up against the stubborn limits to structural reform imposed by politics. Stolypin had to initiate his bold agrarian transformation with the Fundamental Law's emergency Article 87, during a Duma recess, and the changes sparked deep resistance among the propertied establishment. They, as well as others, blocked Stolypin's related modernization efforts.[40]

Russia's prime minister would attempt not just to rearrange peasant landholdings and credit and introduce workers' accident and sickness insurance, but also to expand local self-government to the empire's Catholic west, lift juridical restrictions on Jews, broaden civil and religious rights, and overall invent a workable central government and general polity.[41] But his government found it had to bribe many of the elected conservative Duma deputies for votes on bills. And even then, Stolypin could not get the votes for his key legislation. Only the agrarian reforms and a watered down version of worker insurance made the statute books. Conservatives circumscribed Stolypin's room for maneuver. He was partly the victim of his own success: he had garroted the 1905–6 revolution and, the next year, emptied the Duma of many liberals and socialists, thereby making possible a working relationship between the quasi-parliament and the tsar's appointed government, but the urgency had vanished. At a deeper level, he had miscalculated. In Stolypin's June 1907 new franchise, the societal groups that had the most to gain from his reform programs were either excluded from the Duma or outnumbered in it by traditional interests—the landholding gentry— that had the most to lose but that Stolypin's electoral coup had entrenched.[42] To put the matter another way, the political interests that most accepted autocracy least accepted modernizing reforms.

## RUSSIA'S PROTO-FASCISM

That the Russian autocracy would experience severe difficulties developing a political base is not self-evident. The number of Social Democrats shot up from a mere 3,250 in 1904 to perhaps 80,000 by 1907—a vault, to be sure, but less impressive in relative terms. The Social Democratic Workers' Party achieved little success among Ukrainian speakers, especially peasants, publishing next to nothing in the Ukrainian language. On the territory of what would become Ukraine, the party had no more than 1,000 members.[43] The leftist Jewish Labor Bund drew most of its membership not from the empire's southwest (Ukraine) but the northwest (Belorussia, tsarist Poland). Be that as it may, even adding the Bund—with whom most Russian Social Democrats did not desire a close relationship—and adding the empire's separate Polish and Latvian Social Democrat-equivalent parties as well as the semiautonomous Georgian Social Democrats, the combined Social Democratic strength in imperial Russia probably did not exceed 150,000.[44] By comparison, the classical liberal (proprivate property, proparliament) Constitutional Democrats—said to have no real social base in Russia—grew to around 120,000, and another constitutionalist party (Octobrists) just to the right of the Cadets enrolled 25,000 more.[45] The Socialist Revolutionaries who aimed to represent the agricultural proletariat, failed to achieve mass peasant support in 1905–7, though the SRs did attract urban workers and attained a formal membership of at least 50,000.[46] Dwarfing them all, however, was the staunchly monarchical and national chauvinist Union of the Russian People, founded in November 1905, with rallies under the roof at the Archangel Michael Riding Academy as a church choir sang "Praise God" and "Tsar Divine"; already by 1906, it had ballooned to perhaps 300,000, with branches across the empire—including in small towns and villages.[47]

During the revolutionary uprising, in which liberal constitutionalism was pushed to the forefront, while socialism emerged as an empirewide aspiration, the rise of the illiberal Union of the Russian People constituted a remarkable story. Until 1905, self-styled patriotic elements faced legal limitations in expressing themselves publicly, having to be content with religious processionals, military-victory commemorations, imperial funerals and coronations. That revolutionary year, moreover, most conservatives found themselves caught out, unwilling to enter, let alone master, the political arena. But the Union of the Russian People was different.[48] As the most prominent of many upstart rightist organizations in Russia, the Union brought together courtiers, professionals, and churchmen—including many from the young Stalin's old Tiflis seminary—with townspeople, workers, and peasants. Drawing in the disaffected and the disoriented, as well as the patriotic, the Union managed to sweep in the lower orders and middle strata "for Tsar, faith, and fatherland," stealing a march on the left.[49] The tsarist regime, stymied by rightist establishment opposition in the Duma and State Council, appeared to have the option of grassroots mobilization.

The Union of the Russian People helped invent a new style of right-wing politics—novel not just for Russia but for most of the world—a politics in a new key oriented toward the masses, public spaces, and direct action, a fascism avant la lettre.[50] The Union's members and leaders, such as the grandson of a Bessarabian village priest, Vladimir Purishkevich—who liked to exclaim, "To the right of me there is only the wall"—were antiliberal, anticapitalist, and anti-Semitic (the triad being redundant, in their eyes).[51] They emphasized the uniqueness of Russia's historical trajectory, rejected Europe as a model, preached the need for Orthodox primacy over Jews and Catholics (Poles), and demanded "restoration" of Russia's traditions. The Union disdained the Russian government's cowardly preoccupation with its own security, which they saw as indicative of a lack of will to crush the liberals (and socialists). The Union also abhorred the modernizing state as tantamount to socialist revolutionaries. Union members held that the autocrat alone must rule, not the bureaucracy, let alone the Duma. Unionists overlapped with right-wing vigilantes known as Black Hundreds, who became notorious for pogroms against the Jews in the Pale of Settlement and for fighting alongside imperial troops in crackdowns against rebellious peasants and workers. Russian rightists of all stripes, after a slow start, mobilized to a stunning degree, widely disseminating pamphlets and newspapers, organizing rallies in the name of defending autocracy, Orthodoxy, and nationality against Jews and European encroachments such as Western-style constitutionalism.

The empire's socialists did not shrink from confronting the rightist upsurge. The socialists often forced the Union of the Russian People to hold rallies indoors, under the threat of leftist counterdemonstrations, and then, to use ticket checkers to keep out leftist terrorists who would blow the rightists to smithereens. The left also drew considerable strength and cohesion of its own from Karl Marx and his "Song of Songs" *Communist Manifesto* (1848). Still, Russia's rightists possessed real Biblical scripture and what should have been genuinely *electrifying* material—a Russian right-wing newspaper had introduced the world to the so-called *Protocols of the Elders of Zion*. This fabricated transcript of a purported Jewish organization's meetings portrayed Jews as a global conspiracy—visible yet somehow invisible—preying on Christians while plotting to dominate the world.[52] It was first published in Russian, serialized over nine days (August 28 through September 7, 1903), in *Znamya* (St. Petersburg), which was financed by Interior Minister Vyacheslav von Plehve and published by the anti-Semitic Moldavian Pavalachii Cruşeveanu (b. 1860). Known as Pavel Krushevan, he not only oversaw the text's compilation in 1902–3 but instigated the major pogrom in Kishenëv (Chişinau) in 1903 and founded the Bessarabian branch of the Union of the Russian People in 1905.[53] Anti-Semitism, whether in earnest or in cynicism, could serve as a political elixir: everything that went awry could be, and was, blamed on the Jews. In the Pale of Settlement and western borderlands (Volhynia, Bessarabia, Minsk), the rightists nearly took the entire peasant vote, and in the central agricultural heartland (Tula, Kursk, Oryol), site of major agrarian disturbances, rightists won around half the peasant vote.[54] In fact, across the expanse of imperial Russian, sympathy for the political right was there to be galvanized.[55]

Just as the autocracy had refused to use the word "constitution" (or even "parliament"), from the start, the "Union" of the Russian People had abjured the designation "political party" and presented itself as a spontaneous movement, an organic union of the people or folk (*narod*). Even so, senior government officials in St. Petersburg were unwilling to accept the movement on a permanent basis. Stolypin maintained the expedient of surreptitiously financing the rightist organizations and their anti-Semitic publications, among many newspapers that his government funded, but Stolypin's deputy in the interior ministry from 1906 to 1911, Sergei Kryzhanovsky, who handled the disbursements to the Union of Russian People and similar organizations, saw no distinction between the political techniques and social program of the far right—redistribution of private property from plutocrats to the poor—and that of the leftist revolutionary parties.[56] The government had not created these mass movements and remained wary of them. Thus, even if the far right's calls for social leveling seemed mostly bluff, the policy of the *okhranka* was still to treat right-wing organizations as another revolutionary movement. Some factions inside the *okhranka* ignored or subverted this policy. But mostly, *okhranka* operatives deemed the far right's leaders "uncultured" and "unreliable" and kept them under close surveillance, with good reason. Exactly like the radical left, the Union of the Russian People compiled lists of current and former government officials to be assassinated.[57] Stolypin was one of their targets.[58] His influential top domestic adviser, a former rabbi converted to Orthodoxy, was an anti-Semite, but the prime minister also tried to ease residence, occupational, and educational restrictions on Jews, for both principled and instrumentalist reasons, to diminish the perceived cause of Jewish radicalism and improve Russia's image abroad.[59] Stolypin succeeded in enraging the hard right.

Many rightist movements, refraining from hyperinflammatory rhetoric or arming vigilante "brotherhoods" to combat leftists and Jews and assassinate public figures, were considerably less volatile than the Union of the Russian People. And yet, Nicholas II and others throughout the regime continued to look askance on large public gatherings *by supporters*. The tsar and most government officials, including Stolypin, frowned on the public "disorder" of political mobilization, and wanted politics to return from the street to the corridors of power. This rebuff of the street held even though the supportive conservative movements pushed not for a right-wing revolution but, mostly, for a restoration of the archaic autocracy that had existed prior to the advent of the Duma.[60] No less fundamentally, many rightist organizations themselves would have refrained from mobilizing patriotic social constituencies on behalf of the regime even if they had been permitted, or encouraged, to do so: After all, what kind of *autocracy* needed help? The autocracy's very existence in a sense handcuffed the Russian right, both moderate and radical.[61]

Most rightists wanted an autocracy without asterisk—that is, a mystical unity of monarch and folk—and they rejected anything more than a consultative Duma, but the autocrat himself had created the Duma. This circumstance confused and divided the right. Almost all rightists believed that autocracy ipso facto ruled out opposition, which of course ruled out their own opposition. "In the West, where the government is elected, the concept of 'opposition' makes sense; there it refers to 'opposition to the government'; this is both clear and logical," explained the editor of the rightist Petersburg weekly *Unification*. "But here, the government is appointed by the monarch and invested with his confidence. . . . To be in opposition to the imperial government means to oppose the monarch."[62] Still, many rightists despised Stolypin merely for his willingness to engage with the Duma, even though that was the law and the prime minister's manipulations of the Duma were government triumphs. For some, including Nicholas II, the mere existence of a prime minister was an affront to autocracy.[63]

In August 1906, assassins dressed in state uniforms nearly killed Stolypin by dynamiting his state dacha where he received petitioners. "Everywhere one could see shreds of human flesh and blood," one witness recalled of the twenty-seven instant deaths. Another witness observed how Stolypin "came into his half-demolished study, with plaster stains on his coat and an ink spot on the back of his neck. The top of his writing desk had been lifted off by the explosion, which took place in the hall at a distance of about thirty feet from the study, and the inkstand had hit his neck." A few months later, a time bomb was discovered in former Prime Minister Witte's home, although it failed to detonate (the clock had stopped). Both acts against proautocratic, conservative prime ministers went unsolved; circumstantial evidence pointed to possible involvement of right-wing circles.[64]

Stolypin gained in stature from the failed assassination, thanks to his display of composure and resolve, but he felt constrained to move his family into the Winter Palace (near his offices), which was considered more secure than the prime minister's official residence on the Fontanka Canal. Even then, the police compelled the Russian prime minister to constantly alter the exits and entrances he used. Unsafe leaving or entering the Winter Palace! Many disgusted rightists, at a minimum, hoped Stolypin would be replaced by Durnovó or another hard-liner who would emasculate or outright abolish the Duma. At the same time, other diehard monarchists—who in principle were no less against voting and political parties—found themselves organizing to compete in the elections they rejected if only to deny use of the Duma to the "opposition" (liberals and social-ists, lumped together). But the rightists who accepted the Duma became anath-ema to the rest. Modern street politics fractured the Russian right.[65] The gulf between the politics of parliament participation and of assassination was never bridged.[66]

## A PUNDIT

When first subjected to Durnovó's ferocious assault, the factionalized Social Democrats had tried to close ranks. In the two weeks before the first Duma opened, between April 10 and 25, 1906, the Russian Social Democratic Workers' Party convoked its 4th Congress under the slogan of "unity." Held across the border in the safety of Stockholm, which allowed émigrés to attend, the gathering brought together, at least physically, the recently divided Mensheviks (62 delegates) and Bolsheviks (46 delegates), as well as the separate parties of Latvian and Polish Social Democrats and the Bund.[67] Among Caucasus Social Democrats, the second most numerous contingent in the empire after the Russian Social Democrats, there was already near unity because Caucasus Bolsheviks were so few.[68] Unity, however, proved elusive in policy. Jughashvili turned out to be the only Bolshevik among the eleven Caucasus delegates in Stockholm, but, taking the congress podium to speak on the vexing agrarian question, he boldly rejected the Bolshevik Lenin's proposal for complete land nationalization as well as a Russian Menshevik call for land municipalization. Instead, the future collectivizer of agriculture recommended that *the peasants get the land*. Land redistribution, Jughashvili argued, would facilitate a worker-peasant alliance, an unacknowledged tip of his hat to his Georgian Menshevik adversaries. More than even that, Jughashvili argued, reiterating the comment of another speaker, offering the land to the peasants would rob the peasant Socialist Revolutionary Party—the Social Democrats' competition on the left—of its platform.[69] What impression these suggestions made at the 4th Congress remains unclear. [70] For the time being, among Russian Social Democrats, the decisive issue of a land redistribution to the peasants—in the overwhelmingly peasant Russian empire— would go unresolved.

What could not be left unresolved was the survival of their party. In 1905, both Menshevik and Bolshevik factions had concurred on the need to form combat squads for self-defense: after all, the unjust tsarist system used terror. The factions also agreed, in order to obtain weapons and party funds, on conducting "expropriations," often in concert with the criminal underworld.[71] As a result, the Russian empire became even more of a cauldron of political terrorism after it had become a quasi-constitutional order.

Until this time, imperial Russia's regular police had been remarkably few and far between. In towns the police presence was often sparse, and outside the towns in 1900 Russia had fewer than 8,500 constables and sergeants (*uriadniki*) for the rural population of nearly 100 million. Many constables (assisted by a handful of sergeants) "oversaw" 50,000 to 100,000 subjects, over more than 1,000 square miles. In 1903, the state created the position of guardsmen (*strazhniki*), deploying some 40,000 in the countryside, which brought the ratio of state officers to rural inhabitants only to roughly 1 for every 2,600 inhabitants. Salaries rose but remained low, as did levels of education and training. Abusive, arbitrary behavior, and graft, rendered the police profoundly unpopular. The regular police routinely brought criminal cases or detained people without incidence of a crime, and resorted to physical abuse in what they called "the law of the fist." Peasant-born sergeants acted like petty tyrants toward villagers, boasting of their power, under the theory that the more severe they were, the greater would be their authority.[72]

The mass revolts beginning in 1905 precipitated a vast increase in police personnel. But between 1905 and 1910, more than 16,000 tsarist officials, from village policemen up to ministers, would be killed or wounded by terrorist-revolutionaries (including in many cases by Menshevik assassins).[73] Countless carriage drivers and railway personnel—proletarians—perished as well. One top police official complained that the details of bombmaking "became so widespread that practically any child could produce one and blow up his nanny."[74]

This leftist political terror instilled fear throughout tsarist officialdom, but the regime fought back savagely.[75] Stolypin "seized the revolution by the throat." His government deported tens of thousands to forced labor or internal exile. It also introduced special field courts that used summary justice to send more than 3,000 accused political opponents to the gallows, strung up in demonstrative public executions, a deterrent that became known as the Stolypin necktie.[76] No regime could let go unanswered the pervasive assassination of its officials, but the courts bore little resemblance to due process. Be that as it may, people got the point. Lenin, who named Stolypin Russia's "hangman-in-chief," and other prominent revolutionaries fled, having only just returned to Russia in 1905's (briefly) freer circumstances.[77] The would-be revolutionaries rejoined some 10,000 expatriates already resident in Russian colonies around Europe as of 1905. The émigré leftists fell under the surveillance of the 40 operatives and 25 informants in the *okhranka*'s foreign department, run out of Russia's Paris embassy, which amassed dramatic documentation on the exiles' often pathetic endeavors.[78]

Koba Jughashvili was among those committed socialists who did *not* seek to flee abroad. In Stockholm, he had met not only Klimenty "Klim" Voroshilov, a lifelong acquaintance, but also the Polish nobleman and Bolshevik Felix Dzierżyński and the Russian Bolshevik Grigory Radomylsky (better known as Zinoviev). And Jughashvili had encountered his old Tiflis seminary nemesis Seid Devdariani, by now a Georgian Menshevik. From Stockholm Jughashvili returned to the Caucasus in spring 1906. He wore a suit with a real hat, and carried a pipe, like a European. Only the pipe would last.

Back home, in a pamphlet in Georgian (1906) reporting on the Stockholm Congress, Jughashvili stridently dismissed Russia's first-ever legislative body. "Who sits between two stools betrays the revolution," he wrote. "Who is not with us is against us! The pitiful Duma and its pitiful Constitutional Democrats got stuck precisely between two stools. They want to reconcile the revolution with the counter-revolution, so that the wolves and the sheep can pasture together."[79]

Jughashvili also got married.[80] Ketevan "Kato" Svanidze, then twenty-six, was the youngest of the three Svanidze sisters of Tiflis, whom Jughashvili had met either through the Svanidzes' son, Alyosha, a Bolshevik (married to a Tiflis opera singer), or through Mikheil Monoselidze, an old seminary friend who had married another Svanidze sister, Sashiko.[81] The Svanidzes' apartment stood right behind the South Caucasus military district headquarters, in the heart of the city, and thus was considered an ultrasafe shelter for revolutionaries: no one would suspect. In the hideaway, the scruffy Jughashvili wrote articles, regaled the sisters with talk of books and revolution, and brazenly received members of his small revolutionary posse. Koba and Kato also evidently met for lovemaking in the Atelier Madame Hervieu, the private salon where the sisters, all expert seamstresses, worked. Sometime during that summer of 1906, Kato informed him she was pregnant. He agreed to marry her. But because Jughashvili had false papers and was wanted by the police, a legal marriage faced complications. They lucked upon a former seminary classmate, Kita Tkhinvaleli, who had become a priest and agreed to perform the ceremony, in the dead of night (2:00 a.m., on July 15–16, 1906). At the "banquet" for ten, where the bridegroom showed off his voice and charm, the honored role of toastmaster (*tamada*) was performed by Mikho Tskhakaya, the former Tiflis seminarian and Bolshevik elder statesmen (then aged thirty-nine). Jughashvili seems not to have invited his mother, Keke, though it could hardly escape notice that the old woman shared a given name— Ketevan (Ekaterina in Russian)—with the young bride.[82] In fact, just like Keke, Kato was devout, and she, too, prayed for Jughashvili's safety, but unlike Keke, Kato was demure.

The beautiful and educated Kato—a world away from the Chiatura manganese dust—was a class above the future Stalin's usual girlfriends, and she evidently pierced his heart.[83] "I was amazed," Mikheil Monoselidze observed, "how Soso, who was so severe in his work and to his comrades, could be so tender, affectionate and attentive to his wife."[84] That said, the shotgun marriage did not alter his obsession with revolution. Almost immediately after the conspiratorial summer 1906 wedding, he took off on underground business, abandoning his pregnant wife in Tiflis. As a precaution, she had not recorded the marriage in her internal passport as required by law. Still, the gendarmerie, somehow tipped off, arrested Kato on a charge of sheltering revolutionaries. She was four months pregnant. Her sister Sashiko, appealing to the wife of a top officer whose gowns the girls made, managed to get Kato released—after a month and a half in jail—into the custody of the police chief's wife. (The Svanidze sisters made her gowns, too.) On March 18, 1907, some eight months after her wedding, Kato gave birth to a son. They christened the boy Yakov, perhaps in honor of Yakov "Koba" Egnatashvili, Jughashvili's surrogate father. The future Stalin was said to be over the moon. But if so, he continued to be rarely home. Like other revolutionaries—at least those still at large—he was constantly on the run, rotating living quarters and battling his leftist rivals. The Georgian Mensheviks controlled most of the revolutionary publications in the Caucasus, but he came to play an outsized role in the small-circulation Bolshevik press, becoming editor of Georgian Bolshevik periodicals one by one. On the eve of Yakov's birth, Jughashvili, together with Suren Spandaryan (b. 1882) and others, established the newspaper *Baku Proletarian*. He had found a calling in punditry.

Stolypin's resolute campaign of arrests, executions, and deportations crippled the revolutionary movement, however. Instead of the grand May Day processionals of recent years, displays of proletarian power, leftists had to content themselves with collecting pitiful sums for the families of the legions who were arrested, and staging "red funerals" for the prematurely departed. Among those lost to the struggle was Giorgi Teliya (1880–1907). Born in a Georgian village, Teliya completed a few years of the village school and, in 1894, at age fourteen, made his way to Tiflis, where he was hired by the railway and, still a teenager, helped organize strikes in 1898 and 1900. He was fired, then arrested. Like Jughashvili, Teliya suffered lung problems, but his proved far more serious: having contracted tuberculosis in a tsarist prison, he succumbed to the disease in 1907.[85] "Comrade Teliya was not a 'scholar,'" the future Stalin remarked at the funeral in Teliya's native village, but he had passed through the "school" of the Tiflis railway workshops, learned Russian, and developed a love for books, exemplifying the celebrated worker-*intelligentsia*.[86] "Inexhaustible energy, independence, profound love for the cause, heroic determination, and an apostolic gift," Jughashvili said of his martyred friend.[87] He further divulged that Teliya had written a major essay, "Anarchism and Social Democracy," which remained unpublished supposedly because the police confiscated it. Georgian anarchists had made their appearance in late 1905, early 1906—yet another challenge on the fractious left—and the topic of how to respond was widely discussed.[88] From June 1906 to January 1907, Jughashvili published his own articles under a nearly identical rubric as Teliya, "Anarchism or Socialism?," and for the very same Georgian periodicals.

"Anarchism or Socialism?" was nowhere near the level of *The Communist Manifesto* (1848) or *The Eighteenth Brumaire of Louis Bonaparte* (1852), which the pundit Karl Marx (born in 1818) had written when similarly youthful. Still Jughashvili's derivative antianarchist essays dropped a plethora of names: Kropotkin, Kautsky, Proudhon, Spencer, Darwin, Cuvier, in addition to Marx.[89] It also showed that in Marxism he had found his theory of everything. "Marxism is not only a theory of socialism, it is a complete worldview, a philosophical system," he wrote. "This philosophical system is called dialectical materialism."[90] "What was materialism?" he asked in the catechism style for which he would later become famous. "A simple example," he wrote: "Imagine a cobbler who had his own modest shop, but then could not withstand the competition from big shops, closed his and, say, hired himself out to the Adelkhanov factory in Tiflis." The goal of the cobbler, Jughashvili continued, without mentioning his father, Beso, by name, was to accumulate capital and reopen his own business. But eventually, the "petit-bourgeois" cobbler realized he would never accumulate the capital and was in fact a proletarian. "A change in the consciousness of the cobbler," Jughashvili concluded, "followed a change in his material circumstances."[91] Thus, in order to explain Marx's concept of materialism (social existence determines consciousness), the future Stalin had rendered his father a victim of historical forces. Moving to the practical, he wrote that "the proletarians worked day and night but nonetheless remain poor. The capitalists do not work but nonetheless they get richer." Why? Labor was commodified and the capitalists owned the means of production. Ultimately, Jughashvili asserted, the workers would win. But they would have to fight hard—strikes, boycotts, sabotage—and for that they needed the Russian Social Democratic Workers' Party and a "dictatorship of the proletariat."[92]

Here we see more than a glimpse of the future Stalin: the militancy, the confident verities, the ability to convey, accessibly, both a worldview and practical politics. His ideational world—Marxist materialism, Leninist party—emerges as derivative and catechismic, yet logical and deeply set.

Right after the essay series appeared, Jughashvili stole across the border to attend the 5th Russian Social Democratic Workers' Party Congress, held between April 30 and May 19, 1907, in north London's Brotherhood Church. Congress luminaries were lodged in Bloomsbury, but Jughashvili stayed with the mass of delegates in the East End. One night, utterly drunk, he got into a pub scrape with a drunken Brit, and the owner summoned the police. Only the intercession of the quick-witted, English-speaking Bolshevik Meir Henoch Mojszewicz Wallach, known as Maxim Litvinov, saved Jughashvili from arrest. In the capital of world imperialism, the future Stalin also encountered Lev Bronstein (aka Trotsky), the high-profile former head of the 1905 Petrograd Soviet, but what impression the two might have made on each other remains undocumented. Stalin did not speak from the dais; Trotsky maintained his distance even from the Mensheviks.[93]

According to Jordania, Lenin was pursuing a back-room scheme: if the Georgian Mensheviks would refrain from taking sides in the Bolshevik-Menshevik dispute among the Russians in the party, Lenin would offer them carte blanche at home at the expense of Caucasus Bolsheviks. No other evidence corroborates this story of Lenin's possible sellout of Jughashvili, who had expended so much blood and sweat fighting for Bolshevism in the Caucasus.[94] Lenin often proposed or cut deals that he had no intention of honoring. Whatever the case here, Jordania, in later exile, was trying to distance Stalin from Lenin. What we know for sure is that when shouts at the congress were raised because Jughashvili, along with a few others, had not been formally elected a delegate—which provoked the Russian Menshevik Martov to exclaim, "Who are these people, where do they come from?"—the crafty Lenin, chairing a session, got Jughashvili and the others recognized as "consultative" delegates.

## GEOPOLITICAL ORIENTATION

Alongside everything else, Stolypin had to work diligently to keep Russia out of foreign trouble. Tensions with Britain were particularly high, and Britain was a preeminent global power. Britons invested one fourth of their country's wealth overseas, financing the building of railroads, harbors, mines, you name it—all outside Europe. Indeed, even as American and German manufacturing surpassed the British in many areas, the British still dominated the world flows of trade, finance, and information. On the oceans, where steamship freighters had jumped in size from 200 tons in 1850 to 7,500 tons by 1900, the British owned more than half of world shipping. In the early 1900s, two thirds of the world's undersea cables were British, affording them a predominant position in global communications. Nine tenths of international transactions used British pounds sterling.[95] Reaching an accord with Britain seemed very much in the Russian interest, provided that such a step did not antagonize Germany.

In the aftershock of the defeat by Japan in 1905–6, Russia had undergone a vigorous internal debate about what was called foreign orientation (what we would call grand strategy). St. Petersburg already had a defensive alliance with Third Republic France, dating to 1892, but Paris had not helped in Russia's war in Asia. By contrast, Germany had offered Russia benevolent neutrality during the difficult Russo-Japanese War, and Germany's ally, Austria-Hungary, had refrained from taking advantage in southeastern Europe. A space had opened for a conservative reorientation away from democratic France toward an alliance based on "monarchical principle"—meaning a Russian alliance with Germany and Austria-Hungary, something of a return to Bismarck's old Three Emperors' League. Arrayed against this, however, stood Russia's Constitutional Democrats, Anglophiles who wanted to preserve the alliance with republican France and achieve rapprochement with liberal Britain in order to strengthen Russia's Duma at home.[96] In August 1907, just two months after Stolypin's constitutional coup d'état introducing narrower voting rules for the Duma, he opted for an Anglo-Russian entente.[97] Stolypin was something of a Germanophile and no friend of British-style constitutional monarchy, but in foreign policy, the Constitutional Democrats, his sworn enemies, had gotten their way because rapprochement with Britain seemed Russia's best path for securing external peace while, in Stolypin's mind, not precluding friendly relations with Germany, too.[98] This was logical enough. And the content of the 1907 Anglo-Russian Entente was modest, mostly just delimitation of spheres of influence in Iran and Afghanistan.[99] But without a parallel treaty with Germany, even on a symbolic level, the humble 1907 Anglo-Russian Entente constituted a tilt.

Nicholas II, in fact, had signed a treaty with Germany: A scheming Wilhelm II, on his annual summer cruise in 1905, which he took in the Baltic Sea, had invited Nicholas II on July 6 (July 19 in the West) to a secret rendezvous, and Nicholas had heartily agreed. The kaiser aimed to create a continental bloc centered on Germany. "Nobody has slightest idea of [the] meeting," Wilhelm II telegrammed in English, their common language. "The faces of my guests will be worth seeing when they behold your yacht. A fine lark . . . Willy."[100] On Sunday evening July 23, he dropped anchor off Russian Finland (near Vyborg), close by Nicholas II's yacht. The next day the kaiser produced a draft of a short secret mutual defense accord, specifying that Germany and Russia would come to each other's aid if either went to war with a third country. Nicholas knew that such a treaty with Germany violated Russia's treaty with France and had urged Wilhelm to have it first be shown to Paris, a suggestion the kaiser rejected. Nicholas II signed the Treaty of Björkö, as it was called, anyway. The Russian foreign minister as well as Sergei Witte (recently returned from Portsmouth, New Hampshire) went into shock, and insisted that the treaty could not take effect until France signed it, too. Nicholas II relented and signed a letter, drafted by Witte, for Wilhelm II on November 13 (November 26 in the West), to the effect that until the formation of a Russian-German-French alliance, Russia would observe its commitments to France. This provoked Wilhelm II's fury. The German-Russian alliance, although never formally renounced, was aborted.[101]

This fiasco inadvertently reinforced the importance of Russia's signing of the entente with Britain, which seemed to signal a firm geopolitical orientation and, correspondingly, the defeat of the conservatives and Germanophiles. Moreover, given that Britain and France already had concluded an entente cordiale, Russia's treaty with Britain in effect created a triple entente, with each of the three now carrying a "moral obligation" to support the others if any went to war. And because of the existence of the German-led Triple Alliance with Austria-Hungary and Italy, the British-French-Russian accord gave the impression of being more of an alliance than a mere entente. Events further solidified this sense of the two opposed alliances. In 1908, Austria-Hungary annexed the Slavic province of Bosnia-Herzegovina from the Ottoman empire, and although Austria had been in occupation of Bosnia-Herzegovina since 1878, apoplectic Russian rightists denounced the failure of a strong Russian response to the formal annexation, calling it a "diplomatic Tsushima" (evoking the ignominious sinking of Russia's Baltic fleet by Japan).[102] But Stolypin, despite being charged by some rightists with abandoning Russia's supposed "historic mission" in the world, had told a conference of Russian officials that "our internal situation does not allow us to conduct an aggressive foreign policy," and he held firm.[103] Still, given the Anglo-German antagonism as well as the opposing European alliance system, Russia's entry into the Triple Entente carried risks driven by world events beyond its control.

In Asia, Russia remained without help to deter possible further Japanese aggression. The British-Japanese alliance, signed in 1902 and extended in scope in 1905, would be renewed again in 1911.[104] The two Pacific naval powers, although wary of each other, had been thrust together by a British sense that their Royal Navy was overstretched defending a global empire as well as a joint Anglo-Japanese perception of the need to combat Russian expansion in Asia, in Central Asia, and in Manchuria. And so, when the Japanese had promised not to support indigenous nationalists in British India, Britain had assented to the Japanese making Korea a protectorate, or colony. Besides Korea, which bordered Russia, the Imperial Japanese Army had also pushed as far north as Changchun during the Russo-Japanese war, conquering southern Manchuria (provinces of China). Even though the United States had acted as something of a constraining influence in the Portsmouth treaty negotiations, Japan had nonetheless gotten Russia evicted from southern Manchuria and claimed the Liaodung region (with Port Arthur), which the Japanese renamed Kwantung Leased Territory, and which commanded the approaches to Peking. Japan also took over the Changchun–Port Arthur stretch of the Chinese Eastern Railway, which the Russians had built and which was recast as the Southern Manchurian Railway. The Japanese civilian population of both the Kwantung Leased Territory and the Southern Manchurian Railway zone would increase rapidly, reaching more than 60,000 already by 1910. Predictably, a need to "defend" these nationals, the railroad right of way, and sprouting economic concessions spurred the introduction of Japanese troops and, soon, the formation of a special Kwantung army. China's government was forced to accept the deployment of Japanese troops on Chinese soil, hoping their presence would be temporary. But as contemporaries well understood, Japan's sphere of influence in southern Manchuria would be a spearhead for further expansion on the Asian mainland, including northward, in the direction of Russia.[105]

Thus did foreign policy entanglements pose a dilemma at least as threatening as the autocracy's absence of a reliable domestic political base. In combination, each dilemma made the other far more significant. Both of Russia's effective strategic choices—line up with France and Britain against Germany, or accept a junior partnership in a German-dominated Europe that risked the wrath of France and Britain—contained substantial peril. Stolypin had been right to ease tensions with Britain while trying to avoid a hard choice between London and Berlin, but in the circumstances of the time he had proved unable to thread this needle. Japan's posture compounded the Russian predicament. After 1907, Britain carried no obligations toward Russia should the Japanese ramp up their aggressiveness, but Russia was on the hook should the Anglo-German antagonism heat up. Stolypin's determined stance of nonintervention in the Balkans in 1908 did not alter the underlying strategic current toward foreign imbroglio.

## DEAD-END BANDITRY

Having arrived back in Baku, in May 1907, Jughashvili reported on the 5th Congress of the Russian Social Democratic Workers' Party in the pages of the Bolshevik-faction underground newspaper *Baku Proletarian*. He noted that the congress had been dominated by Mensheviks, many of whom were Jews. "It wouldn't hurt," he wrote in the report, recalling another Bolshevik's remarks at the congress, "for us Bolsheviks to organize a pogrom in the party."[106] Such a remark—which had been made by someone from the Russian empire's Pale of Settlement, and which Jughashvili was repeating—indicated the animosities and high level of frustration that by 1907 accompanied the now frayed unity hopes of 1905. Significantly, this was the future Stalin's first signed article in Russian; he would never publish anything in the Georgian language again. The historical record contains no explanation for this shift. One hypothesis may be the future Stalin's desire for assimilation. The great triangle of social democracy encompassing the Russian empire's northwest—St. Petersburg down to Moscow, and over to tsarist Poland and Latvia—was European in culture and physiognomy. Below that, in the southwest (lower half of the Pale of Settlement), social democracy was largely absent; farther south, it was strongly present, in the Caucasus, but predominantly of the Menshevik persuasion. The upshot was that every time Jughashvili attended a major Party Congress in the company of his Bolshevik faction, he would be confronted with a thoroughly Europeanized culture, against which his Georgian features and heavy Georgian accent stood out. The Jews among the Bolshevik faction of Social Democrats were often deeply Russified, as were many of the Poles (some of them Jewish) and the Latvians; but even when the latter were not deeply Russified, they were still recognizably European. Thus, although the other non-Russian Bolsheviks also stood apart from the ethnic Russians to an extent, Jughashvili was a recognizable Asiatic. That may explain why he returned from the 1906 Party Congress in a European suit. More enduringly, this circumstance may have motivated his 1907 abrupt abandonment of the Georgian language in favor of Russian in his punditry.

Asiatic pedigree was not the only way this Caucasus Bolshevik stood out, or tried to stand out. The Menshevik-dominated Social Democratic Workers' Party 5th Congress in 1907 was notable for a decision to change tactics. Even though the autocracy continued to prohibit normal legal politics—beyond the very narrow-suffrage Duma, which hardly met—the Mensheviks argued that the combat-squad/expropriation strategy had failed to overturn the existing order. Instead, the Mensheviks wanted to emphasize cultural work (workers' clubs and people's universities) as well as standing for Duma elections. Martov observed that the German Social Democrats had survived Bismarck's antisocialist laws by engaging in legal activities in the Reichstag and other venues.[107] Five Caucasus Social Democratic representatives would get elected to the Duma, including the patriarch Noe Jordania. In the meantime, a resolution to ban "expropriations" was put to a vote at the 5th Congress. Lenin and thirty-four other Bolsheviks voted against it, but it became party law. Still, just as Lenin had refused to abide the 1903 vote won by Martov on party structure, now Lenin plotted with Leonid Krasin, an engineer and skilled bomb maker, as well as with Jughashvili, on a big expropriation in the Caucasus in violation of party policy.[108]

On June 13, 1907, in broad daylight in the heart of Tiflis, on Yerevan Square, two mail coaches delivering cash to the Tiflis branch of the State Bank were attacked with at least eight homemade bombs and gunfire. The thieves' take amounted to around 250,000 rubles, a phenomenal sum (more than Durnovó had gotten in a prize the year before for having saved tsarism). The scale of the brazen heist was not unprecedented: the year before in St. Petersburg, Socialist Revolutionaries had stormed a heavily guarded carriage en route from the customs office to the treasury and looted 400,000 rubles, the greatest of the politically motivated robberies in 1906.[109] Still, the 1907 Tiflis robbery—one of 1,732 that year in the province by all groups—was spectacular.[110]

Koba Jughashvili did not risk coming out onto the square himself. Nonetheless, he was instrumental in plotting the heist. The brigands (up to twenty) included many members of his squad from the bang-bang Chiatura days, and in some cases, before that. On the square that day the man who took the lead was Simon "Kamo" Ter-Petrosyan (b. 1882), a half-Armenian, half-Georgian gunrunner, then twenty-five, whom the future Stalin had known since Gori days.[111] Kamo was said to be "completely enthralled" by "Koba."[112] That June 13, 1907,

Kamo's "apples" blew to pieces three of the five mounted Cossack guards, the two accompanying bank employees, and many bystanders. At least three dozen people died; flying shrapnel seriously wounded another two dozen or so.[113] Amid the blinding smoke and confusion, Kamo himself seized the bloodstained loot. Traveling by train (first class) disguised as a Georgian prince with a new bride (one of the gang), Kamo delivered the money to Lenin, who was underground in tsarist Finland. (According to Lenin's wife, Nadezhda Krupskaya, Kamo also brought candied nuts and a watermelon.)[114] The bravado and defiance of Social Democratic party policy notwithstanding, the robbery resembled an act of desperation, threatening to elide completely the Social Democrats' cause with banditry. No less important, the Russian State Bank had been prepared: it had recorded the serial numbers of the 500-ruble notes and sent these to European financial institutions. How much—if any—of the Yerevan Square loot proved useful to the Bolshevik cause remains unclear. "The Tiflis booty," Trotsky would write, "brought no good."[115]

Stool pigeons eager to ingratiate themselves with the tsarist authorities offered up a welter of conflicting theories about who had perpetrated the theft, but the *okhranka*, rightly, surmised that the plot went back to Lenin. Feeling the heat, Lenin would flee his sanctuary in tsarist Finland back into European exile in December 1907, seemingly for good. Several Bolsheviks, such as Maxim Litvinov, whom Lenin tasked with fencing the stolen rubles in Europe on the party's behalf, were arrested.[116] That arrest provoked three different Russian Social Democratic Workers' Party investigations, which lasted years. The inquisitions were sponsored by the Mensheviks, who saw an opportunity to strike at Lenin's leadership. Jordania led one internal investigation. Silva Jibladze, the old Jughashvili nemesis from the Tiflis and Batum days, led another. The Mensheviks obtained the testimony of a bribed tsarist postal clerk who had provided inside information on the mail coach schedule and fingered Jughashvili. The future Stalin may have been expelled temporarily from the party. Into old age, he would smart from the rumors of having been a common criminal and suffered party expulsion.[117] Whatever the outcome of the purported party disciplinary hearing, Jughashvili would never reside in Tiflis again. He decamped to Baku, with his wife, Kato Svanidze, and infant son, Yakov.[118]

Baku was Chiatura all over again, only on a far grander scale. Situated on a peninsula jutting out into the Caspian, the oil port offered a combination of spectacular natural amphitheater, labyrinthine ancient Muslim settlement, violent boomtown of casinos, slums, vulgar mansions—one plutocrat's villa resembled playing cards—and oil derricks.[119] By the early 1900s, tsarist Russia was producing more than half the global oil output, much of it in Baku, and as the oil bubbled up, and the surrounding sea burned, staggering fortunes were made. East of Baku's railway station lay the refineries built by the Swedish Nobel brothers, and farther east lay the Rothschilds' petroleum and trading company. Workers toiled twelve-hour shifts, suffering deadly chemical exposure, rabbit-hutch living quarters, and miserly wages of 10 to 14 rubles per month, before the "deductions" for factory-supplied meals. By Caucasus standards, the oppressed proletariat in Baku was immense: at least 50,000 oil workers. That mass became the special focus of radical Bolshevik agitators like Jughashvili.[120]

Jughashvili's Baku exploits included not just propagandizing and political organizing, but also hostage taking for ransom, protection rackets, piracy, and, perhaps, ordering a few assassinations of suspected provocateurs and turncoats.[121] How distinctive was he in this regard? Even by the wild standards of the 1905–8 Russian empire, political murder in the Caucasus was extraordinary. That said, the majority of Caucasus revolutionary killings were the work not of Bolsheviks but of the Armenian Dashnaks. The Dashnaks—the Armenian Revolutionary Federation—had been founded in Tiflis in the 1890s, initially to liberate their compatriots in the Ottoman empire, but soon enough they rocked the Russian empire as well.[122] The *okhranka* also feared the anarchists. Still, even if the future Stalin's mayhem was hardly the most impressive, he would recall his Baku bandit days with gusto. "Three years of revolutionary work among the workers of the oil industry forged me," he would observe in 1926. "I received my second baptism in revolutionary combat."[123] The future dictator was fortunate not to be treated to a "Stolypin necktie."

"On the basis of the Tiflis expropriations," Trotsky would write, Lenin "valued Koba as a person capable of going or conducting others to the end." Trotsky added that "during the years of reaction, [the future Stalin] belonged not to those thousands who quit the party but to those few hundreds who, despite everything, remained loyal to it."[124]

Baku's toxic environment, meanwhile, exacerbated his young wife Kato's frailty and she died a frightful death in December 1907 from typhus or tuberculosis, hemorrhaging blood from her bowels.[125] At her funeral, the future Stalin is said to have tried to throw himself into her grave. "My personal life is damned," one friend recalled him exclaiming in self-pity.[126] Belatedly, he is said to have reproached himself for neglecting his wife, even as he abandoned his toddler son, Yakov, to Kato's mother and sisters for what turned out to be the next fourteen years.

As for his exhilarating revolutionary banditry, it was over, quickly. Already by March 1908, Jughashvili was back in a tsarist jail, in Baku, where he studied Esperanto—one fellow inmate recalled him "always with a book"—but was again dogged by accusations of betraying comrades (other revolutionaries were arrested right after him).[127] By November, he was on his way, once more, to internal exile, in Solvychegodsk, an old fur-trading post in northern Russia and "an open air prison without bars."[128] There, hundreds of miles northeast of St. Petersburg in the taiga forest, every tiresome argumentative political tendency, and every variety of criminal career, could be found among the 500-strong exile colony living in log houses. Nearly succumbing to a serious bout of typhus, Jughashvili romanced Tatyana Sukhova, another exile, who would recall his poverty and his penchant for reading in bed, in the daytime. "He would joke a lot, and we would laugh at some of the others," she noted. "Comrade Koba liked to laugh at our weaknesses."[129] Comrade Koba's life had indeed become a sad, even bitter affair following the failed 1905 experience of a socialist breakthrough. His beautiful, devoted wife was dead; his son, a stranger to him. And all the exploits of the heady years—Batum (1902), Chiatura (1905), Tiflis (1907), and Baku (1908), as well as the Party Congresses in Russian Finland (1905), Stockholm (1906), and London (1907)—had come to naught. Some, such as the mail coach robbery, had boomeranged.

In summer 1909, Jughashvili found himself dependent on Tatyana Sukhova to escape woebegone Solvychegodsk by boat. He was always something of a brooder, like his father Beso, and increasingly took to nursing perceived slights. Grigol "Sergo" Orjonikidze, who would come to know his fellow Georgian as well as anyone, remarked upon Stalin's "touchiness" (*obidchivy kharakter*) many years before he had become dictator.[130] (The hothead Orjonikidze knew whereof he spoke—he was one of the touchiest of all.) Jughashvili seems to have been prone to outbursts of anger, and many contemporaries found him enigmatic, although none (at the time) deemed him a sociopath. But brooding, touchy, and enigmatic though the future Stalin might have been, his life was unenviable. Not long after his escape, on August 12, 1909, his father, Beso, died of cirrhosis of the liver. The funeral service was attended by a single fellow cobbler, who closed Beso's eyes. The father of the future dictator was buried in an unmarked grave.[131]

And what had the younger Jughashvili himself achieved?

Soberly speaking, what did his life amount to? Nearly thirty-one years of age, he had no money, no permanent residence, and no profession other than punditry, which was illegal in the forms in which he practiced it. He had written some derivative Marxist journalism. He had learned the art of disguise and escape, whether in hackneyed fashion (female Muslim veil) or more inventive ways, and like an actor, he had tried on a number of personas and aliases—"Oddball Osip," "Pockmarked Oska," "the Priest," "Koba."[132] Perhaps the best that could be said about Oddball, Pockmarked Oska, and Koba the Priest was that he was the quintessential autodidact, never ceasing to read, no doubt as solace, but also because he remained determined to improve and advance himself. He could also exude charm and inspire fervid loyalty in his small posse. The latter, however, were now dispersed, and none of them would ever amount to much.

Just as the older vagrant Beso Jughashvili passed unnoticed from the world, his son, the fugitive vagrant Iosif Jughashvili made for St. Petersburg. He took refuge that fall of 1909 in the safe-house apartment of Sergei Alliluyev, the machinist who had been exiled to Tiflis but then returned to the capital where he would often shelter Jughashvili. (Sergei's daughter, Nadya, would eventually become Stalin's second wife.) From there, Jughashvili soon returned to Baku, where the *okhranka* tailed him for months—evidently to trace his underground network—before rearresting him in March 1910. Prison, exile, poverty: this had been his life since that day in March 1901 when he had had to flee the Tiflis Meteorological Observatory and go underground, and it would remain this way right through 1917. But Jughashvili's marginal existence was not a personal failing. The empire's many revolutionary parties all suffered from considerable frailty, despite the radicalism of Russia's workers and the volatility of its peasants.[133] But the *okhranka* had managed to put the revolutionary *parties* on a short leash, creating fake opposition groups to dilute them.[134] The infiltrated Socialist Revolutionaries, especially their terrorist wing, had declined precipitously by 1909. (Their most accomplished terrorist, Evno Azef, a former embezzler nicknamed "Golden Hands," was unmasked as a paid police agent.)[135]

Later, the failures and despondency would be forgotten when, retrospectively, revolutionary party history would be rewritten, and long stints in prison or exile would become swashbuckling tales of heroism and triumph. "Those of us who belong to the older generation . . . are still influenced up to 90 percent by the . . . old underground years," Sergei Kostrikov, aka Kirov, would later muse to the Leningrad party organization that he would oversee. "Not only books but each additional year in prison contributed a great deal: it was there that we thought, philosophized, and discussed everything twenty times over." And yet, details of Kostrikov's life demonstrate that the underground was at best bittersweet. Not only were party ranks riddled with police agents, but blood feuds often ruined personal relations, too. The biggest problem was usually boredom. After a series of arrests, Kostrikov settled in Vladikavkaz, in the North Caucasus (1909–17), which is where he adopted the sonorous alias Kirov—perhaps after the fabled ancient Persian King Cyrus (Kir, in Russian). He managed to get paid for permanent work at a legal Russian-language newspaper of liberal bent (*Terek*), whose proprietor proved willing to endure many police fines, and he mixed in professional and technical circles while reading some Hugo, Shakespeare, Russian classics, as well as Marxism. Kirov was arrested again in 1911, for connections to an illegal printing press discovered back in Tomsk (where he had originally joined the Social Democrats), but acquitted. He later confessed that prior to 1917 he felt remote from the intellectual life of the rest of the empire and suffered terrible ennui—and he was not even in some frozen waste but in a mild clime, and drawing a salary, luxuries of which the forlorn Jughashvili could only dream.[136]

## PARALLEL SELF-DEFEAT

Thanks to the *okhranka*, the years between 1909 and 1913 would prove relatively peaceful, certainly compared with the madness of the preceding few years.[137] Social Democratic party strength, which had peaked at perhaps 150,000 empire-wide in 1907, had fallen below 10,000 by 1910. Members of the Bolshevik wing were scattered in European or Siberian exile. A mere five or six active Bolshevik committees existed on imperial Russian soil.[138] At the same time, by 1909, the Union of the Russian People had splintered, and the entire far right had lost its dynamism.[139] That year, Stolypin began to align himself overtly with Russian nationalists and to promote Orthodoxy as a kind of integrating national faith. He did so out of his own deep religious conviction as well as political calculation. Imperial Russia counted nearly 100 million Eastern Orthodox subjects, some 70 percent of the empire's population. But Eastern Orthodoxy did not unite to a sufficient degree. "The mistake we have been making for many decades," Sergei Witte recorded in his diary in 1910, "is that we have still not admitted to ourselves that since the time of Peter the Great and Catherine the Great there has been no such thing as Russia: there has only been the Russian empire."[140] To be sure, non-Russian nationalist and separatist movements remained relatively weak; armed rebellion had largely been confined to the Poles, who in retribution lost their separate constitution, and the Caucasus mountain tribes. Imperial loyalties remained strong, and Russia's loyal ethnically diverse elites constituted an enormous asset, even in the global age of nationalism. But the very constituency to which Stolypin appealed, Russian nationalists, caused the greatest political disruption precisely for wanting to compel non-Russians to become a single Russian nation. In aiming for a single "Russian" nation defined in faith (Orthodoxy)—imagined to comprise Great Russians, Little Russians (Ukrainians), and White Russians (Belorussians)—the nationalists had imposed severe prohibitions against Ukrainian language and culture. Predictably, this only stoked Ukrainian national consciousness further—and in the guise of opposition, rather than loyalty. These were the same detrimental processes that we have seen at work in the Caucasus at the Tiflis seminary and elsewhere, whereby hard-line Russifiers infuriated an otherwise loyal, and largely cultural, nationalism. It was the Russian nationalists, more than non-Russian nationalisms, who helped destabilize the Russian empire.[141]

Stolypin's turn to Orthodoxy as nationalism, after his reform efforts had stalled, testified to weakness and reconfirmed the lack of an effective political base for the regime. Bismarck had managed for more than two decades to wield control over the legislative agenda, despite the growing power of Germany's middle and working classes and the absence of his own political party. Stolypin's herculean efforts at forging Bismarck-like parliamentary coalitions without his own political party failed. But if Stolypin's ambitious (for Russia) modernization schemes were stymied by the Duma, they had ultimately depended abjectly on the whim of the autocrat. To be sure, notwithstanding Bismarck's shrewdness vis-à-vis the Reichstag, the Iron Chancellor's handiwork, too, had ultimately hung on his relationship with a single man, Wilhelm I. But Bismarck, a master psychologist, had managed to make the kaiser dependent on *him* for twenty-six years. ("It's hard to be kaiser under Bismarck," Wilhelm I once quipped.)[142] Stolypin had to operate within a more absolute system and with a less-qualified absolutist, a figure more akin to Wilhelm II (who dismissed Bismarck) than Wilhelm I. Nicholas II and his German wife, Alexandra, were jealous of the most talented official who would ever serve them or imperial Russia. "Do you suppose I liked always reading in the papers that the chairman of the Council of Ministers had done this... the chairman had done that?" the tsar remarked pathetically to Stolypin's successor. "Don't I count? Am I nobody?"[143] With Stolypin gone, "the autocrat" would reassert himself, appointing lesser prime ministers, and encouraging Russia's ministers to obviate their own government. These actions flowed, in part, from Nicholas II's personality. Whereas Alexander III would flatly state his faltering confidence to any given official, Nicholas II would say nothing but then secretly intrigue against the objects of his displeasure. He invariably sought escape from the incessant ministerial disputes even as he egged them on. Such behavior provoked officials' quiet, and sometimes not so quiet, fury, and eroded their commitment not just to him personally but to the autocratic system.[144] Nonetheless, the deeper patterns were systemic, not personal.

Nicholas II could not act as his own prime minister in part because he was not even part of the executive branch—the autocrat, by design, stood above all branches—while the Russian government he named, oddly, was never an instrument of his autocratic power, only a limitation on it. Nor had Nicholas begun the practices of deliberately exacerbating institutional and personal rivalries, encouraging informal advisers (courtiers) to wield power like formal ministers, playing off courtiers against ministers and formal institutions, in loops of intrigues, and making sure jurisdictions overlapped.[145] The upshot was that some Russian ministries would prohibit something, others would allow it, intentionally stymying or discrediting each other. Russian officials even at the very top chased the least little gossip, no matter how third hand or implausible; those trafficking in rumors allegedly from "on high" could access the most powerful ears. Everyone talked, yet ministers, even the nominal prime minister, would often not know for sure what was being decided, how, or by whom. Officials tried to read "signals": Were they in the tsar's confidence? Who was said to be meeting with the tsar? Might they soon obtain an audience? In the meantime, as one high-level Russian official noted, the ministries felt constantly impelled to enlarge their fields of sway at others' expense in order to get anything done at all. "There was really a continually changing group of oligarchs at the head of the different branches of administration," this high official explained, "and a total absence of a single state authority directing their activities toward a clearly defined and recognizable goal."[146]

During Stolypin's ultimately futile effort to impose order on the government, let alone the country, Koba Jughashvili experienced a long stretch of squalor, years full of disappointment, and often desperation. To be sure, thanks to the Party

Congresses or the common fate of exile, the future Stalin had come to know nearly everyone high up in the Bolshevik revolutionary milieu—Lenin, Kamenev, Zinoviev—and numerous others, such as Feliks Dzierżyński. But Stalin's dabbling in banditry in 1907 in Tiflis had afforded him notoriety of a mostly negative sort, which he would have to work hard to suppress, and led to his decampment to Baku. There, in 1910, he had tried but failed to obtain permission in time to marry a woman, Stefania Petrovskaya, evidently in order to remain legally resident in the city; instead, he was deported north back to internal exile in Solvychegodsk. In late 1911, the landlady of his latest exile hut, the widow Matryona Kuzakova, gave birth to a son, Konstantin, likely Jughashvili's.[147]

By then, the future Stalin was already gone from Solvychegodsk, having been allowed to relocate to Vologda, the northern province's "capital," where he continued to chase peasant skirts. He took up with another landlady's divorcée daughter, the servant Sofia Kryukova, and briefly cohabitated with Serafima Khoroshenina, until her exile sentence ended and she left. Jughashvili bedded the teenage school pupil Pelageya Onufrieva as well. He further busied himself collecting postcards of classical Russian paintings. Vologda, unlike Solvychegodsk, at least had a public library, and the police observed him visiting the library seventeen times over a stretch of 107 days. He read Vasili Klyuchevsky, the great historian of Russia, and subscribed to periodicals that were mailed to him in Siberia.[148] Still, thinning from a meager diet, hounded by surveillance, humiliated by surprise searches, the "Caucasian"—as the Vologda police called him—led a destitute existence. The *okhranka*'s handiwork had reduced the future Stalin's life, yet again, to the offerings of a provincial library as well as an underaged girl (born 1892), to whom he moaned about his dead wife Kato. Young Pelageya—known in *okhranka* code as "the fashion plate"—was actually the girlfriend of Jughashvili's closest Vologda comrade, the Bolshevik Pyotr Chizikov, whose period of exile had ended but who had stayed behind with her. Chizikov not only "shared" his girlfriend, he was tasked by the higher-ups with assisting "Comrade Koba's" escape.[149] In September 1911, carrying Chizikov's legal papers, Jughashvili slipped out of Vologda and again made his way to St. Petersburg. In the boondocks of Vologda (or Siberia), tsarist police surveillance was laughable, but in the capital and large cities, such as St. Petersburg, Baku, or Tiflis, the *okhranka* proved vigilant and effective. In the capital, the *okhranka* tailed Jughashvili immediately, and arrested him three days after his arrival.

That same September 1911, while Jughashvili was being rearrested in St.

Petersburg, farther south, at the Kiev Opera House during a performance of Nikolai Rimsky-Korsakov's *The Tale of Tsar Saltan*, Mordekhai "Dmitry" Bogrov, a twenty-four-year-old lawyer and anarchic terrorist—in the clandestine pay of the *okhranka*—assassinated Stolypin. Russia's top statesman, by then in near isolation, amid rumors of his imminent transfer to the Caucasus or Siberia, had followed the imperial family southward for the dedication of a monument to Alexander II.[150] Stolypin had been forewarned, again, of plots against him, yet he traveled anyway, without bodyguards, which he never used, or even a bullet-proof vest (such as they were at the time). "We had just left the box," Nicholas II wrote to his mother of the second intermission, "when we heard two sounds as if something had dropped. I thought an opera glass might have fallen on somebody's head, and ran back into the box to look." When the tsar glanced down into the orchestra, he saw his prime minister standing in a bloodstained uniform; Stolypin, upon seeing Nicholas II, raised his hand to motion the tsar away to safety, then made the sign of the cross. He died a few days later in a hospital. This was the eighteenth attempt on Stolypin's life. His assassin, Bogrov, was convicted and hanged in his jail cell ten days after the shooting. It became public knowledge that Bogrov had been suspected of police collaboration by his leftist terrorist colleagues and that he had entered the premises with a police-supplied pass, delivered to him a mere one hour before the performance. These circumstances fomented speculation that via the *okhranka*, Russia's far right had finally dispatched the conservative prime minister they reviled. This unproven yet widely believed account testified to the fact that the prime minister never found the conservative political base he sought for the autocratic regime. Even before he was killed, Stolypin had been politically destroyed by the very people he was trying to save.[151]

As the tsarist government's incoherence proceeded apace in Stolypin's absence, and Russia's still unreconciled political right wing continued to denounce the "constitutional monarchy," Koba Jughashvili had been deported back to internal exile by December 1911.[152] He found himself, once again, in remote Vologda. But suddenly the Georgian revolutionary rose to the pinnacle of Russian Bolshevism (such as it was), thanks to yet another underhanded internal party action. In January 1912, the Bolsheviks called a tiny party conference—not a congress—in Prague, where Lenin's faction managed to claim eighteen of the twenty delegates; aside from two Mensheviks, most of the non-Bolshevik faction of Social Democrats refused to attend. On the dubious grounds that the party's old Central Committee had "ceased to function," the conference assigned itself the powers of a congress and named a new (and all-Bolshevik) Central Committee.[153] In effect, the Bolshevik faction formally asserted a claim over the entire Russian Social Democratic Workers' Party. Immediately thereupon, at the first plenum of the new Central Committee, Lenin decided to co-opt Jughashvili (in Vologda exile) in absentia as a new Central Committee member. The Prague gathering also created a Central Committee "Russia bureau" (for those located on Russian territory), which Stalin had been insisting upon, and on which he was now placed. Stalin became one of twelve top Bolshevik insiders, and one of three such from the Caucasus.[154] Lenin's motives in promoting him are not well documented. Given their different places of exile (Western Europe versus eastern Russia), they had seen little of each other in the six odd years since their first meeting in December 1905. But already in 1910, when Stalin was part of the Baku underground, the Bolshevik leadership in exile had wanted to co-opt him into the Central Committee. For whatever reason it did not happen then. In 1911, Grigol Urutadze, the Georgian Menshevik who had once sat in prison with Jughashvili, poured poison into Lenin's ear about Jughashvili' s illegal expropriations and his supposed past expulsion from the Baku organization. "This means nothing!" Lenin is said to have exclaimed. "This is exactly the kind of person I need!"[155] If Lenin said it, he was praising how Stalin recognized few if any limits on what he would do for the cause. The 1912 elevation to the Central Committee would become a momentous breakthrough in Stalin's rise, allowing him to join the likes of Zinoviev, Lenin's shadow in Genevan exile, as well as Lenin himself.

Splittism and a hard line against "reformist" socialists were not peculiar to Lenin.[156] The young Italian socialist radical Benito Mussolini (b. 1883), the son of an impoverished artisan who named his boy for a Mexican revolutionary, relocated in 1902 to Switzerland, where he worked as a casual laborer, and might have met Lenin; Mussolini certainly read some Lenin.[157] But he came up with his rejection of Italian economic anarcho-syndicalism and parliamentary socialism on his own. In 1904, Mussolini called for "an aristocracy of intelligence and will," a vanguard to lead workers (a position that would remain with him into fascism).[158] He pounded this theme in newspapers. At the Italian Socialist Party Congress in July 1912, a few months after Lenin had forced through the formation of a self-standing Bolshevik party, Mussolini, a delegate from the small town of Forlì who was not yet thirty years old, catapulted himself into the Italian Socialist Party leadership by leading the expulsion of moderate reformist socialists (Mussolini's supporters, known as intransigents, included Antonio

Gramsci).[159] "A split is a difficult, painful affair," Lenin, hailing Mussolini's action, wrote in *Pravda* (July 15, 1912). "But sometimes it is necessary, and in such circumstances every weakness, every 'sentimentality'... is a crime.... When, to defend an error, a group is formed that spurns all the decisions of the party, all the discipline of the proletarian army, a split becomes indispensable. And the party of the Italian socialist proletariat has taken the right path by removing the syndicalists and Right reformists from its ranks."[160] Outré radicalism, whether Bolshevik or incipient fascist, was both political program and an impatient street-fighting disposition.

Stalin's vault from godforsaken Vologda to the pinnacle of the new all-Bolshevik Central Committee in 1912 would have been unthinkable without Lenin's patronage. And yet, it must be said, Lenin was a user, using absolutely everyone, Stalin, too, as a non-Russian to afford his faction appeal. The rash of arrests, furthermore, made promotion of some people a necessity. Still, Stalin's elevation went beyond tokenism or expediency. Stalin was loyal as well as effective: he could get things done. And, also important, he was a Bolshevik in the heavily Menshevik Caucasus milieu. True, two other Caucasus figures, Sergo Orjonikidze and the truly infamous womanizer Suren Spandaryan (about whom it was said, "all the children in Baku who are up to three years old look like Spandaryan"), were also in the top Bolshevik stratum at this time. Orjonikidze served as Lenin's chief courier to Bolsheviks in the Russian empire, and he was the one who was tasked in early February 1912 with informing Koba of his Central Committee membership and his new 50-ruble monthly party allowance—a sum, however welcome, that would not free Jughashvili from continuing to scrounge and beg for handouts.[161] Be that as it may, Stalin would come to dominate Orjonikidze; Spandaryan would die an early death. Consider further that Ivan "Vladimir" Belostotsky, a metalworker and labor-insurance clerk, was co-opted to the Bolshevik Central Committee at the same time, but he soon disappeared.[162] Stalin, in other words, contrary to what would later be asserted, was no accidental figure raised up by circumstances. Lenin put him in the inner circle, but Stalin had called attention to himself and, moreover, would go on to prove his worth. He endured.

Predictably, Lenin's socialist opponents—Bundists, Latvian Social Democrats, Mensheviks—denounced the Prague conference for the illegitimate maneuver that it was. Equally predictably, however, their own efforts to answer with their own Party Congress in August 1912 disintegrated into irreconcilable factionalism.[163] Later that very same month, Jughashvili escaped Vologda again, returning to Tiflis, where by summer 1912 there were no more than perhaps 100 Bolsheviks. Nearly his entire adult life had been consumed in factional infighting, yet now even he took to advocating for unity among Social Democrats "at all costs" and, what is more, for reconciliation and cooperation with all forces opposed to tsarism.[164] His head-snapping about-face testified to the dim prospects of all the leftist parties. In fairness, though, even the political forces nominally *supporting* the autocracy could not come together.

From the height of mass disturbances of only five years before, Stolypin's left-right political *demobilization* of imperial Russian had been breathtakingly successful, but at the expense of establishing an enduring polity. On the latter score, many observers, especially in hindsight, have attributed Russia's lack of a polity to an inherent inability to forge a nation. Ethnic Russians made up just 44 percent of the empire's 130 million people, and even though the Orthodox numbered close to 100 million, they divided into Russian, Ukrainian, and Belorussian speakers—and they were not concentrated territorially. Every would-be internal nationalist mobilization inside Russia had to somehow manage substantial internal national minorities, too. But Stalin's regime would find a way to cultivate loyalties through and across the different language groups of a reconstituted Russian empire. The biggest problem for imperial Russia was not the nation but the autocracy.

The autocracy integrated neither political elites nor the masses, and, meanwhile, the waves of militancy that Durnovó and Stolypin had crushed erupted again in a remote swath of deep Siberian forest in late February 1912. More than 1,000 miles north and east of Irkutsk on the Lena River—the source of Lenin's pseudonym from his Siberian exile days—gold-mine workers struck against the fifteen-to-sixteen-hour workdays, meager salaries (which were often garnished for "fines"), watery mines (miners were soaked to the bone), trauma (around 700 incidents per 1,000 miners), and the high cost and low quality of their food. Rancid horse penises, sold as meat at the company store, triggered the walkout. The authorities refused the miners' demands and a stalemate ensued. In April, as the strike went into its fifth week, government troops subsidized by the gold mine arrived and arrested the elected strike committee leaders (political exiles who, ironically, wished to end the strike). This prompted not the strike's dissipation but a determined march for the captives' release. Confronted by a peaceful crowd of perhaps 2,500 gold miners, a line of 90 or so soldiers opened fire at their officer's command, killing at least 150 workers and wounding more than 100, many shot in the back trying to flee.

The image of workers' lives extinguished for capitalist gold proved especially potent: among the British and Russian shareholders were banking clans, former prime minister Sergei Witte, and the dowager empress. Word of the Lena goldfields massacre spread via domestic newspaper accounts—overwhelming, in Russia, news of the *Titanic's* contemporaneous sinking—and spurred empirewide job actions encompassing 300,000 workers on and after May Day 1912.[165] The vast strikes caught the beaten-down socialist parties largely by surprise. "The Lena shots broke the ice of silence, and the river of popular resentment is flowing again," Jughashvili noted in the newspaper. "The ice has broken. It has started!"[166] The *okhranka* concurred, reporting: "Such a heightened atmosphere has not occurred for a long time. . . . Many are saying that the Lena shooting is reminiscent of the January 9 [1905] shooting" (Bloody Sunday).[167] Conservatives lashed out at the government for the massacre, as well as at the gold company's Jewish director and foreign shareholders. A Duma commission on the goldfields massacre deepened the public anger, thanks to the colorful reports provided by the commission chairman, a leftist Duma deputy and lawyer named Alexander Kerensky.

## TRAGIC SECRET

Even as rightists demanded unconditional obedience to the autocrat, behind closed doors some of them took to fantasizing about his assassination. They contemplated regicide despite the fact that Nicholas II's son, Alexei, was a toddler—Russian law required a tsar to be sixteen—and most rightists viewed the regent, the tsar's younger brother, Grand Duke Mikhail Aleksandrovich, as no better, and probably worse than Nicholas II.[168] But by 1913, when the empire celebrated three centuries of Romanov rule with spectacular pageantry, the frail dynasty was the only overarching basis for loyalty that the autocracy permitted. The tercentenary celebrations opened on February 21 with a twenty-one-gun salute from the cannons of the Peter and Paul fortress—the same guns that had announced Tsarevich Alexei's birth nine years earlier. Next came an imperial procession from the Winter Palace to Our Lady of Kazan Cathedral. Amid the clattering hoofs, fluttering banners, and peeling church bells, the noise grew deafening at sightings of the emperor and little Alexei riding in an open carriage.

At the Winter Palace ball that evening, the ladies wore archaic Muscovite-style gowns and *kokoshniks,* the tall headdresses of medieval Russia. The next night at the capital's storied Mariinsky Theater, the conductor Eduard Napravnik, the lyric tenors Nikolai Figner and Leonid Sobinov, and the ballerinas Anna Pavlova and Matylda Krzesińska (a one-time teenage lover of Nicholas II), joined in a glittering performance of Mikhail Glinka's *A Life for the Tsar.*

Public involvement in the tercentenary was kept conspicuously slight. The celebrations, moreover, focused not on the state (*gosudarstvo*) but on the grand Romanov personages who had ruled (*gosudar*). At the same time, Russia's immense size was the main device used to burnish the dynasty. At the Kazan Cathedral—decorated with more than 100 of Napoleon's state symbols captured by Russia—the Orthodox services had been accompanied by an imperial mani-festo, read out at all the empire's churches. "Muscovite Rus expanded and the Great Russian Empire now stood in the ranks of the first powers of the world," proclaimed Nicholas II, the eighteenth Romanov.[169] On the tercentenary Easter egg manufactured by special order in the workshops of Peter Carl Fabergé, double-headed eagles as well as diamond-framed miniature portraits of all eigh-teen Romanov rulers graced the outer shell. The tiny egg's customary "surprise" proved to be an interior rotating globe, which contrasted Russia's boundaries of 1613 with the much-expanded empire of 1913.[170] Whether the Romanov House was up to defending that patrimony, however, was widely doubted.

After Easter 1913, the imperial family devoted a celebratory fortnight to retrac-ing the route of the first Romanov, Mikhail Fyodorovich, in reverse, from Moscow through the heartland to the ancient Romanov patrimony of Kostroma, and back to a triumphal entrance to Moscow. The face of the Our Lady of St. Theodore icon in Kostroma, the Romanov dynasty's patron icon, had become so badly black-ened, the image was nearly invisible, a terrible omen.[171] But Nicholas II, embold-ened by the renewal of seventeenth-century roots, renewed his scheming to end the constitutional autocracy by canceling the Duma's legislative rights, ren-dering it purely advisory "in accordance with Russian tradition." He shrank, how-ever, from attempting what he and so many conservatives desperately craved.[172] Amid the cult of autocratism, moreover, disquiet spread among the monarchy's staunchest advocates. Despite the pageantry, many people in Russia's upper and lower orders alike had come to doubt Nicholas II's fitness to rule. "There is autoc-racy but no autocrat," General Alexander Kireev, the Russian courtier and pundit, had complained in a diary entry as early as 1902, a sentiment that over the years had only widened, like a rock-thrown ripple across the entire pond of the empire.[173] An imperial court hofmeister observing the Romanov processional to the Kazan Cathedral concluded that "the group had a most tragic look."[174] The immense Russian empire was ultimately a family affair, and the family appeared doomed. It was not simply that Nicholas II, a traditionally conservative man of family, duty, and faith, was piously committed to the "autocratic idea" without the personal wherewithal to realize it in practice. Had the hereditary tsar been a capable ruler, the future of Russia's dynasty still would have been in trouble.[175]

Because of a genetic mutation that the German princess Alexandra had inherited from her grandmother Britain's Queen Victoria, the Russian tsarevich Alexei came into the world with hemophilia, an incurable disease that impaired the body's ability to stop bleeding. The tsarevich's illness remained a state secret. But secrecy could not alter the likelihood that Alexei would die at a relatively early age, perhaps before fathering children. Nor was there a way around the improbability that a boy walking on eggshells, subject to death from internal bleeding by bumping into furniture, could ever serve as a vigorous, let alone autocratic, ruler. Nicholas II and Alexandra remained in partial denial about the dynasty's full danger. The hemophilia, an unlucky additional factor piled on the autocracy's deep structural failures, was actually an opportunity to face the difficult choice that confronted autocratic Russia, but Nicholas II and Alexandra, fundamentally sentimental beings, had none of the hard-boiled realism necessary for accepting a transformation to a genuine constitutional monarchy in order to preserve the latter.[176]

CONSTITUTIONAL AUTOCRACY was self-defeating. Nicholas II worked assiduously not just to stymie the realization of the parliament he had granted, but even to block the realization of a coordinated executive branch, as an infringement on autocracy. "Autocratic government" constituted an oxymoron, a collision of unconstrained sacral power with legal forms of administration, a struggle among functionaries to decide whether to heed the "will" of the autocrat or act within the laws and regulations.[177] Blaming the failings of imperial Russia on "backwardness" and peasants, therefore, is misguided. Stolypin was undone primarily by the autocracy itself as well as by Russia's uncomprehending elites. He wielded an arsenal of stratagems and possessed tremendous personal fortitude, but he met relentless resistance from the tsar, the court, and the rightist establishment, including from Sergei Witte, who now sat in the State Council.[178] The establishment would not allow Stolypin to push through a full program of modernization to place Russia on the path of strength and prosperity in order to meet the array of geopolitical challenges. "I am certainly sorry for Stolypin's death," Pyotr Durnovó, another Stolypin nemesis in the State Council, remarked at a meeting of rightist politicians in 1911. "But at least now there is an end to the reforms."[179] True enough: reform died. At the same time, it was notable that Stolypin had not for the most part attempted to outflank the recalcitrant establishment by appealing directly to the masses, despite his eventual promotion of a broad Eastern Orthodox "nation." Devoted to the monarchy, he sought to fuse divinely ordained autocratic power and legitimate authority, caprice and law, tradition and innovation, but he relied upon a deliberately antimass-politics Duma, aiming for a regime of country squires (like himself). In the emigration in 1928, a refugee forced to flee Russia would celebrate Stolypin as Russia's Mussolini, the first "Eastern Orthodox fascist," a national social leader.[180] Not in the least. Stolypin's contradictory five-year premiership lacked a radical ideology, and he remained a corridor politician even when he went out to address the people.

In international affairs, Stolypin had been unable to avoid a de facto posture of alignment with Britain against Germany. True, he did achieve an improbable and important policy victory at conservative expense, and despite lacking formal foreign affairs jurisdiction, by restraining Russian passions over the Balkans and elsewhere.[181] That hard-won restraint, however, was destined not to last. Beginning just three years after Stolypin's death, a world war would break out that, when combined with Russia's alienated conservatives and the Romanov's secret hemophilia, would sweep aside Russia's constitutional autocracy and, in very short order, Russia's constitutionalism entirely. Even then, a Russian fascism would not take hold.[182] If anyone alive had been informed during the Romanov tercentenary celebrations of 1913 that soon a fascist right-wing dictatorship and a socialist left-wing dictatorship would assume power in different countries, would he or she have guessed that the hopelessly schismatic Russian Social Democrats dispersed across Siberia and Europe would be the ones to seize and hold power, and not the German Social Democrats, who in the 1912 elections had become the largest political party in the German parliament? Conversely, would anyone have predicted that Germany would eventually develop a successful anti-Semitic fascism rather than imperial Russia, the home of the world's largest population of Jews and of the infamous *Protocols of the Elders of Zion*?[183]

A focus not on leftist revolutionary activity but on geopolitics and domestic high politics reveals the central truth about imperial Russia: The tsarist regime found itself bereft of a firm political base to meet its international competition challenges. That circumstance made the regime more and more reliant on the political police, its one go-to instrument for every challenge. (Alexander Blok, the poet, who would study the files of the tsarist police after the revolution, deemed them Russia's "only properly functioning institution," marveling at their ability "to give a good characterization of the public moods.")[184] Indulgence of the police temptation did not result from any love of the *okhranka* or of police methods; on the contrary, the tsar and others roundly despised their ilk.[185] Rather, the overreliance on the political police stemmed from an irreconcilable antagonism between the autocracy and the Constitutional Democrats, and from the tsarist system's profound distaste for street mobilization on its behalf. In modern times, it was not enough to demobilize opponents; a regime had to mobilize proponents. A system deliberately limited to the narrow privileged strata, backed by police and a peasant army, was, in the modern age, no polity at all, certainly not for a would-be great power competing against the strongest states. A modern integrated polity needed more than gonfalons, processionals holding icons, polyphonic hymns ("Christ Is Risen"), and the retracing in 1913 of a pilgrimage to Moscow originally undertaken in the seventeenth century. Durnovó, in leading the rescue of the autocracy in 1905–6, had proved able to reset the political moment in Russia, but unable to alter the fundamental structures. Stolypin, equally ready to wield repression yet also far more creative politically, bumped up against tsarism's political limits. Of all the failures of Russia's autocracy with regard to modernity, none would be as great as its failure at authoritarian mass politics.

Autocratic Russia's discouragement of modern mass politics would leave the masses—and the profound, widespread yearning among the masses in Russia for social justice—to the leftists. The latter, for their part, including the Russian Social Democratic Workers' Party, were riven by extreme factionalism, and crippled by the state's severe repression. Under the autocracy, not just a Russian fascism but also opposition leftist parties largely failed. And yet, within a mere decade of Stolypin's demise, the Georgian-born Russian Social Democrat Iosif "Koba" Jughashvili, a pundit and agitator, would take the place of the sickly Romanov heir and go on to forge a fantastical dictatorial authority far beyond any effective power exercised by imperial Russia's autocratic tsars or Stolypin. Calling that outcome unforeseeable would be an acute understatement.

## PART II

# DURNOVÓ'S REVOLUTIONARY WAR

The trouble will start with the blaming of the
government for all disasters. In the legislative institutions
a bitter campaign against the government will begin,
followed by revolutionary agitation throughout the
country, with socialist slogans, capable of arousing and
rallying the masses, beginning with the division of land
and succeeded by a division of all valuables and property.
The defeated army, having lost its most dependable men,
and carried away by the tide of primitive peasant desire for
land, will find itself too demoralized to serve as a bulwark
of law and order. The legislative institutions and the
intellectual opposition . . . will be powerless to stem the
popular tide, aroused by themselves.

Pyotr Durnovó, February 1914 memorandum to Nicholas II,
on the consequences of a possible war against Germany

BETWEEN 1905 AND 1911, revolutions broke out in Mexico, Qajar Iran, the
Ottoman empire, China, and Portugal, as well as Russia—countries that together
accounted for one quarter of the earth's population. Each led to the introduction
of constitutions. It was a global moment, akin in some ways to the 1780s, when
revolutions broke out in the United States, France, and the Caribbean. But the
early-twentieth-century constitutional experiments were quickly undermined or
reversed in every single case. (Only Portugal's lasted a bit longer, through thirty-
eight prime ministers, until a 1926 military coup.) Liberty exerted a powerful

pull, but institutionalizing liberty was another matter. The push for constitutionalism usually entailed intellectual types—such as the leader of Russia's Constitutional Democrat Party (Cadets), Paul Miliukov—coming to power and then looking to wield the state as an instrument to modernize what they perceived as backward societies. But the dream of an intellectual-led, classically liberal leap to modernity ran into a social wall made up of urban laboring populations and communally oriented rural majorities. In the tantalizing examples of Britain and the United States, classical liberal orders were institutionalized long before the dawn of mass politics.[1] By the early twentieth century, the introduction of constitutionalism proved too narrow to satisfy the masses. The positive aspects of the changes involved in constitutionalism were often discredited by social disorder. (Russia recorded some 17,000 peasant disturbances between 1910 and 1914 just in the European part of the empire.)[2] Furthermore, even though liberalizing intellectuals were inspired by the advanced countries of Europe, the European powers helped suppress the political openings, aiding the "forces of order" in China, Mexico, Iran, and elsewhere. In the Ottoman empire, the would-be modernizers backed away from liberalization. China's constitutional experiment yielded to warlordism; Mexico erupted into civil war.[3] In Russia, too, there was de facto civil war (1905–7), which was won by the forces of order.

If Russia stood out at the dawn of the twentieth century, it was because its forces of order were demoralized in victory: they hated the outcome, "constitutional autocracy," and had come to disrespect the tsar, even though they were joined to him at the hip.[4] At the same time, Russia's would-be radical socialist revolution was mired in perhaps even greater disarray than the fraught constitutionalism. Socialists were dragged down by a harsh police regime and their own factionalism. More fundamentally, most Russian socialists supported the constitutionalism ("bourgeois" democracy) rather than socialism, as a necessary stage of history, while despising the bourgeoisie.

"Socialism," concretely, meant a life in Siberia. True, thanks to the Romanov three-hundredth jubilee amnesty in 1913, many were released from internal exile. Lev Rozenfeld (Kamenev) returned to St. Petersburg to take up the editorship of *Pravda*. The newspaper had been established at the Bolshevik-dominated party conference in Prague in January 1912 and had commenced publication on April 22, 1912; Koba Jughashvili had written the lead article in the first issue, calling for "proletarian unity no matter what."[5] Jughashvili, newly a member of the illegally formed all-Bolshevik Central Committee, had illegally sneaked back to St.

Petersburg after escaping internal exile. The day of his article's appearance, however, the *okhranka* ambushed him, and by summer he was deported to the remote far northern Siberian village of Kolpashëvo, near Narym ("marsh" in the Khanty language).[6] In September 1912, before winter set in, he escaped by boat and made his way to Lenin in Habsburg Krakow, carrying the passport of a Persian merchant. Lenin considered himself one of the party's top experts on national affairs. But Jughashvili surprised him with his own work on the nationalities, prompting Lenin to write to Gorky, "We have a marvelous Georgian who has sat down to write a big article for *Enlightenment,* for which he has collected all the Austrian and other materials."[7] "Marxism and the National Question," not unlike Jughashvili's only other lengthy publication ("Anarchism or Socialism?"), was partly derivative, defining "a nation" in terms of three characteristics borrowed from the German Karl Kautsky (common language, territory, and economic links), and one from the Austrian Marxist Otto Bauer (common national character).[8] But the work was significant for confronting a crucial aspect of revolution in the polyglot Russian empire and largely repudiating the views of the Austro-Marxists and their Georgian Menshevik emulators. It was also significant for its signature—"Stalin" ("Man of Steel").[9] That strong, sonorous pseudonym was not only superior to Oddball Osip, Pockmarked Oska, or the very Caucasus-specific Koba, but also Russifying. By the time the essay came out in Russia, in the March-May 1913 issue of the journal *Enlightenment,* "Stalin" had again returned to St. Petersburg. There, at a fund-raising ball for International Women's Day, he was ambushed yet again, betrayed by another member of the Bolshevik Central Committee, Roman Malinowski, a thief who had risen to head of the metalworkers' union but who was also a secret *okhranka* agent.[10] Stalin was deported back to Siberia, where Kamenev, too, would end up.

Malinowski became the only high-level Bolshevik inside Russia left at liberty. Lenin had placed him in charge of directing the entire apparatus of Bolshevik activity inside the Russian empire.[11] The Bolshevik leader's vision of a party membership restricted to professional revolutionaries, a narrowness supposedly necessary in conditions of illegality—a stance Stalin, too, supported—had failed spectacularly. In fairness, the *okhranka* also ran the similarly hyperconspiratorial Socialist Revolutionary terror organization.[12] Russia's increasingly paranoid revolutionaries "looked in the mirror," the Bolshevik Nikolai Bukharin would later recall, "and wondered if they themselves were provocateurs."[13]

Despite the *okhranka*'s virtuosity, however, the autocracy remained under threat of nitroglycerine. In connection with the Romanov tercentenary, the St. Petersburg *okhranka* had bulked itself up while forbidding any appearance of crowds, fearing they would morph into demonstrations of workers carrying red flags, and that the tsar, like his grandfather Alexander II, might be assassinated.[14] "The city," recalled the chief of the Corps of Gendarmes, "was literally turned into an armed camp." An "autocrat" unsafe in his own capital? The unseemly clampdown in the capital cast a pall over the celebrations. Despite the wide acclaim during the 1913 Romanov jubilee for the first-ever exhibition of Russian icons, the revivals of Modest Mussorgsky's operas *Boris Godunov* and *Khovansh-china,* and the gala culmination of the tercentenary in Moscow in May 1913, elites understood full well that the autocrat could not go about in public.

GERMANY'S WILHELM II—who was Nicholas II's cousin—launched his own "festive year" of pomp in 1913. It was the kaiser's fifty-fourth birthday, the silver jubilee of his reign, and the centenary of the Prussian defeat of Napoleon. Never mind that it had been the Russians who had vanquished Napoleon and occupied Paris. Germany wanted to showcase its dynasty and impressive modernity.[15] The combination of German power on the continent and terror dread in St. Petersburg was uppermost in the mind of the man who in 1905–6 had saved the Romanov dynasty.

Pyotr Durnovó viewed foreign affairs through the eyes of a policeman.[16] Back in 1904, at the outbreak of what he had dismissed as the "senseless" Russo-Japanese War, he told his predecessor as Russia's interior minister, "A naïve idea: to fix internal disorder with a foreign success!"[17] After Durnovó's April 1906 dismissal from the interior ministry, he served as leader of the rightist bloc in Russia's upper house (State Council), a perch from which he went about subverting the post-1905 constitutional experiment (such as it was), and affording special grief to Stolypin.[18] Durnovó became well known for expressing unwelcome views to people's faces, rather than just behind their backs—and this applied even to the tsar.[19] In February 1914, he submitted a long memorandum to Nicholas II, and some fifty recipients in the upper elite, seeking to reorient Russian policy.[20] Durnovó scoffed at those who asserted that mere displays of Russian power and Anglo-French-Russian unity would deter Germany.[21] "The central factor of the period of world history through which we are now passing is the rivalry between

England and Germany," he explained, adding that between them "a struggle for life and death is inevitable." He argued that what had originally been just a Russian "understanding" (entente) with England had somehow become a formal alliance, and that taking the side of Britain in its confrontation with Germany was unnecessary, because there was no fundamental clash of interests between Germany and Russia. Further, unlike the foreign ministry personnel far removed from the roiling class hatreds that this ex-policeman had confronted, Durnovó emphasized how a war would be catastrophic domestically and the government blamed. "In the event of defeat," he wrote in the February 1914 memorandum to Nicholas II, "social revolution in its most extreme form is inevitable." Durnovó specifically forecast that the gentry's land would be expropriated and that "Russia will be flung into hopeless anarchy, the issue of which cannot be foreseen."[22]

The analysis—an avoidable war against a too-powerful Germany; Russia's defeat; Russian elites heedlessly pressuring the autocracy only to be engulfed by extreme social revolution—was as hard-boiled as it was blunt. Nothing penned by Vladimir Lenin, not even his later celebrated polemic *State and Revolution* (August 1917), approached the clairvoyance of Durnovó. "Tsarism was victorious," Lenin would write of the years prior to 1917. "All the revolutionary and opposition parties were smashed. Dejection, demoralization, schisms, discord, desertion, and pornography took the place of politics."[23] That was essentially correct as far as the revolutionaries went. But although the police had contained the revolutionary parties, the socialist militancy of the workers (revived during the Lena massacre of 1912) and especially the waves of peasant land-hunger unrest (which affected the army) constituted an ongoing, far greater threat. This was something the archconservative Durnovó saw better than the would-be professional revolutionaries. From 1900 through 1917, except for two years (1905–7), Lenin lived entirely outside Russia, mostly in Switzerland. Trotsky was in foreign exile from 1902 to 1903 and 1907 to 1917. Kamenev and Grigory Radomylsky (Zinoviev) each spent long stretches of the pre-1917 period in prison, Siberia, or Europe. The same was true of the diehard opponents of Lenin among the Social Democrats, such as Martov and Pavel Axelrod. Victor Chernov—the leader of the Socialist Revolutionary Party, Russia's most populous party on the left—was in emigration without interruption from 1899 until 1917. Durnovó knew the tsarist system not from Geneva, Paris, or Berlin, but from the inside, and in particular from inside the interior ministry. He understood better than outsiders or even most insiders that the autocracy was hollowing out.[24] Equally important, while members of Russia's establishment dreaded a new "Pugachev-style" riot from below, Durnovó condemned Russia's *upper classes,* especially the Constitutional Democrats, who pushed for political rights against the autocracy without realizing, as he saw it, that the militant masses would be incited to go much further and deluge them all.[25]

But what did the prescient Durnovó propose? Instead of autocratic Russia's "unnatural alliance" with parliament-ruled Britain, he was urging a birds-of-a-feather alliance with Germany, a conservative monarchy, as part of an eventual continental bloc that would also include France (somehow reconciled to Germany) and Japan.[26] But how was that to happen? The German kaiser was set on imposing German control over the Turkish Straits, through which passed up to 75 percent of Russian grain exports, the key to the empire's prosperity.[27] Moreover, domestically, Durnovó inclined toward a new state of emergency, which he had enforced in 1905, but at the time of his memorandum, some two fifths of the Russian empire's 130 million subjects *already* lived under martial law or special regime ("reinforced protection"). True to his principles, Durnovó had refused the temptation of a rightist populism to win over the peasants with property redistributions, not because, like most members of the State Council or Duma, he owned generous land allotments (he did not), but because he feared the disorder.[28] Nor would he condemn democracy outright, allowing that it might be appropriate for some countries. Still, he argued that democracy would bring disintegration to Russia, which needed "firm authority."[29] But his strategy of keeping a lid on—retaining as much centralized power as possible, refusing cooperation with the Duma, waiting for a real autocrat to take charge—was a policy of stasis.[30] He himself grasped the core dilemma: The government needed repression to endure, yet repression alienated ever more people, further narrowing the social base of the regime, thereby requiring still more repression. "We are in a blind alley," Durnovó had lamented in 1912. "I fear that we all, along with the tsar, will not succeed in getting out."[31]

If it came to war against Germany, not even the tsarist regime's greatest living policeman could rescue the autocracy a second time.[32] Stolypin, too, not just Durnovó, had been warning that another major war would "prove fatal for Russia and for the dynasty."[33] Durnovó understood, still more fundamentally, that a downfall *during* a world war would shape everything that followed.[34] Just as he prophesied, the new war, against Germany, did become a revolutionary war, which did redound to the socialists, and did produce anarchy. "However paradoxical it sounds," recalled the Menshevik Social Democrat Fyodor Gurvich (aka Fyodor Dan), "the extreme reactionaries in the Tsarist bureaucracy grasped the movement of forces and the social content of this coming revolution far sooner and better than all the Russian 'professional revolutionaries.'"[35]

NOSTALGIA FOR TSARIST RUSSIA, however understandable, is misplaced: "constitutional autocracy" was never viable and not evolving into something better, and the development of civic associations could never substitute for Russia's missing liberal political institutions or overcome the illiberal ones.[36] When a rush of political parties had suddenly sprung into being, illegally, the leftist ones had come first: the Revolutionary Armenian Federation (Dashnaks) (1890), the Polish Socialist Party (1892), the Jewish Bund (1897), the Russian Social Democratic Workers' Party (1898), which split into Bolsheviks and Mensheviks (1903), the Jewish Social Democratic Workers' Party or Poale-Zion (1900), the Socialist Revolutionary Party (1901). In 1905 were born the Constitutional Democrats or Cadets (classic liberals) and the Union of the Russian People (proto-fascists), among others.[37] All of these organized parties, even the anti-socialists, were anathema to the autocracy, and the autocracy's intransigence stamped them all, including the constitutionalists. The wartime radicalization would further tilt Russia's peculiar political spectrum further left, while furnishing a cornucopia of violent practices. "The Bolshevik Revolution," one scholar shrewdly observed, "fixed the near-ubiquitous, but transitory practices of the trans-European 1914–21 catastrophe as a permanent feature of the Soviet state." Of course, as that scholar adds, those violent practices, that state building, would be driven by ideas.[38] And not just any ideas, but visions of remaking everything, from top to bottom, ushering in the socialist kingdom of heaven on earth. The transcendentally powerful ideas, in turn, were carried forward by new people thrust onto the political landscape by revolution, such as Stalin.

For a Georgian from small-town Gori—via Tiflis, Chiatura, Baku, and Siberian exile—to rise anywhere near the summit of power, and seek to implement Marxist ideas, the whole world had to be brought crashing down. And it was. Stalin had little role in those momentous events. Unlike the wild years of 1905–8, or the period after March 1917, his life story from 1909 through early 1917 contains few moments of note. Most accounts either embroider these years, rendering them more dramatic than they were, or skip them. But this long stretch of time, in which Stalin did little or nothing, was colossally significant for Russia, and indeed the world. To make sense of Stalin's role in the sudden, stunning episode of 1917, and above all to understand his entire later regime, the momentous history in which he had little noteworthy part must be described and analyzed in depth. But once Stalin did get near power, he battled indefatigably, like a man with a sense of destiny, and demonstrated revolutionary talents that proved especially apt in the Eurasian setting.

Modern revolutions are spectacular events, awesome in the millions who rise up and stake a claim to control their destiny, exhilarating in their new solidarities and sense of unlimited possibility. But revolutions are also signs of decay and breakdown, the cracking of one ruling system and the untidy formation of another. Whatever does or does not happen in the streets, the barracks, the factories, the fields, it is in the corridors of power, centrally and provincially, where the revolution finds an outcome. One must therefore study the high politics and the nitty-gritty of institutional formation, the practices and procedures of governance, the ways of thinking and being that inform the exercise of power. High politics is, of course, shaped by social forces, by the actions and aspirations of the broad masses, but politics is not reducible to the social. Indeed, although born of the most popular revolution in history, the new regime in the former Russian empire became unaccountable to the people, and even to itself. A mass participatory revolutionary process not only can, but frequently does, culminate in a narrow regime, and not because the revolution has "degenerated," or because good intentions and a good beginning are ruined by malefactors or unlucky circumstances, but because the international situation impinges at every turn, institutions are formed out of the shards of the old as well as the maw of the new, and ideas matter. Dictatorship can be seen by revolutionaries as criminal or as an invaluable tool; human beings can be seen as citizens or chattel, convertible foes or congenital enemies; private property can be seen as the cornerstone of freedom or of enslavement. A profound, genuine upsurge for social justice can—depending on the overarching ideas and accompanying practices—institutionalize the gravest injustices. A successful revolution can be a tragedy. But tragedies can still be grand geopolitical projects. Russia's revolution became inseparable from long-standing dilemmas and new visions of the country as a great power in the world. That, too, would bring out Stalin's qualities.

## CHAPTER 5

# STUPIDITY OR TREASON?

What is it, stupidity or treason? (*A voice from the left*:
"Treason!" [*Someone else*]: "Stupidity!" Laughter.)

> Paul Miliukov, leader of the Constitutional Democrats
> (Cadets), speech in the Duma, November 1916[1]

As a rule, a regime perishes not because of the strength of
its enemies but because of the uselessness of its defenders.

> Lev Tikhomirov, Russian conservative theorist, 1911[2]

IN 1910, AFTER THEODORE ROOSEVELT met Kaiser Wilhelm II, the former American president (1901–9) confided in his wife, "I'm absolutely certain now, we're all in for it."[3] After the death of the kaiser's predecessor and grandfather (at age ninety-one), the inexperienced Wilhelm II had dismissed the seventy-five-year-old chancellor Otto von Bismarck.[4] The young kaiser, who proved to be both arrogant and insecure, proceeded to plot coups against Germany's constitution and parliament, and to engage in a blustering foreign policy, exacerbating the paradox of Bismarck's unification: namely, that Germany seemed to threaten its neighbors while itself being vulnerable to those neighbors on two fronts. Wilhelm II—known as All Highest Warlord—had declined to renew Bismarck's so-called German-Russian Reinsurance Treaty, thereby unwittingly spurring Russian reconciliation with France, and raising the prospect for Germany of a two-front war.[5] Wilhelm II's belated attempt to correct this mistake, by manipulating Nicholas II into the Treaty of Björkö, had failed. Then there was the kaiser's naval program. As of 1913, Britain accounted for 15 percent of international trade, but Germany came in second at 13 percent, and in this increasingly interdependent world of global trade, especially of vital food imports, Germany had every right to build a navy.[6] But Wilhelm II and his entourage had unleashed a sixty-battleship fantasy for the North Sea.[7] This had spurred Britain's reconciliation with France—despite a near Franco-British war in 1898 over colonies—and even with autocratic Russia. "The kaiser is like a balloon," Bismarck had once remarked. "If you do not hold fast to the string, you never know where he will be off to."[8]

It took two to tango, however, and the "sun-never-sets" global position that Great Britain sought to defend was itself aggressive. Britain had reluctantly ceded naval hegemony in the Western hemisphere to the rising United States and in the Far East to upstart Japan, at least temporarily. (Even then, spending on the Royal Navy consumed one quarter of state revenue.) At the same time, British foreign policy had been most immediately fixated on containing perceived Russian threats to its empire in Persia, Central Asia, and China. Many viewed Russia, because of its European, Middle Eastern, and Far Eastern geography, as the only potential global rival to Britain's global empire.[9] Still, even before the Anglo-Russian Entente of 1907, the ascent of German power was the more immediate and explosive circumstance as far as the British were concerned. Anglo-German economic and cultural ties were strong.[10] But the clash of interests was strong as well, and unlike in the cases of the United States and Japan, Britain was not inclined to accommodate German power. "In my opinion," Lord Curzon had written in a private letter on September 25, 1901, "the most marked feature in the international development of the next quarter of a century will be, not the advance of Russia—that is in any case inevitable—or the animosity of France—that is hereditary—but the aggrandizement of the German Empire at the expense of Great Britain; and I think that any English Foreign Minister who desires to serve his country well, should never lose sight of that consideration."[11] To manage the fundamental antagonism between the dominant status quo power and a Germany seeking to secure a place in the world order rising on Britain's continental doorstep, exceptional statesmanship, on both sides, was required.[12] Instead, the antagonism was allowed to spur an arms race and two hostile systems of alliance (or understanding): the Triple Entente of Britain, France, and Russia, versus the Central Powers of Germany and Austria-Hungary.

Alliances by themselves never cause war; calculation and miscalculation do.[13] For Germany, the road to victory against Britain was judged to go through Russia. Just as British imperialists had been obsessed with Russia's expansiveness in Asia, Germany's top military had become fixated on a supposed Russian "threat" in Europe. Between the 1860s and 1914, Russia's GDP had fallen further behind Germany's: Russian steel production in 1914, for example, was no more than 25 percent of Germany's. But in that same interval, Russia's economy expanded fourfold.[14] And German military planners—whose job it was to prepare for possible war—harped as well on Russia's gigantic population (around 178 million versus Germany's 65 million) and Russia's recently announced Great Military Program for rearmament, intended to be completed by 1917.[15] The German army brass argued that an industrializing Russia, along with Europe's other land power—and Russia's ally—France, should not be left to choose a propitious time to attack on two fronts, and that Russia was a near-future threat that had to be attacked preemptively. "To wait any longer," German chief of staff Helmuth von Moltke the Younger (b. 1848) complained to the Austrian chief of staff in May 1914, would entail "a diminishing of our chances; it was impossible to compete with Russia as regards quantity."[16] Germany was eager for the conflict in supposed self-defense against a weak Russia that was deemed on the brink of becoming invincible.[17]

British miscalculations were of longer standing. Britain offered the promise of global order, a Pax Britannica, without the desire or wherewithal to enforce it, while Britain's much envied imperialism inspired rival imperialisms, which, in turn, struck fear in the British geopolitical imaginary. "It was the *rise* of Athens and the *fear* that this inspired in Sparta that made war inevitable," the ancient Greek historian Thucydides wrote. Back in the fifth century B.C., a clash among peripheral states, Corinth and Corcyra, sparked a showdown between the powers Athens and Sparta, a showdown that each had sought and that each would come to regret. Bismarck called such decisions rolling "the iron dice." In the case of 1914, the British did not reckon fully with the consequences of the rivalry they had helped set up. But while the Anglo-German antagonism was the underlying cause of the Great War and Russia the critical complicating factor, the detonator was supplied not by rivalries over African colonies, where the leftists and others expected it, but in Eastern Europe, where Bismarck had warned in 1888 that war might happen over "some damned foolish thing in the Balkans."[18] Here, as the Ottoman empire contracted, the other big land empires—Austria-Hungary, Russia, Germany—ground up against one another like tectonic plates, which is how the fault line of tiny Serbia precipitated a world war and, on the eastern front, a revolution in the Russian empire.

## SARAJEVO AND STATE PRESTIGE

Serbia had emerged out of the Ottoman realm in the early nineteenth century, and a century later enlarged itself in two Balkan wars (1912–13), but neither Balkan war had resulted in a wider war. True, Austria-Hungary had annexed Bosnia-Herzegovina (from the Ottoman empire) and thereby vastly increased its South Slav (Yugoslav) population of Serbs, Croats, and Bosnian Muslims. This 1908 annexation, which Russia failed to prevent, spurred numerous plots to advance the cause of South Slav independence by Young Bosnia, a terrorist group dedicated to the Yugoslav cause. In 1914 the latter resolved to murder the Austrian governor in Sarajevo, Bosnia-Herzegovina's capital. But then its members evidently read in the newspaper that the heir to the Habsburg throne, Archduke Franz Ferdinand, would be visiting—exact day and location specified—and they decided to murder him instead. Happenstance had made the archduke, Kaiser Franz Josef's nephew, Austria-Hungary's next in line: the kaiser's son had killed himself. Many observers hoped that the eighty-four-year-old Franz Josef—in power sixty-six years—would at some point give up the ghost and that the fifty-year-old Franz Ferdinand would have a go at reorganizing and stabilizing the realm's internal politics. After all, in 1913, the archduke, who had a Slavic (Czech) wife, had criticized Austria's top military commander for "a great Hurrah-Policy, to conquer the Serbs and God knows what."

On Sunday, June 28, 1914—the couple's wedding anniversary but also Serbia's sacred St. Vitus's Day—the royal pair, as announced, entered Sarajevo. The local Habsburg governor had deliberately selected the Serbian holy day for the visit. It commemorated 1389, when, in losing the Battle of Kosovo, ending the Serbian empire, a Serb had nonetheless managed to assassinate the Ottoman sultan in his tent (the guards then decapitated the assassin).[19] As Franz Ferdinand made his publicly preannounced processional in an open motorcar, the first of the six Young Bosnia terrorists spaced out along the route failed to act. A second did hurl his small bomb at the archduke's car, but it bounced off, and despite an explosion under the car that was behind, which wounded two officers, the heir was able to proceed on his way; the remaining conspirators were still in position but none acted. The Habsburg heir delivered his speech at Sarajevo's Moorish town hall. The daring assassination plot had been botched.

At the town hall, after the speeches and ceremonies were complete, the archduke decided to alter his itinerary in order to visit the bomb victims in the hospital. Gavrilo Princip, a nineteen-year-old Bosnian Serb member of Young Bosnia and one of those who had not acted that day, had tried to recover by taking up a position on Sarajevo's Franz Josef Street near Moritz Schiller's Delicatessen, hoping to catch Franz Ferdinand on the rest of his tour. The archduke's driver, unfamiliar with the new plan to go to the hospital, made a wrong turn toward Franz Josef Street, heard shouts of reprimand, and began to back up, but stalled the car—some five feet from Princip. Six of Princip's eight siblings had died in infancy, and he himself was consumptive, a wisp of a human being. He had dreamed of becoming a poet. Suddenly point-blank with history, he took out his pistol and shot the Austrian heir, conspicuous in a helmet topped with green feathers, as well as his wife (intending to strike the governor). Both died nearly instantly.

Serbia had just fought two Balkans wars, losing at least 40,000 dead, and the last thing the country needed was another war. But after the Young Bosnia terrorists, all Austro-Hungarian subjects, were captured, some testified that they had been secretly armed and trained by Serbia's military intelligence, a rogue actor in that rogue state.[20] Serbia's prime minister had not been an initiator of the assassination plot, but he did not repudiate it, and he proved unable to tamp down Serbia's domestic euphoria, which intensified the fury in Vienna. "The large area in front of the War Ministry was packed," wrote Lev Trotsky, who was living in Viennese exile and working as a correspondent for a newspaper in Kiev. "And this was not 'the public,' but the real people, in their worn-out boots, with fingers gnarled. . . . They waved yellow and black flags in the air, sang patriotic songs, someone shouted 'All Serbs must die!'"[21] If in response to the "Sarajevo outrage" Kaiser Franz Josef did nothing, that could encourage future acts of political terror. But what *level* of response? The Habsburgs had almost lost their state in 1740 and again in 1848–49; in 1914 they faced a dilemma unlike anything even the multinational Russian empire faced: of Austria-Hungary's eleven major nations, only five were more or less exclusively within the realm; in the case of the other six, a majority lived outside the empire's boundaries.[22] Austrian ruling circles decided to smash Serbia, even at the great risk of provoking a pan-European war, in effect risking suicide from fear of death.

A Viennese envoy visited Berlin on July 5 to solicit Germany's backing for a reckoning with Serbia, and returned with Kaiser Wilhelm II's "full support." There was still the matter of consent from the leaders in Budapest, the Hungarian half of Austria-Hungary. On July 23, after internal discussion with

Hungarian leaders (who came on board by July 9), as well as intense military preparations, Vienna cabled an ultimatum to Belgrade listing ten demands, including assent to a joint investigatory commission to be supervised on Serbian soil by Austrian officials. Except for the latter stipulation—an infringement on its sovereignty—and one other, Serbia's government accepted the demands, with conditions. Even now, Kaiser Franz Josef could have pursued a face-saving climbdown. "Almost no genius," wrote the great historian Jacob Burckhardt of Europe's greatest family, the Habsburgs, "but goodwill, seriousness, deliberateness; endurance and equanimity in misfortune."[23] No longer: with a sense that the monarchy was in perhaps fatal decline and running out of time, Vienna, on July 28, declared war—for the first time in history—by telegraph.[24]

A wider conflict did not ensue automatically. Escalation—or not—lay principally in the hands of two men, cousins by blood and marriage, "Willy" and "Nicky." Wilhelm II had a low opinion of Nicholas II, telling Britain's foreign secretary at Queen Victoria's funeral in 1901 that the tsar was "only fit to live in a country home and grow turnips."[25] The kaiser had no insight into Russian grand strategy. Nicholas II, for his part, temporized, observing that "war would be disastrous for the world, and once it had broken out would be difficult to stop."[26] During the first half of 1914, more strikes had rocked St. Petersburg and other parts of the empire, like the Baku oil fields, than at any time since 1905, and in July 1914 workers became particularly menacing, partly out of desperation in the face of repression. The Duma, before its early June summer recess, was rejecting significant parts of the government budget, including funds for the interior ministry tasked with the domestic repressions. As for Russian military might, Russia's allies France and Britain overestimated it, while Germany and Austria-Hungary underestimated it—but not as much as the Russians themselves did.[27] What is more, Russia and Serbia did not even have a formal alliance, and Cousin Nicky would never go to war out of some supposed Pan-Slavic romantic nonsense.[28] Russian officials instructed the Serbs to respond reasonably to Austria. Nonetheless, the bottom line was that Russia would not allow German power to humiliate Serbia because of the repercussions for Russia's reputation, especially following Russia's inability to prevent Austria's annexation of Bosnia-Herzegovina back in 1908.[29] Nicholas II was determined to deter Austria-Hungary, which had begun mobilization, *for the sake of Russia,* not Serbia.

The German leadership in late July momentarily reconsidered, in an eleventh-hour initiative, but Austria-Hungary rejected the peace feeler idea—and Germany acceded. Had Wilhelm II backed off and curbed his dependent Austro-Hungarian ally, Nicholas II would have backed down as well. Instead, facing the belligerence of his cousin, domestic pressure from elites to stand tall, and unrest at home, the tsar ordered, then rescinded, and finally ordered again, on July 31, a full mobilization.[30]

Russia was no innocent victim, however. The perpetual machinations to have the tsar abolish the Duma, or downgrade it to a mere consultative body, had heated up. In effect, the decision for war was Nicholas II's sideways coup against the Duma he despised. War would allow his reclamation of an unmediated mystical union between tsar and people (a prolongation of the Romanov tercentenary of the year before). The tsar did suffer genuine pangs of conscience over the innocent subjects who would be sent to their deaths, but he also felt tremendous emotional release from the distasteful political compromising and encroachments on the autocratic ideal. Nicholas II also fantasized about a domestic patriotic upsurge, "like what occurred during the great war of 1812."[31] Conveying such delusions, a provincial newspaper wrote about the war that "there are no longer political parties, disputes, no Government, no opposition, there is just a united Russian people, readying to fight for months or years to the very last drop of blood."[32] There it was, the grand illusion: the hesitant, dubious war to uphold Russia's international prestige was imagined as a domestic political triumph—throngs kneeling before their tsar on Palace Square. Visions took flight of further imperial aggrandizement as well: a once-in-a-century opportunity to seize the Turkish Straits and the Armenian regions of Ottoman Anatolia; annex the Polish- and Ukrainian-speaking territories of Austria; and expand into Persia, Chinese Turkestan, and Outer Mongolia.[33]

Nicholas II was not alone in suddenly inverting the traditional link in Russia between war and revolution—no longer causative but somehow preventative.[34] In Berlin, too, insecurities fed fantasies of foreign expansion and domestic political consolidation. Germany's two-front vulnerability had produced a defense scheme to *conquer the continent*. Known to history as the Schlieffen Plan, for the general Count Alfred von Schlieffen (1833–1913), and originally conceived partly as a bold way to lobby for more war resources, the scheme, reworked by Helmuth von Moltke the Younger, had come to entail wheeling huge armies through Belgium into France in a giant arc, while also readying to smash Russia. Germany could, it was hoped, overcome numerical disadvantage by tactical surprise, mobility, and superior training.[35] The German general staff, in bouts of pessimism, expressed fewer illusions about a short war than sometimes recognized, but could not admit that war had ceased to be an effective policy instrument—to them, war still promised a decisive resolution of multiple state problems, and the civilians did not disagree. Thus, Germany would violate Belgian neutrality in order to support Austria against Russia, with the larger aim of avoiding losing the arms race to Russia, which also meant war with Britain.[36]

Less well known is the fact that the British Admiralty, the equivalent of the German general staff, had been planning to fight a war by precipitating the rapid collapse of Germany's financial system, thereby paralyzing its economy and its military's ability to wage war—the formula of a quick victory, at supposedly very low cost, and the British equivalent of the Schlieffen scheme. The Admiralty's plan for Germany's demise was worked out in a committee on trading with the enemy headed by Hamilton "Ham" Cuffe (1848–1934), known as Lord Desart. It not only extended war far beyond military considerations but presupposed massive state intervention in the laissez-faire market economy. The Admiralty sought control over the wartime movements of British-flagged merchant ships and the private cargoes they carried, censorship over all cable networks, and supervision over the financial activities of the City of London. Because Britain had the greatest navy and wielded a near monopoly over the global trading system's infrastructure, the Admiralty fantasized that it could somehow manage the effects of the chaos on Britain's own economy. All of this contravened international law. The British cabinet had endorsed the Admiralty's plan in 1912, and even predelegated the authority to enact it when hostilities broke out. The internal war debate in Britain took place over whether Britain could avoid also becoming entangled in strictly military actions (sending troops to the continent) while denying Germany access to shipping, communications, and credit.[37]

Britain and Germany almost pulled back from the brink. Wilhelm II did not give the full go-ahead for war until told that Russia had mobilized.[38] The kaiser signed the mobilization order on August 1, 1914, at 5:00 p.m., but a mere twenty-three minutes later, a telegram arrived from the German ambassador in London. The British foreign secretary, Sir Edward Grey, "has just called me upon the telephone," wrote the German ambassador, "and asked me whether I thought I could give an assurance that in the event of France remaining neutral in a war between Russia and Germany we should not attack the French."[39] Was this a parallel to Pyotr Durnovó's (unheeded) advice to Nicholas II to keep out of the Anglo-German quarrel: namely, an expression of London's dream of escaping war by directing German might eastward, against Russia? Details out of London were sketchy. The conversation between Grey and the German ambassador had lasted a mere six minutes. But the telegram seemed to have broached the core question that would drive world politics throughout the first half of the twentieth century and would become the main dilemma of Stalin's regime—whither German power?

To an elated German kaiser, the August 1 telegram from London seemed a godsend: the splintering of the Triple Entente, and one less front. Grey *seemed* to be proposing that Britain and even France could remain neutral in Germany's support for Austria against Serbia and thus in Germany's quarrel with Russia. A nearly apoplectic von Moltke protested the great security risk and chaos involved in halting Germany's precision war plan and (somehow) shifting entire armies from west to east—"Your majesty, it cannot be done. The deployment of millions cannot be improvised"[40]—but when a follow-up telegram arrived seeming to confirm British neutrality if Germany attacked only Russia, Wilhelm II ordered champagne. The kaiser also cabled King George V, another cousin, to give his word that German troops, although continuing to mobilize in the west (for protection), would not cross the French frontier. It looked like a deal. But that very same night, the British king sent a stupendous reply. Drafted by Grey, it called the conversations between Grey and the German ambassador a "misunderstanding."[41] Was it British treachery? No, just stupidity. Paris would never acquiesce in a German annihilation of Russia because that would drastically alter the balance of power on the continent to France's detriment, and in any case France had formal treaty obligations to Russia. Grey—who deemed Germany a battleship without a rudder but was himself acting inexplicably—belatedly specified that for Berlin a deal to avert war required that Germany had to hold back from attacking Russia, too. A livid Wilhelm II ordered a relieved von Moltke to resume the occupation of Belgium. His revised "Schlieffen Plan" was on.[42]

Germany declared war against Russia and France; Britain declared war against Germany.[43] German officials managed through clever propaganda to make the German war order appear a necessary response to the "aggression" of Russia, which had mobilized first.[44] (Stalin would later come to share the general conclusion, fatefully, that any mobilization, even in deterrence or self-defense, led inexorably to war.)[45]

Lord Desart's plan was on as well, at least initially, even though financial groups, the department of trade, and other interests had vehemently opposed this grand strategy. But July 1914 had brought a stunning financial panic from a loss of confidence: London banks began calling short-term loans and disgorging their immense holdings of bills of exchange, freezing the London market; interest rates jumped. In New York, European investors dumped American securities and demanded payment in gold. Fear of war pushed insurance rates so high, however, that gold stopped being shipped even though the global financial system was based upon the metal. "Before a single shot had been fired, and before any destruction of wealth, the whole world-fabric of credit had dissolved," a managing director of the firm Lazard Brothers would observe in fall 1914. "The Stock Exchange was closed; the discount market dead; . . . commerce at a standstill throughout the world; currency scarce; the bank of England's resources highly strained." The United States, which was neutral, would not tolerate closing down the global economic system by Britain in its quarrel with Germany. The British government would soon back off attempting to collapse the German economy in toto and would instead improvise a piecemeal effort at economic blockade. It would fail. The transoceanic flow to Germany of goods and raw materials financed by British banks and carried on British ships would increase.[46] Meanwhile, Britain had sent a land army to the continent.

World war looks inexorable. Over decades, imperial German ruling circles had lacked elementary circumspection about their newfound might; imperialist Britain lacked the visionary, skillful leadership needed to accept and thereby temper Germany's power. Elements in Serbia plotted murder with disregard for the consequences. Austria-Hungary, bereft of its heir, opted for an existential showdown. German ruling circles looked to shore up their one ally, a beleaguered Austria, while being fundamentally insecure about an inability to win the arm's race against the great powers on either side of Germany, especially with the growing military prowess of a weak Russia, and therefore developed a defensive plan that entailed the conquest of Europe.[47] Russia risked everything, not over a dubious pan-Slavic interest in Serbia, but over what a failure to defend Serbia would do to Russia's prestige.[48] And, finally, Britain and Germany tried but failed to collude in a last-minute bilateral deal at Russia's expense. (The thought would persist.) As if all that was not sufficient cause, it was summertime: Chief of Staff von Moltke was on a four-week holiday at Karlsbad until July 25, his second extended spa visit that summer for liver disease; German grand admiral Alfred von Tirpitz was at a spa in Switzerland; the chief of the Austro-Hungarian staff, Field Marshal Baron Franz Conrad von Hötzendorf, was in the Alps with his mistress; both the German and Austrian war ministers were on holiday as well.[49] Additional structural factors—an overestimation of the military offensive—also weighed heavily in the march toward Armageddon.[50] But if St. Petersburg had possessed irrefutable proof of Serbian intelligence's complicity in the archduke's assassination, the tsar's honor might have been offended to the point that he refused standing up militarily for Belgrade.[51] If Princip had quit and gone home after he and his accomplices botched the assassination, or the archduke's driver had known the revised plan to visit the hospital, world war might have been averted. Be that as it may, launching a war always comes down to decision makers, even when those decision makers are themselves the products, as much as the arbiters, of armed state structures. Across Europe in 1914, with few exceptions—a shrewd Pyotr Durnovó, a bumbling Edward Grey—politicians, military men, and particularly rulers hankered after territory and standing and believed (or hoped) that war would solve all manner of their international and domestic problems, reinvigorating their rule, at what each believed was, for them, a favorable moment.[52] In other words, when contingencies such as the wrong turn of a driver on a Sarajevo street confronted a tiny handful of men with the question of world war or peace, they hesitated yet chose war, for the sake, in varying combinations, of state prestige, state aggrandizement, and regime revitalization.[53]

## THE SUMMONS TO LENIN

The conflict of August 1914 escalated into a world war partly because of the expectation that states were vulnerable to conquest, but it was protracted because of the circumstance that they were not.[54] Already by late fall 1914 the Great War had become a stalemate: Britain, and to a lesser extent Russia, had foiled Germany's attempted preemptive conquest of France. From that point—and every day thereafter—the further choice, for all belligerents, could not have been starker: Negotiate an end to the stalemate, admitting that millions of soldiers had been hurled to futile deaths; or continue searching for an elusive decisive blow while dispatching millions more. Each belligerent chose the latter course. To put the matter another way, if the decision for war was, in the first instance, Austria-Hungary's, then Germany's, then Russia's, then Britain's, the decision to prolong the agony was everyone's. Belligerent states ran out of money yet they persisted in the fight. During fifty-two months of war, the rulers of the world's most educated and technologically advanced countries would mobilize 65 million men. Up to 9 million were killed, more than 20 million wounded, and nearly 8 million taken prisoner or missing—in all, 37 million casualties.[55]

For two years, the British had mostly allowed the French and Russians to absorb the brunt of Germany's blows.[56] But in July 1916, during the bloodbath at Verdun—launched by the Germans in a new strategy of attrition to overcome the stalemate by bleeding the French to death—the British countered with an offensive on the Somme farther west in France. At least 20,000 British soldiers were killed and another 40,000 wounded *during the first twenty-four hours*. This was the greatest loss of life—working class and aristocrat—in British military history. Before the Battle of the Somme, just like Verdun, ended in stalemate, it would claim 430,000 British killed and mutilated (3,600 *per day*), along with 200,000 French and perhaps 600,000 Germans.[57] On the western front overall, 8 million of 10 million battlefield deaths were caused not by "industrial killing" but by long established technologies: small arms and artillery.[58] Still, artillery barrages now shredded men on impact from more than twenty-five miles away (territorial gains were measured in yards). Machine guns had not only become easily portable but could now fire 600 rounds per minute, and for hours on end without pausing, a hail of metallic death.[59] Poison gas seared the lungs of the troops in trenches, until shifting winds often brought the lethal clouds right back against the side that had launched the chemical weapons. (Of all the belligerents, the Russian army suffered the worst from the chlorine and mustard gas because of insufficient masks.)[60] In the Ottoman empire, which had joined the side of Germany and Austria-Hungary, Armenian subjects were accused en masse of treason—collaborating with Russia to break away eastern Anatolia—and were massacred or force-marched away from border areas, resulting in 800,000 to 1.5 million Armenian civilian deaths. In Serbia, losses were fully 15 percent of the population, a monstrous price even for a heedless assassination; Serbian incursions into Habsburg territories, meanwhile, failed to ignite a South Slav uprising, demonstrating that the fears in Vienna that had prompted the showdown were exaggerated.[61] And what of that vaunted German navy, whose construction had done so much to incite the British and drive Europe toward the precipice? During the entire Great War, the German fleet fought a single engagement against Britain, in summer 1916, off the Danish coast, where the British lost more ships, but the Germans withdrew and chose not to risk their precious navy again.

The war itself, not the subsequent bungled Peace of Versailles, caused the terrible repercussions for decades. "This war is trivial, for all its vastness," explained Bertrand Russell, a logician at Cambridge University and the grandson of a British prime minister. "No great principle is at stake, no great human purpose is involved on either side. . . . The English and the French say they are fighting in defence of democracy, but they do not wish their words to be heard in Petrograd or Calcutta."[62] Beyond the murderous hypocrisy, it was the fact that men could dispose of the destiny of entire nations that Lenin, leader of the Bolsheviks, now assimilated. But whereas European rulers and generals knowingly sent millions to their deaths for God knows what, Lenin could assert that he was willing to sacrifice millions for what now, thanks to the imperialist war, looked more than ever like a just cause: peace and social justice. Marx, in *The Communist Manifesto*, had celebrated the intense dynamism of capitalism, but Lenin emphasized its limitless destructiveness: the war, in his view, showed that capitalism had irrevocably exhausted whatever progressive potential it once had. And Europe's Social Democrats who had failed to oppose the war, despite being Marxists, became similarly irredeemable in his eyes.[63] Among socialists internationally, Lenin now stood out, radically. "I am still 'in love' with Marx and Engels, and I cannot calmly bear to hear them disparaged," Lenin wrote from Zurich to his mistress Inessa Armand in January 1917. "No really—they are the genuine article. One needs to study them." He concluded the letter by disparaging "Kautskyites," that is, followers of Karl Kautsky, the German Social Democrat and towering figure of the socialist Second International (1889–1916), which the war destroyed.[64]

Lenin added a politics of imitative war techniques to his Marxist ideology, which the wartime slaughterhouse helped to validate in ways that the prewar never did.[65] His propaganda work would be almost too easy. With the war raging, he wrote his foundational *Imperialism: The Highest Stage of Capitalism* (1916), adapting the ideas of the Brit John Hobson and the Austrian Rudolf Hilferding, arguing that capitalism was doomed but for its recourse to exploitation abroad. But it was hardly necessary to read Lenin to appreciate the link between the Great War and colonial rapaciousness. Between 1876 and 1915, gigantic swaths of the world's territory had changed hands, usually violently.[66] France had amassed a global empire 20 times its size, and Britain 140 times, colonizing hundreds of millions of people. Outside Europe, only Japan had managed to stave off the European onslaught and, with its own overseas colonies, emulate Europe's rapaciousness. In German-controlled South-West Africa, when the colonized Herrero rebelled (1904–7), suppression escalated into extermination—and almost succeeded: Germany wiped out up to 75 percent of the natives.[67] The most noto-rious of all was tiny Belgium's empire—80 times its size—which, in the pursuit of rubber and glory, enslaved, mutilated, and slaughtered perhaps half of Congo's population, as many as 10 million people, in the decades before 1914.[68] But this was the thing about the Great War: even in countries that practiced rule of law, politicians and generals used their own citizens no better, and often worse, than they had their colonial subjects. The British commander at the Somme, General Sir Douglas Haig, demonstrated no concern for human life, neither the enemy's nor that of his own men. "Three years of war and the loss of one-tenth of the manhood of the nation is not too great a price to pay in so great a cause," Haig wrote in his diary. When British casualties were too low, the general saw a sign of loss of will.[69] Of the 3.6 million men under arms in 1914 in democratic France—the only republic among the great powers—fewer than 1 million remained by 1917. Some 2.7 million had been killed, wounded, taken prisoner, or gone miss-ing. Civilians died en masse, too. No large European city was laid waste—mostly, the Great War was fought in villages and fields—but state "security" now meant the destruction of the enemy culturally, as the Germans had demonstrated from the outset in Belgium: libraries, cathedrals, and the civilians who embod-ied the enemy nation were made targets of bombing and deliberate starvation.[70] "This is not war," a wounded Indian soldier wrote home from the carnage of France in 1915, "it is the ending of the world."[71]

## CONSCRIPTS AND THE AWOL

Stalin missed the war. That summer of 1914, at age thirty-six, he was serving the second year of a four-year term of internal exile in the northeastern Siberian wastes of Turukhansk. This was the longest consecutive term of banishment he would serve, wallowing near the Arctic Circle right into 1917. This time, the authorities had moved him too far beyond the railhead for escape. While two generations of men, the flower of Europe, were fed into the maw, he battled little more than mosquitoes and boredom.

None of the top Bolsheviks saw action at the front. Lenin and Trotsky were in comfortable foreign exile. In July 1915, Lenin wrote to Zinoviev, "Do you remem-ber Koba's name?" Lenin obviously meant Koba's real name or surname. Zino-viev did not recall. In November 1915 Lenin wrote to another comrade, "Do me a big favor: find out from Stepko [Kiknadze] or Mikha [Tskhakaya] the last name of 'Koba' (Iosif J—??). We have forgotten. Very important!" What Lenin was after remains unknown.[72] He was soon busy wrongly attributing the conquest of 85 percent of the globe to inexorable economic motivations. Trotsky, who dashed from country to country during the conflict, was writing journalistic essays about trench warfare and the war's sociopsychological impact, political life in many European countries and in the United States, and the politics of socialist movements in relation to the war, calling for a "United States of Europe" as a way to halt the conflict.[73] But Stalin, Trotsky would later observe, published absolutely nothing of consequence during the greatest conflict of world history, a war that roiled the international socialist movement. The future arbiter of all thought left no wartime thoughts whatsoever, not even a diary.[74]

Extreme isolation appears to have been a factor. Stalin wrote numerous letters from godforsaken Siberia to Bolsheviks in European exile begging for books that he had already requested, particularly on the national question. He contemplated assembling a collected volume of his essays on that topic, building on his 1913 article "Marxism and the National Question." Before the war commenced, in early 1914, Stalin completed and sent one long article, "On Cultural Autonomy," but it was lost (and never found).[75] He wrote to Kamenev (in February 1916) that he was at work on two more, "The National Movement in Its Historical Development" and "War and the National Movement," and provided an outline of the content. He was aiming to solve the relationship between imperialist war and nationalism and state forms, developing a rationale for large-scale multinational states.

> "Imperialism as the political expression [. . .] The insufficiency of the old frameworks of the 'national state'. The breaking up of these frameworks and the tendency to form states of [multiple] nationalities. Consequently the tendency to annexation and war. [. . .] Consequently the belief in nat[ional] liberation. The popularity of the principle of nat. self-determination as a counterweight to the principle of annexation. The clear weakness (economic and otherwise) of small states . . . The insufficiency of a completely independent existence of small and medium-sized states and the fiasco of the idea of nat. separation [. . . ] A broadened and deepened union of states on the one hand and, on the other, autonomy of nat. regions within states. [. . .] it should express

itself in the proclamation of the autonomy of a nat. territory within multinational states in the struggle for the united states of Europe."[76]

These thoughts predated publication of Lenin's *Imperialism: The Highest Stage of Capitalism,* and dovetailed somewhat with Trotsky's writings on a United States of Europe (which Lenin had attacked). But Stalin's promised wartime articles, which he told Kamenev were "almost ready," never materialized.

Severe isolation cannot be the whole explanation. In Siberian exile Stalin made the acquaintance of a future rival, Yankel "Yakov" Sverdlov (b. 1885), the son of a Jewish engraver from Nizhny Novgorod, who had completed four years of gymnasium. Like Stalin, Sverdlov had been co-opted in absentia into the Bolshevik Central Committee after the 1912 party gathering in Prague. The two had been betrayed by the same *okhranka* agent within Bolshevik ranks, Malinowski, and overlapped for several years in Turukhansk, including in remote Kureika, a settlement of perhaps thirty to forty inhabitants. During the war in remote Siberia, Sverdlov managed to complete a pamphlet history titled *Mass Exile, 1906–1916* and a number of articles: "Essays on the History of the International Worker Movement," "Essays on Turukhansk Region," "The Downfall of Capitalism," "The Schism in German Social Democracy," "The War in Siberia."[77] He also wrote letters that revealed a rivalry with Stalin. "My friend [Stalin] and I differ in many ways," Sverdlov wrote in a letter postmarked for Paris on March 12, 1914. "He is a very lively person and despite his forty years has preserved the ability to react vivaciously to the most varied phenomena. In many cases, he poses new questions where for me there are none any more. In that sense he is fresher than me. Do not think that I put him above myself. No, I'm superior [*krupnee*], and he himself realizes this. . . . We wagered and played a game of chess, I checkmated him, then we parted late at night. In the morning, we met again, and so it is every day, we are our only two in Kureika." For a brief time, they roomed together. "There are two of us" in a single room, Sverdlov wrote to his second wife, Klavdiya Novogorodtseva. "With me is the Georgian Jughashvili, an old acquaintance . . . He's a decent fellow, but too much of an egoist in everyday life." Soon enough, Sverdlov could not take it anymore and moved out. "We know each other too well," he wrote on May 27, 1914, to Lidiya Besser, the wife of an engineer revolutionary. "The saddest thing is that in conditions of exile or prison a man is stripped bare before you and revealed in all petty respects. . . . Now the comrade and I are living in different quarters and rarely see each other."[78]

Stalin took to indulging in the desolate circumstances of his profound isolation. When a fellow Siberian exile drowned, Stalin seized the man's library for himself alone, violating the exiles' code, and cementing his reputation for self-centeredness. Stalin also continued to engage in the exiled revolutionary's pastime of seducing and abandoning peasant girls. He impregnated one of his landlord's daughters, the thirteen-year-old Lidiya Pereprygina, and when the police intervened he had to vow to marry her, but then betrayed his promise; she gave birth to a son, who soon died. (Stalin would later recall his dog in Siberia, Tishka, but not his female companions and bastards.) During Turukhansk's eight months of winter, the future dictator cut holes through the river ice to fish for sustenance, like the indigenous fur-clad tribesmen around him, and went on long, solitary hunts in the dark, snowed-in forests. ("If you live among wolves," Stalin would later say, "you must behave like a wolf.")[79] Sudden, blinding snowstorms nearly took his life. Ever the agitator and teacher, he also harangued the local indigenous people, Yakut and Evenki, in his cold, cramped rented room, whose windows had no glass, vainly trying to recruit them to the revolutionary struggle. He had an audience but few genuine interlocutors, let alone followers. (Stalin's supposed Caucasus gang, never more than a tiny band of irregular followers, had long ago dispersed, never to be assembled again.) He did manage to turn the pitiful gendarme assigned to guard him into a subordinate who fetched his mail and accompanied him on unsanctioned trips to meet fellow exiles in the scattered settlements.[80] And his Armenian fellow exile, Suren Spandaryan, accompanied by his girlfriend, Vera Schweitzer, did make a long trek northward on the frozen Yenisei River to visit. But, dirt poor, Stalin mainly wrote to everyone he knew begging for money as well as for books. "My greetings to you, dear Vladimir Ilich, warm-warm greetings," he wrote to Lenin. "Greetings to Zinoviev, greetings to Nadezhda! How are things, how is your health? I live as before, I gnaw my bread, and am getting through half my sentence. Boring—but what can be done?" In his supplication to the Alliluyev sisters (in Petrograd), Stalin complained of "the incredible dreariness of nature in this damned region."[81] He fathered a second son by Lidiya, Alexander, who survived—his second surviving bastard—but, like his first, Konstantin, in Solvychegodsk, he left the boy behind.

In late 1916, Stalin received a draft notice. But in January 1917, after a six-week trip by reindeer-pulled sleds from Turukhansk through the tundra down to the induction center at Krasnoyarsk in southern Siberia, the future dictator was disqualified from army service because of his physical deformities.[82]

What was the tsarist state doing trying to induct riffraff like Stalin and his fellow internal exiles? Russia, like most of the Great Powers, had mandated universal conscription in the 1870s. For some time thereafter, states did not wield the governing capacity or financial wherewithal to realize such complete mobilizations. In France, half the second-year call-ups would be given noncombatant jobs, while in Germany about half the possible conscripts were often missing from the ranks. In Russia, two thirds of the eligible pool had been exempted from conscription. As the Great War approached, the imperatives heightened to fulfill the universal call to the colors, but states still fell short.[83] Still, at the war's outbreak Russia fielded the world's largest force, 1.4 million in uniform. Britain and France referred to their ally's mass army as "the steamroller." Despite draft riots, moreover, another 5 million Russian subjects were conscripted in the second half of 1914 alone.[84] But just as the war killed or wounded nearly the entire 1914 officer corps, it chewed through conscripts. At least 2 million Russian troops met death over the course of hostilities.[85] The tsarist authorities were forced to dig ever deeper.[86] Of imperial Russia's 1914 estimated population of 178 million, nearly 18 million were eligible for service, and 15 million of them would be conscripted. This was a huge number, but proportionately smaller than in France (8 million of 40 million) or Germany (13 million of 65 million). To be sure, during the war, hired labor on Russian farms fell by almost two thirds, and Russian factories were frequently emptied of skilled labor, too. The call-ups also took away half of Russia's primary schoolteachers (who were not in abundance to start with). And yet, the relative limits in Russian numbers indicated limits to the tsarist regime's reach over the vast empire. Russia could not manage to take full advantage of what had so terrified the German high command: namely, the gigantic population.[87]

That said, once on the battlefield, Russian troops and field officers acquitted themselves well, despite initial shortages—more severe than suffered by the other belligerents—of shells, rifles, bullets, uniforms, and boots.[88] Between August and December 1914, Russian armies drove into Germany's eastern flank and over time managed to crush Austria-Hungary. Against Ottoman armies, Russia did far better than the British, emerging victorious after the Ottomans had invaded Russia in winter 1914–15 expecting, erroneously, to ignite Russia's Muslims. The problem, however, was that the Germans recovered to repel Russia's early advances and encircle Russian troops at Tannenberg (southeast of Danzig), then forced a 300-mile Russian retreat.[89] By late 1915, German-led forces had not only reversed the Russian conquests of the previous year in

Habsburg Galicia, but had overrun Russian Poland, with its vital industry and coal mines; much of Belorussia; and Courland (on the Baltic), thereby threatening Petrograd. Nonetheless, from 1914 to 1916, the Russian army tied down more than 100 Central Powers' divisions on the eastern front; until 1917, Russia captured more German prisoners than Britain and France combined.[90]

## AUTOCRACY PREPARES A REVOLUTION

Russia had gone to war with a non-binding constitution tacked on to the autocracy, and neither side in the Duma-autocracy antagonism understood or had any sympathy for the other.[91] Nicholas II clung to autocracy even though it afforded him no personal pleasure and he proved incapable of living up to the role.[92] That said, the tsar often outmaneuvered the constitutionalists: the Duma was scarcely being summoned into session. It met for a day on July 26, 1914, to approve war credits (a formality), and for three days on January 26–29, 1915.[93] Following the 1915 retreat, which was cast as a terrible rout, even though its orderliness impressed (and stymied) the Germans, Nicholas II did recall the Duma to session, and in August 1915, Paul Miliukov, head of the Constitutional Democrat party, emerged as the leader of the six-party Progressive Bloc. The latter comprised almost two thirds of Duma deputies and aimed to improve the war effort with what the deputies called a government of confidence.[94] At one level, this connoted a cabinet appointed by the tsar that had the Duma's positive appraisal. But the interior minister, suspecting that the constitutionalists really sought a genuinely parliamentary order—a government reflective of electoral majority—denounced Duma president Mikhail Rodzyanko as "stupid and bombastic," adding, "You just want to get together and put forth various demands: ministers answerable to the Duma and, perhaps, even a revolution."[95] Russia's conservatives, meanwhile, sought to counter the Progressive Bloc with a Conservative Bloc, but in August 1915 the rightists lost one of their foremost leaders, Pyotr Durnovó, who suffered a fit of apoplexy, fell into a coma, and died.[96]

Even more important than that loss, Nicholas II continued to discourage rightist political parties organizing on his behalf as attempts to "interfere" in his autocratic prerogatives.[97] He refused even a private secretary to organize his vast responsibilities and ensure implementation of his decisions, because he feared falling under any secretary's sway; so the "autocrat" opened all his own correspondence. Later, Trotsky would observe that a debilitated autocracy got the enfeebled autocrat it deserved. That was true, to a point. The much-missed Alexander III had managed to project will and authority; had he not died prematurely of illness, he would have been sixty-eight years old in 1914. Still, everything about his reign indicates that he, too, would have held fast to the autocracy and its incoherence. The autocrat alone retained the prerogative of ministerial appointments, without parliamentary recommendation or confirmation, and if a tsar allowed perceived loyalty and lineage to trump competence, there was nothing to be done. Between July 1914 and February 1917, Russia saw a parade of four different prime ministers and six interior ministers, all of whom became laughingstocks.[98] (Able officials, in many cases, increasingly chose to keep their distance.) The ministers' initial response to the 1915 war crisis was depression. The generals Nicholas II appointed, meanwhile, often blamed scapegoats for the problems they themselves caused.[99] Nicholas II, predictably, reacted to the 1915 crisis by suspending the Duma he reviled. At the same time, the tsar imagined he could inspire the troops, and the people more broadly, by naming himself frontline supreme commander.[100] In September 1915, Nicholas II relocated to staff headquarters at the town of Mogilyov, displacing his strapping first cousin Grand Duke Nicholas, who was known in family circles as Nikolasha—and, among the masses, as Nicholas III.

Nearly everyone in Russia's establishment who was high enough to do so advised against the move. That included eight of the tsar's own twelve ministers *in writing*—two more concurred orally—who feared that the monarch and monarchy could now be directly tarnished by a sagging war effort. Their pleading was in vain: even an overwhelming majority of the top state officials was powerless to correct the will of an autocrat. Other than an autocrat's own (rare) about-face, the tsarist system provided no corrective mechanisms.

The tsar's notorious personal shortcomings were on full, and fatal, display. At Mogilyov, some 490 miles from the maddening Russian capital, Nicholas II finally seemed to find that elusive world he craved of "no political parties, no disputes, no Government, no opposition . . . just a united Russian people, readying to fight for months or years to the very last drop of blood." Recalling his extended escapes from St. Petersburg in Crimea, Nicholas II took long strolls with his English setters, rode into the countryside in his Rolls-Royce, listened to music, played dominoes and solitaire, and watched motion pictures. The tsar occasionally had Alexei brought to Mogilyov for visits, and the heir "marched about with his rifle and sang loudly," interrupting the war councils. True, although Nicholas II loved the romance of military pageantry, he knew next to nothing of strategy and tactics, but then again, neither had Nikolasha, a graduate of the General Staff Academy, nor German Emperor Wilhelm II. But as chief of staff, Nicholas II had appointed the gifted General Mikhail Alexeyev, a relatively small man but "a gigantic military force."[101] At the same time, the domestic mobilization for the war and domestic politics had to be taken care of, but Nicholas II's escape to Mogilyov had, in effect, left his wife, rather than a strong political figure like Witte or Stolypin, in charge of the wartime empire's capital.[102] Described by the French ambassador as "constant sadness, vague longing, alternation between excitement and exhaustion, . . . credulousness, superstition," Alexandra did not shrink from making personnel and policy recommendations, and from presenting her husband "the autocrat" with faits accomplis.[103] "Do not fear what remains behind," she wrote to him. "Don't laugh at silly old wify, but she has 'trousers' on unseen."[104] For Russia's state officialdom and the officer corps, fighting a monumental war for the very survival of the motherland, what they observed or heard about the wartime regime felt like daggers to the heart.

Whatever Nicholas II's personal shortcomings, Alexandra was several magnitudes below even him as would-be autocrat. To boot, she was German. The German-sounding St. Petersburg had been renamed Petrograd, but spy mania had already broken out in Russia. "There is not one layer of society that can be guaranteed free of spies and traitors," thundered the military prosecutor, who arrested hundreds, including long-serving war minister General Vladimir Sukhomlinov. He was innocent of treason, but his public trial broadcast damaging revelations about deepset corruption and incompetence, which was cast as sedition (a dangerous obfuscation that prefigured aspects of Bolshevism in power).[105] Alexandra, too, incessantly wrote to Nicholas of "traitor-ministers" and "traitor-generals." But soon, the rumors of "dark forces" boomeranged onto her and her entourage, which included Grigory Rasputin (Novykh). Born in Western Siberia in 1869, the son of a poor peasant, not educated and unable to write proper Russian, Rasputin, known to the tsaritsa and tsar as "our Friend," was a religious wanderer and pretend monk who had made his way into the heart of power. He was rumored to smell like a goat (from failing to bathe), and to screw like one, too. He identified with the outlawed sect of Khylsty, who taught rejoicing (radenie), or "sinning in order to drive out sin"; Rasputin advised followers to yield to temptations, especially of the flesh, asking, "How can we repent if we have not first sinned?"[106] Tales of a court harem spread, conveyed in cartoons of Rasputin's manipulative hands emanating from a naked Alexandra's nipples. That was myth. Still, in public, as the *okhranka* noted, he approached female singers in a restaurant and exposed his penis while striking up a conversation. The faux "Holy Man" accepted sexual favors from noblewomen seeking his influence at court and sent half-literate policy memoranda to top ministers. Officials became afraid to incur his displeasure—he never forgot a slight—and paid him regular cash gifts, but a few fought back. A would-be female assassin, connected to a rival monk, behind whom stood high figures at court, had taken a knife to the mystic's stomach on June 29, 1914—the day after Archduke Franz Ferdinand was killed in Sarajevo—but Rasputin, his entrails hanging out, survived.[107]

Throughout the war, the highest Russian government ministers tried but could not manage to evict the "Siberian tramp" from the capital. Alexandra was immovable.[108] Why? Why did she permit a debauched phony and rumored German agent the run of Russia's corridors of power? The answer was twofold. First, despite all the talk that Rasputin was running state affairs through Alexandra, it was the tsaritsa who used the pretend monk, having him voice her personnel and policy preferences as "God's will," thereby rendering what she wanted more palatable to the pious Nicholas II. Rasputin's sway began when Alexandra lacked an opinion, but he held no definite, enduring political views of his own.[109] Second, the heir's hemophilia posed a daily threat to his life from possible internal bleeding into joints, muscles, and soft tissue, and no cure existed, but Rasputin could somehow alleviate the "Little One's" symptoms.

Nicholas II's family certainly seemed bedeviled. His first brother (and next in line), Alexander, had died of meningitis in infancy (1870). His next brother, Grand Duke Georgy, Nicholas II's childhood playmate, died in 1899 aged twenty-eight (the tsar kept a box of jokes uttered by Georgy that he had written down and could be heard laughing in the palace by himself). That is how Nicholas II's younger brother Mikhail became heir, until the birth of Alexei in 1904 displaced him to second in line and regent for the minor, should Nicholas II die before Alexei's maturity (in 1920). Then, the incurable hemophilia was diagnosed. Back in the autumn of 1912, at an imperial hunting preserve just below tsarist Warsaw, the-then eight-year-old Alexei had bumped his thigh exiting a boat. This mundane occurrence caused vast internal hemorrhaging and a bloody tumor near his groin, which became infected and produced spiking fevers (105°F). Death appeared imminent, yet an operation was out of the question: the blood flow from surgery would be unstoppable. Nicholas and Alexandra prayed to their most revered icons. They also appealed to Rasputin. "God has seen your tears and heard your prayers," he telegrammed while traveling back in Siberia. "The Little One will not die." Miraculously, following the telegram, the bleeding stopped, the fever subsided, and the tumor was reabsorbed.[110] The doctors were stunned; the royal couple became attached still more unshakably to the magical Holy Man. Grand Duke Mikhail also did his part to bond Nicholas and Alexandra to Rasputin. At the time of the whispers in the fall of 1912 that Tsarevich Alexei had been given last rites, Mikhail, the next in line, evaded the *okhranka* and eloped in Vienna with his lover, Natalya Wulfert, a commoner and a divorcée, thereby appearing deliberately to forfeit his right to the throne. This left no one except the precarious boy.[111] Alexei's life-threatening incidents continued—falling off a chair, sneezing hard—yet each time Rasputin's ramblings calmed the boy (and the boy's mother) and halted the bleeding.

Mysticism and the occult were rampant among Russia's privileged orders—as everywhere in Europe's aristocratic circles—but Nicholas and Alexandra's anxiety for the dynasty's future was entirely legitimate. And yet, among Europe's monarchies secrecy in court affairs was the norm, and Russia's royals refused to reveal the state secret that explained everything—and that might have elicited mass sympathy. Not even top generals or government ministers knew the truth about Alexei. In the resulting information vacuum, a public bacchanalia flourished about the pretend monk's debauch with Alexandra and his malignant court camarilla. These tales were widely published, and sabotaged the monarchy in ways that all the alleged spies (like Sukhomlinov) never did. Street hawkers helped burn the Romanovs in figurative effigy with such pamphlets as *The Secrets of the Romanovs* and *The Life and Adventures of Grigory Rasputin*, in print runs of 20,000 to 50,000. And for the illiterate, picture postcards, skits, easily remembered verses, and jokes spread the stories of the monarchy's moral decay and treason.[112] "What's the use of fighting," soldiers at the front began to say, "if the Germans have already taken over?"[113]

The supreme paradox was that despite everything, by 1916 the Russian state, assisted by self-organizing public associations tightly intertwined with the state's agencies, had immensely improved the wartime economy.[114] Until that year, Russia had to purchase most of its weapons abroad, and Russian soldiers were often hard pressed to match ammunition with their weapons—Japanese Arisakas,

American Winchesters, British Lee-Enfields, on top of ancient Russian Berdans.[115] The frontline troops were short of shells, short of rifles, short of uniforms, and short of boots (the army demanded a quarter-million pairs of boots *per week*).[116] But after two years of war, Russia began producing ample quantities of rifles, ammunition, wireless sets, aircraft.[117] Russia's economy in 1916 was humming: employment, factory profits, and the stock market were way up. Taking advantage of the manufacturing surge, as well as new aerial reconnaissance of enemy positions, General Alexei Brusilov launched a bold offensive in June 1916. Technically, he was only conducting flanking support against Austria-Hungary as part of a Russian offensive against Germany to relieve the pressure against France and Britain (which were bogged down in the Verdun and Somme slaughterhouses). But in just weeks, Brusilov, adapting a crude form of an advanced technique—artillery combined with mobile infantry—while attacking on a wide front, broke through Austro-Hungarian defenses and devastated its rear. His forces annihilated nearly two thirds of Austria-Hungary's eastern-front army: 600,000 enemy dead and wounded, 400,000 captured.[118] A shattered Austrian chief of staff warned that "peace must be made in not too long a space, or we shall be fatally weakened, if not destroyed."[119] Instead, the German field marshal Paul von Hindenburg was sent to assume direct command over Habsburg forces—he called it the "worst crisis the eastern front had known."[120]

"We have won the war," boasted the Russian foreign minister, who added that "the fighting will continue for several more years."[121] In the event, Russia's own generals undermined Brusilov. One insubordinate general even marched the elite Imperial Guards—"physically the finest human animals in Europe"—into bogs, rendering them sitting ducks for German planes.[122] Betrayed, in addition, by the railroad, Brusilov ran out of supplies. Brusilov himself had sacrificed a staggering 1.4 million Russians killed, wounded, and missing, and left himself no reserves. The final indignity came courtesy of Romania, which joined the Entente precisely because of Brusilov's successes, but then had to be rescued when its catastrophic army went into battle. Nonetheless, Brusilov had mounted the Entente's single best performance of the entire war, and optimists in Russia looked forward to 1917 as the year when military victory would be at hand. Politically, however, things looked increasingly shaky. "In our monarchy," one former justice minister observed in 1916, "there is only a handful of monarchists."[123]

Soon enough, not victory but political implosion came to seem more likely. In fall 1916, a clutch of mutinies broke out, some involving whole regiments, in Petrograd's outskirts, where rear units had swelled with untrained call-ups who fraternized with workers.[124] Nicholas II heaped fuel onto the bonfire that was the dynasty's image by transferring the accused traitor Sukhomlinov—known to be championed by Alexandra—from prison to house arrest. On November 1, 1916, the respected Paul Miliukov, speaking from the rostrum of the Duma, lit into the government, punctuating his indictment of war mismanagement with the ringing phrase "Is this treason, or is it stupidity?" Many deputies chanted "stupidity," others "treason," and quite a number shouted "Both! Both!" Miliukov elicited an ovation.[125] The incendiary speech was banned from publication, but a disillusioned monarchist in the Duma, Vladimir Purishkevich, a prominent member of the Union of the Russian People, had it illegally distributed in thousands of copies at the front. Purishkevich himself, in the Duma, denounced government ministers as "Rasputin's marionettes." Hours before the Duma's holiday recess, Purishkevich helped murder Rasputin, in a plot led by Prince Felix Yusupov with the tsar's cousin Grand Duke Dmitri Pavlovich, as well as British intelligence officials. The mutilated and bullet-riddled corpse was found floating in the capital's icy river a few days later, on December 19, 1916.[126] Nicholas II was both quietly relieved and revolted.[127] But many members of the establishment, cheering the sensational demise of the "internal German," nonetheless continued to sound the alarm. Grand Duke Alexander Mikhailovich wrote to his cousin the tsar after Rasputin's murder, "Strange as it may sound, Nicky, we are witnessing a revolution promoted by the government."[128]

An autocrat strangely absent from the wartime capital, a pseudomonk in the autocrat's absence inexplicably running wild at court, a government of nobody ministers who came and went anonymously, tales of treason on every newspaper's front page, every street corner parliament, and in the Duma—the autocracy's image became wrecked beyond repair. "I am obliged to report," Maurice Paléologue, ambassador of France, Russia's closest ally, telegraphed Paris in January 1917, "that at the present moment the Russian empire is run by lunatics."[129] Open gossip about pending palace coups speculated whether Nicholas II and Alexandra would both be murdered or just the latter.[130] At staff headquarters, General Alexeyev and the brass discussed how they had managed the Brusilov offensive on their own, and began to think the once unthinkable. But what if a putsch against Nicholas II from the left came first?

## LAST LAST STRAW

Revolutions are like earthquakes: they are always being predicted, and sometimes they come. Throughout 1916 and into early 1917, almost every branch of the *okhranka* was warning of pending revolution (as well as anti-Jewish pogroms).[131] No top revolutionary leaders were in Russia—Lenin, Martov, Chernov, Trotsky were all abroad—and the *okhranka* had neutralized many of the lesser socialist leaders who were resident in Petrograd, if the latter had not already neutralized themselves by political mistakes.[132] On January 9, 1917, the twelfth anniversary of Bloody Sunday, 170,000 strikers massed in the capital, shouting "Down with the government of traitors!" and "Down with the war!" but the day passed without revolution, thanks to numerous arrests. On February 14, 1917, up to 90,000 workers in the capital went on strike, and again the police made mass arrests.[133] Strikes persisted; a February 22 lockout over wages at the Putilov Works sent thousands of men into the streets.[134] A number of factories ceased operating for want of fuel, idling more workers. As fortune would have it, after a frigid January, the weather in Petrograd had turned unseasonably mild. On February 23, International Women's Day—March 8 by the Western calendar—some 7,000 low-paid women left Petrograd's textile mills to march, shouting not only "Down with the tsar!" and "Down with the war!" but also "Bread!" Why were marchers on International Women's Day demanding bread? Contrary to myth, the tsarist state had managed to cope with most exigencies of the war, as Brusilov's well-supplied offensive demonstrated (by the end of 1917, the shell reserve would reach a total of 18 million.)[135] But the tsarist state fumbled the organization of the food supply.[136] The state's food supply emergency emerged as a kind of last last straw.

Prewar Russia had fed both Germany and England, accounting for 42 percent of global wheat exports. The empire functioned as a giant grain-exporting machine, from silos to railways, moving harvests over very long distances in large amounts to far-off markets, until the war shut down foreign trade—which, in theory, meant more food for Russia's domestic consumption (whose norms were low).[137] True, sown acreage declined slightly as peasants moved to the front or cities, and western territories fell under foreign occupation. Moreover, the army, made up of men who had previously grown grain, were now consuming it—half of the country's marketable grain in 1916.[138] But that was not the key problem. Nor was the problem *primarily* the transportation system, which nearly everyone scapegoated. True, the rail network was not organized to circulate grain to markets *within* the empire. More fundamentally, however, many peasants refused to sell their grain to the state because the prices were low, while prices for industrial goods peasants needed (like scythes) had skyrocketed.[139] Perhaps even more fundamentally, wartime state controls, driven by a deep anticommercial animus, had squeezed out the maligned but essential middlemen (petty grain traders), and failed to serve as an adequate substitute, thereby disorganizing domestic grain markets.[140] Thus, although Russia had food stocks, by late January 1917, grain *shipments* to the capital in the north, from grain-producing regions in the south, did not even reach one sixth of the absolute lowest daily-consumption levels.[141] The government had long resisted rationing, fearing that an announcement of rationing would bring expectations for supplies that could not be met. Finally, on February 19, however, the government belatedly announced that rationing would commence on March 1. This attempt to calm the situation induced panicked shelf stripping. Bakery windows were smashed. Bakery personnel were observed hauling off supplies, presumably for speculative resale. Petrograd's inhabitants also learned through word of mouth that although many bakeries, lacking flour, remained open just a few hours a day, freshly baked white bread was uninterruptedly available in high-priced dining establishments.[142] An *okhranka* agent surmised that "the underground, revolutionary parties are preparing a revolution, but a revolution, if it takes place, will be spontaneous, quite likely a hunger riot."[143]

A mere four days after the tsarist government's announcement of impending rationing was when the women had marched through Petrograd demanding bread; within seven days of their march, the centuries-old Russian autocracy was dissolved.

In the winter of 1917, Russia did not suffer famine, as the empire had in 1891 or 1902, two episodes that were within living memory and had not caused the political regime's overthrow. (The 1891–92 famine had claimed at least 400,000 lives.)[144] During the Great War, food shortages in Germany—partly caused by a British blockade designed to starve civilians and break Germany's will—had already provoked major urban riots in late fall 1915, and such riots continued each year, but the German state would hold up until the German regime would lose the war in 1918. Neither food marches nor even general strikes constitute a revolution. It is true that socialist agitators had been swarming the factories and barracks, finding receptive audiences.[145] Revolutionary songs—like the ones

Stalin had sung each May Day in Tiflis—new forms of address ("citizen" and "citizenness"), and above all, a compelling story of senseless wartime butchery and high political corruption had conquered the capital, filling the symbolic void that had opened up in tsarism and empowering the people with solidarity.[146] Some Petrograd demonstrators took to looting and drinking, but many others placed towels, rags, and old blankets inside their jackets to face the anticipated whip blows of Cossack cavalrymen. The raucous crowds that seized hold of Petrograd's streets in late February 1917 were brave and determined. Still, protesting crowds are often resolute and courageous, and yet revolution is very infrequent. Revolution results not from determined crowds in the streets but from elite abandonment of the existing political order. The food demonstrations as well as strikes *revealed* that the autocratic regime had already hollowed out. Almost no one would defend it.

Critically, it was not just the women in the streets: General Brusilov was warning that the army had no more than ten days' supply of foodstuffs—and there could be no doubt that he, and the rest of the brass, blamed the autocracy. "Every revolution begins at the top," wrote one tsarist official, "and our government had succeeded in transforming the most loyal elements of the country into critics."[147] Desperate high-level plots to unseat the tsar proliferated, even among the Romanov grand dukes. Already in late 1916, Alexander Guchkov, a former president of the Duma, in cahoots with the deputy Duma president, initiated discussions with the high command to (somehow) force out Nicholas II in favor of Alexei under the regency of Grand Duke Mikhail Alexandrovich, and appoint a government answerable to the Duma. (One of Guchkov's ideas involved "capturing" the tsar's train.) In a parallel plot, General Alexeyev, chief of staff, discussed with Prince Georgy Lvov arresting Alexandra and, when Nicholas II objected, forcing him to abdicate in favor of Grand Duke Nikolasha (by then in Tiflis). Still more seriously, in January 1917, before the food demonstrations and strikes, Lieutenant General Alexander Krymov—highly decorated for valor— requested a private meeting with Duma president Mikhail Rodzyanko as well as select deputies and told them, "The feeling in the army is such that all will greet with joy the news of a coup d'état. It has to come . . . we will support you."[148] It can never be known, of course, whether one of the palace coup schemes against Nicholas II would have come to fruition even if the workers had not gone on strike. But with the masses having seized the capital's streets, elites seized the opportunity to abandon the autocrat.

## CRACKDOWN AND DESERTION

On the eve of the women's bread march, Nicholas II had made a short visit home to the Alexander Palace at Tsarskoe Selo, just outside the capital, but on February 22 he returned to his Mogilyov sanctuary. There he buried himself in a French history of Julius Caesar's conquest of Gaul. (Never mind that France was Russia's ally.) "My brain feels rested here—no ministers & no fidgety questions to think over," the tsar wrote to Alexandra on February 24–25.[149] During those days of no fidgety questions, half of Petrograd's workforce, up to 300,000 angry people, went on strike and occupied the Russian capital's main public spaces. Alexandra— among the key sources informing the tsar about the disturbances—dismissed the strikers as "a hooligan movement, young boys & girls running about & screaming that they have no bread," assuring her husband the disturbances would pass, along with the unseasonably warm weather.[150] But the tsar had other sources of information. And although he has been nearly universally derided as indecisive, Nicholas II, from the front, issued an unequivocal order for a crackdown.

The previous mass uprising in the capital, in connection with the Russo-Japanese War, had been terrifying, but it had failed.[151] Nicholas II's apparent lack of grave concern may have been related to the successful use of force back in 1905–6.[152] Of course, that had been under Pyotr Durnovó, and before the agonies of Stolypin's five strenuous years had ended in failure, and before the debacle of Rasputin had stripped the autocracy of its remaining shreds of legitimacy. This time, Major General Sergei Khabalov, head of the Petrograd military district, oversaw security in the capital. Admittedly, he was a desk general who had never commanded troops in the field. Khabalov was assisted by people like Major General Alexander Balk, who had been displaced from Warsaw by the German occupation and whom Nicholas II named Petrograd city commandant only after all other candidates had fallen through. A favorite of Alexandra and Rasputin, Balk, in turn, reported to Interior Minister Alexander Protopopov, Russia's fifth interior minister in thirteen months. Erratic, voluble, smitten with serial manias, he had previously driven his textile business to near bankruptcy, and now followed advice at séances with the spirit of the deceased Rasputin.[153] Nicholas II had had immediate second thoughts and had wanted to dismiss Protopopov, but could not overcome the resistance of Alexandra, to whom he had written: "I feel sorry for Protopopov; he is a good and honest man, but a bit hesitant. It's risky to leave the ministry of the interior in such hands nowadays. I beg you not to drag Our Friend in this. This is only my responsibility and I wish to be free in my choice."[154]

Instead, the dubious interior minister Protopopov was handed near dictatorial powers—"Do what is necessary, save the situation," the tsar told him. But Protopopov was no Durnovó. Later, the cronyism in Protopopov's appointment—a favorite not just of Alexandra and Rasputin, but also of Rodzyanko and other government officials—would be scapegoated for the February Revolution.[155] But Khabalov and Balk had been preparing for a crackdown. True, Russia, universally viewed as a police state, had a mere 6,000 police in the capital in 1917, far too few to forestall the mass gatherings. But Russia maintained gigantic army garrisons in the rear for political as well as military purposes: Petrograd alone garrisoned at least 160,000 soldiers, with another 170,000 within thirty miles. That was double the peacetime number.[156] In 1905, when the regime survived, the entire St. Petersburg garrison had numbered a mere 2,000[157]; 1917's bloated soldiery in the rear included mere school cadets and untrained conscripts, but the majority of the capital garrison comprised cavalry (Cossacks) and elite guard units. It was a formidable force. Indeed, a Petrograd military district had been separated from the northern front in early February 1917 precisely in order to free up troops for quelling anticipated civil disorders.[158] Now those demonstrations were at hand: on the morning of February 24, people again marched for bread.

Around 9:00 p.m. on February 25, Nicholas II telegrammed Khabalov, "I order you to suppress the disorders in the capital at once, tomorrow. These cannot be permitted in this difficult time of war with Germany and Austria."[159] Khabalov and Balk had already observed some Cossacks hesitating to confront the crowds in Petrograd. "The day of February 25 was lost by us in every sense," Balk would later recall, noting that "the crowd felt the weakness of authority and got impudent."[160] Now, with the tsar's order to hand, Khabalov and Balk informed a meeting of government ministers toward midnight on February 25–26 about the next day's coming crackdown. Doubts ricocheted around the private apartment where the government meeting took place. Hearing of the impending crackdown, the foreign minister advised that they all "immediately go to the Sovereign Emperor and implore His Majesty to replace us with other people." A ministerial majority inclined toward trying to find "a compromise" with the Duma.[161] But in the wee small hours, the *okhranka* went ahead and swept up more than 100 known revolutionaries, and later that day (February 26), at the

ABOVE: Japan's rise and the first signs of catastrophe: Russian Pacific fleet flagship *Petropavlovsk* after striking two mines off Port Arthur, Russo-Japanese War, March 31, 1904. To make up for the loss, Russia dispatched its Baltic fleet around the world, but its ships, too, were promptly sunk in battle.

LEFT: Sergei Witte, New Hampshire hotel, August 1905. Witte's support for construction of the Trans-Siberian Railway had been partially responsible for provoking the war with Japan, but after Russia's defeat, he negotiated an advantageous peace at Portsmouth, New Hampshire. Nicholas II appointed him Russia's first ever prime minister, but could not stand him.

Ceremonial opening of the State Duma (the lower house), Tsar Nicholas II presiding, Winter Palace throne room, April 27, 1906. The tsar instantly regretted conceding the creation of Russia's first-ever legislature and schemed to emasculate or abolish it.

Pyotr Durnovó. Interior minister whose political crackdown rescued the autocracy in 1905–6. A fellow official recalled him as "small, all muscle and nerves." This caricature by Zinovy Grzhebin formed part of a series ("Olympus") of biting portraits of high officials.

Pyotr Stolypin (second from the right, in white), who succeeded Witte as prime minister and, concurrently, Durnovó as interior minister, in Kiev, August 1911, as Nicholas II greets peasants of Kiev province. Stolypin would shortly fall to an assassin in the Kiev Opera House.

A metaphor for the hollowing autocracy: Stolypin's state dacha, August 12, 1906. During this earlier assassination attempt, twenty-eight people died, including the prime minister's fifteen-year-old daughter. Photographed by Karl Bulla.

Queen Victoria (lower center) and her royal relatives: German Kaiser Wilhelm II (lower left, looking up), the future Russian tsar Nicholas II (bowler hat), at the Coburg Palace, Germany, April 21, 1894, two days after the wedding of Victoria's grandchildren Princess Victoria Melita ("Ducky") of Saxe-Coburg/Edinburgh and Ernst Ludwig of Hesse, Germany. Alix of Hesse, another grandchild and the sister of the groom, had just acceded to Nicholas's proposal for marriage and soon became Alexandra of Russia.

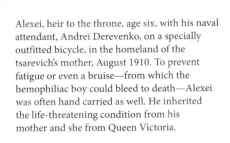

Alexei, heir to the throne, age six, with his naval attendant, Andrei Derevenko, on a specially outfitted bicycle, in the homeland of the tsarevich's mother, August 1910. To prevent fatigue or even a bruise—from which the hemophiliac boy could bleed to death—Alexei was often hand carried as well. He inherited the life-threatening condition from his mother and she from Queen Victoria.

Besarion "Beso" Jugashvili.
The only known image of what is thought
to be Beso, Stalin's father.

Ketevan "Keke" Geladze, Stalin's mother.

ABOVE: Stalin's birth house, Gori, Georgia.

RIGHT: Yakobi "Koba" Egnatashvili, Gori tavern owner, falsely rumored to have been Stalin's father. He paid for Stalin's education.

Gori church school, students and teachers, 1892;
young Ioseb Jugashvili, age thirteen, is in the last row, dead center.
This is the first known photograph of Stalin

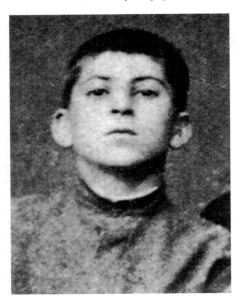

Tiflis Orthodox seminary students and teachers, 1896;
Jugashvili (last row, second from the left) is clean shaven.

Neoclassical seminary building, dubbed the Stone Sack,
where for a time Stalin lived as well as studied under a regimen of surveillance and snitching.

Lado Ketskhoveli (1877–1903), Stalin's first mentor in Marxism and revolution. Lado was killed by prison tsarist officials, a fate that befell many leftists and could have befallen Stalin.

Meteorological Observatory in Tiflis, where Stalin worked from December 1899 through March 1901 (photographed by TASS in 1939). His stint as a meteorologist was, essentially, the only legal paid employment he held until being named a people's commissar in 1917, at age thirty-nine.

A close-up of Stalin from a group photograph, Kutaisi prison (Georgia), 1903.

Misfortune and misery: Stalin at the bier of Yekaterina "Kato" Svanidze (b. 1885), who had captured his heart, but who died in agony from disease, December 1907. They had just married the year before. Stalin left their infant son, Yakov (b. March 1907), to be raised by her relatives.

Tsarist police mug shots of Stalin, Baku, March 30, 1910. Stalin generally spent his time in prison reading books, studying Esperanto, and denying rumors that he was a police informant, which, although unsubstantiated, would never desist.

Sarajevo, capital of Bosnia-Herzegovina, in Austria-Hungary, June 28, 1914. Archduke Franz Ferdinand, heir to the Habsburg throne, in a car approaching the corner near Schiller's Delicatessen, where the nineteen-year-old Gavrilo Princip was waiting, after an assassination plot had failed. The archduke had altered his itinerary, but the driver had not been informed, started to turn down the wrong street, and stalled the car.

Princip, circa 1915, serving life in prison.

The village of Kureika in Siberia, just below the Arctic Circle, where Stalin would spend most of the Great War. Its bleak isolation is evident even during the short season without snow drifts and icy winds.

Siberian exiles in Monastyrskoe, administrative center of Turukhansk region (which was larger than Britain, France, and Germany combined), July 1915. Sverdlov, in glasses, is seated in the front row, next to him in a hat is Hryhory Petrovsky. Stalin is in the back row in a black hat. To Stalin's right is Lev Kamenev and to his left is Suren Spandaryan, who died in these frozen wastes at age thirty-four. Kamenev was being subjected to a party "trial" for contradicting Lenin's view that the Bolsheviks sought a Russian military defeat.

Lavr Kornilov, imperial Russia's supreme military commander, 1917. Kornilov, Kerensky wrote, "spent little time in fashionable drawing-rooms, although their doors were always open to any officer of the General Staff. . . . He was regarded as rather shy and even somewhat of a 'savage.'" In fact, Russian patriots looked to Kornilov for salvation.

Alexander Kerensky versus Vladimir Lenin. Lenin was photographed by Pavel Zhukov, who, like these two political adversaries, also happened to be a native of Simbirsk.

Matylda Krzesińska, Polish-born prima ballerina of Russia's Imperial Mariinsky Theater, and former mistress of Nicholas II, St. Petersburg, 1900. Her elegant mansion was seized in 1917 and served as the first Bolshevik headquarters until July. (The ballerina emigrated to France, married one of her two Romanov grand duke lovers, and lived to just shy of one hundred years old.) Photograph by Yakov Steinberg.

Exterior of the art nouveau mansion, strategically situated across the river from the Winter Palace. Lenin would thunder from the small balcony.

ABOVE: Seizure of Power: Second Congress of Soviets, banners proclaiming "All Power to the Soviets," Tauride Palace, Petrograd, second night of the coup, October 26, 1917. Photographed by Pavel Otsup. "When I entered the hall," wrote the chronicler Nikolai Sukhanov, "there was a bald, clean-shaven man I didn't know standing on the podium and talking excitedly in a rather hoarse, stentorian voice, somewhat guttural and with a spectacular emphasis at the end of his phrases. Ha! It was Lenin."

RIGHT: Julius Tsederbaum, known as Martov, who had led the Mensheviks out of the congress hall on the first day, in protest of the Bolshevik coup. He would attack Stalin in 1918, and serve as the source of ill will between Stalin and Lenin.

ABOVE: Bolshevik government (Council of People's Commissars), Smolny, Petrograd, Lenin in the center, Stalin, hand on face, standing against the wall, early 1918, during the brief time when Left SRs, such as Prosh Proshyan, commissar for posts and telegraphs (to Lenin's right), joined the Bolshevik-dominated government. Trotsky is absent (likely at the negotiations with Germany at Brest-Litovsk).

LEFT: Maria Spiridonova, famed terrorist, leader of the Left SRs, Petrograd, 1917. Spiridonova could have put an end to Lenin's rule in July 1918 but did not.

Иосиф Виссарионович
Сталин
( 1915 г )

Надежда Сергеевна
Аллилуева
( 1917 г )

Page from Stalin's photo album, showing himself in 1915 and Nadya Alliluyeva in 1917; they were married in 1918, and that spring Stalin took her to Tsaritsyn as his secretary. In Tsaritsyn in 1918, Stalin created a local, personal dictatorship that foreshadowed his assumption of power over the whole country.

Leather-clad Trotsky, war commissar and newly named chairman of the Revolutionary Military Council of the republic, on the Volga near Kazan, September 1918. Lenin had just been shot, and Trotsky returned to the front to save the situation, after a lightning visit to Moscow.

sound of bugles, imperial troops fired on civilian demonstrators, in some cases using machine guns. Around 50 people were killed and 100 or more wounded (in a city of 3 million).[162] The show of force appeared to puncture the festive crowds. It also stiffened the government ministers' spines.[163] On the evening of February 26, 1917, the chief of the *okhranka* phoned Petrograd city commandant Balk to report that he expected "a decline in the intensity of disorders tomorrow." As in 1906, the crackdown seemed to have worked.[164]

Such confidence was misplaced, however. Correctly, *okhranka* analysts had concluded that back in 1905–6 only the loyalty of the troops had saved the tsarist regime. And now, surmised one *okhranka* agent, "everything depends upon the military units. If they do not go over to the proletariat the movement will die down quickly."[165] Ominously, however, one elite guards regiment—the Pavlovsky Guards reserve battalion—had tried to stop the killing of civilians. Another guards unit, the Volhynian, had carried out its orders.[166] But those Volhynian Guards stayed up overnight discussing their killing of unarmed civilians, and on February 27, when street crowds defiantly massed again, the Volhynians—24,000 soldiers—went over to the protesters.[167] The suddenly rebellious Volhynians visited the nearby billets of other units, too, recruiting the rest of the capital garrison to mutiny. Giddy insurgents ransacked and set aflame the *okhranka* headquarters.[168] They also emptied the prisons of criminals and comrades— many arrested only days before in *okhranka* sweeps—and broke into arsenals and weapons factories. Armed men started careering about Petrograd in commandeered trucks and armored carriers, wildly shooting in whatever direction.[169] "I'm doing all I can to put down the revolt," Khabalov telegrammed staff headquarters. Yet he also begged them "to send reliable troops from the front at once." Later that evening he informed staff headquarters that "the insurrectionists now hold most of the capital."[170] Khabalov contemplated bombing Russia's own capital with airplanes.[171] He turned out to be far out of his depth, but even a well-executed crackdown is only as good as the political authority behind it— and tsarist political authority was long gone.[172]

Events moved rapidly. Duma president Rodzyanko, ambitious for himself and fearful of the crowds, was frantically telegraphing staff headquarters in Mogilyov about "the state of anarchy" in the capital, urging that the tsar reverse his prorogue order so the Duma could legally meet and form a Duma-led government. "Again, this fat Rodzyanko has written to me lots of nonsense, to which I shall not even deign to reply," Nicholas II remarked.[173] While waiting in vain for the tsar, the Duma leaders refused to break the law and assemble on their own. But two socialist Duma deputies goaded some 50 to 70 of the 420 Duma deputies to gather for a "private" meeting in the Duma's regular building, the Tauride Palace, but outside their usual venue of the ornate White Hall. These deputies declared themselves not a government, but a "Provisional Committee of the State Duma for the Restoration of Order."[174] In the very same Tauride Palace at the same time, hundreds of leftists—including many freed from prison that morning—met to reconstitute the 1905 Petrograd Soviet of Workers' and Soldiers' Deputies.[175] The Provisional Committee had competition. The ministers of the government, for their part, telegrammed Mogilyov headquarters with their resignations, which the tsar refused to accept, but the ministers began to make themselves scarce anyway. "The trouble was that in all that enormous city [Petrograd], it was not possible to find a few hundred people sympathetic toward the government," recalled one rightist deputy in the Duma. "In fact, there was not a single minister who believed in himself and in what he was doing."[176] The autocracy was deserted not just in the capital's streets and in the capital garrison, but also throughout the corridors of power.

### TREASON

From police reports, Nicholas II knew that the British in Petrograd—the embassy of his ally, for whom he had gone to war—were assisting the Duma opposition against him.[177] At staff headquarters that February 27, he received urgent messages, including from his brother Grand Duke Mikhail, the regent for the underage Alexei, pleading that he announce a new "Government of confidence" comprising Duma deputies.[178] Instead, blaming Khabalov for botching the crackdown, the tsar made two decisions: first, early the next morning, he would return to the capital (a fourteen-to-sixteen-hour train ride)—actually to the capital's outskirts, Tsarskoe Selo—where he and Alexandra lived with the children; second, an expeditionary force from the front (800 men) commanded by General Nikolai Ivanov would ride to the capital "to institute order."[179] General Alexeyev, the chief of staff, ordered many additional units—at least eight combat regiments—to link up with Ivanov's expedition. Nicholas II granted the sixty-six-year-old General Ivanov dictatorial power over all ministries.[180] But the tsar himself never made it back to the capital. Deliberate disinformation spread by a wily representative of the Duma's Provisional Committee exaggerated the extent of worker disorders on the railroad, which made the tsar's train shunt to and fro for nearly two days. He finally alighted on the evening of March 1 at the staff headquarters of the northern front in Pskov. General Ivanov easily reached Tsarskoe Selo, but in the meantime, his superior, General Alexeyev, had changed his mind and telegrammed Ivanov not to take action in the capital. Instead, amid reports of the formation of the Duma's Provisional Committee and of diminished anarchy in Petrograd, Alexeyev now began to urge Nicholas II to concede a Duma-led government.

The commander of the northern front in Pskov, General Ruzsky, had already come out in favor of a Duma-led government well before Alexeyev; now, with Alexeyev's urging, Ruzsky pressed this idea on his unexpected guest—the sovereign.[181] Nicholas II agreed to allow Duma president Rodzyanko to form a government, but insisted that it would report to him, not to the Duma. Later, after more telegrams from Alexeyev, however, the tsar finally granted a government responsible to the Duma. Nicholas II also personally instructed Ivanov, at Alexeyev's request, to "please undertake no action" (for the time being)—and then Nicholas II retired to the sleeping car.[182] Having conceded a real constitutional monarchy and parliamentary regime after so many years of tenacious resistance, the tsar stayed awake in torment.[183] Unbeknownst to a sleepless Nicholas II, beginning around 3:30 a.m., and for the next four hours, Ruzsky communicated with Rodzyanko in the capital over the torturously slow direct wire, or Hughes apparatus (which was capable of transmitting about 1,400 words per hour). Rodzyanko shocked the general with the news that it was already too late for a constitutional monarchy, at least for Nicholas II, given the radicalism in the capital.[184]

Alexeyev, informed by Ruzsky, now took it upon himself to contact all the front commanders and urge them to support Nicholas II's abdication "to save the army." Each commander—sharing a general staff esprit de corps—was to telegraph his request for Nicholas to step down directly to Pskov, with copies to Alexeyev. Later that morning of March 2, 1917, General Ruzsky, as per Alexeyev's instructions, reported to the tsar's imperial train carrying the tapes of the conversation with Rodzyanko urging abdication in favor of Tsarevich Alexei and Grand Duke Mikhail as regent.[185] Nicholas II read, walked to the carriage window, went silent, then stated he "was prepared, if necessary for Russia's welfare, to step aside." Nothing was decided. Around 2:00 p.m., however, the telegrams arrived from the front commanders—Brusilov and all the rest, plus Alexeyev—unanimously urging abdication; Ruzsky took them to the tsar, who made the sign of the cross and soon emerged to request that HQ prepare an abdication manifesto. Whether Nicholas II would have renounced his sacred calling had he made it to Tsarskoe Selo and the arms of Alexandra can never be known. ("And you, who are alone, no army behind you, caught like a mouse in a trap, what can you do?" Old Wify cabled him on March 2.)[186] Stoic, as ever, the now-former tsar was quietly anguished. "All around me," Nicholas II confided to his diary, "there is nothing but treason, cowardice, and deceit!"[187] The tsar's diaries indicate that only the urging of his generals persuaded him to abdicate.[188]

And so, in the guise of patriotism, it had come to treason after all.

In violating their oaths—sworn to the tsar, after all—the high commanders could imagine they were saving the army. Desertions were running at 100,000 to 200,000 per month, swelling the ranks of protesting crowds and criminal bands, and clogging the critical railroad stations.[189] In addition, the February rebellion had spread from Petrograd to Moscow and the Baltic fleet, threatening the front.[190] As far back as the disturbances during the Russo-Japanese War, Alexeyev had concluded that "a revolution from above is always less painful than one from below."[191] But though "military dictatorship" crossed the lips of many civilian elites, and contemporary examples existed—General Ludendorff, de facto, in Germany; the young Turk officers in the Ottoman Empire—Alexeyev and Russia's military men refrained from claiming power themselves.[192] It cannot be that Russian generals lacked confidence in their ability to take over civilian affairs (they had already usurped much civilian operational authority to manage the war). Moreover, Alexeyev had very good information from the general staff and the naval staff in the capital about the incompetence and prevarication of Russia's civilian leaders. But the officers detested the dirty work of serving as an auxiliary police force and crushing domestic rebellion, a task that undermined the army's military function and tarnished it in society. Steeped in their military general staff ethos, moreover, they had not developed broad political horizons.[193] And so, needing to quell the disorders engulfing the wartime capital and save the army and war effort, Alexeyev saw—or imagined—a solution in the Duma's Provisional Committee, aided by the figurehead of a new tsar, Aleksei, a darling-looking boy.[194] Their calculations were destined to be upended.

RUSSIA WAS a genuine great power, but with a tragic flaw. Its vicious, archaic autocracy had to be emasculated for any type of better system to emerge.

Unmodern in principle, let alone in practice, the autocracy died a deserving death in the maelstrom of the Anglo-German antagonism, the bedlam of Serbian nationalism, the hemophilia bequeathed by Queen Victoria, the pathology of the Romanov court, the mismanagement by the Russian government of its wartime food supply, the determination of women and men marching for bread and justice, the mutiny of the capital garrison, and the defection of the Russian high command. But the Great War did not break a functioning autocratic system; the war smashed an already broken system wide open.

Not knowing that the military brass had already successfully pressured Nicholas II into abdicating, the self-appointed Provisional Committee of the Duma had sent two deputies to Pskov to do so. The emissaries were both lifelong monarchists, and inveterate palace coup plotters: Alexander Guchkov and Vasily Shulgin. They were unshaven; Shulgin in particular was said to resemble a convict.[195] "Having given my consent to abdication, I must be sure that you have considered what impression this will make on all of the rest of Russia," Nicholas II said to the pair. "Will this not carry dangerous consequences?"[196] Consequences there would be.

By February 1917, Pyotr Durnovó was a year and a half in his grave, but his February 1914 prophecies were already on their way to fulfillment: the constitutionalists' revolt against the autocracy was accelerating a mass social revolution. Lenin—for the time being—lived outside Russia, behind German lines, in neutral Switzerland. Stalin was holed up in the Siberian backwater of Achinsk, one of myriad internal political exiles. There, as almost everywhere in the Russian empire (including in his native Georgia), the February Revolution arrived by telegraph ("All is in the hands of the people"). On March 3, a local soviet assumed power in Krasnoyarsk city, the regional center, and began arresting local tsarist officials. Stalin—suddenly a free man, for the first time in nearly seventeen years—boarded the Trans-Siberian Railway bound for Petrograd. It was some 3,000 miles away. He traveled in the company of fellow Bolshevik exile Lev Kamenev as well as his own latest girlfriend, Vera Schweitzer, the widow of the Bolshevik Central Committee member Suren Spandaryan, who had perished in the wastes of Stalin's place of exile, Turukhansk, Siberia, at age thirty-four of lung problems. The future dictator arrived in the imperial capital on March 12, 1917, wearing Siberian *valenki* (felt boots) and carrying little more than a typewriter.[197]

## CHAPTER 6

# KALMYK SAVIOR

Some comrades said it is utopian to advance the question
of the socialist revolution, because capitalism is weakly
developed with us. They would be correct if there were no
war, if there were no disintegration, if the foundations of
the economy were not shattered.

Iosif Stalin, Bolshevik Party Congress, late July 1917[1]

Save Russia and a grateful people will reward you.

A shout-out to General Lavr Kornilov, supreme commander,
by a Constitutional Democrat, August 1917[2]

"IT'S STAGGERING!" exclaimed one exiled revolutionary at the newspaper
reports of the February downfall of the monarchy in Russia. "It's so incredibly
unexpected!"[3] That exile was forty-seven years old and named Vladimir Ulyanov, better known as Lenin. For nearly seventeen years straight he had been
living outside Russia. After tsarism's coercive and corrupt rule, its narrow privilege and pervasive poverty, and above all its relentless denial of human dignity,
hope for new horizons understandably soared. The entire empire, while at war,
became embroiled in one gigantic, continuous political meeting, with a sense
anything might be possible.[4] The removal of tsar and dynasty during the monumental war, it turned out, would exacerbate nearly every governing problem it
had been meant to solve. The downfall of any authoritarian regime does not ipso
facto produce democracy, of course. A constitutional order must be created and
sustained by attracting and holding mass allegiance, and by establishing effective instruments of governance. The Provisional Government, which replaced the
tsar, would achieve none of that.

As both anarchy and hope erupted in the war-torn land, new and transformed
mass organizations proliferated.[5] These included not just revolutionary move-

ments, such as the Bolsheviks and others, and not just grassroots soviets and soldiers' committees but, even more basically, the army and navy. In 1914, imperial Russia's population of 178 million had been dispersed across 8.5 million square miles of territory, but the war recruited some 15 million imperial subjects into a mass organization—the Russian "steamroller." This unprecedented concentration would permit, once the tsar had vanished, an otherwise unattainable degree of political activity, right up to full-fledged congresses of elected deputies at the front itself. In mid-1917, some 6 million troops were at the front. Additionally, 2.3 million thoroughly politicized soldiers were deployed in sprawling rear garrisons, in almost every urban center of the empire.[6] To these millions, the February Revolution meant "peace"—an end to the seemingly endless Great War—and the dawn of a new era.

Well before 1917, ordinary people readily accepted the idea of an irreconcilable conflict between labor and capital, but rather than speak of classes per se, they tended to speak of light versus darkness, honor versus insult. A trajectory of suffering, redemption, and salvation was how they made sense of the struggle with their masters, not capital accumulation, surplus value, and other Marxist categories.[7] This would change as languages of class came to suffuse all printed and spoken public discourse in revolutionary Russia, from farms and factories to the army, fleet, and corridors of power. Even the classically liberal Constitutional Democrats, who strove to be above class (or nonclass), fatally accepted the definition of February as a "bourgeois" revolution.[8] This step conceded, implicitly, that February was not in itself an end, but a way station to an eventual new revolution, beyond liberal constitutionalism. As 1917 saw the mass entrance into politics of soldiers and sailors, brought together into a giant organization, Russia's army would steamroll not Germany but the country's own political system.

Given the role that the army had played in 1905–6 in saving the regime, and given the role it could be expected to have to play again, the tsar's decision to roll the iron dice had been an all-in gamble on the masses' patriotism. The fatal flaw of the tsarist regime had proven to be its inability to incorporate the masses into the polity, but the widespread politicization of the masses by the war meant that the constitutional experiment of 1917—if it was to have any chance whatsoever of surviving—needed to incorporate not just any masses, but mobilized soldiers and sailors. But if the Great War in effect restructured the political landscape, vastly deepening social justice currents that had already made visions of socialism popular before 1917, the Provisional Government proved no match for that challenge. On top of its feeble governing structures, its entire symbolic universe failed miserably, from the use of a tsarist eagle, uncrowned, as state symbol to its new national anthem, "God Save the People," sung to the Glinka melody of "God Save the Tsar." Caricatures of the Provisional Government were accompanied by popular pamphlets, songs, and gestures that discredited all things bourgeois, attacking the educated, the decently dressed, the literate, as fat cats, swindlers—even Russia's *Stock Market Gazette* poked fun at the bourgeoisie.[9] At the same time, in 1917, far more even than in 1905–6, Russia's constitutional revolution was deluged by a multifaceted leftist revolutionary *culture* enacted in evocative gestures and imagery: the "Internationale," red flags and red slogans, and a vague yet compelling program of people's power: "All Power to the Soviets." The potent hammer-and-sickle symbol appeared in spring 1917 (well before the Bolshevik coup), and it would soon capture the linkage—or the hoped-for linkage—between the aspirations of urbanites and the aspirations of country folk, joined in possibilities for social justice (socialism). The political mood in 1917, as one contemporary observer rightly noted, was characterized by "a general aspiration of a huge mass of Russians to declare themselves, no matter what, to be absolute socialists."[10]

How "socialism" came to be Bolshevism, and how the Bolsheviks came to be Leninist, are separate questions. Lenin and the Bolsheviks neither invented nor made broadly popular in Russia European socialism's long-developing symbolic repertoire, to which the war and then the February Revolution added profound extra impetus. But if the Russian empire experienced a mind-and-spirit mass socialist revolution—in the city streets and villages, at the front and in the garrisons, in the borderlands and even in adjacent regions beyond the state border—well before the Bolshevik coup in October 1917, the Bolsheviks in 1917 (and beyond) would manage to claim the socialist revolutionary repertoire, indeed, relatively quickly, almost to monopolize it. "The revolution" came to Lenin, and he proved ready to seize it, even against much of the Bolshevik inner circle.

Stalin's role in 1917 has been a subject of dispute. Nikolai Sukhanov (Himmer), the ubiquitous chronicler of revolutionary events who was a member of the Socialist Revolutionary Party and had a Bolshevik wife, forever stamped interpretations, calling Stalin in 1917 "a grey blur, emitting a dim light every now and then and not leaving any trace. There is really nothing more to be said about him."[11] Sukhanov's characterization, published in the early 1920s, was flat wrong. Stalin was deeply engaged in all deliberations and actions in the innermost circle of the Bolshevik leadership, and, as the coup neared and then took place, he was observed in the thick of events. "I had never seen him in such a state before!" recalled David Sagirashvili (b. 1887), a fellow Social Democrat from Georgia. "Such haste and feverish work was very unusual for him, for normally he was very phlegmatic no matter what he happened to be doing."[12] Above all, Stalin emerged as a powerful voice in Bolshevik propaganda. (For all the talk, most of it negative, about his involvement in expropriations during the wild days of 1905–8, in the underground, from the very beginning, he had really been an agitator and propagandist.) On May Day 1917, he noted that "the third year approaches since the rapacious bourgeoisie of belligerent countries dragged the world into the bloody slaughterhouse"—one of his typically incendiary editorials.[13] To party circles as well as public audiences, he delivered speech upon speech, many of which were published in the press. Stalin wrote often in the main Bolshevik newspaper, while editing and shepherding into print far more.[14] Between August and October—the critical months—he authored some forty lead articles in *Pravda* and its temporary replacements *Proletariat* or *Workers' Path*.[15] This outpouring—a sharp contrast to his silence during the first nearly three years of the war—stressed the need to seize power in the name of the soviets, which to Lenin meant in the hands of the Bolsheviks.

The reestablishment of functional institutions and a new authority to fill an immense void was a staggering task, which the ongoing war made still vaster, narrowing the possible political options. All this might appear to have rendered the onset of a new dictatorship a foregone conclusion. But countries do not *descend* into dictatorship any more than they burst into democracy. A dictatorship, too, must be created, and sustained. And modern dictatorship—the rule of the few in the name of the many—requires not only the incorporation of the masses into a polity but a powerful symbolic repertoire and belief system, in addition to effective instruments of governance and well-motivated repression.[16] Amid the kind of state breakdown Russia underwent in 1917, the idea—or fear—that a strong modern dictatorship would be created out of the rampant chaos could only seem farfetched. One key to Bolshevik power, however, lay in the Russian establishment's tireless search for a savior. Diverse efforts to stave off the triumph of Bolshevism, particularly those centered on Supreme Commander General Lavr Kornilov, would end up having the perverse effect of decisively strengthening Bolshevism. The outcome of the mass participatory process after February 1917 remained dependent on the war and the fundamental structure of soldiers' moods, but also the specter of counterrevolution, analogized from the French Revolution after 1789. For the Bolsheviks, the idea of counterrevolution was a gift.

## FREEDOM VERSUS FIRM AUTHORITY

Russia's constitutional revolution got a second chance, this time, unlike 1905–6, without the autocrat. Mishap and illegitimacy, however, shadowed the Provisional Government from its birth. Nicholas II had agreed to abdicate in favor of thirteen-year-old Alexei and to name Grand Duke Mikhail, his brother, as regent. The high command and Duma president Rodzyanko—monarchists all—counted on the cherubic Alexei to rally the country, while affording them a free hand. But the tsar, conferring once more with his court physician, heard again that hemophilia was incurable and that once the fragile boy took the crown, Nicholas would have to part with him and go into exile, and so, the fatherly tsar impetuously renounced Alexei's right to the throne, too, naming Mikhail outright.[17] By the 1797 succession law, however, a tsar could be succeeded only by his rightful heir, in this case Nicholas II's firstborn son, and a minor such as Alexei had no right to renounce the throne.[18] Beyond the illegality of naming Grand Duke Mikhail, no one had bothered to consult him; on March 3, a hasty summit took place with him in Petrograd. Paul Miliukov, leader of the Constitutional Democrats (Cadets), argued for retention of the monarchy, stressing tradition and the need to preserve the state; Alexander Kerensky, then a Duma deputy of the left, urged Mikhail to renounce, stressing popular moods.[19] Mikhail listened, mulled, and decided not to accept unless a forthcoming Constituent Assembly (or constitutional convention) summoned him to the throne.[20] Thus, what the generals had started—Nicholas II's abdication—the politicians finished: namely, Russia's de facto conversion into a republic. Two jurists hastily drafted an "abdication" manifesto in which Mikhail transferred "plenary powers" to the Provisional Government, even though the grand duke had no such authority to convey. In the chaos of regime change, the "abdication" manifesto of non-Tsar Mikhail Romanov provided the only "constitution" that would ever undergird the unelected Provisional Government.[21]

Revolution, by definition, entails violation of legal niceties. But in this case, eleven men—essentially handpicked by the fifty-eight-year-old Miliukov, who took the foreign ministry—replaced not just the hollowed-out autocracy but also the Duma, whence they emerged.[22] This was not because the Duma had become illegitimate. Among most frontline troops as of March 1917, acceptance of, if not confidence in, the Duma remained.[23] The Duma, for all its flaws, had earned some stripes by clashing with the autocracy over the years. After being prorogued, some members had convened in defiance of the tsar. But a draft protocol of the Provisional Government's first session (March 2) indicates that the group of assembled men contemplated resorting to the infamous Article 87 of the tsarist Fundamental Laws to rule without a parliament, a move for which the constitutionalists had viciously denounced Stolypin. The first meeting protocol also specified that "the full plenitude of power belonging to the monarch should be considered as transferred not to the State Duma but to the Provisional Government."[24] In fact, the Provisional Government laid claim to the prerogatives of both legislature and executive: the former Duma (the lower house) as well as the State Council (the upper house, abolished by government decree); the former Council of Ministers (the executive, dismissed by Nicholas II's order of abdication) and, soon, the abdicated tsar. Initially, the Provisional Government met in the Duma's Tauride Palace but quickly relocated to the interior ministry and then settled in the gilded imperial Mariinsky Palace, where the Council of Ministers and the State Council had held formal sessions. Poorly attended "private" meetings of the Duma (with Mikhail Rodzyanko still president) would continue through August 20, 1917, and from time to time, ministers of the Provisional Government would trek over to the Tauride to chat privately with members of the aimless Duma. But there was no legislature. Duma members pleaded to have the legislature legally reinstated, but Miliukov and the rest of the Provisional Government refused.[25]

What was this? The Provisional Government was not a well-intentioned but hapless bunch that would be undone by unprecedented economic collapse and Bolshevik sedition. The rebellious old-regime insiders had long claimed to want a constitutional monarchy with a "responsible" government, by which they meant a government rooted in parliamentary majorities, but in their great historical moment, they immediately created another central government suspended in the air. When Miliukov had first publicly announced the membership of a Provisional Government in the Tauride Palace's columned Catherine Hall on March 2, one person had interjected, "Who elected you?" "The Russian Revolution elected us," Miliukov answered, and vowed to step aside "the moment representatives, freely elected by the people, tell us they wish to give our places to others more deserving of their confidence."[26] No one had elected them, and, crucially, no one would be given the opportunity to un-elect them. To be sure, the self-assigned government did promise the "immediate preparation for the convocation of the Constituent Assembly on the basis of universal, equal, direct and secret ballot, which will determine the form of government and the constitution of the country." The government added that it had not "the slightest intention of taking advantage of the military situation to delay in any way the realization of the reforms and measures." Such a universal-suffrage Constituent Assembly—which is what rendered their government "provisional"—might seem to have made the Duma superfluous.[27] But over the eight months of the Provisional Government's existence, through four iterations (March, May, July, September), it would fail to bring a constitutional convention into being. Difficult circumstances cannot account for this failure. (In 1848, when France's July Monarchy fell, a Constituent Assembly was convened within four months.) Rather, Miliukov and the Cadets deliberately stalled on elections for the Constitutional Assembly, privately fearful of the votes by "war-weary" soldiers and sailors, to say nothing of the peasant mass.[28] The constitutionalists, who had no constitution, avoided the ballot box. The February Revolution was a liberal coup.

All through the war, some classical liberals in Petrograd as well as Moscow had been clamoring to take power for themselves—and now they had it, or so it seemed.[29] The one socialist in the initial Provisional Government, the thirty-six-year-old Kerensky—who served as justice minister, then war minister, and finally prime minister, having held no significant executive office before 1917—would later write that "with abdication of the emperor all the machinery of apparatus of Government was destroyed."[30] True, but Kerensky had been the keenest inside proponent for an end to the monarchy. In addition, the Provisional Government deliberately abetted the Russian state's disintegration. On March 4, 1917, rather than try to salvage a police force out of the dissolving tsarist police, whose offices in the capital had been ransacked, the Provisional Government formally abolished the Department of Police and *okhranka,* while reassigning Special-Corps-of-Gendarmes officers to the army. But the newly formed "citizen militias" that were supposed to replace the police failed miserably: looting and social breakdown spread, thereby hurting the poor as much as the rich, and staining the cause of democracy.[31] (Some militias, predictably, were headed by former convicts who escaped or were released from prison in the chaos.) On

March 5, 1917, the Provisional Government dismissed all governors and deputy governors, almost all of them hereditary nobles, in an attack on "privilege" and preemption of "counterrevolution." Some of these provincial executives had resigned of their own accord and some had been arrested locally. Still, most governors had participated in ceremonies to inaugurate the new Provisional Government, only to be treated as, ipso facto, disloyal.[32] The Provisional Government never acquired local branches, and the "commissars" it dispatched to local governing bodies could be ignored. Those local bodies, meanwhile, took time to get up and running, then often succumbed to economic and governance chaos. The sole major institutions of the "old regime" to survive were the ministerial bureaucracy and the army. But the influence of central state functionaries cratered and, under Kerensky, the Provisional Government would fatally wreck the all-important army, too.[33]

The new Russia had one organizing principle that could not be ignored and was up for grabs: the lodestar of "the revolution." Miliukov's decision not to root the government in the Duma invited the elected Petrograd Soviet to fulfill that crucial parliamentary role. The Soviet, whose reemergence had prompted the Provisional Government into existence, came to occupy more and more of the rooms in the Tauride, symbol of opposition to tsarism and of elected representation.[34] And yet, as a hybrid of both representative and direct democracy (like a Jacobin club), the Soviet—eventually with more than 3,000 members—struggled mightily, and, as we shall see, ultimately unsuccessfully, to live up to its popular mandate amid ever more radicalized expectations.[35] Indeed, even before the announcement of the Provisional Government's formation, garrison soldiers, when ordered by the Duma's Military Commission to return to their nearby barracks and submit to discipline, had stormed into a session of the Soviet on March 1, 1917, and laid out demands. The angry garrison soldiers had first tried to present their case to the Duma, but were rebuffed.[36] "I don't know whom to deal with, whom to listen to," one soldier deputy to the Petrograd Soviet complained of military authority that day. "Everything is unclear. Let's have some clarity."[37] What became known as Order No. 1 authorized "committees of representatives elected from the lower ranks" to adjudicate relations between soldiers and their officers, effectively terminating formal discipline in the army. De facto, such a state of affairs already obtained in the rebellious garrison, but now soldiers and sailors at the front, de jure, would have to obey their officers and the Provisional Government only "to the extent that" orders were deemed not to contradict decrees of the Soviet.[38] On March 9, the new war minister, Alexander Guchkov, one of the two monarchist Duma representatives sent to obtain Nicholas II's abdication, had been asked by the tsar whether such abdication would have consequences. Now, Guchkov learned of Order No. 1 for the army only upon its publication. He telegraphed General Alexeyev at front headquarters, reporting that "the Provisional Government has no real power of any kind and its orders are carried out only to the extent that this is permitted by the Soviet," which controls "the troops, railroads, postal and telegraph services." Guchkov suggested that the government resign en masse to acknowledge its lack of authority.[39]

The Provisional Government would last all of 237 days, 65 of which were spent trying to form a cabinet (that was more time than any of its four different cabinets would last). Here was the further rub: the *effective* authority of the Soviet, too, was widely overestimated. Soldiers' committees did not see themselves as subordinate to the Soviet. On March 5, the Provisional Government and Soviet had jointly issued Order No. 2, expressly denying the rumored right to elect officers and reaffirming the necessity of military discipline—to no avail.[40] Trotsky would famously dub this situation "dual power," but it more resembled "dual claimants to power": a Provisional Government without a legislature or effective executive institutions, and a Petrograd Soviet amounting to an unwieldy quasi-legislature that was not legally recognized as such.

A third grouping existed as well: the political right, which initially accepted the head-turning Provisional Government's replacement of the failed autocracy but which lived in fear as well as hope.[41] Around 4,000 officials of the "old regime" suffered arrest during the February Revolution, many turning themselves in to escape being torn to pieces by the crowds. In fact, bloodshed had been relatively minor: perhaps 1,300 wounded and 169 deaths, mostly at the naval bases of Kronstadt and Helsinki, where the rank-and-file lynched officers (amid rumors of their treasonous activities). Still, the post-February press stepped up the vilification of rightist organizations, and revolutionaries assaulted the offices of the most notorious far right group, the Black Hundreds. (The Petrograd Soviet seized some rightist printing presses for its own use.) Within weeks of Nicholas II's abdication, Vladimir Purishkevich—cofounder of the 1905 right-wing Union of the Russian People, and coassassin of Rasputin—had allowed in a pamphlet, which circulated widely in typescript, that "the old regime cannot be resurrected."[42] By July 1917, however, the extreme right would regain its footing, and Purishkevich would be pointedly listing Russia's revolutionary Jews by their real names and demanding dissolution of the Petrograd Soviet as well as a "reorganization" of the "cowardly" Provisional Government.[43] Over on the less radical right, many believed, with cause, that they had played a significant role in the downfall of Nicholas II and ought to have a place in the new order, but the varied associations of nobles and landowners, business elites, church officials, tsarist state functionaries, rightist military officers and self-styled patriots of all stripes had grave difficulty being accepted into the new order after February 1917. On the contrary, merely for exercising their legal right to organize, traditional conservatives were subjected to charges of "counterrevolution."[44] These accusations against an establishment mostly desirous of continuing to support the February Revolution but essentially not allowed to do so would become a self-fulfilling prophecy.

And then there was the empire. Upon the removal of the multinational institution of the tsar, many of the imperial borderlands declared themselves national units (not provinces) with "autonomy in a free Russia," but their streams of urgent telegrams to the Provisional Government in the capital often went unanswered, and the borderlands began edging toward de facto independence— Finland, Poland, Ukraine, the Caucasus, the Baltics. "Everybody agrees," wrote Maxim Gorky in June 1917, "that the Russian state is splitting all along its seams and falling apart, like an old barge in a flood."[45]

Of course, to many people this weakening was liberating. Between May 1 and 11, 1917, the Muslim caucus of the defunct Duma convened the first All-Russia Congress of Muslims, an act of religious and communal solidarity, with some 900 attendees (double the number expected) from across the country and political spectrum—only the tiny handful of Bolshevik Muslim activists refused to attend. It opened with recitation of a verse from the Qu'ran, then Professor S. A. Kotlarevsky, head of the foreign religions bureau in the Provisional Government's interior ministry, made a speech promising freedom of conscience and national educational development, while calling for a single, unified country, rather than federalism based upon ethnoterritorial units. Many Muslim delegates expressed disappointment. Some, especially Tatars, advocated for a single state for all Turkic peoples (under Tatar domination); a few pan-Turkic delegates refused to speak Russian, although no single Turkic language was intelligible to all the delegates. The final resolution on state organization entailed a compromise: "The type of governmental structure that will serve the best interests of the Muslim peoples of Russia shall be a united (federal) republic based on territorial autonomy; for Muslim peoples with no territorial claims, a people's republic based on national cultural autonomy shall be secured." Although more than 200 delegates signed a petition of protest over the vote for women's equal right to inheritance and against polygamy, it passed—making Russia the first country with a large Muslim population to do so.[46]

Certainly the freedom was intoxicating.[47] All the subjects of imperial Russia had broken through to an unprecedented degree of civic liberties that were independent of social station: freedom of association and the press, equality before the law, universal suffrage elections to local bodies, rights that the Provisional Government, dominated by lawyers and intellectuals, fixed in obsessive legal detail.[48] Kerensky would jubilantly proclaim Russia the "freest country in the world"—transformed from Europe's last autocracy to its "most democratic government"—and he was right.[49] But freedom without effective governing institutions is, ultimately, not enduring. It is an invitation to all manner of adventurists and would-be saviors.[50] February's delirium of freedom, in just a few months, metamorphosed into a desperate longing for "firm authority."[51] By summer 1917, many prominent classical liberal Constitutional Democrats would join figures on both the traditional right and the radical right in seeing a redeemer in General Lavr Kornilov, the Russian army's supreme commander.

Kornilov, forty-seven years old in 1917, though very short, thin, and wiry, with Mongol facial features, had much in common with the medium-height, thick-set thirty-nine-year-old Jughashvili-Stalin. Kornilov, too, was a plebeian—in contrast to the minor nobles Lenin and Kerensky—and Kornilov, too, had been born on the imperial periphery, in his case in Ust-Kamenogorsk (Oskemen) on the banks of the Irtysh (a tributary of the Ob). His father was a Cossack, his mother a baptized Altai Kalmyk (a mix of Turkic, Mongol, and other tribes conquered by Mongol overlords); he was raised an Orthodox Christian among the nomad-herders of the empire's Qazaq steppes. But whereas Stalin sought to downplay his full Georgianness and blend into his Russian environment, Kornilov, who was half Russian, played up his exoticism, surrounding himself with red-robed Turkmen guards who wore tall fur hats, carried curved swords, and called their leader Great Boyar in Turkic (a language Kornilov spoke fluently). In further contrast to Stalin, Kornilov had attended the Russian empire's military schools. He, too, was an excellent student, and, after postings on the border with Afghanistan—whence he led expeditions to Afghanistan, Chinese Turkestan, and Persia—Kornilov graduated from the General Staff Academy in St. Petersburg. In 1903–4, when Stalin was in and out of Caucasus prisons and Siberian exile, Kornilov was posted to British India, where, under the pretext of language study, he prepared a sharp-eyed intelligence report on British colonial troops. During the Russo-Japanese War, when Stalin was raising hell in Georgian manganese mines, Kornilov was decorated for bravery in land battles in Manchuria, after which he served as Russia's military attaché in China (1907–11). There he again traveled widely on horseback in exploration and met the young Chinese officer Jiang Jieshi, better known as Chiang Kai-shek, who later would unify China after a failed constitutional revolution and rule for some two decades. Intelligent and brave, Kornilov appeared cut from the same cloth as Chiang Kai-shek. During the Great War, Kornilov commanded an infantry division and was promoted to major general. While covering for Brusilov's retreat in 1915, Kornilov fell captive to the Austro-Hungarian forces, but in July 1916, he managed to escape and return to Russia, to wide acclaim and an audience with the tsar. "He was always out front," Brusilov noted of his subordinate on the battlefield, "and in this he won over his men, who loved him."[52]

Kornilov's star rose in inverse relation to Kerensky's. The latter's family hailed from Simbirsk, in central Russia, the same town as the Ulyanov family. "I was born under the same sky" as Lenin, Kerensky wrote. "I saw the same limitless horizons from the same high bank of the Volga." Kerensky's father was a schoolteacher and briefly headmaster at the high school where Lenin and Lenin's brother Alexander studied; Lenin's father, in turn, was a school inspector for the province and knew Kerensky père, before the latter moved his family to Tashkent.[53] But whereas Lenin looked set to follow in his father's footsteps, studying for a law degree (Kazan University) to become a state functionary, only to drop out, Kerensky, eleven years Lenin's junior, finished his law degree (St. Petersburg) and obtained a real job, serving as legal counsel to victims of tsarist repression in 1905, when he joined the Socialist Revolutionary Party. In the Provisional Government, Kerensky, almost alone, did not fear the masses. He bred a monarchist-like cult of himself as the "leader of the people" (*vozhd' naroda*), a kind of citizen king. "In his best moments he could communicate to the crowd tremendous shocks of moral electricity," wrote Victor Chernov. "He could make it laugh and cry, kneel and soar, for he himself surrendered to the emotions of the moment."[54] The kneeling soldiers and others kissed Kerensky's clothing, cried, and prayed.[55] He took to wearing semimilitary attire—the style Trotsky and Stalin would adopt—yet Kerensky likened himself not to Napoleon but to Comte de Mirabeau, the popular orator who had sought a middle way during the French Revolution. (When Mirabeau died of illness in 1791, his burial inaugurated the Panthéon; by 1794, however, he was disinterred and his tomb given over to Jean-Paul Marat.) But as Russia descended into anarchy, Kerensky, too, began to speak of the need for "firm authority." Under him, the Provisional Government would begin to backtrack on civil liberties and release and reengage many of the arrested tsarist interior ministry officials, but "firm authority" remained elusive.[56] Hence the spiking fascination with Kornilov. The talk of a "man on horseback," the Napoleon of the Russian Revolution, alighted upon the Kalmyk savior.[57] In the event, the *idea* of a military "counterrevolution"—an expression of hope on one side, dread on the other—would prove more potent than its actual possibilities.

## LENIN'S HELPMATES

Lenin's faction of Bolsheviks showed themselves in 1917 to be a disorganized yet tough street-fighting group.[58] The Bolsheviks now claimed some 25,000 members, a number impossible to verify (membership was often not formalized), but hard-core activists numbered closer to 1,000, and the top insiders could fit around a conference table (if they were not in exile or jail). Still, after February, Bolshevism had become a mass phenomenon in the capital: in the armaments and machine factories along Petrograd's Lesser Neva River, in the huge Franco-Russian shipyard, in the sprawling Putilov Works, in the Petrograd neighborhood known as the Vyborg side, there were large concentrations of industrial workers and they fell under a barrage of Bolshevik agitation. Workers' radical moods, in other words, were tied to radical stances of the Bolshevik Party. The Vyborg district especially became, in effect, an autonomous Bolshevik commune.[59]

Bolshevik party headquarters, where Stalin was also holed up, was initially established at a "requisitioned" art nouveau mansion whose chandeliered interiors and excellent garages were perfectly situated—not only close to the Vyborg district, but right across from the Winter Palace. The compound had been seized from the Polish-born prima ballerina of Russia's Imperial Mariinsky Theater, Matylda Krzesińska, who had acquired the property thanks to her lovers, Nicholas II (before his marriage), and then, simultaneously, two Romanov grand dukes.[60] (She later claimed to have spotted the Bolshevik Alexandra Kollontai in the mansion's garden wearing her left-behind ermine coat.)[61] Such house seizures were illegal but difficult for the policeless Provisional Government to reverse. The Federation of Anarchist-Communists, sprung from prison, seized the former villa of the deceased Pyotr Durnovó in a beautiful park abutting the factories of the Vyborg side.[62] Beyond Vyborg, Bolshevism developed key strongholds in the Baltic fleet, stationed in Helsinki and Kronstadt near Petrograd and accessible to Bolshevik (as well as anarchist-syndicalist) agitators. Where Bolshevik agitators did not reach—factories in Ukraine, the Black Sea fleet—the socialist-leaning masses did not identify with the party. In the vast countryside, Bolshevism achieved little presence through most of 1917 (of the 1,000 delegates to the First All-Russia Congress of Peasants' Deputies, perhaps 20 identified as Bolsheviks).[63] And in 1917 there were between one and two dozen Muslim Bolsheviks in all of Russia.[64] Still, Bolshevik strongholds were strategic—the capital, the capital garrison, and the front near the capital.

The Bolsheviks had to earn their standing, and in pockets they did so. For those within earshot of the message that Stalin and others were tirelessly propagating, Bolshevism possessed nonpareil recruiting tools: the absolutely hated war and the all-purpose explanation of class exploitation of haves and have-nots, which resonated beyond anyone's wildest imagination. That said, the war did not inevitably provide for Bolshevik triumph. The Provisional Government, as we shall see, chose not just to remain in the war but to launch a catastrophic offensive in June 1917.[65] This decision became an opportunity for those most radical, and Lenin had set up the Bolshevik party to benefit from it.

In exile, living in Zurich, in a single room, near a sausage factory, Lenin had been calling for the defeat of his own country in war, but suffered no legal consequences. On the contrary, he fell under the Provisional Government's March 1917 general amnesty for victims of tsarism. But he had no official permission to return and, in any case, was trapped behind German lines.[66] To get back to Russia he quietly solicited Germany's help through intermediaries, thereby risking charges of being a German agent—the devastating accusation that had fatally punctured the tsarist autocracy.[67] Berlin was showering money on Russia's radicals, especially the Socialist Revolutionaries, in order to overturn the Provisional Government and force Russia out of the war on German terms, and was sold on assisting the fanatical Bolshevik leader, too—referred to as "a Tatar by the name of Lenin."[68] Both sides, however, aimed to blunt accusations of serving the enemy Germans and so Lenin traveled through German lines to Russia on what has been called a sealed train—that is, his carriage was locked and neutral Swiss intermediaries handled all contact with German authorities en route. The train departed Zurich on March 27, 1917 (by the Russian calendar), for Berlin and then the Baltic coast with thirty-two Russian émigrés, nineteen of them Bolsheviks (including Lenin, his wife, Nadzehda Krupskaya; his onetime French mistress, Inessa Armand; and Zinoviev with wife and child) as well as other radicals.[69] The Menshevik Social Democrats Martov and Axelrod chose not to risk treason charges by accepting a German deal without having obtained the permission of the Provisional Government (the Mensheviks ended up traveling on a later train).[70] Lenin's only obligation in the bargain was to agitate for release of Austrian and German civilians held in Russia. He had no compunction about availing himself of imperial Germany's logistical assistance and finances in order to subvert Russia; he anticipated revolution in Germany, too, as a result of the war. Lenin never admitted the truth about receiving German money, but he was not a German agent; he had his own agenda.[71] Lenin had the Bolsheviks discuss how they would conduct themselves in the event they were taken into custody at the Russian border on orders of the Provisional Government and subjected to interrogation, fears that did not materialize.[72] (Karl Radek, who held an Austro-Hungarian passport, was denied entry into Russia as a subject of an enemy country.) The worried ambassador of France, Russia's ally, listening to Foreign Minister Miliukov—who could have blocked Lenin's return—saw the Bolshevik leader's arrival as a radical new danger.[73] But Lenin was not arrested at Petrograd's Finland Station (in the Vyborg district "Bolshevik Commune"), where he arrived at 11:10 p.m. on April 3, 1917, the day after Easter Sunday. Lenin climbed atop an armored vehicle, illuminated by specially wheeled-in spotlights, to speak at the station to a sizable crowd of workers, soldiers, and sailors, who were seeing him for the first time.

In the vast expanses of the Russian empire very few had any knowledge of Lenin.[74] Many of the hundreds of thousands of villages had not learned of the February Revolution until April and the spring thaw. Lenin's April 3 return coincided with the onset of mass land seizures in Russia, a phenomenon unknown in the French Revolution of 1789. On the eve of the Great War, Russia's peasants had owned roughly 47 percent of the empire's land, including forests and meadows, having purchased land from nobles in the four decades following emancipation, often as a collective (commune), sometimes individually, especially beginning with Stolypin's 1906 reforms.[75] But if gentry holdings had been reduced to roughly equal that of peasant holdings, the peasantry still composed 80 percent of the population, the gentry a mere 2 percent.[76] Peasant expectations of a total land redistribution were intense, and the wartime tsarist government had helped spur them, confiscating land from ethnic Germans living in imperial Russia, which was supposed to be redistributed to valiant Russian soldiers or landless peasants. The army, on its own, promised free land to winners of medals, spur-ring rumors that all soldiers would receive land at war's end.[77] Total tsarist *government* confiscations of agricultural land during the war—which was seized with minimal or zero compensation from some of the empire's most productive farmers, and contributed to the severe shortage of grain in 1916 and the bread riots in 1917—amounted to at least 15 million acres.[78] Now, the peasants began to follow suit, seizing crop lands, draft animals, implements, in what they called the Black Repartition. The Provincial Government tried to resist, arguing that deci-sions on land reform had to await the forthcoming Constituent Assembly. Indeed, even after the seizures became a mass phenomenon, and even though it could never muster the force to prevent or reverse such seizures, the Provisional Gov-ernment refused to accede to uncompensated peasant expropriation of land.

Years of colossal peasant effort to realize Stolypin's dream of a stratum of inde-pendent, well-off yeoman on large enclosed farms vanished nearly overnight in 1917–18, without resistance; on the contrary, many peasants deliberately reduced the size of their farms.[79] Even smaller enclosed farms underwent redistributions. The commune reasserted itself.[80] Even as peasants engaged in illegalities, they employed a vocabulary of rights and citizenship.[81] Gentry-owned estates were the main targets. They had in many cases survived during the Great War only because of an ability to call upon the labor of 430,000 prisoners of war and, in peasant logic, after February 1917, if an estate had been deprived of peasant labor and was idle, its takeover was legitimate.[82] Indeed, many of the land seizures did not occur in one fell swoop; rather, peasants spoke of "excess" gentry lands and of putting "idle" land to the plow—and took more and more. But because most peasant land seizures were carried out collectively, as a village, in which all shared responsibil-ity and all divided up the plunder into their carts, the assembled peasants usually became as radical as the most radical members present. Invariably, the radicals urged their country folk to carry off still more and even to burn down the valuable manor houses. Harvesters and winnowing machines were too big to cart off and were left behind, sometimes vandalized. As for animals, often peasants heated the oven, butchered the sheep, geese, ducks, and hens, and laid on a feast.[83] But in the end, far from all peasants ended up with their own dreams fulfilled: around half of peasant communes gained no land at all from the revolution, while much of the land peasants did "obtain" they had already been leasing. One scholar has estimated that around 11 percent of gentry landowners would remain into the 1920s, tending remnants of their lands.[84] Still, that means the vast majority were expropriated. Peasants stopped making payments to the big landowners, and collectively expropriated around 50 million acres of gentry land.[85]

Compared with this immense upheaval—the peasants' own revolution—Lenin was a single person. And yet, his role in 1917 was pivotal. Marxist theory held that history moved in stages—feudalism, capitalism, socialism, communism—such that before advancing to socialism, it was necessary to develop the bourgeois-capitalism stage. Almost all Bolsheviks expected that the revolution would move toward socialism eventually, but the issue was when: they argued vehemently about whether the "bourgeois" or "democratic" revolution phase was complete or had to go further in order to prepare the way for the socialist revolution. Lenin was not proposing an immediate leap into socialism, which would have been blasphemy, but an acceleration of the move toward socialism—what he would call "one foot in socialism"—by not waiting for the full development of the bourgeois revolution and instead seizing political power now.[86]

In Petrograd, the Bolshevik Russia Bureau—"Russia" as opposed to foreign exile (Lenin)—was led by the thirty-two-year-old Alexander Shlyapnikov and the twenty-seven-year-old Vyacheslav Molotov, and they (especially Molotov) had been dismissive of the Provisional Government as counterrevolutionary. By contrast, Stalin and Kamenev called for *conditionally* supporting the "democratic" revolution, meaning the Provisional Government, in order that the democratic revolution would go through to the end. When the pair had returned from Siberia to Petrograd on March 12, 1917, neither was invited to join the Russia Bureau, although Stalin was offered "advisory status." (He was rebuked for "certain personal features that are basic to him," evidently negative personal behavior toward fellow Siberian exiles.)[87] The next day Molotov, an early and lifelong hard-liner, like Lenin, was elbowed out, and Stalin became a proper member of the Russia Bureau, while Kamenev became editor of *Pravda*.[88] Kamenev and Stalin immediately turned *Pravda* away from absolute repudiation of the Provisional Government toward opportunistically working with it, arguing that it was doomed but in the meantime had significant historical work to carry out. This provoked Lenin's ire from afar. His first angry missive was printed in *Pravda* with distorted editing, his second was suppressed entirely.[89] But then he showed up.

Lenin had greeted Kamenev at the border in smiling rebuke: "What's this you're writing in *Pravda*?"[90] Even now, the Bolshevik organ refused to publish its own leader's theses. An April 6, 1917, Bolshevik Central Committee meeting outright rejected Lenin's theses. After all, the bourgeois-democratic revolution had only *just begun,* the country needed land reform, an exit from the war, economic reform, and how would the proletariat, by overturning the Provisional Government, advance all that? (As one Bolshevik commented, "How can the democratic revolution be over? The peasants do not have the land!")[91] Kamenev especially pointed out that the bourgeois classes in the towns and the better-off peasants had a great deal of historical work still to bear on behalf of the socialist revolution, by carrying the bourgeois-democratic revolution through to the end.[92] Stalin deemed Lenin's theses "a schema, there are no facts in them, and therefore they do not satisfy."[93] *Pravda* finally published the ten "April Theses" (some 500 words) on April 7, under Lenin's name, but accompanied by an editorial note by Kamenev distancing the party from its leader.[94]

If the top Bolsheviks had not been inclined to force a seizure of power, the same was even truer of the Petrograd Soviet. Before Lenin's arrival back in Russia, in late March, representatives of the Soviet had gathered to establish a new seventy-two-person All-Russia central executive committee, as well as various departments for food supply, the economy, foreign affairs, thereby asserting the Petrograd Soviet's writ over the whole of Russia. The Soviet also pledged conditional support for the "bourgeois" Provisional Government (about half the Bolshevik delegates voted in favor).[95] At the Finland Station on April 3, Nikoloz "Karlo" Chkheidze, the Georgian Menshevik Social Democrat who had become chairman of the Petrograd Soviet, had greeted Lenin on behalf of that body in the former tsar's reception room. Outside, after Lenin denounced the Petrograd Soviet's cooperation with the Provisional Government, concluding "Long live the world socialist revolution!," he had ridden the armored vehicle to Bolshevik HQ at the Krzesińska mansion. There, well after midnight, he gave a "thunder-like speech" to about seventy members of his faction, arranged on chairs in a circle.[96] The next day, at a meeting of the Petrograd Soviet in the Tauride Palace, he reiterated his radical "April Theses," arguing that the pathetic Russian bourgeoisie was incapable of carrying through its historical tasks, which compelled Russia to accelerate from the bourgeois-democratic toward the proletarian-socialist revolution.[97] One Bolshevik took the floor to liken Lenin to the anarchist Bakunin (who had fought bitterly with Marx). Another speaker called Lenin's theses "the ravings of a madman."[98] Even Lenin's wife, Nadezhda Krupskaya, who had known him since 1894, observed according to a friend that "I am afraid it looks as if Lenin has gone crazy," one reason perhaps that he ceased to use her as his principal secretary.[99] Yet another Bolshevik advised that "after Lenin becomes acquainted with the state of affairs in Russia, he himself will reject all these constructions of his."[100] When Irakli Tsereteli, the chairman of the Soviet's central executive committee (and a Georgian Menshevik), offered a reasoned refutation of Lenin's views while extending an olive branch—"however irreconcilable Vladimir Ilich may be, I am convinced we'll be reconciled"—Lenin leaned over the balustrade and shouted, "Never!"[101]

Lenin browbeat his inner circle relentlessly, while also occasionally addressing outdoor crowds from the Krzesińska mansion balcony. By the end of April 1917, at a Bolshevik party conference, a majority voted for Lenin's resolutions, thanks partly to the voices of the sometimes more radical provincials who were brought to the fore, as well as to other loyalists who supported their leader.[102] Despite Lenin's formal policy victory in late April, however, the Bolshevik inner circle remained divided over when, and even whether, to push for soviet power as opposed to completing the bourgeois-democratic revolution. As Lenin continued to press his views for embracing the moment, he insisted that the Bolshevik Central Committee lagged far behind the masses. (That would prove true: the mobilization of the masses did mobilize would-be elites, including the Bolshevik leadership.)[103] Meanwhile, Stalin, initially an ally of Kamenev, emerged as a crucial ally of Lenin.

Stalin has wrongly been dismissed as the man who "missed" the October Revolution. True, he does appear to have missed Lenin's arrival at the Finland Station (perhaps because he was at a meeting trying to convert left-wing Mensheviks to the Bolshevik side.)[104] Also, Stalin initially resisted Lenin's heretical April 3 radicalism (for which he would publicly apologize in 1924).[105] But at the late April conference, Stalin gave his first-ever political report to an official Bolshevik gathering and broke with Kamenev and sided with Lenin. "Only a united party can lead the people to victory," Stalin wrote of the April conference in *Soldiers' Pravda*.[106] Stalin did not buckle under abjectly, however: whereas Lenin sought land nationalization, Stalin insisted the peasantry get the land—a position that eventually won out.[107] Stalin also rejected Lenin's slogan of turning the "imperialist war" into a "European civil war," reasoning that besides land, the masses desired peace—and Lenin, too, now called for an immediate peace.[108] Thus

Stalin managed to become loyal to Lenin while defending positions that he, among others, held to. When Stalin's candidacy for a new nine-member party Central Committee came under criticism from Caucasus comrades who claimed to know him well, Lenin vouched for him. "We've known Com. Koba for very many years," Lenin told the voting delegates. "We used to see him in Krakow where we had our Bureau. His activity in the Caucasus was very important. He's a good official in all sorts of responsible work."[109] In the Central Committee elections, Stalin claimed the third most votes, 97, behind only Lenin and Zinoviev (both of whom would soon become fugitives). Stalin also replaced Kamenev as editor of *Pravda*.

As editor and pundit, Stalin revealed a talent for summarizing complicated issues in a way that could be readily understood. He evidently apologized to Molotov for stabbing him in the back in March—"You were nearest of all to Lenin in the initial stage"—and then took advantage of their communal-style living arrangements to steal Molotov's girlfriend.[110] Soon, though, Stalin would move into the apartment of the Alliluyev family, bringing all his worldly possessions: his typewriter as well as books and some clothes in the same wicker suitcase with which he had returned from Siberia. The Alliluyev daughter Nadya had turned sixteen, and she returned to the apartment in late summer 1917 for the pending school year. Stalin had known the Alliuluyevs since 1900 (Tiflis days), the year before Nadya was born. He treated her like a daughter, reading stories by Chekhov ("Chameleon," "Dushechka") to her, her sister Anna, and their friends.[111] Charming the girls right through their nightshirts, Stalin turned the boredom, loneliness, and despair of his Siberian exile into dramatic tales of revolutionary exploits. They called him Soso, and he reciprocated with nicknames for them. Their mother, Olga Alliluyeva, was fond of Stalin—they may have had a liaison— but not fond of her teenage daughter falling for the thirty-eight-year-old widower.[112] Nadya could be defiant, including to Stalin, but she was also, he noticed, attentive to housework. Within ten months, their courtship would become public.[113] All that was in the future, however. For now, Stalin had become a proto-apparatchik and defender of the Leninist line. Even Trotsky would allow, later, that "Stalin was very valuable behind the scenes in preparing the [Bolshevik] fraction for balloting," adding, condescendingly, that "he did have the knack of convincing the average run of leaders, especially the provincials."[114]

Alongside Stalin, though, another Central Committee figure emerged that April: the thirty-two-year-old Yakov Sverdlov, whom Lenin had finally met in person on April 7, 1917, and began to assign various tasks, which Sverdlov managed handily. Born in 1885, wispy, with a scraggly goatee and glasses, he had joined the Russian Social Democrats in 1902 in Nizhny Novgorod and taken part in the 1905 events while in the Urals. In 1917, Sverdlov, even more than Stalin, remained almost entirely behind the scenes. Not an orator, he nonetheless possessed an authoritative basso voice, and a steely demeanor. Lenin placed him in charge of a small "secretariat" formally created at the April 1917 party conference.[115] During Sverdlov's years in tsarist jails or Siberian exile (1906–17), he had proved able to memorize the real names, noms de guerre, locations, and characteristics of scattered fellow exiles, putting nothing incriminating to paper. He had also twice shared quarters with Stalin (in Narym and Kureika), which resulted in sharp personal conflicts and a certain rivalry.[116] Now, however, the two worked side by side. In fact, the younger Sverdlov provided a kind of school in party building for Stalin as they left the speechifying to the orators, such as Zinoviev. With a mere half dozen female clerks at the Krzesińska mansion, Sverdlov, assisted by Stalin, worked to coordinate far-flung party organizations. He received a parade of visitors and, in turn, sent emissaries to Bolshevik committees in the provinces, to jump-start local periodicals and membership, demonstrating a deft touch with provincials. Sverdlov obsessed over details, *forcing* everything to come to his attention, while placing a premium on concrete actions. Of course, like all political movements in 1917, Bolshevism incarnated bedlam. The organizing was not—and could not have been—directed at producing a centralized, let alone "totalitarian," party in the conditions of 1917, but at effecting majorities at the gatherings of party representatives in the capital on behalf of Lenin's positions. In other words, through manipulation of rules, suasion, and favors, Sverdlov showed his helpmate Stalin how to organize a loyal Leninist faction.[117]

## ZEALOTRY

Lenin's zealotry became an instant (and everlasting) legend, but nearly everyone on Russia's political scene lived under the tyranny of idées fixes. Miliukov, having fought tooth and nail in the Duma against the autocracy's poor conduct of the war, mulishly clung to the notion that the February Revolution signified a universal desire to conduct the war more successfully. He therefore opposed land reforms and convocation of a constituent assembly before military victory, and even refused to allow revision of tsarism's imperialist war aims, which secretly entailed annexation of Constantinople and the Turkish Straits, German and Austrian Poland, and other foreign territories. The damage from this zealotry proved as severe as the damage from his March 1917 ditching of the Duma. Leaders of the Menshevik wing of the Social Democrats, for their part, stubbornly stuck to the notion that the Revolution was "bourgeois" in character and therefore they refused to push for socialism, despite insistent prodding from the broad masses they supposedly represented. The Mensheviks soon joined the Provisional Government, in coalition with the Cadets, as did the Socialist Revolutionaries (SRs), the party that added the most members in 1917. Theory alone did not motivate them. Partly the crushing defeat in 1905–6 hung over the moderate socialists, a cautionary tale against provoking "counterrevolution" with radicalism.[118] But the Menshevik leadership adhered to the core Marxist idea whereby socialism had to await the full development of Russian capitalism, for which a "bourgeois revolution" was necessary.[119] They zealously clung to the "bourgeois revolution" and supported the "bourgeois" Provisional Government even as their propaganda often hammered "the bourgeoisie."[120]

Russia's political figure who most embodied the moderate socialist line from the start was Kerensky, who aimed to bridge Russia's "bourgeois" and "proletarian" revolutions, to stand above parties, to balance left and right by tilting one way, then the next. Straining to be indispensable to each side, he came, predictably, to be seen as anathema to both.[121] Bolshevik propaganda spread rumors that Kerensky was addicted to cocaine and morphine, dressed in women's clothing, embezzled from state coffers—a smear campaign that would come to seem plausible (and that took in the British War Office).[122] It bears recalling, however, that initially Kerensky had attracted widespread praise from diverse quarters, including Romanov grand dukes and leaders of the Soviet.[123] Kerensky's political failing in 1917 was partly personal but partly structural: he had thrown in his lot not with the Petrograd Soviet but with the Provisional Government and, as the Provisional Government's impotence became ever more brutally exposed, his own authority disintegrated.[124] Thus did Kerensky acquire a reputation as spineless, a professional "windbag," in the mocking phrase of his nemesis, Lenin, who had little contact with the high-profile leader. Lenin and Kerensky met for the first and only time at the First All-Russia Congress of Soviets (June 3–24, 1917) at a military school in Petrograd. Kerensky showed himself to be under the spell, if not the tyranny, of the French Revolution.[125] "How did 1792 end in France? It ended in the fall of the republic and the rise of a dictator," Kerensky said in response to Lenin at the Congress of Soviets, referring to the episode of Robespierre's self-defeating terror and the rise of Napoleon. "The problem of the Russian socialist parties and of Russian democracy is to prevent such an outcome as there was in France, to hold on to the revolutionary conquests already made; to see to it that our comrades who have been released from prison do not return there; that a Lenin, who has been abroad, may have the opportunity to speak here again, and not be obliged to flee back to Switzerland. We must see to it that historic mistakes do not recur."[126]

## ROLLING THE IRON DICE

Kerensky could certainly feel confident. In the elections to the June 1917 First Congress of Soviets, the Bolshevik party won a mere 105 of the 777 delegates with a right to vote, versus 285 by Socialist Revolutionaries and 248 by Mensheviks.[127] Only something extremely dramatic could have possibly reversed Bolshevik fortunes. But just such a head-spinning turnabout transpired right in the middle of that First Congress of Soviets: namely, a Russian military offensive.

Perhaps the central riddle of 1917 is why the Provisional Government decided in June to attack the Central Powers. Russia's towns overflowed with the maimed; the countryside had begun to suffer starvation in places from the disorganization of agriculture, the incomprehensible sacrifice of so many males, and grain requisitions. One might think that for Provisional Government officials, especially classical liberals like the Cadets who sincerely believed in liberty, the use of state power for soldier conscription and coercive grain extraction to feed the army would have been abhorrent.[128] But one would be wrong. Nor did the Provisional Government's relentless invocation of democracy entail following soldiers' antiwar sentiment, which had been universally on display since the downfall of the tsar and "Order No. 1." Still, one would expect that the politicians would at least heed careerist self-interest. Paul Miliukov had been forced on May 2 to quit the Provisional Government that he himself had named (leaving Kerensky preeminent in the cabinet) just for stating that Russia "has no desire to enslave or degrade anyone" in the war but would nonetheless "fully stand by its obligations to our allies."[129] Even the most successful allied offensive of the entire war, Brusilov's in 1916, had ultimately failed.

And the German high command planned no new military actions on the eastern front in 1917. How did anyone in their right mind imagine that the Russian army should—or could—undertake an offensive in 1917?

No small part of the offensive's rationale had been inherited. Back in November 1916, at a meeting in France, the Western Allies had, once again, pressured the government of the tsar to commit to an offensive, in this case for spring 1917, to relieve pressure on the western front.[130] Nicholas II had agreed, and the Provisional Government, which shared the values of and indeed looked up to the rule-of-law Allies, resolved to honor this commitment. By now, however, the French themselves were no longer capable of an offensive: in late May 1917, following a failed attack on the German lines, the French army suffered a full-scale mutiny, affecting 49 infantry divisions out of 113. General Philippe Pétain, the newly appointed commander, restored discipline, but he recognized that the French rank and file and field officers would continue to defend the homeland, but no more.[131]

Even without the incongruous Allied pressure, however, Kerensky would likely have gone forward. Just before France's mutinies, Russia's supreme commander Mikhail Alexeyev—who had pushed to make Kerensky war minister—toured his own front, finding a collapse of discipline, with desertions running at more than 1 million (out of 6–7 million).[132] But Alexeyev, underscoring Russian obligations to its allies, also wrote in a confidential memorandum summarizing the views of the top commanders, which he shared, that "disorder in the Army will have no less a detrimental effect on defense than on offense. Even if we are not fully confident of success, we should go on the offensive."[133] Kerensky nonetheless dismissed Alexeyev as a "defeatist" and replaced him with General Brusilov, the hero of 1916, but then Brusilov toured the front and found the selfsame demoralization.[134] To be sure, hope springs eternal. Russian intelligence surmised that the Austro-Hungarian army was highly vulnerable, and that even the German army could not survive another winter, so a knockout blow might be possible. And if that was true, Russia did not want to be left out of the presumed Central Powers defeat, in order to have a say in the peace: a good Russian show on the battlefield would force the Allies to take Russia's diplomatic notes more seriously.[135] Still, Kerensky's chief motivation appears to have been domestic politics: he as well as some Russian generals thought—or hoped—that an offensive would restore the collapsing army and squelch the domestic rebellion. In other words, the very collapse of Russia's army served as the key rationale for the offensive.[136] "War at the front," went the saying, "will buy peace in the rear and at the front."[137]

Thus did the Provisional Government willingly make the tsar's fatally unpopular war its own. Kerensky, then merely the war minister, departed for the front, to rally the army like Nicholas II had done, making himself hoarse with harangues of the troops about the offensive for "freedom." More than one soldier interjected, "What's the point of this slogan about land and freedom if I have to die?" Lenin's Bolshevik agitators swarmed the regiments at the front, along with some thirty urban garrisons, to undermine the army but also to trump their main targets: Menshevik and Socialist Revolutionary agitators. Bolsheviks flooded highly receptive soldiers and sailors with easily digested radical materials characterizing the war as a sacrifice of Russian blood for English and French moneybags.[138] "A single agitator," lamented one Russian frontline general, "can set back on its heels an entire regiment with the propaganda of Bolshevik ideals."[139] And where Bolsheviks did not reach, German propaganda did. "The English," one Russian soldier read aloud from a Russian-language German newspaper, the *Russian Messenger,* "want the Russians to shed the last drop of their blood for the greater glory of England, who seeks her profit in everything."[140] Not just the horrendous war, which had precipitated the downfall of the autocracy, but the military offensive enabled the Bolsheviks to associate their party with the moods in the country's single biggest mass organization, the 6–7 million soldiers at the front, achieving a spectacular breakthrough to "trench Bolshevism."[141]

It would be easy to pin all the domestic blame on Kerensky. His insistence on a military offensive against the external foe in order to defeat the internal foe rendered him, the "revolutionary democrat," no better than the tsar and the "reactionaries" who had begun the slaughter in 1914. No less stunning, however, the Petrograd Soviet, controlled by a Menshevik-Socialist Revolutionary bloc, as well as even the elected soldiers' committees, supported the June military offensive, and did so against the wishes of the soldiers and sailors they claimed to represent. Irakli Tsereteli, the Georgian Menshevik, had risen to the top of the Soviet by putting forward a position he had called "revolutionary defensism": if Russia's army would (somehow) continue to fight, the Soviet would (somehow) organize a negotiated peace "without annexations" by pressuring the public in the Allied countries.[142] Victor Chernov, head of the Socialist Revolutionaries, signed on, and so did prominent Mensheviks in the Soviet (though not the skeptical Yuly Martov). But a proposed international conference in Stockholm of socialists for peace in June 1917 failed to take place: Britain and France had no interest in a "democratic" peace, they wanted Germany defeated.[143] Without the "peace" part,

Tsereteli's position, despite his repudiation of annexations, amounted to a continuation of the war, the same policy as the Provisional Government's. *Pravda* relished publishing figures for the wartime profits of privately owned factories and placing the Soviet alongside the Provisional Government as "executive organ" of "Messieurs capitalists and bankers."[144] To the masses, the position of the Petrograd Soviet and the soldiers' committees became incomprehensible: the war was imperialist yet should continue?[145] But worse, a majority in the Soviet agreed that Russia ought to *attack*? The moderate socialists clung to the principle of cooperating with "the bourgeois revolution," that is, with the Provisional Government and Constitutional Democrat Party. Partly, too, in their minds the offensive would help increase Russia's bargaining power vis-à-vis recalcitrant Britain and France.[146] The non-Bolshevik socialists were lethally wrong.

Because the Allies refused to negotiate an end to the meat-grinder war short of an elusive decisive victory, a posture of strategic defense was the only survivable policy for both the Provisional Government and the Soviet. Simultaneously, the Russian government could have stolen the thunder of the extreme left by attempting to negotiate an acceptable separate peace with Germany. If such an effort failed, the Germans would have been blamed, buying the government some legitimacy for nominally staying in the war. But even if a consensus in the Russian establishment could not be reached to break with the Allies and approach Germany separately, a *threat* of doing so could have been wielded as a bargaining chip to force the Allies to accept the Provisional Government's belated desire, as publicly professed at least, for a formal inter-Allied conference to discuss and perhaps redefine war aims.[147]

Back in September-October 1916, after the momentum of the Brusilov offensive had been broken, tsarist Russia and Germany had held secret talks for a separate peace in Sweden, Denmark, Switzerland, and Kovno (a territory of imperial Russia under German occupation). Britain and France, after catching wind of the Russo-German talks, had moved to sign new financial agreements with Russia, finally conceding some long-standing Russian requests.[148] Russia depended on its Allied partners for finance and matériel, but Russian leverage was perhaps even greater in 1917. Be that as it may, a strictly defensive posture would have allowed a wait-and-see respite while the U.S. entry on the western front got into high gear.

Instead, the lunatic gamble of the Kerensky-Soviet offensive commenced on June 18 (July 1 in the West) with the greatest artillery barrage in Russian history to that point: two nonstop days, drawing on a colossal supply of heavy guns and shells produced by Russia's working classes (80 percent of whom worked in war production). Despite some initial success, especially by troops under General Kornilov's command, many Russian units refused to advance; some sought to kill their commanders, while others held meetings to discuss how to escape the inferno.[149] The main Russian thrust aimed at the "soft target" of Austria-Hungary—a lesson from the 1916 Brusilov offensive—but the awakened beast of the German army counterattacked mercilessly.[150] Russia's gratuitous offensive drew the Germans much farther onto Russia's territory—Germany seized Ukraine—while tearing Russia's army to pieces.[151] The offensive also shattered the authority of the moderate socialist representatives in the Soviet and the soldiers' committees.[152] In trying to cajole soldiers to obey orders and return to battle, members of the Soviet Executive Committee were beaten and taken into custody, including Nikolai Sokolov, one of the drafters of Order No. 1. "The whole of 1917," one historian has aptly written, "could be seen as a political battle between those who saw the revolution as a means of bringing the war to an end and those who saw the war as a means of bringing revolution to an end."[153]

## KERENSKY'S FIRST FAILED COUP

In the spring of 1917, after he had arrived back in Russia, Lenin occupied the fringe in Russia's politics—the fringe of the left—sniping at Kerensky, badmouthing the other Marxists in the Soviet, but the June 1917 offensive—launched by Kerensky, supported by the Soviet—vindicated Lenin's extremism, which was no longer extreme. Tellingly, even the talented Lev Trotsky signed on.

Trotsky was a shooting star. Nearly Stalin's exact contemporary, he hailed from a different corner of the empire—southern Ukraine, in the Pale of Settlement, 200 miles up from the Black Sea port of Odessa. His father, David Bronstein, was illiterate but by dint of hard work had become such a successful farmer that by the time his son was born, the family owned 250 acres outright and leased another 500.[154] Trotsky's mother, Aneta, also a loyal subject of the tsar, was a cultured woman who chose the life of a farmer's wife and imparted a love of learning to her four children (survivors of eight births). The young Leib—Lev in Russian—had been sent to a heder, a Jewish primary school, even though he did not know Yiddish, but he was switched to a German school attached to a Lutheran Church in Odessa, where he studied at the top of his class, despite being suspended for a year as a result of a student imbroglio with a French teacher from Switzerland. At his next school, in the city of Nikolayev, he devoted himself to literature and mathematics; eyewitnesses recalled him having no close friends. "The fundamental essence of Bronstein's personality," explained G. A. Ziv, who knew him then, "was to demonstrate his will, to tower above everyone, everywhere and always to be first."[155] Around age seventeen, Bronstein became a revolutionary. Like Stalin, he was arrested when still a teenager (in 1898) and exiled to Siberia. In 1902 he adopted the family name of one of his jailers, becoming Trotsky, and escaped, meeting Lenin and Martov, then allies, in London as a twenty-three-year-old. The next year, at the fateful 2nd Congress of the Russian Social Democratic Workers' Party, Trotsky sided with Martov in the controversy over party organization and soon blasted Lenin in print. Still, Trotsky never drew especially close to the Mensheviks: he had kept his distance from all groups. For long stretches he lived in Europe, where he contributed to German Social Democrat periodicals and enjoyed the company of the Marxist pope, Karl Kautsky, whom he called "a white-haired and very jolly little old man," and with whom he famously polemicized on the necessity of terror ("Terror can be a very effective weapon against a reactionary class that does not want to leave the scene").[156]

By chance in New York when the tsar fell, Trotsky had set off for Russia in April 1917, was released from arrest en route in Canada—thanks to then-foreign minister Miliukov—and arrived at Petrograd's Finland Station on May 4, a month later than Lenin.[157] Immediately, the muscular, spirited, intransigent Trotsky, with pince-nez, became a sensation, making the rounds of the biggest factories as well as the garrison barracks, ending up most nights at the capital's Cirque Moderne, across the river from the Winter Palace, electrifying huge crowds with political oratory. The "bare, gloomy amphitheater, lit by five tiny lights hanging from a thin wire, was packed from the ring up the steep sweep of grimy benches to the very roof—soldiers, sailors, workmen, women, all listening as if their lives depended upon it," wrote John Reed, the former Harvard cheerleader.[158] Trotsky recalled that "every square inch was filled, every human body compressed to its limit. Young boys sat on their fathers' shoulders; infants were at their mothers' breasts. . . . I made my way to the platform through a narrow human trench, sometimes I was borne overhead."[159] One Social Democrat commented at the time, "Here's a great revolutionary who's arrived and one gets the feeling that Lenin, however clever he may be, is starting to fade next to the genius of Trotsky."[160]

In fact, on May 10 Lenin had asked Trotsky to join the Bolsheviks.[161] Having mocked Lenin mercilessly for years, and during the war grown intellectually further apart from him, in summer 1917 Trotsky agreed to join the Bolsheviks, converting to Leninism—that is, to an immediate transfer of power to the soviets.

Underlying structural shifts were still more momentous. The splintering off of large parts of the Russian imperial army accelerated, with the formation of de facto national armies—especially Ukrainian and Finnish, but also Estonian, Lithuanian, Georgian, Armenian, Crimean Tatar—thereby prefiguring the empire's dissolution.[162] The Provisional Government had become even more of a shell. The Petrograd Soviet and especially soldiers' committees had been deeply discredited. But in July 1917, even as the political scene continued to move swiftly toward Lenin, the Bolshevik party was almost annihilated. The Constitutional Democrats resigned from the coalition Provisional Government on July 2; between July 3 and 5, amid rumors that the capital garrison would be deployed to the front, a confused uprising took place in Petrograd involving a machine-gun regiment and Kronstadt sailors. The soldiers and sailors, working with radical lower-level Bolsheviks under the slogan "All Power to the Soviets," managed to seize key junctions in the capital. Hundreds were killed or wounded. Kerensky was at the front. On July 4, a huge crowd at the Tauride Palace demanded a meeting with a leader of the Soviet; when the Socialist Revolutionary Party leader Victor Chernov emerged, a sailor shouted, "Take power, you son of a bitch, when it's handed to you." The rebels took Chernov into custody and he had to be rescued.[163] But an early evening blinding downpour dispersed the crowds.[164] Top Bolsheviks had hesitated to seize the moment, and Kerensky swiftly counterattacked, charging them with treason for the armed insurrection and for receiving funds from a foreign enemy. It was a brilliant move, taking advantage of a situation he did not create.

That the Bolsheviks were receiving smuggled German funds is beyond doubt. Somehow, the party managed to publish newspapers with a combined print run of more than 300,000 per day; *Pravda* alone circulated 85,000 copies. Compared with the bourgeois press (1.5 million per day in the capital), or the combined SR-Menshevik press (700,000), Bolshevik publications could look like small change, but the party also published scores of pamphlets and hundreds of thousands of leaflets, which required financing.[165] Documents showing Lenin and other Bolsheviks in the pay of the Germans appeared on July 5 in Russian newspapers. "Now they are going to shoot us," Lenin told Trotsky. "It is the most advantageous time for them."[166] On the morning of July 6, the Provisional Government's

Counter-Espionage Bureau smashed *Pravda*'s editorial offices and printing presses. Russian troops raided the Bolshevik "fortress" (Krzesińska's mansion) where some 400 Bolsheviks, despite being heavily armed inside, surrendered. Andrei Vyshinsky, the chief of the citizens' militia in central Moscow—and Stalin's future hangman judge in the terror—signed arrest warrants for 28 of the highest-level Bolsheviks, including Lenin.[167] Tipped off, Lenin fled, slipping away to the Alliluyev family flat with Stalin's assistance, then on to Russian Finland with Zinoviev. The folklore has it that Stalin personally shaved Lenin's beard so he would look like a Finnish peasant.[168] Lenin requested that his notebooks be brought to him, and in this sanctuary he wrote *State and Revolution;* he would complete the text in August-September 1917. It argued that all states were instruments for the domination of some classes over others, so that any new class power (like the working class) needed to create its own state form—"the dictatorship of the proletariat"—to suppress the remnants of the old ruling classes and distribute resources during the transition.[169] Meanwhile, two agencies of the Provisional Government gathered volume upon volume of case materials in preparation for a public trial of Lenin and his comrades for treason.[170]

Thus, notwithstanding the disaster of War Minister Kerensky's military offensive, July 1917 looked like a turning point, thanks to Kerensky's offensive against the Bolsheviks. He was going to snatch victory from the jaws of defeat. Altogether, nearly 800 Bolsheviks and radicals would be imprisoned, including Kamenev, who was nearly lynched, but not Stalin (for reasons that remain unclear).[171] On July 6, the war minister returned from the front to the capital, amid the publicized arrests, and the next day took over the entire government when the nominal prime minister, Prince Georgy Lvov, resigned. Lvov observed that "in order to save the country, it is now necessary to shut down the Soviet and shoot at the people. I cannot do that. Kerensky can."[172]

Lvov, who disappeared into a Moscow sanitorium, was wrong, however: Not Kerensky's but Lavr Kornilov's moment had arrived. On July 7, Kerensky promoted Kornilov to command the southwestern front. On July 12, Kerensky announced the restoration of the death penalty at the front for indiscipline, and two days later the tightening of military censorship. Who might enforce these measures remained unclear, but on July 18, Kerensky sacked General Brusilov and proposed Kornilov as army supreme commander. Before accepting Kerensksy's offer, Kornilov consulted the other generals. Back in March 1917, when Kornilov had replaced the arrested Sergei Khabalov as Petrograd military district commander, it had fallen to him to implement the order to arrest the tsaritsa Alexandra, but in April 1917, when Kornilov tried to use troops to quell disturbances in the capital, the Soviet forced him to reverse his order, claiming sole right to command the garrison; disgusted, Kornilov had requested a transfer to a command at the front. There, enlisted men issued demands to their officers, and his June 1917 success in punching a hole through the Austrian lines vanished when Russian troops refused to advance. Resorting to terror at the front against Russia's soldiers had spiraled into looting, atrocities against civilians, and even greater indiscipline.[173] Nonetheless, Kornilov now put forward demands to emasculate the soldiers' committees and reinstitute the death penalty in the rear garrisons. Kerensky had already heard similar demands even from moderates on the general staff at a conference at headquarters on July 16.[174] Kornilov further demanded complete autonomy in military operations and in personnel decisions, as well as a war mobilization plan for industry, just as General Ludendorff had in Germany.[175] On July 21, Kornilov's ultimatum-like terms were leaked to the press—and his popularity on the political right soared.[176] Verbally, Kerensky assented to Kornilov's conditions, so the latter took over supreme command, but when the war ministry drew up the documents to meet Kornilov's conditions, Kerensky delayed signing them, dragging the process into August, raising Kornilov's ire and suspicions, even as Kerensky's own fears of the man he had promoted escalated.[177]

The Bolsheviks convoked a Party Congress between July 26 and August 3, 1917, their first since 1907. (It was the sixth overall, counting the founding Russian Social Democrat Party Congress in Minsk in 1898, which had been the last to take place on Russian territory.) Some 267 attendees, including 157 voting delegates, many from the provinces, assembled under threat of arrest in the sanctuary of Petrograd's factory-laden Vyborg district. With Lenin and Zinoviev in hiding and Kamenev and Trotsky in prison, Sverdlov, assisted by Stalin, organized the gathering. They did yeoman work, turning out representatives from nearly thirty front-line army regiments and ninety Petrograd factories and garrison units, whose moods were radical. Stalin gave the opening greeting and the main political report, the highest profile assignment. "He had on a gray modest jacket and boots, and was speaking in a low, unhurried, completely calm voice," noted one eyewitness, who added, of Stalin's Georgianness that another comrade in the same row "could not suppress a slight smile when the speaker uttered a certain word in a somehow especially soft tone with his special accent."[178] Stalin admitted the severe damage done by the "premature" July uprising. Defiantly, however, he asked "What is the Provisional Government?" and answered, "It is a puppet, a miserable screen behind which stand the Constitutional Democrats, the military clique, and Allied capital—three pillars of counterrevolution." There would be explosions, he predicted.

On the final day of the congress, in the discussion of the draft resolution following from his report, Stalin objected to a proposal by Yevgeny Preobrazhensky that they include a reference to revolution in the West. "The possibility cannot be excluded that Russia will be the country that blazes the trail to socialism," he interjected. "No country has hitherto enjoyed such freedom as exists in Russia; none has tried to realize workers' control over production. Besides, the base of our revolution is broader than in Western Europe, where the proletariat stands utterly alone face to face with the bourgeoisie. Here the workers have the support of the poorest strata of the peasantry. Finally, in Germany the machinery of state power is functioning incomparably better than the imperfect machinery of our bourgeoisie. . . . It is necessary to give up the antiquated idea that only Europe can show us the way. There is dogmatic Marxism and creative Marxism. I stand by the latter."[179]

This remarkable exchange evidenced a level of astuteness almost always denied to Stalin. His argument carried, and an amendment on the victory of socialist revolution in Russia "on condition of a proletarian revolution in the West" was voted down.

Thanks to Stalin's shrewd analysis as well as his generally high regard for Russia, which Lenin did not share, Lenin's militancy was ascendant even in his absence.[180] Lenin still faced the threat of a trial, however, and when Stalin had told the congress delegates that under certain conditions Lenin along with Zinoviev might submit to the courts, he was roundly rebuked. But the promised trial of the Bolsheviks would never materialize. Kerensky allowed his duel with Kornilov to eclipse his battle with Lenin.[181]

## KERENSKY'S SECOND FAILED COUP

In mid-July, Kerensky had put out the call for a state conference for mid-August in Moscow, the ancient capital, with invitations to industrialists, landowners, all former Duma representatives, local governing bodies, higher education institutions, representatives of soviets and peasant bodies, and the military brass—some 2,500 participants, who met inside the Bolshoi Theater.[182] And grand theater it was. Kerensky's opening-day speech on August 12 made a powerful impression, seeming to confirm his authority. He appears to have intended the conference to "consolidate" Russia's political forces, although newspapers half-joked that he arrived in Moscow, site of tsarist coronations, "to crown himself." The newspaper of the Soviet, employing class markers, complained that "morning coats, frock coats, and starched shirts predominate over side-fastening Russian [folk] shirts."[183] But the Soviet, for its part, had excluded the Bolsheviks from its allotted delegation for the latter's refusal to promise to abide by the Soviet's collective decisions (including whether or not to walk out). Moscow workers defied the Soviet, undertaking a one-day wildcat strike on opening day, for which the Bolsheviks claimed credit.[184] "The trams are not running," *Izvestiya* reported, "coffee shops and restaurants are closed"—including the buffet inside the Bolshoi. Gas workers struck, too, and the city went dark.[185]

Kornilov arrived in the light of day from the front on August 13, a Sunday. At the Alexandrovsky (later Belorussian) Station, his red-robed Turcomans leapt out onto the platform with sabers drawn, forming eye-catching rows. Amid a sea of smart-looking military cadets and Russian tricolor flags, the diminutive Kornilov emerged in full-dress uniform and was showered with flowers. Like a tsar, he received waiting ministers, soldiers, dignitaries, after which his twenty-sedan motorcade—the general in an open car—paraded through the city, sparking ovations, including when he stopped to pray to the Mary, Mother of God, icon at the Iverskaya shrine (as all tsars had done). In the evening, a further cavalcade of well-wishers—former chief of staff and supreme commander General Alexeyev, Cadet leader Miliukov, far right-wing leader Purishkevich—were received by Russia's ethnic Kalmyk supreme commander.[186]

The moment was riveting: a state assembly of Russia's entire battered establishment, representatives of the left who themselves had ostracized the Bolsheviks, a motherland in genuine danger of foreign conquest, and rival would-be saviors.

At the August 14 session, Kerensky, in the chair, invited the supreme commander to the rostrum. An intentionally inflammatory speech by a Kornilov Cossack ally had been staged to make Kornilov appear eminently reasonable.[187] "We have lost all Galicia, we have lost all Bukovina," the Kalmyk savior told the hall, warning that the Germans were knocking at the gates of Riga, on a path to the Russian capital. Kornilov demanded strong measures.[188] The right-side aisles in the Bolshoi exploded in ovation, while the left kept silent or made catcalls. This could have been the opportunity to reverse Russia's slide and consolidate the establishment: Some industrialists wanted the State Conference to become a permanent body. Members of the Soviet supportive of order and authority could have been targeted for co-optation and a split of the left. Back on August 9, Stalin, writing in the periodical *Worker and Soldier*, had warned that "the counterrevolution needs its own parliament," a bourgeois-landowner organ, formed without the peasant vote and intended to displace the still-unsummoned Constituent Assembly, "the single representative of the entire laboring people."[189] Four days later, on the opening day of the Moscow State Conference, Stalin had written that "the saviors' make it seem that they are calling a 'simple gathering,' which will decide nothing, . . . but the 'simple gathering' little by little will be transformed into a 'state gathering,' then into a 'great assembly,' then into . . . a 'long parliament.'"[190] Kerensky, however, had no strategy for the Moscow State Conference other than three days of speechifying.[191] Nothing institutional endured.

Even symbolically it failed. Instead of a show of patriotic unity, the State Conference (as Miliukov would observe) confirmed "that the country was divided into two camps between which there could be no reconciliation."[192] Worse, not just Stalin but the entire leftist press—observing the display of assembled nobles, industrialists, and military men—sounded even more hysterical alarms over a supposedly heightened threat of imminent "counterrevolution." Kerensky, the person behind the gathering, drew the same conclusion. "After the Moscow Conference," he would recall, "it was clear to me that the next attempt at a coup would come from the right, and not the left."[193]

Kerensky had himself to blame for raising expectations for bold solutions that were instantly dashed. A full collapse at the front continued to threaten the very survival of the Russian state, and many constitutionalists—Miliukov, Lvov, Rodzyanko—leaned toward a military coup by Kornilov, even if they worried he lacked mass popular support and ignored the practical aspects of power. The idea, or fantasy, was to have Kornilov "restore order" by force, possibly with a military dictatorship and, later, to summon a constituent assembly under favorable conditions.[194] Similar thoughts of imposing order had occurred to General Alexeyev, Vice Admiral Alexander Kolchak (commander of the Black Sea fleet until June), and others who were in conversations with Kornilov. The latter certainly contemplated a coup against both the Provisional Government and the

Soviet in order to suppress an anticipated Bolshevik coup, hang Lenin and his associates, disband the Soviet, and maybe install himself in power, at least temporarily.[195] But this appeared to be a worse option. A would-be military conspirator had no secure communications: chauffeurs, orderlies, telegraph operators would report suspicious activities to the soldiers' committees and the Soviet.[196] So Kornilov worked *with* the Provisional Government. The latter, he rightly concluded, was incapable of mastering the situation. Still, Kerensky did tell Kornilov he wanted a "strong authority," and working with the government allowed the legal movement of troops. Back on August 6–7, with Kerensky's approval, Kornilov had ordered Lieutenant General Alexander Krymov, commander of the Third Cavalry Corps, to relocate his troops from the southwest (Romanian front) up to Velikie Luki (Pskov province). Krymov's troops, some of whom were known as the Savage Division, included Muslim mountaineers from the North Caucasus (Chechens, Ingush, Dagestani) who were viewed as the most reliable in the whole army, and had been used for political enforcement at the front.[197] On August 21, Riga fell—just as Kornilov had warned at the Moscow State Conference—and Kerensky authorized Kornilov to move the frontline troops near Petrograd to defend the capital and suppress an anticipated coup by the Bolsheviks, presumed agents of the Germans. This action remained secret.

The moderate socialists were still arguing for neither/nor: neither truck with the extreme right counterrevolution, nor truck with the extreme left seizure of power.[198] But the Bolsheviks embraced the polarization as welcome and inevitable. "Either, or!" Stalin wrote on August 25, 1917. "Either with the landlords and capitalists, and then the complete triumph of the counterrevolution. Or with the proletariat and the poor peasantry, and then the complete triumph of the revolution. The policy of conciliation and coalition is doomed to failure."[199]

The movement of Krymov's troops, at Kornilov's command, with Kerensky's apparent approval, in order to preempt a presumed Bolshevik coup and strengthen political authority in the name of the hopelessly limp Provisional Government, erupted in a showdown between Kerensky and Kornilov. From the moment it was under way, between August 26 and 31, 1917, and ever since, analysts have divided over two ostensibly opposed interpretations.[200] First, that it was a putsch by Kornilov to make himself dictator, under the guise of protecting the Provisional Government. Second, that it was a monstrous provocation by Kerensky to oust Kornilov and make himself dictator. Both interpretations are correct.[201]

Around midnight on Saturday, August 26—after a series of very convoluted messages, messengers, and pseudo-messengers between Kerensky and Kornilov—the prime minister called an emergency cabinet meeting and requested "full authority [*vlast'*]" to fight off a counterrevolutionary plot. The Provisional Government ministers all resigned.[202] Right about then, on Sunday, August 27, at 2:40 a.m., Kornilov telegraphed the government to the effect that to put down the anticipated Bolshevik rising in the capital, as agreed, Lieutenant General Krymov's army "is assembling in the environs of Petrograd toward evening August 28. Request that Petrograd be placed under martial law August 29."[203] At 4:00 a.m., Kerensky telegraphed Kornilov, dismissing him. At headquarters, the general staff viewed the order either as a forgery or a sign that Kerensky had been taken hostage by extreme leftists. Kornilov had Krymov speed up. In the capital, various naïve personages sought to mediate the "misunderstanding," but Kerensky rejected them. On August 27–28, the newspapers published special editions with an accusation of treason on the part of the supreme commander signed by Kerensky.[204] Enraged, Kornilov telegrammed all frontline commanders, branding Kerensky a liar who was acting under Bolshevik pressure "in harmony with the plans of the German general staff." The public counterappeal by Kornilov pointedly called himself "the son of a peasant Cossack" and asserted a desire "only to save Great Russia. I swear to lead the people through victory over the enemy to the Constituent Assembly, where it will decide its own destiny and choose its new political system."[205] Kerensky turned to the Soviet to muster forces to subvert the "counterrevolution." On the rail lines, workers and specially dispatched Muslim agitators harassed Krymov's Savage Division forces. Trotsky would write that "the army that rose against Kornilov was the army-to-be of the October Revolution."[206] In fact, no fighting took place.[207] Krymov entered Petrograd by automobile on the night of August 30–31 under a guarantee of personal safety from Kerensky, and answered a summons by the prime minister, who told him to report to a military court. Krymov then went to a private apartment and shot himself.[208]

Stalin rejoiced at the "breaking of the counter-revolution," but warned that its defeat remained incomplete. "Against the landowners and capitalists, against the generals and bankers, for the interests of the peoples of Russia, for peace, for freedom, for land—that is our slogan," he wrote on August 31. "The creation of a government of workers and peasants—that is our task."[209] In captivity, the ex-tsar Nicholas II privately expressed disappointment in the failure of Kornilov to establish a military dictatorship. "I then for the first time heard the tsar regret his abdication," recalled the court tutor Pierre Gilliard.[210] In any attempted coup, even many on the inside remain confused and uncertain, and support mostly materializes if and when the coup begins to appear successful.[211] The entente, on August 28, indicated it would support efforts in Russia to "unify" the country as part of the joint war effort; Russian business interests would have backed Kornilov. But Kornilov never even left front headquarters at Mogilyov.[212] It was an odd military coup that depended on the cooperation of Kerensky, who effectively betrayed Kornilov before Kornilov had any chance to betray him.[213] But Kerensky's August move against Kornilov constituted his own second failed coup, following his aborted July coup against Lenin and the Bolsheviks.

Whether a genuinely mass movement on the right existed in summer 1917 to be galvanized and perhaps eventually consolidated can never be known. Still, some insight about the masses may lie in the story of a rightist periodical, the *Little Newspaper* (for the "little" or ordinary person), founded in 1914 and published by Aleksei A. Suvorin (Poroshin), the son of a famous conservative Russian pundit. A vulgar and grammatically challenged broadsheet that delivered brilliant real-life chronicles in real-life prose, the *Little Newspaper* won a mass following among Petrograd's lower orders: workers, soldiers, war invalids, the jobless, those lacking rent money, those shortchanged by traders—in short, much of the wartime capital. Bringing readers to tears of laughter over sketches of quotidian life, but also skewering political cowardice among elites, the *Little Newspaper* opposed Russia's socialist parties and demanded Lenin's arrest before the Provisional Government had issued a warrant. It hammered the Provisional Government and Kerensky for ineptitude and gutlessness, blustered about even bolder war annexations and demanded that government leadership pass to strongmen (especially Vice Admiral Kolchak). It also published the percentages of Jews in soviets, using familiar code like "Rabinovich." The Petrograd Soviet deemed the *Little Newspaper* a "pogrom-publication" and urged print workers not to print it. But by June 1917, the *Little Newspaper*'s circulation rose to 109,000, more than *Pravda*'s, and reached readers in the capital's garrison, nearby naval bases, and factories. That said, it remains impossible to know whether its popularity derived primarily from its scurrilous entertainment or its calls for a "strong hand."[214]

After the Kornilov flameout, the broadsheet lost its popularity. Even before then, however, the *Little Newspaper* had started to label itself "socialist," almost like proto-national socialists, albeit without much conviction in terms of the socialism. This telling, if halfhearted embrace demonstrated that any aspiring movement on the right now had to be "socialist." Socialism in some form was an unavoidable structure in the political landscape. Socialism was also one of the prime evils that motivated Kornilov and others on the political right, however. The war that helped make the aspiration for socialism nearly universal vastly narrowed the Russian right's options. And the very instrument that Kornilov wanted to use to restore order—the army—was now more than ever the key instrument of socialist revolution.[215]

## THE VANISHING ACT

Unhappy Kerensky. Despite comprehending the dire necessity of strengthening central authority, he had played a double game that forced him into a devil's choice: embrace either the general staff (indispensable to prevent a leftist coup) or the democratically elected Soviet (meaning, in his mind, the masses, whose favor he so craved).[216] With his embrace of the Soviet and disgracing of Kornilov, however, establishment figures abandoned the Provisional Government for good; a few even began to hope for a foreign intervention to save Russia.[217] Two generals at frontline headquarters declined Kerensky's urgent requests to replace the dismissed Kornilov. The utterly bankrupt prime minister—without even his own government, let alone a parliament—was compelled to direct the Russian army to obey Kornilov's orders. "A Supreme Commander, accused of treason," Kornilov observed of himself, "has been ordered to continue commanding his armies because there is no one else to appoint."[218]

Some insiders urged Kerensky to resign in favor of General Alexeyev. Instead, the thirty-six-year-old lawyer appointed himself military supreme commander and named General Alexeyev—whom Kerensky had recently dismissed as "defeatist"—to the position of chief of staff. This was the same arrangement that had obtained under Nicholas II. Alexeyev took three days to assent to Kerensky's request; nine days after appointing Alexeyev, Kerensky sacked him.[219] The original eleven-man suspended-in-the-air Provisional Government had narrowed to just one man. Kerensky appointed himself head of a new Council of Five, evoking the five-person Directory of the French Revolution (1795–99) that had aimed to occupy the political middle against far right and far left; Russia's pretend "Directory" would nominally last a few weeks.[220] Kerensky's actions beginning in June 1917, particularly his military offensive, and now in August 1917 had shifted the entire political landscape, pulverizing the right, energizing the left, and helping to shove the entire left much further leftward.

Back in July, Bolshevism had sunk to a low ebb.[221] The newly minted Bolshevik Trotsky, like Kamenev, was in prison, while Lenin, like Zinoviev, was in a Finnish barn. That left Sverdlov and Stalin. Whether this duo—without the hiding Lenin and the imprisoned Trotsky—could have led the Bolshevik party to power seems doubtful. Stalin wrote for and edited *Workers' Path,* the Bolshevik mouthpiece that had replaced the shuttered *Pravda,* while Sverdlov worked to keep an organization together, cajoling provincials to submit concrete examples of their party work (copies of leaflets, membership details), then sending them instructions.[222] But leading the entire revolution, which was a street and trench phenomenon?

There could be no doubt about the policital direction of events. Despite the successful staging of the 6th Party Congress in late July and early August, the slogan "All Power to the Soviets" had been shelved, but then—poof: the long-anticipated "counterrevolution" had suddenly materialized in late August.[223] The slogan "All Power to the Soviets!" was reinstated in a summons to change the class power. The ruling classes were said to be failing to drive the bourgeois-democratic revolution (necessary for socialism); on the contrary, they were now openly counterrevolutionary. Generals would not bring peace. Bankers would not bring economic reforms. Landowners would not bring land redistribution. The bourgeoisie was turning out to be too weak. Class power would have to be seized, or all the gains, the entire revolutionary process, would be lost. Workers and peasants would have to lead the revolution.[224] The leftmost wings of the Socialist Revolutionaries and even of the Mensheviks, for the first time, now accepted this program, too. "In the days of Kornilov," *Workers' Path,* edited by Stalin, would explain, "power had already gone over to the soviets."[225]

The Kerensky-Kornilov debacle completely reversed the Bolshevik slide.[226] Even as Kornilov and many other high-ranking officers submitted to arrest at Mogilyov headquarters, virtually all imprisoned Bolsheviks who did not break out on their own were freed, including, most crucially, Trotsky (released on 3,000 rubles' bail on September 3). On September 25—the same day that Kerensky's ridiculous "Directory" idea was retired—Trotsky became chairman of the Petrograd Soviet. This ascension, from prison to the top of the popular organ, reflected the stunning newfound Bolshevik majority in that body. (The Bolsheviks also achieved a majority of delegates in the Moscow soviet.) No less striking, a great many of the 40,000 guns Kerensky had ordered distributed to resist Kornilov went to factory workers—before this, workers by and large had not been armed—and many of these "Red Guards" would now end up on the Bolshevik side. Stalin, writing on September 6, 1917, publicly acknowledged the gift of the Kerensky-Kornilov affair: "Marx explained the weakness of the 1848 revolution in Germany with the absence of a powerful counter-revolution that might have whipped up the revolution and strengthened it in the fire of battle."[227] In Russia, Stalin underscored, the appearance of counterrevolution in the person of Kornilov had confirmed the need for "a final break with the Cadets," meaning the Provisional Government. On September 16, in yet another lead editorial, Stalin issued a full-throated demand for the immediate transfer of all power to the soviets. "The fundamental question of revolution is the question of power," he explained. "The character of a revolution, its path and outcome, is completely determined by which class is in power," so in the name of the proletariat class, the socialists ought to seize the direction of Russia's revolution.[228]

After the bitter failure of the "July Days," after which Bolsheviks had been subjected to mass arrests, many lacked confidence in any sort of insurrection, fearing possible complete destruction. From hiding in Finland, however, Lenin sent manic directives demanding an immediate coup, arguing that "a wave of real anarchy may become stronger than we are."[229] Russia's stock market had crashed. Deserters and criminals pillaged. "In Rostov the town hall is dynamited," explained one Moscow newspaper that fall. "In Tambov province there are agrarian pogroms. . . . In the Caucasus there are massacres in a number of places. Along the Volga, near Kamyshinsk, soldiers loot trains. . . ."[230] Long queues reappeared for bread, as in February 1917.[231] Food supply officials discussed demobilization of the army, because they could not feed it.[232] Kerensky, along with a nominally revived Provisional Government cabinet of ministers, relocated to the more secure setting of the Winter Palace, availing himself of the former apartments of Alexander III, sleeping in the tsar's bed and working at his desk; his personal affectations became subject to still greater ridicule, and not just by the livid right, which spread false stories of his Jewish origins and clandestine work for the Germans.[233] Soon there were also rumors, Rasputin style, of an affair between Kerensky and one of Nicholas II's daughters. (Kerensky had separated from his wife.) All this incited Lenin. "We have thousands of armed workers and soldiers in Petrograd who can seize *at once* the Winter Palace, the General Staff building, the telephone exchange and all the largest printing establishments," he insisted again on October 7. "Kerensky will be compelled to *surrender*."[234] Stalin reproduced Lenin's message for public audiences, hammering on the point that the workers, peasants, and soldiers had to expect a new Kerensky-Kornilov strike. "The counter-revolution," Stalin urged in an article published on the morning of October 10, "is mobilizing—prepare to repulse it!"[235]

The Central Committee was stalling, however, and Lenin risked the trip from Finland to Petrograd sometime between October 3 and 10; on the latter day, in a safe-house private apartment, wearing a wig and glasses, and without his beard, he attended his first meeting with the Central Committee since July. Of its twenty-one members, only twelve were present. Sverdlov gave the report, citing supposedly widespread popular support for an insurrection. After nearly all-night browbeating, Lenin won the votes of ten of the twelve for an immediate coup; Kamenev and Zinoviev opposed. Stalin joined Lenin in voting for the resolution, written with pencil on a sheet of paper torn from a children's notebook, to the effect that "an armed uprising is inevitable and the time for it is fully ripe." No date was set, however. ("When this uprising will be possible—perhaps in a year—is uncertain," Mikhail Kalinin would note on October 15.)[236] On October 18, Zinoviev and Kamenev, in a small-circulation newspaper, published word of their opposition to a coup—essentially revealing one was being planned.[237] Lenin wrote a furious letter, calling them "strike breakers" and demanding their expulsion.[238] Stalin, in the main Bolshevik newspaper he edited, allowed Zinoviev to publish a conciliatory response, and appended an editorial note. "We, for our part, express the hope that with the declaration by Zinoviev . . . the matter may be considered closed," the anonymous note stated. "The sharp tone of Lenin's article does not alter the fact that, fundamentally, we remain of one mind."[239] Zinoviev and Kamenev were perhaps potential allies to counteract Trotsky's newfound power.

Lenin had no telephone at his hideaway, the apartment of Madame Fofanova, although Krupskaya went back and forth with Lenin's paper and oral messages pressuring the Central Committee.[240] Between October 10 and 25, Lenin would see Trotsky only once, on October 18, in the private apartment where he was hiding, but that once was enough; Trotsky, at the Central Committee on October 20, harshly condemned Stalin's attempt at internal party peacemaker, and the members voted to accept Kamenev's resignation. Trotsky, even more than the

Central Committee, became the key instrument of Lenin's will. Kerensky, for his part, had expelled the Bolsheviks from the Krzesińska mansion ("the satin nest of a court ballerina," in Trotsky's piquant phrase). They had taken up residence in a finishing school for girls of the nobility, Smolny Institute, even farther out on the eastern edge of the capital than the Tauride Palace. The Soviet, expelled from the Tauride, had relocated to Smolny as well. There, the Soviet's central executive committee had approved—by a single vote (13 to 12)—the formation of a defensive Military Revolutionary Committee (MRC), which the full Soviet approved on October 12.[241] The rationale for the armed body—originally proposed by the Mensheviks—was to calm the roiling garrison and defend the capital against a German attack. But Trotsky, urged on by Lenin, would use the MRC on behalf of the Bolsheviks to shunt aside the carcass of the Provisional Government. Now, everything broke Lenin's way.

The Second All-Russia Congress of Soviets had been scheduled for October 20—a colossal stroke of lucky timing, and Trotsky hatched the brilliant idea of having a seizure of power simultaneously with the congress, appropriating a source of critical legitimacy while imposing a fait accompli on all other socialists.[242] Many delegates seemed unlikely to make it to Petrograd on time, and on October 17–18, moderate socialists forced the Soviet's central executive committee to postpone the congress until October 25—crucial for the Bolsheviks, who gained time to undertake coup preparations.[243] (The Military Revolutionary Committee only held its first meeting on October 20.)[244] "The Soviet government will annihilate the misery of the trenches," Trotsky told an audience of soldiers and sailors on October 21, according to the eyewitness Sukhanov. "It will give the land and it will heal the internal disorder. The Soviet government will give away everything in the country to the poor and to the troops in the trenches. If you, bourgeois, have two fur coats, give one to a soldier. . . . Have you got a warm pair of boots? Stay at home. A worker needs them." Sukhanov added: "A resolution was proposed that those present stand for the workers' and peasants' cause to their last drop of blood. . . . Who's in favor? As one, the thousand-man audience shot their hands up." A similar scene took place the next day, at the Cirque Moderne, where Trotsky enjoined the crowd to swear an oath of allegiance: "If you support our policy to bring the revolution to victory, if you give the cause all your strength, if you support the Petrograd Soviet in this great cause without hesitation, then let us all swear our allegiance to the revolution. If you support this sacred oath which we are making, raise your hands."[245] On the eve of the Second

Congress of Soviets, on October 23, the Trotsky-led MRC asserted its exclusive claim to command the capital garrison and, through its commissars posted to garrison regiments, ordered them "to combat readiness."[246] Still, the MRC remained uncertain as to its next moves.

Stalin, on the afternoon of October 24, informed a gathering of Bolshevik delegates who had arrived for the congress that two possible courses of action divided the MRC: one held that "we organize an uprising at once"; the other advised "that we consolidate our forces." A party Central Committee majority, he indicated, tilted toward the latter, meaning wait and see.[247] Kerensky came to the rescue, again, ordering the arrests of top Bolsheviks—people he had released following the Kornilov debacle—and shuttering two Bolshevik newspapers: *Workers' Path* and *Soldier* (two rightist papers were also to be closed, in a balancing act). On October 24, in Stalin's presence, a handful of military cadets and citizens' militia destroyed the freshly printed newspaper copies and damaged the presses, but Stalin's staff ran to Smolny with news of the attack and the MRC dispatched forces and got the presses rolling again.[248] Preparations for defense of the revolution became offense. Rumors of "suspicious" troop movements in the city—"Kornilovites!"—goaded the Red Guards to occupy the rail stations, control the bridges, and seize the telegraph. When the government disconnected the phone lines to Smolny, the MRC seized the telephone exchange, had the lines reconnected, and disconnected the Winter Palace. When the lights in Smolny seemed to be experiencing trouble, Red Guards seized the electricity generating station. Trotsky would later quip that "it was being left to the government of Kerensky, as you might say, to insurrect."[249]

In fact, the Bolsheviks would have laid claim to power anyway—nothing stood in their way. They managed to be thoroughly confused and still seize power because the Provisional Government simply vanished, just as the vaunted autocracy had vanished.[250] Red Guards—described as "a huddled group of boys in workmen's clothes, carrying guns with bayonets"—met zero resistance and by nightfall on October 24 already controlled most of the capital's strategic points.[251] During that night, Kerensky sacked the commander of the Petrograd military district, Colonel Georgy Polkovnikov, but the latter ignored his own dismissal and used military channels to wire the general staff at headquarters: "I report that the situation in Petrograd is menacing. There are no street demonstrations or disorders, but systematic seizure of institutions and railroad stations, and arrests are going on. No orders are being carried out. The military school cadets are abandoning their posts without resistance . . . there is no guarantee that attempts will not be made to capture the Provisional Government."[252] The colonel was right, but just how many garrison troops and irregulars the Bolsheviks mustered that night remains unclear, perhaps as few as 10,000.[253] General Alexeyev would later claim he had 15,000 officers in Petrograd, of whom one third were immediately ready to defend the Winter Palace, but that his offer was not taken up. (In the event, the officers got drunk.)[254] The Petrograd garrison did not participate en masse in the Bolsheviks' coup, but more important, they did not defend the existing order.[255] General V. A. Cheremisov, commander of the nearby northern front, hounded by a military revolutionary committee formed near his headquarters, rescinded the orders previously given to the reinforcements who were supposed to relieve the Winter Palace.[256] All that the hollow Provisional Government managed to muster in its defense were women and children: that is, an all-female "Death Battalion" (140 strong) and a few hundred unenthusiastic young military cadets, who were assisted by a bicycle unit; some stray Cossacks; and forty war invalids whose commander had artificial legs.[257]

## LENIN AND TROTSKY

In October 1917 Russia counted 1,429 soviets, including 455 of peasant deputies, a formidable grassroots movement, but their fate to a great extent rested in the hands of two men. Lenin had headed for Smolny around 10:00 p.m. on October 24—in violation of a Central Committee directive to remain in hiding—donning a wig with fake bandages around his face. A military cadet patrol stopped him and his lone bodyguard, but, looking over the deliberately rumpled Bolshevik leader, decided not to detain what appeared to be a drunk. Without a pass, Lenin had to sneak his way into Smolny; once inside, he started screaming for an immediate coup.[258] He was wasting his breath: the putsch was already well under way. But the next night, the Second Congress of the Soviets was delayed while Military Revolutionary Committee forces sat on their hands outside the largely unguarded Winter Palace; the congress could not wait any longer and finally opened at 10:40 p.m. Smolny's colonnaded hall, formerly used for school plays, had filled up with between 650 and 700 delegates, who were barely visible through the haze of cigarette smoke. Somewhat more than 300 were Bolsheviks (the largest bloc), along with nearly 100 Left SRs, who leaned toward the

Bolshevik side. More than 500 delegates recognized the time had come for "all power to the soviets," but, confronted with a Bolshevik fait accompli, many were angry, especially the moderate socialists.[259] A frail and awkward Yuly Martov, leader of the Mensheviks, in a trembling and scratchy voice—signs of his tuberculosis (or the onset of cancer)—offered a resolution calling for a "peaceful solution" and immediate negotiations for an inclusive "all-democratic government." Martov's resolution passed unanimously, amid "roaring applause."[260] But then vociferous critics of Bolshevism rose to condemn their conspiracy to arrest the Provisional Government "behind the back of the Congress" and foment "civil war," thereby prompting most Menshevik and Socialist Revolutionary delegates to demonstrate their disapproval of the Bolsheviks by walking out. "Bankrupts," Trotsky shouted at their heels. "Go where you belong—onto the trash pile of history."[261]

"Martov walked in silence and did not look back—only at the exit did he stop," recalled his fellow Menshevik Boris Nicolaevsky. A young Bolshevik firebrand from the Vyborg district stunned the Menshevik leader by saying, "And we among ourselves had thought, Martov at least will remain with us." Martov replied: "One day you will understand the crime in which you are complicit," and waved his hand as he departed the hall in Smolny.[262]

After months of open discussion in newspapers, barracks, factories, street corners, and drawing rooms, the Bolshevik putsch was over and done before the vast majority of the population knew it had happened. On October 25, trams and buses in Petrograd operated normally, shops opened for business, theaters put on their productions (Fyodor Chaliapin sang *Don Carlos*). Around the empire, whether in Kiev or Vladivostok, people had little or no inkling of events in the capital. Still, the flow of power to the soviets had long been unmistakable: already in summer 1917, the Kronstadt naval base had become a de facto minirepublic ruled by a soviet. The Tashkent soviet, while refusing to accept Muslims (98 percent of the local population) as members, had seized power before the Bolshevik coup in Petrograd.[263] By September 1917, at the very latest, the issue was never the survival of the ghostly Provisional Government, but what would replace it in the capital? One contender might have been the August 1917 Moscow State Conference, a potentially (unelected) Constituent Assembly of the establishment, but such an opportunity, to the extent it had existed, was squandered. This left replacement by the Petrograd Soviet. In that regard, the critical issue was *who* would wield the upper hand at the Soviet? There, the climb in Bolshevik fortunes had been stunning. In Petrograd, as in most other towns with huge wartime garrisons, Kerensky's suicidal June offensive, and his August encouragement and then betrayal of Kornilov, delivered the Soviet to the Bolsheviks. That meteoric political gain was consolidated by Trotsky's idea to use the recently formed Military Revolutionary Committee to present the Second Congress of Soviets with the fait accompli of a Bolshevik seizure of power.[264] But the socialist opponents of the Bolshevik coup unwittingly did the rest in their abandonment of the congress hall.[265]

Later, much would be made of the "art of insurrection," especially by Trotsky. Sometime after 2:00 a.m. that first night of the Congress of Soviets (October 25–26)—at a parallel special session of the Petrograd Soviet held during the congress—he announced that forces of the Petrograd Soviet's Military Revolutionary Committee had finally located the Provisional Government ministers inside the Winter Palace, seated around a table waiting to be arrested. (Kamenev—the Bolshevik opponent of the Bolshevik coup—would inform the Congress of Soviets of the arrests.) Lenin had written out a proclamation on the transfer of power (signed "Military Revolutionary Committee of the Petrograd Soviet"), which the grandiloquent Anatoly Lunacharsky read aloud to the congress, while repeatedly being interrupted by riotous cheers. After discussion the Left SRs in the hall agreed to support the decree with a minor change; a delegate of the Menshevik Internationalists, who had returned to the hall, asked for an amendment calling for a government of the broadest possible elements, but he was ignored. Around 5:00 a.m., the primarily Bolshevik and Left SR delegates remaining in the hall overwhelmingly approved the transfer of power: just 2 voted against, and 12 abstained.[266] Around 6:00 a.m., some seven hours into the opening session, the delegates adjourned to get some rest. There was no functioning government. The MRC Bolsheviks had frog-marched the ex-ministers into the damp cells of the Peter and Paul Fortress, which until the Kornilov-Kerensky affair had been full of Bolsheviks.[267] Red Guards, however, had never actually "stormed" the Winter Palace: they, finally, had just climbed unopposed through unlocked doors or windows, many going straight for the storied wine cellars, history's most luxurious.[268] Each new Red Guard detachment sent to prevent a ransacking instead got drunk, too. "We tried flooding the cellars with water," the leader of the Bolshevik forces on site recalled, "but the firemen . . . got drunk instead."[269]

Crucially, however, Kerensky's vainglorious relocation of himself and the ersatz "ministers" into the Winter Palace forever linked the Provisional Government with the seat of oppressive tsarism. This symbolic link would facilitate depictions of the October Bolshevik coup—via tales of a mythical storming of the Winter Palace—as a continuation of the overthrow of the old regime, thereby eliding the February and October revolutions.

Lenin had still not even appeared at the Congress of Soviets. He finally emerged—to thunderous applause—around 9:00 p.m. on the night of October 26, after the opening of the second (and last) session, still in the ragtag disguise he had used to evade capture while crossing the capital to Smolny. (As part of his disguise, Lenin had taken to donning a worker's cap, which he never relinquished, even as he continued to wear "bourgeois" suits.)[270] "Lenin—great Lenin," recorded John Reed. "A short, stocky figure with a big head set down on his shoulders, bald and bulging . . . dressed in shabby clothes, his trousers too long for him."[271] He was not widely recognized. Lenin was predominantly an ethnic Russian, but had German, Jewish, and Kalmyk ancestry as well. Born the same year as Kornilov, Lenin by now was solidly middle-aged. He "is short, broad-shouldered, and lean," the St. Petersburg writer Alexander Kuprin observed. "He looks neither repellant, militant, nor deep-thinking. He has high cheekbones and slanting eyes. . . . The dome of his forehead is broad and high, though not as exaggerated as it appears in foreshortened photographs. . . . He has traces of hair on his temples, and his beard and moustache still show how much of a fiery redhead he was in his youth. His hands are large and ugly. . . . I couldn't stop looking at his eyes . . . they are narrow; besides which he tends to screw them up, no doubt a habit of concealing short sight, and this, and the rapid glances beneath his eyebrows, gives him an occasional squint and perhaps a look of cunning."[272] Gleb Kryżanowski, a Bolshevik, recorded a similar impression of Lenin's short stature and eyes ("unusual, piercing, full of inner strength and energy, dark, dark, brown"), but found his visage startlingly distinct, "a pleasant, swarthy face with a touch of the Asiatic."[273] Not as Asiatic in appearance as the diminutive Kornilov, nor as wiry, Lenin's face was nonetheless partly Mongol.

Lo and behold: *here* was Russia's Kalmyk savior.

The Bolshevik zealot read out a decree on immediate peace "to peoples and governments of all the warring powers," interrupted by stormy applause and a singing of the "Internationale."[274] Lenin also read out a decree on land endorsing the peasants' private and collective land seizures, instead of a state nationalization. To objections that the land decree contradicted the long-standing Bolshevik platform and had been lifted from the Socialist Revolutionaries—no longer present in the hall—Lenin replied, "Who cares who drafted it. As a democratic government we cannot ignore the feelings of the lower orders [*narodnye nizy*] although we do not agree with them."[275] The land decree was adopted without discussion.

Lev Kamenev, the chairman of the Soviet's central executive committee, had deftly withdrawn Trotsky's sharply worded resolution condemning the Mensheviks and SRs for walking out at the first session of the congress. Before Lenin's appearance, in between the first (October 25–26) and second (October 26–27) sessions of the Congress of Soviets, Kamenev strenuously worked to agree a coalition government with the Left SRs, but the latter had balked at the exclusion of all the other socialists. And so, near the very end of the Congress of Soviets' second and final session, around 2:30 a.m. (October 27), Kamenev announced the formation of a "temporary" exclusively all-Bolshevik government. Boris Avilov, a Menshevik Internationalist, stood up and predicted that an all-Bolshevik government could neither solve the food supply crisis nor end the war. He further predicted that the Entente would not recognize a Bolshevik-monopoly government and that the latter would be compelled to accept a separate and onerous peace with Germany. Avilov proposed inviting back those elected Soviet delegates who had walked out and, with them, forming an all-socialist democratic government. Avilov's proposal failed, garnering only a quarter of the votes (150) of those present in the hall (600), despite considerable sympathy for this stance even among many Bolsheviks.[276] It was Trotsky who most vehemently spoke against a deal with the "traitors."[277]

Trotsky cut an inordinately dashing figure—the shock of wild dark hair and the blue eyes, the pince-nez of an intellectual, and the broad shoulders of a Hercules—but he wielded his public charismatic power on behalf of Lenin. Lenin's power was uncanny. "I felt somewhat surprised that a person who—irrespective of one's views of his ideology—had had such a far-reaching influence on the fate of his huge fatherland should make such a modest impression," remarked one Finnish visitor to Smolny. "His speech was very simple and unforced, as was his manner. If one did not know him, one could never have been able to comprehend the strength that he must have possessed. . . . The room was in no way different from any of the other rooms in Smolny. . . . The walls were painted white, there was a wooden table and a few chairs."[278] Lenin's political instruments were not imposing architecture, a bureaucracy, a telephone network. They were ideas and personality. "The whole success of Lenin . . . to assume dominion over a hundred and fifty millions," an acute foreign observer would note, "is plainly due entirely to the spell of his personality, which communicated itself to all who came into touch with him."[279] Lenin in 1917 was rarely a physical presence. Alexander Shlyapnikov, the head of the Bolshevik party inside the country at the time of Lenin's return in spring 1917, spent the entire period before, during, and immediately after the October coup in the hospital (he had been hit by a tram); he had no effect on events. But Lenin did have an effect, even though he did not visit crews on board battleships or troops in trenches in 1917; most sailors and soldiers nonetheless knew his name. He had sometimes delivered public speeches, such as from the Krzesińska mansion balcony, or harangues at the Petrograd Soviet, and in May, militant workers held banners that proclaimed, "Long Live Lenin!" But having arrived in Russia on April 3, 1917, after an absence of nearly seventeen years, the Bolshevik leader had soon been forced to seek refuge in tsarist Finland.

From early July 1917, when the warrant had been issued for his arrest, Lenin remained underground, hiding, for almost four consecutive months, right through October 24.[280] During that crucial period, he almost never even met the Bolshevik inner circle face to face, let alone the masses. Here was the equivalent of a catacomb Christian who, in a single lifetime, would suddenly emanate from the caves to become pope. Most political figures who succeed on a dizzying trajectory almost always do so by cobbling broad coalitions, often with very unlikely bedfellows, but not Lenin. He succeeded despite refusing cooperation and creating ever more enemies. Of course, he cultivated allies among the class of professional revolutionaries, loyalists such as Trotsky, Sverdlov, and Stalin. Lenin's torrent of polemical theses further enhanced his power, first among revolutionaries, who in turn popularized Lenin's intellectual as well as political standing among the mass. Lenin proved a master of the abusive, pithy phrase, and of the crude, sweeping analysis of developments and rationale for revolution.[281] But whatever Lenin's charisma and encapsulation talents, much of his power would derive from events going his way. Again and again, he stubbornly insisted on what appeared to be a crazy course of action, which then worked to his advantage. Lenin seemed to incarnate political will.

Later, Trotsky, for all his Marxist invocation of the supposed laws of history, would feel constrained to admit that without Lenin, there would have been no October Revolution.[282] Lenin, for his part, never made explicit that the same held true for his indispensable handmaiden Trotsky. But others did so. "I tell you what we do with such people," the despairing military attaché of liberal Britain, General Alfred Knox, had said of Lenin and Trotsky to an American Red Cross official. "We shoot them." This was on October 20, the eve of what turned out to be the predicted Bolshevik coup. The Red Cross official, ostensibly wiser, had replied, "But you are up against several million. General, I am not a military man. But you are not up against a military situation."[283] In fact, the Red Cross official was wrong: he confused the assumption of power by the Second Congress of Soviets, which had become unavoidable, with the assumption of power by the Bolsheviks alone. The Bolshevik putsch could have been prevented by a pair of bullets.

"THE RUSSIAN REVOLUTION," observed Rosa Luxemburg, "is the mightiest event of the world war."[284] Whether a prewar transition to a constitutional monarchy—from constitutional autocracy—would have been enough to incorporate the masses into a stable polity can never be known. What we do know is that the long, stubborn refusal, not just of Nicholas II but of almost the entire Russian establishment, to abandon the autocracy in order to save the monarchy ensured that the dysfunctional autocracy's downfall would precipitate a disintegration of state institutions as well. Freedom and state breakdown became synonymous and, in that context, the classical liberals got their chance. The February 1917 liberal coup, nominally against the autocracy but really against the Duma, presaged the Bolshevik October 1917 coup, nominally against the Provisional Government but really against the Soviet. Each appeared to spearhead the mass sentiment of the moment; each brought a far narrower group to power than mass sentiment preferred. That mass sentiment, moreover, did not stand still: the world war vastly accelerated the radicalization of popular mood. To be sure, the history of revolutions indicates that an inevitable failure to satisfy millenarian hopes naturally radicalizes the populace. The surprise in Russia, if there was one, lay not in the deepening popular radicalization but in the debilitating weakness of the establishment and upper military.[285]

Russia had always been a police state that relied predominantly on the army for its heaviest policing, but not only had Russia lost its police in March 1917, after that it lost its army as well. "The Seizure of power by 'force' in a modern State," noted the historian Adrian Lyttelton, apropos of Italy, but equally applicable to Russia, "is never possible, except when the army or police carries out the coup, unless the will to resist of the Government forces has been undermined."[286] The world war, and especially the 1917 military offensive, did more than hasten popular radicalization: it also defanged the army as a force of order. Wartime radicalism in the army and fleet—from Vyborg and Helsinki to Pskov, which the Provisional Government called the "rotten triangle"—served as the indispensable scaffolding for Bolshevism. "October may have been a 'coup' in the capital," one historian has written, "but at the front it was a revolution."[287] The politicized armed forces were made up predominantly of peasants, and whether they served in the army or not, they carried out their own revolution. "A country of boundless territorial expanse, with a sparse population, suffered from a shortage of land," the Constitutional Democrat Duma representative Vasily Maklakov would remark in hindsight. "And the peasant class, elsewhere usually a bulwark of order, in Russia in 1917 evidenced a revolutionary temper."[288] But whereas the revolution of the soldiers and sailors consciously linked up with Bolshevism, the peasant revolution only happened to coincide with it. Soon enough, the peasant revolution and Bolshevism would collide.

Inside the Bolshevik party, the way that the Petrograd coup had unfolded would have lasting repercussions. The opposition to the coup by Kamenev and Zinoviev was a stain they would bear for the rest of their lives. When Stalin's mediation efforts were slapped down by Trotsky, Stalin's resentment at the upstart, high-profile intellectual Trotsky boiled over. Stalin, in a huff, had announced his intention to quit as editor of the party newspaper. "The Russian revolution has overthrown not a few authoritative types," Stalin wrote with disdain on the day of his proffered resignation. "The revolution's power is expressed in the fact that it has not bowed before 'famous names,' but has taken them into service or, if they refused, consigned them to oblivion."[289] The Central Committee rejected his resignation, but even after the successful coup, the bitterness would rankle.[290] Later, in exile, Trotsky would call Sverdlov "the general secretary of the October insurrection"—a poke in the eye of (by then) General Secretary Stalin. Trotsky would also defend Kamenev, the opponent of the putsch, for having played a "most active part in the coup," pointedly adding that Stalin had played no noticeable role.[291] This was patently false. To be sure, Trotsky, Kamenev, Lenin, and Lunacharchy all spoke at the historic Second Congress of Soviets, while Stalin did not. But Stalin gave a speech to the Bolshevik delegates to the Soviet before the congress met, on October 24, demonstrating clear familiarity with the military and political preparations for the coup. Throughout 1917, moreover, his punditry and editorial work were prodigious, especially in the summer and fall.[292]

Stalin's publications explained the revolution in simple, accessible terms, including during the Congress of Soviets. "In the first days of the revolution the slogan 'All Power to the Soviets' was a novelty," he wrote in *Pravda* (October 26, 1917), referring to the period beginning in April 1917. "At the end of August the scene changed very radically" with "the Kornilov Rebellion. . . . The soviets in the rear and the soldiers committees at the front, which were in a moribund state in July-August, 'suddenly' revived and took power in their hands in Siberia and the Caucasus, in Finland and the Urals, in Odessa and Kharkov. . . . Thus, 'Soviet power' proclaimed in April by a 'small group of Bolsheviks in Petrograd' obtains almost universal recognition of the revolutionary classes at the end of August." He differentiated the move to Soviet power from the endless changes in the Provisional Government that had brought socialists into the cabinet. "Power to the Soviet means the thorough purging of every government office in the rear and at the front, from top to bottom. . . . Power to the Soviet means the dictatorship of the proletariat and the revolutionary peasantry . . . open, mass dictatorship, exercised in the eyes of all, without ploys and behind-the-scenes work; for such a dictatorship has no reason to hide the fact that no mercy will be shown to the lock-out capitalists who have intensified unemployment . . . or to the profiteering bankers who have increased the price of food and caused starvation." Certain classes brought on the misery; other classes would bring salvation. "This is the class nature of the slogan 'All Power to the Soviets.' Events at home and abroad, the protracted war and the longing for peace, defeat at the front and defense of the capital, the rottenness of the Provisional Government . . . , chaos and famine, unemployment and exhaustion—all this is irresistibly drawing the revolutionary classes of Russia to power." How "classes" exercised power remained to be seen.

Stalin's Georgian Social Democrat compatriot David Sagirashvili had known him since 1901, when Sagirashvili was fourteen and the future Stalin twenty-three. His upbringing had been similar to Stalin's—absent father, immersion in tales of Georgian martyrs and national poets, loathing for imperial Russian administrators and soldier-occupiers, admiration for Georgian outlaws who fought for justice, and membership in a circle of revolutionaries—but he had become a Menshevik. Still, when Sagirashvili, after the coup, refused to join his Menshevik colleagues in boycotting the Bolshevik-dominated Soviet, Stalin, in a

Smolny corridor, "put his hand over my shoulder in a most friendly manner and [began] to talk to me in Georgian."[293] The Georgian Jughashvili-Stalin from the Russian empire's periphery, the son of a shoemaker, had become part of a new would-be power structure in the capital of the largest state in the world, thanks to geopolitics and world war, to many fateful decisions and multiple contingencies, but also to his own efforts. On the list of Bolsheviks voted to a new Soviet central executive committee, Stalin's name appeared fifth, right before Sverdlov, and after Lenin, Trotsky, Zinoviev, and Kamenev.[294] Still more pointedly, Stalin was one of only two people whom Lenin gave permission to enter his private apartment in Bolshevik headquarters at Smolny, a proximity and confidence that would prove pivotal.

## CHAPTER 7

# 1918: DADA AND LENIN

Let us try for once not to be right.

> Samuel Rosenstock, aka Tristan Tzara ("sad in my country"),
> a Jewish Romanian poet, "Dada Manifesto" 1918[1]

Lunacharsky was clutching his head, his forehead against
the window-pane, standing in an attitude of hopeless
despair.

> Kremlin commandant Pavel Malkov, August 30, 1918[2]

FEW STREET CELEBRATIONS had accompanied or immediately followed the
October Bolshevik coup, in contrast to the giddy days during and after February-
March 1917, but within a week Lenin was posing for sculptors. And yet, few
thought this crazy putsch would last even before it had happened. Throughout
the summer of 1917, Russia's press, nearly across the political spectrum, had
spread the idea (as Paul Miliukov recalled in 1918) that "the Bolsheviks either
would decide not to seize power as they lacked hope of retaining it, or, if they did
seize it, they would endure only the shortest time. In very moderate circles, the
latter experiment was even viewed as highly desirable for it would 'cure Russia of
bolshevism forever.'"[3] Many on the right had openly welcomed a Bolshevik coup,
imagining that the leftists would quickly break their own necks, but not before
first clearing away the despised Provisional Government.[4] When the coup happened, it still surprised. Then Lenin opted for a cabinet government rather than
abolishing the state and the Second Congress of Soviets—at least those who
remained in the hall—approved the formation of the all-Bolshevik government. Admittedly, the Council of People's Commissars was made up not of
"bourgeois" ministers but "commissars," a name derived from the French *com-
missaire* and originally the Latin *commisarius*, signifying plenipotentiaries of a

higher authority (in this case, from "the people").[5] But would it last? The "provisional" men of February who had dared to replace the tsar (Miliukov, Kerensky) had been pushed aside.[6] Top army commanders had fallen to incarceration or despair, such as Lavr Kornilov and Mikhail Alexeyev, the longest-serving and most successful chief of staff in the war (who was compelled to arrest Kornilov). Would-be political replacements among non-Bolshevik socialists, such as Victor Chernov and his socialist revolutionaries and Yuly Martov and his Mensheviks, appeared to have been trampled underfoot. But in 1918—which as a result of a calendar change in February from the Julian (eastern orthodox) to the Gregorian (western) was the shortest year in Russia's thousand-year history[7]—the Bolsheviks, too, looked destined for oblivion.

The would-be "regime" consisted, at the top, of just four people: Lenin, Trotsky, Sverdlov, and Stalin, each of whom had a criminal record for political offenses and none of whom had any administrative experience. (The fifteen members of the Council of People's Commissars had spent a collective two centuries in tsarist prison and exile.) Ensconced in the stale air of Smolny, the eighteenth-century finishing school for girls of noble lineage, they commanded a few tables and ratty couches. Opposite Lenin's small, dirty room was a larger space where members of the Council of People's Commissars came and went; initially they held no formal meetings. The room had an unpainted wooden partition to conceal a typist (the chancellery) and a cubbyhole for a telephone operator (the communications network). The former headmistress still occupied the room next door. A sailor, designated by Sverdlov as the new Smolny commandant, hastily organized a perimeter around the campus and began to purge the building room by room.[8] But Lenin's first official car, a magnificent Turcat-Méry of 1915 make (formerly belonging to the tsar), was stolen from Smolny by members of a fire brigade looking to profit by selling it in Finland. (Stepan Gil, a first-class auto professional and conversationalist, who had driven the tsar and became Lenin's principal driver, led a hunt that managed to retrieve the vehicle).[9] "Nobody knew Lenin's face at that time," Krupskaya would recall. "In the evening we would often stroll around Smolny, and nobody would ever recognize him, because there were no portraits then."[10] The thirteen commissars set up "offices" inside Smolny and attempted to visit and assert authority over the ministries they sought to supersede.[11] Stalin, announced as the commissar for nationalities, had no tsarist or Provisional Government ministry to try to take over.[12] His deputy, Stanisław Pestkowski—part of the Polish Bolshevik contingent that had seized the central telegraph during the October coup—stumbled across an empty table in Smolny, over which he tacked up a handwritten sign: "People's Commissariat of Nationalities."[13] According to Pestkowski, the room was close to Lenin's, and "in the course of the day," Lenin "would call Stalin an endless number of times and would appear in our office and lead him away."[14] Lenin, perhaps preferring to remain behind the scenes, is said to have offered the chairmanship to Trotsky, who refused.[15] Instead, Trotsky became "foreign affairs commissar" and got a room upstairs, the quarters of a former "floor mistress" for the girls. Sverdlov continued to oversee Bolshevik party matters.[16]

That such lowly beginnings would soon become one of the world's strongest dictatorships is beyond fantastic. Lenin was essentially a pamphleteer. In 1918 he was identified as "Chairman of the Council of People's Commissars and journalist," and earned more money from publication honoraria (15,000 rubles) than from his salary (10,000 rubles).[17] Trotsky was a writer as well, and a grandiloquent orator, but similarly without experience or training in statecraft. Sverdlov was something of an amateur forger, thanks to his father's engraving craft, and a crack political organizer but hardly an experienced policy maker. Stalin was also an organizer, a rabble-rouser, and, briefly, a bandit, but primarily a periodicals editor—commissar of nationalities was effectively his first regular employment since his brief stint as a teenage Tiflis weatherman.

Now, these four products of autocratic Russia issued a torrent of paper decrees: "abolishing" social hierarchy in law, civil ranks, and courts; declaring "social insurance for all wage workers without exception, as well as for the city and village poor"; announcing the formation of a Supreme Council of the Economy and a determination to enforce a state monopoly in grain and agricultural implements. The decrees were suffused with terminology like "modes of production," "class enemies," "world imperialism," "proletarian revolution." Published under the name Vladimir Ulyanov-Lenin—and signed for him by Stalin, among others—the decrees were proclaimed to have the "force of law."[18] In the meantime, the regime had no finances or functionaries. Trotsky failed in multiple efforts to take over the ministry of foreign affairs' building and personnel.[19] His first arrival there, at Palace Square, 6, on November 9 was greeted with derision, followed by mass desertion. True, his minions eventually found some petty cash in the ministry's safe, and Stalin, to fund his own "commissariat," had Pestkowski sponge 3,000 rubles from Trotsky.[20] Pestkowski soon let on that he had studied some economics in London and was decreed "head of the State Bank."[21] The employees laughed him away, which is how he instead ended up working for Stalin.

The decree naming the unemployed Pestkowski as central bank governor, and many similar pronouncements, had an absurdist quality reminiscent of the provocations of the new performance art known as Dadaism. A perfectly apt nonsense term, Dada had arisen in neutral Switzerland during the Great War, largely among Jewish Romanian exiles, in what they called the Cabaret Voltaire, which, coincidentally, lay on the same street in Zurich (Spiegelgasse, 1) as Lenin's wartime exile apartment (Spiegelgasse, 14). Tristan Tzara, a Dada poet and provocateur, and Lenin may have played chess against each other.[22] Dada and Bolshevism arose out of the same historical conjuncture. Dada's originators cleverly ridiculed the infernal Great War and the malevolent interests that drove it, as well as crass commercialism, using collage, montage, found objects, puppetry, sound poetry, noise music, bizarre films, and one-off pranks staged for the new media they mocked. Dada happenings were also transnational, and would flourish in Berlin, Cologne, Paris, New York, Tokyo, and Tiflis. The Dada artists—or "anti-artists" as many of them preferred to be known—did not conflate, say, a urinal repurposed as a "fountain" with a new and better politics.[23] Tzara composed poems by cutting newspaper articles into pieces, shaking the fragments in a bag, and emptying them across a table. Another Dadaist read a lecture whose every word was purposefully drowned out by the shattering noise of a train whistle. Such tactics were a world away from the pedantic, hyperpolitical Lenin: He and his decrees about a new world order were issued without irony. But Bolshevik decrees were also issued into Dada-esque anarchy.

If the collapse of the tsarist order was a revolution, the revolution was a collapse. The immense vacuum of power opened up by the tsar's wartime abdication had stunned the Provisional Government like a blow to its professorial head. "General Alexeyev characterized the situation well," a Provisional Government finance official wrote in his diary on the eve of the Bolshevik coup. "The essence of the evil lay not in the disorder but *in the absence of political authority [bez-vlastii]*."[24] After October, organizations *claiming* broad authority proliferated, just as before, but the "absence of authority" worsened. Bolshevism, too, roiled with deep internal fractures, riotousness, and turnover, and Lenin's superior political instincts—when compared with other leaders of Russia's revolution—could not overcome the functional equivalent of the Dadaist's deafening train whistle: namely, the man-made destruction and chaos that brought the Bolsheviks to nominal authority. Some powerful groups, notably the railway workers union, would insist on a government without Lenin and Trotsky; Germany, militarily victorious on the eastern front, looked to be on the verge of completely conquering Russia; the chief of the new Bolshevik political police would be taken hostage in a near leftist coup against Bolshevism; and an assassin would pump two bullets into Lenin. By summer 1918, armed insurrection against the regime would open on four fronts. And yet Lenin and his inner circle of Trotsky, Sverdlov, and Stalin had already managed to assert a Bolshevik political monopoly.

The Bolshevik dictatorship was not an utter accident, of course. Russia's political landscape had become decisively socialist, as we have seen. The right-wing ranks of the army and officer corps were weaker in Russia than in every other predominantly peasant country, and unlike everywhere else, Russia lacked a non-socialist peasants' party, a circumstance partly derived from the intransigence and sheer daftness of the old rightist establishment on the land question. Russia's other socialist parties, moreover, contributed mightily to the Bolsheviks' opportunities to monopolize the socialist cause. Lenin was not a lone wolf among political sheep. He sat atop a large, centrally located Bolshevik political base in the biggest cities and the Russian heartland. That said, the Bolsheviks' dictatorship did not arise automatically, even in the parts of imperial Russia that nominally fell under their jurisdiction. The dictatorship was an act of creation. That creation, in turn, was not a reaction to unforeseen crisis, but a deliberate strategy, and one that Lenin pursued against the objections of many top Bolsheviks. The drive for dictatorship began well before the full-scale civil war—indeed, the dictatorial drive served as a cause of the armed conflict (a fact universally noted by contemporaries). But in no way should any of this be taken to mean the Bolsheviks established effective structures of governance. Far from it: the Bolshevik monopoly went hand in hand with administrative as well as societal chaos, which Lenin's extremism exacerbated, causing an ever-deepening crisis, which he cited as justification for his extremism. The catastrophic collapse of the old world, however debilitating for millions of real people, was taken as progress by the Bolsheviks: the deeper the ruin, the better.

One would think the bedlam would have been more than enough to topple the playacting government. Food supply problems alone had helped precipitate the autocracy's downfall and revealed the Provisional Government's hollowness. But monopoly and anarchy proved compatible because the Bolshevik monopoly entailed not control but denying others a role in presiding over chaos.[25]

Bolshevism was a movement, a capacious, freewheeling, armed anarchy of sailors and street squads, factory hands, ink-stained scribes and agitators, would-be functionaries wielding wax seals. Bolshevism was also a vision, a brave new world of abundance and happiness, a deep longing for the kingdom of heaven on earth, accompanied by absurdist efforts at enactment. In 1918, the world experienced the pointed irreverence of Dada as well as an unintentionally Dada-esque Bolshevik stab at rule, performance art that involved a substantial participatory audience. At the center, Lenin persisted in his uncanny determination, and Stalin hewed closely to him. Stalin assumed the position of one of Lenin's all-purpose deputies, prepared to take up any assignment.

## MONOPOLY

Marxism's theory of the state was primitive, affording little guidance beyond the Paris Commune (1870–71), which Marx had both praised and denigrated. The Commune, which lasted all of seventy-two days, had inspired the idea of the dictatorship of the proletariat (in the 1891 preface to a reissue of the *Civil War in France,* Engels had written, "Do you want to know what this dictatorship looks like? Look at the Paris Commune. That was the Dictatorship of the Proletariat").[26] The Commune also afforded inspiration because of its mass participatory character. Still, Marx had noted that the Communards had "lost precious time" organizing democratic elections when they should have been busy gathering forces to finish off the "bourgeois regime" in Versailles, and had failed to seize the French National Bank to expropriate its vaults; the money was moved to pay for the army in Versailles that crushed the Commune.[27] Lenin, at a gathering in Geneva in 1908 on the thirty-seventh anniversary of the Commune, and the twenty-fifth of Marx's death, had reiterated Marx's point that the Commune had stopped halfway, failing to extirpate the bourgeoisie.[28] Nonetheless, its romantic allure persisted. In 1917 and into early 1918, Lenin imagined a "state of which the Paris Commune was the prototype," with "democracy from below, democracy without an officialdom, without a police, without a standing army; voluntary social duty guaranteed by a militia formed from a universally armed people."[29] This, too, constituted a part of the unintentional resemblance to Dadaism. As late as April 1918, Lenin would be urging that "all citizens must take part in the work of the courts and in the government of the country. It is important for us to draw literally all working people into the government of the state. It is a task of tremendous difficulty. But socialism cannot be implemented by a minority, by a party."[30] Once the sense of siege set in that the Bolshevik coup had itself precipitated, however, Lenin ceased to uphold the Commune as inspirational model, and that episode became solely a cautionary tale about decisively eliminating enemies.[31] And there was no end to enemies.

Behind their winning slogans about peace, land, bread, and all power to the Soviets, and their machine guns, Lenin and the adherents of Bolshevism felt perpetually under threat. On the morning of the coup during the Second Congress of Soviets on October 25, 1917, Alexander Kerensky, nominally aiming to return with reliable units from the front, had fled Petrograd in a pair of automobiles, one "borrowed" from in front of the nearby U.S. embassy.[32] "Resist Kerensky, who is a Kornilovite!" Bolshevik appeals proclaimed; in fact, at the front Kerensky found only a few hundred Cossack troops of the Third Cavalry Corps of Lieutenant General Krymov—the very Kornilov subordinate whom Kerensky had accused of treason and who, after a conversation with Kerensky, had committed suicide.[33] On October 29, in combat outside Petrograd, at least 200 were killed and wounded—more than in either the February or October revolutions—but the demoralized remnant cavalry proved no match for the several thousand motley Red Guards and garrison soldiers mustered by the Petrograd Military Revolutionary Committee.[34] Kerensky narrowly evaded capture and fled again, into foreign exile.[35] Other anti-Bolsheviks had rallied military school cadets in the capital who seized the Hotel Astoria (where some top Bolsheviks resided), the State Bank, and the telephone exchange, but the schoolboys, too, were easily beaten back.[36] Still, the Bolsheviks never stopped fearing "counterrevolution," on the example of the French Revolution, especially the episode in August 1792 when external aggression appeared to facilitate internal subversion.[37] "I can still remember," recalled David Sagirashvili, "the anxious faces of the Bolshevik leaders . . . whom I saw in the corridors at the Smolny Institute."[38] That anxiety only deepened.

Despite the formation of an all-Bolshevik Council of People's Commissars, a majority of Russia's socialists continued to favor the formation of an all-socialist government, a sentiment also evident among many Bolsheviks. Lev Kamenev, a member of the Bolshevik Central Committee, had become the new chairman of the Soviet central executive committee, the standing body of the Congress of Soviets, in whose name power had been seized. During the coup, Kamenev had sought to bring the most left-leaning Socialist Revolutionaries and possibly other socialists into a revolutionary government, and he continued to do so afterward, fearing that a Bolshevik-only regime was doomed. The latter prospect heightened on October 29, when the leadership of the Union of Railroad Employees laid down an ultimatum, backed by the threat of a crippling strike, demanding an all-socialist government to prevent civil war.[39] This occurred during the uncertainty of a possible Kerensky return. A rail strike had paralyzed the tsarist authorities for a time in 1905 and it would stymie Bolshevik efforts to defend themselves. At a meeting of garrison troop representatives, also on October 29, Lenin and Trotsky rallied support against "counterrevolution" from the twenty-three units that were represented that day (out of fifty-one).[40] But Kamenev, joined by Zinoviev and other top Bolsheviks, formally agreed to allow Socialist Revolutionaries and Mensheviks into the Council of People's Commissars.[41] While the Menshevik Central Committee agreed to negotiations for an all-socialist government with Bolsheviks in it by a single vote, the railway union insisted on a government entirely without Trotsky and Lenin. Kamenev and his allies proposed to the Bolshevik Central Committee that Lenin would remain in the government but yield the chairmanship to someone like the leader of the Socialist Revolutionary party, Victor Chernov. The Bolsheviks would keep only minor portfolios.[42]

Lenin appeared to be losing his grip on the party. On November 1, 1917, the lead editorial in a Bolshevik-controlled newspaper announced "agreement among all factions" across the socialist left, adding that "the Bolsheviks" always understood "revolutionary democracy" to mean "a coalition of all socialist parties . . . not the domination of a single party."[43] Kamenev stood ready to yield what, in Lenin's mind, were the fruits of the October coup. But Trotsky, Sverdlov, and Stalin enabled Lenin to beat back the challenge. Also on November 1, at the autonomous Petersburg Committee of Bolsheviks—which, unusually, was attended by Central Committee members—Lenin condemned Kamenev's efforts to ally with the SRs and Mensheviks as treasonous, saying, "I can't even talk about this seriously. Trotsky long ago said such a union was impossible. Trotsky understood this and since then there hasn't been a better Bolshevik." Lenin had once divided the Social Democrats, and now threatened to divide the Bolsheviks. "If there is to be a split, let it be so," he said. "If you have a majority, take power . . . and we shall go to the sailors."[44] Trotsky proposed negotiating only with the left wing of the Socialist Revolutionaries, who were in the process of splitting off to form a separate party, and could be junior partners to the Bolsheviks. "Any authority [*vlast'*] is force," Trotsky thundered. "Our authority is the force of the majority of the people over the minority. This is unavoidable, this is Marxism."[45] That same day, at a follow-up meeting of the Bolshevik Central Committee—with Moscow still not in Bolshevik hands but with the threat (more apparent than real) of a Kerensky-led Cossack march on Petrograd having subsided—Lenin exploded at Kamenev for carrying out coalition negotiations in earnest, rather than as cover to send military reinforcements to seize power in Moscow. Lenin demanded that the negotiations cease altogether, and that the Bolsheviks appeal directly to the masses. Kamenev retorted that the railway union had "huge power." Sverdlov argued against breaking off the negotiations, from a tactical point of view, but also recommended arresting members of the railway union leadership.[46] (Stalin did not attend the November 1 meeting; he did appear later that night at a delayed meeting of the Soviet's central executive committee, where the battle continued.)[47]

Lenin's uncompromising stance was strengthened on November 2, 1917, when pro-Bolshevik forces definitively seized the Moscow Kremlin in the name of "soviet power." The back-and-forth week-long armed clashes in the central district of Moscow involved a tiny fraction of the overall population, perhaps 15,000 on each side; the Bolshevik side lost 228 killed, more than in any other locale, while government defenders lost an unknown number. "Artillery fire directed on the Kremlin and the rest of Moscow is not causing any damage to our troops but is destroying monuments and sacred places and is bringing death to peaceful citizens," observed their cease-fire proclamation, which amounted to surrender.[48] The next day, back in Petrograd, Kamenev and Zinoviev got the Soviet's central executive committee to endorse continued negotiations on an all-socialist government, but with Kerensky turned back and Moscow in hand, Lenin met individually with Trotsky, Sverdlov, Stalin, Dzierżyński, and five others, getting them to sign a resolution denouncing as "treason" the efforts of a Bolshevik Central Committee "minority" to relinquish monopoly power.[49] Accusing close comrades who had spent years in the underground, prison, and exile of treason over policy differences was typical Lenin.

History might have been different had Kamenev called Lenin's bluff and told him to go to the sailors. But instead of denouncing Lenin as a deranged fanatic, seizing control over the Central Committee, and himself trying to rally the factories, streets, local Bolshevik party organizations, and other socialist parties in behalf of the overwhelmingly popular idea of an all-socialist government, Kamenev yielded his place on the Bolshevik Central Committee. Zinoviev and three others resigned as well.[50] Several Bolsheviks resigned from the Council of People's Commissars, including Alexei Rykov (interior affairs commissar). "We stand for the necessity of forming a socialist government of all soviet parties," they declared. "We submit that other than that, there is only one path: the preservation of a purely Bolshevik government by means of political terror."[51] And so, Lenin's Bolshevik opponents ceded two key institutions—the Central Committee and the government—to him.

There was still the Petrograd Soviet central executive committee, which Kamenev chaired and which many saw as the new supreme body: Lenin himself had drafted a resolution, approved by the Second Congress of Soviets in October 1917, subordinating the Council of People's Commissars to the Soviet.[52] But on November 4, Lenin went to the Soviet central executive committee to tell its members they did not legally have jurisdiction over the Council of People's Commissars. The vote to decide the matter was set to go against Lenin, but suddenly he insisted that he, Trotsky, Stalin, and one other people's commissar in attendance would also vote. The four people's commissars voted yes, on what was essentially a vote of confidence in their own government, while three moderate Bolsheviks abstained, allowing Lenin's motion to pass 29 to 23.[53] Thus did the all-Bolshevik government free itself from legislature oversight. Lenin was not finished: on November 8, at the Bolshevik Central Committee, he forced Kamenev to resign as chairman of the Soviet's central executive committee.[54] (That same day, Zinoviev recanted and rejoined the Bolshevik Central Committee. Before the month was out, Kamenev and Rykov would also recant, but Lenin would not accept them back right away.) Lenin quickly maneuvered to have Sverdlov nominated as the new Soviet chairman; Sverdlov won the critical post by a mere five votes.

Sverdlov emerged more than ever as the indispensable organizational man. He now served simultaneously as secretary of the Bolshevik party and chairman of the Soviet central executive committee, and deftly transformed the latter into a de facto Bolshevik organ, "orienting" its meetings to obtain the desired results.[55] At the same time, Sverdlov managed what Kamenev had been unable to do: he coaxed the Left Socialist Revolutionaries into a Bolshevik-controlled Council of People's Commissars, in a minority role, with the aim of dividing the anti-Bolshevik socialists.[56] The meteoric rise of the Left SRs between the end of 1917 and early 1918 was perhaps second only to that of the Bolsheviks in summer and fall 1917. The reason was obvious: the imperialist war continued, and so did the lurch toward ever more radical leftism. There were even rumors in December-January that some leftist Bolsheviks wanted to join the Left SRs in a new coup, arrest Lenin and form a new government, perhaps under the Left Communist Grigory "Yuri" Pyatakov. The Left SR entrance into the Council of People's Commissars robbed the railway workers union of a united front opposed to Bolshevik monopoly, and its efforts to force a genuine all-socialist coalition fizzled. The Left SR entrance into the central government also buttressed the Bolshevik position in the provinces.[57] The Bolsheviks essentially had had no agrarian program when they lifted that of the SRs in October 1917; Sverdlov flat out admitted that prior to the revolution the Bolsheviks had "conducted absolutely no work among the peasantry."[58] In this context the Left SRs offered not just immediate tactical advantage but far-reaching political promise.[59]

Most Left SRs recognized themselves as junior partners, not as members of a genuine coalition, and they largely occupied positions in the Cheka (All-Russia Extraordinary Commission for Combating Counter-revolution and Sabotage) or as military commissars in the army. Lenin's monopolistic political offensive, meanwhile, continued unabated, targeting the public sphere. Before the October coup, he had denounced censorship as "feudal" and "Asiatic," but now he deemed the "bourgeois" press "a weapon no less dangerous than bombs or machine guns."[60] Lenin bullied shut some sixty newspapers in late October and November 1917. True, in a cat-and-mouse game—as Isaiah Berlin quipped—*Day,* the liberal newspaper, was shuttered, briefly reappeared as *Evening,* then as *Night,* then *Midnight,* and finally *Darkest Night,* after which it was shuttered for good.[61] Recognizably leftist newspapers were also targeted. "History repeats itself," complained the Right Socialist Revolutionary newspaper the *People's Cause,* which had been closed down under tsarism.[62] Some Left SRs also joined the cries of outrage at Bolshevik press censorship. According to the Bolshevik decree, the repressions were "of a temporary nature and will be removed by a special degree just as soon as normal conditions are reestablished," but, of course, "normal" conditions never returned.[63]

## STATELESSNESS

Trotsky would unabashedly recall that "from the moment the Provisional Government was declared deposed, Lenin acted in matters large and small as the Government."[64] True enough, but even as Lenin maniacally imposed political monopoly in the Petrograd neighborhood containing Smolny and the Tauride Palace, authority in the wider realm fragmented still further. The coup accelerated the empire's disintegration. Between November 1917 and January 1918, chunk after chunk of imperial Russia broke off like an iceberg collapsing into the sea—Finland, Estonia, Latvia, Lithuania, Poland, Ukraine, Georgia, Armenia, Azerbaijan. The conversion of these former borderland provinces into self-declared "national republics" left a truncated "Soviet Russia" in uncertain relation to most of the realm's most developed territories. Stalin, as nationalities commissar, was drawn into trying to manage this dissolution, signing, for example, a treaty fixing a border with newly independent Finland (the frontier ran precariously close to Petrograd). Inside the Russian heartland, too, provinces declared themselves to be "republics"—Kazan, Kaluga, Ryazan, Ufa, Orenburg. Sometimes, this was pushed from above, as in the case of the Don Soviet Republic, which, it was hoped, would forestall German assertions of military intervention on the basis of "self-determination."[65] Whatever their origins, province republics hardly ruled their nominal territories: counties and villages declared themselves supreme. Amid the near total devolution, copycat "councils of people's commissars" proliferated. A Moscow "council of people's commissars" showed no intention of subordinating itself to Lenin's Council of People's Commissars and claimed jurisdiction over more than a dozen surrounding provinces. "Due to parallel commissariats, people and [local] offices do not know where to turn and have to do business with the two levels simultaneously," one observer complained, adding that petitioners "regularly appeal to both province and central commissariats, accepting as legal whichever decision is more beneficial."[66]

While basic governing functions were taken up by very local bodies—or not at all—the nominal central authorities hunted for money. Already on the afternoon of October 25, and multiple times thereafter, Wiaczeysław Mężyński, another Polish Bolshevik (normally Russified as Menzhinsky), had taken an armed detachment over to the Russian State Bank.[67] Mężyński, who had for a time worked as a bank teller for Crédit Lyonnais in Paris, was the new "people's commissar for *finance ministry affairs*"—as if there would be no enduring financial commissariat in the new order, just confiscations. His actions prompted finance ministry and Russian State Bank personnel to strike.[68] Private banks shut their doors, too, and, when forced by armed threats to reopen, refused to honor checks and drafts from the Bolshevik government.[69] Mężyński finally just robbed the State Bank and laid 5 million rubles on Lenin's table in Smolny.[70] His heist inspired Bolshevik officials—and impostors—to seize more bank holdings. Holders of deposit boxes, meanwhile, under threat that their valuables would be confiscated, were compelled to appear for "inventories," but when they showed up with their keys, their valuables were confiscated anyway: foreign currency, gold and silver, jewelry, unset precious stones.[71] As of December 1917, bond interest payments (coupons) and stock dividends essentially ended.[72] By January 1918, the Bolsheviks would repudiate all tsarist internal and external state debt, estimated at some 63 billion rubles—a colossal sum, including about 44 billion rubles in domestic obligations, and 19 billion foreign.[73] Whatever the ideological fulminations, they were wholly incapable of servicing the debt.[74] Shock waves hit the international financial system, the ruble was removed from European markets, and Russia was cut off from international financing. The country's financial system ceased to exist. Credit to industry was shut off.[75] A paper money "famine" soon plagued the country.[76]

All the while, Russia's hundred-million-plus peasants were engaged in a redistribution of lands owned by gentry, the imperial household, the Orthodox Church, and peasants themselves (beneficiaries of Stolypin's reforms, many of whom were now expropriated).[77] Boris Brutzkus, a contemporary Latvian-born economist in Russia, deemed the 1917–18 peasant revolution "a mass movement of an elemental fury, the likes of which the world has never seen."[78] On average, however, peasants seem to have acquired a mere one extra acre of land. Some showed canny skepticism regarding the new strips, keeping them separate from their previous holdings, in the event someone came to take them away. (Sometimes they had to travel such distance to work the new allotments that they gave them up on their own.)[79] Still, peasants ceased paying rent and had their debts to the peasant land bank canceled.[80] Overall, the upheavals strengthened the redistributive commune and the ranks of middling peasants who neither hired others nor sold their own labor.[81] How much credit the Bolsheviks received for the land redistribution remains uncertain, even though Lenin had expediently lifted the popular Socialist Revolutionary Land Decree. (The SRs, serving in coalition with the Cadets in the Provisional Government, had essentially abandoned their plank for immediate land redistribution.) The Bolshevik agriculture commissar, pronouncing the Land Decree in "the nature of a battle cry intended to appeal to the masses," revealingly added that "the seizure is an accomplished fact. To take back the land from the peasants is impossible under any condition."[82] The decree was trumpeted in all the newspapers and published as a booklet (soldiers returning to native villages were given calendars with their copies, so that they would have something other than the Land Decree for rolling cigarettes).[83] But the greatest concentrations of private land in the Russian empire were in the Baltic areas, the western provinces, Ukraine, and North Caucasus, all of which fell outside Bolshevik control. It would take a lot more than paper decrees to push the peasants toward Bolshevism.

Rural tumult and violence worsened the already severely war-disrupted urban food supply. Petrograd, which lay distant from the main farming regions, and even Moscow were forced onto starvation rations, some 220 grams of bread per day.[84] Fuel and raw materials started to vanish altogether, prompting workers to go from helping run their factories to taking them over ("workers' control"), if only just to try to keep them operating, acts that more often than not failed. The entire proletariat—dwindling from its peak of perhaps 3 million—was dwarfed by at least 6 million internal refugees, a number that ballooned to perhaps 17 million when counting soldier deserters and POWs.[85] This immense transient population frequently morphed into armed bands that pillaged small towns as well as the countryside.[86] In the cities, Red Guard irregulars and garrison troops continued to incite public disorder—and Bolshevism had no police force, other than the Red Guards. Frontline soldiers were supposed to receive around 5 rubles per month, while Red Guards were paid 10 rubles *per day*, about the daily wage of factory workers, but many factories had closed and ceased paying wages. And so the ranks of Red Guards—factory workers who were handed rifles or just looted arsenals—swelled.[87] With or without red armbands, looters targeted the wine cellars of the capital's countless palaces; some "suffocated and drowned in the wine," an eyewitness recorded, while others went on shooting sprees.[88] On December 4, 1917, the regime announced the formation of the Commission Against Wine Pogroms under a tsarist officer turned Bolshevik, Vladimir Bonch-Bruevich. "Attempts to break into wine-cellars, warehouses, factories, stalls, shops, private apartments," the Soviet's newspaper threatened, "will be broken up by machine-gun fire without any warning"—a stark indication of the uninhibited violence.[89]

But the regime discovered a greater threat: the functionaries of the old regime were rumored to be plotting "a general strike." Many holdover officials were already on strike, as were telephone workers, even pharmacists and schoolteachers; mostly just cleaning people and doormen were showing up for work at ministries.[90] On December 7, the Council of People's Commissars created a second emergency force, the "temporary" All-Russia Extraordinary Commission for Combating Counter-revolution and Sabotage, known by its Russian acronym as the Cheka, and headquartered at Gorokhovaya, 2. "It is war now—face to face, a fight to the finish, life or death!" the Cheka head, Felix Dzierżyński, a Polish Bolshevik of noble lineage, told the Council of People's Commissars. "I propose, I demand an organ for the revolutionary settlement of accounts with counterrevolutionaries."[91] Dzierżyński (b. 1877) had endured eleven years in tsarist prisons and Siberian exile, emerging with few teeth, a partially paralyzed face with a lopsided smile, and a burning passion for justice.[92] Within its first two weeks, the Cheka arrested some thirty alleged plotters said to belong to a "Union of Unions of State Functionaries" and used their confiscated address books to make additional arrests. Other functionaries—whose wages, apartments, food rations, and freedom were on the line—reconsidered their opposition to the new government.[93] The Bolsheviks then spent much of January debating whether to allow these "tools of capitalism" and "saboteurs" to resume their state positions.

Most of Russia's revolutionaries, even many hard-core Bolsheviks, found the new political police anathema.[94] Many unscrupulous types, including criminal elements, joined the Cheka and they often became preoccupied not solely or exclusively with political repression. The Cheka had added combating "speculation" to its mandate, but the agency itself emerged as a grand speculator.[95] "They looked for counterrevolutionaries," wrote an early eyewitness to Cheka raids, "and took the valuables."[96] Warehouses filled up with goods seized as "state property," coercively acquired without recompense, which were then distributed as favors to officials and friends or sold. In mid-May 1918, a Cheka was established in Bogorodsk, a center of the tanning industry on the Volga with a population of 30,000, but on May 29 an attack destroyed the Cheka building. A detachment from Nizhny Novgorod, the provincial capital, arrived and conducted executions. "We confiscated two hundred thousand rubles' worth of gold and silver articles and one million rubles' worth of sheep wool," the Cheka reported. "The factory owners and the bourgeoisie are in flight. The Commission decided to confiscate the property of those who fled and sell it to workers and peasants."[97]

("Workers and peasants" could include party bosses and police officials.) When the Cheka and the Bolshevik authorities were accused of looting, they often issued blanket denials, although Lenin hit upon the convenient slogan, "We loot the looters."[98]

The Cheka was far from alone in wheeling and dealing. "Everyone who wished to 'nationalize' did so," recalled one official in the new Supreme Council of the Economy.[99] The chaos of seizures and speculation in some ways proved more destabilizing than any genuine plots of counterrevolution. The Cheka's role in providing security, meanwhile, remained doubtful. Back in January 1918, Lenin's car was strafed from behind (two bullets passed through the windshield) and Smolny was subjected to bomb scares.[100] By February, the Cheka proclaimed the power of summary execution against "the hydra of counter-revolution"—a declaration that looked like panic, as much as contempt for "bourgeois" liberties.[101] A secret mid-1918 Cheka self-assessment would observe that "we did not have the strength, ability, or knowledge, and the [Extraordinary] Commission's size was insignificant."[102]

## BALLOTING

Such was the Bolshevik monopoly in the stateless anarchy: idle factories, gun-toting drunks and marauding Red Guards, a deliberately shattered financial system, depleted food stocks, an ambiguous junior partnership for the Left SRs, and an ineffectual secret police busy with property theft and the very speculation it was supposed to combat—and on top of it all, the Provisional Government, just before its death, had finally set elections for a Constituent Assembly to begin on November 12, 1917.[103] The ironies would be rich: Russia's Constitutional Democrats had hesitated to allow democratic elections to go forward, fearing the consequences of a vote by peasants, soldiers, sailors, and workers, but now the dictatorial Lenin decided to let the democratic elections proceed.[104] The prospect of a pending constitutional convention would blunt some of the fiercest socialist opposition to the all-Bolshevik Council of People's Commissars and, anyway, not a few top Bolsheviks imagined they might win. The party certainly tried, suppressing the propaganda of other contenders and, in their own press, ripping into the alternatives, denouncing the Socialist Revolutionaries ("wolves in sheep's clothing"), the Menshevik Social Democrats ("slaves of the bourgeoisie clearing the path for the counterrevolution"), and the Constitutional Democrats ("capitalist pillagers"). The stage seemed set for mass intimidation and fraud. Incredibly, however, Russia experienced its first ever genuine universal-suffrage elections.

Work to organize the vote proved to be immense, perhaps the largest civic undertaking in the realm since the peasant emancipation half a century before. A genuinely independent sixteen-member All-Russia Election Board oversaw the process, with local supervision performed by regional, county, and communal boards staffed by representatives of the judiciary, local government bodies like tsarist-era *zemtsvos* but also the soviets, as well as by members of the voting public. The town, township, and county election boards drew up lists of voters: everyone, male and female, above twenty years of age.[105] Around 44.4 million people voted by secret paper ballot, across vast distances, during wartime, in seventy-five territories, as well as at the front and naval fleets (nearly 5 million soldiers and sailors voted). No voting took place in territories under German occupation (tsarist Poland, Finland, the Baltic littoral), or in woefully undergoverned Russian Turkestan, and returns from some regions ended up lost. As of November 28, 1917, the original date for convocation, the balloting remained incomplete, so the announced opening was postponed, which provoked defenders of the Constituent Assembly to march that day on the Tauride Palace. Lenin responded by proposing a decree to arrest the main Constitutional Democratic politicians as "enemies of the people" (a term that Bolshevik opponents had first applied to Lenin's gang) even before they had taken up their seats.[106] Lenin's resolution against the Cadets on November 28 was supported by every member of the Bolshevik Central Committee except one—Stalin.[107] Stalin's reasons remain obscure. Be that as it may, the next day the Bolshevik Central Committee—characteristically using a secret decree—formalized the new political order by awarding Lenin, Trotsky, Sverdlov, and Stalin the right to decide "all emergency questions."[108] And what was not an emergency?

Despite the repression and assertion of dictatorial powers, however, the election produced an expression of popular will.[109] To be sure, taking in the full measure of Eurasia, beyond the two capitals, one scholar has argued that through mid-1918 most people remained far more committed to particular institutions (soviets, soldiers' committees, factory committees) than to specific parties.[110] This was changing, however, for in the voting the populace was presented choices of parties. The four fifths of the population who lived in the countryside, and who had no non-socialist farmers' party to vote, cast their ballots for the peasant-oriented Socialist Revolutionaries in a strong plurality, just under 40 percent of the total ballots recorded, nearly 18 million, while another 3.5 million voted for the Socialist Revolutionaries of Ukraine. Another 450,000 voted for Russia's Left Socialist Revolutionaries (they had split off only after the electoral lists had been formed). The overall SR vote proved strongest in the most fertile agricultural territories and in villages overall, where turnout proved extraordinarily high: 60 to 80 percent, versus around 50 percent in cities. The SRs won their highest percentage in Siberia, a land of farming and little industry.

The SRs had won the election. But the split in the SR Party showed the strong trend moving still more toward the radical socialist variant (the SRs in Ukraine were already further left than their counterparts in Russia). The Social Democratic vote was substantial, too, though not for the Menshevik wing; only the Georgian Mensheviks did well, amassing 660,000 votes (30 percent of the ballots in the Caucasus); Russia's Mensheviks won just 1.3 million votes, under 3 percent of the total vote. By contrast, around 10.6 million people voted for the Social Democrat-Bolsheviks—24 percent of the votes counted. Eight provinces voted more than 50 percent Bolshevik. The Bolsheviks and SRs split the military vote, each taking about 40 percent, but tellingly, the Black Sea fleet, distant from Bolshevik agitation, voted 2 to 1 SRs over Bolsheviks, while the Baltic fleet, reached easily by Bolshevik agitators, went 3 to 1 Bolshevik. The Bolsheviks overwhelmingly won the Western Army Group and the Northern Army Group, as well as the big urban garrisons, reaching 80 percent among the soldiery stationed in Moscow and in Petrograd. Thus, the votes of soldiers and sailors (peasants in uniform) in and near the capital saved Bolshevism from an even more overwhelming defeat by the SRs, as Lenin himself later admitted.[111]

The non-socialist vote came in at only 3.5 million, some 2 million of which went to the Constitutional Democrats. That put the Cadets under 5 percent. Significantly, though, almost one third of the Cadet vote was recorded in Petrograd and Moscow—around half a million ballots. The Bolsheviks garnered nearly 800,000 votes in the two capitals, but the Cadets came in second there (while besting the Bolsheviks in eleven of thirty-eight provincial capitals). Thus, the supreme strongholds of Bolshevism were also strongholds of the "class enemy," a source of unrelenting Bolshevik anxiety about imminent "counterrevolution."[112] And perhaps the most important fact of all: organized right-wing politics were nowhere to be seen. Amid the atmosphere of "revolutionary democracy," land redistribution, and peace, Russia's electorate overwhelmingly voted socialist—socialist parties of all types collectively garnered more than 80 percent of the vote.[113]

Bolshevism did better than non-Bolsheviks expected. In one sense, around half the former Russian empire voted for socialism but against Bolshevism: the electorate seemed to want people's power, land, and peace without Bolshevik manipulation. In another sense, however, the Bolsheviks had secured an electoral victory in the strategic center of the country (Petrograd and Moscow), as well as among crucial armed constituencies (capital garrisons and Baltic sailors). For Lenin, that was sufficient. Other parties and movements remained slow to take his full measure, and even more important, this mass political power of Bolshevism (already visible at the front in summer 1917). "Who cannot see that what we have is nothing like a 'Soviet' regime, but is instead a dictatorship of Lenin and Trotsky, and that their dictatorship relies on the bayonets of the soldiers and armed workers whom they have deceived," the Socialist Revolutionary Nikolai Sukhanov lamented in November 1917 in the newspaper he edited, *New Life,* which Lenin soon shut down.[114] But it was not primarily deception, even though Bolshevik prevarication and legerdemain were bountiful. In fact, Lenin's dictatorship shared with much of the mass a popular maximalism, an end to the war come what may, a willingness to see force used to "defend the revolution," and an unapologetic class warfare of the have-nots against the haves—positions that were divisive, but also attractive. Lenin drew strength from the popular radicalism.[115]

On January 5, 1918, at 4:00 p.m., the long-awaited Constituent Assembly opened in the old White Hall of the Duma's Tauride Palace, but in a menacing atmosphere. The Bolsheviks had flooded the streets with armed loyalists and artillery. Rumors spread that the electricity would be turned off—Socialist Revolutionary delegates had come with candles—and of paddy wagons en route. Inside, the spectators' gallery overflowed with raucous sailors and provocateurs. Ear-splitting heckling, clanking rifle bolts, and snapping bayonets punctuated the speechifying.[116] Close to 800 delegates had won seats, including 370–380 for Socialist Revolutionaries, 168–175 for Bolsheviks, another 39–40 for Left SRs, as well as 17 each for Mensheviks and Constitutional Democrats, but the latter were outlawed and not seated, and many of the Mensheviks did not attend.[117] Crucially, the Ukrainian SRs stayed away. Because of these no-shows and arrests, actual attendees numbered between 400 and 500.[118] Lenin observed from the curtained seclusion of the former government box.[119] On the floor, the Bolshevik caucus was led by the thirty-year-old Nikolai Bukharin, well described by John Reed as "a short red-bearded man with the eyes of a fanatic—'more left than Lenin,' they said of him."[120] The delegates elected SR party chairman Victor Chernov as Assembly chairman; the Bolsheviks backed the Left SR Maria Spiridonova, a renowned terrorist, who won an impressive 153 votes, 91 fewer than Chernov. A Bolshevik motion to limit the scope of the Constituent Assembly failed (237 to 146). Lenin had one loyalist, the leader of the Baltic sailors, announce that Bolshevik delegates were walking out; the Left SR delegates, including Spiridonova, walked out later.[121] Some twelve hours in, around 4:00 a.m., a sailor of the Baltic fleet mounted the stage, tapped Chernov's shoulder (or pulled his sleeve) and bellowed that the Bolshevik navy commissar "wants those present to leave the hall." When Chernov answered, "That is for the Constituent Assembly to decide, if you don't mind," the sailor responded, "I suggest you leave the hall, as it's late and the guards are tired."[122] Chernov rushed through snap votes on laws and adjourned at 4:40 a.m. Later that afternoon (January 6), when delegates arrived to resume, sentries refused them entry.[123] Russia's Constituent Assembly ended after a single day, never to meet again. (Even the original of the meeting protocols would be stolen from Chernov's émigré residence in Prague.)[124]

Bolshevik threats had been no secret.[125] "We are not about to share power with anyone," Trotsky wrote of the Constituent Assembly before it opened. "If we are to stop halfway, then it wouldn't be a revolution, it would be an abortion . . . a false historical delivery."[126] The Socialist Revolutionary Party had carried the Southwestern, Romanian, and Caucasus fronts decisively, yet the SR leadership failed to bring troops to the capital or even to accept an offer of armed aid from the Petrograd garrison.[127] Some SR leaders abjured the use of force on principle; most fretted that attempts to mobilize willing soldiers to defend the elected legislature would serve as a pretext for the Bolsheviks to close it down, which the Bolsheviks did anyway.[128] No imperative to defend the Constituent Assembly was felt in the countryside, where the peasant revolution had helped sweep away the full panoply of tsarist officialdom, from provincial governors to local police and the land captains, who were replaced by peasant self-governance.[129] In the capital, tens of thousands of protesters, including factory workers, marched to the Tauride Palace to try to save the Constituent Assembly, but Bolshevik loyalists fired on them.[130] This was the first time civilians in Russian cities had been gunned down for political reasons since February and July 1917, but the Bolsheviks got away with it.

The Petrograd Soviet's existence helped diminish popular attachment to a Constituent Assembly.[131] Lenin characterized the Bolshevized Soviet as a "higher form" of democracy, not the procedural or bourgeois kind celebrated in Britain and France, but the democracy of social justice and (lower class) people's power. This view resonated widely in Russia, even if far from everyone accepted Lenin's tendentious equation of the overwhelmingly socialist Constituent Assembly with "bourgeois" democracy.[132] Reinforcing the point, the Sverdlov-dominated central executive committee of the Soviet had prescheduled a Third All-Russia Congress of Soviets for January 10, which happened to be immediately after the Constituent Assembly would be dispersed.[133] Many of the delegates boycotted the gathering in protest, but those present retroactively legalized the forced closure of the Constituent Assembly.[134]

## TROTSKY'S FAILURE

Peace! Immediate, universal peace, for all countries, for all peoples: Bolshevism's popularity had been propelled, above all else, by a promised extrication from the hated war. At the Second Congress of Soviets, however, Lenin had suddenly equivocated. "The new power would do everything," he promised, "but we do not say that we can end the war simply by sticking our bayonets in the ground . . . we do not say that we shall make peace today or tomorrow."[135] (Newspaper accounts of his remarks omitted these words.) The "Decree on Peace"—which mentioned England, France, and Germany, but not the United States, "as the mightiest powers taking part in the present war"—by the congress had invited all belligerents to observe a three-month armistice and negotiate a "just democratic . . . immediate peace, without annexations and without indemnities." (Other Bolshevik proclamations invited citizens of those belligerents to overthrow their governments.)[136] Lenin and Stalin radioed instructions to Russia's troops—hardly necessary—to desist from fighting. Lenin sent German military headquarters an uncoded offer of unconditional cease-fire, knowing that the Entente, too, would receive the message (when they did, they felt confirmed in their belief he was a German agent). Britain and France refused to recognize the Bolshevik regime and did not respond either to the Peace Decree or to formal notes from Trotsky. The Entente did send communiqués to Russia's military field headquarters.[137] A sailor working for Trotsky, meanwhile, was rifling Russian foreign ministry vaults and located the secret annexationist tsarist war treaties with Britain and France; Trotsky published the documents damning the Entente, referred to as "the imperialists."[138] (Newspapers in the Allied countries almost universally failed to reproduce the exposed texts.)[139] What, if anything, could be done about the ever more proximate German army remained unclear.

Russia's high command at Mogilyov, 400 miles southwest of Petrograd, had taken no part in the October coup, but they had been devastated by the revolution they had accelerated with their request in February 1917 for the tsar's abdication. On November 8, 1917, Lenin and Trotsky had radioed Russia's acting supreme commander, forty-one-year-old General Nikolai Dukhonin—Kornilov's former chief of staff—to enter into separate peace negotiations with the Germans. Dukhonin refused the order to betray Russia's allies. Lenin had the correspondence distributed to all units to show that the "counterrevolution" wanted to continue the war. He also dismissed Dukhonin in favor of thirty-two-year-old Nikolai Krylenko, who heretofore had held the lowest rank in Russia's officer corps (ensign).[140] On November 20, 1917, he arrived at Mogilyov with a trainload of pro-Bolshevik soldiers and sailors. Dukhonin duly surrendered to him.[141] Having chosen not to flee, Dukhonin had nonetheless not prevented the escape of General Kornilov and other top tsarist officers who had been held in the nearby monastery prison since they had surrendered to Kerensky's people (in September 1917). Upon discovering the escape, furious soldiers and sailors shot and bayoneted Dukhonin while he lay face down on the ground, and then for several days used his naked corpse for target practice.[142] Krylenko was either unable or unwilling to stop them. Unlike generals Alexeyev and Brusilov before him, the ensign did not tour the full battlefields. But he got the picture nonetheless: the Russian army was not demoralized; it effectively no longer existed.

Germany also had reasons to seek accommodation, however. Self-negotiated cease-fires between German and Russian soldiers began to spread up and down the eastern front. Some experts were predicting food shortages and civil unrest on the German homefront that winter of 1917–18, troubles that loomed even more gravely for Austria-Hungary. The ferocious battles against France and Britain on the western front continued, now with the United States having joined the Entente. Ludendorff had decided to gather all his forces for a great spring offensive in the west—and troops that were, presumably, released from the east would come in handy. All of these considerations, and a desire to consolidate its immense gains on the eastern front, induced the Central Powers on November 15, 1917 (November 28 in the West) to accept the Bolshevik offer of armistice as a prelude to negotiations.[143] Although the Bolsheviks had advocated for a general, not a separate, peace, the Entente repeatedly refused to participate in talks, and that same day Trotsky and Lenin announced that "if the bourgeoisie of the Allied countries force us to conclude a separate peace [with the Central Powers], the responsibility will be theirs."[144] For the site of negotiations, the Bolsheviks had proposed Pskov, which remained under Russian control (and where Nicholas II had abdicated), but Germany chose the Brest-Litovsk fortress, in a tsarist territory now serving as a German command site.[145] The armistice was quickly signed there on December 2 (December 15 in the West). (In immediate violation of the terms, Germany moved six divisions back to the western front.)[146] One week later the peace talks opened.

Upon arrival, the Bolshevik Karl Radek—born Karl Sobelsohn in Habsburg Lemberg (Lwów)—had hurled antiwar propaganda out the train window at rank-and-file German soldiers, urging them to rebel against their commanders.[147] Seated across the table from the German state secretary for foreign affairs, Baron Richard von Kühlmann, and the chief of staff of German armies in the East, Major General Max Hoffman, Radek leaned forward and blew smoke. At the opening dinner in the officers' mess, one member of the Russian delegation, a Left SR, kindly reenacted her assassination of a tsarist governor for the meeting's host, Field Marshal Prince Leopold of Bavaria. The head of the Bolshevik delegation, Adolf Joffe—whom the Austrian foreign minister, Count Ottokar Czernin, pointedly noted was a Jew—observed that "I very much hope that we will be able to raise the revolution also in your country."[148] Thus did the leftist plebes of the Russian Pale of Settlement and Caucasus square off against titled German aristocrats and warlords of the world's most formidable military caste.[149] After some initial misunderstandings, it soon became evident that the Bolshevik demand for "peace without indemnities and annexations" would never be met; the German and Austrian delegations, invoking "self-determination," demanded Russian recognition of the independence of Poland, Lithuania, and western Latvia, all of which the Central Powers had occupied in 1914–16.[150] The Bolsheviks' only salvation appeared to be waiting for war strains to precipitate revolution in Germany and Austria-Hungary (if the war did not cause the Entente homefronts to collapse first).[151] For a second round of "negotiations," Lenin sent Trotsky to

grandstand and stall.[152] The Bolsheviks had gotten the Germans to permit publicity about the talks, which encouraged much public posturing, and Trotsky's
performance at Brest-Litovsk catapulted him to international renown. Smiling
through a long German diatribe about Bolshevik repression of political opponents, Trotsky, at his turn, unloaded: "We do not arrest strikers but capitalists
who subject workers to lock-outs. We do not shoot peasants who demand land,
but arrest the landowners and officers who try to shoot peasants."[153]

Trotsky soon telegrammed Lenin to advise that the talks be cut off without
a treaty. "I'll consult with Stalin and give you my answer," Lenin cabled. The
answer turned out to be a recess in early January 1918, during which Trotsky
returned to Petrograd for consultations.

The Bolshevik Central Committee met on January 8 to discuss Germany, two
days after the forcible dispersal of the Constituent Assembly and right after an
official report, delivered by Mikhail Bonch-Bruevich, the brother of Lenin's fixer
Vladimir, warning that "the onset of total famine in the army is a matter of the
next few days."[154] Back when Lenin had pushed for a coup he had insisted that
Germany stood close to revolution, but now he changed his tune: the world revolution remained a dream, he observed, while Russia's socialist revolution was a
fact; to save the latter, he urged accepting whatever terms the Germans offered.[155]
Trotsky countered that Germany would not resume fighting, obviating any need
to capitulate. But a self-styled leftist Bolshevik group led by Nikolai Bukharin
and including Dzierżyński, Mężyński, and Radek, argued for a *Russian* resumption of hostilities. They deemed Lenin's position defeatist. Thus the Central
Committee split three ways: capitulation (Lenin); stall and bluff (Trotsky); revolutionary partisan warfare to accelerate revolution in Europe (Bukharin). Of the
sixteen voting Central Committee members present on January 9, only three—
most prominently Stalin—sided with Lenin.

Stalin objected that "Trotsky's position is no position," adding "there is no
revolutionary movement in the West, nothing exists, only potential, and we cannot count on potential. If the Germans begin an offensive, it will strengthen the
counter-revolution here." He further noted that "in October we spoke of a holy
war, because we were told that merely the word 'peace' would provoke a revolution in the West. But this was wrong."[156] Bukharin, by contrast, came around to
conceding that "Trotsky's position"—waiting for the workers in Berlin and
Vienna to strike—"is the most correct." Trotsky's proposal ("end the war, do not
sign a peace, demobilize the army") carried the day, 9–7.[157] After the meeting,

Lenin wrote that the majority "do not take into consideration the change in conditions that demand a speedy and abrupt change in tactics."[158] That was Lenin for you: rabidly against any concessions whatsoever to moderate Russian socialists, but demanding the Communists make abject concessions to German militarists.

A Third Congress of Soviets assembled on January 10, 1918 (lasting until the eighteenth), with Bolshevik delegates in a slight majority (860 of 1,647 by the end, as more delegates kept arriving). Meeting at the Tauride Palace, it passed a resolution to erase all references in any future compendia of Soviet decrees to the recently dispersed Constituent Assembly. Stalin gave a report as commissar of nationalities, and the congress formally established the Russian Soviet Federated Socialist Republic (RSFSR). Commenting on the Constituent Assembly, Stalin concluded, "In America they have general elections, and the ones who end up in power are attendants of the billionaire Rockefeller. Is that not a fact? We buried bourgeois parliamentarism, and the Martovites want to drag us back to the period of the February Revolution. (Laughter, applause.) But as representatives of the workers, we need the people to be not merely voters but also rulers. The ones who exercise authority are not those who elect and vote but those who rule."[159] Trotsky reported on Brest-Litovsk. "When Trotsky ended his great speech," one British enthusiast reported, "the immense assembly of Russian workmen, soldiers and peasants rose and . . . sang the Internationale."[160] Despite a mood for revolutionary war, however, the congress avoided a binding resolution one way or the other. Trotsky returned to Brest-Litovsk on January 17 (January 30 in the West) to stall further.

In Petrograd the next day, the Bolshevik Central Committee argued over whether to summon a party conference to discuss a possible separate peace. "What party conference?" Lenin snapped. Sverdlov deemed it impossible to organize a full party conference quickly enough and proposed consulting with representatives of the provinces. Stalin lamented the lack of clarity in the party's position, and, reversing himself somewhat, suggested that "the middle view—the position of Trotsky—had given us a way out of this difficult situation." Stalin proposed to "give the spokesmen for different points of view more chance to be heard and call a meeting to reach a clear position."[161] Trotsky had a point: Russia's war effort was not the only one disintegrating. The Central Powers, too, were under colossal strain: in Germany a strike wave was suppressed, but mass deprivation from a British blockade persisted; Austria was begging Germany, and even Bulgaria, for emergency food.[162] In the meantime, however, the Germans turned up a trump card: a delegation from the Ukrainian government, known as the Central Rada—socialist but non-Bolshevik—had showed up at Brest-Litovsk. The lead German civilian politican called the group of people in their twenties "young ladies" (*Bürschchen*), but on January 27 (February 9 in the West), Germany duly signed a treaty with them.[163] Never mind that, by this point, Red Guards from Russia had deposed the Central Rada in Kiev.[164] The Central Rada representatives promised Germany and Austria Ukrainian grain, manganese, and eggs in exchange for military assistance against Bolshevik forces and the establishment of a Ruthenian (Ukrainian) autonomous region in Austrian Galicia and the Bukovina. (Austria's Czernin called it the Bread Peace.)[165] Whatever the aspirations of Ukrainian intellectuals and political figures, independent Ukraine, for Germany, was a tool to subdue Russia and support the Reich's war effort in the West.[166]

With Ukraine seemingly in their pocket, the German delegation felt triumphant. The next day (January 28, February 10 in the West), Trotsky arrived to deliver a long indictment of "imperialism," which the German delegation took as a windy prelude to Bolshevik capitulation. It had been some fifty days since the Brest-Litovsk talks commenced; the Russian army had essentially evaporated. But instead of bowing before these realities, Trotsky ended his speech by proclaiming a policy of "neither war, nor peace." That is, Russia was exiting the war while refusing to sign a treaty. After a silence, German Major-General Hoffmann, architect of the great victory at Tannenberg, muttered, "Unheard of."[167] The Bolshevik delegation exited to board a train. "On the return trip to Petrograd," Trotsky recalled, "we were all under the impression that the Germans would not start an offensive."[168] An ambiguous telegram from Brest about "peace" to the Soviet capital had sparked telegrams from Petrograd to the front, where soldiers broke out in song and ceremonial firing of guns, to celebrate "the peace."[169] Trotsky arrived back at Smolny amid jubilation on January 31, 1918. (The next day in Russia would be February 14, thanks to the introduction of the Western Gregorian calendar.) A skeptical Lenin wondered if Trotsky might have pulled off a magician's trick. A diplomatic cable from Brest-Litovsk to Vienna prompted preparations for a victory celebration in the exhausted Habsburg capital: huge crowds filled the streets and bunting started to go up.[170]

But the Germany brass insisted that they would never get the promised Ukrainian grain without a military occupation. At a German war council on

February 13—the same day that Trotsky had arrived back at Smolny—Field Marshal Hindenburg pointed out that the armistice had failed to result in a peace treaty and therefore no longer held; he urged a policy to "smash the Russians [and] topple their government." The kaiser agreed.[171] Some 450,000 Central Power troops entered Ukraine, with the deposed Central Rada's permission. (Angry riots erupted among Polish speakers over the promises to Ukraine in Galicia; Polish troops entering Ukraine under Habsburg command broke off into their own armed force.)[172] A parallel German force (fifty-two divisions), beginning on February 18—eight days after Trotsky's coup de théâtre—would waltz 125 miles through northern Russian territory in two weeks, capturing Minsk, Mogilyov, and Narva, putting the Germans on an unobstructed path to Petrograd. "This is the most comic war I have experienced," Hoffmann noted of his operation (named Thunderbolt). "One puts on the train a few infantry with machine guns and one artillery piece, and proceeds to the next railroad station, seizes it, arrests the Bolsheviks, entrains another detachment, and moves on."[173]

## QOQAND MASSACRE

Events elsewhere on the former Russian imperial space followed a dynamic dictated neither by the geopolitics of Germany versus the Entente nor by the acrimonious duets of Trotsky and Lenin. The Soviet in Tashkent, comprising primarily Slavic colonists and garrison troops, had succeeded in seizing power on its second try on October 23, 1917, even before the Bolshevik coup in Petrograd. In mid-November, a local Congress of Soviets gathered essentially without any indigeneous members.[174] "The soldiers sent thither from the interior provinces of Russia, the peasants settled therein by the old regime on the lands confiscated from our people, and the workers accustomed to regard us haughtily from above—these were the people who were at this moment to decide the fate of Turkestan," recalled Mustafa Choqai-Beg, a Muslim leader.[175] The Tashkent Congress of Soviets voted 97 to 17 to deny Muslims governmental posts.[176] Muslim scholars who composed the ulama and who took it for granted that they spoke for the mass, were gathering simultaneously in their own congress, in another part of Tashkent, and, being accustomed to petitioning the colonial authorities, voted overwhelmingly to petition the Tashkent Soviet to form a more representative local political body, given that "the Muslims of Turkestan . . . comprise 98 percent of the population."[177] At the same time, a different group of Muslims, self-styled modernists known as the Jadid, saw an opportunity to outflank the traditional ulama and, in early December 1917, assembled in Qoqand, a walled city that had been captured by the Russians only thirty-four years earlier. With nearly 200 representatives, including 150 from the nearby populous Ferghana valley, this congress resolved on December 11 to declare "Turkestan territorially autonomous in union with the Federal Democratic Russian Republic," while vowing to protect local national minorities (Slavs) "in every possible way."[178] They constituted a Provisional Government and elected a delegation to the Constituent Assembly, reserving one third of the seats for non-Muslims. The congress also debated whether to seek an alliance with the anti-Bolshevik steppe Cossacks, a proposition that divided the delegates but seemed inescapable as the only path to continuing to import grain: local farmers had almost all been switched by the tsarist regime to growing cotton.

Qoqand Autonomy representatives went to Tashkent on December 13 to announce their existence on the Soviet's territory. It was a Friday (the Muslim holy day) and, as it happened, Muhammad's birthday. Tens of thousands of men, many wearing white turbans and carrying green or light blue flags, marched toward the Russian quarter of the city. Even many ulama joined, as did some moderate Russians. The marchers demanded an end to household searches and requisitions, and stormed the prison, freeing the inmates incarcerated by the Tashkent Soviet.[179] Russian troops fired at the crowd, killing several; more died in a resulting stampede.[180] The prisoners were recaptured and executed.

Dominated by Muslim intellectuals educated in imperial Russia, the Qoqand Autonomy's leaders petitioned the Bolshevik authorities in the Russian capital "to recognize the Provisional Government of autonomous Turkestan as the only government of Turkestan" and to authorize the immediate dissolution of the Tashkent Soviet, "which relies on foreign elements hostile to the native population of the country, contrary to the principle of self-determination of peoples."[181] Stalin, as nationalities commissar, issued the reply. "The soviets are autonomous in their internal affairs and discharge their duties by relying on their actual forces," he wrote. "Therefore, it will not behoove the native proletarians of Turkestan to appeal to the central Soviet authority with petitions to dissolve the Turkestan Council of People's Commissars." He added that if the Qoqand Autonomy felt that the Tashkent Soviet had to go, "they should themselves dissolve it by force, if such force is available to the native proletarians and peasants."[182] Here was naked admission both of the central Bolsheviks' powerlessness and of the role of force in determining revolutionary outcomes. But, of course, the Tashkent Soviet commanded the arms inherited from the tsarist-era colonial garrisons. The Qoqand Autonomy tried but failed to form a people's militia (it managed three score volunteers). It lacked the wherewithal to levy taxes and its diplomatic missions to the steppe Qazaqs and the emirate of Bukhara yielded nothing. After the Bolsheviks' dispersal of the Constituent Assembly, Qoqand tried to coax the Tashkent Soviet into convening a Turkestan Constituent Assembly—which, of course, would have returned an overwhelming Muslim majority. On February 14, the Tashkent Soviet mobilized local garrison troops, other soldiers from the Orenburg steppes, Armenian Dashnaks, and armed Slavic workers to crush the "counterfeit autonomy," setting siege to Qoqand's old city. Within four days they breached the walls and set about massacring the population. An estimated 14,000 Muslims were slaughtered, many of them machine-gunned; the city was looted, then burned.[183] The Tashkent Soviet used the moment to step up requisitions of food stocks, unleashing a famine, in which perhaps 900,000 people would perish, as well as mass flight toward Chinese Turkestan.[184] Stalin and the Bolsheviks would have their work cut out in marrying the revolution and the anti-colonial question in practice.

## CAPITULATION

No reliable Bolshevik forces stood in the path of Major General Max Hoffmann's eastward-marching German army. "For us, as well as from the international socialist point of view, the preservation of the [Soviet] republic stands above all else," Lenin argued at a Central Committee meeting on February 18, the very day Hoffmann had renewed the German advance.[185] For Lenin, ceding territories that the Bolsheviks did not rule anyway—and, in his mind, ceding them only temporarily, until the world revolution—constituted a price worth paying. Initially, however, Lenin again failed to muster a Central Committee majority. Stalin stood by Lenin once more. "We want to talk straight, go straight to the heart of the matter," Stalin said at the Central Committee on February 18. "The Germans are attacking, we have no forces, the time has come to say that negotiations must be resumed."[186] This statement constituted an unambiguous repudiation of Trotsky's position. Trotsky, throughout, had been the swing figure, and he remained so now. Sometime before he had returned to Brest-Litovsk in mid-January, Lenin had held a confidential tête-à-tête with him; each man evidently held to his arguments, but Lenin pointedly asked Trotsky what he would do if in fact the Germans did resume their offensive, and no revolutionary uprisings in Germany's rear broke out. Would the capitulatory peace have to be signed? Trotsky had evidently agreed that if those circumstances were to come to pass, he would not oppose Lenin's call for accepting a punitive peace on German terms.[187] And now, Trotsky kept his word, rescinding his no vote. This gave Lenin a 7 to 5 majority (with one abstention) for immediate capitulation, against the advocates for "revolutionary war."[188]

A radiogram under the signatures of Lenin and Trotsky agreeing to the original terms was dispatched to the Germans.[189] But the Germans did not respond; and Major General Hoffmann continued his march. On February 21, German forces began intervening in the Finnish civil war, where the October coup had split officers of the imperial Russian army. (German troops would help nationalist Finns led by General Carl Gustav Mannerheim rout Red Guards and overthrow a Bolshevik-backed Finnish Socialist Workers Republic.)[190] The failure to have accepted German terms immediately now looked like a far larger gamble. Aside from Ukraine and the southern Cossack lands (4.5 million people), "Soviet power" had everywhere seemed triumphant, but the silence out of Berlin made the February 18, 1918, resumption of a German military attack on the eastern front seem a potential turning point in the socialist revolution.[191] This proved to be among the bloodiest single episodes of the war in per capita terms. More desperate than ever, Lenin had Trotsky put out feelers to the Entente, trying to appeal to French imperialists to save the socialist revolution from German imperialists.[192] "We are turning the party into a dung hill," Bukharin, in tears, exclaimed to Trotsky.[193] "All of us, including Lenin," Trotsky recalled, "were of the impression that the Germans had come to an agreement with the Allies about crushing the Soviets."[194] For that, both Trotsky and Bukharin would have borne the responsibility.

Finally, on the morning of February 23, the German response to the Bolshevik capitulation arrived by courier: It took the form of an ultimatum whose terms were far more onerous than before Trotsky's posturing of neither war, nor peace. That same afternoon the Central Committee grimly assembled. Sverdlov detailed the German conditions: Soviet Russia would also have to recognize the independence—under German occupation—of the breadbasket of Ukraine, as well as the oil of the Caspian Sea and the strategic Baltic ports of Finland and Estonia, all to be dominated by Germany. Further, the Bolsheviks would have to disarm all Red Guards, decommission their navy, and pay a colossal indemnity. In other words, the Germans were continuing to place a large bet on Bolshevism, while at the same time containing it and extracting advantage. To accept, the Bolsheviks were given forty-eight hours, much of which had already passed while the German document was in transit. Lenin stated that "the terms must be accepted," otherwise, he would resign, a threat he put in writing (in *Pravda*).[195] Sverdlov backed Lenin. But Trotsky and Dzierżyński urged rejection. So did Bukharin. Another hard-line leftist called Lenin's bluff, stating, "There is no reason to be frightened by Lenin's threat to resign. We must take power without V.I. [Lenin]." Even Stalin—among Lenin's staunchest allies throughout Brest-Litovsk—blinked. He suggested that "it's possible not to sign, but to begin peace negotiations," adding that "the Germans are provoking us into a refusal." This could have been a breakthrough moment, when Stalin tipped the balance, breaking Lenin's hold on power. But Lenin countered that "Stalin is mistaken," and repeated his insistence on accepting the German diktat to save the Soviet regime. Stalin's brief vacillation ended. Partly that was because Trotsky swung Lenin's way. Trotsky pointed out that the terms "were best of all when Kamenev made the first trip [to Brest-Litovsk] and it would have been better if Kamenev and Joffe had signed the peace" back then. Anyway, "now things were quite clear." Thanks to four abstentions—including, crucially, Trotsky—Lenin, supported by Sverdlov and Stalin, won the Central Committee vote: 7 to 4.[196]

Over at the Tauride Palace, where the central executive committee of the Soviet was in session and included non-Bolsheviks such as a large Left SR faction and some Mensheviks, the arguments resumed late at night and continued into the morning of February 24, when the German ultimatum would expire at 7:00 a.m. Jeers of "Traitor!" greeted Lenin when he mounted the dais. "Give me an army of 100,000 men, an army which will not tremble before the enemy, and I will not sign the peace," he replied. "Can you raise an army?" At 4:30 a.m., capitulation to the German diktat passed 116 to 85, with 26 abstentions: the Left SRs provided much of the opposition.[197] Lenin hurried to have a note dispatched to the Germans from the special radio transmitter at Tsarskoe Selo.[198] Neither Trotsky nor anybody else in the inner circle wanted to return to Brest-Litovsk to sign the humiliating treaty. The task fell to Grigory Sokolnikov, who had evidently suggested Zinoviev and then was himself "volunteered."[199] The Bolshevik delegation arrived back in Brest-Litovsk, but had to cool their heels while the German army seized Kiev on March 1–2, 1918, reinstalling the Central Rada government, and presented new Turkish demands for still more Russian territorial concessions in the Caucasus. The signing took place on March 3. "It is your day now," Radek snapped bitterly at Major General Hoffmann, "but in the end the Allies will put a Brest-Litovsk treaty upon you."[200] Radek was right: the Allies did become convinced, largely as a result of Brest-Litovsk, that imperial Germany was incapable of moderation and a negotiated peace, and needed to be defeated.

Trotsky—too clever by half—had miscalculated, and he now resigned as foreign affairs commissar (Lenin would appoint him commissar of war instead). But Lenin had been the one who had maniacally pushed for the October coup, and he was the one now vilified for the captiulatory peace.[201] Russia was compelled to renounce 1.3 million square miles of territory—lands more than twice the size of Germany, and lands imperial Russia had spilled blood and treasure to conquer over centuries from Sweden, Poland, the Ottoman empire, and others. The amputation removed a quarter of Russia's population (some 50 million people), a third of its industry, and more than a third of its grain fields.[202] Germany now sat in titular command of a vast eastward wedge, stretching from the Arctic to the Black Sea. Equally spectacular, subjects of imperial Germany and Austria-Hungary received exemptions from Bolshevik nationalization decrees, meaning they could own private property and engage in commercial activities on Soviet Russian soil, and German nationals who had lost property from tsarist confiscations were now owed compensation. The Bolsheviks became duty bound to demobilize their army and navy and cease international propaganda (the Germans considered Bolshevik propaganda far more dangerous than any Russian troops).[203] No Russian government had ever surrendered so much territory or sovereignty.

Doom enveloped Petrograd. A year had passed since the heady days of Nicholas II's abdication, on March 2, 1917, when the tsar had pointedly asked two Duma representatives, "Would there not be consequences?" A mere five months had lapsed since Boris Avilov, a Menshevik Internationalist, had stood up on October 27, 1917, at the Second Congress of Soviets during the Bolshevik coup and predicted that an all-Bolshevik government could neither solve the food supply crisis nor end the war, that the Entente would not recognize a Bolshevik-monopoly government, and that the Bolsheviks would be compelled to accept a separate and onerous peace with Germany. That day had come. On top of everything, Russia's wartime allies now instituted a de facto economic blockade, and soon would seize Russia's assets abroad.[204]

Lenin's party was divided and demoralized.[205] At the 7th (Extraordinary) Party Congress in the Tauride Palace on March 5–8, 1918, a mere 46 delegates turned up (compared with the nearly 200 at the last Party Congress in the summer of 1917). The self-styled Left Communists, who had been among the strongest supporters of Lenin's putsch in 1917, rejected Brest-Litovsk. Bukharin and other leftist Bolsheviks even established a new periodical, *Communist,* expressly to denounce the "obscene" treaty, and at the congress took the floor to urge "revolutionary war" against imperial Germany. Lenin put through a name change from Russian Social Democratic Workers' Party (Bolsheviks) to Russian Communist party (Bolsheviks) and pleaded for party acceptance of Brest-Litovsk. The recriminations raged over three days. Lenin pointed out that his opponents had caused the catastrophe by refusing to accept the initial, better German offer. He won the vote 30 to 12, with 4 abstentions (including, again, Trotsky).[206] And yet, this vote was in many ways merely an exercise in affirming the leader's authority: Lenin insisted on signing the treaty, but he had already ceased to believe that even the Brest-Litovsk concessions would be enough to halt the German advance on Petrograd. On February 24, the day Lenin telegrammed acceptance of German terms, Major General Hoffmann seized Pskov, 150 miles southwest from, and on the direct rail line to, the Russian capital. On February 26, Lenin had approved a secret order to abandon the capital of Russia's revolution. It was a rich irony. After Kerensky's Provisional Government had decided to relocate from Petrograd to Moscow for safety in early October 1917, the Bolshevik newspaper *Workers' Path*—edited by Stalin—had accused Kerensky of treason for surrendering the capital to the Germans.[207] Kerensky had backed down.[208] But now—again, just as Lenin's accusers had long predicted—he had not only handed the Germans everything but was preparing to desert the Russian capital.

## FLIGHT AND ENTRENCHMENT

Bolshevik evacuation preparations, rumored on newspaper front pages for months, could not be concealed. Already in late February 1918, the American and Japanese diplomatic missions had relocated for safety to Vologda, while the French and British sought to exit Russia entirely via Finland to Sweden: only the British got through; the French ended up stranded at Vologda, too (where Stalin had been in exile). Vladimir Bonch-Bruevich, chairman of the government's "intelligence operations"—a room in Smolny—used ruses to ensure Lenin's security: freight stamped "Council of People's Commissars" was loaded in plain sight at a central passenger station, while under cover of darkness, at a derelict depot south of Petrograd, a train of former imperial carriages was secretly assembled. Bonch-Bruevich sent two teams of agents unknown to each other (*okhranka* style) to maintain surveillance on the disused spur, eavesdrop on nearby "tea" houses, and spread rumors of a train being prepared for doctors heading to the front. Some cars were loaded with wood fuel, typewriters, and telephones; flatbeds were added for automobiles. Bonch-Bruevich had also filled two cars just with Bolshevik party literature (not including his own personal library).[209] On the evening of Sunday, March 10, the secret train—carrying Lenin, his sister and wife, the poet Yefim Pridvorov (aka Demyan Bedny), Sverdlov, Stalin, Cheka head Dzierżyński with a single briefcase, and a detachment of guards—departed with the lights off. Two trains carrying the Soviet's central executive committee (many of whom were not Bolsheviks) followed at a distance, not knowing what was in front of them. Anxiety was high: seventy-five miles southeast of Petrograd, Lenin's train was delayed when it unexpectedly crossed paths with a train carrying demobilized armed troops. Only when Lenin's train pulled within three station stops of Moscow did Bonch-Bruevich alert the Moscow soviet of the train's existence. Arriving at 8:00 p.m. on March 11, Lenin was greeted by a small party of "workers," addressed the Moscow soviet, and took up residence in the gilt National Hotel, where an accompanying team of telegraphists was also billeted.[210]

What arrived on the main train was the "state" as of March 1918: Lenin's person, a handful of loyal lieutenants, Bolshevik ideas and some means to spread them, an armed guard.

The armed guard was especially unusual. A desperate call to form a defense force "from the class-conscious and best elements of the working classes" had been issued in mid-January 1918, during the Brest-Litovsk talks, when the Germans were marching eastward without obstacle, but nothing came of the summons.[211] On the train escorting the revolution to the new capital of Moscow were the Latvian Riflemen of the tsarist army. Before the Great War, the Russian imperial army had refused to countenance expressly national units; only in 1914–15 had the authorities permitted Czechoslovak, Serbo-Croatian, and Polish volunteer "legions," made up of POWs who wanted to return to fighting to help liberate their compatriots under Habsburg rule. Finns were denied such permission, but in August 1915, Russia allowed all-volunteer Latvian brigades, aiming to exploit their antagonism to Germany. By 1916–17, the two Latvian brigades had ballooned to some 18,000 troops in eight regiments (eventually ten), each named for a Latvian town, but also including ethnic Hungarians, Finns, and others. After heavy casualties in winter 1916–17 fighting, they had turned against the tsarist system. Most were landless peasants or small tenant farmers, and they leaned heavily Social Democratic. By 1917, their homeland had broken off from Russia, under German occupation. Still, it was the decision of their authoritative commander, Colonel Jukums Vācietis (b. 1873), the sixth son among eight children of a landless peasant family from tsarist Courland, whose Russian teacher had been a radical student Populist, to bring the soldiers over to the Bolshevik side.[212] The Latvians guarding Lenin's train were the only disciplined, all-purpose force standing between Bolshevism and oblivion.

Other trains to Moscow hauled storehouses of valuables: the naval staff took files, maps, office equipment, furniture, curtains, rugs, mirrors, ashtrays, stoves, kitchen appliances, dishes, samovars, towels, blankets, and holy icons—1,806 enumerated items in all.[213] A foreign affairs commissariat train carted off "gold goblets, gilt spoons, knives and the like" from the imperial vaults.[214] But what Moscow held in store remained to be seen. "Bourgeois circles are gleeful about the fact that by a strange twist of fate we are realizing the Slavophiles' timeless dream of returning the capital to Moscow," Zinoviev remarked. "We are profoundly convinced that the change of capital will not last long and that the difficult conditions dictating its necessity will pass."[215] The Moscow Council of People's Commissars was taking no chances, having promptly declared its "independence" the day the Petrograd government arrived. Lenin appointed a commission of himself, Stalin, and Sverdlov to take down what they called the parallel "Muscovite Tsardom."[216]

In the meantime, an armed quest for usable property drew in all. Moscow resembled an overgrown village, with narrow, dirty streets of rough cobblestone—nothing like the straight, wide avenues of baroque Petrograd—and lacked an accumulation of administrative edifices.[217] The Moscow soviet central executive committee had already claimed the Governor's Mansion; the Moscow soviet itself was left to fight for the once grand, now dilapidated Hotel Dresden (across the street from the Governor's Mansion). Some members of the soviet's central executive committee moved into the National Hotel (rechristened the House of Soviets No. 1), but more ended up at the Hotel Lux, on Moscow's main artery Tverskaya Street.[218] Most state agencies found themselves widely dispersed: the new Supreme Council of the Economy, set up to counteract anarchosyndicalist tendencies in industry, would claim eighty structures, virtually none of them originally built as offices.[219] The war commissariat took over the unluxurious Hotel Red Fleet, also on Tverskaya Street, but additionally claimed the Alexander Military School, the Trading Rows on Red Square, and prime spaces in Moscow's Kitaigorod, the walled inner merchant ward near the Kremlin. The Trade Union Council got an eighteenth-century neoclassical foundling home out along the Moscow River as well as some plush reception space in Moscow's former Nobility Club. The Cheka appropriated the property of two private insurance companies, Yakor (Anchor) and Lloyd's Russian branch, on Bolshaya Lubyanka.[220] Predictably, the scramble was shameless: When members of the Moscow party committee went to occupy a facility they had obtained in a barter deal, they discovered that the kitchen equipment and phone cables had been ripped from the walls, and the lightbulbs were gone.

Moscow's grandest hotel, the Metropole, was an art nouveau jewel that had originally been intended as an opera house. The structure was commissioned by the railway industrialist and arts patron Savva Mamontov (1841–1918), but he was jailed on fraud charges, after which the project changed, resulting in the hotel that opened in 1905. The war altered it nearly beyond recognition and with the revolution, the property was nationalized, rechristened the Second House of the Soviets, its 250 rooms overrun by new regime parvenus. The entrance was barricaded by guards and a pass system was initiated; the interior crawled with bed bugs and higher ups, along with their relatives, cronies, and mistresses. Yefraim Sklyansky, Trotsky's top deputy at the war commissariat, had commandeered several apartments on different floors for his "clan." Bukharin lived here, as did his future lover Anna Larina, then a child (they met when she was four and he, twenty-nine). Foreign Affairs Commissar Georgy Chicherin and many foreign affairs personnel were particularly well ensconced; many had offices here, too. The commissariat of trade got a two-room junior suite with bathtub. Yakov Sverdlov had his public reception for the Soviet central executive committee upstairs, while formal sessions of that body took place in the disused banquet hall–restaurant. Amid the darkness and severe cold of a capital without fuel, the former opulent hotel degenerated into a filthy wreck. Child residents relieved themselves on the luxury runners in the hallways, on which adults threw lit cigarette butts. The toilets and grand baths were particularly execrable. Fierce scrums broke out over the irregularly distributed state food packets (*payok*) for the elite residents. Packets could include clothes, even coveted overcoats. The "administration" of the Second House of the Soviets, meanwhile, stole everything removable.[221] An opera house it had belatedly become.

But the center of power formed elsewhere. To accommodate the Council of People's Commissars, among the options considered were a hostel for patrician women near the city's medieval Red Gate, or the medieval Kremlin, which, however, had been neglected, physically and politically—the clock on the Savior Gate Tower overlooking Red Square was still chiming "God Save the Tsar" every hour.[222] Whatever the Kremlin's associations with ancient Muscovy or its disrepair, it had high walls and lockable gates, and a unique central location. After a week in the National Hotel, Lenin moved his operations into one of the Kremlin's masterpieces. Catherine the Great had commissioned a residence for the times she was in Moscow; the resultant neoclassicial structure, instead, was built for the Imperial Senate (the Russian empire's highest judicial body), whose spacious, luxurious offices were later given over to the Courts of Justice. Lenin, a lawyer manqué, set up shop on the upper (third) floor in the former suite of the state procurator.[223] The riding stable (manège) just outside the Kremlin gates became the government garage, though most officials made their way in sledges and droshkies commandeered from the populace.[224] The Smolny commandant, Pavel Malkov, a Sverdlov protégé, became the new Kremlin commandant and set about clearing out the nuns and monks from the monastery and nunnery just inside the Savior Gate. Malkov also furnished Lenin's office, found a tailor to clothe the regime, and began stockpiling foodstuffs.[225] For living quarters, Lenin got a two-room apartment in the Kremlin's Cavalry Building in the former residence (now divided up) of the cavalry commander. Trotsky and Sverdlov, too, moved into the Cavalry Building. "Lenin and I took quarters across the corridor, sharing the same dining room," Trotsky later wrote, bragging that "Lenin and I met dozens of times a day in the corridor, and called on each other to talk things over." (They dined on suddenly plentiful red caviar, whose export had ceased.)[226] By the end of 1918, some 1,800 new people (including family members) would obtain Kremlin apartments.

Stalin also took part in this struggle over space. For his nationalities commissariat, he schemed to seize the Grand Siberian Hotel, but the Supreme Council of the Economy had squatted in the building. ("This was one of the few cases," Pestkowski gently noted, "when Stalin suffered defeat.")[227] Instead, Stalin secured a few small, private detached houses, after the Cheka had left them for the insurance buildings. Right before the relocation to the capital, meanwhile, in late February or early March, he appears to have married sixteen-year-old Nadezhda "Nadya" Alliluyeva, the daughter of the skilled worker Sergei Alliluyev, who in the prerevolutionary years had long sheltered Stalin in Tiflis and St. Petersburg.[228] She was still a girl, and remarkably earnest. ("There's real hunger in Petrograd," she wrote to the wife of another Bolshevik on the eve of her wedding to Stalin. "They hand out only an eighth of a pound of bread every day, and one day they gave us none at all. I've even cursed the Bolsheviks.")[229] Her relatives observed the couple quarreling already during the initial "honeymoon" phase of the marriage.[230] Stalin addressed her in the familiar ("ty"); she used the formal ("vy"). He hired her as his secretary in the commissariat (the next year she would shift over to Lenin's secretariat and join the party).[231] The couple obtained a Kremlin apartment, for some reason not in the Cavalry Building with Lenin, Trotsky, and Sverdlov, but in an even more modest three-story outbuilding that serviced Moscow's Grand Kremlin Palace. Their rooms on the second floor of the servants' quarters, in the so-called Frauleins' Corridor, with three opaque windows, carried the new address Communist Street, 2.[232] Stalin complained to Lenin about the noise from the communal kitchen and the vehicles outside, and demanded that Kremlin vehicles be banned from driving beyond the arch where the residential quarters began after 11:00 p.m. (a sign, perhaps, that Stalin was not yet the insomniac he would become).[233] Stalin also acquired a government office inside the Imperial Senate building, like Lenin and Sverdlov, but the Georgian was rarely there.

## CRUELEST MONTHS: SPRING 1918

Ten days after Brest-Litovsk nominally ended hostilities on the eastern front, the German army captured Odessa, way down on the Black Sea coast. Beginning the next day, March 14, the Fourth All-Russia Congress of Soviets convened in Moscow to ratify the treaty. The Soviet's central executive committee had voted to recommend approval—amid shouts of "Judases . . . German spies!"—only thanks to Sverdlov's manipulations, and even then, just barely (abstentions and noes constituted a majority).[234] At the congress, ratification was also fraught. "Suppose that two friends are out walking at night and they are attacked by ten men," Lenin tried reasoning with the delegates. "If the scoundrels isolate one of them, what is the other to do? He cannot render assistance, and if he runs away is he a traitor?"[235] Running from a fight hardly seemed persuasive. Still, of the 1,232 voting delegates—including 795 Bolsheviks and 283 Left Socialist Revolutionaries—784 voted in favor of ratification, 261 against, with the remainder, some 175, abstaining or not voting.[236] The Left Communists were the ones who abstained. But the Bolshevik junior partner Left SRs voted no en masse, declaring their party "not bound by the terms of the Treaty" and quitting the Council of People's Commissars (which they had joined only two months earlier). And Lenin had not even dared to divulge the full treaty provisions before the vote. "We are asked to ratify a treaty the text of which some of us have not seen, at least neither I nor my comrades have seen it," complained the Menshevik leader Yuly Martov. "Do you know what you are signing? I do not. . . . Talk about secret diplomacy!"[237] Martov did not know the half of it: Unbeknownst to the Congress of Soviets delegates, Lenin had authorized Trotsky to conspire with American, British, and French representatives in Russia to obtain pledges of Entente support against the Germans, for which Lenin had promised to sabotage ratification of Brest-Litovsk.

Still viewing Lenin and Trotsky as German agents, Entente governments failed to respond to the offer.[238] But a British Navy squadron, a token force, had landed at the port of Murmansk, on Russia's northwest (Arctic Ocean) coast, on March 9, with the express aim of countering German and Finnish forces threatening Russia's Murmansk Railway as well as military storehouses. More broadly, the British and French wanted to prevent Germany from transferring eastern front divisions to the western front by reviving an eastern front. This desire was vastly heightened as the Central Powers began to occupy and extract the riches of Ukraine. The British, in other words, were intervening initially not to overthrow Bolshevism but to mitigate the Central Powers' newfound war advantages.[239] But what had started out largely as a preemptive move to deny Germany Russian military stores would become, over time, an underfunded campaign against the supposed threat that Communism posed to the British empire in India.[240]

Lenin and Trotsky, for their part, had welcomed the Entente's military landing on Russian soil as a counter to Germany. Stalin, at a Council of People's Commissars meeting on April 2, 1918, with the Germans about to capture Kharkov, proposed shifting policy to seek an anti-German military coalition with the Ukrainian Central Rada, which the Bolsheviks had overthrown just two months before, and which Germany had restored one month before.[241] Stalin's proposal was complementary to Trotsky's about-face negotiations with agents of the Entente to help organize and train a new Red Army, along with railroad operators and equipment. Three days later, Japanese troops, on the pretext of "protecting" Japanese nationals, landed at Vladivostok. Lenin and Trotsky vehemently objected—this was a military intervention they did not invite.

Germany, which was eager to break Japan's alliance with Britain, had encouraged the Japanese intervention against Russia, a landing that raised the prospect of a west-east flanking occupation, based on a common interest, to reduce Russia to a colonial dependency. Lenin, notwithstanding all the fog of his class categories, well understood the possibility of a German-Japanese alliance, just as he had grasped the antagonism of state interests between Germany and Britain on the one hand and, on the other, Japan and the United States.[242] But Lenin struggled to induce Britain and France, let alone the far-off United States, to align with Communist Russia against Germany and Japan. Despite the 1917 rupture, Soviet Russia's strategic position bore resemblance to imperial Russia's. A big difference between past and present, however, was that parts of imperial Russia had broken off, and they could be used by hostile foreign powers against Russia.

Stalin was busy with these lost territories. On March 19, 1918, he wrote to Caucasus Bolsheviks urging them to strengthen the defenses of Baku, and a week later an article of his appeared in *Pravda* denouncing non-Bolshevik leftists ("South Caucasus Counter-Revolutionaries under a Socialist Mask").[243] On March 30, Stalin spoke on the Hughes apparatus to the head of the Tashkent Soviet about developments in Turkestan. On April 3–4, *Pravda* carried an interview with him on a draft constitution on which he was working, based upon a proposed federal structure and new name for Soviet Russia—the Russian Soviet Federated Socialist Republic (RSFSR).[244] On April 9, Stalin dispatched a message, published in *Pravda,* to the soviets of Kazan, Ufa, Orenburg, and Tashkent, indicating that the principle of self-determination had "lost its revolutionary meaning" and could be overridden. On April 29, the Council of People's Commissars appointed Stalin RSFSR plenipotentiary to negotiate a peace treaty with the Ukrainian Central Rada. That same day the Germans, further improvising in the East, betrayed their Ukrainian Central Rada treaty partners, installing a puppet Ukrainian "Hetmanate," a deliberately archaic name, under General Pavlo Skoropadskyj. But his misrule, alongside the Austro-German occupation, provoked peasant insurrections and a many-sided armed conflict.[245] "When the German forces entered Ukraine they found absolute chaos," a German official reported. "Not infrequently, one came across neighboring villages surrounded by trenches and fighting each other for the land of the former landlords."[246] The promised grain stocks that had lured a nearly half-million-man German occupation army failed to materialize.

Stalin had no better success organizing pro-Bolshevik actions on the territory of Ukraine, but in a sign of his increasing visibility and importance—and of Yuly Martov's frustration at Lenin—Martov revived accusations of Stalin's complicity in the spectacular 1907 Tiflis mail coach robbery and the 1908 robbery of a steamship, writing in a Menshevik periodical that Stalin "had been expelled by the party organization for his involvement in expropriations."[247] Stalin sued Martov for slander in a Revolutionary Tribunal and, on April 1, denied the charges in *Pravda*, stating "that, I, Stalin, was never called before the disciplinary committee of any party organization. In particular, I was never expelled." He added—in exquisite irony—that "one has no right to issue accusations like Martov's except with documents in one's hand. It is dishonest to sling mud on the basis of mere rumors."[248] The tribunal convened on April 5 before a full house. Martov was denied a shift to a civil court with jury trial, but he went on the offensive, requesting time to produce documents, explaining that for conspiratorial purposes, no written party records had been kept, but witnesses could back up his claims, and so he would gather affidavits from Georgian Bolsheviks such as Isidor Ramishvili, who had headed the disciplinary body for Stalin's case in 1908, regarding Stalin's participation in a 1908 steamship armed robbery and the near-fatal beating of a worker familiar with Stalin's murky past. Stalin objected that there would be insufficient time to wait for the witnesses. Still, the court postponed its proceedings against Martov for a week and, by some accounts, the Menshevik Boris Nicolaevsky went to collect testimony in the Caucasus, returning with affidavits from Ramishvili as well as Silva Jibladze and others. Once back in Moscow, however, Nicolaevsky is said to have discovered that all other records of the case had vanished. Sverdlov as well as Lenin—who admired Martov, for all their differences—had helped to close out the inquiry.[249] On April 18, 1918, the tribunal found Martov guilty of slander, but only assessed him a reprimand; before the month was out the verdict had been annulled.[250] On May 11, Sverdlov, who oversaw the Martov case from behind the scenes, did have the Soviet's central executive committee approve closure of the Menshevik newspaper for generally printing false information.[251] But Stalin's bandit past would never go away.[252]

## CZECHOSLOVAK LEGION REVOLT

General Alexeyev, Nicholas II's former chief of staff and then supreme commander, had formed a clandestine network of officers after February 1917; following the Bolshevik coup, he summoned them to constitute a Volunteer Army among the Don Cossacks at Novocherkassk.[253] The Volunteer Army began with a mere 400 to 500 officers. Among them was Kornilov, himself of Cossack pedigree, who, upon release from the prison near Mogilyov, traveled south disguised in peasant rags with a forged Romanian passport.[254] Because the sixty-one-year-old Alexeyev had cancer, he assigned the military command to the forty-eight-year-old Kornilov, even though the two never really got along. Kornilov's forces—former tsarist officers, Cossacks, military school cadets (teenagers)—came under heavy assault from mid-February 1918. He sought sanctuary, marching a few thousand Volunteers southeastward toward the Kuban through heavy snow and barren steppes with little shelter or food other than what they plundered. Volunteers taken prisoner had their eyes gouged out—and they responded in kind. ("The more terror, the more victories!" Kornilov exhorted.)[255] After the frightful "ice march," 700 miles in eight days, wearied survivors arrived near Yekaterinodar, the Kuban capital, only to discover it was held not by the Cossacks but by Reds in superior numbers. One general (Kaledin) had already shot himself. Kornilov was killed when a shell struck his headquarters in a farmhouse on April 12, 1918, and buried him under the collapsed ceiling. "A cloud of white plaster streamed forth," one staff officer recalled of Kornilov's room; when they turned the general over, they saw shrapnel lodged in his temple.[256] The Whites quickly decamped, and pro-Bolshevik units exhumed his shattered body, dragged it to Yekaterinodar's main square, and burned it on a rubbish pile.[257] "It can be said with certainty," an elated Lenin boasted, "that, in the main, the civil war has ended."[258] Russia's civil war was about to begin.

Kornilov's was not the only notable death that month: Gavrilo Princip passed away at the Habsburg's Terezin Fortress prison (the future Nazi Theresienstadt), where he was serving 20 years for the murder of the Austrian heir. The tubercular Princip, weakened by malnutrition, disease, and blood loss from an amputated arm, weighed eighty-eight pounds and was 23 years old. The 700-year-old Habsburg empire would outlive him by just a few months.[259]

As for Russia's civil war, it was precipitated from utterly unexpected quarters. In the Great War, Russia had captured around 2 million Central Power prisoners, mostly Austro-Hungarian subjects.[260] Later in the Great War, in anticipation of gaining a new Czechoslovak homeland in an Entente victory, the Czechoslovak Legion, which came to comprise some 40,000 POWs as well as deserters, served the tsar and took part in Kerensky's June 1917 offensive. In December 1917 they had been placed under French command.[261] Trotsky schemed to use the Legionnaires (who leaned Social Democratic) as the nucleus for a new Red Army, but Paris insisted that the Legionnaires be transferred to France, on the western front.[262] Russia's closest port in the west, at Arkhangelsk (750 miles north of Petrograd), was ice bound in March, so the armed troops were sent via Siberia to Vladivostok, whence they were supposed to sail to France.[263] But Germany had demanded that the Bolsheviks halt and disarm the Czechoslovak Legion, an obligation inserted into Brest-Litovsk. The Entente, for its part, requested that the troops who had not yet reached Omsk, in Western Siberia, be turned around and sent northwest to Murmansk and Arkhangelsk after all, to fight off the Germans nearby. The Japanese suddenly refused to transport Legionnaires from Vladivostok on boats for the west, assisting the Germans and keeping Siberia for themselves. The Legionnaires, for their part, wanted only to fight the Austrians and Germans, and were understandably wary about the meaning of all the back and forth. Amid suspicions, trouble broke out in Chelyabinsk (eastern Urals) on May 14, 1918, when a Russian train with ethnic Hungarian POWs of Austria-Hungary pulled up alongside a train of the Czechoslovak Legion troops. Insults flew. A Hungarian threw a metal object, wounding a Czech; the Czechs assaulted the other train and strung up the Hungarian object thrower. The Chelyabinsk soviet detained several Czechs and Slovaks in an investigation. On May 25, Trotsky cabled: "Every armed Czechoslovak found on the railway is to be shot on the spot."[264] That stupid order could never have been carried out. Still, suspecting the Bolsheviks intended to turn them over to Germans, the Czechoslovak Legion seized Chelyabinsk and then one town after another: Penza (May 29), Omsk (June 7), Samara (June 8), Ufa (July 5), Simbirsk (July 22), and so on, until they held the entire Trans-Siberian Railway as well as much of the Volga valley, more than two thirds of the former Russian empire.[265] They conquered more territory than anyone else in the Great War.[266]

The Czechoslovak Legion had harbored no special desire to fight or overthrow the Bolsheviks, but in the vacuum opened up by their self-defense conquests, more than a dozen anti-Bolshevik movements, from late May through June 1918, proclaimed their existence throughout the Volga region and Siberia.[267] Governments also sprouted in the tsarist lands under German occupation and those not under German occupation, including the Caucasus, where the British landed an expeditionary force near the oil fields. With the Germans in possession of Ukraine; the Czechoslovaks, Western Siberia; the Cossacks, the Don; and the Volunteer Army, the Kuban, the heartland of Russia, where the Bolsheviks were ensconced, had run out of food—and the fall harvest remained a long way off. On May 29, the Council of People's Commissars appointed Stalin a special plenipotentiary for South Russia to obtain food for the starving capitals Moscow and Petrograd. "He equipped an entire train," recalled Pestkowski. "He took with him a Hughes apparatus, airplanes, cash in small notes, a small military detachment, some specialists. I accompanied him to the station. He was in a very jolly mood, fully confident of victory."[268] On June 6, Stalin arrived in Tsaritsyn, on the Volga. If anti-Bolshevik forces captured Tsaritsyn, they could cut off all food and establish a united front from Ukraine through the Urals and Siberia.[269] The assignment would entail a vast expansion from his managing contacts with the various non-Russian nationalities, and a transformation of his role in the Bolshevik regime. But in the meantime, with the Czechoslovak Legion revolt, and the absence of any genuine Bolshevik army, the regime's survival seemed ever more in doubt.

## NON-COUP

Alone among the powers, Germany recognized the Bolshevik regime and maintained a real embassy in Moscow in a luxury private residence once owned by a German sugar magnate, on a quiet lane near the Arbat. On April 23, 1918, the forty-seven-year-old Count Wilhelm Mirbach (b. 1871), who had been in Petrograd to negotiate prisoner exchanges with the Bolsheviks and had worked at the embassy in the tsarist period, arrived back in Moscow as ambassador with a mission to ensure that no Russian rapprochement with the Entente took place. Mirbach had been reporting that the Bolshevik regime was "not for long," and that all it would take to sweep it away would be "light military pressure" by German forces sent via Estonia. The count openly courted monarchist groups as Bolshevik replacements, and behaved as if Moscow were already under German occupation.[270] Most Bolsheviks responded in kind. "The German ambassador has arrived," *Pravda* wrote, "not as a representative of the toiling classes of a friendly people but as plenipotentiary of a military gang that, with boundless insolence, kills, rapes, and pillages every country."[271] On May 1, International Workers' Day, German troops reached the Sevastopol naval base in Crimea, headquarters of the Black Sea fleet. On May 8, the Germans seized Rostov, in the Don River basin, where they abetted the gathering anti-Bolshevik forces. Pro-Bolshevik forces had to evacuate; they managed to transfer to Moscow confiscated gold coins, jewels, and other valuables that filled three wooden crates, one metal container, and six leather pouches.[272] Two days later, at a Central Committee meeting attended by a mere half a dozen members, Grigory Sokolnikov, signatory of Brest-Litovsk, argued that Germany's post-Brest offensive had violated the treaty and urged a renewed Anglo-French formal alliance.[273]

Germany occupied seventeen former tsarist provinces as well as tsarist Poland. Amid rumors of secret clauses in Brest-Litovsk and of Germans dictating Soviet government policies, newspapers warned of an imminent German conquest of Moscow and Petrograd. In fact, the German high command did consider a narrow thrust for the two capitals feasible. At this point, however, mid-May 1918, when they stood fewer than 100 miles from Petrograd (at Narva), and 300 miles from Moscow (at Mogilyov), the Germans stopped advancing.[274] Why? Lenin's continued appeasement of Berlin played a part. Equally important, German ruling circles deemed an invasion superfluous: Bolshevism seemed doomed. Mirbach, received by Lenin in the Kremlin on May 16, reported that same day to Berlin that the Bolshevik leader "continues to maintain his inexhaustible optimism," but, Mirbach added, Lenin "also concedes that even though his regime still remains intact, the number of its enemies has grown. . . . He bases his self-confidence above all on the fact that the ruling party alone disposes of organized power, whereas the other [parties] agree only in rejecting the existing regime." On Mirbach's May 16 report of Lenin's difficulties, Kaiser Wilhelm II wrote: "He is finished."[275]

In this context Yakov Sverdlov sought to drive a revival of the Communist party, which appeared to be atrophying. On May 18, 1918, he circulated a resolution that urged "the center of gravity of our work be shifted somewhat towards building up the party," and stipulated that "all party members, irrespective of their employment or their positions, are obliged to participate directly in party organizations and must not deviate from party instructions issued by the relevant party center."[276] Subordination to the center, however, remained elusive. In the meantime, Lenin's strategy was to impress a cost-benefit analysis on Berlin. "If the Germans-merchants take economic advantages, comprehending that via war they will get nothing from us, that we will burn everything, then your policy will be successful," he instructed the new Soviet envoy to Berlin, Adolf Joffe, on June 2, 1918. "We can supply raw materials."[277] But for the German government, which had already claimed Ukraine's breadbasket, the grand prize remained Paris. The German embassy in Moscow warned Berlin on June 4 that the Bolsheviks might tear up the Brest-Litovsk agreement ("These people's actions are absolutely unpredictable, particularly in a state of desperation"), yet the embassy's chief message was that Bolshevism was at the end of its rope ("famine is encroaching upon us. . . . Fuel reserves are waning. . . . The Bolsheviks are terribly nervous, probably feeling their end approaching, and therefore the rats are beginning to flee from the sinking ship. . . . It may be they will attempt to flee to Nizhny Novgorod or Yekaterinburg. . . .").[278] German diplomats were contacting political has-beens of both the tsarist regime and the Provisional Government about a restoration.[279] On June 25, in another note to Berlin, Mirbach again predicted Bolshevism's imminent demise.[280]

Mirbach's high-handed antics in Moscow, meanwhile, were more than matched by the Bolsheviks in Berlin. Thanks to Brest-Litovsk, the hammer and sickle flew on Unter den Linden, 7, the old tsarist embassy. Joffe, the son of a rich merchant and himself a firebrand Left Communist, had refused to present his credentials to the kaiser, held dinners on embassy territory for the Spartacus League and other German leftists, and funneled money to German Social Democrats, openly aiming to bring down the imperial German regime. The Soviet embassy amassed a staff of several hundred, including agitators listed as attachés who fanned out to meetings of German socialist organizations. Joffe spread weapons, too, often imported via diplomatic pouch.[281] General Ludendorff, for his part, on June 28 again urged that the Bolsheviks be cleared out of Russia so that Germany could set up a puppet regime. Never mind that the Germans lacked reserves even for the western front. A more sober-minded German foreign ministry argued against such cockamamie recommendations: the Bolsheviks already supported Brest-Litovsk, what more did Berlin need? And, the foreign ministry personnel added, the various anti-Bolshevik forces inside Russia did not conceal their sympathy for the Entente. What was Ludendorff's alternative for a pro-German group with which to replace the Bolsheviks? The kaiser declined Ludendorff's pleadings and even permitted the Bolsheviks to redeploy many of their Latvian Riflemen against internal enemies to the east, in the Volga valley.[282] Lenin's German loyalties paid off.[283] But in Moscow people knew nothing of the kaiser's decision to rebuff Ludendorff against an invasion to finish off Bolshevism. What people in Moscow saw was the imperious Mirbach, physical symbol of detested partnership with German militarism—a circumstance that provoked the Left Socialist Revolutionaries to action.

The Left SRs had resigned over Brest-Litovsk from the Council of People's Commissars, but not from their perches in the Cheka or from the Soviet's central executive committee. On June 14, 1918, the Bolsheviks had expelled the handful of elected Mensheviks and Right Socialist Revolutionaries from the central executive committee, and shuttered their newspapers. "Martov, swearing at the 'dictators', 'Bonapartists', 'usurpers', and 'grabbers' in his sick, tubercular voice, grabbed his coat and tried to put it on, but his shaking hands could not get into the sleeves," recalled one Bolshevik eyewitness. "Lenin, white as chalk, stood and looked at Martov." But a Left SR just burst into laughter.[284] The splinter party claimed a relatively robust membership in excess of 100,000.[285] This was considerably less than the Bolshevik membership of more than 300,000; both were microscopic in a country of some 140 million. Despite the Bolshevik numerical advantage, however, many contemporaries hoped, or feared, that the Left SRs—on the basis of their increasingly resonant anti-Brest-Litovsk stance—might command a majority of the elected delegates to the upcoming Fifth Congress of Soviets, scheduled to open June 28. Was there an option on the radical socialist left besides the Bolsheviks?

The Left SR Central Committee resolved to introduce a resolution at the congress denouncing Brest-Litovsk and calling for (quixotic) partisan war, such as was under way in Ukraine against the German occupation.[286] On June 24, Sverdlov delayed the congress's opening until early July while he manufactured more Bolshevik delegates. (On a pretext, Sverdlov had also expelled all Mensheviks and Right SRs from the Soviet's central executive committee.) The Left SRs held their 3rd Party Congress June 28 to July 1, and resolved to fight against German imperialism and for Soviet power by eliminating Councils of People's Commissars, so that Soviet executive committees could rule.[287] Meanwhile, Sverdlov, chairman of the central executive committee, did produce hundreds of suspicious soviet delegates, beyond the already extra weight afforded to worker voters over peasants (the Left SRs constituency). When the congress opened at Moscow's Bolshoi Theater on the evening of July 4, there were 1,035 voting attendees, including 678 Communists, 269 Left SRs, and 88 mostly unaffiliated others.[288] (Non-voting delegates, some 200 each for Left SRs and Communists, brought the attendees to 1,425, of whom two thirds were between twenty and thirty years of age; collectively, the attendees had spent 1,195 years in prison for political reasons.)[289] The evident fraud was hardly the only source of anti-Bolshevik anger: delegates from Ukraine, Latvia, and South Caucasus described the terrors of German imperialism's occupation and exploitation of their resources. "Down with Mirbach!" "Down with Brest!" Left SRs shouted with Germany's ambassador seated as an honored guest in a front box. Provocatively, Trotsky countered that all "agents of foreign imperialism" who were trying to provoke renewed war with Germany "be shot on the spot."[290]

Maria Spiridonova, the Left SR party's highest profile leader, had been a strong proponent of coalition with the Bolsheviks, but for her the last straw had already come in June 1918, when the Bolsheviks sent armed detachments to villages to "requisition" grain. She rose to denounce Bolshevik policies.[291] Lenin flat out stated that "we probably made a mistake in accepting your socialization of the land in our law [decree] of October 26 [1917]."[292] When the fraud-enhanced Bolshevik majority voted down the Left SR resolution to renounce the treaty with imperial Germany, Lenin baited the Left SRs: "If these people prefer walking out of the Congress, good riddance."[293] But he was in for a surprise: The Left SR leadership, knowing that their anti-Brest resolution might fail, had resolved to arouse the masses and provoke a breach in German-Soviet relations by terrorist acts "against high-profile representatives of German imperialism."[294] Thus did the occasion of the Fifth Congress of Soviets serve as the motivation for Left SR action, just as the Second Congress had for a Bolshevik coup.

Spiridonova, on the evening of July 4, had tasked twenty-year-old Yakov Blyumkin with assassinating German ambassador Count Mirbach.[295] The son of a Jewish shop assistant in Odessa, Blyumkin had arrived in Moscow in April 1918 and, like many Left SRs, had worked in the Cheka, one of about 120 employees at that time (including chauffeurs and field couriers).[296] He served in counterintelligence and among his responsibilities was the German embassy. On July 5, Spiridonova took the stage at the Bolshoi, accused the Bolsheviks of murdering the revolution and, with Lenin audibly laughing behind her, vowed she would "take up again the revolver and the hand grenade," as she had in tsarist times.[297] Pandemonium! A grenade exploded in one of the Bolshoi's upper tiers, but Sverdlov, presiding, kept the hall from stampeding for the exits.[298]

The next day, with the Congress of Soviets scheduled to resume later that afternoon, Blyumkin arrived at the German embassy accompanied by Nikolai Andreyev, a photographer, with credentials signed by Felix Dzierżyński authorizing them to request an urgent meeting with the ambassador. At the embassy, First Secretary Kurt Riezler, a noted philosopher as well as a diplomat, indicated he would meet with them on the ambassador's behalf. (Riezler had been among the key German foreign ministry personnel who had handled the secret negotiations to send Lenin in the sealed train back to Russia in 1917.)[299] Mirbach, however, came down to meet the pair; Blyumkin removed a Browning from his briefcase and opened fire three times—missing. As Mirbach ran, the photographer shot at the ambassador from behind, evidently striking the back of his head. Blyumkin hurled a bomb and the two assassins leaped out a window to a getaway car. Mirbach died around 3:15 p.m.[300]

Spiridonova and the Left SRs expected the political murder would provoke a German military response, forcing the Bolsheviks back into the war. With the congress set to resume at 4:00 p.m., and Lenin strategizing with Trotsky, Sverdlov, and Stalin, the telephone rang at the Kremlin. Bonch-Bruevich transmitted the news about an attack at the German embassy; Lenin ordered him to the scene.[301] Radek, the new foreign affairs commissar Georgy Chicherin, and Dzierżyński also went. The Germans demanded Lenin. The Bolshevik leader arrived with Sverdlov around 5:00 p.m., learned details of the murder, and offered condolences. The German military attaché thought Lenin looked frightened.[302] Perhaps Germany would respond with a military assault?

Lenin now learned that the very organization established to protect the Bolshevik revolution, the Cheka, was involved in a conspiracy against them. Blyumkin had left behind his credentials, and Dzierżyński, without a guard detail, drove to the Cheka military barracks on Grand Three-Holies Lane where Blyumkin had previously been seen. There the Cheka leader discovered the entire Left SR leadership, who made clear that Blyumkin had acted on their orders. "You stand before a fait accompli," they told Dzierżyński. "The Brest Treaty is annulled; war with Germany is unavoidable. . . . Let it be here as in Ukraine, we will go underground. You can keep power, but you must cease being lackeys of Mirbach."[303] Dzierżyński, although he had opposed Brest-Litovsk at the Bolshevik Central Committee, ordered them all arrested; instead, they took *him* hostage.[304]

At news of the capture of the Cheka head, Lenin "turned white as he typically did when he was enraged or shocked by a dangerous, unexpected turn of events," according to Bonch-Bruevich.[305] Lenin summoned the Chekist Mārtiņš Lācis, a thirty-year-old Latvian born Jānis Sudrabs, to take Dzierżyński's place.[306] When Lācis showed up at the main Cheka headquarters on Bolshaya Lubyanka—guarded, as always, by the Left SR–controlled Cheka Combat Detachment—the sailors wanted to shoot him. Only the intercession of the Left SR Pyotr Alexandrovich Dmitrievsky, known as Alexandrovich, a deputy to Dzierżyński, saved Lācis' life.[307] Had Lācis, and perhaps Dzierżyński as well, been shot "on the spot"—in the words of Trotsky's outburst from two days before—the Bolshevik regime might have been broken. As it was, Lenin and Sverdlov contemplated abandoning the Kremlin.[308]

Spiridonova went to the Bolshoi, for the evening resumption of the Fifth Congress of Soviets, to announce that Russia had been "liberated from Mirbach." Dressed in black, she wore a scarlet carnation upon her breast and carried a small steel Browning pistol in her hand.[309] The opening was delayed, however, and confusion reigned. Around 8:00 p.m. that night (July 6), the entire Left SR faction, more than 400 people, including guests, moved upstairs to discuss the situation, amid rumors that armed Latvians had surrounded the Bolshoi. The Bolshevik faction retreated to other quarters (some may have been let out of the theater).[310] "We were sitting in our room waiting for you to come and arrest us," Bukharin told one Left SR. "Since you did not, we decided to arrest you instead."[311] The Left SRs in the Cheka, for their part, had sent sailors out into the streets to take Bolshevik hostages, grabbing more than two dozen from passing automobiles, and still held Dzierżyński and Lācis. Lenin discovered that the Moscow garrison was not going to defend the Bolsheviks: most soldiers either remained neutral or sided with the anti-German Left SRs. "Today around 3 p.m. a Left SR killed Mirbach with a bomb," Lenin telegrammed Stalin at Tsaritsyn. "The assassination is clearly in the interests of the monarchists or of the Anglo-French capitalists. The Left SRs . . . arrested Dzierżyński and Lācis and started an insurrection against us. We are about to liquidate them tonight and we shall tell the people the whole truth: we are a hair's breadth from war" with Germany.[312] Stalin would write back the next day that the Left SRs were "hysterics."[313] He was right.

But the counterattack was not assured. Many of the few reliable Red units had been sent eastward to counter the Czechoslovak rebellion. Around midnight on July 6–7, Lenin summoned the top Latvian commander, the squat, stout Colonel Jukums Vācietis. "The Kremlin was dark and empty," Vācietis recalled of the Council of People's Commissars' meeting room, where Lenin finally emerged, and asked, "'Comrade, will we hold out until morning?' Having asked the question, Lenin kept staring at me."[314] Vācietis was taken aback. He sympathized with the Left SRs and could have decided, at a minimum, to be neutral, thereby perhaps dooming the Bolsheviks. But his own experience fighting the Germans during Christmas 1916 had produced colossal casualties, and resuming the war held no appeal. (There was, in any case, no Russian army to do so.) Furthermore, he expected the imperial German regime to collapse from the war, just as Russia's had, so why sacrifice men for nothing? What Vācietis did not know was that Lenin did not even trust him: a half hour before receiving him that night, Lenin had called in the two political commissars attached to the Latvians to get reassurances about Vācietis's loyalties.

Nor was it clear that the Latvian rank and file would fight for the Bolsheviks. The Left SRs had been waiting, on July 6 for the arrival of Lieutenant Colonel Mikhail Muravyov (b. 1880), an ethnic Russian militant Left SR and another commander of the Latvian Rifles, but he failed to show in the capital.[315] Still, although Vācietis's counterassault on the Left SRs was planned to begin a few hours after he saw Lenin, in the wee hours of July 7, to take advantage of the darkness, this happened to be St. John the Baptist's Day, a Latvian national holiday, and the riflemen had decided to celebrate with an outing to Khodynka Field on Moscow's outskirts.[316] No Latvians, Red Guards, or, for that matter, anyone mustered at their jumping-off points.[317] The attack would have to wait, instead, for daylight. The Cheka military units were under command of a Left SR former Baltic sailor Dmitri Popov; lodged in Moscow's inner walled Kitaigorod, they numbered 600 to 800 men total, mostly sailors. Against them, Vācietis later claimed to have assembled perhaps 3,300 men (fewer than 500 of them Russians).[318] The Latvians would recall that Popov's unit was better armed than they were, with heavy guns, scores of machine guns, and four armored cars. "The Popovites had seized a row of houses," Vācietis explained, "and fortified them." In fact, Popov, whose unit included many Finns as well as sailors, had been busy trying to recruit more fighters to his side, and expected the Bolsheviks to negoti-ate. Instead, Vācietis ordered a 152 mm howitzer brought in to reduce the Popov-Cheka stronghold to rubble—even with Dzierżyński inside.[319] When the shelling started to wreck the building, as well as its neighboring structures, Popov and his men began to flee (they left Dzierżyński behind). Sources conflict on the duration of the skirmish (perhaps many hours, perhaps forty minutes). The two sides sustained around ten fatalities and about fifty wounded. Hundreds of Left SRs were taken into custody.[320] Thirteen or so, including Spiridonova, were transferred to prison cells in the Kremlin. At 4:00 p.m., the Council of People's Commissars confidently pronounced "the uprising . . . liquidated."[321]

The Cheka initiated an immediate countercoup against the Left SRs, solidify-ing the Bolshevik monopoly.[322] The Cheka raided the editorial offices and smashed the printing facilities of non-Bolshevik periodicals.[323] Blyumkin escaped to Ukraine. But many Left SRs in Bolshevik custody, including Alexandrovich—the savior of Lācis—were executed immediately without trial; the Bolsheviks publicly announced that some 200 had been shot.[324] The vast majority of Left SRs across the country simply switched to the Bolshevik party. In the meantime, without the Left SR delegates, the Congress of Soviets resumed on July 9, and Trotsky regaled the delegates with details of "the Uprising."[325] In fact, one Left SR, Prosh Proshyan, had gone to the Central Telegraph Office around midnight on July 6 and proclaimed, "We killed Mirbach, the Council of People's Commis-sars is under arrest." Proshyan—who briefly had been commissar of posts and telegraph—dispatched a series of confused telegrams around the country, one referring to the Left SRs as "the presently governing party."[326] But this individual initiative aside, there had been no Left SR coup. The Left SR leadership had made plain many times, before and during the events, that they were prepared to defend themselves with force but not to seize power: theirs was an uprising on behalf of Soviet power "against the imperialists" (Germany), not against the Bolsheviks.[327]

The Left SR episode put in sharp relief Lenin's coup seven months earlier in October 1917. Just as in 1917, so in summer 1918, power was there for the seizing: The Left SRs enjoyed no worse prospects against Lenin and the Bolsheviks than Lenin had had against Kerensky. The Left SRs served in and had seized full con-trol over the Cheka, won over much of the garrison by agitation, and possessed Kremlin passes, including to the Imperial Senate, where Lenin had his office.[328] But the Left SRs lacked something critical: will. Lenin was fanatically committed to seizing and holding power, and his will had proved decisive in the Bolshevik coup, just as its absence now proved decisive in the Left SR non-coup.

Lenin had relentlessly pursued personal power, though not for power's sake: he, too, was moved by visions of social justice via revolution, as well as an allegedly scientific (Marxist) conviction in his rightness, even as he continued to strike many contemporaries as mad.[329] But all along, Lenin had gotten lucky with his socialist opponents: Victor Chernov of the populous Right SRs, who had shrunk from offers of force by the capital garrison to protect the Constituent Assembly; Yuly Martov of the Mensheviks, who had clung to the "bourgeois phase" of history even without a bourgeoisie; Lev Kamenev, who had opposed the Bolshevik coup and tried to displace the Bolshevik monopoly with an all-socialist coalition government, then begged to be readmitted to the Bolshevik Central Committee. And now, Maria Spiridonova, who also proved no match for Lenin.[330] Spiridonova, just thirty-four years old in 1918 but the only widely known Left SR leader, happened to be the only female head of any political force in 1917–18, and as such, was long subject to condescension ("a tireless hysteric with a pince-nez, the caricature of Athena," one German journalist remarked).[331] But she certainly did not lack gumption. At age twenty-two, in 1906, she had shot a tsarist police general for suppressing a peasant rebellion in 1905, for which she received a sentence of lifetime penal labor in Eastern Siberia. In prison and in transit, she suffered beatings and sexual assault, the least of which involved cigarettes extinguished on her bare breasts. She possessed courage. She could also be politically clear-eyed: unlike the vast majority of Left SRs, and the self-styled Left Bolsheviks, Spiridonova had supported Brest-Litovsk. "The peace was signed not by . . . the Bolsheviks," she had shrewdly noted, but "by want, famine, the lack of desire of the whole people—suffered out, tired—to fight."[332] But time and again, Lenin and Sverdlov had manipulated her earnestness. Now, in July 1918, she unexpectedly had them in her grasp, but did not evolve her initial strategy and seize the opportunity.

The Bolshevik counterassault on the Left SRs, meanwhile, would culminate in a secret "trial" against the party. Spiridonova would be sentenced to just one year, and then amnestied.[333] But a once powerful political force was now neutered.[334] Without the Left SRs, the Congress of Soviets, on its final day (July 10), approved a constitution declaring that "all central and local power belongs to soviets" and calling for "abolition of all exploitation of man by man, the complete elimination of the division of society into classes, the ruthless suppression of the exploiters, the establishment of a socialist organization of society, and the victory of socialism in all countries."

## ASSASSINATION AND NEAR ASSASSINATION

The Romanovs were still alive—and offered a potential rallying point, whether for the Bolsheviks in a public trial or for the anti-Bolsheviks to spring free. Nicholas's brother Grand Duke Mikhail had been arrested by Kerensky and later deported by the Bolsheviks to a prison in the Urals (Perm). There, in the wee hours on June 13, 1918, five armed men of the Cheka, led by an old terrorist who had served time in tsarist prisons, staged an escape of the grand duke in order to execute him. Mikhail's bullet-ridden body was burned in a smelter. The Bolsheviks shrank from admitting the execution, and circulated rumors Mikhail had been freed by monarchists and vanished.[335] As for Nicholas, the Provisional Government had decided to exile him and his family abroad, but the Soviet had objected, and in any case, British king George V—who was a cousin to both Nicholas and Alexandra—rescinded an offer to shelter them.[336] So Kerensky had sent the Russian royals to house arrest in the Tobolsk governor's mansion (Nicholas's train was disguised as a "Red Cross mission" and flew a Japanese flag).[337] The symbolism of Siberian exile resonated. But as rumors spread of the ex-tsar's comfortable existence and of monarchist plots to free him, the Urals soviet resolved to bring Nicholas to Yekaterinburg. But in April 1918, Sverdlov sent a trusted agent to fetch him from Tobolsk to Moscow. As the train for the former tsar traveled through Yekaterinburg, Urals Bolsheviks kidnapped him and placed him in the requisitioned mansion of a retired army engineer, Nikolai Ipatyev, around which they erected a palisade, and kept a large guard detail. In Moscow, Lenin had minions gather materials to put Nicholas on trial, a development mooted in the press, but the trial kept being "postponed."[338] "At the time," Trotsky wrote of the closely held trial discussions, "Lenin was rather gloomy."[339]

By July 1918, the Czechoslovak Legion was advancing on Yekaterinburg and the Bolshevik military commissar of the Urals went to Moscow to discuss the Urals defense and presumably, Nicholas and his family. On July 2, the Council of People's Commissars appointed a commission to draft a decree nationalizing Romanov family property. Two days later, the newly formed Yekaterinburg

Cheka displaced the local soviet as the royal family's guards. Nicholas lived in evident bewilderment; he discovered the *Protocols of the Elders of Zion*, the infamous anti-Semitic tract forged in imperial Russia about a global Jewish conspiracy, which he now read aloud to his German wife and daughters; perhaps Communism was a Jewish conspiracy?[340] Soon the Cheka forged a crude monarchist letter in French purporting to be a conspiracy to free and restore the tsar. On this pretext, in the dead of night July 16–17, 1918, without formal charges, let alone a trial, a "sentence" of death by firing squad was carried out against Nicholas, Alexandra, their son, Alexei (aged thirteen), their four daughters (aged seventeen to twenty-two), the family physician, and three servants. Yakov Yurovsky, the eighth of ten children of a Jewish seamstress and a glazier (and suspected thief), led the eleven-person execution squad. Their hail of pistol bullets ricocheted off the brick walls around the half basement, and burned the executioners (some would become deaf). Alexei survived the barrage—he let out a moan—but Yurovsky went up and shot him point blank. Some of the daughters, whose bodies held concealed jewels that repelled the bullets, were bayoneted to pieces. Yurovsky's squad buried the bodies off a dirt road at a village (Koptyaki) twelve miles north of Yekaterinburg. They poured sulfuric acid over the corpses to disfigure them beyond recognition, and burned and separately buried the corpses of Alexei and a daughter mistaken for Alexandra. That same day, July 19, Yurosovky left for Moscow to report.[341] The central Bolshevik government never admitted its responsibility, and the act was attributed to the Urals Bolsheviks.[342] The day the Bolshevik government published an announcement of the tsar's death—falsely reporting the survival of Alexei and Alexandra—it also published the decree nationalizing Romanov family property (approved six days earlier).[343] "There was no sign of grief or sympathy among the people," noted ex-tsarist prime minister Vladimir Kokovtsov, who on the day of the announcement rode in a Petrograd tram. "The report of the Tsar's death was read aloud, with smirks, mockeries, and base comments." Some passengers said, "High time!"[344]

The Romanovs' summary execution, and the failure to mount a public political trial, indicated desperation. The Bolsheviks had no military force capable of genuine combat, and the attempts to form some sort of army floundered, as soldiers scattered in search of food, turning into robber bands. Even the reliable Latvians were looking for other options. "At the time it was believed that central Russia would turn into a theater of internecine warfare and that the Bolsheviks would hardly hold on to power," recalled Vācietis, the Latvian commander, of the summer of 1918. He feared for the "complete annihilation of the Latvian Rifles" and entered into secret talks with the irrepressible Riezler, the deceased Mirbach's temporary replacement as chargé d'affaires. Riezler, fearing the Bolsheviks would fall and be replaced by a pro-Entente regime, secretly urged a coup to install a government in Moscow similarly friendly to Berlin by bringing in a battalion of German grenadiers to "guard" the embassy.[345] Lenin refused to allow them (he did consent to the arrival of some Germans in small groups without uniforms).[346] In any case, Riezler's superiors at the German foreign ministry in Berlin saw no need to abandon Lenin, who had paralyzed Russia and remained loyal to Germany.[347] Still, Riezler hoped to undo the Bolsheviks by obtaining the defection of the Latvian Riflemen, whose units guarded the Kremlin, and he found a receptive group eager to return to their homeland, which was under German occupation. If the Latvians were repatriated, Vācietis promised they would remain neutral in any German-Bolshevik showdown.[348] General Ludendorff, however, undercut Riezler's negotiations, arguing that Latvia would be contaminated by Bolshevik propaganda if the Rifles were repatriated. The Reichswehr helped save Bolshevism, yet again.

The Czechoslovak Legion and anti-Bolshevik forces seized Yekaterinburg on July 25, 1918, less than a week after Nicholas had been buried there.[349] "The Entente has bought the Czechoslovaks, counter-revolutionary uprisings rage everywhere, the whole bourgeoisie is using all its strength to sweep us out," Lenin wrote the next day to Klara Zetkin, the German revolutionary.[350] In August 1918, the British, against Bolsevik wishes, shifted from Murmansk (where the Bolsheviks had invited them to land) to the larger port of Arkhangelsk, as a better base of operations, hoping to restore an eastern front against Germany by linking up with the Czechoslovak Legion. Rumors spread that Entente forces would march on Moscow, 750 miles to the south.[351] Panic erupted on the jerry-built northern railroad. "Among us no one doubted that the Bolshevks were doomed," wrote an agent (sent to Moscow by former tsarist General Mikhail Alexeyev) who had managed to get himself appointed deputy trade commissar. "A ring had been established around Soviet power, and we were sure that the Bolsheviks would not escape it."[352] To the north were the British and soon the Americans (with different agendas); to the east, the Czechoslovak Legion and other anti-Bolshevik forces, who captured Kazan (August 7); to the south, anti-Bolshevik forces aided by Germany and advancing on Tsaritsyn, poised to link up with the anti-Bolshevik forces in the east. And to the west stood the Germans, who occupied Poland, Ukraine, and the Baltic littoral, and kept a force in Finland at its government's request. Lenin and the inner circle contemplated abandoning Moscow for Nizhny Novgorod, in the deeper interior.[353] Bolshevik officials also began requesting diplomatic passports and travel documents for Germany for their families; money was transferred to Swiss banks.[354]

Might Lenin go back whence he came? "The Bolsheviks were saying openly that their days were numbered," reported a new German ambassador, Karl Helfferich (appointed above Riezler), who was urging Berlin to break off relations with the doomed Bolsheviks, and who for safety reasons did not venture out of his Moscow residence.[355]

Lenin, however, came up with his boldest, most desperate maneuver yet. The same day that the British landed the expeditionary force at Arkhangelsk, where a local coup put a non-Bolshevik figure in power, he dispatched his foreign affairs commissar to the German embassy to request what the Bolshevik leader had long feared—a German invasion toward the Russian imperial capital of Petrograd. "In view of the state of public opinion, an open military alliance with Germany is not possible; what is possible is parallel action," Georgy Chicherin told Helfferich. The people's commissar asked the Germans not to occupy Petrograd but to *defend it,* by marching on Murmansk and Arkhangelsk against the Entente forces. Furthermore, in the south, Chicherin requested that the Germans stop supporting the anti-Bolshevik forces and instead move troops in to attack them. "Chicherin," Helfferich reported to Berlin, "made clear that the request for German troops in the north and in the south came directly from Lenin.[356] Despite inconclusive wrangling over whether the Germans could, or could not, occupy Petrograd itself, the upshot would be a new, even more oppressive treaty, "supplementary" to Brest-Litovsk, signed in Berlin on August 27, 1918. Lenin agreed to renounce Estonia and Livonia (Lithuania); sell Germany 25 percent of the output of the Baku oil fields; afford Germany use of the Black Sea fleet; and make reparations of 6 billion marks, half in gold reserves. Germany promised to send coal, rifles, bullets, machine guns, and evacuate Belorussia, promises from a depleted Germany not worth the paper on which they were printed.[357] Three secret clauses—never mind the Bolshevik condemnation of capitalists' "secret diplomacy"—provided for German action against Allied forces on Russian soil in the north and in the south, and expulsion of the British from Baku, a task for which Germany obtained the right to land there.[358]

Lenin clung to imperial Germany like sea rust on the underside of a listing ship. If during the wild rumors of 1914–17, the imagined treason of the tsarist court to the Germans had never been real, in 1918, the abject sellout to the Germans by the Bolsheviks was all too real. The August 27 treaty was a worse capitulation than Brest-Litovsk, and one that Lenin voluntarily sought. He was bribing his way to what he hoped was safety from German overthrow as well as the right to call upon German help against attempted Entente overthrow. "There was a coincidence of interests," Lenin wrote by hand—avoiding secretaries—to the Bolshevik envoy to Sweden. "We would have been idiots not to have exploited it."[359] The Germans, for their part, were no less cynical, determined, as the foreign secretary expressed it, "to work with the Bolsheviks or to use them, as long as they are in the saddle, to our own best advantage."[360] The Bolsheviks' first installment of promised payment, 120 million gold rubles, was remitted in August (more payments would be made in September).

Colonel Vācietis, the Latvian commander, had been dispatched to the city of Kazan to help clean up the Red mess and salvage the situation. On August 30, 1918, Lenin wrote to Trotsky that if the city of Kazan was not retaken, Vācietis was to be shot.[361] Later that evening, a Friday, the Bolshevik leader went to the Mikhelson Machine Factory in the heart of Moscow's worker-saturated factory district to give a speech. Fridays were "party day" in Moscow and officials dispersed around town to address mass meetings of workers and soldiers in the evenings. Lenin addressed some 140 such meetings in Moscow and its immediate environs between his arrival in March and July.[362] He went to Mikhelson, his second public speech of the day, without a guard detail, aside from his chauffeur (who remained with the car). The idea of assassinating top Bolsheviks crossed many a mind. In 1918, members of the British Secret Service Bureau evidently asked a Russian-born British spy to invent a pretext for an interview with Stalin in order, once inside, to assassinate him (the Brit claimed he refused the request).[363] On that morning of August 30, the head of the Cheka in Petrograd, Moisei Uritsky, yet another former Menshevik who had thrown in his lot with the Bolsheviks, was assassinated in the old tsarist general staff headquarters on Palace Square (the square would be renamed after him). Dzierżyński departed Moscow to oversee the investigation.[364] Lenin had spoken at Mikhelson four times previously. That evening, the venue—the hand grenade shop—was jammed. But Lenin was running very late and at 9:00 p.m. two hours after the scheduled start, a substitute speaker was finally sent out to the crowd. Some forty-five minutes later Lenin's car pulled up and he took the stage immediately. "Comrades, I won't speak long, we have a Council of People's Commissars meeting," he began, then delivered an hour-long harangue on the theme of "Bourgeois Dictatorship versus Proletarian Dictatorship." The audience had many tough questions (submitted as per custom in written form), but Lenin claimed no time to answer them. "We have one conclusion," he summed up, calling them to take up arms to defend the revolution. "Victory or Death!"[365]

Lenin made his exit, but just before entering his waiting vehicle, he fell to the ground, shot in the chest and the left arm (the bullet passed into his shoulder). His driver, Stepan Gil, and some members of the factory committee placed him in the backseat of his car. Lenin was white as a sheet, blood still pouring out despite tourniquets; he also suffered internal bleeding.[366] They drove to the Kremlin. When the call came in to the Kremlin, Commandant Malkov gathered pillows from the tsars' collection at the Grand Kremlin Palace and took them over to Lenin's apartment in the Imperial Senate, where the wounded leader had been brought. No one knew how to stop the bleeding, and Lenin passed out from blood loss and pain.[367] The head of the Kremlin garage rushed out to find oxygen tanks: one tank was rented from the A. Bloch and H. Freiman pharmacy on nearby Tverskaya Street for 80 rubles, another at a different pharmacy farther down for 55 rubles. (The automobile department head, in his report, wrote that "since the money was paid out of my own pocket, I would ask that it be returned to me.")[368] The first person a prostrate Lenin asked for was Inessa Armand, his former mistress, who arrived with her daughter.[369] Bonch-Bruevich ordered the Kremlin guard to high alert.[370] Sverdlov summoned a famous doctor; meanwhile, Bonch-Bruevich's wife, Vera, a doctor, checked Lenin's pulse and injected him with morphine.[371]

Back at Mikhelson, a fleeing Feiga Roidman (aka Fanya Kaplan) had been detained at a nearby tram stop as the presumed shooter.[372] A twenty-eight-year-old Right Socialist Revolutionary, she confessed at her initial interrogation and insisted no one else had been involved, although she was nearly blind and it was dark where Lenin had been shot. (The would-be assassin may have been an accomplice, Lidiya Konopleva, an Anarchist SR and a Kaplan rival, or someone else.)[373] Sverdlov, in the name of the Soviet central executive committee, denounced the Right SRs as "hirelings of the British and French."[374] Bonch-Bruevich sent telegrams to Trotsky (then at the southeastern front, in Sviyazhsk) concerning Lenin's temperature, pulse, and breathing.[375] Trotsky rushed back to Moscow immediately. On September 2, 1918, he addressed the Soviet central executive committee, calling Lenin not merely "the leader of the new epoch" but "the greatest human being of our revolutionary epoch," and while admitting that Marxists believed in classes, not personalities, acknowledged that Lenin's loss would be devastating. Trotsky's speech would be published in the press and as a widely distributed pamphlet.[376] The same day, the regime declared the formation of the Revolutionary Military Council of the Republic, headed by Trotsky. The next day Sverdlov ordered Kremlin commandant Malkov to execute Kaplan, which he did, then burned the body in a metal drum in the Kremlin's Alexander Garden.[377] On September 4, Vācietis, instead of facing a firing squad, was promoted to Red commander in chief. The rank-and-file Latvian Riflemen were becoming disillusioned over Bolshevik dictatorial behavior.[378] Vācietis again approached the Germans seeking repatriation of his men to Latvia, but he was again rebuffed.[379] ●

FROM THE OUTSET, the survival of the Bolshevik escapade had been in doubt, even as the new regime set about ripping tsarist insignia off buildings and taking down old statues, such as Alexander II inside the Kremlin and Alexander III outside Christ the Redeemer Cathedral. Lenin and others, using ropes, ceremoniously pulled down the large Orthodox cross inside the Kremlin for Grand Duke Sergei (Romanov), the Moscow governor general assassinated in 1905.[380] In their place would go up statues to Darwin, Danton, Alexander Radishchev, and others in the leftist pantheon. "I am exasperated to the depths of my soul," Lenin wrote to enlightenment commissar Anatoly Lunacharsky on September 12, 1918, days after having been shot. "There is no outdoor bust of Marx. . . . I scold you for this criminal negligence."[381]

The Bolsheviks had begun renaming Moscow's streets: Resurrection Square would become Revolution Square; Old Basmannaya Street, Karl Marx Street; Prechistenka, Kropotkin Street; Grand Nikita Street, Alexander Herzen Street.[382] That year of 1918, on Moscow's grandest artery, Tverskaya, at the junction between Bolshoi and Maly Gnezdnikov Lanes, Café Bim-Bom buzzed with freneticism. It belonged to the founding member of the clown pair Bim and Bom, Iwan Raduński (who at this time was teamed with Mieczysław Staniewski as Bim). The celebrated duet dated to 1891 and specialized in biting satire accompanied by musical numbers. Bom's café was a crazy anthill in the new Bolshevik capital, frequented by all types, from the political (Menshevik leader Yuly Martov, a young Left SR Yakov Blyumkin) to the artistic (writer Ilya Ehrenburg, performing clown Vladimir Durov). Inevitably, the café also attracted Moscow's criminal element, including one figure who had pocketed the proceeds from the sale of the former Moscow governor-general's mansion, which was located on the same street as the café, by pretending the property was his own residence. When the irreverent satirists began to mock the new Bolshevik regime, however, Latvian Riflemen in the audience shot up the premises and began to chase Bim and Bom. The audience laughed, assuming it was part of the act. The clowns would be arrested.[383]

Despite such reflexive repression and the grandiose plans, the would-be regime had hit a nadir in 1918. Rumors flew around Moscow that Lenin had died and been buried in secret. Zinoviev spoke of Lenin in a public speech on September 6, 1918, as "the greatest leader ever known by humanity, the apostle of the socialist revolution" and compared Lenin's famous *What Is to Be Done with the Gospels,* sacralizing imagery, that, intentionally or not, sounded ominous.[384] Bonch-Bruevich hastily arranged to film Lenin—against his wishes—outside on the Kremlin grounds, the first ever documentary of him, which proved he was alive.[385] At the same time, the Bolsheviks proclaimed a Terror "to crush the hydra of counter-revolution."[386] Zinoviev, for effect, would announce that 500 "hostages" had been shot in Petrograd, executions of imprisoned former tsarist officials that were staged in public places.[387] There were at least 6,185 summary executions in the Red Terror of 1918—in two months. There had been 6,321 death sentences by Russian courts between 1825 and 1917, not all of them carried out. To be sure, executions in tsarist Russia are not easy to calculate: the repression of the Polish uprising in 1830, for example, was often outside the judicial system, while the courts-martial of 1905–6 were generally not counted in the "normal" statistics. Still, the magnitude of the Red Terror was clear.[388] And the public bragging of its scope was designed to be part of its effect. "The criminal adventurism of Socialist Revolutionaries, White Guards, and other pseudo-socialists, forces us to reply to the criminal designs of the enemies of the working class with mass terror," Jēkabs Peterss, deputy chief of the Cheka, thundered in *Ivzestiya.* The same issue carried a telegram from Stalin calling for "open, mass, systematic terror against the bourgeoisie."[389]

Bolshevism's core convictions about capitalism and class warfare were held to be so incontrovertible that any and all means up to lying and summary executions were seen as not just expedient but morally necessary. The demonstrative Red Terror, like its French precedent, would make an indelible impression, on enemies and (newfound) supporters of the Bolsheviks alike.[390] Faced with extinction, the Bolsheviks wielded the specter of "counterrevolution" and the willingness of masses of people to risk their lives defending "the revolution" against counterrevolution in order to build an actual state. What in summer and fall 1918 looked for all the world like political Dadaism would soon become an enduring, ambitious dictatorship.[391]

## CHAPTER 8

# CLASS WAR AND A PARTY-STATE

The world war formally ended with the conclusion of the armistice. . . . In fact, however, everything from that point onward that we have experienced and continue to experience is a continuation and transformation of the world war.

Pyotr Struve, Rostov-on-the-Don
(held by the Whites), November 1919[1]

Every military specialist must have a commissar on his right and on his left, each with a revolver in his hand.

Lev Trotsky, Commissar of War, 1918[2]

BEYOND THEIR MONOPOLY OF 1917–18, the Bolsheviks created a state in 1918–20. The distinction is often lost. Forcibly denying others a right to rule is not the same as ruling and controlling resources. The new state took shape by means of the predation, confiscation, and redistribution of material things (grain, buildings, valuables) as well as the intimidation or conscription of people, refracted through notions of revolutionary class warfare. The resulting regime, one scholar observed, "necessarily also meant a burgeoning bureaucracy, needed both to expropriate the old owners and to administer the newly expropriated property."[3] In many cases, the bureaucrats, even when they themselves were not holdovers, continued to use the letterhead of the tsarist regime or Provisional Government. That said, this was a very particular state: an armed political police that resembled criminal bandits; a sprawling food procurement commissariat, which bested numerous rivals in a battle for bureaucratic aggrandizement; a distribution apparatus to allocate the spoils and to feed off them itself; an immense desertion-beset Red Army; an inefficient but—thanks to the aura of emergency—increasingly hierarchical party hydra, which absorbed and deployed personnel;

and a propaganda machinery, with an estimated 50,000 activists already in 1918, wielding newspapers, posters, skits, films, and agitation trains, albeit largely confined to the towns and the army.[4] Despite the existence of soviets as well as revolutionary tribunals, this was almost entirely an executive-branch state, but it roiled with rival executive claimants to power, as "commissars" went up against "commissars," nationally and locally, those who were appointed and those self-appointed. Above all, the new state owed its existence to civil war, as most states do, but it remained in peacetime a counterinsurgency.[5] Civil war was not something that deformed the Bolsheviks; it formed them, indeed it saved them from the Dada and near oblivion of 1918.[6] To be sure, even before the onset of full-fledged civil war, the Bolsheviks had not been shy about expropriation and terror. But the civil war provided the opportunity to develop and to validate the struggle against "exploiting classes" and "enemies" (domestic and international), thereby imparting a sense of seeming legitimacy, urgency, and moral fervor to predatory methods.[7] "The ruling class," as Lenin explained, "never turns its power over to the downtrodden class."[8] And so, power had to be claimed by force in an ongoing, not one-off, process. The "seizure of power" would be enacted anew, every day.[9]

Stalin, like Lenin, is rightly seen as an admirer of the grand trappings of statehood, but an idolatry of the state did not initially drive Bolshevik state building.[10] Nor was the driver the shattering conditions of world war and revolution. Rather, it was a combination of ideas or habits of thought, especially profound antipathy to markets and all things bourgeois, as well as no-holds-barred revolutionary methods, which exacerbated the catastrophe in a self-reinforcing loop.[11] Plenty of regimes justify martial law, summary shootings, roundups, and confiscations by citing emergency circumstances, but they do not, as a rule, completely outlaw private trade and declare industry nationalized, ration food by class (workers versus "non-laboring elements"), summon "poor peasants" and workers to dispossess "kulaks," and try to subvert major world powers because they are capitalist ("imperialists"). Bolshevik state building was launched with desperate measures to address inherited, and then severely aggravated, urban food shortages, but *every* challenge was cast as a matter of counterrevolution, on the part of someone, somewhere. "In the name of saving the revolution from counter-revolution": so began countless documents from the period, followed by directives to "requisition" flour, petrol, guns, vehicles, people.[12] "Today is the first year anniversary of the Revolution," remarked one former tsarist official (referring to the February Revolution). "A year ago nearly everyone became revolutionaries; and now, counterrevolutionaries."[13] The idea of counterrevolution was the gift that kept on giving.

Pitiless class warfare formed the core of Lenin's thought—the Great War, to his mind, had irrevocably proven that capitalism had forfeited its right to further existence—but a Soviet state was not born fully armed from Lenin's forehead. Among the broad masses there was an intuitive antibourgeois ethos—exploiters versus the exploited, haves versus have-nots—which could both motivate and justify an all-out mobilization to combat counterrevolution and defend the revolution. Consider a revolutionary episode in late summer 1918 in Kamyshinsk, on the Volga, a merchant town of sawmills, windmills, and watermelons. "The Cheka has registered all the big bourgeoisie, and at the moment they are being kept on a barge," proudly proclaimed a group that had constituted itself as the local political police. "During the day the [prisoners] work in town." No one had to explain to these local defenders of the revolution who the "bourgeoisie" were or why they were the enemy. And when members of the "bourgeoisie" on the Kamyshinsk barge suddenly fell ill, and the Cheka consented to an inspection by a physician from nearby Saratov, who prescribed better rations and release from forced labor, the suspicious Chekists decided to investigate the doctor's background and discovered he was an impostor. "Now," the operative gloated, "he too is on the barge."[14] Such prison barges for "class aliens" arose up and down the Volga—none more impressive than under Stalin at Tsaritsyn—as did barge equivalents all across the former Russian empire.[15] The ideologically inflected practices that generated the barges enabled tens of thousands of new people in thousands of locales to entrench a new unaccountable power.[16] (Apolitical gangsters and profiteers got into the act, too, to rob the "bourgeoisie.") Violent actions against "counterrevolution" that flowed from the logic of socialist revolution also provoked outrage. "To whom does power in the provinces belong?" one angry commissariat official asked in fall 1918. "To the soviets and their executive committees, or to the Chekas?"[17] The answer could not have been plainer: when villagers in Samara Province, also in the Volga valley, revealed that they wanted to hold a new election for the local Cheka's leadership, the Chekists readied their weapons. As a frightened peasant ran away, a sixteen-year-old Chekist shot him in the back. "Pay special attention to this and write in the newspaper," one peasant urged, "that here is a fellow who can kill whomever he wants."[18]

Here was the eureka moment: from bottom to top, and places in between, the ideas and practices of revolutionary class war produced the Soviet state. Marx had written about emancipation, freedom—but he had also written about class war. For the revolution to succeed, for humanity to break free and advance, everything connected to "the bourgeoisie" and to capitalism had to be smashed. Everything that hindered annihilation of the bourgeosie and capitalism also had to be cleared away, including other socialists. True, far from everyone leapt into the mayhem. The vast majority of inhabitants just sought to survive by scavenging, finagling, uprooting. At the same time, substantial numbers of people also sought to *live* the revolution right here and now, organizing communes, building children's nurseries, writing science fiction. "All aspects of existence—social, economic, political, spiritual, moral, familial—were opened to purposeful fashioning by human hands," wrote Isaac Steinberg. "Everywhere the driving passion was to create something new, to effect a total difference with the 'old world.'"[19] But within the utopia, the class principle, fundamentally, was intolerant. Many Bolsheviks who were bursting with conviction to serve humanity began to see that their dedicated efforts to end suffering and level social hierarchies were producing the opposite. This realization proved shattering for some, but for most it constituted a way station on the ladder of revolutionary career advancement.[20] True believers mixed with opportunists, revolutionary ascetics with swindlers, and together, in the name of social justice and a new world of abudance, they drove ineptitude, corruption, and bluster to heights scarcely known even in tsarist Russia.[21]

Peasant partisan armies fighting against Bolshevism forcibly requisitioned grain from villages under their control, while denouncing the injustices of the market, and instituted an organization similar to that of the Red Army, right down to the formation of units for deployment against the civilian population and the use of political commissars to ensure loyalty. The anti-Bolshevik Whites, too, had internal-order battalions, grain requisitioning, political commissars, and terror, as civilians lamented.[22] But the Bolsheviks, unlike their enemies, boasted that they had an all-encompassing, scientific answer to everything, and they expended considerable resources to disseminate their ideology. Party thinking equated Bolshevism with the movement of history and thereby made all critics into counterrevolutionaries, even if they were fellow socialists. Meanwhile, in trying to manage industry, transport, fuel, food, housing, education, culture, all at the same time, during a time of war and ruin, the revolutionaries came face to face with their own lack of expertise, and yet the solution to their woes struck them with ideological horror: They had to engage the class enemy—"bourgeois specialists"—inherited from tsarist times, who often detested socialism but were willing to help rebuild the devastated country. "These people," Alexander Verkhovsky, tsarist general and Provisional Government war minister, presciently wrote of the Bolsheviks immediately after the October coup, "while promising everything, will give nothing—instead of peace, civil war; instead of bread, famine; instead of freedom, robbery, anarchy and murder."[23] But Verkhovsky soon joined the Red Army. This provides a striking contrast to the extreme hesitancy of almost any German old-regime holdovers to cooperate with the Weimar Republic. But the cooperative tsarist experts were not trusted even if they were loyal, because they were "bourgeois." Dependency on people perceived as class enemies shaped, indeed warped, Soviet politics and institutions. The technically skilled, who were distrusted politically, were paired with the politically loyal, who lacked technical competence, first in the army and then in every institution, from railroads to schools.[24] The unintentional upshot—a Communist watchdog shadowing every "bourgeois expert"—would persist even after the Reds were trained and became experts, creating a permanent dualist "party-state."

The revolutionary state became ever more powerful without ever overcoming its improvised, chaotic nature. Supervision was ad hoc, intermittent. Steinberg, a Left Socialist Revolutionary who served as justice commissar during the short-lived coalition government of 1918, tried but failed to curb the arbitrary power of the Extraordinary Commission for Combating Counter-revolution, Sabotage, and Speculation. Bureaucratic infighting alone did not defeat him, however. When the capital had shifted to Moscow in March 1918, the central Cheka had a mere 131 employees, 35 of whom were rank-and-file soldiers, 10 chauffeurs, and many others who were secretaries or couriers, leaving no more than around 55 operatives.[25] They carried the "budget" around in their pockets and holsters. Moreover, the carving out of a separate Cheka for Moscow came at the expense of the central apparatus. True, as of August 1918, even after the mass eviction from the Cheka of the Left SRs, the political police in the capital had grown to 683.[26] But more important, by summer's end 1918, *Izvestiya* would report the existence of local Chekas in 38 provinces and, lower down, in 75 counties (*uezd*).[27] Also, a separate Railroad Cheka took shape to battle "counterrevolution" across the far-flung rail network, and Cheka "special departments" arose for security in the Red Army. No one coordinated or controlled these political policemen. The local Chekas and the sundry parallel Chekas formed largely on their own. One example was that Kamyshinsk barge, another, the Yekaterinburg Cheka, which "was quartered at No. 7 Pushkin Street; a two-story building of no great size, with a deep cellar into which the prisoners were stuffed," wrote one operative who served there. "White Officers and priests [were] packed sardine-wise along with peasants who had concealed their grain against the requisitions. Every night we had a 'liquidation' of 'parasites'"—that is, the prisoners were brought up from the dungeon, made to cross a courtyard, and gunned down. This operative added that, as a result of confiscations from "the bourgeoisie," "there was a great mass of miscellaneous stuff: jewelry, banknotes, trinkets, garments, provisions. We brought it all together into one place and divided it up."[28] Overall, the political police were a mess, corrupt and at cross-purposes.[29] But "the Cheka" constituted not just a formal state agency; it was also a deadly mind-set, a presupposition of the existence of class enemies and an injunction to employ any and all means in their eradication.[30] Socialist critics of the political police, like Steinberg, were invariably told that the summary executions were "temporary," until the class war had been won, or the world revolution had taken place, or some other point on the horizon had been attained. In the meantime, Chekists said, history would forgive an excess of harshness but not of weakness. Lynch law and self-dealing—otherwise known as class war—simultaneously discredited the cause and galvanized militants. Violent chaos was a form of "administration," driven by a zealously held vision.

The fracturing of the imperial Russian geopolitical space, as well as the simultaneity of many civil war events from one end of Eurasia to another, militates against ease of narration. (Einstein once said that "the only reason for time is so that everything doesn't happen at once.") Below we take up the dictatorship of Stalin in Tsaritsyn (1918), the founding of the Communist International (1919), the Versailles Treaty (1919), the leftist revolutions or near revolutions in Germany, Hungary, and Italy (1919), and the shifting combat between Reds and Whites (1918–20). The next chapter continues the civil war story with examination of the Soviet-Polish War (1919–20), the Congress of the Peoples of the East (1920), the reconquest of Turkestan (1920), the mass peasant uprisings in Tambov and elsewhere (1920–21), the Kronstadt sailor revolt (1921), the 10th Party Congress, the war of reconquest in Georgia (1921), and the creation of the first Soviet satellite in Mongolia. Even all that—a vast panaorama—falls short of a comprehensive account of what transpired. A single Russia ceased to exist, replaced by a proliferation of states, in which would-be governments rose and fell (Kiev changed hands nineteen times). What knit together the fractured space were the reconstitution of state authority, deep legacies of Russification, ideas, and accompanying intrigues and personal networks. Here we shall see Stalin emerging as the dominant force in the regime, second only to Lenin. "There is no doubt," Trotsky later wrote, "that Stalin, like many others, was molded in the environment and experiences of the civil war, along with the entire group that later enabled him to establish a personal dictatorship . . . and a whole layer of workers and peasants raised to the status of commanders and administrators."[31] Russia's civil war produced a surge of people, institutions, relationships, and radicalism. Inside the whirlwind could be discerned the possibilities of Stalin's future personal dictatorship.

## WHITES AND REDS, OFFICERS AND GRAINS

After General Lavr Kornilov's death in April 1918, one of his ex-jail mates, Lieutenant General Anton Denikin (b. 1872), had assumed military command of the Volunteer Army. The son of an ethnic Polish seamstress and an ethnic Russian serf whose "emancipation" had come in the form of military conscription (for the usual term of twenty-five years), Denikin had served as chief of staff in succession to generals Alexeyev, Brusilov, and finally Kornilov. Initially he sought to keep the charismatic Kornilov's demise a secret from the Volunteers, fearing mass defections.[32] But the forces under Denikin, now numbering more than 10,000, held together and secured the southern Kuban River basin as a base. After the cancerous Alexeyev also died (October 8, 1918), Denikin catapulted to political command, too. His ascent in the south was paralleled in the northwest by that of General Nikolai Yudenich (b. 1862), the son of a minor court official, who was a former commander of Russian forces against the Ottoman empire, and "a man five foot two inches in height weighing about 280 pounds, [his] body shaped like a coupe, with unnoticeable legs."[33] Yudenich took advantage of sanctuary in breakaway Estonia to set up a second, smaller anti-Bolshevik base. Finally, there was Alexander Kolchak (b. 1874), the son of a major general in the artillery and himself the youngest vice admiral in Russian history (promoted in 1916), a man of valor and patriotism whose favorite reading was said to be the *Protocols of the Elders of Zion*.[34] In 1918, he returned from a futile mission to the United States via Vladivostok, but, as he was en route to joining the Volunteer

Army in the south, on November 16 a coup in Omsk (Western Siberia) brought Socialist Revolutionaries to power. Two days later, Siberian Cossacks arrested the socialists and invited Kolchak to take charge as "Supreme Ruler" of Russia. Kolchak did so, calling his new duties "a cross," but he promoted himself to full admiral—3,500 miles from the nearest port, and without a fleet.[35]

Kolchak (east), Denikin (south), and Yudenich (northwest) led three separate anti-Bolshevik groupings, vilifying the "commissars" as German agents and Jews, desecrators of all that was dear to Russian patriots and Orthodox believers. The Bolsheviks, in turn, pilloried their foes as "Whites," evoking the color of supporters of monarchical restoration against the revolution in France after 1789. None of the "White" leaders sought to restore the monarchy.[36] But they did seek to turn back the socialist revolution.

The White leaders' task of forming an army might have seemed within reach, but they had to attract officers who were utterly unlike them. Entering the Great War in 1914, the Russian officer corps had been dominated by General Staff Academy graduates (like Alexeyev, Kornilov, Denikin), as well as by the elite Imperial Guards, and 87.5 percent of the generals and 71.5 percent of the staff officers had been descendants of noble families. (Never mind that most owned no property.)[37] But Russia lost more than 60,000 officers during just the first two years of the Great War. At the same time, the officer ranks of imperial Russia, and then the Provisional Government, swelled to a quarter million. Both the replacements and the new recruits came overwhelmingly from the peasants and urban lower orders.[38] (Jews excluded, just about any male of military age in Russia who had the slightest bit of formal education could become an officer.)[39] Many of these tsarist officers of humble origin morphed into petty tyrants who abused the common soldier worse than had upper-class military men.[40] But their social backgrounds meant they were not preternaturally inclined to an antisocialist orientation. In other words, the Great War catastrophe had not only made possible the far-fetched Bolshevik coup, it had also rendered conservative armed opposition to Bolshevism more difficult. At the same time, the Whites greatly complicated their difficult task by refusing to acknowledge peasant land seizures, thereby alienating their potential mass base. Had it not been for the Cossacks, who eventually supported Denikin in numbers but remained reluctant to fight beyond their home territories of the Don and Kuban; the Czechoslovak Legionnaires, who remained reluctant to leave the Urals and Siberia unless it was for home but sometimes fought for Kolchak; and the Entente, which supplied military aid, there would have been no White movement.

Everything about the Red Army's birth proved difficult, too.[41] The Bolsheviks had wanted no part of peasant conscripts, a class they distrusted, and initially sought to recruit only workers, a fantasy that had to be relinquished.[42] In addition, the vast majority of Bolsheviks wanted no part of former tsarist officers: the revolution had been launched by soldiers and sailors in revolt against their authority. In fact, leftists in the Communist party, as well as Menshevik critics, repudiated a standing army with "a Bonaparte," calling for a democratic militia loyal to the soviets.[43] But Trotsky—who became the new war and naval commissar, and who had no special training in the military arts (he had never served in the army)—came out strongly in favor of a professisonal army led by real military men.[44] Trotsky would deem the famously democratizing Order No. 1 of 1917 "the single worthy document of the February Revolution," but he afforded no quarter to democracy in a Red Army.[45] The soldiers' committees that had brought down the tsar were formally abolished in March 1918.[46] Trotsky also issued a service appeal to former tsarist officers, even generals (March 27), and stated in a newspaper interview published the next day that "the tsarist legacy and deepening economic disarray have undermined people's sense of responsibility. . . . This has to stop. In the army as in the Soviet fleet, discipline must be discipline, soldiers must be soldiers, sailors sailors, and orders orders."[47] He also continued to insist that "we must have teachers who know something about the science of war."[48] Stalin would be among the most emphatic in rejection of these "military specialists." But Lenin shared Trotsky's view on the necessity of expertise, making it official policy.[49] Stalin and other opponents of bourgeois experts, however, continued the fight.[50]

Thus, the keys to the possibility of Red victory—military experts and peasant conscripts—remained under suspicion of treason. In the event, while the peasant revolution in many ways structured the entire civil war, the fraught incorporation of former tsarist officers structured the entire Soviet state.

Most former tsarist officers who took part in the civil war gravitated toward the anti-Bolshevik forces, some 60,000 to Denikin, 30,000 to Kolchak, and 10,000 to other commanders.[51] But by the end of the fighting, around 75,000 were serving in the Red Army, composing more than half the Bolsheviks' officer corps of approximately 130,000. Even more strikingly, around 775 generals and 1,726 other officers of the tsarist general staff would serve in the Red Army at one time or another.[52] Their motives varied from patriotism, preservation of the military establishment, and generous pay and rations, to concern for their family members kept as hostages. Would they be loyal? This question had prompted the Provisional Government to introduce "commissars" alongside the inherited tsarist officer corps to prevent counterrevolution, and the Bolsheviks expanded the practice.[53] Every commander at every level was supposed to be paired with at least one commissar, alongside of which were instituted appointed "political departments" for clerical and propaganda work.[54] Bolshevik political commissars' powers included "preventing any counterrevolutionary move, wherever it might come from" and arresting "those who violate the revolutionary order."[55] The officers alone were supposed to make all operational decisions, but in practice these began to be considered as valid only with both the commander's and the commissar's signatures, opening the way to commissar involvement in purely military matters.[56] Both political and military tensions became endemic.[57]

An odd civil war it would be, then: Whites pushing peasants away and attempting to recruit officers from the lower orders to fight the socialists; Reds giving command posts to tsarist officers, albeit only under armed guard and recruiting peasants only reluctantly. Had the Whites embraced the peasant revolution, or the Reds driven all former tsarist officers into White hands, Lenin, Trotsky, Stalin, and the rest would have been delivered back into exile or hung from the lampposts.

Within this electrified political atmosphere, Russia's civil war was in many ways a war of town against country, a scramble for grains (wheat, rye, oats, barley).[58] Neither food supply failures nor even recourse to requisitioning originated with Bolshevism, however. The tsarist agricultural ministry, back in fall 1916, had introduced a grain-quota system (*prodrazverstka*), under which quotas at fixed prices were assessed on provincial authorities, who in turn assessed the county authorities, down to the villages. Predictably, this failed. In March 1917, after marches for bread helped precipitate the tsar's downfall, the Provisional Government had founded a stand-alone ministry for the food supply and declared a state "grain monopoly" over distribution, except for a fixed minimum to be left with the growers, but provincial and district supply committees could not extract the grain, while inflation debased the currency offered to peasants (in any case, consumer goods were largely unavailable for purchase).[59] Petrograd ate, meagerly, only because bagmen flouted the monopoly and jammed the river ports, roads, and rail lines, often forced to ride dangerously on the roofs of the train cars, to haul foodstuffs back from villages for resale. In late August 1917, during the Kerensky-Kornilov showdown, the Provisional Government suddenly doubled the price its state agents paid to the peasants for grain, a concession internal critics called a "complete capitulation," but supplies of paper money, not to mention sacks and railcars, were insufficient. The Provisional Government found itself dependent on peasant cooperation to feed the cities and army, but unwilling to indulge peasant desires on the land question.[60] On October 16, 1917, normally a month of abundance following the harvest, a desperate-sounding (last) minister of food supply for the Provisional Government observed, "We must cease our attempts at persuasion . . . a shift to compulsion is now absolutely necessary."[61] War and attempted state administration of food supply had pushed toward still greater clumsy state action in the form of confiscations and distributions.[62]

The Bolsheviks, who had even less tolerance for private traders, resolved to enforce the Provisional Government's failed state grain monopoly, while reinventing it in class terms, seeking to enlist "poor" peasants in locating grain stores. The poor peasants did not rise to the summons, but the Bolshevik ability to enforce compulsion proved far more vigorous.[63] Still, the underlying policy of assigned delivery quotas at artificially set prices to be exchanged for nonexistent industrial goods was not going to feed the cities and army. The Red Army grew from nonexistent in early 1918 to a staggering 600,000 troops already by December of that year, at least in terms of the rations being requested; idled people were hungry.[64] The promise of food helped drive recruitment, but delivering on the promise was another matter. In the event, many soldiers and most ordinary people ate because much of the population was turned into illegal private traders (not always willingly).[65] A non-Bolshevik newspaper, wryly noting that "hundreds of thousands of members of different committees have to be fed," offered a logical suggestion: legal restoration of free trade and free prices in grain.[66] That indeed would have been the answer, but it remained heresy.

Lenin understood next to nothing of Russian agriculture, land utilization, migrant labor, or the actual operations of the peasant commune, let alone market incentives. In late January 1918, he had appointed Trotsky chairman of a short-lived Extraordinary Commission for Food and Transport; not long thereafter a food commissariat was established, and on February 25 Alexander Tsyurupa, an agricultural academy graduate, was appointed commissar. Lenin suggested that all peasants be compelled to deliver grain by name, and that those who failed to do so "be shot on the spot." Tsyurupa and even Trotsky balked.[67] Lenin continued to fulminate (May 9, 1918) against "those who have grain and fail to deliver it to properly designated rail stations and shipping points," declaring them to be *"enemies of the people."*[68] That same month the regime proclaimed a "food dictatorship" and "a great crusade against grain speculators, kulaks, bloodsuckers, disorganizers, bribe-takers," who had grown "fat and rich during the war" and "now refuse to give bread to starving people."[69] Dzierżyński and Lunacharsky warned this assault would imperil Bolshevik relations with the peasantry, but Lenin ignored their objections.[70] By winter, with civil war in full swing, the Bolsheviks would climb down from an *official* policy of war against kulaks and speculators back to one of obligatory delivery quotas of foodstuffs at fixed prices in exchange for industrial goods.[71] Still, in practice, they continued to employ blocking detachments to interdict private traders and to requisition food at gunpoint in the name of class warfare, a platform for Stalin's blossoming.[72]

## MORE THAN A BARGE: STALIN IN TSARITSYN (1918)

No region would prove more decisive in the civil war than the Volga valley, a premiere source of food and recruits as well as the strategic separator between the two large White armies of Kolchak (Urals-Siberia) and Denikin (Don-Kuban).[73] No locale better encapsulated the class warfare revolutionary dynamic than Tsaritsyn, on the confluence of the Volga and the Tsaritsa rivers. It had become the largest industrial center in Russia's southeast (population 150,000) and had traced the revolution in telescoped fashion, going from an absence of Bolsheviks (February 1917) to domination by Bolsheviks (September 1917) even before the coup in Petrograd.[74] Red Tsaritsyn was a critical rail junction for grain and raw materials linking the Caucasus and Moscow, but it lay just east of the expansive Don and Kuban valleys, Cossack lands where the Volunteer Army-White southern base formed.[75] The military situation around Red Tsaritsyn had grown precarious, but workers in Moscow and Petrograd were receiving just four ounces of bread every other day, and Tsaritsyn, situated amid grain-growing regions, looked like a solution. To lead a southern food expedition, Lenin selected a tough worker Bolshevik, Alexander Shlyapnikov, the labor commissar. Tsyurupa, who had become close to Lenin, suggested sending along Stalin as well. In the event, Shlyapnikov became bogged down in Moscow, and Stalin ended up going without him, departing Moscow with 460 armed men on June 4,

1918, and arriving two days later at Tsaritsyn's train station.[76] His role, in essence, was Bolshevik bandit-in-chief in the south to feed the northern capital. Already a top member of the central government (or Council of People's Commissars), Stalin was concomitantly named "director for food affairs in South Russia." The food crisis, and Stalin's chance appointment as sole head of an armed expedition to relieve it, enabled him to reprise his exploits at Batum (1902), Chiatura (1905), and Baku (1907), but this time with greater consequence.

Lenin had already appointed someone as Red Tsaritsyn's supreme military commander: Andrei Snesarev (b. 1865), a tsarist staff officer who had risen to the rank of lieutenant general under the Provisional Government and volunteered to the Reds. He had arrived in Tsaritsyn on May 27, 1918, with a Council of People's Commissar mandate signed by Lenin as the newly named head of the new Military Commissariat of the North Caucasus. With Red forces melting away, Snesarev set about creating a real army out of ragtag local partisan warfare units, many of which had recently been driven from Ukraine by the advancing Reichswehr and resembled roaming bandits. His first report to the center (May 29) indicated a dire need for more tsarist military specialists.[77] But on June 2, a political commissar in Tsaritsyn informed Moscow that locals "have heard little about the formation of a Red Army. . . . Here we have a mass of staff headquarters and bosses, beginning with basic ones right through extraordinary ones and supreme command ones."[78] It was four days later that Stalin arrived.

Stalin set up residence not in the local Hotel France, but in a parked railway carriage and like a commander, donned a collarless tunic—the quasi-military style of attire made famous by Kerensky—and ordered a local cobbler to fashion him a pair of high black boots.[79] Stalin also had his teenage wife, Nadya, in tow; she wore a military tunic and worked in his traveling "secretariat." Already on his first workday, June 7, he boasted to Lenin that he would send eight express trains loaded with grain as he "pumped out" the fertile region, adding, "Be assured, our hand will not tremble." At the same time, Stalin complained, "If our military 'specialists' (cobblers!) had not been asleep or idle, the railway line would not have been cut, and if the line is restored, it will not be because but in spite of them."[80] On June 10, Lenin issued a proclamation "to all toilers" reporting that food help was on the way: "People's Commissar Stalin, located in Tsaritsyn and leading all food provisioning from the Don and Kuban, has telegraphed us about the immense grain reserves he soon hopes to send northwards."[81] In fact, within a few weeks, Stalin dispatched the first trainloads of grain northward, said to be about 9,000 tons, although how much total grain Stalin managed to forward northward overall remains unclear. Still, he spared nothing and no one in trying. His frequent telegrams to Lenin promised further food shipments, and dripped with venom against other regime officials operating in parallel, whom he depicted as saboteurs.[82]

Among the key instruments of the swaggering cobbler's son was a Tsaritsyn Cheka, which had just announced its existence in May 1918 when it took over a two-story mansion overlooking the Volga. It made the top floor into offices and living quarters, and partitioned the lower floor into cells, which were soon stuffed with prisoners beaten unconscious to "confess." Targets included "bourgeois," clergy, intelligentsia, and tsarist officers, many of whom had answered a local appeal to join the Red Army. Workers and peasants were also arrested as counterrevolutionaries if they dared to criticize the arbitrary arrests and torture, or if someone said they had.[83] Rumors of atrocities constituted part of the Cheka's mystique: the Kharkov Cheka was said to scalp victims, the Yekaterinoslav Cheka to stone or crucify them, and the Kremenchug Cheka to impale them on stakes.[84] In Tsaritsyn, the Cheka was said to cut through human bones with handsaws.[85] Alexander I. Chervyakov (b. 1890), who had emerged as the regional Cheka boss in Tsaritsyn, conducted himself like a tyrant, and he and his leather-clad thugs settled their own scores, including with other Cheka operatives, but now they answered to Stalin.[86] An eyewitness, the Bolshevik Fyodor Ilin, who had taken the name Raskolnikov from the Dostoevsky character, recalled that "Stalin in Tsaritsyn was everything"—de facto boss of the regional Cheka, and soon, of the regional Red Army.[87]

Snesarev had built a local Red Army of 20,000 and organized the defenses of Tsaritsyn's perimeter as fighting raged along the Tsaritsyn-Yekaterinodar railway.[88] Stalin, however, was angling to displace the former tsarist officer. On July 10, he telegrammed Lenin that "there is plenty of grain in the South, but in order to get it, we need a functioning apparatus that does not meet obstacles on the part of [military] echelons, commanders, and such." Therefore, Stalin concluded, "For the good of the cause, I need military powers. I have already written about this, but have received no reply. Very well. In that case, I shall myself, without formalities, dismiss army commanders and commissars damaging the cause. . . . The absence of a paper from Trotsky will not stop me."[89] Here was brazen insubordination of the war commissar's authority, which Trotsky took surprisingly well. He telegrammed Stalin on July 17 indicating that Snesarev ought to be retained as commander (*voenruk*), but that "if you consider it undesirable to retain Snesarev as military commissar, inform me and I will remove him. Your Trotsky."[90] Stalin leapt at the offer. On July 19, approval came for the replacement of Snesarev and his Military Commissariat of the North Caucasus by a local Revolutionary Military Council consisting of three people: Stalin; the top Tsaritsyn Bolshevik, Sergei Minin, who was the son of a priest and, like Stalin, a former seminary student; and one other local official. The order from Moscow bore the notation: "The present telegram is sent with Lenin's approval."[91] Lenin needed food.[92] Stalin wanted autonomy from Trotsky.

Stalin now expropriated Snesarev's operations department: a July 22 inventory yielded typewriter (Remington), one; telephone (city line), one; telephone (Tsaritsyn HQ), one; desks, four; wicker chairs, seven; pens, three; pencils, five; folders, one; trash can, one.[93] Stalin had forced Snesarev, whom he viewed as Trotsky's man, to unite two armies under the command of Klim Voroshilov.[94] Born in Lugansk, the same Donbass coal-mining hometown as Alexander Chervyakov of the Tsaritsyn Cheka, Voroshilov had met Stalin at the 4th Party Congress in 1906 (they shared a room). His origins were similarly humble: the son of a washerwoman and a peasant who worked the mines and railways. Voroshilov had ended his formal schooling at age eight, tended animals, and trained as a locksmith. In August 1917, he took over the Lugansk City Duma from Chervyakov, heading it through February 1918, when the Germans began to overrun Ukraine and he turned to partisan warfare, which constituted his first military experience.[95] He had retreated from Ukraine to Tsaritsyn with other Red Guards. Although a fine horseman and marksman, and a genuine proletarian, which garnered him some popularity with rank-and-file troops, he was no strategist. "Personally Voroshilov does not sufficiently possess the characteristics necessary for a military chief," Snesarev had written to Trotsky in July 1918, adding that he "does not observe elementary rules of commanding troops."[96] But Stalin, with Voroshilov, pushed a defense plan that stipulated removing troops from Tsaritsyn's northern defenses to its southern and western side for an offensive. It was duly launched on August 1. Within three days Tsaritsyn had lost contact with Moscow; units had to be transferred back to the city's north. Stalin wrote to Lenin (August 4) blaming his "inheritance" from Snesarev.[97]

Stalin had Snesarev and various tsarist-era military men arrested, part of a sweep of "military specialists" that included the entire local artillery directorate down to the scribes.[98] They were imprisoned on a barge moored in the river in front of Cheka HQ. Trotsky sent an aide, the Siberian Alexei Okulov, to investigate, and he freed Snesarev (who was reassigned elsewhere), while criticizing Stalin and Voroshilov. Trotsky also sent a stern telegram ordering Tsaritsyn to allow tsarist officers to do their jobs, but Stalin wrote on it, "Take no account."[99] Many of the 400 or so arrestees crammed onto the barge would die of starvation or a bullet to the neck that summer of 1918.

Stalin was conducting a parallel incandescent intrigue against a high-level fuel expedition. Fuel, too, was scarce in Moscow and Lenin had tasked the Bolshevik K. E. Makhrovsky of the Supreme Council of the Economy with mounting an expedition to the Grozny refinery in the North Caucasus with 10 million rubles in cash to secure petroleum. Accompanied by the non-Communist technical expert N. P. Alekseev of the transport commissariat, as well as Sergei Kirov, head of the Terek province (North Caucasus) soviet, Makhrovsky's special tanker train reached Tsaritsyn around July 23, passing through on its way to Grozny. Stalin informed them that the rail lines farther south had fallen into the hands of rebellious Chechens and Terek Cossacks. Makhrovsky, after also failing to lay claim even to the fuel supplies he spotted in Tsaritsyn, returned to Moscow to report, leaving behind his empty fuel train and the 10 million rubles in a locked suitcase with his wife and the non-party specialist Alekseev. On August 13, Kirov accosted Makhrovsky's wife and demanded the money, in Stalin's name. She refused, then privately discussed with Alekseev how to hide it at a new location. Makhrovsky arrived back in Tsaritsyn on August 15. After further back and forth about the 10 million and related matters, on the night of August 17–18, Stalin had Alekseev arrested and driven to the Cheka, accompanied by Makhrovsky, to face charges of masterminding a wide conspiracy to seize power. His coconspirators were said to be, variously, ex-tsarist officers, Serbian officers, Socialist Revolutionaries, trade unionists, one of Trotsky's "generals," ex-Provisional Government officials.[100] "All specialists," the Cheka chief Chervyakov is said to have remarked, "are bourgeois and most are counterrevolutionary."[101]

Makhrovsky, too, found himself under arrest. Tsaritsyn's Cheka refused to recognize his government mandate signed by Lenin. "Comrade, give up talking about the center and the necessity of the localities' subordination to it," the interrogator Ivanov told Makhrovsky, according to the latter's account (submitted to Lenin). "In Moscow they do things their way, and here we do it all afresh in our own fashion. . . . The center cannot dictate anything to us. We dictate our will to the center, for we are the power in the localities."[102] Later that same month, when the local soviet sought to investigate unfounded arrests and summary executions by the Tsaritsyn Cheka, the latter fended them off by claiming that their mandate came from the center. In fact, they followed Stalin's orders. Stalin would eventually let Makhrovsky go, but he got what he sought: the fuel expedition's money, vehicles, and all other property.[103]

Stalin had his prisoner barge, like his local counterparts up and down the Volga, but he had more than a barge. With fanfare, the Stalin-directed Tsaritsyn Cheka proclaimed the discovery of millions of rubles aimed at funding counterrevolution; mass arrests followed, and the execution of twenty-three leaders of an "Alekseev counter-revolutionary-White Guard plot of Right SRs and Black Hundred officers."[104] No trial took place. Alekseev was beaten to a bloody pulp, then shot, along with his two sons (one a teenager); others in custody for whatever reason, or for no reason, were rolled into the "plot." Stalin made energetic use of the press, having changed (on August 7) the local newspaper *News of the North Caucasus Military District* into the mass-oriented *Soldier of the Revolution;* the foiling of the Alekseev "conspiracy" was duly proclaimed in an "extra" edition (August 21, 1918). "Stalin placed high hopes on agitation," wrote Colonel Anatoly Nosovich, a former tsarist officer and a member of the command staff in the Red Army in Tsaritsyn. "He frequently remarked in arguments over the military arts that everything being said concerning the necessity of the military arts is fine, but if the most talented commander in the world lacked politically conscious soldiers properly prepared by agitation, then, believe me, he would not be able to do anything against revolutionaries who were small in number but highly motivated."[105]

When news of the grand "Alekseev plot" broke, General Pyotr Krasnov, the recently elected ataman (leader) of the Don Cossacks, and his army had surrounded Tsaritsyn, but Stalin's executions did not flow from panic.[106] Many *were* panicking at the prospect of the Cossacks' entrance into the Red city, but Stalin was enacting a strategy, wielding the specter of "counterrevolution" to galvanize the workers and intimidate would-be anti-Bolsheviks. In a political spectacle, the Cheka forced "the bourgeoisie" to dig defense trenches around the city, and conspicuously frog-marched inmates from "the barge" to the prison, accompanied by whispers they were being led to their deaths. Informants were said to be everywhere.[107] Above all, the Stalin-directed Cheka's extermination of "enemies" was given a strong propaganda message: it was said that while Krasnov's White forces surrounded Tsaritsyn, the internal foes of the revolution were planning to stage an uprising to enable the Cossacks to capture the city.[108] (Later, this would be called a fifth column.) Here, in tiniest embryo, was the scenario of countless fabricated trials of the 1920s and 30s, culminating in the monstrous terror of 1937–38.

So entrenched was Stalin's class-inflected modus operandi that he sought to restore make-or-break rail lines by the arrest or summary execution of the few technical specialists who actually knew something about rail lines, because they were class aliens, saboteurs by definition. Admittedly, he was not so improvident as to be against all former tsarist officers.[109] But he relied on upstarts, those who, like himself, had emerged from "the people," so long as they remained loyal to him. The proletarian Voroshilov (b. 1881) showed no inclination to pursue his own ambitions at Stalin's expense. Voroshilov would deem Stalin's actions "a ruthless purge of the rear, administered by an iron hand"—hardly a vice among Bolsheviks.

Around this time (August 1918), after Kazan had fallen to the Whites, Trotsky had gone to Sviyazhsk, near Kazan, where he got to know the former tsarist colonel and Latvian commander Jukums Vācietis, whom he promoted to Red supreme commander (a position that had been vacant).[110] Trotsky also got to know Fyodor Raskolnikov, commander of the Volga Flotilla, and two commissars, Ivan Smirnov (the "Siberian Lenin") and Arkady Rozengolts, a Kazan-battle group that would form something of Trotsky's counterpart to Stalin's Tsaritsynites.[111] To save the collapsing front, Trotsky ordered that "if any unit retreats of its own accord, the first to be shot will be the commissar, the second, the commander . . . cowards, self-seekers, and traitors will not get away from a bullet."[112] Trotsky's objections about Stalin did not, therefore, involve the latter's excess of inhumanity, but his military amateurism and insubordination. Stalin, for his part, bristled at the military orders from afar, which, to him, took no account of "local conditions." He was illegally diverting supplies sent from Moscow for the Caucasus front farther south, locking up and shooting military specialists, and aiming to have armed workers hold the city, Red Guard style.

In Tsaritsyn, Stalin revealed himself in depth: rabidly partisan toward class thinking and autodidacts; headstrong and prickly; attentive to political lessons but militarily ignorant. Trotsky perceived the martial dilettantism, willfulness, and prickliness, but little else. Few besides Voroshilov caught the full Stalin. But one person who "got" Stalin was the former tsarist officer Nosovich (b. 1878), a descendant of nobility who had joined the Reds in 1918 and escaped Stalin's guillotine for class aliens and critics by defecting to the Whites that fall, an act that reconfirmed Stalin in his view about military specialists.[113] "Stalin does not hesitate in the choice of paths to realize his aims," Nosovich (under the pseudonym A. Black Sea Man) wrote in his real-time exposé of the Red camp. "Clever, smart, educated and extremely shifty, [Stalin] is the evil genius of Tsaritsyn and its inhabitants. All manner of requisitioning, apartment evictions, searches accompanied by shameless thievery, arrests, and other violence used against civilians became everyday phenomena in the life of Tsaritsyn." Nosovich correctly explained the true nature of the Georgian's assignment—grain at any cost—and the real threats Red Tsaritsyn faced. He captured not only Stalin's thirst for absolute power but his absolute dedication to the cause: Stalin stole 10 million rubles and a fleet of vehicles from his own (Red) side not for personal luxuries, but for defense of the revolution; he was executing "counterrevolutionaries" without proof or trial, not from sadism or panic, but as a political strategy, to galvanize the masses. "To be fair," Nosovich concluded, "Stalin's energy could be envied by any of the old administrators, and his ability to get things done in whatever circumstances was something to go to school for."[114] Nonetheless, Tsaritsyn hung by a thread.

## STALIN'S RECALL AND CLOSE CALL

When Lenin was shot at the Mikhelson factory in Moscow on August 30, 1918, Stalin exchanged telegrams with Sverdlov about his patron's precarious condition.[115] With Stalin and Trotsky absent from Moscow, Sverdlov took charge; slight in physical stature yet with a booming baritone, he was authoritative in a meeting hall but commanded nothing of the stature of a Lenin. Trotsky had the highest profile after Lenin, while Stalin's profile was growing, but the two had developed deep mutual enmity; Sverdlov could neither resolve their differences nor rise above either of the two. All three had to pray for Lenin's recovery: Bolshevik survival depended on it.

As Lenin convalesced, Trotsky and Stalin deepened their antagonism. On September 11, 1918, a "southern front" replaced the North Caucasus military district and Sverdlov summoned Stalin to Moscow; he arrived on September 14 and the day after that had an audience with Sverdlov and Lenin. Trotsky, at a session of the Revolutionary Military Council of the Republic on September 17, which

Stalin attended, appointed Pavel Sytin, a former major general in the tsarist army, above Voroshilov as commander of the southern front (not merely a place, but like an army group).[116] Stalin arrived back in Tsaritsyn on September 24; three days later, he complained to Lenin that Tsaritsyn wholly lacked ammunition and nothing was arriving from Moscow ("some kind of criminal negligence, outright treachery. If this persists, we will for sure lose the war in the South.")[117] That same day, Stalin demanded from the military a load of new weapons and 100,000 full sets of uniforms (more than the number of troops locally), and, in purple ink, threatened, "we declare that if these demands (which are the minimum considering the number of troops on the Southern Front) are not met with the utmost urgency, we shall be forced to cease military action and withdraw to the left bank of the Volga."[118]

Major General Sytin arrived in Tsaritsyn on September 29, 1918; immediately Stalin and Minin obstructed his prerogative to name commanders or issue operational orders, and objected to his plan to ensure contact with Moscow by moving the front headquarters outside Tsaritsyn.[119] On October 1, Stalin formally requested that Sytin be replaced by Voroshilov.[120] Sverdlov telegrammed sternly that same day: "All decisions of the Revolutionary Military Council of the Republic"—Trotsky—"are binding on the Revolutionary Military Councils of the front."[121] Trotsky complained to Sverdlov (October 2), and sent a direct order (October 3) to Stalin and Voroshilov not to interfere in military matters.[122] That same day, Stalin wrote to Lenin excoriating his nemesis at length. "The point is that Trotsky generally speaking cannot get by without noisy gestures," Stalin wrote. "At Brest-Litovsk he delivered a blow to the cause by his far-fetched 'leftist' gesturing. On the question of the Czechoslovaks he similarly harmed the cause by his gesturing with noisy diplomacy. . . . Now he delivers a further blow by his gesturing about discipline, and yet all that this Trotskyite discipline amounts to in reality is the most prominent leaders on the war front peering up the backside of military specialists from the camp of 'nonparty' counter-revolutionaries."[123] In fact, although Trotsky argued that revolution would radically change everything, even speech, he insisted that revolution had not changed war: the same operational tactics, logistics, basic military organization still held.[124] On military matters, Stalin was the leftist, waging relentless class warfare against former tsarist officers, regardless of their behavior. Disingenuously, Stalin concluded his October 3 telegram to Lenin, "I am no lover of noise and scandal," and "right now, before it's too late, it's necessary to bridle Trotsky, bringing him to heel." Sverdlov counseled diplomacy, but on October 4, Trotsky, from elsewhere in the south, telegrammed Sverdlov, with a copy to Lenin, "I categorically insist on Stalin's recall."[125]

And so the clash had come to its logical conclusion: Trotsky and Stalin each appealing to Lenin for the other's removal.

In his incredulous fury, Trotsky pointed out that the Red Army outnumbered the Whites three to one on the southern front, yet Tsaritsyn remained in grave danger.[126] "Voroshilov could command a regiment, but not an army of 50,000 soldiers," Trotsky wrote in his October 4 telegram demanding Stalin's recall. "Nonetheless, I will leave him [Voroshilov] as commander of the Tenth Tsaritsyn Army on the condition that he is subordinated to the [overall] Southern Front Commander Sytin." Trotsky threatened that "if this order is not implemented by tomorrow, I will remand Voroshilov and Minin to court martial and publish this fact in an order to the army. . . . No more time for diplomacy. Tsaritsyn should either follow orders or get out."[127] On October 5, Sverdlov again directed Stalin, Minin, and Voroshilov to fulfill Trotsky's orders.[128]

Lenin acceded to Trotsky's demand to recall Stalin—Tsaritsyn could not be lost—but refused Trotsky's demand to punish Stalin. "I received word of Stalin's departure from Tsaritsyn for Moscow," Sverdlov telegrammed Trotsky (October 5). "I consider maximum caution necessary right now regarding the Tsaritsyn-ites. There are many old comrades there. Everything must be done to avoid conflict without retreating from conducting a hard line. Needless to say I am communicating only my opinion."[129] Sverdlov had tactfully revealed his judgment of Stalin, while imposing limits on Trotsky. On October 6, Stalin departed for Moscow, meeting Lenin on the eighth.[130] In Tsaritsyn, on October 7, an assembly of more than fifty local party, soviet, and trade union activists chaired by Minin approved a resolution recommending "a national congress to reexamine and assess the policy of the center" on hiring former tsarist military brass. This act—provincials calling upon the Central Committee to reverse policy—demonstrated both the decentralization of power in 1918 and the locals' confidence in having a "roof" (or protector) in Stalin.[131] In Moscow, however, Stalin failed to get his way: he was relieved of his post on the southern front, although he was appointed a member of the central Military Council of the Republic, an obvious attempt to mollify him.[132] Stalin would now have to communicate with Trotsky by addressing telegrams to the "Chairman of the Military Council" from "Member of the Military Council Stalin."[133]

Stalin returned to Tsaritsyn around October 11, evidently in the company of Sverdlov, who aimed to impose a local diplomatic resolution on the daggers-drawn Red camp.[134] The Whites reached Tsaritsyn's outskirts on October 15, 1918, a day on which the situation was described as "catastrophic" in a telegram sent by Red supreme military commander Vācietis to Voroshilov, with copies to Sytin and Trotsky; Vācietis blamed Voroshilov's refusal to cooperate with his superior, Sytin.[135] Stalin departed Tsaritsyn for good on October 19–20, in the heat of the decisive battle. Trotsky arrived to replace him and salvage the city's defense.[136]

Tsaritsyn would be saved—just barely—not by Trotsky but by Dmitry Zhloba, whose "Steel Division" of 15,000 men had left the Caucasus front, covered 500 miles in sixteen days, and surprised the Whites' unguarded rear.[137] On October 25, the Steel Division pushed the Cossacks back across the Don.[138] Four days later, Stalin reported to a plenum of the Moscow soviet how dicey the situation had been.[139] Indeed, had Tsaritsyn fallen that autumn of 1918, he might have faced a government inquiry and disciplinary action, as well as permanent reputational damage.[140]

## A WORLD TURNING
## (NOVEMBER 1918-JANUARY 1919)

Lenin was hardly the only high stakes gambler. Germany's high command had attempted one immense gamble after another: the Schlieffen Plan (1914) to win a war of mobility; Verdun (1916) to bleed the enemy white in a new strategy of attrition; unrestricted U-boat warfare (1917) to break the stranglehold of the British naval blockade; sending Lenin home to foment chaos and knock Russia out of the war; and, following a German victory on the eastern front, an all-out offensive on the western front launched March 21, 1918.[141] By June, the German army in the west had come within thirty-seven miles of Paris, close enough to strike it with Big Bertha heavy artillery. But the Reichswehr failed to take the French capital, after suffering one million casualties.[142] United States troops, provoked into the war by the U-boats, had begun arriving in France at the rate of 120,000 per month (the United States had entered the war in early 1917 with 150,000 men under arms *total*). Canada, Australia, New Zealand, India, and

South Africa, meanwhile, put even more men into military action on behalf of Britain than would the United States, and in August 1918, the reinforced Allies counterattacked. True, thanks to Brest-Litovsk—or rather, to Berlin's willingness to violate its own treaty prohibitions—Germany shifted half a million troops to the western front, increasing its strength there to 192 divisions from 150.[143] But by September 28, 1918, Deputy Chief of Staff General Erich Ludendorff, the man responsible for the western offensive, informed his superior, Field Marshall Paul von Hindenburg, that the Reich had no prospect of winning: Germany lacked reserves to send into battle. What Ludendorff did not say was that during the western offensive, nearly a million Reichswehr soldiers were bogged down in a disorganized occupation of the east that instead of extracting resources consumed them.[144] (Germany had to export 80,000 tons of coal just to get railways in Ukraine restarted.) Ludendorff would scapegoat Bolshevism and its "infection" of German troops, lamenting, "I often dreamed of this [Russian] revolution, which would so lighten the burden of our war, but today the dream is suddenly realized in an unanticipated way."[145] But as one scholar explained, "The man who defeated Ludendorff the soldier, was not so much [Allied Supreme Commander] Marshal Foch, as Ludendorff the politician."[146]

Meanwhile, to salvage the retreating Reichswehr—which was everywhere on foreign soil, from France to Ukraine—a broken Ludendorff proposed importuning the Allies for an immediate cease-fire, but the civilians in a new German cabinet refused while contemplating an all-out mobilization of the civilian population for a last stand—exactly the opposite of the future stab-in-the-back legend.[147] Ludendorff soon changed his mind about begging for an armistice and resigned; the cabinet never managed the civilian mobilization.

On November 9, inside the neoclassical Bolshoi Theater, Lenin crowed to the delegates to the Sixth All-Russia Congress of Soviets, "we have never been so near to international proletarian revolution as we are now."[148] That same day, as it turned out, the staunch monarchist Hindenburg and others in the German high command, fearing a domestic version of the kind of revolution they had sent Lenin to incite in Russia, pressed the kaiser to abdicate. Wilhelm II had his imperial train shunted across the border into the Netherlands and, once in personal safety, signed a formal abdication.[149] (Unlike his executed cousin Nicky, Willy would live a long life and die peacefully in exile.) An armistice followed on November 11, 1918, signed in Marshal Foch's railway carriage in a French forest near the front lines. The armistice called for the immediate withdrawal of German troops everywhere, except in the former Russian empire, where the Germans were to remain until further instructed by the Entente.[150] Two days later, Moscow unilaterally repudiated the Brest-Litovsk Treaty as well as the August 1918 Supplementary Treaty (wih its 6 billion ruble indemnity, already partially paid).[151] (The victorious Allies would soon compel Germany to renounce Brest-Litovsk.) After fifty-two gruesome months, the Great War was over. Lenin was in such a good mood he released non-Bolshevik socialists from prison and, on November 30, 1918, relegalized the Menshevik party.[152]

The repercussions of the war were immense, and enduring. Wartime GDP had increased in the United States and in the United Kingdom, but in Austria, France, the Ottoman empire, and Russia it cratered by between 30 and 40 percent.[153] The Great War required unprecedented levels of taxation and state economic control across belligerent countries, most of which would not be rolled back.[154] Beyond the 8.5 million war dead and the nearly 8 million taken prisoner or missing, an influenza epidemic would infect 500 million people globally and kill at least 50 million, fully 3 percent of the global population (some estimates range up to 100 million).[155] Some 20 million people returned home maimed in some fashion. One and a half million Brits were crippled (the disabled received compensation: 16 shillings a week for a lost right arm, 11 shillings sixpence for a lost right hand and forearm, 10 for a lost left arm, nothing for a disfigured face). In Germany, around 2.7 million people returned with war-related disabilities, alongside half a million war widows and 1.2 million orphans. In the interest of maintaining public order, let alone to repay a debt, soldiers and widows were granted war-related pensions. Other war-influenced emergency social policies included emergency housing decrees, which willy-nilly introduced permanent government regulation. Unemployment insurance, cash sickness benefits, birth and burial grants were expanded into a proto-welfare state, spurred by warfare. The Russian empire lost 2 million dead and 2.5 millon wounded.[156] An estimated 2.4 million Russian subjects contracted disease, while 3.9 million were taken prisoner, a massive surrendering equal to all the POWs of other belligerents combined.[157] It was in such a context that Trotsky scorned "papist-Quaker babble about the sanctity of human life," and Lenin approvingly quoted Machiavelli to the effect that "violence can only be met with violence."[158]

Lenin's big gambles—accepting imperial German aid to return to Russia; the coup in Petrograd; the capitulatory separate peace with Germany—had paid off. Russia and Germany, on opposing sides in the war but now both vanquished, provided an illuminating contrast. He would admit that "the war taught us much, not only that people suffered, but that those who have the best technology, discipline, and machinery come out on top."[159] Contemporaries widely remarked on the similarities in the methods of Ludendorff (b. 1865) and Lenin (b. 1870), as well as wartime German and Bolshevik policies generally.[160] The German military occupiers of Eastern Europe had resorted to population registration, property confiscation, conscription, and promiscuous issuance of decrees, claiming an unlimited mandate while foundering in self-made administrative chaos. But unlike Bolshevism, German wartime rule in Eastern Europe did not organize the populace politically and culturally. No native-language newspapers or native-language schools had been established to involve and shape the local societies. Instead, the Germans obsessed over how to keep their German staff awash in *Kultur,* lest they go native. If not for the local Jews who spoke Yiddish and adapted quickly to German as translators, the German overlords would have been unable to communicate.[161] The Germans put forth no narratives of overarching purpose that elicited mass involvement, and they did not build mass organizations. Germany's experience in Eastern Europe demonstrated not only how much Bolshevism owed to the Great War, but how much Bolshevism transcended a military-style occupation.[162] In addition, contrasting Ludendorff's private kingdom in Lithuania, western Belorussia, and Latvia with Stalin's in Tsaritsyn, we can see that Stalin exhibited the exact opposite talents of Ludendorff: military amateurism but political cunning.

Voroshilov, Stalin's protégé, was hanging on as commander of the Tenth Army in Tsaritsyn.[163] At first, Supreme Commander Vācietis wanted him sacked, but Trotsky, while insisting on the immediate removal of Sergei Minin ("conducts extremely harmful policies"), allowed Voroshilov to remain, provided someone competent could be assigned alongside him.[164] Soon, however, Trotsky telegrammed Sverdlov demanding Voroshilov's removal, too ("shows no initiative, trivialities, talentless").[165] Vācietis, meanwhile, had softened, indicating he was not strongly against Voroshilov being appointed to a Red Army command in Ukraine (he may have had no other candidate for the post).[166] Trotsky exploded. "A compromise is necessary but not a rotten one," he pleaded to Lenin (January 11, 1919). "Essentially, all the Tsaritsyn-ites have assembled in Kharkov. . . . I consider Stalin's protection of the Tsaritsyn tendency a dangerous ulcer, worse than the betrayal and treason of military specialists. . . . Voroshilov, along with Ukrainian partisan warfare-ism, a lack of culturedness, demagoguery—that is something we cannot have under any circumstances."[167]

The enmity between Voroshilov and Trotsky rendered the former that much more valuable to Stalin. Voroshilov, Minin, and their subordinates engaged in a revenge whispering campaign against Trotsky, spreading word that the war commissar was in bed with tsarist generals and sending Communists to the firing squad—a whiff of treason.[168] (Stalin could pour his anti-Trotsky poison directly into Lenin's ear.) Left Communists, such as Nikolai Bukharin, who edited *Pravda,* used the Tsaritsynites to further their own anti-Trotsky campaign to "democratize" military organization.[169] Impelled to respond, Trotsky in early 1919 derided "the new Soviet bureaucrat, who, trembling over his job," envious of the competent, unwilling to learn, sought a scapegoat for his own shortcomings. "This is the genuine menace to the cause of communist revolution . . . the genuine accomplices of counter-revolution."[170] Here was the gist of Trotsky's future critique of Stalinism.

Lenin continued to show confidence in his Georgian protégé despite having abruptly removed him from Tsaritsyn, and in January 1919, he sent Stalin to a new hotspot, Vyatka, in the Urals, to investigate why Perm and the surrounding region had fallen to Admiral Kolchak.[171] Stalin traveled together with the Cheka's Dzierżyński and was again accompanied by his wife, Nadya, as well as her sister Anna Alliluyeva (b. 1896); Dzierżyński's personal secretary, Stanisław Redens (b. 1892), another Pole, fell in love with and would soon marry Stalin's sister-in-law. As for the Red debacle in Perm, Stalin and Dzierżyński issued three separate reports, noting the Reds' abject disorganization and the local population's hostility to the regime (over food requisitioning), but shifting the blame each time, first impugning Trotsky, then Vācietis. Their reports pointedly listed the former tsarist officers on the Red side who had defected to the Whites. They also allowed that the Bolshevik regime should avoid posting as overseers of tsarist-era commanders comrades who were "too young" or party "demogogues," a slight backtracking on Stalin's earlier hard line, evidence perhaps of Lenin's intervention.[172] Lenin, meanwhile, on January 19, a Sunday, heading out to meet Krupskaya convalescing in the fresh air and woods outside of Moscow, had his Rolls-Royce hijacked by three armed men. The revolution's leader, his sister, driver (Stepan Gil), and one bodyguard trudged the rest of the way on foot.[173]

## VERSAILLES 1919: THE ANOMALY

Few peace treaties have gone down in history less favorably than that of Versailles. The talks opened in Paris on January 18, 1919, the anniversary of Germany's unification, and concluded in Versailles' Hall of Mirrors—where the German Reich had been proclaimed—on June 28, 1919, five years to the day after Archduke Franz Ferdinand's assassination. Thirty-seven countries sent delegations (some more than one); myriad expert commissions worked on ethnic and territorial claims; and 500 journalists reported on the proceedings, but just three people determined the outcome: David Lloyd George (Britain), Georges Clemenceau (France), and Woodrow Wilson (United States), a former Princeton professor who became the first sitting American president to travel to Europe. The seventy-eight-year-old Clemenceau aimed to counteract Germany's superior economic might and population; Lloyd George to attain Britain's colonial and naval aims at German expense; and Wilson to imagine a secure permament peace, though he abetted the French imposition of punishment on Germany. The final text contained 440 clauses, the first 26 of which concerned a new League of Nations, while the remaining 414 took up Germany's alleged sole war guilt. Germany was forbidden to maintain more than 100,000 troops or any military aircraft, and lost 13 percent of its territory, including Alsace and Lorraine to France, its foreign colonies, and its merchant fleet. France had wanted to detach the Rhineland, too, but Lloyd George objected; the Rhineland was instead demilitarized. A newly reconstituted Poland was awarded most of German West Prussia, while Danzig, predominantly ethnic German, was made a "free city" and a so-called Polish Corridor was created between German territories, isolating German East Prussia. To fund the reconstruction of French and Belgian territory, and the British war-loan debt to the United States, Germany was ordered to pay 132 billion gold marks, then equivalent to $31.4 billion or £6.6 billion. (Approximately $440 billion in 2013.)[174]

Germany's imposition of Brest-Litovsk on Russia served as one rationale for the expressly punitive Versailles Peace—exactly as the impudent Bolshevik Karl Radek had predicted to Germany's Brest negotiators. Versaillies' terms, meanwhile, were publicly assailed even in the West. France's Marshall Foch commented, "This is not a peace; it is an armistice for twenty years."[175] Still, unlike imperial Russia under Brest-Litovsk, Germany was not dismembered. (Lloyd George remarked of Germany, "we cannot both cripple her and expect her to

pay.") Moreover, the treaties that followed with the other defeated belligerents—
St. Germain with Austria (September 10, 1919), Neuilly with Bulgaria (November 27, 1919), Trianon with Hungary (June 4, 1920), Sèvres with Turkey (August 10, 1920)—were in some ways harsher. (The Turks alone, taking up arms, managed to revise their treaty terms.) The victors' Peace of Versailles certainly had flaws, irrespective of its attribution of sole war guilt to Germany. It enshrined self-determination and the nation while promoting territorial revisionism: Versailles and its sister treaties approved the award to 60 million people of states of their own, while making another 25 million into national minorities. (There was also a jump in the number of stateless persons.) Edvard Beneš and Tomáš Masaryk managed to extract extra territory, at the expense of Hungary, for the new Czechoslovakia, even though both had fought on the losing Austrian side. Romania obtained significant ethnically mixed lands at Hungarian expense. But if Hungary was the legitimate homeland of the Hungarians, according to national self-determination, why were so many Hungarians stuck elsewhere? Jews had no separate homeland, becoming a minority in every state. Self-determination did not apply to any of the colonial peoples under the British and French empires, both of which expanded: in 1919 the British empire alone grew to one quarter of the earth. Many war spoils were colonial: new mineral-rich possessions in Africa, new oil fields in the Middle East. Masaryk, who served as the first president of the new Czechoslovakia, dubbed the Versailles Peace Conference a "laboratory built over a vast cemetery."

Whatever Versailles' deep flaws on principle, it failed utterly in terms of power politics: the United States would go home, the British would back away, and the French—who shared a land border with Germany—could not bear the burden of enforcing the treaty provisions.[176] A punitive peace is punitive only if there is the unity of will to enforce it, which was lacking. All that was fatal enough, but even before the powers bailed on the Versailles structure, it was being erected on the basis of a temporary anomaly: the simultaneous disintegration of both German power and Russian power. *Both* of those conditions could not last; in the event, neither would.

Russia's contribution to the Allied effort in the Great War (through 1917) remained unacknowledged. The British had imagined that to defeat Germany, the Russian "steamroller," together with France, would do the bulk of the fighting (and dying), leaving supply and finance to Britain, but the treatment of Russians as British mercenaries and cannon fodder had to be abandoned, even as it generated lasting resentment.[177] At the same time, Britain had found itself in what was an unaccustomed dependence on its allies' strategic imperatives and, in the postwar, London would seek an arm's-length grand strategy, derived from long-standing preferences (to have others fight) and priorities (the empire), as well as the Great War experience.[178] As for Bolsevik Russia in the here and now, the Allies were at a loss. While Foch argued for a preemptive war, Clemenceau advocated containment (a cordon sanitaire); while Lloyd George imagined moderating Bolshevism through trade, other British political figures wanted to roll back the leftist menace.[179] Some British imperialists, for their part, smiled upon the forced retreat of Russian sovereignty from the Caucasus and hoped to consolidate Ludendorff's policy of imperial partition in the East, but other Brits, with a wary eye on Germany, preferred a reunified Russia as a counterweight. In the end, for all the talk of the possible spread of the "Bolshevik bacillus," Versailles showed itself far less concerned with Russia than with Germany. Still, the two turned out to be inseparable.[180] Much of Germany's political class would refuse to accept the verdict of Versailles; Soviet Russia's exclusion from the peace conference—delegations were received from Georgia, Azerbaijan, Armenia, Ukraine—gave Moscow additional grounds for treating the result as illegitimate. Directed against Germany and in disregard of Russia, Versailles would push the two pariahs into each other's arms, as each would strive to resurrect its world power, forming a foundation of Stalin's world.[181]

## LIGHTNING ROD COMMISSAR

The Bolsheviks attempted to counter Versailles immediately. On January 24, 1919, a letter of invitation was issued by wires to the world and on March 2 a semi-international group of some fifty Communists and other leftists attended a gathering in Moscow that became the Third (Communist) International or Comintern. The floors in the long, narrow Mitrofanov Hall of the Kremlin's Imperial Senate were covered in extravagant carpets and the windows in brilliant drapes, but the stove heaters in the frigid space sat idle for lack of fuel. Some fifty guests from the Moscow party organization sat in a kind of gallery. "The delegates took their seats on flimsy chairs at rickety tables obviously borrowed from some café," recalled a French Communist. "On the walls were photographs: the founders of the First International Marx and Engels; the still honored leaders of the Second, mostly those no longer with us."[182] Travel to Soviet Russia had proved difficult because of the Allied blockade and the civil war's disruptions; a mere nine delegates made it from abroad. Several leftist parties extended "mandates" to individuals already resident in Moscow. Even so, just thirty-four attendees held credentials to represent Communist parties, or almost Communist parties, from about twenty countries (many of which had once been part of the tsarist empire). Lenin, Trotsky, Stalin, Chicherin, Bukharin, and Zinoviev were made voting delegates (six people sharing five votes; Stalin signed their mandates).[183] "Anyone who had attended the old Congresses of the Second International," a Russian Communist observed in *Pravda*, "would have been quite disappointed."[184] As more attendees showed up, however, the assembly boldly voted itself the founding congress of the Comintern. Trotsky's pen let out a burst of rapture. "The tsars and the priests, ancient rulers of the Moscow Kremlin, never, we must assume, had a premonition that within its gray walls would one day gather the representatives of the most revolutionary section of modern humanity," he wrote on the Comintern Congress's closing day (March 6), adding that "we are witnesses to and participants of one of the greatest events in world history."[185] Lenin had planned to hold the assembly openly in Berlin, but the German Social Democrats were hostile.[186] In Moscow, Lenin made Zinoviev (who spoke some German) chairman of an executive committee, which also included Radek, who had been educated at German and Swiss universities and influenced by Rosa Luxemburg, before turning against her, then turning back to her to help establish the German Communist party.[187] The "delegates" approved Lenin's theses denouncing "bourgeois democracy" and upholding "proletarian dictatorship"—precisely the point of dispute with the German Social Democrats. That rift on the left, now institutionalized globally, would never be healed.[188]

The 8th Congress of the Russian Communist Party, meanwhile, had been planned to commence right after the Comintern gathering, on the evening of March 16, with a half session, so that the delegates could attend a commemoration of the 1871 Paris Commune, but Yakov Sverdlov returned to Moscow from a trip to Oryol on March 8 with a raging fever; he never properly recovered. Conflicting rumors had him either giving a speech to workers outside in the cold, or killed by a blow to the head with a heavy object administered by a worker at a factory—revenge against Bolshevik deprivation and repression. In fact, Sverdlov died of typhus or influenza.[189] From his Kremlin apartment, Lenin, according to Trotsky, phoned the war commissariat on March 16: "'He's gone. He's gone. He's gone.' For a while each of us held the receiver in our hands and each could feel the silence at the other end. Then we hung up. There was nothing more to say."[190]

Sverdlov was buried on Red Square, near the Kremlin Wall, in the Bolsheviks' first major state funeral. His death prompted the cancellation of the Paris Commune tribute and a two-day delay in the Party Congress. It opened in the evening after the funeral, on March 18, in the Imperial Senate's rotund Catherine Hall (which would be renamed for Sverdlov). Trotsky, too, was absent: he had obtained Central Committee permission to return to the front, given the "extremely serious" situation. Although he had also wanted all Red Army delegates returned to the front, the soldiers protested and were allowed to decide for themselves; many stayed at the Congress.[191] Lenin's opening night speech hailed Sverdlov as "the most important organizer for the party as a whole." Everyone stood.[192] Thanks partly to Sverdlov's skills, but also to the formation of a Red Army, the party had doubled in size since the previous congress a year before. In attendance were invited guests, 301 voting delegates, and 102 non-voting delegates, representing 313,766 party members in Soviet Russia (220,495), Finland, Lithuania, Latvia, Belorussia, and Poland, which were not under Soviet rule.[193] A survey of the 500-plus attendees established that 17 percent were Jewish and nearly 63 percent Russian—information that did little to alter perceptions.[194] The Whites and other Bolshevik opponents slurred the regime as "Kike Bolshevik" with a "Kike" Red Army (Trotsky).[195]

Among the principal agenda items at the congress was the widespread employ of former tsarist officers, a controversial policy identified with Trotsky, whom Lenin had to defend over his absence. Debate was prolonged and heated (March 20–21).[196] Lenin had explained the matter on the opening day. "Military organization was completely new, it had not been posed before even theoretically," he stated on March 18, adding that the Bolsheviks were experimenting, but that "without an armed defense the socialist republic could not exist."[197] Soviet Russia, therefore, needed a regular, disciplined army, and it needed knowledgeable military specialists. Lenin knew he would have to sway the hall full of Communists, whose class ideology he shared but whose flexibility he greatly exceeded. And so, the Bolshevik leader had instructed one person whom he tasked with reporting to the congress to employ the word "threatening [*grozno*]" for the situation at the front, illustrate it with a large color-coded map visible to the whole auditorium, and blame informal partisan-warfare tactics.[198] Even so, the talk was of the treason committed by former tsarist officers admitted into Red ranks (a handful of cases, among tens of thousands of serving officers).[199]

Moreover, Trotsky had published several defenses of using former tsarist officers, but their brutal logic came across as politically tone deaf, and further incensed opponents. ("So, can you give me ten divisional commanders, fifty regimental commanders, two army commanders and one front commander—today? And all of them Communists?")[200] Trotsky had also published "theses" on the eve of the congress defending military policy and now tapped Grigory Sokolnikov to defend them; Vladimir Smirnov, a Left Communist, offered the rebuttal.[201] Sokolnikov tried to argue that the danger lay not in former tsarist officers but in the peasantry. The critics, dubbed the "military opposition," could offer up few proletarians—other than Voroshilov—to substitute for former tsarist officers in command posts, and instead proposed strengthening the role of commissars and the Communist party in the Red Army, a point that Trotsky, through Sokolnikov, conceded. The policy issue, therefore, subtly shifted to whether stronger commissars meant merely greater political control, or in the words of Smirnov, "a larger part in the direction of the armies."[202] Despite this narrowing of the disagreement, inflamed speeches of principle (for and against use of "military specialists") continued to dominate the sessions.[203]

Stalin allowed Voroshilov to bear the brunt of criticism for Tsaritsyn, then took the floor to aver that Europe had real armies and "one can resist only with a strictly disciplined army" as well as "a conscious army, with highly developed political departments." Not long ago, none other than Kornilov, at the Moscow State Conference in August 1917, had insisted to wide applause that "only an army welded together by iron discipline" could save Russia from ruin.[204] Second, Stalin revealed a hostile attitude toward the peasantry, stating "I must say that the nonworker elements, which constitute a majority of our army, peasants, will not fight for socialism, will not! Voluntarily they will not fight."[205] In accentuating discipline and dismissing the peasantry, he had assumed a position close to Trotsky's. But Stalin did not mention him by name.[206]

Lenin took the floor again on March 21, 1919. "Sometimes he took a step or two forward toward the audience, then stepped back, sometimes he looked down at his notes on the table," one witness recalled. "When he wanted to punctuate the most important point or express the unacceptability of the military opposition's position, he raised a hand."[207] Lenin conceded that "when Stalin had people shot at Tsaritsyn I thought it was a mistake." This was a telling observation—a mistake, not a crime.[208] But now, upon further information, Lenin conceded that Stalin's Tsaritsyn executions were not a mistake. Still, Lenin rejected Stalin's insinuation that the war commissariat had persecuted Voroshilov, and rebuked Stalin's protégé by name: "Comrade Voroshilov is guilty for refusing to relinquish the old partisan warfare [*partizanshchina*]."[209] Lenin's offensive threw the "military opposition" on the defensive, and probably turned the tide in the vote. On March 21, 174 voted for the Central Committee theses (drafted by Trotsky and backed by Lenin) and 95 for the military opposition theses, with 3 abstentions.[210] After the vote, victory in hand, Lenin formed a five-person reconciliation commission—3 from the winning side, 2 from the losing side—who together confirmed some tweaks to Trotsky's theses on March 23.[211]

Stalin had voted with Lenin.[212] Stalin also signed the telegram (March 22–23) informing Trotsky at the front that his theses had been approved, a sign no doubt of Lenin's efforts at reconciling the two.[213] The policy compromise had been foretold by a party official from Nizhny Novgorod named Lazar Kaganovich, in an article in his local press that was summarized in *Pravda*, which rebuked critics of military specialists but also cautioned against "an excessive faith" in them, proposing they be watched closely by the party.[214] Kaganovich, an early admirer of Trotsky, would soon become one of Stalin's most important lieutenants.

Military controversy almost eclipsed another major issue at the Congress: the lack of fuel or food. Opponents were deriding Bolshevism as banditry, as well as "the socialism of poverty and hunger." Suren Martirosyan (known as Varlaam Avanesov), newly named to the collegium of the Cheka, told the delegates that "now the broad masses . . . demand not that we agitate about bread but that we provide it."[215] Food extracted from a radically contracting economy was going mostly to two "armies": one in the field and one behind desks.[216] Ration cards stipulated a right to specific amounts of food, on a class basis, but often the provisions were unavailable: the Bolshevik food commissariat did not attain the level of food procured by the tsarist state in 1916–17.[217] However much grain might be procured by state agents, ruined railways could not transport it all to the cities, labor was insufficient to unload the grain that did get transported, and functioning mills were too few. At the same time, perhaps 80 percent of the grain requisitioned in the name of the state was being diverted for private sale to black markets.[218] In a mass exodus for survival, Moscow's population, which had swelled during the Great War to 2 million, declined to under 1 million.[219] Even so, urban food shortages remained chronic.[220] Remaining urbanites had little choice but to try to obviate the blocking detachments and venture into the countryside to purchase and haul back food, which was known as "bagging." (When the historian Yuri Gothier, an official at Moscow's Rumyantsev Museum—later the Lenin Library—returned from a series of lectures in Tver in 1919, he recorded "the balance for the trip" in his diary as "30 pounds of butter.")[221]

Illegal petty private trade kept the country alive, but bureaucratic self-dealing threatened to smother it. Viktor Nogin, a member of the Central Committee, tried to call the Congress delegates' attention to "horrifying facts about drunkenness, debauchery, corruption, robbery, and irresponsible behavior of many party workers, so that one's hair stands on end."[222] The Congress authorized a new commissariat for state control (it would be renamed the workers' and peasants' inspectorate); a few weeks after the Congress, Stalin would be appointed its commissar, concurrent with his post as nationalities commissar, with broad investigatory powers to oversee state administration centrally and locally.

The Congress, as the highest organ of the party by statute, also elected a new Central Committee, the party's executive between Congresses. The new Central Committee consisted of nineteen members—Lenin was listed first, the rest in alphabetical order—as well as eight candidate members. The Congress adopted a new party statute (which would endure to 1961). Fully fifty delegates voted against Trotsky's inclusion in the Central Committee, a number far exceeding the negative votes of any other nominee.[223] One of his closest loyalists, Adolf Joffe, was not reelected (and would never again serve on the Central Committee). Trotsky had emerged as a lightning rod, and the antagonism to his imperious "administrative-ness" would extend beyond the delegates in the hall, cropping up in discussions at primary party organizations.[224]

The Congress also formalized the existence of a small "political bureau" (politburo) and party secretariat, alongside a recently created larger "organization bureau" (orgburo). As Lenin explained, "the orgburo allocates forces [personnel], while the politburo decides policy."[225] The politburo had five voting members—Lenin, Trotsky, Stalin, Lev Kamenev, Nikolai Krestinsky—and three candidate (non-voting) members: Zinoviev, Kalinin, Bukharin.[226] Krestinsky replaced Sverdlov as secretary of the party. Sverdlov's fireproof safe, meanwhile, was delivered to the Kremlin commandant warehouse, still locked. It contained tsarist gold coins in the amount of 108,525 rubles, gold articles, and precious jewels (705 items in total), tsarist banknotes in the amount of 750,000 rubles, and nine foreign passports, one in Sverdlov's name, as if the Bolsheviks feared they might have to flee the Whites.[227]

# FORCES OF ORDER

All during the cacophony of Versailles, the world was shifting, and it would shift still more, in ways that escaped the major protagonists of France, Britain, and the United States. As 1919 dawned, war-induced inflation obliterated middle-class savings, prompting many to barter the family furniture, down to the piano, for sacks of flour or potatoes, even as war veterans loitered outside restaurants, begging for scraps. "Councils" (soviets) formed in Berlin and dozens of cities in Central Europe, mostly with the aim of reestablishing public order and distributing food and water, but revolution was in the air, too.[228] People dreamed not just of getting something in their empty stomachs but of an end to militarism and war, police batons and political repression, extremes of obscene wealth and poverty. A German Communist party was founded in December 1918, from the Spartacist movement, led by Rosa Luxemburg, a Polish-Jewish revolutionary born in tsarist Russia.[229] From Germany's Breslau Prison, just before being released and helping found the German Communists, she attacked Lenin and Bolshevism, writing that "freedom only for the supporters of the government, only for members of one party—however numerous they may be—is no freedom at all. Freedom is always and exclusively freedom for one who thinks differently."[230] But Luxemburg went after the reformism of the German Social Democrats with even greater verve.[231] She never had the opportunity to show how her rhetorical commitment to freedom would work in practice as a result of socialist revolution. In January 1919, worker actions, joined by the German Communists, led to a general strike—half a million workers marched in Berlin—and then a controversial armed uprising, which provoked a crackdown; Karl Liebknecht, who had pushed for the armed uprising, and Luxemburg, who had opposed it, were assassinated. This reminds us that Lenin and Trotsky were *not* assassinated in 1917. The executioners of the two leading German Communists were so-called Freikorps, a right-wing nationalist militia of returning frontline soldiers called in by the shaky postkaiser government against the leftists. Altogether, around 100 people were killed; 17 Freikorps members died as well.

By contrast, in Munich, Kurt Eisner, a German journalist of Jewish extraction, attempted to reconcile the new grassroots councils-soviets with parliamentarism, Kerensky style, but he, too, failed. Instead, on April 7, 1919, a new party that broke away from the Socialist Democrats, joined by groups of anarchists, declared a Bavarian Soviet Republic. Six days later, German Communists took it over, emptied the prisons, began to form a Red Army (recruiting from the unemployed), and sent telegrams of victory to Moscow. On April 27, Lenin replied with greetings and advice: "Have the workers been armed? Have the bourgeoisie been disarmed? . . . Have the capitalist factories and wealth in Munich and the capitalist farms in its environs been confiscated? Have mortgage and rent payments by small peasants been cancelled? Have all paper stocks and all printing-presses been confiscated? . . . Have you taken over all the banks? Have you taken hostages from the ranks of the bourgeoisie?"[232] In very short order, however, beginning on May Day 1919, some 30,000 Freikorps, together with 9,000 regular German army troops crushed the Bavarian Soviet Republic.[233] More than 1,000 leftists were killed in bitter fighting. (Eisner was assassinated by a right-wing extremist). Instead of a Bolshevik-style far-left revolution, Germany convened a Constituent Assembly in Weimar (February to August 1919) that produced a center-left parliamentary republic. Antiliberal rightist forces continued their mobilization.[234]

A related scenario unfolded in Italy, which, though nominally a Great War victor, had suffered casualties totaling 700,000 of 5 million men drafted to the colors and a budget deficit of 12 billion lira, saw mass strikes, factory occupations, and, in some cases, political takeovers in northern cities. This spurred an embryonic movement on the right called fascism—a closely knit combat league to defend the nation against the socialist threat. In rump Hungary, which was undergoing severe territorial truncation, a Soviet Socialist Republic was declared on March 21, 1919, under the leadership of the Communist Béla Kun [Kohn], who had been in Russia as a POW and met Lenin. Kun and the nucleus of a Hungarian party had been brought together a few months before in a Moscow hotel, but upon return to Hungary he and other leaders had been thrown into prison. Hungary's Social Democrats, appointed to form a government, decided to merge with the Communists in hopes of obtaining military aid from Russia in order to restore Hungary's pre-1918 imperial borders. Kun "walked straight from the cells into a ministerial post," one observer wrote. "He had been badly beaten while incarcerated and his face showed the wounds that he received and fully intended to avenge."[235] Lenin hailed the Hungarian revolution, and, on May Day 1919, the Bolsheviks promised that "before the year is out the whole of Europe will be Soviet."[236] The Budapest government issued a welter of decrees nationalizing or socializing industry, commercial enterprises, housing, transport, banking, and landholdings greater than forty hectares. Churches and priests, manor houses and gentry, came under assault. The Communists also established a Red Guard under Mátyás Rákosi, which the police and gendarmerie joined, and Kun attempted a coup in Vienna (his mercenaries managed to set fire to the Austrian parliament). But when Kun sought formal alliance with Moscow and Red Army troops, Trotsky replied that he could not spare any.[237] No matter: Kun had the Red Guard invade Czechoslovakia to reclaim Slovakia, and Romania to reclaim Transylvania. A foreign correspondent noted, "again and again, he [Kun] rallied the masses by a hypodermic injection of mob oratory."[238] But the "revolutionary offensive" failed, and the Communists resigned on August 1, 1919. Kun fled to Vienna. The 133-day Communist republic was over. ("This proletariat needs the most inhumane and cruel dictatorship of the bourgeoisie to become revolutionary," Kun complained, just before fleeing into exile.) Romanian forces entered Budapest on August 3–4. Rear Admiral Miklós Horthy, in landlocked Hungary (like "Admiral" Kolchak in Siberia), formed an embryonic National Army, whose units instituted a White Terror against leftists and Jews, killing at least 6,000 in cold blood. As the departing Romanians cleaned out everything, from sugar and flour to locomotives and typewriters, Horthy soon styled himself "His Serene Highness the Regent of the Kingdom of Hungary" and formed a right-wing dictatorship.[239]

## WHITE OFFENSIVE OF 1919— FALL AND RISE OF TROTSKY

Russia's would-be forces of order, the three different armies of the Whites in the east, south, and northwest, fought with one hand, sometimes both, behind their backs. Just like the Bolsheviks (and the *okhranka* before them), the Whites formed "information departments" to compile reports on the prevailing political mood from secret informants—refugees, actors, railway employees, obstetricians—but they made no effective use of the intelligence.[240] They "neither understood nor showed any interest in societal problems," one White political activist complained. "All of their interests were on military power, and all of their hopes were focused on military victory."[241] Under the slogan "Russia, One and Indivisible," the Whites refused to acknowledge the aspirations of national minorities in whose territories they operated, precluding an alliance with Ukrainian or other anti-Bolshevik forces.[242] Anti-Semitic outrages perpetrated by Denikin's army, and especially by Ukrainian anti-Bolshevik troops, stamped the White movement.[243] Between 1918 and 1920 in Ukraine alone, more than 1,500 pogroms resulted in the deaths of up to 125,000 Jews, who "were killed on the roads, in the fields, on trains; sometimes whole families perished, and there was no one left to report on their fate."[244] The Whites acted self-righteously toward their British and French patrons, and never moderated their hostility to Germany.[245] Additionally, the Whites were arrayed outside the heartland in a 5,000-mile interrupted loop—from the Urals and Siberia, westward across the southern steppes, up to Petrograd's outskirts—which presented immense logistical and communications challenges. The two main fronts, Denikin's south and Kolchak's east, never linked up.[246] Denikin and Kolchak never met.

And yet, despite their lack of unity, alliances, or popular support, the Whites mounted an offensive in 1919 that threatened the Bolshevik grip on the Muscovite heartland.[247] The offensive occurred in three separate advances: Kolchak's from the east toward Moscow in spring 1919; Denikin's from the south, also toward Moscow, in spring-summer 1919; and Yudenich's from the north, toward Petrograd, in fall 1919. Each effort commenced only after the preceding one had fallen short.

Kolchak commanded around 100,000 men and even though the admiral lacked familiarity with land operations, his forces managed to advance westward, surprising the Reds by seizing Ufa in March 1919, splitting the Bolsheviks' eastern lines, and threatening Kazan and Samara in the Middle Volga. (This is why Trotsky had received permission to skip the 8th Party Congress and return to the front.) Kolchak's advance was halted by May 1919, however, thanks to Mikhail Frunze, a thirty-four-year-old millworker turned commander, who reestablished discipline and led a counterattack.[248] But right then, Denikin, whose Volunteer Army—now renamed the Armed Forces of South Russia—had increased to 150,000 with the Cossacks as well as conscripted peasants in Ukraine, and whose supplies came from the Entente, made his move.[249] A staff officer, Denikin had never commanded a large army in the field, but he proved a formidable soldier. On June 12, 1919, his forces captured Kharkov, in Ukraine. On June 30, they captured Tsaritsyn. ("The hordes surrounded it," howled *Pravda* [July 1, 1919]. "The English and French tanks captured the worker fortress. . . . Tsaritsyn fell. Long live Tsaritsyn.")[250] All told, in 1919, Denikin would annihilate Red armies numbering close to 200,000 poorly led and equipped and in many cases starving troops. After Denikin triumphantly entered Tsaritsyn and attended services in its Orthodox cathedral, on July 3, he "ordered our armed forces to advance on Moscow."[251] Trotsky, as always, blamed Red partisan-warfare tactics for the establishment of an anti-Bolshevik front from the Volga to the Ukrainian steppes. And he had a point. Although he had issued a decree forbidding Voroshilov from commanding an army again, in June 1919 Voroshilov had received command of the Fourteenth Army in Ukraine—and promptly surrendered Kharkov to Denikin's forces. This prompted Voroshilov's remand to revolutionary tribunal, which would conclude that he was unfit for a high command. ("We all know Klim," Moisei Rukhimovich, the military commissar in Ukraine and a Voroshilov friend, noted, "he's a brave guy, but come on with commanding an army. A company, at most.")[252] As for captured Tsaritsyn, it had been Voroshilov's recent previous command. But the twin setbacks against the Whites only emboldened Voroshilov's clique—that is, Trotsky's Bolshevik enemies.

Trotsky was rarely seen at the war commissariat, which was managed by Yefraim Sklyansky, a graduate of the Kiev medical faculty and a chain-smoker, still in his twenties, who proved an able administrator, and remained in constant contact with the front via the Hughes apparatus.[253] ("One could call at 2 or 3 in the morning, and find him at his desk," Trotsky would write.)[254] Trotsky lived on his armor-plated train, which had been thrown together in August 1918 when he raced to Sviyazhsk.[255] It required two engines and was stocked with weapons, uniforms, felt boots, and rewards for valiant soldiers: watches, binoculars, telescopes, Finnish knives, pens, waterproof cloaks, cigarette cases. The train acquired a printing press (whose equipment occupied two carriages), telegraph station, radio station, electric power station, library, team of agitators, garage with trucks, cars, and petrol tank, track repair unit, bathhouse, and secretariat. It also had a twelve-person bodyguard detail, which chased down food (game, butter, asparagus). Trotsky's living quarters, a long and comfortable carriage, had previously belonged to the imperial railroad minister. Conferences were held in the dining car.[256] The men were clad in black leather, head to toe. Trotsky, then with jet black hair to go with his blue eyes, wore a collarless military-style tunic (now known as a *vozhdevka*). While on board, he would issue more than 12,000 orders and write countless articles, many for the train's newspaper (*En Route*).[257] Stalin, too, spent virtually the entire civil war in motion, and he too had a train, but without cooks, stenographers, or a printing press. Trotsky's train would log 65,000 miles, mobilizing, imposing discipline, boosting morale.[258] It also evolved into an independent military unit (taking part in combat thirteen times), and took on mythic status. "News of the arrival of the train," Trotsky would recall, "would reach the enemy lines as well."[259] Trotsky's arrival, however, also meant a cascade of orders often issued without even informing, let alone consulting, the local Red commanders.[260] Voroshilov was far from the only person with whom Trotsky clashed.[261]

Matters came to a head at a rancorous Central Committee plenum on July 3, 1919, the same day Denikin issued his order to advance on Moscow.[262] Stalin had been clamoring for the dismissal of Jukums Vācietis, the Red supreme commander who had become close to Trotsky. On the Petrograd front in late May–early June 1919, Stalin unmasked a "conspiracy" of military specialists, a claim that helped set the July plenum in motion.[263] Vācietis, for his part, was angered by the incessant accusations that former tsarist officers like himself were saboteurs, but he also clashed with another former tsarist colonel, Sergei Kamenev (no relation to Lev), who had his own ambitions. Kamenev, as the Red commander of the eastern front, had wanted to pursue a retreating Kolchak into Siberia, while his superior Vācietis, supported by Trotsky, feared being lured into a trap. Trotsky had Kamenev removed as eastern front commander, but after his replacement, a former tsarist general, changed the direction of the main attack five times over ten days, Trotsky agreed to reinstate Kamenev.[264] (On the larger strategy issue, Trotsky would later admit that Kamenev had been correct.) Now, it was Vācietis who was sacked. Trotsky evidently suggested as his replacement Mikhail Bonch-Bruevich, but he lost the vote. Sergei Kamenev became the new commander in chief.[265] Unlike the Latvian Vācietis, Kamenev was an ethnic Russian and eight years younger. Lenin also unilaterally overhauled the Revolutionary Military Council of the Republic, sharply reducing its membership, from around fifteen to six, relocating its headquarters to Moscow from Serpukhov (sixty miles south of the capital), so that he could assert greater control; and expelling its ardent Trotsky supporters. Stalin, too, was taken off. Trotsky was to remain as chairman, and Sklyansky as deputy chairman; the additions were Sergei Kamenev; Yakov Drabkin, known as Sergei Gusev, a Kamenev man and, initially, a Stalin nemesis; Ivar Smilga (another Latvian); and Alexei Rykov, Lenin's deputy.[266] Having lost the fight over the commander in chief, and having had the body under his chairmanship purged without his consultation, Trotsky submitted his resignation from all military and party posts. On July 5, the Central Committee refused to accept it.[267]

Sergei Kamenev's promotion took effect on July 8, 1919.[268] The next day,

Trotsky, by then back at the front (in Voronezh), was notified that Vācietis had been arrested—nearly one year to the day after the Latvian saved the Bolshevik regime from the Left SRs. Whereas Stalin's surrogate, Voroshilov, had been disciplined for cause (surrendering Kharkov), Vācietis, Trotsky's surrogate, had been arrested for murky accusations of White Guard associations. Vācietis was soon released—someone at the top thwarted Stalin's machination—but the shot across Trotsky's bow had been delivered.[269] It was an extraordinary added humiliation.[270]

Trotsky liked to portray himself as above it all, as if politics in the Bolshevik regime did not involve constant backbiting and smearing. A top Cheka official, Wiaczesław Mężyński, had confidentially informed Trotsky on a visit to his armored train that Stalin was "insinuating to Lenin and to some others that you are grouping men about you who are especially hostile to Lenin." Instead of recruiting the powerful, sympathetic Chekist on the spot—as Stalin would have done—Trotsky claims he rebuked Mężyński.[271] Be that as it may, Stalin was hardly the sole intriguer badmouthing Trotsky by pointing out that former tsarist officers were deserting the Red Army and taking their troops along. Denunciations of the war commissar flowed to Moscow, incited by his personal haughtiness and strident defense of old-regime officers' supremacy in military decision making, which seemed to betray the absence of a class outlook.[272] Trotsky even managed to anger the very tsarist officers he was accused of championing in his disdain for their proceduralism and narrow intellectual horizons, compared with his.[273] Summer 1919's battlefield crisis had enabled Trotsky's opponents to claw back from their defeat only four months before at the 8th Party Congress, thanks to Lenin; belatedly, he got the Central Committee, if not to subordinate the military to the party, at least to affirm the party-military dual command as a special achievement of the revolution.[274] But if Lenin sensed that his war commissar had gotten too big for his britches, the Bolshevik leader continued to give every indication that Trotsky remained indispensable. Trying to win over a skeptical Maxim Gorky in 1919, for example, Lenin said, "Show me another man able to organize almost a model army within a single year and win the respect of the military specialists. We have such a man."[275] Had Lenin allowed Stalin and his band a complete victory over Trotsky in July 1919, the outcome of the other battle—the civil war against the Whites—might have turned out differently.[276]

Trotsky rushed to the faltering southern front against Denikin as Sergei

Kamenev, a graduate of the imperial General Staff Academy, devised a plan of counterattack down the Don toward Tsaritsyn, to outflank and cut Denikin off from his main base. Vācietis, supported by Trotsky, had argued for a drive down through the Donetsk coal basin, more hospitable territory (full of workers as well as railroads), rather than through the Cossack lands, where a Red offensive would rally the population against Bolshevism. The politburo, including Stalin, had supported Sergei Kamenev's plan. The upshot was that Denikin seized Kiev and captured nearly all of Ukraine, even as he was advancing against the Red Army's weakened center on Moscow. On October 13, Denikin's forces seized Oryol, just 240 miles from the capital (about as far as from the German border to Paris, giving a sense of the distances involved in Russia). On October 15, the politburo reversed itself, belatedly endorsing the original battle plan of Vācietis and Trotsky; Stalin, too, now agreed that Trotsky had been right.[277] With the engagement north of Oryol in full force, Trotsky rallied the Red side, which was twice as numerous, and began to take advantage of White overextension and other vulnerabilities. Right then, Yudenich's forces, 17,000 troops along with six British-supplied tanks, advanced from Estonia on Petrograd, capturing Gatchina (October 16–17) and then Tsarskoe Selo, on the outskirts of Petrograd. The city, frozen and famished, had seen its population dive from 2.3 million to 1.5 million as workers fled idle factories for villages.[278] The famed working-class Vyborg district, the "Bolshevik Commune" of 1917, had withered from 69,000 to 5,000 people.[279] "Squads of half-ragged soldiers, their rifles hanging from their shoulders by a rope, tramped under the red pennants of their units," one eyewitness said of Petrograd in 1919. "It was the metropolis of Cold, of Hunger, of Hatred, and of Endurance."[280] Lenin proposed the former capital be abandoned so that Red forces could be swung to Moscow's defense; he was supported by Petrograd's party boss, Zinoviev. Trotsky, along with Stalin, insisted that "the cradle of the revolution" be defended to the last drop of blood, with hand-to-hand combat in the streets, if necessary.[281]

Crucially, Admiral Kolchak, the White "supreme ruler," refused to recognize Finnish independence, and so the Finnish leader Karl Mannerheim refused to provide troops or a Finnish base of operations for Yudenich's assault on Petrograd, while the Entente withheld support as well.[282] Trotsky rushed to the northwest, followed by reinforcements—Yudenich's forces had failed to secure the rail line—and halted the Whites' offensive. "Trotsky's presence on the spot at once showed itself: proper discipline was restored and the military and administrative agencies rose to the task," explained Mikhail Lashevich (b. 1884), a leading polit-ical commissar. "Trotsky's orders, clear and precise, sparing nobody, and exact-ing from everybody the utmost exertion and accurate, rapid execution of combat orders, at once showed that there was a firm directing hand.... Trotsky pene-trated into every detail, applying to every item of business his seething, restless energy and his amazing perseverance."[283] Yudenich went down to defeat, his troops driven back into Estonia, disarmed, and interned. He himself emigrated to the French Riviera.[284] Denikin, despite having 99,000 combat troops, could muster just 20,000 to spearhead the assault on Moscow, and with his entire front distended—700 miles, from their base in the Kuban—great gaps had opened when his men advanced.[285] Near Oryol, Denikin's overextended, all-out gamble for Moscow went down to defeat as well.[286] By November 7, 1919, the revolution's second anniversary, Trotsky, having just turned forty, was suddenly, resplen-dently triumphant. His colleagues fêted both his armored train and his person-age with the Order of the Red Banner, Soviet Russia's highest state award. Lev Kamenev, according to Trotsky, proposed that Stalin receive the same distinc-tion. "For what?" Mikhail Kalinin objected, according to Trotsky. Following the meeting, Bukharin took Kalinin aside and said, "Can't you understand? This is Lenin's idea. Stalin can't live unless he has what someone else has." Stalin did not attend the ceremony at the Bolshoi, and at the announcement of his Red Banner award almost no one clapped. Trotsky received an ovation.[287]

## WHITE FAILURES

Petrograd and Moscow were held. Kolchak was taken prisoner in Irkutsk (East-ern Siberia) and, without trial, executed by firing squad at 4:00 a.m. on February 7, 1920, his body kicked down a hole cut in the frozen Ushakovka River, a tribu-tary of the Angara—a watery river grave for the admiral.[288] The "supreme ruler" would be the only top White leader captured. With Kolchak disappeared impe-rial Russia's gold. Tsarist Russia had possessed some 800 tons of gold on the eve of the Great War, one of the largest reserves in the world, which had been evacu-ated from the State Bank vaults beginning in 1915 to Kazan and other locations for safekeeping, but the bulk of it was seized by the Czechoslovak Legion in 1918. (Trotsky summarily shot the Red commander and commissar who had surren-dered Kazan and the imperial gold.) Eventually, the cache had made its way into

Kolchak's custody—480 tons of ingots as well as coins from fourteen states, more than 650 million rubles' worth, shipped in thirty-six freight cars to Omsk, Siberia. Rumors had it sunk in Lake Baikal or seized by the Japanese government.[289] In fact, Kolchak had chaotically doled out nearly 200 million rubles' worth on his campaigns; most of the rest was spirited out via Vladivostok to the Shanghai Bank, and would be consumed in the emigration.[290] Denikin had made no move to try to rescue Kolchak. His own armies, following their trouncing north of Oryol, undertook an uninterrupted retreat southward, and by March 1920, they had straggled onto the Crimean peninsula, salvaging a rump of perhaps 30,000 troops. Denikin, compelled to relinquish command to Lieutenant General Baron Pyotr Wrangel, fled to Paris. The baron, from a family with German roots, until relatively recently had commanded only a cavalry division. Tall and lanky, he theatrically wore a *cherkeska,* the North Caucasus long black caftan with bullet cartridges across the outside. Despite the change in leadership and the (temporary) Crimean refuge, the Whites were spent.

On this last foothold of the White movement, Stalin reported to Trotsky that a directive would be issued for a "total extermination of the Wrangelite officer corps." The order was issued and carried out. An Order of the Red Banner was awarded to a Red commander for "having cleansed the Crimean peninsula of White officers and counterintelligence agents who had been left behind, removing up to 30 governors, 50 generals, more than 300 colonels and as many counterintelligence agents, for a total of up to 12,000 of the White element."[291] Overall, no reliable casualty counts exist for the Red-White skirmishes. Red deaths from combat have been estimated to have been as high as 701,000; White deaths, anywhere from 130,000 to many times that.[292] The absence of reliable figures is itself indicative of the nature of the antagonists, not just the low value they placed on human life but also the severe limits of each side's governing capacities.

The Red military victory cannot be attributed to impressive strategy; mistakes were plentiful.[293] Nor did intelligence win the war.[294] Nor did victory derive from homefront production. To revive military industry and supply, the Bolsheviks formed innumerable "central" commissions, which underwent perpetual reorganization, often deepening the ruin.[295] They had mocked tsarist supply problems, but the tsarist state had equipped a force ten times larger than the Red Army in the field—and the tsarist state supplied the Red Army, too. Anywhere from 20 to 60 percent of the old regime's accumulated 11 million rifles, 76,000 machine guns, and 17,000 field guns survived the Great War, an invaluable inheritance, almost all of which came into Red hands.[296] In 1919, Soviet Russia manufactured just 460,000 rifles (compared with 1.3 million by tsarist Russia in 1916), 152 field guns (versus 8,200 in 1916), and 185,000 shells (versus 33 million in 1916).[297] As of 1919, the Red Army possessed perhaps 600,000 functioning rifles, 8,000 machine guns, and 1,700 field guns. The Tula plant (founded by Peter the Great) was producing around 20 million rounds of ammunition monthly, while Red forces were firing 70 to 90 million.[298] A keen Polish observer of Soviet affairs, Józef Piłsudski (whom we shall meet in the next chapter) correctly told the British ambassador, before the major Red-White clashes of 1919, that the armies of both sides were of similarly low quality, but that the Reds would nonetheless push the Whites back toward the Black Sea.[299]

Crucially, the Bolsheviks needed only to hold on; the Whites needed to dislodge them.[300] Railroad junctions, depots, barracks, and the central administrative core of the old tsarist army were located in the Red-held capitals and heartland.[301] In addition, the Whites fielded fewer than 300,000 soldiers (160,000 in the south, not quite 20,000 in the north, and perhaps 100,000 in the east), while Red combatants at peak reached 800,000. True, perhaps up to half of Soviet Russia's registered population for mobilization—5.5 million, including 400,000 in so-called labor armies—failed to report or deserted between 1918 and 1920, but conscripts defected not to the other side but from the war (particularly at harvest time).[302] Moreover, the Red Army could replenish because, occupying the heartland, it drew upon some 60 million people, a majority of them ethnic Russian, a greater population at the time than any state in Europe. The Whites, mostly in the imperial borderlands, had perhaps 10 million people underfoot, including many non-Russians.[303] As for the British, French, and U.S. interventions, they did not send enough soldiers to overturn Bolshevism, but the fact that they did send troops proved a propaganda boon for Bolshevism.[304]

The Red rear also held. Many people anticipated strong efforts to subvert the regime, especially the regime itself. In summer 1919, through informants and perlustration, the Cheka had belatedly hit upon an underground network known as the National Center, comprising former politicians as well as tsarist officers in Moscow and St. Petersburg who were plotting on behalf of Denikin.[305] Lenin, when informed of the National Center's discovery, instructed Dzierżyński "to capture [suspects] rapidly and energetically and *widely*."[306] On September 23, 1919, the Cheka announced the executions of 67 spies and saboteurs.[307] Two days later, two bombs crashed through the ballroom window of the Moscow party

HQ, a two-story mansion on Leontyev Lane, the former Countess Uvarova mansion, which the Bolsheviks had seized in 1918 from the Left SRs after the latter's failed pseudo-coup; some 120 Communist party activists and agitators from around the city's wards were gathered for a lecture about the unmasking of the National Center. By some accounts Lenin was due to show (he did not). Twelve people (including the Moscow party secretary Vladimir Zagorsky) were killed and 55 wounded (including Bukharin). The Cheka immediately suspected White Guard revenge, and on September 27 announced executions in connection with a "White Guard conspiracy." The Cheka soon discovered the bomb culprit was an anarchist (assisted by a Left SR familiar with the building). A vast sweep took place to root out anarchist hiding places throughout the capital, accompanied by exhortations to the working class to maintain vigilance.[308] The mass internal subversion never materialized.

Red leadership, too, made a contribution, albeit in a complicated way. Lenin never once visited the front. He followed the civil war with maps, the telegraph, and the telephone from the Imperial Senate.[309] He refrained from assuming the title of supreme commander and generally kept out of operational planning, yet he managed to commit or support several of the biggest mistakes. No one attributed the victory to him. But Lenin's crucial leadership in the struggle against the Whites was felt at three significant moments: his support for Trotsky's recruitment of former tsarist officers, including those of high rank, beginning in early 1918; his refusal to allow Trotsky to destroy Stalin definitively in October 1918; and, above all, his refusal to allow Stalin to rout Trotsky definitively in July 1919.[310] As for Trotsky, his contribution, too, was equivocal. He committed mistakes when he intervened in operational questions, and his meddling angered many commissars and commanders alike, but he also organized, disciplined, and inspired the fighting masses.[311] Trotsky excelled at agitation, and in the agitation he loomed large, which, however, became a source of resentment among insiders, but provided tremendous strength to the regime.[312] Stalin's role remains a tangle. Despite the Tsaritsyn shambles, Lenin still sent him on critical troubleshooting assignments (the Urals, Petrograd, Minsk, Smolensk, the south). Genuine shortcomings and bottlenecks were rampant, but in Stalin's reports it became impossible to sort fact from exaggeration or invention. Each time he unmasked anti-Soviet "conspiracies"; each time he disobeyed direct orders from Moscow; each time he criticized everyone save himself, while nursing grievances as if he were the victim of miscomprehension and slander. That said, Trotsky would recall asking another Central Committee member in the Revolutionary Military Council of the Southern Front if they could manage without Stalin. "No," came the reply, "I cannot exert pressure like Stalin."[313] "The ability 'to exert pressure,'" Trotsky would conclude, "was what Lenin prized so highly in Stalin"—a back-handed, yet accurate compliment.[314]

When all is said and done, however, White political failings were epic.[315] The Whites never rose above the level of anarchic warlordism, worse even than General Ludendorff's occupation.[316] "Politicians," in the White mental universe, signified the likes of Kerensky: bumblers, betrayers.[317] Kolchak formed a "military dictatorship" that reaffirmed tsarist state debts and tsarist laws, condemned "separatism," and ordered factories returned to their owners and farm lands to the gentry.[318] But there was no government, military or otherwise, as cliques of officers and politicians engaged in political murders and self-dealing.[319] "In the army, disorganization," wrote one observer of Kolchak's abysmal 1919 offensive, "at the Supreme Headquarters illiteracy and hare-brained schemes; in the Government moral decay, discord, and the dominance of the ambitious and egotistical; . . . in society panic, selfishness, graft and all kinds of loathesomeness."[320] Yudenich only belatedly formed any government at all in the northwest under intense British pressure, and produced an ideological Frankenstein of monarchists and socialists (Mensheviks and Socialist Revolutionaries, who distrusted each other, let alone the monarchists). Denikin's political vision consisted of "temporary" military rule aiming to stand above politics; 1917 had convinced him that in Russia democracy equaled anarchy (the Constituent Assembly, he said, had arisen "in the days of popular insanity").[321] The British mission— Denikin's patron—told him in February 1920 that it would have been a "complete shipwreck if you had reached Moscow, because you would have left behind you an occupied area which would not have been consolidated."[322] Only Wrangel, when it had become too late, appointed genuine civilian ministers, supported local self-government, formally recognized the separatist governments on former imperial Russian territory, and acknowledged peasant ownership of the land—but his land decree (May 25, 1920) required that tillers pay his government for land they already controlled.[323]

A debilitating absence of government machinery was compounded by White failure in the realm of ideas. Red propaganda effectively stamped the Whites as military adventurists, lackeys of foreign powers, restorationists. The Whites mounted their own propaganda, military parades, and troop reviews blessed by

Orthodox priests. Their red, white, and blue flags, the national colors of pre-1917 Russia, often had images of Orthodox saints; others had skulls and crossbones. The Whites copied the Bolshevik practice of the agitation trains. But their slogans—"Let us be one Russian people"—did not persuade.[324] Elsewhere, when leftist revolutions or minirevolutions had erupted—Roman Catholic Bavaria, Hungary, and Italy—these places shifted rightward, galvanized partly by the specter of Bolshevism. Indeed, across Europe, the forces of order, including Social Democrats opposed to Communism, were ascendant. Clearly, the keys to political outcomes were not wartime ruin, the downfall of a monarchy, military mutinies, strikes, the formation of local soviets, or direct-action efforts by the left to seize power, but the strength, or weakness, of organized rightist movements and reliable peasant armies. The outnumbered Whites, despite thoroughly alienating the peasants, had counted on popular uprisings to join them.[325] But unlike in Italy, Germany, and Hungary, the Whites failed even to try to reinvent an antileftist movement on the basis of right-wing populism, and not even a Horthy, emerged among them. "Psychologically, the Whites conducted themselves as if nothing had happened, whereas the whole world around them had collapsed," observed Pyotr Struve. "Nothing so harmed the 'White' movement as this very condition of psychologically staying put in previous circumstances, circumstances that had ceased to exist . . . in a revolution, only revolutionaries can find their way."[326]

## FUNCTIONARIES SHALL INHERIT THE EARTH

Lenin, in notes for a speech he would not be able to deliver, embraced the civil war: "The Civil War has taught and tempered us (Denikin and others were good *teachers*; they taught seriously; all our best functionaries [*rabotniki*] were in the army)."[327] Lenin was right. Authoritarianism, moreover, was not a by-product. The sad fate of the factory committees, grassroots soviets, peasant committees, trade unions and other structures of mass revolution can hardly be considered mysterious. Bolshevik types worked strenuously to take over or crush grassroots organizations, in an energetic *Gleichschaltung* (as one historian of early Bolshevik state building aptly dubbed the process, analogizing to the later Nazi regime).[328] Even many delegates elected to the soviets came to see the elected grassroots bodies as hindrances to administration.[329] But the targeting of grass-roots and often independent forms of political expression was rooted in core beliefs. Lenin's regime set as its raison d'être not maximizing freedom but maximizing production. "The dictatorship of the proletariat," as Trotsky thundered, "is expressed in the abolition of private property in the means of production"— not in workers control over industry or other participatory forms of decision making.[330] The very meaning of *contrôle*, a French word adapted into Russian, shifted from spontaneous workers' control over factory operations to bureaucratic control over factories and worker.[331] The driving idea was transcendence of capitalism and construction of socialism; the nonpareil instrument was centralized state power.

The administrative machine was created from chaos, and in turn fomented chaos. The striving for hierarchy, to a great extent, stemmed from a desire for regularization, predictability. The regime was having a trying time not just governing but managing itself. At the finance commissariat more than 287 million rubles disappeared in a single robbery in October 1920, a heist accomplished with the aid of insider employees.[332] A regime created by confiscation had begun to confiscate itself, and never stopped. The authors of *Red Moscow,* an urban handbook published at the conclusion of the civil war, observed that "each revolution has its one unsightly, although transient, trait: the appearance on the stage of all kinds of rogues, deceivers, adventurists, and simple criminals, attaching themselves to power with one kind of criminal goal or another. Their danger to the revolution is colossal."[333] The line between idealism and opportunism, however, was often very fine. The revolution was a social earthquake, a cracking open of the earth that allowed all manner of new people to rise up and assume positions that otherwise they would have waited decades to fill, or never been able to fill at all, and the revolutionary mission overlapped their sense of their own destiny.

The reconstitution of functioning state power turned out to be the primary task after the Bolshevik coup, and what saved the Bolsheviks from oblivion, but the upkeep of the beneficiaries consumed a substantial part of the state budget, independent of their self-dealing. Around 5,000 Bolsheviks and family members had taken up residence in the Kremlin and the best hotels in the heart of Moscow. Collectively, they acquired a sizable service staff and swallowed considerable resources during the civil war. Their apartments, not just Lenin's, were heated by furnaces even though fuel was hard to come by. Inside the Kremlin they enjoyed access to a children's nursery, club, ambulatory, and bathhouse as well as "closed" distribution centers for food and clothing. (Trotsky claimed that he found Caucasus wines in the Council of People's Commissars "cooperative" in 1919 and tried to have them removed, since the sale of alcohol was technically banned, telling Lenin, in Stalin's presence, but Stalin supposedly retorted that the Caucasus comrades could not make do without wine.)[334] Compared with the tsarist royal court and high nobility, Bolshevik elite perquisites were hardly extravagant—an apartment, a dacha, a motor car, food packets—but amid the rubble and penury, such advantages were significant and conspicuous.[335] Privileges for functionaries became a sore point well beyond the central regime. "We have cut ourselves off from the masses and made it difficult to attract them," a Tula Bolshevik wrote to Lenin in July 1919. "The old comradely spirit of the party has died completely. It has been replaced by a new one-man rule in which the party boss runs everything. Bribe-taking has become universal: without it our Communist cadres would simply not survive."[336]

There was abundant idealism in the apparatus, too, but the epidemic of "bureaucratism" shocked revolutionaries. Suddenly, "bureaucrats" were everywhere: boorish, spiteful, prevaricating, embezzling, obsessed with crushing rivals and self-aggrandizing.[337] But one of the many revolutionary paradoxes was that although all "social forces" were understood in class terms—whether alien (bourgeoisie, kulaks, petit bourgeois) or friendly (workers and sometimes peasants)—the one class that could not be so called was the one in power.

SYMBOLICALLY, A RED-WHITE BINARY—Bolsheviks against everyone else, including those who made the February Revolution and the non-Bolshevik socialists—defined the new regime. This was dramatically captured on the revolution's third anniversary (November 7, 1920) in a reenactment of the "storming of the Winter Palace" staged in Petrograd, which involved far more people than the original event—around 6,000 to 8,000 participants and 100,000 spectators. In the show, on the immense square in front of the baroque edifice, one of the world's grandest public spaces, two large stages (red and white) were set, and connected by an arching bridge. At 10:00 p.m., trumpets announced the beginning of the action and an orchestra of perhaps 500 played a symphonic composition titled "Robespierre," which segued into "La Marseillaise." Floodlights shone on the right platform, revealing the Provisional Government, Kerensky on a throne (!), and various ministers, White generals, and fat-cat capitalists. Gesticulating, Kerensky gives a windy speech and receives large sacks of money. Suddenly searchlights illuminate the left platform, showing the masses, exhausted from factory work, many maimed from the war, in a chaotic state, but to cries of "Lenin" and strains of the "Internationale," they cluster around a Red flag and form into disciplined Red Guard units. On the connecting bridge, an armed struggle commences, during which the Reds gain the upper hand. Kerensky flees in a car toward the Winter Palace, bastion of the old regime, but is pursued by Red Guards—and the audience. He escapes, dressed as a woman, but the masses "storm" the Palace. Some 150 powerful projector lights illuminate the Winter Palace, through whose colossal windows can be seen pantomime battles, until the lights in every window glow red.[338] Those who questioned any aspects of that glow might find themselves, like Kerensky and the moderate socialists, in the White camp, which proved to be ever expandable.

Institutionally, the Bolshevik monopoly regime not only formed a state, but with the mass assimilation of former tsarist officers, became a party-state. "The institution of commissars" in the Red Army, Trotsky had explained of the political watchdogs, was "to serve as a scaffolding. . . . Little by little we shall be able to remove this scaffolding."[339] That dismantling never happened, however, no matter how often commissars themselves called for their own removal.[340] On the contrary, soon Vyacheslav Molotov, a central apparatchik, bragged in a pamphlet about how the task of governing had rendered the Soviet Communist party distinct from others. Among other innovations, he singled out the implantation of political commissars alongside technical experts—and not solely in the Red Army, but throughout the economic and administrative apparatus as well.[341] Nothing like the party-state had existed in tsarist Russia. The Red expert dualism would endure even after the overwhelming majority of state officials, army officers, or schoolteachers were party members, becoming an added sourge of bureaucratic proliferation and waste.

Traditionally, Russia's civil war, even more than the October coup, has been seen as Trotsky's time. He was ubiquitous in the public imagination, and his train encapsulated the Red Army and its victory. But the facts do not bear out the long-held notion that Trotsky emerged significantly stronger than Stalin.[342] Both Stalin and Trotsky were radicals to the core, but on the issue of former tsarist officers Stalin pushed a "proletarian" line, infuriating Trotsky (Trotsky's rage was Stalin's inspiration). To be sure, Stalin did not reject all military specialists, just "class aliens," which for him included those of noble descent and those who had attained a high rank before 1917, while Trotsky, in turn, also advocated for the training of former non-commissioned officers as well as pure neophytes from the bench.[343] In that connection, Trotsky claimed that in 1918 former tsarist officers composed three quarters of the Red commanding and administrative staffs, by civil war's end they composed, according to him, only one third.[344] Whatever the precise totals, however, the engagement of former tsarist officers, and of "bourgeois" specialists in other realms, helped focus the widely gathering negativity about Trotsky, who became a lightning rod, widely disliked inside the regime that he helped bring to victory, much earlier than usually recognized, right in the middle of his civil war exploits. At the same time, Stalin's role in the civil war—knocking heads—was substantial, as even Trotsky acknowledged.[345] And the Tsaritsyn episode of 1918, in what had been a desperate situation for the Reds and for Stalin personally, provided a preview of Stalin's recourse to publicizing conspiracies by "enemies" and enacting summary executions in order to enforce discipline and rally political support.

Trotsky was Jewish but, like almost all intellectuals and revolutionaries in the Russian empire, wholly assimilated into Russian culture, and to boot, he had striking blue eyes and an unprominent nose, yet he claimed to feel his Jewishness as a political limitation. Peasants certainly knew he was a Jew.[346] America's Red Cross chief in Russia called Trotsky "the greatest Jew since Christ." White-Guard periodicals roiled with evocations of "Kike-Bolshevik commissars" and the "Kike Red Army" led by Trotsky.[347] In 1919, Trotsky received a letter from an ethnic Korean member of the Russian Communist party concerning rumors that "the motherland has been conquered by Yid commissars. All the country's disasters are being blamed on the Jews. They're saying the Communist regime is supported by Jewish brains, Latvian rifles, and Russian idiots."[348] The London *Times* asserted (March 5, 1919) that three quarters (!) of the leading positions in Soviet Russia were held by Jews. Many Soviet Communists themselves could be overheard to say Shmolny for Smolny (Jewish "sh") or prezhidium (Jew-sidium) for presidium.[349] Trotsky kept a copy of a 1921 German book of drawings of all the Jewish Bolsheviks, with a preface to the text by Alfred Rosenberg, in his files.[350] Peasants, too, knew he was a Jew.[351] Retrospectively, he would cite the perception of him as a Jew to explain why he had declined Lenin's proposal in 1917 to become commissar for the interior (i.e., regime policeman).[352] All the same, he had accepted other high-profile appointments, and the degree to which his Jewishness constituted a genuine handicap remains unclear. At the top, only the Georgian Jughashvili-Stalin was not partly Jewish. The Jewishness of Lenin's maternal grandmother was then unknown, but other leaders were well known to be Jews and it did not inhibit them: Zinoviev had been born Ovsei-Gershon Radomylsky and used his mother's surname Apfelbaum; Kamenev, born Lev Rozenfeld, had a Jewish father; both had Jewish wives.[353] Trotsky-Bronstein managed to be a lightning rod not just in his Jewishness but in all ways.

Stalin, unlike Trotsky, had not made so bold as to challenge Lenin publicly in high-profile debates, such as Brest-Litovsk, as if he were Lenin's equal, provoking Lenin's ire. True, Stalin often engaged in disruptive political mischief.[354] But Lenin could not have been put off by Stalin's use of indiscriminate terror designed to deter enemies and rally the worker base because Lenin was the principle promoter of shoot first, ask questions later as a way to impart political lessons. (Lenin backed Trotsky's severe measures of shooting deserters, even if they were party members.) Lenin also was not naïve: he saw through Stalin's self-centered, intrigue-prone personality, but Lenin valued Stalin's combination of unwavering revolutionary convictions and get-things-done style, a fitting skill set for all-out revolutionary class warfare. Stalin's role for Lenin was visible in the regime's internal groupings. "All Bolsheviks who occupied high posts," recalled Arkady Borman, a deputy trade commissar, "could be divided into two categories: Lenin's personal protégés and the rest. The former felt firm and secure in the intraagency clashes and always held the upper hand."[355] Stalin was both the highest ranking member of Lenin's grouping and the belated builder of his own faction, which overlapped Lenin's. A parallel Trotsky faction did not overlap Lenin's and instead became a target of the Bolshevik leader. (The ambitious Zinoviev had his own grouping, in Petrograd.) Appealing to Lenin, Stalin managed during the civil war to escape subordination to Trotsky despite the latter's position as chairman of the Revolutionary Military Council. Going forward, as we shall see, the tables would be turned, and Trotsky would find himself appealing to Lenin to try to escape subordination to Stalin in the party. Stalin's aggrandizement was already well advanced, yet only really beginning.

## CHAPTER 9

# VOYAGES OF DISCOVERY

I know Russia so little. Simbirsk, Kazan, Petersburg, exile, and that's about it!

> Lenin, Island of Capri, responding to someone talk about the Russian village, c. 1908, in reminiscences of Maxim Gorky[1]

The isolated existence of separate Soviet republics is unstable and impermanent in view of the threats to their existence posed by the capitalist states. The general interests of defense of the Soviet republics, on the one hand, and, on the other, the necessity of restoring productive forces destroyed by the war, and, as a third consideration, the necessity of the food-producing Soviet republics to supply aid to the grainless ones, all imperatively dictate a state union of the separate Soviet republics as the sole path of salvation from imperialist yoke and national oppression. . . .

> 10th Party Congress resolution based upon Stalin's report, March 15, 1921[2]

REVOLUTION AND CIVIL WAR had broken out in the Russian empire, a startlingly heterogeneous state spanning two continents, Europe and Asia. That said, this realm had not presented an especially difficult governing challenge from the point of view of nationalism. Imperial Russia had had no "republics" of Georgia or Ukraine; officially, Ukrainians did not even exist (they were "Little Russians"). True, imperial Russia had countenanced two so-called protectorates (Bukhara, Khiva), while Finland had enjoyed a measure of self-rule, but the rest of the empire was divided into governorships (*gubernii*). Then the world war, German military occupation, and civil war midwifed an independent Finland,

Poland, Lithuania, Latvia, and Estonia, none of which the Red Army managed to reconquer. World war, occupations, and civil war also helped create Ukraine, Belorussia, Georgia, Armenia, and Azerbaijan, all of which the Red Army did reconquer, but even after falling to Red forces, those national republics retained important attributes of statehood. Nation was suddenly central.

The Great War irrevocably altered the political landscape, helping dissolve all three major land empires, but unlike Austria-Hungary and the Ottoman empire, Russia was resurrected, albeit not in toto, and not in the same form. What set Russia apart, and transformed its civil war into a partly successful war to recover territories of the former Russian empire, was a combination of instruments and ideas: the Communist party, Lenin's leadership (actual and symbolic), the Bolsheviks' belated discovery of the device of federalism, the vision of world revolution—not just a Russian revolution, which made "self-determination" a flexible concept—and Stalin's machinations. An extremely broad spectrum of imperial Russian political figures, from tsarist statesman Pyotr Stolypin and others on the right to Stalin and others on the left, with the Constitutional Democrats in between, had alighted upon the necessity of forms of local-national autonomy, but only under the aegis of a strong state (*gosudarstvennost'*).[3] The story of how Stalin arrived at that point is a lesser known aspect of his civil war odyssey; it is also one of the uncanny successes of Bolshevik state building.

"From the very beginning of the October Revolution," Lenin had remarked in November 1918, "foreign policy and international relations became the main issue before us."[4] Bolshevism was not just a state-building enterprise but an alternative world order. The Bolshevik recourse to federation recognized a formal right to succession of the dependent peoples in Soviet Eurasia, in a clarion call for colonial peoples everywhere.[5] State structure, domestic minority policy, colonial policy, and foreign policy became indistinguishable.

Germany, Russia's former nemesis, had recognized the new Soviet state but then collapsed, while Britain and France, Russia's former allies, were now antagonists: they recognized the new independent republics of Azerbaijan, Armenia, and Georgia, without recognizing Soviet Russia. But Greater Poland and Greater Romania, two big winners at Versailles, emerged as the most immediate Soviet antagonists to the West. On the other flank, the former Russian Far East fell under the occupation of Japanese troops, partly as a result of American president Woodrow Wilson's request to Japan to supply troops to a planned eleven-country, 25,000-man expedition to rescue the Czechoslovak Legion and safeguard military storehouses in Siberia. Initially, the Japanese had declined to intervene militarily in Russia, but in 1918 sent even more troops than were requested, motivated by a desire to reverse historic territorial losses as well as anti-Communism. Japan's occupation of the Soviet Far East grew to more than 70,000 troops, entangled against many different enemies, and turned out to be domestically divisive and costly, perhaps 12,000 dead and nearly 1 billion yen. Nonetheless, after the Americans left Vladivostok in 1920, the Japanese stayed.[6] The upshot was that Japan, Poland, Romania, and Britain combined to constitute a kind of ring around the Soviet Socialist Republics, although, as we shall see, Soviet revolutions poked through briefly in Iran, thanks to the reconquest of the South Caucasus, and enduringly in Mongolia.

By 1921, with the outcomes of the wars of reconquest more or less clear, the population of the Soviet republics amounted to perhaps 140 million, including about 75 million Russians and, among the 65 million non-Russians, around 30 million Turkic and Persian speakers. Around 112 million of the total Soviet-area population were peasants. The national question was also ipso facto the peasant question: they comprised the vast majority of people in every nation in Russian Eurasia.

Not peasants per se but Communist party members undergirded the Red victory against the Whites.[7] During a purge in 1919, nearly half the party's paper membership was expelled; in 1920, during a renewed purge, more than a fourth was kicked out, but the party had kept growing.[8] The party expanded from 340,000 (March 1918) to more than 700,000 by civil war's end, while party members in the Red Army grew from 45,000 to 300,000. But even if peasants were not decisive, they made up, often reluctantly, three quarters of the Red Army troops at any given time. Peasant soldiers often deserted with their army rifles. They also availed themselves of hunting rifles and homemade weapons. In 1920–21, at least 200,000 peasants in the Ukraine, the Volga, Don, and Kuban valleys, Tambov and Voronezh provinces, and especially Western Siberia took up arms against Bolshevik misrule, a revolt fed by the onset in September 1920 of Red Army demobilization. The regime replied with notable brutality, but also major concessions. In 1921, the peasants forced an end to requisitioning upon Lenin and he, in turn, forced upon the 10th Party Congress a so-called New Economic Policy (NEP), which allowed peasants to sell much of what they grew. Confiscations did not cease: a state that was built upon the idea and practices of class warfare took time to adjust to a NEP. But the civil war outcome across much of

Eurasia—the creation of the Bolshevik monopoly party-state—went hand in hand with a federation that acknowledged national identity and with legalized markets that acknowledged the parallel peasant revolution.

Kaleidoscopic does not begin to capture the civil war in Eurasia, particularly in the years 1920–21. Eurasia needs to be understood geographically. In Russian, as well as German and English, the term "Eurasia" had arisen in the late nineteenth century to denote Europe plus Asia, but in the early twentieth century its meaning had shifted to something distinct from either, something mystical.[9] A tiny group of inventive intellectuals, who had been cast abroad by the revolution, and happened to be Ukrainian-Polish-Lithuanian in heritage, suddenly declared that the geographic and ethnic composition of the dissolved Russian empire had fused eastern Christianity and steppe influences into a transcendent new synthesis. "Russians and those who belong to the peoples of 'the Russian world' are neither Europeans nor Asiatics," the exiles who had fled westward wrote in their manifesto *Exodus to the East* (1921). "Merging with the native element of culture and life which surrounds us, we are not ashamed to declare ourselves *Eurasians*."[10] Their Eurasia, ruled from Moscow, economically self-sufficient and politically demotic (of the people but not democratic), was allegedly some sort of symphonic unity.[11] Nothing could have been further from the truth, as we shall see, and as Stalin fully recognized, because he was managing the diversity. Despite his admiration for the Great Russian nation and the Russian working class, and his persistent preference for centralized authority and party rule (class) over national interests, he recognized the necessity of fashioning appeals and institutions to accommodate different nations.[12] Early on he made linguistic equality and nativization of administration the centerpiece of his views on the national question.[13] Of course, the flip side of the Russian Communist party's attempt to capture natives' allegiance by embracing national states was that nationally inclined Communists in those states obtained vehicles for their aspirations. Had there really been a "Eurasian" synthesis the way the émigrés fantasized, Stalin's life would have been far simpler.

Russia's civil war amounted to a kind of "voyages of discovery," even if, unlike Christopher Columbus and Vasco da Gama, the voyagers did not cross literal oceans. A bewildering cast of characters dance across this stage: the Polish marshal Józef Piłsudski and the Polish Bolshevik Józef Unszlicht; the mustachioed leader of the Red Cossacks Semyon Budyonny and the Armenian horseman Haik Bzhishkyan, known as Gai Dmitrievich Gai, who rode Mikhail Tukhachevsky's flank; the two Tatar Muslim Communists Sahib Garei Said-Galiev and Mirsäyet

Soltanğäliev, who wanted to kill each other, and a Bashkir non-Communist, Akhmetzaki Validi, who blocked Soltanğäliev's Tatar imperialism; Danzan and Sükhbaataar, two Mongol nationalists who cooperated until drawing daggers against each other; Mirza Kuchek Khan, the mild-mannered would-be liberator of Persia from foreign influence, and Reza Khan, the ruthless leader of a rightist putsch in Tehran; the Belorussian Jew Georgy Voldin, known as Safarov, a commissar in Turkestan, and the Latvian Jēkabs Peterss, an old-school Chekist in Turkestan who nearly destroyed the career of the great proletarian commander Mikhail Frunze; the peasant rebels' leader Alexander Antonov and his Bolshevik nemesis Vladimir Antonov-Ovseyenko, who had stormed the Winter Palace and arrested the Provisional Government but could not subdue Tambov peasant fury; the workerist Bolsheviks Alexander Shlyapnikov and Alexandra Kollontai, who led a Communist party internal opposition; the nationally inclined Ukrainian Communist Mykola Skrypnyk and nationally inclined Georgian Communists Pilipe Makharadze and Budu Mdivani; the forgettable former tsarist major general Alexander Kozlovsky on the Kronstadt island fortress and the unforgettable former tsarist Cossack officer Baron Roman von Ungern-Sternberg, a Baltic German riding in the footsteps of Chinggis Khan. And yet the principal character, even more than Lenin, turned out to be the Georgian reincarnation of Stolypin in the national sphere. Stalin pursued a statist agenda that sought to combine retention of a grand unitary state with provision for national difference, and an iron fist for separatism, even though Stalin, both in appearance and fact, was a quintessential man of the borderlands.[14]

The unexpected significance of the national question in the civil war proved to be yet another issue that empowered Stalin, and brought him into a close working relationship with Lenin. The two, often in the face of hostility from both hard-line Bolsheviks opposed to nationalism at all and national-minded Bolsheviks opposed to centralization, groped toward a workable federalism consonant with Marxist tenets, faits accomplis on the ground, and geopolitics.[15]

## ACCIDENTAL FEDERALISTS

Four watchwords had accompanied the coup in 1917: peace, land, and bread, but also national self-determination, yet the latter notion had long vexed the left. "The nationality of the worker is neither French nor English nor German, it is labor," Marx wrote in his early years. "His government is neither French nor English nor German it is capital. His native air is neither French nor German nor English it is factory air."[16] But as a result of the Irish Question, Marx later in life changed his position; a right to self-determination had been included in the program of the First International.[17] Karl Kautsky's essay "Modern Nationality" (1887) constituted the first major Marxist effort to elaborate the orthodox position that capitalist commodity relations had produced nations, which would presumably disappear with capitalism (the essay was translated into Russian in 1903). A hard-line Marxist position on nations had been outlined in 1908–9 by Rosa Luxemburg, who also argued that capitalism had generated nationalism, dividing the international proletariat by tying it to its ruling classes, but who denied self-determination except for the exploited working class, a position that attracted class-fixated leftists in polyglot Eastern Europe.[18] Then a countervailing Marxist view emerged in Austria-Hungary, where Otto Bauer and others argued for an elaborate program of "national cultural autonomy" independent of territory to reconcile nation with class.[19] Stalin's essay "The National Question and Social Democracy" (1913) rejected what he saw as the Austro-Marxist attempt to substitute "bourgeois" nationality (culture) for class struggle (Luxemburgism), questioning, for example, who had appointed the Muslim beys and mullahs to speak for Muslim toilers, and noting that many "cultural" practices (religion, bride kidnapping, veiling) would have to be eradicated. Stalin especially targeted the Caucasus echoes of Austro-Marxist "national cultural autonomy" (Jordania and the Georgian Mensheviks), insisting that autonomy should only be territorial (i.e., not extended to nationals outside their homelands). Still, he concluded that nationalism could serve the worldwide proletariat's emancipation by helping win over workers susceptible to nationalist appeals.[20] Lenin—who has wrongly been credited with commissioning Stalin's refutation of the Austro-Marxists—targeted Luxemburg's dismissiveness of nationalism in an essay in a Russian émigré journal in Geneva in 1914.[21] He distinguished between the nationalism of an oppressor nation and the nationalism of the oppressed (such as the Irish cause that had influenced Marx), and partially accepted a right to self-determination not merely for tactical reasons, à la Stalin, but also for moral political reasons: emancipation of the toilers of oppressed nations.[22] In Lenin's mind, one could not be both for socialism and for imperialism (national oppression by a big state).

Such, then, was the Marxisant corpus, polemics written for one another— orthodox Kautsky (a majoritarian citizen of Germany), hard-line Luxemburg (a

Pole assimilated into Germany), and soft-line Bauer (an Austro-Hungarian multinationalist) versus Stalin (a Georgian assimilated into imperial Russia) versus Lenin (a majoritarian subject of Russia). These ideas became an even greater battleground in the real context of Russia's civil war.

Bolshevik ranks embodied the wildly multinational character of imperial Russia (as the names, given in this book in the original, demonstrate) but the Bolsheviks were thoroughly Russified, too (as shown by the more typical spellings of their names). Still, they were conscious of the difference between ethnic Russia and imperial Russia. Trotsky, a Russified Jew, painted Russia in profoundly negative cultural terms, demanding a "final break of the people with Asianism, with the seventeenth century, with holy Russia, with icons and cockroaches."[23] Lenin, vehemently excoriating Great Russian chauvinism as a special evil that "demoralizes, degrades, dishonors and prostitutes [the toiling masses] by teaching them to oppress other nations and to cover up this shame with hypocritical and quasi-patriotic phrases," still allowed that a popular nationalism could emerge among ethnic Russians.[24] Stalin had once been a passionate critic of Russification. "Groaning under the yoke are the oppressed nations and religious communities, including the Poles, who are being driven from their native land . . . and the Finns, whose rights and liberties, granted by history, the autocracy is arrogantly trampling," he had written in Georgian, in the periodical *Brdzola* (November–December 1901). "Groaning under the yoke are the eternally persecuted and humiliated Jews who lack even the miserably few rights enjoyed by other subjects of Russia—the right to live in any part of the country they choose, the right to attend school, the right to be employed in government service, and so forth. Groaning are the Georgians, Armenians, and other nations who are deprived of the right to have their own schools and be employed in government offices, and are compelled to submit to the shameful and oppressive policy of *Russification*."[25] But Stalin had quickly shed this Georgian nationalism, denying in *Proletariatis Brdzola* in September 1904 that national characteristics or a national spirit existed.[26] By 1906, still writing in Georgian language, he was arguing that national autonomy would sever "our country [Georgia] from Russia and link it to Asian barbarism."[27] Thus, whereas Lenin railed against Russian chauvinism, Stalin worried about non-Russian backwardness and came to see Russian tutelage as a lever to lift other nations up—an echo perhaps of his personal experience in Russian Orthodox schools.[28] This difference would prove consequential.

As the recognized expert in the party's innermost circle on the national question, by virtue of his Georgian heritage and 1913 essay, Stalin emerged as the most significant figure in determining the structure of the Soviet state. It was no accident that the first Bolshevik government included a commissariat of nationalities, headed by him.[29] The Russian empire's dissolution in war and revolution had created an extraordinary situation in which the revolution's survival was suddenly inextricably linked to the circumstance that vast stretches of Russian Eurasia had little or no proletariat. In order to find allies against "world imperialism" and "counterrevolution," the party found itself pursuing tactical alliances with "bourgeois" nationalists in some territories, especially those without industry, but even those where a proletariat did exist. The first efforts in this regard had involved Polish-speaking lands: already in November 1917 the nationalities commissariat set up a Polish suborgan to recruit Polish Communists and retain Poland as a part of the Soviet Russian space. Never mind that the regime controlled no Polish territory at this time, and that serial rhetorical promises made by the competing Great War belligerents had continually upped the ante for an independent Poland. Stalin's ethnic Polish deputy commissar Stanisław Pestkowski oversaw the plans to Sovietize Poland, and his unreconstructed Luxemburgism did little more than intensify splits in the Polish left and generate friction between local soviets and local-branch ethnic Polish committees.[30] Poland, events would show, was not just a nation but a geopolitical factor in its own right. Similar suborgans in the nationalities commissariat emerged for Lithuania, Armenia, Jews, Belorussia, and so on, but the commissariat, and Stalin's attention, became especially absorbed by the Muslim territories of Russian Eurasia and the search for tractable Muslim collaborators. A Muslim suborgan was established, but its leaders pursued their own agenda: an "autonomous" Tataria encompassing nearly all Muslims in former tsarist Russia. Stalin had initially supported this Greater Tataria in May 1918 as a way to assert some political control, but very soon he undermined it as a dangerous vehicle at odds with Bolshevik monopoly and a threat to winning the allegiance of non-Tatar Muslims.[31] Stalin, despite his greater familiarity with Eurasia, had a learning curve, too.

Federalism, Stalin's key instrument, had started out with little support among Bolsheviks. Whereas in the American Revolution the federalists were those who argued for a strong central government, in the French Revolution, against an absolutist state, federalists wanted to weaken central power. It was the French understanding that influenced Marx, who rejected federalism. (The anarchists were the ones who supported looseness, decentralization, federalism.)[32] Lenin had written (1913) that "Marxists are of course hostile to federation and decentralization," further explaining in a private letter the same year that he stood "against federation in principle" because "it weakens the economic link and is an unsuitable form for a single state."[33] Stalin in March 1917 had published "Against Federalism," arguing that "federalism in Russia does not and cannot solve the national question, [but] merely confuses and complicates it with quixotic ambitions to turn back the wheel of history."[34] But the wheel had turned, and quickly. In 1918, in power, Stalin conceded federalism—not "forced unification" as under the tsars, but a "voluntary and fraternal union of the working masses of all nations and peoples of Russia"—as a necessary but temporary expedient, a "transitional" phase toward socialism.[35] A constitutional commission for Soviet Russia was hastily thrown together on April 1, 1918, with Stalin as the only member also in the Council of People's Commissars; he wrote the theses that served as the basis for the draft document published on July 3, when it was submitted for approval to the Central Committee. Formally, the constitution was adopted at the Congress of Soviets, which took place July 4–10—the one that occurred during the Left SR quasi-coup in Moscow.[36] Soviet Russia, officially, became the Russian Soviet Federated Socialist Republic, or RSFSR.[37] The term "federation" occurred in the constitution's title and initial principles, but not in the body of the text specifying the governing machinery, that is, the federation in practice.[38] Nonetheless, even as most of the "self-governing" entities that comprised the RSFSR quickly fell to White occupation armies and other anti-Bolshevik forces, Soviet Russia remained a federation.

Stalin was the one who developed the Bolshevik rationale for federalism, which, in his description, entailed a way to bind the many peoples into a single integrated state. "Soviet power has not yet succeeded in becoming a people's power to the same extent in the border regions inhabited by culturally backward elements," he wrote in *Pravda* (April 9, 1918). He saw the Bolshevik task as splitting the masses from "bourgeois" nationalists by promoting "schools, courts, administrations, organs of power and social, political, and cultural institutions in which the laboring masses . . . use their own language."[39] In other words, Stalin's understanding went beyond mentorship: even if Great Russia as a higher culture extended a helping hand to the various peoples, the latter still needed education and propaganda in their native tongues and participation in managing their own affairs. Here was the Communist version of a discovery that had been made by Russian Orthodox missionaries in remote areas of the empire: namely, that the Bible had to be taught in the empire's vernacular languages, in order to get non-Christians to read it and convert. So it would be with Communism. This was not a question of a direct Orthodox missionary influence on Bolshevism, but of structurally similar circumstances leading to similar approaches.[40] Stalin showed himself to be a missionary de facto.

The first major party discussion of the national question occurred at the 8th Party Congress in March 1919. This was also the congress that reaffirmed the use of tsarist officers, whose presence necessitated political commissars, which solidified the basic structure of a dualist party-state. On the national question, Bukharin, Pyatakov, and other leftist Communists at the congress demanded a hard-line Luxemburgist position (an end to the slogan of self-determination for nations).[41] After all, federalism was the stance of the Mensheviks, the Jewish Bund, the Armenian Dashnaks, and non-socialist Ukrainian nationalists. Lenin responded that nations existed "objectively" and that "not to recognize something that is out there is impossible."[42] He prevailed in the vote, which acknowledged nationalism as a "necessary evil." The congress even wrote the principle of self-determination into the Communist party program, albeit only after rejecting Stalin's formulation ("self-determination for the working masses") in favor of what was called self-determination from the "historical class viewpoint." In fact, Stalin could live with this formulation, which meant that if a nation was moving from bourgeois democracy to soviet democracy, then the proletariat was the class deserving of self-determination, but if from feudalism to bourgeois democracy, then "bourgeois" nationalists could be engaged in political coalition.[43] But what was most consequential about the 8th Congress was a resolution establishing the strictly non-federal nature of the party. "All decisions of the Russian Communist Party are unconditionally binding on all branches of the party, regardless of their national composition," the resolution stated. "The Central Committee of the Ukrainian, Latvian, Lithuanian Communist parties enjoy the rights of regional committees of the party and are wholly subordinated to the Central Committee of the Russian Communist Party."[44] Thus, the 8th Congress, while retaining a federal state, confirmed a non-federal party. Federalism, in other words, had to be kept subordinate to "the proletariat."

## SUPREMACY IN EASTERN EUROPE

Poland did not exist between 1795 and 1918. Józef Piłsudski (b. 1867), a descendant of nobility, a graduate of the same Wilno gymnasium as Felix Dzierżyński, and a former political terrorist against tsarism on behalf of Polish independence, had fought in the Great War on the side of the Central Powers but refused to swear an oath to Germany, which got him imprisoned. On November 8, 1918, three days before the armistice, the Germans released him; he returned on a train to Warsaw, not unlike Lenin's return to Petrograd the year before. As Poland returned to the map 123 years after the partitions, its borders remained undetermined. Six worthless currencies, not to mention bureaucrats of three defunct empires (Austria, Germany, Russia), remained in circulation; crime, hunger, and typhus spread.[45] Piłsudski, the new head of state, negotiated the evacuation of the German garrison from Warsaw as well as other German troops from Ludendorff's kingdom of Ober Ost (many left their weapons to the Poles). He also set up an espionage-sabotage unit called the Polish Military Organization, and with French assistance, began improvising an army. "Literally everything needs to be rebuilt, from the bottom to the top," wrote one French trainer, Charles de Gaulle, fresh from a German POW camp.[46] Beginning in early 1919, against expansionist-minded Bolsheviks as well as local nationalists, the makeshift Polish legions under Piłsudski conquered parts of tsarist Belorussia, Lithuania, and Ukraine, including the Galician oil fields.[47] By fall 1919, the Poles offered to take Moscow for Britain, with an army of 500,000, at a proposed cost of anywhere from £600,000 to £1 million per day; no one proved willing to pay (the British were still backing Denikin).[48] In December 1919, Piłsudski put out feelers to Paris for support of a major Polish offensive against Bolshevism; France saw in Poland the eastern bastion of the Versailles Order, but offered only an ambiguous reply.[49] The Soviets also appealed to France, and fantasized about obtaining German military help against Poland from the circle around Ludendorff.[50] In the end, Poland and Soviet Russia would fight a war largely on their own.

The Polish-Soviet War of 1919–20 mirrored neighboring armed border skirmishes—Romania with Hungary over Transylvania, Italy with Yugoslavia over Rijeka/Fiume, and Poland with Germany over Poznań/Pomerania and with Czechoslovakia over Silesia. Greater Romania especially, with its monarchy intact, emerged as a new power on the southwestern Soviet frontier. But the Warsaw-Moscow conflict was larger, a full-scale battle for supremacy in Eastern

Europe that would profoundly shape the interwar period.[51] It would also shape Bolshevik internal politics.

Lenin and Piłsudski had lived in Habsburg Krakow on the same street and at the same time as exiles from tsarist Russia. Piłsudski had even been arrested in the same plot to assassinate Alexander III that had led to the execution of Lenin's brother. But overlapping maps of the Polish-Lithuania Commonwealth (1569–1795), once the largest state in Europe and of the Russian empire, the largest state in world history, gave inspiration to two competing imperialisms.[52] In power, Lenin and Piłsudski issued mostly bad-faith peace proposals to the other and claimed they were undertaking military actions defensively, even as they harbored grandiose ambitions. Lenin viewed "bourgeois" Poland as the key battleground for the revolution against the Versailles Order: either an Entente springboard for intervention in socialist Russia—which had to be prevented—or a potential corridor for Bolshevik fomenting of revolution in Germany.[53] Piłsudski, a Social Democrat and Polish nationalist who now added the title of marshal, sought a truncated Russia and a Greater Poland in the form of a Polish-dominated "federation" with Belorussia and Lithuania, allied with a small independent Ukraine.[54]

Historic Ukraine—at different times and in different ways part of both Poland-Lithuania and imperial Russia—had seen its own opening from the dissolution of the three major land empires in 1918, yet unlike the case of Poland, the decision makers at Versailles had refused to recognize Ukraine's independence. Puppet governments of Germany, Bolshevik Russia, and Poland, not to mention General Denikin, rose and fell, but amid the competing claims, the countryside remained ungovernable to any would-be rulers. In April 1920, the deposed Ukrainian nationalist leader Symon Petliura, whose so-called Directory controlled very little Ukrainian territory and who was in asylum in Warsaw, signed a military alliance with Piłsudski, known as the Treaty of Warsaw. In exchange for Polish assistance in battling for an independent Ukraine against the Bolsheviks, Petliura relinquished claims to eastern Galicia (centered on Lwów/Lviv), for which the Ukrainian-speaking majority there roundly denounced him. Piłsudski faced uproar from Polish nationalists opposed to Ukraine's existence at all, but he argued that Polish forces could not garrison all of a huge Ukraine and that given the history of Russian imperialism, "there can be no independent Poland without an independent Ukraine." At the same time, he claimed territories for Poland with large western Ukrainian-speaking populations.[55] The latter included his native Wilno/Vilna/Vilnius, which was also sought by Lithuania and Belorussia. The Poles, additionally, had captured Minsk, also claimed by Belorussia and even by some Lithuanians. (Belorussia, in its greatest form, encompassed the imperial Russian provinces of Grodno, Vilna, Minsk, Mogilyov, and Vitebsk; Brest-Litovsk was in Grodno province.)

In Moscow, amid these weighty considerations, an anti-Poland demonstration scheduled for April 22, 1920, was postponed so that Soviet Russia could instead celebrate Lenin's fiftieth birthday. The regime's two principal newspapers were devoted almost exclusively to the Bolshevik leader, with encomia by Trotsky, Zinoviev, Bukharin, and Stalin, who hailed Lenin's extirpation of enemies.[56] But at the regime gathering on April 23, Stalin made so bold as to recall Lenin's political errors, including his vociferous demands, not indulged, that the October coup be carried out before the Congress of Soviets had met. "Smiling and cunningly looking at us," Stalin noted, "he said, 'Yes, you were probably right.'" Lenin was not afraid to acknowledge his mistakes.[57]

The same day, Lenin submitted a peace offering to Poland to cede all of Belorussia and much of Ukraine.[58] This proposal would make any Polish military advance farther eastward resemble an unprovoked aggression. Had the Polish marshal called the Bolshevik bluff by accepting Lenin's peace offer, Piłsudski would either have exposed it as a fraud, when the Bolsheviks failed to live up to the proposed terms, or obtained a Polish border far to the east without having to fight. Instead, on April 25, citing a supposed need to preempt a Bolshevik offensive, Piłsudski rolled the iron dice, sending some 50,000 Polish troops into historic Ukraine.[59] Assisted by Ukrainian nationalist forces, Piłsudski's army captured Kiev on May 7, 1920, announcing the liberation of Ukraine from Russia. In fact, the Bolsheviks had abandoned the eastern Slav mother city without a fight, seeking to inflame Russian feeling against the Poles and to conserve Red forces, which were massing to the north.

Lenin saw in Piłsudski's eastward march not a messianic Polish nationalist drive but a contrivance of world imperialism, and in Bolshevik propaganda, this was a class-based conflict. "Listen, workers, listen, peasants, listen Red Army soldiers," Trotsky proclaimed. "The Polish *szlachta* [gentry] and bourgeoisie have attacked us in a war. . . . Death to the Polish bourgeoisie. On its corpse we have concluded an alliance with worker-peasant Poland."[60] But Trotsky himself privately warned not to expect a supportive Polish worker uprising.[61] Stalin, ever attentive to the power of nationalism, also voiced early skepticism. While

Denikin and Kolchak had possessed no rear "of their own," he wrote in *Pravda* (May 25 and 26, 1920), "the rear of the Polish army appears to be homogenous and *nationally* knit together. . . . Surely the Polish rear is not homogenous . . . in the class sense, [but] the class conflicts have not reached such intensity as to damage the feeling of national unity." National feeling trumping class among the Poles: heresy but true. Stalin agreed with Lenin on one point, though: he, too, saw the hand of the Entente behind Poland.[62] Indeed, Piłsudski's very reckless-ness seemed prima facie evidence of this supposed backing. Furthermore, the British War Office would end up shipping rifles and artillery to Piłsudski; these had been contracted for the previous year, but in the new context they looked like British support for Polish "aggression." In fact, the British, as well as the French, were irritated at Piłsudski's eastern offensive in spring 1920.

Whatever the clash's national and international versus class dimensions, this began as a Great War military surplus clash. Perhaps 8 million Poles had fought for the Central Powers in the Great War; 2 million fought in the tsarist army.[63] Now the Poles were still wearing their Austrian or German gear, to which they affixed a white eagle pin. Many Poles who had become POWs in the West got French uniforms. The Red troops in many cases wore tsarist uniforms, to which they affixed red ribbons, as well as pointed hats with red stars. Some Poles, too, wore their old tsarist Russian uniforms.

As for the field of battle, it resembled a triangle, with points at Warsaw in the west, Smolensk in the north, and Kharkov in the south. Inside the triangle lay the Pripet Marches, meaning that an advance westward could take place only on either side of the forested bogs: via the northern Smolensk-Wilno-Grodno-Warsaw axis (Napoleon's route, in reverse); or via the southern Kiev-Rivne/Równe-Lublin-Warsaw axis (which the Soviets designated the Southwestern Front). These two lines eventually met up, but they lacked a single base in their rear or a single headquarters, complicating Red military operations.[64] But the Polish dash to Kiev had put them far from home, overextended, and vulnerable to counterattack. In a battlefield innovation, the Russian side fielded the First Cavalry Army, formed in fall 1919 to counter the Cossacks. The leader of these Red Cossack equivalents was Semyon Budyonny, a tall, big-boned, and breath-taking horseman, holder of the St. George Medal for Bravery in the tsarist army, where he had been a sergeant major. Voroshilov served as the First Cavalry Army's political commissar, meaning their higher patron was Stalin. They grew to 18,000 sabers—former Cossacks, partisans, bandits—and in their ranks could be found young commanders such as Georgy Zhukov (b. 1896) and Semyon Timoshenko (b. 1895). Trotsky, typically, was condescending: after visiting the cavalry force, the war commissar called it "a horde" with "an Ataman ringleader," adding "where he leads his gang, they will go: for the Reds today, tomorrow for the Whites."[65] But Budyonny and his army, formed to counter the Whites' devastating Cossack cavalry, had pushed Denikin's forces into the sea at Novorossiysk in the southeast in February 1920. Their tactics combined supreme mobility with mass: they probed for enemy weak spots, then concentrated all forces upon that point to smash through and wreak havoc deep in the enemy rear, thereby forcing a panicked enemy retreat, which they savagely converted into a rout. To reach the southwestern front from Novorossiysk, the Red's First Cavalry Army traveled westward more than 750 miles on horseback.[66] In late May 1920, Polish intelligence, from an airplane, spotted the dust storm that the Red cavalry's horses were kicking up en route.[67]

Before the Red cavalry swept across Ukraine, on April 29, 1920, Sergei Kamenev, Red supreme commander, had written to Lenin requesting that Mikhail Tukhachevsky be placed in overall charge of the army in the field for a Polish campaign.[68] Tukhachevsky was not merely an aristocrat; he could trace his ancestry back to a twelfth-century noble clan of the Holy Roman Empire that had served the princes of Kievan Rus. His mother was a peasant. He was graduated first in his class at the Alexander Military School in 1914 and chose the Semenov Guards, one of the empire's two oldest and most prestigious regiments, which were attached to the court. "He was a well-proportioned youth, rather presumptuous, feeling himself born for great things," recalled a friend.[69] Another classmate recalled that Tukhachevsky behaved despotically toward underclassmen and that "everyone tried to avoid him, being afraid." (Three younger cadets he disciplined were said to have committed suicide.)[70] During the Great War, Tukhachevsky fell captive to the Germans in June 1915, becoming one of 5,391 Russian officers held as POWs. Unlike General Lavr Kornilov, who quickly escaped, Tukhachevsky languished two and a half years in Ingoldstadt, a camp outside Munich (the same place de Gaulle had been interned). He made it back to Russia just days before the Bolshevik seizure of power, volunteered for the Red Army early, and even joined the party (April 1918).[71] In summer 1918, White forces had captured him in Simbirsk but the young Bolshevik activist Jonava Vareikis rescued him.[72] In fall 1918, Tukhachevsky smashed the Whites at Simbirsk (Lenin's hometown), and in 1919 he triumphed in the Urals uplands, chasing Kolchak's army into Siberia, where it would be annihilated.[73] By the time he spoke at the General Staff Academy in December 1919, outlining a theory of "revolutionary war," he was recognized as the top Red commander. In spring 1920 his star rose higher still when, as the commander of the Caucasus front, he helped smash Denikin's army. Twenty-seven years old in 1920, the same age as his idol Napoleon during the fabled Italian campaign, he arrived at western front headquarters in Smolensk the week that Kiev had fallen to the Poles, and began to amass forces for a major strike to the northwest.

Another former tsarist officer, Alexander Yegorov (b. 1883)—a metalworker and lieutenant colonel who had taken over Tsaritsyn from Voroshilov and lost it, then lost Oryol to Denikin, but then initiated a spectacularly successful counteroffensive—was named top commander of the southwestern front. This is where Stalin had recently been appointed commissar. The southwest's responsibilities included mopping up Wrangel's White remnants in Crimea, but also, now, assuming a secondary part of the counterattack against Poland. On June 3, 1920, Stalin telegrammed Lenin demanding either an immediate armistice with Wrangel or an all-out offensive to smash him quickly. Lenin wrote to Trotsky aghast ("This is obviously utopian"). Trotsky was affronted that Stalin had bypassed his authority as head of the Revolutionary Military Council of the Republic and gone to Lenin. "Possibly this was to make mischief," Lenin admitted. "But the question must be discussed urgently."[74] No immediate decision was made on Wrangel. On June 5, in Ukraine, Budyonny's cavalry ruptured Polish lines. "We have taken Kiev," Trotsky gloated on June 12, adding that "the retreating Poles destroyed the passenger and freight rail stations, the electric station, the water mains, and the Vladimir Cathedral." He advised publicizing these stories to exert international pressure on the Poles to stop destroying more infrastructure as they retreated.[75] The advancing Reds, meanwhile, would loot and desecrate everything in their path: churches, shops, homes. "The universal calling card of a visit by Red soldiers," one writer explained, "was shit—on furniture, on paintings, on beds, on carpets, in books, in drawers, on plates."[76]

Stalin publicly expressed doubts about mission creep in the Polish campaign to a newspaper at southwestern front HQ in Kharkov on June 24, 1920. "Some of them are not satisfied with the successes on the Front and shout, 'March on Warsaw,'" he observed, in words evidently aimed at Tukhachevsky. "Others are not satisfied with the defense of our republic against enemy attack, and proudly proclaim that they can make peace only with 'a red Soviet Warsaw.'"[77] But such doubts were lost in the euphoria spurred by battlefield successes. "Soldiers of the workers revolution!" Tukhachevsky stated in a directive issued at western front HQ in Smolensk (his hometown) on July 2, cosigned by western front commissars Ivar Smilga and Józef Unszlicht. "The time for payback has arrived. Our soldiers are going on the offensive across the entire front. . . . Those taking part smashed Kolchak, Denikin, and Yudenich. . . . Let the lands ruined by the Imperialist War testify to the revolution's blood-reckoning with the old world and its servants. . . . In the West will be decided the fate of the world revolution. Across the corpse of White Poland lies the way to world conflagration. On our bayonets we will carry happiness and peace to laboring humankind. . . . To Vilna, Minsk, and Warsaw—march!"[78]

Eight days later, in the south, Budyonny, having completely rolled Polish forces back, occupied what had been Piłsudski's field headquarters at the launching-off point of his Ukrainian campaign, the town of Rivne/Równe, and its richly symbolic Hotel Versailles.[79] (Lenin liked to denounce Poland as the "bastard child" of Versailles.) The Red Army now stood upon the Bug River, the rough divide between mostly Polish-speaking territories and mostly Ukrainian-speaking ones.[80] Even though Tukhachevsky had already called for a march on Warsaw, strategy remained undecided in the Red camp. Trotsky, Stalin, Dzierżyński, and Radek—just back from a year in a Berlin prison, and considered well informed on Polish affairs—argued that an offensive on Warsaw would never succeed unless the Polish working class rose in rebellion, a remote prospect.[81] Stalin added, in a public warning in *Pravda* (July 11, 1920), that "it is laughable to talk about a 'march on Warsaw' and more broadly about the solidity of our successes while the Wrangel danger is not liquidated."[82] That very day, however, Minsk fell to forces directed by Tukhachevsky. Poland's government again appealed to the Allies. The French government, still angry at Piłsudski's recklessness, nonetheless suggested an anti-Bolshevik operation; the British government, on July 11, sent the Bolsheviks a note signed by Foreign Secretary Lord Curzon proposing an armistice on western territorial terms favorable to Soviet Russia, an armistice with Wrangel and a neutral zone in Crimea (Wrangel's sanctuary), accompanied by a stern warning not to cross into "ethnographical" Polish territory. The note seemed to establish a Polish-Soviet boundary some fifty miles east of the Bug (essentially the 1797 border between Prussia and imperial Russia); it would become known as the Curzon Line.[83] The Poles were taken aback: the British appeared to be giving away eastern territories the Poles viewed as their "historic" patrimony (whoever might be living there as of 1920).[84] To Lenin, it looked like the British wanted, Gibraltar style, to annex the Crimean peninsula, pointing a dagger, like White Poland, at the Reds; on July 12–13, he urged "a frantic acceleration of the offensive against Poland."[85]

Battlefield momentum helped fulfill Lenin's wishes: the First Cavalry Army had already advanced into ethnic Polish lands. Isaac Babel (b. 1894), a city boy from Odessa attached to one of Budyonny's divisions, kept a diary that he later used to write short stories collected in *Red Cavalry*, making poetry out of their savagery.[86] Tukhachevsky's parallel northerly advance was also led by horsemen, the Third Cavalry Corps, under Haik Bzhishkyan. Known as Gai Dmitrievich Gai (b. 1887), he had been born in Tabriz, Persia, the son of an Armenian father and Persian mother who had emigrated from the Caucasus but in 1901 had returned to Tiflis; Gai fought for Russia in the Great War. Although just half the size of the First Cavalry Army, on which it was modeled, and without a Babel to immortalize its exploits, Gai's Third Cavalry Corps would manage to cover twice the ground at twice the speed of Budyonny's sabers, and against the main Polish concentrations, whose lines they pierced repeatedly. Gai personally could not match Budyonny in horsemanship, but he did so in terror tactics and, what is more, he knew how to employ cavalry as a spearhead for infantry.[87] (This would be the last significant reliance on cavalry in European history.) Impatiently, Lenin instructed foreign affairs commissar Georgy Chicherin, who was negotiating a treaty with Lithuanian nationalists (signed July 12), that "all these concessions are unimportant. . . . We must occupy and Sovietize. . . . We must ensure that we first Sovietize Lithuania and then give it back to the Lithuanians."[88] In fact, Gai chased the Poles from Wilno/Vilna, entering the city on July 14, ahead of the Lithuanian nationalists.[89] The next day Gai received his second Order of the Red Banner.[90]

Sergei Kamenev, on July 14, advised war commissar Trotsky that whatever position the regime adopted toward the Curzon Note, with the Poles on the run, "it would be more desirable to enter peace negotiations without ceasing combat operations."[91] Two days later, the Central Committee assembled to discuss the Curzon Note, among other issues; Stalin, at southwestern front headquarters in Kharkov, was the only politburo member absent. Trotsky urged negotiations, arguing that the Red Army and the country were exhausted from war.[92] But the majority followed Lenin in rejecting Entente mediation and continuing the military action.[93] On July 17, Lenin telegraphed the two top frontline commissars, Stalin and Smilga (western front), crowing about his policy victory and instructing them, "Please expedite the order for a furiously ramped up offensive."[94] Already on July 19, Gai's forces seized Grodno. Red Supreme Commander Sergei Kamenev arrived in Minsk, the new western front HQ, to survey the situation; around midnight on July 22–3, he directed Tukhachevsky that Warsaw be captured no later than August 12, 1920, a mere six weeks into the Red Army campaign.[95]

Lenin had ridden to power by denouncing the "imperialist" war. Had he accepted the Curzon Note as a basis for a peace settlement—whether of his own volition or, because the unthinkable happened and Trotsky and Stalin teamed up to impose their well-founded skepticism upon the politburo—then the Poles reluctantly would have been forced to accept the Curzon Note as well. This would have put Ukraine, most of Belarus, and Lithuania in Soviet hands. Instead, Lenin dreamed of igniting a pan-European revolutionary blaze. He rolled the iron dice.

## LENIN'S FLIGHT OF FANCY

Moscow formed a "Polish Revolutionary Committee" on July 23 consisting of a handful of Polish Bolsheviks, including the Chekists Dzierżyński and Unszlicht. That same day, Stalin's southwestern front redirected its forces from the Lublin-Warsaw salient farther south, toward Lwów/Lviv, Galicia's eastern capital.[96] Partly this was because the northern-salient offensive was going so well. In addition, Greater Romania, the power in southeastern Europe, whose forces had crushed the Hungarian Soviet republic, had occupied tsarist Bessarabia and clashed with Soviet troops; Stalin sought to deter Romanian forces.[97] Trotsky, too, was worried Romania might go on the offensive now that the Red Army had crossed the Curzon Line. Occupying Lwów/Lviv, therefore, could secure the Soviet flank with Romania and furnish a base for the offensive military revolutionizing in Central Europe that Lenin sought. Lev Kamenev, negotiating with the British in London for recognition of the Soviet Union, had written to Lenin on the urgency of capturing Lwów/Lviv, because Curzon had acknowledged it as Russia's and because it was a gateway to Hungary.[98] On July 23, a giddy Lenin wrote to Stalin of a Sovietization thrust all the way to the Italian peninsula: "Zinoviev, Bukharin, and I, too, think that revolution in Italy should be spurred on immediately. . . Hungary should be Sovietized, and perhaps also the Czech lands and Romania." Stalin, indulging Lenin, responded the next day from Kharkov that it would indeed be "sinful not to encourage revolution in Italy. . . . We need to lift anchor and get under way before imperialism manages little by little to fix its broken-down cart . . . and open its own decisive offensive." Stalin also observed that Poland essentially was already "defeated."[99]

Full speed ahead: On the northern Smolensk-Warsaw axis, on July 30, the Polish Revolutionary Committee set up HQ in a commandeered noble palace overlooking Białystok/Belostok, which happened to be a majority Yiddish-speaking city.[100] Here the handful of imported Polish Bolsheviks pronounced themselves a "provisional" government for a socialist Poland.[101] Local government and community organizations were dissolved. Factories, landlord property, and forests were declared "nationalized." Shops and warehouses (mostly Jewish owned) were looted.[102] "For your freedom and ours!" proclaimed the Polish Revolutionary Committee's manifesto.[103] On August 1, Tukhachevsky's armies, slicing through Polish lines, seized Brest-Litovsk, richly symbolic and just 120 miles from Warsaw. His shock attacks, designed to exert psychological as well as military pressure, were encircling the enemy, with Gai bounding ahead on the right flank to annihilate any Polish soldiers in retreat. Gai's cavalry soon dashed to the vicinity of Toruń, northwest of Warsaw, a mere 150 miles from Berlin, but he was under orders not to cross the German border.[104] At the same time, the advancing Red Army was forced to live off the land, and its ranks were diminishing. "Some were barefoot, others wore bast leggings, others some kind of rubber confections," one observer commented of the Red rank-and-file. A parish priest in a Polish town, hardly pro-Soviet, observed of the Red Army invaders that "one's heart ached at the sight of this famished and tattered mob."[105] Furthermore, once the stubborn Tukhachevsky fully acknowledged how badly his headlong charge had exposed his left flank, he and Sergei Kamenev belatedly sought to cover it by hastily shifting the southwestern front forces under Yegorov and Stalin northward, and transferring them to Tukhachevsky's command.[106] But the shift and transfer from the southwestern front to the western Polish front never took place.

The Bolsheviks were divided about whether to press on while the battlefield was fast-moving. The British government was threatening military intervention or sanctions against the Bolsheviks and on August 2, the politburo (in Stalin's absence) discussed the possibility of concluding a peace with "bourgeois Poland." But for Lenin Poland as well as Crimea were of a piece—two toeholds for world imperialism, at the pinnacle of which he saw London. And so, it was now decided that the fight would continue, but the southwestern front should be divided, with a part diverting to the southern front (against Wrangel) and the rest folding into

Tukhachevsky's western front (against Piłsudski). Stalin and Yegorov resisted, however. On August 3, Lenin wrote to Stalin, "I do not fully understand why you are not satisfied with the division of the fronts. Communicate your reasons." Lenin concluded by insisting on "the accelerated liquidation of Wrangel."[107] The next day Lenin asked for Stalin's assessment. "I do not know, frankly, why you need my opinion," Stalin replied testily (August 4), adding "Poland has been weakened and needs a breathing space," which should not be afforded by peace talks. The offensive into Poland, though not his idea, was now on.[108] A Central Committee plenum met on August 5 and again endorsed the politburo decision to continue the military operations; Sergei Kamenev passed on the orders.[109]

But the key forces under Stalin that were ordered northward, Budyonny's now battle-scarred First Cavalry Army, had been encircled near Lwów/Lviv, far from Warsaw. They broke out on August 6, but were said to be "collapsing from exhaustion, unable to move," and sought several days' respite to lick their wounds. Also, Budyonny intended to resume the siege on Lwów/Lviv and complete its capture.[110] In addition, Yegorov and Stalin, who were supposed to fight Wrangel, simply did not want to give up their prize cavalry to Tukhachevsky.[111] Lenin telegrammed Stalin on August 7 that "your successes against Wrangel will help remove the vacillation inside the Central Committee" about continuing military operations against Poland, but he added that "much depends on Warsaw and its fate."[112] Already on August 10, Tukhachevsky's forces approached Warsaw's outskirts.[113] The imperative to send Budyonny to link up with Tukhachevsky seemed diminished. The next day, Lenin again telegrammed Stalin: "Our victory is great and will be greater still if we defeat Wrangel. . . . Make every effort to take all of the Crimea with an immediate blow whatever the cost. Everything depends on this."[114] On August 11 and 12, Kamenev repeated his orders to redirect southwestern front units from Lwów/Lviv toward Lublin.[115] Stalin ignored both Sergei Kamenev's orders (about Lublin) and Lenin's instructions (about Wrangel), in apparently blatant insubordination.[116]

What was Stalin thinking? Trotsky would speculate that because Tukhachevsky was going to capture Warsaw, Stalin at least wanted Lwów/Lviv, and therefore "was waging his own war."[117] Whatever Stalin's vanity, however, *not* taking Lwów/Lviv, at that moment, seemed idiotic. Soviet reports had the western front march on Warsaw proceeding splendidly on its own, while the transfer orders for the southwestern front were close to pointless, given that it was near impossible for Budyonny or others to fight their way up near Warsaw in time to make a difference (the Reds now envisioned the Polish capital's capture on or about August 16).[118] Moreover, Lenin, had initially approved Stalin's capture of Lwów/Lviv in order to acquire a revolutionary springboard. Still, on August 13, Sergei Kamenev repeated the transfer order.[119] Stalin and Yegorov replied that their units were deep in battle for Lwów/Lviv and that altering their battle tasks was "already impossible."[120] On August 14, Stalin was summoned to Moscow to clear up the dispute face to face. (Budyonny would finally abandon the siege of Lwów/Lviv, reluctantly, on August 20—a strategic blunder—only to be shifted one direction one day, another direction the next.)[121]

But here was the most intriguing piece of all: Tukhachevsky was ordered not to attack Warsaw directly, but to circle around to its northwest, partly in order to block the Entente from supplying the Poles from Danzig and the Polish Corridor, but mainly to turn those territories over to Germany. Politically, Germany vacillated between loathing Communism versus looking for international aid against Poland. One Polish official observed that the German government "found it impossible to reconcile its foreign policy, which demanded the annihilation of Poland, with its domestic policy, which was very largely directed by the fear of a Spartacist revolution."[122] In fact, the German government was committed to border revisionism, but only by peaceful means; the Red Army, of all instruments, was voluntarily going to restore Germany's 1914 borders—in order to strike a death blow at the Versailles Order. Frontline Red commanders even told German observers they were prepared to march with Germany on France.[123]

What was Lenin thinking? All during the key decision making regarding operations in Poland, from July 19 through August 7, 1920, Lenin had been exultantly preoccupied with the Second Congress of the Communist International, which had drawn more than 200 attendees, far more than the pitiful founding congress back in March 1919.[124] Arriving in Petrograd, site of the first socialist breakthrough, they were treated to a sumptuous meal in Smolny's Great Hall, participated in a march with workers, then, at the former stock exchange, watched a costume drama performed by a cast of thousands titled *Spectacle of the Two Worlds*. Lenin in his opening speech prophesied that the Versailles Treaty would meet the same fate as Brest-Litovsk.[125] When the delegates traveled to Moscow, to continue, the Bolshevik authorities assembled what they claimed were 250,000 workers in the Red capital to greet them (workers were granted paid time off to appear, followed by mini-banquets in canteens).[126] The proceedings resumed in the former Vladimir's Hall, a throne room of the medieval Kremlin. (The delegates were housed at the Delovoi Dvor, a former Moscow merchant hotel emporium.) Lenin's *"Left-Wing"*

*Communism: An Infantile Disorder,* which criticized almost all non-Bolshevik socialists and was written in April 1920, came out in June in Russian and, in July, in German, English, and French; each delegate received a copy. More immediately, the congress sessions transpired under an oversized map of Poland on which Red Army advances were recorded as each news flash arrived. This was the context in which Lenin had enthused to Stalin, in the telegram of July 23 about going beyond Poland, gushing that "the situation in the Comintern is superb."[127]

The Comintern Congress came on the heels of mass demonstrations against colonialism in Korea and China and although the largest non-Russian delegations were from Germany, Italy, and France, compared with the First Comintern Congress, whose meager Asian representation had included only a few Chinese and Korean émigrés, the Second Congress had at least 30 Asian delegates. Lenin stressed that "the whole world is now divided into a large number of oppressed nations and a very small number of oppressor nations that are enormously rich and strong in the military sense," and that Soviet Russia was leading this struggle. What he did not say outright at the Comintern Congress was that Germany—his ally since 1917—was supposed to help smash world imperialism and Versailles.

Here was the source of Tukhachevsky's harebrained military maneuver to regain Danzig and the Corridor for Germany. Egged on by Lenin, Tukhachevsky's troops north of Warsaw entered a void, without reserves, and with a still utterly exposed left flank (the one closest to Warsaw). He had to assume, or hope, that the retreating Piłsudski would not manage to regroup. Piłsudski had pulled back all Polish forces to the very gates of Warsaw, facilitating Tukhachevsky's heady advance, but also buying time. Still, the Polish marshal enjoyed nothing of his subsequent prestige, having led his pre-1914 political party to division, his legions in the Great War to internment, and his invasion of Ukraine to an invasion of Poland. The Entente had given him up for a political and military corpse—just as Lenin and Tukhachevsky did. But on the very morning of the day the Bolsheviks expected Warsaw to fall (August 16), Piłsudski launched a counteroffensive: five divisions shot through a nearly 100-mile gap on Tukhachevsky's left wing, advancing 40 miles in twenty-four hours without encountering the Red Army. Piłsudski, beginning to suspect a trap, toured the front in his car in search of the enemy. By nightfall, the Poles, deep in Tukhachevsky's rear, had seized the heavy Soviet guns that were being moved up to hammer Warsaw.

Shock! As late as August 17, an oblivious *Pravda* was still reporting that "Polish white troops flee backward under the strikes of the Worker-Peasant fist."

That same day, Stalin, in Moscow as a result of his recall from Kharkov, requested to be relieved of all his military duties. Tukhachevsky, at HQ in Minsk, belatedly became aware of the Polish breach of his left wing and ordered a retreat. "Years on he would say of that day that he had aged ten years," one contemporary observed.[128] Sergei Kamenev called Minsk just after midnight on August 18–19, demanding to know why the Polish counterattack had come as such a surprise, showing his own profound ignorance.[129] On August 19, Lenin desperately begged Radek, who had just been added to the Polish Revolutionary Committee "government" preparing for installation in Warsaw, to "go directly to Dzierżyński and insist that the gentry and the kulaks are destroyed ruthlessly and rather more quickly and energetically," and "that the peasants are helped effectively to take over estate land and forests."[130] Already the next day, however, Lenin informed Lev Kamenev in London, "It is unlikely that we will soon take Warsaw."[131] *Pravda* (August 21) lamented: "Just a week ago we had brilliant reports from the Polish front." Kamenev responded that "the policy of the bayonet, as usual, has broken down 'owing to unforeseen circumstances'"—an undisguised rebuke of Lenin.[132]

Piłsudski scored a spectacular victory, the "miracle on the Vistula." In the ensuing rout retreat, Tukhachevsky lost three of his five armies, one to annihilation and two to flight; the other two were severely maimed.[133] It was a staggering defeat, the likes of which often end military careers. Gai fled with his celebrated cavalry into German East Prussia, where they were disarmed and arrested.[134] Finger-pointing was inevitable. Because the total strength of the Red Army in the final assault on Warsaw had been 137,000, and Red operations in Crimea and Lwów/Lvov combined had numbered 148,000, those troops were viewed as the decisive missing factor. And Yegorov and Stalin had failed to transfer them.[135] Never mind that the transfer of Budyonny's cavalry in time was no simple task. An order had been given. On September 1, 1920, the politburo accepted Stalin's resignation from his military posts.[136] The way was open to scapegoat his insubordination. And Piłsudski's army was still on its eastward march.

## PEOPLES OF THE EAST

In the South Caucasus (known in Russian as Transcaucasia), following the simultaneous breakup of the Ottoman and Russian empires (and, in the case of Armenia, following military clashes with the Ottomans), eastern Armenia, northern

Azerbaijan, and Georgia emerged as independent states. But on April 27, 1920, without a fight, the Bolshevik Red Army captured Baku, capital of the Musavat or nationalist Azerbaijan government, whose flag combined blue for Turkic civilization, green for Islam, and red for European socialism. The Georgian Bolshevik Grigol "Sergo" Orjonikidze (the main political commissar) and none other than Tukhachevsky (the military commander) had found an opportune moment to attack when the Azerbaijanis decided to send 20,000 units of their 30,000-troop army to respond to communal clashes between Armenians and Azeris in a disputed mountain region known as Karabakh.[137] Additionally, Baku—uniquely in Muslim-populated areas—had a substantial population of industrial workers, some of whom belonged to the Bolshevik party and welcomed a Red invasion. Indeed, Baku, in one of the instances when Stalin and Trotsky agreed, became a springboard. At dawn on May 18, 1920, a Soviet naval force of perhaps thirteen gunboats, which amalgamated Soviet sailors, Soviet Azerbaijan infantry and cavalry, and ethnic Iranian longshoremen from Baku, invaded Iran, in pursuit of Russian ships and ammunition formerly controlled by the White military leader Denikin and now in the hands of a British military occupation of Iran.[138]

The landing was led by Fyodor Raskolnikov as well as Orjonikidze, who reasoned the British might try to reequip the ships and send them back into action against the Reds. But now the British military handed everything over and retreated inland toward Tehran. "English colonial policy was confronted with the real forces of the Workers' State at Anzali and experienced a defeat," wrote the Soviet journalist Larissa Reisner, who was married to Raskolnikov.[139] On May 24, Mirza Kuchek Khan (b. 1880), leader of a long-standing anticolonial and constitutionalist movement in northern Iran's Gilan forest, who opposed both Russian and British involvement, was persuaded to take advantage of the Red incursion and, citing the Bolshevik claim to be anti-imperialist, declared himself head of a Persian Soviet Socialist Republic in Gilan province.[140] Lev Karakhan, a foreign affairs official accompanying the invasion force, telegrammed Moscow that "the toilers and the bourgeois democrats should be made to unite in the name of Persia's liberty and be instigated to rise up against the British and expel them from the country," though he cautioned against full Sovietization given the underdevelopment.[141] But Georgy Chicherin, foreign affairs commissar, complained bitterly to Lenin, dismissing the episode as "Stalin's Gilan republic."[142]

Kuchek's coalition—ultraleftists and constitutionalists, anarchists and Kurdish chieftains, anti-imperialists and Russians—was unstable, and he abjured the role of Lenin-style autocrat; in fact, he departed the province's capital (Resht) back to the forest in July 1920, allowing Soviet operatives and Iranian Communists to take over.[143] Bolsheviks in Iran contemplated combining their motley 1,500-person guerilla force of Iranian forest partisans, Azerbaijanis from both sides of the border, Kurds, and Armenians with Red Army reinforcements in a march on Tehran. This never came to pass, owing to Iranian counterforces. But flush with success in northern Iran, Orjonikidze helped suggest and plan, beginning in late July 1920, what would be a weeklong Congress of the Peoples of the East to take place in Baku, now the Caspian showcase for Moscow's appeal to Muslims.[144]

The Congress of the Peoples of the East, the largest ever gathering under the Comintern aegis, opened on September 1, 1920, not long after the Bolshevik debacle in the West against Poland. The Comintern aimed the gathering at the "enslaved masses'" of Turkey, Armenia, and Persia, and as if on cue, the August 20, 1920, Treaty of Sèvres that the Entente imposed on the defeated Ottoman empire showcased the British and French diktat over the Near East: Entente oil and commercial concessions in Ottoman lands were confirmed, German property there was taken by the Entente, and the partitioning of Ottoman lands—one of the Entente's secret war aims—was begun with the declaration of mandates and protectorates. In Baku, meanwhile, nearly 1,900 delegates massed, about 60 of whom were women; the largest contingents were Turkic and Persian speakers, followed by Armenians and Russians, then Georgians. Delegations also arrived from India (15 attendees) and China (8). A substantial number, perhaps a majority of the attendees, were not Communists but radical nationalists.[145] The congress's manifesto demanded "liberation of all humanity from the yoke of capitalist and imperialist slavery."[146] Russian speeches were translated into Azerbaijani Turkish and Persian instantaneously. Karl Radek, the Hungarian exile Béla Kun, and the American John Reed gave speeches, but the featured orator was Zinoviev, Comintern chairman. "Brothers," he thundered, "we summon you to a holy war, in the first place against British imperialism!" *(Tumultuous applause, prolonged shouts of "Hurrah." Members of the Congress stand up, brandishing their weapons. The speaker is unable to continue for some time. All the delegates stand up and applaud. Shouts of "We swear it.")*[147]

Comintern policy in fact was divided over the colonial world. Lenin had argued that given the limited size of the colonial proletariat, Communist parties there needed to enter coalitions with bourgeois nationalists in order to emancipate colonial peoples from imperialist powers. But others, such as Manabendra

Nath Roy, from Bengal, insisted that Communists in colonial settings should prepare to seize power themselves. Some delegates thought the first strategy did not preclude a shift to the latter at the opportune moment.[148] But Roy refused to attend the Baku congress, dismissing it as "Zinoviev's circus."[149]

Stalin did not attend Baku—the Polish war was still on—but by virtue of being nationalities commissar, he had had more contact with the national minority Communists of Soviet Russia than any other top Bolshevik figure.[150] Not that he relished the interminable squabbles among national representatives nursing bottomless grievances and boundless claims. His deputy, Stanisław Pestkowski, recalled of the commissariat that Stalin "would suddenly disappear, doing it with extraordinary skill: 'just for a moment' he would disappear from the room and hide in one of the recesses of Smolny, and later the Kremlin. It was impossible to find him. In the beginning we used to wait for him. But finally we would adjourn."[151] Later, during the civil war, Stalin was almost always away at the front.[152] Even when he did make an appearance at the commissariat, he tended to undercut staff efforts to regularize a policy-making process (his non-consultative decision making provoked them to complain to the Central Committee).[153] The commissariat had no jurisdiction over places like Azerbaijan, Belorussia, or Ukraine, all of which, even when re-Sovietized, were formally independent of Soviet Russia. Nor did the commissariat's writ extend to the majority of Soviet Russia's population (the Russians); rather, it was concerned with the 22 percent in the RSFSR who were national minorities. In that connection, however, Stalin had cultivated a coterie of Muslim radicals, jokingly called "Soviet sharia-ites," in particular the ethnic Bashkir Akhmetzaki Validi (b. 1890) and the ethnic Tatar Mirsäyet Soltangäliev (b. 1892).

Tatars and Bashkirs, who lived north of the Caspian Sea—they were the world's northernmost Muslims—were both Turkic-speaking peoples, but the Tatars were sedentary, and far more numerous, while the Bashkirs remained seminomadic. They intermingled with each other. The Tatar Soltangäliev, born in a village near Ufa (Bashkiria), was the son of a teacher at a *maktaba*, where he studied by the "new method" (Jadid) of the self-styled Muslim modernizer Ismail Gasprinski. In addition to Tatar and Arabic, Soltangäliev's father taught him Russian, which allowed him to enter the Pedagogical School in Kazan, an incubator of the Tatar elite, including most of the Tatar Bolsheviks.[154] In 1917, responding to fellow Muslims who accused him of betrayal for cooperating with Bolsheviks, Soltangäliev explained that "they also declared war on English imperialism, which oppresses India, Egypt, Afghanistan, Persia and Arabia. They are also the ones who raised arms against French imperialism, which enslaves Morocco, Algiers, and other Arab states of Africa. How could I not go to them?"[155] He helped organize the defense of Kazan against the Whites, and though he was an undisguised Tatar imperialist inside Russia and a pan-Turanian whose ambitions stretched from Kazan to Iran and Afghanistan, Turkey and Arabia, Stalin made him Russia's highest profile Muslim Communist, appointing Soltangäliev head of the Central Bureau of Communist Organizations of the Peoples of the East. Informally, he was known as the chairman of the Muslim Communist party, even though no such entity existed. As for the Bashkir Validi, a Turcologist, he was not a Communist but a moderate socialist and Bashkir patriot who took a different path into Stalin's patronage: during the dark days of the civil war against Kolchak, Validi offered to desist from leading his 6,500 Bashkir troops against the Reds alongside the Whites and instead to turn their weapons against the admiral. Stalin, in connection with the negotiations with Validi in Moscow, published an ingratiating article in *Pravda,* "Our Tasks in the East" (March 2, 1919), noting that the 30 million Turkic- and Persian-speaking inhabitants of Soviet Russia "present a rich diversity of culturally backward peoples, either stuck in the middle ages or only recently entered into the realm of capitalist development.... Their cultural limitations and their backwardness, which cannot be eliminated with one stroke, allowed themselves to be felt (and will continue to let themselves be felt) in the matter of building Soviet power in the East." This was a challenge to be addressed.[156]

The Stalin-Bashkir talks coincided with the First Comintern Congress and then the 8th Party Congress, and in Moscow, Validi discovered that compared with the hard-line antinationalist Luxemburgists he met, "Lenin and Stalin really did seem like very positive people." Validi also met with Trotsky, and noticed that Stalin and Trotsky hated each other (and competed for his favor). He further came to see that Stalin was a provocateur. Validi would recall how, a bit later, in Ukraine, Stalin invited him to his civil war train, a carriage from the tsarist era. "We drank Georgian wine and ate grilled chicken," Validi wrote. "Stalin was affectionate. Getting close to my soul, he said that he was an Easterner, that he worked exclusively for us eastern people, representatives of small, downtrodden nations. All our misfortunes derived from Trotsky, whom he called a Jewish internationalist. He [Stalin] understood us well, because he was the son of a Georgian writer and himself had grown up in a national milieu. He accused the Russians of chauvinism and cursed them. He, like Lenin, said that I should work on an all-Russia level, and not get too involved in the management of a small nation: all nations will gradually acquire rights."[157] This Asiatic pose was a side of Stalin almost no one saw.[158]

Validi's reward for betraying Kolchak on the eve of the Whites' planned spring offensive was the creation of the Bashkir Autonomous Soviet Socialist Republic (ASSR), with a treaty signed on March 20, 1919—the third day of the 8th Party Congress (Lenin had been rushing to get the agreement as a showpiece for the congress). The Bashkir military commanders who had been White Guards suddenly were constituted as a Bashkir Revolutionary Committee—a turnabout neither side viewed with trust.[159] (Validi would admit that he hid the negotiations with the Soviet authorities from his men.)[160] The Bashkirs, under imperial Russia, had never been serfs and had been able to maintain their own army, and numbered perhaps 2 million, spread across the southwestern slopes of the Urals. Validi, who drew the map of their autonomy, maximized not territory but ethnic population, and in such a way that he would minimize inclusion of Russian colonists. The result was a Lesser Bashkiria.[161] All the same, Tatar nationalists erupted in fury: their dream of a Greater Tataria enveloping Bashkiria had suffered a mortal blow.[162]

Stalin's creation of a Bashkir republic in 1919—just like the earlier failed Tatar-Bashkir expediency—did not derive from a thought-through strategy of national divide and rule; rather, it was an improvisation aimed at dividing anti-Bolshevik forces.[163] On the ground, however, disaster ensued. A flood of Russian and other non-ethnic-Bashkir Communists entered the area, and they directly and indirectly sabotaged the autonomy: they were fighting to create a world of Communism, not for some small nation's "rights." Local Red Army officers, meanwhile, understood the agreement as a surrender, and proceeded to disarm and imprison the Bashkir fighters, provoking revolt. The Red cavalry horde, moreover, engaged in mass pillage, murder, and rape. Their top commander, none other than the cavalryman Gai, tried to rein in the indiscipline to little avail (later he was blamed as an Armenian likely to have been deliberately anti-Muslim).[164] Gai refused Validi's entreaties to allow the Bashkir units to remain intact, but the result was that the Bashkir First Cavalry regiment managed to reconstitute itself—on the side of Kolchak. Validi desperately telegrammed Stalin about the misunderstandings and atrocities. (Stalin, far away in Moscow, invited him for discussions.)[165] Only a White advance put a stop to the Red Army bacchanalia of violence, but after the Whites were driven out again, the Reds enacted "revenge" on the Bashkirs. The bloodshed and bitter recriminations became a matter of national debate, prompting the politburo in April 1920 to appoint a Bashkir commission headed by Stalin. Validi was summoned to Moscow and told he was needed there, evidently to separate him from his base in Bashkiria. Stalin told him that Trotsky was the one who had decided to detain him in Moscow, and that Trotsky and Dzierżyński were worried about Validi's growing authority in the eastern provinces.[166] Validi met with the Bashkir "commission" and Kamenev told him they were expanding Bashkiria to include Ufa and other regions, which happened to have Russian majorities.[167] Severe restrictions on Bashkir autonomy were promulgated on May 19, 1920: the Bashkir military, supply, finance, and much more were subordinated directly to the RSFSR.[168] The politburo felt constrained to declare that the Bashkir Autonomous Republic "was not a chance, temporary phenomenon . . . but an organic, autonomous part of the RSFSR"—indicative of the doubters, on all sides.[169]

Bashkiria's circumscribed "autonomy" became a model. Between 1920 and 1923, the RSFSR would establish seventeen autonomous national republics and provinces on its territory.[170] The immediate next one was Tataria. Even without Bashkiria (for now), Soltangäliev tried once more to get Lenin to accept a grand Turkic state of Tataria, linked to Turkestan and the Qazaq steppe, under Tatar leadership, something resembling Piłsudski's imagined Polish-led federation over Belorussia and Lithuania. Instead, a small Tatar Autonomous Soviet Socialist Republic was declared on May 27, 1920. It included only 1.5 million of the 4.2 million Tatars in Russia (not only were three quarters of the country's Tatars left out, but Tatars had been made a majority in Bashkiria).[171] Moreover, rather than Soltangäliev, Stalin made Sahib Garei Said-Galiev (b. 1894) head of the Tatar government, a man with far less of a following among Muslims outside Tataria, less nationalist, more obedient, and a diehard enemy of Soltangäliev. Said-Galiev soon accused Soltangäliev of attempted assassination; the latter responded that the alleged assassination was simulated to discredit him; a Moscow investigation proved inconclusive, except to establish that Said-Galiev spent a great deal of time sitting around drinking tea and bickering.[172] Soltangäliev and his supporters remained determined to use all levers at their command to transform Kazan into a Muslim capital for the East.[173] By contrast, Validi and his supporters secretly plotted to quit their official posts and oppose the Soviet regime by force. In June 1920, they disappeared underground, joining the "Basmachi" in

Turkestan. (The epithet likely derived from the Turkic *basmacı* and connoted frontier freebooters or brigands, analogous to Cossacks; Russian speakers generally applied it to any Muslims conducting partisan war or other resistance against the Bolshevik regime.) In the Bashkir ASSR, furious Russian Communists—who had let the counterrevolutionaries escape—purged the remaining ethnic Bashkir officials and instituted another anti-Bashkir terror.[174] The defections raised a scandal that could potentially damage Stalin politically: after all, Validi was seen as his protégé.

In September 1920, when the Baku Congress of the Peoples of the East opened, Mirsäyet Soltangäliev—who had been one of the original proponents and invited to speak—was nowhere to be found; Stalin had blocked him from even attending. But Validi eluded a Cheka manhunt, traveled all the way from Turkestan by rail and other means to Baku and took part in the Congress of the Peoples of the East even though the political police were combing Baku for him.[175] On September 12 Validi wrote a letter to Lenin, Stalin, Trotsky, and Rykov, condemning Soviet national minority policy as tantamount to tsarist colonial practice, and complaining that Stalin had tricked him. He deemed the Georgian "an insincere, masked dictator who plays with people." Stalin tried to lure Validi to Moscow, supposedly getting a message to him that noted how he was "much smarter and more energetic than Soltangäliev," how he was "an extraordinary, powerful person, with character, with willpower, a do-er," who had proven he "could create an army from the Basmachi." Validi would never be caught.[176]

## A CENTRAL ASIAN ARK

In former tsarist Turkestan, multiple centers of would-be authority had arisen. Bolshevik rule among the Turcomans had been quickly overthrown in 1918, in revulsion, and been replaced by an anti-Bolshevik Transcaspian government, which was largely proletarian, but its desperate need to requisition grain also sparked revolt, and the Transcaspian "government" was reduced to a shadowy presence in the cities. It was swept aside by Red Army troops battling Kolchak's forces in Siberia who swooped in and conquered Merv and Ashkhabad (July 1919), Kizil Arvat (October 1919), and finally the Turcoman capital of Krasnovodsk (February 1920). Farther inland, a second major center of power, Tashkent, was controlled by the Slavic-dominated local Soviet, which, as we saw, had massacred the Muslim Qoqand Autonomy in February 1918. The Tashkent soviet survived an internal putsch in January 1919 by its own commissar of war, who managed to execute fourteen top local Communists, but then "proceeded to get drunk," according to a British eyewitness, and was undone by a detachment of lingering Hungarian POWs.[177] A showy Red Terror killed an estimated 4,000 victims, on top of deaths from food shortages, even as Stalin instructed the Tashkent soviet on February 12, 1919, "to raise the cultural level of the laboring masses and rear them in a socialist manner, promote a literature in the local languages, appoint local people who are most closely connected with the proletariat to the Soviet organizations and draw them into the work of administering the territory."[178] Red Army troops from without arrived in Tashkent, under the command of Mikhail Frunze, a peasant lad who had a Russian mother and a Moldavian father, an army nurse who had served in tsarist Turkestan, where the boy was born. Frunze possessed no special military training, but in November 1919, he set about strengthening the counterinsurgency against Basmachi resistance.[179] Turkestan's final centers of authority were the two small "emirates" of Khiva and Bukhara, which had enjoyed special status in tsarist Russia and after 1917 had not come under Red control. They resembled jewels sparkling under poorly protected glass in front of well-armed thieves.

Bukhara had iconic status in the Inner Asian Muslim world as a center of traditional Islamic learning and of Sufi masters, and some Bolshevik insiders warned of the consequences of forcible seizure.[180] "I think that in the military sense, it would not be difficult to crush their army," Gersh Broido, the outgoing foreign affairs representative of the Turkestan Commission, wrote to Lenin in spring 1920, "but that would create a situation of prolonged war, in which the Red Army would turn out to be not the liberator but the occupier, and Bukharan partisan warriors will emerge as defenders. . . . Reactionaries will use this situation." A military takeover, he warned, might even broadly unite Muslim and Turkic peoples against the Soviet regime.[181] Frunze, however, would not be deterred. Khiva was seized first, after which, in June 1920, the Khorezm People's Soviet Republic was declared. Then, on July 24, 1920, Frunze wrote to Lenin explaining that in connection with Bukhara, waiting for revolution from within would take forever, and instead urged "revolution from without."[182] Preparations to storm Bukhara were simultaneous with the Red Army's final advance on

Warsaw. Beginning on August 30, 1920, after a small group of Turkic Communists staged an "uprising" and summoned "help," Red Army forces assaulted the Bukharan emirate with about 15,000 troops. The Bukharans had at least twice that number, including irregulars, but the Reds had superior weapons, including eleven airplanes, and they bombed the old city's ancient mosques and minarets, caravansaries, shrines, and tombs. On September 2, the Reds seized the emir's massive Ark fortress, after which large-scale fires and mass looting ensued—silk caftans, jewels, even stones. The fate of the harem is anybody's guess. On September 4, Frunze issued an order to halt the pillaging, threatening soldiers with execution, but he helped himself to fine swords and other trophies. The greatest haul was said to come from the emir's vaults, which the dynasty had accumulated over the centuries and were estimated to hold up to 15 million rubles' worth of gold; the treasure was loaded for "transfer" to Tashkent. The emir, for his part, escaped to Afghanistan, and may have carted away some portion of his treasure.[183] He was the last direct descendant of the twelfth-century Mongol Chinggis Khan to rule anywhere in the world.

Frunze was transferred to Crimea, to lead the operations that would soon expel Baron Wrangel's White army into exile, ending the Whites' resistance for good, and garnering the Red commander surpassing military honors. But Frunze's transfer out of Turkestan was shadowed by reports to Moscow of his troops' shameful looting and gratuitous ruination of Bukhara.[184] Word of the pillaging of the gold spread throughout the East, damaging the Soviets' reputation.[185] Jēkabs Peterss, the Cheka plenipotentiary in Turkestan, wrote to Dzierżyński and Lenin, behind Frunze's back, about military misbehavior. All across Eurasia, the Reds were battling among themselves over the spoils of war and prerogatives of unaccountable power—police operatives against army officers, party apparatchiks against the police, central plenipotentiaries against regional potentates. Denunciations swamped Moscow; "inconvenient" people were disgraced or simply shot. But rarely did such score settling reach the level that it did in Turkestan, and rarely did it seem to involve high principle.

Peterss, an ethnic Latvian (b. 1886) from a region on the Baltic Sea in the country's far northwest, went up against Frunze, an ethnic Moldovan, from a region on the Black Sea in the country's far southwest, who had been born (1885) in Pishpek in the shadows of the Pamir Mountains, in the deep east. Peterss was no calculating careerist trying to climb the greasy pole: he was already at the absolute top, carrying the prestige of being a founder of the Cheka; he had even briefly replaced Dzierżyński as Cheka chairman (during the Left SR fiasco when Dzierżyński was taken hostage). True, Peterss was not above shaving the truth, claiming in his party autobiography, for example, to be the son of a poor peasant while earlier he had divulged to an American journalist that his father had plenty of land and hired labor, but everyone did that. (Inevitably, the woman found him "an intense, quick, nervous little chap with a shock of curly black hair, an upturned nose that gave his face the suggestion of a question mark, and a pair of blue eyes full of human tenderness.")[186] Nor was Peterss the least squeamish about prosecution of the revolution and class warfare: he had conducted mass executions in 1919 Petrograd of former old regime personages, identifying them via the phone book and sending men to their door. Corruption, though, he would not tolerate: he was old school. After the sack of Bukhara, he arrested the Red field commander, Belov, who turned out to be in possession of a sack of gold, silver, and money.[187] This induced Peterss to have his Chekists stop and surround Frunze's train. "Yesterday evening," Frunze wrote in a rage to Tashkent on September 21, 1920, "the entire corps, except for myself and [Gleb] Boki, were subject to searches, discrediting me in the eyes of subordinates."

Frunze insisted that the authorities in Tashkent had a list of all the Bukharan valuables he had confiscated and put on his train, and that Peterss had a copy. It took Moscow party secretary Vyacheslav Molotov's handiwork to kill the revolutionary tribunal that Peterss had raised by burying the matter in the party's Central Control Commission. Nonetheless, Dzierżyński would ask one of his most trusted operatives "to put together a list, secretly, not alarming anyone, of where and how (to whom and how much) the Bukharan emir's gold was distributed."[188] The results remain unknown.

A Turkestan "Autonomous Soviet Socialist Republic" was ceremoniously proclaimed on September 24, 1920.[189] A Bukharan People's Soviet Republic, paired with Khorezm, followed on October 8. Stalin had played next to no role in these Turkestan events—but soon his actions would be decisive for Central Asia's fate. In the meantime, an uncanny number of high officials in his future personal dictatorship had launched or furthered their careers in the Turkestan conquests. Valerian Kuibyshev, for example, the future head of the party Control Commission under Stalin, was chairman of the Turkestan commission in spring-summer 1920, working to implant Bolshevik rule more deeply and plan the emirate conquests. Boki, the future head of the key secret cipher department under Stalin, served alongside Frunze. In the Turkestan Army's political directorate, an unknown young operative headed the registration-information department—Alexander Poskryobyshev, Stalin's future top aide, who would man the inner workings of the dictatorship for decades. Another young Communist operative, Lazar Kaganovich, was dispatched as a high-level party apparatchik official to Turkestan in September 1920.[190] That same month, Grigory Sokolnikov (aka Girsh Briliant) replaced Frunze as the head of the Turkestan front and the Communist party Turkestan bureau. In Tashkent, Sokolnikov went on to introduce a local monetary reform, getting rid of the worthless local currency, presaging a countrywide monetary reform he would oversee as future finance commissar under Stalin in Moscow. In Turkestan, Sokolnikov also repealed requisitioning in favor of a tax in kind—what would be called, in Moscow, the New Economic Policy. Turkestan was a policy laboratory, and an Ark for Bolshevik careers.

## NO GLORY

Lost wars always ripple through political systems. With the defeat in the Polish war still raw, Lenin delivered a rambling report on it at the opening of the 9th party conference in Moscow on September 22, 1920, to 241 delegates (116 with voting rights). He averred that because the Reds had defeated the White armies, those stooges of the Entente, "the defensive period of the war with worldwide imperialism was over, and we could, and had an obligation to, exploit the military situation to launch an offensive war." The "probe with bayonets" had been intended to reveal if revolution had genuinely ripened in Poland, "the center of the entire current system of international imperialism," as well as in Germany, but as it happened, "readiness was slight." Nonetheless, Lenin happily concluded that "we have already undermined the Versailles Treaty, and we will smash it at the first convenient opportunity," because "despite the complete failure in the first instance, our first defeat, we will keep shifting from a defensive to an offensive policy over and over again until we finish all of them off for good."[191] Lenin's political report would not even be voted upon (a first at a party gathering since the assumption of power), and he would not even bother to attend the closing session (September 25).[192] *Pravda*'s account of Lenin's September 22 speech omitted talk of "an offensive war" or of having tried to "Sovietize Poland," to say nothing of "catastrophic," "gigantic," "unheard-of defeat."[193] In the conference discussion, Radek expressly blamed Lenin, prompting others to do so as well. It fell to Stalin to defend the Central Committee's revolutionism. Suddenly, Trotsky laced into Stalin for having misled the Central Committee—in reporting that the Polish army in retreat had lost all fighting capacity—and for sabotaging the campaign by failing to implement troop transfer orders. Lenin piled on, attacking his Georgian protégé viciously.

On the second day (September 23), Stalin insisted on replying to Trotsky and Lenin, and divulged to the conference that he had voiced doubts about a campaign into Poland.[194] In truth, the march on Warsaw had been the work of Tukhachevsky and Sergei Kamenev. But of course Lenin was the prime mover behind the debacle, and now he pulled the rug out from under Stalin, shifting the blame from his own too-optimistic reading of the revolutionary situation to the excessive pace of the military advance.[195] In fact, had Tukhachevsky made it to Warsaw just three days earlier, his mad-dash battle plan might have caught the Polish camp in disarray.[196] But what would Warsaw's capture have brought?[197] Tukhachevsky faced no greater prospect of holding on to Warsaw than Piłsudski had had of holding on to Kiev. The Red Army had known beforehand that it could not have garrisoned the whole land and had not intended to, but Lenin's justification for the war—to spark a Polish worker uprising—had failed.[198] The Reds had picked up very few deserters from the Polish side; even ethnic Ukrainians and Belorussians did not join the Red side in numbers. As for the Polish Communist party, its membership was minuscule, and it had to compete for worker allegiance—to say nothing of the alliance of the majority peasants—with the Jewish Bund, the Poale Zion, the Social Democrats, and Poland's large self-standing trade union movement.[199] Grassroots Polish Revolutionary Committees were established only in the Białystok/Belostok region, and existed for less than a month.[200] Even the head of the central Polish Revolutionary Committee in Białystok/Belostok had warned against hoping to instigate a workers revolution in Poland, given national solidarities.[201] Lenin had ignored their warnings.

Privately at least, Lenin could show contrition.[202] But Tukhachevsky would remain unrepentant years on.[203] "The struggle between capitalist Poland and the Soviet proletarian revolution was developing on a European scale," he would allege in lectures on the war, one section of which bore the title "Revolution from Abroad [izvne]." "All the verbiage about the awakening of national sentiment in the Polish working class in connection with our offensive is merely due to our defeat. . . . To export revolution was a possibility. Capitalist Europe was shaken to its foundations, and but for our strategic errors and our defeat in the field, the Polish War might have become the link between the October Revolution of 1917 and the revolution in Western Europe."[204] Tukhachevsky would avoid blaming Stalin by name.[205] But others, notably Boris Shaposhnikov, a tsarist staff officer who soon became Red chief of staff, would expressly blame the southwestern front—Yegorov and Stalin—for going "against the reciprocity of the two fronts."[206]

So there it was: Lenin madly miscalculating; the tsarist aristocrat Tukhachevsky helping blunder Soviet Russia into an offensive war to ignite "revolution from abroad," then claiming years later it had not been a blunder; and the proletarian Stalin, having warned against such adventurism, scapegoated for insubordination.[207]

Back on the battlefield, the Soviets got lucky. Polish forces recaptured Wilno, Piłsudski's hometown, on October 7, 1920, but Tukhachevsky managed to stabilize the Red retreat at the site of Great War trenches ("attacking Warsaw, I retreated to Minsk," he later noted).[208] The exhausted sides agreed to an armistice in Riga on October 12, 1920 (to take effect on the eighteenth), with a border about 125 miles east of the Curzon Line. That same day, Zinoviev, head of the Comintern, was in Halle, Germany, attending the special Congress of the Independent Social Democrat Party, aiming to split them and annex their left wing to the small party of German Communists. At this time there were 103 Independent Social Democrats in the Reichstag, as against 278 Social Democrats and 2 Communists. Zinoviev was vigorously rebutted by Rudolf Hilferding and Lenin's old Menshevik rival Martov, but in a hall decorated with Soviet emblems, the vote went Moscow's way.[209] "We go forward to the complete elimination of money," Zinoviev explained. "We pay wages in commodities. We introduce trolleys without fares. We have free public schools, free, if temporarily poor, meals, rent-free apartments, free lighting. We are realizing all this very slowly, under the most difficult conditions. We have to fight ceaselessly, but we have a way out, a plan."[210] The German authorities, incredibly, had granted Zinoviev a visa but now promptly deported him. By December, however, around 300,000 of the 890,000 Independent Social Democrats would join the German Communists, bringing the latter to 350,000.[211] Suddenly, there was a mass Communist party in the heart of Europe.[212] At the same time, German Social Democracy had been profoundly weakened, with consequences to follow.

With Romania, there were no further immediate military clashes, but on October 28, 1920, in Bucharest, the Entente powers recognized Greater Romania's annexation of Bessarabia; Soviet Russia rejected the treaty and called for a plebiscite, a demand that was ignored.[213]

Against the Poles the Reds lost some 25,000 dead and seriously wounded; the Poles, perhaps 4,500 dead, 22,000 wounded, and 10,000 missing.[214] Another 146,000 Red Army men fell prisoner in Poland and Germany; how many of them died in Polish captivity remains a matter of dispute, perhaps 16,000 to 18,000 (1,000 refused to return). Of the 60,000 Polish POWs in Soviet Russia, about half returned alive (some 2,000 refused to return).[215] Lenin tried to take solace in the claim that "without having gained an international victory, which we consider the only sure victory, we have won the ability to exist side by side with capitalist powers."[216] Of course, nothing like that had been won. As for Piłsudski—who after so many victims, had also ended up in roughly the same place he had been before his invasion of Ukraine—he dismissed the campaign in which tens of thousands of people died and were maimed as "a kind of children's scuffle."[217]

The Red Army, meanwhile, without waiting for spring, transferred large formations from the Polish front southward, to go up against Wrangel. On November 7, 1920, the third anniversary of the revolution, 135,000 troops overseen by Mikhail Frunze attacked the Crimean peninsula in a complex maneuver. "Today, we can celebrate our victory," Lenin said at the anniversary celebration in the Bolshoi.[218] Soon enough, indeed, Wrangel ordered a total evacuation toward the Turkish Straits and Constantinople. Between November 13 and 16, from Sevastopol, Yalta, and other Crimean ports, 126 ships carrying almost 150,000 soldiers, family members, and other civilians departed Russia; Wrangel left aboard the *General Kornilov*.[219] The Cheka rampaged among those who stayed behind, executing thousands, including women.[220] And so, not long after "White" Poland's ambitions to displace Soviet Russia as the great power in Eastern Europe had been checked, the Whites inside Russia had been definitively vanquished. There was no glory for Stalin: he had originally been assigned Wrangel's destruction, but had resigned his military posts over the Polish campaign.

## WINTER OF DISCONTENT (1920-21)

The Whites in many ways served as unwitting Bolshevik handmaidens by alienating the peasants even more, but once the Whites had ceased to be a battlefield threat in 1920, the Bolsheviks were left face to face with the angry majority of the populace. Paradoxically, as one historian observed, "the conclusion of peace with Poland and the elimination of Wrangel were psychologically disadvantageous, from the standpoint of the Communists."[221] These developments removed the immediate threat while exposing the regime's aggressive incompetence. Thus, whereas the crisis of 1918 had been overcome by mobilization for civil war, and the battlefield crises of 1919–20 had been met largely thanks to White political failures, a new, and in many ways deeper, crisis broke out that fall-winter of 1920–21: Soviet Russia's people were not only freezing, starving, and disease ridden, but they were also embittered. Like all extreme violence, war, and particularly civil war, transforms individual choices and behavior, such that notions of political "support," adapted from peacetime circumstances, cannot be applied so easily.[222] But the deprivation and to an extent the disillusionment may have been even worse than they had been four years earlier under Nicholas II, on the eve of the February Revolution.

Peasants were invaded from all sides and compelled to choose allegiances, at least until armies moved on. "The Whites would come and go, and the Reds, and many others without any color," as the writer Viktor Shklovsky poetically recapped.[223] Of course, peasants well understood the Whites wanted to restore the old barons and denied national difference, but the peasants also detested Bolshevism's conscription and forced grain requisitions. Across Eurasia already in mid-1918 peasant resistance to Bolshevik grain seizures had emerged on a wide scale.[224] Requisitioning detachments began to use not just rifles but machine guns and, in some cases, bombs. Still, peasants fought back. "Many of the villages are now well armed, and seldom does a grain expedition end without victims," one newspaper reported. "A band of hungry 'partisans' had attacked a food train," *Pravda* reported of Ufa in 1918. "They first tore up the tracks and then opened fire on the train guard."[225] The obvious alternative would have been to allow a market-incentive system that encouraged peasants to solve the food supply crisis by paying a fixed tax and keeping the profits from their hard work. But when peasants demanded free trade, Bolshevik agents perceived darkest ignorance.[226] Still, the peasants kept reminding everyone that they had made their own revolution.

In August 1920—while Lenin was fantasizing about overturning the entire Versailles Order through conquest of Poland, and Tukhachevsky lost his army in a void north of Warsaw—a peasant rebellion had begun in Tambov, 350 miles southeast of Moscow. It started with just a few rebels who killed some members of a requisition squad, then beat back attempted Bolshevik reprisals; by fall 1920, local rebel forces mushroomed to 8,000. Their leader, Alexander Antonov (b. 1889), had conducted expropriations in prerevolutionary days to fund the Socialist Revolutionary Party (he was caught and got hard labor in Siberia); under Bolshevik tyranny, he reverted to underground terrorism. Many of the peasant rebels had served in the tsarist army or the Red Army, from which they deserted (the troops garrisoned in small towns might as well have been prisoners of war, so meagerly were they provisioned). The rebels formed a cross-village network they called the Union of the Toiling Peasantry, infiltrated the Tambov Cheka, employed guerrilla tactics against regime personnel and installations, sometimes wearing Red Army uniforms, and developed an operational headquarters staffed by people chosen in secret ballot, with excellent reconnaissance and a strong agitation department. A congress of Tambov rebels formally abolished Bolshevik authority, calling for the "victory of the genuine socialist revolution," with unmolested peasant land ownership.[227] Perhaps the single most interesting aspect of the Tambov peasants' demands was for "the political equality of all without regard to class."[228] The regime only faintly understood what was going on. Supreme Commander Sergei Kamenev had reported to the government that thousands of starving peasants in Tambov, as well as Voronezh and Saratov provinces, were pleading with local authorities for seed grain from grain-collecting stations. In some cases, Kamenev reported, "the crowds were being shot with machine guns."[229] Notwithstanding such moments of comprehension as Kamenev displayed, the scope of the rural catastrophe was still clouded in Moscow by class-war idées fixes as the regime reflexively labeled the peasants' legitimate grievances "an uprising of kulaks, bandits, and deserters."

A plenipotentiary, Vladimir Antonov-Ovseyenko—who in 1917 led the storming of the Winter Palace—had arrived in February 1921 to overhaul the demoralized local Cheka and intensify efforts to encircle and annihilate the peasant army, but repression alone was not going to rescue the situation. The harvest was turning out to be poor, and political disturbances had already forced the food supply commissariat to "suspend" grain procurements in thirteen provinces.[230] On February 9 came reports of yet another immense wave of armed unrest in rural Siberia, cutting off rail links and food shipments.[231] Four days later, a Cheka team noted of Tambov that "the current peasant uprisings differ from the previous ones in that they have a political program, organization, and a plan."[232] Vasily Ulrich, a top official of the deadly Revolutionary Tribunal dispatched to Tambov in early 1921, reported to Moscow regarding the hated grain detachments that "there is nothing more they can achieve other than to arouse more animosity and provoke more bursts of rebellion." No softie, Ulrich nonetheless recommended that peasants who demonstrated loyalty to the Soviet regime be rewarded, in order to "silence those Socialist Revolutionary agitators who claim that Soviet power only takes from the peasant."[233] As a result, that February 1921 in Tambov the policy of obligatory grain quotas to be delivered at fixed prices was replaced by a tax-in-kind that allowed the peasants to retain much of their grain for sale—a very significant concession, so far in one province.[234]

## "SOVIETS WITHOUT PARTIES"

Rural rebellion was paralleled by significant urban strikes.[235] In shops there were just one-fifth the consumer goods that had been available in 1913. Workers who had remained in Petrograd were being press-ganged into unremunerated extra "labor duties" [*povinnost'*]. Then, on February 12, 1921, the authorities announced the temporary closing of 93 factories, including even the famous Putilov Works, for lack of fuel, threatening nearly 30,000 workers with unemployment and the complete loss of rations (however meager).[236] When many of the plants reopened ten days later, work collectives walked out on strike, openly demanding an end to Communist dictatorship and the return to soviets with genuinely free elections.[237] Menshevik and Socialist Revolutionary groups issued their own anti-Bolshevik proclamations; the Cheka wrongly blamed the non-Bolshevik socialists for inciting the strikes, as if the workers themselves were not capable of opposing the regime's oppressive policies and failures. On February 24, as crowds of several thousand started to appear in the streets, Grigory Zinoviev, Petrograd party boss, and the Petrograd Cheka arrested non-Bolshevik socialists en masse (some 300 Mensheviks and Socialist Revolutionaries), sent young military student cadets to disperse the marches with warning shots fired into the air, and proclaimed martial law—just as tsarist General Khabalov had done under Nicholas II in the same city, four years earlier almost to the day. The striking workers were locked out. At the same time, however, extra rations were suddenly released to the city, and the detachments blocking travel to and from the countryside for food were removed. Still, word of the martial law, on top of rumors of bloodshed, reached the nearby Kronstadt fortress, twenty miles from Petrograd on an island in the Gulf of Finland and the HQ of the Baltic fleet.[238]

On Kronstadt in 1917, during the Provisional Government, there had never been "dual power," just soviets as the island fortress became a socialist ministate. In 1921, the island garrison contained 18,000 sailors and soldiers as well as 30,000 civilians, and on March 1 around 15,000 of them gathered on Kronstadt's Anchor Square and overwhelmingly approved a fifteen-point resolution stipulating freedom of trade as well as "freedom of speech and the press for all workers and peasants, anarchists and left socialist parties"—that is, not for the bourgeoisie or even rightist socialists. The sailors also demanded "All power to the soviets and not to parties."[239] Only two Bolshevik officials present voted against the resolution, while Mikhail Kalinin—the chairman of the All-Russia Soviet (head of state)—who had come to address the sailors, was shouted down, and lost a vote on whether he could resume. A socialist regime was faced with determined socialist rebellion among its armed forces.

Later that night of March 1, the sailors formed a Provisional Revolutionary Committee to oversee order on the island and prepare free and fair, multicandidate, secret ballot elections to the Kronstadt soviet. The next day, in the House of Enlightenment (the former Engineers' School), Stepan Petrichenko (b. 1892), a clerk on the battleship *Petropavlovsk,* who had been a Communist but in a "reregistration" had lost his party status, opened a gathering of 202 delegates whose presidium consisted solely of non-party people. Communists at the fortress arrived at party HQ requesting 250 grenades, but that evening, most party members and Cheka operatives evacuated across the ice to the mainland—the Revolutionary Committee had come to power without bloodshed. The next day the regime in Moscow issued a statement, signed by Lenin and Trotsky, denouncing the rebellion as a "White Guard Conspiracy" incited by French intelligence and adopting "Socialist Revolutionary-Black Hundred" resolutions.[240] Some Cheka operatives accurately reported the sailors' demands as "freedom of the press, the removal of barring detachments, freedom of trade, reelections to the soviets with a universal and secret ballot."[241] But the Bolshevik political police seized sailors' wives and children in Petrograd as hostages, cut off all communication in a blockade of the island, and dropped leaflets from an airplane: "You are surrounded on all sides. . . . Kronstadt has no food, no fuel." "You are being told fairy tales, like how Petrograd stands behind you. . . ."[242] The sailors, unlike in 1917, had no means to communicate the truth about their insurrection. The regime used its press monopoly to slander the rebels and rally stalwarts to suppress proletarian sailors and soldiers in the name of a higher proletarian goal of defending the revolution. Moreover, the authorities, unlike in 1917, possessed a reliable instrument of repression—the Cheka.

Inside the Kronstadt republic, heated discussions broke out about whether to go on the attack, seizing Oranienbaum, on the mainland to the south, and Sestroretsk, on the mainland to the north, in order to extend the island's defense perimeter; the Revolutionary Committee rejected the idea. The sailors behaved transparently, living the ideals they professed, publishing almost all Soviet government notices without shortening in the Kronstadt newspaper (edited by the chairman of the 1917 Kronstadt soviet), and sending delegations to Petrograd to negotiate; the Bolshevik authorities arrested the negotiators (they would be executed), instituted a vicious smear campaign, and issued an ultimatum to surrender—acting just like the repressive tsarist regime, as the sailors pointed out.[243] On March 5, 1921, the politburo secretly assigned the task of "liquidating" the uprising to Tukhachevsky, and set the date of attack as March 8, the opening of the 10th Party Congress (which had been postponed from March 6). On the afternoon of March 5, Trotsky arrived on his armored train in Petrograd, where only months before he had vanquished Yudenich; the war commissar was accompanied by Tukhachevsky as well as Sergei Kamenev.[244] On the night of March 7 an artillery barrage hit Kronstadt, and in the morning at 5:00 a.m. a multiprong crackdown began as Red Army infantry (many wearing white sheets) crossed the frozen white Gulf of Finland. The heavy assault across several miles of ice was turned back, however. "The sailors' position is defended and they answer artillery with fire," Tukhachevsky sheepishly reported to Sergei Kamenev.[245] Trotsky telephoned for an explanation.[246] The news was shocking: even specially chosen, archreliable Red Army units had vacillated.[247]

On the same morning of March 8 nearly 900 delegates (694 with voting rights), representing more than 700,000 Communist party members, gathered in Moscow for the 10th Party Congress underneath red banners proclaiming the victory of "the proletariat."[248] The Bolshoi Theater's expansive parterre and five tiers of boxes were crammed to bursting. The Whites had been scattered—in the ground, prison, or exile—but large-scale industry had fallen 82 percent since 1913, coal output was one quarter of the 1913 level, electricity, one third.[249] Combat with Poland had exposed the limits of the Red Army's economic base, demanding a respite to rebuild, somehow.[250] Politically, the non-agricultural labor force had declined since the October coup from 3.6 million to 1.5 million, and more than one third of the latter were artisans, leaving just 950,000 industrial workers in the workers state.[251] That contrasted with perhaps 2.4 million functionaries. Workers in Petrograd and elsewhere, as well as sailors of the Baltic fleet, were demanding the same program urged upon them by Bolshevik agitators in 1917—"All Power to the Soviets!"—but now expressly without Bolshevik party members. Peasants, too, had taken up arms in the name of a genuine people's power. World revolution had failed to materialize; on the contrary, the attempted revolutions surrounding Soviet Russia had been crushed. And to top it all off, Lenin faced organized opposition within party circles. Of course, party opposition to him had been constant: in the underground days, Martov and the Mensheviks opposed Lenin's vision of the party and tactics; in 1917, Zinoviev and Kamenev opposed the seizure of power; in 1918, Bukharin and the Left Communists opposed Brest-Litovsk; in 1919, the military opposition opposed tsarist officers. But now, a self-styled Workers' opposition, headed by two stalwart Bolsheviks, Alexander Shlyapnikov and Alexandra Kollontai, were demanding "party democracy" and real trade unions to defend workers' rights.

Lenin was infuriated at the Workers' opposition, but after all, he himself had allowed it ample opportunity to air its critique. By Central Committee decision, the party press had been carrying nasty polemics over trade unions since November-December 1920.[252] This *public* debate beyond the halls of party meetings, so uncharacteristic, might actually have been a provocation by Lenin to make Trotsky discredit himself by broadcasting his unpopular turn-up-the-screws approach. Trotsky was demanding that unions become an arm of the state. Lenin seems to have conspired with Zinoviev to bait and then counterattack Trotsky (whom Zinoviev despised); Stalin counterattacked Trotsky, too.[253] At the congress, Lenin won the policy battle: unions were neither merged into the state (Trotsky) nor afforded autonomy (Shlyapnikov). And yet, Lenin proved a sore winner.[254] "Comrades," he noted in his opening greetings, "we allowed ourselves the luxury of discussions and debates within our party."[255] The implication was that this "luxury" was going to end. Lenin also flashed his anger, telling Shlyapnikov that the fitting response to his criticism ought to be a gun.[256] And although Trotsky, unlike Shlyapnikov, had refused his supporters' urgings to form a formal faction for the congress, Lenin did not take kindly to his grandstanding. "Comrades, today comrade Trotsky polemicized with me especially politely and reproached or called me hyper-cautious," Lenin told the delegates on

March 14, in one of his milder outbursts. "I ought to thank him for the compliment and express regrets that I lack the opportunity to return it."[257]

## RELATIONS AMONG SOVIET SOCIALIST REPUBLICS

Stalin's responsibility at the 10th Party Congress, predictably, was the national question. The battle against Denikin and other Whites in 1919–20 had allowed the Red Army to reconquer Ukraine in the name of Soviet power, but the Russian Soviet Federated Socialist Republic felt constrained to sign a so-called union treaty with the Ukrainian Soviet Socialist Republic, one of the many such treaties with the different Soviet republics, on December 28, 1920.[258] Despite the treaty's name, however, the RSFSR and Ukrainian SSR did not establish an overarching union citizenship or supreme organs of rule above those of the member states, and they both continued to act separately in international relations. Soviet Ukraine, like Soviet Russia, would go on to sign a plethora of state-to-state treaties—with Poland, Austria, Lithuania, Latvia, Estonia—right through late 1921.[259] Ukraine maintained missions abroad in Prague, Berlin, Warsaw, Vienna, often in the same building as the RSFSR missions; Ukraine also had a representative office in Moscow.[260] On the eve of the Party Congress, Stalin published theses on relations among the non-integrated Soviet republics. He argued that the treaty approach, essentially just begun, was already "exhausted," demanding a new approach. "Not one Soviet republic taken separately can consider itself safe from economic exhaustion and military defeat by world imperialism," he wrote. "Therefore, the isolated existence of separate Soviet republics has no firm basis in view of the threats to their existence from the capitalist states. . . . The national Soviet republics that have freed themselves from their own and from the foreign bourgeoisie will be able to defend their existence and conquer the united forces of imperialism only by joining in a close political union."[261] Such an integrated state, however, would require significant concessions by the non-Russian republics such as Ukraine.[262]

Amplifying these theses at the Party Congress in a report on March 10, Stalin called for "a federation of Soviet republics" and held up the RSFSR, a federation, as the model. He criticized Chicherin, the foreign affairs commissar, who was emerging as a rival, and praised "the state-ness in Ukraine, Azerbaijan, Turkestan and other borderlands," but warned of pan-Islam and pan-Turkism as a "deviation" rooted in national oppression of the past, rather than a forward-looking program to be embraced.[263] The impact of Stalin's speech appears to have been underwhelming. Trotsky and Zinoviev were absent, in Petrograd, taken up with the Kronstadt rebellion. From the rostrum the Georgian spoke slowly, in his characteristically accented and soft voice—there were no microphones yet. After polite applause, Klim Voroshilov, the Stalin loyalist assigned to preside over his session, recommended a break. "If we do not break," Voroshilov admonished the delegates, "we must forbid here in the strictest way the milling about, reading of newspapers and other acts of impertinence."

Voroshilov further announced that because of scheduling changes related to the Kronstadt situation, the delegates would have the night off and could go to the Bolshoi Theater. "Today," he informed them, "the Bolshoi has 'Boris Godunov,' only without Chaliapin."[264] Voroshilov could have sung the part himself, but he was soon to depart for Kronstadt.

Forty delegates, apparently of the Turkestan delegation, had signed a petition demanding a coreport on nationalities by Georgy Voldin, known as Safarov (b. 1891). A half Armenian-half Pole born in St. Petersburg who alternated British-style pith helmets with a worker's cap, he had arrived in Turkestan along with Frunze and was soon named to the Turkestan party bureau. Now he offered a rambling coreport, admitting that "in the [eastern] borderlands we did not have a strong revolutionary movement," and that "in Turkestan the Communist party arose only after the October Revolution," his way of explaining why it was full of rogues.[265] Safarov demanded "corrections" to Stalin's theses. In the discussion one of those given the floor, Anastasy Mikoyan, an ethnic Armenian party official in Azerbaijan, also challenged Stalin, objecting that "in the theses of comrade Stalin nothing is said about how we should approach classes in the borderlands, how precisely we should determine the class structure of these nationalities." Again and again and again, even in cases when people, such as Mikoyan, urged that local conditions had to be accommodated, the Bolsheviks were trying to think and act through the ideology.[266]

When discussion was abruptly cut off, Mykola Skrypnyk (b. 1872), a Communist from Ukraine six years Stalin's senior, interjected from the floor, "The national question is important, painful; comrade Stalin in his report did not in the least degree resolve this question."[267] But the Stalin tormentor Skrypnyk was not given the podium. Nor was Safarov allowed a closing statement. Stalin got the last word, and attacked an array of objections. "Here I have a written note to the effect that we, Communists, supposedly artificially forced a Belorussian nation," he stated. "This is false, because a Belorussian nation exists, which has its own language, different from Russian, and that the culture of the Belorussian nation can be raised only in its own language. Such speeches were made five years ago about Ukraine, concerning the Ukrainian nation. . . Clearly, the Ukrainian nation exists and the development of its culture is a duty of Communists. One cannot go against history."[268]

The congress voted to adopt Stalin's theses in toto as a basis and to form a seventeen-person commission for further action. His fundamental point—that "the national Soviet republics . . . will be able to defend their existence and conquer the united forces of imperialism only by joining in a close political union"— pointed toward resolute action on his part.[269] Shortly after the Party Congress, on April 11, 1921, Stalin would have the Turkestan Autonomous Soviet Socialist Republic annexed by the Russian Soviet Federated Socialist Republic.

## "PEASANT BREST-LITOVSK," PARTY "UNITY"

After trade unions and the national question, the 10th Party Congress turned to the question of the ruined, seething countryside. Siberia's delegation had set out for Moscow "armed to the teeth," as one delegate recalled, needing to cross territories overrun by rebellious peasants with primitive weapons.[270] On Lenin's initiative, on the morning of March 15, after the elections to the new Central Committee had taken place, the congress took up a resolution to concede a tax in kind not just in Tambov but across Soviet Russia. The tax was to be lower than the most recent obligatory quotas, and whatever grain the peasants would have left over after paying the tax they would be able sell at market prices—which presupposed the legalization of private trade.[271] "There is no need for me to go into great detail on the causes of the reconsideration," Lenin explained to the congress, adding "there is no doubt that in a country where the immense majority of the population belongs to the petty land-holding producers, a socialist revolution is possible only via a whole host of transition measures, which would be unnecessary in a developed capitalist country."[272]

Illegal private trade already accounted for at least 70 percent of grain sales. But opposition to legalization persisted. The relative merits of obligatory quotas versus taxation and private trade had been debated on and off since 1918, nearly always ending with affirmations of the proletariat needing "to lead" the peasantry (signifying grain requisitioning to feed the cities).[273] Trotsky, in February 1920, had proposed a tax in kind that would incentivize more planting, meaning that successful farmers (kulaks) would not be penalized, but he did not mention accompanying free trade, instead writing of "goods exchange" (*tovaroobmen*) and "labor obligations" (*povinnost'*). His *dirigiste* theses had been rejected.[274] True, as a result of the uprising in Tambov, even the leftist hothead Bukharin had come around to the need for concessions.[275] But for the majority in the hall, Lenin's proposal came as a stunning blow because he admitted, unlike Trotsky in 1920, that introduction of the tax necessitated legal private trade.[276]

The need for a new policy was obvious, but demoralizing all the same. "How is it possible for a Communist party to recognize freedom of trade and transition to it?" Lenin asked himself in front of the delegates. "Are there not here irreconcilable contradictions?" He did not answer, only calling the questions "extremely difficult."[277] But whatever the theoretical morass, Lenin belatedly insisted that the war-torn country absolutely had to have a breathing spell. His leadership was crucial in breaking what he had helped to create: namely, the militant vicious circle of requisitioning whereby a dearth of grain supplied to cities induced ever more gun-point requisitioning, resulting in ever less grain.[278] Lenin caught a break at the evening session that same day (March 15) when David Ryazanov, a respected Marxist theoretician, felicitously dubbed the shift to a tax in kind and free trade a "peasant Brest-Litovsk."[279] The Brest-Litovsk Treaty with Germany had been widely opposed in the party, of course, but it had quickly proved Lenin right. Lenin again got his way.

Lenin's peasant Brest-Litovsk went hand in hand with an absolute refusal of concessions to political critics. On March 16, the last day of the 10th Party Congress, a surprise took place that was no less consequential than the shift to legal private trade: Lenin took the floor again, and spoke in support of a resolution "on party unity." It required immediate dissolution of groups supporting separate platforms on pain of expulsion from the party. (Ironically, the emergence of the Workers' opposition had resulted from a decision to allow public discussion of the trade union question and elect congress delegates by "platform.") In other words, the archfactionalist Lenin now wanted an end to all factions (besides his own). "I do not think it will be necessary for me to say much on this subject," he again disingenuously remarked when introducing the unity resolution, which in effect rendered "opposition" illegal.[280] The congress delegates present voted 413 in favor and 25 against, with 2 abstentions.[281] Karl Radek, in his characteristic out-of-the-mouths-of-babes fashion, stated that "in voting for this resolution I feel that it can well be turned against us." Nonetheless, he supported "on party unity," saying, "Let the Central Committee in a moment of danger take the severest measures against the best party comrades, if it finds this necessary."[282]

The 10th Party Congress was of monumental significance across the board, including for its glimpses of Stalin's aggrandizement. He could not hope to achieve the high profile that Trotsky commanded at the Party Congress, but he grasped the nettle of one of the most consequential issues before the party—the ambiguous relations among the various Soviet republics—and showed himself ready to force those relations toward a more integrated structure. Stalin also hewed closely to Lenin politically on the big issue of trade unions and, overall, bested his rival Trotsky organizationally. When Lenin wrote up the slate for the new Central Committee, he denied several Trotsky supporters nomination for reelection: Ivan Smirnov, Nikolai Krestinsky, Leonid Serebryakov, Yevgeny Preobrazhensky. They were replaced by Molotov, Voroshilov, Orjonikidze, Yemelyan Yaroslavsky, Hryhory "Grigory" Petrovsky—all people congenial to Lenin, but also very close to Stalin. Sergei Kirov, Valerian Kuibyshev, and Vlas Chubar, similarly close to Stalin, became candidate members of the Central Committee. When the new Central Committee convened right after the congress, it would elect a politburo of Lenin, Stalin, Trotsky, Zinoviev, and Kamenev, with Molotov now listed as "responsible secretary," a potential linchpin functionary.[283] Thanks to Trotsky's relentless propensity to polemicize and exasperate, Lenin was helping to form an anti-Trotsky faction at the pinnacle of power that would fall into Stalin's hands. Insiders on the upper rungs of the regime were using the expression "Stalin faction" (*stalinisty*) as a contrast to the "Trotsky faction" (*trotskisty*).[284]

## WHITE GUARDS, IMPERIALISTS, SOCIALIST REVOLUTIONARIES

All of this was worlds away from the Kronstadt sailors. By the time the Party Congress was winding down, their non-party "Kronstadt republic" had turned fifteen days old. The regime mobilized and armed around 1,000 armed Communists from several provinces and sent a special train from Moscow with more than 200 Party Congress delegates led by Voroshilov, part of a new counterinsurgency force of 24,000.[285] Also, rumors reached the mobilized delegates that hundreds of military-school cadets trying to storm the fortress had died on the ice. There was fear.[286] On March 16, the day the "party unity" resolution was being passed, Tukhachevsky launched a second crackdown with an artillery bombardment, followed by a furious infantry assault. After intense street fighting, the town fell to regime forces by the morning of March 18. Several days earlier the sailors' leadership had requested asylum from the Finnish government, and—despite a warning to Helsinki from Trotsky conveyed by Chicherin—received a quick affirmative response, allowing 8,000 rebel sailors to escape by ship.[287] How many Kronstadters perished in the fighting remains unknown.[288] The Red Army lost 1,200 dead; two congress delegates were killed and 23 wounded.[289] The Finnish and Soviet governments shared responsibility for removal of the corpses from the ice surface of the frozen Gulf of Finland. A revolutionary tribunal on Kronstadt would issue 2,103 death sentences; another 6,459 sailors got terms in labor camps.

On March 18, the Bolsheviks in Moscow celebrated the fiftieth anniversary of the Paris Commune—whose suppression had led to perhaps 30,000 immediate executions. Whether anyone remarked upon the irony remains unknown.[290]

A few days later at a politburo session, Lenin exchanged private notes with Trotsky about abolishing the Baltic fleet, a gluttonous consumer of fuel and food and a likely political nuisance in future; Trotsky defended the need for a navy.[291]

On the very day Kronstadt's destruction began (March 16, 1921), after protracted negotiations, Soviet Russia and Britain signed a trade agreement.[292] The Soviets had shown some diplomatic muscle. Reza Khan in Persia, who had seized power in Tehran in a putsch on February 21, 1921, with the aid of White Cossack troops and British assistance, promptly denounced the existing Anglo-Persian Treaty and signed a Soviet-Persian Treaty of Friendship, which specified both Soviet and British troop withdrawals. Independent Afghanistan signed a treaty with Soviet Russia, too, as insurance against a renewed British invasion. And Ataturk's Turkey began talks with the Soviets, which would result in a pact three weeks later.[293] All three treaties—Persia (February 26), Afghanistan (February 28), and Turkey (March 16)—conveyed diplomatic recognition on Soviet Russia. British intelligence employed one of the leading cyptanalysts of tsarist Russian and could read Moscow's codes, so that when Chicherin denied Soviet involvement in Persia, Britain knew he was lying. Lenin was intercepted saying, "That swine Lloyd George has no scruples of shame in the way he deceives. Don't believe a word he says. . . ."[294] Nonetheless, the British cabinet had concluded by mid-March that "despite the events in Russia"—Kronstadt, Tambov—"the position of the Soviet government without any qualification is firm and stable."[295] Moscow took the preliminary trade deal as de facto political recognition by the leading imperialist power. British goods, too, were coveted to help get peasants in Soviet Russia to sell their grain (so there would be something to buy).[296]

Following the British trade agreement, on March 18, the Soviets finally signed a peace treaty with Poland in Riga, which also entailed diplomatic recognition.[297] The Treaty of Riga did not, however, resolve the historic or the more recent Russian-Polish grievances or alter their aspirations regarding Eastern Europe.[298]

Eight countries now recognized the existence of Soviet Russia in the international state system: Iran, Afghanistan, Turkey, Poland, Lithuania, Latvia, Estonia, and Finland. The RSFSR also had treaty relations with other Soviet Socialist Republics, such as Ukraine. German diplomatic recognition would come soon, but in the meantime, Zinoviev and Bukharin in the Comintern, egged on by the Hungarian Béla Kun, who was resident in Germany on behalf of the Comintern, had decided to play with fire: On March 21, 1921, German Communists were spurred to undertake a lunatic seizure of power.[299] The insurrection was smashed.[300] Some 4,000 sentences were handed down in newly established special courts. German Communist party membership fell by almost half to 180,000. The Bolsheviks in Moscow blamed the fiasco on "counterrevolutionaries," including the German Social Democrat Hilferding, who months before had struggled in vain against Zinoviev's call for the desertion of the Independent Social Democrats to the German Communists.[301] The Comintern Congress would conclude on July 12 in the full subordination of the (for now) crippled German Communist party to the Russian.[302]

Enemies became even more a Bolshevik obsession. Lenin had told the 10th Party Congress that the Kronstadt revolt was led by White generals and SRs and that "this petit-bourgeois counter-revolution is doubtless more dangerous than Denikin, Yudenich, and Kolchak taken together, because we are dealing with a country in which the proletariat is a minority."[303] The centerpiece of counterrevolution charges against the sailors became the one tsarist major general on the island, Alexander Kozlovsky, a distinguished staff officer and artillery specialist serving the Reds, whom Baltic fleet commander Fyodor Raskolnikov had awarded a watch "for courage and feat of arms in the battle against Yudenich."[304] The Cheka had correctly reported that Major General Kozlovsky was not a member of the Kronstadt Revolutionary Committee yet still insisted, absurdly, that "he is the main leader of the movement."[305] Kozlovsky escaped to Finland (where he became a Russian-language teacher in Vyborg). Soon Lenin would warn of the presence of 700,000 Russian émigrés in Europe and of how "no country in Europe was without some White Guard elements."[306] The Bolsheviks, of course, were the ones who had 75,000 former tsarist officers in their ranks, including hundreds of former tsarist generals, and who had restored capitalist free trade. The Cheka proved unable to stage a large show trial of Socialist Revolutionaries and "Entente spies" over Kronstadt.[307] Nonetheless, Dzierżyński concluded in a secret internal assessment that "while Soviet Russia remains an isolated hearth of communist revolution and is in capitalist encirclement, she will need to use the iron hand to put down White-Guard escapades."[308]

Menshevik leader Yuly Martov, a cofounder with Lenin of the original Russian Marxist émigré broadsheet *Spark,* had left Russia in October 1920 to attend the fateful Halle conference of German leftists and had not been permitted to return; he was mortally ill and would soon repair to a Black Forest sanitorium, but he continued his withering criticism in a new émigré newspaper he founded in early 1921, *Socialist Herald.* Martov underscored how Lenin's foolhardy attempted sovietization of Poland had resulted in the "surrendering to Polish imperialism of a number of non-Polish territories, against the interests of the Russian laboring classes."[309] He tore into Lenin over Kronstadt as well.[310] Above all, he pointed out that the Mensheviks had been right all along—socialist revolution in Russia had been premature, as demonstrated by Lenin's mistakes, recourse to political repression, and policy shifts over the peasantry.[311] And yet, Martov was back in exile, while Lenin sat in the Kremlin. "Anyone who wants to play at parliamentarism, at Constituent Assemblies, at non-party conferences, go abroad to Martov," Lenin thundered in April 1921 in his pamphlet *On the Tax in Kind.* "We are going to keep the Mensheviks and SR—both open ones and those disguised as 'nonparty'—in jail."[312]

In Tambov, meanwhile, even after the tax-in-kind concession had been granted, the peasant rebels had not desisted, employing conscription and seeking new adherents by crossing into neighboring provinces (Saratov, Voronezh), while raiding arms depots. They seized grain and livestock, as well as people, and increased their forces to more than 20,000.[313] In April 1921, the beefed-up partisans managed to defeat the Red Army in a number of battles. Plenipotentiary Antonov-Ovseyenko, in his reports, beseeched Moscow for more troops. Yefraim Sklyansky advised Lenin on April 26 "to send Tukhachevsky to crush the Tambov uprising"; Lenin concurred.[314] Tukhachevsky's failure to capture Warsaw had not diminished him.[315] The politburo gave him a month to "liquidate" the Tambov rebellion.[316] He set up HQ at a gunpowder plant just outside Tambov on May 6, and announced preparations for a "shock campaign" of clear-and-hold pacification, employing mobile forces to exterminate the rebels, then infantry to occupy cleared villages so as to deny sanctuary. More than 100,000 mostly urban Red Army troops were deployed, along with special Cheka detachments. After public executions, hostage taking, and conspicuous deportations of entire villages to concentration camps, by the third week of June 1920 only small numbers of rebel stragglers had survived.[317] Tukhachevsky was flushing rebel remnants out of the forests with artillery, machine guns, and chlorine gas "to kill all who hide within."[318] At least 11,000 peasants were killed between May and July; the Reds lost 2,000. Many tens of thousands were deported or interred. "The bandits themselves have come to recognize . . . what Soviet power means," the camp chief noted of his reeducation program.[319] Lenin's deputy Alexei Rykov, alerted to the savage campaign by concerned Communists in Tambov, sought to have Tukhachevsky reined in so as not to alienate the peasantry, but Sergei Kamenev urged perseverance: "On the whole, since the appointment of comrade Tukhachevsky to the command in Tambov, all measures that have been undertaken have proven entirely appropriate and effective."[320]

Alexander Antonov, the rebel leader, escaped. The Cheka, knowing that he dreamed of unifying Right and Left Socialist Revolutionaries and Constitutional Democrats, had let out word of a "congress" of all anti-Bolshevik partisan movements, which opened on June 28, 1921, in Moscow. Three "delegates" of the Right SRs, two of them Cheka agents, insisted Antonov should join the congress. He did not show, but the ruse congress enabled mass arrests of Antonovites. (Antonov, hiding in swampy woods for almost a year, would finally be located, as a result of a pharmacist's tip, and killed in a village shootout in June 1922; he would be buried at local Cheka HQ—a Tambov monastery.)[321]

## ABSORBING GEORGIAN NATIONALISM

Stalin arrived in Baku in November 1920, two months after the Congress of Peoples of the East, and on the eighth telegrammed Lenin: "One thing is not in doubt. It is necessary to move troops rapidly to Armenia's borders with the necessity of entering with them to Yerevan. Orjonikidze is undertaking preparations in this spirit." This was before Orjonikidze had received operational authorization from Moscow.[322] In fall 1920, Turkish troops had invaded former tsarist Armenia, which nominally was ruled by the Armenian nationalists known as Dashnaks but beset by more than half a million refugees, epidemics, and starvation.[323] On November 28, Orjonikidze and Stalin conspired to send troops across Russia's border with Armenia, stage an "uprising," and declare an Armenian Soviet Republic ("by the will of the toiling masses of Armenia"). The Dashnaks, like the Musavat in Azerbaijan, surrendered.[324] The Soviet conquest of Armenia would nearly provoke war with Turkey, but the most immediate consequences of Armenia's reconquest were felt in Georgia.

Stalin's homeland had been ruled since 1918 by Georgian Social Democrats of Menshevik tilt, who governed not via soviets, which they abolished, but a parliament, under the proviso first the democratic (bourgeois) revolution.[325] Menshevik Georgia's prime minister, Noe Jordania, had been the person who, in 1898, had told a then twenty-year-old Stalin eager to join the socialist movement, to return to his studies, and, in 1904, had humiliated Stalin again, forcing him to recant from "Georgian Bundism," that is, advocacy for a formally separate Georgian Social Democratic Party and an independent Georgian state.[326] But then came world war, revolution, and imperial dissolution, and voilà—Georgian Menshevism had morphed into a vehicle for Georgian nationalism.[327] Lenin and Chicherin, as part of their pursuit of formal recognition from Britain, had recognized the independent Georgian Menshevik state with a treaty on May 7, 1920, pledging noninterference in its affairs.[328] In exchange, however, the Georgian government—in a codicil that remained secret—agreed to legalize Communist party activity on its territory, and Bolshevik agents in the Caucasus, including a young operative named Lavrenti Beria, promptly set about subverting the Menshevik state.[329] It was while the Georgians in Moscow were awaiting the final version of the treaty to sign that the Red Army had captured Azerbaijan. After Armenia's turn, Bolshevik forces had Menshevik Georgia essentially surrounded.

Lenin and other top Bolsheviks regarded Mensheviks with a mixture of contempt and fear. True, Russian Mensheviks were not barred from attending the Eighth Congress of Soviets (the last one they would attend), which was held December 22–29, 1920, and was where, in the unheated, dimly lit Bolshoi Theater, Lenin unveiled a fantastic scheme for the electrification of Russia.[330] But Trotsky—who had already consigned Mensheviks and Right Socialist Revolutionaries to the trash pile of history at the Second Congress of Soviets in October 1917—informed the 2,537 delegates that "now that the civil war is over, the Mensheviks and SRs are especially dangerous and must be fought with particular ruthlessness," a point echoed by Dzierżyński. Fyodor Dan, a Menshevik leader, pointed out that Lenin, in his speech, had given a long list of countries with which Soviet Russia had signed peace treaties, but omitted one—Georgia.[331] In fact, Lenin was secretly urging extra caution in dealing with Georgian national feelings, evidently chastened by the fiasco over Poland. Lenin explicitly ordered Orjonikidze "not to self-determine Georgia."[332]

Trotsky and Stalin, however, agreed, just as they had about using Baku as a revolutionary springboard, on the necessity of seizing Georgia militarily.[333] Indeed Stalin showed none of the hesitation over Georgia that he had repeatedly voiced over Poland. On top of his grudge against the Georgian Mensheviks, he articulated a strategic rationale for a forward policy. "The importance of the Caucasus for the revolution is determined not only by the fact that it is a source of raw materials, fuel, and food supplies," he told *Pravda* (November 30, 1920), "but also by its position between Europe and Asia, and in part between Russia and Turkey, as well as the presence of highly important economic and strategic roads."[334] Above all, Stalin argued, Menshevik Georgia provided "a zone of foreign intervention and occupation"—a stepping zone for aggressors to attack the Soviet heartland, lending apparent urgency to the matter.[335]

Many Bolsheviks anticipated that the Georgian Menshevik government would collapse under the weight of its own unpopularity and incompetence and therefore advised to wait for a popular uprising. Still, the Communists in Georgia numbered only 15,000, not really an indigenous force to be reckoned with, while the Mensheviks had at least 75,000 and could claim more worker support.[336] And as accusations flew about the Menshevik government's perfidiousness—for example, in supporting anti-Soviet rebels in the North Caucasus—opposition in Moscow to military action softened. On February 14, 1921, Lenin dropped his caution and Orjonikidze finally extracted permission for a takeover. In fact, on

February 11–12, Orjonikize, on the spot, with the collusion of Stalin in Moscow as well as Trotsky, had sent units of the Red Army from Armenia into Georgia and staged an "uprising" by Armenian and Russian rebels in the disputed mixed-ethnic Lori district, a pretext for full Red Army invasion.[337] On February 15, a full Red incursion was launched from Azerbaijan into Georgia. On February 16, the Georgian Bolshevik Pilipe Makharadze pronounced the formation of a Georgian Soviet Republic, and appealed to Soviet Russia for "aid." Already, on February 25, the Red Army entered Tiflis (abandoned to spare it from shelling).

Orjonikidze had done in his native Georgia what Frunze had done in his native Turkestan. "Long Live Soviet Georgia!" Orjonikidze exulted in a telegram to Moscow. Stalin, too, was triumphant at the destruction of the handmaidens of the Entente. But Lenin—who had threatened to resign over allowing other socialists in Russia into the revolutionary government in 1917—now instructed Orjonikidze to try to form a *coalition* with the defeated Georgian Mensheviks.[338] Lenin appears to have been motivated by a sense that the political base for Bolshevism in "petit-bourgeois" Georgia was weak. Also, he seemed sensitive to the fact that the Red Army invasion had cast a pall on the Soviets' international reputation: Georgia emerged as a cause célèbre among Social Democrats in Europe. A baffled Orjonikidze, on March 3, 1921, telegrammed Lenin: "Everything possible is being done to promote contact and understanding with the Georgian intelligentsia."[339] But Orjonikidze felt that walking on eggshells was a losing policy.[340] In any case, the Georgian Mensheviks refused Lenin's offer of a coalition.

Georgia was not Poland, certainly not in the military sense, and the three small, unstable republics of the South Caucasus lacked a Poland equivalent on whose coattails they could have ridden to independence, as happened in the case of the three small Baltic republics. The Georgian Mensheviks had been oriented toward London and Paris, but the Entente powers did not come to their aid. France had promised only to turn over rusted carbines and machine guns that had been abandoned by the Whites and were sitting in an Istanbul warehouse. Georgian ministers were in Paris still imploring the French government for military help the very day Tiflis fell.[341] The British had had their eyes on Caspian oil, and had sent an expeditionary force to deny the petroleum to Germany, but then hit up against the expense and complexity of a prolonged Caucasus occupation. "I am sitting on a powder-magazine, which thousands of people are trying to blow up," the British commissioner wrote to his wife from Tiflis.[342] Foreign Secretary Curzon was urging his government to retain the costly British military

presence in the South Caucasus, as well as in northern Persia, in order to prevent Russian reconquest, but War Secretary Winston Churchill—no less anti-
Bolshevik than Curzon—argued that a further partitioned Russia raised the
specter of a future German reaggrandizement all across Eastern Europe and
maybe the Levant, too.[343]

The British had evacuated from Baku and Tiflis, making their way west to the
port of Batum, then left the Caucasus for good (July 7, 1920). Georgians had celebrated Britain's departure as a triumph over imperialism, covering Batum with
Georgian flags, but British withdrawal, on top of French hesitation, had left Moscow and Ankara to determine the Georgians' fate.[344] Turkey's Mustafa Kemal
prioritized annexation of Armenian-inhabited provinces (Kars, Ardahan) over
aiding the brethren Azerbaijani Turks, and he saw an ally in Soviet Russia against
Versailles (a parallel to the emerging German-Soviet rapprochement).[345] As the
Red Army invaded Georgia from the east and north, the Turks had advanced
from the south, their eyes set on grabbing the port of Batum, where the Georgian
leadership had fled advancing Red Army forces. Already on March 11, 1921, the
French ship *Ernest Renan* carried Georgian gold stocks, church treasures, and
archives to Istanbul, for transshipment to France.[346] Five days later Turkey pronounced its annexation of Batum. But Menshevik Georgia's 10,000 troops managed to disarm Batum's small 2,000-troop Turkish garrison.[347] The Red Army,
with Menshevik connivance, entered the port on March 22 to hold it from Turkey.[348] Three days later, French and Italian ships carried the Menshevik government, military command, and refugees to Istanbul from the same port whence
they had waved off the British.[349]

Stalin, meanwhile, suffered a debilitating illness and was placed on a special
diet. On March 15, 1921, Nadya Alliluyeva wrote to Kalinin that "15 chickens
(exclusively for Stalin), 15 pounds of potatoes and one wheel of cheese were
included in the monthly food packet," but "10 chickens have already been consumed and there are still 15 days to go. Stalin can only eat chickens in connection with his diet." She requested that the number of monthly chickens be
increased to 20, and the potatoes to 30 pounds.[350] On March 25, Stalin underwent an operation to remove his appendix.[351] Lenin ordered an assistant to send
Stalin "four bottles of the best portwine. It's necessary to strengthen Stalin before
his operation."[352] But Stalin was suffering other maladies, perhaps related to
typhus, perhaps to chronic, non-active tuberculosis, which he had contracted
before the revolution (Sverdlov, with whom Stalin bunked in a single room in

Siberian exile, had tuberculosis; in the era before penicillin there was no cure). In April 1921, the politburo ordered Stalin to a spa, and he spent May through August 1921 at Nalchik in the North Caucasus.[353] Lenin sent several telegrams to Orjonikidze inquiring of Stalin's health and the opinion of the doctors.

Stalin's medical holiday coincided with continued political upheaval across the mountains, in the South Caucasus. On April 10, 1921, at a meeting of some 3,000 workers' representatives and workers in the Tiflis Opera House on Rustaveli Avenue, an assembly approved a resolution urging the Bolshevik Revolutionary Committee to defend Georgia's right to self-determination and independence, and called for legalization of all socialist organizations not dedicated to overthrowing the regime and even for the formation of a separate Georgian Red Army. Such sentiments only deepened. Orjonikidze became desperate for assistance in getting his countrymen to knuckle under their new Bolshevik masters, and he invited Stalin to cross the mountains down to Tiflis. Stalin obliged, and participated in a Caucasus bureau plenum July 2–3, 1921, where Orjonikidze gave a report on the political situation.[354] On July 5, at another mass meeting with workers in the Tiflis Opera House, Stalin began by "greeting the Tiflis workers in the name of the Revolution, stressing their leading role," but the hall greeted him with jeers of "Traitor" and "Murderer." The main speaker, the Georgian Marxist elder Isidor Ramishvili, accused Stalin and the Bolsheviks of forcible conquest and received an ovation. Alexander Dgebuadze, a leader of the Tiflis workers, said of Stalin, "Who asked you to come here? What happened to our Treaty? At the orders of the Kremlin, blood is shed here and you talk about friendship! Soso, you give us both a laugh!"[355] The audience sang Georgian freedom songs.[356]

That night, after his public humiliation on his home Georgian turf, Stalin had the Cheka arrest more than a hundred local Social Democratic Mensheviks, including Ramishvili and Dgebuadze, filling up the tsarist-era Metekhi Prison as well as the newer lockup below. (When Stalin discovered that his childhood friend Soso Iremashvili, now a Georgian Menshevik, had been arrested, he arranged to have him released and invited him to meet, but Iremashvili refused—deeming Stalin a traitor—and emigrated, taking with him intimate knowledge of the young Stalin from Gori days.)[357]

On July 6, Stalin made for local Bolshevik party HQ, where he laced into the Georgian leadership (Pilipe Makharadze, Mamiya Orakhelashvili, Budu Mdivani) and addressed a general meeting of the Tiflis Communist party. "I remember the years 1905–17, when only complete brotherly solidarity could be observed among the workers and toiling people of the South Caucasus nationalities, when the bonds of brotherhood bound Armenian, Georgian, Azerbaijani, and Russian workers into a single socialist family," Stalin is recorded as having said. "Now, on my arrival in Tiflis, I am astounded by the absence of the former solidarity among the workers of the South Caucasus. Nationalism has arisen among the workers and peasants, and there is a strong feeling of distrust toward their other-national comrades." He blamed this "spirit of aggressive nationalism" on the three years of government by Georgian Mensheviks, Azerbaijan Musavat, and Armenia Dashnaks, and summoned the Georgian Bolsheviks to a "merciless struggle with nationalism and the restoration of the old brotherly international bonds." Stalin also broached the idea of the South Caucasus Federation to contain the three nationalisms, which met strenuous objection.[358] Georgian Bolsheviks proved no less nationalistic than the deposed Mensheviks. Indeed, with Poland, Finland, and the Baltic states out, it would be the nationalism of the Georgians, along with that of the Ukrainians, which would prove the most difficult to tame. The political and spiritual conquest of Stalin's Georgian homeland *after* 1921 would dramatically shape his personal dictatorship, too.

## FIRST SOVIET SATELLITE

When biographers write about Stalin, projecting backward in time an early psychopath and murderer, they are, in effect, describing the Stalin contemporary, Baron Roman von Ungern-Sternberg.[359] The savage, demented baron had been born in Austria in the 1880s to a German aristocrat mother and a Baltic German father from an ancient noble family, but the boy, like his crusading ancestors, grew up on imperial Russia's Baltic littoral. He served in the imperial Russian army, including in multiethnic Cossack formations in the eastern Baikal and Amur regions, and won a plethora of decorations for valor in the Great War. He was also disciplined for willfulness. Brave and cruel, he patterned himself partly after the crusading Teutonic knights, but he was also said to have boasted to friends that one day he would become emperor of China and perhaps even restore the grand Mongol empire of Chinggis Khan across Eurasia. The baron married a nineteen-year-old Manchu princess, which afforded him a second, Manchurian, title. He was a staunch monarchist and hater of Bolshevism's sacrileges, and assembled a so-called Savage Division of east Siberian Cossacks, Tatars, Mongols, and Tibetans, among others, to crusade against the Reds in the civil war, but after Kolchak's defeat he sought refuge in Manchuria. In October 1920, the baron marched his small Savage Division of 800 men from Manchuria several thousand miles into Outer Mongolia, which had been a province of China until 1911, when it became de facto independent as a result of the fall of the Qing dynasty, but which in 1919 had been reoccupied by Chinese troops who conducted a reign of terror. The Chinese had deposed the Bogd Gegen, a Living Buddha, third after the Dalai Lama (in Lhasa) and the Panchen Lama in the Lamaist Buddhist hierarchy and Mongolia's temporal ruler, whom the baron aimed to restore. But in late October and early November 1920, Ungern-Sternberg failed to take the Chinese-held Mongol capital of Urga, guarded by up to 12,000 garrison troops. Killing his deserters, he retreated to eastern Mongolia, where he picked up more White Army stragglers from Eastern Siberia, recruited additional Mongol and Tibetan troops to liberate the Buddhist land, plundered caravans to and from China, fed his opium addiction, and burnished his reputation for bravery and butchery. Men whom he whipped until their flesh fell off were taken to hospital, to recuperate, so that they could be whipped again. Sometimes the baron had a bound victim's hair set on fire; other times, he had water poured through nostrils and turpentine through rectums.[360]

In early February 1921, Ungern-Sternberg renewed his assault on Urga, with around 1,500 men against at least 7,000 Chinese, but this time, on the auspicious lunar New Year (February 4), he triumphed.[361] It took several days to clear the corpses, some 2,500, most with cavalry saber wounds. Looting ensued. Chinese reinforcements from afar were interdicted, yielding hundreds of camels' worth of weapons, supplies, and silver.[362] On February 21—the same day Reza Khan, the future shah, staged a right-wing coup in Tehran, four days before Orjonikidze seized the Georgian capital of Tiflis from the Mensheviks, and seven days before the Kronstadt uprising began—Ungern-Sternberg ceremoniously reinstalled the Bogd Gegen in the Mongol capital.[363] Basking in Mongol and Tibetan adulation, the baron embarked on a rampage against Bolshevik commissars, Jews, and anyone with physical defects. A list was compiled of 846 targets, 38 of them Jews, who were summarily executed.[364]

Russian merchants and adventurers had long penetrated Outer Mongolia as a gateway to China. Now the Bolshevik regime sent Sergei Borisov, an ethnic Altaian (Oirot) and the head of the Comintern's Mongolian-Tibetan department, to Urga with a small group of "advisers."[365] Borisov, from a shamanistic people whom the Buddhists had once tried to convert (he himself went to a Russian Orthodox school), aimed to forge an alliance with Mongol nationalists, who had already made contact with the Soviets in Buryatia in Eastern Siberia. The Mongol nationalists comprised two groupings. One, the East Urga group, was led by Danzan (b. 1885), a low-ranking customs official and the illegitimate son of a poor woman, and included Sükhbaatar (b. 1893), who at nineteen had become commander of a machine-gun regiment in Bogd Gegen's army. The other group, known as Consular Hill (the section of Urga occupied primarily by Russians), was the more radical and was led by Bodoo (b. 1895), a Mongolian language teacher at a Russian school, and included Choybalsan (b. 1895), a former lama and the illegitimate son of an impoverished woman who had fled a monastery; in the course of working at menial jobs, he had met the director of a Russian translators' school, where he enrolled before going on to further education in Irkutsk, the capital of Eastern Siberia.[366] On June 25, 1920, the two Mongol groups had joined forces in Danzan's tent to form a Mongolian People's Party in order "to liquidate the foreign enemy which is hostile to our religion and race; to restore lost rights and truly revive the state and religion; . . . to give total attention to the interests of the poor and lowly masses; and to live neither oppressing nor oppressed."[367] They agreed with Borisov to send a delegation to Moscow to request aid.[368] In November 1920, a seven-person Mongol delegation arrived in in the Soviet capital, meeting Lenin and Stalin.[369]

By this time, the Bogd Gegen had been restored as khan, and Urga had fallen under Ungern-Sternberg occupation. Between March 1 and 3, 1921, a conference of the Mongolian People's Party took place in Troitskosavsk (Kiakhta), on the Soviet side of the frontier, with perhaps twenty-six delegates by the final day.[370] To unseat Ungern-Sternberg, they constituted a Provisional Revolutionary Committee and a People's Revolutionary Army of around 400 horsemen, which assembled in southeastern Siberia; then, on March 18—the same day the Soviets signed a peace treaty with Poland—they crossed the Soviet-Mongol frontier, trailed by Red Army units.[371]

There was no "revolutionary situation" in Mongolia, to use the Comintern argot, but Baron Ungern-Sternberg's occupation proved to be a godsend, providing the pretext for Bolshevik invasion and a revolutionary putsch. By the time of the spring 1921 Mongol-Soviet offensive against the "counterrevolutionary base" in Mongolia, Ungern-Sternberg's army, which was living off extravagant "requisitioning" of Mongol herders, was itself on the move. On May 21, he issued a proclamation summoning Russians in Siberia to rise up against Bolshevism in the name of "the lawful master of the Russian Land, all-Russia Emperor Mikhail Alexandrovich," while vowing "to exterminate commissars, communists, and Jews."[372] (Never mind that Grand Duke Mikhail, Nicholas II's brother, had been executed in Perm in 1918.) On June 16, the politburo belatedly approved a "revolutionary onslaught." An official "request" for Soviet military assistance was cooked up. Sükhbaatar and the Red Army forces took Urga on July 5–6, 1921.[373]

Stalin was away from Moscow on holiday and being shouted down as a Bolshevik imperialist in the Georgian capital of Tiflis. Simultaneously with events in Georgia and Mongolia, the Third Congress of the Comintern happened to be taking place in Moscow, and one of its key themes was national liberation. "I would like to emphasize here the significance of the movement in the colonies," Lenin told the 605 delegates from more than 50 countries on July 5. "It is quite clear that in the coming decisive battles of the world revolution the movement of the great majority of the population of the globe, which will be directed first at national liberation, will turn against capitalism and imperialism and, perhaps, play a much greater role than we expect." Backward countries suddenly would be revolutionary leaders ("animated approval"). And just as Soviet Russia offered "a strong bulwark for the Eastern peoples in their struggles for their own independence, so the Eastern countries are our allies in our common struggle against world imperialism."[374] On July 11, Mongol independence was declared anew. Ungern-Sternberg's forces, meanwhile, had conveniently captured or driven out large numbers of Chinese on the way to Siberia, while failing to spark the anticipated anti-Soviet uprising in Siberia itself, and he was on the run; a Comintern report characterized his men as "speculators, morphine addicts, opium-smokers . . . and other dregs of counter-revolutionary elements."[375] According to an eyewitness of his final march, the baron, "with his head dropped to his chest, silently rode in front of his troops. He had lost his hat and most of his clothes. On his naked chest numerous Mongolian talismans and charms were hanging on a bright yellow cord. He looked like a reincarnation of a prehistoric ape man."[376]

Ungern-Steinberg survived an assassination conspiracy (his tent was strafed), but he was captured and handed over to the Red Army on August 22, 1921, and revealed his identity to his captors.[377] His Mongol counselor evidently absconded with 1,800 kilos of gold, silver, and precious stones that had been hidden in a river bottom. A convoy escorted the baron to Novonikolaevsk, capital of Western

Siberia, where interrogations established that he "was by no means psychologically healthy."[378]

Lenin, on the Hughes apparatus from Moscow, ordered a public trial, which was supposed to take place in Moscow, but Ivan Smirnov, known as the Siberian Lenin, insisted that the effects would be greater if he were tried locally.[379] On September 15, 1921, a trial was staged in front of several thousand in the wooden summer theater of Novonikolaevsk's main park on the banks of the Ob River. The baron appeared in his yellow Mongol outer caftan, with his imperial Russian St. George's Cross pinned to his chest. After some six hours, he was pronounced guilty of working in the interests of Japan to create a Central Asian state, trying to restore the Romanovs, torture, anti-Semitism, and atrocities. He denied only the connection with the Japanese.[380] He was executed the same evening or in the wee hours after midnight by the local Cheka.[381] Others would reap the rewards of his lunacy. The baron had not only chased out the Chinese troops from Mongolia, on behalf of the Mongols, but his marauding and savagery had helped drive out Chinese peasant settlers, who had numbered perhaps 100,000 as of 1911, but had dropped to 8,000 by 1921.[382] On September 14, 1921, the Mongolian government issued a statement that it did not recognize Chinese suzerainty.[383] Chicherin on behalf of Soviet Russia issued a two-faced statement that did not expressly deny Chinese claims of suzerainty but in effect recognized Mongolia's independence.[384]

Von Ungern-Sternberg's contribution was historic both to Mongol independence and the creation of the first Soviet satellite—long before post–World War II Eastern Europe—for after his defeat, the Red Army stayed.[385] A Mongolian delegation headed by Danzan and including the twenty-six-year-old Sükhbaatar arrived in Moscow in September 1921, surprising the Soviet foreign affairs commissariat (which was in the midst of trying to establish diplomatic relations with China). The Mongols sought assistance with finances, infrastructure, and weapons, and wanted to discuss territorial disputes with Soviet Russia and lingering imperial Russian economic concessions.[386, 387] Five sessions were held, beginning October 26, 1921, at the Metropol. Boris Shumyatsky, a Comintern official from Buryatia, explained to Lenin on November 2 that they would be lucky to see a bourgeois revolution, let alone a socialist one, for Mongolia lagged Soviet Russia by two centuries: nearly half the male population was composed of monks in lamaseries, and the only figure of authority was the Bogd Gegen, a Living Buddha. But Shumyatsky added that "Sükhbaatar is the war minister, a plebeian, the offspring of the new arising in Mongol relations. Uncommonly brave, though a young man . . . One of the most active figures in the Mongol People's Party and the best orator. . . . Fully oriented toward Soviet Russia. Speaks a little Russian."[388] On November 5, the Soviet government, having renounced tsarist Russia's secret treaties, signed its own unequal treaty with Outer Mongolia.[389] Red Army troops were "asked" to stay and the two governments—not the two states, so as not to overly antagonize China—recognized each other. Shumyatsky made a documentary (he would go on to head the film industry under Stalin). With the Bogd Gegen retained as nominal ruler, Mongolia became a constitutional monarchy but also a "people's democracy of a new type."[390]

No other civil war in history took place across such an immense expanse. Compared with the Great War, none of the military battles in Russia's civil war or wars of territorial reconquest were significant in scale, but nonetheless, 8 to 10 million people would perish here between 1918 and 1923. Probably nine tenths were civilians. Typhus, typhoid, cholera, influenza, and hunger may have killed more than enemy fire. Countless soldiers wounded on the battlefield perished because of an absence of field doctors, medicines, transport, or hospitals. Additionally, up to 200,000 people fell victim to Red Terror, and at least 50,000 to White Terror. Wealth destruction, too, was epic. In 1921, economic output did not even reach one sixth of the pre-1914 level; the 1921 grain harvest came in at one half of the 1913 level.[391] Russia would go from world grain exporter (1913) to cannibalism (1923).[392] Additionally, doctors, scientists, teachers, artists, and others emigrated en masse, perhaps 1.5 million total, most of whom (unlike France after 1789) would not return—extending the civilization of Russian Eurasia across the globe and shaping Soviet Russia's foreign policy. Inside the country, not one but two powerful structures had emerged: the peasant revolution, upon which the Whites broke their teeth, and the Bolshevik dictatorship, which was compelled to concede a "peasant Brest-Litovsk." With the latter, Lenin, an inveterate gambler, had gambled yet again. He would later call the "economic defeat" of spring 1921 "more serious" than the military defeats inflicted by Kolchak, Denikin, or Piłsudski.[393] Sadly, however, Lenin's belated concession of a tax in kind and of legal private trade at the 10th Party Congress in March 1921, over considerable party opposition, had come too late to spare the country mass death from famine (a subject of chapter 10), although not too late to rescue the regime.

The Russian-Eurasian combat was also an economic war, as each battlefield advance brought spoils: grain, moonshine, clothes, boots, kerosene, or in the case of Bukhara, gold. Seized by soldiers or other armed personnel, the trophies would usually show up on newly sprouted black markets. Freelancing banditry flourished as well. All manner of Red Army military contraband (rifles, machine guns, artillery shells) were for sale at the markets on Red-controlled territory. Sometimes the weaponry came not from the battlefield but straight from warehouses or train depots, bribery of officials and guards being merely a cost of doing business. The revolution to stamp out the market turned the whole country, regime included, into practitioners of illegal market exchange. "The New Economic Policy," observed an official of the state planning commission, "did not fall from heaven, but grew out of the guilty soil and developed out of the 'sins' of October against the capitalist system."[394] There was something passing strange about establishing legal markets with an avalanche of decrees, which flowed in April, May, June, and July 1921, granting grudging permission for this or that private activity. (A decree on August 9, 1921, enjoined state agencies to implement the decrees.)[395] Legacies of forced dispossession, however, were not quickly surmounted.[396] The NEP's property laws, in many ways, remained entangled in the unresolved ambiguities of market relations under Communist party rule.

National policy proved to be a similarly immense tangle. Stalin showed himself to be the Bolshevik in ruling circles who time and again best demonstrated an appreciation for the panoply of Russian Eurasia. He had strong ideas about nationalities, and was confident enough to instruct Lenin in this area.[397] But Lenin ignored Stalin's warnings about Polish nationalism and forced an ill-fated western military offensive to instigate revolution from abroad.[398] Poland's crushing 1920 defeat of Soviet Russia imparted an overt geopolitical dimension to the "necessary evil" of embracing nationalism: the Ukrainian Soviet Republic as well as the Belorussian Soviet Republic—which Stalin had a hand in creating—now appeared as counterweights to Polish aggrandizement.[399] But while Polish nationalism had become an external problem with internal repercussions, Georgian nationalism, also strong, had been ingested, thanks in considerable measure to Stalin's machinations. Figuring out how to curb such nationalism and use it for Communist aims preoccupied him. He was at heart a class intransigent, but he was also convinced of the need to find a modus vivendi with national minority Communists, even if he was not going to brook separatism when he felt the territory could be used by the Soviet Union's external enemies to weaken and perhaps invade the Soviet state.[400]

Lenin developed a very different preoccupation: the condescension and outright discrimination, not to say violence, that prevailed in Great Russian relations with the smaller peoples, which in his view showed Soviet Russia in a bad light. Adolf Joffe sent Lenin a troubled telegram on September 9, 1921, asserting that in Turkestan, policy differences between two Bolshevik officials had ignited animosity between Russians and indigenes. Responding on September 13, Lenin demanded more information ("facts, facts, and facts"), and concluded, "For our entire *Weltpolitik* it is desperately important to win over the trust of the indigenes; thrice and four-times win over; prove that we are not imperialists, that we will not abide a deviation in that direction. This is a world-level matter, without exaggeration world-level. . . . This affects India, the East, here we cannot joke, here we need to be 1000 times cautious."[401]

Around this time Lenin had begun to make asides of monumental theoretical significance. In 1921, he observed that the Bolsheviks had only managed to carry out a bourgeois democratic revolution; they had not yet gotten to socialism.[402] The question of when, and especially how, socialism in Russia would actually be built had only become more acute with the surprise failure of the world revolution, and the civil war "voyages of discovery" revelations about the depth of backwardness and despair across now shattered Eurasia.

Stalin continued to puzzle out the larger picture of the revolution's global prospects, including the relationship of war to revolution. On a copy of a 1920 work by Radek, he wrote, "In Russia the workers and soldiers joined up (because peace had not been achieved), but in Germany they did not because there *peace* had already been attained."[403] On a 1920 copy of Zinoviev's *War and the Crisis in Socialism*, Stalin wrote, "Without this defeat [of Russia by Japan in 1905] there would not have been a Russian revolution either."[404] These sentiments were expressed just before the Red Army managed to serve as an instrument of revolution, reconquering the former imperial borderlands—Ukraine, Turkestan, the South Caucasus—as well as Mongolia. But Stalin as yet offered no comprehensive statements about the relationship of the Red Army to revolution.[405] He revealed a certain pessimism in private exchanges he had with Chicherin. "Your objections to my letter about economic policy for Eastern countries, based on extreme pessimism in the question of our own economic condition, supposes that Entente capital will now penetrate into eastern countries and that in connection with this we are powerless," Chicherin wrote to him (November 22, 1921). "But this is not so. We are talking about a rather prolonged process, during which we will not be standing in place. Even in those countries that are organically connected to western capital, the national bourgeoisie will not capitulate so quickly in the face of an Entente-capital onslaught, and between them there will be a prolonged struggle." Chicherin named Romania, Turkey, Persia, and Egypt. But Stalin was unpersuaded. "Of course we will crawl out from economic ruin at some point, and when we do, we can talk about economic actions in these states." In the meantime, however, the ruble's exchange value was falling, Soviet Russia had nothing to export, its trade balance was not good, and it lacked sufficient gold. Stalin argued that it was better for Soviet Russia to develop the parts of the country that bordered on the East—Turkestan, Siberia, Azerbaijan.[406]

Stalin publicly revealed his pessimism in late 1921. "Gone on the wing is the 'fear' or 'horror' of the world bourgeoisie in the face of the proletarian revolution, which had seized [the world bourgeoisie], for example, in the days of the Red Army advance on Warsaw," he wrote in *Pravda* (December 17, 1921). "And with it has passed the boundless enthusiasm with which the workers of Europe used to receive almost every piece of news about Soviet Russia." In geopolitical terms, Russian power in the world was much diminished overall by the civil war. The hard-won trade agreement with Britain was a barbed laurel. "We should not forget that commercial and all other sorts of missions and associations, now flooding Russia to trade with her and to aid her, are at the same time the best spies of the world bourgeoisie, and that now it, the world bourgeoisie, knows Soviet Russia with its weak and strong sides better than ever before—circumstances fraught with extremely serious dangers in the event of new interventionist actions," Stalin wrote. He singled out Poland, Romania, and Finland, but even Turkey and Afghanistan, as well as Japan, as formidable challenges.[407] The victorious Soviet state had emerged surrounded, penetrated. Its tense efforts at a temporary modus vivendi with the capitalist powers went hand in hand with its fraught internal rapprochement with capitalism in the New Economic Policy. Durnovó's revolutionary war had yielded a paradoxical outcome.

## PART III

# COLLISION

"Lenin was born for revolution. He was a genuine genius
of revolutionary explosions and the greatest master of
revolutionary leadership. Lenin never felt himself freer or
happier than in the epoch of revolutionary shocks."

Stalin, January 1924[1]

"The truth is that the Socialist revolution has ended in pure
individualism. . . The great achievement of the Bolshevik
class has been the creation of a peasant class intensely
conscious of the value of private ownership of land."

Max Sering, German scholar of Russian
agriculture, 1921[2]

ONCE IN A BLUE MOON THE FUTURE can be foreseen—as when former tsarist
interior minister Pyotr Durnovó predicted, in the event of a lost war against Germany, mass social revolution and catastrophe—but mostly clairvoyance is impossible. Into the latter category falls the fact and consequences of Vladimir Lenin's health. He was a singular political figure. The nightmarish Great War and all-encompassing breakdown rendered even more unlikely that a rule-of-law order would replace the intransigent tsarist autocracy, but Lenin's malign contribution should not be underestimated. In August 1917, even before the Bolshevik coup, he had belligerently observed that "who does not know that the world history of all revolutions shows that class struggle turns not accidentally but inevitably to civil war."[3] Once in power, Lenin elevated political violence to

principle.[4] Moderate socialists, in his mind, were more dangerous than open counterrevolutionaries, whom the moderates abetted with their "ornate Socialist-Revolutionary and Menshevik phraseology about a people's government, a constituent assembly, liberties, and the like. . . . He who has not learned this from the whole history of the 19th century is a hopeless idiot."[5] Behind mundane disagreement he saw not legitimate opinion but malevolent forces. His conception of politics did not even allow for politics.[6] Lenin railed against the idea that every society was made up of multiple interests that deserved competitive political representation and balancing as naively inviting in the "wrong" interests ("bourgeois" or "petit bourgeois").[7] He repudiated any separation of powers among executive, legislative, and judicial branches as a bourgeois sham.[8] He rejected the rule of law as an instrument of class domination, not a protection against the state.[9] He dismissed the self-organization of society to hold the state in check.[10] The upshot was a brutal intensification of tsarism's many debilitating features: emasculation of parliament, metastasizing of parasitic state functionaries, persecution and shakedowns of private citizens and entrepreneurs—in short, unaccountable executive power, which was vastly enhanced in its grim arbitrariness by a radiant ideology of social justice and progress. But then, Lenin fell fatally ill.

Rarely in world history has one man played such an outsized role and, suddenly, been sidelined—an outcome evocative, in very different political ways, of Abraham Lincoln's civil war victory and emancipation of the slaves, followed by his assassination. Lenin's early departure was an unintentional revolutionary shock second only to the seizure of power, and it unexpectedly cleared a path for Stalin to supreme power.

Lenin's poor health had affected him longer than almost anyone knew. He endured a variety of ailments common to the time, including typhoid, influenza, and erysipelas (a skin disorder), but he also suffered blinding headaches, sleeplessness, and blackouts—on a hunt during the civil war, for example, he suddenly slumped down on a tree stump unable to move ("pins and needles," he said). In winter 1920–21, his insomnia and headaches became still more frequent, which stumped his battery of physicians. "Unfortunately I am very ill," Lenin wrote to Clara Zetkin in German in February 1921, during the tense days of the Tambov rebellion and Petrograd worker strikes. "My nerves are *kaputt*."[11] During the 10th Party Congress the next month, he continued to complain about feeling debilitated. His nerves were on edge in July 1921, when his Kremlin apartment was being remodeled: he directed that the walls between rooms be rendered "absolutely soundproof, and the floors absolutely free of squeaks."[12] In summer 1921, the politburo several times decreed, to no avail, that Lenin should take a month-long break; finally, in August, he relented.[13] In mid-September 1921, when Lenin sought to resume a full workload, he proved unable to do so. In October he blacked out several times.[14] In December 1921, even a severely curtailed workload proved too much; the politburo decreed another six-week holiday, and on December 6 Lenin departed for the countryside, where he was supposed to be restricted to a maximum of just one hour per day for telephone conversations on priority business. He returned to the Kremlin on January 13, 1922, but his condition had not improved, and he returned to the Moscow countryside, resolving to come to the capital only for politburo and government meetings. But even that became less and less the case. On March 1, 1922, Lenin came back to the Kremlin, but the next day his family and staff noted a periodic loss of speech and of feeling on his right side.[15] On March 4, Lenin told one of his doctors that "his song had been sung, his role played, and he needed to pass on his cause to someone."[16]

Lenin never named a successor. But in a momentous act in March 1922, he created a new post, "general secretary" of the party, expressly for Stalin. Stories would be invented, for understandable reasons, about how Lenin had never *really* intended to give Stalin so much power. These stories, however, are belied by the facts. Lenin had been taking Stalin into his confidence across a wide range of matters, and already in August-September 1921 he had moved Stalin nearly full-time to overseeing party affairs; Stalin took to preparing politburo meeting agendas and appointing officials.[17] True, there were two other Central Committee secretaries at that time, but Stalin was senior to both. Despite that seniority, Lenin still chose to underscore Stalin's predominant position in an appointment announced at the 11th Party Congress March 27-April 2, 1922, and formalized at an April 3 Central Committee plenum—both of which Lenin attended.[18] Stalin was voted "general secretary" at the congress by 193 votes in favor, 16 against; the rest (273), more than half the voting delegates, effectively abstained.[19] This was Lenin's initiative, and he certainly knew what he was doing. Just before the opening of the 11th Congress in the Kremlin, he had organized a conspiratorial meeting in a side room, gathering his most reliable followers, 27 people, to ensure election to the Central Committee of his preferred candidates against Trotsky's followers; Stalin's name was marked on Lenin's list as "general secretary."[20] At the congress itself, where all 27 names on Lenin's list were duly elected, one delegate (Preobrazhensky) questioned how Stalin could hold so many concurrent positions, but Lenin stoutly defended his protégé.[21]

Lenin had by no means intended to hand over *supreme* power to Stalin. Some insight into how Lenin might have envisioned Stalin's new position can be gleaned from the circumstance that the politburo had acceded to Zinoviev's request for creation of a Comintern "general secretary" to run its day-to-day affairs, appointing Otto Kuusinen, a Finnish Communist resident in Moscow, while Zinoviev (in Petrograd) remained chairman (*predsedatel'*).[22] In similar fashion, Lenin remained chairman of the government (Council of People's Commissars), while Stalin became general secretary of the (party) apparatus.[23] Of course, the Russian Communist party far outweighed the Comintern as a power base, and Stalin's "chairman" was not well.[24] Still, no one dreamed Lenin would become utterly incapacitated, and so quickly. In March 1922, Stalin had imported two German doctors, Otfried Förster (a neurologist) and Felix Klemperer (a lung specialist), at a cost of 50,000 gold rubles each.[25] The latter judged Lenin's severe headaches to be caused by lead poisoning from the bullets, which, following the attempted assassination four years earlier, were still lodged in his body (one in the neck, one, which had pierced his lung, in the left collarbone).[26] April 22 was Lenin's birthday—he turned 52—and the next day he underwent surgery to remove the neck bullet: it turned out to be three millimeters from his carotid artery.[27] After his surgery, on May 19, in good cheer, Lenin composed a playful note to Stalin.[28] Doctors in the hospital, however, recorded "a general nervousness, . . . neurasthenia," which they attributed to "overwork." On May 23, 1922, Lenin went back to the countryside to continue his post-surgery recuperation.[29] There, catastrophe struck: on the night of May 26-27, he suffered severe memory lapse, partial loss of speech, and partial paralysis of his right leg and right arm. The regime issued a bulletin to the effect that Lenin had a stomach ailment.[30] In fact, he had suffered a massive stroke—a mere seven weeks after having elevated Stalin to general secretary.

LENIN'S ILLNESS became another avenue for Stalin to draw closer to him. The stroke, a state secret (like the hemophilia of Tsarevich Alexei), exposed Lenin's dearth of close confidantes and protectors. He had no children, who might be considered possible heirs, and no Praetorian Guard, whose leader might have sought to mount a coup, as so often happens in a dictatorship. He did have a po-litburo, but Molotov, who worked very closely with Lenin and knew him well, would recall that "Lenin had no friends in the politburo."[31] One reason may have been Lenin's relentless disparagement of his colleagues.[32] He did have an extremely loyal service staff, which included a business manager and a number of secretaries, one of whom, the most junior, was Nadya Alliluyeva, Stalin's wife.[33] But after the death of Lenin's mistress Inessa Armand (in fall 1920), he was left with just two trustworthy intimates: his unwed younger sister Maria Ulyanova (b. 1878), who worked at *Pravda*, and his wife Nadezhda Krupskaya (b. 1869), who worked in the commissariat of enlightenment; both of them lived with Lenin.[34] Stalin was well-positioned as Lenin's right hand and all-purpose fixer.

Unbeknownst to the world, Lenin had retreated to the thick woods outside Moscow, where, in the southeast, lay the Gorki estate, a 16th century property that had changed hands a number of times and fallen into disrepair by the early 1900s, when a two-time widow (of both a leading art collector and the second-to-last Moscow governor-general) had the main building remodeled in gaudy "Russian Empire" style. This produced a yellowish baronial manor fronted by six white columns, which the Bolsheviks nationalized. Lenin first went to Gorki on September 25, 1918, about a month after the near fatal attempt on his life.[35] (To prolong the restless leader's recuperation, Yakov Sverdlov began to refurbish a new Kremlin apartment for Lenin in the Imperial Senate: three bed-rooms, one each for Lenin, Krupskaya, and Ulyanova, as well as a service kitchen and a small dining room formed out of a former hallway, but, conspicuously, no parlor room to receive guests.)[36] As Lenin's health further deteriorated, he spent more and more time at the estate: all told, about two-and-a-half of the next five years after his initial visit. Gorki acquired a staff, including the worker-cook Spiridon Putin (grandfather of Vladimir Putin), a large library, and a direct tele-phone line to Moscow. Leonid Krasin, the former top salesman in tsarist Russia for the German company Siemens and now the Bolshevik foreign trade commis-sar, purchased a Rolls-Royce "Silver Ghost" in 1921, so Lenin could be driven around, while a film projector enabled him to watch newsreels of Bolshevik anniversaries and Henry Ford's assembly lines.[37] Nonetheless, Lenin came to feel isolated in his second home, imprisoned by incapacitating illness.[38] Stalin visited Gorki more than any other person in the inner circle—twelve times—and was observed by Lenin's sister Maria Ulyanova to cheer Lenin up, cracking wise, mockingly impersonating others in the regime, sharing jokes about police surveillance on Lenin's doctors.[39] Stalin would use these visits to advantage, arriving from Gorki to politburo meetings, passing on "greetings from Ilich," and orally transmitting the leader's directives.

Lenin's medical issues did not stem from the lead in the bullet or overwork (nor, for that matter, from syphilis: Lenin's tests had come back negative, although he was nonetheless injected with arsenic, the remedy of the day).[40] On May 27, 1922, Professor V.V. Kramer, a neuropathologist, definitively concluded not only that Lenin's migraines, acute anxiety, and insomnia stemmed from brain disease, but that "the basis of his illness is actually not only overstrain of the brain, but also severe disorder of the blood vessels in the brain." The diagnosis was inadequate supply of blood to the brain caused by a clogging of the arteries with fibrous plaque (athereosclerosis). Kramer noted that his patient "has lost the ability to recall even a few short phrases, while retaining his intellect in full"—a grim dynamic that intensified Lenin's anxieties about becoming paralyzed.[41] "When the first obvious signs of brain disease appeared," Ulyanova would recall, "Lenin spoke about it with Stalin, asking him for poison, since his further existence would be pointless. Stalin promised to fulfill Lenin's request, should it become necessary, while treating [the likelihood] rather skeptically."[42] On May 29, after proving unable to fulfill the doctor's request to multiply 12 by 7, the Bolshevik leader "determined . . . that it was over for him and demanded we summon Stalin for the briefest interval." Lenin's other Russian doctor, A.M. Kozhenikov, advised against the meeting, but Lenin was adamant. Stalin arrived on May 30 with Nikolai Bukharin, who remained outside Lenin's room, leaving Stalin alone with Lenin for perhaps five minutes. Stalin, walking back to the car with Bukharin and Ulyanova, divulged that Lenin had reminded him of his request for cyanide "to help him leave the stage should he become paralyzed" and stated "now that time had come." The three evidently decided to send Stalin back in to say he had conferred with the doctors and they did not consider Lenin's condition irreversible, a blatant lie.[43] Kozhevnikov recorded in his notebook: "Stalin visited. Conversation about *suicidium*."[44] Had Stalin wanted to poison Lenin, the Bolshevik leader himself had furnished him a golden opportunity to do so, as a humanitarian gesture, with reliable witnesses. Stalin did no such thing.

Lenin's illness also had an impact on his relations with Trotsky. No one had given him more grief. Once, at a politburo meeting, Trotsky was sitting studying the English language, then paused briefly to criticize the politburo's poor organization—causing Lenin to lose his composure. At another politburo meeting Trotsky was said to have called the Bolshevik leader "a hooligan," inducing him to turn "white as chalk."[45] In March 1921 Lenin had deemed Trotsky "a temperamental man . . . as for policy [*politika*], he hasn't got a clue."[46] In summer 1921, Lenin had taken part in a scheme to transfer Trotsky to Ukraine, a move that Trotsky, in breach of party discipline, resisted; Lenin backed down.[47] Still, in violation of party rules, "Lenin proposed that we gather for the politburo meetings without Trotsky," Molotov recalled. "We conspired against him." Molotov, whose recollections comport with the archival record, added that "Lenin's relations with Stalin were closer, albeit on a business footing."[48] But now, in 1922, Lenin appears to have tried to reconcile and balance Stalin and Trotsky. In summer 1922, Lenin miraculously seemed to improve—a circumstance celebrated in *Pravda*—and on July 11 Stalin visited him.[49] "Ilich greeted him in friendly manner, joked, laughed, demanded that I afford Stalin hospitality, I brought wine and such," recalled Ulyanova, who added that "during this and subsequent visits they spoke about Trotsky. . . . They discussed inviting Trotsky to visit Ilich." She maintained that the invitation "had the character of diplomacy," denoting mere mollification, but it appears to have been genuine.[50] Trotsky, although duly invited, never once came to see Lenin in Gorki in 1922.[51] On July 14, Stalin telegrammed Orjonikidze, apropos of his own Gorki visit, that "for the first time after a month and a half the doctors permitted Lenin visitors. Today we already have written directives from him. The doctors think that in a month he'll be able to return to work in the old way."[52] Stalin—writing to an intimate—showed himself unafraid of Lenin's return, a sign of confidence in his position and perhaps affection for Lenin—or of dissembling. On July 18, Lenin wrote Stalin, gleefully, "Congratulate me! I got permission *for newspapers!*"[53] That same day Lenin wrote again to Stalin to make a note for himself and Kamenev inquiring whether Kamenev had not forgotten, as he had agreed, to answer Lenin about Trotsky."[54] Lenin may have been urging them to desist from ganging up.

Lenin's efforts to reconcile and balance Trotsky and Stalin did not come easily. The party that Lenin had founded and Stalin now led wielded too much power. On July 20, for example, when the entire politburo, Trotsky included, resolved that "Lenin should have absolutely no meetings" without that ruling body's permission, they tasked Stalin with overseeing enforcement.[55] Stalin tried not to overdo it. At the 12th party conference (August 4–7, 1922), the first major gathering since his appointment as general secretary—which he and his staff organized—he was observed behaving with arch-humility. "Such conduct," recalled Anastas Mikoyan, a delegate, "raised Stalin's prestige in the eyes of the delegates."[56] Lenin's continuing confidence in Stalin's management of party affairs is copiously documented in the archives, but so is Lenin's continued desperation to do something about the Council of People's Commissars and the regime's future more broadly. On September 2, 1922, he evidently discussed with his sister Maria the ages of the leading figures and noted it would be good to have people of various age cohorts in the Central Committee, to ensure longevity.[57] On September 11, Lenin wrote to Stalin (for the entire politburo) proposing an expansion of his formal deputies by adding Trotsky to the Council of People's Commissars and Kamenev to the Council of Labor and Defense (a parallel, if smaller, top executive body).[58] Lenin's motives remain unclear: He was proposing to move Trotsky near the top of the government, but rather than offering him the economy portfolio, which was Trotsky's preference, Lenin seems to have wanted him to take up ideology and education, as well as second-order questions of international affairs.[59] Was Lenin, who had just browbeaten the party to swallow the legalized markets of the New Economic Policy, concerned about Trotsky's obsession with state planning? Or was he trying to elevate Trotsky's position? It is impossible to say for sure, but it is likely Lenin had both considerations in mind: containment of Trotsky's anti-NEP impulses and balancing of Stalin's power.

Lenin's proposal presented an immense opportunity for Trotsky to begin to lay claim to Lenin's government mantle.[60] Stalin put Lenin's proposal before the seven members of the politburo (likely the very day he received it) for vote by telephone. Stalin, Rykov, and Kalinin ("do not object") voted with Lenin; Kamenev and Mikhail Yefremov, known as Tomsky, abstained. One person voted against Trotsky's appointment—Trotsky himself: "I categorically refuse."[61] Trotsky's most outstanding biographer surmised that he refused because he "had no doubt that even as Lenin's deputy he would depend at every step on decisions taken by the General Secretariat which selected the Bolshevik personnel for the various government departments and by this alone effectively controlled them."[62] Dependency on Stalin was indeed anathema to Trotsky. But equally important, Trotsky seems to have been holding out for a major overhaul of the administration to allow planning of the entire economy under his leadership. On September 12, Stalin went to see Lenin in Gorki, evidently to discuss the situation. Trotsky's stance meant that, at a politburo meeting on September 14, Kamenev alone was added to the ranks of deputies at both the Council of People's Commissars and the Council of Labor and Defense, which meant he also chaired politburo meetings. "The politburo," stated its September 14 protocols, "records the categorical refusal of comrade Trotsky with regret."[63] Trotsky's refusal—like his failure to visit Lenin at Gorki in 1922—was a choice.[64]

Immediately after Trotsky's refusal to become Lenin's deputy in the government, *Pravda*, the organ of the party apparatus that Stalin controlled, spotlighted Stalin's September 1922 visits to Gorki in an illustrated supplement (September 24) intended to demonstrate how well Lenin was doing. Stalin was quoted enumerating the plethora of matters he and Lenin had supposedly discussed: "the internal situation . . . the harvest . . . the condition of industry . . . the ruble exchange rate . . . the budget . . . the external situation . . . the Entente . . . France's behavior . . . England and Germany . . . America's role . . . the SRs and Mensheviks . . . the White press . . . the emigration . . . the far-fetched legends about Lenin's death."[65] In effect, Stalin was enumerating his own limitless responsibilities. The article, in addition, carried a photograph, taken by Ulyanova, of a happy Lenin with Stalin outdoors at Gorki seated side by side, smiling, conveying Lenin's supposed ruddy health as well as Stalin's proximity to him, for the entire party, the country, and the world.[66] The succession struggle was on, but the prospects for Lenin's recovery had not been extinguished and, on October 2, 1922, after a four-month absence, he returned to Moscow, presiding the next day over the Council of People's Commissars. "The meeting was populous, fifty-four people attended," recalled the head of Lenin's secretariat, Lidiya Fotiyeva. "Everyone wanted to see Lenin, as soon and as closely as possible."[67] But the Trotsky question lingered. Around this time, Lenin reacted sharply to efforts by Kamenev and Stalin to reduce Trotsky's position. "You write, '(the Central Committee) is casting or is preparing to cast a healthy cannon overboard'," Lenin observed in a letter to Kamenev. "To cast Trotsky overboard—which is what you're hinting at, there's no other interpretation—would be the height of absurdity. If you do not consider me to have become hopelessly stupid, then how can you think of such a thing!!!" Lenin went so far as to close with a quotation from Pushkin's *Boris Godunov* warning about "bloody children before the eyes"—a clear allusion to the wages of betrayal for the sake of political ambition.[68]

Hopes that Lenin might beat his health troubles were raised on October 31, when, in his first public address since the stroke, he delivered the closing speech to a session of the Soviet central executive committee, which incited a prolonged ovation.[69] The euphoria did not last, however. Lenin declined an invitation for November 7, 1922, the fifth anniversary of the October Revolution, to return to the Mikhelson factory, now renamed for him, where he had been shot in 1918.[70] On November 13, he did speak at the Fourth Comintern Congress, for an hour, in German, but he was drenched in perspiration and told people that during the speech he had "forgot what he had already said, and what he still had to say."[71] On November 20, Lenin delivered a public speech to the Moscow soviet at the Bolshoi Theater. "Long Live Ilich!" the audience shouted upon spotting him, applauding until their hands ached. When, finally, Kamenev introduced Lenin as speaker, a prolonged ovation erupted again.[72] But, one witness recalled, Lenin "seemed to me even more exhausted than at the Fourth Comintern Congress."[73] A French Communist eyewitness noted that "those who were seeing him for the first time said, 'This is still the same Lenin!' But for the others no such illusion was possible; instead of the alert Lenin they had known, the man before them now was strongly affected by paralysis, his features remained immobile . . . his usual simple, rapid, confident speech was replaced by a hesitant, jerky delivery."[74] Lenin himself stated in the speech that "he had lost his ability to work for a rather long time."[75] The next day (November 21, 1922) a "diary of duty secretaries" was launched to monitor Lenin; the first entry was made by Alliluyeva (Stalin's wife).[76] Four days later, Lenin was walking along the corridor when his legs erupted in spasms, which caused him to fall. He rose only with great difficulty. In consultation with his doctors, he had to cancel meetings and speeches. On November 30, a day Lenin missed a politburo session, he wrote "retain on the shelf," meaning do not return to the library, on a copy of Engels's *Political Testament* (Moscow, 1922).[77] Perhaps Lenin would compose his own political testament?

FEW ISSUES IN SOVIET HISTORY involved more intrigue than Lenin's so-called Testament, which is dated to December 1922-January 1923, but which, as we shall see, Lenin might not have dictated at that time—contrary to entrenched scholarship—or even dictated at all. Whatever its provenance, however, the document gravely threatened Stalin's embryonic personal dictatorship, and became an enduring, haunting aspect of his rule. Usually adduced in connection with delegitimizing Stalin's position as Lenin's successor, the Testament is important as a key to Stalin's psyche and behavior. The Testament helped bring out his demons, his sense of persecution and victimhood, his mistrust of all and sundry, but also his sense of personal destiny and iron determination. None of this is intended in any way to affirm Stalin as Lenin's legitimate successor. But it bears reminding that the assertion that Stalin "usurped" power has an absurdist quality. Beyond the fact that Stalin's ascendancy inside the regime owed a great deal to Lenin's actions, the Communist regime had come into being as a result of a coup, and, while claiming to rule in the name of the proletariat, executed proletarians who dared to question the party's self-assigned monopoly. It was the party that had usurped power. In effect, those scholars who intentionally or unintentionally echo Trotsky and his supporters are accusing Stalin of stealing what had already been stolen.[78]

Likewise, assertions of a Bolshevik collective leadership predating Stalin ring hollow. Lenin's secretariat took on an essentially limitless range of issues, setting a precedent, and no one did more than Lenin to establish a living example of one-man rule at the top. (When the other "collective leaders" disagreed with Lenin, he threatened to expel them or, failing that, to quit the party and form a new one.) Beyond the red herring of Stalin's alleged usurpation and supposedly unprecedented unilateralism, Trotsky and other critics of Stalin's regime also asserted that his triumph reflected no special abilities, just special circumstances. This is manifestly false. Still, we must be careful not to err in the opposite direction and lionize him. He was brilliantly adept at administration and manipulation, but we shall observe Stalin learning on the job, and often failing. That was not merely because of his plentiful shortcomings but also because Lenin had helped conjure into being both an ideologically blinkered dictatorship and a costly global antagonism. Managing the severely difficult challenge of Russian power in the world, now further complicated by the Leninist Communist dictatorship, would have confounded any would-be successor. Stalin's efforts were strenuous but the results decidedly mixed.

Part III will examine Stalin's creation of a personal dictatorship within the Bolshevik dictatorship, and the ways he put that remarkable power to use. It was Stalin who formed the Union of Soviet Socialist Republics, helped make the recuperative New Economic Policy work, and spelled out the nature of Leninism for the party mass. Stalin not only managed to implant and cultivate immense numbers of loyalists, but also to invent for himself the role of Lenin's faithful pupil. Stalin's role as guardian of the ideology was as important in his ascendancy as brute bureaucratic force. In the 1920s, Communist party plenums, conferences, and congresses constituted the core of Soviet political life and of Stalin's biography; the political brawling shaped not just his methods of rule, but also his character, and image. To an extraordinary extent, it was skirmishes over *ideas* not solely personal power that preoccupied him and his rivals in the struggle to define the revolution going forward. Ideology was Bolshevik reality: The documents, whether those made public at the time or kept secret, are absolutely saturated with Marxist-Leninist ways of thinking and vocabulary—the proletariat, Bonapartism, the petit bourgeoisie, imperialism, capitalist encirclement, class enemies, military specialists, NEPmen, kulaks, socialism. Mastery and control over the ideology turned out to be a key to unlocking ultimate power, but at the same time the content of the ideology proved to be tragically for real, in domestic and foreign affairs.

The Bolshevik dictatorship was not the only outcome of the revolution and civil war. What had emerged on the ground was two parallel revolutions: one in the northern cities, where an expanding functionary class—the regime's social base—and proliferating, overlapping institutions scratched and clawed among themselves for power and spoils; and another in the countryside, where small-holding peasant households had seized the land, still by far the country's principal source of wealth. ("The revolution," Molotov would recall later in life, "had taken place in a petty-bourgeois country.")[79] These two revolutions were set on a collision course. The entrenched peasant revolution could not hold back entrenchment of the Communist dictatorship, but, no less than the international environment, it acted as a severe constraint on Bolshevik ambitions. Accommodation to the peasant, in turn, proved extremely difficult to stomach for many party stalwarts. Indeed, over time, exactly as the militants feared, the forced accommodation of the New Economic Policy would begin to change the composition and political mood in the Communist party, much to Stalin's alarm. His collision with Trotsky in the wake of Lenin's illness would turn out to be mere prelude. More profoundly, the stage was set for one of the truly manifold collisions in Russian and indeed world history—between Stalin's personal dictatorship and the entire Russian-Eurasian peasantry.

That Stalin would end up launching a violent reversal of the peasant revolution was literally fantastic. A perspicacious German scholar of Russian agriculture, Max Sering, had concluded in an analysis in 1921 that "a regime in Russia under which the peasants would not independently own the land they cultivate is now *inconceivable*."[80] Sering erred in that the peasants did not, de jure, own the land, but they did assume that their usage rights were tantamount to ownership, and overturning that did seem inconceivable. Stalin, however, would prove Sering, as well as a mostly disbelieving Communist party, wrong. Collectivization and the violent expropriation of better-off farmers (dekulakization)—Stalin's revolutionary shock of 1928–30—would turn out to be significantly more ramified even than Lenin's shock coup of 1917. What stands out in Stalin's action is not just his desire to launch a socialist transformation of the countryside, which all Bolsheviks expected to see eventually, but the fact that when the gamble met mass resistance and caused unfathomable ruin, Stalin *saw it through to completion.* No one else in or near the Bolshevik leadership, Trotsky included, could have stayed the course on such a bloody social-engineering escapade on such a scale. The personal dictatorship that Stalin painstakingly built, he would, beginning in January 1928, use to enact a vision of anti-capitalist socialism, utterly transforming and shattering Eurasia.

## CHAPTER 10

# DICTATOR

This was a time when we worked initially on Vozdvizhenka, and then relocated to Old Square. We would work together until midnight, 12:30 am, 1:00 am, and then we'd walk on foot to the Kremlin along Ilinka St. Me, Molotov, Kuibyshev, others. We were walking along the street, I recall, one winter, he [Stalin] wore a hat with earflaps, his ears flapping. . . . We laughed and laughed, he would say something, we would respond, tossing jokes at one another . . . totally free [*volnitsa*]. . . . Those watching off to the side would ask: who were this company? We had practically no bodyguards. Very few. Maybe one or two people walking, that was it. . . . It was a happy time of life. And Stalin was in a good mood.

Lazar Kaganovich, reminiscing about the period 1922–24[1]

Everything in the Soviet Union depends in the last resort on the harvest.

British diplomatic report, December 1924[2]

STALIN'S CREATION OF A DICTATORSHIP within the dictatorship was unforeseen. Lenin was undisputed leader (*vozhd'*) and no one imagined he might become incapacitated. When that suddenly happened, most everyone assumed collective leadership would prevail: even if other top Bolsheviks believed in their heart of hearts they might be Lenin's equal, they understood no one else would perceive them as such. Also, Stalin's considerable political gifts were underappreciated or even contemptuously scorned. Trotsky, in a brilliant phrase, would dismiss Stalin as the "outstanding mediocrity of our party," while Kamenev, according to Trotsky, deemed Stalin "a small-town politician."[3] Finally, there was one other lesser known factor that made a Stalin ascendancy appear unlikely: several individuals had preceded him as head of the party and, after the first one died, skepticism set in that anyone could cope with the job, to say nothing of transforming it into the focal point of the entire regime.

Yakov Sverdlov, the party's original lead administrator or "secretary" (from April 1917), had been renowned for the fact that, as one official gushed, "he knew our party better than anyone else."[4] In fact, with a staff of just six, Sverdlov had had his hands full as party committees mushroomed around the vast country, from under 600 in 1917 to 8,000 by 1919, and he simultaneously served as chairman of the Soviet central executive committee (head of state), manipulating relations with non-Bolshevik socialists.[5] When Sverdlov died in 1919 at age thirty-three—having spent twelve of those years in tsarist prisons and exile—Lenin despaired of finding a replacement.[6] For the central executive committee of the Soviet, Lenin even proposed returning Kamenev, the person he had shunted aside from that post in 1917. In the event, Mikhail Kalinin, an ethnic Russian, the son of a poor peasant, and a peasant in visage, got the nod, but the Soviet central executive committee had already ceased to be a locus of power.[7] At the party apparatus, Yelena Stasova, a code specialist, took over as secretary, but after a few months "judged herself insufficiently competent in political questions" and in late 1919, stepped aside.[8] Her replacement, the third Stalin predecessor, was Nikolai Krestinsky, a graduate of the law faculty of St. Petersburg University and the finance commissar. Krestinsky was an original member of both the politburo and the orgburo, positions he held concurrently while taking over the secretariat, a unique commanding position atop the party. He had a legendary memory, but the scope of the work seems to have overwhelmed him.[9] In April 1920, Leonid Serebryakov and Yevgeny Preobrazhensky were added alongside Krestinsky, charged with improving contact with local party organizations.[10] But no one in the threesome proved adept or diligent, as demonstrated by runaway complaints in the party press (something similar dogged Krestinsky at the finance commissariat).[11] Files piled up unexamined, and officials lamented that nasty scrums over power (*skloki*) paralyzed party work nearly everywhere.[12] Rather than their incompetence, however, the Krestinsky-Serebryakov-Preobrazhensky trio was done in by its support for Trotsky in the trade union row of 1920–21. Lenin cleaned house, ensuring at the 10th Party Congress that none of the three was even reelected to the Central Committee.[13]

As the party's new "responsible secretary," Lenin elevated Vyacheslav

Molotov, the fourth Stalin before Stalin. "Unexpectedly for me in 1921," Molotov would recall, "I became a Central Committee secretary."[14] Two others were appointed alongside him, Yemelyan Yaroslavsky and Vasily Mikhailov, both middling organizers. Neither lasted. The hours were long and the work tough: the secretariat was besieged with both reports of functionaries' drunkenness, bribe taking, and political illiteracy, and requests to supply competent cadres, while appointees or prospective appointees showed up in droves looking for guidance, permissions, or favors. The party secretariat reported that in 1921 it issued passes for 254,468 visitors to its offices, or an average of nearly 700 per day, including weekends.[15] But when Lenin made Stalin "general secretary" in April 1922, in place of Yaroslavsky and above Molotov, he was compensating for the redoubtable Molotov's lack of sufficient political heft and looking for high-level leadership as well as efficiency.[16] "The power [*vlast'*] of the Central Committee is colossal," Lenin wrote in spring 1922, just before promoting Stalin. "We dispose of 200,000–400,000 party functionaries, and through them thousands upon thousands of nonparty people. And this gigantic Communist cause is utterly befouled by foggy bureaucratism!" Lenin demanded rising above "trifles, push them onto aides and deputy aides," and taking on the really surpassing challenges.[17] Stalin now became the only person simultaneously in the politburo, orgburo, and secretariat—and he endured.

Explanations for Stalin's aggrandizement have rightly pointed to notable qualities of the Communist party, particularly its centralized appointments and conspiratorial secrecy, which afforded incomparable sway over information, agendas, links to the grassroots, and supervision of every state body.[18] Certainly all of that *could* be used for institutional and personal aggrandizement, but those mechanisms had to be further built up and taken advantage of. Trotsky famously wrote that "Stalin did not create the apparatus. The apparatus created him."[19] This was exactly backward. Stalin created the apparatus, and it was a colossal feat.[20] To be sure, we shall see him learning on the job, committing significant mistakes, and it would be a while before he emerged as the recognized Leader (*vozhd'*) not just of the party but of the country. But he demonstrated surpassing organizational abilities, a mammoth appetite for work, a strategic mind, and an unscrupulousness that recalled his master teacher, Lenin.[21] Stalin proved capable of wielding the levers he inherited, and of inventing new ones. Admittedly, too often his power, including over personnel, has been viewed as that of an impersonal machine. What Trotsky and others missed or refused to acknowledge was that Stalin had a deft political touch: he recalled names and episodes of people's biographies, impressing them with his familiarity, concern, and attentiveness, no matter where they stood in the hierarchy, even if they were just service staff. Stalin, in his midforties, found his calling at the party apparatus: he was, for all his moodiness, a people person, a ward-boss-style politician, albeit one in command of instruments beyond a ward boss's dreams—the Communist party's reach, discipline, and radiant-future ideology.

But what stands out most about Stalin's ascendancy is that, structurally, he was handed the possibility of a personal dictatorship, and he began to realize that potential just by fulfilling the duties of general secretary.

Stalin had exceptional power almost instantaneously. When he took over in 1922, the Central Committee apparatus, secretariat and orgburo, already numbered some 600 people, up from just 30 two years before. No one else commanded anything like this personal staff: Lenin's chancellery in the Council of People's Commissars numbered 102.[22] Unlike the government, the party was not merely an executive body, but a mass organization, and one deliberately intended to shadow all other institutions. Stalin's impact on this machine was immediate. Molotov had instituted important improvements, such as a rudimentary catalogue of party personnel, but Stalin would see all this vastly expanded.[23] All through spring and summer 1922, he brought in energetic people from the provinces, and obliged local party organizations to send bimonthly reports in the form of two-page personal letters. In the six months from May 1, 1922, through January 15, 1923, the apparatus recorded receiving 13,674 local meeting protocols, 1,737 summary reports, 324 reports on the political mood, and 6,337 other pieces of information, while itself sending out 141 directive circulars.[24] At the 12th Party Congress (1923), the first after Stalin's appointment, speakers marveled at how the secretariat had vastly improved.[25] Stalin had a phenomenal memory, like Krestinsky, but Stalin banged heads and brought order. He *liked* the job. Above all, he *did* the job. "Ilich has in him unquestionably the most reliable Cerberus, fearlessly guarding the gates of the Central Committee," Stalin's first top aide, Amayak Nazaretyan, an Armenian whom he imported from the Caucasus, wrote to Sergo Orjonikidze in Tiflis (August 9, 1922). "The work of the Central Committee has significantly mutated now. What we encountered here was indescribably bad. And what were the views in the locales about the Central Committee apparatus? Now everyone has been shaken up."[26]

The regime's very physical geography spoke to the stunning strengths of Stalin's position. The addresses in themselves appear to mean little—Vozdvizhenka, 5, and then Old Square, 4; Znamenka, 23; Bolshaya Lubyanka, 2; Blacksmith Bridge, 15; Ilinka, 9—but they reveal the crucial lines of contact among the security police and the military.[27] Scholars long ago established that the provincial party machines became a cornucopia of recruits for the central apparatus and of Stalin loyalists in locales, but we shall also see how early Stalin, as head of the party, began to exercise his authority via the secret police, bringing some of them into the party apparatus and maintaining very tight contact with the police over at Lubyanka. Stalin also imposed effective control over the military. After the politiburo or Central Committee meetings took place, whatever might be decided, Stalin went back to his office and implemented the decisions—or chose not to do so. From his party office he initiated schemes outside meetings via party apparatchiks and secret police operatives. He achieved a free hand in making appointments to his own staff.[28] But he also implanted his loyalists everywhere else, and found or cultivated enemies for them, too, in order to keep loyalists under watch. This went well beyond just fulfilling the duties of the general secretary position, but again, this was structurally baked into that position. Stalin would have had to show uncommon restraint, deference, and lack of ambition not to build a personal dictatorship within the dictatorship.

A geography of authority, however, also exposes limits to the power of the regime and of Stalin's personal dictatorship, particularly the near absence of the party in the vast countryside, where four fifths of the population lived. On the eve of the October coup, the Bolsheviks had counted a mere four rural party cells and 494 peasant members, in a two-continent country.[29] By 1922, after mass demobilizations of the Red Army soldiers back to their native villages, the number of party members in the countryside reached 200,000, out of 515,000 total Communists.[30] But of the total rural population of nearly 120 million, party members were still less than one tenth of 1 percent. Only one of every twenty-five or so villages had a party cell. Provincial capitals were festooned with red flags and Communist slogans, but just ten minutes' walk beyond a city's limits, an observer would have been hard pressed to find visible evidence of the regime.[31] This did not mean party rule in the cities was all well. In elections to urban soviets, the regime felt constrained to switch from secret to open balloting, with secret police monitors present, and the results were predictable, as shown in December 1922 at Moscow's Guzhon Works (soon renamed Hammer and Sickle): Bolshevik candidates were elected by a margin of 100 votes to 2—with 1,900 abstentions.[32] Beyond intimidation, the regime co-opted workers into administration, offering regular salaries, housing, special shops, and other perquisites, but also tasking them with conducting the harangues of workers riled by perceptions of Communist privilege and corruption.[33] The Communist regime's social base was itself. That meant the expanding regime was itself a society, and this society's center was Stalin.

Unlike Nazaretyan, the aide, most everyone who managed to encounter Stalin in the 1920s caught mere glimpses. Marina Ryndzyunskaya, a sculptress at the Museum of the Revolution commissioned to craft a likeness, noted that he was a man "of medium height" and that his gait was odd. "With his left hand tucked into his pocket, he moved forward all at once," she wrote. "When he turned, he turned not gradually, head, neck, and then body, but completely, like a soldier."[34] But what *moved* him? Even those who worked with Stalin usually failed to take his measure. Alexander Barmine, then a twenty-three-year-old general staff officer, first glimpsed Stalin in 1922 at the Fourth Congress of the Comintern in the Kremlin's St. George's Hall and claimed to have seen him "not only as he is on dress parade before delegations or admiring audiences, but in his office at work." Stalin "looks coarser and more common, and also smaller" in person, Barmine later wrote. "His face is pockmarked and sallow. . . . His eyes are dark brown with a tinge of hazel. His expression tells nothing of what he feels. There is to me a curious heaviness and sullenness about him. The man seems neither European nor Asiatic, but a cross between the two." At meetings, Barmine noted, Stalin sat off to the side, smoked a pipe that he stuffed with cigarette tobacco, and doodled, but he accumulated power because of his "strength of will, patience, slyness, ability to perceive human frailties and play upon them with contempt, and the supreme gift of pursuing a chosen goal inflexibly and without scruple."[35] It was a simplistic assessment—master psychologist, iron will—that came to be widely held, especially retrospectively, but it overlooked Stalin's immersion in Marxism, a key source of his power. And it left open the question of why so many people proved susceptible to him.[36] Naked careerism was one reason they sought to attach themselves to the general secretary, but many were attracted to Stalin because of his tenacious dedication to the revolutionary cause and to the state's power.

## FROM VOZDVIZHENKA TO OLD SQUARE

Before Lenin took ill, the regime revolved around his physical location: the dacha at Gorki or the office and apartment in the Kremlin's Imperial Senate, between which the regime had its principal meeting space, used by both the Council of People's Commissars and the politburo.[37] Central Committee offices were less grand, and located outside the Kremlin walls. Initially, the party staff set up shop inside a rooming house, where the "apparatus" squeezed into a single apartment, though soon it knocked down the wall, linking to a second. Stasova, then Krestinsky, then Molotov had offices here. It was located on Vozdvizhenka, a radial street that ran from just outside the Kremlin walls, from the Trinity Gate-Kutafya Tower westward to the Arbat. (The address was Vozdvizhenka, 4, although on the building's other side it was listed as Mokhovaya, 7.)[38] In 1920, the expanding apparatus relocated across the street, to Vozdvizhenka, 5, a more august structure built in the late eighteenth century by Matvei Kazakov, the architect of the Kremlin's Imperial Senate, but just a fraction of the size of the latter.[39] "The anterooms were crowded with callers; numerous clerks, mostly young girls in abbreviated skirts and high-heeled lacquered shoes, flitted about with arms full of documents," wrote a Russo-American anarchist of a visit in 1920, adding that the functionaries themselves "looked pale, with sunken eyes and high cheek bones, the result of systematic undernourishment, overwork, and worry."[40] Vozdvizhenka, 5, was near the historic location of a monastery that had been burned down in the fires that had helped drive out Napoleon. Before that, it had been the site of Ivan the Terrible's Oprichnina. Here, in the jammed neoclassical edifice, Stalin would have his inaugural general secretary's office.[41]

That the party's *service* apparatus would become almighty was something of a surprise, but not an accident.[42] Lenin had chosen a ministerial form of government, but the busy people's commissars sent proxies to the supposedly deliberative Council of People's Commissars' meetings, which, in any case, Lenin dominated, whoever might be present.[43] More fundamentally, Lenin had insisted that the party, mainly the politburo but to an extent the Central Committee, serve as the top policy-making body. This choice was reinforced by the circumstance that neither the Council of People's Commissars nor individual commissariats had local branches and depended on local party organizations for implementing decisions, as well as for supplying personnel perceived to be loyal.[44] Technically, the party was not a state organ, so its decisions had to be formulated as decrees of the Council of People's Commissars or laws of the Soviet central executive committee, and this redundancy bred confusion, with some suggesting that the party be abolished, others that the soviets be abolished.[45] Nothing was eliminated. Departments of the central party apparatus came to parallel the structure of the Council of People's Commissars. Not all Central Committee staff were full-fledged functionaries (or *otvetstvennye rabotniki*); many were stenographers, accountants, drivers—indeed, around 240 of the 600 staff members were non-party members; 340 were female.[46] (Here, as elsewhere, the typing and most of the filing were done by Bolshevik wives, mistresses, or "bourgeois ladies.")[47] Nonetheless, the apparatus of the party-centric regime attracted talented people, who developed areas of special expertise, touching on nearly every possible sphere of administration: personnel, propaganda, communications, army, navy, foreign policy, security, finance.[48]

Pinched for space, the central party apparatus relocated in late December 1923 to the inner-city trading quarter of Kitaigorod (whose high walls and gate towers dated from medieval times), where it took over Old Square, 4, a grand former trading house of the Moscow Merchant Association dating to 1915.[49] Of the wintertime move, the functionary Alexei Balashov recalled that "the staff themselves loaded and unloaded the furniture and documents on sleds, forming a long train."[50] Stalin took an office in the combined modernist-neoclassical structure built by merchant capital on the top floor, with access only through two other offices, which accommodated his main aides and a special document courier. Stalin's suite was spacious and orderly, with a door at the back that opened to an ample conference room, where he and Molotov often conferred (behind this meeting room was Molotov's office).[51] To the left inside Stalin's office stood a large table that could accommodate twenty people; to the right, in the far corner, stood his writing desk, along with a smaller table holding telephones, and his personal safe. He was not the night owl he would become. "Stalin arose usually around 9:00 a.m., and arrived at the Central Committee on Old Square by 11:00," according to a long-serving bodyguard. "Stalin frequently worked until late at night, especially in those years after Lenin's death when he had to conduct an active struggle against the Trotskyites."[52] After work, he walked home the short distance down to Red Square and through the Savior Gate (the one with the clock), often with Molotov, who also lived in the Kremlin.

Stalin had an office in the Kremlin's Imperial Senate building, too, a result of his government post (people's commissar for nationalities), but he seems to have used that office sparingly. But the Kremlin was also the location of the twice weekly politburo meetings. As of 1922, there were only seven full members (Lenin, Stalin, Trotsky, Zinoviev, Kamenev, Rykov, Tomsky) and three candidate or non-voting members (Bukharin, Kalinin, Molotov), although Stalin would soon add a fourth (Jānis Rudzutaks). But politburo sessions were sprawling affairs, including numerous technical personnel from the apparatus, as well as various Central Committee members, Central Control Commission members, and others invited to attend parts of the meetings based upon pertinent agenda items. Central Committee plenums were even larger, and took place once or twice a month.[53] But the orgburo, which handled personnel decisions, met far more frequently than any party body, and its sessions sometimes lasted whole days—they were known as orgies. And the party secretariat was essentially in continuous session. In addition, central party apparatchiks could command the assistance of the staff of entire commissariats when gathering information and preparing politburo and Central Committee agendas, reports, or recommendations for Stalin.

Stalin's emerging dictatorship within the dictatorship, despite having no link, physical or personal, to the old regime in the old capital, nonetheless resembled tsarism in an important respect. Before 1917, the locus of power had been the imperial chancellery, nominally a service apparatus, which reported directly to the tsar and eventually merged with the tsar's own personal chancellery.[54] "The head of the chancellery," wrote one of its long-serving heads, "was completely independent and not subordinate to the chairman of the Committee of Ministers."[55] Ministers were often less informed than chancellery functionaries, who alone developed a bird's eye view on the state, accumulating vast power thanks to the size and complexity of the realm as well as their own aspirations and skills. All this could be said of the central Communist party apparatus vis-à-vis the Council of People's Commissars or the Soviet central executive committee. But whereas the imperial chancellery never succeeded in fully subordinating the ministries—bureaucratic infighting had thwarted the tsars' efforts to transform the chancellery into a personal watchdog over the entire state—in the Soviet case, every institution far and wide, except peasant communes, had a party organization that enabled the party to serve as a watchdog over the state, and the society.[56] The ubiquitous party cells were empowered by a potent worldview and belief system. Stalin's machine was not tsarist autocracy redux, in other words, but a modern one-party dictatorship.[57]

Old Square, 4, the heart of the Soviet regime, came to present a formidable contrast for those who knew the informal days of 1917. Alexander Ilin, known as the Genevan, recalled the original "headquarters" of the Central Committee in Petrograd "as a serene family scene," with "everyone sitting at the dining table and drinking tea." Now there was "a gigantic building with a labyrinth of sections and subsections. An immense number of functionaries are on every floor, hurrying about."[58] Ilin viewed this bureaucratic metamorphosis as inevitable yet sad. What he did not seem to appreciate was that inside the new "gigantic building," there was still intimacy and camaraderie. Functionaries rode in the elevator with Stalin; some ran into him in the corridor. His office door was unlocked. "Sometimes I took a book from his library to the reading lounge," the functionary Balashov recalled. "There, there were cupboards with a splendid library. Stalin was sent two copies of every book published by the central publishers, often signed copies. Many authors themselves sent their books. Stalin passed one copy on to us and we divided them among ourselves." Stalin did not lock his desk. "At night he turned or locked in the safe all secret documents," Balashov explained. "At the reception area someone stood duty, and further on were guards, so what did he have to fear?"[59]

## NOMENKLATURA AND CONSPIRACY

Power accrued to Stalin's apparatus in the first instance thanks to leverage over personnel. The vast majority of party members held full-time jobs, whether in factories or commissariats, their party activities being seen as voluntary, but a small number were paid to engage exclusively in party work (apparatchiks), such as running party organizations, and although such officials were supposed to be elected, during the civil war elections had taken a backseat. As fighting wound down, many officials insisted on reversion to elections, prompting Lenin, at the 11th Party Congress (March-April 1921), to counter that "if the Central Committee is deprived of the right to distribute personnel, it will be unable to direct policy."[60] Stalin, on June 6, 1922, dispatched a circular on the prerogative of Central Committee overseers to nominate the candidates (usually just one) for election to local party posts.[61] Would-be regional potentates were seeking to impose their will over other locals, partly out of personal ambition, partly out of frustration at the proliferation of agencies and power centers, and the central apparatus took sides, rotating out local officials of the side it did not back. This enabled some regional officials to consolidate authority as provincial party bosses, who, in turn, centralized their power by intervening lower down, having their people "elected" as county party bosses.[62] Stalin could never centralize the whole country himself, but he could effectively centralize the bosses who were centralizing their own provinces.[63]

Stalin's success remained circumscribed by the country's great distances and by mutual protection rackets (*semeistvennost'*), but the central apparatus compelled locals to submit ever more personnel data, forced through periodic campaigns of verifications or "purges," and managed to register all party members in the country.[64] Stalin's functionaries incited local apparatchiks to denounce each other to the center, and sent traveling commissions to break up or at least manage local cliques.[65] Here was a hoary cat-and-mouse game in sprawling Russia— far-off locales struggling to evade or otherwise cope with central commands—but now the center had the potent mechanism of the party and party discipline. What stands out is not that local party organizations often managed to reject candidates to top party posts proposed by the center, but that the central apparatus managed to impose itself to a high degree. The orgburo made at least a thousand appointments just between April 1922 and March 1923, including no fewer than forty-two new provincial party bosses.[66] Stalin could hardly know every one of the cadres being moved about.[67] But the desire for promotion made provincials eager to please, if they could not deceive, him. In September 1922, Stalin created a commission to promote standout local functionaries to Moscow. In confidential written evaluations that year of forty-seven secretaries of provincial party committees, one official in the Urals (Leonid) was deemed "unable to lead either soviet or party work. Falls under alien influence. . . . A functionary below provincial level." But another, Nikolai Uglanov of Nizhny Novgorod, was said to show "initiative. He is able to unite functionaries to achieve the work. Authoritative."[68] In 1923, Stalin named Uglanov a voting member of the Central Committee, and the next year he would promote him to the capital as second secretary of the Moscow organization, and soon, first secretary.[69]

Appointments and transfers of senior functionaries were systematized with the development, on the initiative of Stalin's orgburo, of a "nomenklatura" (from the Latin *nomenclatura,* for a list of names). Functionaries occupying a position on the nomenklatura could not be removed without approval from the central apparatus. The initial list (November 1923) contained some 4,000 positions/officials: first secretaries of republics, provinces, and counties; people's commissars and their deputies; military district commanders; ambassadors.[70] Especially notable was application of the party-controlled nomenklatura process to state-run industry. Sorting all these appointments out entailed no small amount of work, and Stalin sought to reduce the number of positions for which the central apparatus would be responsible.[71] Provincial party organizations emulated the center with their own nomenklatura of appointments under their control. Tensions persisted between the practice of appointment and the principle of election and between central and local prerogatives, but the invention of the nomenklatura system, and its demand for up-to-date personnel data, was a remarkable patronage mechanism in energetic hands. Stalin put a premium on competence, which he interpreted in terms of loyalty. "We need to assemble functionaries so that people who occupy these positions are capable of implementing directives, comprehending those directives, accepting those directives as their own and bringing them to life," he observed at the 12th Party Congress (April 1923).[72] Fulfillment of Central Committee directives became Stalin's mantra, and suspicion of non-fulfillment, his obsession.[73]

Stalin's apparatus wielded additional instruments. Ivan Ksenofontov, a founding member of the Cheka, who had overseen the Supreme Revolutionary Tribunal during the civil war, was placed in charge of the party's business directorate, which managed mundane matters such as party member dues and the party budget, but also controlled offices and furnishings, apartments, food packets, medical care, cars and drivers, trips abroad.[74] The business directorate had the power to grant or withhold favors, affording Stalin enormous leverage. Yet another key device was the government phone system. Worried that switchboard operators could listen in on calls, the regime developed a "vertushka," so named because it had dials, then a novelty. At first, the self-dialed government network linked around sixty people, but soon it grew to a few hundred, and served as a mark of power (or lack thereof for those without).[75] One defector claimed that Stalin oversaw installation of the vertushka system and as a result connived a way to eavesdrop on it.[76] This is plausible but not corroborated by other evidence, at least for this early period.[77] What we can say is that most of the vertushka phones were at Old Square and reinforced the party apparatus as a nodal point.[78] The regime also established a special cipher unit, which, though nominally a division of the Cheka, in practice was autonomous, so that politburo telegrams did not pass through the secret police leadership.[79] Run by Gleb Boki, an ethnic Ukrainian born in Tiflis who had studied math and physics at the St. Petersburg

Mining Institute—and who had also founded a colony for wife swapping and drunken orgies—the cipher specialists coded and decoded hundreds of telegrams per day for regional party organizations, embassies abroad, and officials on holiday.[80]

Only Stalin, in the name of the Central Committee, could issue directives to every locale and institution, while anything sent to the politburo or Central Committee from commissariats, secret police, or the military went to the party secretariat. The Old Square mail room resembled a military operation with secret police couriers gluing, sewing, sealing, and unsealing envelopes; couriers also had to carry clean, well-oiled, loaded weapons, and to check and recheck the identity of recipients.[81] But complaints of leaks and violations became constant, and officials were perpetually admonished.[82] In July 1922, Yaroslavsky, who had been shifted to the party's Siberian Bureau, lost his briefcase in which he had a codebook and notebook. The authorities offered a 100 million ruble reward—obviously, with no intention or possibility of paying; the briefcase was found, but without its contents.[83] As of April 1923, it was forbidden to put in writing anything relating to state security; instead, security matters were to be discussed first in Stalin's secretariat, before being brought to the attention of the politburo.[84] On August 19, 1924, the politburo issued a resolution "on conspiracy in handling documents of the CC," with an appendix laying out the "rules in handling the conspiratorial documents of the CC." Many of the instructions demanded that officials "observe absolute conspiracy in the handling of documents" in terms of who saw them and how they were kept; any official who pursued a secret document had to sign it. Many had to be returned after reading.

Hypersecrecy became an unquenchable thirst that strengthened Stalin's grip. Out of the business directorate he and his functionaries carved out a separate entity named the "secret department," which took charge of denunciations and investigations, the party archives, and the contacts with the secret police. Modest in size at first, the secret department would expand to several hundred staff by the mid-1920s and acquire affiliates in local party branches, the military, factories, and state agencies—eventually, all major institutions. These secret departments constituted a parallel information system, a regime within the regime, that could be used to intimidate: officials did not know what was being recorded and reported in these parallel channels. The central secret department was physically cordoned off by steel doors. "The sanctum sanctorum in the grey building on the old Square is the secret department," wrote one Soviet official after he defected. "One goes up by lift, then along a seemingly endless corridor. Meetings are held in the evenings. The building is thus in semi-darkness, empty and silent. Each step taken gives off a resounding and lonely echo. Then one is face-to-face with the inner guard posts. One's special pass is checked. Finally one passes through the steel door separating this department from the rest of the building. And then one approaches the last door."[85]

No small degree of the apparatus's power flowed from its mystique. Ryndzyunskaya, the sculptress, wrote of the rarely glimpsed interiors of Old Square that "the first thing that amazed me in this facility was the striking cleanliness and some kind of taciturn reticence, if one can speak that way. Reticence of words, reticence of movement, nothing superfluous." The next time she met Stalin, in her studio, she told him of being unnerved by the scary (*zhutko*) feeling at Central Committee HQ. "I am very, very pleased," Stalin is said to have replied, smiling, "that's the way it should be."[86] But of all the apparatus's secrets, the biggest one was that runaway decree-ism, obsessive demands for written reports, and endless traveling commissions exacerbated the roiling administrative chaos across the party-state, and buried Old Square, too, in paper. Dictatorship unwittingly imposes limits on itself. Orgburo staff studied manuals by the prolific Platon Lebedev, known as Kerzhentsev, such as *Principles of Organization*, whose first two editions had sold out in a matter of months; the third edition (1924) was issued in a print run of 5,000. Aiming to deliver "concise practical leadership for rank and file organizers in whatever sphere they worked," Kerzhentsev cited American and British writings, and reproduced illustrations of a British card file system for personnel—index cards for each employee—which he urged be compiled not just by alphabet but also by occupation and geography.[87] But his brief for clearly specified directives, follow through, and then intelligent adjustments neglected to acknowledge the tendency of dictatorships to incur, or even promote, multiple jurisdictions and other deliberate inefficiencies as a way to ensure political control.

The conspiracy to seize power behaved like a conspiracy in power.[88] The apparatus in theory was supposed to be transparent to the wider party; Lenin had insisted that a sign-in sheet hang inside the party complex with Stalin's name on it, in alphabetical order, for his office hours.[89] That said, Lenin's own written orders were often distributed only under the proviso that they be returned to him or immediately destroyed after reading. He constantly urged, as he wrote in 1919 referring to Bolshevik subversion of Turkestan, that things had to be carried out "in an extremely conspiratorial manner (as we knew how to work under the tsar)."[90] The origins and perpetuation of conspiracy, in other words, had little to do with Stalin's personality, even if, by nature, Stalin was an archconspirator, and now the principal beneficiary.

### ZNAMENKA, 23

West of the Kremlin, parallel to Vozdvizhenka, was Znamenka Street, named for an ancient church (Signs of the Holy Virgin). Znamenka, 23, the former Alexander Military School, was appropriated by the Revolutionary Military Council of the Republic, the war commissariat, and the Bolshevik General Staff.[91] During the civil war, Znamenka was a power center, but that shifted precipitously with the victory and demobilization, as the Red Army shrank from around 5 million to 600,000 troops by the end of 1923. (Desertions drove a significant part of the reductions.) Equally important, the army was honeycombed by Communist party "political departments" in all its units, which fell under a self-standing army Political Administration—but that became a Stalin target. In 1923, the orgburo commissioned a "study" of party work in the army, ostensibly to ascertain whether such work was conducted in accord with orgburo instructions; the orgburo further mandated that representatives of the party apparatus be present at discussions of party-organizational activities in all military districts, and that the army's political administration report regularly to the Central Committee. By fall 1923, the orgburo had instituted the equivalent of a party-controlled nomenklatura for top army positions, including members of the Revolutionary Military Councils of the center and regional military districts, as well as their aides; the main military commands; key staff of the army political administrations; military procurators and military academies.[92] Every top Bolshevik official, including Trotsky, the war commissar, recognized the supremacy of the party.

If the military was politically weak in the Soviet party-state, unlike the case in most dictatorships, the military also suffered from the weak condition of society. The regime hoped to use the Red Army as a "school for socialism," and Trotsky took a very active role in driving political training.[93] Stalin, predictably, sought to seize this issue, telling the 12th Party Congress that whereas others tended to see the Red Army through the lens of military offense and defense, he saw "a collection point of workers and peasants."[94] Around 180,000 peasants would be conscripted annually during the 1920s.[95] A 1924 study revealed that the call-ups were clueless about "the Bolshevik party line, the party's struggle with Menshevism, and with other alien groups."[96] Another survey revealed that nearly nine tenths of the army's political educators had no more than two years of primary schooling. Meanwhile, newspapers and lectures were overrun with incomprehensible foreign words, neologisms, and jargon.[97] "Let's be frank," one army educator noted, "when we speak about banks, stock exchanges, parliaments, trusts, finance kings, and democracies, we are not being understood."[98] In some ways, the Red Army rarely rose above being a Russian language remedial course for the multinational conscript populace, not exactly a political power base. Nor was the army a bulwark for Soviet security.[99] "If God does not help us . . . and we get entangled in a war," Stalin remarked in 1924, "we'll be thoroughly routed."[100] That said, the general secretary's subordination of the military to the party apparatus was very far along, with the exception that Trotsky remained its nominal head. Already in late 1923, however, the workers' and peasants' inspectorate—controlled by Stalin—had pointed out, accurately, that Trotsky did not really manage the everyday work of the war and navy commissariat.[101]

## LUBYANKA, 2

Lubyanka, a Moscow neighborhood, owed its name to Ivan III's conquest of medieval Novgorod ("Lubyanits" had been a name for a district in that town brought to Moscow by those forced to relocate). In spring 1918, the central Cheka, arriving from Petrograd, had commandeered Bolshaya Lubyanka, 11 (site of Dzierżyński's first Moscow office), as well as no. 13, near the city's main commercial quarter. As the staff expanded and a separate Moscow region Cheka was established, in fall 1919, the Cheka Special Department overseeing security in the army grabbed Bolshaya Lubyanka, 2, where the narrow street opened onto Lubyanka Square. These premises consisted of an elegant five-story rectangular building with a clock on the top front façade that had been built in 1900 by the All-Russia Insurance Company, and like the solid structure occupied by the party apparatus nearby at Old Square, reflected the ample finances and tastes of Moscow merchant capital. The insurance company had rented out Bolshaya Lubyanka, 2's ground-floor storefronts (a bookstore, sewing machine shop, bed store, beerhall) as well as some twenty apartments of up to nine rooms each, but the residents had already been evicted, the storefronts emptied, and the building earmarked for Soviet trade unions when the Cheka swooped in. In 1920, an internal prison was outfitted here (later it would be enlarged, when two stories were added to the building). "From the outside it looks like anything but a prison," one cellmate reported. The Cheka also appropriated additional nearby buildings and as a result, wrote one observer, it "occupies a whole neighborhood in the center of the city . . . here are located the endless administrative sections and subsections: 'secret operations,' 'investigation,' 'statistical,' 'data and graphs,' and other functions. . . . It is an *entire city within the city*, working . . . day and night."[102]

Lubyanka, 2 was effectively subordinated not to the civilian government, but to Lenin and the politburo, which meant that this instrument, too, fell under Stalin's purview in his capacity as head of the party apparatus.[103]

The Cheka's staff was smaller than it seemed.[104] As of March 1921, Lubyanka, 2, budgeted for 2,450 staff, yet managed to hire just 1,415, with genuine operatives composing only about half that total, although by January 1922, the central staff had grown to 2,735, a number it would more or less maintain. As of November 1923, the secret police also commanded 33,000 border troops, 25,000 internal order troops, and 17,000 convoy guards.[105] The number of secret informants on the rolls declined from a reported 60,000 in 1920 to 13,000 by the end of that year.[106] Provincial Cheka branches varied in the size of staff, with around 40 total people in most cases, only half of them operatives, to cover vast swaths of territory with often limited transportation options. The Cheka relied on its fearsome reputation. *Pravda* carried reports of Cheka victims being flayed alive, impaled, scalped, crucified, tied to planks that were pushed slowly into roaring furnaces or into containers of boiling water. In winter, the Cheka was said to pour water over naked prisoners, creating ice statues, while some prisoners were said to have their necks twisted to such a degree their heads came off.[107] True or not, such tales contributed to the Cheka mystique. But if an unsavory reputation served as a force multiplier, it also provoked revulsion.[108] In May 1919, on Dzierżyński's initiative, the Cheka was ordered to report weekly to the-then newly established orgburo—that is, to Stalin. Dzierżyński was added to the orgburo in 1920.[109] Dzierżyński also named the operative Mikhail Kedrov to head a commission that traveled the country by armored train to root out Cheka impostors and malfeasance. But sadists and riffraff who got purged for discrediting the regime turned up elsewhere in different regional branches. Kedrov, a half-trained physician and virtuoso pianist, was himself notorious for butchery, and was said to have briefly sought psychiatric care.[110]

The Cheka made no bones about using the tsarist inheritance of prisons, rebuilding, for example, the tsarist-era Verkhne-Uralsk "Isolator" expressly for "politicals." Rumors circulated that the Cheka ranks overflowed with veterans of the hated *okhranka*, which was false—the Cheka mounted manhunts for them—but damaging to its reputation all the same.[111] Whatever operatives' origins, "people are beginning to look upon us as *okhranniki*," fretted a Cheka deputy chairman, the Latvian known as Mārtiņš Lācis.[112] Nor did it help reputationally that a substantial proportion of Soviet Russia's jailers, interrogators, and executioners were non-ethnic Russians, often Poles and Jews, a circumstance derived partly from the categories of those who had been oppressed under tsarism, and partly from methods of recruitment (Jews and Poles recruited their own).[113] Proposals to curb Cheka abuses and authority were under discussion throughout 1921—after all, the civil war had been won, so why were the secret police continuing to carry out summary executions? Kamenev, the leading politburo proponent of a police overhaul, told a meeting of metalworkers that year that "there are people who justly hate the Lubyanka."[114] He proposed limiting the Cheka's writ to political crimes, espionage, banditism, and security on railroads and at warehouses, while ceding everything else to the justice commissariat. Lenin supported Kamenev.[115] So did Stalin. Dzierżyńsk balked at relinquishing the Cheka's expansive extrajudicial powers.[116] But Lenin held his ground, and on February 6, 1922, the Cheka was replaced by the so-called State Political Administration (GPU), with functions that were duly circumscribed, albeit not to the full degree of Kamenev's proposal.[117]

Conversion to the GPU was not enacted in February 1922 in the South Caucasus, where the threat of uprisings was deemed too great, indicating that the reform was intended as a genuine reduction in power, but this intention would be subverted, and by Lenin himself.[118] On February 20, 1922, he wrote to the justice commissar demanding a "strengthening of the repression against political enemies of Soviet power and the agents of the bourgeoisie (in particular the Mensheviks and Socialist Revolutionaries)," and urged "a series of demonstration trials" in the big cities, "exemplary, noisy, educational trials," with "an *explanation* of their significance to the popular masses through the courts and the press."[119] There had already been various public trials, from that of Countess Sofia Panina (1918) to cases involving the State Bank, the state department store, the textile trust, as well as some staged in the worker-saturated Donbass to rally the proletariat and send a shot across the bow of non-party economic managers.[120] But this latest trial was the biggest to date. Lenin, in Gorki, despite his stroke in May 1922, examined the arrest dossiers.[121] From June 8 to August 7, 1922, thirty-four putative members of the Right Socialist Revolutionary Party stood in the dock in the Hall of Columns of the House of Trade Unions. Every one had been imprisoned by the tsarist regime for revolutionary activity, but now, according to Pravda, they were "traitorous lackeys of the bourgeoisie." The GPU used captured archives of the SR Central Committee to try to authenticate the charges. (Dziga Vertov made a propaganda film, The SR Trial.)[122] Grigory "Yuri" Pyatakov, the presiding judge, handed down predetermined death sentences.[123] But an uproar arose abroad, and Kamenev found a clever compromise, proposing the executions be stayed for the time being but be implemented in the event of further "criminal" actions by the SR party.[124] Sitting in Lubyanka, the death-row SRs in effect became hostages.[125]

Lenin's crusade against fellow socialists vitiated the police reform. In August 1922, the GPU obtained the formal power to exile or sentence people to a labor camp without trial or court conviction, and by November was granted this prerogative even for cases lacking a specific anti-Soviet act, solely on the basis of "suspicion."[126] A subversion of secret police reform would likely have happened in due course anyway: a siege mentality was baked into Bolshevism, and the GPU occupied the same building as the Cheka, with the same personnel.[127] Still, Lenin personally also forced through the deportation in fall 1922 of theologians, linguists, historians, mathematicians, and other intellectuals on two chartered German ships, dubbed the Philosophers' Steamers. GPU notes on them recorded: "knows a foreign language," "uses irony."[128] A far larger number of what Pravda (August 31, 1922) called "ideological Wrangels and Kolchaks" were deported internally to remote labor camps, such as Solovki, officially the Northern Camps of Special Designation, at the site of a former monastery on an island in the White Sea.[129]

The ideologized class division of the world empowered the secret police without end. "Those elements we are dispatching or will dispatch are in themselves politically worthless," Trotsky told a leftist foreign journalist, Louise Bryant, widow of John Reed, who published the interview in Pravda (August 30, 1922). "But they are potential weapons in the hands of our possible enemies. In the event of new military complications . . . we would be compelled to shoot them according to the regulations of war." Here is the view later attributed to Stalin that the Soviets could not tolerate *potential* enemies in their midst, because their presence would encourage and facilitate foreign intervention.[130]

Stalin was inundated with materials from the secret police. The GPU claimed in the mid-1920s to have more than 2 million Soviet inhabitants under permanent watch.[131] The *okhranka* had produced the "tsar's briefing" (*tsarskii listok*), a compilation of observations concerning "the opposition," as well as natural disasters, explosions, and sensational non-political crimes, which was issued weekly and added up to as many as 600 pages annually, and which Nicholas II read and marked up. But the Soviet secret police compiled extensive summaries of the political mood (*svodki*) far more regularly, relying upon informants from nearly every institution and settlement, down to villages.[132] Around 10,000 people were also engaged in perlustrating mail for the Soviet state, compared with 50 for the tsarist state in 1914.[133] Each copy of the secret police mood summaries was numbered, and sent to Lenin and Stalin, Trotsky and his deputy Sklyansky at the military, but not to Zinoviev or Kamenev, though the latter soon were included.[134] Additionally, however, Stalin, in the name of the Central Committee, pursued special firsthand reports outside normal channels, recruiting his own networks of informants.

## BLACKSMITH BRIDGE AND HOTEL LUX

Down the street from GPU headquarters at Lubyanka sat the enormous premises of the foreign affairs commissariat, at Blacksmith Bridge, 15. The name (*Kuznetskii most*) was derived from a long gone stone crossing over the long ago filled-in Neglinnaya River. Before the revolution, the elegant street had been known for fashion houses, bookshops, photography workshops, and restaurants, and the commissariat's home was an opulent, semineoclassical, six-story accordion of a building built in 1905–6 with two symmetrical wings, and seized from the All-Russia Insurance Company in 1918.[135] It had resplendent residences (Yagoda, a deputy chief of the GPU, happened to live here) as well as offices. Among tsarist-period ministries after the coup, foreign affairs underwent the greatest turnover as the diplomatic corps filled with a combination of returning old Bolshevik émigrés and young firebrands. "Well, what are we Soviet diplomats?" Leonid Krasin liked to say. "I'm an engineer, Krestinsky, a teacher. That's what sort of diplomats we are." The Soviets refused to use the "bourgeois" term "ambassador" and called their envoys "plenipotenitiary representatives," but in 1923 the foreign affairs commissariat distributed to envoys abroad "Short Instructions on following the rules of etiquette observed in bourgeois societies."[136] Pyotr Voikov, the envoy to Poland, even tried to impress upon fellow young diplomats the value of ballroom dancing. "He said, for instance that the greatest diplomatic victories had been won in conservatories," one pupil recalled. "I will not quote the examples he cited in support of this astonishing theory; it is enough to say that the most recent example he cited referred to the Congress of Vienna" of 1815.[137] As of 1924, when the commissariat numbered 484 persons in positions of responsibility, fully 33 percent were university graduates, a far greater proportion than in the central party apparatus.[138] Fewer than half of commissariat personnel were ethnic Russians.[139]

Not far from Blacksmith Bridge was the Hotel Lux, at Tverskaya, 36, known, not without irony, as the "headquarters of world revolution" after it was given over to the Comintern. It was the place where every affiliated party could be criticized—except one.[140] For the Third World Congress of the Comintern (June-July 1921), the Lux housed some 600 delegates from fifty-two countries in its small rooms.[141] The premises were honeycombed with undercover GPU agents who enticed or entrapped foreigners into informing on one another. Contacts with Soviet inhabitants would become strictly regulated.[142] Still, the Lux had art deco elegance to go with hot water once a week. Comintern offices proper were located elsewhere, in the two-story mansion that had belonged to the sugar baron Sergei Berg and had served as the inaugural German embassy (where Mirbach had been assassinated) on Money Lane. In 1921, when Lenin summoned Otto Kuusinen (b. 1881), the former chairman of the Finnish Social Democrats and the founder of the Finnish Communists, from Stockholm to untangle the mess of day-to-day Comintern operations as general secretary, the Finn, in turn, engaged a personal assistant, Mauno Heimo (b. 1896), who arrived in Moscow in 1924 and took over day-to-day Comintern operations. "There is no proper organization in the Comintern and you and I must create one," Kuusinen was said to have told him. "There is no proper staff and no proper delineation of responsibilities. Fifteen hundred people are being paid for their work, but no one knows who his superior is or what authority he has or what he is actually supposed to be doing."[143] Heimo's first order of business was to procure better premises. He lit upon Mokhovaya, 6 (also known as Vozdvizhenka, 1), a five-story building just outside the Kremlin's Trinity Gates-Kutafya Tower.[144] On the building's inaccessible top (fifth) floor, the GPU held sway, overseeing the real work: illegal money transfers to foreign Communist parties, forged visas, and stolen foreign passports doctored for reuse.

Comintern funds invariably vanished, presumed stolen; it was also rumored to be penetrated by foreign intelligence. Other Soviet agencies tended to despise the organization ("thousands of Comintern parasites were on the Soviet payrolls," noted one Soviet intelligence operative).[145] "To understand the workings of the Comintern one must realize two things," wrote Kuusinen's wife: "Firstly, it was always being reorganized, and secondly, a great deal of activity was fictitious."[146] Foreign affairs commissar Chicherin pushed to separate the functions of his commissariat and the Comintern, which he would call his "internal enemy No. 1" (the "GPU hydra" only got second place). But none other than he had issued the invitation to the Comintern's founding congress in 1919, where he was a delegate.[147] Although only Comintern agents were supposed to conduct illegal work abroad, in practice, embassy personnel did so as well.[148] Comintern personnel (known as "foreigners") usually had offices under flimsy cover right inside Soviet embassies, which also housed the GPU ("close neighbor") and military intelligence ("distant neighbor"). Moreover, the public rhetoric of top Soviet officials, including politburo members who sat on the Comintern executive committee, nearly always aligned with "the oppressed" against the governments of putative diplomatic partner countries. Still, the foreign affairs commissariat issued endless memoranda reminding the politburo that the Comintern's high profile and the GPU's summary executions reduced the Soviet room for maneuver internationally: foreign governments did not trust such a regime to engage in legitimate business, and if they did take the risk, invariably a scandal broke apart about underhanded Soviet-Comintern machinations.

Beyond Moscow's two-faced foreign policy, aiming to foment revolution in the very countries they were trying to have normal relations and trade with, lay the debilitating class-based worldview. Lenin argued that the international "bourgeoisie" could never accept the permanent existence of a workers' state, but the truth was the opposite: although Western hostility toward the Soviet regime was often intransigent and some Western individuals were committed to Soviet overthrow, Western *government* hostility was mostly "sporadic, diffused, disorganized," as George Kennan explained. He added that while "many people in the Western governments came to hate the Soviet leaders for what they *did,*" the Communists "hated the Western governments for what they *were,* regardless of what they did."[149] Thus, Moscow could view a Labour government and a Tory government as in essence identical: both imperialist and, therefore, both perfidious. Entente hostility toward Soviet Russia, in other words, no more caused Bolshevik Western antagonism than Entente accommodation would have caused a friendly, hands-off Bolshevik disposition. Lenin argued that if capitalists accommodated the Soviet regime on something, it was only because they had been forced to do so, whether by their own workers' militancy or their dependence on chasing new markets (such as Russia's).[150] Stalin accepted this line in toto, and explained that when the moment was propitious, the capitalists would intervene militarily again, aiming to restore capitalism.[151] In the meantime, in negotiations for new trade deals and long-term credits, the capitalists invariably demanded repayment of repudiated tsarist-era state debt and compensation for nationalized foreign-owned property as a precondition.[152] Although Lenin allowed the foreign affairs commissariat to announce Soviet readiness to enter into discussions about tsarist debts contracted before 1914, he would spurn the opportunities that would result.[153]

Prime Minister Lloyd George, a liberal in the classic nineteenth-century sense of laissez-faire and free trade, advanced the idea of an international conference to rehabilitate Russia and Germany in an improved peace settlement aiming at European economic reconstruction, which could profit Britain and perhaps shore up his fragile coalition government with a bold act.[154] In early 1922, the Soviets accepted an invitation to attend the conference, scheduled to open April 10 in Genoa, where thirty-four countries would be represented.[155] Lenin would not personally attend, allegedly out of security concerns (the Cheka reported that the Poles were planning to assassinate him in Italy); in fact, Lenin, after returning from exile in 1917, never left Russia again.[156] Still, he dictated the Soviet posture. When Foreign Affairs Commissar Georgy Chicherin, preparing for Genoa, inquired, "Should the Americans strongly press for 'representative institutions' do you not think we could, in return for some decent compensation, make some minor changes in our constitution?" Lenin wrote "madness" on the letter, had it circulated to the politburo, and added "this and the following letter show clearly that Chicherin is sick and very much so."[157] (The Americans ended up declining to attend Genoa.) "This is ultrasecret," Lenin wrote to Chicherin a bit later. "It suits us that Genoa be wrecked . . . but not by us, of course."[158] Whether in the end the political establishments of the great powers were ready for a full détente with Moscow remains uncertain.[159] But instead of their manifest ambivalence, Lenin saw a concerted attempt at a united capitalist front against the Soviets, even though this was a conference expressly designed to help Russia with diplomatic recognition and trade.[160]

Lenin was not alone in sabotaging Lloyd George's effort. French prime minister Raymond Poincaré, who did not deign to attend, forced the removal from the agenda of any opportunity for the Germans to discuss their reparation grievances. Poincaré viewed Lloyd George's effort to amend Versailles ("neither victors nor vanquished") as coming at French expense, but his hard-line strategy backfired. Back at Versailles in 1919, France had inserted a clause, Article 116, granting Russia—a post-Bolshevik Russia, it was assumed—the right to obtain German reparations for the war, and now the Soviets hinted they would do so. Walther Rathenau, the newly appointed German foreign minister, who was oriented toward rapprochement with the West, nonetheless felt constrained to order bilateral talks with Russia to remove the Article 116 sword of Damocles.[161] When rumors circulated that during the Genoa opening sessions the Soviets were engaged in separate Anglo-French talks in Lloyd George's private villa without Germany, Rathenau requested meetings with the British prime minister but was rebuffed. At 1:15 a.m. on April 16, the Soviets accepted the Germans' suggestion of a meeting that day.[162] Rathenau's staff again tried to alert the British, but Lloyd George's assistant did not take at least two calls. The British prime minister's diplomatic amateurism unwittingly amplified the French prime minister's unrealistic inflexibility as well as Lenin's ultrasecret treachery.[163] In the driving rain the German delegation drove over to the Soviet delegation at their Genoa quarters, the Hotel Imperiale, on the road between the small Ligurian seaside resort of Santa Margherita and the larger town of Rapallo, and by early evening that same day, Easter Sunday, a bilateral treaty was signed. Terms had been set out the week before in Germany (Chicherin had traveled to Genoa via Berlin), but only now did Rathenau agree to them.[164]

The Rapallo Treaty, for the second time, made Germany the first major power to formally recognize the Soviet state—the other had been the abrogated Brest-Litovsk Treaty—and this resumption of diplomatic ties came without the need for tsarist debt repayment or domestic concessions such as softening the Bolshevik dictatorship. The Germans accepted the validity of Soviet expropriations of German property, and the Soviets renounced all claims under Article 116. The two sides agreed to trade under what would later be called most-favored-nation status.[165] Rathenau, who in addition to his government post was the general director of AEG, the German electrical conglomerate, could well understand Russia's economic value as a supplier of raw materials to and a customer of Germany, especially with the New Economic Policy and restoration of the market. (Rathenau, the first Jew to serve as German foreign minister, would be assassinated by right-wing ultras within two months.) Rapallo reconfirmed the centrality to Bolshevik fortunes of Germany, and it seemed to preempt Lenin's suspicions of an across-the-board coalition of the powers against the Soviet regime. The French refusal to acknowledge German grievances, the British inability to tame the French, and the Soviets' manipulation of Article 116—a French invention— had led to France's nightmare and Lenin's fantasy: an apparent Soviet-German axis.[166] Rapallo was accompanied by rumors of secret protocols about military obligations amounting to an alliance, which Chicherin categorically denied in a note to France.[167] In fact, ties between the Red Army and the Reichswehr were already intimate and on August 11, 1922, the two countries signed a secret formal agreement on military cooperation. Obviating Versailles restrictions, the German army would obtain secret training facilities for its air and tank forces inside the Soviet Union, in exchange for Soviet access to German military industrial technology, in plants that were to be built on Soviet soil and supply each country's armed forces.[168] That, anyway, was the promise.

Lenin was running foreign affairs as a personal fief. He probably had more telephone conversations with Chicherin than anyone else, and considerable direct contact with him, too, but he treated his foreign affairs commissar like an errand boy. Even after the Rapallo Treaty, Chicherin and the Soviet delegation wanted to sign the Genoa agreement and began going slightly beyond their brief to discuss repudiated wartime debts, seeing no way to rebuild ravaged Russia other than with Western help, but Lenin condemned his negotiators for their "unspeakably shameful and dangerous vacillations."[169] In the event, no tsarist debts were repaid and no nationalized property compensated to the Entente, and as a result, no investment consortium for Russia was formed and no peace treaty with Russia signed.[170] Lenin believed that the capitalist powers would be compelled to revive the Russian economy by the logic of global capitalist development, and thus he had allowed the unique moment for a possible reintegration of Russia into the European community to be lost. (The next such gathering for the Soviets would be at Helsinki in 1975.) At the same time, the Weimar Republic and the Bolshevik dictatorship were not kindred regimes and their cooperation would be fraught as Germany continued to seek rapprochement with the West.[171]

How the Soviets would acquire advanced technology on a large scale remained hanging. Once Lenin became incapacitated, Stalin became the central figure in foreign policy, inheriting all these challenges of the intransigent Leninist legacy. In international relations, Stalin was anything but a dictator.

## OLD SQUARE, 8

When Stalin was handed the opportunity to build a personal dictatorship, not only did Lenin suffer a stroke, but Soviet Russia was prostrate, having lost millions of people to war, political terror, and emigration. The extreme dislocation was exacerbated by the orgy of Bolshevik grain requisitioning, then by a severe drought, intense heat, and hot winds that turned the black earth into a dustbowl. Sown area had already shrunk, but now 14 million of the mere 38 million acres sown failed to produce crops, causing a famine whose scale had not been seen since the eighteenth century. Peasants were reduced to eating poisonous concoctions boiled from weeds, ground bones, tree bark, or straw from their roofs, as well as dogs, cats, rats, and human flesh.[172] Upward of 35 million people suffered intense hunger—the entire Volga valley (the epicenter), the southern Urals and the Tatar and Bashkir republics, the North Caucasus, large parts of southern Ukraine, Crimea. An estimated 5 to 7 million people lost their lives between 1921 and 1923 from starvation and related diseases, amounting to 50,000 deaths per week.[173] In the worst famine-stricken areas, the GPU would post guards at cemeteries to prevent the starving from digging up corpses to eat. Just in the Volga valley and Crimea, the authorities registered more than 2 million orphans, miracle survivors, albeit often with hollow eyes, distended stomachs, matchstick legs.[174]

Lenin—having beaten back demands to repeal the NEP—now dispatched a food procurement plenipotentiary to steppe regions, which were put under martial law. When the plenipotentiary advised that fulfilling the grain quotas 100 percent would leave regions without even seed grain, he was ordered to proceed as originally instructed.[175] In early 1922, Lenin sent Felix Dzierżyński on a food expedition to Siberia, whose harvest, unaffected by the severe drought elsewhere, was more or less normal.[176] Dzierżyński lived in his train carriage, civil war style, writing to his wife Zofia Muszkat in despair of the enormity of the tasks and the inadequacy of his leadership as concurrent commissar of railroads ("Only now, in winter, do I clearly understand the need to prepare in summer for the winter"). His stay was prolonged—it was while Dzierżyński was in Siberia, on February 6, 1922, that the Cheka had been abolished and replaced by the GPU—and eye-opening. "The Siberian experience has demonstrated to me the fundamental shortcomings of our system of management," he wrote his wife again in February. "Even the best thoughts and directives from Moscow do not make it here and hang in the air."[177] The GPU, meanwhile, reported out of one Siberian province (February 14) that "abuses by procurement agents reach utterly stunning proportions. . . . Everywhere arrested peasants are locked in icy granaries, flogged with whips [nagaiki] and threatened with shooting." Peasants, fleeing to the woods, were "chased and trampled upon with horses first. Then they were stripped naked and shut in granaries with no heat. Many women were beaten unconscious, buried naked in the snow, raped."[178]

Fixated on extracting food for its hungry northwest cities, the regime's response to the rural regions in starvation had been slow and ineffective.[179] Lenin refused to seek help from "imperialist" governments, but the exiled writer Maxim Gorky, with Lenin's connivance, issued a private appeal to "all honorable persons," and Herbert Hoover, the American secretary of commerce, replied affirmatively just two days later. Hoover (b. 1874), the son of a Quaker, had been orphaned as a child, had gone on to be part of the inaugural graduating class of Stanford University as a mining engineer, and during the Great War had founded the American Relief Administration (ARA), initially a government agency that was converted into a private body with government funding. In heeding the summons to help Soviet Russia, he laid down two conditions: that American relief personnel be allowed to operate independently, and that U.S. citizens in Soviet prisons be released. Lenin cursed Hoover and acceded. In a monumental triumph of philanthropy and organization, Hoover mustered more than $60 million worth of foreign food support, primarily in the form of corn, wheat seeds, condensed milk, and sugar, much of it donated by the United States Congress, some of it paid for by the Soviet regime with scarce hard currency and gold (melted down from confiscated church objects and other valuables). Employing 300 field agents who engaged up to 100,000 Soviet helpers at 19,000 field kitchens, the ARA at its height fed nearly 11 million people daily.[180] Gorky wrote to Hoover that "your help will enter history as a unique, gigantic achievement, worthy of the greatest glory, which will long remain in the memory of millions of Russians . . . whom you have saved from death."[181]

Stalin applied pressure on the foreign affairs commissariat to look after foreign grain purchases, and took part in instituting surveillance of foreign aid workers.[182] He also proposed that the ARA be charged for the cost of transporting its emergency food supplies on Soviet territory.[183] Thanks to the foreign donations and the purchases abroad of seed grain, as well as a return of favorable weather and peasant survival instincts, the 1922 harvest turned out to be robust. Additional alleviation was provided by the belated effects of the New Economic Policy's incentives for peasants, so that from 1923 a recovery commenced.[184] The regime, grudgingly, played a part, too. It passed the Land Code, which forbade the sale and purchase of land and restricted the legality, and to an extent the reality, of land leasing and the hiring of non-family farm labor, but it allowed peasants legally to grow any types of crops, raise any type of livestock, and build any type of structures on the land; women were recognized as equal members of the peasant household. Above all, the Land Code allowed peasant households to exercise real choice in legal land tenure: communal-repartitional, collective farm, even consolidated homesteading (i.e., Stolypinism).[185] The Land Code did not use the term "commune," substituting instead "land society," but the regime was compelled to acknowledge that the commune had self-governing authority.[186] The regime also found itself compelled to drastically reduce financial support for collective farms, which shrank to an even smaller part of the arable land (under 1 percent). The turnabout was stunning: peasants, whether communal-repartitional or homesteader, obtained far-reaching economic freedom.

The size and timely collection of the harvest remained the key determinant of the country's well-being, and the peasant revolution that paralleled the Bolshevik seizure of power was strong enough to reshape the Soviet state. The civil war commissariat of food supply, the "requisitioning commissariat," yielded its predominant position to the agriculture commissariat, a kind of "peasants' commissariat" inside the proletarian dictatorship. Punctuating the shift, Alexander Smirnov (b. 1898), a party loyalist with a practical bent, was shifted from deputy food supply commissar to deputy agriculture commissar, on his way to assuming the top position in 1923. The "requisitioning commissariat" had been located at the Upper Trading Rows right on Red Square; the "peasants' commissariat" was located, of all places, at Old Square—N. 8, just down from Communist party HQ—in the former Boyarsky Dvor Hotel and business complex built in 1901–3 in art nouveau style.[187] In the famine, agricultural commissariat personnel found a raison d'être, concluding that peasant farming was perpetually on the edge of the abyss because peasants were ignorant of modern farming's best practices.

Therefore, peasants needed to be educated by agronomists and other specialists.[188] The agriculture commissariat would grow into the regime's largest, with
more than 30,000 staff in central and regional offices, plus another 40,000 working on forestry. This eclipsed in size even the internal affairs commissariat, that
is, the combined regular police-GPU, as well as the second biggest—the finance
commissariat.[189]

## ILINKA, 9

That a finance commissariat existed under a Communist regime was a surprise.
During the civil war the regime had collected no taxes, funding itself by confiscating grain and other goods and printing paper money.[190] Confusion enveloped
the country's monetary base. The populace still used *nikolaevki* (rubles under
Nicholas II), *dumskie* (rubles associated with the Duma period), and *kerenki*
(rubles under Kerensky and the Provisional Government), which the Soviet
regime itself printed for a time without the crown on the double-headed eagle, as
well as foreign currency, which circulated illegally and at ever steeper exchange
rates.[191] The Whites in territories they controlled had accepted Soviet-printed
*kerenki,* but not Soviet rubles (*sovznaki*) on which the Whites stamped "money
for idiots."[192] The resulting runaway inflation made vodka a major means of
exchange and store of value, as barter took over the economy. Things were not as
bad as Weimar Germany's hyperinflation, where the Mark went from 60 to $1 in
1921 to 4.2 trillion to $1 two years later, but a top tsarist-era economist estimated
that between 1914 and 1923 the ruble depreciated by 50 million times.[193] Some
Bolshevik fanatics asserted that the hyperinflation constituted a form of class
war, and one called the printing presses the "machine-gun of the finance commissariat." Ideologues also asserted that the "end of money" marked an advance
in the stages of civilization, toward Communism.[194] But by 1924, the Soviet currency would be stabilized and the economy remonetized, a stunning turn of
events achieved by a rebuilt finance commissariat.

The finance commissariat had seized the grand premises of the Moscow offices
of the expropriated St. Petersburg International Bank, at Ilinka, 9. The street's
name derived from an ancient monastery named for Ilya (Elijah) the Prophet, but
Ilinka was jammed with enclosed trading rows, banks, and exchanges, and had
served as prerevolutionary Moscow's financial hub inside the walled commercial

quarter known as Kitaigorod. Also situated on Ilinka were the foreign trade commissariat (N. 14) and the workers' and peasants' inspectorate, which Stalin had merged with the party's Central Control Commission (N. 21), where many a Communist was summoned to be disciplined. The Red Army, besides its main complex at Znamenka, had seized a second structure for the army political administration, Ilinka, 2, the former wholesale Middle Trading Rows, right near Red Square, where it would publish its newspaper *Red Star*. Ilinka connected Old Square and Red Square, and was the street Stalin walked down every day to and from work with his party comrades who also lived in Kremlin apartments. Without the macroeconomic achievements of Ilinka, 9, Stalin would not have enjoyed the stability that rescued the Soviet regime and enabled him to concentrate on building his personal dictatorship. The finance commissar was Grigory Sokolnikov (b. 1888), who had replaced the hapless Nikolai Krestinsky in 1922, not long after Stalin had filled Krestinsky's former position atop the party apparatus.

Sokolnikov had a spectacular revolutionary biography.[195] He grew up in bourgeois privilege in a Moscow Jewish family: his father, a physician, owned a building where the family occupied eight rooms on the upper floor and operated a lucrative pharmacy on the ground floor. Grigory, their eldest son, had German and French governesses, attended a classical gymnasium in the Arbat neighborhood (with Nikolai Bukharin and Boris Pasternak), and joined the Moscow Bolsheviks in 1905 (he may have derived his *nom de révolution* from the city's Sokolniki ward). He ended up in Siberia, then in foreign exile, where he completed a doctorate in economics at the Sorbonne. Sokolnikov returned to Russia on the sealed train with Lenin and in July 1917 was elected to the small Bolshevik Central Committee, working closely with Stalin as one of the key editors of the party press and taking part in the key votes in favor of a coup, which he helped carry out.[196] Afterward, Sokolnikov oversaw bank nationalization.[197] He replaced Trotsky as head of the Brest-Litovsk delegation, at age twenty-nine, and signed the treaty.[198] During the civil war, despite lacking formal military training, Sokolnikov served not as a political commissar but as a commander, earning an Order of the Red Banner.[199] In 1920, Stalin requested that Sokolnikov be dispatched to him on the southern front against the Poles.[200] Instead, Sokolnikov was given charge of reconquered Turkestan, where, as we saw, he organized a counterinsurgency and introduced the NEP tax in kind earlier than would be done in the country as a whole, legalized private markets, and carried out a monetary reform.[201] In Moscow, following surgery in Germany (he had a liver condition, among other ailments), Sokolnikov relied on a team of prerevolutionary financial professionals, forced through a restoration of the State Bank, and prevented the deportation of Professor Leonid Yurovsky, who spearheaded the creation of a new currency called the chervonets, a "hard" ruble to be limited in the scale of issue and backed by gold bullion and foreign reserves.[202] Sokolnikov supplemented the chervonets with gold coins issued with a portrait of the murdered Nicholas II.

Sokolnikov achieved his macroeconomic reforms in the face of widespread resistance and incomprehension in the party.[203] Hard currency and gold reserves had essentially been depleted to finance emergency grain imports, but the good harvest of 1922 allowed renewed exports, which delivered a shock windfall that rebuilt gold reserves from 15 million gold rubles in January 1923 to 150 million a year later, and enabled the takeoff of the chervonets.[204] Regular Soviet rubles (*sovznaki*) underwent three bouts of replacement at severely depreciated levels, while the chervonets grew to around 80 percent of the currency in circulation.[205] Sokolnikov enforced balance of payments discipline as well, and by 1924 the Soviets would manage a trade surplus.[206] Sokolnikov oversaw introduction of a regular budgetary system, with revenues from customs duties, transport, and especially direct taxation (the agricultural tax in kind, an income tax), but also new excise taxes on common items such as matches, candles, tobacco, wines, coffee, sugar, and salt. Taxing salt had been abolished as far back as 1881, making its revival by Sokolnikov extraordinary. The regime, in 1923, also reintroduced the monopoly on vodka sales (the tsars' derided "drunken budget"), bringing in significant revenues.[207] The GPU undercut Sokolnikov's work—the politburo approved Dzierżyński's proposal to expel all "speculators," including currency dealers, from Moscow and other big cities—but Sokolnikov fought back.[208] "The more financing your operatives receive," Sokolnikov is said to have told Dzierżyński, "the more manufactured cases there will be."[209] The industrial lobby, too, battled Sokolnikov tooth and claw, claiming that his tight money was strangling Soviet industry.[210] But Sokolnikov gave no quarter, taunting them by declaring, "Money-printing is the opium of the economy."[211] Mikhail Lurye, known as Yuri Larin, a pundit, charged in 1924 that the finance commissariat was imposing its own "dictatorship."[212] In effect, Sokolnikov helped teach Stalin macroeconomics, the relationship between the money supply, inflation, balance of payments, and exchange rates. Stalin backed him.[213]

## "UNDER STALIN'S WING"

Stalin's power flowed from attention to detail but also to people—and not just any people, but often to the new people. The Society of Old Bolsheviks came into being on January 28, 1922, and Stalin spoke at their inaugural meeting.[214] Members had to have joined the party before 1905 and expected recognition of their hard labor stints and exile under tsarism and their seniority. But though the regime resolved to reserve the position of provincial party secretaries for party members who had joined at least before the February Revolution, in practice the guideline was violated. Old Bolsheviks were proportionally overrepresented in administration, but in a preponderance of lower-level posts, the politburo excepted.[215] The Old Bolsheviks, especially those who had lived in European emigration, often looked askance at the newcomers as crude simpletons, but the latter viewed the Old Bolsheviks as suspiciously bourgeois. Each group had gone through the same civil war experience and the younger ones came out confident they did not need to know multiple foreign languages or be university educated to get things done. Stalin, although of course an Old Bolshevik himself, favored the upstarts. Many came from the workers and the peasants, but far from all.[216] Fully one quarter of party members as of 1921 *admitted* to white-collar origins. These were not, however, predominantly figures who had served in tsarist institutions; many were products of the February Revolution, having joined various bodies of the Provisional Government. After October, they grafted themselves onto the new regime.[217] "The new political elite was not predominantly proletarian in origin," one scholar has written. "It was, however, predominantly plebeian."[218] The revolution was carried by the partially educated who often continued to study at night after long hours on the job.[219] Stalin identified with them; they were younger versions of himself. Still, the people closest to him presented an eclectic mix.

The most important was Vyacheslav Skryabin (b. 1890), better known as Molotov ("the Hammer"), perhaps the regime's first pure apparatchik (Krestinsky had concurrently been party secretary and finance commissar). The son of a shop clerk, he had managed to enroll in the St. Petersburg Polytechnic Institute, but joined the party and became an editor of *Pravda* after it was briefly legalized. In 1915, he adopted his party pseudonym, later explaining that "Molotov" was easier to pronounce than "Skr-ya-bin" for someone who stuttered, as he did, and that "Hammer" sounded proletarian, industrial, and could impress workers, who did not overly love party members of the intelligentsia.[220] (Molotov, like Lenin, preferred a bourgeois suit and tie.) Like Stalin, Molotov had spent some time in prerevolutionary exile in Vologda, where he earned his keep by playing violin in a restaurant to entertain drunken merchants. He and Stalin may have first met in St. Petersburg, in 1912, at a dentist's quarters that doubled as a safe house.[221] Elbowed from the top position by Stalin twice (in 1917 at *Pravda* and in 1922 at the party secretariat), Molotov could have nursed a grudge and connived to undercut Stalin. Instead, he hitched his wagon to the Georgian, acceding to Lenin's wishes and Stalin's eleven-year seniority. Trotsky mocked Molotov as "mediocrity personified," but Lenin, intending a compliment, called his protégé "the best filing clerk in Russia."[222] Boris Bazhanov, who worked in the apparatus in the early 1920s, also came away impressed. "He is a very conscientious, not brilliant but extremely industrious bureaucrat," he wrote of Molotov. "He is calm, reserved. . . . With everyone who approaches him he is correct, a person utterly approachable, no rudeness, no arrogance, no bloodthirstiness, no striving to humiliate or crush someone."[223] Bazhanov's words said as much about Bolshevik political culture as about Molotov.

Valerian Kuibyshev (b. 1888), an ethnic Russian and native Siberian, was from a hereditary military family. He studied at the Omsk Cadet School, then moved to the capital to enter the Military Medical Academy, but in 1906 was expelled for political activity and fled likely arrest. He managed to enter the Tomsk University Law Faculty but left after a year, went into the Bolshevik underground, and was arrested and exiled numerous times, including to Narym (from 1910) and Turukhansk (from 1915), places where Stalin had been exiled. Kuibyshev was a practiced musician like Molotov and a poet like Stalin. He took part in the 1917 Bolshevik coup in the Volga city of Samara and during the civil war served on the southern front, and then had a commanding role in the reconquest of Turkestan. Precisely when he first caught Stalin's eye remains unclear. Stalin made him a full member of the Central Committee and a Central Committee secretary in 1922. In late 1923, Stalin named him the head of the party's Central Control Commission, which had been established as a neutral court of appeal, but under Stalin became a bludgeon to punish party members.[224] Kuibyshev viciously went after local resistance, perceived and real, to central directives and lined up officials behind Stalin in the regions and the center.[225] Trotsky dubbed Kuibyshev "the foremost violator and corruptor of party statutes and morals."[226] Kuibyshev's loyalty to Stalin was absolute.[227] He also appears to have played a role in bringing to Moscow yet another indispensable functionary in Stalin's faction—Lazar Kaganovich.

Kaganovich (b. 1893) hailed from a village in the tsarist Pale of Settlement near the small town of Chernobyl, and embodied the rough plebeian cohort. His father was an uneducated farm and factory laborer; his mother gave birth to thirteen children, six of whom survived. Lazar spoke Russian and Ukrainian, with a smattering of Yiddish, and he briefly attended a heder attached to a synagogue. But his family could not afford to educate him and he apprenticed to a local blacksmith, then moved to Kiev and joined one of his brothers at a scrapyard. At age fourteen, Kaganovich started laboring at a shoe factory—what Stalin might have become, had he had fewer options in Gori and Tiflis—joined the party in 1912 in Kiev, fought in the Great War, and, following the Bolshevik coup, in January 1918, as a twenty-four-year-old went to Petrograd as a Bolshevik delegate to the Constituent Assembly.[228] During the civil war, he served in Nizhny Novgorod and Voronezh, where Trotsky's people predominated. But during the controversy over trade unions, Kaganovich, then a trade unionist, sided with Lenin against Trotsky. Just two months after Stalin became general secretary, Kaganovich was hired in the central apparatus and put in charge of the Organization and Instruction Department, which soon absorbed the Records and Assignment Department—and would oversee the nomenklatura system. Kaganovich's attachment to the charismatic Trotsky may have extended beyond the civil war (according to an aide in the apparatus, Kaganovich "for a rather long time tried to look like Trotsky. Later everyone wanted to copy Stalin").[229] But soon he would infuriate Trotsky with slashing ad hominem attacks. He was indisputably proletarian and, like Stalin, distrusted intellectuals and "bourgeois specialists."[230] Kaganovich was a fine speaker and natural leader, with immense energy and organizational muscle. "He is a lively fellow, no fool, young and energetic," wrote Bazhanov.[231] In 1924, Stalin made Kaganovich a Central Committee secretary.[232]

Stalin's faction had tentacles around the country. He picked up a number of loyalists united by their common service, whether former or current, in Ukraine, the key republic after Russia. Other figures around him hailed from the Caucasus: the Georgian Orjonikidze (b. 1886), party boss in Georgia; the Russian Sergei Kirov (b. 1886), party boss in Azerbaijan; and the Armenian Anatas Mikoyan (b. 1895), party boss in the North Caucasus. Another figure who ended up close to the dictator was Mikhail Kalinin (b. 1875), three years Stalin's senior, who had similarly spent time in the Caucasus during the underground years.[233] Stalin got his civil war loyalist Klim Voroshilov named head of the North Caucasus military district (1921–24); he turned out to be the only loyalist from the Tsaritsyn "clan" who remained close to Stalin.[234] Other figures from the civil war–era southern front—above all, those associated with the First Cavalry Army—would see their fortunes rise with Stalin, including the First Cavalry commander Semyon Budyonny as well as Alexander Yegorov. Still, in the early 1920s, Molotov, Kuibyshev, and Kaganovich constituted the innermost core of Stalin's political clan. Observers began to say these men walked "under Stalin's wing" (*khodit' pod Stalinym*).[235]

Stalin's team of aides was highly capable. Amayak Nazaretyan, the ethnic Armenian, was the son of a merchant, had studied at (but not graduated from) the law faculty at St. Petersburg University and was judged to be "a very cultured, clever, well-meaning and well-balanced man," as well as among the very few, like Voroshilov and Orjonikidze, who addressed Stalin by the familiar "thou" (*ty*).[236] Additionally, there was Ivan Tovstukha (b. 1889), who had studied abroad and resembled a professorial type; in the Parisian emigration he gave lectures on art to a group of Bolsheviks at the Louvre. (Stalin is supposed to have told him, according to Bazhanov, "My mother kept a billy-goat who looked exactly like you, only he didn't wear a pince-nez.")[237] After the revolution Tovstukha worked for Stalin in the nationalities commissariat, and in 1922, immediately upon becoming general secretary, Stalin brought him into the party apparatus. Known to be taciturn, Tovstukha had tuberculosis and only one lung, but he would soon replace Nazaretyan as Stalin's top aide.[238] Stalin also brought in the Odessa native Lev Mehklis (b. 1889), the scion of a minor tsarist official and himself a prerevolutionary member of the Paole Zion party. Mekhlis came over from the workers' and peasants' inspectorate, which Stalin nominally headed; there, Mekhlis had overseen reductions in state employees and expenditures, especially of hard currency, and fought against embezzlement, bragging on a 1922 questionnaire how he had "straightened out the [state] apparatus."[239] Mekhlis moved into House of Soviets no. 1 (on Granovsky), one notch down from a Kremlin apartment. He was severe and unsocial. "Conversations between Mekhlis and his subordinates went like this: 'Do the following. Is that clear? Dismissed.' Half a minute," the apparatchik Balashov recalled. Whereas Stalin addressed Tovstukha respectfully, he tended to be abrupt with Mekhlis. "Stalin could say, for example, 'Mekhlis, matches!' or 'Pencils!'" Balashov observed. "Not to Tovstukha. [Stalin] was very respectful toward him, listened to him. [Tovstukha] was a reserved person, dry, spoke little, but very smart. He was a good leader." But although "Mekhlis had a difficult personality," Balashov concluded, "Stalin valued him for such qualities, believing that Mekhlis would implement any assignment, no matter what."[240]

Countless new people entered Stalin's circle in these early years, some who would fall by the wayside, some who would make remarkable careers, such as Georgy Malenkov (1902–1988), the son of a railroad civil servant, an ethnic Macedonian, who studied at a classical gymnasium and then at Moscow Technical College, and Sergei Syrtsov (b. 1893), who hailed from Ukraine, joined the party at the St. Petersburg Polytechnique (which he did not finish) and served as a political commissar in the civil war responsible for forcible deportation of Cossacks. Syrtsov also participated as a 10th Party Congress delegate in the crackdown against Kronstadt in 1921, and was appointed head of personnel in the Central Committee apparatus that same year before being moved to head of agitation and propaganda in 1924.[241] Stalin's apparatchiks included Stanisław Kosior (b. 1889), whom the general secretary appointed party boss of all Siberia, Andrei Zhdanov (b. 1896), who got Nizhny Novgorod province, and Andrei Andreyev (b. 1895), whom Stalin kept in the central apparatus as a Central Committee secretary. These and other examples show that Stalin promoted not only the uneducated. This especially applied to the worldly Sokolnikov, a master of the Russian language, as well as six foreign languages, and an accomplished musician, who was a genuine *intelligent,* the opposite of Kaganovich (who had worked under Sokolnikov in Turkestan).[242] But Sokolnikov, no less than Kaganovich, was an extremely effective organizer.[243] Sokolnikov helped transform Lenin's NEP from a slogan into a reality, and yet Lenin, typically, disparaged him.[244] Stalin, however, was solicitous. True, Sokolnikov lived outside the Kremlin (he and his young third wife, a writer, had an apartment in the secondary elite complex on Granovsky), but in 1924, Stalin would elevate Sokolnikov to candidate member of the politburo.

## LOOKING FOR LEVERAGE

Many appointments Stalin had not made. Georgy Chicherin (b. 1872), for example, an aristocrat and a distant relative of Alexander Pushkin, was a Lenin appointee.[245] It was Chicherin, not Stalin, who was the regime's original night owl: he lived in an apartment adjacent to his office at Blacksmith Bridge, 15, and worked through the wee hours, being known to telephone subordinates at 4:00 or 5:00 a.m. to request information or convey directives. (To wind down, Chicherin played Mozart on the piano.) For leverage, Stalin looked to Chicherin's principal deputy, Maxim Litvinov (b. 1876), who despite being from a wealthy banking family in Bialystok, as a Jew had been refused admission to gymnasium and then university.[246] Litvinov never became reconciled to the fact that Chicherin, who had joined the Bolsheviks only in January 1918, rather than himself, an original member of the Russian Social Democrats dating to 1898, had been named foreign affairs commissar. (Both men had been in London when the summons to Chicherin came).[247] Lenin told Litvinov he was an indispensable "party militant" in the commissariat, and Litvinov did carry a certain confidence based on his long-standing party service.[248] But he was also perceived as suspicious and mistrustful, angling to advance himself, given to putting on airs yet suffering an inferiority complex, craving to be liked, manipulative.[249] His antagonism with Chicherin became legendary. "Not a month would go by without my receiving a note marked 'strictly confidential, for politburo members only,' from one or the other of them," the inner-sanctum functionary Bazhanov wrote. "In these notes Chicherin complained that Litvinov was rotten, ignorant, a gross and crude criminal who should never have been given diplomatic duties. Litvinov wrote that Chicherin was a homosexual, an idiot, a maniac, an abnormal individual."[250]

The politburo required Chicherin to bring Litvinov to its sessions on Western issues, and as a counter Chicherin elevated Lev Karakhanyan, known as Karakhan, an Armenian born in Tiflis (1889), as his deputy for the East.[251] Karakhan had belonged to Trotsky's group of internationalists, joining the Bolsheviks with him in the summer of 1917, and initially Stalin pushed to replace the Armenian, insisting that the regime needed a Muslim more amenable to Eastern peoples. Soon, however, Stalin's correspondence with Karakhan would become obsequious. ("How's your health and how are you feeling? You must miss [the USSR]. . . . Don't believe Japanese diplomats for a second; the most treacherous people. . . . My bow to your wife. Greetings. I. Stalin. P.S. So far I'm alive and healthy. . . ."). Karakhan answered in kind ("I grasp your hand. With heartfelt greetings. Your L. Karakhan"). It seems that Karakhan ingratiated himself with Stalin, who, in turn, was on the lookout for his own person inside the commissariat. But Litvinov, too, competed for that role by conspicuously aping Stalin's views.[252] This dynamic could be seen all across the Soviet system—Stalin looking for personal animosities to manipulate to his benefit; officials appealing for his favor against political rivals.

## SECRET WEAPON

Three men formed the inner core of the Cheka-GPU, and each would develop close relations with Stalin. First was Dzierżyński, who had been born in 1877 near Minsk in the borderlands of Lithuania-Belorussia, one of eight children in a family of Polish nobility landowners. He was orphaned, and zealously studied for the Catholic priesthood.[253] "God is in my heart!" he is said to have told his elder brother. "And if I were ever to come to the conclusion, like you, that there is no God, I would shoot myself. I couldn't live without God."[254] As a schoolboy, he converted to Marxism, was expelled two months before graduation from the Wilno gymnasium and, in his own words, became "a successful agitator" who "got through to the utterly untouched masses—at social evenings, in taverns, and wherever workers met."[255] But he ended up spending eleven years all told in tsarist prisons, in internal exile, and at hard labor in penal colonies, and he became consumptive.[256] "His eyes certainly looked as if they were bathed in tears of eternal sorrow, but his mouth smiled an indulgent kindness," observed the British sculptor Clare Sheridan, who in 1920 made a bust of him. (Dzierżyński told her that "one learns patience and calm in prison.")[257] Dzierżyński had a certain political vulnerability, having joined the Bolsheviks only in April 1917 and then opposed Lenin over Brest-Litovsk (1918) and trade unions (1921), but he won plaudits as the scourge of counterrevolutionaries and for living like a revolutionary ascetic, sleeping in his unheated office on an iron bed, subsisting on tea and crusts of bread.[258] He reported to Lenin personally and once Lenin became incapacitated, got still closer to Stalin. Stalin was neither threatened by Dzierżyński nor fully dependent on him for secret police favors.

Wiaczesław Mężyński, another Pole, had become Dzierżyński's first deputy and, because his boss was simultaneously railroad commissar (and from 1924 would concurrently chair the Supreme Council of the Economy), ran the secret police. He had been born in St. Petersburg, the son of a Polish nobleman and teacher who converted to Eastern Orthodoxy, and graduated from the St. Petersburg law faculty.

He lived in European emigration for 11 years, working as a bank clerk (in Paris) or teaching at a Bolshevik school (in Bologna), while painting and publishing sonnets. In Smolny in 1917 he was said to play Chopin waltzes on the grand piano of the former girls' finishing school, and came across as a banker or a dandy in his three-piece suit. After his brief stint as the original commissar for finance and then some diplomatic work—Mężyński knew a dozen or so languages—Dzierżyński promoted him in the Cheka, considering him unfailing in operational instincts.[259] The two lived in the Kremlin and had dachas near each other in Arkhaneglskoe (Gorki-6). Legends about Mężyński abounded: that he conducted interrogations lying on a settee draped in Chinese silks, dyed his finger- and toenails red, wore gold-framed pince-nez, and married a former governess to the Nobel family (she left him and took the children). Lenin called him "my decadent neurotic."[260] In fact, Mężyński did receive people while lying on a couch. An automobile accident in Paris had severely damaged his hearing and nerves, leaving him with degenerative osteoarthritis of the spine. In addition, he had contracted scarlatina and diphtheria in his youth and typhus at age 28, and suffered acute angina, arteriosclerosis, an enlarged heart, migraines, breathing arrhythmia, and an infected kidney. He stood 5'9" but weighed 200 pounds, smoked 50 to 75 cigarettes daily, and managed no more than 5 hours of sleep because of insomnia.[261] Although Mężyński had warned Trotsky during the civil war about Stalin's incessant intriguing behind Trotsky's back, Stalin and Mężyński, both former poets, got along. In any case, Mężyński's profusion of ailments rendered him unthreatening, while enabling Stalin to work around him.

The most consequential official in the secret police for Stalin was Jenokhom Jehuda, better known as Genrikh Yagoda, which he pronounced Yagóda, although Stalin cheekily called him Yágoda (berry). (Maxim Gorky would call him "Little Berry" [Yágodka]). Yagoda had been born in 1891 to a Polish-Jewish family in Yaroslavl province, one of eight children, but the next year his family settled in Nizhny Novgorod; his father was a jeweler, his mother, the daughter of a watchmaker. Yagoda's father was a cousin of Yakov Sverdlov's father. The young Yagoda studied at gymnasium, learning German and statistics, but in 1907 became active in revolutionary politics, mostly as an anarchist. One of his sisters was an anarchist and a pharmacist's apprentice and he apprenticed for six months as a pharmacist in 1912; that May he was arrested in Moscow, apparently for theft and fencing stolen goods, including weapons and dynamite. Yagoda also apprenticed as an engraver to Sverdlov père, and was rumored to have stolen all the tools, set himself up on his own, failed, come back and apologized, and then did it all over again. In the Great War he was conscripted (one of his brothers was executed for refusing to serve), and in 1915 he married a niece of Sverdlov's, who provided his future entrée into the regime: He became head of the Cheka business directorate in November 1919, though in his party autobiography he stressed his military exploits "on almost all the fronts," with "the most varied duties, up to shooting."[262] In late 1920, Yagoda was granted the right to sign directives in Dzierżyński's absence. In September 1923, he became second deputy GPU chairman, filling the vacuum created by Dzierżyński's multiple responsibilities and Mężyński's illnesses. Yagoda, no master of foreign languages, made his mark in economic management and intrigue.[263] Direct reports from him to Stalin date from summer and fall 1922, a circumstance reflecting Stalin's new position as general secretary, but also Stalin's cultivation of police operatives.[264]

Yagoda became Stalin's secret weapon, but the dictator took no chances. He cultivated Yagoda's enemies inside the secret police, such as Artur Fraucci. The latter had been born (1891) in Tver province to an ethnic Italian cheesemaker father from Switzerland and an Estonian-Latvian mother, becoming fluent in German and French and graduating from gymnasium with a gold medal, after which he completed the St. Petersburg Polytechnique. Fraucci went often to the opera to hear the basso Fyodor Chaliapin, and he himself could sing as well as play the piano and draw. He had gotten into the Cheka through connections (one of his mother's sisters married Mikhail Kedrov), changed his name to Artur Artuzov (easier on the Russian ear), and was handed counterintelligence in July 1922.[265] At Lubyanka HQ, struggles often took place among rival Cheka clans as much as against "counters" (counterrevolutionaries), and Artuzov and his professional staff disdained Yagoda and his people for their limited counterintelligence tradecraft. (Never mind that Polish intelligence, which knew Soviet personnel and Russian-Soviet police methods intimately, penetrated Soviet intelligence.)[266] Besides Artuzov, Stalin had a close relationship with Józef Unszlicht, who would run military intelligence.

Yagoda also made it easy for Stalin to manage him by his high living and compromising activities. Yagoda complained to the ascetic Dzierżyński that police officials had "no money or credit, no foodstuffs, no uniforms, the most necessary things are lacking," leading to "demoralization, bribe-taking and other flowers blooming luxuriantly on this soil." Karelia, Yagoda noted, lacked even stationery to write about the lack of everything.[267] But Yagoda himself took up residence in the elite building at Blacksmith Bridge, which he had reconstructed at state expense, acquired an immense dacha complex, and convoked GPU meetings over crêpes and caviar washed down with vodka in private apartments. He also built up a coterie of shady characters. In one case, more than 200 bottles of confiscated brandy and rum vanished from the care of one of Yagoda's bagmen.[268] An even more notorious associate, Alexander "Sasha" Lurye, fenced "confiscated" valuables abroad in exchange for hard currency, nominally on behalf of the GPU, gave Yagoda a cut from his diamond business, and procured fine foreign wines and dildos. Yagoda acquired the foul odor of a *commerçant*, and his ultimate boss, Stalin, could closely track the disreputable machinations by the likes of Lurye—it was dictator's insurance.

## "THE POINT IS ABOUT LEADERSHIP"

Which brings us to the regime's focal point, the dictator himself. Stalin's character would become a central factor in world history, an outcome that would color all assessments. One scholar observed characteristically that a "politics of permanent emergency" generated by war, revolution, and civil war proved well suited to Stalin's personal qualities. True enough, but this was applicable to the vast majority of Bolsheviks.[269] Retrospective "insight" into Stalin's character can be deeply misleading. He identified himself the way most top revolutionaries did: In 1920, in the space provided for "profession" on a party questionnaire, Stalin had inserted "writer (pundit) [*publitsist*]."[270] Lenin, on a similar party questionnaire the year before, had written "man of letters" [*literator*]; Trotsky, when admitted to the Society of Former Political Prisoners, gave as his profession "writer-revolutionary."[271] (Of course, writing and editing were among the few legal activities for revolutionaries in tsarist Russia.) But while Stalin was proud of his immersion in the Marxist and Russian intelligentsia traditions, he was also a self-styled *praktik*: a practitioner, a doer, the closest a non-proletarian revolutionary could get to assuming the identity of a proletarian. That said, Stalin returned again and again to the touchstone of Lenin's writings. The fundamental fact about him was that he viewed the world through Marxism.

Probably the most pervasive characterization of Stalin, particularly among intellectuals, pegged him for an inferiority complex. "Because of his enormous envy and ambition," Trotsky would assert, "Stalin could not help feeling at every step his intellectual and moral inferiority."[272] Trotsky would gather every morsel of hearsay that depicted Stalin's inferiority. "I am doing everything he has asked me to do, but it is not enough for him," Avel Yenukidze said, according to Leonid Serebryakov, who told Trotsky, "He wants me to admit that he is a genius."[273] But how well Trotsky understood Stalin remains doubtful. The two did not socialize. ("I was never in Stalin's apartment," Trotsky admitted, which, however, did not inhibit his assurances that he had Stalin figured out.)[274] Beyond doubt, Stalin possessed a searing ambition to be a person of consequence; indeed, he worked at it relentlessly. Stalin subscribed to a substantial number of periodicals, and soon he would instruct Tovstukha to organize his enormous library according to sub-jects: philosophy, psychology, sociology, political economy, Russian history, his-tory of other countries, diplomacy, military affairs, belles lettres, literary criticism, memoirs. This was not for demonstration but for work.[275]

Assertions regarding Stalin's sense of inferiority reveal at least as much about others' sense of superiority—and not just in the case of Trotsky. Consider Boris Bazhanov, who had a university education and possessed an exalted sense of self, and who after having emigrated would belittle Stalin's intelligence, observing that "very often he didn't know what to do or how to do it, but he didn't show it. I often saw him hesitate, preferring to follow events rather than direct them." Supposedly, this behavior demonstrated that Stalin was uneducated, uncultured, unread.[276] And yet, in an interview, Bazhanov condescendingly ended up putting Stalin's circumspect inclinations in a positive light. "Stalin had the very good sense never to say anything before everyone else had his argument fully devel-oped," Bazhanov said. "He would sit there, watching the way the discussion was going. When everyone had spoken, he would say: Well comrades, I think the solution to the problem is such and such—and he would then repeat the conclu-sions towards which the majority had been drifting. And, as time passed, it came to be said of Stalin that . . . he had a fundamental wisdom of sorts which led him to propose the right answers to difficult questions."[277]

Episodes that show Stalin in an ungenerous light are many, but scarcely remarkable. Consider the following: Lenin perhaps did his intellectual nemesis Yuly Martov an unintended favor in late 1920 by denying him reentry to Soviet Russia after he had attended a conference in Germany, thereby allowing Martov to avoid a future trial that would befall the Mensheviks. As it happened, Martov had consumption and two years later Lenin requested that Stalin transfer party funds to pay for Martov's medical care in Berlin. Stalin, no doubt remembering Martov's accusations of banditry in 1918, which resulted in a court case for libel, refused. "What, start wasting money on an enemy of the working class?" Stalin is said to have answered Lenin. "Find yourself another [party] secretary for that!"[278] Martov died on April 4, 1923; Rykov attended the funeral in Berlin on behalf of Lenin. But this can hardly be cited as evidence of Stalin's special penchant for vengeance. Stalin was far from alone in his ill will toward Martov. Radek, who wrote the obituary for *Izvestiya,* dismissed Martov as "the most sincere and selfless representative of the once revolutionary petit-bourgeoisie."[279] Trotsky was no kinder, calling Martov "the Hamlet of democratic socialism."[280] Martov's critics from the right, including the Constitutional Democrats, even his own Menshevik party, correctly accused him of having been doctrinaire and politically myopic.[281] And Lenin, Martov excepted, pursued not just the political but the physical extirpation of the Menshevik Social Democrats.

Stalin played favorites, warming to some, intriguing against many. (Budyonny, the Red cavalry commander, recalled that Stalin would privately bring up doubts about this or that person whom Budyonny had appointed.)[282] But in the early 1920s, there is no hard evidence of epic depravity. Trotsky related the following anecdote, evidently from 1922, attributed to Bukharin: "I have just come from seeing Koba. Do you know how he spends his time? He takes his year-old boy from bed, fills his own mouth with smoke from his pipe, and blows it into the baby's face. 'It makes him stronger,' Koba says. . . . 'That's barbaric,' I said. You don't know Koba. He is like that—a little peculiar."[283] This story rings true, but it would be read in a more sinister light only later. According to a high official of the food supply commissariat, Lenin said to him in a meeting in 1921, "When I look you in the eyes, you seem to agree with me and say 'yes,' but I turn away and you say 'no.'"[284] Had this anecdote been told about Stalin, it would be taken as prime evidence of clinical paranoia.

A very few people figured Stalin out early on. "Am I satisfied with my work?" Amayak Nazaretyan wrote to his close friend Orjonikidze (June 14, 1922) back in Tiflis. "Yes and no. On the one hand, I have gone through a grand school and course of all Russian and world affairs, I am going through a school of discipline, learning exactitude in work, and from this point of view I am satisfied. On the other hand, the work is utterly paper-oriented, laborious, subjectively little-satisfying, manual labor, swallowing so much time that it's impossible to sneeze and breathe, especially under the iron hand of Koba." Nazaretyan added that "there is much to learn from him. Getting to know him close-up, I have developed unusual respect for him. He has a character that can only be envied. I cannot take offense. His severity is accompanied by attention to the staff."[285] Nazaretyan had caught Stalin to a T: both solicitous and demanding, and above all doggedly hardworking. That was not all. "He is sly," Nazaretyan wrote in another letter to Orjonikidze (August 9, 1922). "Hard like a nut, you do not crack him open right away."[286] Stalin's enemies, predictably, viewed his combined solicitude-slyness in dark terms.[287]

Stalin could be very closed and inaccessible, yet he could also switch on the charm, and he proved to be a loyal patron to those "under his wing."[288] Mikoyan, who had met Stalin in 1919, captured well the impression Stalin made on those he favored. Mikoyan would recall how in 1922, when he was serving as party boss in Nizhny Novgorod, Stalin summoned him to his Kremlin apartment in connection with regional delegate elections for the 11th Party Congress—and how Lenin walked right in. "Stalin gained in my eyes," Mikoyan recalled. "I saw that he was the right hand of Lenin in such important internal party matters." In summer 1922, Stalin transferred Mikoyan to head the party's southeast bureau (headquartered in Rostov). "After the 11th Party Congress Stalin energetically started to gather cadres, organize and rotate them in the provinces and in the center," Mikoyan continued. "And I liked what he did, as far as I knew, and what was connected to my work." Stalin quickly grasped the concerns Mikoyan brought and never once rejected one of the provincial's recommendations. "All this strengthened my trust in Stalin and I started to turn to him often and during my trips to Moscow I would visit him." Mikoyan added that "Stalin at that time worked with all his strength. . . . He was in top form, which elicited respect, and his manner and behavior elicited sympathy."

Mikoyan—manifestly ambitious—was clearly paying close attention, from his own careerist calculations, to a rising political force. "In spring 1923, I think in May, being in Moscow, I stopped by his apartment," he continued. "He lived then in the first building to the right from the Kremlin's Trinity Gate, on the second-floor of a two story building. The rooms were simple, not especially expansive, except for the dining room. His office was very small." (Later, when Stalin upgraded his Kremlin residence and moved Mikoyan to Moscow, he gave him this apartment.) "Stalin exited his home office with his arm in a sling. I saw this for the first time and, naturally, inquired what was the matter." Stalin: "My arm hurts, especially in spring. Rheumatism, it seems. Eventually it'll go away." Stalin's arthritic problems had likely begun in childhood and worsened over time, especially during his Siberian exile; the periodic flaring was accompanied by quinsy and flu.[289] (In 1904, when Stalin was twenty-six, the tsarist police noted "a distinctive trait: the movement of his left arm is circumscribed as a result of a long-ago dislocation." This was clearly recorded from Stalin's own words.)[290] When Mikoyan asked why Stalin did not seek treatment, he answered: "And what will doctors do?" But Mikoyan consulted with physicians and managed to get Stalin to go south for treatment under the care of physicians, beginning in 1923, at the medicinal baths near Matsesta.[291] The sulfur waters worked, alleviating the pain in Stalin's joints, and he started to holiday down south every year. "Stalin liked Sochi so much," Mikoyan concluded, "he went there even after he no longer needed to go to the Matsesta baths."[292] (In fact, the aches persisted.)

Another privileged gathering place was Stalin's dacha outside Moscow. This country home in Usovo on the left bank of the Medvenka River had belonged to Levon Zubalov [Zubalashvili], one of four brick dachas the now deceased Baku oil magnate had built on an expansive plot of land for himself and family members, in thick woods behind high brick walls.[293] The main house (designated Zubalovo-4) had two stories; Stalin and his wife had separate rooms on the upper floor, where Stalin also had an office. Nadezhda (b. 1901), or Nadya in the diminutive, his second wife, whom he had bounced on his knee when she was a toddler and wed when she was a teenager, worked in Lenin's secretariat. She wanted a career, not to be known as the wife of the ruler, but she suffered severe headaches and down moods.[294] The lower floor was used by a constant stream of relatives and hangers-on: the extended clans of the Alliluyevs as well as the Svanidzes (the family of Stalin's deceased first wife), with broods of sisters-in-law, brothers-in-law, and spouses. The same year that Vasya was born, Stalin's abandoned son from his first marriage, Yakov, then fourteen, was sent from Tiflis to live with him in Moscow. Stalin had abandoned him to be raised by his mother's sister and uncle in Georgia; the move to Moscow was a difficult transition, given that he did not know Russian or, for that matter, his father. Stalin treated Yakov with hostility, calling him "my fool" in front of others, perhaps partly because he reminded his father of the lovely Georgian wife he had lost. For a time, the Stalin household had another young member, Artyom Sergeyev, who had been born nineteen days after Vasya in the same hospital, and whom Stalin took in after the boy's father, a close civil war comrade, died in the crash of an experimental high-speed railcar fitted with an aircraft engine.

Zubalovo was located a good eight miles beyond Moscow and lacked a direct road; in winter one needed chains on a vehicle's wheels or an auto sled (a car body with tank treads). Stalin traveled out infrequently, mostly on Sundays. Still, the dacha had a player piano, left over from the old Zubalov days—miraculously, it still functioned—which Stalin enjoyed, being exceedingly fond of music. Also, he tended a vegetable garden on the grounds, as well as geese, chickens, guinea fowl, and a small apiary. From the nearby state farm he occasionally borrowed a horse-drawn sled—like scenes from Chekhov, one of Stalin's favorite authors. "In the evenings," Artyom recalled, "Stalin really loved to ride the sleds."[295] Here was a Stalin few saw. Trotsky's dacha—known as Headquarters—was grander, located just north of Moscow in the settlement of Arkhangelskoe at the nationalized Yusupov Palace, an estate formerly owned by the Golitsyns and before that the Sheremetevs, where the art still hung on the walls: Tiepolo, Boucher, Fragonard; it was not known as a social gathering spot. By contrast, the Orjonikidzes and, later, Sergei Kirov, perhaps Stalin's closest friend, would visit Stalin at Zubalovo. The Mikoyans and their four boys would occupy an even larger Zubalovo dacha (Zubalovo-2), where the Voroshilovs also obtained a dacha.[296] Stalin would sometimes arrive at Zubalovo in a dark mood, however, and set to quarreling with Nadya. Their marriage was strained over different conceptions of the wife's role.

Lidiya Fotiyeva, under whom Nadya worked, recalled Stalin's wife as being "very beautiful" and having "Georgian eyes" (her grandfather was Georgian), but Fotiyeva also noted that "Stalin was very rude with her," although he did not raise his voice ("Stalin always spoke softly"). While Nadya was working in Lenin's secretariat, Stalin sometimes had her take his own dictation, too, but mostly he wanted her to play hostess to his guests at their apartment. When she was pregnant with Vasya (1920–21), Stalin became determined that she quit her work outside the home. Fotiyeva claimed that when she reported Stalin's pressure on Nadya to quit to Lenin, he asked to be kept informed; when Stalin backed down, Lenin nonetheless remarked, "Asiatic." On December 10, 1921, eight months after Vasya's birth, Nadya—the wife of a politburo member and a personal secretary to Lenin—was expelled during a party purge for political "passivity."[297] She wrote an appeal to Lenin. Who would have had the temerity or the power to purge her? Only one person, who was evidently trying to force his wife back into the home. Lenin dictated a note over the telephone to the head of the party's Central Control Commission urging Nadya's reinstatement.[298] Nadya was restored to candidate status, but regained full membership only in 1924.[299] She would take up secretarial work at *Revolution and Culture*, part of *Pravda*'s publishing empire, not wanting to be known or treated as the general secretary's wife. Nadya could be extremely difficult, prone to migraines and depression. At the same time, Stalin was a self-centered, patriarchal husband and poor father.

This, then, was the person at the center of the regime in the early 1920s: personable yet secretive, charming yet dissembling, solicitous yet severe, sociable yet malevolent toward the wife who sought his love. But within the "family" of apparatchiks, Stalin was the supreme patron. "Notwithstanding all his intelligent wildness of disposition, if I may use such an expression," Nazaretyan concluded of Stalin's peculiarities, "he is a soft person, has a heart, and is capable of valuing the worth of people."[300] Ultimately, what stood out most about Stalin was his command inside the apparatus. "Working alongside Stalin was not easy, especially for the leaders of the secretariat and the closest aides," recalled Alexei Balashov, a functionary. "Very great tension was felt around him. . . . You had to work round the clock, without exaggeration, going home only to sleep." They all became exhausted, and dreamed of getting leave to study. One time, according to Balashov, they held a meeting of what they called the "true Leninists"—otherwise known as the 20—and "Stalin said, 'Comrade Dzierżyński, [Grigory] Kanner here petitioned to be released to study. What do you think about that?' All the aides became intently quiet. 'That's terrific,' Dzierżyński answered, 'I have a free cell. Let him sit there and study.' We all went cold."[301] (Kanner, described as "a small man" who had "curly black hair" resembling "sheep's fleece," had joined Stalin's apparatus early in May 1922, and developed a reputation for getting tasked with the nastiest assignments.)[302] Balashov added that "there was no fear. There was respect for [Stalin's] tenacity, industriousness, and exactitude. I considered that there was a lot to learn from him on how to become a good leader-organizer."[303]

Balashov made an additional point, though: the general secretary lived inside the apparatus bubble. "I did not like that Stalin was an apparat functionary, an apparatchik," Balashov noted. "The management of the party and country flowed from us in chancellery fashion, without advice from the masses. Of course, he [Stalin] met with many different people, took part in meetings of village correspondents, for example, specialists. But that all happened in the office. It was as if people were smoking tobacco [*makhorka*] and nothing was visible in the smoke cloud."[304] But if Stalin had limited contact with the masses, he had an extraordinary degree of contact with young regime functionaries. Whereas Trotsky openly mocked functionaries for perverting the revolution, Bukharin later supposedly told the Menshevik Fyodor Dan that Stalin "is like the symbol of the party, the lower strata trust him."[305] Balashov, who was a Kaganovich protégé but who through an uncle saw Trotsky in private settings, noted that in all the years he (Balashov) worked in the central apparatus (1922–26), Trotsky showed up only once.[306] Stalin identified with these people, he listened to their concerns and, although perhaps not capable of genuine empathy, worked to enable mid- and lower-level functionaries to raise their abilities, to master Marxism and administration. Stalin developed a romantic view of the Soviet system that he would hold his entire life. "What must the dict[atorship] *of the party* signify?" he wrote in a copy of a 1923 work by Lenin. "A state power resting on force? No, that's rubbish! Unlimited rights by the party? Not that either! The point is not about rights, the point is about trust in the party, and trust does not at all presuppose unlimited rights of the party as its necessary condition. The point is about leadership."[307] Thrust into power, Stalin found himself on a lifelong quest not only for personal glory but also for deciphering the secrets to ruling over men and things in order to further Russian power in the world.

VOZDVIZHENKA AND THEN OLD SQUARE became the hub in the vast wheel of Stalin's kingdom. Like its imperial Russian predecessor, the Soviet state emerged as a labyrinth of patron-client relationships that cut across formal institutions. But Stalin's patron-client relations were strongly institutional: the Communist party machine, for all its inefficiencies and frictions, was something that the tsarist regime just did not have. Because of the party, the vast collection of personal followings that composed the party-state converged on a single person, the party's leader.[308] In a remarkably short time, Stalin had people everywhere that mattered, and the extent to which functionaries serving the cause understood themselves also to be serving him personally was extraordinary. People were surprised by this breathtaking power because they underestimated Stalin. But if such a degree of political control had been established that quickly even by a person immediately recognized as one of the great political figures of all time, it still would have surprised contemporaries. To be sure, the capacity of the dictatorship as of 1922–24 was limited, but it was greater than that of tsarism, for unlike the autocracy, the Soviet regime actively promoted mass mobilization on its behalf. And yet, the Soviet state, too, had failed so far to discover the secret to fully integrating the mobilized masses into an authoritarian polity.

The regime's political and even physical arrangements reflected the dual revolutions of 1917–18, Bolshevik and peasant, which faced each other warily. Additionally, the two governmental pillars of the New Economic Policy—at Old Square, 8 (agriculture) and Ilinka, 9 (finance)—flanked the central party apparatus. All three bodies were ensconced smack in the heart of Moscow's prerevolutionary commercial and financial quarter (Kitaigorod), and all three were architectural embodiments of merchant capital and aspirations. How cognizant Stalin was of being housed in Moscow's prerevolutionary capitalist epicenter, while running the Communist party and presiding over a Communist indulgence of capitalism (NEP), remains unclear. What is clear is that he was marinated in Communist ideology. Lots of regimes have a secret police and hunt for enemies. What differentiated this regime was its special single-party structure and a transcendent idea, the vision of a new world of abundance, social justice, and peace. Many were committed to building that world within the framework of the one-party system, but others became disappointed that that world had not yet materialized. Talk circulated of the New Economic Policy as a Thermidor, the French revolutionary name for the month of July, when, in 1794, a counterrevolution had occurred and the Jacobins were overthrown. To be sure, the Bolsheviks themselves had introduced the NEP and remained in power.[309] Still, some observers foresaw an inevitable forced denationalization of industry, with corresponding changes in the political system. The NEP, in such thinking, was merely the first concession.[310]

Lenin had confessed in November 1922 that "we still do not know where and how we must restructure ourselves, reorganize ourselves, so that after the retreat we may begin a stubborn move forward."[311] It would fall to Stalin to provide an answer. Before that, though, he had to deal with Trotsky. Every dictatorship needs a ubiquitous "enemy," who threatens it from within. For that role, Trotsky was tailor-made, a gift to Stalin, once he figured that out. It was not Trotsky, let alone Zinoviev or Kamenev, but Stalin's principal patron, Lenin—or at least, dictation attributed to Lenin—who would prove to be the gravest threat to the absolute power inherent in the general-secretary position, and to Stalin's psychic balance.

## CHAPTER 11

# "REMOVE STALIN"

> Comrade Stalin, having become general secretary, has
> concentrated boundless power in his hands; and I am not
> sure that he will always be able to use that power with
> sufficient caution.
>
> Dictation attributed to Lenin, given a date of December 24,
> 1922, and brought forward in late May 1923[1]

> Stalin is too rude and this defect, although quite tolerable
> in our midst and in relations among us Communists,
> becomes intolerable in a general secretary. That is why I
> suggest the comrades think about a way of removing
> Stalin.
>
> Dictation attributed to Lenin, given a date of January 4,
> 1923, and brought forward in June 1923[2]

STALIN FOUND HIMSELF in a position of supreme power before most people knew of him, let alone of his power. Trotsky, in fall 1922, seems to have been among the first to recognize how, with Lenin sidelined, Stalin held uncanny power. By summer 1923, Zinoviev and Bukharin, as we shall see, were stunned at how much wherewithal Stalin had to act. Examining the instruments at Stalin's command in the central apparatus, as we did in the last chapter, his path to absolute rule looks like a cakewalk. But even as the means to build a dictatorship within the dictatorship had fallen right into his hands, the most astonishing thing took place: Lenin appeared to call for Stalin's removal. Stalin's vast power fell under siege, just as he was energetically building it up. The general secretary's cakewalk was more like a treacherous bivouac through enemy territory.

Lenin's vexation by Trotsky was amply documented over a long period, but Lenin's alleged exasperation with Stalin emerged all of a sudden in cryptic documentary form, in spring and summer 1923. The centerpiece would become known as Lenin's Testament (*zaveshchanie*) and was brought forth by Lenin's wife, Nadezhda Krupskaya, with the assistance, or collusion, of the women working for Lenin, especially Maria Volodicheva and Lidiya Fotiyeva, the head of Lenin's secretariat. There are no extant originals of the most important documents attributed to Lenin (which had no such title as "testament," indeed no title at all when they first surfaced). Their authenticity has never been proven, as one Russian scholar has demonstrated in a scrupulously detailed examination. He argues, correctly, that unless persuasive documentary evidence comes forward corroborating Lenin's generation of this dictation, we must treat his authorship with caution.[3] That said, whether or not and, if so, in what form the documents might have derived from Lenin's own words, they became a reality in Soviet political life, and particularly in Stalin's life. We shall analyze the documents attributed to Lenin not by their alleged dates of dictation, but by the dates and the context in which they were brought forth, and above all, by their consequences. Their key phrase—"remove Stalin"—would eventually haunt Soviet Eurasia and the world beyond, but in the first instance would haunt Stalin himself.

Developments in 1922–23 were quite bizarre. The trigger of Stalin's potentially mortal political troubles turned out to be none other than Georgia, the homeland he'd left behind but had colluded in reconquering for the Bolshevik regime. The specific event in Georgia that set in motion a vast wheel of intrigues in Moscow against Stalin's continuation in the position of general secretary of the Communist party was a slap in someone's face. Stalin had no role in that act—he was busy with the herculean task of forcing into being a functioning state out of the loose, ambiguous, hardly even confederal structures among the various Soviet republics that had emerged from civil war. His mastery of the complex national brief, not just his position as general secretary, remained a key source of his supremacy. But not long after the heavy assignment of banging together what would become the Union of Soviet Socialist Republics, Stalin got caught up in a delirious plot by Zinoviev to instigate a "German October," or Communist coup, in the one country across the entire hostile capitalist world that had already promised the Soviet Union clandestine military cooperation and technology transfer. Moreover, the Soviet regime, claiming to perceive a "revolutionary situation" in Germany, was itself beset by waves of strikes by the workers in whose name it ruled.[4] And the New Economic Policy, expected to bring recuperation, brought a confounding gulf between prices in the country-side for foodstuffs and prices for manufactures made in the towns. All the while, Lenin was suffering a succession of massive strokes.

Often this period is narrated in terms of the formation of a ruling triumvirate of Stalin, Kamenev, and Zinoviev arrayed against Trotsky. There is truth to this, even though, for many years, the erroneous judgment held sway that Stalin was the junior partner. But the triumvirate against Trotsky was shadowed by the circumstance that even as it was getting operational, a conspiracy took place against Stalin, initiated by Zinoviev and Bukharin, with the latter trying but failing to serve as self-appointed go-between between Zinoviev and Trotsky. The triumvirate narrative should not be allowed to eclipse the far more important story: namely, the attempts in the Bolshevik inner circle to overcome the unforeseen yet inbuilt structural circumstance of the ability of the party's general secretary to build a dictatorship within the dictatorship. Those efforts, in turn, generated a new reality, overlaid on the first: Stalin's sense of grievance and betrayal. If in the previous chapter, wielding the levers of power, he came across as charming and confident, if occasionally peculiar, in this chapter, battling Zinoviev, Trotsky, and especially the dictation attributed to Lenin, Stalin will come across as distrustful and self-pitying, a potentate who viewed himself as a victim.

The life of the Communist—congresses, Central Committee plenums, politburo meetings (Stalin's life)—did not encompass even a fraction of rank-and-file party members, let alone define the rhythm of life in the vast country. To most peasants, who continued to compose the overwhelming majority of the inhabitants, the party was just a greedy adversary, concealing its tax-collecting and conscripting activities behind elaborate rhetorical camouflage. (Party meetings were closed to the public, not least for fear that non-party people would lash out at members from the floor.) Peasants were preoccupied with surviving the famine and tilling the land; with the size and health of their herds, if they had them; with weeds and weather; obtaining and maintaining their implements; warding off disease and rodents; making sure their spouses did not all of a sudden seek to take advantage of new Communist laws on divorce. The land of socialism was a hardscrabble one, struggling to emerge from devastation. Soviet per capita income in the early 1920s, at least in terms of recorded economic activity, was probably no more than around 70 rubles, annually. What follows, therefore, is not a portrait of the life of the country, which Stalin viewed mostly through the twisted top secret reports brought to him by telegraph and field courier, but a portrait bookended by the formation of the USSR and a would-be "German October," of a dictatorship with circumscribed capacities but grandiose ambitions, and of a man at the center of it all who was skillfully enlarging those dictatorial state capacities while constantly glancing over his shoulder.

## UNION OF SOVIET SOCIALIST REPUBLICS—AND A SLAP IN TIFLIS

The grand story of the formation of the USSR is saturated in misapprehension, with Lenin cast as defender of the nationalities and Stalin as Russian chauvinist and archcentralizer.[5] Stalin did propose forging a unitary state by having the Russian Soviet Federated Socialist Republic (RSFSR) absorb the other Soviet republics, but he also proposed granting them "autonomy" in most domestic affairs, and initially Lenin had accepted Stalin's plan. Trotsky's reaction had been similar: "Comrade Stalin's proposal presents itself as very alluring from the point of view of simplicity."[6] This framework gained impetus in mid-1922, when Georgian Communists permitted the Ottoman Bank, funded by British and French capital, to open a branch in Tiflis, inciting an angry Grigory Sokolnikov, finance commissar for Soviet Russia, to demand the bank's charter for operations in Georgia be rescinded, which in turn provoked the fury of the Georgian Communist Central Committee.[7] But could the genie of national states unleashed by the Great War really be put back in the bottle? Stalin thought so.

As head of an orgburo commission on state structure, Stalin drafted theses calling for "unifying [the Soviet republics] in a single federation, folding in military and economic matters and external connections (foreign affairs, foreign trade) into one whole, keeping for the republics autonomy in internal affairs."[8] But the formal proposal for the RSFSR to absorb Ukraine, Belorussia, Georgia, Armenia, and Azerbaijan was accepted only by the Central Committees of Azerbaijan, which faced an Iranian state that used to rule it, and Armenia, which faced Turkey, where Armenians had been massacred. The Georgian Central Committee agreed solely to "the unification of economic strength and general policy, but with the retention of all the attributes of independence." The Belorussian Central Committee requested the same treaty relations as currently existed between Soviet Ukraine and Soviet Russia—ambiguity cum de facto independence—while the Ukrainian Central Committee did not even discuss the new draft.[9] Only an extraordinary effort by an extraordinary figure was going to produce a functioning integrated state.

Stalin's most dogged opponent initially was the-then head of Ukraine's government, Kryasto Stanchev, known as Cristian Rakovski, a respected official whose calls for the weakest possible central authority amounted to confederation. Stalin would not be so easily stopped, however: on September 23 and 24, while Rakovski and others happened to be on holiday, he had the commission approve his plan for a unitary state with autonomy.[10] The Moscow party secretariat immediately circulated the paperwork to the members of the Central Committee of Soviet Russia even before the politburo had met. Stalin also privately lobbied Lenin on the extreme urgency of his plan, noting that the RSFSR apparatus found itself constantly revisiting decisions of the republics, while republics protested the "illegal" interference of Soviet Russia. He presented a stark choice: either genuine independence ("a divorce"), "or the real unification of the Soviet republics into one economic whole with formal extension of the powers of the Council of People's Commissars, Council of Labor and Defense, and central executive committee of the RSFSR over [those] of the independent republics." The latter, he noted, would still retain "real autonomy . . . in the areas of language, culture, justice, internal affairs, agriculture." Stalin warned Lenin that "independentists among the Communists," emboldened by "Moscow's liberalism" during the civil war, would only grow if not brought to heel.[11] Lenin received Stalin's letter on September 25, after the orgburo commission had approved it. The next day, Stalin went out to Gorki for a long private meeting. He would never again visit Gorki (Lenin returned to Moscow the next week.) By one account, Stalin was observed departing Gorki in bad temper.[12]

Lenin nixed the idea of the unitary state, instructing Stalin to switch from "enter" the RSFSR to "formal unification together with the RSFSR in a Union of Soviet Socialist Republics of Europe and Asia." Lenin's counterproposal presupposed that the units, including Soviet Russia, would be equal members, and that as more countries underwent socialist revolutions, they could join the federation as well. Stalin conceded the change, allowing Lenin to crow to Kamenev that day about "the significance of [Stalin's] concession."[13] Lenin insisted that the RSFSR central executive committee of the Soviet not become the one for the single state, contradicting Stalin, but Lenin also proposed having Union commissariats where Stalin had proposed republic-level ones (finance, food, labor).[14] Moreover,

Lenin, in the way he behaved as head of the RSFSR government, taking decisions for all the Soviet republics, was hardly a genuine federalist.[15] But in the letter to Kamenev, Lenin insisted that "it is important not to give grist for the mill of the 'independence lobby,' not to destroy their independence, but to create a new level, a federation of equal republics." Stalin, however, also felt the issue involved principle, complaining that in Lenin's plan, some republics—Ukraine, Belorussia—were being treated equally with Russia but others, the various autonomous republics currently inside the RSFSR, were not. He argued that his plan of autonomy for *all* the national republics was actually fairer, which certainly held for Bashkiria, Tataria, or Turkestan, which in Stalin's scheme would be equal to Ukraine or Belorussia. At the same time, in Stalin's version the Russian republic would be the mother ship, which was Lenin's objection.

Lenin had never set foot in Georgia, or even Ukraine, for that matter; Stalin had far greater firsthand experience of the varied realm, and, while cognizant of the need to indulge nationalism in order to secure political allegiance, recognized a state need to tame nationalism. Unlike Lenin, who viewed Georgians as a small-nation victim of imperial Russia, Stalin knew that Georgian national chauvinism oppressed the other peoples of the Caucasus.[16] More than that, Stalin rightly suspected the Georgian Communists' agenda was really de facto Georgian independence through mere confederation. Polikarp "Budu" Mdivani, a member of the orgburo commission as well as of the Georgian Central Committee, had managed to get a letter through to Lenin—Bukharin passed it on—that hurled accusations at Stalin as well as Orjonikidze, the highest-ranking Bolshevik in the South Caucasus.[17] On September 27, right after seeing Stalin, Lenin received Mdivani.[18] That same day, Stalin exploded, writing an irate letter to all members of the politburo accusing Lenin of "national liberalism" as well as "hurriedness." No top party official had ever used such an intemperate tone in written communications with the Bolshevik leader.[19] Stalin, however, knew Lenin was being inconsistent: earlier in 1922 the Bolshevik leader had accused Ukraine's Communists—"the people there are sly"—of trying to evade party directives in a struggle against Moscow's centralism.[20] That was precisely what Stalin understood his fellow Georgians to be doing now; hence his explosion. Nonetheless, the plan that Stalin circulated for the October 5–8, 1922, Central Committee plenum corresponded entirely to Lenin's version of a federal Union of Soviet Socialist Republics. Even though Lenin was too ill to attend the plenum, Stalin made sure Lenin's plan carried.[21]

Stalin's absorption-by-Russia proposal faced fatal obstacles—not just Lenin and the Georgian nationalist Communists, but also the Bolshevik leaders of Ukraine, including Rakovski, an ethnic Bulgarian raised in Romania, as well as Ukrainian national Communists who fought tooth and nail in the orgburo commission.[22] Indeed, lost in the confusion generated by Mdivani was the fact that opponents of a unitary state had won. (Objections were raised to the designation "of Europe and Asia"—what if revolutions took place in Africa or the Americas?—so the geographical marker was dropped.) The Soviet state became a federation. Also lost in the swirling passions was the circumstance that Stalin was the would-be centralizer in Eurasia, but Lenin was the centralizer globally. He had wanted during the Polish War not just to Sovietize but also to incorporate a number of states on the heels of a Red Army sweep westward into Europe. Stalin had responded that "for the nations that formed part of old Russia, we can and should consider our (Soviet) type of federation as an appropriate path to international unity," but not so for "a future Soviet Germany, Poland, Hungary, Finland. These peoples . . . would scarcely agree to enter straight into a federative bond with Soviet Russia on the Bashkir or Ukrainian model." Instead, he had deemed "confederation (a union of independent states) as the most appropriate form of drawing together."[23] Stalin had also set Finland and Poland apart as unsusceptible to federation with Soviet Russia even though they had been constituents of "old Russia."[24] Lenin's reply, if there was one, has been lost or destroyed, but its gist was captured in a summary by Stalin: Lenin scorned Stalin's proposal for European confederation as "chauvinism, nationalism," insisting "we need a centralized world economy, run from a single organ."[25] Stalin had no such delusions.

Further lost in the Georgian-generated confusion of 1922 was the circumstance that any federal state structure in Eurasia would be fettered even before coming into being. That was because although the Russian Communist party had authorized the creation of national Communist parties, in connection with the USSR's formation the non-federal nature of the party that had been set down at the 8th Congress in 1919 was not rescinded. It took a lot of head banging to implement the strict subordination to Moscow of republic Communist parties in practice, but in the last analysis, as Marxists liked to say, the party trumped the state. Indeed, that is how nationalist Communists such as Mdivani could be called to account: they were subject to Communist party discipline, meaning the rule of the Stalin-controlled apparatus in Moscow.

Even as the Ukrainians and Georgians managed to hold the line against annexation into Russia, the Georgians remained deeply unsatisfied: they were not being afforded the same status in the Union as Ukraine, for which they blamed Orjonikidze. Sergo Orjonikidze, thirty-six years old in 1922, had been born in western Georgia to a non-serf family, and studied medicine in Tiflis, qualifying as a medical orderly, while also joining the Bolsheviks (1903). In 1907 he had met Stalin, aka Koba, in cell number 3 of the Baku prison.[26] In 1920–21, colluding with Stalin, Orjonikidze had seized back Armenia, Azerbaijan, and Georgia militarily, raising Georgians' ire. Only Lenin's forceful intervention had spared Orjonikidze being dropped from the Central Committee. "What can I do?" Orjonikidze had pleaded. "I'm a hot-tempered person. Maybe when I turn fifty I'll mellow a bit, but in the meantime I can't do anything about it."[27] Not long after this, in November 1921, Orjonikidze, over the objections of his fellow Georgian Bolsheviks, had set in motion the formation of a South Caucasus Federation.[28] Georgians were forcibly driving the large Armenian population from Tiflis, directly or indirectly, and the Georgian Council of People's Commissars issued instructions for citizenship in Soviet Georgia based upon ethnic criteria.[29] Armed territorial disputes, customs barriers, and other acts of "chauvinist poison" also argued for federation.[30] After Orjonikidze's latest fait accompli, Lenin, writing to Stalin (November 28, 1921), deemed the formation of a South Caucasus Federation premature but accepted it.[31] The formal treaty for the South Caucasus Federation was signed on March 12, 1922.

The Georgian Central Committee had refused to accede. "Dear Iosif!" Alyosha Svanidze, Stalin's brother-in-law from his deceased first wife, Kato, wrote to him in despair. "Not a single Central Committee meeting has taken place lately that did not start and end with stormy scenes between Sergo and Budu. . . . Teach them to treat each other with respect. P.S. I shall be boundlessly grateful to you for tearing me out of this milieu and giving me the chance to work in some mission abroad."[32] Mdivani, also the offspring of west Georgian nobility, was himself stubborn and hotheaded, but the intense personal animosity between him and Orjonikidze flowed from significant policy disagreements over Georgia's place in the Union.[33] Orjonikidze's federation plan was passed at a Georgian Party Congress with the support of rank-and-file delegates.[34] Orjonikidze also had behind him Stalin, who made none of the arguments on behalf of national "equality" for the Georgians that he had made for the Bashkirs and Tatars. This derived partly from grudges—Stalin and Mdivani had long known and detested one another—but also from Georgia's borderland position. Stalin reasoned that as the case of Georgian Menshevism had proven, socioeconomic "backwardness" spawned "opportunists" who, wittingly or even unwittingly, used nationalism to separate territories from Soviet Russia, which played into the hands of the international bourgeoisie by creating "a zone of foreign intervention and occupation."[35] Mdivani and his supporters complained to Lenin about an influx of non-Georgians to Georgia, Moscow's concession of Georgian territory to Turkey, and the abandonment of Georgian territorial claims vis-à-vis Armenia and Azerbaijan.[36] In Stalin's mind, this behavior was no different from that of the Georgian Mensheviks.

As the formation of the USSR entered its final stage, Orjonikidze erupted in fury, vowing to purge the "chauvinist rot" from the Georgian Central Committee. On October 21, 1922, at 2:55 a.m., Mdivani called from Tiflis to the Kremlin on the Hughes apparatus and unleashed a long stream of invective against Orjonikidze to Avel Yenukidze, an ethnic Georgian in Moscow and the secretary of the Soviet central executive committee presidium. Yenukidze responded sharply that if the situation in Georgia had deteriorated, the "soil had been prepared by the Georgian Central Committee majority."[37] Lenin, too, had now had his fill of them, sternly rebuking Mdivani in a telegram later that same day, defending Orjonikidze, and proposing that the dispute go to the party secretariat—meaning Stalin.[38] In Tiflis, the local Central Committee met in the presence of Orjonikidze as well as Rykov (who happened to be down south), yet a majority voted up a resolution to join the USSR not in the form of a South Caucasus Federation but as the Georgian republic, against the decision of the Central Committee of Soviet Russia—a blatant flouting of party discipline. The Georgians were instructed to resign and on October 22 nine of the eleven Georgian Central Committee members did so. Orjonikidze had achieved his purge.[39] But the Georgians still refused to desist, and one Mdivani supporter leveled formal party charges against Orjonikidze for going after him with a marble paperweight as well as a knife and threatening to have him shot; Orjonikidze denied the accusations.[40]

Although the South Caucasus Federation had been settled by majority Georgian vote, the accusations could not be ignored and the politburo decided on November 25, 1922, to send a three-person investigatory commission headed by GPU chief Dzierżyński, who was on holiday near Tiflis in Sukhum on the Black Sea.[41] Lenin, for whatever reason, did not participate in the telephone vote confirming the commission's composition, but he may have asked Rykov, who was also on holiday in Sukhum, to be his eyes and ears. Rykov stayed in Orjonikidze's Tiflis apartment, where he arranged to meet a former Siberian coexile, Akaki Kabakhidze, who belonged to the Mdivani group. It is likely the parties were drinking. Kabakhidze accused Orjonikidze of keeping a fine white horse at state expense. Orjonikidze's friend Mikoyan would later explain that the animal had been a gift from mountain tribesmen in the Caucasus—such a gift could not be declined—and that Orjonikidze had turned it over to the state stables, riding it occasionally.[42] Orjonikidze struck Kabakhidze. Rykov separated the men, and reported to Moscow that the altercation had been personal, not political.[43] But the slap would reverberate, and form the basis of a challenge to Stalin's dictatorship.

## FAILED QUEST FOR ECONOMIC DICTATORSHIP

While Stalin had his hands full trying to forge a functioning state across Eurasia, Trotsky was busy trying to seize command over the economy. Just before the 11th Party Congress in spring 1922—the one at which Stalin was appointed Communist party general secretary—Trotsky had sent a critical note to Lenin complaining that provincial party organizations were concerning themselves with economic issues such as the agricultural sowing campaign or the leasing of factories. "Without the emancipation of the party, as a party, from direct governing and supervision, it is impossible to cleanse the party from bureaucratism and the economy from dissoluteness," Trotsky wrote, urging that the party confine its attention to questions such as the rearing of youth in matters of theory.[44] Lenin wrote on the note: "to the archive."[45] Trotsky, however, continued his struggle to forge an "economic dictatorship" by proposing to vastly expand the powers of the tiny state planning commission, which did not do economic planning, only ad hoc consultation with managers.[46] But the kind of planning Trotsky desired was incompatible with the NEP. Whereas Trotsky warned of a revolution drowning in an ocean of petit bourgeois peasants, Lenin warned that the peasants were the "judges" of the Bolsheviks: rural toilers were extending the Bolsheviks political "credit" and would cease to do so if the Bolsheviks failed to raise living standards.[47] Lenin called a working class "alliance" (smychka) with the peasantry a necessity "insofar as there is not yet a possibility to rely on the victorious working class of Europe."[48] At Lenin's initiative, the 11th Congress reaffirmed the NEP as well as the party's predominance in all spheres, including the economy.

Following his defeat at the 11th Party Congress, Trotsky took to criticizing Lenin regarding the likely ineffectiveness of his proposals to improve the state's performance.[49] Their exchanges heated up when Trotsky declared in a speech in October 1922 that if world capitalism managed to stand another ten years, it would be "strong enough to put down the proletarian revolution once and for all throughout the world, and of course, in Soviet Russia, too."[50] There can be no doubt that Trotsky was trying to change Lenin's version of the NEP, and that he provoked Lenin to respond. On November 20, 1922, at the Moscow soviet—in what would turn out to be his final public appearance—Lenin declared that "we never doubted that we should . . . attain success alone." He tried to stress that "socialism is now not a question of the far-off future," suggesting rivalries among the capitalist powers would provide an opening, but overall he was stumped: "We dragged socialism into everyday life and here we need to figure it out." Workers were organizing production at factories themselves, peasants were forming cooperatives, maybe socialism, or at least its seeds, lay in that.[51] Trotsky persisted in exposing the despair of Lenin's position, demanding immediate industrialization through planning. Lenin in effect was saying be patient: the regime was fully secure for now and in time would win out if it performed its job of regulating capitalist relations. Trotsky was saying build socialism in the economy now, or else the opportunity would be lost forever.[52]

## SECOND STROKE

Lenin's poststroke return to public life, after a long, slow, and partial convalescence, would turn out to be brief: only from October 2, 1922, through December.[53] On December 7, after departing a politburo meeting early, he was ushered back to Gorki, where he was visited two days later by Rykov, just returned from Tiflis.[54] Lenin insisted on returning to the Kremlin, which he did on December 12, but, after discussions with his government deputies in his Kremlin office during the day, and in the evening receiving Dzierżyński to hear about the Georgian events, Lenin retired to his apartment down the corridor, feeling extremely unwell.[55] It would prove to be his last working day in his Kremlin office. The next morning he suffered two attacks. "He is having paralytic attacks every day," the doctors' journal noted. "Vladimir Ilich is upset and worried by the deterioration in his condition."[56] Still, Lenin met with Stalin in the apartment from 12:30 p.m. for more than two hours.[57] That same day, however, he conveyed to his deputies that he was compelled to take another holiday after "liquidating" the issues he was working on.[58] On December 14 and 15, Lenin continued working in his apartment, lobbying several officials, including Trotsky, to forestall dilution of the state monopoly on trade.[59] On December 15, Lenin wanted to dictate a letter on the national question but did not manage to do so.[60] Nonetheless, he sent a letter to Stalin reporting that he had finished the "liquidation" of pressing matters, and reminded him that Trotsky would be defending his position on the trade monopoly at the upcoming plenum, warning against any backsliding.[61]

This letter would serve, in Trotsky's memoirs, as evidence that Lenin had proposed that he and Trotsky form a "bloc" on the trade monopoly, and that Lenin and Stalin suffered a break in relations over this question, on top of their national question contretemps.[62] But in an exchange of letters around this time, both Lenin and Trotsky underscored not just their partial agreement (trade monopoly) but their continuing differences (planning).[63] Moreover, on the trade monopoly, just as on the USSR structure, Stalin readily acceded to Lenin's wishes. There was no bloc and no break.

Before Lenin could depart for Gorki to renew his convalescence, in the wee hours of December 15–16 he suffered what may have been a series of lesser strokes. "His condition has worsened," the physicians wrote. "He can write with difficulty, but what he writes is illegible, the letters overlapping each other. . . he could not touch the tip of his nose with the tip of his finger."[64] Lenin would never write again.[65] Despite migraines, spasms, memory loss, speech impairment, bouts of paralysis, and despair, Lenin somehow managed to dictate a letter to his three deputies (recorded in Krupskaya's hand) instructing that Rykov should be given the state planning commission.[66] Sometime between December 16 and 18, Lenin dictated a letter to Stalin conveying that just days ago (December 14) he had received Kamenev and had "a lively political conversation. Slept well, felt wonderfully. Then, on Friday [December 15], paralysis. I demand your appearance immediately, to tell you something in the event the illness worsens."[67] Lenin feared the onset of total paralysis and wanted poison. Stalin is not recorded in the visitors' book for Lenin's office but, like Kamenev, could have gone to the apartment.[68] On December 18, 1922, a Central Committee plenum voted to make Stalin responsible for "the isolation of Vladimir Ilich in terms of personal relations with staff and correspondence," as per doctors' orders, based on a diagnosis of strain from overwork.[69] Visits to Lenin were forbidden, beyond immediate family members, physicians, orderlies, and secretaries, and those few allowed contact were forbidden to agitate him by discussing current affairs.[70]

The physicians' journal records no activities by Lenin for December 19–22.[71] Trotsky claimed that on December 21 Lenin dictated a warm letter to him ("with the very best comradely greetings") via Krupskaya, thanking Trotsky for winning the battle on the foreign trade monopoly.[72] But the alleged letter in Trotsky's archive is not an original but a copy of a copy; the copy in Lenin's archive is a copy of *that* copy.[73] Lenin certainly had reason to be pleased: the December 18 Central Committee plenum had voted to uphold his position on keeping the state foreign trade monopoly—the draft resolution is in Stalin's hand.[74] The plenum had also voted for Lenin's preferred version of the new state structure, a USSR, which Stalin arranged. Finally, the plenum had rejected Trotsky's insistence on a reorganization of economic management under the state planning commission.[75] Further doubts about the December 21 dictation are connected with Krupskaya's manufacture of an incident on December 22 whereby Stalin, having supposedly learned of Lenin's alleged congratulatory dictation for Trotsky the day before, phoned to berate her.[76] Stalin would indeed get angry at Krupskaya, but that would take place a month later, and, as we shall see, the difference in timing is crucial. What we know for sure is that on December 22, Lenin managed to dictate a formal request (through Lidiya Fotiyeva) to Stalin for cyanide "as a humanitarian measure."[77] Right then, Lenin's worst fears were realized: during the night of December 22–23, he suffered his second massive stroke.[78] "Absolutely no movement," the doctors wrote, "neither of the right arm nor of the right leg."[79]

We also know for sure that on the evening of December 23, Lenin wheedled permission for five minutes' dictation with a stenographer, "since," according to the doctors' journal, "he is anxious about one question and worried that he won't be able to fall asleep." After a tiny bit of dictation, "he calmed down." The original of the dictation of December 23 appears to be in Nadya Alliluyeva's hand.[80] If so, this was the last time Stalin's wife would be summoned to take dictation.[81] The short dictation was a personal letter to Stalin, as is clear from the fact that it was addressed with a capital "You" (for a person), not lower case (for a group); the subject matter comported with Stalin's role as head of the party:

namely, a proposal for expansion of the Central Committee from the then 27 to 50 or even 100.[82] Lenin's dictation to Stalin also called for granting law-making but not executive functions to the state planning commission and noted he was prepared to "move toward Trotsky's position to a certain degree and under certain conditions." Lenin was furiously insisting that he be able to continue dictation, spurring the politburo subcommittee responsible for him (Stalin, Kamenev, Bukharin) to hold a conference with his doctors on December 24; they resolved that "Vladimir Ilich has the right to dictate every day for 5 to 10 minutes, but this cannot have the character of correspondence, and Vladimir Ilich may not expect to receive any answers"—restrictions that, far from soothing Lenin, provoked his ire, undercutting their ostensible medical purpose.[83] The injunction also deepened Lenin's already near-paranoiac suspicions that his politburo colleagues were hiding political decisions from him that contradicted his instructions.

Stalin evidently informed Trotsky straightaway of Lenin's December 23 letter, including the unspecified concession to Trotsky on the economy.[84] Trotsky seems to have been emboldened, for on December 24 and 26, 1922, he sent two letters to the Central Committee relitigating his proposal for a grandiose reorganization of executive institutions, insisting that the matter be placed on the upcoming Party Congress's agenda.[85] In the letters, Trotsky effectively sought a merger of the state planning commission and the Supreme Council of the Economy under himself.[86] Lenin received a copy of the letters, and expressly rejected Trotsky's proposal for a super ministry to run the economy and, against Trotsky's criticisms, defended state planning commission chairman Gleb Kryżanowski, a respected, soft-spoken specialist.[87] Lenin's staff passed his December 27 dictation to Stalin, for the politburo, in real time.[88]

On December 30, 1922, in the Bolshoi Theater, the USSR was formally acclaimed by the Tenth Congress of Soviets, which now became the First USSR Congress of Soviets. Constituent republics were awarded control over commissariats of justice, education, land, health, and social security, while the Union government in Moscow controlled the commissariats of war, foreign affairs, foreign trade, and finance, as well as the GPU—now rechristened the "united" or OGPU. Lenin had missed both the October 1922 and the December 1922 Central Committee plenums when the form of the new state had been discussed, and had not been able to attend and speak at the Tenth Congress of Soviets, but the USSR state structure conformed to his vision of a federation of equal members. True, because of the party, the federative nature of the USSR was overridden, but the fact that, as Lenin insisted, the Soviet Socialist republics such as Ukraine formed a joint federation with the RSFSR would have immense consequences one day. The USSR would dissolve into its constituent republics, but the RSFSR would remain intact. Lenin's preferred form of a USSR was ultimately a bet on world revolution, while Stalin's proposal—annexation into the RSFSR—would have been a bet on historic Russia, without excluding world revolution.

## FIRST RECOGNITION

On the recommendation of doctors, Trotsky was granted a six-week holiday from January 6, 1923, but he stayed in Moscow. That same day, Stalin addressed a letter to the Central Committee proposing that Trotsky be made chairman of the Supreme Council of the Economy and a deputy chairman of the government, a proposal Stalin attributed, properly, to Lenin.[89] Trotsky declined. On January 15, Trotsky detailed why he had already refused to become deputy prime minister at Lenin's suggestion back in September 1922, writing that he disliked both the practice of a "deputies' collegium," which took people away from running their respective commissariats, and the policies of the party apparatus (under Stalin). For example, decisions on military affairs were being taken "de facto against the interests of the institution and even behind its back," so "I do not consider it possible to take on still more responsibility for still other institutions." Trotsky claimed that Lenin had proposed forming a commission to examine the selection, training, and promotion of cadres—Stalin's bailiwick—but it had never been formed because Lenin's illness worsened.[90] On January 17, Stalin proposed that Trotsky become head of the state planning commission as well as deputy chairman of the government.[91] Trotsky refused this, too.[92] By refusing to become Lenin's top deputy with Lenin seriously ill, Trotsky in effect was refusing to take over the government. It seems inexplicable. One part of the explanation consists of Trotsky's continued insistence on replacing Sokolnikov's "dictatorship of finances" (as Trotsky wrote in this exchange of letters) with a "dictatorship of industry," which, however, Lenin adamantly refused. No less fundamentally, Trotsky understood that Stalin, as head of the party, could control the government (through the nomenklatura process, among other levers), and he was just not going to take a position subordinated to Stalin, even if Trotsky refrained from saying as much explicitly.

Trotsky's desire for a dictatorship of industry and an end to the party's oversight of the economy had both a policy aspect (planning, super industrialization) and a political aspect: it was his answer to Stalin's dictatorship of the party apparatus. But Stalin, who did not like the NEP any more than Trotsky did, crucially, like Lenin, and because of Lenin, understood the necessity of flexible tactics for the greater cause: Stalin accepted the NEP. To put the matter another way, in 1922, Stalin could have his party dictatorship and Lenin's NEP. Trotsky could not have his economic dictatorship and the NEP. This means that the charges of Trotskyism that Stalin would level, with all manner of distortions, nonetheless had some basis: Trotsky on the economy was forcefully pushing against Lenin's foundational policy. This episode also shows that, with Lenin incapacitated, Trotsky recognized the sudden vastness of Stalin's power.

But Stalin suddenly became vulnerable over that slap in Tiflis. Lenin now saw his bête noire—Great Russian chauvinism—in the persons of a Georgian (Orjonikidze) and a Pole (Dzierżyński), whom he suspected of whitewashing Georgian events.[93] On January 25, 1923, without Lenin, the rest of the politburo met—even Trotsky took part, though on holiday—and heard from the Dzierżyński commission as well as Mdivani, then voted to approve Dzierżyński's findings exonerating Orjonikidze and removing the four leading Georgian Communists from Georgia.[94] No one was supposed to be keeping Lenin informed about party affairs, on doctors' orders, but on January 24, Lenin's secretariat recorded that he directed Maria Volodicheva to request the materials of the Dzierżyński Commission from Stalin or Dzierżyński, so that his secretariat could study them and report to him in order that he could prepare a report to the upcoming 12th Party Congress (scheduled for spring 1923).[95] His innate suspiciousness was intensified by his illness and prescribed treatment of reduced political involvement. He began to accuse Fotiyeva, his head secretary, of "intriguing" against him, according to the doctors, because she had discovered that Dzierżyński was away from Moscow but reported that when he returned, she would ask him for the dossier.[96] Sometime around now, in late January, Stalin and Krupskaya had a confrontation over the telephone. The sources indicate the conflict was sparked by the request for the Dzierżyński report, which Lenin's secretariat formally made to Stalin on January 29.[97]

The request struck Stalin as prima facie evidence that someone, presumably Krupskaya, had been informing Lenin about party and state affairs against the strict prohibition set down by the politburo at the instruction of the doctors.

Molotov, who knew Stalin extremely well, recalled late in life that "Stalin was irritated: 'Why should I get up on my hind legs for her? To sleep with Lenin does not necessarily mean to understand Leninism!' Stalin told me something like this: 'Just because she uses the same bathroom as Lenin, do I have to appreciate and respect her as if she were Lenin?' He was too coarse and rude."[98] Krupskaya would characterize Stalin's rudeness over the phone as extraordinary, but this is not corroborated by any other source. Maria Ulyanova, an eyewitness—the telephone was in the corridor just outside Lenin's room in Gorki—would recall that Stalin had pointed out Krupskaya's violation of the politburo decision "in a rather sharp manner" and that Krupskaya had descended into hysterics: "She completely did not resemble herself, she screamed out, she rolled around on the floor, and so on." Perhaps Krupskaya was deliberately trying to stage a memorable incident. Ulyanova would further recall that Krupskaya had told Lenin about the incident "after several days" and that she (Krupskaya) and Stalin had reconciled.[99]

The fact that the rudeness incident took place in late January—not, as most accounts assert, on December 22—helps explain why, on February 1, 1923, Stalin read out a statement at the politburo requesting to be "relieved of the responsibility for overseeing the regime established by the doctors for comrade Lenin." The politburo unanimously rebuffed his request.[100] That same day, Stalin also turned over the Dzierżyński Commission materials to Lenin's secretariat. The request was unorthodox, given that the materials were supposed to be re-examined by a new "commission," which no party body had authorized, and which was made up of mere technical personnel with no standing.[101] The next day, the politburo discussed, once again, Trotsky's insistence on concentrating economic authority in the state planning commission and opening the sluices to finance industry; the issue was tabled.[102] His proposals were turned over to the whole Central Committee and, ultimately, the 12th Party Congress.[103] Trotsky persisted in his quest for economic dictatorship as a counter to Stalin's party dictatorship.

## SUSPICIOUS DICTATION

Maria Glasser, Lenin's secretary who handled politburo matters, recalled that between December 1922 and March 1923, the Bolshevik leader, "having only a half hour each day, rarely more, and sometimes less, hurried frightfully to say

Gersh Brilliant, known as Grigory Sokolnikov (third from right), commander of the Turkestan front, with his subordinate Lazar Kaganovich (second from right) and indigenous members of the Bolshevik Turkestan Commission, fall 1920. Kaganovich would become a Stalin protégé in the central apparatus. Sokolnikov would become USSR finance commissar under Stalin and oversee the New Economic Policy.

Baron Roman von Ungern-Sternberg, the would-be restorer of the great Mongol empire who instead unwittingly delivered Outer Mongolia into Soviet hands, photographed during his interrogation by Bolshevik capturers and wearing an imperial Russian St. George's Cross for bravery on his Mongol caftan. He was said to rip out the hearts of those he captured and place them in bowls of skulls as offerings to the Tibetan Buddhist gods.

Red Army bayonets, celebrating victory over Baron Pyotr Wrangel, the last of the White armies, Crimea, 1920.

Golgotha. What imperial weakness and vaulting ambition, epic miscalculation and idées fixes hath wrought—famine victims, Tsaritsyn, winter 1921–22. In 1925, the city would be renamed Stalingrad.

Stalin and Lenin at Gorki, just outside Moscow, September 1922. Photograph by Maria Ulyanova, Lenin's sister. Stalin had images of his visit published to show Lenin's supposed recovery—and his own proximity to the Bolshevik leader. This pose was not among those published.

12th Party Congress, April 1923, Stalin, among some of the more than eight hundred attendees at the Grand Kremlin Palace, without entourage. Lenin did not attend. Almost immediately afterward, Krupskaya suddenly brought forward dictation, attributed to Lenin, calling for Stalin's removal as general secretary.

Lenin, Gorki, 1923, one of his last photos, with doctor and nurse, taken by Maria Ulyanova.

Lenin's funeral, Stalin and Molotov with the casket, a frigid January 27, 1924.

Sculptor Sergei Merkurov fashioning Lenin's death mask, which would find its way into Stalin's office.

Stalin's bestseller, *On Lenin and Leninism* (Moscow, 1924). Mastery of the ideology, not just the apparatus, undergirded Stalin's power.

ABOVE: **Old Square, 4:** Communist party headquarters (to the right of the white tower), and Old Square, 8, the agricultural commissariat (to the left of the tower), both behind the Kitai-gorod wall enclosing Moscow's commercial quarter. From Old Square, 4, Stalin controlled the police, military, and foreign affairs as well as the party.

RIGHT: **Blacksmith Bridge, 15:** foreign affairs commissariat.

**Znamenka, 23:** the Alexander military school, which became the war commissariat and headquarters of the general staff.

**Lubyanka, 2:** headquarters of the Cheka-GPU-OGPU.

Innermost staff of Stalin's dictatorship within the dictatorship, Old Square, 1924: Amayak Nazaretyan (seated far right), Stalin's top aide; Ivan Tovstukha (standing, second from left), also a top aide; Grigory Kanner (standing, far left). Notwithstanding the anarchist commune resemblance, the functionaries were highly qualified.

Stalin and the military: 14th Party Conference, Moscow, April 1925. Left to right: Mikhail Lashevich (a deputy war commissar), Mikhail Frunze (war commissar), Alexander Smirnov, Alexei Rykov, Klimenty Voroshilov (Moscow military district commander), Stalin, Mykola Skrypnik, Andrei Bubnov (head of the Red Army political department), Grigol "Sergo" Orjonikidze, Józef Unszlicht (a deputy war commissar). Frunze, who had replaced Trotsky, would be dead before the year was out. Stalin would promote his man Voroshilov.

Felix Dzierżyński, Soviet secret police chief, on a recuperative holiday, Sukhum, Abkhazia, Black Sea coast, 1922. Long in ill health and overworked, he would die of a heart attack in summer 1926.

Bearing Dzierżyński's body, July 1926.
Right to left: Unszlicht out front, Yenukidze, Bukharin, Rykov, Stalin, and Voroshilov (in cap).

**OGPU HIERARCHS:** TOP LEFT: Wiaczesław Mężyński, who replaced Dzierżyński but was himself very ill. TOP RIGHT: Jenokhom Jehuda, known as Genrikh Yagoda (new first deputy chief), Stalin's secret agent in the secret police. BOTTOM LEFT: Artur Fraucci, known as Artuzov (head of counterintelligence), Yagoda's nemesis. Dzierżyński called Artuzov "the absolute cleanest comrade." BOTTOM RIGHT: Yefim Yevdokimov, North Caucasus OGPU chief, who, while visiting Stalin at the dacha in Sochi, brought the gift of fabricated industrial sabotage.

A caricature mocking Grigory Zinoviev's supposedly opportunistic criticisms of the party's New Economic Policy, December 1925. By Valery Mezhlauk. Caption: "Masha, tonight is the Central Committee plenum; take out the kulak and NEPman puppets and, after I return, cover them again with mothballs, we won't need them until autumn."

Stalin with newly installed Leningrad party boss Sergei Kirov, who replaced Zinoviev, Smolny, April 1926. Left to right: Nikolai Antipov, new Leningrad second secretary; Stalin; Kirov; Nikolai Shvernik, outgoing Leningrad second secretary, moving to the Central Committee apparatus; Fyodor Sobinov, known as Nikolai Komarov, head of the Leningrad soviet.

Three Caucasus Musketeers, summer 1926:
Mikoyan, Stalin, Orjonikidze, in a retouched photograph published in the newspaper.

LEFT: Poteshny Dvorets (Amusement Palace), triangles on the roof dating from the seventeenth century, the only surviving Boyar residence inside the Kremlin, where Stalin and his family lived. Alexei Rykov lived here, too. The double-headed eagles on the Kremlin towers would be removed only in the 1930s.

BELOW: Zubalovo-4, in the secluded, leafy western outskirts of Moscow, the Stalin family dacha from 1919, formerly owned by the ethnic Georgian Levon Zubalashvili [Russified to Zubalov], a Baku oil magnate.

Vasily Stalin (b. 1921, left) and Artyom Sergeyev, Yalta, 1926. Artyom was born a few months after Vasily and, after his father was killed that year in a civil war accident, was informally adopted into the Stalin household.

Nadya and newborn Svetlana, 1927. Portrait by Moscow's renowned private studio photographer Nikolai Svishchov-Paola. Photo album of Sergei Alliluyev, Stalin's father-in-law.

Yakov Jugashvili (b. 1907), Stalin's first child from his marriage to Kato Svanidze, circa 1927.

Karolina Til (left), who managed the Stalin household, and Aleksandra Bychkova, Svetlana's nanny.

Polish marshal Józef Piłsudski, victor of the Soviet-Polish War, on a state visit to Romania, Poland's military ally, September 1922. Poland, particularly in alliance with Romania, was the foremost threat in Soviet military intelligence reports.

Chiang Kai-shek, March 13, 1927, on the eve of the massacre of his political allies, the Chinese Communist party. After learning his assault was proceeding, Chiang confided in his private diary that his heart was "lifted" and the Communists were "worthy of being killed." Yet Stalin felt constrained to stick with the Chinese strongman as a bulwark against British and Japanese influence in China.

The Red Army on bicycles, parading across Red Square in front of Lenin's cube mausoleum, May 1, 1926. Photographed by Pyotr Otsup. The Soviet military, which rode bicycles on maneuvers, too, was in no position to fight a major war.

At the height of triumph, 15th Party Congress, December 1927. To Stalin's left is Minei Gubelman, known as Emelyan Yaroslavsky, an all-purpose functionary. Before and after the congress, Stalin again demanded to be relieved of the post of general secretary.

Enemies' row: foreign military attachés at the May Day Parade, Red Square, 1928.

Stalin, Barnaul, Siberia, January 22, 1928. Many of these Siberian officials, including regional party boss Sergei Syrtsov (on Stalin's right), opposed a policy of forced collectivization, which Stalin had proclaimed in an epochal closed-door speech in Novosibirsk two days earlier. "Now," Stalin said to those in this photo from Barnaul, apropos of forcing collectivization, "we will see who is a true Communist and who just talks like a Communist.... We possess all the power we want, but we lack the ability to exercise our power."

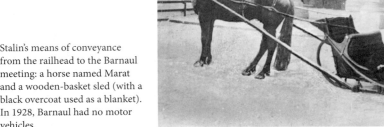

Stalin's means of conveyance from the railhead to the Barnaul meeting: a horse named Marat and a wooden-basket sled (with a black overcoat used as a blanket). In 1928, Barnaul had no motor vehicles.

Shakhty trial, spring 1928, Hall of Columns in the House of Trade Unions, foreign journalists. The trial was filmed and accorded intense publicity. Stalin used Shakhty to stir a frenzy and mobilize the masses.

Interrogation protocols, the only "evidence" produced in court.

Class in the village, Vyatka province, 1928, on the eve of dekulakization: a "kulak" (rich peasant) with leather boots, depicted watching as a poor peasant, with feet wrapped in towels and bast sandals, does the work. In fact, most peasants who hired labor themselves also worked.

Nikolai Bukharin Stalin caricature, February 20, 1928. Stalin had treated Bukharin, his political ally, as a younger brother, but before the year was out Stalin would turn against him in a way that displayed his political virtuosity and exceptional malice. "He is maneuvering in order to portray us as culprits of a schism," Bukharin complained to Kamenev of Stalin on July 11, 1928.

and do everything necessary."[104] But Professor Kramer, in February 1923, noted that "Vladimir Ilich was finding it hard to recall either a word he wanted or he was unable to read what he had dictated to the secretary, or he would begin to say something completely incoherent."[105] Despite the strict prohibition on conveying political information to him, all regime materials were still being sent to his secretariat, and Lenin, confined to his small room in the Kremlin apartment, cajoled his secretaries into divulging information about current events and making phone calls on his behalf. It was these loyal women, Fotiyeva, Volodicheva, and above all Krupskaya, who assumed the task of interpreting his nearly unintelligible words and half-paralyzed pantomime.[106] On February 14, he was said to have instructed a secretary to "convey to someone of the insulted [Georgians] that he is on their side." Lenin added, "Did Stalin know? Why did he not respond?"[107] The doctors recorded that on February 20 Krupskaya withheld from Lenin the protocols of the Tenth Congress of Soviets, which happened to show that Stalin had implemented Lenin's will.[108] Fotiyeva recorded on March 3, that she passed to Lenin their dossier on Georgia, which refuted the Dzierżyński Commission report article by article.[109]

The counterdossier was blatantly tendentious. Just one example: it omitted the salient fact that Pilipe Makahradze's secret letter to the Central Committee, with Kamenev's response, had been leaked to the émigré Menshevik *Socialist Herald*—i.e., the Georgians had divulged state secrets.[110] The counterdossier also rendered political judgments about the slap in Tiflis ("the differences carry a political character and should be raised at the next Party Congress"). Who inserted these assessments remains unclear. Trotsky's involvement has been suggested.[111] But feeling under the weather, he was holed up in his Kremlin apartment, in a different building from Lenin's. "Neither Lenin nor I could reach the telephone; furthermore, the doctors strictly forbade Lenin to hold any telephone conversations," Trotsky would write, adding that Lenin's secretaries shuttled back and forth between the two with messages. The latter included a note, dated March 5, 1923, which purported to be from Lenin, beseeching Trotsky's "to undertake the defense of the Georgian affair at the Central Committee of the party. That affair is now under 'prosecution' at the hands of Stalin and Dzierzynski and I cannot rely on their impartiality. Indeed, quite the contrary!"[112] That same day, Trotsky called Lenin's secretariat and spoke to Volodicheva, complaining he was too ill to do as Lenin requested. Trotsky added that Orjonikidze's behavior in the incident was an aberration.[113]

The circumstances point to Krupskaya as the shaper of the anti-Dzierżyński dossier and of the note to Trotsky. Another purported Lenin dictation, also said to be have been taken by Volodicheva, was for Stalin and reached him the next day.[114] It was typed; no stenographic handwritten copy survives. Nor did the staff of Lenin's secretariat make the usual obligatory notation that a letter had been dispatched. The typescript demanded an apology for mistreatment of Krupskaya and threatened a break in relations. Copies, for some reason, went to Zinoviev and Kamenev. Stalin had already apologized to Krupskaya, but the incident was now revived. On March 7, Stalin answered in writing: "Around five weeks ago [i.e., late January] I had a conversation with comrade N. Konstantinova, whom I consider not only your wife but also my old party comrade, and told her (over the telephone) approximately the following: 'Doctors forbid giving Ilich political information, considering that such a regimen was a very important means of healing him, and you, Nadezhda Konstantinova, turn out to violate that regimen; it's not allowed to play with Ilich's life' and so on." Stalin continued: "I do not consider that one could find something rude or impermissible undertaken 'against' you in these words, for I pursued no goal other than your returning to health. Moreover, I considered it my duty to oversee implementation of the regime. My explanations with N. Kon[staninova] confirmed there was nothing here, and could be nothing here, other than a trivial misunderstanding. Still if you consider that in order to maintain 'relations' I must 'take back' the words I said as above, I can take them back, but I refuse to understand what it was about, where my 'guilt' lies, and what is really wanted of me."[115]

Yet another purported dictation from Lenin, this one a telegram dated March 6, was addressed to Mdivani and Makharadze: "I am with you in this matter with all my heart. I am outraged at the rudeness of Orjonikidze and the connivance of Stalin and Dzierżyński. I am preparing notes and a speech for you."[116] Only a few months before, Lenin was admonishing Mdivani and Makharadze sternly. It was not clear Lenin was in any condition to dictate letters. On March 6, the physicians recorded the following: "When he awoke, he summoned a nurse, but he could almost not converse with her, he wanted the nurse to summon Nadzehda Konstantinova, but he could not say her name. . . . Vladimir Ilich lay with a confused visage, the expression on his face was frightening, his eyes were sad, his look questioning, tears came down from his eyes. Vladimir Ilich is agitated, he tries to speak, but cannot find the words, and he adds: 'Ah the devil, ah the devil, such an illness, this is a return to the old illness' and so on. After measures were taken, 'his speech improved,' V.I. Lenin calmed down and fell asleep."[117]

It is noteworthy that Trotsky later would write that "Lenin entered into clandestine contact with the leaders of the Georgian opposition (Mdivani, Makharadze, and others) against the faction of Stalin, Orjonikidze, Dzierżyński, *through Krupskaya*" (italics added).[118] Perhaps Krupskaya, interpolating Lenin's intentions, concocted all three March letters. Perhaps she first mouthed the words to Lenin and he mouthed them back. Perhaps he mumbled versions of them himself. We shall likely never know. Whatever their provenance, the letters had consequences. On March 7, Kamenev, writing to Stalin, divulged Lenin's support for the "national deviationists" in Georgia; writing to Zinoviev, Kamenev assigned himself the role of peacemaker.[119] By this time, Lenin's illness had taken a sharp turn for the worse: he suffered a seizure on the night of March 6–7.[120] (The journal kept by Lenin's secretaries ends in midsentence on March 6.)[121] Stalin's March 7 apologetic response to Lenin over Krupskaya was recorded as "not read" by Lenin. These three March letters were the last documents that would be attributed to Lenin by the dates assigned to them, but not the last ones that would emerge in his name.

## THIRD STROKE AND FAKE ARTICLE

On the night of March 9–10, 1923, Lenin suffered another massive stroke, which resulted in "complete loss of speech and complete paralysis of the right extremities," according to Professor Kramer, the neurologist.[122] The physicians' duty journal for March 11 recorded that "he kept trying to say something, but only quiet, disjointed sounds emerged.... Today, especially towards evening, his comprehension of what was being said to him was worse, sometimes he replied 'no' when he should have said 'yes.'" The next day the physicians wrote: "He cannot understand what he is asked to do. He was shown a pen, his spectacles, and a paper-knife. When he was asked to give the spectacles, he gave them, when he was asked for the pen, he gave the spectacles again."[123] On March 11, Stalin sent a cipher to all provincial and republic party organizations: "More than ever, the provincial committees need to be informed about the moods of the masses so as to allow no confusion." Moscow in the 1920s was generally roiled by rumors and leaks and Soviet newspapers conducted polemics with émigré periodicals, so keeping anything totally under wraps was out of the question. Lenin's illness was publicly disclosed in a special edition of *Pravda* on March 12, albeit with utmost caution: "some weakening of the movement functions of his right hand and leg," "some upset in his speech."[124] This published note, signed by German doctors, was enough for sharp readers to deduce that Lenin had suffered partial paralysis.[125]

That same day the OGPU sent ciphers to the regional branches instructing them to intensify activity: "The state of comrade Lenin's health is critical. A fatal end is possible. Immediately set up a secret 'troika' in order to take all necessary measures to prevent anti-Soviet disturbances."[126] Dzierżyński worried that émigrés in France would lobby that country and perhaps Poland to take advantage with a military intervention. The politburo contemplated introducing martial law. A partial mobilization occurred on March 14. Of the discussion to disclose Lenin's illness to the public, Trotsky would soon state in a speech, "I think, comrades, you can imagine the mood in which this meeting of the politburo took place. . . . We asked ourselves with genuine alarm how those outside the party would receive the news—the peasant, the Red Army man."[127]

Everything was being filtered through the prism of the succession. *Pravda* began issuing special bulletins concerning Lenin's health from March 14, 1923. That issue happened to be the twenty-fifth anniversary of the party's official founding, and the twentieth of the 2nd Party Congress, when the Bolshevik faction had been constituted, and it carried commemorative essays. One stood out: "Lev Trotsky—Organizer of Victory," by Karl Radek, who deemed Trotsky "the first leader [*vozhd'*]," and used soaring language to laud Trotsky's "genius," praising even controversial subjects, such as "his courageous determination to utilize military specialists for creating the army."[128] Rumors circulated that Lenin had designated Trotsky his successor.[129] Within a short period the OGPU submitted a report on eavesdropped conversations, with coverage of workers in cities and peasants right near cities or along the rail lines, because "the news about Lenin's illness had barely begun to penetrate the genuine village." Some people did not believe the reports of illness, others expressed concern for Lenin. According to the OGPU, people discussed possible successors for Lenin by name, mentioning Trotsky, purportedly "without particular sympathy," which the OGPU attributed to "anti-Semitism of the masses." Others named as possibilities to become chairman of the Council of People's Commissars included Kamenev, Bukharin,

Zinoviev, and Dzierżyński.[130] Stalin was not mentioned. In the country at large, in spring 1923, he was poorly known. But the OGPU report was submitted to him.

Lenin was frantically trying to get the nurses to give him cyanide or summon Stalin to do so. On Saturday, March 17, Krupskaya herself summoned Stalin, telling him Lenin was in a "horrible" state and demanding poison again.[131] Stalin went over to Lenin's Kremlin apartment, and that same day wrote an explanatory note to Kamenev and Zinoviev, following up four days later with a note to the full politburo. Stalin was not admitted to Lenin's room; Krupskaya transmitted Lenin's poison request and Stalin's answer, a vague promise that "at the necessary time, I will implement your request without vacillating." But he told the politburo that "I do not have the strength to fulfill this request of V. Ilich and must refuse the mission, since it is not humane and necessary." The politburo members supported Stalin's stalling tactics.[132] Also on March 21, Lenin's secretariat ceased to receive regime documents, a cutoff only Stalin could have ordered.[133]

Kamenev, meanwhile, had acted upon his self-assigned peacemaker role for Georgia and, along with Kuibyshev (Central Control Commission), had gone to the Second Georgian Party Congress, which opened in Tiflis on March 14.[134] The Georgian party delegates refused to reinstate Mdivani and seven other "national deviationists" in the new twenty-five-member Georgian Central Committee, but the Muscovite emissaries insisted.[135] Orjonikidze perceived Kamenev as playing both sides.[136] On March 21, Stalin telegrammed Orjonikidze to admonish him that he had learned from Kamenev and Kuibyshev that the South Caucasus Federation constitution was "wrong and illegal," because the economic commissariats of the three individual republics lacked genuine operational functions. "This mistake must be corrected obligatorily and immediately."[137] Suddenly, on March 23, Trotsky, belatedly taking up the cause of the Georgian Central Committee, lobbied the politburo to remove Orjonikidze, but only one other member voted with him. Kamenev and Kuibyshev returned to Moscow and reported to the politburo on March 26 on mistakes of "both sides" in Georgia. Trotsky kept up the attack.[138] On April 1, he tried to get Bukharin to write a prominent article on the national question before the upcoming Party Congress (which had been postponed from March 30 until April 17). Nothing appeared in *Pravda* by Bukharin.[139] But then, something extraordinary happened: on April 16, Lidiya Fotiyeva telephoned Kamenev to report that there was a new article by Lenin on nationalities.

Fotieya then telephoned Stalin with the same information. Stalin refused to receive the "article," stating he would "not get involved."[140] The article, titled "Notes on the Question of Nationalities," departed significantly from Lenin's lifelong and even recent views on nationalities, advocating confederation.[141] The "Notes" also had Lenin stating that "I think that Stalin's haste and his infatuation with pure administration, together with his spite against the notorious 'nationalist-socialism,' played a fatal role here," meaning in the bad blood aroused in Georgia. "In politics spite generally plays the basest of roles."[142]

Lenin's alleged "Notes" were dated December 30–31, 1922, and Fotiyeva later observed that the long article had been dictated in two fifteen-minute sessions.[143] The typescript lacked a signature or initials. The existing evidence strongly points to a maneuver by Krupskaya, and the staff in Lenin's secretariat, to forge what they interpreted as Lenin's will. They knew he was exercised over the Georgian affair; indeed, they egged him on over it. Trotsky might also have been complicit by this point. Controversy ensued over his claim that he had received Lenin's "Notes on the Question of Nationalities" before the Central Committee had—and, supposedly, before Lenin's third stroke—but had inexplicably held on to them.[144] Lenin's purported dictation happened to dovetail with views Trotsky published in *Pravda* (March 20, 1923).[145] Even more telling, Lenin's secretaries had kept working on the counterdossier on Georgia, for a report by Lenin to a future Party Congress, even after he had his third massive stroke and permanently lost his ability to speak. Their material contains the following note (dated March 12): "Group the material not so much in defense of the [national] deviationists as in the faulting of the great power chauvinists"—meaning Stalin. In fact, their counter-Dzierżyński Commission dossier reads like a first draft of the "Notes on the Question of Nationalities." On April 16, when Fotiyeva set the "Notes" in motion, Trotsky belatedly adduced the alleged Lenin letter, supposedly dictated March 6, to Mdivani. Rumors were spreading that "Lenin had expressed confidence in Trotsky and gave him some kind of important tasks and prerogatives."[146]

## ABSENT LENIN

The 12th Party Congress, which took place April 17–25, 1923, in Moscow, with 408 voting delegates among 825 attendees, was the first that Lenin would miss since the 6th in summer 1917, when he was in hiding. Initially, the politburo, as usual, had assigned Lenin the main political report, but that now fell to Zinoviev.[147] "You remember with what thirst we always listened to this speech, a thirst like that of a man who, on a sultry summer day, falls upon a deep clear spring to drink his fill," Zinoviev remarked, raising expectations, then failing to meet them.[148] Stalin, in his organizational report, boasted that "for the past six years the Central Committee has never before prepared a congress the way it has prepared this one."[149] In fact, the opening was postponed because the delegate elections were annulled and new elections held in far-flung locales with "representatives" of the Central Committee present. The garrulous Zinoviev later admitted that "people could say to us: the party's Central Committee, right before a congress at which the Central Committee was going to be criticized, . . . has gathered its own delegates, curtailing the electoral rights of members. . . . But we had to do this from the point of view of the interests of the revolution. From the point of view of the benefits to the revolution, [we decided] to allow voting only by those who are the genuine party guard."[150] Translation: Trotsky supporters were culled. Some sense of the acrimony can be gleaned from the anecdote that when Voroshilov saw Radek at the congress walking behind Lev Trotsky, he called out something to the effect of "There goes Lev [Lion] and behind him his tail." Radek got to work and, a few moments later, produced a riposte: "Oh, Klim, you empty head,/Stuffed full of manure,/Better to be Lev's [Lion's] tail/Than Stalin's ass."[151]

Trotsky's appearance, amid blazing lights and rolling movie cameras, provoked a thunderous ovation.[152] He delivered a long, intricate speech that introduced a brilliant metaphor to capture a major crisis bedeviling the regime's economic policy. Soviet industry, slower to recover than farming, was producing insufficient goods leading to higher prices (a situation exacerbated by the organization of the industrial economy into trusts that engaged in monopoly price gouging); at the same time, prices for farmers' output were falling, and the price differential inhibited peasants from marketing their grain. Trotsky adduced a sensational graph that showed the rising prices for manufactured goods and falling prices for agricultural goods, which he likened to the opening of scissor blades.[153] His speech culminated in a paean to planning. "Our New Economic Policy was established seriously and for a long time, but not forever," he stated, calling the market a "diabolical phenomenon" and drawing applause.[154] Trotsky did not specify how a transition to planning might happen, but he did indicate how he would pay for it: "There may be moments when the state does not pay a full wage or pays only a half, and you, the worker, give a credit to your state at the expense of your wages." A few voices called Trotsky out on this call for exploitation of labor, but the members of the leadership, for the most part, avoided engaging his speech, which was followed by applause.[155] What did Trotsky then do? "As soon as he had finished he left the hall," one student admirer remarked. "There was no personal contact in the corridors."[156]

Stalin delivered a second report, on nationalities, and being unable to outdo Trotsky in theatrics, concentrated on substance and delivered the speech of his career to that date. He refrained from stating that Lenin's "Notes on the Question of Nationalities" was a forgery, but he did allow that "comrade Lenin forgot, he forgot a great deal recently. He forgot that with him we passed the fundamentals of the Union (Voice: he was not at the plenum)."[157] Stalin proceeded to refute the arguments of the "Notes" point by point. Stalin knew his Lenin. He painstakingly proved that Lenin himself had spurned the confederation argument, accurately citing his own correspondence with Lenin as well as Lenin's many other writings. Stalin demonstrated that Lenin stood for a federation, which is how the recently formed Union had been designed and approved; Lenin stood for a single, integrated economy; "for Lenin the national question is a question subordinated to a higher question—the workers' question."[158] Stalin further proved that Lenin had been an early backer of a South Caucasus Federation to tamp down nationalist excess.[159] Stalin drove home the point by noting that the Georgians oppressed national minorities, and not just the tribals (Abkhazians and Ossetians), but also Armenians—look at Georgian officials' efforts to deport local Armenians and "transform Tiflis into a real Georgian capital."[160] Great Russians, in other words, had no monopoly on chauvinism. Anyway, not chauvinism but backwardness and the need for development were the salient issues. The party needed to employ the instruments of regional autonomy and native language education, which would now consolidate the nations, so that they could be developed, a policy confirmed at the congress as "indigenization" (korenizatsiia).[161]

Dissenting voices tried to rally. Rakovski decried usurpation of republic prerogatives and a creeping "administrative, apparatus, bureaucratic psychology," and sought to marshal Lenin against Stalin, but Stalin mounted a strong rebuttal with an accurate account of his 1920 exchange with Lenin, during the

Polish War, quoting himself and Lenin's answer to show that Lenin was the arch-centralizer; Stalin, the one who acknowledged difference.[162] Ukraine's Skrypnyk characterized Great Russian chauvinism as "sucked in with their mother's milk," so that it had become "instinctual in many, many comrades"—including, somehow, in the Georgian Stalin—while Mdivani denounced the South Caucasus Federation as "artificially established." No one tried to use Lenin's alleged letter to Mdivani—not Trotsky, not even Mdivani. The latter did try to use Lenin's alleged "Notes on the Question of Nationalities" article, but Kamenev, who was presiding, cut him off.[163] Only Bukharin joined Rakovski in supporting a confederation (after the Union federation had already been formed).[164] The vast majority of the delegates lined up with Stalin. "The thunder of applause from everywhere was heard," Bukharin admitted.[165] Even Yevgeny Preobrazhensky—the person who had challenged Lenin at the previous congress a year earlier over Stalin holding so many concurrent positions—allowed that "comrade Stalin's report was extremely substantive, I would say that it was a very intelligent report."[166]

Stalin enjoyed a moment of high visibility and a smashing victory.[167] Trotsky himself, by putting before the Party Congress the choice of Lenin's authority versus his (Trotsky's) on the matters of the New Economic Policy and the Union federation, had allowed Stalin to demonstrate that he was the one faithful to Lenin. Kamenev, too, had thundered that "the NEP could be terminated with a single decree of yours or of any higher organ of Soviet power, and this would not cause any political tremors," while Zinoviev remarked that "it is not the turn of NEP right now."[168] Stalin was leery of "the corrupting influence of NEP elements" on the party, and even blamed NEP and private capital for growth in Great Russian chauvinism and "Georgian, Azerbaijan, and Uzbek and other nationalisms," but at the top of the regime Stalin was the one who defended Lenin's NEP.[169] He was reconfirmed as general secretary. In the elections to the new Central Committee, Trotsky came in thirty-fifth place in the total number of positive votes, as opposed to second, where he had stood in the elections at the previous Party Congress. Kamenev came in twenty-fourth, Zinoviev thirty-second, and Stalin tied for first (384 votes out of 386) with Lenin.[170] Trotsky would not even have remained a member of the Central Committee if Stalin had not now radically expanded that body, as Lenin had proposed in his December 23 dictation for Stalin.

## MIRACULOUS DICTATION

On May 15, 1923, Lenin was transported at a snail's pace from the Kremlin to Gorki with a team of doctors. On top of paralysis, he suffered insomnia, lost appetite, stomach troubles, fevers, and memory loss. He was desperately trying to regain the power of speech, mostly by reciting the alphabet and singing the "Internationale."[171] But his speech was limited to a handful of words—"congress," "peasant," "worker"—and when he repeated the words Krupskaya said to him, it was not clear he understood their meaning. Physicians observed how he was "given dried bread chips, but for a long time he could not put his hand straight onto the plate and kept putting it around it."[172] He had bouts of weeping and raged at the doctors, as if they were at fault. It was abundantly clear that he would never again play any role in political life. From May 16, no more official bulletins appeared about his health. The strain on Krupskaya was enormous.[173] Lenin's life work, the fate of the revolution, would have to be carried forward by others, and while she spent her days with a hopeless invalid, Stalin had emerged as successor.

But then the heavens crackled and a lightning bolt flashed across the sky: sometime in late May 1923, Krupskaya brought forth a very short document purporting to be dictation from Lenin. She handed it to Zinoviev, with whom she had developed close relations dating back to the emigration in Switzerland.[174] Volodicheva, again, was said to have taken the dictation, over several sessions, recorded as December 24–25, 1922.[175] But the purported dictation had not been registered in the documents journal in Lenin's secretariat. It was a typescript; no shorthand or stenographic originals can be found in the archives. Lenin had not initialed the typescript, not even with his unparalyzed left hand.[176] According to Trotsky, the typescript had no title.[177] Later, titles would be affixed—Lenin's Testament or "Letter to the Congress"—and an elaborate mythology would be concocted about how the dictation had been placed in a wax-sealed envelope with Lenin's instructions that it be opened only after his death. Of course, Krupskaya had given the typescript to Zinoviev while Lenin was still alive.

These were extraordinary pieces of paper, consisting of barbed evaluations of six people. (When Stalin was handed and read the dictation, he is said to have exclaimed of Lenin, "He shit on himself and he shit on us!"[178]) Several top officials were omitted, however, including Rykov, Tomsky, and Kalinin, all full members of the politburo, and Molotov, a candidate member of the politburo and someone who worked very closely with Lenin.[179] By contrast, Bukharin, another politburo candidate member, was mentioned, as was Pyatakov. Lenin saw these two in Gorki and he was preoccupied with next-generation cadres; the purported dictation called them "the most outstanding best forces (among the youth forces)." Still, the document drove a stake through both of them:

> Bukharin is not only a most valuable and major theorist of the party; he is also rightly considered the favorite of the whole party, but his theoretical views can be classified as fully Marxist only with great reserve, for there is something scholastic about him (he has never made a study of dialectics, and, I think, never fully understood it). . . . As for Pyatakov, he is unquestionably a man of outstanding will and outstanding ability, but shows too much zeal for administrating and the administrative side of the work to be relied upon in a serious political matter.

The dictation urged Bukharin, then thirty-four, and Pyatakov, then thirty-two, to "find occasion to enhance their knowledge and amend their one-sidedness." This seemingly fatherly advice had to sting.

But the immediately preceding comments in the typescript, about Zinoviev and Kamenev, were still more damning:

> The October episode with Zinoviev and Kamenev was, of course, no accident, but neither can the blame for it be laid upon them personally, any more than non-Bolshevism can upon Trotsky.

That was it: a single sentence about two of the most important regime figures, an apparent pardon for their opposition to the October coup in the form of a devastating reminder of it.

What preceded the dismissal of Kamenev and Zinoviev, however, was nothing short of earth-shattering:

> Comrade Stalin, having become general secretary, has concentrated boundless power in his hands, and I am not sure whether he will always be able to use that power with sufficient caution.

Stalin had somehow acquired "boundless power" himself, as if Lenin had not made him general secretary. The immediate next line was eye-popping as well:

> Comrade Trotsky, as his fight against the Central Committee in connection with the issue of the people's commissariat of railways proved, is distinguished by the highest abilities. He is personally perhaps the most able man in the present Central Committee, but he has displayed excessive self-assurance and shown excessive preoccupation with the purely administrative side of matters.[180]

The dictation warned that "these two qualities of the two outstanding leaders of the present Central Committee"—Stalin's incaution, Trotsky's self-assured political daftness—"can inadvertently lead to a schism, and if our party does not take steps to avert this, the schism may come unexpectedly."[181]

Although the text raised doubts about all six, as well as others who had not merited a mention, Trotsky emerges as the central figure, called the ablest, pardoned for his grievous non-Bolshevism up to 1917, and mentioned even when others were being dealt with. Before, during, and after the 12th Party Congress, Trotsky was under relentless, scurrilous assault. Anonymous opposition pamphlets had appeared demanding the removal from the Central Committee of Stalin, Zinoviev, and Kamenev, but a far greater number of "underground" works emerged against Trotsky, such as *A Small Biography of a Big Man* (rumored to have been authored by Stalin's minion Tovstukha) and *What Ilich Wrote and Thought About Trotsky* (which dredged up Lenin's nasty comments).[182] Conspicuously, all the phrases of the supposedly late December 1922 dictation correspond with either the anonymous pro-Trotsky hectographs or with the pro- and anti-Trotsky speeches during the congress: the threat of a schism, the need to remove the triumvirate or leading group, Trotsky's non-Bolshevism (mentioned by Zinoviev), Stalin's rudeness. A veritable rough draft of the dictation appeared in the form of the congress speech by the trade unionist Vladimir Kosior (brother of Stanisław Kosior), who pointed a finger at the "triumvirate," the "secretariat," and the "leading party organs" as having interests different from those of the party as a whole and as threatening a schism.[183] Overall, there is a strong sense that the author of the dictation supposedly made in December 1922 had studied the speeches of the 12th Party Congress in spring 1923.[184]

No one at the congress—which ended on April 25—Krupskaya included, had hinted at the existence of Lenin's alleged dictation. Why did Krupskaya not choose to show this document to the 12th Party Congress? She had brought forth the "Notes on the Question of Nationalities," a blatant forgery that had failed to gain any attraction.

One cannot exclude the possibility that Lenin dictated the untitled typescript with evaluations of six personnel, despite the absence of corroborating evidence. It is also possible that someone, knowing Lenin's thoughts, rendered some barely audible but genuine words and gestures into this form. But it may be that the intermediaries interpolated Lenin without specific dictation. The timing of late May 1923 closely fits a circumstantial case that the alleged Lenin dictation was produced as part of the struggle in the party in connection with the outcome of the 12th Party Congress—Stalin's triumph, Trotsky's rout. The document's appearance also followed Lenin's removal from the Kremlin to Gorki and the termination of official bulletins about his health, indicating a certain hope-lessness about his condition.[185] Furthermore, on or just before June 2, 1923, Krupskaya handed Zinoviev what was said to be a Lenin dictation on the state planning commission that, wondrously, now supported Trotsky's long-standing desire to achieve economic dictatorship, against which Lenin had fought tooth and nail right through his second massive stroke.[186]

One thing is indisputable: the miraculous dictation could not have emerged from Lenin's innermost sanctum without the involvement of Krupskaya.[187] But why would she support Trotsky? She and Stalin had been at daggers drawn for some time, yet her acrimony with Trotsky dated back far longer.[188] After she had become not only Lenin's wife but also secretary in 1898, she had found herself in the middle of bitter polemics that would produce the Bolshevik-Menshevik split, and in her own letters of the time she wrote sharp barbs not just against Martov but Trotsky, too, calling one of his brochures "the most scandalous perversion of the revolutionary movement in years."[189] More recently, Krupskaya was keenly aware of Lenin's deep exasperation at Trotsky's constant public polemics with him during the civil war and early NEP. It is wrong to see her as on Trotsky's side, just as it is wrong to see Maria Ulyanova on Stalin's.[190] Both women sought not to favor someone but to attain a balance.[191] Krupskaya, in her quarter century by Lenin's side, had undergone a master class of political intrigue, and no doubt she believed in her heart she knew Lenin's wishes. From deep inside the regime, she could see Stalin's "boundless power," and her gambit, if that is what it was, seems designed to deny the Georgian the status of Lenin's sole successor.

## OPERATION PARLIAMENT-2
## (SOLTANĞÄLIEVISM)

Stalin, right after the 12th Party Congress, was unfolding a cunning manipulation of his own, aimed at national-minority party cadres he suspected of disloyalty. It began with the OGPU Eastern Department, which carried responsibility for Muslims and Buddhists, whether abroad or on Soviet territory. The Eastern Department, founded and headed by the Latvian Jēkabs Peterss, had instituted close surveillance over Soviet Muslim Communists, tracking everything from political views to sexual liaisons. In an operation code-named Parliament-2, a particular target was the Tatar Mirsäyet Soltanğäliev, a Stalin protégé and rare bird. Tataria had a mere 3,483 party members, of whom just 28.5 percent were Tatars.[192] Here was a literate Muslim Communist with a mass following among a difficult constituency (as Stalin knew well from his time agitating among Muslims in Batum and Baku), but Soltanğäliev had taken to consistently criticizing Stalin at party forums over such matters as the inclusion of Muslim Turkestan as part of the RSFSR rather than as a self-standing republic of the Union.[193] He called the Muslim peoples of the Volga valley, southern Urals, Central Asia, and Caucasus the springboard of the world revolution, battled the writ of the RSFSR agricultural commissariat over land in Tataria, sponsored glorification of the medieval Tatar Khanate, and pushed to impose Tatar as the language for Muslims across Soviet Russia. Casually, in spring 1923, Stalin approached Soltanğäliev and informed him he had been shown a conspiratorial letter from the Tatar to a comrade in Baskhiria, which indicated the existence of an underground organization, and warned him to be careful. Whether by design or not, this warning prompted Soltanğäliev to write in code to one of his correspondents to ask that his previous letters be destroyed.[194] This letter was intercepted by the OGPU and sent to Kuibyshev, chair of the party Central Control Commission, where, in early May 1923, Soltanğäliev was summoned, expelled from the party for pan-Turkism, pan-Islamism, and nationalism, and arrested.[195]

Although the 13th Party Congress had just discussed the national question in depth, the expulsion of a member of the central government (nationalities commissariat collegium) seemed sufficient for the politburo to summon a special meeting of national Communists, fifty-eight of whom attended, along with two dozen members and candidate members of the Central Committee. On June 9, 1923, with Kamenev chairing, and the Muslim attendees aware that Soltanğäliev was sitting at Lubyanka internal prison, Kuibyshev opened the four-day gathering with a report containing excerpts from the incriminating Soltangäliev letter asking that his previous letters be destroyed as well as from his interrogation testimony. Kuibyshev asserted that Soltangäliev had admitted writing the secret correspondence, called his own arrest "lawful," and allowed that "it would also be lawful to apply the highest measure of punishment to me—execution. I say this sincerely." Kuibyshev concluded that Soltangäliev had committed grave transgressions but could be released, because he had admitted his actions; otherwise, despite the proof just presented (in this secret forum), the Tatar might become a martyr.[196] Much of the ensuing discussion was taken up by those who had worked closely with Soltangäliev and were trying to explain themselves. But Orjonikidze observed that in Turketsan, where he had been recently, the infighting took the form of Sunnis versus Shiites, Turks versus Persians, not national Communism, while in the Caucasus, students in the Azerbaijan Muslim-teachers school wore badges featuring Turkey's Mustafa Kemal. He called for training national-minority Communists as internationalists (like himself). By contrast, Skrypnyk, the Ukrainian Communist, remarked that someone was trying to use this incident "to shift policy" toward a harder line against national Communists (Trotsky shouted out: "Completely correct").[197] Skrypnyk, along with Rakovski, was giving Stalin fits on the constitutional commission to finalize the governing structures of the Union.[198]

Stalin spoke in the discussion after Kuibyshev's report, even though his own report was scheduled for that evening. "Nationalism is the fundamental idea-obstacle on the path to growing Marxist cadres, a Marxist avant-garde, in the borderlands," he stated, equating Muslim nationalists to Mensheviks, "a bourgeois ideology" and platform for reviving a bourgeoisie in conditions of the NEP. Before the four-day meeting, he may have been contemplating a revolutionary tribunal culminating in a death penalty.[199] But now, Stalin agreed with his minion Kuibyshev on the need to release Soltangäliev. "The guy admitted all his sins and sought forgiveness," Stalin stated, as if being magnanimous. "He has been expelled from the party and of course will not be readmitted. But for what purpose should he be held in prison?" When a voice interjected to ask what work Soltangäliev could do, Stalin answered, "He is not ours, he's alien, but, I assure, you, he is no worse than certain military specialists who conduct very important work in important posts."[200] The equation of a national minority Communist with tsarist military specialists was revealing of Stalin's pervasive suspicions of disloyalty. He made Soltangäliev into an example as a means of intimidation and control. While Zinoviev inadvertently managed to reveal his ignorance of national affairs at the forum, Kamenev, who was in on Stalin's virtuoso manipulation to tighten the political screws, closed the gathering by reminding attendees that internal threats such as Soltangälievism could become a weapon in the hands of Britain, "the greatest imperialist power."[201] On June 14, the OGPU's Mężyński had Soltangäliev released, after forty-five days in prison. (He would end up relegated to working in the country's hunting association.)[202] Stalin had a stenographic account of the gathering quickly distributed for required discussion in all national republic party organizations. The discussion in the Tatarstan party was presided over by the local OGPU chief.[203] There would be "indigenization" of national cadres, as mandated by the 12th Party Congress, but also OGPU surveillance. Here were techniques Stalin could apply beyond Muslim Communists.

## "CAVE MEETING"

On July 10, 1923, Zinoviev and Bukharin left Moscow for an extended holiday in Kislovodsk, the country's celebrated southern spa town of medicinal "acidic waters" (*kislye vody*).[204] Before departing, the pair had become privy to a sensational additional purported Lenin document, what was called "Ilich's letter about the secretary." Supposedly, it had been dictated by the Bolshevik leader on January 4, 1923, as an addendum to the dictations dated December 24–25; Fotiyeva claimed to have taken the addendum dictation.[205] Krupskaya had again approached Zinoviev.[206] Kamenev, who remained in Moscow at this time, also knew about it. The contents were explosive:

> Stalin is too rude, and this defect, while fully tolerable in the milieu and company among us, Communists, becomes intolerable in the post of general secretary. That is why I suggest that the comrades think about a way to transfer Stalin from this post and name a different person who in all other respects differs from Stalin in having only one advantage, namely that of being more tolerant, more loyal, more polite and more considerate toward comrades, less capricious, and so on. This circumstance may appear to be a mere trifle. But I think that

from the standpoint of safeguards against a schism and from the standpoint of what I wrote above about the relationship between Stalin and Trotsky it is not a trifle, or it is a trifle that can assume decisive importance.[207]

Could Lenin have wanted to sack Stalin just fifteen months after having created the post of general secretary expressly for him? If so, why did the dictation not suggest a replacement? And why did the letter also mention Trotsky?

There is no stenographic original of the "Ilich letter about the [general] secretary." In the journal of Lenin's activities kept by the secretarial staff there is no mention of any such "Ilich letter." The physicians' journal for January 4, 1923, recorded that Lenin suffered a sleepless night and a "poor" disposition, and "gave dictation twice and read," but not a single source corroborates the *content* of the January 4 dictation.[208] Also curious is the fact that Zinoviev had not been made privy to the "Ilich letter about the [general] secretary" in late May, along with the evaluations of six regime personnel. The new typescript emerged only in June.[209]

This alleged dictation—perhaps the most momentous document of the entire regime's history until now—should have radicalized the political dynamic. But Zinoviev and Bukharin, in possession of knowledge of Lenin's ostensible instruction to find a way to remove Stalin as general secretary, did not do so. What the pair did do was to hold a "cave meeting," conspiratorially bringing together on the rock cliffs a few other officials who were also on holiday in Kislovodsk or nearby.[210] Attendees, besides Zinoviev and Bukharin, were Grigory Yevdokimov, the trade union head in Petrograd and one of Zinoviev's closest allies; Mikhail Lashevich, the commander of the Siberian military and another close Zinoviev supporter; and Klim Voroshilov, a staunch Stalin supporter and the commander of the local North Caucasus military district headquartered in Rostov, who received a telegram to come to Kislovodsk, some 300 miles away.[211] There were five "cavemen" in total. An invitation had also gone to Mikhail Frunze, commander of the Ukraine and Crimea military district, who was on holiday at Zheleznovodsk, 25 miles away, but he arrived only the day after.[212]

Trotsky also happened to be in Kislovodsk on holiday, but by all accounts he took no part in the cave meeting.[213] He was, of course, no less unhappy than Zinoviev or Bukharin with how Stalin operated the party secretariat, but Trotsky, polemicizing against potential allies, holding himself at a distance, made it exceedingly difficult for anyone to ally with him. That summer he was mostly absorbed in writing, though he did agree to receive the American leftist writer Max Eastman, who came down to Kislovodsk during a twenty-one-month stay in the Soviet Union to talk to Trotsky about writing his biography ("the most universally gifted man in the world to-day," Eastman would write).[214]

Zinoviev would later explain that "all the participants understood that the secretariat under Lenin was one thing, but the secretariat without Lenin altogether something else." Bukharin, who may have spurred the cave process, proposed that they "politicize" the secretariat, that is, turn it into a small politburo by adding (alongside Stalin) Zinoviev and Trotsky, or perhaps Trotsky and Kamenev, or Trotsky and Bukharin. "There were great rows over this," Zinoviev continued in his explanation, "and many (myself included) considered that comrade Trotsky would work with us, and together we would succeed in creating a stable balance of power."[215]

A consolidated "triumvirate" against Trotsky had yet to form in summer 1923; rather, the immediate concern generated by Lenin's three strokes was not Trotsky's power but Stalin's.

Some days after the cave meeting, Sergo Orjonikidze, the head of the South Caucasus regional party committee in Tiflis, who had a previously scheduled trip to Berlin via Moscow for medical treatment, stopped over in Kislovodsk. Zinoviev briefed Orjonikidze, considered a Stalin loyalist, on the cave discussions and handed him a letter (dated July 29) for Stalin and Kamenev.[216] Predictably, Stalin became infuriated. Zinoviev, in the meantime, had received two letters from Stalin (dated July 25 and 27) reporting various actions that Stalin, as general secretary, had taken.[217] The most important, for Zinoviev, entailed Stalin's decision to countermand Zinoviev's Comintern directives for bolder actions by German Communists. This infuriated Zinoviev. On July 30, a white-hot Zinoviev dashed off an accusatory letter from Kislovodsk to Kamenev in Moscow, complaining of the latter's complicity in Stalin's peremptory, non-consultative decision making. "You are in Moscow," Zinoviev wrote. "You have no small influence. And you are simply letting Stalin mock us." Zinoviev cited various examples, then added, "Did Stalin consult with anyone about these appointments? Not with us, of course." Even at sessions of the Comintern, run by Zinoviev (and Bukharin), Stalin was dominant: "Stalin arrives, glances about and decides. And Bukharin and I are 'dead bodies'—we are not asked anything." Then Zinoviev delivered the punch line:

We *shall not* tolerate this anymore. If the party is condemned to go through a period (prob. very brief) of Stalin's one-man-rule [*edinoderzhavie*], so be it. But at least I do not intend to cover up all this swinishness. In practice there is no "triumvirate," there is Stalin's dictatorship. Ilich was a thousand times correct.

The final reference could only denote the "Ilich letter about the secretary."[218]

Zinoviev reminded Kamenev that "you yourself said this more than once," and appeared at once irate ("If you do not answer this letter, I will write no more") and hopeful: "But what surprises me is that Voroshilov, Frunze, and Sergo think almost the same." Here, however, Zinoviev may have been shaving the truth. Frunze's position on Stalin's exercise of power is unclear, though he could have tilted toward a "balancing" strategy, while Orjonikidze, even though Stalin had just saved his political hide over the Georgian affair, was his own man and owed his high position in the party not only to Stalin but also to Lenin.[219] But whatever the dispositions of Frunze and Orjonikidze, Voroshilov certainly opposed Zinoviev.[220] Bukharin, meanwhile, wrote his own letter to Kamenev (on July 30), complaining that in his (Bukharin's) absence and without consultation, Stalin had named a temporary editorial collective to oversee *Pravda*. In fact, the politburo had appointed the Trotsky supporter Preobrazhensky as temporary editor, but he had resigned over the reintroduction of a vodka monopoly (the much-criticized tsarist practice of raising revenue from drunkenness), and this unexpected act compelled Stalin to take alternate temporary action, until Bukharin returned from holiday.[221] Stalin's mundane power to act, in this instance and others, seems to have shocked both Bukharin and Zinoviev. They discovered that Stalin indeed had "boundless power."

Zinoviev saw himself as behaving reasonably—"Don't take it and interpret it badly. Consider it calmly," he wrote to Stalin on July 31—given that there was dictation attributed to Lenin calling for Stalin's *removal* and Zinoviev was merely asking for Stalin to share power.[222] But Stalin did not take kindly to the proposal. Moreover, he had not seen this purported Lenin dictation, and he had to be anxious, perhaps frightened, about what the entire document might contain. Orjonikidze wrote to Voroshilov (August 3, 1923) that Stalin viewed the Zinoviev-Bukharin proposals as akin to the appointment of "political commissars" to watch over him, as if he were as untrustworthy as one of those former tsarist generals. Stalin went on the counterattack that same day (August 3), writing to Zinoviev and Bukharin: "I received your letter [of July 29], I spoke with Sergo. I do not understand what I am supposed to do in order that you don't curse me, or what the problem is here?" Stalin proposed a face-to-face meeting—"If you consider the possibility of further friendly work (for from the conversation with Sergo I began to understand that you, evidently, are not against preparing a break, as something unavoidable)."[223]

Stalin would not let them do to him what he had just done to the Tatar Mirsäyet Soltangäliev. After another Zinoviev-Bukharin letter (August 6), written in a conciliatory tone ("the mention of a 'break' comes from your exhaustion, of course. Such a possibility is excluded"), Stalin exploded. "Why was it necessary to cite Ilich's letter about the [general] secretary, which is unknown to me— is there no proof that I'm not enamored of position and therefore not afraid of letters?" Stalin wrote on August 7. "What does one call a group whose members try to intimidate one another?" Stalin added that decisions were not being taken by the secretariat alone without others and that the agendas were not being decided without input from anyone other than the secretariat. He painted himself as a victim: "You are lucky people: you have the opportunity on holiday to discuss all manner of concoctions, debate them and so on, and meanwhile I am here tugging like a dog on a chain, sputtering, and I turn out to be 'guilty.'" He was doing all the work! Scoffing at their pretense of friendship, he called their bluff: "I favor a change in the [general] secretary, but I'm against instituting political commissars (we have not a few political commissars already: the orgburo, the politburo, the plenum)."[224]

Stalin's response, laced with self-pity, yet forceful—and including an apparent offer to resign—provoked from Zinoviev and Bukharin their sharpest letter yet. "Yes, there exists a letter of V.I., in which he advises the 12th Party Congress not to reelect you as [general] secretary," they wrote on August 10. "We (Bukharin, Kamenev, and I) decided not to talk to you about it yet. For an understandable reason: You already take disagreements with V.I. too subjectively, and we did not want to unnerve you." Unnerve him they had, of course, and their attempt at mollification was strained:

There's no Ilich. The secretariat of the CENTRAL COMMITTEE, therefore, objectively (without evil intentions on your part) begins to play the role in the Central Committee that the secretariat plays in another provincial party organization, that is, in fact (*not* formally), it *decides everything*. This is a fact, which is impossible to deny. No one wants to institute political commissars. (You even deem the orgburo, politburo, and plenum political commissars!) . . . The situation (both with Trotsky and with various "platforms") gets more complicated and dissatisfaction in the party grows (don't look at the surface). Hence, a search for a better form of collaboration.

The document was handwritten by Bukharin yet signed only by Zinoviev. It concluded: "Don't for a minute think that we are conspiring. Take a holiday as you should. All the best. Zinoviev."[225] But the letter was never sent.[226] Stalin was scheduled to depart for Kislovodsk on August 15, 1923, for a one-and-a-half-month holiday, which, however, he put off.[227]

## DELIRIUM

A key issue delaying Stalin's holiday departure was the vision of an October-style revolution in Germany.[228] Germany was far and away the most important country in the world for the USSR. Suffering devastating inflation, Germany had defiantly fallen into arrears in its reparations. France had been bled white in the Great War (fought on its territory), but the British wanted to reduce German obligations, which made the French even more livid. The Reparations Commission declared Germany in default, and France and Belgium militarily occupied the Ruhr valley, site of 80 percent of Germany's steel, pig iron, and coal.[229] This crashed German markets and worsened the rampant inflation (by November 1923, to purchase $1 would cost 130 billion marks).[230] Expressing solidarity with its Rapallo partner, Soviet Russia boldly warned its nemesis Poland not to take advantage of Germany's crisis and seize East Prussia, on the other side of the Versailles-created Polish Corridor.[231] Moscow also urged Latvia and Lithuania to agree to a policy of non-intervention in German affairs. At the same time, Zinoviev and Bukharin had decided the moment was ripe for the USSR to intervene in German affairs by staging a Communist coup d'état. In Kislovodsk, while pondering how to curb Stalin's power, the pair received a letter (dated July 11) from Heinrich Brandler (b. 1881), a former bricklayer and a leader of German Communists who had a quarter-century experience in revolutionary struggle.

Brandler crowed that the German Communists would soon stage a major anti-fascist day rally and that "for every Communist who is killed we shall kill ten fascists."[232]

While Karl Radek warned Brandler to avoid any confrontation that could serve as a pretext for a massive anti-Communist crackdown, Zinoviev took Brandler's letter as a sign of newfound determination and Radek's action as insubordination—Zinoviev headed the Comintern. Stalin supported Radek, expressing skepticism in his exchange of letters with Zinoviev about Germany, just as he had over Poland's alleged ripeness for revolution back in 1920. Brandler, for his part, disregarded Radek's warnings and on July 31 publicly announced German Communists' intention "to win political power." A few days later, he proclaimed the imminent "fall of the bourgeois order" and onset of a "civil war."[233] Stalin continued his skepticism. Although Germany in 1923 had a far larger working class than Russia had had in 1917, in his letter to Zinoviev on August 7 Stalin enumerated special circumstances that had favored the Bolsheviks in 1917, and he emphasized not only or even primarily worker support for Bolshevism, but also that the Bolsheviks had had a people desperate for peace and a peasantry eager to seize the landlords' estates. "At the moment, the German Communists have nothing of the kind," he noted. "They have, of course, a Soviet country as neighbor, which we did not have, but what can we offer them at this time? Should power in Germany, so to speak, topple over now and the Communists seize it, they would end up crashing. That is in the best case. In the worst case they will be smashed to smithereens. . . . In my opinion the Germans should be restrained and not encouraged."[234]

This disagreement was not going to be resolved over the wires and on August 9, Stalin had the politburo formally request that members return from holiday for direct discussion. An affirmative answer came back from Zinoviev and Bukharin on August 12. Trotsky stipulated that the interruption in his course of medical treatment should last "not more than one week."[235]

Mass strikes had engulfed Germany, involving 3 million workers, a scale that surprised even German Communist militants, and, after the hapless German central government resigned, its place was taken by the classical liberal politician Gustav Stresemann in a grand coalition that included German Social Democrats. Even before this, leftist Social Democrats had entered the regional governments of Thuringia and Saxony, Brandler's home state. The evident radicalization in Germany fed Zinoviev's initial zeal; Stalin warned of a likely military intervention by France and Poland against a German workers' government that would also engulf the USSR.[236] On August 21, the politburo resolved to dispatch 1 million gold marks to Germans by underground channels, the onset of a river of money from a poor and ruined country still suffering severe hunger.[237] Two days later a breathtaking discussion took place at the politburo, at which Stalin supported the idea of a coup, but in hypersecrecy. "Stalin's point of view is correct," Trotsky noted. "It cannot seem that we, not only the Russian Communist party but also the Comintern, are orchestrating." Trotsky appeared to be the skeptic, demanding a detailed plan of insurrection, while Stalin stated, lyrically, that "either the revolution in German fails and knocks us off, or there, the revolution succeeds, all goes well, and our situation is secured." There was likely some cold calculation at work here: if Germany did go Communist, and Stalin was on record as having been unsupportive, he would end up looking like Zinoviev and Kamenev in 1917. Still, Stalin's turnaround revealed a degree of enthusiasm unnecessary to a calculated demonstration. He rhapsodized about the USSR needing "a border with Germany," which could be created by trying to "overturn one of the bourgeois border states." When Chicherin asked whether the USSR should work to consolidate the states of Czechoslovakia and Yugoslavia or prepare uprisings in them, voices shouted "of course, both."[238]

The Comintern issued a worldwide appeal on August 25 to trade unionists and socialists of all stripes for unified action in the face of the "fascist" threat. No one answered.[239] That same day, Trotsky instructed his deputy at the Military Revolutionary Committee of the Republic, Yefraim Sklyansky, to prepare the Red Army for a possible Entente attack.[240] Three days later, Central Committee secretary Rudzutaks sent a coded telegram to provincial party committees to the effect that a revolution was imminent in Germany and to expect a bourgeois military intervention against Germany, as had happened to Soviet Russia.[241]

## DREAD EVERLASTING

Stalin knew that his expansive faction would be aggressive in his defense. When he had informed Kuibyshev and Rudzutaks, the other Central Committee secretaries and his staunch loyalists, they supposedly laughed at Zinoviev's intrigues.[242] And yet, this was no laughing matter: an apparent instruction from Lenin to remove Stalin, which lay in the hands of politburo members. Powerful indirect testimony to the fear Stalin felt appeared in the journal *Proletarian Revolution*. In its ninth issue for 1923, which came out in September, Lenin's letters of spring 1917 to Karpinsky and Ganetsky were published, the very letters that the Provisional Government police had intercepted and used to charge Lenin with treason as a German agent in July 1917.[243] One might expect such incriminating documents, published from police copies, to appear in an émigré periodical aiming to discredit Lenin, but in a Soviet journal, and one prepared for publication in August 1923? It could have been a bizarre coincidence. But it seems highly likely that Stalin, who controlled Lenin's archives, set in motion the publication, aiming to strike a blow at Lenin's reputation.[244] If so, it was an act of desperation. Precisely when Stalin first read the "Ilich letter" remains unknown. One would expect to find a copy of it, with his pencil marks, in his archive, but no such copy is extant. Who showed it to him, when, under what circumstances, and with what reaction, may never be known. We can guess, however, that when Zinoviev and Bukharin returned to Moscow around August 20, 1923, Stalin demanded to see it. But it is possible that Krupskaya had not handed a copy to Zinoviev but only let him read it, which would only have augmented Stalin's terror.

Stalin blunted the cave-meeting initiative with a clever proposal, accepted by the others, to add two politburo members, Zinoviev and Trotsky, to the orgburo—not, as originally proposed, to the secretariat—as full members, along with two new candidate orgburo members, Ivan Korotkov (a regional party boss promoted to Moscow) and Bukharin (listed second). Predictably, Trotsky and Bukharin would never attend a single meeting of the labor-intensive orgburo; Zinoviev would claim he attended once or twice.[245]

Part of the failure of the cave-meeting machinations derived from Trotsky's behavior. Bukharin would explain that "I personally wanted to unify the biggest figures into an upper stratum of the Central Committee, namely Stalin, Trotsky and Zinoviev. . . . I tried with all my might to bring peace inside the party. . . . Comrade Zinoviev vacillated, and soon he took the position of a merciless attack against Trotsky, ruining this plan. Comrade Trotsky, for his part, did everything possible to aggravate relations."[246] True enough, but an even greater factor was Kamenev's position.[247] Kamenev, because he ran meetings efficiently, developed a reputation for business-like practicality, but those who knew him better understood he was an inveterate intriguer. His thinking at this moment is undocumented. He knew Zinoviev well and perhaps did not have as high opinion of him as Zinoviev had of himself. Similarly, Kamenev had known Stalin a very long time, since the early 1900s, in Tiflis, and in 1917 the two had returned from Siberian exile to Petrograd together, then worked together. Kamenev certainly understood that Stalin was no angel—thin-skinned, two-faced, a nasty provocateur—but Kamenev clearly did not see Stalin as a *special* danger, for otherwise he would have joined the action against him. Here is an indicator that, in 1923 at least, the monstrous later Stalin either did not yet exist or was not visible to someone who worked with him very closely. On the contrary, Kamenev appears to have viewed Stalin as manageable. He told Orjonikidze that the complaints of Zinoviev and Bukharin were exaggerated.[248] Kamenev also likely appreciated the heavy load that Stalin was carrying as general secretary. The draft USSR constitution was ceremonially approved by the Soviet central executive committee on July 6, 1923, in the Grand Kremlin Palace—the nationalities commissariat was abolished, so that Stalin no longer had a formal government position—but the USSR structure still had to be implemented, and in that Stalin was indispensable.[249] Whatever Kamenev's precise calculations, or miscalculations, his siding with Stalin was deliberate and crucial to the general secretary's political survival.

Zinoviev and Bukharin had misjudged Kamenev, who in turn misjudged Stalin, but Zinoviev's behavior is the grand mystery. Everyone understood that Zinoviev had designs on being number one.[250] And in that summer of 1923, Krupskaya had handed him a letter from Lenin advising that they remove Stalin. But Zinoviev did no such thing. He had been afforded an opportunity to alter the course of history, and did not seize it. To be sure, the views of Rykov, Kalinin, and Tomsky, as well as Molotov, remained to consider; and Kamenev's siding with Stalin—even on a proposal well short of removal—had been a ghastly surprise for Zinoviev. Trotsky, moreover, had been his usual aloof self in connection with the admittedly inchoate feelers Zinoviev appears to have delivered via Bukharin. Nonetheless, Zinoviev could have forced the issue to remove Stalin from the pivotal position of general secretary by demanding that Lenin's will be enforced. He could have demanded a Central Committee plenum on the subject, even an extraordinary party congress. Instead, Zinoviev had called a meeting in a cave, then signed his name to some letters to Stalin Bukharin wrote, then did not even send one of them. Given the fact that Stalin's personality would prove to have momentous consequences, Zinoviev's failure to act upon his own blatant ambition and force the issue of Stalin's removal—even more than Kamenev's hesitation merely to curb some of Stalin's powers—was arguably the most consequential action (or inaction) by a politburo member after Lenin had become irreversibly sidelined.

Krupskaya setting in motion in summer 1923 the "Ilich letter about the [general] secretary" turned out to be a turning point that did not turn. For Stalin, however, the episode was hardly over. He likely suspected Zinoviev would return to Lenin's purported dictation, and perhaps reveal it to the Central Committee and maybe beyond. And would not Trotsky, too, become involved? And how long would Kamenev's backing last? And what about Bukharin's prominent role in the cave intrigue? Stalin's biggest concern, though, remained Lenin, even though the Bolshevik leader could neither speak nor write. Out at Gorki, he was being walked around the grounds in imported wheelchairs, struggling to scratch out some words with his left hand ("mama," "papa"), and listening as Krupskaya read to him as to a baby.[251] Lenin was never going to return to public life. But documents attributed to him had been coming forward piecemeal, months after they were allegedly dictated. Through the OGPU, Stalin could maintain close surveillance on the comings and goings at Gorki, under the guise of security, but he could not control Krupskaya, and he could not be sure what other documents purporting to be instructions from "Ilich" might yet be brought to light. Finally, Stalin appears to have departed for Kislovodsk in late August.[252] But one wonders what kind of "holiday" it could have been with the sword of Damocles hanging over his head. In any case, the dubious respite was brief, for he was attending meetings in the capital by the third week of September.

## HUMILIATION

Revolutionary fever swept Moscow in September 1923. Brandler had arrived in late August and by mid-September other German Communists had arrived to find the city strewn with banners proclaiming the imminent "German October," while factories held meetings on how Soviet workers could aid their German counterparts.[253] But the German Communists were at each other's throats, riven into left, right, and center factions, and Brandler was begging for either Zinoviev or Trotsky to lead the insurrection. That September, a Comintern-pushed uprising in Bulgaria, aimed at overthrowing a government that itself had recently come to power in a coup d'état, was crushed, after which the Bulgarian forces of order went on a reprisal spree, killing 2,000 Communist activists and agrarians, but this, too, did nothing to slow the plans for Germany.[254] Zinoviev pursued a German breakthrough to blot out the stain of having opposed the October 1917 seizure of power. Stalin was not to be outdone by him. "The forthcoming revolution in Germany is the most important world event of our day," he wrote on September 20, in response to a request for an article from the editor of *Die Rote Fahne,* the Communist organ in Germany. "The victory of the revolution in Germany would have more substantive significance for the proletariat of Europe and America than the victory of the Russian Revolution six years ago. The victory of the German proletariat would undoubtedly shift the center of the world revolution from Moscow to Berlin."[255]

Meetings of the politburo or its German commission took place from September 21 through 23.[256] One key agenda item was what to do about the German Social Democrats. If they agreed to be junior partners to the Communists, cooperating with them would be helpful, Stalin argued; if they refused, this would expose the Social Democrats in front of the German workers—even better.[257] Right in the middle of these sessions, Avel Yenukidze, secretary of the Presidium of the central executive committee, formally approved a USSR coat of arms with a hammer and sickle resting on a globe depicted in sun rays, with the inscription "Workers of the world, unite!" in six languages (Russian, Ukrainian, Belorussian, Georgian, Azeri, Armenian).[258] Zinoviev enlarged upon the possible formation of a United States of Worker-Peasant Republics of Europe.[259] Trotsky published an overview of revolutionary tactics in the French and Russian revolutions in *Pravda* (September 23, 1923), which he intended as instructions to the Communist forces in Germany. What effect the article, which was republished in German in Berlin, had on the German Communist organizers is unclear, but it did draw an official protest from the German ambassador in Moscow.[260] Zinoviev was beside himself with zeal and sat night after night with Trotsky in the latter's war commissariat offices at Znamenka, 23, posing operations questions about Germany to Sergei Kamenev, the Red Army military commander-in-chief.[261] Brandler boasted to a Party Congress of the Polish Communist party held in Moscow's immediate countryside that the German Communists had more than 350,000 members, and would be able to field 200,000 armed workers, weapons for the equivalent of fifteen divisions of 5,000 troops each, and 330 partisan groups for behind-the-lines warfare—numbers that were eye-popping, or eye wash.[262]

From September 23 to 25, a Central Committee plenum took place in the

Grand Kremlin Palace with fifty-two participants. The opening day saw two reports, one by Zinoviev on the international situation, which concerned Germany, and another by First Deputy Head of government Rykov on the defense of the country and the creation of a special reserve fund.[263] The plenum approved a date for the German coup of November 9, the anniversary of the kaiser's abdication and the "bourgeois" revolution (i.e., the founding of the Republic).[264] Kuibyshev reported on changes in the composition of the Revolutionary Military Council, headed by Trotsky. In other words, instead of a discussion of Lenin's apparent demand to find a way to remove Stalin—the "Ilich letter about the [general] secretary"—Trotsky was ambushed by a scheme, developed without his consultation, to enlarge and stuff the Revolutionary Military Council with partisans of Stalin, Zinoviev, and Kamenev. Trotsky announced his intention to resign from every one of his posts—including his politburo and Central Committee membership—and requested to be sent abroad "as a soldier of the revolution" to assist the German Communists in the planned coup.[265] When one attendee from Petrograd, Fyodor Sobinov, known as Nikolai Komarov—the son of poor peasants and himself a former factory worker—suddenly asked why Trotsky "put on such airs," Trotsky exploded. He shot up, stated "I request that you delete me from the list of actors of this humiliating comedy," and stomped out, resolving to slam the cast-iron door—a massive metal structure not given to demonstrative slamming. He could only manage to bring it to a close slowly, unwittingly demonstrating his impotence.[266]

Whether by design or dumb luck, Stalin, Zinoviev, and Kamenev had humiliated Trotsky.

A delegation was dispatched to his nearby apartment to coax him back, but he refused and the plenum continued and officially rebuked his behavior.[267] The protocols further noted: "Send excerpt to comrade Trotsky immediately." In his absence, the plenum voted to add several Central Committee members to the Revolutionary Military Council.[268] This was the second time its composition had been altered against Trotsky; the first had been by Lenin, in March 1919, which had also precipitated Trotsky's announcement of his resignation. Back then, his resignation had been rejected, and Lenin mollified him. This time, too, Trotsky's resignation was rejected, but without Lenin to smooth things over and balance the personalities.

It was only now that the other top members of the politburo began to act concertedly as a triumvirate. At one of the subsequent politburo sessions, when a ruckus erupted between Trotsky and Zinoviev, the latter burst out, "Can't you see you're in a ring [*obruch*]? . . . Your tricks no longer work, you're in a minority, you're in the singular." From this point, whenever Zinoviev and Kamenev secretly came over to Stalin at the secretariat to prearrange issues before polit-buro meetings, their three-way clandestine gatherings acquired the secret catch-phrase "the ring."[269] Their ring around Trotsky provoked him.

## LEFT OPPOSITION

NEP's grudging legalization of markets had done nothing to alleviate the blatant squalor of workers in whose name the regime ruled. Industry had been reorga-nized in giant trusts (metalworking, cotton) and those enterprises deemed most important, known as the commanding heights, had been placed under the aegis of the state, but this had not shielded many factories from being shuttered or leased, sometimes to their former capitalist owners. Redundant workers were being laid off, while those not fired saw their wages linked to output quotas, just as under the old regime.[270] Engineers and "specialists," meanwhile, enjoyed con-spicuous privileges, also as if no revolution had happened. "The specialist lives better, gets paid better, he gives the orders, makes demands; the specialist is an alien, the specialist did not make the October Revolution," Mikhail Tomsky, the head of the trade unions, explained, in summarizing worker views.[271] When lectured that the country was poor, workers snapped that officials should go to the city's restaurants, where party bosses did not seem to be experiencing pov-erty.[272] This combustible situation had erupted in strike waves at the biggest fac-tories beginning in spring 1923 and continuing through the fall.[273] Soviet and British intelligence independently noted a linkage between hopeful rumors of impending war and of the Soviet regime's downfall.[274] The OGPU conducted sweeping arrests, but workers often struck again to free their comrades, accord-ing to the secret reports sent to party headquarters. Matters resembled a Kron-stadt dynamic: only fanatics ("special purpose units") would bash in the heads of proletarians.[275]

Bolshevik propaganda sought to explain away worker unrest by references to an alleged "dilution" of the proletariat by recent arrivals from the countryside and by women, or sophistry. "Although there are several workers' parties there is only one proletarian party," Zinoviev asserted in a series of lectures on the history of the party in connection with its twenty-fifth anniversary in 1923. He added that "a party can be a workers' party in its composition and yet not be proletarian in its orientation, program, and policy."[276] In other words, the regime's "proletariat" was no longer even a partly sociological entity, but a wholly ideological one.

The secret police vigorously enforced the ban on independent trade unions and on non-Communist worker movements, but an ostensible alternative within the single party emerged around Trotsky, and became known as the Left opposition. Trotsky in fall 1923 began demanding "inner party democracy," decrying how "the bureaucratization of the party apparatus has developed to unheard of proportions by means of the method of secretary selection [appointment]" and how "a very broad stratum of functionaries has been created who, upon entering into the apparatus of the government of the party, completely renounce their own party opinion, at least the open expression of it."[277] Of course, it was hardly surprising that Bolshevik assaults on private property and the rule of law had not resulted in the formation of a supple, efficient, responsive civil service. Apparatchiks supposed to engage in merciless class warfare with summary executions on one side, were not likely, on the other, to make way for a Greek polis. Unaccountable bureaucratic satrapies, political intimidation, and runaway self-dealing were inescapable consequences of Trotsky's own commitment to Communism. Moreover, even as he was railing against bureaucratic "degeneration," he was proposing a super bureaucracy of specialists (preferably led by him) to "plan" the economy. The Left opposition's positive program promised next to nothing for working people on strike. In fall 1917, Trotsky had shown himself to be a political magician, able to popularize even the most difficult ideas for the working man, raising enormous crowds to fever pitch as they swore sacred oaths to the positions he argued, but in fall 1923 he was writing not about the plight of real workers and their families who needed jobs or housing but abstractly about "crisis." Wage arrears and forced deductions for state "loan" subscriptions were tailor-made for Populist appeals, but Trotsky made no concerted effort to demagogue them.

Still, Trotsky's critique had considerable impact on the apparatus. On October 12, 1923, a mere four days after Trotsky had sent a blistering missive to the Central Committee, Molotov dispatched to all party organizations a secret circular that enumerated "excessively luxurious" apartments, "stables with race and riding horses," "heavy expenditures at restaurants," and on and on. "At the disposal of the Central Committee are a series of facts indicating both the central and provincial party organizations . . . maintain fleets of automobiles and horse-drawn carriages without any work-related need," the circular read. "It has come to our attention that very often special railcars have been dispatched to southern resorts for the sole purpose of delivering one passenger. . . . At state expense, entire freight railcars were dispatched to the southern resorts transporting automobiles."[278] Reports were flooding the apparatus of inebriated, power-hungry, thieving officials who were "cut off from the masses," as the jargon had it—unless they were trying to rape them.[279]

Trotsky forced a public debate upon the triumvirate in fall 1923, but its contours were strikingly narrow—furious polemics about a monopoly party's *procedures* for discussion of the complexities of modern society in terms of class, with no sense of common humanity.[280] On top of its sterile program, as far as the non-party masses were concerned, the Left opposition was severely handicapped by regime structure. Bolshevism itself was nothing if not a faction, a minority, which, back in 1903, had broken off and called itself majoritarians (Bolsheviks) while tagging its opponents as minoritarians (Mensheviks), but after the resolution on party unity at the 10th Party Congress, there was no way for like-minded party members to criticize regime policies without risking expulsion from the party. A so-called Declaration of the 46—a disparate group of policy critics—tried to turn the tables, demanding "the factional regime" of the central party apparatus be "replaced by a regime of comradely unity and internal party democracy."[281] Neither Trotsky nor several of his highest profile supporters had affixed their names to the text. Nonetheless, the triumvirate mobilized party bodies to condemn the document, as well as Trotsky's own letter, as illegal factionalism.[282] Regime failures were so blatant, however, that Left opposition resolutions were carrying votes in protest at meetings of primary party organizations in Moscow. Stalin's top aide, Nazaretyan, threw the winning tallies in the trash and reported false returns for publication in *Pravda*. Nazaretyan's aide, however, felt a pang of conscience and confessed. Both would both be transferred out of the central apparatus, but the distorted vote counts were not redone.[283] The anti-Trotsky struggle accelerated institutionalization of the party's violation of its own rules.[284] When the French and Polish Communist parties initiated protests of the vilification of Trotsky, Stalin had Trotsky charged with attempting to split the Comintern.[285] The prime mover of the French action, Boris Lifschitz, known as Souvarine, would later write an excellent condemnatory biography of Stalin.[286]

## CONFRONTATION

Trotsky united instead of divided his enemies with a relentlessly condescending personality.[287] By nature aloof as well, he was clueless about the consequences, even in hindsight, as when he would recall that he had refused to socialize with others in the ruling group because he "hated to inflict such boredom on myself. The visiting of each other's homes, the assiduous attendance at the ballet, the drinking-parties at which people who were absent were pulled to pieces, had no attraction for me. . . . It was for this reason that many group conversations would stop the moment I appeared."[288] Nonetheless, Trotsky did at times fight hard.[289] He suffered a physical setback, however. As he would tell the story, one Sunday that October 1923, while hunting for geese, curlew, snipe, and ducks north of Moscow in the marshes of Tver province, he stepped into a deep bog of cold water, proved unable to warm himself in the car, and came down with flu symptoms.[290] Whatever the cause, his fevers were real, and he was confined to bed by doctors' orders. In deference, at Kamenev's suggestion, the politburo meeting on October 16 took place in the study of Trotsky's Kremlin apartment in the Cavalry Building. This was the meeting that decreed an immediate investigation of Trotsky by the Central Control Commission for "factionalism." The war commissar, according to his wife, "came out of his study soaked through, and undressed and went to bed. His linen and clothes had to be dried as if he had been drenched in a rainstorm."[291]

With Trotsky under political assault and feverish, a bizarre event occurred: On October 18, 1923, Lenin showed up at the Kremlin, where he had not been for five months.[292] It went like this: following the usual late afternoon meal at Gorki, Lenin demanded to be pushed in his wheelchair to the garage, used his orthopedic shoes to climb into his Silver Ghost, and refused to get out, insisting—by his demeanor—that he was going to Moscow. Staff talked him into shifting to a closed vehicle, and he departed around 4:00 p.m. with Krupskaya, Maria, and nurse attendants, while others, including his doctors, Professors Osipov,

Rozanov, Priorov, and a bodyguard detail, traveled in accompanying vehicles. Upon arrival at the Imperial Senate, Lenin looked over his Kremlin apartment, took tea and lunch. He stayed overnight. He visited his Kremlin office on October 19, where he retrieved books from his library (three volumes of Hegel, works of Plekhanov). He insisted on being pushed around the Kremlin grounds— where, of course, people recognized him—but a driving rain forced him instead to take a car ride around central Moscow, including to the All-Russia Agricultural and Handicraft Exhibition, which would soon close and which Lenin had avidly followed in the press, but which he saw only through the vehicle windows because of the downpour. He agreed to return to Gorki in the early evening, exhausted.[293] "News of Vladimir Ilich's arrival spread around the Kremlin, and people were looking out from all the windows and doors," Lenin's driver recalled.[294] It is inconceivable that Stalin did not know, because OGPU channels would have alerted the party secretariat to Lenin's movements. Also, Lenin's drivers reported to the head of the Special Purpose Garage, who was Stalin's principal driver. Trotsky, as war commissar, would have received word from the Kremlin garrison and Moscow military district. Strangely, however, by all accounts Lenin did not meet with Stalin, Trotsky, Zinoviev, Kamenev, or anyone else from the leadership.

On October 18 and 19 (a Thursday and Friday), the usual politburo and Council of People's Commissars meeting space next to Lenin's office and apartment proved to be empty. Whether Lenin expected to catch meetings there remains unknown. "Did he [Lenin] wish to see one of the comrades on this visit?" wrote Maria Ulyanova, later, in recollections of the trip. "I think not. I'm judging by the fact that, shortly before his trip, when he asked for something and no matter how much we strained our heads we could not understand what he wanted, I asked him would he not like to see someone from among his comrades. I named a few names, but he shook his head bitterly—he had no cause to see them, since he had been deprived of the opportunity to work."[295] Be that as it may, sources agree that when the car from Gorki with Lenin had first gotten within sight of Moscow's golden-dome skyline, he excitedly pointed with his finger, a by now familiar gesture that was taken to mean: "That's it, that's it, that's it, that's iiiitttt!"[296] Lenin remained in high spirits during the entire time in Moscow. Back at Gorki, he became manifestly sad. His trip seems to have fulfilled a long-standing wish to set his eyes on Moscow once more. He would never set foot in the Kremlin again.

If Lenin had been looking for the Bolshevik "conspiracy in power," he did not find it because, though a politburo meeting did take place on October 18, by twist of fate it was convened in feverish Trotsky's apartment in the Cavalry Building, a different building from Lenin's apartment in the Imperial Senate. (The meeting might also have finished before Lenin arrived from Gorki.) On the agenda was the dire need to send grain to Germany, anticipating likely civil war over the planned Communist coup, and the possible behavior of Germany's neighbors. "I think that it's better to refrain from sounding out the Poles and instead sound out the Latvians—the Latvians can be intimidated, put up against the wall, and so on," Stalin wrote on a piece of paper during the meeting. "You cannot do that with the Poles. The Poles must be isolated, we will have to fight with them. We'll never ferret them out, just reveal our cards. . . . The Poles to be isolated. The Latvians to be bought (and intimidated). The Romanians to be bought. But with the Poles we wait."[297] For Stalin, a German revolution, in addition to everything else, recommended itself as a means of addressing the existence of the newly independent states that were arrayed in whole or in part on former tsarist territories.

On October 19, with Lenin walking the Kremlin grounds and Trotsky holed up in the Cavalry Building, the politburo collectively answered Trotsky's critical letters to the Central Committee in a long text composed primarily by Stalin—it was typed up and distributed from the party secretariat on Vozdvizhenka. "If our party does not compel comrade Trotsky to repudiate those monstrous mistakes he has made in his 'letter-platform' of October 8, 1923, then not just the Russian Communist party but also the USSR and the German revolution will suffer colossal damage," the politburo response stated.[298] The politburo scheduled a further meeting (in Trotsky's apartment), as well as a joint plenum of the Central Committee and Central Control Commission for October 25–27. On the opening evening of October 25, immediately after Stalin's report, Trotsky got the floor for forty-five minutes. A so-called joint plenum was something of another Stalin trick to add more loyalists from the apparatus. He stacked the deck even beyond that, inviting not just the now punitive (instead of impartial) Control Commission personnel but "representatives" of ten major "industrial" party organizations who turned out to be provincial party bosses whom Stalin's orgburo had appointed to their posts. At the same time, just twelve of the forty-six signatories of the Declaration were asked to appear, and only on the second day.[299] The second day was given to discussion, culminating in summations, first by Trotsky (10:33 p.m. to 11:25 p.m.), then by Stalin (11:25 p.m. to 12:10 a.m.). Stalin had the politburo recording secretary, Boris Bazhanov, secretly compile résumés of the speeches, anticipating using them against Trotsky.[300]

This was the first direct confrontation, absent Lenin, between Stalin and Trotsky at a party forum, and those present had to understand the stakes.

Trotsky, on the attack, acknowledged that he was being accused of recidivism, given his role in the trade union debate two years ago, but he charged that now "within the politburo there is another politburo and within the Central Committee there is another Central Committee, so that I was effectively sidelined from the discussion . . . as a result I only had this path." In trying to explain the seemingly inexplicable—why he had refused Lenin's request to become a deputy head of government—he revealed that in 1917 he had declined Lenin's request to serve as interior minister. "The fact is, comrades, there is one personal aspect of my work, which although playing no role in my personal life and my day-to-day existence, is nonetheless of great political significance," he stated. "This is my Jewish origin. . . . I firmly turned down his offer on the grounds, as before, that we should not give our enemies the opportunity to say that our country was being ruled by a Jew."[301] More recently, when Lenin proposed that he become his deputy in the government, Trotsky said, he refused on the same grounds. This revelation is hard to credit. Trotsky accepted other high-profile appointments in the government.

In his speech to the plenum, Trotsky conceded that he and Lenin had disagreed about economic policy and that relations had become strained. But he stressed, again, that the party should take up ideology and party life, while economic experts ran the economy. "If I were removed from other work and sent to the state planning commission, I would not object," he said. "The state planning commission is our most important organ," but the current institutional architecture did not suit him. "I return to the question: 'What would I do at the Council of People's Commissars, if the state planning commission were not reorganized?'" He claimed his character was such that "I cannot abide sloppiness, unthought-through-ness." In closing, Trotsky pleaded with those assembled not to condemn him for factionalism. "Comrades, . . . try to think about and understand my situation. I was in extremely tragic circumstances"—the party press and a whispering campaign accused him of being anti-Lenin, of creating

"Trotskyism"; others were meeting behind his back, he was enclosed in a ring: "I had to break out."[302]

Stalin, in his speech, displayed contempt. "Could anyone be against improvement of the state planning commission?" he stated. "It's laughable to build a platform around the necessity of improving the state planning commission.... Instead of discussing these serious questions, you go around with platforms. In all the statements of the oppositionists I did not find one single concrete proposal." To their concrete calls for party democracy, he answered, "the Central Committee implements the decisions of party congresses," adding that "democrats tell the congress that we do not need distancing from the influence of the NEP. Let's see if the congress will agree with you." To the complaint of an attendee that "there is no discussion," Stalin likened him to "Chekhov's Lady, 'give me atmosphere.' There are times when it's not a matter of discussion." Bald-faced, he added that "there has never been a case when someone came to the Central Committee proposing to discuss a question and the Central Committee refused." He accused the group of 46 and Trotsky of taking their accusatory statements about the Central Committee's "mistakes" outside proper party channels, appealing directly to the party mass. Stalin averred that "a discussion in the center right now would be especially dangerous. Both the peasants and the workers would lose their trust in us, enemies would regard it as weakness. We experienced such discussion in 1921. At that time we lost out frightfully.... Trotsky started it back then, refusing to abide by Lenin's suggestion to limit the discussion in the trade union commission.... Trotsky has repeated that step, which had threatened us with schism."[303] In fact, in 1921 Lenin had deliberately provoked Trotsky into public debate; and now, in 1923, Trotsky had not appealed to the party mass—he had no such possibility because Stalin controlled the party press.

After Stalin spoke, no rebuttal was allowed. Notwithstanding Trotsky's gobbledygook about his refusals to become Lenin's deputy and his continuing obsession with planning, he had not had to resort to naked lies. Stalin was desperately making up spurious arguments, and showed himself to be thin-skinned, an intellectual bully. Of course, the room had already been prepared: in the voting on a long resolution condemning Trotsky and the Left opposition for factionalism and schism, 102 votes were recorded as in favor, with just 2 against and 10 abstentions. In violation of party rules, non-Central Committee members—the twenty "representatives" of the ten big "industrial" party organizations invited by Stalin—had been permitted to vote.[304] Such manipulation was a sign of weakness. Stalin never used the secretly recorded transcript of this confrontation with Trotsky.

Stalin's other principal nemesis, Krupskaya, who had taken part in the "joint" plenum, on October 31 sent a strongly reproachful letter to Zinoviev. She had voted with the majority against Trotsky, but now, privately, she insisted that Trotsky was not the sole person to blame for party divisions and that "the workers would severely judge not just Trotsky but us" even though what was going on in the party "was being kept hidden" from them. "The moment is too serious to create a schism and make it psychologically impossible for Trotsky to work." She criticized the "intemperate language," "the personal quarrels and squabbles," and took particular umbrage at the "abuse of Vladimir Ilich's name. . . . References to Ilich were uncalled-for and insincere. . . . They were mere hypocrisy." She seemed especially incensed at insinuations that Trotsky's letter writing to internal party bodies had exacerbated Lenin's illness ("I should have shouted that this was a lie"). She reminded Zinoviev of Lenin's dictation warning of a schism because of Stalin.[305] And yet, Krupskaya, who, uniquely, could speak with the authority of Lenin's purported wishes, had failed to express any of this at the plenum, where it would have mattered. She had relied on Zinoviev, who was drunk with world revolution and just not up to the task of curbing Stalin's power.

The OGPU and Comintern had flooded Germany with agents and money, and worked hand in glove with the foreign affairs commissariat, borrowing its cipher codes and the diplomatic pouch, with the approval of Chicherin.[306] But Brandler's wild claims about the vast forces the German Communists commanded were now exposed: Mátyás Rákosi (b. 1892), a Hungarian Comintern agent in Germany, reported to Moscow that the ratio of the forces of order to armed Communists was twenty to one. Contrary to Brandler's earlier boasts, Saxony had a mere 800 rifles, not 200,000.[307] Comintern agents who were supposed to purchase and stockpile weapons either failed to manage the difficult task or stole the funds. But the deepest failing was that German Communists held a majority in a mere 200 of the 1,400 local trade union committees and just 5,000 of the 70,000 factory committees.[308] German workers were overwhelmingly members of the Social Democrats. There were, in effect, two Communist conspiracies over Germany in fall 1923: one against the German government, one against the German Social Democrats. Stalin had proposed a "united front" against the German right as mere tactics, designed to split the German Social Democrats and discredit their left wing, leaving the entire revolutionary space to the Communists. The German Social Democrats—as the Communists discovered and reported to Moscow—issued their own secret circular calling for cooperation with German Communists only in the event of absolute necessity against the right, while secretly forming combat units for defense against expected attacks on Social Democrats by the Communists.[309] Rather than discrediting the Left Social Democrats—Stalin's prediction—in the eyes of the workers, Stalin's strategy of a phony "united front" utterly exposed the German Communists.[310]

The empty arsenals, German Communist unpreparedness, and the Social Democrats' cold shoulder prompted the Soviet squad on the ground to call off the uprising at the last minute. "I well remember the evening of 22 October [1923] in our apartment in the Lux Hotel, where Otto [Kuusinen], [Osip] Pyatnitsky and [Dmitry] Manuilsky sat waiting for a telegram from Berlin which was to inform them that the revolution had broken out," recalled Kuusinen's wife Aino, one of the many Soviet military intelligence officers under Comintern cover. "They remained for hours in Otto's study, smoking and drinking coffee. There was a direct telephone line to Lenin's sick-bed at Gorki, and this was kept open all night: Lenin could not speak except to mumble a few syllables, but his mind was fully alert." No telegram from Berlin arrived and the threesome dispersed at dawn. "The Comintern leaders were besides themselves with fury and disappointment, and could not wait to discover what had gone wrong and, no less important, whose fault it was."[311] In Hamburg, however, Germany's second largest city, 300 Communists rose up on their own initiative between October 23 and 25, 1923, assaulting police stations and seized plenty of weapons, but reinforcements crushed them; an estimated 90 people were killed and hundreds wounded.[312] In Moscow, the politburo was shocked at both the postponement and the massacre.[313] In Germany, the Soviet agents were shocked at the divisive anti-Trotsky politics at home, threatening to abandon their work in Germany.[314] Stalin was trying to puzzle out what happened. "If Ilich were in Germany, he would say: 'I think that the main enemy of the revolution is the Social Democrats, especially their left wing,'" he wrote to the Soviet agent group in Berlin (November 8, 1923).[315] The very next day, in a sign of his confusion, he reversed, writing that the Social Democrat "leftists were right in many ways": German Communists did not have the workers' support and a seizure of power would fail.[316] The Communists were not the only political group in fiasco, however: on

November 8, Adolf Hitler, along with Hermann Göring, Rudolf Hess, and a squadron of Brownshirts, marched on Munich's Townsmen's Beer Hall.[317]

THE BOLSHEVIK REGIME was suffocating the country and itself in paperwork and red tape, presiding over mass embezzlement amid impoverishment, hostile to, yet dependent upon, the market, fearful not only of peasants' political leanings but of workers' as well. Inside the roiling mess, however, Stalin was building a personal dictatorship. His was a life of theses and countertheses, compilation and dissemination of meeting protocols, intense orgburo drudgery of the expanding personnel machine, and absorption of the denunciations and secret reports forwarded by and about the OGPU, the military, foreign embassies, newspaper correspondents. More than anyone he had brought the USSR into being. It was he who schemed to bring to heel the Muslim Communists of the populous East. He was the one who defended the anathema of Lenin's New Economic Policy. Objectively, no one was more central to the Communist enterprise on a day-to-day basis, a conclusion Stalin likely reached himself. But during these years, his power was gravely threatened by a sheet of paper calling for his removal. Volodicheva's and Fotiyeva's memoirs, composed after Stalin's death (for obvious reasons), contain a number of implausible or outright impossible details. Lenin's doctors also never clarified the origins of the dictation.[318] Krupskaya, as far as the record indicates, never publicly explained the specific circumstances of the dictation's generation. Molotov would recall that "Krupskaya had a big grudge against Stalin. But he had a grudge against her, too, because Lenin's signature to his Testament was supposedly affixed under Krupskaya's influence. Or so Stalin believed."[319] This was an odd formulation because the dictation lacks Lenin's signature, but it indicated that Stalin believed Krupskaya was complicit in the content, and possibly even the very existence, of the documents.

Maria Ulyanova does not appear to have been directly involved in any aspect of the key dictation, but she saw her brother nearly every day during his illness, and singled out two incidents relating to Stalin that had disturbed Lenin. One was the time in 1921 when the Menshevik leader Yuly Martov had taken ill and Stalin had refused Lenin's request to transfer funds for Martov's medical treatment. The other was the Georgian affair in 1922, which was far more consequential. "One morning Stalin summoned me to Lenin's office," she explained a few years later. "He had a very depressed and sorry look. 'I did not sleep the whole night,' he said to me. 'Who does Ilich take me for, how does he treat me! As if I am some kind of traitor. I love him with all my soul. Tell him this sometime.'" Ulyanova recalled that she "felt sorry for Stalin. It seemed to me he was sincerely aggrieved." Stalin's immense power was at stake. Ulyanova conveyed to her brother Stalin's message that he loved him, but, she recalled, Lenin received this coldly. Ulyanova then told her brother that "after all Stalin is intelligent," prompting Lenin to frown and state, "He is not at all intelligent." Ulyanova added that this had been uttered not out of anger but matter-of-factly, and accorded with what she knew to be her brother's long-held view—a devastating observation. She added, trying to soften but instead sharpening the blow, that Lenin "valued Stalin as a practical type." This had to sting. Ulyanova praised Stalin's dedication and hard work, but concluded that Lenin had wanted to have Stalin's peculiarities held in check, which is why he had called for Stalin's removal as general secretary.[320]

Without proving her brother's authorship or precise date of generation of the dictation, Ulyanova—no enemy of Stalin—corroborated that the dictation captured something of Lenin's views. Equally telling, Molotov, a lifelong Stalin loyalist and admirer, validated the dictation's criticisms. "I think Lenin was right in his evaluation of Stalin," Molotov recalled. "I said it myself right after Lenin's death, at the politburo. I think Stalin remembered it because after Lenin's death we got together at Zinoviev's in the Kremlin, about five of us, including Stalin and me, and talked about the 'Testament.' I said I considered all of Lenin's evaluation of Stalin to have been right. Stalin, of course, did not like this. Despite this we remained close for many years. I think he appreciated me because I spoke out about certain matters in a way others hypocritically avoided, and he saw that I addressed the matter of the 'Testament' forthrightly."[321] Stalin himself never publicly voiced suspicions about the authenticity of Lenin's dictation. He could not escape the fact that Lenin's dictation—however it was produced—comported with a widespread view of his own character. In other words, even if it was partly or wholly concocted, the dictation rang true. Stalin's leadership, as we saw in the previous chapter, went a long way toward holding the whole sprawling regime together, but he could be malevolent and possessed too much power.

Although Stalin blamed Krupskaya, the dictation may have had an effect on his feelings for Lenin. Direct evidence of Stalin's emotional state in 1922–23 is slight. Reminiscences from his closest colleagues, such as Kaganovich, recalled these years at party headquarters fondly, a gregarious Stalin laughing and joking, exuding warmth ("It was a happy time of life. And Stalin was in a good mood").[322] But the record also includes Stalin's written remarks in the letter to Zinoviev in Kislovodsk, reinforced by observations of others in his inner circle at the time, of his sense of victimhood and self-pity. And the role of the dictation was only beginning.

## CHAPTER 12

# FAITHFUL PUPIL

Departing from us, comrade Lenin enjoined us to hold
high and safeguard the purity of the great title of a
member of the party. We vow to thee, comrade Lenin,
we shall fulfill thy behest with honor!

Departing from us, Comrade Lenin enjoined us to
safeguard the unity of the party as the apple of our eye.
We vow to thee, comrade Lenin, that we shall fulfill with
honor this, thy behest, too!

Stalin, January 26, 1924[1]

SUCH WERE THE PARADOXES of Stalin's vertiginous ascent: he had "boundless power" early, from spring 1922, when appointed general secretary of the
party and the next month Lenin suffered his first major stroke, but only one year
later, in spring 1923, out popped a sheet of paper calling for Stalin's removal. This
supremacy-insecurity dyad defined his inner regime, and shaped his character. It
also paralleled the Bolshevik dictatorship's own fraught relationship to the
outside world: the supposed global inevitability of the revolutionary cause amid
perilous capitalist encirclement. Of course, such a combination of aggressive
ambition and siege mentality was well known from the long sweep of Russia's
history, a great power whose aspirations always seemed to exceed its capabilities
in that complicated Eurasian space. But this predicament also derived from
Lenin's handiwork—a monopoly party's seizure of power and a cynical approach
to international relations. Both the revolution as a whole, and Stalin's personal
dictatorship within it, found themselves locked in a kind of in-built, structural
paranoia, triumphant yet enveloped by ill-wishers and enemies. The revolution's
predicament and Stalin's personality began to reinforce each other, and form
into a kind of Mobius strip under the pressure exerted by the Lenin dictation.

Lenin would always remain the single most important relationship in Stalin's life, a relationship of protégé, not merely in fact but, crucially, in self-conception. Stalin proved spectacularly successful in 1924 in positioning himself as Lenin's heir, as we shall see, but, again paradoxically, this would only raise the stakes of the existential threat posed by the dictation.

Stalin got help in easing his dilemma from none other than Trotsky. Uniquely for those at the very top of the regime, Trotsky was not a longtime Bolshevik and the lateness of his conversion (July 1917) made him vulnerable to charges of being an interloper—a Menshevik, not a true Leninist. Trotsky's own pen provided a cornucopia for this charge. In August 1904, following the Bolshevik-Menshevik split, Trotsky had denounced Lenin as "a slipshod attorney," a "Robespierre" who sought "a dictatorship *over* the proletariat." The fusillade of epithets included "hideous," "dissolute," "demagogical," "malicious and morally repulsive." Such over-the-top, if accurate, denunciation by Trotsky continued through the years.[2] Lenin returned the invective, in writings that were similarly preserved in amber. "A new pamphlet by Trotsky came out recently . . . a pack of brazen lies," Lenin wrote in October 1904.[3] In August 1909, he wrote that "Trotsky behaves like a despicable careerist and factionalist. He pays lip-service to the party and behaves worse than any other of the factionalists."[4] In a private letter of October that same year, Lenin coined the pejorative term "Trotskyism."[5] In January 1911, he referred to "Judas Trotsky."[6] As late as early 1917 he wrote (to Inessa Armand), "That's Trotsky for you!! Always true to himself = twists, swindles, poses as a leftist, helps the rightists while he can. . . ."[7] Stalin's minions in the central apparatus who had taken possession of Lenin's archive had little difficulty dredging up his anti-Trotsky gems.[8] Nothing had to be invented, although much would be fabricated or lifted out of context. Trotsky, however, magnified the effects by presenting himself as Lenin's equal and even, in some ways, his superior. Trotsky did not seem to comprehend that his relationship to Lenin was a question not of fact but of positioning.[9]

That Stalin was fortunate in his rivals, from Trotsky on down, has long been understood.[10] To be sure, Kamenev and Zinoviev, both five years younger than Stalin, had better political skills than usually credited to them, especially Zinoviev, who built a formidable machine in Leningrad. That said, scholars have correctly noted that Kamenev was widely perceived as a deputy rather than a leader in his own right and that Zinoviev's personality aroused widespread enmity (the Italian Communist Angelica Balabanoff deemed him, "after Mussolini . . . , the most despicable individual I have ever met").[11] But what may be less well appreciated is that Trotsky proved to be less the obstacle to than the instrument of Stalin's aggrandizement. Just as the Bolshevik regime needed the civil war to form a state, so Stalin needed "opposition" to consolidate his personal dictatorship—and he found it. Compared with Trotsky's delight in polemicizing against this or that regime policy, which lent itself to accusations of schism and factionalism, Stalin presented himself as the faithful defender of the Central Committee and Lenin's legacy. At the same time, Stalin was the one with the pronounced physical features, including the protruding nose, and the thick accent, but Trotsky turned out to be the alien.[12] Compared with the preening Trotsky, Stalin could appear as the revolution's hardworking, underappreciated foot soldier. Compared with Trotsky's popularity among Russia's small cosmopolitan intelligentsia, as the master of multiple European languages and author of fluent works about culture as well as politics, Stalin could be the representative of the far vaster middling sort, whose aspirations he captured like a tuning fork.[13] Stalin walked into a golden opportunity to become the orthodox Leninist as well as a household name by battling, and besting, the world-renowned Trotsky.

Stalin certainly showed guile, maneuvering always to seize the orthodox middle ground and to drive his critics into the position of apparent schismatics and factionalists, while employing the classic device of changing political alliances to his advantage, but such textbook stratagems ultimately have their limits. The succession was a brawl not just over raw power but also ideas and narratives. Nothing is more powerful than a compelling story, especially in the framework of a revolution, which entails a struggle to create new symbols, new vocabularies, new ways of looking at the world, new identities, new myths.[14] In 1924, Stalin produced a greater written output than even in 1917. His major work of the year, and of his life to that date, "Foundations of Leninism," was plagiarized.[15] It proved to be a striking success, reflecting not just dishonesty but diligence and even sound judgment: he chose an excellent text, and appears to have sharpened it. Additionally, Stalin produced a second major work, *Socialism in One Country*, which was his own and, contrary to received wisdom, had nothing to do with abandoning world revolution and everything to do with imagining a viable Marxist approach to geopolitics. As Lenin's would-be faithful pupil, Stalin emerged in 1924–25 as both an ideologue ("capital," "the bourgeoisie," "imperialism") and an embryonic geostrategic thinker.

## REVELATION

On January 8, 1924, *Pravda* divulged that Trotsky was ill, a statement, according to OGPU informants, the rank and file took as a sign of his imminent removal.[16] He was suffering raging fevers, migraines, chest pains, catarrh in the upper respiratory organs, enlargement of the bronchial glands, and loss of appetite and weight. Some specialists thought he had a paratyphoid infection; the Kremlin doctors diagnosed influenza.[17] Trotsky supporters kept up the fight.[18] But with Trotsky convalescing in a village outside Moscow, Stalin ripped into him at a two-day Central Committee plenum (January 14–15, 1924), and was even more relentless in his report to the 13th party conference (January 16–18) attended by 350 delegates, most of them non-voting, an obvious packing of the gallery for maximum hostility.[19] Stalin scolded party members who "fetishized" democracy as "possible always and under all conditions," as if "only the evil will of 'apparatchiks' prevents its introduction." He demanded to know why ordinary workers had to submit to party discipline, while Trotsky "imagines himself to be a superman standing above the Central Committee, above its laws, above its decisions."[20] Then Stalin pulled out the truncheon: "I think the time has come when we must publicize the clause of the resolution on party unity made at the suggestion of comrade Lenin, adopted by the 10th Congress of our party, but which was not subject to disclosure": namely, the penalty of expulsion from the Central Committee by two-thirds vote for forming an illegal faction.[21] Stalin appears to have found it a lot easier to get the better of Trotsky in the latter's absence.[22] The 13th conference demonized the Left opposition as "not only a direct turn away from Leninism, but a manifest expression of petit bourgeois deviation."[23] After Stalin's withering speech to close out the gathering, an Italian journalist observed that most "people consider the political role of comrade Trotsky over."[24]

Trotsky appears to have been thrown into depression by the unremitting opprobrium, laced with smears, from the very party to which he had devoted his whole being. Of course, he had been no slouch at condemning and smearing the Mensheviks, SRs, or revolutionary Kronstadt sailors, but none of that lessened the impact on him.[25] "The pages of *Pravda* seemed endless, and every line of the paper, even every word, a lie," observed his wife, Natalya Sedova. "L.D. kept silent.... In the family we avoided talking about the persecution, and yet we could talk of nothing else."[26] Trotsky's most trusted physician, Fyodor Guetier, prescribed a prolonged rest in the Soviet subtropics, and so, on January 18, 1924, the same day as Stalin's party conference–ending speech, Trotsky retreated southward to the Black Sea. The timing proved momentous.

Lenin was dead to the regime but still alive. Soviet newspapers were spreading false hopes about his disposition.[27] During intermissions at the 13th conference, Maria Ulyanova told delegates crowded around her that he was better and had attended Orthodox Christmas festivities at Gorki.[28] Krupskaya, meanwhile, sought to alleviate her husband's torment and on January 19 read a tale aloud to him out of Jack London's *Love of Life* (1906) about a Canadian gold prospector in the wilderness bereft of food who is followed by a wolf waiting for him to die. The next day, Lenin woke up feeling poorly; that evening, he began pointing to his eyes. An oculist summoned from Moscow arrived around 10:00 p.m. but detected nothing other than nearsightedness in one eye. On Monday, January 21, Lenin was examined by his doctors; minutes after they left, he began convulsing. Bukharin, as usual, had been staying at the Moscow party organization's facility in Gorki near Lenin's estate, and although usually only allowed to observe Lenin from afar, this time a doctor appears to have summoned him.[29] "When I ran into Ilich's room, stuffed full of medicines and doctors, Ilich made his last breath," Bukharin would claim. "His face turned backwards, and went horribly pale, a wheeze was heard, hands shook."[30] Krupskaya recalled that with Lenin's chest gurgling, his bodyguard-nurse held him in his arms, and that Lenin "occasionally moaned quietly, a tremor ran through his body, at first I held his hot, damp hand, but then just watched as the towel turned red with blood, and the stamp of death settled on his deathly pallid face."[31] The doctors applied artificial respiration. He died at 6:50 p.m.[32]

Maria Ulyanova phoned the Kremlin, and her call was redirected to the presidium of the Eleventh All-Russia Congress of Soviets in the Bolshoi Theater's smaller Beethoven Hall; she asked for Stalin or Zinoviev. Evidently, Stalin took the phone.[33] The news shattered the hall. "I had never before seen that many crying men," recalled a then seventeen-year-old Communist Youth League eyewitness in the Bolshoi.[34] The members of the inner circle repaired to Zinoviev's Kremlin apartment, and around 9:30 p.m. they departed on vehicles outfitted with sled tracks for Gorki.[35] Rykov was ill, and Trotsky was en route to the Soviet subtropics. Molotov and Rudzutaks remained at party headquarters to prepare public statements; Dzierżyński also stayed behind in Moscow to oversee public order. At Gorki, Stalin is said to have entered the room first, theatrically. "He moved heavily, gravely, decisively, holding his right hand behind his semi-military jacket," wrote one eyewitness, who added that at parting, "Stalin, impulsively, emotionally, suddenly approached Lenin's head: 'Farewell, farewell, Vladimir Ilich. . . . Farewell!' And he, pale, took Lenin's head in both his hands, lifted it, bringing it almost to his breast, to his heart, and firmly, firmly kissed him on the cheeks and on the lips. . . . He waved his hand and stepped back sharply."[36] Kamenev, Zinoviev, and Bukharin also pronounced their farewells, and the sculptor Sergei Merkulov composed a gypsum cast of Lenin's hands and a death mask, which would find a place in Stalin's Old Square office.[37]

The inner circle, returning to Moscow in the wee hours, at 2:30 a.m. on January 22, convened a meeting of the presidium of the Soviet central executive committee to approve a funeral commission and discuss arrangements.[38] At Gorki an autopsy commenced, during which Lenin's brain was opened, revealing fatty deposits blocking the arteries supposed to carry blood (and oxygen) to the brain, a condition for which there was no cure. Some arteries were so calcified a human hair could not have passed through. The pressure built and the arteries finally burst, which resulted in a vast river of blood on his brain. The destroyed vessels happened to be in the part of the brain controlling the respiratory function, so Lenin stopped breathing.[39] The public reports were obsessive, minutely detailing even the precise weight of his brain (1,340 grams).[40] Privately, Professor Kramer, the neurologist, recorded that Lenin's illness "lasted all in all about two and a half years, and its general characteristics harbored signs that all the neurologists, whether Russian or foreign, dwelt on as something that did not conform to the conventional disease of the nervous system."[41] Lenin's father had apparently died in his early fifties of a brain hemorrhage, perhaps brought on by a clogging of arteries. The condition had affected Lenin's moods: elation, followed quickly by depression; laughter for no reason; extreme irritability.[42]

Lenin had been incapacitated for more than a year, but now the regime had to confront his eternal absence. Kalinin, on January 22, asked the delegates to the Eleventh All-Russia Congress of Soviets to rise as the orchestra struck up a funeral march. "Comrades," he started, tears streaming down his face, "I must tell you some frightful news. Vladimir Ilich's health. . . ." Screams pierced the hall. Some delegates erupted into sobs. Kamenev, Zinoviev, Budyonny, and other members of the presidium wept. Avel Yenukidze, secretary of the Soviet central executive committee, cut in and imposed quiet, Kalinin broke down again. Mikhail Lashevich stepped to the dais to announce the details of the viewing and burial. The congress was suspended.[43] There is no reliable record of Stalin's emotional state. On the day before Lenin's sudden death, one functionary who visited Stalin's small Kremlin apartment in the Grand Kremlin Palace's outbuilding noted "an abundance of books."[44] That is how Stalin had and would always relate to Lenin: through his writings, and how Stalin would express himself. On the morning of January 23, Lenin's casket was transported from the manor house to Moscow, arriving around 1:00 p.m. to the accompaniment of the Bolshoi orchestra playing a dirge. The casket, draped in red cloth, made a five-mile processional to the House of Trade Unions, and was placed in its Hall of Columns (where Sverdlov had lain in state).[45] The catafalque, in the middle of the grand space, was surrounded by countless wreaths, fragrant lilies, and a rotating honor guard. That evening at 7:00 p.m., the doors were thrown open to the public. Already in spring 1923, when Lenin had become deathly ill, regional military commanders had received a secret telegram to prepare to put down uprisings.[46] Now, Dzierżyński sent instructions via OGPU channels to "pay the main attention to Black Hundreds, monarchists, White Guardists," while making sure "to maintain complete calm and preempt panic, giving no pretext for panic by outward behavior or unfounded mass arrests."[47]

If one read the OGPU political mood summaries delivered to party headquarters, as Stalin did, one would have thought the USSR was overrun by monarchists and "former" people, priests and mullahs, hostile intelligentsia, sullen workers, property-loving peasants, Red Army malcontents.[48] Dzierżyński again and again complained to Yagoda that "these summaries produce a very depressing impression, utterly dark without any ray of light." (Yagoda would invariably respond that "our task is to illuminate the shadowy side. . . . Thus it is natural that our summaries produce dark impressions.")[49] In January 1924, reports from the countryside suggested that without Lenin, peasants expected the regime to collapse and imperialist powers to take advantage and intervene again.[50] Thus did the Soviet regime prove wholly unprepared for the emotional outpouring: Over the course of three days, between half a million and one million people passed by Lenin's open coffin in the Hall of Columns at the House of Trade Unions, enduring queues a mile and a half long in outside temperatures of −28 degrees F. (Delegations from state or party agencies could visit outside the queue at appointed times.) Certainly many rejoiced at seeing Lenin dead. But a large number seem to have believed he was better than the other Communists, if only for having introduced the NEP, an admission of error and a humane policy.[51] "An enormous proportion of the population," wrote one eyewitness to the scene at the bier who was not part of the regime, "reacted to Lenin's death with unshakeable grief."[52]

## POLITICAL PARALYSIS
## VERSUS HOLY OATHS

Four days after departing Moscow for the Soviet subtropics of Abkhazia, Trotsky's train had pulled into the station in Tiflis early on Tuesday, January 22, with the last leg to the Black Sea coast still pending. But a messenger came to their railcar with a decoded telegram, sent via secret police channels: "Tell comrade Trotsky. On January 21 at 6:50 p.m. comrade Lenin died prematurely. Death followed from paralysis of his respiratory center. Burial on Saturday January 26. Stalin." Trotsky telegrammed back: "I consider it necessary to return to Moscow." The train was held at the station. An hour later, came Stalin's reply: "The funeral will take place on Saturday, you will not make it in time. The politburo considers that in your state of health you should continue on to Sukhum. Stalin."[53] Trotsky claimed that once in Sukhum, convalescing under blankets on an outdoor veranda, he would learn that the funeral was delayed for a day, until Sunday, proving that Stalin had tricked him.[54] Certainly Stalin was devious. But special trains were continuing to pour into the capital, some from farther away than Tiflis, so that the funeral commission, chaired by Dzierżyński, announced only on January 25 that Lenin's funeral would take place one day later, on Sunday (January 27).[55] (Also, workers had dynamited the frozen ground in front of the Kremlin Wall but were still furiously constructing a temporary wooden crypt.) Even with Stalin's original timetable, Trotsky had almost 100 hours to retrace the 1,000 miles back to Moscow. When Lenin had been shot, in September 1918, Stalin had remained in Tsaritsyn, but Trotsky had rushed back from the far-off eastern front of the civil war, reaching Moscow on only the second day after the shooting. That was when the regime had established a Revolutionary Military Council of the Republic, which in January 1924 Trotsky still led. If he feared his train might not make it back to Moscow on time, he could have commandeered whatever military or civilian aircraft were to hand in the South Caucasus military district, headquartered right there in Tiflis.

Trotsky was not the only top official to miss the funeral: Rykov, who had influenza, had gone to Italy with his wife for a rest cure for a few months under a false name, but his absence had no effect on his political career; after all, Rykov was Lenin's deputy and potential successor only bureaucratically. Everyone in Moscow was expecting Trotsky. "For the last three days there had been a report that he was returning from the Caucasus where he was ill," wrote the *New York Times* reporter. "More than once crowds assembled to greet him at the station, and official photographers were sent to wait chilly hours before the Hall of Columns to film his entry. To the last many believed he would come."[56] Trotsky's disconsolate seventeen-year-old son, Lev Sedov, who had his own fever well above 100 degrees F., rose from his sickbed in Moscow to pay his respects to Lenin in the Hall of Columns, unable to comprehend his father's absence.[57] Trotsky would also be missing from the newsreel shown to the masses and the world.[58] Decades later, he would lament, "I should have come at any price."[59] True enough, but he would also later write that on that January 22, when his train was being held in the station in Tiflis after news of Lenin's death had been delivered to him, he had wanted to be left alone. Beseeched by a delegation of local officials, Trotsky had hurriedly composed a short tribute: "And now Vladimir Ilich is no more. The party is orphaned. The working class is orphaned. Such was the very feeling aroused by the news of the death of our teacher and leader. How will we go forward, will we find the way, will we not go astray? . . . Our hearts are stricken with boundless grief, all of us who by the great grace of History were born contemporaries of Lenin, who worked alongside him, who learnt from him. . . . How shall we go ahead? With the lamp of Leninism in our hands."[60] Eloquent, and perhaps indicative of Trotsky's own feelings of being orphaned.

After being demoralized by the skullduggery of the Stalin-manipulated January 1924 party gatherings censuring him for factionalism, Lenin's death offered Trotsky a potential breakout moment to reverse the setbacks of the closed-door sessions, to outshine them all on the biggest stage, Red Square. He could have arrived dramatically from afar, like Lenin had once done at the Finland Station, and used his powers to capture the prevailing grief of Lenin's death, electrify the crowds, embody the revolution in its next phase. It was none other than Trotsky who had written breathlessly about the "art of the insurrection," and now he could try to use that art to smash "the ring" around him formed by those he regarded as pygmies. In the name of the greater cause of safeguarding the revolution, he could have violated party discipline by reading aloud on Red Square from Lenin's purported dictation, using as his mantra Lenin's summons to "remove Stalin" as general secretary, then flown from factory to factory to rally workers, just as in 1917—let them arrest him. Of course, to do all that, Trotsky needed to perceive Lenin's death as a strategic opportunity, and he needed a persuasive story line about how the grand socialist dream could be revived, why all those harsh exchanges he had had with Lenin were incidental, and why he (Trotsky) was uniquely qualified to carry forward the sacred Leninist cause. A tall order, to put it mildly. But who could doubt that if Lenin had found that others were conspiring against him, he would have mounted a coup against his own party? Stalin, in Trotsky's position, would have been incapable of dramatic street actions to win over the masses. Of course, Stalin did not have to accomplish that: he already held the levers of power, ensconced at Old Square. Indeed, Stalin relocated to the new party headquarters at Old Square precisely in January 1924.

For Stalin, Lenin's death presented a different kind of opportunity, and he seized it. With more than 2,000 delegates inside the Bolshoi on January 26, the Second USSR Congress of Soviets opened, devoting its first day to Lenin's memory. After Kalinin (head of state) and Krupskaya (widow), Zinoviev took the floor, marveled at the crowds that had come to pay their respects, and advised everyone always to ponder, "What would comrade Lenin do if he were in my place?" But what would Zinoviev do in Lenin's place? Unclear. Next up Stalin, who evoked a mystical calling. "Comrades, we Communists are people of a special mold," he stated, in his first known remarks on Lenin's passing. "We are made of special stuff. We are those who constitute the army of the great proletarian strategist, the army of comrade Lenin. There is nothing higher than the honor of belonging to this army. There is nothing higher than the title of member of the party whose founder and leader was comrade Lenin. It is not given to everyone to be a member of such a party." Now those afforded such an honor would be tested. "Departing from us, comrade Lenin enjoined us to hold high and safeguard the purity of the great title of member of the party. We vow to thee, comrade Lenin, we shall fulfill thy behest with honor!" Stalin said. "Departing from us, Comrade Lenin enjoined us to safeguard the unity of the party as the apple of our eye. We vow to thee, comrade Lenin, that this behest, too, we shall fulfill with honor!" And on and on went the collective vows: to safeguard the dictatorship of the proletariat, the worker-peasant alliance of the New Economic Policy, the Union of Soviet Socialist Republics, the Communist International. Each time he intoned the collective promise: "We shall fulfill this bequest with honor!"[61] Stalin's liturgical incantations stood out starkly not just from the drab content offered by Zinoviev, normally a surpassing orator, but from everyone's remarks.[62] When the speeches were published in *Izvestiya,* however, the editor excised the religious aura of Stalin's speech.[63] Perhaps some Communist sensibilities were offended. But Stalin, as general secretary, had *Pravda* republish the speeches three days later in full.[64] Within days of Lenin's death, the ex-seminarian had unveiled the winning formula he would pursue: zealously dedicating his life and the entire party to fulfillment of Lenin's sacred "behest."

Delegates at the Congress of Soviets voted to rename Petrograd Leningrad, erect Lenin monuments around the Union, and publish his works in millions of copies, then adjourned for the outdoor funeral, which took place the next day, January 27, and lasted six hours in bitter cold of −30 degrees F.[65] At 4:00 p.m., as the coffin was placed in a temporary wooden crypt, all radios and telegraphs broadcast a single message: "Stand up, comrades. Ilich is being lowered into the grave!" All factories and transport were halted as the whole country came to a dramatic standstill, with five minutes of silence. At 4:06 radios sent a new message: "Lenin has died—Leninism lives!"

The quest for retrospective precedence in proximity to the deceased Lenin was in full swing.[66] Stalin gave another speech on January 28, this time to Kremlin military cadets, and asserted he had received a "simple but deeply significant letter" from Lenin in 1903, which he did not produce, but which advanced by two years their actual acquaintance.[67] Trotsky supporters, for their part, were printing copies of Lenin's purported dictation to distribute to the party members who had arrived in Moscow from around the country for the funeral. The Trotsky people affixed the written appellation "Testament" (*zaveshchanie*), which the written document carried for the first time. The Central Control Commission expressly banned circulation of the Lenin documents on January 30.[68] That same evening, the Second USSR Congress of Soviets resumed and, the next day, ratified the new Constitution of the USSR.[69] Rykov was formally named chairman of the USSR Council of People's Commissars, but in the traditional gathering space on the third floor of the Imperial Senate, Lenin's chair, directly in front of the door to his old office, was left empty.[70] Still, many details testified to Stalin's ascendancy, including the fact that he had taken charge of the regime's Special Purpose Garage. Nothing spoke power more than the allocation of scarce state cars. Automobiles also happened to be a special interest of Stalin's, from the six-cylinder 1914 Vauxhall purchased in England for Nicholas II's mother (and used by Paul Miliukov after the February Revolution), to the twelve-cylinder Packard Twin Six (originally purchased for the tsarist military) that Stalin had in Tsaritsyn. Stalin would soon decide to purchase a suite of American-made cars for the regime: Lincolns, Cadillacs, Buicks, and for himself, a Packard. Packards would remain Stalin's preferred machine for decades—heavy yet fast.[71] Meanwhile, with Lenin buried, in early February 1924 Stalin took a holiday.

Oddly enough, it was Trotsky's holiday that testified to Stalin's ascendancy. That winter of 1924 was the Trotskys' first visit to Abkhazia and its capital, Sukhum, on the balmy Black Sea. Trotsky seems to have been entranced by his escape. They were put up at a villa, the Sinop (Synoptic), located in the outskirts on a hill enveloped by a botanical park with hundreds of varieties of flora and fauna that the prerevolutionary owner had imported from around the world.[72] "In the dining room of the rest house there were two portraits on the wall, one— draped in black—of Vladimir Ilich, the other of L.D. [Trotsky]," Natalya Sedova wrote.[73] Their host was the diminutive Nestor Lakoba, who was nearly deaf—the sound amplifier he used helped little—but Trotsky took a shine to the man-of-the-people demeanor of a Communist beloved among his countrymen of Abkhazia (jokingly known as Lakobistan).[74] Lakoba visited Trotsky nearly every day, bringing oranges, tangerines, and lemons, sitting for long discussions. His Caucasus hospitality, however, had a further purpose: Dzierżyński had sent a telegram the day of Trotsky's Moscow departure noting that the war commissar's rest trip to Sukhum "has become widely known even abroad, and so I am concerned that the White Guards do not attempt an assassination." Ah, yes, those White Guard terrorists: Dzierżyński requested that Trotsky be kept in splendid isolation. That same day Lakoba also received a letter from Tiflis, written by the South Caucasus party boss Orjonikidze, asking him to "take care" of Trotsky and adding that in Tiflis "matters are going splendidly well. The Left opposition has been smashed to its foundation."[75]

Relieved by the exemplary Caucasus hospitality, Trotsky appears not to have suspected the ulterior motives behind it on what was, after all, Stalin's home turf.[76] Already on the day Trotsky had landed in Sukhum, January 23, a very young police operative (b. 1899) who had already become deputy head of the Georgian Cheka wrote to Yagoda in Moscow that he had visited Trotsky. The ostensible reason for the visit was to inform Trotsky he had to deliver a speech (still feverish, Trotsky promised to write an article). The real reason was a personal initiative to size up Trotsky's thinking. "The death of Ilich has affected him greatly," the secret police interlocutor reported. "He thinks that at this moment what's needed is a closing of ranks [*splochennost'*]. . . . Lenin can only be replaced by a collective. Comrade Trotsky does not feel well."[77] The precocious Georgian Chekist humbly asked Yagoda, his superior in Moscow, to share the requested report with Stalin immediately. The name of the secret police operative was . . . Lavrenti Beria.

Trotsky's political quarantine was broken by Krupskaya, who sent a warm note (January 29) stressing how, about a month before, "as he was looking through your book, Vladimir Ilich stopped at the place where you sum up Marx and Lenin, and asked me to read it over again to him: he listened very attentively, and then looked it over himself. And there is another thing I want to tell you: the attitude of V.I. toward you at the time you came to us in London from Siberia did not change right up to his death. I wish you, Lev Davidovich, strength and health, and I embrace you warmly."[78] This was the same Krupskaya who, earlier that same month, had repudiated Trotsky's recent writings, denying the party was alienated from the masses and underscoring that his charges of bureaucratism came without practical solution, other than substituting Trotsky supporters for sitting officials.[79] But now Krupskaya had undertaken a demonstrative political act, to counterbalance Stalin.[80] Stalin, however, sent a delegation, led by Mikhail Frunze, to inform Trotsky that he Frunze would replace Trotsky's loyal first deputy at the war commissariat, Yefraim Sklyansky.[81] In Abkhazia, Trotsky had become well enough to hunt, the avid avocation that had afflicted him with the fevers in the first place. Lakoba, a top marksman, gushed to the major local newspaper, *Dawn of the East,* that Trotsky "kills ducks in flight; in the outskirts of Sukhum, not a single lake or swamp that contained game escaped his eye."[82] It was Trotsky who did not escape Lakoba's eye until mid-April 1924, when Trotsky finally disembarked for Moscow.


## LENINISM


Lenin's mummification for viewing in a crypt near the Kremlin Wall may look inevitable, but many, perhaps most, members of the inner circle objected to the idea; the decision was pushed by Dzierżyński, the funeral commission chairman, who had once studied for the Catholic priesthood and was backed by Stalin the seminarian. Dzierżyński argued that "if science can preserve a human body for a long time, then why not do it," adding that "the tsars were embalmed just because they were tsars. We will do it because he was a great person, unlike any other."[83] Preservation of Lenin as a viewable holy relic required an extraordinarily high level of scientific technique, which did not emerge immediately; the lead scientist eventually hit upon a novel solution mixing glycerin, alcohol, water, potassium acetate, and quinine chloride, which managed to restore the body.[84] For a more permanent mausoleum to replace the original jerry-built crypt, the regime commissioned the architect Alexei Shchusev, noted for his art nouveau Kazan railway station in Moscow, who would come up with an alluring design of three cubes arranged horizontally and connected by corridors, based upon ancient Mayan motifs.[85] Inside, Lenin would be laid in a red-lined sarcophagus covered with airtight glass, dressed not in his usual bourgeois suit but a khaki tunic, his posthumously awarded Order of the Red Banner pinned to his chest.[86] Leonid Krasin had proposed inclusion of a terrace from which the masses could be addressed, an idea that Shchusev adopted, albeit only on the flanks, not across the top front.[87] The mausoleum's formal public opening would take place later in 1924.[88] "The body is in a perfect state of preservation," Walter Duranty of the *New York Times* would enthuse, noting that the Soviet professors boasted to him that unlike Egyptian pharaoh mummies, not only the body but the entire face was preserved. Duranty would add that "the embalmers have even contrived to impart a smile."[89] The lifelike mummy of a saintlike figure would prove of incalculable value to the regime.

Unexpectedly, the Soviet regime had acquired a potent sacred space on Red Square. (Many visitors to Lenin adopted a superstitious pose.)[90] Meanwhile, the Lenin Museum had already been established.[91] Some items there were not on public view. The artist Yuri Annenkov, invited to select photographs for a book, noticed a glass jar in which sat "Lenin's brain preserved in alcohol . . . one hemisphere was healthy and full-sized, with clearly defined convolutions; the other, which hung as it were by a ribbon, was wrinkled, crumpled, crushed, and no larger than a walnut."[92] Publicly, the museum humanized Lenin with photographs of his childhood, alongside heroic episodes of the revolution. "In a glass case is the revolver with which he was shot in 1918," wrote a professor from Chicago of an early visit. "The extracted bullet, with the signed reports of the doctors who performed the operation, is also exhibited."[93] Codification of Lenin's written legacy was also well under way. The informal Lenin Institute had emerged on the initiative of the Moscow party organization, but Stalin took it under the wing of the central apparatus, partly to put it on better financial footing, but mostly to ensure his control.[94] He implanted his Marxist-scholar aide, Ivan Tovstukha, as the person in charge of day-to-day operations.[95] Stalin would commission a new five-story building in modernist style, at Soviet Square, 1/3 (formerly Tver Square), one of the first large public buildings to be built after the revolution.[96] Kamenev remained editor of Lenin's *Collected Works,* but Tovstukha oversaw the immediate publication, or suppression, of key Lenin documents.[97] Everyone who had known Lenin was required to send the Lenin Institute their reminiscences.[98] Krupskaya sent hers to Stalin for comments; he would have the text published without running his editing by her.[99]

*Pravda*'s portrait, likely penned by Bukharin, gave voice to the emerging orthodoxy: Lenin's modesty, intense force of logic, fidelity to principle, faith in the masses, perseverance and will.[100] Unmentioned was his extreme cruelty. Lenin loved people only "in general," the self-exiled writer Maxim Gorky nicely summarized in a short book in 1924. "His love looked far ahead, through the mists of hatred."[101] Molotov, who worked intimately with both Lenin and Stalin, would famously judge Lenin "the more severe" and "harsher."[102] Lenin had liked to see himself as Marx's equal (once, when a factory worker asked him for a photograph as a memento of their meeting, Lenin pulled from his pocket a small badge with Marx's portrait). But although Lenin's and Marx's portraits in giant size hung side by side on Red Square for the major holidays, many were calling Marx the theorist, and Lenin the (mere) practitioner.[103] It was Stalin who would resolve their equality. In April 1924, he went into the mouth of the tiger, the Sverdlov Communist University, where the Trotsky Left opposition had carried the vote at a party meeting in fall 1923.[104] Stalin's lectures would be serialized in April and May 1924 under the title "Foundations of Leninism."[105]

Stalin had long carried the stamp of an organizer, not a theoretician.[106] Few knew that he had plagiarized whole cloth his "Anarchism or Socialism?" (1906–7) from the deceased Giorgi Teliya. Now, for his "Foundations of Leninism," he plagiarized *Lenin's Doctrine of Revolution,* a manuscript by the still-living Filipp Ksenofontov (not to be confused with the unrelated Ivan Ksenofontov, the Cheka operative). Ksenofontov (b. 1903), a journalist and editor, was suddenly packed off to Tashkent amid rumors that he had protested Stalin's borrowings. (In a private letter to Ksenofontov, Stalin expressed gratitude for his help; later Stalin would deny Ksenofontov permission to cite this letter.)[107]

While in Tashkent in 1924, Ksenofontov published a book on the tenth anniversary of the Great War, *Lenin and the Imperialist War 1914–1918*, in which his presentation of Leninism tracked closely with that published under Stalin's name.[108] Leninism, Ksenofontov wrote, was not merely Marxism in practice, as many suggested, but "the science of the revolutionary politics of the working class in conditions of imperialism, i.e. the theory and practice of the proletarian revolution."[109] Stalin's "Foundations of Leninism" had a punchier version: "Leninism is the Marxism of the epoch of imperialism and of the proletarian revolution."[110] Stalin also made abundantly clear that Lenin, not Trotsky (and not Stalin), had been the reason for victory in 1917.

Trotsky's parallel effort, a May 1924 compilation of older materials and current recollections, adopted a stance very different from Stalin's discipleship.[111] His *On Lenin* was, as expected, less about Lenin than Trotsky's supposed special closeness to him (as emphasized in the fawning book review by a Trotsky supporter).[112] But Trotsky made himself the coleader of the revolution, the very stance that had gotten him into trouble time and again while Lenin was still alive. In fact, Lenin in October 1917 was depicted as *taking advice from Trotsky*. The outrage was intense. Molotov hammered Trotsky for portraying Lenin as mistake prone (fallible).[113] Zinoviev lashed out at Trotsky for equating his (Trotsky's) Brest-Litovsk blundering in 1918 with Lenin's failed Polish War in 1920.[114] But Zinoviev, whose vanity may have exceeded even Trotsky's, in his own reminiscences included passages no one else would have been stupid enough to set down in print. "In Paris once we were drinking to the success of his new book and we sat in the café till the small hours (though, to be honest, I could not imagine who would read the book, apart from a handful of Social Democrats)," he wrote.[115] More often, Zinoviev went to the other extreme of embarrassing obsequiousness, even by the standards of the emerging hagiography: "As mighty as the ocean; as stern and inaccessible as Mont Blanc; as tender as the southern sun; as great as the world; as humane as a child."[116] For all his oratorical prowess, on the written page Zinoviev tended to be diffuse, the opposite of Stalin.

Already in spring 1924 it was evident that Stalin had won the battle over presenting Leninism.[117] "Stalin's book is, without doubt, so far the best text on Leninism, although it does not bear a loud and pretentious title, unlike other such publications," noted a signed review in *Bolshevik*. The reviewer, Alexander Slepkov (b. 1899), was a product of the Sverdlov Communist University, where the lectures had been delivered, as well as of the Institute of Red Professors

(1924), the first institution of higher learning founded on the basis of Marxism across all subjects, from literary criticism to natural science. He embodied Stalin's target audience.[118] Slepkov made some criticisms—of a work by the general secretary—but he singled out for special praise the book's overall conceptualization, the organization and exactitude of each chapter, the economy of expression, and the clarity of the core principle of the party "as an expression of the historical interests of the proletariat."[119]

## "LETTER TO THE CONGRESS"

The 13th Party Congress took place May 23–31, 1924, in the Grand Kremlin Palace, and was attended by 1,164 delegates (748 voting), who represented 736,000 party members. Only around 150,000 lived outside of a town, and of the latter, 61,000 lived in the central regions of the Russian republic and Ukraine. All of Soviet Belorussia had only about 3,000 party members, the Soviet Far East, about the same.[120] Even as the regime had continued to grow, it had remained remarkably narrow. For the congress, the triumvirate had taken no chances: the Left opposition was limited to only non-voting delegates and from their ranks only Trotsky had been elected to the forty-two-person congress presidium.[121]

Everyone knew this congress would be unusual, with Lenin gone forever, but delegates were still in for a shock. Krupskaya had been negotiating for months to publish the dictation, which was now being called Lenin's "Letter to the Congress."[122] A few late Lenin dictations had already been published, but not the explosive six evaluations of possible successors or the "Ilich letter about the secretary" calling for Stalin's removal.[123] Trotsky, who alone argued in favor of publication, made notes of the discussion. Kamenev: "It cannot be published: it is a speech unspoken at the politburo. It is nothing more." Zinoviev: "N.K. [Krupskaya] was also of the opinion that it should only be given to the Central Committee. I did not ask about publishing it, for I thought (and think) that is excluded." Stalin: "I suggest there is no necessity to publish, especially as there is no authorization for publication from Ilich."[124] On the evening of May 21, at the customary Central Committee plenum on the eve of a congress, Kamenev delivered a report on behalf of a special commission for the Lenin documents.[125] No transcript is extant. According to the apparatchik Bazhanov, Kamenev read aloud the dictation, after which Zinoviev rose to defend Stalin, a message Kamenev reinforced as he presided over discussion.[126]

Stalin offered to step down. "Well, yes, I am definitely rude," Trotsky quoted Stalin as saying. "Ilich proposes to you to find another person who differs from me only in external politeness. Well, ok, try to find such a person." But in a hall packed with Stalin loyalists, a voice shouted out: "It's nothing. We are not frightened by rudeness, our whole party is rude, proletarian."[127] A neat trick, but the moment was extraordinary all the same. Back during the cave meeting episode in summer 1923, Stalin had testily intimated he could give up the general secretary position, but that was in a mere private letter.[128] This was a plenum, which had the power to remove him. But Stalin escaped: the precongress plenum retained him.[129]

On May 23, the 13th Congress opened with a parade of Young Pioneers, an organization for children aged ten to sixteen, at Lenin's wooden tomb on Red Square.[130] That day, Stalin inscribed a copy of his Lenin book for the party boss of Azerbaijan in language he used for no one else: "To my friend and dear brother Kirov." Zinoviev delivered the main political report, just as he had at the 12th Congress, and demanded the Left opposition recant publicly.[131] Trotsky rose to speak, and his appearance aroused prolonged applause, just as it had at the previous congress. Afforded an opportunity to go on the offensive and read aloud Lenin's dictation, Trotsky did not do so. Nor did he recant. Instead, he sought to disarm his critics with conciliation. "Comrades, none of us wishes to be nor can be right against our party," he stated. "In the last analysis the party is always right, because the party is the unique instrument given to the proletariat for the fulfillment of its fundamental tasks. . . . I know it is impossible to be right against the party. It is possible to be right only with the party and through the party, because history has created no other paths to the realization of what is right." Trotsky paraphrased the English saying—"my country, right or wrong"—to conclude "this is still my party."[132] The gesture backfired. Even Krupskaya rebuked him, observing that if the party was always right, he should never have instigated the now half-year-long debate for a new course.[133] A formal resolution again condemned the Left opposition as a "petit bourgeois deviation." Rumors spread that Trotsky had come in fifty-first out of the fifty-two members elected to the new Central Committee, perhaps a Stalin-instigated defamation, because the regime conspicuously broke tradition and did not announce the voting totals.[134]

The precongress plenum had resolved to present the "Letter to the Congress" not at the congress sessions, but to each delegation individually.[135] This meant that the congress stenographic record—controlled by Stalin's secretariat—could omit how these discussions went. Still, memoirs offer an indication. "They read the letter, and everyone was shocked," recalled Alexander Milchakov (b. 1903), a Communist Youth League official, who noted that his North Caucasus delegation asked that the text be read again. "After a repeat reading the readers proposed the following: taking into account the difficult situation in the country and party, the condition of the Comintern, and the fact that comrade Stalin promises to take comrade Lenin's criticisms into consideration, there is a proposal to ask comrade Stalin to remain in the post of general secretary. The North Caucasus delegation agreed with this."[136] Similar affirmations occurred at the May 25 gathering of the delegations from the central industrial region and Volga valley (presided over by Isai "Filipp" Goloshchokin and Nikolai Uglanov, Stalin supporters) and the May 26 gathering of Urals, Siberia, Far East, Bashkiria, and Vyatka province delegates (presided over by Mikhail Lashevich, the staunch Zinovievite). These well-orchestrated gatherings accepted assurances that Stalin had acknowledged Lenin's criticisms and promised to modify his behavior, as well as assertions that he had already improved, that he was shouldering a colossal burden, and that anyway, whatever Lenin had been worried about, time had shown Stalin had not abused his power because of his character.[137] The new post-congress Central Committee voted unanimously to reelect him general secretary.[138] Even the cave meeting addition of Zinoviev and Trotsky to the orgburo was formally rescinded.

If, contrary to myth, Lenin's dictation was widely read and discussed, many revealing documents were suppressed. A group of unemployed workers, for example, had written a letter to Comrades Zinoviev, Kamenev, Stalin—in Russian alphabetical order—stating that "no one, comrades, is seriously talking about the army of a million unemployed."[139] Requesting in vain that their letter be read to the congress, the writers added, "We ask, give us work, give us a hunk of bread, let us earn our keep so that our families do not die of starvation there where there is 'splendor.'"[140] Anger in villages was hardly less raw. "You Red butchers ought to know that the steam boiler of peasant patience may explode one day," one outraged villager shouted at an agitator in 1924, according to a police summary. "You ought to know that the peasants curse you usurpers in their morning prayers. . . . Where is truth? Where is justice? Why did you fool us with words such as freedom, land, peace, and equality?"[141]

## FASCISM'S LESSONS

Fascism constituted the other major Great War-era mass revolt against the constitutional liberal order besides Bolshevism. Back in 1922, Benito Mussolini, despite the fact that his fascist party had won just 35 seats out of 500 in its best showing in open elections, was demanding to be made prime minister, threatening to march on Rome with hordes of Blackshirts known as *squadristi*. The squads were lightly armed, their numbers exaggerated.[142] The proposed "march" was a colossal bluff, an exercise in psychological warfare, and King Vittorio Emanuele III seemed ready to summon the army to disperse the ruffians. But the king backed off from the anticipated bloodshed, and the well-equipped army did not act on its own.[143] On the contrary, the brass, as well as influential business circles, the pope, and even some constitutionalists thought Mussolini should be given a chance to "restore order," as an antidote to the left. The vacillating king telegraphed Mussolini to ask him to become prime minister in a coalition (with just those 35 fascists in the Chamber of Deputies).[144] On October 30, 1922, the thirty-nine-year-old fascist leader arrived in a luxury sleeping car, alighting at the last station before Rome, which he then entered as if on a march. Mussolini had almost lost his nerve; a comrade bucked up his resolve.[145] Only after he had been made prime minister did about 20,000 fascist marchers enter Rome. Many of them had failed to muster at appointed locations, and many of those who did show arrived short of weapons or food. After the *squadristi* paraded around Rome like conquerors, paying tribute at the Tomb of the Unknown Soldier and at the palace of the king, whom they saluted in ancient Roman style (right arm outstretched), Mussolini sent them home.[146] But their presence in Rome created a myth of a successful coup d'état.

Fascism puzzled the Communists in Moscow. From Rome, Yemelyan Yaroslavsky—the prosecutor of the mad sadist and would-be conqueror of Mongolia, Baron von Ungern-Sternberg—had written to Lenin on October 3, 1922, predicting that Italian fascism stood on the verge of seizing power, pointing out that their organizational abilities were influencing workers "who are impressed by the fascists' strength," and adding that "our Italian colleagues" (i.e., the Italian Communists) "have something to learn from the fascists."[147] But Yaroslavsky's prescient surmise that fascism was a movement on the right capable of attracting workers and peasants made little impression in Moscow. Instead, *Izvestiya*, beginning on October 31 and for several days thereafter, had reprinted Comintern speeches highlighting Mussolini's origins as a socialist (not a Communist) and linking Italy's Socialist party to the fascist triumph.[148] Mussolini, the apostate socialist, would enhance the appearance of an ostensible socialist-fascist link by soon taking to wearing tailcoats, wing collars, and spats, like a bourgeois class enemy. This superficial impression made in connection with Mussolini's biography and dress was reinforced in Communist thinking by the allegiance of German workers to the Social Democrats, particularly during the fall 1923 Communist putsch fiasco. But in reality, fascism and Social Democracy were implacable enemies. (In fact, as one historian noted, both "Bolshevism and fascism were heresies of socialism."[149]) Moreover, the traditional right, not Social Democrats, had brought fascism to power in Italy, while Communists had divided the left and galvanized the right in Italy and in Germany.

Stalin's inability to understand fascism was sorely evident. He followed Lenin, who had insisted that the non-Bolshevik left—Mensheviks, SRs, other moderates—were the most dangerous of all counterrevolutionaries, because they hid behind the mask of socialism. This chasm on the left undergirded the misinterpretation of fascism, and was institutionalized globally at the Fifth Comintern Congress, which met from June 17 to July 8, 1924, in the ornate Andreyev Hall of the Grand Kremlin Palace, with 504 delegates from 46 parties and 49 countries. The congress was held under the explicit slogan of "Bolshevization," which meant member parties were ordered to organize along Leninist lines to combat "petit-bourgeois deviation," and which meant Russification, facilitating an enlargement of Stalin's Comintern role (he did not speak German).[150] Stalin took over Trotsky's seat on the Comintern executive committee.[151] During the interminable denunciations of Trotsky and his foreign "stooges," one delegate from French Indochina interrupted: "I feel that the comrades have not yet sufficiently grasped the idea that the destiny of the proletariat of the whole world . . . is closely tied to the destiny of the oppressed nations in the colonies." His name was Nguyen Ai-Quoc, better known as Ho Chi-Minh.[152] Despite the acrimonious atmosphere, the delegates closed the proceedings by collectively singing the "Internationale." Congress delegates also visited Lenin's mummy and a session of the congress was staged on Red Square, with speakers perched on the cube.[153] But the Fifth Congress was most notable for institutionalizing the analysis, as Zinoviev said in his speech, that "the fascists are the right hand and the Social Democrats are the left hand of the bourgeoisie." Stalin, in his speech, reiterated the point, arguing that the Comintern needed "not a coalition with Social Democracy but lethal combat against it as the pillar of fascist-ized power."[154]

If Italian fascism offers a crucial lesson on the fateful limits of Stalin's thinking, its story holds another transcendent lesson: on how dictatorships take root. In April 1924, Prime Minister Mussolini's national list won 66.3 percent of the vote, against just 14.6 for the socialists and Communists and 9.1 percent for the Catholics. This gave the fascists 374 of 535 seats. On May 30, Giacomo Matteotti, the son of a wealthy family from the Veneto, a graduate of the law faculty in Bologna, and the leader of the United Socialist party, who had persistently criticized Mussolini and carried tremendous prestige, accused the fascists of intimidation and outright fraud, and demanded that the elections be annulled. "I've said my piece," he concluded. "Now you prepare my funeral speech."[155] Eleven days later he was bundled into a car, stabbed multiple times with a carpenter's knife, and beaten to death. His corpse was found two months later, on August 16, in a shallow grave some twenty miles from Rome. The motive for his murder remains murky.[156] But fascist complicity was established early: five thugs with ties to the fascist secret police had been arrested almost immediately. Mussolini's complicity or at least foreknowledge became a matter of speculation; it was never proven or disproven, but the murder sabotaged his secret intrigues to broaden his coalition and pushed his government to the point of collapse. Anti-fascist demonstrations occurred in the streets, a general strike was bruited, and many centrist supporters of Mussolini in the Chamber removed their fascist party badges. (Toscanini refused to play the fascist youth anthem "Giovinezza" at La Scala, saying the opera house was "not a beer garden.")[157] Mussolini seemed evasive under questioning. By December 1924, it was widely thought he would have to resign. The king refused to dismiss Mussolini, and so the anti-fascist deputies in parliament, to pressure him, quit the Chamber, heading for the Aventine Mount, where in ancient Rome the plebeians had exacted revenge against the patricians.[158] Their foolish act was reminiscent of the Mensheviks and SRs who in October 1917 abandoned the Congress of Soviets.

The leader of the anti-fascists in the Italian Senate "was in favor of arresting Mussolini by a *coup de main*," one historian explained, but most anti-fascists refused to employ extralegal means.[159] In the meantime, Mussolini was galvanized by fascist hard-liners who condemned the idiotic murder of Matteotti, called for a bottom-up fascist renewal, and threatened him with a coup in a new march on Rome.[160] On January 3, 1925, Mussolini rose in the Chamber, stating "I declare here, before this solemn assembly and before the whole Italian people, that I, and I alone, assume political, moral and historic responsibility for all that has happened." He dared those assembled to prosecute him. They did not. Already on January 10, by decree he outlawed all parties but the fascists and curbed the press. He also refused to let his opponents back in the parliament and pronounced their mandate forfeited as a result of their secession. Only now was Italy transformed from a constitutional monarchy into a one-party dictatorship. A fascist party card became a prerequisite for employment in universities, schools. Soon, Mussolini started calling himself *duce*. This turnaround of the Matteotti crisis against his opponents, not the 1922 march on Rome, was the fascist seizure of power.

There are moments in history that could have been turning points but did not turn or turned in the opposite direction, such as happened in 1924 simultaneously in fascist Italy, thanks to the parliamentary secession as well as the king, and in the Soviet Union, thanks to Zinoviev and Kamenev. A congress was one of Stalin's few vulnerable moments—and he had asked to be removed at the precongress plenum, so Zinoviev and Kamenev could have had the measure placed on the congress agenda. They could not have been unaware of Stalin's ambitions.[161] Perhaps they were content in the belief that he had been wounded by revelation of the dictation. Still, opportunism alone could have dictated that they seize on Lenin's purported dictation and take down the general secretary. In the case of Italy, Mussolini's political destruction might have allowed the rickety parliamentary system to survive the pressure of the street squads and the king's fecklessness, although Mussolini's demise might instead have facilitated the rise of the likes of Roberto Farinacci, the toughest, nastiest of the fascist local bosses, who could have pushed through an even more radical fascist social revolution. In the case of the USSR, the removal of Stalin might have proven temporary, given the lackluster qualities of his rivals; or for that same reason, it might have precipitated an eventual dissolution of the one-party rule that he was holding together.

Just as Mussolini had triumphed over his Matteotti crisis, Stalin did so over the Lenin dictation, but Stalin had not walked away unscathed. The nearly 1,200 delegates to the 13th Party Congress had witnessed his humiliation. Many of them doubtless brought back stories to the three quarters of a million party members they represented. Mention of the Lenin dictation appeared in the Paris-based Menshevik émigré newspaper *Socialist Herald* (July 24, 1924).[162] The whole world was beginning to learn: Lenin had called for Stalin's removal.

## SOVIET GEOPOLITICS

In Moscow there were no easy answers for the circumstance that the USSR was a would-be alternative global order, but the existing order had not gone away.[163] By the mid-1920s, around twenty countries, including almost all the major powers—Germany, Britain, France, Italy (but not the United States)—as well as Japan and Poland would recognize the Soviet state, but none saw a close, reliable partner in the Communist dictatorship. How could they, given Soviet behavior?[164] In one sense, the USSR was no different from all countries of the day, working to intercept and decode foreigners' radio signals and mail. A special cryptology department proved able to read the ciphered telegrams of foreign embassies from Moscow to Berlin and to Ankara from 1921, while Polish codes were broken in 1924 (in 1927 Japanese codes would be broken); access to this traffic fed an already deep Soviet cynicism about "diplomatic relations" as intercourse with the enemy.[165] At the same time, the British had broken Soviet codes and could compare internal Communist discourse with the external prevarication, which shredded already low Soviet credibility. Stalin, however, unlike his prying foreign counterparts, had little understanding of or interest in the simultaneous need for trust building in international affairs. While foreign embassies on Soviet soil were treated as Trojan horses of imperialism—even vital trade pacts were dogged by assumptions of spying and subversion by "agents of imperialism"—Soviet embassies abroad were headquarters for instigating Communist coups abroad, even as the USSR was conducting diplomatic and economic relations with those same countries.[166]

Mongolia occupied a special place as the sole other country to have had a Communist-style "revolution." At Lenin's death, the German ambassador Count Ulrich von Brockdorff-Rantzau had laid a wreath in the name of the entire diplomatic corps in Moscow, but the Mongolian ambassador laid a separate wreath "to the world leader of the toilers, friend and defender of the lesser peoples."[167] In 1924, the Bogd Gegen, the quasi-monarchical head of state, died; he was fifty-five. No traditional determination of his reincarnation was allowed. Instead, the Soviets oversaw proclamation of a "Mongolian People's Republic."[168] Soviet "advisers" were already pulling the strings behind nominal Mongol leaders.[169] Following the establishment of a Mongol version of the OGPU, membership in the Mongol party shrank by half from purges; many mysterious deaths ensued, including those of several of the original Mongol revolutionaries who had sought Soviet aid. A German foreign ministry official, on a visit, found Mongolia to be "practically on the way to becoming a Russian province."[170] Although Soviet-led attempts to create a single centralized trade cooperative failed and a mere 400 Mongol children were enrolled in schools, instruments of political indoctrination were being created: on November 10, 1924, the first issue of a Mongol-language newspaper, the organ of the Mongolian People's Party, was published—in Irkutsk, Siberia.[171] Building a socialist order in a nation of shepherds and monks presented profound problems for Communist ideology as well as practice. Most immediately, though, the Mongolian satellite was meant to serve Soviet security interests as a forward base of national liberation in Asia.

For Europe, the dream of additional Communist coups had not died in the German and Bulgarian fiascos. Pēteris Ķuzis, known as Jan Berzin, a former member of the Latvian Riflemen and the head of Soviet military intelligence, had infiltrated some threescore operatives into Estonia in spring 1924 to prepare a seizure of power with Estonian Communists.[172] Estonian counterintelligence had stepped up infiltration of the local Communist underground, however, and in a November 10–27, 1924, trial, 149 indigenous Communists stood accused of participation in a clandestine Communist organization (the party had been banned) and of being agents of the USSR. Seven were acquitted but for those convicted sentences were severe: one got death; thirty-nine, life; twenty-eight, fifteen years.

Moscow's putsch went ahead anyway.[173] Before dawn on Monday, December 1, a few hundred men in small squads—underground Baltic Communists, armed longshoremen from the Soviet merchant marine, Soviet consulate personnel—assaulted strategic positions in Tallinn, the Estonian capital.[174] The putschists chased half-dressed military men around their barracks in the darkness, threw grenades without having pulled the pins, and climbed into tanks not realizing the exits of the tank garages were blocked.[175] Still, the squads managed to occupy the main railway station for almost two hours, where they killed the railway minister (who arrived to investigate the commotion), and seized the residence of the head of government (state elder) and a military airfield. But the accompanying worker uprising never materialized. By 10:00 a.m. the coup was over.[176] Officially, 12 of the more than 250 putschists were killed in the fighting; more would die and around 2,000 would be arrested during a multimonth manhunt. Some escaped to the USSR. The Soviet press wrote fancifully of a rising of Estonian workers put down by a "White Guardist bourgeois clique."[177]

Right at this time, Stalin issued yet another anti-Trotsky broadside in *Pravda* (December 20, 1924), which he republished as the preface to his collection *On the Path to October* (January, 1925), with the title "Socialism in One Country," pointing out that the latter was possible.[178] Stalin had already said as much at the 6th Party Congress in August 1917, and now, essentially, was just affirming the seven-year existence of the Soviet Union. Lenin had quietly come around to the view that, if necessary, socialism could be built in one country.[179] Even Trotsky, in an unpublished lecture at the Sverdlov Communist University in spring 1923, had stated that "if the whole world collapsed except for Russia, would we perish? . . . No, we would not perish, given our resources, given the circumstance that we constitute a sixth of the earth."[180] True, Stalin's "Foundations of Leninism," when serialized in *Pravda* back in April and May 1924 and published in stand-alone form as *On Lenin and Leninism* (May 1924), had contained a passage denying the possibility of socialism in one country, but that was excised in a second edition in late 1924.[181] Stalin, moreover, was only declaring the possibility of socialism in one country *first,* for he noted that the "final" victory of socialism required the help of the proletariat of several countries and that world revolution would still occur, most likely as a result of uprisings in countries under the yoke of imperialism, and they could expect help from the USSR. This meant that the victory of socialism in one country actually "bore an international character," and that Russia had a special mission, now in revolutionary guise.[182] The essay became his most misunderstood piece of writing, but when initially published, aroused no controversy.[183]

The Menshevik newspaper in Europe *Socialist Herald* would later sensationalize Stalin's position as "A fig for Europe—we shall manage by ourselves."[184] Such a sentiment did have deep roots in Russia. Imperial Russia's international posture had vacillated between the pursuit of validating Western alliances and pursuit of a special, messianic mission in a space all its own, as heir to both the Byzantine empire and the grand Eurasian empires of the Mongols. Stalin's statement on socialism in one country superficially looked like just such a declaration of independence—the Soviet Union could go forward without waiting for revolution in the West—and therefore like an indulgence of the old saw of the expansive self-contained space. But hunkering down did not actually emancipate Russia from the West: the latter remained stronger, and therefore a geopolitical threat, while also possessing the advanced machines indispensable to Russia (and now the USSR). A "fortress Russia" stance had never worked, despite the temptation, as Stalin, no less than Trotsky, knew. The key to his "socialism in one country" article lay not in some imagined nose-thumbing of the West, but in a passage in which he explained the relative ease of the Bolshevik victory with reference to three conditions, all related to the Great War: the existence of two "imperialist blocs, the Anglo-French and Austro-German," whose all-out clash distracted them from giving serious attention to the revolution in Russia; the hated war's spawning in Russia of a profound longing for peace, which made proletarian revolution seem the pathway out of the conflict; and the war's spurring of strong movements of workers in imperialist countries who sympathized with the revolution in Russia.[185] In other words, even as Stalin had shown a primitive understanding of fascism derived from class analysis, he achieved an ideological breakthrough in linking revolution to war, rather than just class.

Additionally, Stalin recognized that world revolution afforded the Soviet Union a tool to pursue a special global mission and to break out of its enclosed geopolitical space. From the days of ancient Muscovy, Russia had expanded at the expense of weaker neighbors (Sweden, Poland, the Ottoman empire, China), always in the guise of seeking security amid wide-open frontiers. What had smacked of pure adventurism—the thrust into Central Asia and then Manchuria, where Russia had built a railroad to shorten the route to Vladivostok—could be seen as the logical completion of an advance that otherwise would have had to stop in the middle of nowhere.[186] Bolshevik instigation of world revolution, in a way, was the ultimate "defensive" expansionism. But while the tsarist borderlands had been vulnerable to foreign powers stirring up trouble among the *domestic* enemies of tsarism, now many of the borderlands were full-fledged anti-Soviet states: Estonia, Latvia, Lithuania, Finland, Poland, Romania. Known in Soviet parlance as the "limitrophe," they imposed the burden on the great powers of securing small state cooperation for any repeat military intervention in the USSR, but in Soviet eyes, this made the small states nothing more than playthings in the designs of world imperialism. Part of Stalin's calculation for the putsch in Estonia had entailed a desire to deny anti-Soviet forces a base of operations in the Baltics.[187] One Soviet intelligence analysis reported that Finland had held a conference in 1924 with the three Baltic countries to exchange intelligence about the USSR, relying upon the listening posts in Helsinki, Riga, Tallinn (Revel), Lwów, and Wilno, and recruiting agents among émigrés' family members who hoped to join their loved ones in emigration.[188] (Such intelligence reinforced the inclination to see as illegitimate the independence of the former imperial Russian territories.)[189] Considerations of Russia's position in the world had also motivated Stalin's otherwise inexplicable wild enthusiasm for the Communist coup in Germany, which he saw as a strike against independent Poland and the Baltics as well.

Stalin made revealing remarks about the failed coup in Estonia at a January 19, 1925, Central Committee plenum in a discussion of the defense budget. He had inserted the question of Trotsky's continuation as war commissar and head of the Revolutionary Military Council on the plenum's agenda.[190] Trotsky, not waiting to be sacked, had submitted his resignation on January 15 and departed for subtropical Abkhazia again.[191] Kamenev slyly proposed that Stalin replace Trotsky in the military; Stalin was not about to move out of or dilute his command of the party apparatus.[192] Mikhail Frunze, a recently named candidate member of the politburo and already the day-to-day operations head of the war commissariat, was promoted from first deputy to commissar.[193] But the plenum was no less noteworthy for the Estonia analysis. Stalin argued that "people there began to take action, made some noise, and tried to gain something, but all facts show that without the presence of the Red Army, standing united and vigilant and creating facts [on the ground], nothing serious will be achieved." He added that "our banner, as of old, remains the banner of peace, but if war begins, then we must not sit with folded arms—we must act, but act last. And we will act in order to throw the decisive weight on the scales, a weight that might be dominant. Hence my conclusion: be ready for everything, prepare our army, shoe and clothe it, train it, improve its technology, improve its chemical weapons, aviation, and in general lift our Red Army to the requisite heights. This is demanded of us by the international situation."[194]

Stalin reiterated his war-revolution theme following the anniversary of Lenin's death (January 21, 1925), when the Red Army Political Administration, just days after ceasing to report to Trotsky, issued a list of recommended readings with Stalin's *On Lenin and Leninism* as number one.[195] "This may seem strange but it is a fact, comrades," Stalin told a Moscow party conference on January 27. "If the two main coalitions of capitalist countries during the imperialist war in 1917 had not been engaged in mortal combat against each other, if they had not been at one another's throat, not been preoccupied and lacking in time to enter a contest with the Soviet regime, the Soviet regime would hardly have survived then. Struggle, conflicts, and wars between our enemies are, I repeat, our greatest ally."[196] Soviet geopolitics had been born.

## BRUSHING OFF EUROPEAN RAPPROCHEMENT

That Stalin would be enticed by a vision of an opportunistic windfall dropping into his arms from an intracapitalist war is understandable. The Communists seemed to be staring into the very dilemma that had bedeviled tsarist Russia's foreign policy: namely, whether to seek a German orientation, the way Durnovó had advocated, or an Anglo-French one, the path the ill-starred tsarist regime had chosen.[197] Like Lenin, Stalin saw Britain as the principal pillar of global imperialism, refracting a familiar imperial-Russian Anglophobia through the prism of Marxism-Leninism. Moreover, a reprise of the Franco-Russian alliance waned not only because the Communist regime was anathema to France, but Russia's strategic value had declined thanks to the resurrection of a Polish state on the other side of Germany; to contain Berlin, Paris set its sights on partnership with Warsaw. Stalin, for his part, worried less about containing German power, the rationale for the tsarist alliance with France, than benefitting from Germany as a source of solidarity against Versailles and technology transfer. But Stalin was in for a nasty surprise: the two opposing blocs that had offered tsarist Russia a fateful choice snatched that choice away from the USSR.

First came some Soviet maneuvering. Stalin despised the demands of the capitalist powers, especially the British, for such things as anti-propaganda clauses in bilateral agreements—the British incessantly propagandized against internal Soviet politics such as the repressions, as if their police did not beat striking workers—but the Soviets swallowed and symbolically foreswore Comintern propaganda in the British empire.[198] This secured coveted diplomatic recognition in February 1924 and, on August 8, 1924, the agreement of Britain's first ever Labour government to a draft commercial treaty that afforded British goods most-favored-nation status in exchange for which the USSR was to receive significant loans, albeit only after successful conclusion of negotiations over the status of tsarist debts.[199] Before the latter deal was sealed, on October 29 Britain held parliamentary elections and Labour lost (covertly subverted by the British intelligence services). The Tory Stanley Baldwin became prime minister and the new British foreign secretary Austen Chamberlain delivered an official note to Moscow stating, "The government of his majesty finds that it cannot recommend these treaties for consideration by parliament or propose them to the king for ratification by his majesty." A forged letter attributed to Zinoviev surfaced seeming to confirm Comintern subversion on the British Isles as well as Labour's political flirtations with Moscow.[200] While anti-Communist interests were at work in the UK, in the USSR far from all Communists appreciated the value to be gained from repaying the debts to blood-sucking British capitalists incurred by the bloody tsarist regime.[201] Still, the power of the major capitalist countries could not be wished away.[202] The West had the technology.

Moscow had also achieved commercial relations with Berlin, which were capped by diplomatic recognition, and the prospect loomed of modernizing Soviet industry with German help, but here, too, the Comintern cast a long shadow, especially the attempted Communist putsch in Germany.[203] While Berlin deplored how German Communists secretly trucked with German right-wing nationalists against the Weimar Republic, the Soviets were maddened by German pursuit of Western rapprochement. Pro-Western elements in Germany, in a secret document captured by Soviet military intelligence, asserted that "without doubt Moscow is prepared to sacrifice the interests of Germany."[204] But there was also an "Eastern School" of German diplomacy, represented by the German ambassador to Moscow, Count Ulrich von Brockdorff-Rantzau, who had supported Kolchak and other anti-Bolshevik forces, but even before their final defeat sought to make the most of the Bolshevik regime.[205] Back when he was Weimar Germany's first foreign minister, Brockdorff-Rantzau had led the German delegation to the Versailles talks in 1919 and publicly declared that a German admission of sole guilt would constitute a lie and warned that the Versailles terms would generate a German combination of nationalism and socialism.[206] He saw close ties with the Soviets as a way to overcome France's Versailles diktat and revive Germany's special mission in the world. To be sure, he was disgusted by Bolshevism, but he resented everything French, save cognac, and worried that his colleagues in Berlin would align Germany with Britain, thereby pushing the Soviets into the arms of France, a repeat of the fatal Great War two-front scenario. The count and Chicherin, also an aristocrat, found common cause, even observing similar nocturnal schedules (the two often met after midnight).[207] Most important, the Chicherin–Brockdorff-Rantzau pas de deux fit Stalin's Leninist Anglophobic, Germanophile inclinations.

A hidden dimension to German-Soviet ties entailed clandestine military cooperation, initiated under Lenin.[208] Versailles had imposed severe restrictions on the German military's size, training, weapons production, and even the ability to send military attachés abroad, but the Soviets offered to allow Germany to violate these restrictions. Major German manufacturers (Blohm & Voss, Krupp, Albatrosswerke) were able to build submarines, aircraft, and artillery on Soviet territory, and the Reichswehr obtained secret training facilities. The Soviets, for their part, sought to attract German firms through leases, or concessions, to take over and revive moribund weapons factories. Moscow welcomed an "unofficial" German military mission in the form of a commission for the verification of German economic concessions on USSR territory, known as Moscow Center in secret documents, and headed by Oskar von Niedermeyer, a Lawrence of Arabia type who had led missions during the Great War to Afghanistan and the Ottoman empire to rally tribes against the British. The Germans used the Moscow Center to gather intelligence as well as to cooperate, but Junkers did reopen an airplane plant just outside Moscow (at Fili).[209] And Germany held out the promise of coveted advanced and financial credits for Soviet industrial purchases well beyond the military sphere. Chicherin, knowing that von Brockdorff-Rantzau reported directly to the German chancellor, in fall 1924 offered the ambassador an enlargement of the Rapallo partnership into a "continental bloc" with France against Britain, emphasizing the clash of Soviet and British interests in Asia.[210]

Back in Berlin, where distrust of the Soviets lingered, the consensus was that Germany needed Britain for its Versailles revisionism against France; Germany declined the Soviet offer.[211] Rebuffed on the continental bloc, Chicherin, with the full backing of the politburo, proposed a bilateral Soviet-German alliance.[212] The German side did not immediately reject the idea, given the mutual enmity and mutual claims against Poland, but on the latter score the Soviet side hesitated, at least as presented by Chicherin, who sought a security guarantee against an aggression by or from the territory of Poland but not a new Polish partition.[213] The Soviets, for leverage, had not ignored France, which also recognized the USSR (October 1924), but conservatives in France voiced extreme disgust at the red flag flying over the reestablished embassy. Karl Radek, the Comintern official, published word of Soviet negotiations with France in German newspapers, but it did not move Berlin. Notwithstanding the Rapallo Treaty breakthrough, the German-Soviet dalliance resembled a marriage of convenience, in which each partner cheated on the other. Stalin was waxing on about how "the struggle between Britain and America for oil, for Canada, for markets, the struggle between the Anglo-American bloc and Japan for Eastern markets, the struggle between Britain and France for influence in Europe, and, last, the struggle between enslaved Germany and the dominant Entente—all these are commonly known facts that indicate that the successes capital has achieved are transient, that the process of capitalism's 'recovery' contains within itself the germs of its inherent weakness and disintegration." And German foreign minister Gustav Stresemann put out feelers for normalization with the Entente.[214]

Britain, prioritizing its empire, remained wary of committing significant resources to continental Europe and therefore was eager to integrate Germany politically and economically to remove the presumed basis for war, and perhaps even have Germany to manage the Soviet Union. Britain's Foreign Secretary Austen Chamberlain, unusually for a top London official, was sensitive to French security concerns, but keen to pry Germany away from the Soviet Union. Stresemann, for his part, remained keen to retain German-Soviet military cooperation, however. An agreement to open an aviation school was signed April 15, 1925, and ground broken in the Soviet city of Lipetsk (it would go into full operation within two years).[215] In August 1925, Reichswehr officers observed Red Army maneuvers for the first time (they arrived disguised as German worker Communists). A group of Red Army officers, disguised as Bulgarians, reciprocated, going to Germany to observe fall maneuvers. "The German command made sure that we did not come into contact with soldiers," Mikhail Tukhachevsky, head of the delegation, reported to Moscow on October 3, 1925, adding that "secret observation was established." (German drivers for the Soviets, predictably, pretended not to know Russian when they did.) Tukhachevsky was particularly struck by how "discipline in the mass of soldiers is firm and profoundly inculcated. I did not observe officer's rude treatment of soldiers, but I did by the unter-officers. . . . One notices the immense proportion of aristocrats among the officers in the field command and the general staff."[216] Still, right at this time, Stresemann's Western feelers yielded results.

The Locarno Peace Pact consisted of a clutch of seven agreements negotiated at a resort on Lake Maggiore (October 5–16, 1925) between Britain, France, Italy, Belgium, and Germany as well as Poland and Czechoslovakia. Germany recognized its borders in the west (the Rhineland frontier), effectively ceding Alsace-Lorraine to France, and agreed to vague arbitration over its borders to the east, effectively allowing for future revision. Germany was given a path to admission into the League of Nations, shedding its pariah status. "The gates of war are closed," declared France's foreign minister Aristide Briand (who had headed the government back during the siege of Verdun). But no comparable non-aggression pledges or mutual guarantees were issued for Germany's relations with its smaller eastern neighbors. Polish foreign minister Józef Beck would complain that "Germany was officially asked to attack the east, in return for peace in the west." The retired former head of state Józef Piłsudski observed that "every honest Pole spits when he hears this word [Locarno]."[217] Still, all three principals (Briand, Stresemann, and Chamberlain) would be awarded Nobel Prizes. The Soviets, who had not been invited, were alarmed that Germany had apparently been drawn back into the western orbit as part of a presumed British-led anti-Soviet coalition. Chicherin did get Stresemann to promise that Germany would not participate in sanctions against the USSR or seek a frontier rapprochement with Poland.[218] But suspicions about Germany's motives lingered. The Soviet press wrote of "a united anti-Soviet imperialist bloc."[219]

Locarno's implications—the two capitalist blocs making agreements—threatened to upend Stalin's theory of a pending Soviet windfall from an intra-capitalist war. Was this a capitalist "stabilization"?[220] Stalin tried to puzzle out Locarno's significance in notes to himself for a speech he would deliver before the end of 1925. "They want to repeat the history of 'guaranteed pacts' that existed before the Franco-Prussian War," he wrote. "Then and now, the grouping of forces for a new war is hidden under the phrase securing peace (guarantee of peace)." But in the old days, Stalin continued, Russia had been fodder for the imperialist cliques, while now "Russia cannot and will not be either a weapon, or a reserve, or cannonball fodder for bourgeois states." He also stressed the games of British conservatives, whom he suspected of scheming to use Poland against the USSR.[221] In other observations of 1925, Stalin characterized the international situation as analogous to the time right before the Great War.[222] He refused, in other words, to accept the notion of an *enduring* capitalist stabilization. Despite the Locarno shock, Stalin persisted in foreseeing a fratricidal war between imperialist blocs, with the USSR as the potential beneficiary and revolutionary outbreaks as a potential consequence. Believing otherwise implied the necessity of deep Soviet concessions to the capitalist powers on core principles, up to granting domestic political pluralism. Either innate rivalry among the capitalist powers for markets and colonies led to fratricidal war or Leninism was wrong and the USSR in trouble.

## A DUUMVIRATE

Stalin's apparatus, along with Zinoviev's in Leningrad, deluged the public domain with tendentious pamphlets undoing Trotsky's heroics in the October coup and civil war and blackening his image ("For Leninism, Against Trotskyism").[223] Stalin had the wherewithal to make this line ubiquitous throughout the provincial press.[224] Still, he had a way to go to extirpate Trotsky's renown, especially internationally: in a February 1925 report intercepted by the OGPU, a British diplomat deemed Trotsky—after his sacking—"the most powerful figure in Russian Bolshevism" and even "the most significant individual in socialist revolutionary Europe." A copy went to Stalin.[225] But Trotsky was no longer Stalin's sole target. Already in late 1924, Stalin had begun to move against his allies Kamenev and Zinoviev. He replaced a Kamenev protégé as Moscow party boss and Central Committee secretary with his own new loyalist, Nikolai Uglanov.[226] Uglanov had originally worked under Zinoviev in Leningrad, but the two had clashed and Stalin had found Uglanov, promoting him from Nizhny Novgorod to the capital; in Moscow, Uglanov fended off Zinoviev's blandishments.[227] Most important, Nikolai Bukharin had been promoted to fill the politburo slot vacated by Lenin's death, which kept the full (voting) members at seven—and Stalin became very solicitous of him. From August 1924, the prepolitburo gatherings of the triumvirate had been expanded to a "septet": Bukharin, Rykov, Tomsky, and Kuibyshev, in addition to Zinoviev, Kamenev, and Stalin—that is, all members of the politburo except Trotsky, plus the head of the Central Control Commission (Kuibyshev).[228] But Stalin was already working on a new configuration, an alliance with the thirty-six-year-old Bukharin as well as Rykov and Tomsky.[229]

Trotsky assisted Stalin's scheme, inadvertently but decisively. In late 1924, from the spa town of Kislovodsk, recuperating from fevers again, he detonated another written bomb, "Lessons of October."[230] It recounted the opposition by Zinoviev and Kamenev to the 1917 coup, which Trotsky labeled "desertion" and "not at all accidental"—a phrase straight out of the Lenin dictation. (Stalin went unmentioned, as if he had not been around in 1917.) Trotsky, being himself, also could not resist demonstrating that at times he had corrected Lenin. Still, he scored a spectacular strike against the triumvirate. Stalin mobilized the full anti-Trotsky forces: at least thirty articles denouncing "Trotskyism" appeared in *Pravda* over two months, including those by Bukharin, Kamenev, Zinoviev, even Sokolnikov.[231] In a single issue, *Pravda* printed a long dilatory attack by Kamenev and a concise, devastating one by Stalin.[232] Krupskaya's rebuttal praised Trotsky's "colossal energy" but deemed him weak in "Marxist analysis" and inclined to "a purely 'administrative' and utterly superficial" approach to the party's role, similarly echoing Lenin's dictation.[233] But the damage to Zinoviev and Kamenev was severe: most of the party mass had no idea about the pair's opposition to the 1917 coup, and Trotsky joined it to the failure of the German coup in 1923, warning that such "cowardice" would be dangerous going forward.

Stalin's shifting political alliance to undercut rivals—with Zinoviev and Kamenev against Trotsky; with Bukharin, Rykov, and Tomsky against Zinoviev and Kamenev—hardly constituted evidence of special genius: it was no more than Personal Dictatorship 101. Nonetheless, his elementary tactics surprised his erstwhile partners. Zinoviev, Kamenev, and Krupskaya, still living in the apartment she had shared with Lenin, had taken to meeting in a threesome on their own. At the same time, Stalin's provocations of them were also evident: Molotov, at the party secretariat, stopped inviting Zinoviev supporters to the semiclosed party sessions without Trotsky, perhaps to induce the Leningraders to meet on their own, thereby giving the appearance of an illegal faction. Additionally, Trotsky later claimed, plausibly, that Stalin's minions spread rumors that their boss was looking to reconcile with Trotsky, and had even sent emissaries to him in Abkhazia in March 1925. (The plane carrying the emissaries crashed.) "Stalin, without entangling himself," Trotsky wrote, "was merely trying to sow illusions among the 'Trotskyites,' and panic among the Zinovievites."[234] And the coup de grâce? When Zinoviev and his Leningrad party organization supporters aggressively demanded Trotsky's expulsion from the politburo, Central Committee, and even the party, Stalin would *defend* Trotsky against their attacks.[235] As for Bukharin, having savaged Trotsky, he turned his fluent viciousness against Kamenev and Zinoviev with gusto. Wholly under Stalin's patronage, Bukharin became half of an emerging duumvirate.

## "ENRICH YOURSELVES"

Not Bukharin the ideologist but Grigory Sokolnikov the finance commissar made the New Economic Policy work. Sokolnikov did not strike the typical leather-clad Bolshevik pose. "An effeminate looking gentleman, he had the face of an Indian maharajah," noted his wife Galina Serebryakova. "His refined gestures, clean aristocratic face with direct, proud nose, oblong dark eyes, tall, unusually contoured lips and wonderful ears—all his bearing of a well-developed and physically powerful person of the English peerage."[236] But Sokolnikov was tough. He campaigned to raise apparatchiks' salaries and eliminate the cash envelopes ("bonuses"), special food packets, special fashion ateliers, the state-supplied dachas, personal automobiles, and all the rest. These perquisites became entrenched, even as the salaries would rise, but in his strenuous efforts to separate the state budget from apparatchiks' personal finances, Sokolnikov lived what he preached. "He could not abide gifts from people unknown to him and steadfastly took nothing from his subordinates," his wife maintained. "He saved Soviet power's every kopeck, and not only did not spend the money given him for foreign travel, but, as a rule, returned the greater part of his advances." Abroad he always traveled third class and stayed in the cheapest hotels.[237]

Sokolnikov drew lessons for the USSR from postwar European capitalist experience. In a speech delivered in July 1924, for example, he reasoned that in France and Germany the "bourgeoisie" had wielded inflation at the expense of workers and peasants to support *privately* owned industry. State-owned industry, he believed, was preferable, but nonetheless he warned that the *interests* of state industry might conflict with the interests of "the state as a political organization." In other words, if state industry got its way, the resulting inflation would be paid for by the peasants, who could not turn over their money quickly and would see it devalued. Sokolnikov also deduced from European inflation that absent a stable currency, the Soviet state could be engulfed in political crisis, as had happened in France, to say nothing of Weimar Germany. Sokolnikov concluded that even if the Soviet state *tried* to use inflation to underwrite industry, it would be forced to retreat, just as "the bourgeoisie" in Europe had been.[238] But many Communists remained incredulous that gold was a guarantor of value under socialism and that the USSR needed to accumulate reserves of capitalist currencies, even if they took comfort in the fact that the party controlled the "commanding heights" (heavy industry, railways, foreign trade).[239] Soviet industrial trusts were struggling just to pay wage arrears, let alone invest in the future. "There is in the Soviet Union a very great shortage of capital," a secret British diplomatic report observed in December 1924. "The need for re-equipment of the factories is great, but where are the resources to pay for this equipment?"[240]

Industrial production in 1925 on average was less than half of what it had been in 1913, and Sokolnikov's opponents in the Soviet industrial lobby screamed that he was strangling the very "material base" the country needed to build socialism. Most prominently, the left economist Yevgeny Preobrazhensky presented a scientific paper titled "The Fundamental Law of Socialist Accumulation," which, building on Marx's idea of primitive capitalist accumulation, argued for a stage of forced "expropriation of surplus product," meaning pumping resources out of the countryside and artisanal labor at low prices.[241] But Sokolnikov's monetary reforms and stringent budgets had paid dividends—by 1924, a tax in money had replaced the tax in kind and the economy had been remonetized—but in state industry, costs were rising and labor productivity was not, while mismanagement and waste were rampant. State trusts were largely shielded from market discipline: perversely, those that performed better received lower budget allocations, while the worst could count on bailouts instead of bankruptcy.[242] Sokolnikov's hesitation was fully warranted. He pressed the point by writing books and articles characterizing the USSR system as "state capitalist" and arguing that capitalist methods were essential in a transition period for the benefit of the proletariat and that the country could revive economically only if reconnected to the world economy.[243]

What tripped up Sokolnikov, however, was that the harvest in 1924 had been poor, and in some regions famine had not ended. Foreign currency–earning grain exports would be suspended entirely that hungry summer.[244] The head of the government, Alexei Rykov, and the OGPU's Yagoda toured the Volga valley accompanied by journalists. ("Comrade Yagoda," the Soviet journalist Mikhail Koltsov remarked, "did it ever occur to you that without horns you simply do not look your part?" Everyone guffawed, Yagoda included.) Rykov addressed an enormous crowd on the central square of Saratov, his hometown, where twelve years earlier, under the old regime, he had been beaten during a May Day demonstration. "These very stones ran red with our blood," he said. "In those days we dreamed of a Russia redeemed from the blight of tsarism. That dream is fulfilled. But to destroy absolutism was only part of our task. Our aim today is to build a truly free, socialist Russia." The square erupted in applause. But as Rykov made the rounds of villages, peasants asked him, "What is a kulak? Can it be a muzhik who owns a horse, a cow, and some poultry?" Rykov tried to calm the peasants, but answered, "If we let kulaks thrive, we shall soon revert to the old system—a few rich peasants in each village and the rest destitute. Do you want those exploiters?"[245] Of course, Rykov knew full well that the danger was incompetent, corrupt governance.[246] But the party debate about agricultural policy became consumed with arguments about class differentiation amid reports that kulaks had seized control over cooperatives and village soviets.[247]

The state, as in tsarist times, could not "see" all the way down to the self-governing villages. The peasant revolution had strengthened the communes, rechristened "land societies," which the regime saw as survivals of a backward era. Under the commune system, livestock was usually held individually (by household), albeit often pastured in common, and the land was worked by household rather than collectively (except for some scything in meadows). But the commune as a collective bestowed the usage rights to the land, allocating each household a number of strips of varying size and location, which the commune periodically redistributed according to shifting household size and other considerations. Improving one's assigned strips with manure or other means made little sense because they could be reallocated. In regions of black soils, the number of strips typically ran twenty to thirty per household; in areas of non-black earth, fifty to eighty. Some strips could be as narrow as seven to fifteen feet wide and a mere seventy feet long. They could also lie as far as ten miles or more away, and sometimes peasants declined to farm them. Some of the arable land was lost to access paths, while the redistributions could be time-consuming, requiring measurements in situ and volatile meetings. Soviet legislation tried to restrict redistributions as inefficient, but efforts to place villages under rural soviets often failed. Communes generated their own income—they collected the taxes—while rural soviets required subsidies from above (and spent the funds on administrative salaries).[248] Peasants could quit the commune, Stolypin style, and in the northwest, Ukraine, or Belorussia, enclosed farms rather than communes predominated, but here, too, the party and soviet were just an occasional presence. In 1924, the party's theoretical journal mockingly referred to the NEP as the new "Stolypin-Soviet" policy as well as a "kulak deviation."[249]

Sokolnikov insisted that the chief instrument of struggle against the "kulak danger" had to be economic—progressive taxation—but the Bolsheviks needed more grain, immediately. The politburo was compelled to approve grain imports, costing vital hard currency. Even then, in several provinces, including in the Volga valley visited by Rykov, peasants would still be consuming food surrogates into 1925. Herds were increasing in size, consumption was going up, and sown acreage finally attained the 1913 level, but yields per acre were substantially lower, and grain marketings overall seemed to be declining.[250] Agricultural prices rose precipitously, from 102 kopecks per *pud* (36 pounds) of rye to 206 kopecks, and reports circulated of kulaks' buying up and holding grain stocks in anticipation of further price rises. *Pravda* blamed private capital for "disorganizing" the internal grain market.[251] The regime was forced to spend more budget revenue on higher wages for the workers at state factories so they could buy bread. At the same time, the imports threatened Sokolnikov's strong currency and budget discipline: the grain imports would push the country back into a trade deficit. Agriculture's "backwardness" took the blame for multiple dilemmas of unfortunate weather, poor governance, and policy errors.

Stalin's position was a Lenin-style combination of flexible tactics and unshakable core beliefs. He urged party officials to earn the trust of the peasant, kulaks excepted, following to the letter the late Lenin's dicta regarding the NEP. He also asserted that a capitalist path of development would impoverish Soviet peasants, producing an underclass of wage slaves condemned to toil on latifundia, and that private traders would gouge the peasants, so he stressed mass peasant membership in agricultural and trade cooperatives, also true to Lenin's vision of the NEP.[252] But on November 7, 1924, the revolution's seventh anniversary, Stalin visited the Moscow factory Dynamo and offered a glimpse into his deeper thinking. "I wish for the workers of Dynamo, and the workers of all Russia," he wrote in the visitors' book, "that our industry expands, in order that the number of proletarians in Russia in the near term climbs to 20-30 million, that collective agriculture flourishes in villages and subordinates to its influence private farming." Stalin's words that day—a leftist manifesto—were not published until several years later.[253] In January 1925, this time in a public setting, Stalin did reveal something of his otherwise closely held views. "[The peasantry] is at our side, we are living with it, we are building a new life together with it, whether that's good or bad," he said at a meeting of the Moscow party organization. "This ally, you know yourselves, is not a very strong one, the peasantry is not as reliable an ally as the proletariat of the developed capitalist countries." But Stalin had also been relentlessly accusing Trotsky of underestimating the peasantry, and in the speech characterized "Trotskyism" as the "disbelief in the forces of our revolution, disbelief in the alliance [smychka] between workers and peasants," which was indispensable to the success of the NEP and the revolution's ultimate triumph.[254] Attacks on Trotsky, in other words, translated into strong support for the NEP.

Such was the background to the 14th party conference in April 1925, when, continuing to adhere to Sokolnikov's advice on the need for fiscal discipline and currency stability, while also indulging Bukharin's insistence on conciliation on the peasant question, Stalin oversaw a doubling down on the NEP's concessions. The Central Committee reduced the agricultural tax and cost of farm machinery, expanded the rights to lease land and hire labor, enhanced loan programs, and softened the restrictions on small-scale trade.[255] These measures, it was hoped, would bring in a bumper harvest both to feed the country and, via exports, to finance a higher tempo of industrialization.[256]

Stalin relished demonstrating his superior leadership skills with people, not least because the others at the top viewed him as inferior. Once, for instance, the politburo discussed uniting the commissariats of foreign and domestic trade and appointing as the single head Alexander Tsyurupa, Lenin's former deputy, so Kamenev went to talk to him. "He waved his hand, went white and became so obviously resentful that I ditched the conversation," Kamenev, giving up, wrote to Stalin. But Stalin answered: "I also spoke with him (he himself asked). Outwardly he protested against his candidacy, but his eyes were smiling. I told him that, in that light, he is agreed, obviously. He stayed silent. I think he'll do."[257] On matters of international political economy, too, Stalin revealed himself as a quick study and adept. The Soviet Union operated in a capitalist financial world, which, for better or worse, had seen the reintroduction of a quasi-gold standard and the institutionalization of convertible currency reserves, but hardly anyone in the Central Committee grasped these issues.[258] Stalin would invariably take the floor to explain matters, employing his canonical style (first point, second point, third point). In deliberations about prices, for example, he illuminated why trade margins were still operative even though this was socialist trade. He also reinforced Sokolnikov's point about the causal link between monetary emissions and inflation, and admonished that expenses had to be held in check, which meant enduring high levels of unemployment and lower rates of economic expansion, just as the capitalists did for the same reasons.[259] But it was Bukharin who, with Stalin's blessing, seized the spotlight to explain this deepening of the NEP.

On April 17, 1925, in a memorable speech to a meeting of the Moscow party active, Bukharin chastised those who were dismissive of the village, for "nothing is more harmful than the lack of understanding that our industry depends on the peasant market," that is, on peasant demand and ability to pay for manufactured goods. But, he lamented, "the well-off upper stratum of the peasantry and the middle peasant who strives to become well-off are now afraid to accumulate. The situation is created such that a peasant is afraid to mount a metal roof over his house so as not to be called a kulak; if he purchases machinery he does so in a way that the Communists do not see. Higher technology becomes conspiratorial." Poor peasants, meanwhile, complained that Soviet power hindered their hiring by the better-off peasants. (Most peasants who hired labor themselves worked; they were not rentier landlords.) Party attitudes were holding down production on which the state's well-being and industrialization hopes rested. Bukharin dismissed the fantasy of collective farms, because the peasants were just not joining them. "That we should in all ways propagandize among the peasants formation of collective farms is true, but it is not true when people maintain that there is a highway to the movement of the peasant mass toward the path of socialism," he stated. Rather, the answer was to benefit from economic incentives. "It is necessary to say to the entire peasantry, to all its strata: 'Enrich yourselves, accumulate, develop your farms,'" he told the party activists. "Only idiots can say that we should always have the poor; now we need to conduct policy in such a way that the poor would vanish."[260]

Bukharin's typically inflammatory rhetoric notwithstanding, he was merely drawing the logical conclusions of the regime's own policy: Did the Communists want a smaller harvest? Should peasants be encouraged to produce less just to avoid appearing to be kulaks? Fury at Bukharin's aggressive logic, however, exploded. Also, it was now that furious critiques were belatedly launched against Stalin's "socialism in one country," demagoguing Stalin's arguments as antiworld revolution, a rare taste of his own medicine.[261] The combination of Bukharin's incautious speech and Stalin's deliberately misconstrued article afforded a significant opportunity for critics of the new duumvirate. Zinoviev, in May 1925, stated that "the worst thing that can happen to a revolutionary party is to lose its [revolutionary] perspective."[262] He was acutely aware of the rising discontent over disparities of wealth and privilege based upon his knowledge of Leningrad, where workers repeatedly engaged in slowdowns and strikes, and in that context a doubling down on the NEP would be perceived as, and indeed was becoming, a wager on the kulaks.[263] He viewed Bukharin's advocacy as unwittingly paving the way for the very capitalist restoration predicted by émigré critics when they said the Bolsheviks would be forced to make ever greater concessions to capitalism. Zinoviev would state that 14 percent of the peasantry produced 60 percent of the grain, while earning half a billion rubles.[264] Behind closed doors, in June 1925, Stalin stated that "the slogan 'get rich' is not our slogan," adding, "our slogan is socialist accumulation."[265] Bukharin had to publicly repudiate his summons of enrichment, over and over, even as the opposition continued to bash him with it.

But all the questions about the New Economic Policy remained. Lenin himself had warned of the dangers of a self-inflicted capitalist restoration in the "peasant Brest-Litovsk," but whereas the original Brest-Litovsk had been overturned with Germany's defeat in the war on the western front, it remained unclear what, if anything, would overturn the NEP. How long was the retreat? Lenin's statements were highly ambiguous ("seriously, and for a long time" "a long period, measured in years," "not less than a decade, and probably more," "25 years is too pessimistic").[266] The only clarity was that the NEP had not been intended to last forever. In the meantime, was it leading to socialism or full restoration of capitalism? And how was the NEP facilitating the imperative to industrialize? Leftists such as Preobrazhensky insisted that the NEP would never produce the "surplus" necessary to fund industrialization; therefore, why indulge the kulak?[267] Stalin himself wrote in *Pravda* in May 1925 that "we need 15-20 million industrial proletarians," at a time when the country had perhaps 4 million.[268] Was this feasible? It was all well and good to talk about wielding the contradictions among the imperialists, but how was socialism going to survive without modern machine industry? If kulak farms were to be harassed and contained, how would petty-peasant farming serve to build up the country, in conditions of capitalist encirclement? How would NEP Russia become socialist Russia? "The main thing now is not at all to ignite the class struggle in the village," Stalin said, contra Zinoviev's line, in a summary of the 14th party conference in May 1925, while adding emptily that "the leadership of the working class is the guarantee that the construction proceeds along the path to socialism."[269]

Police, party, and journalistic channels continued to report deep resentment in villages of kulaks, while largely ignoring the anger at officials.[270] The regime directed its own ire at private traders, disparaged as "NEPmen." The vast majority of privateers were small-fry hawkers of what they themselves had planted or fabricated (or of their possessions), but OGPU operatives periodically made a show of swooping in on the bazaars and throwing a dragnet. "There was a very fine line between permissible profits and illegal speculation," wrote one eyewitness of the arrests, a process known as skimming the NEP. "The cook knows how to skim the fish soup but I doubt whether all the NEPmen understood which they were: the scum or the fish."[271] A few NEPmen did achieve scale, using their wealth to open restaurants, billiard houses, bathhouses, recreational facilities, in other words, points of public congregation, where people traded news, rumor, and ideas, and a few exercised influence over the strategic rail network, paying bribes to underpaid officials. There was even a private airline based in Ukraine, one of only three airlines in the country, which served Kharkov (the capital), Rostov, Odessa, Kiev, and Moscow.[272] But no NEPman could rise and remain above the others without the complicity of the authorities, especially the OGPU, which commandeered the choice rooms in those restaurants.[273] Outside the thick ideological soup, the Soviet Union's greatest challenge was neither kulaks nor NEPmen, but the "Enrich yourselves" behavior of officials engaged in shakedowns and massive embezzlement.[274]

## TESTAMENT REPUDIATED

Stalin had an additional worry: the damned Lenin dictation, which Trotsky's supporters had labeled the Testament. Someone had passed a copy to the writer Max Eastman, who knew some Russian, having married Yelena Krylenko, sister of Nikolai (lately, deputy justice commissar). In spring 1925, Eastman published *Since Lenin Died,* which retailed Trotsky's analysis of a bureaucratic deformation under Stalin, carried excerpts from Lenin's purported dictation, and made reference to the warm private letter Krupskaya had sent to Trotsky immediately following Lenin's death. Because Cristian Rakovski, the Soviet envoy to France (a form of exile), had read Eastman's manuscript, the American took it as Trotsky's approval. In Moscow that May, Trotsky had tried to explain himself and claimed he had had no contact with Eastman for more than a year and a half and had never passed him any secret documents. But Eastman's book was being cited in the "bourgeois" press and spurring questions among Communists abroad.[275] Stalin's apparatus made a Russian translation, and he wrote a long letter on June 17, 1925, citing many specific passages as "slander" against Lenin and the party, demanding that Trotsky refute them in print. Trotsky was summoned before the politburo the next day and ordered to denounce Eastman's book. Stalin rejected Trotsky's first draft response, which was published in France, after being leaked by the Comintern operative and Stalin loyalist Manuilsky, in order to blacken Trotsky with more leaking.

Stalin personally edited Trotsky's final text.[276] The long note appeared in English in the *Sunday Worker* (July 19) and then in Russian in the Soviet party's main theoretical journal. "In certain parts of his short book Eastman says that the Central Committee 'concealed' a number of extremely important documents from the party that had been written by Lenin in the last period of his life," Trotsky's text stated. "This cannot be called anything other than slander of the Central Committee of our party." Trotsky's text further averred that Lenin, contrary to Eastman's assertions, had not intended these documents for publication, and that they merely offered "advice of an organizational nature," and even that "Lenin did not leave behind any 'Testament,' and the very nature of his relations to the party, like the nature of the party itself, exclude such a 'Testament.'"[277] Trotsky's text also stated that the Lenin document had not been concealed but "examined by the 13th Party Congress in the most attentive way."[278] Trotsky concluded that Eastman's "little book could only serve the vilest enemies of Communism and the revolution, and constitutes, in that sense, an objective counterrevolutionary weapon."[279] Trotsky's supporters, who had been circulating the Testament underground at personal risk, were dumbfounded. "He has made himself despicable," one commented on what he saw as the lies that Trotsky signed his name to.[280] But the politburo had voted on the wording, and Trotsky was subject to party discipline.[281]

Krupskaya, as Lenin's widow, was also summoned to repudiate Eastman, and her remarks were published in the *Sunday Worker* (August 2, 1925) and in the party theoretical journal as well.[282] "All delegates of the congress familiarized themselves with the letters, just as Lenin had wanted," her text averred. "They are being called a 'testament' incorrectly, since Lenin's Testament in the true sense of the word is much more extensive—it includes his last articles and touches on the foundations of party and soviet work." She condemned how the "enemies of the Russian Communist party are trying to use the 'Testament' to discredit the current leaders of the party, to discredit the party itself." She also repudiated Eastman's use of her January 1924 private letter to Trotsky: "This letter in no way should be interpreted as it was interpreted by Max Eastman. One cannot conclude from this letter that Lenin considered Trotsky as his deputy."[283] There is no record of Stalin's reaction.[284] But if he imagined this gift from his enemies had driven a stake through the Testament, he was mistaken. It would never die.

## VOROSHILOV'S ASCENT

Stalin's theory of geopolitics presupposed a robust Red Army, but this instrument gave the regime trouble. Even before Frunze's promotion to commissar, he had headed a military commission, which by September 1925 pushed through a reform that combined the existing (and inadequate) territorial militia system with a regular peacetime army, improved living conditions and supply, and increased the army's party membership and Communist Youth League support groups.[285] Frunze envisioned wholesale replacement of former tsarist officers with Red commanders (such as himself), and rapid industrialization to transform the military's material base, which remained painfully below the level of 1916 (during the Brusilov offensive), even as Western military production had advanced. In conditions of the NEP, however, Frunze barely succeeded in retaining dedicated military factories: Red militarism was not merely a dirty word but expensive.[286] The intrigues around former tsarist officers, meanwhile, had not subsided, even though their number had been trimmed from the peak of 75,000 (including noncoms) to fewer than 2,000.[287] Former tsarist officers dominated military education institutions, including the General Staff Academy, while no more than about 6 percent of the Red Army belonged to the Communist party.[288] Even Trotsky, the person most responsible for their mass recruitment, in a 1925 publication divided former tsarist officers into a minority who had consciously chosen to fight the Whites and an "unsteadfast, convictionless and cowardly" majority who had sided with Bolshevism but might yet turn back the other way.[289] It is hard to know which threatened the army more: the primitive material base or the paranoid class politics.

OGPU reports portrayed former tsarist officers as a tightknit caste with shared values, capable of acting as a collective body, lying in wait for an opportunity, while Soviet foreign intelligence was organized almost entirely to penetrate émigré circles, especially those with a military aspect.[290] The OGPU special departments in the army set up false anti-Soviet conspiracies, using former White officers in Cheka employ as provocateurs to expose anti-Soviet moods, while abroad an elaborate OGPU operation known as the Trust (or the Syndicate) was created around a false underground monarchist "center" that supposedly united former tsarist officers, high tsarist officials, and expropriated industrialists serving the Bolshevik regime while secretly plotting against it.[291] Agents of the Trust smuggled abroad some genuine documents, thereby entering into confidences, enabling them to feed disinformation about the status and plans of the Red Army.[292] Even skeptical émigrés clued in to OGPU methods wanted to believe their homeland could somehow be seized back from the godless, barbaric Bolsheviks, and speculated endlessly about a Napoleon figure to lead a patriotic movement, mentioning most often Mikhail Tukhachevsky: noble by birth, megalomaniacally ambitious, and rumored to "imitate Napoleon in everything and constantly to read his biography and history."[293] One émigré publication, which derided Tukhachevsky as "a typical adventurist, in love with himself, self-reliant, striving for one thing only: career and power," allowed that he "might be determined" to follow in the footsteps of the French general who had massacred the Paris Communards. After all, Tukhachevsky had done it at Kronstadt to the sailors and at Tambov to the peasants, what were the Communists to him?[294] Soviet intelligence fostered these fantasies about Tukhachevsky's concealed disloyalty, feeding it through multiple channels, such as the OGPU-sponsored Russian-language journal *War and Peace* in Berlin, which held him up as an anti-Bolshevik nationalist savior linked to foreign intelligence circles.[295] At home, Tukhachevsky was under close police surveillance.[296]

An additional source of anxiety was Frunze's fragile health. Despite an operation in 1916 for a perforated ulcer, he continued to endure chronic inflammation, and doctors had warned him his internal organs were utterly frayed, counseling a surgical excision, the only known treatment at the time, but he would only agree to less invasive treatments. Thus it went for years until summer 1925, when his internal bleeding worsened considerably; in early September, the politburo mandated a seven-week holiday. Frunze left for Yalta with his wife, Sofia, but on September 29 he returned to enter the Kremlin hospital. No fewer than twelve leading internists and surgeons examined him in two rounds, concurring on the need for surgery.[297] "I now feel completely healthy and it's laughable even to contemplate, let alone undergo an operation," Frunze wrote to Sofia, still in Crimea, on October 26. "Nevertheless, both sets of consultations decided to do it. I'm personally satisfied with this decision. Let them once and for all make out what's there and try to establish a genuine treatment."[298] Two days later, he was transferred to the country's best facility, Soldatyonkov Hospital, where Lenin had been operated on, and the next afternoon a team led by Dr. V. N. Rozanov, who had treated Lenin, performed an operation. A day and a half later, in the wee hours of October 31, 1925, Frunze died of what the newspaper reported to be heart failure provoked by anesthesia.[299] It seems he had been administered a heavy dose of chloroform, which might have provoked dystrophy in the muscles of his vital organs.[300] Frunze was buried near the Kremlin Wall on November 3.[301] Pishpek, Kyrgyzia, where he had grown up, was renamed for him.

Rumors were instigated that Trotsky's people had killed the proletarian commander in revenge for taking his place, while Trotsky's acolytes turned the tables, accusing Stalin.[302] Beyond these false accusations, Bolshevik susceptibility to illnesses became the talk of the day as a psychoneurologist presented a grim report about pervasive "revolutionary exhaustion and attrition."[303] Nearly half of all visits by top party figures to medical clinics were for nervous disorders (with tuberculosis well behind, at around one quarter).[304] Two German specialists were imported to examine a list of fifty regime figures, beginning with Dzierżyński and Mężyński and working through to Rykov and Stalin, with what results remains unknown, but the internal discussions indicate acceptance, including by Trotsky, of the fact that Frunze had died of natural causes, even if better medical care might have saved him.[305] For Stalin, Frunze's demise presented yet another opportunity. Tukhachevsky, during a moment of the usual gossip, voiced support for Sergo Orjonikidze—which was duly reported—but the handwriting was on the wall: Stalin appointed his close associate Voroshilov.[306]

Voroshilov, after his checkered civil war role, had written to Stalin begging to be let out of the army ("you should pity me"), but Stalin had ignored his pleas.[307] In May 1924, he had promoted him to Moscow military district commander, in place of Trotsky's associate Nikolai Muralov. Absent Frunze, Voroshilov was the next highest "proletarian" commander. Zinoviev's man, Mikhail Lashevich, became first deputy war commissar.[308] Tukhachevsky became the chief of the general staff, the so-called brains of the army, and a vivid rival to Voroshilov, who began to circumscribe the general staff chief's powers, removing military intelligence from his purview. Tukhachevsky complained bitterly in writing, but Voroshilov remained unmoved.[309] Probably no one despised Trotsky more than Voroshilov, not even Stalin himself, but the Voroshilov-Tukhachevsky animosity would reach operatic dimensions. This afforded Stalin tight control, but did nothing to elevate fighting capacity. "The situation with the Red Army is very difficult," Tukhachevsky reported. "If enemies learn about the situation, they may want to attempt something."[310]

## DZIERŻYŃSKI'S MUDDLE

Kamenev, though close to Stalin, had joined Zinoviev's Leningrad opposition and, from September 1925, his speeches began to disappear from the press and even from the "stenographic" records of party meetings.[311] Kamenev had no political machine and publishing house, unlike Zinoviev in Leningrad, but he had skill at intrigue and he managed to recruit Finance Commissar Sokolnikov to protest the Stalin-Bukharin duumvirate's leadership. Together with Krupskaya, they produced a "platform of the four" that, though unpublished, circulated to members of the Central Committee and Central Control Commission, where it was discussed at a plenum October 3–10.[312] Sokolnikov, unlike the other signatories, stood by the NEP's conciliatory peasant policy but he objected to the throttling of internal party debate and bullying tactics. The wily Kamenev had even courted the head of the OGPU, Dzierżyński, and not without success: On the night of October 5–6, Dzierżyński sent an abject letter to Stalin, which he also addressed to Orjonikidze (but in the end not to Krupskaya, indicating she, too, may have played a role in recruiting him). "I ask that you acquaint a meeting of the faction of Leninists with the following letter from me," Dzierżyński began, divulging the existence of "a plot" by Zinoviev and Kamenev, a "new Kronstadt within our party," which, he noted, was especially alarming because "the peasantry in the majority is not with us, though they are not against us—we have not yet organized the peasantry to our side." After explaining that a schism in the party would open the doors to enemies and make Thermidor unavoidable, Dzierżyński confessed that he had joined the conspiracy before coming to his senses. "I am not a politician, I am unable to find a solution or to propose one, perhaps in judging me you will find the fragment of a solution. But I am leaving the [opposition] faction, remaining a Leninist, for I do not wish to be a participant in a schism, which brings death to the party." Expecting to be relieved of his post, Dzierżyński offered to take up any work he might be given.[313]

Stalin had to wonder who else in the OGPU might have been recruited to the side of the opposition. Dzierżyński, as head of the political police and someone whose stout reputation made him invulnerable to removal, occupied a potentially decisive position. Stalin, of course, made no move to remove him; public revelation of a rift between them would have been damning.

Dzierżyński had been a staunch Left Communist who hung a portrait of the Polish-German leftist martyr Rosa Luxemburg in his Lubyanka office, but his experience of practical work as concurrent head of the Supreme Council of the Economy, where he employed an army of "bourgeois" economists, had made him a staunch defender of the NEP.[314] Already in 1923, he denounced "the rise of ever newer apparatuses, monstrous bureaucratism of all kinds, mountains of paper and hundreds of thousands of scribblers, the seizure of huge buildings and facilities, the automobile epidemic," and what he dubbed "legal *kormlenie*"—that is, functionaries living parasitically off those they were supposed to serve, as in ancient Muscovy.[315] He predicted the overweening bureaucracy and pilferage would bankrupt the system, but offered no practical solutions.[316] Stalin, who called him "Felix" in his confidential letters to Molotov (when he called everyone else by their last names), knew Dzierżyński was overworked and had a heart condition. Dzierżyński had suffered his first heart attack back in late 1924, but ignored doctors' warnings that he limit his work hours.[317] In summer 1925, Dzierżyński had submitted his resignation.[318] Stalin had already left for Sochi and wrote to him (July 25, 1925), "I implore you not to do that," asking for patience.[319] That same day, Stalin wrote to Bukharin: "Dzierżyński is just jittery, he's drowning. It'll pass."[320] In August 1925, when Tovstukha wired Stalin to ask if Dzierżyński, who was going south on vacation, could visit him in Sochi, Stalin wrote back, "With pleasure I'll receive Dzierżyński and his friends from work. Stalin."[321] Not long thereafter Dzierżyński was approached by Kamenev, who was aware of the OGPU's frustrations with economic policy.

Although Dzierżyński quickly went back on Kamenev and Zinoviev, the opposition did not relent, taking the offensive in rival regional party conferences, including one of the Moscow organization, which opened on December 5, 1925 (and ran until the thirteenth), and one of the Leningrad organization, which started and ended earlier. In Leningrad the delegates attacked Bukharin and his slogan "Enrich yourselves"; in Moscow, Bukharin hysterically mocked Zinoviev and his supporters as "hysterical young ladies," and forced through a resolution condemning the Leningrad party organization's behavior as "antiparty."[322] Besides the policy dispute over the NEP's seeming prokulak bias, the Leningrad party fought to uphold its autonomy. But the New opposition amalgamated contradictory tendencies, as the Menshevik émigré newspaper pointed out.[323] Sokolnikov, in his speech, extolled market relations, which he called different from capitalism, and cultured farmers, whom he called different from kulaks. Such a formulation had the potential to render markets compatible with socialism, at least in the countryside. Sokolnikov, however, also put his finger on the fundamental problem at the heart of the NEP: "We are encouraging the middle peasant up to a certain limit and then we begin strangling him." Politics, in other words, limited economic growth. Another speaker, Yakov Yakovlev, founder and editor of *Peasant Newspaper,* flat out proposed that the regime allow peasants to register the land they farmed as private property, to be bought, sold or inherited, arguing that legal ownership, instead of mere user rights, would boost output because peasants would be able to pass on the fruits of their hard work to their children.[324]

As for Dzierżyński, on December 12 he sent Stalin a long letter enumerating the intractable problems in the economy, citing his inability to manage them, pointing to his health, his nerves, and asking to be allowed to resign from the Supreme Council of the Economy: "I am sure that if Vladimir Ilich were alive he would honor my request."[325] Stalin again refused the request. But Stalin also found out that sometime in late 1925, with the 14th Party Congress looming, a number of leading figures gathered in the apartment of Petrovsky, the Ukrainian Communist, and without Dzierżyński's participation, discussed having him replace Stalin as general secretary.[326] But unlike secret police chiefs in most dictatorships, he did not aspire to supreme power. In fact, Dzierżyński would not speak at the 14th Congress.

## BIRTHDAY DENUNCIATIONS

Stalin had twice postponed the 14th Party Congress, and by the time it met (December 18–31, 1925), eighteen months had elapsed since the previous one, the longest interval yet. The Leningrad delegation arrived early, on December 14, fanning out to factories and urban ward party organizations to argue their case. Back at the previous congress, when Stalin was still in alliance with Zinoviev, the two had agreed to hold the next one in Leningrad, but in October 1925, Stalin's new politburo majority voted to annul this as "out of date." The congress assembled 1,306 delegates (665 voting), representing 1,088,000 party members and candidates. Stalin for the first time since before the revolution delivered the main political report. But on the opening day, Zinoviev had fired an advance salvo in *Leningrad Pravda*. "They fight against the kulak, but they offer the slogan 'Enrich yourselves!'" he charged. "They proclaim the Russia of NEP as a socialist country." Stalin, in his speech, cunningly made no mention of disagreements with Zinoviev and Kamenev, ensuring that the opposition would be viewed as causing the dissension. Sure enough, the Leningrad delegates petitioned that Zinoviev be allowed to deliver a coreport, which took place on the evening of the second day, ran for four hours, and targeted Bukharin with a vengeance.[327] After a break, Bukharin was given the floor, and droned on even longer.[328] The atmosphere was belligerent. Krupskaya, on behalf of the opposition, omitted mention of Stalin but assailed Bukharin's "Enrich yourselves" slogan as unsocialist, while scolding the delegates for their "shameful" heckling of Zinoviev. She cited the Stockholm Party Congress of 1906, when the Mensheviks had a majority, to imply that the current Zinoviev, Kamenev, Krupskaya group, though a minority, were the real Bolshevik-Leninists.[329] But the congress sensation turned out to be, of all people, Kamenev, who was known for equivocating, but delivered a sharply worded oration on December 21.[330] This happened to be Stalin's birthday (officially he was forty-six).

Kamenev began by referring to his responsibilities as nominal director of the Lenin Institute, which was intended to assert Leninist credentials, then took aim at "rosy" portrayals of Lenin's New Economic Policy.[331] "I have reproached comrade Stalin at a number of conferences, and I repeat it at the congress: 'You do not really agree with this [pro-NEP] line, but you protect it, and this is where you are at fault as a leader of the party,'" Kamenev said. "'You are a strong man, but you do not allow the party strongly to reject this line, which a majority of the party thinks incorrect.'" He called Stalin "a prisoner of this incorrect line, the author and genuine representative of which is comrade Bukharin." But Kamenev went far beyond separating Stalin from Bukharin.

> We are against creating a "leader" theory, we're against building up a "leader." We are against the idea that the secretariat, by combining both policy and organization in practice, should stand above the main political organ, that is, the politburo. . . . Personally, I suggest that our general secretary is not someone who is capable of unifying the old Bolshevik headquarters around himself. . . . Precisely because I have

spoken on numerous occasions with Comrade Stalin, precisely because I have spoken on numerous occasions with a group of Lenin's comrades, I say here at the Congress: I have come to the conclusion that Comrade Stalin cannot perform the function of unifying the Bolshevik headquarters.

Kamenev, as he uttered these remarkable words, was interrupted repeatedly, and the jeering became nearly deafening:

"Untrue!" "Nonsense." "So that's what they're up to." "Stalin! Stalin!" The delegates rise and salute Comrade Stalin. Stormy applause.... "Long live Comrade Stalin." Prolonged stormy applause. Shouts of "Hurrah." General commotion.

The published stenogram continued: "Yevdokimov, from his seat: 'Long live the Russian Communist Party! Hurrah! Hurrah!' (The delegates stand and shout 'Hurrah!' Noise. Stormy, long-sustained applause) (Yevdokimov, from his seat) 'Long live the central committee of our party! Hurrah!' (The delegates shout 'Hurrah!') 'The party above all! Right!' (Applause and shouts, 'Hurrah!')"[332]

Stalin never had a birthday like this (nor would he again).

Tomsky was given the floor for repudiation: "It is ridiculous to speak as some comrades have spoken here, attempting to represent someone as having concentrated power in his hands. . . . How could this happen?"[333] The answer to Tomsky's question was, in part, Kamenev himself, who had abetted Stalin nearly every step of the way.

Stalin's birthday celebration was not over: That same evening, Sokolnikov got the floor. Stalin relied on him utterly for the NEP. "Garya's relations with Stalin . . . were friendly," his wife, Galina Serebryakova would recall, referring to her husband by a diminutive of his real first name (Gersh). "I heard their conversations often on the vertushka. There was never any tension or inequality in tone or interaction. . . . Before the congress, according to what Garya told me, Stalin met with him and implored him not to support Krupskaya and Klavdiya Nikolaeva, not to speak of Lenin's Testament and the need to elect a different general secretary. But Garya would not agree. 'You'll be sorry, Grigory,' Stalin warned him and later that same night called him on the vertushka, asking for his support and not to mention the Testament in his speech." Sokolnikov refused to back down.[334] At the congress, speaking for nearly an hour, he cited Lenin against Bukharin, stated that the USSR was "state capitalist," and called not for dispossessing the kulaks but raising the level of agriculture in order to have more grain for export to pay for imports of machinery, which in turn would develop agriculture in a virtuous circle, the only realistic path to industrialization. But though Sokolnikov backed the Stalin-Bukharin Central Committee majority against the opposition in economic policy, he backed the latter against the Central Committee in their critique of the absence of party democracy and the concentration of Stalin's power.[335]

The published stenogram carried only the bare bones of Sokolnikov's speech, but the unpublished version contains the details. Of the tendentious characterizations of Zinoviev and Kamenev in official resolutions and the party press, he said, "since when did you start throwing around such accusatory expressions?" Sokolnikov was interrupted repeatedly—"Give us facts!"—but he persisted, stating he could not imagine the politburo without Kamenev and Zinoviev, and demanding the politburo, not the secretariat, run the country. He further stated that Stalin, as general secretary, should not concurrently sit in the politburo. "I have absolutely no feelings of hostility, personal or political, toward Comrade Stalin—absolutely none," Sokolnikov stated. "I must say this because people are claiming that our relationship is dictated by personal hostility. It is not, and I do not doubt that for the entire party, the work of Comrade Stalin brings the most enormous benefit." Against accusations that talk of changing the general secretary amounted to a coup, Sokolnikov stated matter-of-factly, "Could it be that at the congress we cannot discuss a question that any provincial party organization can discuss: namely who will be the secretary?" Sokolnikov concluded with a challenge: if "comrade Stalin" wants to enjoy "the kind of trust comrade Lenin had," then "Win that trust, comrade Stalin!"[336]

Stalin's power—its extent and legitimacy—dominated much of the rest of the congress. Voroshilov stated that "it is clear either nature or fate allows Comrade Stalin to formulate questions more successfully than any other member of the politburo. Comrade Stalin—and I confirm this—is the principal member of the politburo."[337] Zinoviev spoke again, and invoked the Testament. "Without Vladimir Ilich it became clear to everyone that the secretariat of the Central Committee would acquire absolutely decisive significance," he stated, in the language of the letters he had sent to Stalin from the cave meeting. "Everyone thought, how could we do things . . . so that we had a well-known balance of forces and did not commit big political mistakes. . . . At that time, some kind of personal confrontations ripened—and rather sharp confrontations—with comrade Stalin."[338] This allowed Stalin to quip, "And I did not know that in our party to this day there are cave people!"

Sycophants leapt to dismiss talk of a Stalin personal dictatorship.[339] "Now—about that 'boundless power' of the secretariat and the general secretary," said Sergei Gusev, whom Stalin named to head the central apparatus department overseeing newspapers. "Look what experience says about this. Was there abuse of this power or not? Prove even one fact of abuse of this power. Who put forward such a fact of abuse? We, the members of the Central Control Commission at the meetings of the politburo systematically watch over the work of the politburo secretariat and, in part, the work of the general secretary. Did we see abuse of this 'boundless power'? No, we did not see such abuses of power."[340] When a delegate from Leningrad complained of the pervasiveness of denunciations, such that "a friend cannot tell his closest friend the thoughts in his soul," Gusev shot back: "Lenin taught us that every party member should be a Chekist, that is, should observe and denounce. . . . If we suffer from anything, it is not denunciations but non-denunciations."[341]

Momentous policy issues were also broached. Stalin's report invoked "peaceful coexistence" with the capitalists, a phrase that had been born with the regime itself, but whereas some figures, such as Litvinov, deputy foreign affairs commissar, took it to connote joint efforts toward the prevention of any war—socialism as peace for all—Stalin maintained that because international conflicts were at bottom economic, he expected, indeed hoped, the capitalist powers would clash among themselves. The congress resolution alluded to only "a certain period of 'peaceful coexistence' between the world of the bourgeoisie and the world of the proletariat."[342] Meanwhile, the Soviet Union was hemorrhaging gold to import machinery and food and support the exchange rate of the chervonets, policies that were unsustainable; Stalin played both sides, echoing Skolonikov's insistence on "a positive trade balance, restraint in the pace of industrialization and the importance of avoiding inflation," but accusing the finance commissariat of trying to keep the Soviet Union in economic dependence on the West.[343] Stalin's corrections to Bukharin's text for the congress stressed a vague coming technical rearmament of agriculture with machines and mysterious "all-encompassing support" among peasants for collectivized agriculture. Stalin's version was approved at the congress.[344] The congress also resolved to create, somehow, a world-class military industry.[345]

Stalin's concluding speech, on December 23, was priceless, asserting that Zinoviev and Kamenev "demand the blood of comrade Bukharin," but "we shall not give you that blood." He continued: "We did not agree with Zinoviev and Kamenev because we knew that a policy of cutting off members was fraught with great dangers for the party, that the method of cutting off, the method of bloodletting—and they were asking for blood—is dangerous and contagious. Today one person is cut off, tomorrow another, the next day a third—but what will remain of the party? (Appaluse)"[346]

A resolution condemned the Leningrad delegation for "the attempts to undermine the unity of our Leninist party."[347] Congress delegates supported Stalin not only because he had appointed them, ward-boss style, and they could recognize his commanding power, but also because back home they had a common foe—"oppositionists" (i.e., rivals to themselves)—and Stalin proactively helped them solidify their power locally.[348] In the elections to a new Central Committee, there were 217 votes against Kamenev, 224 against Zinoviev, 87 against Stalin, and 83 against Bukharin.[349] Trotsky was not on the slate. He would never attend another Party Congress. Beforehand, some of his supporters had been advocating a bloc with Zinoviev and Kamenev against Stalin—after all, Zinoviev and Kamenev now admitted that the "Trotskyites" had been right all along—but other Trotsky loyalists urged keeping a distance from either side. Trotsky had met secretly with Zinoviev and Kamenev, but nothing resulted.[350] Hearsay accounts have Stalin, just prior to the congress, seeking the assistance of Trotsky's faction to destroy Zinoviev.[351] If true, it was not because Stalin needed Trotsky's help, but to sow further discord among the oppositionists. At the congress Stalin loyalists (Mikoyan, Yaroslavsky) praised Trotsky against Zinoviev and Kamenev. Trotsky, for his part, said nothing when Zinoviev invoked Lenin's Testament. Sitting in the congress presidium, he kept silent even when addressed directly. Over the nearly two weeks of sessions, he made a single intervention. Most remarkably, Trotsky failed to react to Kamenev's bold, courageous denunciation of Stalin's personal dictatorship. "The explosion was absolutely unexpected by me," Trotsky would write. "During the congress, I waited in uncertainty, because the whole situation had changed. It appeared absolutely unclear to me."[352]

## AND NOW, ONE

In January 1926, Voroshilov, without having served as a candidate politburo member, became a full member, the only military man under Stalin ever to do so. Molotov and Kalinin were promoted to full membership as well, raising the voting members to nine. Kamenev was demoted to candidate member, joining Dzierżyński and three Stalin protégés (Rudzutaks, Petrovsky, Uglanov). Stalin removed Sokolnikov as a candidate politburo member and finance commissar. Sokolnikov's wife, Serebryakova, observed that "Stalin did not once and for all break relations with Sokolnikov. They saw each other less often."[353] Sokolnikov's policies of tight money and accumulation of gold reserves were formally reconfirmed at a politburo meeting, but without him to fight tooth and nail against the industrial lobby, monetary emissions appear to have jumped.[354] Kamenev was named commissar of trade over his vehement objections ("I do not know this stuff," he wrote to the Central Committee), payback for his volcanic speech.[355] Zinoviev's machine in Leningrad presented a bigger challenge, and Stalin sent in an expansive commission led by Molotov and Voroshilov, as well as squads of Communist Youth League activists. Raucous party meetings were held at Leningrad's universities and big factories. "Yesterday I was at the Three Angle Factory, a collective of 2,200," Sergei Kirov, Stalin's appointee to take over the Leningrad party, wrote to his close friend Orjonikidze on January 16, still using the letterhead of the Azerbaijan party. "There was an incredible fracas, such as I had not seen since the October [1917] days. I did not even imagine that a meeting like that of party members was possible. At times it got to the point of real smashing of faces. I'm telling you, I'm not exaggerating."[356] To ensure passage of the anti-Zinoviev resolutions, Molotov spewed threats: "son-of-a-bitch, saboteur, counterrevolutionary, I'll turn you into dust, I'll force you before the Central Control Commission."[357]

Kirov begged Stalin to allow him to return to Baku, but he was indispensable to Stalin in Leningrad.[358] During his first year there, Kirov would go out to almost every single Leningrad factory—more than 180 total—admit he was weak in theory, and win people over with his simplicity and directness. "I discovered for the first time that Kirov was a wonderful orator," one eyewitness wrote, adding that Kirov's oratory "was not distinguished by particular depth, but it was full of allegory, metaphors, comparisons, folk sayings. I sensed that he spoke sincerely."[359]

Kamenev clung to a compromise from Stalin's side, telling a March 18, 1926, politburo meeting, "At the congress, when I used the phrase that Stalin cannot unite around his person the Bolshevik general staff and when the congress noisily protested this and gave Stalin a standing ovation, I could have cut off this ovation if I had said that I was only repeating the words of Ilich." Stalin interjected: "Why did you not say it?" Kamenev: "Because I did not want to employ such methods."[360] And to think this was the Bolshevik who in 1904 had given Stalin a copy of Machiavelli in Russian translation. Kamenev was almost as much a gift to Stalin as Trotsky, and even more than Zinoviev.

To sow additional discord Stalin went so far as to meet one on one with Trotsky, even as the calumnies continued to rain down on Trotsky in the party press under Stalin's control.[361] Kamenev, in parallel, invited Trotsky to a private meeting in his Kremlin apartment with Zinoviev, their first such gathering in three years, and flattered him: "It is enough for you and Zinoviev to appear on the same platform, and the party will find its true Central Committee."[362] They found common cause mimicking Stalin's accent and body movements, and wrote nearly apologetic statements to each other. But a Trotsky supporter recalled objecting, "How could we sit at the same table with the bureaucrats who had hunted and slandered us, who had murdered the principles and ideas of the party?"[363] Trotsky, for his part, traveling incognito (he shaved his goatee), picked up and left for two months of medical treatment in Berlin.[364] Many years later, commenting on the machinations of early 1926, he would quote one of his supporters: "Neither with Stalin nor with Zinoviev; Stalin will cheat, and Zinoviev will run."[365]

Stalin traveled to liberated Leningrad himself, and on April 12 delivered a report to the local party on a recent Central Committee plenum. The journalist Pyotr Boldovkin, known as Chagin, was summoned to Kirov's apartment, where he found Stalin, too. Chagin handed over the proofs of Stalin's speech he was working on and made to depart, but Kirov and his wife, Maria Markus, invited him to stay for supper, along with the others. Chagin recalled that Kirov said, "'It would be hard without Lenin, of course, but we have the party, the Central Committee, the politburo and they will lead the country along the Leninist path.' Stalin paced the room and said, 'Yes, this is true—the party, the CC, the politburo. But consider, the people understand little in this. For centuries the people in Russia were under a tsar. The Russian people are tsarist. For many centuries the Russian people, especially the Russian peasants, have been accustomed to one person being at the head. And now there should be one.'"[366]

## MENACING TURNS

Three years of clandestine military cooperation with Germany had done little to boost Soviet weapons production, but in yet another push for a breakthrough, Józef Unszlicht, the deputy military commissar for armaments and a German-speaking Pole, led a delegation to Berlin in spring 1926 seeking a vast expansion of joint German-Soviet production on Soviet territory: tanks, heavy artillery, machine guns, precision optics, field telephones, radios.[367] But at a grand reception on March 30, 1926, at the Soviet embassy on Unter den Linden, attended by the German chancellor, foreign minister, and army commander in chief, the German government seemed hesitant, according to the Soviet report, wanting "to reduce their role to that of intermediaries between private German companies and Soviet organizations."[368] German private companies, in turn, preferred to sell weapons, not help potential competitors manufacture them. Herbert von Dirksen, a German foreign ministry official, warned his government that Moscow viewed enhanced military cooperation as "the most persuasive evidence of our wish to continue our relationship with them."[369] But even though the German establishment had become less hopeful about the degree of Versailles Peace revisionism the British would allow, the German government still did not want a deal with Moscow that could be perceived as anti-British, while the continuing illiberal nature of the regime in Moscow, despite the NEP, aroused antipathy in Germany.[370] Still, the German nightmare was losing the East without winning the West, and a compromise emerged: the German-Soviet Neutrality and Non-Aggression Pact of April 24, 1926, also known as the Treaty of Berlin, which affirmed the earlier Rapallo agreement: the two states pledged neutrality in the event one was subject to an unprovoked attack by a third party. It sounded like something, but amounted to little, essentially a pledge by Germany not to grant transit rights to another power hostile to the USSR.[371] As long as Germany entertained hopes of Western rapprochement, the USSR was a means to that end.[372]

Stalin had not excluded a deal with Britain, even though he saw it as the bulwark of the global imperialist order, but the global political economy got in the way of resumed trade negotiations. Europe's collective decision to return to gold at the pre-Great War sterling-gold parity meant a return to the sterling-dollar exchange rate ($4.86), which made British exports expensive. An overvalued currency led to balance-of-payment deficits and an outflow of gold, which tamped down domestic economic activity. Critics saw this as sacrificing industry on the altar of gold, but the obvious solution, devaluation of the pound, was viewed in London's financial district as tantamount to filing for bankruptcy or inflicting fraud on creditors. Winston Churchill, chancellor of the exchequer, had wondered why the Bank of England governor "shows himself perfectly happy in the spectacle of Britain possessing the finest credit in the world simultaneously with a million and a quarter unemployed," and claimed he "would rather see Finance less proud and Industry more content."[373] (This provides insight into the debates inside the Soviet Union between Sokolnikov, backed by Stalin, and the industrial lobby of Pyatakov.) The gold standard and fiscal austerity hit British mining especially hard. The Great War had hindered exports and allowed other countries to develop their domestic coal industries, while Germany was exporting "free" coal to pay its Versailles Treaty obligations, leading to a drop in world prices at a time when British productivity was declining at overworked seams. A major structural adjustment to remove excess capacity was unavoidable, but British miners and their families constituted perhaps 10 percent of Britain's population, and their pay had already fallen. Some mine owners were ready to compromise, others were eager to abolish the national bargaining framework hammered out in the Great War and impose terms; the Conservative Tory government ended up colluding with the more intransigent owners and, on May 1, 1926, around 1 million miners were locked out. Dealt an unwinnable hand, British miners decided to fight rather than settle.[374] In solidarity, more than a million and a half other British workers launched the first (and only) general strike in British history on May 3, which disrupted the entire economy, including food production and distribution.[375] On May 4, the politburo resolved to support the British workers financially, with a notice published in the press.[376] Zinoviev, in *Pravda,* enthused about "great events" in Britain.[377] But the general strike fizzled, and though the miners' strike would drag on for months, it would end with the wage cuts in place. The Soviet Union had gone out on a limb and in the bargain risked dashing hopes for resuming talks toward an improved bilateral trade deal.

Events in Poland were the most directly menacing. Its parliamentary system saw a parade of no less than fourteen different cabinets up to May 1926, when the zloty, the Polish currency, collapsed.[378] The Soviet-German Treaty of Berlin, despite its modesty, raised the nightmare scenario in Warsaw of a return to partitioning at the hands of powerful neighbors. With Dzierżyński away, finishing up a holiday in early May and about to travel to Ukraine for a month—he instructed Yagoda in Moscow to keep an eye on the lowly émigré Alexander

Guchkov, the former war minister in the Provisional Government—the retired Polish marshal Józef Piłsudski, a private citizen, left his home on the morning of May 12, rendezvoused with troops loyal to him, and marched on nearby Warsaw.[379] The marshal expected his show of force and peacock-feather prestige to compel the president to dismiss the week-old center right government; instead, the president arrived to confront Piłsudski on the bridge into Warsaw. The intended bloodless coup degenerated into skirmishes. Piłsudski, unnerved, lucked out: on May 13, the commander of government forces, rather than press his tactical victories to decisive conclusion, waited for reinforcements, a blunder made fatal when Piłsudski's former associates in the Socialist Party—not the army he relied upon—conspired with railroad workers to stymie troops loyal to the right-wing government from arriving while shepherding through reinforcements loyal to Piłsudski. On May 14, the president and prime minister stepped down. Piłsudski had been dismissive of the idea of enacting a coup. "If I were to break the law, I would be opening the door to all sorts of adventurers to make coups and putsches," he had told a journalist some years back, in remarks that were published on May 27.[380] Now he was master of Poland again. The Assembly elected him president, but he declined, instead reigning as commander in chief and war minister. Political parties, trade unions, and the press endured as Poland's semidemocracy became a soft dictatorship.

The British government, which had not been involved in the coup, mostly welcomed it.[381] Already strained Soviet-Polish relations worsened.[382] Tukhachevsky was dispatched to Minsk and Alexander Yegorov to Kharkov to be at the ready should Piłsudski suddenly repeat his eastward march of several years back, while the Soviet press agency TASS denied rumors of Red Army troop massing near Polish frontiers as a typical Polish provocation.[383] The marshal insisted to the Soviet envoy in Warsaw that the Russians must consider him stupid if they believed he wanted a war, from which Poland could gain nothing.[384] Truth be told, it did seem improbable that Poland could fulfill the role of a significant European power when sandwiched between a hostile Germany and hostile Soviet Union, itself antagonistic to Lithuania, scornful of Czechoslovakia, cool even to its ally France, and discriminatory against its large ethnic Ukrainian and Belorussian populations, while harboring territorial designs on Soviet Ukraine and Soviet Belorussia. But Foreign Affairs Commissar Chicherin deemed Piłsudski "unpredictable." Greater Romania, too, was a worry, as the Romanian national project radicalized amid the addition of many minorities as a result of the Great

War. It acquired the third most powerful fascist movement after Italy and Germany, and its antiurban, anti-Semitic nationalist ideology folded in anti-Bolshevism.[385] Romania refused even to grant diplomatic recognition to the USSR. To be sure, Romania was just a 17-million peasant nation and Poland just a 32-million peasant nation. But they signed a treaty of mutual aid in 1926, and the combination of the two implacably anti-Soviet states, in alliance with France—or egged on by some other more furtive imperialist machination—set Moscow on edge.

Stalin also had to worry about an exposed eastern flank. Japan had agreed in 1925 to diplomatic recognition and to vacate northern Sakhalin, while holding on to the southern half of the island and receiving an extensive lease for oil and coal extraction in the north, while the Soviet Union confirmed Japanese supremacy in Manchuria.[386] But protracted negotiations over fishery convention and timber concession highlighted the fundamental lack of comity, and in Moscow few doubted Japan would take advantage of any possible complications in the Soviet Union's international situation. In the Soviet Far East, the population of ethnic Koreans, whose homeland had been annexed into the Japanese empire, had almost tripled to nearly 170,000 by 1926, reaching one quarter of the total population of the USSR's strategic Vladivostok region.[387] The Soviets knew the Japanese cultivated spies among this enormous East Asian population on its soil. Stalin permitted formation of a Korean national district and scores of Korean national townships, with Korean-language schools, but the regime also began discussing deportation of the concentrated Koreans away from the border, indicating the feeling of vulnerability.[388] In the European part of Soviet territory, the number of ethnic Poles was estimated at between 2.5 and 4 million, and at least some of the many disaffected among them were assumed to be collaborating with Polish intelligence.[389] Additionally, there were ethnic Finns on the Soviet side of the border with Finland. The USSR was hardly alone in suspecting disloyalty among its ethnic population with coethnics on the other side of an international border, but Soviet borders were incomparably vast.[390]

LENIN'S DEATH brought him back to life for the regime, and especially for Stalin. Trotsky's political position showed itself to have been dependent on Lenin being physically around.[391] But even had Trotsky been more adept politically, his biography (a former Menshevik, an intellectual), his personality (condescending, aloof), and his position (war commissar) afforded him little chance to succeed Lenin, especially against a formidable rival. Of course, in Trotsky's mind Stalin was a deformation conjured into being by "the tired radicals, by the bureaucrats, by the NEPmen, the kulaks, the upstarts, the sneaks, by all the worms that are crawling out of the upturned soil of the manured revolution."[392] This, of course, was exactly how Stalin would characterize his nemesis. Had there been no Trotsky, Stalin would have had to invent him. Or more precisely, Stalin invented the Trotsky he needed, a task that looks simple only in hindsight. Stalin defeated Trotsky on the plane where the Georgian was perceived as most vulnerable yet proved strong—ideology. His propagation of a persuasive, accessible Leninism, which also happened to afford him the role of guarantor, was virtuoso, if unscrupulous in its plagiarism. Stalin certainly marshaled all his bureaucratic advantages and maneuvered with skill, but he also studied assiduously. "I must add a few words to try to explain Stalin's effectiveness as a writer and orator, which gave him an edge over other orators and writers who were more skilled," one contemporary Soviet literary critic remarked. "Kamenev, Zinoviev, Bukharin, even Trotsky were much less familiar with the texts of Lenin's writings than Stalin.... Unlike them, Stalin studied Lenin's texts and knew the printed Lenin intimately. He had no trouble selecting a quotation from Lenin if he needed it."[393]

Stalin positioned himself as honoring Lenin's "behest." He could have made a different choice, like Trotsky, and presented himself as Lenin's equal. Stalin had the ego for that, too. But he opted for the more strategic stance, the appearance of humility, the mere pupil, and excelled at its realization.[394] Strange to say, Stalin demonstrated a far better capacity for empathy than Trotsky as well. Later, Trotsky would viciously mock the functionary and Stalin loyalist Lazar Kaganovich, failing to appreciate the uneducated Kaganovich's immense organizational talents and perspicacity. Kaganovich—who had once admired Trotsky—showed himself to be the more incisive person, sizing up Trotsky as supremely talented in public speaking and even organization (referring to the civil war), but woefully inferior to Stalin in strategy.[395] Stalin was indeed a strategist, improvising dexterously in the face of sudden opportunities, thereby seizing the advantage, including in the case of the colossal opportunity presented by upstart self-made types like Kaganovich and countless other new men like him. But Stalin emerged a victor with a grudge, roiling with self-pity, resentment, victimhood. Many scholars have attributed such feelings to an inferiority complex, an assertion that may or may not be true. But what is certain is that he exercised his personal dictatorship amid a profound structural hostility: Stalin was the disciple of a man who seemed to have called for his removal. This state of siege mirrored the position of the revolution as a whole.

Stalin's geopolitical vision of a Soviet Union able to avoid entanglement in what he saw as the inevitable next intraimperialist war, which would produce new revolutions, was put in doubt by the apparent rapprochement of the two capitalist blocs at Locarno, as well as by the hostile posture of newly independent Poland, Finland, Estonia, Latvia, Lithuania, expanded Romania, and Japan. Stalin entered the summer of 1926 amid profound disquiet over close-neighbor enmity, to say nothing of the ambiguous trajectory of the New Economic Policy. And the cursed Testament continued to hound him.

## CHAPTER 13

# TRIUMPHANT DEBACLE

Comrades! It is already three years that I am asking you
to relieve me of the duties of the general secretary. The
plenum has refused me each time. . . . I'll allow that there
was a necessity, despite the known letter of comrade Lenin,
to keep me in the post of general secretary. But those
conditions are gone now. They are gone because the
Opposition is crushed. . . . Now it is time, in my view, to heed
Lenin's instructions. Therefore I ask the plenum to relieve
me of the post of Central Committee general secretary.
I assure you, comrades, the party will only gain from this.

Stalin, Central Committee plenum, December 19, 1927[1]

STALIN'S APARTMENT WAS LOCATED on the second floor of the Kremlin's
Amusement Palace (Poteshny Dvor), a modest, three-story former boyar residence immediately inside the Trinity Gate. Most recently it had been the quarters of the Kremlin commandant. The apartment had six rooms, including an
oval-shaped dining room, two children's bedrooms, one main bedroom, and an
office, as well as a small telephone room. Stalin got the bedroom, his wife, Nadezhda "Nadya" Alliluyeva, one of the children's bedrooms. Five-year-old Vasily
("Vasya") and Artyom, the boy born the same year whose father had died in the
civil war, shared the other. Stalin's first child, Yakov, now nineteen years old,
slept in the dining room. Nadya's room had a window that looked out onto the
Alexander Gardens and the Kutafya Tower, the Kremlin's only surviving draw-
bridge tower.[2] But overall the apartment was hardly luxurious. Still, it marked an
improvement: This was the family's second Kremlin apartment, the first having
been in a noisy outbuilding of the Grand Kremlin Palace.[3] After Stalin had complained to Lenin, Abram Belenky, the chief of the leadership bodyguard detail,
suggested Stalin relocate to rooms in the Grand Kremlin Palace itself. Trotsky's

wife, Natalya Sedova, a museum director, had objected, insisting that the palace fell under museum jurisdiction.⁴ She relented, offering to yield museum offices for the proposed residence, but instead Stalin had displaced the commandant.⁵ In the aftermath, Belenky tried to indulge Stalin, but it backfired. "In the move to the new apartment, it turns out that someone from the central executive committee business department, perhaps comrade Belenky of the GPU, took it upon himself to order new furniture at state expense for my apartment," Stalin complained. "This capricious operation was carried out against my decisive statement that the old furniture fully satisfied me." He asked that the head of the Central Control Commission investigate and punish the culprit, and that the newly bought furniture be immediately removed to the warehouse or wherever it was needed.⁶ Regime personnel had a hard time navigating the fine line between Stalin's sincere commitment to modest living and the sycophancy sprouting all around him.

Stalin did not play much of a paterfamilias role. The Kremlin apartment was obviously cramped. The Zubalovo two-story Gothic dacha just outside Moscow had twelve rooms and 5,000 square feet, but Stalin's Sunday appearances there were irregular, even in summer. His widowed mother, Keke Geladze, continued to live in Georgia and did not visit Moscow; Nadya kept in touch ("We send you greetings from Moscow. We're living well, all are healthy. The children are growing . . .").⁷ Nadya's parents, Sergei and Olga Alliluyeva, had moved to Leningrad. Stalin's in-laws from his first marriage to the deceased Kato Svanidze lived in Moscow and saw him on occasion, but how often remains unclear; he barely saw his wife. Stalin's marital life was hardly bliss. He appears to have loved Nadya, yet he was inattentive, and when he did pay her mind, he often became abusive, shouting obscenities at her, or what may have been more difficult to endure, refusing to speak with her at all.⁸ She suffered debilitating migraines and isolation. "I decidedly have nothing to do with anyone in Moscow," Nadya wrote in early 1926 to Maria Svanidze, the wife of Stalin's brother-in-law from his first wife, who was in Berlin and complaining of boredom. "Sometimes it's even strange: after all these years not to have a single close friend but, evidently, it's a question of character. Oddly enough, I feel closer to people outside the party (with women, of course). This is obviously because they are simpler." Nadya had little interest in indulging the role and perquisites of the wife of the leader. On the contrary, she expressed anxiety that she would not be taken seriously if she did not work outside the home, but at the same time, she wanted to be qualified for any position she obtained. When she wrote to Svanidze, she was in the last stages of pregnancy with their second child and added, "I am very sorry to have tied myself down with yet more family bonds."[9]

A daughter, Svetlana, was born on February 18, 1926; her nursery was set up in Nadya's room. In all the voluminous documentation that Stalin left behind, there is no record of his reaction. He could be very attentive to the children, when he was home, usually at late lunches, and when he had time, asking about their affairs, presenting them with books, sending them to the theater, disciplining them in a way that would impart life lessons. Responsibility for the children and the household largely devolved onto the head servant, Karolina Til, who also retrieved the family's meals from the Kremlin canteen. However much Stalin may have loved Nadya, the woman whom he had married as a teenager was not the cheerful, submissive hostess he now sought, given his patriarchalism and his position as leader. At least once Nadya whisked herself, Vasily, and Svetlana to her parents' home in Leningrad.[10] Kremlin gossips faulted *her* for "deserting" him.[11] Fatefully, she returned. Yakov's kindness enabled him to become close to his stepsiblings as well as his stepmother (a mere six years his senior), with whom he shared the cruelty of Stalin's domestic tyranny.[12] When Yakov graduated from an electromechanical high school and, instead of entering university, announced his intention to marry a sixteen-year-old schoolmate, Zoya Gunina, Stalin exploded. Alone, Yakov put a gun to his heart in the kitchen of the Stalin family's Kremlin apartment in the Amusement Palace, missing that vital organ by inches but wounding himself. Stalin, writing to Nadya, branded Yakov "a hooligan and blackmailer, who does not have and could not have anything more to do with me."[13] Yakov's act, in Stalin's eyes, was not a cry of despair at his father's relentless disapproval, but an effort to exert pressure. Yakov would marry Zoya, however, and Nadya would move the couple into her parents' apartment. Zoya would give birth to a daughter—Stalin's first grandchild—but the baby would die in infancy from pneumonia.[14]

Even Stalin's absolute power did not delight him absolutely. He exulted in it, yet it roused his self-pity. He thrilled to being the center of attention, the decision maker, the successor to Lenin, the leader, but it ate at him that everyone knew Lenin's Testament called for his removal. The giddy pleasure and the torment, the long-held ambition and the current burden, the paradoxes of his power, weighed on him. After the rigmarole of staging the huge 14th Party Congress, and much else besides, he was exhausted. "I'm thinking about going on a short holiday in two weeks, I'm really tired," he had written on February 1, 1926, to Orjonikidze in Tiflis. But Stalin's boundless power continued to besiege him: meetings with the State Bank chairman, state statistical administration personnel, the central consumer cooperative chairman, the railways, Ukrainian officials, Bashkir officials, Belorussian officials, Dagestanis, Kazakhstanis, Buryat Mongols, the health commissar, managers of state trusts, this local party boss, that local party boss, worker delegations, trade union functionaries, newspaper editors, university rectors, foreign affairs staff, ambassadors, foreign Communists, secret police, military brass, youth organizers, final negotiations for the disappointing treaty with Germany, women's organizers, the May Day parade and receptions, the first ever general strike in Britain. Finally, however, he escaped. "I'll be near Sochi in a few days," he wrote again to Orjonikidze on May 16. "How are you planning to spend your holiday? Koba."[15] Stalin arrived on May 23. Almost immediately he sent a ciphered telegram to Molotov, who was minding the store in Moscow (Monday, May 24): "I got here Sunday evening. The weather is lousy. . . . Belenky told me that 1) Trotsky was back in Moscow [from Berlin] as early as Wednesday morning; 2) Preobrazhensky went to visit him in Berlin (for a rendezvous?). Interesting."[16] Yes, even on holiday.

Some four years after Stalin had been named general secretary his personal rule was secure even when he was far from Moscow. That said, the survival of his power still depended upon maintaining a majority in the politburo. Through January 1926, changes in the composition of the full (voting) members of that body had been rare: Yelena Stasova had served only briefly, following Sverdlov's death, July-September 1919; Lenin had removed Nikolai Krestinsky in 1921, promoting Zinoviev in his place; Bukharin had taken the deceased Lenin's place in 1924. As of 1926, Zinoviev and Trotsky were still full members. But in January 1926, while demoting Kamenev to candidate (non-voting) member, Stalin had managed to promote Voroshilov, Molotov, and Kalinin to full members. Stalin's voting majority in the nine-person body comprised those three, as well as the trio of Rykov, Bukharin, Tomsky. The worn-down Dzierżyński was another of the five candidate members, as were the Stalin protégés Nikolai Uglanov, Moscow party boss, Jānis Rudzutaks, a Central Committee secretary on Old Square, and Petrovsky, a Ukrainian state official after whom Yekaterinoslav, the country's tenth biggest city, was renamed Dnepropetrovsk in 1926. In other words, many of Stalin's loyalists had non-voting status. True, beginning in the summer of 1926, he would manage to change the politburo composition still more, to his advantage. But it would take him through the end of 1927, when the 15th Party Congress would finally be held, to drive the Zinoviev-Trotsky opposition out of the party entirely and into internal exile. And all the while, the nasty political brawling would go on and on and on, party forum after party forum, dragging in all those around Stalin and impinging on his psyche.

Stalin's complete political triumph over the opposition in December 1927, moreover, would follow debacle after debacle in his policies. Almost all the problems could be traced to the source of the regime's strength: Communist ideology. Bolshevik socialism (anticapitalism) attracted and gave meaning to the shock-troop activists, supplied the vocabulary and worldview of millions in the party and beyond, and achieved a monopoly over the public sphere, but this same politically empowering ideology afforded no traction over the international situation or the faltering quasi-market domestic economy. On the contrary, the ideology made those formidable challenges still less tractable. The seizure of power had resulted in a narrow set of options for managing Russia's power in the world, rendering it orthogonal to the great powers abroad and to the majority population peasants at home. Reinforcing this sense of siege was a personal dynamic whereby Stalin's political victory only whetted his thirst for vindication. Benevolence was beyond him. Toward vanquished rivals he showed only false magnanimity. Dedicated revolutionaries, longtime comrades in arms, became presumed traitors for questioning his personal rule or regime policies. This demonization inhered in Bolshevism, of course, and it closely paralleled Lenin's behavior, but Stalin carried it further, applying it to Communists. After Stalin crushed his party rivals, they became alleged terrorists plotting to kill him and collude with foreign powers.

The problems of the revolution brought out the paranoia in Stalin, and Stalin brought out the paranoia inherent in the revolution. The years 1926–27 saw a qualitative mutual intensification in each, which was related to events as well as to the crescendo of the opposition. Insiders arrayed around Stalin, however, appear not to have perceived him as a criminal tyrant. Certainly they had come to understand he tended to be thin-skinned and vindictive, but they also saw a driven, inexhaustible, tough-minded, and skilled workhorse leader of the party and the cause, whose moods and caprice they hoped to contain, using the politburo as their key mechanism. Whether anyone on the inside had genuine insight into the depths of his character even by December 1927, however, remains an open question.

## A JAUNT THROUGH THE CAUCASUS

No sooner had Stalin arrived in Sochi then the clever Anastas Mikoyan, the thirty-year-old party boss of the adjacent North Caucasus territory, ambushed him on May 26. Mikoyan, whose letters were intimately addressed "Dear Soso"— the diminutive Stalin's mother used for her son—had been the one to talk Stalin into trying the medicinal sulfur baths at Matsesta, near Sochi, which had led to these annual holidays down south.[17] Now Mikoyan talked Stalin into a romp through his native South Caucasus. They departed the Black Sea coast by train that very day, in the direction of Tiflis. Stalin took along only underwear and a hunting rifle. "First I'll mess around a bit, then I'll attend to my health and recuperation," Stalin remarked.[18] Tovstukha telegrammed on May 28 that at a politburo meeting, Trotsky and Molotov had been at daggers drawn over a foreign concession contract that Molotov found disadvantageous; Trotsky had signed it months before, but only now had the details come to light. Well, let Molotov muck it up with Trotsky. That same day, a staff member of Stalin's entourage wrote back to Tovstukha, "The Master is in a very good mood."[19]

"The Master" (khoziain), a patrimonial term derived from a lord of the manor, was more and more becoming a nickname for Stalin, but down south, to his longtime compatriots, he was still Koba, the avenger. He and Mikoyan visited Borjomi, land of famed mineral waters; Kutaisi; even Gori. (One can only imagine the commotion.) At some point during the trip Stalin met up with Peti "Pyotr" Kapanadze, an old friend from the Tiflis seminary whose photograph had hung on Stalin's wall and who had actually gone on to become a priest.[20] In Tiflis, Stalin took in an opera, going backstage, as he liked to do, to greet the performers and director. In the Georgian capital he and Mikoyan stayed at Orjonikidze's apartment, where Sergo's elder brother, Konstantin, remembered Stalin singing a bawdy Georgian song.[21] Here was Stalin's preferred company. Only their mutual close friend and honorary Caucasus compatriot Kirov, now in Leningrad, was absent.

In Moscow, in Stalin's absence, the politburo gathered on June 3, 1926, to discuss the strikes in Britain. Trotsky would publicly argue against continued

Soviet support for Britain's establishment trade unions in order not to strengthen the forces of collaboration with the bourgeois regime, which he argued would weaken the British Communist party and leave the British working class unprepared for the imminent crisis-opportunity for a revolutionary breakthrough.[22] The politburo session, with forty-three people in attendance, lasted six hours. The day it met, in a telegram of instructions to Molotov, Stalin correctly intuited that the general strike had been a "provocation by the British Conservatives"— that is, "capital, not the revolution, was on the attack." He added that "as a result, we do not have a new phase of stormy onslaught by the revolution but a continuing stabilization, temporary, not enduring, but stabilization nonetheless, fraught with new attempts by capital to make new attacks on the workers, who continue to be forced to defend themselves." He condemned the radical posturing of Trotsky as well as Zinoviev, which, with no revolution in the offing, only threatened to split the British trade union movement.[23] Stalin viewed Soviet support for British trade unions and striking workers as a deterrent to renewed aggression against the USSR. Still, he wanted to complete the bilateral trade negotiations of 1924 that had been left hanging. During the general strike, the British chargé d'affaires in Moscow had made yet another private plea to London to restart the talks for "a settlement of one kind or another with Russia."[24] But with the Soviet announcement of money transfers to the strikers, on top of clandestine Soviet efforts to spread revolution in the colonies, British government plans to reopen the trade negotiations would be put on ice.[25]

Neither Genoa (1922), the idea of reintegration of the Soviet Union and Germany into the international order, nor Rapallo (1922), the idea of a mutual rogues' special relationship with Germany, had delivered a viable Soviet security policy. And now British conservatives spearheaded a vocal public campaign for reprisals against the Soviet Union, even though the general strike was over and had failed. Trotsky, at the politburo meeting, complained that the general strike had never been discussed internally, which was untrue: the politburo had discussed it on May 4, 6, and 14, and formed a dedicated commission, led by the head of Soviet trade unions, Tomsky (Trotsky was not a member of the commission). Those assembled on June 3 rejected Zinoviev's Comintern theses on the lessons of the British strikes. The already deeply acrimonious atmosphere was worsened by near constant jeering. Kamenev sardonically asked the menacing hecklers speaking while he was speaking: "Why are you all helping me?" Trotsky cut in: "'Collective leadership' is precisely when everyone hinders each other or everyone attacks each other.' (Laughter)." Trotsky may have been trying to ease the tension.[26] *Collective leadership—ha!* Stalin would get a full report.

In the Caucasus, Stalin was on home turf in a way he had not been in a long time. On June 8, he met with a delegation of the Tiflis Main Railway Shops, where more than two decades ago he had been a youthful agitator. "I must say in all conscience, comrades, that I do not deserve a good half of the flattering things that have been said here about me," he modestly suggested, according to the local newspaper. "I am, it appears, a hero of the October Revolution, the leader of the Communist Party of the Soviet Union, the leader of the Communist International, a miraculous warrior-knight, and whatever else could be imagined. This is nonsense, comrades, and absolutely unnecessary exaggeration. It is the sort of thing that is usually said at the graveside of a departed revolutionary. But I have no intention of dying yet. . . . I really was, and still am, one of the pupils of the advanced workers of the Tiflis railway workshops." While maintaining this *faux* humble posture, Stalin went on to outline how he had risen in the revolutionary underground, from his first workers' "circle" in 1898, when he became a "pupil of the workers," to 1917, when he became a pupil of "my great teacher—Lenin." No fancy-pants intellectual, but a hardworking revolutionary laborer closely linked to the workers and to the Founder. "From the title of novice (Tiflis), through the title of apprentice (Baku) and the title of one of the foremen of our revolution (Leningrad)—that, comrades, is the school of my revolutionary university. . . the genuine picture of who I was and who I became, if one speaks without exaggeration, and in good conscience. (Applause turning into an ovation.)"[27]

A far cry from the hissing and cursing Stalin had undergone five years earlier in Tiflis, when he had left a meeting hall with his head between his legs. This time, Orjonikidze and his men had evidently pulled out all the stops, taking no chances. But Stalin's presentation of self at the railway shops that day was not published for a national audience, and neither were his accompanying observations on foreign affairs. Particularly salient were his comments on the coup d'état the previous month in Poland. He retrospectively, demagogically denounced the Polish Communist party for having supported Piłsudski's action (against a conservative government), then outlined with precision the political differences between the Piłsudski forces and their domestic rightist rivals, the National Democrats, predicting that although the former were stronger militarily, the latter would win out: Poland would turn further rightist and chauvinistic. In the meantime, Stalin called Piłsudski "petit-bourgeois" but not fascistic, a view he would later change as Piłsudski himself would move in the very direction Stalin had attributed to the war minister's domestic rivals.[28] Thus, while Georgian nationalism seemed on its way to being tamed, national sentiment in independent Poland was another matter entirely.

In Moscow the bitterness flowed and flowed. At another politburo meeting on June 14 in Stalin's absence, when Dzierżyński, back from his trip through Ukraine, asserted that it was a "crime" to record their inner deliberations (a legal request made by the opposition), Trotsky shot back: "We should direct the GPU to stop us from talking; this will simplify everything."[29] Dzierżyński remained in high dudgeon over the death grip of bureaucracy, telling his subordinates at the Supreme Council of the Economy that June that the Soviet administrative machine was "based on universal mistrust," and concluding, "We must junk this system." The metastasizing apparatus, he added, was "eating the workers and peasants out of house and home, those who by their labor create real things of value."[30] To Rykov he wrote, "I do not share the policy of this Government. I do not understand it and I do not see any sense in it."[31] To Kuibyshev, he wrote that even good administrators were "drowning in interagency coordination, reports, papers, commissions. The capitalists, each one of them has his means and core responsibility. We now have the Council of Labor and defense and the politburo answering for everything. . . . This is not work, it is agony." At the same time, Dzierżyński feared that his criticisms might "play into the hands of those who would take the country to the abyss—Trotsky, Zinoviev, Pyatakov. . . . If we do not find the correct line and pace of development our opposition will grow and the country will get its dictator, the grave digger of the revolution irrespective of the beautiful feathers on his costume. Almost all dictators nowadays are former Reds—Mussolini, Piłsudkski."[32]

## AILMENTS APLENTY

The three Caucasus musketeers wound down their jaunt: Orjonikidze accompanied Stalin and Mikoyan on the return train all the way to Poti, the Black Sea port, and from there, Stalin and Mikoyan took a boat up to Sochi, arriving on June 15, 1926. One gets the feeling that if Stalin could have just stayed the whole year at Sochi, running the regime from there, he might have been content. He read regime documents for pleasure not just work, played skittles (*gorodki*), and gardened. "He liked to go on picnics," recalled the daughter of Stalin's chief bodyguard, the Lithuanian Ivan Jūsis. "Usually we headed up the mountains and looked for an interesting spot, and there arranged to stop. We always took along a white tablecloth. We were sure to have kebabs and different open-faced sandwiches: with caviar, with fish—sturgeon, salmon. There were also cheese and herbs, especially cilantro. My father knew how to make sausage out of bear meat, Lithuanian style, which Stalin loved."[33] Jūsis appears to have been particularly close to Stalin. In Moscow, he had moved from Varsonefyev Lane (near the Lubyanka), where elite Chekists lived, into the Grand Kremlin Palace, taking one of the apartments formerly occupied by ladies-in-waiting. Dzierżyński lived at the end of the same corridor; the celebrated proletarian poet Demyan Bedny lived one floor up, in a sumptuous dwelling, as did Voroshilov. In Sochi, Jūsis was no mere bodyguard but a companion.

Stalin had come down with food poisoning from a rotten fish, and the doctors forced him onto a diet. They also managed to conduct a serious medical examination of him, perhaps the most detailed record of his health up to then. Ivan Valedinsky, newly appointed scientific director of the Matsesta sanitorium near Sochi, and three other physicians examined Stalin in a small room at dacha no. 4, where he was staying. "Comrade Stalin entered from the balcony wing, sat across from us doctors and carried himself very simply," Valedinsky recalled. "We doctors felt at ease." Stalin was found to have chronic, albeit non-active tuberculosis. His intestines gave him trouble, as if he had been poisoned. (Actually, in his youth he had contracted typhus, which leaves ulcers on the walls of the stomach.) He suffered bouts of diarrhea. He had chest pain caused by insufficient blood to the heart, which he self-treated using lemons. He complained of pain on the fingers of his left hand. His joints were inflamed and red. The doctors noted the beginnings of muscular atrophy in his left preshoulder. "Myalgia and arthritis of the left upper extremity," they wrote. (Myalgia or muscle pains, if not caused by a trauma, often results from viral infections.) The doctors also observed eruptions of chronic quinsy (peritonsillar abscess), which produced sore throats and swelling. Stalin's breathing was heavy, but the cause, pathologies in his right lung (pleural effusion or excess fluid), would not be discovered until many years later. This might have been the cause of the softness of his voice: even after microphones were introduced, he could sometimes barely be heard.

Valedinsky would write that during an objective examination of Stalin's internal organs, no elements of any pathological changes were found. Still, the examination appears to have led to a diagnosis of Erb-Charcot syndrome—fatigue, cramps, and a progressive wasting.[34] Whatever the correct diagnosis, Stalin's left arm with the suppurated elbow had continued to deteriorate and was barely usable. He also felt a permanent crunch in his knees, as well as in his neck when he turned. His aching muscles showed some signs of dystrophy, perhaps also symptoms of Erb-Charcot, although this might have been a genetic ailment.[35] The doctors recommended a dozen Matsesta sulfur baths. "Upon departing from the examination Stalin asked me, 'How about a bit of brandy?'" Valedinsky answered that "on Saturdays it's possible to get somewhat stirred up and on Sundays to really relax, but on Mondays to go to work with a clear head." He added, using a sly Communist code for a convivial occasion, that "this answer pleased comrade Stalin and the next time he organized a 'voluntary Saturday' [subbotnik] that was very memorable for me."[36] Stalin clearly took a shine to Valedinsky, the son of a priest who himself had completed seminary, and then, with his father's permission, had gone on to Tomsk for medical training, after which he'd earned a Ph.D., served in the Great War, and got himself named to the Kremlin sanatorium. Stalin could be spectacularly charming when he wanted to be, particularly with service personnel. And the relief that Sochi-Matsesta brought may well have influenced Stalin's moods for the better.

Despite the lingering effects of the rotten fish, there was delightful news: the besieged opposition had served up yet another unwitting gift for the dictator they despised. Grigory Belenky, a Left oppositionist who had managed to hold his position as party boss of Moscow's Krasnaya Presnya ward, organized a meeting at a dacha in the woods around twenty miles outside Moscow. Perhaps seventy people attended. They aimed to organize supporters at the big factories, higher educational institutions, and state agencies.[37] "Even if there were only one chance in a hundred for regenerating the Revolution and its workers' democracy, that chance had to be taken at all costs," one participated asserted.[38] Belenky estimated the support of sixty-two party cells in his ward. "If we can take Krasnaya Presnya, we can take everything," he supposedly said.[39] This was all delusion. Who was going to stick their necks out for *them*, with OGPU goons sitting conspicuously in party cell meeting halls and voting by means of an open show of hands? To the meeting in the woods, Belenky had invited Mikhail Lashevich, first deputy war commissar, who, when asked whether the oppositionists were organizing in the army, supposedly replied, "Here, the situation is excellent."[40] At least one participant informed on the group, and already on June 8–9 interrogations began.[41] A clandestine opposition meeting in the woods, involving the first deputy commissar of war: manna from heaven.

With Tovstukha telegramming Sochi, on June 24, that given Stalin's continued absence he would put off the Central Committee plenum in Moscow until July 12, Stalin moved to take full advantage of the opposition's latest "conspiracy," writing back on June 25 "to Molotov, Rykov, Bukharin, and other friends" that the "Zinoviev Group" must have been involved in this "Lashevich Affair." Zinoviev had not been present in the woods that day, but, after all, *everything was linked*. Stalin added some tendentious remarks about how the bounds of "loyal" opposition had, for the first time, been breached, and demanded not only that Lashevich be sacked from the war commissariat but that Zinoviev be removed from the politburo and, by extension, from the Comintern. "I assure you," Stalin concluded with evident glee, "in the party and the country no one will feel sorry for Zinoviev, because they know him well."[42]

Pure joy. One functionary accompanying Stalin reported to his superiors in Moscow that the poet Demyan Bedny "comes by often. He regales us with bawdy jokes." Still, it was past time to coax the dictator back to the capital. Molotov, on July 1, 1926, wrote insistently, "We consider necessary your arrival on July 7." Molotov's correspondence reveals appreciation for Stalin's strong leadership, and affection. Stalin departed for Moscow no earlier than July 6.[43] No sooner did he arrive back in the capital than Dzierżyński wrote asserting that Britain had been behind Piłsudski's coup in Poland. "A whole host of data show with indubitable clarity (for me) that Poland is preparing a military attack against us with the aim of breaking off Belorussia and Ukraine from the USSR," Dzierżyński asserted. "All the work of Piłsudski is concentrated on this. . . . In short order Romania is set to receive a huge mass of weapons from Italy, including submarines." At the same time, he noted "an enlivening of activity of all White Guards in the limitrophe"—Finland, Estonia, Latvia, Lithuania, and Poland. Almost immediately after Piłsudski's coup, the Soviet Union had proposed nonaggression pacts to Estonia and Latvia, but neither responded affirmatively.[44] Dzierżyński maintained that only domestic political considerations held Piłsudski back and that to mount his invasion, all he needed was to galvanize public opinion. Dzierżyński wanted the Central Committee to check the Red Army's combat readiness, supply, mobilization and evacuation capability.[45] Welcome back to Moscow, comrade Stalin! (The relentless greeting at every encounter which rang in his ear.)

## TESTAMENT, AGAIN

The delayed Central Committee plenum opened on July 14 (it met through the twenty-third). On the second day, outside the plenum, Dzierżyński instructed Yagoda to remove local OGPU archives from the frontier regions closest to Poland and Romania. He also suggested transferring out the spies, White Guards, and bandits held in prisons near the western borders.[46] To the plenum, Dzierżyński gave a report on July 20. Having recently instructed Yagoda to clear speculators from Moscow and other cities, now Dzierżyński complained that the provincial OGPU "arrested, exiled, imprisoned, pressured, and blackmailed private traders (who meanwhile were prepared to work 14–16 hours a day)."[47] He called the Trotsky supporter Pyatakov, deputy chief of the state planning commission, "the single biggest disorganizer of industry." To Kamenev, who had recruited Dzierżyński into the opposition, he said, "You are engaged in intrigue [*politikantsvo*], not work." Dzierżyński stated that had he known about the opposition's secret gatherings outside Moscow beforehand, he would "not have hesitated to take two companies of OGPU troops with machine guns and settle matters." Sweating profusely, pale, he barely managed to finish before returning to his seat. Soon he was helped from the hall and placed on a divan outside the meeting hall. Someone administered camphor. Dzierżyński began to make his way back to his apartment in the nearby Grand Kremlin Palace but collapsed. Forty-nine years old, he was dead. He had evidently suffered a heart attack during his plenum speech. The autopsy revealed advanced arteriosclerosis, especially in the blood vessels to the heart.[48] "After Frunze, Dzierżyński," Stalin observed in brief remarks at the funeral on July 22. "'The terror of the bourgeoisie'—that's what they called him."[49]

The plenum continued. Trotsky read a statement on behalf of himself, Zinoviev, and Kamenev announcing their common struggle against the tyranny of the apparatus, defense of worker interests against the NEP, the need for tax increases on kulaks, collectivization of agriculture, and rapid industrialization. Stalin had the "Lashevich affair" in his pocket, but the opposition was circulating Lenin's Testament, and without the lines about Trotsky's non-Bolshevism. Stalin grabbed the Testament nettle and read it aloud, in its entirety. Trotsky later wrote that Stalin was choking back anger, and suffered repeated interruptions calling out his distortions. "In the end he completely lost his equilibrium and, rising on tiptoe, forcing his voice, with a raised hand started to shout, hoarsely, crazy accusations and threats, which dumbfounded the whole hall," Trotsky claimed. "Neither before nor after have I ever seen him in such a state."[50] But the declassified record of the discussion shows the opposition on the defensive and Stalin on the attack.

"It is incorrect to call Lenin's letter a Testament," Stalin noted in a long speech on July 22, going on to observe that "Lenin's letter mentions six comrades. Of three comrades, Trotsky, Kamenev, and Zinoviev, it says they had errors of principle that were not accidental. I think it would not be immodest if I observed here the fact that there is not one word in the 'testament' about the mistakes of principle of Stalin. Ilich scolds Stalin and notes his rudeness, but in the letter there is not even a hint that Stalin has errors of principle."[51] Stalin added that he had taken the criticisms into account, while Trotsky, Zinoviev, and Kamenev had ignored them. Trotsky's method, Stalin asserted, was to attack with rumors, and above all to make everything a matter of personalities. "The letter says that we should not blame Trotsky 'personally' for his non-Bolshevism . . . from this it follows that comrade Trotsky needs to be cured of 'non-Bolshevism,'" Stalin said. "But from this it does not follow that comrade Trotsky has been afforded the right to revise Leninism, that we should nod our heads in agreement, when he revises Leninism." Trotsky interjected "past" concerning his non-Bolshevism, to which Stalin answered, "The letter does not say 'past,' it only says non-Bolshevism. . . . Two different things. The 'non-Bolshevism' of Trotsky is a fact. The impossibility of blaming comrade Trotsky 'personally' for the non-Bolshevism is also a fact. But Trotsky's non-Bolshevism exists and the struggle against it is necessary—that's also a fact, beyond doubt. Lenin should not be distorted."[52] Stalin dismissed Lenin's "Notes on the Question of Nationalities" as a matter of the leader's weakening memory, and asserted that Mdivani and the Georgians deserved far more serious punishment than he (Stalin) had meted out: after all, they had created a faction, which was illegal. Stalin conceded nothing but his own rudeness, which, in light of the fight against Trotsky's seeming non-Leninism, could indeed appear trifling.[53]

Stalin did not overlook the "October episode" of Zinoviev and Kamenev either, which, echoing the Testament, he called "non-accidental," an ongoing, chronic, endemic, defining characteristic, like Trotsky's non-Bolshevism. "The 'episode' could be repeated. Do you not think, comrades that a repeat of the October mistakes of Zinoviev and Kamenev, a certain recidivism of these mistakes was demonstrated in front of us at the 14th Party Congress?" Stalin answered his rhetorical question: "This is true. From this the conclusion follows that comrades Kamenev and Zinoviev did not take into account Lenin's directives."[54] Zinoviev, when he got a chance to respond, admitted, "I made many mistakes.... My first mistake in 1917 is known to all.... My second mistake I consider even more dangerous because the 1917 mistake was done under Lenin, and Lenin corrected it, and so did we with his help after a few days, but my mistake in 1923 consisted in . . ." At this point Orjonikidze cut him off: "What are you doing, taking the whole party for a fool?" Orjonikidze had allowed himself to be caught up in the summer 1923 cave meeting intrigue and did not want the plenum members to find out.

Thus did Stalin not only neutralize their main weapon—the damned Testament—he flagellated them with it.[55] All the while he remained the humble servant, executor of the party's will. "Delegations of the 13th Congress discussed this question and I do not consider it a lack of humility if I report that all delegations without exception spoke out for the retention of Stalin in the post of general secretary. I have these resolutions right here and I can read them aloud, if you want." Voice: "Unnecessary." Stalin: "Despite this fact immediately after the 13th Party Congress, at the first plenum of our Central Committee, I offered my resignation. Despite my request to be removed, the plenum decided, and as I recall, unanimously, that I should remain in the post of general secretary. What could I have done comrades? I am a person not of free will and I subordinated myself to the plenum's decision."[56]

Zinoviev was voted out of the politburo entirely. "Down with factions and factional struggle," read the resolution. "Long live the unity and cohesion of the Leninist party."[57] And yet, Stalin managed to maintain his pose as the moderate, noting that against the insistence of Zinoviev and Kamenev, he had refused to have Trotsky removed from the politburo.

Stalin had Rudzutaks promoted to full member of the politburo, assuming Zinoviev's place, while the Caucasus duo Mikoyan and Orjonikidze were named candidate members, along with Kirov in Leningrad, Kaganovich, and Andrei Andreyev. A few days later Stalin informed Mikoyan, party boss in the North Caucasus, that he was being transferred to Moscow to replace Kamenev as commissar of trade. Mikoyan balked, but Stalin forced him.[58] As Dzierżyński's replacement as head of the Supreme Council of the Economy, Stalin named Valerian Kuibyshev, which opened a hole at the party Central Control Commission. Stalin summoned Orjonikidze from Tiflis to head it, warning him "not to buck," but the transfer required considerable arm-twisting.[59] Before the year was out, Stalin would have two new key allies in the capital (Mikoyan, Orjonikidze), to go with his key ally in Leningrad (Kirov).[60]

Dzierżyński's office became a shrine to the incorruptible ascetic. "A simple desk, an old screen hiding a narrow iron bed . . . he never went home to his family except on holidays," one of his old-school colleagues observed.[61] The man who had insisted on preserving Lenin's mummy was honored with a lesser version: an effigy made from the death masks of Dzierżyński's face and hands was placed in his uniform under a glass case in the OGPU officers' club.[62] A cult of Dzierżyński would buttress the police regime. He was said to pluck flowers while carefully avoiding trampling on a nearby anthill—but woe to enemies of the revolution.[63] Mężyński was formally promoted to chairman of the OGPU. "Everyone was surprised that there was nothing military about him," recalled Raisa Sobol, an operative. "He spoke quietly, and could be heard only because the hall was tensely silent. And his manner of speech was not command-style but contemplative. The chairman, strangely, resembled a teacher."[64] But the physically ailing Mężyński, also depressed by Dzierżyński's death, went south to Matsesta for six weeks of sulfur baths.

Testament unpleasantries extended beyond the sitting of the plenum. Zinoviev had charged that "in a private letter to comrade Stalin Lenin broke comradely relations with him."[65] Stalin responded in written form. "Lenin never broke comradely relations with me—that is the slander of a person who has lost his head. One can judge Lenin's personal relations with me by the fact that Lenin, while ill, turned to me several times with such important assignments, the kind of assignments with which he never once tried to turn to Zinoviev or Kamenev or Trotsky. Politburo members and comrades Krupskaya and Maria Ilinichna [Ulyanova] know about these assignments."[66] (Stalin refrained from specifying that these were requests for poison.) On July 26, 1926, Ulyanova lent her authoritative status as Lenin's sister to Stalin's defense in the Testament controversy, signing a formal letter to the presidium of the just concluded joint plenum; the archives contain a draft for her by Bukharin (she worked at *Pravda*, where he was editor). "V. I. Lenin valued Stalin highly," her letter stated, using her brother's initials. "V.I. used to call him and would give him the most intimate instructions, instructions of the sort one can only give to someone one particularly trusts, someone one knows as a sincere revolutionary, as a close comrade. . . . In fact, during the entire time of his illness, as long as he had the possibility of seeing his comrades, he most frequently invited comrade Stalin, and during the most difficult moments of his illness Stalin was the only member of the Central Committee he invited." She allowed that an incident had occurred, "of a purely personal character without any connection to policy," because Stalin had upheld the doctors' prohibition against Lenin's engaging in political matters while ill. "Comrade Stalin apologized and with that the incident was exhausted. . . . Relations were and remained the closest and most comradely."[67]

Not long thereafter, evidently feeling pangs of guilt, Ulyanova wrote a second letter, for which no one supplied a draft, noting that she had been reflecting on those days more broadly, not just in the context of blocking the intrigues of Kamenev and Zinoviev, and found her original letter incomplete: Lenin had indeed wanted to curb Stalin's power, removing him as general secretary because of his personal traits.[68] But Ulyanova's second, private letter, unlike her first, was not circulated to members of the joint plenum. Krupskaya, a member of the joint plenum and thus, presumably, a recipient of Ulyanova's original letter, does not appear to have moved to contradict her.[69] Krupskaya still wanted to publish the Testament, but Stalin had pointed out that only a congress, the party's highest organ, had the right to remove the prohibition on publication that had been placed by the 13th Party Congress. "I regret that the joint plenum of the Central Committee and Central Control Commission does not have the right to decide to publish these letters in the press," he stated. "I deeply regret this and I shall get it done at the 15th Party Congress of our party."[70] Mention of the Testament was included in the plenum transcript circulated to party organizations countrywide.[71] A dark cloud accompanied every hard-earned advance over the opposition.

## RUSSIA'S NEW RULER
## (EYE ON AMERICA)

Zinoviev was still, nominally, chairman of the Comintern, but the days were long passed when Stalin conducted Comintern affairs with him. Kuusinen, the Comintern secretary general, who referred to Zinoviev behind his back as the satrap, had been reporting all serious business to Stalin.[72] Stalin had Kamenev named ambassador to Italy. The short-lived trade commissar surreptitiously brought 600,000 gold rubles to finance the Italian Communist party. In the one known meeting between Kamenev and Mussolini, the *duce* was disgusted to receive as an envoy a man who was not only a Communist but disgraced by his own government. Kamenev, for his part, told Mussolini he was "grateful to get away from Russia and from Stalin."[73] The day before exiling Kamenev, Stalin granted an interview—his first ever—to an American journalist. The interviewer, Jerome Davis, was a former YMCA leader in Russia, a labor activist, and a professor at Yale University's Divinity School who arrived in the USSR on an American delegation of some twenty self-described progressives. Davis managed to obtain his audience with Stalin on the pretext of being able to assist with U.S. diplomatic recognition of the Soviet state.[74] Davis would publish a sensational essay, "Russia's New Ruler," as he called Stalin, in the *New York American,* owned by the conservative William Randolph Hearst. "After a hearty handshake," Davis wrote, "I turned out to be seated at a table across from a powerful, magnetic personality with curly black hair, manly moustaches, brown eyes, and a face with visible marks of smallpox, and a welcoming, friendly smile."[75]

Davis filled a vacuum. But the Hearst exclusive passed largely without commentary in the rest of the American press, a circumstance, according to the director of the New York bureau of TASS, that would not have happened had it been the property of the Associated Press or the *New York Times*—a passage Stalin underlined.[76] Still, whatever the disappointment over the dearth of international resonance, the published interview offered something to both sides: it rendered Stalin very articulate (a Soviet plus); it contained interesting details about his life and apparent political views (a Davis achievement).

During the interview, when Davis requested a copy of Stalin's biography, the dictator had handed him a photograph, with a short note. "That's so little," Davis responded. "How did you become a Communist?" Stalin: "That's difficult to say. At first people go over to opposition, then they become revolutionaries, then they choose for themselves a party. We had a lot of parties—SRs, Mensheviks, Anarchists, Bolsheviks." Davis pressed: "Why a Communist?" Stalin: "We had so many Communists because Russian capitalism was the most savage. . . . We had the most severe political system, so that even the most peaceable types went into opposition; and because a simple opposition could not help the oppositionists. From the rich to the laborers, they were sent to exile in Siberia, [so] they strove to create a party that was the sharpest in standing against the government and acted the most decisively. Therefore all those inclined to opposition sympathized with the Bolsheviks and looked upon them as heroes." Stalin related the story of how he had allegedly been expelled from the seminary for reading Marx. He also offered a theory of rule, explaining that the Communist party had 1 million members—a fighting organization, not a discussion club—but an organization even with 1 million could not rule such a large country: once decisions were taken, they had to be implemented. For that, a regime needed a shared sense of mission. Davis pointed to the conspiratorial nature of Bolshevism, and Stalin referred to "shadow committees" in British politics, and asserted that the politburo was newly elected every year.[77] When Davis touched on the peasants, Stalin said, "You cannot do anything with propaganda alone. We hope that we'll attract the peasants because we create the material conditions for pushing the peasants onto the Bolshevik side." Peasants needed affordable consumer goods, credit, aid during famine. "I would not say that they are in ecstasy over the Bolsheviks. But the peasants are practical and, comparing the capitalists, who did not want to talk to them and exploited them, and the Communists, who talk to them, persuade them, and do not rob them, they come to the conclusion that it's better with us. They do not take us for the ideal, but they consider us as better than the others."[78]

While strenuously trying to soften the image of the Soviet state, Stalin's main subject was the puzzle of securing American diplomatic recognition, trade, and foreign investment to advance the Soviet economy. He complained that it remained unclear what more, concretely, he could do; the USSR had made abundant public pronouncements of its desire for normal relations. Davis indicated that for state recognition, Stalin should consider acknowledging tsarist and Kerensky government debt; compensating the majority of Americans who suffered from confiscations; and refraining from using Soviet representatives abroad in propaganda work. Stalin retorted that any agitation against the United States stemmed from its failure to recognize the Soviet state, unlike the other powers. On the commercial side, he pointed to the profits obtained by Averell Harriman in the Lena goldfields, thanks to the Soviet Union's internationally low wages. Davis asked Stalin if the Soviets lived up to their agreements. "Concerning the Bolsheviks, sundry myths are propagated, that they do not eat, do not drink, that they are not people, that they have no families and that they do nothing but fight with each other and depose one another (and then it turns out they are all still there), that night and day they send out directives to the whole world," he responded. "Here that only induces laughter." Stalin did not allow that the United States government might refuse to truck with Communism on moral grounds; after all, when did imperialists have morals? "Germany stands below the United

States in technical level, culture, yet Germany takes more leases [concessions], it knows the market better, it engages more. . . . Why?" Stalin asked. "Germany extends us credit." Stalin craved the same from the United States. "In view of American technical skill and her abundant surplus capital," he said, "no country in the world is better fitted to help Russia. . . . The unsurpassed technology of America and the needs and tremendous population of Russia would yield large profits for Americans, if they cooperated."

What Stalin saw in the United States is not hard to grasp: America's share of global production would soon reach a breathtaking one third. Consider Henry Ford's Model T, whose supply could not keep pace with demand. When Ford had opened a new plant in Highland Park, he had taken advantage of mechanized conveyors to send the automobile frame along a line, along which each worker was assigned one simplified, repetitive assembly task to perform in a system known as mass production. It involved standardization of the core aspects of products and reorganized flow among shops, and allowed replacement of manual labor by machinery. At Ford's River Rouge factory near Detroit, a finished car rolled off the assembly line every ten seconds, and the effects were felt throughout the economy and thousands of communities. River Rouge alone employed 68,000, making it the largest factory in the world, but more than that, its cars required millions of tons of steel alloys, as well as vast amounts of glass, rubber, textiles, and petroleum. Cars also needed roads and service stations. Altogether, nearly four million jobs were connected directly or indirectly to the automobile, in a labor force of 45 million workers. U.S. production and business organization mesmerized the world.[79] And it was only half the story. Already in 1925, one of every six Americans nationally had a car, and one of every two in Los Angeles, a result of the fact that standardization enabled a drop in the price of the Model T to $290, from $850. Ford had further expanded the market for his cars by paying his own workers $5 per day, approximately twice the country's average manufacturing wage. "The necessary, precedent condition of mass production," Ford wrote, "is a capacity, latent or developed, of *mass consumption*, the ability to absorb large production. The two go together, and in the latter may be traced the reasons for the former."[80] In the 1920s, average household income in the United States rose by 25 percent. Eleven million families owned their own homes by the middle of the decade. Stalin understood little of the transcendent might of this *consumer* republic. And the benefits for the USSR of American industrial modernity remained elusive.

## GRAVE DIGGER OF THE REVOLUTION

With Stalin in Moscow that August 1926, people from every imaginable sphere queued on Old Square: local party bosses, party Central Control Commission members, the head of the central consumer cooperative, functionaries from the labor and trade commissariats, the Soviet envoy to Persia, an editor from *Bolshevik,* the acting head of the Communist Youth International, the deputy war commissar, even Filipp Ksenofontov, the original author of Stalin's "Foundations of Leninism."[81] And on and on it went, until in late August, through late September, Stalin returned to his beloved Sochi. There he expressed dismay about the delays in receiving newspaper reports from Britain on the miners' strike. In Moscow, a British delegation was about to arrive, and on August 27, Stalin telegrammed that the striking British miners be supplied a substantial sum, as much as 3 million rubles.[82] Molotov informed Stalin on September 5 that the USSR had dispatched 3 million rubles, which came out of the wages of Soviet workers at state trusts, as a purported act of solidarity, and fed the anti-Communist uproar in Britain.[83] But Stalin would not be intimidated by "finance capital."

Trotsky at this time jotted down some reflections. He wrote that "the slogan of party unity, in the hands of the ruling faction, increasingly becomes an instrument of ideological terror," suppressing internal criticism. More than that, he detected an explicit strategy of "complete destruction of that nucleus which until recently was known as the Leninist old guard, and its replacement by the one-man leadership of Stalin relying on his group of comrades who always agree with him." Trotsky foresaw that "one-man rule in the party, which Stalin and his more narrow group call 'party unity,' demands not just the destruction and removal of the current United opposition, but the gradual removal from the leadership of the more authoritative and influential representatives of the current ruling faction. It is utterly clear that Tomsky, Rykov, Bukharin—by their past, by their authority, and so on—cannot and are incapable of playing the role, under Stalin, played by Uglanov, Kaganovich, Petrovsky, and others." Trotsky predicted a coming phase in which Kaganovich and the rest would go after Rykov, Bukharin, and Tomsky. He even predicted that "opportunistic elements in the party would open fire on Stalin, as too infected by 'left' prejudices and hindering of their quicker, more open ascent."[84] Remarkably, Trotsky proved able, almost uniquely, to discern the direction of the political dynamic, but more remarkably, he failed to understand Stalin as the autonomous driver of a personal dictatorship, seeing him as a mere instrument for larger social forces in a bureaucratic aggrandizement.

Trotsky, Zinoviev, and Kamenev had belatedly formed what they called the United opposition, and by early October 1926 were gathering once more at Kamenev's Kremlin apartment, to discuss strategy, now with Zinoviev expelled from the politburo. Trotsky continued to question Zinoviev about his previously vicious attacks on "Trotskyism," which had generated enduring bad blood.[85] But the threesome, looking at the correlation of forces, decided to offer Stalin a truce, promising to desist from oppositional activity.[86] He dictated the terms: they were to affirm that all Central Committee decisions were binding, publicly repudiate all factional activity, and disavow their supporters among foreign Communists (Ruth Fischer, Arkadi Maslow, Boris Souvarine). *Pravda* published their joint statement, signed also by Sokolnikov and Pyatakov, on October 17.[87] The very next day, however, Max Eastman happened to publish the full Lenin Testament in the *New York Times*, a bombshell that, the USSR excepted, was reprinted in newspapers worldwide.[88] On October 19, Stalin resigned yet again, this time in writing. "A year and a half's joint work in the politburo with comrades Zinoviev and Kamenev after the withdrawal, and then the death, of Lenin have made utterly clear to me the impossibility of honest and sincere joint political work with these comrades in the confines of one narrow collegium," he wrote in a note to the upcoming Central Committee plenum. "In view of that I ask you to consider me to have left the politburo." He added that because a non-politburo member could not head the secretariat and orgburo, he should be considered to have left those posts as well. He asked for a two-month holiday, after which he wanted a posting to godforsaken Turukhansk, Siberia, where he had been stuck in prerevolutionary exile, or remote Yakutia, or maybe abroad.[89]

Stalin gave a pretty good impression of feeling sorry for himself. From his point of view, the *New York Times* Testament publication reinforced his jaundiced view of the oppositionists as traitorous enemies. Of course, neither his politburo majority—including those Trotsky had privately predicted would soon be eclipsed—nor his Central Committee majority accepted his written request to resign. On the contrary, on October 22 *Pravda* published Stalin's "theses" denouncing the opposition, just in time for the 15th party conference.[90] The next day he had the joint plenum of the Central Committee and the Central Control Commission meeting to finalize the party conference's agenda, insert a "special report" on the opposition to be delivered by himself: the truce, not a week old, was dead.[91]

The 15th party conference opened on October 26 (it lasted until November 3) and was attended by 194 voting delegates, plus 640 non-voting, a substantial audience. It was now that Trotsky, belatedly, denounced Stalin's "socialism in one country" as a "betrayal" of the world revolution and guarantee of capitalist restoration in Russia.[92] Zinoviev, too, erupted on this theme. "The theory of final victory in one country is wrong," he stated. "We will win final victory because revolution in other countries is inevitable."[93] (Of course, Stalin had said *final* victory was impossible in one country.) Krupskaya kept silent, evidently abandoning the opposition cause. On November 1, Stalin delivered his report, rehearsing the entire history of the opposition from his viewpoint, and mocking the supposed musicality of Trotsky's writings. "Leninism as a 'muscular feeling in physical labor,'" Stalin quoted, dripping with sarcasm. "New, original, profound, no? Did you understand any of it? (Laughter.) All that is very beautiful, musical and, if you want, even grand. It is only missing a small thing: the simple and human touch of Leninism."[94]

Trotsky rose, turned to the Georgian, pointed his finger and exclaimed, "The first secretary poses his candidacy to the post of grave digger of the revolution!" Stalin flushed with anger and fled the room, slamming the door. The session broke up in uproar.

At Trotsky's apartment in the Cavalry Building, his supporters, arriving before him, expressed apprehension at his outburst. Pyatakov: "Why, oh why, did Lev Davidovich say that? Stalin will never forgive him unto the third and fourth generation!"[95] Trotsky had gotten under Stalin's skin, but whatever satisfaction he might have savored was short-lived; the next day, when the party conference resumed, Stalin had the votes to have Trotsky expelled from the politburo. Kamenev was removed as a candidate member of the politburo, and Stalin put Zinoviev's sacking as Comintern chief on the agenda for the next meeting of that body's executive. Zinoviev and Kamenev turned on Trotsky for having raised Stalin's ire. They all tried to defend themselves against the dictator's calumnies, but they were relentlessly interrupted. Yuri Larin pointed to what he called "one of the most dramatic episodes of our revolution, . . . the revolution is outgrowing some of its leaders."[96] Bukharin's speech was especially vicious, even by his standards, sarcastically quoting Trotsky's "grave digger of the revolution" phrase to turn the tables.[97] Stalin was so delighted with Bukharin's frothing remarks that he interjected, "Well done, Bukharin. Well done, well done. He does not argue with them, he slashes!"[98]

Ah, the sweet satisfaction of violent recriminations. Stalin had the conference's final word, on November 3, and ridiculed Zinoviev, Kamenev, and Trotsky at length, eliciting peals of laughter.[99] In the meantime, a new electoral law of November 1926 deprived still more kulaks and private traders of the right to vote, in a sharpening tilt against the NEP, and several speakers at the party conference warned of a war on the horizon.

## PARSING THE STRATEGIC SITUATION

Nothing whatsoever guaranteed Soviet security and, notwithstanding the regime's pugnacious rhetoric and often aggressive actions, it felt vulnerable. Soviet theories behind a likely casus belli varied, from Moscow's refusals to pay back tsarist-era loans or supply sufficient raw materials to a burning Western desire to continue the breakup of Russia, separating Ukraine, the Caucasus, and Central Asia. Because a supply blockade could choke the Soviet Union, rumors circulated that the imperialists would not even need to launch an attack, but merely blackmail the regime into concessions.[100] A real war, though, could not be excluded and the OGPU reported it could take the form of an allied Polish-Romanian aggression, provoked into attack and supported by Britain and France, which would likely draw in Latvia, Lithuania, Estonia, and Finland, too—the full "limitrophe."[101] Chicherin repeatedly warned the Baltic states that willingly serving as pawns of the Western powers in an anti-Soviet coalition would one day result in loss of their independence. He warned Poland similarly.[102] The OGPU was also convinced hostile foreign powers planned to rally disaffected elements inside Soviet territory—after all, the Entente had used proxies before (the Whites during Russia's civil war).

It was no secret that even without British prodding, the dictatorship in Warsaw coveted those parts of historic Ukraine and Belorussia it did not yet control.[103] Stalin read secret report after secret report about Polish infiltration of Soviet Ukraine and Soviet Belorussia and preparations for sabotage operations on Soviet territory. He had instituted a much-publicized Polish national region inside Belorussia to blunt anti-Soviet sentiments among the Soviet Union's ethnic Poles, but whether that would help at all remained uncertain.[104] To test Piłsudski, in August 1926, the Soviets revived the talks started earlier in the year for a non-aggression pact, but negotiations went nowhere. Poland had planned parallel balancing agreements with Moscow and Berlin, but did not even launch talks with Germany. Rumors were rife of a Polish invasion of Lithuania, where a leftist government had emptied the prisons of political prisoners, including Communists, and on September 28, 1926, signed a non-aggression treaty with the Soviet Union, adding to the outcries of "Bolshevism." Never mind that the previous rightist Lithuania Christian Democrat government had launched the negotiations with Moscow. The Soviet-Lithuanian pact had an anti-Polish edge to it.[105] Over on the USSR's eastern flank, Soviet military intelligence continued to beat the drums about a likely renewed military intervention by Japan. Japan had quit their civil war–era military occupation of Soviet territory later than any of the other interventionist powers. It had annexed Korea and eyed Manchuria and even Mongolia, the Soviet satellite, as its sphere of influence. In August 1926, Tokyo refused Soviet offers of a neutrality pact. The chief of the Siberian OGPU, Henriks Štubis (b. 1894), an ethnic Latvian who used the name Leonid Zakovsky, reported to Mężyński that "Russian White-Guardist circles in China have become significantly enlivened," which, to him, testified not to the émigrés' dynamics but to Japan's plans for a northern aggression. Zakovsky recommended preparing partisan warfare units on the Soviet side of the border to counter a Japanese military occupation.[106]

Britain, however, was the greater preoccupation, as always. The British military attaché was throwing banquets at its Moscow embassy for the Red Army brass, as the OGPU reported to Stalin, using hospitality to take advantage of "our chattiness, loose their tongues . . . our comrades often get drunk at these banquets." Inebriated Soviet officials talked of secret assignments carried out in China, which incited the already hypersuspicious British like the proverbial red flag before a bull.[107] In London, the Inter-Departmental Committee on Eastern Unrest catalogued Bolshevik intrigues in Turkey, Afghanistan, China, Persia, and the jewel in the crown, India.[108] On December 3, 1926, the *Manchester Guardian*, a British newspaper, making use of leaked information, exposed the clandestine German-Soviet military cooperation in violation of the Versailles Treaty. Two days later, the German Social Democrat newspaper republished the report.[109] An uproar ensued in the Reichstag, where Social Democrats denounced the illegal activities of the German army. Chicherin happened to be in Berlin on medical leave and he and Ambassador Krestinsky called on German Chancellor Wilhelm Marx on December 6 to smooth matters over. *Pravda* belatedly acknowledged the scandal on December 16, blaming the leak on "the German Social Democratic lackeys of the Entente." The Soviet newspaper confirmed that the Germans, on the basis of concessions (leases), had helped build facilities on Soviet territory for the production of airplanes, poison gas, and ammunition, but reasserted a Soviet right to defense.[110] Britain internally contemplated severing diplomatic relations, which the Foreign Office opposed for now on pragmatic grounds: such an action would fail to alter Soviet behavior and encourage those in Berlin who wanted an "eastern orientation." Still, British-Soviet relations were on a knife's edge. "The Soviet to all intents and purposes—short of direct armed conflict—is at war with the British empire," one British Foreign Office official wrote on December 10, 1926. "Whether by interference in the strikes at home or by fomenting the anti-British forces in China, in fact, by her action all the world over, from Riga to Java, the Soviet power has as its main objective the destruction of British Power."[111]

A week later the military in Lithuania overthrew the democratically elected government—a left coalition of Social Democrats, Peasant Popular Union, and small parties of ethnic minority Germans, Poles, and Jews. The putschists installed a rightist dictatorship of Antanas Smetona, whose Lithuanian National Union had a membership of 2,000 countrywide and a parliamentary representation of three seats. The Christian Democrats, in the elections that had brought the leftist coalition to power, had failed for the first time to obtain a majority and supported the putsch. Martial law was declared and hundreds of Lithuanian Communists swept up in arrests. Lithuanian-Polish enmity now had to compete with anti-Communist solidarity.

When the head of Soviet military intelligence, Jan Berzin, summarized the international position of the USSR as of the end of 1926, he acknowledged an increase in tensions but deemed an anti-Soviet "military action in 1927 unlikely."[112] But beyond cultivating friendly relations with Turkey, Persia, and China, Berzin's recommendations were almost wholly reactive: hindering Polish-German settlement of Danzig and Upper Silesia, subverting a Polish-Baltic alliance, keeping Germany from passing over to the West, aggravating the tensions between Britain-France and Germany and between Britain and France themselves, as well as between the United States and Japan.[113] Communist boilerplate about the "fragility" of capitalist stabilization, about the gathering revolutionary movement in Europe and the colonial world, was face to face with hard reality. Soviet military expenditures in fiscal 1926–27 reached a mere 41 percent of the 1913 level.[114] The Red Army essentially had no tanks, other than the ancient Western-made ones it had captured from the Whites during the civil war.[115] Red Army soldiers rode bicycles in the holiday parades across Red Square and during war games. One third of the conscripts did not even have uniforms.[116] Neither did the country even have a comprehensive war plan covering the various contingencies in 1926, according to Voroshilov.[117] On December 26, 1926, Deputy Defense Commissar Mikhail Tukhachevsky, as part of the work toward producing a war plan, underscored that in the event of hostilities, "Our miserly combat resources for mobilization would barely last through the first stage of combat." Tukhachevsky was jockeying to be named head of the state planning commission's defense sector and given to dramatization. Still, he was correct. "Our situation would only deteriorate, particularly in the event of a blockade," he continued. "Neither the Red Army nor the country is ready for war."[118]

Suddenly, Stalin resigned again. On December 27, he wrote to Rykov, "I ask you to release me from the post of Central Committee general secretary. I affirm that I can no longer work at this post, that I am in no condition to work any longer at this post."[119] Precisely what prompted this latest fit of self-pity remains unclear. Just four days earlier, Stalin had written to Molotov, who was on holiday down south, "You don't have to hurry back—you could easily remain another week (or even more). . . . Things are going pretty well for us here."[120] Stalin's moods were becoming almost as difficult to parse as the intentions of the Soviet Union's external enemies.

## STATE OF SIEGE

Soviet grand strategy, absent a real military or a single alliance, amounted to a wing and a prayer (intracapitalist war). With the external situation apparently worsening, Voroshilov, in early January 1927, stated at a Moscow province party conference, in a speech carried by *Pravda*, "We must not forget that we stand on the brink of war, and that this war will be far from fun and games."[121] Rykov and Bukharin made similar speeches around this time, conveying that war could come within days, or by spring, or autumn.[122] Such alarms sprang not from specific intelligence but deepening anxieties, combined with a tendency to group disparate events and attribute conspiratorial causes to them.[123] "It becomes clearer every day," a British diplomat in Moscow observed in early 1927, "that the panic that now exists, which is audible in every utterance of public men, and legible in every press leader, is not 'faked,' . . . but indeed represents the feelings and emotions of the Communist party and Soviet government."[124]

Not everything talked about in the Soviet Union related to capitalist encirclement. In mid-January 1927 through late March, Sergei Prokofyev returned from Parisian exile for an exhausting concert tour in Moscow, Leningrad, and his native Ukraine (Kharkov, Kiev, Odessa). He had left in 1918, married a Spanish singer, and become internationally acclaimed, though in Europe he never dazzled quite like Stravinsky. (Stravinsky thought Prokofyev Russia's greatest composer, after himself.) Back in his homeland—Prokofyev had kept his Soviet passport—he heard a twenty-year-old Dmitry Shostokovich play his own First Piano Sonata at a young composers' evening. The music scene in the USSR proved lively, intense, and Prokofyev's opera *Love for Three Oranges* thrilled Soviet audiences. At the same time, his phone was tapped; he failed to obtain the release of an arrested cousin (a childhood playmate); and became worn down by rehearsals, performances, admirers, impresarios, and swindlers ("If that's how things are," he told a clothes cleaner, "perhaps you can tell me why the whole of Moscow isn't ironing trousers for a living?"). Isaak Rabinovich, a stage designer, told Prokofyev that "Moscow looks absolutely disgraceful," and, given how long full reconstruction would take, divulged a personal plan to paint "one street entirely in blue, another one that crosses it in two colors." On the way out to Poland, even the Soviet customs official recognized Prokofyev, asking, "What is in the trunk, oranges?"[125]

Stalin did not receive Prokofyev. Indeed, no musicians, actors, directors, dancers, writers, or painters are listed in the logbooks for his office in 1927. Certainly he had a strong interest in the arts, especially the music world, but only later would he acquire the authority to summon artists at will. For now he saw them when he went out to their performances. Stalin loved attending live theater, where an astonishing run of plays followed one after the other: *The Forest* and *The Mandate* by Alexander Ostrovsky and Nikolai Erdman, respectively, which Vesvolod Meyerhold produced; and *Days of the Turbins* by Mikhail Bulgakov, Stalin's favorite playwright. Stalin also occasionally went to the famed cinema on the roof pavilion of the Nirnzee House, then the tallest building in Moscow, located at Bolshoi Gnezdnikov Lane, 10, up Tverskaya Street from the Kremlin.[126] (Also seen there: Bulgakov and other luminaries in Moscow's beau monde.) During Prokofyev's tour, Stalin did find time to meet Konstantin Gerulaitis-Stepuro, an acquaintance from the prerevolutionary exile days of Turukhansk who did not belong to the party but came to Old Square during office hours on a "personal matter." He was unemployed, a life trajectory that put Stalin's ascent from the same frozen Siberian swamps into stark perspective.[127]

Diverting activity was a luxury, however. Stalin knew that Britain was encouraging Germany to take control over Danzig and the Polish Corridor, compensating Poland with part of (or even all) of Lithuania.[128] Germany was his great frustration. The German military brass, on the very day that the *Manchester Guardian* had exposed clandestine German-Soviet cooperation, gave final approval to sign an agreement in Moscow to open a secret joint tank school in Kazan. For Moscow, however, this fell far below hopes. Unszlicht, in a pessimistic overview, outlined for Stalin all dimensions of the cooperation—the aviation school (Lipetsk), the Tomko (a code name) chemical warfare testing facility (Samara), the Dreise machine guns, the Bersol company's chemical devices, the Junkers airplane concession (Fili), and the tank school (Kazan)—but concluded that "our attempts to attract German investments in our military industry through RWM have failed." Unszlicht recommended "continuing our joint work in the tank school and aviation school and in chemical warfare tests."[129] Others in the Soviet establishment clung to the exchanges. "Every comrade, without exception, who has come here for maneuvers or to attend the academies has found the display of the technological innovations of the Germany army very useful," Krestinsky from Berlin argued to Litvinov on January 18, 1927. "What we are offering to the Germans does not cost us anything, because they pay for everything, while there is no problem finding in the depths of the USSR secret locations for their schools and other smaller military establishments."[130] The goal of strengthening the Red Army's material base, however, remained elusive.[131]

Soviet counterintelligence, meanwhile, intercepted a Japanese document titled "General Strategic Measures Against Russia," which was translated into Russian on February 7. It called for sharpening "the racial, ideological and class struggle in the Soviet Union and especially the internal tensions in the Communist party," and for unifying all Asian nations on Soviet territory against European Russia. As targets it listed non-Russian soldiers in the army, from whom secret information could be obtained about Soviet military plans and operations in the Far East. It also suggested inciting the states on the Soviet Union's western and southern border to preempt the Soviets' ability to shift troops eastward, and sabotaging the USSR's transport and infrastructure, and telegraph and telephone connections.[132]

Stalin was on edge. Maxim Litvinov had delivered remarks at a meeting of the foreign affairs commissariat collegium in mid-January 1927 that were roundly critical of Soviet international posture, and an informant secretly wrote to Stalin with details. Litvinov was said to have argued that "English policy toward us is hostile because we ourselves conduct a hostile policy toward them," and that "England is a great power and in England's foreign policy we play a relatively insignificant role." Litvinov's greatest heresy, as reported, consisted in asserting that "our interests in Europe do not conflict with English interests and it is a great mistake to see the 'hand of England' everywhere." His case in point: the Piłsudski coup in Poland. This contravened Stalin's entire worldview. Even in Asia, noted the informant, Litvinov deemed bilateral British-Soviet interests compatible, and dismissed Soviet policy toward Britain as self-defeating noise making and the Soviet military intelligence and foreign intelligence reports he saw as up to 99 percent Soviet disinformation or agents' fantasy. "Comrade Litvinov kept emphasizing that he was stating his personal opinion, which is in contradiction to our official policy," noted the informant, adding that the deputy foreign affairs commissar even warned that the USSR was blundering toward war.[133] At a Central Committee plenum of February 12, 1927, Voroshilov presented on Soviet military preparedness; the politburo criticized his draft theses: "too little said on adaptation of all industry and the economy in general to the needs of war."[134] Litvinov delivered an assessment of the international situation. Stalin, who of course already knew what Litvinov had been saying, penciled a note to Molotov during the plenum about the advisability of making a corrective statement. Molotov responded that some ironic commentary might be in order, but advised to just let the matter pass. Rykov wrote that "Stalin should make, possibly, a cautious statement."

Litvinov, however, pressed the case, addressing a letter on February 15, 1927, to Stalin, with copies to all politburo members, in which the deputy foreign affairs commissar boldly asserted that the foreign affairs commissariat collegium agreed with his analysis "at least 95 percent, maybe 100, including Chicherin." Litvinov acknowledged there was no threat of war from the East, only a certain vulnerability of the Soviet eastern rear in the event of war in the West, and that the Western threat emanated from Piłsudski, Poland's ally

Romania, and all the limitrophe states except Lithuania (Poland's enemy). But he emphasized that Poland was an independent actor, not a plaything in the hands of the West, yet avowed that it might seek to take advantage of Soviet-Western hostilities. Therefore, Soviet policy should strive not just to prevent a Polish-Baltic alliance but also to avoid creating general conditions for war, such as an artificial British-Soviet conflict, which would also cost the USSR economically. Further, because France had great influence over Poland, Litvinov urged redoubling efforts to secure an agreement with Paris via concessions in the matter of repudiated imperial Russian debts. On additional pages that are not part of the original letter (at least as assembled in the archival file), Litvinov made further comments on Germany, underscoring the likelihood and adverse consequences of Germany's moving away from its expedient flirtations with the USSR more closely toward the West. He copied his letter to some but not all members of the foreign affairs collegium (Boris Stomonyakov, Teodor Rotstein, Rakovski, Krestinsky). "I urge the politburo to discuss the above and to point out to the foreign affairs commissariat which conclusions are incorrect," Litvinov brazenly concluded—as if he had himself just conducted an across-the-board policy review.

Evidently white hot with fury, Stalin drafted a multipage memorandum for the politburo, dated February 19 and finalized four days later, entirely in red pencil. He began by pointing out that, contrary to Litvinov, he (Stalin) had refuted him at the plenum not in his own name but on behalf of the entire politburo, and that Litvinov's assertion of 100 percent support in the foreign affairs collegium was contradicted by the remarks at the plenum by Lev Karakhan (to whom Litvinov had not sent his letter). On substance, Stalin reiterated that the number one enemy was the "English financial bourgeoisie and the conservative government," which "was conducting a policy of encircling the USSR from the East (China, Afghanistan, Persia, Turkey) and from the West (the limitrophe states and so forth)." He mocked Litvinov's assertion "that if relations deteriorate it is primarily the fault of our party press and our party orators, as if it had not been for these sins (extremism of the press and the orators) we would have a pact with England." Britain vigorously worked against the USSR's revolutionary forward policy in China, which, Stalin insisted, was essential for Soviet security and for world liberation. Stalin further argued that Litvinov misunderstood Soviet policy toward Germany, "lumping into one pile all bourgeois states and not differentiating between Germany and other 'great powers.'" Stalin himself seemed to do just that, noting that the Central Committee was abundantly clear that Soviet economic development would spark inevitable conflict with the capitalist states. "We cannot harbor illusions about the possibility of establishing 'good' and 'friendly' relations with 'all' bourgeois states," he wrote. "At some point serious conflict will arise with those bourgeois states that are known to be the most hostile toward us, and this inevitability cannot be obviated either by a moderate tone in the press or by the sagacious experience of diplomats." A socialist state, Stalin concluded, "must conduct a socialist foreign policy," which meant no shared interests "with the imperialist policies of so-called great powers," only "exploiting the contradictions among the imperialists."

Unsurprisingly, the politburo, on February 24, approved its leader's statement on Soviet foreign policy's assumptions and aims, and resolved to compel the foreign affairs commissariat to follow Central Committee's directives as well as to desist from pursuing the debate questioning the British as "the main enemy." As if on cue, that same day the British foreign minister passed to Moscow a sharply worded note, replete with excerpts from Soviet leaders' speeches, demanding the USSR immediately cease anti-British propaganda and military support for revolution abroad. Mirror-image "propaganda" comments on the Soviet Union could have been assembled from the speeches of British political figures, yet, as Litvinov warned, relations were on a knife's edge. Still, the foreign affairs commissariat, following the thrashing by Stalin, responded to London with threats.[135]

Stalin, apparently unintentionally, was driving the USSR into a state of siege. As it happened, the day after the British note, workers at several Leningrad factories went on strike, and the disaffected staged a demonstration on the city's Vasilyev Island demanding freedom of speech and the press, and free elections to factory committees and soviets. Instead of seeing this as an expression of worker aspirations, the regime saw proletarians offering themselves up as accomplices to a foreign intervention by the international bourgeoisie.[136] Amid a swirl of defeatist talk in society reported by the OGPU, Stalin began to try to tamp down the rumormongering. "War will not happen, neither in spring nor fall of this year," he stated to the workers of the Moscow railroad shops, in words carried in *Pravda* (March 3, 1927). "There will be no war this year because our enemies are not ready for war, because our enemies fear the results of war more than anyone else, because the workers in the West do not want to fight against the USSR, and fighting without the workers is impossible, and finally because we are conducting a firm and unwavering policy of peace, and this hinders war with our country."[137] But reports he was getting continued to raise questions about the Soviet homefront. "In the event of external complications," a top official of the central consumer cooperative wrote to Stalin and the politburo that spring, "we do not have a secure peasant rear." His main point was that the current level of exports of agricultural products and raw materials—"less than half the prewar level"—could not pay for the necessary industrialization.[138]

## IMPLOSION

Lenin had taught that capitalism would be weakened, perhaps fatally, if it could be cut off from its colonial and semicolonial territories, from which it extracted cheap labor, raw materials, and markets. He also deemed the colonial peoples a "strategic reserve" for the proletarian revolution in the advanced countries of Europe.[139] Therefore, Soviet strategy would not rely solely or even primarily on Communists in Asia, but befriend the class enemy, bourgeois national parties, and restrain foreign Communists from forming soviets. When the Indian Communist Roy rebuked Lenin and demanded the formation of soviets in the colonial world, too, Lenin continued to insist that on the whole, workers in colonial settings were too few and too weak to seize power, but he conceded that soviets would be appropriate in some cases. Thus, both the prevention of soviets and their formation were fully Leninist.

Stalin's thinking on Asia evolved within the Leninist mold. He believed that Communist parties and workers in colonial settings should support consolidation of independent "revolutionary-democratic national" states against "imperialist forces," a struggle analogous not to the Bolshevik revolution but to Russian events of 1905 and February 1917. "In October 1917 the international conditions were extraordinarily favorable for the Russian revolution," he told the Indonesian Communists in 1926. "Such conditions do not exist now, for there is no imperialist war, there is no split between the imperialists.... Therefore, you must begin with revolutionary-democratic demands."[140] But Stalin also advised that the proposed colonial-world alliance with the bourgeoisie had to be a "revolutionary bloc," a joining of "the Communist party and the party of the revolutionary bourgeoisie." His model was China.

China in the 1920s was still rent by the chaos that ensued after the downfall of the emperor and creation of a republic in 1911. In Peking, the capital, a quasi-government was internationally recognized. But it was really just a local war-lord, one of many holding regional power around the country. In the south, a rival capital in Canton (Guangzhou) had been established by the Nationalists or Guomindang, a movement that sought to appeal to the lower orders, but not on the basis of class; rather, the Guomindang was an umbrella supraclass National-ist movement, which held significant appeal but was diffuse. At the same time, large numbers of Soviet advisers in the country helped transform a loose collection of militant intellectuals into the Chinese Communist party, which became linked to an urban labor movement at cotton mills, docks, power plants, railways and tramways, printing, and precision machine building that spread a political vocabulary and worldview of class alongside nationalism.[141] When the Chinese Communists held their founding congress in July 1921 at a school for girls in the French concession of Shanghai, present were two Comintern officials, one special envoy of a leading Chinese Communist who could not attend, and twelve delegates, representing fifty-three party members in total.[142] (Mao Zedong attended as a delegate from Hunan province in the interior.) By mid-1926, the Chinese Communist party had grown to perhaps 20,000. A mere 120 full-time apparatchiks were on the rolls as of July 1926, mostly in Shanghai, Canton, and Hunan.[143] Still, within one year of July 1926 the party would triple in size to nearly 60,000.[144] But Soviet advisers also helped transform the loose personal webs of the Guomindang into a similarly Leninist-style hierarchical, militarized party. The Guomindang had perhaps 5,000 more members than the Commu-nists, and they were better educated: one fifth had been to a university. But mem-bership in the Guomindang often amounted to a mere status marker: in answer to a questionnaire about their party-related activities, more than one third answered "nothing." Another 50 percent claimed to have engaged in some pro-paganda work. Only 6 percent had participated in mass actions.[145] The Commu-nists were a party of activists. That said, neither party was a genuine mass party: China had nearly 500 million people.

Comintern policy compelled the Chinese Communists to become the junior partner in a coalition with the Guomindang, in order to strengthen the latter's role as a bulwark against "imperialism" (British influence). To that end, beyond creating two parallel, deadly rival parties in forced alliance, Soviet advisers also built a real, disciplined army in China.[146] The Soviets had declined the request of Sun Yat-sen, the founder of the Guomindang, to send Red Army troops to

Manchuria as dangerously provocative, possibly summoning "a Japanese intervention."[147] But the Soviets did furnish him with weapons, finances, and military advisers. The Soviets sent perhaps $100,000 annually, a substantial subsidy, to the Chinese Communist party, but more than 10,000,000 rubles annually in military aid to the Guomindang.[148] Part of that went into the Whampoa (Huangpu) Military Academy near Canton, opened in 1925, which was led by the Sun Yat-sen protégé and chief of staff, Chiang Kai-shek (b. 1887), who had been trained in Japan.[149] After Sun Yat-sen died of liver cancer on March 12, 1925, at age fifty-eight, Chiang won the succession struggle. A Soviet adviser deemed him "conceited, reserved, and ambitious," but nonetheless thought him useful, provided he was "praised in a delicate manner" and treated "on the basis of equality. And never showing that one wants to usurp even a particle of his power."[150] In truth, Soviet advisers on the ground, while overestimating the value of their own expertise and advice, tended to look down upon Chinese officers, and often usurped the positions of Chinese nominally in charge. Still, the Whampoa Academy helped conjure into being the strongest army in China, which Chiang Kai-shek commanded.[151]

Ideologically, Leninism conflated anti-imperialism with anticapitalism, but many Chinese intellectuals, including those who had become Marxists, concluded that the depredations China suffered at the hands of foreign powers made anti-imperialism the bedrock task.[152] Trotsky, in a note to himself, wrote that "the main criterion for us [in China] is not the constant fact of national oppression but the changing course of the class struggle," precisely the opposite of the sentiment in China.[153] Stalin held that world revolution needed the supposedly "bourgeois" Guomindang to defeat the warlords and their imperialist paymasters, thereby uniting China, and that the Communists were to enter an alliance with the "revolutionary bourgeoisie," but prepare for eventual independent action at some point.[154] For Stalin, therefore, the Chinese Communist alliance with the Guomindang presupposed betrayal: Communists were to win positions at the base of the joint movement, and then apply leverage, as in mechanics, from the bottom up.[155] This would enable the Chinese Communists to capture the "revolution" from within. Soviet policy called the Communist alliance with the Guomindang a "bloc within."

Compared with the debacles in Germany, Bulgaria, and Estonia, China long stood out as the Comintern's shining success.[156] Under the surface, however, the multiple Comintern advisers supported their own protégés, fragmenting the

Chinese political scene, and competed to undermine each other. "The other day, in the course of a lengthy conversation with Stalin, it became evident that he believes the Communists have dissolved into the Guomindang, that they lack an independent standing organization, and that the Guomindang is 'mistreating' them," Grigory Zarkhin, known as Voitinsky, complained to Lev Karakhan, the Soviet ambassador to Peking, on April 25, 1925. "Comrade Stalin, expressing his regrets over the Communists' dependent condition, evidently thought that such a situation was historically unavoidable at the current time. He was extremely surprised when we explained that the Communists have their own organization, more cohesive than the Guomindang, that the Communists have the right of criticism within the Guomindang, and that the work of the Guomindang itself to a great degree is being carried out by our comrades." Voitinsky attributed Stalin's misinformed views to the reports of Mikhail Grusenberg, known as Borodin, a Belorussian Jew educated in Latvia who had worked as a school principal in Chicago.[157] But Voitinsky, who was supposed to uphold the bloc-within alliance, instead pushed for independence of the Communists. Events also pulled in this direction.

Perhaps the greatest underlying conflict was Chiang Kai-shek's distrust of the Communists, even as he coveted Soviet military aid. Chiang had headed a mission to Moscow on Sun's behalf in 1923. "Judging by what I saw, it is not possible to trust the Russian Communist party," he had written in a private letter. "What they told us in Soviet Russia we can believe only about 30 percent."[158] On March 20, 1926, he forced the arrest of all political commissars attached to military units, who were mostly Communists, placed Soviet advisers under house arrest, and disarmed worker strike committees. Chiang wanted to suppress trade unions and use punitive expeditions to put down peasant unrest (and seize their rice stocks to feed the army). He also had his security forces torture Chinese Communists to extract information about plots. Communists in China again formally sought Moscow's authorization to withdraw from the bloc within and strike back at Chiang, but Stalin refused. In May 1926, Chiang had the Guomindang Central Executive expel all Communists from senior posts, though he did release the interned Soviet advisers. In Moscow, a politburo commission on May 20 heard a report on Chiang Kai-shek's "coup."[159] But Stalin upheld the bloc within.[160]

Trotsky had paid scant attention to China.[161] He did chair a committee that proposed preempting a feared British-Japanese alliance by declaring Manchurian "autonomy," effectively bribing Japan with the offer of a satellite, the same way the Soviets had obtained Outer Mongolia.[162] But Trotsky went on medical leave to Berlin and publicly remained silent on China. Zinoviev ignited an uproar, however, which infuriated Stalin. Zinoviev had long been the main Comintern spokesperson for the bloc-within policy and had even called the Guomindang "a workers' and peasants' (multiclass) party." As late as February 1926, Zinoviev had been urging acceptance of a Guomindang request to be admitted to the Comintern.[163]

In July 1926, Chiang Kai-shek launched the Northern Expedition against the warlords to expand Guomindang rule over all of China with the planning support of Vasily Blyukher, the chief Soviet military adviser attached to the Guodminang government at Nanjing. While pressing the unification offensive between July and December 1926, the Guomindang split: a leftist faction established its own army at a base in the central city of Wuhan, an agglomeration of Hankow and other cities, in the Yangtze basin, west of Shanghai. During the Northern Expedition, Chiang decided to advance eastward on Shanghai, against the urgings of Borodin. As his army stood outside the city, its Communist-influenced trade unions called a general strike and mobilized their pickets in their third bid to seize Shanghai from its warlord ruler. By the end of March 1927, 500,000 workers had walked out, in a city of nearly 3 million. The uprising in Shanghai was outside the "bloc within" policy; some local Chinese Communist leaders aimed to form a governing soviet. But the Comintern ordered the Communists in Shanghai to put away their weapons and not oppose Chiang's army, which, as a result, entered Shanghai on April 1 unopposed. "Chiang Kai-shek is submitting to discipline," Stalin told some 3,000 functionaries assembled in Moscow's Hall of Columns in the House of Trade Unions on April 5. "Why make a coup d'état? Why drive away the Right when we have the majority and the Right listens to us?" Stalin conceded that "Chiang Kai-shek has perhaps no sympathy for the revolution," but added that the general was "leading the army and cannot do otherwise against the imperialists." The right wing of the Guomindang, Stalin underscored, had "connections with the rich merchants and can raise money from them. So they have to be utilized to the end, squeezed out like a lemon, and then flung away."[164]

Portents of disaster were everywhere, however. On April 6, 1927, at 11:00 a.m., crowds attacked the Soviet embassy in Peking and the metropolitan police, having solicited the consent of the wider foreign diplomatic corps, entered the Soviet compound and hauled off incriminating documents about Soviet-supported subversion in China.[165] In Shanghai, meanwhile, Chiang Kai-shek's head of special services was arranging with the leading gangsters to mount an assault on the Reds. On April 12, irregulars recruited by the gangs as well as Guomindang forces smashed the Shanghai headquarters of the Chinese Communists. Over the next two days, in the pouring rain, they used machine guns and rifles to massacre Communists and labor activists in key Shanghai wards. Several hundred people were killed, perhaps more; thousands of rifles were confiscated from workers; and Communists were rounded up in house-to-house searches.[166] The Comintern ordered workers in the city to avoid conflict with Chiang's forces—who were slaughtering them. The order was not implemented, but it endured in infamy.[167] Communist survivors fled to the countryside.

On April 13, a previously scheduled three-day Soviet Central Committee plenum opened in Moscow. Most of the nasty debate concerned the economy. But a Zinoviev ally proposed that a review of policy on the Chinese revolution be added to the agenda; Stalin kept interrupting him, but then promised discussion. Zinoviev then ambushed the plenum with fifty-plus pages of "theses" condemning Stalin's mistakes on China, arguing that China was ripe for a socialist revolution and the Guomindang under Chiang Kai-shek were fated to become an antisocialist dictatorship such as Ataturk in Turkey, while China's workers and peasants were being forced to fight the Guomindang with the equivalent of bamboo.[168] Trotsky and Stalin, at the April 15 session, exchanged barbs over Chiang's assault:

TROTSKY: So far, this matter has proceeded with your help.
STALIN (interrupting): With your help! . . .
TROTSKY: We did not advance Chiang, we did not send him our
   autographed portraits.
STALIN: Ha, ha, ha.

In fact, Chiang Kai-shek was an honorary member of the Comintern executive committee, and only a few days before his April 12 launch of attacks on Chinese Communists, the Bolshevik upper crust had received autographed photographs of him, distributed by the Comintern (soon letters would arrive requesting that the photos be returned).[169] Stalin's faction shouted out to suspend stenography of the plenum, which adjourned without answering the opposition's charges. Stalin did permit Zinoviev's theses to be appended to the minutes, but a secret circular from the Central Committee press department warned that the plenum had forbidden open discussion of events in China; at the same time, in several provincial party newspapers, articles appeared attempting to refute the opposition's arguments about a debacle in China.[170]

In the terms of the Marxist-Leninist straitjacket, Chiang and the bourgeoisie had "betrayed" the Chinese revolution and thrown in their lot with the feudals and the latter's imperialist paymasters. In fact, he had not succumbed to money interests: he was just anti-Communist. Chiang did allow Borodin and Blyukher to "escape," and continued to seek Moscow's good graces even after his massacre. And truth be told, for Stalin, the strong Guomindang army still seemed the best bet for the unification and stability in China. Chiang continued his drive northward, at great cost, to defeat the warlords and drive out the imperialists. On May Day 1927 Chiang's portrait was carried through Red Square alongside those of Lenin, Stalin, and Marx. But Stalin was accused of standing by the "reactionary" bourgeois and betraying the Chinese revolution. Trotsky, who had made his first public criticisms of China policy only on March 31, 1927, began to argue, mostly retrospectively, that the USSR should have allowed Chinese Communists to exit from the bloc within and form soviets.[171] But it had been only during the Nationalist Northern Expedition to overcome the warlords and unite China that the Chinese Communist party had belatedly become something of a national political force. Still, the opposition critique, even if belated and pie in the sky, highlighted how the bloc within, which had presupposed a Chinese Communist takeover from within, had instead permitted a Guomindang takeover. Thanks to the Soviet Union, the Guomindang had an army; the Chinese Communists did not. No Communist party cells existed in the Guomindang army until very late, and even then they were pathetic.[172]

Stalin had boasted that an eventual betrayal was built into the bloc within, and he was right—but he was not the one to do the betraying. Chiang Kai-shek had beat him to the punch and, in the meantime, Stalin was still wholly dependent on Chiang as the instrument against British influence ("imperialism") in China.

Soviet foreign policy appeared trapped in a cul-de-sac of its own making. Chicherin, on extended medical leave on the French Riviera and in Germany, seeking treatment for his ailments, not all of them psychosomatic (diabetes, polyneuritis), wrote to Stalin and Rykov that Bukharin's idiotic anti-German tirades in the Soviet press had done so much damage that "I am returning to Moscow in order to request that I be relieved of the foreign affairs commissariat position."[173] The more immediate worry, however, was Britain. On May 12, 1927, the British police in London began a massive four-day raid on the premises of the

All-Russia Cooperative Society (at 49 Moorgate), which operated under British law; the same building housed the official Soviet trade mission offices. Safes and strongboxes were cracked open with pneumatic drills and documents hauled away.[174] Cipher personnel were beaten and codes and cipher books confiscated; Lenin's portrait was defaced.[175] A similar incident several years earlier had severely damaged Soviet-German trade; this time, too, Moscow did not "show weakness." On May 13, the politburo resolved to launch a belligerent press campaign and public demonstrations to assail Britain for warmongering.[176]

Around this time Japan declined renewed Soviet feelers for a non-aggression pact.[177] As if this were not enough for Stalin to worry about, Chiang Kai-shek's actions had breathed new life into Trotsky's rants. "Stalin and Bukharin are betraying Bolshevism at its very core, its proletarian revolutionary internationalism," Trotsky complained to Krupskaya (May 17, 1927). "The defeat of the German revolution in 1923, the defeats in Bulgaria and Estonia, the defeat of the [1926] general strike in England, and of the Chinese revolution in April have all seriously weakened international Communism."[178] The next day, the extended eighth plenum of the Comintern opened, with Stalin determined to have his line on China reconfirmed.[179] In his speech on May 24, he ridiculed Trotsky, asserting that he "resembles an actor rather than a hero, and an actor should not be confused with a hero under any circumstances," adding, in reference to the British prime minister, "There comes into being something like a united front from [Austen] Chamberlain to Trotsky."[180] Trotsky shot back: "Nothing has facilitated Chamberlain's work as much as Stalin's false policy, especially in China."[181]

Stalin was on the back foot. The Comintern plenum, unsurprisingly, voted a resolution that "declares the proposals of the opposition (Trotsky, Zinoviev) to be plainly opportunist and capitulationist."[182] But on May 27, the conservative Tory government in Britain stunned the Soviet dictator by breaking off diplomatic relations.[183] Stalin was infuriated: The imperialists gave refuge to anti-Soviet émigré organizations, financed anti-Soviet national undergrounds on Soviet soil (in Ukraine and the Caucasus), sent in swarms of agents, then got on their high horse about alleged subversion by the Comintern?! It was a blow, however. Britain had become one of the Soviet Union's top trading partners.[184] And it looked like the British conservatives might be ginning up their working class for a war against the Soviets. The Soviet press filled with warnings of imminent war and mass meetings were held to discuss war preparations, which unwittingly fanned defeatist talk.[185] Stalin, knowing Britain was not preparing to invade, nonetheless was convinced the imperialists would incite proxies into fighting. Rykov appears to have believed the same.[186] Britain was known to be busily building a broad anti-Soviet bloc out of Romania, Finland, and the Baltic states, while working to reconcile Germany and Poland.[187]

Under immense pressure, Stalin began an about-face on China, sending a long telegram on June 1, 1927, to the Comintern agents in Wuhan at the left Guomindang base, instructing them to form a revolutionary army of 50,000, to subject "reactionary" officers to military tribunal, to outlaw all contact with Chiang Kai-shek—the commander in chief of the existing army, to which all the soldiers and officers had sworn an oath—and to curb peasant "excesses."[188] There was no way to carry out such an order. Manabenda Rath Roy, a recipient, showed the telegram to the left Guomindang leader, who was already inclined to seek reconciliation with the right Guomindang at Nanjing, and now saw evidence of Moscow's own treachery.[189]

## TERRORISM

Notwithstanding the gravity of developments, on June 5, 1927, Stalin began his summer holiday in his beloved Sochi, this time at the grander dacha no. 7, known as Puzanovka, named for the former owner, on a bluff between Sochi and Matsesta. "When we doctors arrived at the dacha, Nadezhda Sergeyevna Alliluyeva greeted us, a very dear and hospitable woman," recalled Ivan Valedinsky. "That year I examined Stalin three times: before he began the course of Matsesta baths, during, and at the end. Just as in the previous year, Stalin complained of pain in the muscles of his extremities." Stalin also underwent X-rays and an electrocardiogram. Nothing abnormal emerged. Even his blood pressure measured normal. "This examination generally showed that Stalin's organism was fully healthy," Valedinsky recalled. "We noted his jolly disposition and attentive, lively look." The warm baths were followed by extended lounging naked, except for a wrap, to allow the blood to flow up to the skin, muscles, and extremities. "This therapeutic device brought warmth to Stalin's hands and feet," Valedinsky noted. Following the course of medicinal baths, Stalin invited Valedinsky and the other physicians on Saturday for a "brandy," which lasted until the wee hours on Sunday. Early in the gathering, Vasya and Svetlana appeared on the terrace. "Iosif Vissarionovich was enlivened, began to play soldiers with them, fired at a target, in fact Stalin fired very accurately."[190]

The day after Stalin began his holiday, a new law on counterrevolutionary crimes was incorporated into the RSFSR criminal code. Counterrevolutionary offenses were already sweepingly and vaguely defined but now they were expanded. Merely trying to "weaken," not overthrow, the Soviet system became counterrevolution; "terrorist acts" against regime personnel or representatives of the workers' movement were placed on a par with an armed uprising, incurring the death penalty; and the penalty for failure to report foreknowledge of a counterrevolutionary crime was raised from one to ten years.[191] This was Stalin's initiative, spurred by exposure of the OGPU double game to entrap émigrés, known as the Trust, and a resulting attempt on June 3 by double agents who were forced by émigrés to set off a bomb in Moscow at a OGPU dormitory (at Lesser Lubyanka, 3/6), which failed.[192] But on June 7, a compartmentalized émigré terrorist outfit that was unknown to the OGPU did manage to detonate a bomb in Leningrad's central party club at Moika Canal, 59, wounding at least twenty-six people; one died of the wounds. The three terrorists involved managed to get back to Finland.[193] An even more spectacular terrorist act occurred that very same day on the platform of the Warsaw train station: a journalist for a Belorussian-language newspaper in independent Lithuania, Boris Koverda, shot the Soviet envoy to Poland, Pyotr Voikov. Émigré monarchists had had their eye on Voikov because he had been the chairman of the Ural soviet that had murdered the Romanovs.[194] But how the nineteen-year-old son of an anti-Communist émigré evaded the plethora of uniformed and plainclothes police at the station remains mysterious; indeed, how Koverda knew Voikov would be at the station that morning remains mysterious as well.[195] (Voikov was there to see off the Soviet diplomatic personnel passing through on their way to Moscow after their eviction from London.) The thirty-nine-year-old Voikov died an hour later in a Polish military hospital.

For Stalin, the suspicious assassination on Polish territory followed hard upon the British raid in London, the British-initiated break in relations, and the blowup in China, where Soviet policy was geared to denying a foothold to the imperialists. "I feel the hand of England," he wrote on the back of a ciphered telegram from Molotov on June 8 regarding Voikov's murder. "They want to provoke (us into) a conflict with Poland. They want to repeat Sarajevo." Stalin recommended staging one or two trials of English spies, and in the meantime ordered that "all the prominent monarchists in our prisons and concentration camps should immediately be declared hostages," with "five or ten" to be shot, accompanied by announcements in the press.[196] Molotov had Stalin's directive formulated as a politburo decree.

That day the OGPU received additional extrajudicial powers, including the reintroduction of emergency tribunals, known as troikas, to expedite cases (formally approved only in some provinces to aid counterinsurgency operations).[197] Molotov wrote back on June 9: "A few comrades hesitated over the necessity of publishing the government communique" on retaliatory repressions, "but now everyone agrees that it was time."[198] On the night of June 9–10, some twenty nobles, who had recently been arrested as part of a monarchist "organization," were accused of plotting "terrorist acts" against Soviet leaders and executed without trial. Five were said to be agents of British intelligence.[199] Party organizations mobilized meetings at hundreds of factories to affirm the executions, and workers were quoted approvingly: "Finally the Cheka got down to business."[200]

"My personal opinion," Stalin wrote from Sochi in a telegram to Mężyński: "the agents of London here are buried deeper than it seems, and they will still surface." He wanted Artuzov, of counterintelligence, to publicize the arrests so as to smash the efforts of the British to recruit agents and to entice Soviet youth into the OGPU.[201] In July, *Pravda* would report the executions of a group of "terrorist-White Guards" supposedly under the direction of a British spy in Leningrad.[202] In Siberia, where not a single espionage case had been initiated in the second half of 1926, many were launched in 1927.[203] Mężyński secretly reported to the politburo that the OGPU had conducted 20,000 house-to-house searches and arrested more than 9,000 people Union-wide.[204] "A big black cloud, fear is suspended over the whole society and paralyzing everything," a Swedish diplomat reported to Stockholm.[205] Stalin's mind and the country's political atmosphere were melding.

## EMPEROR HAS NO CLOTHES

Persistent war rumors incited runs on shops, hoarding, and boasts of refusals to fight or sabotage in the event of conflict that were fixed in the OGPU political mood reports, echoes of the regime's deepest fears.[206] Chicherin returned to Moscow from his extended medical holiday in Europe around June 15. "Everybody in Moscow was talking war," he would tell the American foreign correspondent and Soviet sympathizer Louis Fischer. "I tried to dissuade them. 'Nobody is planning to attack us,' I insisted. Then a colleague enlightened me. He said, 'Shh. We know that. But we need this against Trotsky.'"[207] Chicherin's efforts to defuse international tensions are understandable, but the war scare emerged directly out of the inbuilt structural paranoia of the revolution (capitalist encirclement) combined with the regime's defiant foreign policy.[208] Relations with the enemy (the capitalist powers) could never amount to more than expediency; internal critics, whatever their professed intentions, broadcast disunity, weakened an encircled USSR, and incited external enemies. And party officials, not all sufficiently schooled in Marxism-Leninism, were susceptible to siren songs.

When Stalin wrote to Molotov from Sochi (June 17) that "in order to strengthen the rear, we must restrain the opposition immediately," he was not merely self-serving and not cynical.[209] The struggle with Trotsky was now even more a matter of state security for him, even as it continued to be obsessively personal. After reviewing the transcript of a punitive Central Control Commission session, Stalin angrily wrote to Molotov (June 23) that "Zinoviev and Trotsky, not the commission members, did the interrogating and the accusing. It is odd that some of the commission members did not show. Where's Sergo? Where has he gone and why is he hiding? Shame on him. . . . Will Trotsky and Zinoviev really be handed this 'transcript' to distribute! That's all we need."[210]

Orjonikidze, in fact, had been present: Trotsky had directed a long soliloquy partly at him. "I say that you are set on a course for the bureaucrat, for the functionary, but not for the masses," he stated, through repeated interruptions. "The organization operates as a vast internal mutual support structure, mutual protection."[211] Orjonikidze nonetheless hesitated to bring down the hammer. He remarked of Zinoviev and Kamenev, "they have brought a good deal of benefit to our party."[212] The votes for and against expulsion were more or less evenly divided. Orjonikidze, Kalinin, and even Voroshilov argued that the matter of expulsion of opposition members from the Central Committee should be deferred to the upcoming Party Congress. Stalin insisted that his vote be counted in absentia, while Molotov got Kalinin to switch sides, providing the margin for expulsion.[213] Orjonikidze, however, would substitute a reprimand instead. Trotsky told him all the same that "the extirpation of the opposition was only a matter of time."[214]

Stalin found time to exchange letters from Sochi with a young schoolteacher, Serafim Pokrovsky (b. 1905), who had entered into a written argument with the dictator over whether party policy in 1917 had favored an alliance with the whole peasantry or just the poor peasantry. "When I began this correspondence with you I thought I was dealing with a man who was seeking the truth," the dictator wrote testily on June 23, 1927, accusing the teacher of impudence. "One must possess the effrontery of an ignoramus and the self-complacency of a narrow-minded equilibrist to turn things upside down as unceremoniously as you do, esteemed Pokrovsky. I think the time has come to stop corresponding with you. I. Stalin."[215] Stalin *hated* to be contradicted on matters of theory.

The China debacle had the potential to dominate the upcoming 15th Party Congress, which is why Stalin pushed for expulsion beforehand. On June 27, Trotsky wrote to the Central Committee: "This is the worst crisis since the revolution."[216] Supporters of Stalin's line clung to the left-wing Guomindang faction in Wuhan, where Communists held two portfolios (agriculture, labor), but that same day, Stalin wrote to Molotov, "I am afraid that Wuhan will lose its nerve and come under Nanjing" (i.e., Chiang Kai-shek). Still, Stalin held out hope: "We must insist adamantly on Wuhan not submitting to Nanjing while there is still an opportunity to insist. Losing Wuhan as a separate center means losing at least some center for the revolutionary movement, losing the possibility of free assembly and rallies for the workers, losing the possibility of the open existence of the Communist party, losing the possibility of an open revolutionary press—in a word, losing the possibility of openly organizing the proletariat and the revolution." He proposed that Wuhan be bribed. "I assure you, it is worth giving Wuhan an extra 3–5 million."[217] But Molotov, uncharacteristically, had become panicky. "A single vote will wind up being decisive," he wrote to Stalin on July 4. "I'm increasingly wondering whether you may need to come back to M[oscow] ahead of schedule." Molotov tattled to Stalin that Voroshilov, the definition of a Stalin loyalist, "is going so far as to express sweeping disparagement of 'your leadership over the past two years.'"[218]

Stalin had appointed the provincial party bosses who composed two thirds of the voting members of the Central Committee, but that body could still act against him if he manifestly failed to safeguard the revolution.[219] And yet he showed a lack of alarm. "I'm sick and lying in bed so I'll be brief," he wrote to Molotov from Sochi sometime in early July 1927. "I could come for the plenum if it's necessary and if you postpone it." Then the left Guomindang Wuhan government disarmed the workers in its midst, which caught out Stalin a second time. Still, he continued to pose as nonplussed, writing on July 8, "We used the Wuhan leadership as much as possible. Now it's time to discard them." Was he delusional? "I am not afraid of the situation in the group [his faction]. Why—I'll explain when I come." But the next day, perhaps with the news sinking in, Stalin flashed anger, accusing Molotov and Bukharin of deceiving him (not providing the full bad news about Wuhan) and Voroshilov of seizing a pretext to stop sending defense commissariat funds to Wuhan. "I hear that some people are in a repentant mood regarding our policy in China," he wrote on July 11. "When I come, I will try to prove that our policy was and remains the only correct policy." By July 15, even as the Wuhan regime, too, unleashed a terror against the Communists, Stalin refused to admit mistakes. To do so would in effect be acknowledging that the demonized opposition had a point, that their policy views went beyond personal hatred for him and were not tantamount to treason. Stalin was contemplating making Trotsky disappear by sending him abroad to Japan, evidently as ambassador. But this would have handed Trotsky an opportunity to capitalize on Stalin's failures in Asia policy and the dictator quickly forgot the idea.[220] Still, Stalin was desperate to rid himself of his longtime nemesis.

## ABOUT-FACE

Voroshilov in spring 1927 had reported grimly that existing Soviet industry just could not meet the needs of the Red Army even in rifles or machine guns, let alone advanced weapons.[221] But knowing that fact hardly required a security clearance.[222] "How can we compete with" the imperialists, one Red Army conscript was overheard to say, according to a secret police report. "They have battleships, planes, cannons, and we have nothing."[223] Small wonder that in July 1927, with Stalin still in Sochi, Unszlicht traveled yet again to Berlin to try to win an agreement for joint industrial production, telling the Germans the USSR expected to be attacked by Poland and Romania. The Soviet proposals had grown to staggering scale, and the Germans were wary. The break in British-Soviet relations had sparked an internal debate in the German foreign ministry over, as one participant wrote, "whether Germany's ties with Russia are worth enough to our present and future political interests so that it pays to assume the political expenses and risks involved in maintaining them." Some Germans sensed desperation. "The Soviet government is reckoning with a catastrophe in the near future," a usually sympathetic Count Brockdorff-Rantzau, Germany's ambassador to Moscow, reported.[224] Berlin demurred on Unszlicht's proposals. Germany had emerged as one of the USSR's two top trading partners (the other being Britain), a circumstance analogous to tsarist times, but this was far below Soviet desiderata, and politically, Moscow proved unable to pry Berlin from London and Paris. The Soviets could not afford to see bilateral relations with Germany come wholly unglued, too, however.[225] And Stalin, even now, would not give up on German help for Soviet military industry. Still, the party press lashed out at Germany.

Stalin returned from holiday early, reaching Moscow on Saturday, July 23.[226] The plenum was scheduled to open six days later. On its eve, July 28, *Pravda* published a long-winded attack by Stalin on the opposition at this time of peril. "It is hardly open to doubt that the basic question of the present is the question of the threat of a new imperialist war," he noted. "It is not a matter of some undefined and intangible 'danger' of a new war. It is a matter of a real and genuine threat of a new war in general and of a war against the USSR in particular . . . there is a struggle for consumer markets, for capital export markets, for seas and dry routes to these markets, for a new division of the world." What held the imperialists back, he averred, was fear of mutual weakening, in the face of the revolutionary possibilities represented by the Soviet Union and the international proletariat. "Soviet people will never forget the rape, looting, and military incursions that our country suffered just a few years ago thanks to the kindness of English capital," Stalin continued. "But the English bourgeoisie does not love to fight with its own hands. It always preferred to conduct a war with others' hands," finding useful idiots to "pull its chestnuts out of the fire." Accordingly, he concluded, "our mission is to strengthen the rear and cleanse it of dross, including 'nobleman' terrorists and incendiaries who set fire to our mills and factories, because the defense of our country is impossible without a strong, revolutionary rear." The British, Stalin asserted, were subsidizing an anti-Soviet underground, in Ukraine and the Caucasus, Leningrad and Moscow, financing "bands of spies and terrorists, who blow up bridges, set fire to factories, and commit acts of terrorism against USSR ambassadors."[227] That was the context in which to view the opposition.

At the plenum, Molotov accused Trotsky and Kamenev of disorganizing the country's rear while the external enemy marshaled troops, and stated that such people "should be imprisoned." Voroshilov gave the sharpest speech, turning at one point to Zinoviev to state, "You know absolutely nothing." Trotsky immediately reacted: "This is the one correct thing you can say about yourself." Trotsky accused Voroshilov of having participated in the demotion of military men who were superior to himself (Primakov, Putna). Voroshilov replied that Trotsky had executed Communists during the civil war. Trotsky: Voroshilov "lies like a dishonorable scoundrel." Voroshilov: "You are the scoundrel and the self-styled enemy of our party."[228] And so it went, for days on end. Thirteen members of the Central Committee submitted an "opposition platform" they wanted discussed at the upcoming 15th Party Congress, but Adolf Joffe and others in the opposition objected that the document had been issued without consultation among themselves, behavior resembling the very "apparatus" Trotsky had long criticized.[229] Despite Stalin's vehement insistence that Zinoviev and Trotsky be expelled for factional activity, the plenum accepted the proposal of Orjonikidze, head of the party Central Control Commission, whereby the pair were allowed to declare their loyalty and remain.

China policy remained the greatest thorn in Stalin's side. In late July, *Pravda* had stated, "The slogan of [forming] soviets is correct now."[230] The Comintern now authorized a series of armed actions in China, what would be called the autumn harvest uprisings. Trotsky's critique that Stalin had assumed the bourgeoisie in China could lead a revolution when it was counterrevolutionary stung. In his speech to the joint plenum, Stalin had denied that he had instructed the Chinese Communists to kowtow to the Guomindang or to restrain the peasants from agrarian struggle.[231] During the Moscow plenum, on August 7, the Chinese Communists met in emergency session in Hankow; Stalin had dispatched the Georgian Communist and Youth League functionary Beso Lominadze to rescue the situation. Bukharin had wired instructions to criticize the Chinese Communist leadership for "opportunistic mistakes." The whole thing was a terrible muddle: the outgoing Chinese Central Committee was accused of failing to anticipate the Guomindang betrayal in a bloc within that these same Chinese Communists had detested but been forced into by Moscow; the Chinese Communists who had not been allowed by Moscow to form soviets were accused themselves of having disarmed the workers and peasants. Strangest of all, the Chinese Communists' annihilation by the Guomindang was said to have accelerated the bourgeois-democratic stage of the Chinese revolution.

The decimated Chinese party now had to prepare for suicidal mass insurrections.[232] The Soviet politburo—which no longer included Zinoviev, Kamenev, or Trotsky—quietly directed the Comintern to smuggle $300,000 in hard currency to the Chinese Communists, and Stalin ordered a shipment of 15,000 guns and 10 million cartridges.[233] As Mao Zedong (b. 1893) observed at the Hankow session presided over by Lominadze, "power comes from the barrel of a gun." But the Guomindang, thanks to Stalin, still had far more of them.

## THEATER OF THE ABSURD

Shortages had become endemic and the rift in the understanding of socialism between the masses, for whom it meant freedom, abundance, and social justice, and the party regime, for whom it meant tighter political control and sacrifices for industrialization, filled police surveillance reports. "We need butter, not socialism," workers at Leningrad's Putilov factory demanded on September 6.[234] Two days later, a joint session of the politburo and Central Control Commission presidium was held in connection with the opposition's plan to submit its own "platform" to the upcoming Party Congress. Trotsky and Zinoviev were summoned to the politburo from which they had been expelled. Zinoviev pointed out that at the party plenum, when Kamenev had suggested they would introduce a platform, no one had objected but now it was denounced as a criminal act. After Zinoviev and his former minion Uglanov got into a shouting match and Stalin interrupted again, Zinoviev said to him, "Everything bad that you could do to us you've already done." Molotov bitingly asked Zinoviev if he and Kamenev had been "brave in October 1917?" Zinoviev reminded them that not just Trotsky but Bukharin had opposed Brest-Litovsk in 1918, to which Kaganovich interjected, "Bukharin will not repeat his mistakes." Nikolai Muralov, the Trotsky supporter, called the resolution condemning the opposition for its platform a feuilleton and challenged them to allow all party members to read the platform and decide for themselves. "Mothers come [to party meetings] with babies and the sound of the reader is interrupted by the sound of the baby sucking at the breast," he noted. "Babies with their mother's milk suck in this hatred of the opposition." Bukharin blamed the victims: "I consider that it is the party that is subjected to systematic attacks and aggression by the opposition." Zinoviev: "You are not the party." Bukharin: "Thieves always shout, 'Catch the thief!' Zinoviev is always doing this. (Commotion in the hall. Chairman rings the bell. Inaudible exclamation from Zinoviev.)"[235]

Trotsky showed that he, too, could be vicious. When the Stalin loyalist Avel Yenukidze was given the floor, Trotsky interrupted to point out that in 1917 Yenukidze "had been arguing against the Bolsheviks when I pulled you into the party." After Trotsky persisted, Yenukidze exploded: "Look, I have been in the party since its formation and was a Bolshevik 14 years earlier than you." Later in the meeting, when Rudzutaks took the floor, Trotsky interrupted to point out that behind his back Stalin expressed a low opinion of his administrative abilities. "You saw that in your dreams," Stalin cut in. Rudzutaks responded: "I know you, comrade Trotsky. You specialize in slandering people. . . . You have forgotten the famous telephone that Stalin allegedly installed in your apartment. You have been like a little boy or a school pupil telling lies [about wiretapping] and refused to allow a technical inspection." Trotsky: "That the telephones are eavesdropped is a fact." When Bukharin spoke, Trotsky interrupted as well, stating that Bukharin had wanted to arrest Lenin during the 1918 Brest-Litovsk negotiations with Germany. "Wonderful," Bukharin responded. "You say that that time was ideal, that during the Brest Treaty there was wide discussion and freedom of factions. And we consider that a crime."[236] Trotsky got the floor and went after Stalin, too, bringing up civil war episodes. "Lenin and I twice removed him from the Red Army when he conducted an incorrect policy," Trotsky stated. "We removed him from Tsaritsyn, then from the southern front, where he conducted an incorrect policy." When Stalin interrupted, Trotsky referred to a document he possessed from Lenin: "Lenin writes that Stalin is wrong to speak against the supreme commander, he carps, is capricious. This happened!" Stalin interrupted again. "Comrade Stalin, do not interrupt, you will have the last word, as always." Stalin: "And why not."[237]

When Stalin took the floor, he denied he had been twice removed from the front, alleging it was Trotsky who had been recalled, prompting Trotsky to interrupt him. Stalin: "You speak untruths, because you are a pathetic coward, afraid of the truth." Trotsky: "You put yourself in a laughable situation." When Trotsky pointed out that because the party had made and kept him the head of the Red Army during the civil war, Stalin was effectively slandering the party. "You're a pathetic person," Stalin said again, "bereft of an elemental feeling of truth, a coward and bankrupt, impudent and despicable, allowing yourself to speak things that utterly do not correspond to reality." Trotsky: "That's Stalin in entirety: rude and disloyal. Who is it, a leader or a huckster." Stalin's allotted time ran out, and Trotsky proposed he be given five more minutes. Stalin: "Comrade Trotsky demands equality between the Central Committee, which carries out the decisions of the party, and the opposition, which undermines these decisions. A strange business! In the name of what organization do you have the right to speak so insolently with the party?" When Zinoviev responded that before a congress party members had the right to speak, Stalin threatened to "cleave" them from the party. Zinoviev: "Don't cleave, don't threaten please." Stalin: "They say that under Lenin the regime was different, that under Lenin oppositionists were not thrown out to other locales, not exiled and so on. You have a weak memory, comrades from the opposition. Don't you recall that Lenin suggested exiling Trotsky to Ukraine? Comrade Zinoviev, is this true or not? Why are you silent?" Zinoviev: "I am not under interrogation. (Laughter, noise, the bell of the session chairman.)"[238]

And then, out it leapt again. Trotsky: "And you hide Lenin's Testament? Lenin in his Testament revealed everything about Stalin. There is nothing to add or subtract." Stalin: "You lie if you assert that anyone is concealing the Testament of Lenin. You know well that it is known to all the party. You know also, as does the party, that Lenin's Testament demolishes you, the current leader of the opposition. . . . You are pathetic, without any sense of truth, a coward, a bankrupt, insolent and impudent, who allows himself to speak of things utterly at variance with reality."[239]

One wonders why Stalin subjected himself to this exchange by summoning Trotsky and Zinoviev to the politburo. The politburo resolution, once again, called the opposition platform an effort "to create a Trotskyite party, in place of the Leninist party."[240] To Zinoviev's repeated requests to publish their platform, Stalin's answer was patently feeble: "We are not prepared to turn the party into a discussion club."[241]

The next day, September 9, 1927, Stalin received a delegation of American worker representatives. They wanted to know whether Lenin had revised Marxism in some way, whether the Communist party controlled the Soviet government and trade unions, how they knew whether the Communists had mass support in the absence of party competition. "The delegation apparently does not object to the proletariat of the USSR depriving the bourgeoisie and the landlords of their factories and workshops, of their land and railroads, banks and mines (laughter), but it seems to me that the delegation is somewhat surprised that the proletariat did not limit itself to this, but went further and deprived the bourgeoisie of political rights," Stalin responded, challenging them: "Does the bourgeoisie in Western countries, where they are in power, show the slightest magnanimity towards the working class? Do they not drive genuine revolutionary parties of the working class underground? Why should the proletariat of the USSR be called upon to show magnanimity towards their class enemy? You must be logical." The Americans also asked about the differences between Stalin and Trotsky. Stalin answered that the differences were not personal and had been outlined in publications.[242]

On September 12, Trotsky departed for a rest in the Caucasus, but that very evening Stalin sprung a nasty surprise on him. The opposition had decided to distribute their platform for the upcoming Party Congress without permission and a few of them secretly had it typed out with carbon copies, but OGPU informants and provocateurs had infiltrated the group and, on the night of September 12–13, raided the "underground printing press."[243] One of those involved had been an officer under Baron Wrangel, a "White Guard" connection with military officer status, which facilitated insinuations of a planned putsch.[244] Another of those caught in the "printing press" scandal conveniently "confessed" that his intention had been a military coup, along the lines of Piłsudski in Poland. Stalin had the central apparatus distribute multiple copies of these OGPU materials on September 22 for a meeting of the politburo and the Central Control Commission, after which the "confessions" were sent to all Central Committee members, the Comintern executive committee, and provincial party secretaries.[245] Some members of the Central Committee would remain unconvinced about accusations of a military coup, despite arrests having been made.[246] Moreover, as Mężyński and then even Stalin would admit, the White Guard officer *was* the OGPU informant.[247]

Trotsky interrupted his southern retreat and returned to Moscow to combat the provocation, but what awaited him was a Comintern executive session on September 27, at which the Stalin-appointed goons of all the foreign Communist parties verbally eviscerated and then expelled him from that body. Bukharin, without irony, said to Trotsky's face: "For you there is no Communist International, there is Stalin, or at most Stalin and Bukharin, and the rest are hirelings." Stalin summarized that "the speakers today have spoken so well, especially comrade Bukharin, that there is nothing for me to add," to which Trotsky interjected, "You're lying." Stalin: "Keep your strong words to yourself. You are discrediting yourself with this abuse. You're a Menshevik!" Only Voja Vujović, the Yugoslav who headed the Communist Youth International, sided with Trotsky, and he, too, was expelled.[248] In late September, *Pravda* reported on a case of unmasked "monarchist-terrorists" directed by British and Latvian intelligence services: here was the new meme.[249] Soviet military advisers, led by Vasily Blyukher, returned from China, having had a firsthand look at what could happen to a supposedly revolutionary struggle that had been bungled—seizure by a military figure, like Chiang Kai-shek.[250] After Chinese Communist army units had begun to conduct guerrilla actions against the Guomindang, Stalin formally shifted policy away from supporting the "bourgeois" phase of the revolution. *Pravda* in an editorial (September 30, 1927) welcomed the establishment of a "revolutionary army of Chinese workers and peasants." This looked like an unacknowledged embrace of the defeated opposition line.[251] What effect it might have in China, if any, remained to be seen.

## FRANCO-SOVIET RIFT

Sergei Witte, as tsarist finance minister, had financed Russia's 1890s industrial boom (Western machinery imports) by means of foreign borrowing (long-term loans), which he paid for on the backs of the peasantry (grain exports), and which was undergirded by a political alliance with France (the main supplier of credits), but in 1918 the Bolsheviks had repudiated tsarist-era debts, making propaganda out of necessity (an inability to pay).[252] Subsequently, in nearly every negotiation with the capitalist powers, the need to make good on those debts came up. From 1926, Moscow had entered secret negotiations with Paris offering to pay an indemnity of 60 million gold francs (approximately $12 million) each year for *sixty-two consecutive years,* in exchange for $250 million in credits now. France's government was keen on bondholder compensation, sale of French capital goods, and imports of Soviet oil, but not on using taxpayer money to finance a Communist regime. French conservatives raised hell. After the French coalition government fell for unrelated reasons, its successor added a demand for compensation of French owners of property in Russia that had been nationalized. In April 1927, French counterintelligence, in a widely reported sensation, rolled up more than 100 Soviet military intelligence agents whose handlers had relied on French Communists, who, of course, were under close police surveillance. "Documents found," the French authorities stated, "show that there is in existence a vast espionage organization, far greater than any discovered since the war."[253] Such was the fraught state of play when scandal erupted over the Soviet envoy to Paris, Cristian Rakovski, who had written a short book on the statesman Prince Klemens von Metternich but had obtained the ambassadorship, a form of exile, for supporting Trotsky.[254]

While back in Moscow for consultations in August 1927, Rakovski had signed an opposition declaration that summoned "every honest proletarian of a capitalist country" to "work actively for the defeat of his government" and "every foreign soldier who does not wish to serve the slave masters of his country to cross over to the Red Army."[255] Usually, ambassadors do not publicly call for mass treason among their hosts. But the act went well beyond Rakovski's personal foibles to the heart of the Soviet foreign policy's pretzel logic—simultaneously participating in and working to overthrow the capitalist world order.[256]

Rakovski quickly disavowed the applicability to France of his summons to treason (it still applied everywhere else), and promised a mutual "non-interference" pact, but French opponents of rapprochement fulminated. "Does a house guest promise not to steal the silverware?" the press asked.[257] In September 1927, trying to rescue the situation, the Soviets went so far as to propose a full-fledged non-aggression pact, just shy of an alliance, and even informed the Soviet public of the offer to pay large sums to private French holders of tsarist bonds. "We buy the possibility of peaceful economic relations with one of the capitalist countries in Europe, and France sells us this possibility," *Pravda* explained.[258] But nothing worked. Rakovski was declared persona non grata and, in mid-October, he got in his car and drove back to the USSR.[259] Moscow had vigorously supported its representative while he was in Paris, but at home promptly expelled him from the party for Trotskyism. "The French expelled me from Paris for having signed a declaration of the opposition," Rakovski, wearing a smart Western sports jacket, explained to the French writer Pierre Naville. "Stalin expelled me from the foreign affairs commissariat for having signed the same declaration. But in both cases they let me keep the jacket."[260] (Upon return, Soviet diplomats were required to hand over all goods acquired while abroad, except clothing.) The protracted Franco-Soviet negotiations collapsed. France stopped short of severing diplomatic relations, unlike Britain, and a replacement Soviet ambassador would arrive in Paris, but prospects remained dim for a credit agreement, let alone a Franco-Soviet pact.

## FINAL FACE-TO-FACE

The nasty September 1927 politburo confrontation was repeated at a joint plenum of the Central Committee and the Central Control Commission that took place October 21 to 23. Trotsky, in response to a proposed resolution to expel him as well as Zinoviev from the Central Committee, quoted Lenin's Testament, "Remove Stalin, who may carry the party to a split and to ruin." Stalin loyalists shouted him down: "Liar," "Traitor," Scum," and of course "Grave Digger of the Revolution." Trotsky stretched out one arm and read his text through the insults. "First a word about the so-called Trotskyism," he said. "The falsification factory is working at full steam and around the clock to construct 'Trotskyism.'" He added: "The rudeness and disloyalty about which Lenin wrote are no longer simply personal qualities; they have become the hallmark of the leading faction, they have become its policy and its regime."[261] He was right. When Trotsky revealed that the former Wrangel officer associated with the opposition "printing press" was in fact an OGPU agent, someone shouted, "This is outside the meeting agenda." Kaganovich called out, "Menshevik! Counterrevolutionary!" The chairman of the session rang and rang the bell.[262] One person threw a doorstop volume of economic statistics at Trotsky; another flung a glass of water (just as the right-wing Purishkevich had done at liberal constitutionalist Miliukov in the tsarist Duma). The stenographer recorded the following: "Renewed whistling. A constantly increasing commotion. Nothing can be heard. The chairman calls for order. More whistling. Shouts of 'Get down from the dais.' The chairman adjourns the session. Comrade Trotsky continues to read his speech, but not a single word can be heard. The members of the plenum quit their seats and begin to file out of the hall."[263]

Stalin had prepared thoroughly. He opened his speech on October 23 with his by now customary self-pity: the opposition was cursing him. "Anyway what is Stalin, Stalin is a little person. Take Lenin. Who does not know that the opposition, headed by Trotsky, during the August bloc, conducted a hooligan campaign against Lenin." He then read Trotsky's infamous private letter from 1913 to Karlo Chkheidze denouncing Lenin. "Such language, what language, pay attention, comrades. This is Trotsky writing. And he's writing about Lenin. Can one be surprised that Trotsky, who so unceremoniously treats of the great Lenin, whose boot he is not worthy of, could now vainly curse one of the many pupils of Lenin—comrade Stalin."

Mężyński had spoken about the opposition's criminal activity, citing the testimony of the arrested Wrangel officer as well as non-party intelligentsia about the opposition's illegal printing press and their "bloc" with the anti-Soviet elements, and Stalin referred back to Mężyński: "Why was it necessary to have comrade Mężyński speak about White Guards, with whom some workers of the illegal antiparty printing press were associated? In order to dispel the lie and slander that the opposition is spreading in its antiparty leaflets on this question. . . . What are the takeaways of comrade Mężyński's report? The opposition, in organizing an illegal printing press, tied itself to the bourgeois intelligentsia, and a part of this intelligentsia, in turn, proved to be connected with the White Guards contemplating a military plot."

Stalin turned to the Testament, reminding everyone that it had been read out to the delegates at the Party Congress, and that Trotsky had published a repudiation of Eastman's claim that the Testament had been concealed. He read from

Trotsky's own 1925 repudiation: "Clear, it would seem? Trotsky wrote this." Stalin then read aloud the damning Testament passages about Zinoviev and Kamenev and Trotsky. "Clear, it seems." He commented that "in reality, Lenin in his 'testament' accuses Trotsky of 'non-Bolshevism,' and in connection with Kamenev and Zinoviev during October says that their mistake was not an 'accident.' What does this mean? It means that politically one can trust neither Trotsky . . . nor Kamenev and Zinoviev." Then Stalin read the Testament passage about himself. "This is completely true. Yes, I'm rude, comrades, in connection with those who rudely and treacherously destroy and split the party. I did not and do not hide this." Stalin's rudeness was in *service to the cause*. His rudeness was *zeal*. As for the Testament's call for his removal, "At the first Central Committee plenum after the 13th Party Congress I asked to be released from my duties as general secretary. The congress itself discussed this question. Each delegation discussed this question, and all delegations, unanimously, including Trotsky, Kamenev, Zinoviev, obliged Stalin to remain at this post. What could I do? Desert my post? That is not in my nature. I have never deserted any post, and I have no right to do so. When the party imposes an obligation upon me, I must obey. One year later, I again submitted my resignation to the plenum, but again they obliged me to remain."[264] Yes they had: as ever, the loyal, humble servant. When Stalin asked if the time had not come to acquiesce to the many comrades demanding the expulsion of Zinoviev and Trotsky from the Central Committee, those present erupted in ovation. *Pravda* would publish Trotsky's speech, in garbled form. The same day it would also publish Stalin's, including the passages he had read aloud about himself from Lenin's Testament.[265]

Stalin and Trotsky's first direct confrontation at a party forum had been exactly four years earlier; October 23, 1927, would turn out to be the last time they saw each other. The next day, handed a copy of the "transcript" with the right to make corrections or additions, as per party policy, Trotsky complained: "The minutes do not show . . . a glass was thrown at me from the presidium. . . . They do not show that one of the participants tried to drag me off the podium by my arm. . . . While I was speaking Comrade Yaroslavsky threw a book of statistics at me . . . employing methods that cannot be called anything but those of fascist hooligans."[266]

Hundreds of regime personnel, from regional party bosses to military men and ambassadors abroad, were shown the transcripts of such meetings. These officials, in turn, were to discuss the contents with subordinates, for the transcripts were meant to be didactic. But what could officials trying to clothe and feed the workers, coax the peasants to sell grain, or defend Soviet interests abroad make of the substance of these top-level meetings? Who was running the country? Of course, whatever thoughts officials might have had, given the webs of mutual surveillance and the hyper-suspicious atmosphere Stalin increasingly accentuated, they had to be careful not to express them. The plenum, meanwhile, had approved resolutions at Stalin's behest calling for "a more decisive offensive against the kulak" as well as "the possibility of a transition to a further, more systematic and persistent restriction on the kulak and private trader."[267] The 1926–27 harvest had come in lower than 1925–26 by several million tons as a result of poor weather, which caused crop failures in some regions. Worse, that October 1927 saw a sharp drop in grain procurements to less than half the amount taken in by this time the previous year. Peasants were diverting grain to fodder for livestock and dairy farming, both of which yielded higher prices, but they were also hoarding grain stocks amid the uncertainty of the war scare. They had enough money on hand to pay their taxes and to wait for agricultural prices to rise. Without more grain, the regime faced possible starvation in the northern cities and in the Red Army by spring. The main journal for trade predicted in October 1927 that "a regulated distribution, rationing, extended to the entire population" might be necessary.[268]

## TENTH ANNIVERSARY: PRETEXT FOR REPRESSION

Stalin had advanced the theory that because the opposition's actions demonstrated internal disunity and weakness, they were objectively traitors, willy-nilly inviting foreign intervention, but now a new and sinister twist was added. On November 1, 1927, Molotov, in *Pravda*, called the opposition's "persecution" of Stalin a mask for malicious attacks against the party. "To exacerbate the struggle by personal attacks and denunciations against individuals," he wrote, with no sense of irony, "may serve as a direct incitement to criminal terroristic designs against party leaders." This article might have been the first denunciation of the party opposition as would-be assassins. Further channeling Stalin, Molotov added on November 5, also in *Pravda*, that "a certain Left SR odor exudes from the opposition cesspit."[269] The Left SRs, in the Bolshevik narrative, were coup plotters.

That same day, as the revolution's tenth anniversary approached, Stalin received an eighty-person delegation of sympathetic foreigners from multiple countries, only to have them question him about Soviet secret police powers. He defended the OGPU as "more or less equivalent to the Committee of Public Safety created during the Great French Revolution," in words carried by *Pravda*, and suggested that the foreign bourgeoisie was engaged in slandering the Soviet secret police. "From the point of view of the internal situation, the state of the revolution is secure and unwavering, so we could get by without the OGPU," he allowed, but added that "we are a country surrounded by capitalist states. The internal enemies of our revolution are agents of the capitalists of all countries. The capitalist states offer a base and a rear for the internal enemies of our country. Battling against internal enemies, it turns out we are conducting a struggle against the counterrevolutionary elements of all countries. Judge for yourself whether we could get by without punitive organs along the lines of an OGPU in such conditions." The foreigners were said to have applauded vigorously.[270]

The political regime had tightened appreciably. When Kamenev and Rakovski attempted to address the Moscow party organization, they were shouted down. The orchestrated vote against them was reported as 2,500 to 1.[271] That was the context in which, on November 7, 1927, the revolution's tenth anniversary, Stalin and the rest of the leadership ascended the cube mausoleum at 10:00 a.m. for the annual parade. Film cameras were rolling as first the Red Army units and then workers from the biggest factories marched by in prearranged columns. Inner Moscow was an armed camp, in anticipation that the opposition would try to mount a counterdemonstration on and close by Red Square. Opposition marchers that day were not numerous, and Stalin and the OGPU had readied plainclothes operatives and others to pounce on any opposition banner or speech. A few oppositionists who marched in the ranks with their work collectives tried to hoist portraits of Trotsky as well as Lenin. Some of them briefly managed to disrupt the official proceedings on Red Square, in a corner of the large public space, with impromptu speeches and banners ("Down with the Kulak, the NEPman, and the Bureaucrat!"). But vigilantes guided by plainclothes OGPU officers pummeled and took them into custody.[272] How many marchers knew what was happening remains uncertain. No non-regime newspapers existed to broadcast the opposition's actions.[273] Trotsky and Kamenev toured Moscow's streets by motor car, but on a side street near Revolution Square, they were greeted by disapproving whistles; shots were fired into the air. Regime vigilantes smashed the vehicle's windows.[274] That night Stalin previewed Sergei Eisenstein's film *October* about 1917, and forced him to remove the frames depicting Trotsky and to make alterations in the portrayal of Lenin ("Lenin's liberalism is not timely").[275]

In China, the Guomindang picked this Red holiday to raid the Soviet consulate in Shanghai; a week later, the government in Nanjing would sever diplomatic relations. In Moscow, Stalin moved quickly to capitalize on the opposition's quixotic counterdemonstrations, which empowered him to press his repression of the party opposition over the objections of others in the inner regime. At a joint plenum of the Central Committee and party Control Commission on November 14, 1927, Trotsky and Zinoviev were expelled from the party for incitement to counterrevolution; Kamenev, Rakovski, and others were ejected from the Central Committee.[276] The next day friends helped Trotsky move out of his Kremlin apartment, settling him in with a supporter just outside the Kremlin walls on nearby Granovsky.[277] Beginning on November 16, Zinoviev, Kamenev, Radek, and others were evicted from the Kremlin. The citadel was soon completely closed to non-regime personnel, and tourism was discontinued.[278]

Later that night, in the wee hours of the next morning, Adolf Joffe, the Soviet diplomat, shot himself. Joffe's wife, Maria, who worked at the editorial offices of the newspaper *Signal,* took the call. He had been bedridden with polyneuritis contracted in Japan and although he had previously gone to Austria for medical treatment, more recently the politburo had refused his request to finance treatment in Germany; when Joffe offered to pay for the trip himself, Stalin still refused to let him go. Joffe had known Trotsky since 1910, had joined the Bolsheviks with him in summer 1917, and had signed the telegram, in Lenin's name, appointing Trotsky war commissar. Joffe left a ten-page suicide note, the thrust of which was "Thermidor has begun," which Maria Joffe passed through trusted intermediaries to Trotsky.[279] "My death is the protest of a fighter who has been brought to such a state that he cannot in any way react to such a disgrace," Joffe wrote, adding about Trotsky, "you were always right and you always retreated. . . . I always thought that you did not have enough Leninist immovable obstinacy, his readiness to remain even alone on the path he chose in the creation of a future majority, a future recognition of the correctness of the path."[280]

Funerals of comrades lost in the struggle had been a sacred ritual of the old revolutionary underground, but this was now under their own regime. Joffe's interment took place on November 19, drawing a sizable crowd on a workday. Chicherin, Litvinov, and Karakhan of the foreign affairs commissariat, as well as

Trotsky, Zinoviev, and Lashevich of the opposition accompanied the cortège to the Novodevichy Cemetery, a place of honor second only to the Kremlin Wall. "The composition of the funeral demonstration also made one stop and think, for there were no workers in it," one eyewitness recalled. "The United opposition had no proletarian support."[281] Among the many eulogies, Trotsky spoke last, and briefly. "The struggle continues," he stated. "Everyone remains at his post. Let nobody leave." These words proved to be his last public speech in the Soviet Union. The crowd surrounded Trotsky, blocking his exit for a long time, trying to transform the funeral into a political demonstration. But they were dispersed.[282] That same evening, in a letter from Rykov, Trotsky was relieved of his last official administrative post (chairman of the foreign concessions committee).[283]

The next day, Rykov spoke at the Tenth Congress of the Communist Party of Ukraine and complained of the opposition's usage of the terms "Stalin the Dictator," "Stalinist methods." "All this is an evil and vile slander against the entire party and against comrade Stalin," Rykov stated, adding that in the politburo "not a single question is decided unilaterally by one member."[284] His statement was both true and false. In the politburo, which Rykov had joined the same day Stalin became general secretary, Rykov was a core member of a solid majority. But as he knew better than almost anyone, Stalin predecided a great deal outside the politburo—on Old Square, at his Kremlin apartment, at his Sochi dacha, over the phone with the OGPU.

## 15TH PARTY CONGRESS (DECEMBER 2–19, 1927)

The 15th Party Congress was the largest party forum yet with 1,669 delegates (898 voting). Trotsky and Zinoviev were not among them. The opposition lacked even a single voting delegate.[285] After the ceremonial opening, Stalin delivered the main political report for only the second time as general secretary. At the mere announcement of his name the delegates erupted ("stormy, prolonged applause; an ovation of the entire hall, shouts of 'Hurrah'"). "Our country, comrades, exists and develops in a condition of capitalist encirclement," he began. "Its external position depends not only on its internal forces but also on the state of this capitalist encirclement, on the condition of the capitalist countries that encircle our country, on their strengths and weaknesses, on the strengths and weaknesses of the oppressed classes of the whole world." Accordingly, he presented a detailed assessment of the world economy, trade, and external markets, and what he called the preparations for a new imperialist war to redivide global spoils. "We have all the signs of the most profound crisis and growing instability of world capitalism," he concluded, calling the capitalist stabilization "more and more rotten," and anticolonial movements and worker movements "growing." Stalin then analyzed the USSR's economic development, in industry and agriculture, the expansion of the working class, the rise in the country's overall cultural level, concluding, "Soviet power is the most stable power of any in the world. (Stormy applause.)"[286] After a break for lunch, Stalin returned to the dais and went into high dudgeon over the opposition. Altogether, he spoke for four hours.

The day of Stalin's report (December 3), Kamenev submitted a petition with the names of 121 oppositionists who were slated for expulsion but promised to abide by party decisions.[287] Stalin mocked them and, as Zinoviev had once demanded of Trotsky, demanded of them: "They must renounce their anti-Bolshevik views openly and honestly, before the whole world. They must openly and honestly, before the whole world, brand the mistakes they committed, mistakes that became crimes before the party. Either that or they can leave the party. And if they don't leave, we'll kick them out!" Pandemonium.[288] During the discussion, the few members of the opposition given the floor, such as Grigory Yevdokimov and Nikolai Muralov, were jeered relentlessly, then, after they left the dais, verbally smeared. "No confidence can be placed in these deceivers of the party," intoned Kuzma Ryndin, a delegate from Chelyabinsk (and the future party boss there). "Enough of this mockery of the party: the party and the proletariat will not stand for it. . . . All those who want to prevent us from working—out of the party with them!" Filipp Goloshchokin stated: "If we pussyfoot around with the opposition, we'll be cutting our own throats." When Kamenev observed that opposition members had been imprisoned for their political views, Rykov responded, "despite the situation the opposition has tried to create, there are only a few in prison. I do not think I can give assurances that the prison population will not have to be increased somewhat in the near future. (Voices from the floor: 'Correct!')."[289]

Kamenev had been allowed to attend as a non-voting delegate, and his remarks, again, were memorable, though utterly different from two years earlier when he had denied Stalin's ability to unite the party. "Before us stands the question of choosing one of two roads," Kamenev now explained, through near constant interruptions and accusations of Trotskyism, lying, and worse. "One of these roads is a second party. This road, under the conditions of the dictatorship of the proletariat, is ruinous for the revolution. This is the road of political and class degeneration. This road is forbidden to us, excluded by the whole system of our views, by all the teachings of Lenin. . . . There remains, therefore, the second road . . . to submit completely and fully to the party. We choose this road for we are profoundly convinced that a correct Leninist policy can triumph in our party and through it, not outside the party and against it."[290] It turned out that Stalin had united the party after all: Kamenev's abasement was the proof.

In remarks on December 7 to close out the discussion of his report, Stalin triumphantly stated, "I have nothing of substance to say about the speeches of Yevdokimov and Muralov, as there was nothing of substance in them. The only thing to say about them is, Allah forgive them." The delegates laughed and applauded. He labeled Kamenev's capitulatory speech that of a Pharisee. Stalin called the party a living organism: "The old, the obsolete falls off (applause), the new, grows and develops (applause). Some leave the stage. . . . New forces grow up, at the top and at lower levels, carrying the cause forward. . . . And if now some leaders fall off the cart of revolution, not wanting to sit firmly in the cart, then in that there's nothing surprising. This will only free the party from those who get their legs crossed and prevent the party from moving forward." To those who "fall off from the cart—then that way is their road! (Rousing applause. The whole congress stands and gives comrade Stalin an ovation)."[291]

A resolution condemning the opposition was put to immediate vote and passed unanimously. Then the damnable Testament popped out, yet again.

Stalin had challenged his critics, back in July 1926, to demand at the next Party Congress (which was now) that Lenin's Testament be published. On December 9, Orjonikidze made a formal proposal to that effect, to reverse the decision of the 13th Party Congress. Rykov proposed that the full gamut of late Lenin dictation be published, not solely the part known as the Testament, and that the Testament be included in the 15th Party Congress proceedings. Rykov's proposals passed unanimously.[292] But the Testament did not appear in the published proceedings.[293] Instead, Stalin had it issued during the congress as a separate bulletin "for members of the party only," in a print run of 13,500, nine times the number of delegates. The method of distribution and the number of people who read a copy remain unclear.[294]

Much was glossed over at the congress. Alarming reports were pouring in via secret police channels of a "goods famine" and widespread popular anger. "Queues for foodstuffs and material for clothing have become an everyday phenomenon (the Center, Belorussia, the Volga valley, the South Caucasus), along with crushes and fighting," the OGPU reported. "There have been cases when women have fainted." The police paid special attention to women in food lines, based on historical precedent, and overheard them lamenting it took an entire day to procure flour and that their husbands were coming home from work to find nothing to eat.[295] To appease workers, the regime had announced a seven-hour workday, which did not sit well with peasants already starved for manufactured goods. "Even now there are no goods in shops and with a seven-hour working day there'll be absolutely nothing," one peasant stated, according to the December 1927 country mood report by the OGPU. One "kulak" was reported to have stated, "If the peasants were organized in some kind of organization and could say with one voice that we will not sell you grain at such a price, then the workers would sit with their goods and croak from starvation, then they'd forget about a seven-hour day."[296] The Bolshevik revolution was more and more looking like a triumphant debacle.

Stalin's China policy had not finished imploding. During the Party Congress in Moscow, on December 11, 1927, the Chinese Communists did finally form a soviet in Canton (Guangzhou); it lasted sixty hours before Guomindang forces annihilated its adherents. All told in 1927, the Chinese Communist party had lost perhaps 85 percent of its membership. "The revolution could not develop in Canton, Shanghai, Tientsin, Hankow, or any of those regions where industry was most developed, because there imperialism and the Chinese bourgeoisie held stronger positions," reasoned the Soviet China expert Mikhail Fortus, who went by the name Pavel Mif. He called for a retreat to the remote northwest, where the Communists could gather forces for a subsequent assault on "imperialist strongholds."[297] Mao Zedong had been urging the need to build a rural base and peasant armies rather than try to seize the cities. But it was Chiang Kai-shek who drove the Communists, an urban movement, into the countryside. Soviet peasants listening to newspaper reports being read aloud of the catastrophic Communist defeat in China in December 1927, meanwhile, according to the OGPU, interpreted this to signify the defeat of Communists in Moscow. Wishful thinking.[298]

The United opposition split. On December 10, Kamenev and the Zinovievites Yevdokimov and Bakayev repeated their written appeal for reinstatement, promising to disperse their faction and requesting release of oppositionists who had been arrested.[299] But that same day, the Trotsky supporters Muralov and Rakovski, while announcing their agreement with the impossibility of forming a second party, maintained their right to continue to defend opposing views within the single party.[300] Stalin decided not to accept the Zinovievites' surrender. Instead of merely requiring that they remain silent, as he initially had demanded, now he ordered that they recant publicly and grovel for the rest of the week. On December 17, the expulsions of Trotsky, Zinoviev, and others from the party, which had been voted back at the previous plenum, were confirmed.[301] Two days later, Zinoviev, Kamenev, and others, twenty-three people in total, signed a degrading petition to the congress—which they were not even allowed into the hall to present in person—renouncing their "wrong and anti-Leninist views." Stalin again refused to reinstate them.[302] Orjonikidze engaged in negotiations over the disposition of the highest-profile Trotskyites who sought to continue working in some capacity, but Stalin soon scattered them into internal exile.[303] Whereas in the politburo back in mid-1924, Great Russians accounted for 46 percent, with a third having been Jews and the remaining three a Pole, Latvian, and Georgian, now the politburo became two-thirds Russian (and would retain a Russian majority thereafter).[304] The talk around the congress was that "Moses had taken the Jews out of Egypt, and Stalin took them out of the Central Committee."[305]

The day before the congress adjourned (December 18), the Soviet secret police celebrated their tenth anniversary with a parade of mounted troops and armored vehicles through Red Square, received by First Deputy Chairman Yagoda, the de facto chief, and a gala evening at the Bolshoi showcasing the revolution's "sword and shield." Workers of Moscow's Dynamo factory had fashioned a huge metal sword that was displayed on stage, and workers at the ceremony asked that it remain unsheathed until "all that remains of the bourgeoisie is a memory." On that morning, *Pravda* had declared war on "whoever does not stand on the path of proletarian revolution—the speculator, the saboteur, the bandit, the White Guardist, the spy, yesterday's comrade, today's most vile traitor and enemy."[306] At the Bolshoi, Voroshilov and Bukharin delivered speeches. Kaganovich observed that the "class struggle" was assuming new forms, especially economic pressure, and that NEP had produced classes hostile to the proletariat.[307] The head of the OGPU, Wiaczesław Mężyński, still very ill, offered brief remarks. Photographs and stories of secret police exploits were splashed across the front pages of the newspapers for three days running. "If there is anything to be regretted now," one old-time Chekist wrote, "it is not that we were too cruel, but that we were too lenient to our enemies."[308] Celebrants were distributed around the capital's elite restaurants at the National, the Grand Hotel, and the Savoy, and at each venue Yagoda made a short appearance to be toasted as "the Great Chekist."[309] Orders of the Red Banner, the state's highest award, were awarded not just to him but to nearly every upper member of the caste; about the only one overlooked was Artuzov, Yagoda's bête noire, who lost control of counterintelligence.

Stalin's victory could scarcely have been more total, yet he indulged his feelings of victimization and self-pity. On December 19, at the inaugural plenum of the Central Committee newly confirmed by the congress, he again brought up the Lenin Testament call for his removal as general secretary. He allowed that there may have been reasons that the party had not heeded Lenin's call previously: the opposition had existed. But no longer. "Never before has the opposition suffered such a defeat, for it is not only crushed, it is expelled from the party," Stalin declared triumphantly. "Now we no longer see those bases whereby the plenum would have been thought correct in refusing to honor my request to relieve me of the duties of the general secretary. And moreover we have Lenin's instructions, which we cannot not take into account and which, in my view, it is necessary to put into effect." The orgburo functionary Alexander Dogadov cut in to suggest voting on Stalin's proposal without discussion, perhaps protecting everyone from having to compete in their panegyrics. Voroshilov immediately recommended rejection of Stalin's request. Rykov, who as head of the government chaired these meetings, implemented Dogadov's proposal. Hands went up—Who was in favor of retaining Stalin as general secretary? Who was against? The vote in favor was unanimous, with a single abstention, unidentified.[310]

Rykov had skillfully maneuvered to tamp down the eruption. But then Stalin made a new proposal: "Perhaps the Central Committee will consider it expedient to eliminate the institution of a general secretary. In the history of our party there was a time when that post did not exist." Voroshilov again cut in. But Stalin answered with a quick history of the party before the introduction of a general secretary above the other secretaries serving the Central Committee. "I don't know why it is necessary to preserve this dead institution," he stated. "While at the top no special rights or special duties in practice are connected with the institution of the general secretary, in locales there are deformations and in all provinces there is a brawl because of this institution among comrades who are called secretaries, for example in the national Central Committees. A lot of general secretaries have been introduced and in locales they have special rights. Why do we need this?" He asked that the position be eliminated. "It's easy to do, it is not in the party statute."

Again it fell to Rykov to manage the situation. He stated unequivocally that the Central Committee would keep its post of general secretary, which Lenin had created, and which Stalin had been granted by the votes of everyone, including oppositionists now expelled from the party. Rykov averred that Stalin had fully justified this appointment by his work, both before Lenin had died and after. This time the vote was unanimous. Rykov's actions, like his remarks at the recent Ukrainian Party Congress, indicated that either he was supremely confident he could manage Stalin or that he understood the only option, even for titans like himself, was to stay in Stalin's good graces and hope for the best. Or perhaps Rykov was no more discerning of Stalin than Kamenev had been when he had let slip the chance to remove him. Stalin's menace was far more evident now. But Stalin's menace was also fully enveloped within the regime's vocabulary and worldview—capitalist encirclement, ubiquitous enemies, vigilance, mercilessness—which Rykov shared and himself had been enacting toward the opposition, while conciliating the peasantry, except for the kulaks.

NO ONE COMPELLED STALIN to submit his resignation time and time again. He had resigned so often the ritual could well have become tiresome for those subjected to it. Not including the private hints in the August 7, 1923, letter to Bukharin and Zinoviev, in connection with their initial awkward disclosure of "the Ilich letter about the secretary" following the cave meeting, there had been clear resignation statements on six known occasions: on the eve of and then immediately after the 13th Party Congress in May 1924; in an August 19, 1926, letter to the Central Committee; in a December 27, 1926, letter to Rykov in the name of the Central Committee; and now again, on December 19, 1927. Of the three party congresses since the Lenin Testament had surfaced, Stalin had not resigned only at one (the 14th), which, however, had devolved into shouting matches over his "boundless power." And now, at this first plenum after the 15th Congress, even after Rykov affirmed the existence of position of general secretary, Stalin was not done. "Comrades, during the first vote, concerning my release from the duties of the secretary, I did not vote, I forgot to vote," he interjected. "I ask that you consider my vote against."[311]

What was this, the expression of a deep well of resentment? The voicing of his darkest fears, his removal by the Central Committee? A provocative test of the inner regime? An odd way that Stalin savored his triumph and the opposition's expulsion? A gesture of false modesty by a man who treasured posing as the humble, albeit indispensable, servant of the party? It was perhaps all of the above—supremacy and siege, elation and self-pity, the paradoxes of Stalin's power.

Stalin had attained a position of power that would have exceeded anyone's wildest dreams, except perhaps his own, but power for him entailed responsibility for advancing the Communist victory at home and abroad. No war had broken out in 1927, but rumors spread that this was solely because the Soviet regime had secretly made concessions: turning over grain, gold, horses, ports, coal mines, territory. (Some wags surmised the Western powers refrained from unseating the Soviet regime to give socialists around the world more time to see the full folly of their delusions.) The 15th Congress passed a resolution on industrialization calling, in classical Marxist terms, for production of the means of production, and in the meantime, imports of machinery not being produced in the USSR.[312] How would this be financed? The secret police were reporting increased attacks, up to murder, against Soviet officials, while state grain acquisitions were failing. On December 12, 1927, the Left Communist Valerian Obolensky, known as Osinsky, had addressed a letter to Rykov and Stalin in reaction to Rykov's congress report indicating the lack of a general crisis, only a partial crisis in grain collection. Osinsky, who worked in the Central Statistical Administration and knew agriculture well, called the grain collection process already "completely lost" for this year—stunning words—"even if procurement prices were to be raised. Such an increase is already a defeat, particularly since it could provoke a further withholding of grain in calculation of further price increases." Osinsky had been urging Mikoyan and other top officials, time and again (January 1927, summer 1927, fall 1927), to raise procurement prices and lower prices of industrial goods for peasants. "I believe that the more fundamental causes of the falloff (so far by half) of our procurement campaign, a falloff that will develop into deep general difficulties, is the ratcheting up of our production to tempos, and in a direction, that do not correspond to the real possibilities of our country."[313] Osinsky's letter implied that something drastic would have to be done about grain procurements, or industrialization would become a pipe dream.

Sokolnikov, the former finance minister, again insisted that "American tempos" of industrialization were possible only by developing agriculture, and deemed it idiotic to evaluate peasant reserves of grain as an expression of some kind of kulak war against Soviet power. He called for using economic levers without a return to requisitioning.[314] In the end, the 15th Party Congress had voted up a resolution at Stalin's behest "on work in the countryside," which called for "employing the whole power of economic organs, and relying, as before, upon the poor and middle peasant masses, to develop further the offensive against the kulaks and to adopt a number of new measures limiting the development of capitalism in the countryside and leading the peasant economy along the road to socialism."[315] What those "new measures" entailed remained unclear. But during the vote on the final resolution regarding the countryside, in the waning moments of the congress, an amendment appeared: "At the present time, the task of transformation and amalgamation of small individual farms into large-scale collective farms must be set as the party's fundamental task in the countryside."[316] Collectivization, *at the present time?* The transcript records "Noise in the hall," when the amendment was read; the session chair noted that only twenty minutes remained until the close of the congress and asked delegates to remain seated. The amended resolution was said to have passed unanimously.[317]

After the rebuff of his resignation, Stalin on December 21 celebrated his official forty-eighth birthday.[318] Nearly half a century should have been more than ample for observers to figure him out, but he revealed himself no better than the dark, vast Siberian taiga forest. Even the great biographical scoop of the American YMCA director Jerome Davis was put in doubt: Stalin forbid its republication in the original Russian and, in December 1927, had a foreign commissariat functionary try to get the Associated Press to discredit the Davis interview as a fabrication.[319] Still, in connection with the birthday milestone, Stalin's top aide, Ivan Tovstukha, reworked the biographical material that had been collectively gathered in the central apparatus and, this time, managed to elicit Stalin's assent to publish it—under just Tovstukha's name—in the *Granat Encyclopedia* of some 250 revolutionaries in 1927. The Stalin material also came out as a stand-alone pamphlet in an initial print run of 50,000. Finally, a Stalin *biography.* It reverentially catalogued his passage through the revolutionary stations of the cross: his discovery of Marx, the organizing in the underground, the various early congresses, the bouts of exile and other political punishments. The text ran fourteen pages, in large, bold type.[320]

# A TRIP TO SIBERIA

We cannot live like gypsies, without grain reserves.

Stalin, Central Committee plenum, July 9, 1928[1]

Stalin was an ideological person. For him the idea was
the main thing.

Lazar Kaganovich[2]

STALIN BOARDED a heavily guarded train bound for Siberia. It was Sunday,
January 15, 1928.[3] He rarely traveled, even domestically, other than to the Black
Sea for relief in the sulfur baths from the terrible pain in his muscles and joints.
Siberia, however, he knew well from before the 1917 revolution, having been
deported there countless times by the tsarist regime, most recently during the
Great War. Stalin had fought on the Boredom and Mosquito Front—that is, he
had wallowed for years as a political exile in the alternately frozen or thawed
swamps of the far north. His 1928 trip would keep him to Siberia's southerly
parts, however: Novosibirsk and the Altai breadbasket of Western Siberia, as well
as Krasnoyarsk, in Eastern Siberia, where in early 1917 a tsarist draft board had
rejected him, owing to the webbed toes on his left foot and his suppurated left
elbow that did not bend properly. Now, eleven years later, he was returning to
these remote parts as the country's ruler, the general secretary of the Communist
party. In Novosibirsk, at gatherings with the local higher-ups, Stalin would
demand coercive measures to overcome a state grain procurement crisis. He
would also declare, unexpectedly, the inescapability of pushing forward the collectivization of agriculture immediately. A few days later he would take a branch
line to Barnaul, an administrative center of the richest Siberian grain-growing
region, to meet with officials lower down. Compared with the 20 million motor-
cars in the United States, cars and trucks in the Soviet Union numbered perhaps
5,500, and Barnaul had not a single one. From the terminal, Stalin was ferried to

the meeting in a primitive wooden-basket sled, a means of conveyance that suggested the enormity of what would be involved in remaking peasant life and state power across two continents.

## SELF-FULFILLING CRISIS

Modern Russian power, in its Soviet guise, too, still rested upon wheat and rye. For all the dreams of modernity, by 1928 industry had barely regained 1913 tsarist levels even with the prolonged recuperation provided by the partially legalized markets of the New Economic Policy.[4] By contrast, industry in Britain and Germany was 10 percent greater than in 1913; in France, 40 percent, in the United States, a whopping 75 percent.[5] Russia had lost ground. At the same time, the NEP presupposed peasants' willingness to sell their "surpluses"—that is, the grain beyond what they consumed as food or moonshine—not just to the private traders (NEPmen), but also to state procurement agents at state-set prices. With the agricultural year running from July to June and harvest gathering and state procurements commencing in summer, from July through December 1927 the Soviet state had secured just 5.4 million tons of grain. The target for that interval was 7.7 million tons, leaving a gaping shortfall that threatened Moscow and Leningrad, as well as the Red Army, with starvation in spring. Procurements for November and December 1927 were particularly alarming, just half the total compared with the previous year.[6] Panicky reports arrived from as far as Soviet Uzbekistan, where cotton growers with little food were insisting on switching to crops that could feed themselves, and officials began seizing grain, all of it, from anyone who grew it.[7] In Moscow, the authorities could scarcely afford major unrest—street demonstrations over a lack of bread had accompanied the downfall of the tsarist regime, and shortages had played a part in undermining the Provisional Government.

Longer-term perspectives were even more troubling. Tsarist Russia had fed both England and Germany and grain exports had reached perhaps 9 million tons in 1913, but in 1927 they constituted a measly 2.2 million tons, delivering a lot less hard currency to finance machinery imports and industrialization. At the same time, Stalin received a table showing a drastic falloff in the percentage of the harvest being marketed since tsarist times, from 26 to 13 percent (of smaller harvests).[8] As a result of the peasant revolution, some of the land that had been used for marketed production had been seized and was now occupied by subsistence farming, so that even if the harvests had been of comparable size, less grain would be marketed beyond village borders.[9] To be sure, Soviet agricultural levels surpassed that of China or India. But the USSR competed with Britain, France, and Germany, and despite some improvement in implements and machines, credit, and marketing cooperatives, farming remained decidedly unmodern. Three quarters of all grain was sown by hand, nearly half reaped with sickles and scythes, and two fifths threshed with chains or similarly manual devices.[10] Russian agriculture was just not advancing, while among the great powers, mechanization was well under way. How to boost overall grain production was a deep concern. After the peak harvest under the NEP of 1925–26 (77 million tons), the 1926–27 harvest had disappointed at around 73 million and the 1927–28 harvest would disappoint, too, also officially estimated at 73 million tons, but likely no more than 70 million.[11] These were stubborn facts, and would have challenged any government in Russia, but Bolshevik actions had inexorably undermined the quasi-market of the NEP.[12]

Private industry in the USSR had been squeezed down to less than 10 percent of total output, and its share continued to fall, but the principal producers, state factories organized as giant trusts, had few incentives to reduce their unduly high production costs or even to manufacture saleable goods. A 1927 decree on trusts had stressed output quotas, not profits, as the guiding criteria, which compounded the already perverse incentives of greater subsidies for worse performance.[13] The regime's inability to resist the urge to finance desperately needed industrial expansion by the printing of money resulted in inflation, which, in turn, elicited further clumsy price controls, worsening the market's operation. In other words, applying administrative measures to the economy only exacerbated imbalances and fed the inclination for more administrative measures, in a vicious loop.[14] "If there is a choice between the industrialization program and equilibrium in the market, the market must give way," Valerian Kuibyshev, head of the Supreme Council of the Economy, blustered to the party organization in his bailiwick in January 1928. He allowed that the market "could be one current, but a Communist and Bolshevik has always been and is able to swim against the current," and concluded that "the will of the party can create miracles . . . and is creating and will create miracles despite all these market phenomena."[15] Just a few weeks later, Kuibyshev proclaimed at the presidium of the Supreme Council of the Economy that "the will of the state has smashed the [market] conjuncture."[16] Such idiotic boasts unwittingly exposed the self-inflicted dimensions of the sharply lower state grain procurements.

Some peasants were holding their grain out of fear of a new famine, but experts mostly attributed the diminished marketings to lower per capita production, higher per capita peasant consumption, and above all the gap in prices between grain (low) and peasant-desired manufactured goods (high), those infamous scissors, in Trotsky's metaphor, whose blades opened in opposite directions.[17] Paying peasants substantially higher prices for grain and ruthlessly restricting monetary emissions would have closed the blades, but the former measure would have necessitated charging workers higher prices for bread, while also hurting industrialization (domestic grain purchases at higher prices would reduce earnings from exports); the latter measure would have entailed scaling back ambitions for industrial expansion.[18] Stalin was loathe to make these kinds of political concessions to the peasantry again, given that after doing so the regime was again in the same place. Instead, in 1927, the politburo had mandated a substantial reduction in prices for manufactures, whose implementation Stalin referred to as "beating down the markup, reducing the markup, breaking the resistance of the cooperatives and other trading agencies at all costs."[19] Some years before that maneuver had worked, when there had been unused industrial capacity to revive, but now, even at the higher prices, demand had been going unmet because of limited supply, and the price reduction—in summer, no less, when workers went on holiday and production normally suffered—reinforced the trend toward bare store shelves.[20] "In some districts," the secret police reported in a December 1927 survey of the country's political mood, "the peasants come to the cooperative every day inquiring whether goods have arrived."[21] True, throughout January 1928 textile factories in the Moscow region operated on Saturdays, too, to produce manufactures for grain-growing regions, but the goods famine persisted.[22]

Rumors of pending war also contributed to the peasant reluctance to part with their grain; the Siberian party organization demanded a halt to "the dim-witted agitation in the press" about imminent foreign invasion.[23] On top of everything else, party officials had been distracted. November 7, 1927, brought the revolution's tenth anniversary, a prolonged drinking bender, then came the elections to and the sessions of the 15th Party Congress through much of December. "Nobody in authority bothers about the purchase of grain," a German espionage agent, posing as a journalist, wrote of rural officials in Siberia. "All the party bosses, the authorities, are in Moscow for the party congress, for the jubilee celebrations, for the soviet sittings and other things, and the lower party bosses, the youth organizations and the village correspondents have only the anniversary of the revolution in their heads."[24] But right after the congress, the politburo held a special session devoted exclusively to grain procurement.[25] And *Pravda* began to bang the gong. Suddenly, as a reporter in Moscow for the London *Times* picked up (January 3, 1928), public discussion had broken out on "the most drastic measures to pump the grain from the peasants."

Stalin ratcheted up the pressure on two tracks. One was the secret police, which had been granted the prerogative of imposing sentences outside judicial channels. On January 4, OGPU deputy chief Yagoda directed all regional secret police branches "to arrest immediately the biggest private grain traders . . . conduct the investigations quickly, persuasively. Send the cases to Special Boards. Communicate immediately the resulting influence on the market."[26] Stalin wanted overt secret police involvement minimized ("Cease publication of communiqués regarding our operations in grain collection," OGPU chief Wiaczesław Mężyński directed Vsevolod Balytsky, head of the OGPU in Ukraine, in January 1928).[27] The other track involved the party apparatus: four sharply worded secret circulars were dispatched to all major party organizations over the course of a single month, beginning on December 14 (during the Party Congress).[28] The circulars moved up the deadline to remit rural tax payments to February 15, 1928 (from April 1), and insurance payments to January 15 (from January 31), changes that the authorities compelled the peasants to affirm at mass meetings.[29] But peasants met their cash obligations by selling meat, dairy, or hides, whose prices were predominantly market driven and high because of demand. Grain, which was readily stored, they held back.[30] Internal secret police reports warned of "a strengthening of kulak agitation"—that is, discussions among peasants about holding out until spring in anticipation of better prices.[31]

Politburo members, mindful of possible spring famine and urban unrest if food supplies failed, as well as harm to industrialization without grain to export, had cautiously consented to Stalin's insistence on "emergency measures." His third secret party circular, sent on January 6, 1928, acknowledged that "despite two firm directives of the Central Committee to strengthen grain procurement, no breakthrough has occurred," and announced the formation of a Central Committee commission for grain headed by himself, which afforded him not just de facto but de jure authority to implement the emergency measures he deemed necessary. With this extra authority, Stalin drove the extension of the antispeculation law wielded by the OGPU against private traders—Article 107 of the criminal code—to grain growers for "not releasing goods for the market."[32] Mere non-sale of privately grown grain became subject to up to three years imprisonment and confiscation of property. Hundreds of publicized arrests took place in Ukraine and the North Caucasus, with published reports of sizable storehouses of "hoarded" grain being discovered.[33] In those locales, Stalin relied upon trusted lieutenants such as Kaganovich, party boss in Ukraine, and Andrei Andreyev, another protégé, whom Stalin had just named party boss of the sprawling North Caucasus territory. But even they required him to exert pressure (Andreyev, newly arrived, wrote to his wife in January 1928 that "now, in earnest, I have to issue directives to restrain the zealots," not exactly Stalin's message).[34] Stalin dispatched Mikoyan to the North Caucasus, but together with Ukraine, these regions were far behind producing their usual two thirds of the country's marketed grain, and so Stalin looked to the Urals and Siberia as what he called "the last reserves." On January 9, the politburo resolved to send out his two top associates, Vyacheslav Molotov, who was directed to the Urals, and Sergo Orjonikidze, who was commanded to Siberia. On January 12, however, Orjonikidze was said to have taken ill and his trip was canceled.[35] The next day Stalin summoned officials in agriculture, supply, and trade.[36] He decided to go to Siberia himself.[37]

Stalin would not be the only person in motion that January 1928. In a nasty jolt, a former top aide in the innermost sanctum at Old Square, Boris Bazhanov, fled the country, conniving to escape (January 1) just when border guards were still feeling the effects of the New Year's celebration, and becoming the first major Soviet defector. Bazhanov had gotten reassigned out of Old Square after failing to return borrowed imported sports equipment; he then fathered illegitimate children with two different mistresses, one of whom he took abroad as his "wife" at state expense. He had contemplated trying to sneak across into Romania, Finland, or Poland before conniving to get himself reassigned to Ashkhabad, Turkmenistan, a few miles from the more porous border with Iran. Just twenty-seven years old, Bazhanov carried out secret politburo documents to prove his bona fides. Whether he had help from foreign intelligence services in the act of crossing remains unclear, but once in Persia he was evidently helped over the mountains to India, whence he sailed to Marseilles, leaving behind his mistress, who was caught trying to cross the Soviet-Iran border separately.[38] Bazhanov had joined the party as a teenager in his native Ukraine, and managed to leap into the orgburo at age twenty-two. His embarrassing betrayal, kept secret from the Soviet public, showed that the dream of a radiant future was not only the well-spring of the system's strength but also its principal vulnerability: people could become white-hot with anger at their earlier illusions. Already, from January 2, Georgy Arutyunov, known as Agabekov, an ethnic Armenian and the chief of the Eastern Department of Soviet intelligence, headed a manhunt on foreign soil (until Agabekov himself defected).[39] Bazhanov would sit for extensive debriefings by French intelligence, generating hundreds of pages of material on clandestine Soviet machinations to undermine the Western powers and on Stalin's opaque regime, telling the French, for instance, that Stalin is "extremely cunning, with an unbelievable power of dissimulation and, above all, very spiteful."[40] Soon, Bazhanov published an exposé in French, writing that Stalin "possessed in a high degree the gift for silence, and in this respect was unique in a country where everybody talks far too much."[41]

Mostly, Bazhanov got Stalin wrong, such as when he asserted that the Soviet leader "read nothing and was interested in nothing" and "had only one passion, absolute and devouring: lust for power."[42] Stalin lived for the revolution and Russian state power, which is what impelled him to return to Siberia. His own power was vastly extended beyond Old Square by the telegraph, telephone, newspaper, radio, and Communist ideology, but those levers barely reached into villages. Nor did that power extend abroad. The Soviet refusal to relinquish internationalizing the revolution by supporting worker and national liberation movements abroad ensured that the core tenet of Leninist foreign relations—intercourse with the enemy—had become a self-fulfilling prophecy, but the challenge persisted of somehow obtaining advanced industrial technology from the capitalist powers. Further complicating the Soviet position, global market prices for wheat in 1927–28 cratered, a deflation that also affected other Soviet export commodities (timber, oil, sugar). At the same time, rising tariffs abroad magnified the punch to the gut.[43] Here was the short straw that the unsentimental global political economy allocated to all primary goods producers: to obtain the hard currency it needed to buy machines, the Soviet Union would have to sell its commodities at a loss.[44] Moreover, despite some successes in securing short-term and some medium-term credits to purchase equipment and cover trade deficits from the Austrian and German governments, the Soviets had failed to obtain long-term financing from Paris, London, or even Berlin. Stalin could not abide the fact that the Soviet regime found itself crawling to the international bourgeoisie, rather than relying on the international proletariat, for a lifeline. Just as the peasants were refusing to sell their grain, foreign capitalists, at a minimum, could aim at the Red regime's demise by refusing to sell their advanced technology.

Stalin lived immersed in the grim OGPU summaries of the country's political mood, which his worldview shaped in a feedback loop, and which brimmed with antiregime quotations from eavesdropped conversations and other reminders that the USSR was encircled by hostile forces and honeycombed with internal enemies.[45] Soviet borderlands were suspect: in Ukraine, the North and South Caucasus, Belorussia, and the Far East, the police wrote, "We have some elements on which the foreign counterrevolution could rely at a moment of external complications."[46] Tsarist-era specialists in industry and the military were suspect: "The collapse of Soviet power is inescapable as a system built on sand," former Major General Nikolai Pnevsky, a nobleman and tsarist-era air force chief of staff serving in the Red Army quartermaster directorate, stated in relation to Britain's rupture of diplomatic relations according to a police informant, adding: "This break is a prelude to war, which should, in light of the low level of USSR military technology and internal political and economic difficulties caused by a war, finish off Bolshevism once and for all."[47] Villages were suspect: "I have talked with many peasants, and I can say straight out that in the event of a conflict with foreign states, a significant stratum of peasants will not defend Soviet power with any enthusiasm, and this is also reported in the army," Mikhail Kalinin, who posed as the country's peasant elder, told the politburo.[48] The Russian émigré press contained leaked information about the secret inner workings of the Soviet regime.[49] For Stalin, his inner circle, too, had become suspect. Without consulting them, and with only the vaguest notion of how it would unfold, he embarked in 1928 upon the greatest gamble of his political life.

## EARTH-SHATTERING SPEECH

*Stalin was coming.* Siberia's party boss, Sergei Syrtsov, sped out on a lightning inspection of the Western Siberian breadbasket—Barnaul, Biysk, Rubtsovsk—to ensure that officials were prepared to receive the general secretary.[50] As a veteran of Stalin's inner apparatus in Moscow, where he had passed through a master school of intrigue, Syrtsov had been only in his thirty-third year two years earlier when Stalin had handed him Siberia (in place of the Zinoviev supporter Mikhail Lashevish). On January 17, 1928, just hours before Stalin's arrival, Syrtsov directed the Siberian party to approve a concrete plan for implementation of the Central Committee's directive to employ Article 107 against grain "hoarders": the Siberian secret police would arrest a quota of between four and ten kulaks from each local grain-producing district for "holding large grain reserves and using the bread shortages to speculate and raise prices." "Start the operation immediately!" ordered Siberian OGPU boss Zakovsky.[51] On January 18, some sixty top Siberian officials, representing the local party bureau as well as local grain procurement personnel, found themselves in the presence of Stalin and his phalanx of aides, as well as advance officials he had sent.[52] He told them Siberia had had a bumper harvest and laid down an obligation of just over 1 million tons of grain for shipment to the Center, leaving a mere 400,000 tons for Siberia's own needs.[53] He also demanded that they specify by name who would be responsible in each county for implementation, and ensure that the railroads could cope—no excuses.[54] As expected, Stalin further insisted that Article 107 be applied to anyone refusing to sell grain stocks. Syrtsov unveiled Siberia's already-launched antihoarding operation (from the day before).[55] Stalin embraced this gift, while softening its appearance, shifting implementation of the measure from the political police to the procuracy, which was to explain the policy in the local press, follow the law (v zakonnom poriadke), and prepare public trials of kulaks with simplified procedures in order to induce the rest of the peasants to market grain.[56]

Stalin's aides had assembled a collection of brochures and other materials published in recent years by the Siberian party organization on the village locally, which he read on the long train ride.[57] At cities en route, he had demanded fresh newspapers and noted, for example, that the Ural Worker, published in Sverdlovsk, contained "not one word" on grain procurements; farther on, in Tyumen, he found that the local Red Banner had a great deal on grain procurements—in Ukraine. The January 1928 OGPU political mood report for Siberia would brim with what was labeled kulak agitation ("You want to recreate 1920, take grain from the lads with force, but you won't succeed, we'll sell a cow, we'll sell two, but grain we won't give"). Anti-Soviet leaflets were appended to the extensive report.[58] In Novosibirsk, Stalin sat down and read the entire run of January issues of Soviet Siberia and found that only very recently had the region's flagship newspaper begun to pay attention to procurements. He concluded that the Siberia party was "not conducting a class line."[59] Still, thanks to Syrtsov's fleet-footed preemptive action, Stalin seems to have come away with a positive impression of that January 18 Novosibirsk meeting.[60] In a ciphered telegram (January 19, 8:00 a.m.) to Stanisław Kosior, a Central Committee secretary who was helping mind the shop back on Old Square (and who had once been party boss in Siberia), Stalin wrote: "The main impression of the gathering: nightmarishly late with procurement, very hard to get back what has been lost, can only get back what has been lost via beastly pressure and skill in leadership, the functionaries are prepared to get down to business in order to fix the situation."[61]

Wishful thinking? Stalin had issued some threatening secret circulars, introduced a policy innovation (widened application of the punitive Article 107), and made a personal visit ("beastly pressure"), and voilà—grain for the cities and army would roll in? Intimations of trouble were there: one attendee at the Novosibirsk meeting, Sergei Zagumyonny, the recently appointed head of the Siberian branch of the USSR Agricultural Bank, had the audacity to challenge Stalin's authority. Zagumyonny's verbal objections were not the sole dissenting voice that day; the chairman of the Siberian union of consumers' cooperatives called for skillful agitation, rather than coercion.[62] But the next day (January 19), Zagumyonny saw fit to elaborate his objections in writing to Stalin as well as to Syrtsov, arguing that if kulaks were arrested for merely refusing to sell the grain in their storage sheds, the middle and poor peasants would view it as an end to the NEP, which would result in the country having less grain—the opposite result of the intended policy. "I do not want to be a prophet," Zagyumonny wrote, before prophesizing catastrophe. He even asserted superior knowledge to his superiors, Stalin included: "I know the village well, both from growing up in it and from recent letters from my father, a poor peasant."[63] Stalin took his pencil and underscored several passages or appended mocking comments ("ha ha") to the letter. Whether he fully grasped that Zagumyonny's thoughts were shared by others in that room of officials, and beyond, remains unclear, but Stalin decided to address the Siberian party bureau again, for a second time, on January 20, in a narrower circle.

Apologizing for divulging the existence and contents of a private letter from Zagumyonny, who was not invited to this gathering, Stalin stressed that "those proposed measures I spoke about the day before yesterday will strike the kulak, the market cornerer, so that there will be no price gouging. And then the peasant will understand, there'll be no price rise, it's necessary to bring grain to market, otherwise you'll go to prison. . . . Comrade Zagumyonny says that this will lead to a decrease in grain procurement. How is that clear?" Stalin's understanding of "the market" connoted not supply and demand but the state's ability to get its hands on peasants' output. In Ukraine, he stated, "they smashed the speculators in the head and the market got healthy again."[64] He denied that he was abrogating the NEP, but reminded those present that "our country is not a capitalist country, but a socialist country, which, in allowing NEP, at the same time retained the final word for the state, so we are acting correctly." He added that "argumentation by use of force has the same significance as argumentation by use of economic means, and sometimes greater significance, when the market [grain procurements] has been spoiled and they try to turn our entire economic policy onto the rails of capitalism, which we will not do." Soon, to reinforce his counterargument to Zagumyonny's assertions that middle and even poor peasants would side with kulaks who came under assault, Stalin and the Siberian party bureau would stipulate that 25 percent of any kulak grain confiscated in the public trials be redistributed to poor peasants and "economically weak" middle peasants, thereby linking the latter to the party's grain procurement drive.[65] Zagumyonny's defiance had spurred a sharpening of policy, but it may have accomplished far more. Stalin, who usually played his cards extremely close to his vest, offered a look into his deepest thinking.[66]

Point blank, Stalin suddenly told the circle of Siberian officials that Soviet agricultural development had dead-ended. He recounted how in the revolution, the gentry class had been expropriated and their large farms subdivided, but mostly into small peasant households that failed to specialize, growing a little bit of everything—grain, sunflowers, keeping cows for milk. "Such a mixed economy, the small household variety, is a misfortune for a large country," he argued, a problem that was immense in scale, because if before the revolution there had been some 15 million individual peasant proprietors [edinolichniki], now the figure approached 25 million. Most of them did not avail themselves of machines, scientific knowledge, or fertilizer.[67] "Whence the strength of the kulak?" Stalin asked. "Not in the fact he was born strong, nothing of the kind, but in the fact that his farming is large scale." Size was how the kulak could take advantage of machinery and modernize. "Could we develop agriculture in kulak fashion, as individual farms, along the path of large-scale farms and the path of latifundia, as in Hungary, Eastern Prussia, America and so on?" Stalin asked. "No, we could not. We're a Soviet country, we want to implant a collective economy, not solely in industry, but in agriculture. We need to follow that path." Moreover, Stalin explained, even if the Soviet regime had *wanted* to develop along the path of individual-proprietor large-scale kulak farms, that approach would fail because "the whole Soviet system, all our laws, all our financial measures, all measures to supply villages with agricultural equipment, everything here moves in the direction of limiting individual-proprietor large-scale farming." The Soviet system "cuts the kulak off in every way, which has resulted in the cul-de-sac into which our agriculture has now entered." To get out of the cul-de-sac, he concluded, "there remains only the path of developing large-scale farms of a collective type." Precisely collective farms (*kolkhozy*), not the cooperatives used by small-scale farmers: "Unification of small and tiny peasant household farms into large collective farms . . . for us is the only path."[68]

The *only* path—Stalin was not one to utter idle reflections. Inside the Communist party throughout most of the 1920s, the NEP had been savagely attacked by the Left opposition and then the United opposition. Stalin had defended the NEP against these leftist attacks.[69] But these matters had been discussed endlessly not just at the formal party gatherings. Many an evening, as the Stalin faction converged on the Kremlin after work—Stalin, Molotov, Orjonikidze, and others down Ilinka from Old Square, Voroshilov down Znamenka—they gathered at someone's Kremlin apartment, often Voroshilov's (the grandest), sometimes Stalin's, where they would chew the cud about the plateauing harvest and dire imperative to modernize agriculture, the plethora of enemies, the absence of allies, the army's lack of modern weapons. The hard men of the Stalin faction looked to him to figure out a practical way forward. NEP's dilemma was not merely that the rate of industrial growth seemed too low, making people wonder how long under the NEP it would take before the USSR became a truly industrial country. The dilemma was not merely the unmodernized technical level and small, divided plots of Soviet agriculture, which produced harvests insufficient to support the kind of grain exports necessary to finance imports of machines, including for agriculture. The dilemma was not even just the fact that the regime lacked control over the food supply or the countryside, rendering it hostage to the actions and decisions of the peasantry. All these were profound problems, but the *core* dilemma of the NEP was ideological: seven years into the NEP, socialism (non-capitalism) was not in sight. NEP amounted to grudgingly tolerated capitalism in a country that had had an avowedly anticapitalist or socialist revolution.

Exactly when Stalin had concluded that it was now time to force the village onto the path of socialism remains unclear. Kalinin would look back and call a politburo commission on collective farms established in 1927, and headed by Molotov, a "mental revolution."[70] But not long before embarking for Siberia, Stalin had told a Moscow organization party conference (November 23, 1927) that "to pursue a policy of discord with the majority of the peasantry means to start a civil war in the village, make it difficult to supply our industry with peasant raw materials (cotton, sugar beet, flax, leather, wool, etc.), disrupt the supply of agricultural products to the working class, undermine the very foundations of our industry."[71] In Novosibirsk, in effect, Stalin was arguing against himself. His was not a lone voice. Kārlis Baumanis, an ethnic Latvian known as Karl Bauman (b. 1892) and a high official in the Moscow party organization, had emphatically stated at the same Moscow party forum (November 27) that "there cannot be two socialisms, one for the countryside and one for the city."[72] Still, this was not yet recognized as official policy. True, during the very last minutes of the 15th Party Congress in December 1927, even as the ink was drying on the expulsions from the party of the leftists Trotsky, Zinoviev, and Kamenev, a resolution on "work in the village" had acquired that revealing amendment about large-scale collective farms being set as the party's fundamental task in the countryside. The significance of that Stalin-initiated resolution—worded generally, and lacking a timetable—may have escaped the wider party, let alone the country at large. Large-scale collective farms had gone unmentioned in the four alarmist Central Committee circulars on grain procurements that Stalin had dispatched to all local party organizations between December 14 and January 14, the last one on the day before he departed for Siberia.[73] Molotov and Stalin had offices that adjoined a common conference room and no one saw or talked more with the general secretary, but Molotov's long report to the Central Committee (January 25, 1928) concerning his own grain procurement trip to the Urals, and before that to Ukraine, said nothing about forcing wholesale collectivization.[74] Out in Siberia, moreover, Stalin's speech on January 20 had been confined to the narrowest of circles. Even the mere fact of his trip to Siberia was held in secrecy: No mention appeared in any Soviet newspaper.[75] Nonetheless, the unpublished Siberian speech was earth-shattering.

Nearly eighteen years before, in August 1910, Pyotr Stolypin, the greatest of all tsarist-era officials, had crisscrossed the Western Siberian steppes, sometimes riding more than 500 miles on horseback away from railheads and rivers to meet with peasants, who turned out to acclaim him.[76] Stolypin wrote to his wife, "I have at least seen and learned things that one cannot learn from documents."[77] The tsarist prime minister's bold reforms—to extirpate what he saw as the roots of peasant unrest by encouraging peasants to quit the communes, consolidate land into contiguous farms, and convert these larger holdings into private property—had sought nothing less than the wholesale remaking of Russia. True, Siberia, unlike European Russia, did not have communes, but because a law to extend private-property homesteading to Siberia (introduced on June 14, 1910) had failed to pass, Stolypin worried that his parallel program to spur peasant migration into open lands of Siberia would end up implanting the commune there.[78] He further worried that the strong spirit of peasant egalitarianism he encountered in Siberia would counteract the individualistic yet authoritarian-monarchist values that he sought to inculcate.[79] In the published report of his trip, Stolypin recommended that private property in land be secured in Siberia de jure, not merely de facto, and underscored how Siberia needed not just small-scale agriculture (which was flourishing) but "larger private landholdings."[80] By the time his report was published, however, Stolypin was dead—felled by an assassin in the Kiev Opera House.

Stalin did not make it out to the northwestern Altai near Slavgorod, where Stolypin had been cheered by thousands of peasants out in the open, and where in 1912 they had erected a stone obelisk in his memory.[81] Stalin would not have seen that Stolypin monument anyway: in 1918, it had been destroyed during revolutionary peasant land seizures that reversed much of the Stolypin wave toward consolidated farms, and strengthened communes with their separated strips.[82] But under the NEP, Stolypin's yeomen had reappeared. The Soviet regime supported conversion into consolidated farms with multifield crop rotation for efficiency purposes, without supporting their conversion into de jure private property. But for the entire USSR's land reorganization, there were a mere 11,500 surveyors and other technical personnel, reminiscent of the dearth that to an extent had held back the progress of Stolypin's reforms.[83] Still, consolidated, multifield farms accounted for under 2 percent of arable land in 1922, 15 percent by 1925, and around 25 percent by 1927.[84] But even when consolidation took place, it was largely without mechanization and with a torrent of complaints that rich peasants who could afford to bribe local officials had tilted the work in their favor. Whether Stalin, out in Siberia, met with actual peasants, let alone large throngs of them, as did Stolypin, remains unclear.[85] What is clear is that although Stalin despised Stolypin, he found himself facing Stolypin's challenges—the village as the key to Russia's destiny, peasants as a supposed political problem in opposition to the reigning regime. But Stalin was proposing to force through the diametrically opposite policy: annihilation of the individual yeoman farmer, in favor of collectively worked, collectively owned farms.

Scholarly arguments that "no plan" existed to collectivize Soviet Eurasia are utterly beside the point.[86] No plan *could* have existed because actually attaining near complete collectivization was, at the time, unimaginable in practical terms. Collectivize one sixth of the earth? How? With what levers? Even the ultraleftist Trotsky, in a speech a few years back, had called a "transition to collective forms" of agriculture a matter of "one or two generations. In the near epoch we are forced to take account of the immense significance of petty peasant individual farming."[87] As of 1928, peasants were still not joining collective farms voluntarily. Whereas commercial and trade cooperatives encompassed some 55 percent of peasant households, production-oriented cooperatives were rare. Collective farms constituted no more than 1 percent of the total, enrolled on average only fifteen to sixteen peasant households, and each possessed just eight horses and eight to ten cows—economic dwarfs.[88] At the same time, administratively, the regime had attained only a minimal presence in the countryside: outside the provincial capitals, traces of the red banners, slogans, and symbols of the new order vanished, and dedicated personnel were shockingly thin on the ground. The 1922 party census had reported that party members made up just 0.13 percent of villagers; by 1928, this percentage had doubled, but it was still just 0.25 percent of rural inhabitants, a mere 300,000 rural Communists out of 120 million people.[89] Siberia counted only 1,331 party cells even in its 4,009 village soviets (and far from every village had a functioning soviet).[90] Moreover, what constituted a "party cell" remained unclear: one Orthodox Church soviet in Western Siberia denounced the local party cell for its card playing and careerism; another rural party cell was found to be holding séances to communicate with the spirit of Karl Marx.[91] Could these cadres, already overwhelmed trying to procure a minimum of the harvest, force 120 million rural inhabitants into collective farms?

Could Stalin even win approval at the top for a program of wholesale collectivization? He would have to outflank not just the pro-NEP opponents in the politburo—such as Bukharin, Tomsky, and Rykov—but even his own faction of loyalists, who remained uncertain of such a scheme. Stalin himself did not yet know how, or by whom, wholesale collectivization would be carried out. A "plan," to do the impossible? At the same time, however, Stalin had concluded— as his speech in Novosibirsk demonstrated—that the impossible was a necessity. In his mind, the regime had become caught in something far worse than a price scissors: namely, a class-based vicious circle. The Bolsheviks desperately needed the peasants to produce good harvests, but the better the peasants did, the more they turned into class enemies, that is, kulaks. To put the matter another way, a non-collectivized countryside was politically unthreatening only if the peasants were poor, but if the peasants were poor they produced insufficient grain to feed the northern cities or the Red Army and to export. That is why, finally, scholars who dismiss Stalin's Marxist motivations for collectivization are as wrong as those who either hype the absence of a "plan" or render collectivization "necessary."[92] Stalin had connected the ideological dots, reaching the full logic of a class-based outlook. Everything would be improvised, of course. But Stalin would not improvise the introduction of the rule of law and a constitutional order; he would not improvise granting the peasants freedom; he would not improvise restricting police power. He would improvise a program of building socialism: forcing into being large-scale collective farms, absent private property. We need to understand not only why Stalin did it, but how.

## EXILING THE LEFT, ENACTING LEFTISM

Stalin's January 15, 1928, departure had occurred almost simultaneously with Trotsky's forced deportation from Moscow.[93] Each had come to define himself via the other: two very differently capable disciples of Lenin, both from the imperial borderlands, but one self-consciously intellectual, with a degree from a university in Ukraine, the other largely an autodidact, with several years study at an Orthodox seminary in Georgia. Trotsky was living in the apartment of a supporter, Alexander Beloborodov, the Bolshevik who had signed the order to execute Nicholas II, but lately had been expelled from the party as an oppositionist (he was also suffering angina attacks). Initially, Stalin proposed exiling Trotsky to the southern city of Astrakhan, but Trotsky objected because of its humid climate, fearing its effects on his chronic malaria, and Stalin had altered the destination to Alma-Ata, a provincial settlement in arid southeastern Kazakhstan. By one account, Bukharin called Trotsky to inform him of the destination of his deportation.[94] By other accounts, Trotsky was summoned to the OGPU, where a minor official read out a decree: internal exile, departure set for January 16, pickup at 10:00 p.m. Either way, he began to pack a lifetime of political activity, filling some twenty crates. "In all the corridors and passages," wrote a German newspaper correspondent who managed to interview Trotsky on January 15, "were piles of books, and once again books—the nourishment of revolutionaries."[95] On January 16, the thickset Trotsky, his hair almost white, his complexion sickly, waited for the secret police with his wife, Natalya Sedova, and two sons, the elder of whom, Lev, planned to leave his wife and child in Moscow and accompany his father into exile as his "commissar" of communications and foreign affairs.[96]

The appointed hour passed, however, and the OGPU failed to show. Cristian Rakovski, the recently disgraced Soviet envoy to France and ardent Trotsky supporter, burst into the Beloborodov apartment with news of a crowd that had massed at the Kazan Railway Station, hung a portrait of Trotsky on the rail carriage, and defiantly chanted ("Long live Trotsky!"). Finally, the OGPU called the apartment to say the departure would be delayed for two days. The secret police had comically miscalculated (informing Trotsky of the correct date and time of his departure). It fell to the shop-minding Stanisław Kosior to send a telegram to Stalin's train (en route to Siberia) to report that on January 16, a crowd of 3,000 had gathered at the train station in Moscow and that they had had to postpone Trotsky's banishment for two days because his wife had taken ill (Sedova did have a fever).[97] Kosior further told Stalin that "the crowd attempted to detain the train, shouting, 'Down with the gendarmes!' 'Beat the Jews,' 'Down with the fascists.'" Nineteen people were detained. "They beat several OGPU operatives," Kosior wrote, as if the armed secret police had come under threat. One demonstrator, according to Kosior, had learned of the two-day postponement and summoned the crowd to reassemble on January 18. This seems to have smartened up the OGPU, for agents showed up at the Beloborodov apartment the very next morning (January 17). Tricked, Trotsky refused to budge, but the OGPU forced his fur coat and hat on over his pajamas and slippers and whisked him to the Yaroslavl Station.[98] Kosior added in his ciphered telegram to Stalin that "we had to lift him and forcibly carry him because he refused to go on his own, and locked himself in his room, so it was necessary to smash down the door."[99]

The whole Trotsky business had left a nasty imprint on Stalin's character. Who really appreciated what he had gone through in the prolonged cock fight? The China policy fiasco had been a very close call. But notwithstanding the grief Trotsky had caused, several politburo members had been lukewarm about, or even opposed to, exiling Trotsky.[100] To Kosior, Stalin wrote back laconically: "I received the cipher about the antics of Trotsky and the Trotskyites."[101]

This time, Kosior and the OGPU had made sure the train station had been cleared utterly; machine-gun toting troops and armored cars lined all approaches. Even so, the moment did not pass in lockstep. "I can't forget the days when I served under him at the front," the top-level Chekist Georgi Prokofyev, in charge of the deportation and full of drink at midday, is said to have told a foreign correspondent with Soviet sympathies. "What a man! And how we loved him! He wrought miracles—miracles I tell you. . . . And always with words . . . each word a shell, a grenade." But now, the once mighty leader had been reduced to a pathetic sight. Trotsky, according to the journalist, held aloft in the arms of a OGPU officer, "had the appearance of a patient taken from a hospital bed. Underneath the fur he had nothing on except pajamas and socks. . . . Trotsky was loaded like baggage aboard the train."[102] A single rail coach with him, his family members, and an OGPU convoy pulled out from Moscow—without the twenty crates of books and papers, many of them Trotsky's copies of top secret politburo memoranda. Nearly thirty years earlier, a teenage Bronstein had glimpsed Moscow for the first time: from a prison railcar, on his way from a jail in Odessa to exile in Siberia. Now he had his last glimpse of Moscow, also from a prison rail transport.[103] Trotsky soon arrived at the last station on the Central Asian rail line, Frunze (Bishkek), in Kyrgyzia; incredibly, the crates with his books and even his archive met up with him. A bus laden with the luggage hauled them the final 150 miles across snowy mountains, and arrived in Alma-Ata at 3:00 a.m. on January 25. He and family were billeted at the Hotel Seven Rivers on— what else—Gogol Street.[104]

It was not only Trotsky: On January 20—the day Stalin sprung his ruminations about collectivization on Siberian higher-ups—Soviet newspapers carried a notice of the internal exile from Moscow of dozens of oppositionists, "bawlers and neurasthenics of the Left," as Stalin liked to call them, whom he dispersed eastward (Uralsk, Semipalatinsk, Narym, Tobolsk, Barnaul), northward (Arkhangelsk), or southward (Astrakhan, Armenia).[105] Radek, already in Tobolsk, Siberia, sent the first letter Trotsky received in Alma-Ata.[106] Stalin did not initially prevent the intra-Trotskyite correspondence, since, thanks to secret-police perlustration, he could read it. Trotsky responded to Radek with some advice: "I strongly urge you to organize a proper way of life in order to preserve yourself. Whatever it takes. We are still of much, much use."[107] Trotsky in 1928 had no inkling that he would be the one to fill the enormous vacuum of information about Stalin, with writings that would profoundly shape all views of the dictator, or that Stalin would discover especially sinister "uses" of Trotsky. Trotsky occupied a vast space in Stalin's psyche and, eventually, Stalin would enlarge Trotsky to the same scale in the Soviet political imagination, as the cause and incarnation of all that was evil. In the meantime, having just banished the longtime leader of the "bawlers and neurasthenics of the Left" inside the party, Stalin, in Siberia, immediately began forcing the party and the country to the left.

## COMMUNIST PARTY ON WATCH

Stalin and his entourage wended their way through Siberia. After his startling speech in Novosibirsk on January 20, he set out the next day—the fourth anniversary of Lenin's death, a state holiday—for Barnaul, a silver-mining town on the approaches to the Altai mountains that had been founded with serf labor to serve imperial Russia's military needs. The severe continental climate brought hot, dry winds from Asian deserts in summer and freezing, damp winds from the Arctic during the long winter, with snow drifts that could exceed human height. Ah, but the soil: black-earth or chestnut-brown, it rendered these lands a Russian peasant paradise.[108] Barnaul officialdom turned out a sizable party to greet Stalin and Syrtsov on the platform on January 22. (The OGPU's Zakovsky, overseeing Stalin's local travels, arrived as well.) Wooden-basket sleds jammed the square in front of the rail station. The one earmarked for Stalin, "insulated with a bearskin and a greatcoat so the leader did not freeze," as one eyewitness recalled, was pulled by a horse named Marat (for the French revolutionary), and driven by a local OGPU commandant who would go on to become a prize-winning executioner.[109] Stalin yielded to the requests for a group photograph, but there would be no banquet. In a speech, he allowed that "one of the causes" for the grain procurement crisis was that "the discussion [with the opposition] diverted our attention, then the easy victory at the congress, the holiday moods of those comrades who went their way home after the congress." But he was not there to indulge excuses and roundly dismissed popular local reasons for the shortfall—severe snowstorms, lack of manufactured goods for sale, a supposedly smaller harvest—insisting "the cause is in ourselves, in our organizations." "We're late, comrades," he admonished the officials. "Some functionaries are even surprised: 'How's that,' they say, 'we sent a lot of grain out and, over there in Moscow, they howl.' . . . No excuses and retreats from the targets can be permitted! . . . Exert pressure on this in Bolshevik style (applause)."[110]

After Stalin, Syrtsov reinforced the message, stating that the share of "middle peasants" in grain marketings for January 1928 as compared with a year earlier had declined from 60 to 30 percent. In other words, it was not the kulaks alone hoarding grain. That was why Stalin wanted to send a message to the middle peasants by arresting kulaks—holding grain would not be tolerated.[111] The next day, at Rubtsovsk, another county seat, to which Semipalatinsk officials had also been summoned, Stalin's appearance provoked loud applause, to which he replied: "Excellent folk, you Siberians, you are able to clap your hands in concert, but you are not able to work!"[112] After the gathering, Stalin did partake of some homemade brandy, the pretext evidently being the severe frosts, according to one participant, who added that despite "a minor blizzard" Stalin "was willing to go on foot" back to his special heavily guarded train, where he spent the night.[113]

The Soviet dictator had traveled not to engage in fact-finding but to explain the rationale for the coercive measures and ensure their implementation, and yet the trip was proving to be a revelation. He was learning, for example, that the kulak seemed far stronger than even he had understood. Never mind that peasant wealth was cyclical and that very few households remained well-off through generations so as to form a distinct capitalist class; at any given moment, there *were* kulaks. "The offensive of capital in the Siberian countryside," one of the better-off agricultural regions, had been an obsession of the Trotskyites. Syrtsov had dismissed such talk as "hysterical bawling," but the counterstudy he had commissioned showed farm machinery and credit were in the hands of the well-off.[114] Now Stalin heard firsthand testimony confirming this point. Moreover, instead of combating such developments, he also learned the party in Siberia seemed contaminated by them, a point that also had been a preoccupation of the Left opposition. Lev Sosnovsky, a Left oppositionist journalist exiled to Barnaul, wrote to Trotsky in Kazakhstan of Stalin's secret visit to Siberia (in a letter that would be smuggled out and published in the foreign émigré press, becoming the sole public acknowledgment of Stalin's travels). Sosnovsky concluded that the Siberian party apparatus was "not up to the task of the new approach" (application of coercive measures against peasants).[115] Half of Siberia's Communists had joined the party since 1924, during the New Economic Policy, and one third were still engaged in agriculture, an eye-popping proportion; the Siberian party leadership even viewed industrialization as intended to serve the needs of agriculture, and wanted to prioritize farm implements, grain storage, food processing.[116] Oddly enough, having exiled the Trotskyites, Stalin was discovering that his problem was not the small numbers of oppositionists. It was the party as a whole.[117]

Already the Siberian apparatus was infamous for the bottle. "Drunkenness has become an everyday phenomenon, they get drunk with prostitutes, and take off in their vehicles, even members of the bureaus of party cells," Zakovsky had told a meeting of the party cell inside the Siberian OGPU, noting that his bosses in Moscow had made this point to him. Zakovsky was himself a lover of the dolce vita, juggling multiple mistresses, rarely far from a bottle, and concluded, "It's OK to drink, but only in our narrow circle of Chekists and not in a public place" (presumably including driving around in easily identifiable, scarce vehicles with hookers in view).[118] Drunkenness, however, was not what Stalin scolded them for. "Is it that you are afraid to disturb the tranquility of the kulak gentry?" he asked menacingly of Siberian officials.[119] Many Siberian functionaries, he had discovered, "live in the homes of kulaks, board and lodge with them," because, they told him, "kulak homes are cleaner and they feed you better."[120] Rural party officials were aching to marry kulak daughters. Such anecdotes ignited Stalin's class sensibilities: Soviet officialdom was becoming dependent materially, and hence, in his Marxist mind, politically, on the rural wealthy.

Stalin expected that the supposedly widespread and increasing class polarization in the village would be galvanized by his measures. "If we give a signal to pressurize and to set upon the kulak, [the mass of peasants] will be more than enthusiastic about it," he had privately told Syrtsov during his Siberia trip.[121] And superficially, his coercive measures did appear successful. Already on January 24, Siberia's first public trial under Article 107 (of three kulaks) took place in Barnaul county, and received extensive newspaper coverage the next day.[122] In perhaps the most sensational case, the kulak Teplov in Rubtsovsk county, a septuagenarian patriarch of a large family, was said to possess 3 homes, 5 barns, 50 horses, 23 cows, 108 sheep, and 12 pigs, while "hoarding" 242 tons of grain. "Why should I sell grain to Soviet power when they do not sell me machines," he was quoted as saying. "If they would sell me a nice tractor that would be another matter." Teplov was sentenced to 11 months and lost 213 tons of his grain; much of the rest rotted.[123] All told, nearly 1,400 kulaks in Siberia would be subjected to trials in January and February 1928. Newspaper accounts invariably claimed that courtrooms were jammed with peasant observers.[124] From those convicted the authorities would manage to seize a mere 12,000 tons of grain (under 1 percent of that year's regional grain procurements), but that information was not publicly divulged.[125] Meanwhile, the Siberian procuracy was dragging its feet, refusing to approve a majority of Zakovsky's arrest warrants for individuals on watch lists—former tsarist officers, former Whites from the civil war—under Article 58 (counterrevolution), which brought significantly harsher penalties than for speculation.[126] While Stalin was still in Western Siberia, *On the Leninist Path*, the local party organization's journal, acknowledged not just a "lack of enthusiasm" but a "flood of protests" by members of the legal apparatus even against the party directive to extend Article 107 to grain growers as a violation of Soviet law. Stalin was quoted as responding that "laws written by Bolsheviks cannot be used against Soviet power."[127]

Stalin had far bigger ambitions that application of Article 107, of course. He continued to tiptoe around the fate of the NEP. When asked, he insisted it would continue, much to everyone's relief. But interlocutors failed to comprehend that he had shifted back to the NEP's original formulation as a *temporary* retreat *combined with* a socialist offensive. The same issue (January 31, 1928) of *On the Leninist Path* that published the disagreements over the application of Article 107 wrote that "the small-scale, dispersed, individual farm is by its very nature reactionary. On this basis further development of the country's productive force, which is indispensable for us, is impossible." The editorial concluded: "Countryside—forward to large-scale collective farming."[128] This may have been the USSR's first editorial about the momentous turnabout about to unfold.

But if the Siberian party could not even manage to seize grain from kulaks, how could it implement wholesale socialist transformation of the countryside? Siberia's party hierarchs did put on a vast show of mobilization, reporting an improbable 12,000 meetings of "poor peasants" held between January and March 1928 (supposedly encompassing 382,600 attendees).[129] All this culminated in the first ever

Siberian conference of "poor peasants," which opened March 1, 1928, in Novosibirsk, with 102 delegates and Union-wide coverage. "We need to clarify for everyone in the village," one delegate was quoted stating in *Pravda*, "that the kulak is an evil horder of grain and an enemy of the state."[130] On the front lines, however, in Siberia's county-level party organizations, apparatchiks ordered that new "troikas" set up to expedite grain procurement should operate solely on the party premises, without revealing their existence, "so as not to cause misinterpretations among the population and among a part of the lower party masses."[131] Stalin wanted wide publicity for the tough coercive measures; the party in rural districts wanted to hide.

No one embodied the challenge of carrying out a new revolution more than Syrtsov. He had seen Stalin off after a party gathering in Omsk and returned to Western Siberia HQ at Novosibirsk, where on January 31 he reiterated to the Siberian party organization Stalin's reassurances that the New Economic Policy was not being abrogated.[132] Syrtsov was no liberalizer—he had spearheaded the bloody deportation of Cossacks from his native Ukraine during the civil war—but he viewed collectivization as solely for hapless poor peasants who individually just could not get on their feet. At a conference on rural issues the year before Stalin's visit, Syrtsov had exhorted, "To the middle peasant, the strong farm, and the well off, we say: 'Accumulate and good luck to you.'"[133] Even after Stalin's visit, Syrtsov voiced faith in the benefits for the state of individual peasant success. As he would tell the Siberian Communists at the next major regional party gathering in March 1928, "When a spider sucks blood from a fly, he also works hard."[134] Apologetics for the kulak, and from a Stalin protégé. Syrtsov was hardly alone. Another top official in Siberia, Roberts Eihe (b. 1890), an ethnic Latvian from a poor farming family who had made his early career in the civil war food procurement commissariat, had echoed Syrtsov's views at a regional party conference back in 1927 ("Those comrades who in their fear of the kulak think that by ravaging strong farms we will speed up socialist construction . . . are deeply mistaken").[135] Now, however, Eihe began parroting Stalin's interpretation of pervasive "kulak sabotage." Officials like Eihe—who not only possessed strong stomachs for bloodshed against their own people, but could shift with the new political winds—would rise higher still. In fact, Eihe would soon replace Syrtsov as Siberia's party boss. Zakovsky, too, would further advance his brilliant career.[136] Soaring ambition laced with animal fear would serve as a formidable instrument in Stalin's kit. Still, it would take a lot more than opportunistic top officials to carry out a totalizing transformation of Soviet Eurasia.

As Stalin traveled from Barnaul and Rubtsovsk up to Omsk, and then pivoted eastward to Krasnoyarsk (at Syrtsov's suggestion, but in Eihe's company), his telegrams to Moscow continued to indicate progress on the immediate aim ("The procurement has livened up. A serious breakthrough should begin in late January or early February"). But rather than citing the serious attitude of local officialdom, as before, he stressed how *he* had "wound everyone up, the way it's supposed to be done."[137] In Krasnoyarsk very late on the evening of January 31 he met party higher-ups summoned from around Eastern Siberia—in the district secret police facility. Stalin exhorted them on grain procurements, but also expressly linked the imperative "to curb the kulak" to the circumstance of "capitalist encirclement," and observed that "the future war could break out suddenly, it will be long and demand immense forces." The meeting concluded around 6:00 a.m. on February 1. Stalin telegrammed Mikoyan (still in the North Caucasus) to increase the grain targets for February in Siberia from 235,000 to 325,000 tons. "This will spur procurements," he wrote. "And now it is necessary."[138] On February 2, Stalin set out in the direction of Moscow.[139] The next day, Krasnoyarsk newspapers summoned the populace to "strike the kulak."[140] Before he was back in the capital, Siberia's "grain troika" had raised their own February target to 400,000 tons. What to expect locally in Stalin's absence, however, remained uncertain. The region's February procurements turned out to be 1.5 times greater than January's, but not 400,000 tons. March quotas would be set at 375,000 tons, but Siberia officials were confident of being able to deliver only 217,000 tons a month.[141]

Stalin arrived back in Moscow on February 6, 1928, after three weeks on the road. Back at Old Square he could follow the repercussions from his trip not just via party channels but also secret police reports. On February 10, for example, the OGPU submitted a political mood summary ominously noting that in Siberia "party members relate to the measures for strengthening grain procurements in many districts almost no differently from how the rest of the mass of peasants do." Names were named, county by county, of those refusing to take part in the coercive turn, and some were quoted to the effect that the opposition was right: the Central Committee was leading the country to crisis.[142] On February 13, Stalin dispatched yet another secret circular from Old Square to party organizations across the Union allowing that "we are exiting the crisis of grain procurement," but asserting that the party "had neglected the struggle against the kulak and the kulak danger" and had turned out to be full of people who wanted "to live in peace with the kulak." Ominously, he called them "Communists" in quotation marks.

He demanded that they work "not for the sake of their jobs but for the sake of the revolution," and that top party bosses "check and decisively purge the party, soviet, and cooperative organizations during the course of the procurement campaign, expel alien and hanger-on elements, and replace them with tested party and verified nonparty functionaries."[143] But if the party was so strongly under the influence of NEP capitalism and kulaks, where would the reliable cadres come from?

Still more confounding to the regime, rural conflict was turning out to be not class based but mostly generational and gender based; the regime indirectly admitted as much by complaining that what it called the middle and even poor peasants were "under the sway" of the kulaks.[144] Fomenting major "class warfare" in the village looked like it would require forcing in outsiders. Already in connection with Stalin's Siberia trip, about 100 worker-Communist militants from Moscow and Leningrad had been mobilized to Siberia to galvanize shakedowns of the kulak. Union-wide, Stalin soon mobilized into grain procurement some 4,000 urban party officials from the provincial and county level, "the staunchest and most experienced Bolsheviks," as well as 26,000 "activists" from the lowest levels.[145] Those sent in found some local counterparts, too. Oleg Barabashev, an Odessa-born Communist Youth League activist and journalist (b. 1904) who had been relocated from Leningrad to Siberia, wrote in the newspaper *Siberia* (which he edited) that "Stalin is right in saying that the party is ready for the slogan of dekulakization." Barabashev meant the worker elements in the party. Observing a party cell meeting at a railroad junction near Omsk, he wrote of working-class fear in the face of shortages and price inflation, and of their yearning to see arrests of "kulak speculators."[146] Barabashev might have also pointed out a strong appetite for the heads of tsarist-era engineers and specialists who continued to enjoy conspicuous privilege and power. To indulge these resentments, for Stalin, proved irresistible, and his policy opponents proved unable to stop him.

## RYKOV'S DILEMMA

Alexei Rykov, who ran the government on a day-to-day basis, did not travel out to a region to forcibly collect grain. (Neither did Tomsky or Bukharin.) Rykov regarded the NEP, for all its shortcomings, as preferable to what he viewed as the destabilizing alternative. Of peasant stock and an ethnic Russian from Saratov, where Stolypin had served as governor, Rykov (b. 1881) had never been other than a Bolshevik and occupied the position that Lenin had, chairman of the Council of People's Commissars. (Uncannily, Rykov had failed to complete the same course of studies for a law degree at Kazan University as Lenin had.)[147] Rykov was nearly Stalin's age and a resident of the same building in the Kremlin, but the two did not really socialize. Rykov had never wavered during the infighting against the opposition, but although he had gone along with Stalin's coercive measures to fill state grain coffers, he was taken aback at Stalin's post-Siberia-trip inclination to maintain the "emergency-ism."[148] After all, Trotsky and the United opposition had just been eviscerated, was Stalin now going to implement their program?[149] In arguing for repeal of the coercive measures, Rykov could point to Stalin's own energetic actions, which had averted the immediate crisis: procurements for February would turn out to be the highest ever for a single month (1.9 million tons), allowing overall procurements for the 1927–28 harvest to leap ahead of the previous year's. Rykov similarly fought the increasingly unrealistic industrialization goals pressed by Kuibyshev. On March 7, 1928, following a politburo meeting at which Molotov, a proxy for Stalin, attacked Rykov's draft industrial-financial plan for 1927–28 as insufficiently ambitious, Rykov took a page out of Stalin's book: he sent a letter of resignation to Stalin, Molotov, and Bukharin. Rykov asked to be reassigned to the Urals, the way Stalin had asked to be sent to godforsaken Turukhansk, Siberia, where he had once been an exile. The same day Rykov sent a second letter, to show he meant business.[150]

Stalin did not try to seize upon Rykov's resignation to rid himself of an ostensible potential rival. Stalin relied greatly upon Rykov, particularly in managing the economy, no small assignment. Rather, just as Rykov had done for him, Stalin sought to mollify the government head. "One cannot pose the issue like that: we need to gather, have a little to drink, and talk heart to heart," he wrote in response to Rykov's resignation letter. "That's how we'll resolve all misunderstandings." Not only Bukharin but even Molotov rejected the possibility of Rykov's resignation. Rykov, it seems, had made his point.[151] His authority was not going to be flouted on the big economic decisions, particularly regarding industry and the budget—or they could find themselves someone else to shoulder the immense responsibilities of the chief executive. Rykov's political weaknesses were many, however, beginning with the circumstance that a crucial member of his voting bloc, Bukharin, was not a person of strong character or perspicacity, and ending with the fact that Stalin had many ways to watch over and checkmate Rykov, but Rykov, other than by threatening to resign, had no real levers over Stalin.

Despite the politburo's decision-making power, none of its members had the wherewithal to ensure that Stalin was implementing its formal decisions (and not implementing others). Between meetings, Stalin had formal responsibility for most important matters, such as supervision of all party organizations and state bodies; in practice, his prerogatives were actually far wider, given the regime's geography of power, communications system, and hypersecrecy.[152] Mikoyan relates an incident from the late 1920s when he fought Stalin over a course of action: the politburo backed Stalin's position, yet the decision was never implemented, apparently because Stalin had changed his mind; the politburo, however, never repealed the formal decision.[153] On another occasion, Stalin had chosen not to inform Rykov of riots in the Caucasus, which lasted several weeks, until after he had put them down.[154] Stalin dominated all official channels and established informal sources of information, while his personal functionaries performed tasks often not formally specified.[155] No one else could verify which materials had been received or gathered by the Central Committee yet not made available for politburo members or what instructions had been given to various agencies in the name of the Central Committee. Above all, Stalin alone had the means to secretly monitor the other top officials for their own "security" and to recruit their subordinates as informants, because he alone, in the name of the Central Committee, liaisoned with the OGPU.

## A TOWN CALLED "MINE SHAFTS" (SHAKHTY)

The police connection detonated just three days after Rykov's rejected resignation, on March 10, 1928, when *Pravda,* in an unsigned front-page editorial, trumpeted how the OGPU had unmasked a counterrevolutionary plot by "bourgeois specialists" trained in the time of the tsar who were said to be working on behalf of the prerevolutionary "capitalist" mine owners now living abroad, aiming to sabotage Soviet power and restore capitalism.[156] Their alleged sabotage had occurred in a small mining settlement known as Shakhty, or "mine shafts," population 33,000.[157] But Shakhty's collieries were adjacent to Ukraine's strategic Donetsk basin and the "investigation" would embroil top economic officials in Ukraine and even Moscow as well as relations with Germany. Rykov, in an overview of the Shakhty case in *Pravda* (March 11), stood behind all the charges, but he also warned against excessive "specialist baiting." He further wrote that "the question of the grain crisis has been taken off the agenda." But for Stalin, Shakhty and the "emergency-ism" in the village were of a piece. He was unleashing a new topsy-turvy of class warfare to expand the regime's social base and his own political leverage in order to accelerate industrialization and to collectivize agriculture. Shakhty's origins had come to Stalin at Sochi, on the cliffs overlooking the Black Sea, the one place he managed to relax, in the company of fat packets of top secret documents and his male service personnel. One person Stalin saw there was the long-standing North Caucasus OGPU boss, Yefim Yevdokimov, who bore responsibility for the dictator's security cocoon during the annual stays down south, a mouth-watering opportunity.

Yevdokimov was a phenomenon. He had been born (1891) in a small town in the Kazakh steppe with two churches and a mosque, where his peasant father served in the tsarist army, but had grown up in Chita, Siberia, where he completed five years of elementary school. He had gone on to become an anarchist syndicalist, then made the leap to Moscow, participating in the protracted revolutionary coup there in fall 1917. The next year, after the regime moved the capital to Moscow, Yevdokimov joined the Bolsheviks and the Red Army. In summer 1919, Dzierżyński named him head of all police Special Departments in the Red Army. Yevdokimov was soon dispatched to civil war Ukraine, where he distinguished himself in massacres of White Guards. At the banquet meeting upon his departure, Vsevolod Balytsky, Yevdokimov's replacement, toasted him as the "Republic's first secret department operative" and handed him his second Order of the Red Banner for "energetic combat against banditism."[158] Yevdokimov praised those present as a "well-organized machine," calling himself merely "a lever of that machine, regulating its operation." When transferred to the vast North Caucasus territory in 1923, Yevdokimov had taken with him to Rostov a brother band who worshipped him as a benevolent godfather or Cossack chieftain (ataman).[159] Unlike at those desk jobs back at Lubyanka headquarters, in the North Caucasus the civil war had never ended and Yevdokimov's life entailed relentless, atrocity-laden campaigns against "bandits" in the rugged mountains. After "mass operations" to confiscate some 20,000 rifles in Chechnya, a similar number in Ingushetia and Ossetia, and more than 12,000 in Karachaevo-Cherskesk and Balkaro-Kabarda, Yevdokimov had written to Yagoda that "the people are armed to the teeth and profoundly dark."[160] The North Caucasus trained a generation of GPU operatives, as well as rank-and-file border guards, in hellacious counterinsurgency techniques against civilians.

Yevdokimov had brought a gift to Stalin in Sochi back in summer 1927. Stalin "as usual, asked me how things were," Yevdokimov would later recall at a big meeting in Moscow. "I told him in particular about this affair"—the tale of a "counterrevolutionary plot" in the city of Vladikavkaz. "He listened carefully and asked detailed questions. At the end of the conversation I said the following: 'For me it is clear that we are dealing with people who are consciously undermining production, but it is not clear to me who their leader is. Either it is the general staffs [of foreign powers], in particular the Polish general staff, or it is the company that in the past owned these enterprises, and that has an interest in undermining production, i.e., the Belgian company.'" Stalin, according to Yevdokimov, "said to me, 'When you finish your investigation, send the materials to the Central Committee'"—meaning bypass normal OGPU channels. "I returned, assembled the underworld gang [bratva]—I apologize for the expression—that is, the comrades [laughter], and I said, get moving."[161] Emboldened by his face-to-face sessions with Stalin, Yevdokimov compiled a photograph album with mug shots of seventy-nine civil war "White Guardists" who lived in the North Caucasus territory, which he sent to the local party boss requesting authorization to liquidate them, not because of anything they had done, but because of what they might do. It was "very important to annihilate them," Yevdokimov wrote to the party boss, because they could serve as "a real force against us, in the event of an international conflict."[162] Yevdokimov's photo-album approach to fast-track executions just in case constituted an innovation. He won a nearly unprecedented third Order of the Red Banner. Meanwhile, the city where Stalin had staged his own discovery of a counterrevolutionary plot by "class aliens" and executed nearly two dozen "spies" and "saboteurs" in 1918, Tsaritsyn, had since been renamed Stalingrad.

Yevdokimov's concocted Vladikavkaz case fizzled, but he delivered to Stalin another case, the one from the coal town of Shakhty, which had originated in the atmosphere of the 1927 war scare, when the OGPU reexamined industrial mishaps with an eye toward possible sabotage. This time, some "confessions" were forthcoming.[163] Shakhty case materials fell into Stalin's hands not long after he had returned from his trip to Siberia and confirmed his suspicions that the kulaks were running wild and the rural Communist party was in bed with class enemies.[164] On March 2, 1928, the same day he received a long report on Shakhty with a cover letter from Yagoda, the dictator received Yevdokimov, in Yagoda's presence.[165] On March 8, the politburo approved a public trial.[166] The next day, a group of the politburo examined the draft indictments, which they completely rewrote (much of the document is crossed out), altering dates and other alleged facts. After the public announcement of the accusations, Nikolai Krylenko, the USSR procurator general, would be dispatched to Rostov, the third biggest city in the RSFSR, and Kharkov, the capital of the Ukrainian SSR, and given no more than a month to finish all work.[167] The regime would settle upon fifty-three defendants, a majority of whom (thirty-five) were mining engineers educated before the revolution; others were mechanics or electricians. The trial was ordered transferred from the Donetsk coal region to Moscow for maximum effect.

Shakhty represented a jumble of fact, fabrication, and twisted laws. An investigation of Shakhty's party organization found it inattentive to industry (its main assignment) and preoccupied with infighting between factions from the Don (ethnic Russian) and Kuban (ethnic Ukrainian), with the latter predominant.[168] Still, by 1927–28 the Donetsk Coal Trust, headquartered in Ukraine's capital, had managed to extract 2.5 million tons of coal, exceeding the 1913 levels, an impressive recovery from the civil war collapse. While mechanized extraction accounted for 15.8 percent of coal output Union-wide, the proportion reached 45 percent in the Shakhty-Donetsk district. These were significant achievements, possible only thanks to skilled engineers and managers as well as workers. At the same time, expensive imported equipment was often used improperly, partly because it fit poorly with existing technology or because skilled installers and operators were lacking. The single-minded drive for coal output, alongside incompetent organization, meant that safety procedures were being violated, mines improperly laid and flooded, and explosions occurring. Some Shakhty defendants admitted lowering worker pay and raising work norms—which was regime policy—and there were links to the former mine owners: the Soviet regime had recruited them, in emigration, to lease their properties back and revive them. One accused mining engineer admitted having received "foreign funds" to blow up a mine, but the mine in question (Novo-Azov) had been detonated in 1921 by directive of the Coal Trust, which had lacked sufficient capacity to restore all the mines and sealed some for safety reasons. Rumor and gossip lent additional credence to the charges. The Polish ambassador was convinced German specialists were conducting espionage (information gathering) on behalf of Germany, albeit not sabotage, but the Lithuania ambassador told his German counterpart that a large Polish-financed organization had carried out sabotage near Shakhty.[169]

Sabotage under Soviet law did not have to be deliberate: if someone's directives or actions resulted in mishaps, then counterrevolutionary intent could be assumed.[170] But in Shakhty the regime was alleging intent, which meant the OGPU had to get the defendants to confess, a high-order challenge for which the secret police employed solitary confinement on unbearably cold floors, forced sleeplessness for nights on end ("interrogations" by "conveyor" method), and promises of lighter sentences. This produced comic pirouettes: when one defendant who confessed to everything predicted to his defense lawyer that he would be imprisoned for just a few months, the lawyer informed him he could get the death penalty, which induced a recantation. But the "investigator" refused to record the change of heart, while a codefendant worried the recantation would end up destroying them both. (The defense lawyer resigned.)[171] Stalin insisted that the evil intent was on orders of international paymasters, which raised the interrogators' challenge still higher, for the trial was going to be public and visible to foreigners. OGPU chief Mężyński, suffering intense pain as well as bouts of flu, would soon depart for Matsesta to undergo sulfur-bath treatments; it was not his problem.[172] Yagoda had to take charge in Moscow. Neither he nor Yevdokimov were stupid: they understood there was no deliberate sabotage.[173] Still, Stalin's pressure was intense, and Yevdokimov and Yagoda gave Stalin what he wanted, from stories of "a powerful counterrevolutionary organization operating for many years" in the Donetsk Coal Trust to "the collusion of German and Polish nationals."[174]

## FOREIGN "ECONOMIC" INTERVENTION

Five German engineers, four of whom were employees of AEG who installed turbines and mining machines, had been arrested in connection with Shakhty. (The politburo had decided English specialists were to be interrogated but released.) Soviet accounts explained that the European working class, impressed by Soviet achievements, held bourgeois warmongers back from a military invasion, but the imperialists had turned to invisible war—economic counterrevolution or "wrecking" (*vreditel'stvo*), a new method of anti-Soviet struggle.[175] On March 10, the chairman of AEG's board telegraphed Ambassador Brockdorff-Rantzau in Moscow from the foreign ministry in Berlin asking him to convey that AEG would cease all operations and withdraw all personnel unless their people were released; the next day the ambassador read the telegram to Chicherin. On March 12, Deputy Foreign Affairs Commissar Litvinov telegrammed Stalin and Chicherin from Berlin regarding the terrible impact on Soviet-German relations of the German arrests.[176] Chicherin had tried to limit the damage by giving the German ambassador in Moscow advance warning about an imminent disagreeable event, which, he hoped, could be jointly managed.[177] But for Germany, the timing was surreal. Just one month before the announcement of the "plot," the Soviets had opened new bilateral trade negotiations in Berlin, promising firm orders of 600 million marks, among other inducements, in exchange for a 600-million-mark credit as well as long-term loans. The Soviets were also requesting that German financial markets handle Soviet government bonds.[178] German industrialists and financiers had their own list of demands, but now, all that seemed for naught. Stalin had lost the French credits in the fiasco over Soviet envoy Cristian Rakovski's behavior, but now he was deliberately poking the Germans in the eye. In the March 2, 1928, note to the rest of the politburo, Stalin, along with Molotov, wrote that "the case might take the most interesting turn if a corresponding trial were organized at the moment of elections in Germany."[179]

Germany, on March 15, 1928, indefinitely suspended bilateral trade and credit talks, blaming the provocative arrests of its five nationals.[180] TASS blamed Berlin for the breakdown in negotiations, and the Soviet press, goaded by Stalin's apparatus, had a field day spewing broadsides against German perfidy. Nikolai Krestinsky, Soviet envoy to Germany, sent Stalin a letter from Berlin on March 17 (copy to Chicherin) asking for the release of one of the arrested German nationals, Franz Goldstein. An infuriated Stalin responded four days later, with copy to Chicherin, accusing Krestinsky of disgracefully abetting the German efforts to use the arrests "to pin the blame on us for the breakdown in negotiations." The dictator added: "The representative of a sovereign state cannot conduct negotiations in such a tone as you consider it necessary to do. Is it difficult to understand that the Germans in the most insolent manner are interfering in our internal affairs, and you, instead of breaking off talks with the Germans, continue to make nice with them? The matter has gone so far that the *Frankfurter Zeitung* has published your disagreements with Moscow on the question of the arrested Germans. There's no further to go than that. With Communist greetings. Stalin."[181]

Suddenly, however, Goldstein as well as Heinrich Wagner, both of whom worked for AEG, were released. Goldstein, according to a note counterintelligence specialist Artur Artuzov wrote for Mężyński, had ingratiatingly told his OGPU interrogators that he knew of three White Guard émigrés who worked for AEG in Germany in the Russian department and were extremely anti-Soviet and that he had seen them with a large sum of money. In a further attempt at ingratiation, he indicated his willingness to return to work in the USSR.[182] Debriefed back in Berlin by the foreign ministry, however, Goldstein dismissed the Soviet claims of sabotage, attributing the breakdown of equipment to worker disinterest, non-party specialists' fear of arrest, inept party overseers, and general disorganization. Publicly, he voiced anger at having been arrested on trumped-up charges while trying to rescue Soviet industry, warned other Germans not to make available "their knowledge and ability" to the Soviet regime, and detailed the horrid initial conditions of his confinement in a provincial Soviet prison (Stalino), creating an uproar.[183] Meanwhile, three Germans who had not been released—Max Maier, Ernst Otto, and Wilhem Badstieber (who worked for the mining company Knapp)—were being held incommunicado, in violation of bilateral treaties specifying that German consular officials had a right to see them. That was not all: Chicherin had passed a note from Yagoda to Brockdorff-Rantzau detailing the alleged crimes of a German national whose name matched no one who was in the Soviet Union; someone whose name was close to that of the accused had last been in the USSR in 1927, which reinforced German doubts about the OGPU's "case."[184]

The arrest of German nationals redounded onto Franco-Soviet relations as well, confirming many there, too, in their view that Moscow was not a place to do business. Like France, Germany stopped short of severing diplomatic relations, but some German companies began to pull the rest of their engineers.[185] Stalin continued to hunger for German specialists, German technology, German capital—but on his terms. AEG decided on March 22 to continue its multiple construction projects in the Soviet Union. A week later, twenty-two days after the arrests, the Soviet regime informed the German embassy that the consul in Kharkov could see the German nationals (confined in Rostov); the German ambassador insisted that someone from the Moscow embassy be allowed to visit them, which was granted. The audiences, on April 2, lasted ten minutes per prisoner, in the presence of three OGPU operatives.[186] Five days later the three Germans were relocated to the Butyrka prison in Moscow in preparation for trial.

## INCITING CLASS WARFARE

Stalin was playing with fire. The entire Soviet coal mining industry had perhaps 1,100 educated engineers, and putting 50 of them on trial in just one case was economically perilous, especially as it frightened many others into inactivity and incited workers to verbal and physical attacks.[187] "I know that if there's a desire, one can accuse the innocent, such are the times," read the note of one engineer with no connection to the Shakhty case who committed suicide after being called a "Shakhtyite" and threatened with arrest. "I do not want defamation, I do not want to suffer while innocent and have to justify myself, I prefer death to defamation and suffering."[188] All industry in Leningrad had just 11 engineers per 1,000 workers; Moscow 9, the Urals 4.[189] With the exception of Molotov, the hard-core Stalin loyalists who supported coercion against the peasantry worked to rein in the hysteria Stalin was stirring over Shakhty.[190] Orjonikidze, head of the Central Control Commission workers' and peasants' inspectorate, told a group of recent graduates on March 26 that the Shakhty engineers were atypical, that engineers were vital to Soviet industry, that foreign specialists should be allowed to work in Soviet industry, and that Soviet specialists should go abroad.[191] Kuibyshev, who had been a Left Communist in the civil war opposed to employing tsarist "military specialists," now, as chairman of the Supreme Council of the Economy, told a gathering of industrial managers, in a speech published in the *Trade-Industrial Gazette,* the newspaper of his agency, that "every wrong assertion, every unjust accusation that has been exaggerated out of proportion creates a very difficult atmosphere for work, and such criticism already ceases to be constructive."[192] On March 28, he assured a group of Moscow engineers and scientists that the Shakhty case did not herald a new policy vis-à-vis technical specialists, and that "the government will take all measures to ensure in connection with the Shakhty case that not a single innocent engineer will suffer."[193]

While Stalin's faction opposed Shakhty, his politburo opponents opposed to his coercive peasant policy supported the wrecking accusations. Voroshilov wrote (March 29) to Mikhail Tomsky, head of trade unions, who had just returned from the coal region, expressing alarm: "Misha, tell me candidly, are we not walking right into a board with the opening of the trial in the Shakhty case? Is there not excess in this affair on the part of local officials, including the regional OGPU?" Tomsky, a former lithographer, short and stocky, with horrendous teeth, deaf in one ear, a man who drank to excess and suffered depression, but was also gruffly charming and caustically witty, was the sole pure worker in the politburo (the peasant Kalinin had also worked at factories) and genuinely popular among workers, far more than Stalin.[194] Tomsky had long been gung ho for "workerification" of the apparatus to combat bureaucratism and a regime summons to worker activism was grist for his mill.[195] Tomsky informed Voroshilov that the bourgeois specialists "are running rings around us!" Soviet mining construction plans were being "approved by the French," as a result of the engineers' foreign ties. "The picture's clear," he reassured Voroshilov. "The main personages have confessed. My view is that it would not be so bad if half a dozen Communists were imprisoned."[196] Bukharin, in a speech to the Leningrad party organization (April 13, 1928), not only endorsed the Stalin line on widespread wrecking in the coal industry, but also the likelihood of finding similar "organizations" sabotaging other industries, and seconded the need for "proletarian democracy" in the form of production meetings. Bukharin underscored the correctness of Soviet vigilance by the fact that after the Germans' arrests, a vociferous anti-Soviet campaign had broken out in Western Europe and relations with Germany had deteriorated sharply.[197] Bukharin, as he had written with his coauthor Preobrazhensky in *The ABC of Communism*, was long predisposed to view "bourgeois engineers" as traitors. Bukharin was also looking to avoid giving Stalin a pretext to accuse him of schism and factionalism. But Shakhty was less about a political attack on the party's defenders of the NEP than about Stalin's outflanking his own loyal faction.

Stalin was also appealing directly to the workers, seeking to win them back and mobilize them for industrialization and collectivization. Wage earners in industry, who were spread over nearly 2,000 nationalized factories, reached 2.7 million in 1928, finally edging past the 1913 total (2.6 million).[198] (Another half million workers were employed in construction.) But proletarians were still stuck in cramped dormitories and barracks, and not a few were homeless. Daily life necessities (food, clothes, shelter) consumed three quarters of a worker's paycheck, when he or she had a paycheck: unemployment had never fallen below 1 million during the NEP, and approached 20 percent of the able-bodied working age population. One in four industrial workers even in the capital was unemployed, a shameful circumstance that cried out for explanation or scapegoats.[199] An expensive whoring nightlife, meanwhile, took place right in front of workers' eyes—who was that for, in the land of the proletariat?[200] What had happened to the revolution? Had the civil war been fought and won to hand power over to NEPmen and speculators? History's "universal class" went hungry while kulaks could hoard immense stores of grain with impunity? Workers were sent into mines that collapsed on them—and it was all just accident? "Bourgeois specialists" and factory bosses lived luxuriously in five or more rooms, with running water and electricity, servants and drivers?[201] What was the self-proclaimed workers' state doing for workers? Doubts about the proletariat's steadfastness had induced party officials to look to themselves, the apparatchiks, as the social base of the regime, an awkward circumstance even without the Trotskyite critique of "bureaucracy." Moreover, a vicious public campaign had been depicting workers as shirkers and self-seekers, drunkards and deserters, while "production meetings" with workers organized by trade unions were actually serving as a way to impose higher output quotas. In 1928, however, party committees seized control of these meetings, which now became opportunities for workers from the shop floor to expose mismanagement, waste, and self-dealing.[202]

Shakhty case materials effectively announced that bosses might be traitors.[203] *Pravda*'s revelations also asserted wrecking had been going on for years "under the very noses of 'Communist leaders.'" Thus prodded, younger party members seized the opportunity to harness the pent-up class resentments and class ambitions of young proletarians, not to mention their own. According to police mood summaries, workers following the Shakhty case often pointed to similar phenomena at their places of work. "At our factory there is enormous economic mismanagement, good machines are thrown into a barn," a worker at the Leningrad factory Bolshevik was overheard to say, according to a report dated March 24, 1928. "This is a second [Shakhty]."[204] Such sentiments reached into the countryside. "Where were the party, the trade union forces, and the OGPU such that for ten years they allowed us to be led by the nose?" one village correspondent wrote in a letter to *Peasant Newspaper*, appending complaints about local investigating organs similarly failing to punish "red tapists" and "alien elements" who persecuted peasants.[205]

Worker efforts to form independent organizations continued to be ruthlessly suppressed, but worker resentments would now be stoked, and not just occasionally but in a clamorous campaign against enemies both abroad and at home.[206] Meeting after meeting was convened to "discuss" wrecking in the coal industry and beyond, and some workers at the events demanded the "wreckers" be put to death; engineers and managers who called Shakhty a cynical manufacture of scapegoats reinforced suspicions that the specialists who had not yet been accused might be guilty, too.[207] In places where no scientific-technical intelligentsia existed, such as the backward Mari Autonomous Province on the Volga, the OGPU targeted the humanist intelligentsia (mostly of peasant origin) for the crime of studying and teaching the history of their region and people.[208] Class warfare was back. Forget about Lenin's wager on poor peasants, let alone Stolypin's wager on prosperous peasants, Stalin was going to wager on young, male strivers from the *urban* lower orders to spearhead a socialist remake of the village many of them had only recently left behind. Here was a manifold technique of rule: a "struggle" not only against grain-hoarding kulaks in the village, but also against the class-alien "bourgeois" specialists in the cities, and against the party officials who willingly colluded with enemies or were complacent, which amounted to collusion. It was a mass mobilization whose message was seductive: the regime would not allow worker dreams to be surrendered, lost in a lack of vigilance, sold for Judas coins. But the campaign risked immense disruption, for an uncertain outcome.[209]

## TACTICAL RETREAT (APRIL 1928)

Stalin was no more worried about the ill effects of coercion against peasants than he was about the ill effects of arrests and suicides among engineers in industry. He had written to Kaganovich in Ukraine on the day before he had departed Moscow for Siberia warning that no one should be afraid of using the stick. "Many Communists think they cannot touch the reseller or the kulak, since this could scare the middle peasants away from us," he explained. "This is the most rotten idea of all the rotten ideas that exist in the minds of some Communists. The situation is just the opposite." Coercion promised to drive a wedge between kulaks and middle peasants, Stalin argued: "Only under such a policy will the middle peasant realize that the prospect of raising grain prices is an invention of speculators, . . . that it is dangerous to tie one's fate to the fate of speculators and kulaks and that he, the middle peasant, must fulfill his duty as an ally to the working class."[210] But even by the OGPU's own statistics, actual kulaks were a minority of those who were arrested, and arrests of non-kulaks generated significant pressures against the coercive policy.[211] Justice Commissar Nikolai Yanson had issued a circular categorizing the extraordinary measures as "temporary," indicating they would expire at the end of the current agricultural year (June 1928).[212] But many officials, not just Rykov, wanted the "emergency-ism" terminated immediately. Such was the background to a joint plenum of the Central Committee and the Central Control Commission held between April 6 and 11. On the opening day, the regime announced the "Sochi affair": for three years, party and soviet leaders in the Black Sea resort town were said to have been embezzling state property, wielding official positions for personal gain, and engaging in drunkenness and moral debauchery. The investigation led to a startling 700 expulsions, nearly 12 percent of the Black Sea party organization. Some of the expelled were civil war heroes.[213] Peasants were not the only target of Stalin's intimidation.

On the plenum's agenda were reports on grain procurement (Mikoyan) and the Shakhty case (Rykov), and the combination of these two subjects testified to Stalin's sly strategy. Rykov, on April 9, sought to allay doubts about Shakhty, pointing out, for example, that Nikolai Krylenko of the procuracy had checked into the work of the OGPU (the organizations were rivals) and that Tomsky, Molotov, and Yaroslavsky had gone to the Donbass to check in person. "The main conclusion consists in the fact that the case is not only not overblown, but larger and more serious than could have been anticipated when first uncovered," Rykov noted, adding that some defendants had already confessed: after fighting for Denikin, they had worked for Soviet power, but two-facedly, while enjoying enormous privileges. Whether he believed in Shakhty or merely thought it had use value is unknown, but he was trying to manage it. "We cannot achieve industrialization of the country without specialists," he added. "Here we are unusually behind, and our attention to this question is unusually weak."[214] Sixty people signed up for the discussion during which Kuibyshev spoke against the specialist baiting and Molotov answered with Stalin's hard line.[215]

Stalin took the floor on the morning of April 10 and asserted that bourgeois specialists in the Shakhty case had been financed by the Russian emigration and Western capitalist organizations, calling such actions "an attempt at economic intervention," not industrial accidents. With the opposition smashed, he stated, the party had wanted to get complacent, but it needed to remain vigilant. "It would be stupid to assume that international capital will leave us in peace," he advised. "No, comrades, this is untrue. Classes exist, international capital exists, and it cannot look quietly at the development of a country building socialism." The Soviet Union faced two paths, he said: either continue conducting a revolutionary policy and organizing the world working class and colonial peoples around the USSR, in which case international capital would obstruct them at every turn; or back down, in which case international capital "would not be against 'helping' us transform our socialist country into a 'nice' bourgeois republic." Britain had proposed dividing Persia, Afghanistan, and Turkey into two spheres of influence, could the USSR make such a concession? "Uniform voices: No!" The United States had demanded that the USSR renounce the policy of world revolution—could the USSR make such a concession? "Uniform voices: No!" The USSR could establish "friendly" relations with Japan if it agreed to divide Manchuria with her—could the USSR agree to such a concession? "No!" And on Stalin went. Terminate the state monopoly over foreign trade, pay back the imperialist war debts of the tsarist and Provisional Government? "No!" The USSR's refusal to make such concessions, Stalin averred, had spurred the "economic intervention" by international capital using internal enemies—ergo, Shakhty. It all made sense somehow.

Stalin mentioned that he had seen a play, *The Rails Are Buzzing,* by the young "proletarian" playwright Vladimir Kirshon (b. 1902). The protagonist was a Communist factory director, promoted from the workers, who, when he tried to reorganize the giant factory, discovered that he needed to reorganize people, including himself. "Go see this play, and you'll see that the worker-director is an idealist martyr who should be supported in every way," Stalin advised, adding that "The NEPmen lie in wait for the worker-director, he is undermined by this or that bourgeois specialist, his own wife attacks him, and despite all that, he sustains the struggle."[216]

The plenum voted a resolution in verbatim support of Stalin's Shakhty line on foreign "preparation for intervention and war against the USSR."[217] The party police machinery fell right in line: Ukraine OGPU chief Balytsky secretly wrote to Yagoda that the Shakhty interrogations had fully substantiated "the conclusions of comrade Stalin in his report to the plenum" concerning "preparation of an intervention."[218] Kaganovich, party boss in Ukraine, conveyed the same conclusion to Stalin, and urged that the party "strengthen the role of the GPU" in the industrial trusts by inserting "OGPU plenipotentiaries, something like the [self-standing] GPU organs for transport."[219] Kaganovich knew Stalin only too well.

Stalin, Leninist to the core, pressed his offensive relentlessly on Shakhty, but on grain procurements executed a tactical retreat.[220] His position still depended on holding a majority of politburo votes, and he made concessions to

Rykov—who after all, accepted Shakhty—in order to retain the votes of Voroshilov, Orjonikidze, and Kalinin. The plenum's resolution on the village mentioned "kulak influence" on procurements but stipulated that "at the bottom of these difficulties lay the sharp violation of market equilibrium"—Rykov's line. Complaints were pouring in about excesses related to the emergency measures: by mid-April, arrests totaled 16,000 Union-wide, including 1,864 under Article 58 (counterrevolution), and the plenum resolution terminated application of Article 107 to farmers for not selling grain.[221] More than that: officials who had punished non-kulaks ("violations of the class line") were themselves to be punished; some were tried and even executed.[222] It was a stunning reversal.

Lower-level party officials who scoured newspapers for subtle differences in the published speeches of top leaders had begun to whisper about a schism between Stalin and Rykov. "I think that oppositionists (concealed), who always infiltrate meetings of party actives, write of Rykov and Stalin factions," Stalin wrote on a note to Voroshilov at a politburo meeting in April 1928.[223] That may have been the same meeting (April 23) at which Stalin pressed the issue of forming giant "state farms"—new farms where there had been none before—on virgin lands in northern Kazakhstan, the Urals, Southern Siberia, the North Caucasus, even Ukraine. He took as his model the large-scale mechanized farm (95,000 acres) of Thomas Campbell in Montana, perhaps the largest and most productive single farm in the world.[224] When Kalinin, a state farm proponent, observed that they would be supplemental to existing farms (which would eventually be collectivized), Stalin interjected his approval (twice).[225] Stalin's retreat, in other words, was only partial. He had gotten the plenum to recognize the party's right to reintroduce emergency measures, should the situation call for them. After the plenum, he told the Moscow party organization (April 13) that although "the crisis has been surmounted," if "capitalist elements try again to 'play tricks,'" Article 107 would be back.[226]

Stalin did not have long to wait: April grain procurement numbers would be just one fifth those of March and one tenth those of February; peasants were avoiding state officials and selling at the bazaars for five times the state-offered price. The margin for error in the Soviet economy had diminished as a result of regime missteps and the larger contradiction between a market economy and a socialist regime. Some regions—especially Ukraine and the North Caucasus—had suffered drought and crop failure. In northern Kazakhstan poor weather and a poor harvest had induced many households to try to obtain food for their own consumption at markets, which pushed prices up; but when the harvest collection began, grain for sale disappeared from the markets. Checkpoints had been established on the roads to block grain from being brought into these poor harvest regions, while better-off peasants—the ones who had grain—refused to sell at the low set prices, but they were afraid to sell it at the market high prices. Some poor peasants were asking why kulaks were not being squeezed more.[227] A series of conferences was hastily convened with provincial party bosses, beginning on April 24, with Molotov and Mikoyan chairing and orchestrating: some regional bosses called for renewed application of Article 107 and a reduced definition of kulak from someone who possessed thirty-six tons of grain to twelve or even seven, and criticized proposals for peasant amnesty and prosecution of officials who had managed to secure grain. One provincial secretary demanded an end to the press discussions of "excesses," which he claimed had produced "a demobilized mood."[228] Molotov, parroting Stalin as ever, told them that "often kulaks write Moscow in the guise of poor peasants. You see, kulaks know better than anyone else how to maneuver around Moscow."[229] Not all fell in line: some regional party bosses expressed well-founded skepticism that the required grain was out there for the taking, while behind the scenes a fight was on to steer policy away from coercion.[230] But under the pressure of falling procurements already on April 26, the politburo voted to reinstate the application of Article 107 to growers.[231]

The year 1928 was the year of hoping against hope that Stalin would back down, but evidence of his resolve continued to be visible everywhere. Secret police country mood summaries, right on cue, increasingly moved away from mentions of a price scissors, a manufactured goods deficit, or other facts, to evocations of "sabotage" and "class enemies."[232] Sometimes the signals of Stalin's muscle flexing were comically unintentional. For example, local branches of the OGPU sent some political mood summaries to party committees and soviets in their regions, but on May 16, 1928, Yagoda sent a circular designated "absolutely secret" lamenting how "in the political mood summaries circulated to local institutions, some referred derogatively to functionaries by name," which created the "false impression" that these functionaries were under close surveillance for what they were saying and to whom. "It is necessary to remove not just all mention of functionaries in the external mood summaries but to avoid this even in those summaries of an internal character."[233] Regime functionaries under surveillance by the secret police—a false impression, obviously.

## SHOW TRIAL

Nothing had ever erupted in the Soviet Union quite like the spectacle of the Shakhty trial, which opened on May 18, 1928, in the marble-walled Hall of Columns of the House of Trade Unions and lasted forty-one days.[234] It was the first major Union-wide public trial since 1922 but far exceeded that affair. Other trials in 1928 that were also designed to instill political lessons, such as a military tribunal hearing about an alleged Anglo-Finnish "spy ring" in the Leningrad border zone, failed to acquire anything remotely resembling Shakhty's intensity and significance.[235] It was staged in Moscow for maximum exposure; nearly 100 handpicked foreign and Soviet journalists reported on the proceedings.[236] More than 30,000 Soviet inhabitants would be led through the red-draped courtroom (the party would claim 100,000)—workers, Communist Youth League activists, out-of-town delegations. "Crowds poured in noisily and jockeyed for advantageous seats," wrote one American foreign correspondent. "The boxes gradually filled with diplomats, influential officials and other privileged spectators—much bowing and hand-shaking."[237] Andrei Vyshinsky, the chief judge, stood out in his suit and pince-nez; Nikolai Krylenko, the chief prosecutor, wore a hunting jacket, riding breeches, and puttees. Shakhty was filmed for newsreels and a stand-alone documentary, and Krylenko's shaven head glistened under the Jupiter lights.[238] Radio broadcast the proceedings. Shakhty electrified the country.

Capitalists were gone, of course, so the prerevolutionary engineers and managers had to assume their roles.[239] Of the fifty-three defendants, twenty pleaded guilty, eleven admitted the accusations partially, and the rest maintained their innocence. Those who denied the charges did not conceal their distaste for the Soviet regime, or their disbelief in the dream of building socialism but argued that being professionals, they could still perform their work conscientiously; their admission of hostile views, however, was taken as proof of engagement in sabotage. Krylenko quoted purported worker statements about abuse suffered at the hands of "vampires of the working class."[240] He "played to the gallery from start to finish," one pro-Soviet foreign correspondent would later recall. "He never missed a chance to harangue the police-picked audience and draw their applause. There were times when some of the defendants applauded along with the cheering crowd."[241] But details in the confessions offered different dates for the establishment of the counterrevolutionary "organization." The choreography was further disturbed when the German technician Max Maier (b. 1876) told

Vyshinsky that he had signed his confession only because he was exhausted from the nightly interrogations and did not know Russian (so he did not know what he signed). When Vyshinsky asked Maier to confirm the guilt of the Soviet inhabitant Abram Bashkin, Maier called Bashkin the most conscientious engineer he knew in the Soviet Union, absolutely devoted to the fate of the imported turbines; Bashkin, sitting in the defendant cage, suddenly shouted out that his own earlier confession (minutes earlier) had been a lie. Vyshinsky declared a recess. Some forty minutes later, Bashkin reconfirmed his earlier self-incrimination.[242]

No one who was innocent would confess, it was widely assumed. Underneath the manipulations, moreover, lay concerns that were partly verifiable. Back in March 1927, the head of the foreign concession department for the air force was arrested, accused of deliberately buying poor-quality airplane parts from Junkers, and at inflated cost, netting the German firm a handsome excess profit, pocketing a hefty kickback, and damaging Soviet security. The official also was accused of divulging the state of Soviet aviation industry to German personnel in his private apartment, something that among professionals might look like shop talk but did cross the line over to espionage. Two months after his arrest, the air force foreign concession head was executed along with alleged accomplices. Merely out of mundane pecuniary motives, tsarist-era specialists, colluding with foreigners, could take advantage of the technical ignorance or bribability of poorly educated Soviet supervisory personnel. Of course, a preternaturally distrustful Stalin assumed that hostile class interests, too, motivated them. Either way, bourgeois engineers wielded potentially far-reaching power, and Stalin saw little recourse other than severe intimidation.[243]

The central figures of what was dubbed the Moscow Center were Lazar Rabinovich (b. 1860); Solomon Imenitov (b. 1865), the Donetsk Coal Trust representative in Moscow, who was accused of failing to report his knowledge of counterrevolutionary activity; and Nikolai Skorutto (b. 1877), an official in the Supreme Council of the Economy who was returning from the United States via Berlin and read about the arrests of his colleagues yet had continued on to Moscow anyway. Skorutto informed the court that he had confessed, but, according to a journalist witness, "the courtroom was electrified by an unearthly shriek from the box where the relatives of prisoners sat. . . . 'Kolya,' the woman cried, 'Kolya darling, don't lie. Don't! You know you're innocent.'" Skorutto collapsed. Vyshinsky recessed. After ten minutes, Skorutto spoke again, stating that he had decided to withdraw his confession. "I had hoped that this court would be more lenient with me if I pleaded guilty and accused the others," he stated.[244] Rabinovich, like Imenitov, denied the charges. "I am absolutely not guilty, I repent for nothing, I shall beg for nothing," he stated. None other than Lenin had tasked Rabinovich, as head of the entire Soviet coal industry, with restoring the civil war-ruined coal mines. "I have behind me fifty years of complete trust, respect and honor, as a result of my public and private life. I have been open with everyone. To the extent of my strength, I served the cause of the proletariat, which has viewed me with full trust and helped create a good working atmosphere for me. My work was conscientious to the end. I knew nothing of sabotage."[245] But Rabinovich had graduated from the St. Petersburg Mining Institute and begun his career in 1884; he was also a former Cadet deputy to the tsarist Duma—prima facie evidence of inimical class interests. Rabinovich requested a death sentence. He got six years: "I sleep as soundly in prison as in my own bed. I have a clear conscience and I have nothing to fear."[246] (He would die in prison.)

German ambassador von Brockdorff-Rantzau, whose height was said to help make him the "most conspicuous" dignitary in the foreigners' section, was suffering from throat cancer, but he refused to depart Moscow for urgent medical treatment (he did give up cognac).[247] The count was angry that no French or Polish nationals, only Germans, were in the dock, and lamented that his own advocacy for maintaining relations through thick and thin had made possible such abuse of his country for Soviet ends. Still, *Izvestiya* (May 29), at least, tried to ratchet down Stalin's aggressiveness, writing that "the German Reich does not sit in the dock, neither does German industry nor German companies as such, only individual German citizens." The German elections that Stalin had eyed when he approved the Germans' arrests took place during the trial. The Social Democrats emerged the top vote getters at 9.2 million (30 percent of those cast), while the German Communists also gained, taking 3.2 million, cracking the 10 percent barrier, and coming in fourth place. The Beer Hall Putsch ban against the Nazis had been lifted, but they polled just 2.6 percent. On May 31, Voroshilov wrote to Stalin that the German high command was recommending that eight Soviet officers again this year visit for studies; the Germans would also want six observers at Soviet maneuvers, including General von Blomberg. Voroshilov interpreted this as a desire on the part of Germany to maintain surveillance over the growing power of the Red Army, and wrote that "the Germans consider the Red Army powerful enough to manage a confrontation with Poland and Romania." He recommended accepting the German offer, and appended a list of proposed Red Army officers for reciprocal travel. Stalin agreed.[248] None of this brought him any closer to acquiring financing for industrialization and state-of-the-art technology.

## BULLY PULPIT (MAY–JUNE 1928)

Spring's renewed wave of coerced grain procurements provoked sharp price increases, long queues, and pockets of starvation. Rationing loomed for the big cities.[249] Trying to convey the despair and anger when armed squads, for the second time in a short period, had come looking for "hidden" grain, an official in the Urals reported the story of an old man who had hung himself: "His son had showed the commission all their reserves. They left them, 14 people, just 2 poods [72 pounds] of grain. The 80-year-old decided he would be one mouth to feed too many. . . . I am worried most about the children. What will be their impression of Soviet power when its representatives bring only fear and tears to their homes?"[250]

The OGPU directed its village informants—who numbered 8,596 Union-wide—to pay close attention to "anti-Soviet agitation" at private village pubs and any queues of women.[251] Some localities had begun improvising rationing of what food they had to hand. Syrtsov was writing from Siberia (May 24, 1928) that peasants had no more grain and that Siberia's own cities might face starvation.[252] Stalin dispatched Stanisław Kosior, who took along his aide Aleksandr Poskryobyshev—soon to become Stalin's top aide—to Novosibirsk. At the June 3 Siberian party committee's "grain symposium," for which officials had been summoned from every Siberian region as well as Kazakhstan and the Urals, Kosior emphasized the need to keep pressuring the kulaks with Article 107.[253] Country-wide, grain procurement in the agricultural year through June 1928 would end up down only slightly from the previous year (10.382 instead of 10.59 million tons).[254] But the late April resumption of "extraordinary measures," on top of the drought, had further disorganized internal grain markets.[255] By June, the regime would again begin to import grain. Most troubling, many farmers were unable to acquire seed grain to sow.[256] Others were simply refusing to plant, despite secret circulars and press exhortations.[257]

Stalin would not be deterred. On May 28, 1928, he appeared at the Institute of Red Professors, located in the former Tsarevich Nicholas School, at Ostozhenka, 53; invites had also gone out to select students of the Sverdlov Communist

University, the Russian Association of the Social Science Research Institute, and the Communist Academy, with no mention of the name of the lecturer, which heightened anticipation. In preparation, "cleaning women had given an extra wash and polish to the floors, workmen had cleaned up the courtyard, the librarians had displayed the best books, chimneysweepers had climbed on the roofs, and professors had lined up at the barber's," according to one young Chechen Communist at the Institute, who added that authorities had hung a full-length oil portrait of Stalin in the hall, but "the head, crudely cut out with a blunt instrument, was lying nearby on the floor." The vandals had stuck a sign to Stalin's painted chest, composed of letters cut from a newspaper: "The Proletariat has nothing to lose but Stalin's head. Proletarians of all lands, rejoice!"[258]

A replacement portrait of Stalin seated next to Lenin at Gorki in 1922 was quickly installed. It is unclear who had perpetrated the vandalism. Trotsky and the Left had been enormously popular at the Institute; most student leftists had been expelled. What the students may not have realized, however, was that Stalin was about to make the most aggressive leftist speech of his life. Titled "On the Grain Front," Stalin's lecture reprised the heretofore unknown brave new world of his January 20 peroration in Novosibirsk.

Stalin again outlined a stirring vision of an immediate, wholesale agricultural modernization to large-scale farms—not of the individual kulak variety, but collectivized. Where no farms currently existed to collectivize, there would be newly founded massive scale state farms. "Stalin spoke quietly, monotonously, and with long pauses," the Chechen Communist recalled. "Of course, Stalin had a Georgian accent, which became especially noticeable when he got nervous." He "spoke for about two hours without stopping. He frequently drank water from a glass. Once, when he lifted the carafe, it was empty. Laughter erupted in the hall. A person in the presidium handed Stalin a new carafe. Stalin gulped down nearly a full glass, then turned to the audience and said, with a mischievous laugh: 'There, you see, he who laughs last, laughs best! Anyway, I have welcome news for you: I have finished.' Applause broke out." After a ten-minute recess, Stalin answered written questions, some of which were irreverent: one student evidently inquired about the suicide note of the Trotsky supporter Adolf Joffe, another about why the OGPU had informants in the ranks of the party (these went unanswered). The assembled students also asked about the implications of Stalin's speech for the NEP; Stalin answered with reference to Lenin's dialectical, tactical teachings. "It turned out we were present at an historic event," the

Chechen Communist, in hindsight, would note. "Stalin for the first time set out his plan for the future 'collective farm revolution.'"[259] The speech was published in *Pravda* (June 2, 1928).[260]

Youth, alongside the working class, constituted Stalin's core audience for the accelerated leap to socialism. Membership in the Communist Youth League had risen from 22,000 (in late 1918) to more than 2 million (of nearly 30 million eligible), making it a mass organization. About one third of party members by the late 1920s had once been Youth League members.[261] Stalin's apparatus was dispatching armed Youth League militants, among others, to villages, where they measured "surpluses" by the eye, smashed villagers on the head with revolvers, and locked peasants in latrines until they yielded their grain stores. In parallel, police arrests under Article 107 and Article 58 spiked again in May and June, provoking the onset of a spontaneous "dekulakization." Many peasants fled to nearby cities or other regions; some even joined collective farms, fearful they would starve otherwise. But some peasants began to organize resistance. "The grain reserves in the village will not be turned over to the government," resolved a group of peasants in Western Siberia's Biysk county, where Stalin had secretly visited earlier in the year. Party officials began to try to prevent peasants from meeting, but in Biysk a poor peasant went to the rural soviet and told the chairman, "Give grain to us poor peasants. If not, we will take it by force. We will go first of all to the party secretary, and if he does not give us grain voluntarily, we will kill him. We must take all the grain and establish a clean soviet power, without Communists." Elsewhere others were reported to say, "Let's get our pikes and become partisans."[262] Rumors spread of a foreign invasion, and the return of the Whites. "The peasantry is under the yoke of the bandit Stalin," read one letter received by Rykov's government in June 1928. "The poorest peasant and worker is your enemy."[263]

The siege Stalin was imposing generated evidence of the need for a siege, as the OGPU reported spreading "kulak" moods, Ukrainian "nationalist" moods, and "peasant" moods in the army.[264] The general crisis that Rykov feared was unfolding.

Stalin had stopped speaking to Bukharin, just as he often refused to speak with his wife, Nadya—a silent treatment, which, in Bukharin's case, too, baffled and infuriated someone who thought he was close to Stalin.[265] In May and again in early June 1928, Bukharin sent letters, addressed to "Koba," trying to get through. "I consider the country's internal and external situation *very* difficult," he wrote, adding that he could discern no thought-through plan of action, whether on taxes, manufactured goods, prices, or imports, nothing. Already the next harvest was upon the country. Incredulous, Bukharin stressed what he regarded as the scandalous fact that Jan Sten, a respected Marxist theorist, was saying that "the 15th Party Congress had been *mistaken*, that the Trotskyites had turned out to be right and were vindicated by history." In fact, Bukharin wrote, "our extraordinary measures (necessary) are, ideologically, *already* being transformed, growing into a new political line." He concluded by suggesting that after the upcoming Comintern Congress and Chinese Communist Party Congress in Moscow, "I will be ready to go wherever, without any fight, without any noise, and without any struggle." Bukharin's letter revealed that he just could not believe that Stalin would irrevocably alter the entire strategic landscape in a sharp leftist direction. "Collective farms, which will only be built over several years, will not carry us," Bukharin wrote. "We will be unable to provide them with working capital and machines right away."[266]

Stalin did not respond.[267] But a row broke out at a politburo meeting on June 27 when Bukharin, Tomsky, and Rykov declared party policy in rupture, and Molotov denounced their declaration as "antiparty," an ominous formulation.[268] At this or perhaps at the follow-up politburo meeting, where Stalin formed a compromise commission with himself and Rykov, the worst confrontation yet between Stalin and Bukharin may have taken place. Stalin finally had deigned to receive Bukharin in his office. "You and I are the Himalayas—the others are non-entities," Stalin flattered him, according to the memoirs of Bukharin's wife. Then, at a politburo meeting, when Stalin laced into Bukharin, the latter divulged Stalin's flattery of him, including the line that the others were "non-entities." Livid, Stalin shouted, "You lie. You invented this story to poison the other members of the politburo against me."[269]

## SECOND TACTICAL RETREAT (JULY 1928 PLENUM)

Peasant anger continued to smolder. "The highest level of government is based on swindling—that's the opinion of everybody down below," one peasant wrote on July 4, 1928, to the *Peasant Newspaper,* adding, "The death of Comrade Lenin was a shame. He died early, unable to carry this business through to the end. So, you government comrades, in the case of war, don't rely on the peasants too much. . . . Our grain goes to feed England, France, and Germany, while the peasants sit and go hungry for a week."[270] That same day another joint plenum of the Central Committee and the Central Control Commission opened, with its first few days given over to Comintern affairs. Then, on July 6, Mikoyan delivered a grim report. Foreign trade was in "an extraordinarily strained situation, more strained than in the last two years," he observed. Oil production substantially exceeded domestic consumption, but oil exports could not generate the revenues that grain had (nor could timber, furs, sugar, and cotton exports). Grain exports had undergirded the tsarist industrialization spurt. Mikoyan grimly noted that perhaps no more than one third of tsarist export levels might be realistically attainable, unless Soviet harvests miraculously grew by leaps and bounds.[271] Disquiet coursed through the upper party ranks.[272]

Later that night, at 1:30 a.m. on July 7, Andrei Vyshinsky read out the Shakhty trial verdicts in the Hall of Columns. Four of the fifty-three defendants were acquitted, including the two Germans Ernst Otto and Max Maier. Four more were judged guilty but given suspended sentences, including Wilhelm Badstieber (who was acquitted under Article 58 but convicted under Article 53 for bribery). Otto and Maier, released within two hours, went to the ambassador's residence; Badstieber, also released, had been fired by Knapp and refused to return to Germany. Count Brockdorff-Rantzau finally departed Moscow; no one from the foreign affairs commissariat showed up at the station to see him off.[273] Procurator General Krylenko had demanded twenty-two death sentences, exclaiming "execution" after each name during his summation; in the event, eleven death sentences were pronounced, but six were commuted to prison terms. Altogether, nearly forty people went to prison, the majority with terms of four to ten years, though many got one to three years. Staging such public trials even under censorship and an invitation-only foreign audience had turned out to be no mean feat: the regime never published a stand-alone transcript of the imperfect spectacle.[274] Still, a pamphlet summarizing the trial for agitators spotlighted how the wrecking was ultimately thwarted because the proletariat was strong, and exorted the party to bring the workers closer to production, enhance self-criticism to fight bureaucratism, become better "commissars" watching over bourgeois specialists, and produce new Soviet cadres of engineers.[275] Stalin would assert that the Shakhty trial had helped "to strengthen the readiness for action of the working class."[276]

At the plenum on the evening of July 9, Stalin gave no quarter to critics. The politburo, he stated, had resorted to extraordinary measures only because there had been a genuine emergency—"we had no reserves"—and he credited the coercion with saving the country. "Those who say extraordinary measures are bad under any circumstances are wrong."[277] Then he turned bluntly to grand strategy. Whereas England had industrialized thanks to its colonies, Germany had drawn upon the indemnity imposed as a result of the Franco-Prussian War of 1870–71, and the United States used loans from Europe, the USSR had no colonies, indemnities, or long-term foreign loans, leaving solely "internal resources." On this point no Bolshevik could readily disagree. But Stalin sought to draw the full logic of the Bolshevik position. The peasants "pay the state not only the usual taxes, direct and indirect, but they also overpay in relatively high prices for industrial goods, first of all, and, second, they underreceive in prices for agricultural produce," he explained, matter-of-factly. "This is an additional tax on the peasantry in the interests of raising industry, which serves the whole country, including the peasants. This is something like 'tribute' [dan'], something like a supertax, which we are forced to take temporarily, to preserve and advance the present tempo of the development of industry, to provide for industry for the whole country." Stalin did not seek to prettify: "This matter of which I am speaking is unpleasant. But we would not be Bolsheviks if we glossed over this fact and closed our eyes to this, that without an additional tax on the peasantry, unfortunately, our industry and our country cannot make do."[278] Despite his apparent iron logic, however, his use of the term "tribute"—an expression not published at the time—provoked people in the hall.[279]

Stalin rejected other policy options, such as the calls by Sokolnikov, a plenum member, to raise the price paid to peasants for grain (by 25 percent). "Is it necessary to close the 'scissors' between town and country, all these underpayments and overpayments?" Stalin asked, in his now signature style. "Yes, unquestionably, they should be eliminated. Can we eliminate them now, without weakening our industry and our economy overall? No, we cannot."[280] Such, ostensibly, was the brutal "logic" of accelerated industrialization: "tribute" extraction trumped market concessions, at least for now. Might "tribute" become permanent? Stalin did not say. He did, however, portray the road ahead as still more arduous. "As we advance, the resistance of the capitalist elements will grow, the class struggle will become sharper, and Soviet power, whose forces will increasingly grow, will carry out a policy of isolation of these elements, . . . a policy of suppression of the resistance of the exploiters," he asserted. "It has never been seen and never will be seen that obsolete classes surrender their positions voluntarily, without attempting to organize resistance . . . the movement towards socialism must lead to resistance by the exploiting elements against this movement, and the resistance of the exploiters must lead to an inevitable sharpening of the class struggle."[281]

Lenin during the civil war had hit upon the idea of escalated resistance by implacable foes as their defeat approached.[282] And before that, before anyone had ever heard Stalin's name, Georgi Plekhanov, the father of Marxism in Russia, had noted that once capitalists realized they were a historically doomed class, they would engage in greater resistance.[283] That said, Stalin's assertion of a "sharpening of the class struggle," like his use of the term "tribute," struck many in the hall as unorthodox. But Stalin pointed to the peasant decision not to sell their produce to the state at low fixed prices as a "grain strike," nothing less than "the first serious action, under the conditions of NEP, undertaken by the capitalist elements of the countryside against the Soviet government."[284] More than any other figure, Stalin for years had banged hard on the circumstances of capitalist encirclement, the hostility of the capitalist class elements inside the USSR and the dangers presented by the new NEP-era bourgeoisie (kulaks), the linkages between external and internal enemies, the threat of a renewed "intervention"—in a word, Shakhty. Shakhty was a colossal fait accompli, no smaller than the trip to Siberia. And in one of those uncanny coincidences that always accompany a well-executed strategy—that is, an improvisation in a certain strategic direction—the five Shakhty death sentences were carried out the very day of Stalin's plenum speech.

Still, the Shakhty trial was over and a road back from "emergency-ism" remained. Immediately after Stalin, on the morning of July 10, Bukharin got the floor. Bukharin was still so afraid of falling into the trap of allowing Stalin to accuse him of "opposition" to the Central Committee line that he refused to air his differences, essentially failing to appeal to the large, top-level audience, upward of 160 people, including guests.[285] Bukharin had admitted that kulaks were a threat and needed to be pressured, even expropriated—in other words, that coercion in the countryside was appropriate, up to a point. He had admitted that it was necessary to build socialism, necessary to industrialize the country, necessary to combat wrecking with vigilance. And Stalin, the tactician, had blunted Bukharin's critique by his retreat at the April 1928 plenum, which Stalin took credit for without even having to follow through, thanks to a combination of induced events (coercion producing diminishing returns) and manipulations (Shakhty). Hounded by Stalin loyalists as he tried to speak, Bukharin insisted that the plenum discuss facts, and he told of some 150 major protests across the country, mentioning "a revolt in Semipalatinsk, violence at the Leningrad and Moscow labor exchanges, an uprising in Kabardiya"—all of which, and more, had indeed taken place.[286] In fact, between May 20 and June 15, 1928, thirteen violent conflicts were recorded at labor exchanges in various cities.[287] He cited letters from village and worker correspondents, evidently received by *Pravda,* where he was still nominally editor in chief, but Bukharin also claimed he had only just learned many of these disturbing facts of social unrest, and only because he had gone in person to the OGPU and sat there for two days, reading through the political mood reports (which, normally, were supposed to be presented to the politburo). Kosior shouted out, "For what did you incarcerate him [Bukharin] in the GPU? (laughter)." Mężyński answered: "For panicmongering. (laughter)."

Bukharin insisted, based on the evidence of discontent and social instability, that the extraordinary measures had to be stopped. "Forever?" someone shouted. Bukharin allowed that extraordinary measures might be necessary at times but should not become permanent, otherwise "you'll get an uprising of the peasant, whom the kulak will take on, will organize, will lead. The petit bourgeois spontaneity will rise up against the proletariat, smash it in the head, and as a result of the sharpest class struggle the proletarian dictatorship will disappear." At Bukharin's picture of social crisis and peasant rebellion, Stalin shouted out, "A terrible dream, but God is merciful (laughter)."[288]

Amid the bullying, on July 11, Kalinin reported on state farms, and objected to the forced exile of kulaks, which risked the loss of their grain before new sources came on line. "Will anyone, even one person, say that there is enough grain?" he stated. "All these conversations, that the kulak conceals grain, that there is grain, but he does not give it up—these are conversations, only conversations. . . . If the kulak had a lot of grain, we would possess it." Here was a politburo vote that Rykov-Tomsky-Bukharin might recruit for repeal of the emergency measures. But Kalinin also agreed with Stalin to an extent, calling the grain shortfall a consequence of a "productivity deficit," which "pushes us into the organization of state farms."[289]

Stalin spoke again that afternoon, polemicizing with other speakers, especially Tomsky. (After observing Stalin verbally assault Tomsky, Sokolnikov had another private meeting with Kamenev at which he said Stalin had appeared "dark, green, evil, irritated. A forbidding sight. . . . What struck us most was his rudeness.")[290] Tomsky, like Bukharin (and Rykov), had proposed stepping back from the brink. "You retreat today, retreat tomorrow, retreat the day after tomorrow, retreat without end—that's what he says will strengthen the alliance" between workers and peasants, Stalin said. "No comrades, this is not true. . . . A policy of permanent concessions is not our policy."[291] And then, in a shock, Stalin capitulated: the plenum, unanimously, repealed the "extraordinary measures."[292] Grain prices were soon raised.[293] Unauthorized searches and arrests in pursuit of grain and the closing of bazaars were made punishable offenses; Article 107 cases against poor and middle peasants were discontinued, and those peasants behind bars were released under an amnesty.[294] Stalin's multiple interventions at the plenum could leave no doubt about his deep-set commitment to the line announced in Novosibirsk and reprised at the Institute of Red Professors.[295] But for the second time, he undertook a tactical retreat. Perhaps he wanted to avoid being the one who had forced a split vote and "schism." Stalin also must have known that Bukharin had conducted conversations with other politburo members, including Orjonikidze, Voroshilov, and Kalinin, about removing him as general secretary at the plenum, which called for caution on Stalin's part.[296] That said, it was easier to retreat knowing he could just go back to Old Square and ring the OGPU.

## INTRIGUE OF INTRIGUES?

The short-lived United opposition of Zinoviev and Kamenev with Trotsky had achieved little more than exacerbating their already extreme acrimony.[297] Stalin had exiled Zinoviev and Kamenev internally to Kaluga, about 110 miles from Moscow, in early 1928. Zinoviev continued to beg for reinstatement in the party, writing an abasing article in *Pravda* in May 1928, inducing a pitiless Trotsky to observe, "Zinoviev resembles a wet bird and his voice from the pages of *Pravda* sounds like the peep of a sandpiper from the swamp."[298] Finally, in June 1928, Stalin had allowed Zinoviev and Kamenev, along with about forty oppositionists, to be reinstated.[299] But Stalin's minions appear to have deviously set in motion a false rumor that Bukharin and his allies had voted against Zinoviev's and Kamenev's readmission, whispers that, predictably, sent Bukharin into a tizzy. Grigory Sokolnikov was reasonably close to both Kamenev and Bukharin, and it appears that Kamenev, during a trip from Kaluga to Moscow, told Sokolnikov about the rumor and Sokolnikov separately mentioned this to Bukharin, who in turn asked Sokolnikov to act as a peacemaker. Sokolnikov sent a letter to Kamenev in Kaluga, providing his Moscow phone number; when Kamenev called on July 9, Sokolnikov summoned him to the capital for a meeting with Bukharin.

How much this episode was fully planned by a supremely cunning Stalin, and how much was happenstance he managed to turn to his advantage, remains unclear. What is clear is that Stalin did nothing to tamp down the divisive rumor. Also clear is that any contact with Kamenev in exile would have been perlustrated or tapped by the OGPU. Sokolonikov, however, was scarcely the type willingly to participate in one of Stalin's master intrigues. But Kamenev? He was able to travel unhindered to Moscow. Stalin had not even taken away his Kremlin apartment, where, on the morning of July 11, with the plenum still under way, Kamenev received another call from Sokolnikov. "The matter has gone much farther, Bukharin has had a final break with Stalin," Sokolnikov stated. "The question of Stalin's removal was posed concretely: Kalinin and Voroshilov went back on their word." Here was a bombshell, related—over a tapped line—by a Central Committee member to a non-member, recklessly, fearlessly. Sokolnikov and Kamenev shared a bond—the only two people ever to call for Stalin's removal as general secretary at a Party Congress, and Sokolnikov might not have abandoned that quest. Kamenev likely held on to that dream as well, but he also seems to have been eager, like Zinoviev, to return himself to favor and resume a high position commensurate with his self-perception and past. Shortly after the second phone call, Sokolnikov showed up at Kamenev's apartment with Bukharin. (Sokolnikov would leave before Bukharin.) Kamenev, who had written notes of his conspiratorial conversation with Sokolnikov, did so again, depicting Bukharin as erupting in an emotional rant of disloyalty to Stalin.

"We consider Stalin's line fatal for the whole revolution," Bukharin told Kamenev, according to the notes. "The disagreements between us and Stalin are many times more serious than they had been with you. Rykov, Tomsky, and I unanimously formulate the situation as follows: 'it would be a lot better if in the politburo we had Zinoviev and Kamenev instead of Stalin.'" Bukharin added that he spoke about this openly with Rykov and Tomsky, and that he had not spoken with Stalin for weeks. "He is an unprincipled intriguer, who subordinates everything to the maintenance of his own power. He shifts theory on the basis of who at any given moment he wants to remove." After all these years together, Bukharin still did not know that Stalin was a hard-core leftist and a Leninist of flexible tactics. Bukharin did at least understand that Stalin "had made concessions" at the July plenum "in order to put a knife in us" and that Stalin "was maneuvering to make us into schismatics." Bukharin also revealed that Stalin "had not suggested a single execution in the Shakhty case," instead sitting back while others did it for him, appearing the moderate, while also making ostensible concessions in all negotiations. Still, Bukharin mocked as "idiotic illiteracy" Stalin's two major plenum formulations: "tribute" from the peasantry and the sharpening of the class struggle as socialism grew. Kamenev asked Bukharin to elucidate the extent of his forces, and Bukharin named himself, Tomsky, Rykov, Nikolai Uglanov, some Leningraders, but not the Ukrainians (whom Stalin had "bought off" by removing Kaganovich), adding that "Yagoda and Trillisser"—of the OGPU—"are with us," but that "Voroshilov and Kalinin went back at the last minute." He also said that Orjonikidze "is no knight. He came to me and cursed Stalin, but at the decisive moment he betrayed us," and that "the Petersburg [Leningrad] people . . . got scared when the talk got to the possibility of removing Stalin . . . there is a terrible fear of a split."[300]

What in the world was Bukharin doing spilling his guts out to Kamenev, a non-politburo member and internal exile, about such top secret, weighty matters? Bukharin was hardly naïve. He flat-out warned Kamenev not to call him on the phone, which he knew was eavesdropped (Stalin had evidently once shown him a transcript of an intimate exchange between Zinoviev and his wife).[301] He also told Kamenev they were being tailed. But Bukahrin appears to have been goaded by desperation. Kamenev noted that Bukharin's "lips sometimes shook from emotion. Sometimes he gave the impression of a person who knows he is doomed."[302] And so, Bukharin had taken the risk. But his act also shows he had not abandoned hope. His main purpose appears to have been to deny the rumor that he had voted against Kamenev's reinstatement in order to preempt Kamenev and Zinoviev from being recruited by Stalin against Bukharin, Tomsky, and Rykov. The notion that Stalin would have reinstated the two Kaluga exiles because he needed them boggles the mind, but Bukharin evidently assumed that Stalin could not rule the country by himself.[303] Bukharin also did not believe Stalin's faction contained people of stature (to Kamenev, he referred to the "moron Molotov, who teaches me Marxism and whom we call 'stone ass'"). Thus, if Stalin, moving demonstratively to the left, was going to jettison Bukharin, Tomsky, and Rykov, it seemed to Bukharin that the Georgian would have no choice but to recall Zinoviev, Kamenev, and perhaps even Trotsky. The meeting was based upon sad misapprehension.

Kamenev, for his part, may have entertained similar delusions about Stalin needing his services in the shift to the left, but in Kamenev's case Bukharin could well have been a means to an end.[304] Bukharin told Kamenev that "Stalin knows only one means: revenge, and he puts the knife into your back. Let's recall the theory of 'sweet revenge.'" The latter referred to an anecdote about Stalin, retailed by Kamenev, said to be from a group picnic in the early 1920s, when some-one asked what was the best thing in the world, the kind of question posed in a drunken state. Kamenev had supposedly answered "books," Radek, "a woman, your woman," Rykov, "cognac," and Stalin, revenge against one's ene-mies.[305] Conspicuously, each person in the anecdote—which exists in many variants—was stereotyped: the bookish Kamenev, the womanizing witty Radek, the alleged alcoholic Rykov, the vengeful Stalin. But what if Kamenev was indulg-ing a tinge of revenge himself against Bukharin, who, after all, had venomously ripped him at the 14th and 15th Party Congresses? What if Kamenev was ingra-tiating himself with Stalin? Kamenev was an intriguer of the first order. He had worked hand in glove with Stalin many times, including on the virtuoso intrigue against Mirsäyet Soltangäliev and the Muslim Communists. It is possible Kame-nev set Bukharin up. Kamenev not only wrote down notes of a conspiratorial meeting but mailed them to Zinoviev back in Kaluga.[306]

Kamenev would later claim that he had planned to stay in Moscow awhile, and did not want to wait to tell Zinoviev in person. Perhaps this was true. And yet, could someone like Kamenev, who had spent fifteen years in the Bolshevik underground and who knew intimately the practices of the Soviet secret police, have doubted that such a letter—to Zinoviev—would get through without being intercepted and reported? Then there is the matter of the exceptionally damn-ing portrait Kamenev painted of Bukharin. Bukharin would later complain that Kamenev's notes "are written, to put it mildly, one-sidedly, tendentiously, with the omission and garbling of a number of important thoughts."[307] More precisely, Sokolnikov would observe that Kamenev's notes "represent a specific interest in the sense of an assessment of the sharpness and sharpening of internal relations."[308]

We may never know whether Kamenev meant to avenge himself against Bukharin and rehabilitate himself with Stalin by means of such a bizarre, ten-dentious document. Be that as it may, it was not Kamenev who had initiated the cockamamie tête-a-tête in the territory of the tightly watched Kremlin. Bukharin's conspiracy with Kamenev—which he evidently undertook without the knowledge of his allies Rykov and Tomsky—handed Stalin a gargantuan gift. Bukharin had divulged politburo secrets to a non-member, and admitted an effort to remove Stalin, naming names. Rykov, summoned to a private audience with Stalin, found out that Bukharin was negotiating over secret politburo matters with the disgraced former Trotsky coconspirator Kamenev, in an effort to remove the general secretary. Rykov headed for Bukharin's Kremlin apartment, lacing into him for being a "silly woman, not a politician."[309] Stalin could rely on Molotov and secondly Kaganovich, capable, thuggish organizers and executors of his will; Rykov had what? Tomsky, a tough but overmatched fighter, and Bukharin, who woefully lacked sufficient political calculation for the crucial regime position he occupied. Bukharin, thanks to Kamenev's notes, had also managed to implicate Orjonikidze, perhaps the one Stalin loyalist who did not detest him. Orjonikidze was forced to explain himself before Koba. Yagoda, too, had to submit a written explanation to Stalin concerning Bukharin's mention of OGPU support for removing the general secretary. All that from one false rumor about Bukharin's opposition to Kamenev's and Zinoviev's reinstatement.

## FUTURE BRICKS, PRESENT MALEVOLENCE

Signs of a world turning upside down were unmistakable. On July 12, Molotov closed out the Soviet party plenum with a report on the training of new specialists, pointing out the backwardness of the Soviet science laboratories and technical learning, giving examples of one Moscow school with equipment dating to 1847 and textbooks to 1895. He divulged that the vast Russian Soviet Federated Socialist Republic had a mere 117 students studying for Ph.D.s in technical subjects. Of course, the secret police and press, with Molotov's rabid collusion, were hounding the few genuinely qualified bourgeois specialists.[310] But Stalin was not going to remain beholden to these class aliens. During the Soviet plenum, the Sixth Party Congress of the Chinese Communist Party came to a close in Moscow, the first Chinese congress convened outside of China. Eighty-four delegates attended (Mao stayed home). Moscow formally acceded to the formation of separate Chinese Communist army units, a process already under way, but Stalin still insisted they had to be under the Guomnindang flag, despite Chiang Kaishek's massacres. Chiang, for his part, had continued his military unification campaign, seizing Peking on July 6 from an ex-bandit and warlord (Zhang Zuolin, expecting Japanese protection, had retreated to Manchuria but was killed by a bomb en route). Stalin found himself still stamping out Trotskyite views inside the Chinese Communist party, even as he was now forcing through a version of Trotskyite views at home.[311]

Only the absolute keenest Kremlinologists could penetrate the fog of the regime. After reading the published version of Stalin's speech to the Communist Academy, which recapitulated what the dictator had said in closed session in Siberia, Boris Bakhmeteff, the deposed Provisional Government's ambassador to the United States, wrote in August 1928 to a fellow Constitutional Democrat in exile, Vasily Maklakov, that "the dictatorial regime cannot feel firmly planted and tranquil because the main sphere of the country's economic life—agriculture—depends in the final analysis on the good will of the many millions of individual peasant proprietors." Bakhmeteff deemed Stalin "one of the few remaining incontrovertible fanatics . . . despite the fact that the majority of foreign writers are inclined to see in him only an opportunist, leading Russia back to capitalism," and noted that Stalin had "recognized that Soviet power must have the source of agricultural production in its hands," just as it did industry. Bakhmeteff further pointed out that the farmers who were designated as kulaks—"even though in essence they are just lads possessing two horses and two to three cows and are not exploiters"—had gradually come to perform the function of old gentry agriculture, producing the surplus desperately needed by the governing authorities. Bakhmeteff laughed off Stalin's earlier mid-1920s polemics with Trotsky and others over the NEP because now Stalin himself had begun to strangle these producers-kulaks, and noted that such actions were correct from the point of view of "Marxist logic and Communist doctrine," which in place of private proprietors needed "bread factories, i.e., collective and state farms" that would "render sufficient grain to emancipate the regime from the whims and sentiments of the peasant masses." Bakhmeteff even understood that "inside the party one can detect a current, which is much fiercer and faster than I thought, against Stalin's new course."[312]

But not even Bakhmeteff, indeed not even regime insiders, foresaw that Stalin's momentous turn to force collectivization and rapid industrialization became centered upon a drawn-out, painstakingly sadistic humiliation of Bukharin. On July 17, the Sixth Comintern Congress opened in Moscow (it would run through September 1), with more than 500 attendees from more than fifty Communist parties around the world. No Comintern Congress had met since 1924, an embarrassingly long hiatus. Never mind: Stalin reached for yet another truncheon against his duumvirate partner. Already on the heels of Stalin's return from Siberia, a plenum of the Comintern's executive committee had already unmasked what was called a right deviation. Tomsky, a target, observed of the dirty campaign, "Every day a little brushstroke—here a dab, there a dab. Aha! . . . as a result of this clever bit of work they have turned us into 'rightists.'"[313] Bukharin had stopped turning up at Comintern headquarters, despite still being its de facto nominal head. Now Stalin's agents spread rumors in the corridors of the congress that Bukharin's days in the leadership were numbered, that he was next in line for internal exile to Alma-Ata. Trotsky, from there, made a contribution to paying Bukharin back for all his years of vicious slander, observing that the number of hours Bukharin spoke at the congress was in inverse proportion to his decision-making power.[314] With the congress dragging on through the summer, in August 1928 Stalin inserted Molotov into the Comintern executive committee to ramp up the pogrom against "rightist tendencies."[315]

Stalin did not take kindly to Bukharin's efforts, dating back to the 1923 cave meeting, to curb his powers or even remove him as general secretary, but this was not Trotsky, where the enmity had been ferocious from the moment Trotsky joined the Bolsheviks in summer 1917 and grew to hatred. Stalin had been treating Bukharin like the younger brother he never had, or even like a son, despite the mere decade that separated them.[316] When Bukharin lived in three rooms at the House of Soviets No. 2, that is, the Hotel Metropole, with his widowed father (a retired math teacher), and the residence became a gathering place for young acolytes and political allies, Stalin visited, too. In 1927, Stalin had moved Bukharin into the Kremlin. Esfir Gurvich, Bukharin's second wife, a Latvian Jewish woman with a degree from St. Petersburg, continued to live separately from him back at the Metropole, but she had become close with Nadya Alliluyeva, Stalin's wife. The couple's daughters, both named Svetlana, became boon companions at the Zubalovo-4 dacha. Bukharin rode to and from Zubalovo with Stalin in his Packard, an unheard of privilege. True, Bukharin and Gurvich observed Stalin's abuse of Nadya firsthand, and later rumors circulated that because Gurvich was too well informed about Stalin's private life, he drove a wedge between her and Bukharin. (The couple would soon break up.)[317] But the causes here were significantly deeper, and entailed strategy over the building of socialism. Still, the malice was extraordinary. Stalin compelled Bukharin, the "theorist," to write up the congress program documents, then humiliatingly crossed out and rewrote everything from top to bottom. The declaration of a Comintern surge to the left came out in Bukharin's name.[318] Stalin's malevolence was palpable.

The irreconcilable schism cum civil war of the global left was also on grue-some display. The Sixth Comintern Congress fully institutionalized the slander of socialist (non-Communist) parties as handmaidens of fascists. Palmiro Togli-atti, leader of the Italian Communist party, who had no love for social democ-racy, nonetheless viewed its class base (the working masses) as distinct from that of fascism (petite bourgeoisie and haute bourgeoisie) and objected to the "social fascism" slogan ("We think this formulation is absolutely unacceptable. Our del-egation is decisively opposed to this bending of reality").[319] Bukharin, too, stated that "it would be a mistake to lump social democracy and fascism together."[320] But in the menacing atmosphere, where Molotov and other Stalin stooges held sway, "social fascism" was forced through for the rest of the left, the complement to the "right deviation" inside the Communist party.[321]

Stalin had delayed his regular Sochi holiday, originally scheduled to com-mence June 10, until August 2, during the Comintern Congress. His 1928 holi-day is not well documented.[322] We do know that Dr. Valedinsky brought in the renowned neuropathologist Vasily Verzilov and therapist Vladimir Shchurovsky, but we have no record of their diagnoses. Stalin appears to have voiced the usual complaints, pain in his muscles and joints, which was alleviated in the warm sulfur baths. He also talked with the physicians about agriculture and the need to strengthen state farms, clearly matters on his mind.[323]

Kamenev met with Bukharin at least three more times, although whether for his own purposes or as Stalin's double agent, or both, remains uncertain.[324] Kalinin, a state-farm proponent, in the end had sided with Stalin at the plenum, spurring rumors that Stalin held compromising material over his head (Kalinin's liaisons with ballerinas were infamous). Stalin learned that Tomsky was vigor-ously trying to win over the general secretary's wavering protégé Andreyev, among others. Stalin evidently wrote to Molotov in August 1928 that "under no circumstances should Tomsky (or anyone else) be allowed to 'work over' Kuiby-shev or Mikoyan."[325]

Because of the renewal of grain imports between July and September 1928, the USSR had begun to hemorrhage gold (145 million rubles' worth) and other precious metals (another 10 million rubles' worth). Foreign exchange reserves fell some 30 percent, down to just 330 million rubles. No one would lend money to the USSR on a long-term basis, so the growing trade imbalance could only be financed by short-term credits, whose renewal was costly and unassured. Soviet external debt rose to 370 million rubles.[326] German banks began to question the advisability of rolling over short-term financing; Germany suffered its own decline in the flow of U.S. capital. "Difficulties are observed on two dangerous fronts: foreign-currency/external trade and grain procurements," Mikoyan wrote to Stalin ("Dear Soso") in Sochi on August 23, 1928. He claimed there was an incipient "credit blockade" against the USSR on the part of Germany, the United States, and France, with political and industrial circles agitating against doing business in the USSR because of uncertainties. "This dictates the necessity of cutting down the plan for imports; we'll have to cut where it hurts," Mikoyan wrote. "This year there will be large reductions in our pace of development as far as imports are concerned." He called for greater attention to other exports besides grain. As for the "grain front," he characterized procurements as very tense.[327]

The sense of general crisis was palpable. The geochemist-minerologist Vladimir Vernadsky (b. 1863) recorded in his diary in August 1928 that "when one returns from abroad, the expectation of war and the corresponding press propaganda astonish," and that "in villages they say: war is coming, we'll take revenge: the Communists, the intelligentsia, in a word the city."[328]

Stalin lived in his world. "I think the credit blockade is a fact!" he wrote back to Mikoyan on August 28. "We should have expected this in the conditions of grain difficulties. The Germans are especially harmful to us because they would like to see us completely isolated, in order to make it easier for them to monopolize our relations with the West (including with America)."[329] A few weeks later (September 17), in a better mood perhaps, Stalin wrote to Mikoyan again: "I was in Abkhazia. We drank to your health."[330] Whether Stalin appreciated the full seriousness of the alarming information Mikoyan was communicating remains unclear. Mikoyan also wrote to Rykov—who was on holiday away from Moscow as well—on September 19 about the incipient international financial blockade and the resulting forced reduction in imports. Mikoyan reported that long queues had formed in Leningrad as peasants descended upon the city looking for food, and that the partially failed harvest in Ukraine was causing ripples in all neighboring territories, too, as people roamed in search of provisions. The long letter concluded that Orjonikidze's health had taken a bad turn and the doctors could not even agree on a diagnosis.[331] Orjonikidze was sent to Germany for medical treatment.[332] Rykov, before the month was out, would go to Ukraine to examine food relief efforts in connection with the crop failures there. "For over four years we have been fighting drought in Ukraine," he stated at a speech carried in the local press. "The effectiveness of our expenditures obviously cannot be considered sufficient."[333]

But also on September 19, Valerian Kuibyshev, the zealous super industrializer, told a meeting of the Leningrad party organization that a five-year plan for industry would go forward, and in ambitious fashion. "We are told that we are 'over-industrializing' and 'biting off more than we can chew,'" he remarked dismissively of critics like Rykov. "History, however, will not permit us to proceed more slowly, otherwise the very next year may lead to a series of even more serious anomalies."[334] An irate Bukharin responded in *Pravda* (September 30, 1928) with a broadside titled "Notes of an Economist," which was ostensibly directed at unnamed "Trotskyites"—meaning Kuibyshev and the party's general secretary who stood behind him. Demanding balanced, "crisis-free" industrialization, Bukharin predicted that total elimination of the market alongside forced collectivization of the peasantry would produce unfathomable red tape, overwhelming the party. Of the industrialization "plan," Bukharin mockingly wrote that "it is not possible to build 'present-day' factories with 'future bricks.'"[335]

Building now with future bricks, however, was precisely Stalin's proposition. He began but never finished a written response to Bukharin's "Notes of an Economist."[336] Perhaps he thought better of granting Bukharin a public discussion. Once Stalin returned from Sochi, he had the politburo, over the objections of Rykov, Tomsky, and Bukharin, reprimand *Pravda* for publishing the article without Central Committee authorization.[337] Nothing Bukharin had pointed out softened Stalin's position. "No matter how well the grain procurements might go, they would not remove the basis of our difficulties—they can heal (they will heal, I think, this year) the wounds, but they cannot cure the disease until machinery raises the productivity of our fields, and agriculture is organized on a new basis," Stalin had written to Mikoyan from Sochi on September 26. "Many thought that removing the extraordinary measures and raising grain prices would be the basis of eliminating the difficulties. Empty hopes of empty Bolshevik liberals!"[338]

A third wave of coercive procurements struck villages that fall of 1928 with greater force than the first (January-February) or second (late April-early July) waves.[339] The pressure sparked peasant protests on a scale the regime did not foresee. Before the year was out, the regime formally announced the introduction of bread rationing in the major cities.[340] The higher yields anticipated from improved seeds, fertilizers, tractors and other machinery, as well as the assumption that collectivized farming would outperform private, individual work, were nowhere in sight. Stalin continued to rebuff Bukharin's murmurs about resigning, while publicly smearing the rightists as a grave danger to the party. "Instead of simply telling me, 'We do not trust you, Bukharin, it seems to us that you conduct an incorrect line, let's part ways'—which is what I proposed be done—you did it differently," Bukharin would soon surmise. "It was initially necessary to smear, discredit, trample, then it would no longer be a question of agreeing to my request to resign but instead 'removal' 'for sabotage.' The game is absolutely clear."[341]

PEACEMAKER ORJONIKIDZE, back from medical treatment in Germany, wrote a long letter in November 1928 to Rykov, who was downcast and again contemplating resigning. "A conversation with you and with others (Stalin) persuades me that there are no fundamental differences, and that's the main thing," Orjonikidze wrote, absurdly. Still more absurdly, he added, "I am frankly imploring you to bring about reconciliation between Bukharin and Stalin," as if that were within Rykov's powers. What must Rykov have thought? Orjonikidze was a hard Bolshevik, a Georgian steeped in Caucasus customs, a person who had grown up without a father or mother, a man notoriously prickly and hot-tempered, yet he exhibited none of Stalin's extreme vindictiveness. Orjonikidze, moreover, although as close to Stalin as anyone, seemed not to understand, or want to understand, him at this moment. He attributed the lingering bad blood inside the politburo merely to the recent grain procurement campaign, without acknowledging that such heavy coercion was the new permanent reality, and that Stalin perceived critics of this policy as enemies.[342]

Stalin went after Nikolai Uglanov. A onetime protégé whom he had promoted to boss of the Moscow party machine, and an indispensable persecutor of the Trotskyites, Uglanov had sided openly with Bukharin and was replaced by the all-purpose Molotov in late November. That month, Bukharin finally managed to obtain a long-sought audience with Stalin, which lasted six hours. According to Mikoyan, Bukharin told Stalin that he did "not want to fight, because it will harm the party. If a fight starts, you'll declare us renegades from Leninism." Bukharin added: "But we'll call you organizers of famine."[343] Stalin, however, was immovable: on his Siberia trip he had declared his intention to force the country toward anticapitalism, and since returning to Moscow, he had additionally indulged a chilling malevolence toward close political allies and friends.

# IF STALIN HAD DIED

HE WOULD DO IT. Stalin would force the collectivization of Soviet villages and nomadic steppes inhabited by more than 100 million people between 1928 and 1933, a story taken up in volume II. At least 5 million people, many of the country's most productive farmers or herders, would be "dekulakized," that is, enclosed in cattle cars and dumped at far-off wastes, often in winter; some in that number would dekulakize themselves, rushing to sell or abandon their possessions to escape deportation. Those forced into the collectives would burn crops, slaughter animals, and assassinate officials.[1] The regime's urban shock troops would break peasant resistance, but the country's inventory of horses would plummet from 35 million to 17 million, cattle from 70 million to 38 million, pigs from 26 million to 12 million, sheep and goats from 147 million to 50 million. In Kazakhstan, the losses would be still more staggering: cattle from 7.5 million to 1.6 million, sheep from 21.9 million to 1.7 million. Countrywide, nearly 40 million people would suffer severe hunger or starvation and between 5 and 7 million people would die in the horrific famine, whose existence the regime denied.[2] "All the dogs have been eaten," one eyewitness would be told in a Ukrainian village. "We have eaten everything we could lay our hands on—cats, dogs, field mice, birds—when it's light tomorrow, you will see that the trees have been stripped of bark, for that too has been eaten. And the horse manure has been eaten. Yes, the horse manure. We fight over it. Sometimes there are whole grains in it."[3]

Scholars who argue that Stalin's collectivization was necessary in order to force a peasant country into the modern era are dead wrong.[4] The Soviet Union, like imperial Russia, faced an imperative to modernize in order to survive in the brutally unsentimental international order, but market systems have been shown to be fully compatible with fast-paced industrialization, including in peasant countries. Forced wholesale collectivization only seemed necessary within the straitjacket of Communist ideology and its repudiation of capitalism. And economically, collectivization failed to deliver. Stalin assumed it would increase both the state's share of low-cost grain purchases and the overall size of the harvest, but although procurements doubled immediately, harvests shrank. Over the longer term, collective farming would not prove superior to large-scale capitalist farming or even to smaller-scale capitalist farming when the latter was provided with machinery, fertilizer, agronomy, and effective distribution.[5] In the short term, collectivization would contribute nothing on net to Soviet industrial growth.[6]

Nor was collectivization necessary to sustain a dictatorship. Private capital and dictatorship are fully compatible. In fascist Italy, industrialists maintained tremendous autonomous power. Mussolini, like Stalin, supported efforts to attack inflation and a balance-of-payments deficit despite the negative impact on domestic employment, for he, too, viewed a "strong" currency as a point of regime prestige. But although for Mussolini, too, economics was subordinate to his political power, he was not a leftist ideologue wedded to theories of class struggle and the like. All he needed was industrialists' recognition of his political supremacy. He got that despite a December 21, 1927, upward revaluation of the lira that the industrialists had adamantly opposed—exports declined (and unemployment skyrocketed to at least 10 percent)—because Mussolini rejected demands by fascism's syndicalist wing to force production and consumption under the aegis of the state. Instead, the fascist regime lowered taxes and transport costs for domestic industry, increased the allowances for depreciation and amortization, prioritized domestic producers on government contracts, encouraged the concentration of industry to reduce competition in order to keep profit levels up, increased tariffs, and took on some of the exchange risk associated with debt contracted by Italian industry abroad.[7] The Italian dictatorship did not go about destroying the country's economically successful people, who could be imprisoned quickly if they became foolish enough to hint at political opposition. None of this is meant to uphold Italian fascism in any way as a model, but merely to spotlight that nothing prevented the Communist dictatorship from embracing private capital—nothing, that is, except idées fixes.

Nor did an adverse turn in the world economy compel collectivization.[8] Global deflation in commodity prices did hit the Soviet Union hard, reducing the revenues from the sale abroad of Soviet grain, oil, timber, and sugar, but Stalin, in his grand speech in Siberia on January 20, 1928, made no mention of such conditions as a factor in his decision. If the global terms of trade for primary goods producers had been favorable, would Stalin have said in Novosibirsk that day, Let's develop large-scale privately owned kulak farms with privately hired labor? Look at these high global grain prices, we'll never have to collectivize the peasantry! If the Soviet Union had obtained abundant long-term foreign credits in 1927–28, would Stalin have said, Let's double down on markets at home? So what if we risk the party's monopoly! The pernicious idea that global capitalism caused Stalin's resort to extreme violence and erection of a brutal command system, in order to exercise control over the export commodities needed to finance industrialization, ignores the vast trove of evidence on the salience of ideology, including ideology's role in worsening the USSR's international position in the first place. There was a debate inside the USSR in the 1920s about how to modernize the country, but it was a remarkably narrow debate in which important options were closed off.[9]

For that reason, it will not do to simplify collectivization as just another instance in the Russian state's infamous strong-arming of a predominantly peasant country because its agricultural season—in its northern climate, on a par with Canada—lasted a mere 125 days, perhaps half the length in Europe, where yields per acre were higher. The image of a Russian state through the centuries as a cruel military occupier at home is one-sided: Alexander had emancipated the serfs and Stolypin's peasant reforms were voluntary. And Stalin was motivated by more than competition with more fortunate European rivals. Like Stolypin, Stalin wanted consolidated, contiguous farms, not the separated, small strips of the commune, but he ruled out the Stolypin route of betting on independent yeoman farmers (kulaks). Critics of Bolshevism abroad had urged old-regime professionals to work for the Soviet regime precisely in order to transform it from within, toward a Russian nationalist order and a full capitalist restoration.[10] Such hopes were Stalin's fears. Collectivization would give the Communists control over the vast countryside, a coveted goal no regime in Russia had ever had. But still more fundamentally, collectivization, like state-run and state-owned industry, constituted a form of ostensible modernization that negated capitalism. Thus did Stalin "solve" the Bolsheviks' conundrum of how, in the words of Lenin's last public speech, "NEP Russia could become socialist Russia."[11]

THERE ARE ALWAYS ALTERNATIVES IN HISTORY. The germane question is, was there an alternative within the Leninist revolution? Nikolai Bukharin had set out the magical thinking underlying the NEP when he and Stalin drew close in political alliance. "We had thought it was possible to destroy market relations in one stroke, immediately," Bukharin had written in *The Path to Socialism and the Worker-Peasant Alliance.* "It turned out that we shall reach socialism *precisely through* market relations." Come again? "Market relations will be destroyed as a result of their own development." How, exactly? Well, explained Bukharin, under capitalism, large entities end up crushing small ones in market competition, ergo, in the Soviet Union case, the large companies under state control, as well as amalgamated peasant cooperatives, would just squeeze the small private peasant farms out of existence.[12] Some version of this abracadabra—that the Soviet Union could, somehow, "grow into socialism" via the NEP—had taken hold in many pockets of the party. But Bukharin was also the one who inadvertently had crystallized the impossibility of growing into anticapitalism via markets with his summons for peasants to "Enrich yourselves!"[13] Of course, as any peasant could have told him—and as many did, writing to, among other newspapers, *Pravda,* which Bukharin edited—no sooner did a peasant household manage to achieve some success, then it was squeezed mercilessly by punitive taxation. And in 1928, with the grain procurement shortfall, hardworking peasants were subjected to criminal sanctions. When armed squads confiscated eight bulls, seven cows, four calves, three horses, thirty-six tons of wheat, a cart, a threshing machine, and a mill from B. Bondarenko of Aktyubinsk province, while sentencing him to a year in prison, he asked the presiding judge to provide an explanation for the basis of his conviction because he was not guilty of a crime. "Our goal is to dekulakize you," the judge snapped.[14] Here was the fateful formulation.

NEP, via its own middling success, was producing kulaks who, in turn, were the ones producing the harvest. Kamenev, at their July 11, 1928, encounter, had pointedly asked Bukharin about his plan for procuring grain, recording the following response: "One can persecute the kulak as much as possible, but we must make peace with the middle peasant." But out in the countryside where such decisions were made by officials following the same class analysis, a farmer with three cows in 1925 who had six by 1928 suddenly became registered as a "class-enemy." In Vologda, a dairy center, where Stalin had spent several years of domestic exile under the tsars, between 1927 and 1928 alone the number of kulaks leapt from 6,315 to 8,462, more than 2,000 new "bloodsuckers," at a time when the province counted just 2,500 rural Communists.[15] For marketed grain, the regime had become dependent on just 2 million peasant-household producers who sowed more than eight hectares each.[16] This was a substantial population—not Bukharin's alleged mere 3 to 4 percent of kulaks—which was susceptible to reclassification as class enemies because of their hard work. The class analysis to which all top Bolsheviks subscribed, Bukharin included, effectively ensured that the NEP had to fail if it succeeded.

Bukharin presented no genuine alternative to Stalin, even leaving aside the fact that he lacked political heft or an organizational power base. A figure with a more solid reputation and skill set was Alexei Rykov, far and away the most important proponent of the NEP. It was the authoritative Rykov who chaired politburo meetings, and had opened and closed the 15th Party Congress. A talented administrator, he possessed skills that Kamenev had only to a lesser degree and that Zinoviev and Trotsky lacked almost completely. Rykov "was gregarious and hearty and would often visit his subordinates in their homes, even if they were not Communists," observed Simon Liberman, who knew him from 1906 and worked under him after the revolution. "He loved to take a glass with them and have expansive talks with them. His slight stutter made him a good deal more human than most of his forbidding colleagues."[17] The warmhearted kindly provincial doctor whom Liberman imagined was not the Rykov who had gone after Trotsky with a vengeance and never wavered during the infighting against the opposition. Rykov was rumored to be prone to alcohol abuse—as one nasty joke had it, "Trotsky dictates in his last will that upon his death his brain should be preserved in alcohol with the instruction that the brain goes to Stalin and the alcohol to Rykov"—but it is unclear if this was true. Rykov was a hard Bolshevik but prudent type, favoring fiscal discipline and living within one's means. He did not dispute that in time small-scale farming would have to be replaced by large-scale and mechanized farms and that modernized farms would be "socialist" (collectivized), but he put a premium on the stability engendered by the NEP's class conciliation. His position was less that the NEP would alchemize capitalism into socialism (Bukharin) than that forced collectivization could simply not be done, and that any attempt to do so would merely destroy what progress had been made since the civil war and famine, bringing on renewed catastrophe.

Rykov turned out to be bleakly prescient about forced collectivization's dire, destabilizing consequences, but on the question of what to do instead he had little idea, other than staying the failing course of the NEP. Another figure, however, who worked under Rykov for many years did have some idea—Grigory Sokolnikov. Sokolnikov, who was Bukharin's former gymnasium classmate, was also known for his softness and intellectualism. He belonged to that group of Bolsheviks—Krasin, Chicherin, Rakovski—from well-to-do families, which could be politically problematic. But he had turned out to be nearly perfect for the role of finance commissar. And when Bukharin was allied with Stalin and eviscerating the United opposition, Sokolnikov clashed with the dictator by insisting on open debate within the monopoly Communist party, including the right to open debate for Zinoviev and Kamenev, with whom Sokolnikov disagreed fundamentally on economic policy. Even in the aftermath of the brouhaha over Bukharin's "Enrich yourselves" speech, Sokolnikov had not shrunk from extolling market relations. To be sure, unlike Yakov Yakovlev, the founder and editor of *Peasant Newspaper,* Sokolnikov did not go as far as to advocate that the regime allow peasants to register their de facto possession of land as private property, which could be bought, sold, or inherited. Still, Sokolnikov had insisted that the market, at least in the countryside, was compatible with socialism—not just during the present difficult conjuncture, but permanently. He also insisted that the so-called kulaks were good farmers, not enemies.

Sokolnikov agreed with Rykov's and Bukharin's insistence on a version of industrialization compatible with market equilibrium, but he went much further and explicitly rejected the vision, alluring to almost all Communists, of achieving comprehensive economic planning in practice. (Sokolnikov allowed for the lesser possibility of coordination.)[18] Of course, almost all non-Bolshevik specialists in the finance commissariat and elsewhere were saying this, but Sokolnikov was a member of the Central Committee. He had not argued in favor of capitalism—it is hard to see how any Bolshevik could have done so and survived in a leadership position—and implementing his market socialism would not have been easy. The Soviet party-state lacked much of the institutional capacity necessary to regulate a market economy skillfully (Sokolnikov excepted). This was especially true of the mixed-state market economy of the NEP, which required a subtle understanding of the effects on the country's macroeconomy of price controls and use of state power against private traders.[19] Nonetheless, acceptance of the market and rejection of planning as a chimera were the sine qua non of any alternative path to the one Stalin had proclaimed in Novosibirsk in January 1928.

When Stalin had evicted Sokolnikov from the politburo and finance commissariat in early 1926, he had named him deputy chairman of the state planning commission—aware that Sokolnikov did not believe in planning—but this had not ended Sokolnikov's career. He had been part of a Soviet delegation to a world economic conference in Geneva convened by the League of Nations in May 1927, when he delivered a substantive, businesslike speech on the Soviet economy and socialism that evidently impressed at least some members of the foreign audience. (Sokolnikov, who had a doctorate from the Sorbonne, spoke even better French than Bukharin.) Sokolnikov argued that the Soviet mode of industrialization was distinct because of coordination and the participation of the masses, but he called for trade and cooperation between the capitalist world and the Soviet Union, especially in the form of foreign investment.[20] The applause was said to have emanated from "every seating bench of the parliament of the capitalist economy," as a Swiss journalist sympathetic to the left observed, according to *Pravda*. "Even the English applauded in a sign of approval of Sokolnikov's speech."[21] This favorable assessment in the party organ was followed, in summer 1927, by Sokolnikov's break with the opposition.[22] In December 1927, at the 15th Congress, Stalin allowed Sokolnikov to be reelected to the Central Committee, a nearly unique outcome for a former oppositionist. In spring 1928, Stalin would shift Sokolnikov over to the chairmanship of the oil trust; oil exports began to generate significant budget revenues.

That said, Sokolnikov was a mere individual, not a faction. No top military men were loyal to him; no high GPU operatives worked for him; he had no Kremlin telephone network (the vertushka) at his command, except when he was summoned on it; no power to send out directives in the name of the Central Committee on which he sat. Sokolnikov had enjoyed his greatest influence under Stalin's patronage and now, too, his promarket, antiplanning stance would have required a politically muscular patron—such as Rykov. A Rykov-Sokolnikov political-intellectual leadership would have offered a genuine alternative to Stalin only if Rykov and others in a ruling coalition came around to capitulating on the commitment to anticapitalism in the village. Such an eventuality would have raised weighty questions: Would the regime be able to manage one system (socialism) for the city and another system (petit bourgeois capitalism) for the countryside? Would such an arrangement have even permitted socialism in the city? Would the Communist party have had to surrender its political monopoly eventually and, if so, would a Rykov-Sokolnikov leadership have acceded to or survived that? Would Rykov, who was far closer to Stalin than to Sokolnikov and fundamentally did not understand markets, even have accepted Sokolnikov as a partner?[23]

Of course, the existence of Stalin's personal dictatorship meant that any real alternative to his preferred course—as opposed to a mere intellectual exercise—had to trump his power, either by outvoting him, because members of his faction defected, or by removing him. Bukharin had tried such a maneuver and failed, but when Stalin, by offering to resign, handed Rykov the opportunity, he failed to seize it. Perhaps Rykov acted out of political self-preservation, given Stalin's power and vengeful disposition. But Rykov and others in the politburo had come to see not only a prickly, self-centered, often morose, vindictive person in Stalin, but also an indomitable Communist and leader of inner strength, utterly dedicated to Lenin's ideas, able to carry the entire apparatus, the country, and the cause of the world revolution on his back.[24] Stalin displayed a strategic mind, which had its cruelties—sizing up the weaknesses of Bukharin for sadistic as well as political purposes—but also its payoffs for managing the nationalities and regional party machines. Additionally, the group arrayed around Stalin was incomparably below him. Orjonikidze was no strategist, and in constant poor health; Voroshilov was no military man, and he knew it; Kirov had a public politician's touch but was given to laziness and womanizing; Kaganovich was an organizer of talent but barely educated; Mikoyan worshiped Stalin, not just for careerist reasons, but because he was young; Kalinin was underestimated, but also no Stalin; Molotov could flex some political muscles, but even he operated in Stalin's shadow. Stalin's dark side had become no small matter to manage, but managing entirely without his leadership?

Perhaps, in the end, Rykov clung to the hope that Stalin would see the folly of his coercive turn. But Stalin would charge Bukharin and Rykov with failing to accept the logic of their own Leninism. If the Soviet Union needed to mechanize agriculture on the basis of consolidated farms (it did), and if one believed this should ultimately occur within a socialist (non-capitalist) framework (at the top almost all believed so), and if the peasants were not joining collectives voluntarily (they were not), what was the Leninist conclusion? Either seize the means of production in the countryside or be prepared to sacrifice the party's monopoly in the long run, for, according to Marxism, class was the determinant of politics and the flourishing of a new bourgeoisie would inevitably bring political consequences. Stalin "was incorruptible and irreconcilable in class questions," Nikita Khrushchev, a rising official in the Ukrainian party apparatus at the time of Stalin's trip to Siberia, would recall. "It was one of his strongest qualities, and he was greatly respected for it."[25]

ULTIMATELY, the principal alternative to Stalin was the willing abandonment or unwilling unhinging of the Bolshevik regime—which Stalin himself almost caused, and not just because of collectivization.

Authoritarian rulers the world over were almost never so bold as to stand up to the great powers, putting their personal regimes at risk. They pursued private gain, appointed relatives and cronies, gathered harems, delivered Populist speeches in public about defending the interests of the patria, then sold out their countries to the Europeans or gringos for the enrichment of themselves and their entourages. This was the typical story of Latin American caudillos, for example. The Soviet Union, to be sure, had a conception of itself as a world power, the center of world revolution, but it, too, was a peasant country, and still hurting from civil war and famine, yet standing up to the whole world. The Bolsheviks, with their coup, had created a condition of capitalist encirclement, then proceeded to conduct themselves in a way that reinforced their predicament, attempting coups in countries where they had won hard-fought diplomatic recognition and sought wider trade relations. But if the challenges for Russian power in the world, always great, had grown harder under a Communist regime, which had no alliances or real friends, they grew harder still as a result of Stalin's brazen defiance.

Alongside the previous shocks of Bismarck's unification of Germany and the Meiji restoration in Japan, whose challenges grew, on top of the long-standing competition with the global British empire, had been added a series of new shocks: the anti-Soviet states in former imperial Russian territories—the "limitrophe" of Poland, Finland, and the Baltics, as well as Greater Romania. Moreover, Germany, the United States, Britain, France, even Italy possessed the world's advanced industrial technology, and the Soviets had been appealing to capitalists' greed, offering to pay good money, in the form of technical assistance contracts, for advanced machines and assistance in mounting and operating them. It was not really working. But although he had tried to cut a deal with France by recognizing tsarist debts, Stalin detested the prospect of becoming dependent on foreign bankers, or conceding changes in Soviet domestic political arrangements. Provocatively, he turned to arresting German engineers in the Shakhty fabrication almost immediately after restarting negotiations for major German loans and investments, shocking Berlin and other capitals. The Soviet Union, *Pravda* wrote grimly in late summer 1928, would have to rely "on our own strength without help from abroad."[26] But going it alone was a delusion: the Red Army could be crushed by superior technology.

Had Stalin not only caused the mass loss of the country's most productive farmers and half its livestock in collectivization but also failed to finagle the machinery necessary for Soviet industrialization, including tractors for agriculture, his rule would have risked the destruction of the Leninist revolution. But a fortuitous event rescued his reckless gambling. On September 4, 1929, stock prices began to fall in New York and on October 29 the market crashed. A host of structural factors and policy mistakes transformed the financial dislocation into a Great Depression. By 1933, industrial production would drop by 46 percent in the United States, 41 percent in Germany, and 23 percent in Britain. Unemployment in the United States would reach 25 percent and still higher elsewhere. International trade would drop by half. Construction would come to a virtual standstill. The world's misfortune was Stalin's great, unforeseen fortune.

Of course, in Marxist thinking this was no accident: Capitalism was seen as inherently prone to booms and busts, a market economy produced depressions, misallocation of capital, mass unemployment, for which planning was supposed to be the answer. But there had never before been a capitalist crisis on the scale of the Great Depression (and there has not been since). The timing of the Depression, moreover, could not have been better for Stalin: right after he launched collectivization and dekulakization. The upshot was a windfall. More than one thousand factories would be newly built or overhauled from top to bottom, and nearly every single blueprint and advanced machine came from abroad.[27] The Depression afforded Stalin unprecedented leverage: suddenly, the capitalists needed the Soviet market as much as the Soviets needed their advanced technology. Without the Great Depression would the capitalists have developed such overwhelming incentives to pursue the Soviet market no matter what? Indeed, the capitalist powers not only sold their best technology to the Communist regime, they continued doing so even after the Soviets were found to be violating contracts by purchasing designs for one factory and using them for others, trickery that was amply recorded in indignant internal foreign company records; the capitalist had no other customers for massive capital goods. Scholars who write of Moscow facing an "uncooperative world economy" have it exactly backward.[28] Ideology and the party monopoly were the constraints; the global economy, the enabler. In fact, the global economic crisis was a double gift. Nothing did more to legitimate Stalin's system. But Stalin had no idea that a Great Depression was around the corner, and that it would bring the foreign capitalists on bended knee.

Because of the Great Depression, we forget just how wild was Stalin's gamble— as great or greater than Lenin's October coup, Brest-Litovsk, and the NEP. The Communist party, let alone the country, was not prepared for forced wholesale collectivization. Stalin could use the police to outflank the party, of course, but he also had to mount a high-profile public trial to fan the flames of "class warfare." The mass mobilization campaign launched with the Shakhty trial entailed the arrests of many qualified engineers amid a severe shortage, when they were desperately needed for the regime's ambitious industrialization.[29] The disruption caused by removing supposedly recalcitrant or sabotaging engineers was worse than whatever these alleged wreckers could have caused. Both collectivization and the class warfare campaign also required Stalin to outmaneuver his own inner circle, which looks easy only in retrospect.

The Shakhty trial and related actions seemed to afford Stalin's personal dictatorship the power to overcome resistance among apparatchiks to collectivization, and to root the regime in more than itself. This task was urgent not just to disprove the critique by Trotsky—that Stalin's was a regime of functionaries— but because Stalin genuinely believed in the working-class social base. In addition, many young people, especially those Stalin was now trying to rally, had secretly continued to sympathize with Trotsky.[30] More broadly, in Soviet society disappointment had become pervasive over the failures of the revolution to deliver abundance and social justice. The vast majority of "anti-Soviet" utterances recorded in police summaries in fact had the populace demanding or wishing the regime live up to socialist goals. Nostalgia for "Father Lenin," misguided in the brutal facts of his rule, made sense in terms of a yearning to reclaim the revolution's promise. Shakhty promised a chance to regain the earlier élan. That all this upheaval, from the countryside to the mines and factories, was going to work out in Stalin's favor, however, was hardly guaranteed. He put everything on the line, including his personal power.

SUBJECTS OF BIOGRAPHY often are portrayed as forming their personalities, including their views about authority and obedience—that is, about power—in childhood and especially the family. But do we really need to locate the wellsprings of Stalin's politics or even his troubled soul in beatings he allegedly received as a child in Gori? The beatings likely never took place, certainly not to the extent they have usually been portrayed, but even if they had? Similarly, were the oppressive surveillance, informing, and arbitrary governance at the Tiflis seminary the critical formative experiences of Stalin's life? That training ground for priests was a nest of tyranny and stool pigeons, but so was the entirety of Russia under the autocracy, and many of the softest Georgian Mensheviks came out of the very same seminary as Stalin did. To be sure, his intense relationship with the daring Lado Ketskhoveli, and the latter's early death at the hands of tsarist jailers, made a lasting impression on him, helping to solidify his lifelong Marxist convictions. And Stalin's prolonged struggle as a Bolshevik and Lenin loyalist against the overwhelming Menshevik majority of Georgia's Social Democrats made a lasting imprint, too, sowing or eliciting some of his inner demons. In other words, Stalin's marked personal traits, which colored his momentous political decisions, emerged as a result of politics. This suggestion to explain Stalin's person through politics amounts to more than expediency (in the absence of plentiful, reliable sources on his early life and inner mind). Even though he had inherited the possibility of a personal dictatorship from Lenin, Stalin went through significant psychological ordeals in the struggle to be acclaimed as Lenin's successor.

It had taken Stalin years of angling and stress to rid himself of Trotsky, a bitter rivalry that had ensued already in 1917, intensified during the civil war into near obsession, and dominated the inner life of the party after the onset of Lenin's fatal illness. The Trotsky struggle had exerted a deep influence on Stalin's character. No less profound an impact came in Stalin's struggle with Lenin's dictation. From May-June 1923 on, Stalin was embroiled in several years of infighting during which Lenin's purported Testament appeared suddenly, and kept reappearing, refusing to go away. With his manifold instruments of personal power, he was mercilessly hounding all those who expressed differences of opinion with him, but he was always the victim. Whether this entailed some sort of long-standing persecution complex or one of more recent vintage cannot be established given the extant sources. But we can say for certain that the internecine political warfare with the opposition—not just with Trotsky, Zinoviev, and Kamenev, but also with the Testament—brought this behavior out.

When all is said and done, the "succession struggle" was with a piece of paper—a few typed lines, no signature, no identifying initials. Stalin triumphed over its recommendation, but the Testament continued to broadcast an irrepressible echo: Stalin's personality is dangerous; find a way to remove Stalin. He resigned, again and again. He cut a deal for a truce with them, and they published the Testament in the *New York Times*. He could trust no one. All the while, he was responsible for *everything*. It was all on his back. But did they appreciate this? Let them try to do better. They again affirmed his leadership. But it was never sufficient.

Closed and gregarious, vindictive and solicitous, Stalin shatters any attempt to contain him within binaries. He was by inclination a despot who, when he wanted to be, was utterly charming. He was an ideologue who was flexibly pragmatic. He fastened obsessively on slights yet he was a precocious geostrategic thinker—unique among Bolsheviks—who was, however, prone to egregious strategic blunders. Stalin was as a ruler both astute and blinkered, diligent and self-defeating, cynical and true believing. The cold calculation and the flights of absurd delusion were products of a single mind. He was shrewd enough to see right through people, but not enough to escape a litany of nonsensical beliefs. Above all, he became in the 1920s ever more steeped in conspiracies. But Stalin's increasing hyper-suspiciousness bordering on paranoia was fundamentally political—and it closely mirrored the Bolshevik revolution's in-built structural paranoia, the predicament of a Communist regime in an overwhelmingly capitalist world, surrounded by, penetrated by enemies.

THE RUSSIAN REVOLUTION—against the tyranny, corruption, and, not least, incompetence of tsarism—sparked soaring hopes for a new world of abundance, social justice, and peace. But all that was precluded by the Bolsheviks, who unwittingly yet relentlessly reproduced the pathologies and predations of the old regime state in new forms (even more than had their French Revolution forerunners, as Alexis de Tocqueville demonstrated for France). The reason was not circumstance but intentional political monopoly as well as Communist convictions, which deepened the debilitating circumstances cited to justify ever more statization and violence. To be sure, socioeconomic class was (and remains) undeniable. But the construction of political order on the basis of class, rather than common humanity and individual liberty, was (and always will be) ruinous. All non-Leninist socialists eventually discovered that if they wanted genuine democracy, they had to abandon Marx's summons to negate and transcend capitalism and markets. In the Soviet case, for anyone not hopelessly sunk in the ideological soup, events provided ample opportunity for a rethinking—for recognition of the dire need to exit the Leninist cul-de-sac: abandon the self-defeating class war approach, accept the market as not inherently evil, encourage prospering farmers to continue, and help lift up the others. But such admissions, for almost every Bolshevik of consequence, proved too great.

Still, even within the encumbering Leninist frame, a Soviet leader could have gone out of his way to reduce the paranoia built into the regime's relations with the outside world and its domestic situation. A Soviet leader could have paid the price of partial accommodation, grasping that capitalism was not, in fact, dying out globally and that the capitalist powers were not, in fact, hellbent on overturning the revolutionary regime at all costs. But Stalin was not such a leader. Of course, all authoritarian regimes, in order to suppress dissent and gin up the masses, cynically require profuse "enemies." On top of that, though, Stalin intensified the insanity inherent in Leninism from conviction and personal characteristics, ensuring that the permanent state of war with the whole world led to a state of war with the country's majority population, and carrying the Leninist program to its full end goal of anti-capitalism.

Stalin had not liked the NEP any more than Trotsky had, although like Lenin, and because of Lenin, Stalin appreciated the recourse to pragmatism for the greater cause. But by 1928, immediately upon Trotsky's deportation to Kazakhstan, Stalin acted upon his long-standing leftist core convictions because, like Lenin in 1921, when the NEP had been introduced, Stalin felt the survival of the revolution was at stake, and that he had the political room to act. Stalin could never admit that Trotsky and the Left opposition, in their critique of the NEP, had been, in his view, correct: it was beyond Stalin's character to be genuinely magnanimous, and it would have undermined his rationale for Trotsky's internal exile, provoking calls for his reinstatement. But those who believe Trotsky could have, and would have, done much the same thing as Stalin are mistaken. Trotsky was just not the leader people thought he was, or that Stalin turned out to be.

Without Lenin, Trotsky never again demonstrated the leadership that he had in

1917 and during the civil war under Lenin's authority. On the very uneven playing field of the personal dictatorship that Stalin inherited by dint of his appointment as general secretary and Lenin's stroke, Trotsky was still capable of brilliant polemics, but not of building an ever-wider faction, dividing his enemies, subsuming his convictions to necessary tactical considerations. More than that, Trotsky had never been an indefatigable, nitty-gritty administrator or a strategist capable of ruthlessly opportunistic improvisation. Whatever the overlap between his and Stalin's core beliefs, Stalin's abilities and resolve were an order of magnitude greater.

But what if Stalin had died?[31] He had come down with a serious case of appendicitis in 1921, requiring surgery. "It was difficult to guarantee the outcome," Dr. V. N. Rozanov recalled. "Lenin in the morning and in the evening called me in the hospital. He not only inquired about Stalin's health, but demanded the most thorough report."[32] Stalin had complained of pain, despite a local anesthetic, and Rozanov administered a heavy dose of chloroform, the kind of heavy dose he would administer to Frunze in 1925, who died not long after his own operation.[33] Stalin, who may have also suffered ulcers (possibly attributive to typhus), following his own operation had taken a rest cure—ordered by the politburo—at Nalchik in the North Caucasus from May through August 1921.[34] In December 1921, he was again incapacitated by illness.[35]

Later, Kremlin doctors recorded that Stalin had suffered malaria at some point in his youth. In 1909, in exile, he had a bout of typhus in the Vyatka hospital, a relapse because he had suffered it in childhood. Stalin's elder second brother Giorgy, whom he never knew, had died of typhus. In 1915, in Siberian exile, Stalin contracted rheumatism, which periodically flared, accompanied by quinsy and flu.[36] Stalin also suffered tuberculosis prior to the revolution. His first wife, Kato, died of tuberculosis or typhus. Yakov Sverdlov, with whom Stalin bunked in a single room in Siberian exile, had tuberculosis, and Stalin moved out. Sverdlov appears to have died of TB in 1919. Tuberculosis might have killed off Stalin as well.

Stalin could have been assassinated. The archives record oblique instances when potential assassins had been able to approach him or stage themselves at places he was likely to appear. At the theater one evening, for example, Dzierżyński noticed someone inside the entrance looking at the posted announcements; when Stalin exited, a different person was in the same place, doing the same thing. "If they are not *ours*," he instructed in a note written that same night, "then, for sure, it is necessary to pay attention. Clarify and report."[37]

Mussolini by this time had been the target of four assassination attempts, most recently when a teenager in Bologna shot at him but narrowly missed.[38] On July 6, 1928, during the Soviet party plenum, a bomb was hurled at the office for passes to the OGPU in Moscow. The perpetrators linked to émigré terrorists.[39] Nikolai Vlasik (b. 1896), the son of poor peasants in Belorussia, who worked in the department responsible for leadership security but was on holiday at the time, was summoned back to Moscow and included in a task force charged with reorganizing the security protection for the Cheka, the Kremlin, government dachas, and the movement of leaders between places. According to Vlasik, who would become Stalin's lifelong chief bodyguard, in 1928 the dictator had only his Lithuanian bodyguard Jūsis, who accompanied him on trips to his dachas at Zubalovo and Sochi and the walks to and from Old Square.[40] Stalin was within reach of a determined assassin, to say nothing of a regime insider.

Sokolnikov, in the meetings with Kamenev in summer 1928, citing Bukharin, relayed that Tomsky, while drunk, had come up and whispered into Stalin's ear, "Soon our workers will starting shooting you."[41] This story exists in other versions, often as an incident at Stalin's Sochi dacha where, on someone's birthday, a group was drinking, eating kebabs, and singing Russian folk and revolutionary songs.[42] Whatever the particulars, assassinating Stalin was not beyond contemplation in the politburo.

If Stalin had died, the likelihood of *forced* wholesale collectivization—the only kind—would have been near zero, and the likelihood that the Soviet regime would have been transformed into something else or fallen apart would have been high. "More than almost any other great man in history," wrote the historian E. H. Carr, "Stalin illustrates the thesis that circumstances make the man, not the man the circumstances."[43] Utterly, eternally wrong. Stalin made history, rearranging the entire socioeconomic landscape of one sixth of the earth. Right through mass rebellion, mass starvation, cannibalism, the destruction of the country's livestock, and unprecedented political destabilization, Stalin did not flinch. Feints in the form of tactical retreats notwithstanding, he would keep going even when told to his face by officials in the inner regime that a catastrophe was unfolding—full speed ahead to socialism. This required extraordinary maneuvering, browbeating, and violence on his part. It also required deep conviction that it had to be done. Stalin was uncommonly skillful in building an awesome personal dictatorship, but also a bungler, getting fascism wrong, stumbling in foreign policy. But he had will. He went to Siberia in January 1928 and did not look back. History, for better and for worse, is made by those who never give up.

# NOTES

Full citations can be found in the bibliography.

## PART I: DOUBLE-HEADED EAGLE

1. Kern, *Culture of Time and Space.*
2. Rieber, "Stalin: Man of the Borderlands."
3. "Polozhenie o voenno-polevykh sudakh"; Rawson, "The Death Penalty in Tsarist Russia."
4. Brewer, *Sinews of Power.*
5. Kotkin, "Modern Times."
6. Pflanze, *Bismarck,* I: 82. The famous remark "politics is the art of the possible," which Bismarck is supposed to have uttered to Meyer von Waldeck on August 11, 1867, does not have a direct source. (It is quoted in Amelung, *Bismarck-Worte,* and see also Keyes, *Quote Verifier.*) But the concept runs throughout Bismarck's recorded thoughts.
7. Pflanze, *Bismarck,* I: 242.
8. Pflanze, *Bismarck,* I: 81–5; Steinberg, *Bismarck,* 130–2.
9. Steinberg, *Bismarck,* 198.
10. Bismarck was preternaturally incapable of being content merely to bask in the glory, and his restlessness often got him into unnecessary trouble, as his ceaseless tactical twists and turns diminished his own room for maneuver. He created his greatest difficulties in a gratuitous struggle (*Kulturkampf*) against Germany's Catholics, a burdensome, dubious undertaking. Waller, *Bismarck at the Crossroads.*
11. Steinberg, *Bismarck,* 184, 241 (quoting *Kölnische Zeitung*).
12. Prince S. N. Trubetskoy, quoted in Riabushinskii, *Velikaia,* I: 96.
13. Tucker, *Stalin as Revolutionary.* For a critique, see Suny, "Beyond Psychohistory." The chief source for the blows that an inebriated Beso rained down on his son has been Iremashvili, *Stalin und die Tragödie.* Iremashvili, also from Gori, attended the Tiflis seminary with Stalin, became a Menshevik and, in October 1921, was deported to Germany along with three score others. His book provided the first memoir account of Stalin's childhood and psychologized the future dictator. Tucker's recourse to psychology in his first volume, partly to compensate for inaccessible source materials, was understandable. In Tucker's second

volume, Stalin is portrayed as a ruler with a paranoid personality who identifies with other paranoid rulers, particularly Ivan the Terrible, and who *chooses* from Russian political culture the elements of a paranoid style of rule. Tucker, *Stalin in Power.* Tucker did not complete the projected third and final volume before his death in 2010.
14. RGASPI, f. 558, op. 4, d. 665, l. 14; Stalin Museum, 1955, 146, 1–11 (Elisabedashvili); Dawrichewy, *Ah! ce qu'on,* 82–4. Stalin would return—to collectivize tens of millions of heads of livestock.
15. "In his old age he would send them and some school mates parcels of cash," one scholar noted of Stalin. Rayfield, *Stalin and His Hangmen,* 8.
16. In September 1931, when Stalin would learn that his former history teacher at the seminary, Nikolai Makhatadze, then seventy-three, was in the Metekhi prison in Tiflis, the dictator would instruct Beria to free him. RGASPI, f. 558, op. 11, d. 76, l. 113.
17. Trotsky, *Stalin,* 61–2. Isaac Deutscher, a biographer of Trotsky as well as of Stalin, followed Trotsky by placing Stalin on the "semi-nomad fringe of *déclassés*," that is, below a genuine *intelligent.* Deutscher, *Stalin,* 24–6.
18. Montefiore, *Young Stalin.* Montefiore's book reads like a novel.
19. Wheen, *Karl Marx.*
20. Montefiore, *Young Stalin,* 10.
21. Only Lavrenti Beria's later move to Moscow was utterly dependent on Stalin, but Beria, unlike Stalin, had forged a huge Caucasus machine, which, also unlike Stalin, he brought with him to Moscow and spread throughout the Soviet state.
22. Kun, *Unknown Portrait,* 74–5; Montefiore, *Young Stalin,* 3–16. Of the highway robbery question, Emil Ludwig had written in his 1931 interview with Stalin, "it was the only one he would not answer—except to the extent that he answered it by passing over it." "Iz besedy," *Bol'shevik,* 42–3.
23. Some of the most accomplished practitioners of the craft of biography

regard filling in the gaps as a necessity. See, for example, the meditations by Hermione Lee in *Virginia Woolf's Nose.*
24. The archive of Georgian Social Democracy has gone missing. Van Ree, "The Stalinist Self," 263, n18 (citing Stephen Jones, personal communication, August 2006).
25. Arsenidze, "Iz vospominaniia o Staline," 219. See also Boris Ivanov, a fellow exile in Siberia, in Tucker, *Stalin as Revolutionary,* 160–1.
26. Stalin filled in a questionnaire at the fourth conference of the Ukrainian Communist party in March 1920, in which he claimed eight arrests, seven cases of exile, and six escapes between 1902 and 1913. Later that same year, for a Swedish Social Democrat periodical, Stalin claimed seven arrests, six cases of exile, and five escapes. This became the source of confusion in his official biographies. Ostrovskii, *Kto stoial,* 7. This edition (2004) differs slightly from the earlier one (Olma, 2002).
27. The young Stalin's school years coincided with the rule of Alexander III (r. 1881–94), when all the empire's elementary schools were placed under the Holy Synod in order to magnify the Orthodox Church's influence in education (which was already high). *Istoricheskii ocherk razvitia tserkovnykh.*
28. Rayfield, "Stalin as Poet."
29. De Lon, "Stalin and Social Democracy," 169.
30. Service, *Stalin,* 27; King, *Ghost of Freedom,* 183–4.
31. Pokhlebkin, *Velikii psevdonim,* 76; Iremashvili, *Stalin und die Tragödie,* 18.
32. Ostrovskii, *Kto stoial;* RGASPI, f. 71, op. 10, d. 273 (Vladimir Kaminskii, "An Outline of the Years of Childhood and Youth of Stalin"); Rieber, "Stalin as Georgian: the Formative Years," 18–44; Jones, *Socialism.* A list of Stalin's pseudonyms and aliases can be found in Smith, *Young Stalin,* 453–4. A list of all "the girls"—ten, not including two wives, by 1918—can be found in Montefiore, *Young Stalin,* xxviii.

## CHAPTER 1: AN IMPERIAL SON

1. Ludwig asked the dictator whether he had become a professional revolutionary because of mistreatment as a child. Stalin could scarcely have allowed his commitment to revolution to have derived from childhood resentments, but his denial rings true all the same. "Iz besedy," *Bol'shevik,* 1932, no. 8, reprinted in *Sochineniia,* XIII: 104–23 (at 113).

2. Mitchell, *Maritime History*.

3. Lieven, *Empire*, 204.

4. Blum, *Lord and Peasant*; Raef, *Understanding Imperial Russia*; Hoch, *Serfdom and Social Control*.

5. de Madariaga, *Russia in the Age*; Klier, *Russia Gathers Her Jews*.

6. Bushkovitch, "Princes Cherkasskii."

7. Baddeley, *Russian Conquest*; Allen, "Caucasian Borderland," 230; Gammer, *Muslim Resistance*.

8. Some resettled in the North Caucasus lowlands rather than cross the border. Degoev, *Kavkaz i velikie*; Barrett, *Edge of Empire*; Breyfogle, *Heretics and Colonizer*; Jersild, *Orientalism and Empire*.

9. King, *Ghost of Freedom*, 140. The notorious imperial Russian Caucasus pro-consul, General Aleksei Ermolov (1771–1861), who complained that "the mountains are full of ungoverned people," went about in local costume and enveloped himself in Caucasus artifacts.

10. Avalon, *Prisoedinenie Gruzii k Rossii*; Gvosdev, *Imperial Policies*. See also Allen, *History of the Georgian People*; and Atkin, "Russian Expansion," 139–87.

11. "Georgians," one scholar has written, "had some reasons to be grateful for Russian rule." Rayfield, *Stalin and His Hangmen*, 3. By 1915, the local population had reached 11.5 million people, including both the South Caucasus (Transcaucasus) and North Caucasus.

12. Lang, *Last Years*; Jones, "Russian Imperial Administration." See also Suny, *Georgian Nation*, 70–3.

13. Zubov, *Kartina Kavkazskogo*, I: 151. One early foreign observer called Tiflis "a second St. Petersburg." Van Halen, *Memoirs*, II: 167.

14. For the ways in which Stalin was a man of the imperial borderlands, see Rieber, "Stalin: Man of the Borderlands."

15. *Kavkaz: spravochnaia kniga storozhila*, 60; Azhavakov, "Gorod Gori"; Sidorov, *Po Rossii*, 460–77; Gorkii, "Prazdnik shiitov"; Bukhnikashvili, *Gori*.

16. Mgaloblishvili, *Vospominaniia*, 11, 14.

17. Gogokhiia, "Na vsiu zhizn' zapomnilis' eti dni," 7.

18. An earthquake in February 1920 damaged the town. In the 400-plus-page Caucasus guidebook of 1927, Gori merited slightly more than a page, which singled out the town's ruins and renowned peaches, but made no mention of Stalin's birthplace. Batenina, *Kavkaz*, 395–6.

19. Kun, *Unknown Portrait*, 19, n30.

20. Kaminskii and Vereshchagin, "Detstvo," 24–5.

21. Montefiore, *Young Stalin*, 19 (citing GF IML, f. 8, op. 2, ch. 1, l. 143–6:

M. K. Abramidze-Tsikhitatrishvili). The official marriage date (as opposed to the betrothal) is sometimes given as May 1872, which Montefiore uses (citing GF IML, f. 8, op. 5, d. 213 [no page] and RGASPI, f. 558, op. 4, d. 1, l. 1). But if they were married in 1872, it is puzzling why he writes "just over nine months after the wedding, on 14 February 1875" (22). The official birth date of Stalin's mother in Soviet sources has also varied, sometimes set at 1860. She appears to have been at least two years older, and her obituaries claimed she was four years older (born 1856), evidently to make her appear older at the time of her wedding: sixteen (if 1872) or eighteen (if 1874). *Zaria vostoka*, June 8, 1937.

22. Kaminskii and Vereshchagin, "Detstvo," 24–5 (Elisabedashvili); Montefiore, *Young Stalin*, 21 (citing GF IML, f. 8, op. 2, d. 15, l. 2–15: Keke's unpublished "memoirs"). Keke's reminiscences were recorded by L. Kasradze, in August 1935, when she was nearing eighty. According to Montefiore, the "newly discovered memoirs" remained "untouched" for seventy years. Ostrovskii uses "a conversation" with Keke, which he dates May 1935, in his 2002 edition of *Kto stoial*.

23. On weddings in Gori: Suliashvili, *Uchenicheskie gody*, 24–8.

24. Montefiore, *Young Stalin*, 19–20 (citing GF IML, f. 8, op. 2, d. 15, l. 2–15: Keke's unpublished "memoirs").

25. Stalin later advanced his birth year from 1878 to 1879. RGASPI, f. 558, op. 4, d. 61, l. 1. As late as the end of 1920, he was still giving December 6, 1878, as his birth date, but in 1922, one of his assistants issued a "correction" to December 21, 1879, which became the official date. *Izvestiia TsK KPSS*, 1990, no. 11: 134 (Tovstukha). It remains unclear why Stalin chose a different day as well as a different year. For further discussion of Stalin's birth year, see Kun, *Unknown Portrait*, 8–10, 60; and Rieber, "Stalin, Man of the Borderlands," 1,659.

26. By some hearsay accounts, a girl was born in 1875 and lived a week, but no evidence supports this.

27. Kaminskii and Vereshchagin, "Detstvo," 27–8.

28. Zhukov, *Vospominaniia*, III: 215.

29. RGASPI, f. 558, op. 4, d. 665 (Abramidze-Tsikhitatrishvili).

30. Ostrovskii, *Kto stoial*, 93 (citing Dato Gasitashvili, GF IML, f. 8, op. 2, ch. 2, d. 8. l. 196, 200); Kaminskii and Vereshchagin, "Detstvo," 30 (Elisabedashvili). See also GF IML, f. 8, op. 2, ch. 1, d. 10, l. 23–47 (Goglichidze); and Iremashvili, *Stalin und die Tragödie*, 8–10.

31. Khutsishvili wrote to Stalin in 1939: RGASPI, f. 558, op. 11, d. 722, l. 51.

32. Lobanov, *Stalin v vospominaniakh*,

13–4 (D. Papiashvili); GF IML, f. 8, op. 2, ch. 1, d. 53 (Aleksandr Tsikhitatrishvili); Kaminskii and Vereshchagin, "Detstvo," 26; Ostrovskii, "Predki Stalin." "Besarion was a very odd person," another witness recalled. "He was of middling height, swarthy, with big black mustaches and long eyebrows, his expression was severe and he walked about looking gloomy." RGASPI, f. 8, op. 2, d. 1, l. 48 (N. Tlashadze). In the Stalin museum in Gori hangs a copy of the only known photograph of Beso, depicting him in advanced age, but it may or may not be him.

33. Montefiore, *Young Stalin*, 25–8. Although Montefiore closely tracks with Keke's account of Beso's dissolute behavior, citing her "memoirs" (the interviews), he nonetheless also supplies the evidence of Keke's "earthy mischief," which contradicts her one-sided account.

34. Dawrichewy, *Ah: ce qu'on*, 26–7. (Davrishevi was the son of the Gori policeman.)

35. According to the dubious Sergo Beria (Lavrenti's son), Keke supposedly once told Sergo's grandmother, "When I was young, I cleaned house for people and when I met a good-looking boy, I didn't waste the opportunity." Beria, *Beria My Father*, 21.

36. Dawrichewy, *Ah: ce qu'on*, 30–5.

37. Ostrovskii, *Kto stoial*, 88–9; Service, *Stalin*, 17. Stalin never became a hard drinker and, though he would prove promiscuous as a young adult, he developed a pronounced prudishness.

38. Ostrovskii, *Kto stoial*, 89 (citing "Detskie i shkol'nye gody Iosifa Vissarionovicha Dzhugashvili [Stalina]"; GF IML, f. 8, op. 6, d. 306, l. 13; Gori. d. 287/1, l. 2).

39. Suliashvili, *Uchenicheskie gody*, 9–16.

40. "Yakov was mischievous and restless as a boy," recalled Sverdlov's wife. "He organized games for all the children on the street." Sverdlova, *Iakov Mikhailovich Sverdlov* [1976], 60.

41. Ostrovskii, *Kto stoial*, 99 (citing GF IML, f. 8, op. 2, ch. 1, d. 10, l. 57); Kaminskii and Vereshchagin, "Detstvo," 37 (Goglichidze).

42. Kaminskii and Vereshchagin, "Detstvo," 37 (Elisabedashvili).

43. Ostrovskii, *Kto stoial*, 93–4 (citing GF IML, f. 8, op. 2, ch. 1, d. 10, l. 57; S. Goglichidze; "Detskie i shkol'nye gody Iosifa Vissarionovicha Dzhugashvili," GF IML, f. 8, op. 6, d. 306, l. 13).

44. Ostrovskii, *Kto stoial*, 101 (citing GF IML, f. 8, op. 2, ch. 1, d. 48, l. 14–5: E. K. Jughashvili, May 1935). Goglichidze's recollections have Soso returning to school within two weeks, which is obviously false—why would he have had to repeat the grade?

45. *Pravda*, October 27, 1935. The dates in the memoirs concerning when Beso removed Soso from school are in conflict. For example, Masho Abramidze, Stalin's wet nurse and neighbor, recalled that Beso threatened to remove Soso from school in the second grade, which would have been 1891-2, and that both her husband and Yakov Egnatashvili tried to talk Beso out of it. Kaminskii and Vereshchagin, "Detstvo," 43-5.

46. *Novoe obozrenie*, January 6, 1891; Khoshtaria-Brose, *Ocherki sotsial'no-ekonomicheskoi*, 46-7.

47. The Metekhi fortress dates from the fifth century, but it was wrecked many times, including by the Persian shah in the 1790s, after which the Russian empire rebuilt it as a prison in 1819. It remained a prison under the Soviets until 1934, when it became the Georgian SSR State Art Museum (and later a scientific institute). In 1959 the Metekhi fortress was torn down.

48. Makharadze and Khachapuridze, *Ocherki*, 143-4.

49. Choirmaster Goglichidze, who is cited often on the "kidnapping," and who later took credit for Soso's school career, made it seem that Beso just could not stomach Soso studying: "The thought that his son was going to school and not learning a trade did not give the father peace. And one fine day Vissarion arrived in Gori and gave Soso over to the Adelkhanov factory." Lobanov, *Stalin v vospominaniakh*, 20.

50. Trotsky, *Stalin*, 9.

51. Kaminskii and Vereshchagin, "Detstvo," 45 (Goglichidze).

52. Iremashvili, *Stalin und die Tragödie*, 5-6. Stalin's daughter from his second marriage, Svetlana, who as a child knew Keke but not Beso, later said that Stalin was "much more like her than like his father." Alliluyeva, *Twenty Letters*, 204.

53. Loginov, *Teni Stalina*, 56 (quoting Pavel Rusishvili. Rusishvili first met Stalin in the spring of 1938, at the Zareche dacha just outside Moscow, in the company of other Georgians, including Data Gasitashvili and the Agnatashvilis, as well as Beria. Stalin,

upon entering the villa, said in Georgian, "May God grant health to those of this house" (Loginov, 60-1). Gasitashvili, who waited a long time while in Moscow to be received by Stalin, lived in Gori in a single room with a metal bed (his sons occupied the rest of the modest living space).

54. Ostrovskii, *Kto stoial*, 94-5; RGASPI, f. 558, op. 4, d. 669 (Kapanadze); GF IML, f. 8, op. 2, ch. 1, d. 48, l. 14-5 (E. Jughashvili, May 1935).

55. Mgeladze, *Stalin*, 242 (citing Guram Ratishvili, a grandson of Yakov Egnatashvili).

56. Lang, *Modern History*, 114-5; Tucker, *Stalin as Revolutionary*, 80-81; Montefiore, *Young Stalin*, 63.

57. Iremashvili, *Stalin und die Tragödie*, 18. It is not clear when the young Stalin first read the novel. In 1893, the year before he entered the seminary in the Georgian capital, Qazbegi died penniless in a Georgian insane asylum, but Chavchavadze wrote a prominent obituary.

58. Iremashvili, *Stalin und die Tragödie*, 14; Alliluyeva, *Only One Year*, 360 ("The mother would beat the boy, and her husband would beat her"); and Alliluyeva, *Twenty Letters*, 153-4, 204.

59. Kaminskii and Vereshchagin, "Detstvo," 49-50; on Stalin's participation: RGASPI, f. 71, op. 10, d. 273, l. 86-8.

60. Dawrichewy, *Ah: ce qu'on*, 82; Iremashvili, *Stalin und die Tragödie*, 5; Kaminskii and Vereshchagin, 29-32, 48-50 (B. Ivanter, A. Khakonov). "Those Egnatashvilis were such famed wrestlers, they were known through the whole of Kartli," the future Stalin is said to have recalled. "But the first and strongest was Yakov." Montefiore, *Young Stalin*, 38-9 (citing Candide Charviani, "Memoirs" [unpublished manuscript], 3). On Gori street culture, see Suliashvili, *Uchenicheskie gody*, 41-6.

61. Smith, *Young Stalin*, 28-9 (citing an August 1909 Russian police report at the Hoover Institution Archives); Montefiore, *Young Stalin*, 57, 70. On the Armenian bazaar in Tiflis, near the Maidan, see Nadezhdin, *Kavkazskii krai*, 318-9.

62. Stalin continued: "I recall I was 10 and I was not happy that my father lost everything and I did not know that it would be recorded as a plus for me 40 years later. But this is a plus that I utterly did not earn." RGASPI, f. 558, op. 11, d. 1121, l. 49-50, reprinted in *Istochnik*, 2001, no. 2: 54-5.

63. Ostrovskii, *Kto stoial*, 96 (citing GF IML, f. 8, op. 2, ch. 1, d. 1, l. 228-9, 236-9: Pyotr Adamishvili).

64. Kaminskii and Vereshchagin, "Detstvo," 36 (Elisabedashvili), 41 (Goglichidze); "Neopublikovannye materialy iz biografii tov. Stalina," *Antireligioznik* (Khabelashvili). The young Stalin's language teacher was Vladimir Lavrov.

65. Kaminskii and Vereshchagin, "Detstvo," 41-2; Iremashvili, *Stalin und die Tragödie*, 7-8.

66. GF IML, f. 8, op. 2, ch. 1, d. 10, l. 23-47 (Goglichidze), d. 54, l. 202-15 (Kote Charkviani); Montefiore, *Young Stalin*, 43-4.

67. Kaminskii and Vereshchagin, "Detstvo," 34 (Elisabedashvili).

68. This appears not just in internal memoirs of the Stalin era, but also in the émigré Iremashvili's *Stalin und die Tragödie*, 8. See also Suliashvili, *Uchenicheskie gody*, 13.

69. Rank, *Trauma of Birth*; Horney, *Neurotic Personality*; Horney, *Neurosis and Human Growth*; Erikson, *Young Man Luther*; Tucker, "Mistaken Identity"; Tucker, "A Stalin Biography's Memoir," 63-81.

70. *Tovarishch Kirov*; Kostrikova and Kostrikova, *Eto bylo*; Sinel'nikov, *Kirov*.

71. Rayfield, *Stalin and His Hangmen*, 8.

72. Ostrovskii, *Kto stoial*, 109. Georgia had three seminaries; the third was in Kutaisi.

73. "Neopublikovannye materialy iz biografii tov. Stalina," *Antireligioznik* (Grigory Glurdzhidze).

74. Dawrichewy, *Ah: ce qu'on*, 47, 60. Davrishevi's police chief father sent him to the Classical Gymnasium no. 1 in Tiflis.

## CHAPTER 2: LADO'S DISCIPLE

1. Ostrovskii, *Kto stoial*, (2002), 197.

2. Cameron, *Personal Adventures*, I: 83. See also Wagner, *Travels in Persia*, II: 119.

3. Badriashvili, *Tiflis*; Chkhetia, *Tblisi*. The 1897 census recorded 159,590 people. Of that number there were 47,000 Armenians, but by 1910 Armenians grew to more than 120,000 of 303,000 total people, or more than 40 percent. *Pervaia vseobschaia perepis' naseleniia Rossiiskoi*

*imperii*, xi-xiv; *Kavkaz: Opisanie kraia*; Suny, "Tiflis," 249-82. The city became predominantly Georgian in 1970.

4. Tiflis had six newspapers in Armenian, five in Russian, and four in Georgian. Bagilev, *Putevoditel' po Tiflisu*. On the municipal franchise in the empire, see Seton-Watson, *Russian Empire*, 662-3.

5. Moskvich, *Putevoditel' po Kavkazu*, 246. The Narikala Citadel is said to

date originally from Persian rule in the fourth century, but the name is Turkic and from the Mongol period (thirteenth century); an earthquake leveled the fortress in 1827.

6. Baedeker, *Russia: A Handbook*, 465-71.

7. Anchabadze and Volkova, *Stary Tblisi*, 98-9. In Tiflis it was said that "a Greek will cheat three Jews, but an Armenian will cheat three Greeks."

8. Makharadze and Khachapuridze,

*Ocherki,* 66, 114-7; Khachapuridze, "Gruziia vo vtoroi," 46-66; Suny, *Georgian Nation,* 124-43.

9. Rieber, "Stalin as Georgian: The Formative Years."

10. Tucker, *Stalin as Revolutionary,* 89-90.

11. Iremashvili, *Stalin und die Tragödie,* 16-7. See also Gogokhiia, "Na vsiu zhizn' zapomnilis' eti dni," 14-5.

12. RGASPI, f. 558, op. 4, d. 21, d. 29, d. 665. This is well covered in Kun, *Unknown Portrait,* 26.

13. Kun, *Unknown Portrait,* 27 (citing RGASPI, f. 558, op. 1, d. 4327: petition dated June 3, 1898).

14. Parsons, "Emergence and Development," 268-9. Chavchavadze was murdered in 1907, a crime that remains unsolved.

15. Jones, *Socialism,* 52; "Gruzinskii ekzarkhat," IV: 197-209; Kirion, *Kratkii ocherk*; Agursky, "Stalin's Ecclesiastical Background," 4.

16. Manuil (Lemeshchevskii), *Die Russischen Orthodoxen Bischöfe,* II: 197-207 (at 203); Makharadze, *Ocherki revoliutsionnogo dvizheniia,* 57-8; Lang, *Modern History,* 109. Pelipe (Filipp) Makharadze, one of the leaders of a weeklong strike in 1890, was permitted to graduate. Jibladze was expelled. The student executioner was Ioseb Lagiashvili; the Rector was Pavel Chudetsky.

17. Quoted in Souvarine, *Stalin,* 14-5.

18. Zhordania, *Moia zhizn',* 11-15; Uratadze, *Vospominaniia,* 58-9.

19. "Iz zaiavleniiia," 174-5; Makharadze, *Ocherki revoliutsionnogo dvizheniia,* 57-8.

20. Ostrovskii, *Kto stoial,* 112 (citing GF IML, f. 8, op. 2, d. 52, l. 198-9: I. Tsintsadze).

21. Rayfield, "Stalin as Poet"; *Sochineniia,* XVII: 1-6.

22. Rayfield, *Literature of Georgia,* 3rd ed., 182-3.

23. RGASPI, f. 558, op. 1, d. 655 (Kapanadze).

24. Ostrovskii, *Kto stoial,* 125 (citing GF IML, f. 8, op. 2, ch. 1, d. 12, l. 176: Devdariani); RGASPI, f. 558, op. 4, d. 665, l. 128 (Parkadze); Iremashvili, *Stalin und die Tragödie,* 17. Iremashvili belonged to the Devdariani circle, too. Devdariani, who became a philosopher, was shot in 1937 by Beria's men. His manuscript, "A History of Georgian Thought," evidently vanished. Rayfield, *Stalin and His Hangmen,* 49.

25. Iremashvili, *Stalin und die Tragödie,* 16-7. See also Darlington, *Education in Russia,* 286-8.

26. De Lon, "Stalin and Social Democracy," 170. Sofrom Mgaloblishvili, who had graduated from the Tiflis seminary and returned to Gori in the 1870s, brought back a cache of Georgian-language books, which became a de

facto library. He and others established a Populist circle, which, inevitably, the police infiltrated; in 1878 they carried out arrests. (Just as important, the activists found the peasants unresponsive to the townfolk.) Mgaloblishvili, *Vospominanii,* 120. In Gori, a "military-conspiratorial organisation," with loose ties to the People's Will in St. Petersburg, was also closed down by the police. A less outré "circle of seminarists," inspired by Land and Liberty, endured into the 1890s. Its members included the sons of the town's nobles and one boy of peasant descent, Arsen Kalanadze, who ran the bookstall that welcomed schoolboys from the church school and seminarians. G. Glurdzhidze, "Pamiatnye gody," 18.

27. Kaminskii and Vereshchagin, "Detstvo," 71.

28. In fall 1898, Inspector Abashidze recorded the following: "Jughashvili, Iosif (V. I), during a search of the belongings of certain fifth-grade pupils, several times spoke up to the inspectors, giving voice in his remarks to the discontent over the searches . . ." Kaminskii and Vereshchagin, "Detstvo," 65, 84. See also "Neopublikovannye materialy iz biografii tov. Stalina," *Antireligioznik* (Razmadze).

29. "Iz besedy," reprinted (in further edited form) in *Sochineniia,* XIII: 104-23 (at 113). On the searches, see also Glurdzhidze, "Pamiatnye gody," 20; Kaminskii and Vereshchagin, "Detstvo," 66 (Vano Ketskhoveli).

30. Trotsky, *Stalin* [1946], 10.

31. Jones, *Socialism,* 51, 309, n11. See also Chelidze, *Iz revoliutsionnogo.*

32. Manchester, *Holy Fathers.* The sons of priests (*popovichi*) comprised 1 percent of the empire's population.

33. RGASPI, f. 71, op. 10, d. 273, l. 185; Rieber, "Stalin as Georgian," 34. Davitashvili emigrated to Leipzig.

34. In Gori, Tarasei Mgaloblishvili is said to have organized posses to defend the peasants. Mgaloblishvili, *Vospominaniia,* 35-6, 37-9.

35. Jones, *Socialism,* 22-6.

36. RGASPI, f. 71, op. 10, d. 273, l. 201-2 (Elisabedashvili). The young Stalin helped Elisabedashvili prepare for exams in the summer of 1898.

37. Stalin-era reminiscences reverse the roles: "Neopublikovannye materialy iz biografii tov. Stalina," *Antireligioznik* (Razmadze).

38. Ostrovskii, *Kto stoial,* 139 (citing GF IML, f. 8, op. 2, ch. 1, d. 12, l. 181: S. Devdariani); RGASPI, f. 558, op. 1, d. 665; Iremashvili, *Stalin und die Tragödie,* 21.

39. Iremashvili, *Stalin und die Tragödie,* 5-6.

40. Lado may have been introduced to the Third Group by Aleksandr Tsulukidze, who had joined in 1895. Beriia

and Broido, *Lado Ketskhoveli,* 9-10; Khachapuridze, "Gruziia vo vtoroi," 66; V. Ketskhoveli, "Druz'ia i soratniki tovarishcha Stalina," 75-86.

41. RGASPI, f. 71, op. 10, d. 272, l. 67.

42. *Katalog Tiflisskoi Deshevoi biblioteki,* 15, 17. See also RGASPI, f. 71, op. 10, d. 273, l. 179 (Ignatii Nonoshvili).

43. RGASPI, f. 71, op. 10, d. 273, l. 85 (Parkadze); Uratadze, *Vospominaniia,* 15. On how Lado led Stalin into a life in the underground, see Tucker, *Stalin as Revolutionary,* 89-90.

44. Riasanovsky, *Teaching of Charles Fourier.*

45. Marx and Engels, *Communist Manifesto,* 64-5, 67.

46. Malia, *Alexander Herzen.* See also Randolph, *House in the Garden.*

47. Peasants in Russia existed in three institutional forms: serfs living on privately owned gentry land (around 42 percent), state peasants residing on rented state-owned land (around 53 percent), and court peasants belonging directly to the imperial household with a status somewhere between serfs and state peasants (around 5 percent). Kabuzan, *Izmenenie v razmeshchenii.* See also Crisp, "State Peasants"; Deal, *Serf and Peasant Agriculture.*

48. The land rights awarded to the peasants came in the form of communal allotments, with the commune collectively answering for required redemption payments to the nobility, while rights to forests (fuel) and meadows (livestock grazing) remained under gentry control, a source of enduring anger among peasants. But how much the emancipation actually altered even arable landholding patterns over the long term remains a matter of dispute. Gershenkron, "Agrarian Policies"; Hoch, *Serfdom and Social Control*; Gatrell, *Government, Industry, and Rearmament*; Mironov, *Gosudari i gosudarevy liudi.* State peasant landholding reforms in 1865 allotted them the same land at lower price.

49. Wortman, *Crisis of Russian Populism.*

50. Baron, *Plekhanov*; Baron, "Between Marx and Lenin"; von Laue, "The Fate of Capitalism in Russia."

51. Marx and Engels, *Selected Correspondence* [1944], 354-5. See also Shanin, *Late Marx.*

52. "Tsensura."

53. Liadov, "Zarozhdenie legal'nogo," 107ff.

54. Zhordania, *Moia zhizn',* 8-9, 13, 25, 27.

55. Gorgiladze, "Rasprostranenie marksizma v Gruzii," V: 472.

56. Makharadze, *Ocherki revoliutsionnogo dvizheniia,* 53, 72-3; Ostrovskii,

*Kto stoial*, 141 (citing GARF, f. 124, op. 7, d. 144, l. 1–6).

57. Ostrovskii, *Kto stoial*, 130–1; *Sochineniia*, VIII: 173–4.

58. RGASPI, f. 71, op. 10, d. 273, l. 195–7. Stalin's future father-in-law properly dates his first encounter with workers to 1898. Sergei Alliluev, "Vstrechi s tovarishchem Stalinym," 154.

59. *Sochineniia*, VIII: 174; Rieber, "Stalin as Georgian," 35–9; Jones, *Socialism*, 71–5.

60. Jordania, "Staline, L'Écho de la lutte"; Vakar, "Stalin."

61. Struve would go on to co-found the Constitutional Democrat Party, or Kadets, in October 1905, when political parties became legal.

62. Struve, "Istoricheskii smysl russkoi revoliutsii i natsional'nye zadachi."

63. Of the nine attendees, one would die in 1911; five would leave Russia shortly after the 1917 revolution; one left in 1922; two (including Eidelman) would be executed in Stalin's purges. Medish, "First Party Congress."

64. A second "founding" congress, four years later, in Bialystok—Russian Poland—would fizzle.

65. Carr, *Bolshevik Revolution*, I: 6–7; *Vsesoiuznaia Kommunisticheskaia Partiia (b) v rezoliutsiiakh* (6th ed.), I: 7–10. After Lenin's term of Siberian exile had ended in January 1900, he and his young wife, Nadezhda Krupskaya—they had married in July 1898—relocated to Pskov, but within months they departed for foreign exile in Germany. Service, *Lenin*, I: 80–1; Carr, *Bolshevik Revolution*, III: 3.

66. RGASPI, f. 558, op. 4, d. 53, l. 2, 157 and others unnumbered; d. 60, l. 1–4; Kaminskii and Vereshchagin, "Detstvo," 84–5 (Talakvadze); Ostrovskii, *Kto stoial*, 140–1 (the expelled student was Vasily Kelbakiani).

67. GIAG, f. 440, op. 2, d. 64, l. 7ob; *Dukhovnyi vestnik gruzinskogo ekzarkhata* (June 15–July 1, 1899), no. 12–13: 8; Kaminskii and Vereshchagin, "Detstvo," 86.

68. Stalin entered this claim on a 1932 party questionnaire, and it entered the party canon. RGASPI, f. 558, op. 1, d. 4349, l. 1; Aleksandrov, *Iosif Vissarionovich Stalin*, 10; Yaroslavsky, *O Tovarishche Staline*, 14; *Istoricheskie mesta Tblisi*, 29; Tucker, *Stalin as Revolutionary*, 91. Stalin's mother later sought to take the blame, asserting that she removed him because he had contracted tuberculosis. In fact, Keke was angry at his expulsion. Smith, *Young Stalin*, 54 (citing an interview with Keke by H. R. Knickerbocker, *New York Evening Post*, December 1, 1930); GF IML, f. 8, op. 2, ch. 1, d. 32, l. 258–9 (Mariia Kublidze).

69. These statements were made in 1902 (in Batum prison), in 1910

(Baku), and in 1913. Ostrovskii, *Kto stoial*, 142–3 (citing GIAG, f. 153, op. 1, d. 3431, l. 275; RGASPI, f. 558, op. 4, d. 214, l. 9ob); Montefiore, *Young Stalin*, 73 (citing RGASPI, f. 558, op. 1, d. 635 and f. 71, op. 10, d. 275).

70. Kaminskii and Vereshchagin, "Detstvo," 84; Montefiore, *Young Stalin*, 70–3. Abashidze seems to have tried but failed to achieve Jughashvili's expulsion already in fall 1898. RGASPI, f. 558, op. 4, d. 665, l. 211–2 (Vaso Kakhanishvili); GF IML, f. 8, op. 2, ch. 1, d. 10., l. 141 (Gogokhiia); *Zaria vostoka*, August 12, 1936 (Gogokhiia); GF IML, f. 8, op. 2, ch. 1, d. 47, l. 126–7 (Talakvadze).

71. Abashidze, because of his pro-Russian extremism, had to be recalled from Georgia in 1905. He served in Ukraine (Podolia), Turkestan, and Crimea, where in 1914 he joined the navy as a chaplain for the Black Sea Fleet. In 1918 he refused to recognize the restoration of the Georgian Church's autocephaly. In the civil war he supported the Whites and Wrangel's army, emigrating in 1919. In the late 1920s he surfaced in Kiev, where he had graduated from the Theological Academy many years before (1896), and became a monk-hermit, changing his monastic name to Antoni. He somehow survived the purges in Ukraine that destroyed the clergy and then survived the Nazi occupation, dying a natural death in December 1943 soon after the Red Army retook Kiev. He was buried in the Kievan Caves Monastery with a marble gravestone. Manuil (Lemeshchevskii), *Die Russischen Orthodoxen Bischöfe*, III: 27–8; Agursky, "Stalin's Ecclesiastical Background," 10.

72. Agursky, "Stalin's Ecclesiastical Background," 6 (citing Anonymous, *Iz vospominanii russkogo uchitelia pravoslavnoi gruzinskoi dukhovnoi seminarii* [Moscow, 1907]); and Durnovo, *Sud'ba gruzinskoi tserkvi*.

73. Kun, *Unknown Portrait*, 30.

74. RGASPI, f. 71, op. 10, d. 73, l. 153–4; Kaminskii and Vereshchagin, "Detstvo," 62–6. By 1900, there were said to be just 50 Georgians out of 300 students, and by 1905 just four Georgians were graduated. The Kutaisi Seminary was shuttered in 1905.

75. In 1938, Pasha's husband's aunt wrote to Stalin about her niece; the letter reached Poskryobyshev on April 16, 1938, via the NKVD (V. Ivanov). The letter pointedly mentioned that Stalin's mother knew of the child's existence, and that the dark-eyed Pasha had become bereft after her husband, her own child, and her mother had died. Pasha evidently had tried to visit Stalin in March 1938, handing to his secretariat photographs and copies of her letters to him over the years. She

had been living in Saratov province, but vanished in Moscow—no doubt arrested. Ilizarov, *Tainaia zhizn'*, 284–7 (citing RGASPI, f. 558, op. 11, d. 775, l. 9–13). Stalin had the husband's aunt's letter preserved in his archive. "In his youth Comrade Soso felt some sympathy towards a certain person, but it did not last for too long," recalled an elliptical Grigory Elisabedashvili. RGASPI, f. 558, op. 1, d. 655.

76. Gogokhiia, "Na vsiu zhizn' zapomnilos' eti dni," 13; Montefiore, *Young Stalin*, 72–3.

77. One memoir claims Jughashvili was already absent from the seminary when it reopened after Easter recess, before the exam period even commenced, having gone home to Gori. RGASPI, f. 558, op. 4, d. 665. l. 381 (Talakvadze); GF, f. 8, op. 2, ch. 1, d. 47, l. 126–7.

78. Kun, *Unknown Portrait*, 32–3; Ostrovskii, *Kto stoial*, 146–7 (citing GIAG, f. 440, op. 2, d. 82, l. 59; RGASPI, f. 558, op. 4, d. 65, l. 3–3ob).

79. RGASPI, f. 558, op. 4, d. 65, l. 1–4; Vano Ketskhoveli, "Na zare sozdanii partii rabochego klassa," *Zaria vostoka*, July 17, 1939: 3.

80. Dawrichewy, *Ah: ce qu'on*, 67. Iremashvili claims he tried to talk Jughashvili out of leaving the seminary, because that would mean forgoing a chance at university, but that Jughashvili did not think the authorities would allow him to attend university and that in any case he was committed to revolution as a profession. Iremashvili, *Stalin und die Tragödie*, 23–4.

81. GF IML, f. 8, op. 2, ch. 1, d. 48, l. 164 (Elisabedashvili); d. 12, l. 28–9 (P. Davitashvili).

82. Montefiore, *Young Stalin*, 79; van Ree, "The Stalinist Self," 266, citing G. Elisabedashvili, I. V. Stalin State House Gori—Museum Fund, f. 3, op. 1, d. 1955/146, l. 1–11, 20–31 (in Georgian).

83. GF IML, f. 8, op. 5, d. 429, l. 170 (Vano Ketskhoveli); Vano Ketskhoveli, "Na zare sozdaniia partii rabochego klassa"; "K istorii fabrik i zavodov Tblisi"; Berdzenishvili, "Iz vospominanii"; RGASPI, f. 558, op. 4, d. 651, l. 50–3.

84. Jones, *Socialism*, 91.

85. V. Ketskhoveli, "Druz'ia i soratniki tovarishcha Stalina," 75–86; Jones, *Socialism*, 71–2.

86. Iremashvili, *Stalin und die Tragödie*, 22; Vakar, "Stalin"; Tucker, *Stalin as Revolutionary*, 87–8.

87. RGASPI, f. 71, op. 10, d. 273, l. 240; Vano Ketskhoveli, "Iz vospominanii o Lado Ketskhoveli," *Zaria vostoka*, August 17, 1939: 3; *Lado Ketsokhveli*, 76, 109–10.

88. "Neopublikovannye materialy iz biografii tov. Stalina," *Antireligioznik* (Kitiashvili).

89. Montefiore, *Young Stalin*, 70 (relying on Anna Geladze, Keke's cousin).

90. RGASPI, f. 558, op. 4, d. 72, l. 5; Ostrovskii, *Kto stoial*, 160; Rieber, "Stalin as Georgian," 39; Galoian, *Rabochee dvizhenie i natsional'nyi vopros v Zakavkaz'e*, 10-2.

91. Jones, *Socialism*, 70, 99.

92. Ostrovskii, *Kto stoial*, 161 (citing GF IML, f. 8, op. 2, ch. 1, d. 15, l. 245: N. L. Dombrovskii).

93. *Lado Ketskhoveli*, 24; Jones, *Socialism*, 100-1; Tutaev, *Alliluyev Memoirs*, 49-51.

94. Another key early figure was Viktor Kurnatovsky, then thirty-two years old, whom Stalin met in Tiflis in 1900. Kurnatovsky had met with Lenin. Medvedev, *Let History Judge*, 30.

95. In 1938, Beria attributed the article to Stalin and Ketskhoveli together. Stalin later assumed sole authorship of the essay, which was translated into Russian as "Rossiiskaia sotsial-demokraticheskaia partiia i ee blizhaishie zadachi." *Sochineniia*, I: 11-31 (at 27); Beriia and Broido, *Lado Ketskhoveli*, 17-33. Stalin also falsely claimed authorship of *Brdzola*'s first (unsigned) editorial. *Sochineniia*, I: 4-9; Deutscher, *Stalin*, 56-7; Jones, *Socialism*, 315.

96. "Podpol'naia tipografiia 'Iskra' v Baku (Materialy Vano Sturua)," 137-8; Yenukidze, *Nashi podpol'nye tipografii na Kavkaze*, 24; V. Ketskhoveli, "Druz'ia i soratnikitovarishcha Stalina," 75-86; Lelashvili, "Lado Ketskhoveli," 87-90; Jones, *Socialism*, 72-3. There have been intimations that the tsarist political police paid bonuses for the liquidation of revolutionary printing presses—leading to exaggerations of their number—but one of the political police chiefs claimed he liquidated ten of them and got nothing for it. Martynov, *Moia sluzhba*, 100, 313-4.

97. Makeev, "Bakinskaia podpol'naia tipografiia 'Nina' (1901-1905)," XVII: 90-109; Arenshtein, "Tipografiia Leninskoi 'Iskry' v Baku"; Nalbandian, "'Iskra' i tipografiia 'Nina' v Baku," XXIV: 3-30; Sarkisov, *Bakinskaia tipografiia leninskoi "Iskry."*

98. Faerman, "Transportirovka 'Iskry' iz-za granitsy i rasprostranenie ee v Rossii v 1901-1903 gg.," 54-92; Koroleva, "Deiatel'nost' V. I. Lenina po organizatsii dostavki 'Iskry' v Rossiiu (dekabr' 1900 g.-noiabr' 1903 g.)"; *Podpol'nye tipografii Leninskoi "Iskry" v Rossii*; V. Kozhevnikova "Gody staroi *Iskry.*"

99. Lih, *Lenin Rediscovered*; Carr, *Bolshevik Revolution*, I: 11-22; Ulam, *The Bolsheviks*, 160-216.

100. Arkomed, *Rabochee dvizhenie*, 81-4 (at 84); Talakavadze, *K istorii*, I: 62; Rieber, "Stalin as Georgian," 39; Talakavadze, *K istorii*, 62-3; Jones,

*Socialism*, 106; van Ree, "Stalinist Self," 267 (citing GARF, f. 102, op. 199, d. 175, l. 93). Arkomed (real name was S. A. Kardjian) evidently gave the speech in November 1901 that provoked Stalin's objections to admitting workers. The first edition of Arkomed's book appeared in 1910 in the emigration, but the 1923 version (which differs only in the addition of notes) was published in the Soviet Union and cleverly managed to criticize Stalin without naming him.

101. RGASPI, f. 70, op. 10, d.273, 292. A claim by Stalin's enemies that a party tribunal had expelled him from the Tiflis Committee for intrigues against Silva Jibladze finds no support in extant police surveillance records, which noted that Jughashvili failed to attend a Tiflis Committee meeting on November 25, 1901, but mentioned nothing of any expulsion. In fact, Jughashvili appears to have been co-opted into the Tiflis Committee in November 1901 (one of nine). Ostrovskii, *Kto stoial*, 169-73. On the supposed expulsion, see Vakar, "Stalin"; Jordania, "Staline, L'Écho de la lutte," 3-4; and Uratadze, *Vospominaniia*, 67. Silva Jibladze's grievances against Stalin were especially bitter. In 1921, after Bolshevik forces would reconquer the Caucasus, Jibladze would choose not to emigrate in order to organize a Menshevik underground. He died suddenly in February 1922, evidently of ill health; his comrades removed the body from a "conspiratorial apartment," but the Bolshevik secret police in Tiflis confiscated it. It is said that Beria was involved (Beria was then in the Georgian Cheka, becoming its head in November 1922). Jibladze's gravesite, if any, remains a mystery. Uratadze, *Vospominaniia*, 278.

102. Tolf, *The Russian Rockefellers*. Mantashov had been born in Tiflis and raised in Iranian Tabriz. Esadze, *Istoricheskaia zapiska ob upravlenii Kavkazom*; Mostashari, *On the Religious Frontier*.

103. Arsenidze, "Iz vospominaniia o Staline," 220-1.

104. Not long thereafter, around New Year's 1902, a fire broke out at the mechanized factory, which was followed by a small strike, then a big one. The rumor that the twenty-four-year-old Jughashvili instigated the fire at Rothschild's, and then used a workers' strike to extort funds for revolutionary coffers in exchange for damping down incidents of arson, is fanciful. In fact, the Rothschild workers had put out the blaze, yet only bosses were awarded extra compensation, provoking anger; also, the first big walkout took place at A. I. Mantashov, beginning on January 31, 1902, when a worker got docked pay allegedly for talking on the job

with coworkers. By February 18, 1902, with the workers' demands over work conditions and the punishment regime partly satisfied, Mantashov resumed operation.

105. The military boss of the Caucasus ordered an internal investigation into the workers' living conditions, producing the historical source material: Makharadze and Khachapuridze, *Ocherki*, 137-8 (archival report dated March 28, 1903).

106. A large party of protesting Mantashov workers were deported to their native villages, many in Guria (western Georgia), which magnified a developing peasant movement there from 1902 to 1906. Jones, *Socialism*, 102, 129-58.

107. After the strike began, the Kutaisi province military governor demanded the workers resume operations; they refused. Thirty-two were arrested, pending deportation. Other workers marched to the prison, singing revolutionary songs and demanding either their coworkers' release or the arrest of everyone. These workers were tricked into entering the barracks at the transit prison. Anger seethed, leading to the deadly confrontation. *Batumskaia demonstratsiia*, 9-11, 99-103 (Teofil Gogoberidze), 177-202, 203-41 (at 207); Arkomed, *Rabochee dvizhenie*, 110-8.

108. GARF, f. 102, op. 199, d. 175, l. 47-8.

109. At some point Jughashvili may have returned to Tiflis, to his friend Kamo's apartment, for help in setting up an illegal printing press. "Kamo was a specialist in such things," enthused Grigory Elisabedashvili. Ostrovskii, *Kto stoial*, 174-80; Zhvaniia, *Bol'shevistkaia pechat' Zakavkaz'ia nakanune*, 70; Chulok, *Ocherki istorii batumskoi kommunisticheskoi organizatsii*, 39-52. A railway conductor, Mshviobadze, supposedly smuggled Stalin from Batum to Tiflis, disguised in a conductor's uniform and hat, with a lantern. RGASPI, f. 558, op. 1, d. 655; Kun, *Unknown Portrait*, 4.

110. Van Ree, "The Stalinist Self," 270 (citing RGASPI, f. 124, op. 1, d. 1931, l. 11: Todriia recollections); *Batumskaia demonstratsiia*, 98-9 (Todriia).

111. Rayfield, *Stalin and His Hangmen*, 26; Kun, *Unknown Portrait*, 59; Alliluyeva, *Vospominaniia*, 37, 168.

112. Pokhlebkin, *Velikii psevdonim*, 47-50. Montefiore, employing memoirs, depicts Jughashvili as "the kingpin of Batumi Prison, dominating his friends, terrorizing the intellectuals, suborning the guards and befriending the criminals." Montefiore, *Young Stalin*, 103. Compare the émigré memoir of Uratadze: "When we were let outside for exercise and all of us made for this

or that corner of the prison yard, Stalin stayed by himself and walked backwards and forwards with his short paces, and if anyone tried to speak to him, he would open his mouth into that cold smile of his and perhaps say a few words." Uratadze, *Vospominaniia*, 65.

113. Ostrovskii, *Kto stoial*, 194; RGASPI, f. 558, op. 4, d. 619, l. 172, reprinted in *Sochineniia*, XVII: 7–8.

114. The doctor was Grigol Eliava. In early 1903, awaiting deportation into exile, then aged twenty-five, Jughashvili may have been conscripted into the tsarist army, but then excused owing to the intervention of an influential family friend. Dawrichewy, *Ah: ce qu'on*, 31.

115. Alliluev, *Proidennyi put'*, 109.

116. The atmosphere was further poisoned because his sudden return followed closely on the heels of mass arrests in Tiflis of Social Democrats. Ostrovskii, *Kto stoial*, 212–6; RGASPI, f. 558, op. 4, d. 537, l. 21 (M. Uspenskii); *Perepiska V. I. Lenina*, II: 114–5.

117. Makharadze and Khachapuridze, *Ocherki*, 71; Chulok, *Ocherki istorii batumskoi kommunisticheskoi organizatsii*, 70–2.

118. Ostrovskii, *Kto stoial*, 214 (citing GF IML, f. 8, op. 2, d. 4, l. 53: Makharadze, and ch. 1, d. 6, l. 231: Boguchava); Arsenidze, "Iz vospominanii o Staline," 218.

119. Ostrovskii, *Kto stoial*, 216 (citing GF IML, f. 8., op. 2, ch. 1, d. 43, l. 217: Sikharulidze); Montefiore, *Young Stalin*, 123 (citing GF IML f. 8, op. 2, ch. 1, d. 26, l. 22–6: Sikharulidze, and d. 26, l. 36–9: Sikharulidze).

120. Alliluev, *Proidennyi put'*, 108–9.

121. Machiavelli, *Gosudar'*.

122. Tun, *Istoriia revoliutsionnykh dvizhenii v Rossii*.

123. Makharadze, *K tridsatiletiiu sushchestvovaniia Tiflisskoi organizatsii*, 29.

124. Jones, *Socialism*, 183–4.

125. Davis, "Stalin, New Leader"; Davis, *Behind Soviet Power*, 14. For more on Davis, see chapter 13. In his Stalin biography, Robert Tucker rightly stressed Stalin's Marxist convictions, but abstracted, and dramatized, the conversion to Marxism: "the grand theme of class war . . . [its vision] of past and present society as a great battleground where-on two hostile forces—bourgeoisie and proletariat—are locked in mortal combat." In fact,

just living in imperial Russia, as Stalin himself explained, made many a young person into a Marxist. Tucker, *Stalin as Revolutionary*, 115–21.

126. The first two entries in Stalin's *Collected Works* date to 1901, in Brdzola, but both were unsigned. His first signed published essay, other than his romantic poems, dates to September 1, 1904. *Sochineniia*, I: 3–55.

127. Arsenidze, "Iz vospominaniia o Staline," 235–6.

128. On Lado as "senior comrade," see also Yenukidze, *Nashi podpol'nye tipografii na Kavkaze*, 5, 24; and Rieber, "Stalin as Georgian," 36–7.

129. Alliluev, "Moi vospominaniia," 173–5; Boltinov, "Iz zapisnoi knizhki arkhivista," 271–5; Ulam, *Stalin*, 38. Ketskhoveli's shooting warranted the appearance at the prison of the vice governor. A Cossack detachment evidently removed the body for immediate burial. Beriia and Broido, *Lado Ketskhoveli*, 201–18 (esp. 214).

130. Beriia and Broido, *Lado Ketskhoveli*, published in the Caucasus during Stalin's terror; Guliev, *Muzhestvennyi borets za kommunizm*.

131. RGAKFD, ed. khr. 15421 (1937).

## CHAPTER 3: TSARISM'S MOST DANGEROUS ENEMY

1. Ascher, "The Coming Storm," 150. The attaché, C. Kinsky, served under Ambassador Aloys Lexa von Aehrenthal (1854–1912).

2. Kabuzan, *Russkie v mire*.

3. Hughes, *Peter the Great*, 11.

4. Klyuchevsky, *Peter the Great*, 257, 262–5.

5. Cited in Bushkovitch, *Peter the Great*, 210; translation from the German slightly amended.

6. Peterson, *Peter the Great's Administrative and Judicial Reforms*; Anisimov, *Reforms of Peter the Great*; Zitser, *Transfigured Kingdom*.

7. The 1730 attempt by two noble clans to limit the tsar's power—setting conditions for accession to the throne—failed largely because of opposition from the other clans. Waters, *Autocracy and Aristocracy*.

8. Hellie, "Structure of Russian Imperial History." Under Stalin, this service obligation would be extended beyond state functionaries and military officers to factory managers, collective farm chairmen, scientists, writers, musicians, even ballet dancers.

9. Raeff, "Bureaucratic Phenomenon"; Raeff, "Russian Autocracy"; Cherniavsky, *Tsar and People*, 82–90; Taranovski, "The Politics of Counter-Reform," ch. 5; Lieven, *Aristocracy in Europe*. LeDonne argues that Russia did develop a self-conscious ruling

elite. LeDonne, *Absolutism and Ruling Class*. See also Torke, "Das Russische Beamtentum."

10. As cited in Yanov, *Origins of Autocracy*, vii.

11. Vasil'chikov, *Vospominaniia*, 142–4, esp. 227–8; Lieven, "Russian Senior Officialdom," 221.

12. Vitte, *Vospominaniia* [1960], III: 460.

13. Dickson, *Finance and Government*.

14. Robbins, "Choosing the Russian Governors," 542; Robbins, *Tsar's Viceroys*; Keep, "Light and Shade."

15. *Otchet po revizii Turkestankogo kraia*, 38, 47; Khalid, *Politics of Cultural Reform*, 60. Slavs were often sent to Turkestan as punishment and the region came closest of any to being an outright colony. The tsarist regime sought to make Tashkent city into a showcase of its rule, but in the late nineteenth century it was probably easier to go from London to India than from St. Petersburg to Turkestan.

16. Zaionchkovskii, *Pravitel'stvennyi apparat samoderzhavnoi Rossii v XIX v.*, 221–2; Troitskii, *Russkii absoliutizm i dvorianstvo v XVIII veke*, 212–6; Rogger, *Russia in the Age of Modernization*, 49–50; Figes, *A People's Tragedy*, 46. Doctors, university professors, engineers, and many other professionals were, technically, state officials, leading to imprecision in the figures

and comparisons. By another rendering, as of 1900 there were 524,000 people in the civil service. Freeze, "Reform and Counter-Reform," 170–99 (at 186). As of 1912, Russia was said to have one functionary for every 60 urban inhabitants, and one for every 707 rural inhabitants. Rubakin, *Rossiia v tsifrakh*, 64.

17. Hoetzsch, *Russland*, 270.

18. Häfner, *Gesellschaft als lokale Veranstaltung*. See also Starr, *Decentralization and Self-Government*.

19. Yevtuhov, *Portrait of a Russian Province*.

20. Polovtsov, *Dnevnik*, I: 477; Suvorin, *Dnevnik*, 25, 327; Lamzdorf, *Dnevnik*, 310. See also Rogger, *Russia in the Age of Modernization*, preface.

21. See the observations of Kokovtsov, quoted in Lieven, "Russian Senior Officialdom," 209 (citing TsGIAL, f. 1200, op. 16/2, d. 1 and 2, s. 749); Lieven, *Russia's Rulers*, 292. The nobility fought against the examinations introduced under Alexander I; they were abandoned in 1834.

22. Tatishchev, *Imperator Aleksandr Vtoroi*, I: 140.

23. Baumgart, *Crimean War*; Stephan, "Crimean."

24. Rieber, "Alexander II"; Rieber, *Politics of Autocracy*.

25. Miliukov, *Ocherki po istorii Russkoi kul'tury*, I: 145–9. On Russian

liberalism, see Leontovitsch, *Geschichte des Liberalismus*; Fischer, *Russian Liberalism*; Karpovich, "Two Types of Russian Liberalism," 129–43; Raeff, "Some Reflections"; Pipes, *Peter Struve*; Shelokhaev, *Russkii liberalizm*.
26. Valuev, *Dnevnik P. A. Valueva*, I: 181. One fear was that a parliament would be a springboard for Polish nobility.
27. Pravilova, *Zakonnost' i prava lichnosti*; Wortman, "Russian Monarchy and the Rule of Law." A state functionary (*chinovnik*) could only be indicted and placed on trial with the sanction of his superior. Korkunov, *Russkoe gosudarstvennoe pravo*, II: 552.
28. On the long-term consequences of the failure to introduce a constitution and legislature in the 1860s and again in the 1880s, see George F. Kennan, "The Breakdown of the Tsarist Autocracy," in Pipes, *Revolutionary Russia*, 1–15.
29. Makarov, *Sovet ministrov Rossiiskoi Imperii*, 41.
30. Dolbilov, "Rozhdenie imperatorskikh reshenii."
31. Chavchavadze, *The Grand Dukes*, 128.
32. Lauchlan, *Russian Hide-and-Seek*, 57–74. See also Laporte, *Histoire de l'Okhrana*; Monas, *The Third Section*, 40–1; Hingley, *The Russian Secret Police*; Zuckerman, *The Tsarist Secret Police*; Ruud and Stepanov, *Fontanka 16*; Peregudova, *Politicheskii sysk Rossii*; and Shchëgolëv, *Okhranniki i avantiuristy*.
33. Vasilyev, *Ochrana*, 41, 55, 57. There were seven black cabinets as of 1913. Kantor, "K istorii chernykh kabinetov," 93. The head of *okhranka* cryptology was later employed by the Soviet secret police. Hoare, *Fourth Seal*, 57. The Kiev *okhranka* operative Karl Zivert invented a device to remove letters without unsealing the wax, a technique that would be passed on to the KGB. Kahn, *Codebreakers*. In Tiflis, whose black cabinet was briefly closed in 1905, there were seven people on staff.
34. When Durnovó became interior minister in late 1905, he found a copy of an intercepted letter he had written instructing that his own mail should not be read. Lauchlan, *Russian Hide-and-Seek*, 122. See also Gurko, *Features and Figures*, 109. Mail perlustration was technically illegal under Russian law; the black cabinet staff used code to refer to themselves. But they were outed in 1908, by a former senior employee, M. E. Bakai.
35. Daly, *Autocracy Under Siege*, 105. Russia's most populous police, the gendarmes, numbered between 10,000 and 15,000.
36. Monas, "The Political Police," 164–90. Zubatov, chief of the Moscow

*okhranka*, introduced up-to-date record keeping, anthropometric archives, and provincial branches. He shot himself in 1917. Zhilinskii, *Organizatsiia i zhizn' okhrannago otdeleniia*, 120.
37. Lauchlan, *Russian Hide-and-Seek*, 167, n77.
38. Vasilyev tells the story of one Sletov, who arrived with a group in St. Petersburg to murder Nicholas II. One of Sletov's acquaintances was an *okhranka* informer. But although Sletov's designs were brought to the attention of the highest police authorities, they did not arrest him. The police reasoned that others of his conspiracy might be unknown to the *okhranka*. Instead, the police had someone warn Sletov that he had been found out, thereby hoping to facilitate and observe the flight of the entire band. The immediate danger to the emperor was averted, and though some of the escapees would in the future be able to attempt political assassinations, now at least the police would feel confident that they knew them all. Vasilyev, *Ochrana*, 71–2.
39. Vasilyev, *Ochrana*, 71–2; Lauchlan, *Russian Hide-and-Seek*, 221; Ruud and Stepanov, *Fontanka 16*, 125–51. Vasilyev explained that because recruited agents led a double life, at some point they would snap, so that "police officials were often murdered by agents in their service who had till then proved absolutely trustworthy" (*Ochrana*, 77–8).
40. Lauchlan, *Russian Hide-and-Seek*, 90–1. In 1905, a separate security agency (*okhrana*) was created for the court; the far larger *Okhrannoe otdelenie* (*okhranka*) was not called the *okhrana*. Stalin would meet not only with his police chiefs but even with assassins.
41. Pipes, *The Degaev Affair*. The first official congress of the united Socialist Revolutionary Party did not take place until December 1905 through January 1906, in Russian Finland. Sletov, *K istorii vozniknoveniia partii sotsialistov revoliutsionerov*, 76–8.
42. Levine, *Stalin's Great Secret*; Smith, *Young Stalin*; Brackman, *Secret File*. Despite strenuous efforts, neither Nikolai Yezhov nor Lavrenti Beria seem to have managed to find persuasive compromising documentation on Stalin's alleged *okhranka* work. Meanwhile, others, like Roman Malinowski, were outed for their *okhranka* ties while they were still alive. Montefiore, *Young Stalin*, xxiii.
43. Trotsky would be accused of having betrayed the St. Petersburg Soviet to the police in 1905, and to have been an *okhranka* agent since 1902. Shul'gin, *Chto nam v nikh ne nravitsia*, 281; Volkogonov, *Trotsky*, 40. Stalin did not use the material—reported by

Yezhov and Beria—in the indictment of Trotsky, perhaps because it was too evocative of the rumors about Stalin. Yakov Sverdlov, too, fell under suspicion. Lipatnikov, "Byl li agentom okhranki Sverdlov?" Later, Kamenev would also be accused of *okhranka* ties. Trotsky, *Stalin*, 221; Slusser, *Stalin in October*, 201–4.
44. Vasilyev, *Ochrana*, 96. See also Daly, *Autocracy Under Siege*, 117–23.
45. "The old regime," one scholar aptly summarized, "never came to terms with the needs of a modern industrial economy." Gatrell, *Government, Industry, and Rearmament*, 326. On tsarist economic performance, in comparative terms, see Gregory, *Russian National Income*.
46. Gann, "Western and Japanese Colonialism," at 502.
47. Kotkin, "Modern Times."
48. Fridenson, "The Coming of the Assembly Line to Europe," 159–75; Hounshell, *From the American System to Mass Production*.
49. Conant, *Wall Street and the Country*; Feis, *Europe: the World's Banker*.
50. Davis, *Late Victorian Holocausts*.
51. Cotton, *New India*, 83.
52. Headrick, *Tools of Empire*.
53. Russia's industrial output was a mere 10 percent of that of the United States. Gregory, *Before Command*, 17–22.
54. When William Fuller asks "how and why was the Russian regime so successful in translating its military resources into power in the eighteenth and early nineteenth centuries and so unsuccessful in the very same undertakings thereafter," he seeks an answer in Russian domestic considerations. But in effect, he could be referring to advances among the other great powers. Russia's success or unsuccess, in military terms, too, was always relative. Fuller, *Strategy and Power*, xiv.
55. Kingston-Mann, "Deconstructing the Romance of the Bourgeoisie." In 1893, under a pseudonym, Danielson published his own answer, a Russian interpretation of Marx: Nikolai-on, *Ocherki nashego poreformennogo obshchestvennogo khoziaistva*.
56. *Rossiia: Entsiklopedicheskii slovar'*, 192–209. In December 1903, Arthur Balfour, the British prime minister, noted the obvious, that "Russia's strong point is her vast population and the unassailable character of her territories. Her weak point is finance." Neilson, *Britain and the Last Tsar*, 242.
57. In 1888, annual imperial expenditures for Georgia were estimated at 45 million rubles, against revenues of only 18 million. Kondratenko, *Kratkii ocherk ekonomicheskogo polozheniia Kavkaza po noveishim ofitsial'nym i drugim otchetam*, 77.

58. Hickey, "Fee-Taking"; van de Ven, "Public Finance."

59. Crisp, *Studies in the Russian Economy*, 26–8; Babkov, "National Finances," 184; Dmitriev, *Kriticheskie issledovaniia o potreblenii alkogoliia v Rossii*, 157.

60. Fuller, *Strategy and Power*; Pogrebinskii, *Ocherki istorii finansov dorevoliutsionnoi Rossii*, 176. Military outlays swallowed 30 percent of Russian government spending as of 1913. This was down from 60 percent in the eighteenth century, when the state spent next to nothing on human capital (education, health, etc.). Gatrell, *Russia's First World War*, 8; Kahan, *The Plow*, 336.

61. Rieber, "Persistent Factors," 315–59; LeDonne, *Russian Empire and the World*.

62. Daly, *Autocracy Under Siege*, 108–10; Spiridovich, *Zapiski zhandarma*, 81–2.

63. Aleksander I. Spiridovich, "Pri tsarskom rezhime," Gessen, *Arkhiv russkoi revoliutsii*, XV: at 141. See also Pipes, *Russian Revolution*, 4.

64. Schneiderman, *Sergei Zubatov and Revolutionary Marxism*.

65. Gregory, "Grain Marketings and Peasant Consumption"; Goodwin and Grennes, "Tsarist Russia."

66. Sukennikov, *Krest'ianksaia revoliutsiia na iuge Rossii*.

67. Jones, *Socialism*, 129–58; Shanin, *Roots of Otherness*, II: 103–7.

68. Borzunov, "Istoriia sozdaniia transsibirskoi zhelezno-dorozhnoi magistrali."

69. Westwood, *History of Russian Railways*; Westwood, *Historical Atlas*.

70. Marks, *Road to Power*, 35–41.

71. *Sibir' i velikaia zhelznaia doroga*, 211; Putintsev, "Statisticheskii ocherk Tomskoi gubernii," 83–4. Siberia still accounted for 80 percent of Russian gold in the 1880s, though its share was declining.

72. Marks, *Road to Power*, 184, 217; McCullough, *Path Between the Seas*, 173, 610. Early Soviet planners saw the railroad as a precursor: Grinevetskii, *Poslevoennye perspektivy Russkoi promyshlennosti*, 62.

73. Kann, "Opyt zheleznodorozhnogo stroitel'stva v Amerike i proektirovanie Transsiba," 114–36.

74. Kaufman, "Cherty iz zhizni gr. S. Iu. Witte"; McDonald, *United Government*, 11–30.

75. Yaney, "Some Aspects of the Imperial Russian Government."

76. *Ministerstvo vnutrennykh del; Ministerstvo finansov, 1802–1902*.

77. A Ministry of State Domains (1837–94) became the Ministry of Agriculture and State Domains (1894–1905), and then the Chief Administration of Land Settlement and Agriculture (1905–1915). *Sel'sko-khoziaistvennoe*

*vedomstvo*. Formally, a standalone Ministry of Agriculture existed only during the war (1915–17).

78. Yaney, "Some Aspects of the Imperial Russian Government," 74.

79. Kuropatkin, *Russian Army*, I: 139–40.

80. von Korostowetz, *Graf Witte*, 20.

81. "Dokladnaia zapiska Witte Nikolaiu II"; von Laue, *Sergei Witte*, 1–4; von Laue, "Secret Memorandum."

82. Von Laue, "High Cost."

83. Wcislo, *Tales of Imperial Russia*, esp. 104–11.

84. Gurko, *Features and Figures*, 56–61; Wcislo, *Tales of Imperial Russia*, 144–53; Urusov, *Zapiski tri goda*, 588. See also Harcave, *Count Sergei Witte*.

85. Romanov, "Rezentsiia," 55.

86. Lieven, *Russia's Rulers*, 139 (citing *Novoe vremia*, September 9, 1915: 3).

87. Iswolsky, *Recollections of a Foreign Minister*, 121; Gurko, *Features and Figures*, 259.

88. Romanov, *Rossiia v Man'chzhurii*, 11, n2; Geyer, *Russian Imperialism*, 186–219.

89. Malozemoff, *Russian Far Eastern Policy*. See also Schimmelpenninck, *Toward the Rising Sun*.

90. Williamson, "Globalization," 20.

91. O'Rourke and Williamson, *Globalization and History*.

92. LaFeber, *The Clash*, 67; Aydin, *Politics of Anti-Westernism in Asia*, 81.

93. Gann, "Western and Japanese Colonialism," at 503.

94. Sergeev, *Russian Military Intelligence*, 31–52; Fuller, *Strategy and Power* 328–9. In 1899, one Russian official had lamented: "If Russian diplomatists had been more alert and enterprising, they might have secured a secret understanding with Japan at the time of the [Sino-Japanese] war in 1894–5 for the joint partition of the Far East." Quoted in Lensen, "Japan and Tsarist Russia," at 339, n9.

95. Westwood, *Russia Against Japan*, 22; White, *Diplomacy of the Russo-Japanese War*, 142–3; Nish, *Origins of the Russo-Japanese War*, 241–2.

96. Ferris, "Turning Japanese," II: at 129.

97. Ukhtomskii, *Puteshestvie na Vostok ego imperatorskogo vysohchestva gosudaria naslednika tsarevicha*; Shin, "The Otsu Incident."

98. McDonald, *United Government*, 31–75; Esthus, "Nicholas II"; Gurko, *Features and Figures*, 264; March, *Eastern Destiny*, 173–84.

99. Koda, "The Russo-Japanese War."

100. *Vpered!*, January 1, 1905; Pavlovich, "SSSR i vostok," 21–35.

101. Nicholas recorded in his diary: "Now finally the awful news about the destruction of almost the entire squadron in the two day battle has

been confirmed." *Dnevnik imperatora Nikolaia II* (1923), 201.

102. Lieven, *Empire*, 159.

103. Menning, *Bayonets Before Bullets*, 152–99; Nish, "Clash of Two Continental Empires," I: 70.

104. *Dnevnik Imperatora Nikolaia II* 1991, 315.

105. Trusova, *Nachalo pervoi russkoi revoliutsii*, 28–30; Field, "Petition Prepared for Presentation to Nicholas II."

106. Gapon, *Story of My Life*, 144, 180–8; Gurko, *Features and Figures*, 345; Galai, *Liberation Movement in Russia*, 239; Pankratova, *Revoliutsiia*, IV: 103, 811, n112; Zashikhin, "O chisle zhertv krovavogo voskresen'ia"; Ol'denburg, *Istoriia tsarstvovaniia Imperatora Nikolaia II*, I: 265–6.

107. Heenan, quoted in Askew, "An American View," 43.

108. Savich, *Novyi gosudarstvennyi stroi Rossii*, 11–14; Daly, *Autocracy Under Siege*, 168–9; Verner, *Crisis of Russian Autocracy*, 182–217.

109. Martynov, *Moia sluzhba*, 59.

110. Zhordania, *Moia zhizn'*, 44. Troops were summoned to restore order at least 2,699 times over the first ten months of 1905 (compared with 29 times in 1900).

111. Robbins, *The Tsar's Viceroys*, 230–2 (citing I. F. Koshko, *Vospominania gubernatora* [1905–1914 gg.]: Novgorod, Samara, Penza [Petrograd, 1916], 83–8). In July 1904, Caucasus governor-general Golitsyn had been wounded in a terrorist attack and departed. He was replaced by the energetic Count Illarion Vorontsov, a horse breeder and oil investor, who was close to the tsar and became viceroy (the post was reinstated). In 1905, Vorontsov requested permission to resign in 1905, but was compelled to stay on (until 1915).

112. Westwood, *Russia Against Japan*, 135, 153.

113. Tani Toshio's secret history of the war blamed Japanese intelligence, while Robert Valliant credits Russian efforts at self-defense. Valliant, "Japan and the Trans-Siberian Railroad," 299.

114. Fuller, *Strategy and Power*, 403–4; Steinberg, *All the Tsar's Men*, 121.

115. Geyer, *Russian Imperialism*, 234–6.

116. White, *Diplomacy of the Russo-Japanese War*, 227ff.

117. Aydin, *Politics of Anti-Westernism*, 71–92 (at 73: Alfred Zimmern of Oxford University). See also Barraclough, *Introduction to Contemporary History*.

118. Motojirō, *Rakka ryūsui*. The *okhranka* intercepted his mail and published a pamphlet, "The Seamy Side of Revolution: Japanese Funds and the Armed Uprising in Russia" (1906), documenting the colonel's activities. *Iznanka revoliutsii:*

*vooruzhennoe vozstanie v Rossii na iaponskie sredstva* (St. Petersburg: A. S. Suvorin, 1906), a 10-kopeck pamphlet. Akashi was recalled from Germany and named head of the military police of Japan's Korea colony, where he spearheaded the kind of repression for which he was noted.

119. Roy A. Medvedev, "New Pages from the Political Biography of Stalin," in Tucker, *Stalinism*, 199 (at 200–1). There are 16 vershki in an arshin, which equals 28 inches.

120. Von Laue, *Sergei Witte*, 40.

121. Cited in Makharadze and Khachapuridze, *Ocherki*, 135. See also Chakhvashvili, *Rabochee dvizhenie*, 63.

122. The "Red Hundreds" organizers in the Caucasus included Mikho Tsakakaya, Pilipe Makharadze, Mikho Bocharidze, Budu Mdivani, and the Menshevik Silva Jibladze, as well as Jughashvili. Talakavadze, *K istorii*, 143; Parkadze, "Boevye bol'shevistskie druzhiny v Chiature v 1905 gody," 46–50. See also Montefiore, *Young Stalin*, 112; and van Ree, "The Stalinist Self," 275–6.

123. "Predislovie k pervomu tomu," in *Sochineniia*, I: 10; XVII: 622–37 (Stalin's own account, in notes recorded by Vasily D. Mochalov, at a Kremlin meeting, December 28, 1945); Service, *Stalin*, 54–5 (citing the unpublished Georgian-language memoirs of Sergei Kavtaradze); Tucker, *Stalin as Revolutionary*, 140–1.

124. "Kak ponimaet sotsial demokratiia natsional'nyi vopros?" *Sochineniia*, I: 32–55 (from *Proletariatis Brdzola*, Sept.–Oct. 1904). See also Tucker, *Stalin as Revolutionary*, 140–1.

125. RGASPI, f. 71, op. 10, d. 183, l. 111, cited in van Ree, *Political Thought of Joseph Stalin*, 69.

126. Ramishvili would be assassinated in Paris by a Soviet agent. See Chavichvili, *Patrie, prisons, exil*. Chavichvili (1886–1975) was a Social Democrat journalist who emigrated and worked as a journalist in connection with the League of Nations.

127. Ostrovskii, *Kto Stoial*, 231–6 (citing GF IML, f. 8, op. 5, d. 320, l. 2–2ob); Trotsky, *Stalin*, 59; Tucker, *Stalin as Revolutionary*, 104. At the first conference of Transcaucasus Bolsheviks in Tiflis in late November 1904, Jughashvili was among the twelve delegates. They created a separate "Caucasus Bureau" (it is not clear if Jughashvili was initially included), and discussed the upcoming April 1905 Bolshevik conference in London, called by Trotsky "the Constituent Congress of Bolshevism." The four (Bolshevik) delegates in London from the Caucasus were Kamenev, Tskhakaya, Japaridze, and Nevsky. Jughashvili remained in Chiatura. RGASPI, f. 558, op. 4, d. 651,

l. 226–7 (M. Chodrishvili); *Perepiska V. I. Lenina*, III: 215–22; Taratuta, "Kanun revoliutsii 1905 g. na Kavkaze"; Moskalev, *Bol'shevistskie organizatsii Zakavkaz'ia Pervoi russkoi revoliutsii i v gody stolypinskoi reaktsii*, 72; Ostrovskii, *Kto stoial*, 223.

128. RGASPI, f. 558, op. 4, d. 649, l. 361 (S. Khanoian, *Zaria vostoka*, January 24, 1925); op. 1, d. 938, l. 5–8; Jones, *Socialism*, 122; Talakavadze, *K istorii*, 119–20; Bibineishvili, *Kamo*, 70; Chavichvili, *Patrie, prison, exil*, 68–9, 71–9, 88–9, 92, 113, 116–7; Ostrovskii, *Kto stoial*, 231–6; van Ree, 271; *Sochineniia*, I: 99–103.

129. Getzler, *Martov*, 219, quoting Martov, *Vpered' ili nazad?* (Geneva, 1904), 2.

130. *PSS*, VI: 126–7.

131. "He who has iron has bread," a quotation from Blanqui, appeared on the masthead of Mussolini's early socialist newspaper, *Il Popolo d'Italia*.

132. Lih, *Lenin Rediscovered*. Among Lih's many breakthroughs, he also showed that Lenin was ultimately not so far from Kautsky, who had written in 1899: "Social Democracy is the party of the militant proletariat; it seeks to enlighten it, educate it, to organize it, expand its political and economic power by every available means, to conquer every position that can possibly be conquered, and thus to provide it with the strength and maturity that will finally enable it to conquer political power and overthrow the rule of the bourgeoisie" (87–8).

133. Ulam, *The Bolsheviks*, 169–4.

134. Sapir, *Fedor Il'ich Dan*, 50–5. Fyodor Dan, who with Martov had helped Lenin against the Bund, had also been the one to smuggle into Russia the first copies of Lenin's *What Is to Be Done?* (1902), in the false bottom of a suitcase. Right through the 1940s, Dan, in emigration, saw Bolshevism and Menshevism as complementary, rather than as opposites. See Liebich, "Menshevik Origins." The police also went after the Bund, which between June 1903 and July 1904 had nearly 4,500 members arrested. Minczeles, *Histoire générale du Bund*, 119.

135. Iremashvili, *Stalin und die Tragödie*, 21–3; Arsenidze, "Iz vospominaniia o Staline," 235; and Tucker, *Stalin as Revolutionary*, 99, 133–7. "If there had been no Lenin," Stalin himself would muse in old age, "I'd have stayed a choirboy and seminarian." This was false, of course: Jughashvili had abandoned the choir and seminary long before he knew much, if anything, about Lenin. Mgeladze, *Stalin*, 82.

136. Himmer, "First Impressions Matter." At the November 26–30, 1905, conference of the Caucasus Union of the Russian Social Democratic Workers' Party in Tiflis, the attendees

discussed the need to unify Bolsheviks and Mensheviks, and elected three delegates to the upcoming 5th Party Congress: Jughashvili, Pyotor Montin, and Giorgi Teliya. RGASPI, f. 558, op. 4, d. 655, l. 185 (G. Parkadze). The Congress was supposed to have opened in St. Petersburg, but Interior Minister Durnovó's December 3 mass arrests of Petersburg Soviet members forced a relocation. Ostrovskii, *Kto stoial*, 242–5.

137. In August 1906, Lenin and Krupskaya would retreat to the safety of tsarist Finland, and then back into European exile in December 1907.

138. Stalin, "O Lenine," reprinted in *Sochineniia*, VI: 52–64 (at 54). See also Souvarine, *Stalin*, 82; Trotsky, *Stalin*, 69; Dawrichewy, *Ah: ce qu'on*, 160, 212–3.

139. Medvedev, *Let History Judge*, 97. The precise circumstances of the creation of the Soviet in 1905 are a matter of dispute. Voline, *Unknown Revolution*; Trotsky, *1905* [1922]; Trotsky, *1905* [1971]. See also Samoilov, *Pervyi sovet rabochikh deputatov*.

140. Quoted in Verner, *Crisis of Russian Autocracy*, 234; "Perepiska Nikolaia II i Marii Fedorovny."

141. Maksakov, "Iz arkhiva S. Iu. Vitte" and "Doklady S. Iu. Vitte Nikolaiu II," 107–43, 144–58; Gurko, *Features and Figures*, 396; Verner, *Crisis of Russian Autocracy*, 228–33; Witte, *Samoderzhavie i zemtsvo*, 211. Asked in 1908 about the political changes to the autocracy, Witte is said to have replied, "I have a constitution in my head . . . but as to my heart . . ." at which point he spat on the ground. Pares, *My Russian Memoirs*, 184.

142. Trepov, "Vespoddaneishaia zapiska D. F. Trepova."

143. Mehlinger and Thompson, *Count Witt*, 29–46.

144. Vitte, *Vospominaniia* [1923–24], III: 17, 41–2; Pilenko, *At the Court of the Last Tsar*, 97; "Zapiska A. F. Redigera o 1905 g.," *Krasnyi arkhiv*, 1931, no. 14: 8. The Grand Duke, originally a supporter of repression, had had a change of heart. "Zapiska Vuicha," in Vitte, *Vospominaniia* [1960], III: 22.

145. *Svod zakonov Rossiiskoi imperii*, I: 2; Savich, *Novyi gosudarstvennyi stroi Rossii*, 24–5; Ascher, *Revolution of 1905*, II: 63–71.

146. Borodin, *Gosudarstvennyi sovet Rossii*; Iurtaeva, *Gosudarstvennyi sovet v Rossii*; Korros, *A Reluctant Parliament*; Gurko, *Features and Figures*, 22–3. By the onset of Nicholas II's reign, the State Council had grown to around 100 appointed men (from 35), but fewer than 40 took any active part, and the tsar was under no obligation to consult them. In total, some 215 men would be appointed to the State Council over the full reign of Nicholas

II, more than two thirds of whom depended for their livelihoods on their salary, rather than inherited wealth—not really independent people.

147. McDonald, *United Government*, 83–6 (citing RGIA, f. 1544, op. 1, d. 5, l. 3–9 [Kryzhanovskii] and l. 270 [Witte]). See also Doctorow, "Introduction of Parliamentary Institutions." 148. Brunck, *Bismarck*, 36.

149. On the ministries, see Yaney, *Systematization*, 286–318. Whenever Government ministers spoke to sessions of the State Duma (or the upper house State Council), they opened with the phrase "With the consent of the Emperor," indicating that even the reporting of information was an imperial favor.

150. The drafter was Alexei Obolensky, a member of the State Council. *Iuridicheskii vestnik*, 11/3 (1915): 39 (A. S. Alekseev).

151. Verner, *Crisis of Russian Autocracy*, 434; McDonald, *United Government*, 10.

152. Maslov, *Agrarnyi vopros v Rossii*, II: 159–60; Perrie, "Russian Peasant Movement."

153. McDonald, "United Government," 190–211. Witte, without the

formal powers of a prime ministership, had managed to exert a kind of dominance via forceful personality in the loose Committee of Ministers (dissolved in April 1906).

154. Gerassimoff, *Der Kampf*, 67; Gerasimov, "Na lezvii s terroristami," II: 139–342 (at 183–4); Vitte, *Vospominaniia* [2000], II: 288, III: 74–5, 619. Witte recalls the diplomat as representing Spain.

155. Witte had evidently tried to make Durnovó the deputy interior minister, but Durnovó refused. Urusov, *Zapiski tri goda*, 589–92; Gurko, *Features and Figures*, 180, 406, 411–2; Vitte, *Vospominaniia* 2000, III: 71–2; Daly, *Autocracy Under Siege*, 173–4.

156. Martynov, *Moia sluzhba*, 59. Martynov oversaw the Moscow *okhranka* from 1912 to 1917.

157. Santoni, "P. N. Durnovo," 118–20; Ascher, *Revolution of 1905*, II: 22. Russia's Fundamental Laws of 1906 were modeled on the Prussian and Japanese constitutions, both of which abjured genuine parliamentary rule. Miliukov et al., *Histoire de Russie*, III: 1123–4; Doctorow, "Fundamental State Law."

158. Gerasimov, *Na lezvii*, 52; D. N. Liubimov, "Sobytiia i liudi (1902–1906

gg.))," RGALI, f. 1447, op. 1, d. 39, l. 464; Beletskii, "Grigorii Rasputin" no. 22: 242; Gurko, *Features and Figures*, 410. 159. "Nikolai II—imperatritse Marii Fedeorovne, 12 ianvaria 1906," 187. 160. Keep, *Rise of Social Democracy*, 251–2; Engelstein, *Moscow 1905*. 161. Pankratova, *Revoliutsiia*, V/ii: 76–7.

162. Shanin, *Roots of Otherness*, II: 278–9.

163. Shestakov, *Krest'ianskaia revoliutsiia*, 50.

164. Ascher, *Revolution of 1905*, II: 157–8. Peasants drafted into the army essentially re-entered serfdom: not only under the tyranny of officers, but also forced to farm and fabricate their own clothes and implements.

165. Fuller, *Strategy and Power*, 138–9. 166. Bushnell, *Mutiny amid Repression*. See also Fuller, *Civil-Military Conflict*, 144–55. In May to July 1906, mutinies resumed (again more than 200 total), and the old order seemed doomed, a second time.

167. Gurko, *Features and Figures*, 7. See also Daly, *Autocracy Under Siege*, 176; and Lieven, *Russia's Rulers*, 216.

168. Stepun, *Byvshee i nesbyvsheesia*, 304.

## CHAPTER 4: CONSTITUTIONAL AUTOCRACY

1. Loukianov, "Conservatives and 'Renewed Russia,'" 776 (citing A. I. Savenko to N. K. Savenko, April 28, 1914: GARF, f. 102, op. 265, d. 987, l. 608).

2. Vereshchak, "Stalin v tiur'me"; Tucker, *Stalin as Revolutionary*, 117. The circumstance that these recollections date from January 1928, rather than the 1930s, and that they appeared in an émigré publication, not in an official Soviet publication, adds credibility. 3. Borges, "The New Czar."

4. Gilliard, *Thirteen Years*.

5. Tagantsev, *Perezhitoe*, 35–6. See also Kokovtsov, *Out of My Past*, 129–31. 6. M. A. Taube, "Vospominaniia," 171, ms., Bakhmeteff Archive, Columbia University. On the institutional structure, see Szeftel, *Russian Constitution*; and McKean, *Russian Constitutional Monarchy*.

7. Maklakov, *Pervaia Gosudarstvennaia Duma*, 59–117; Emmons, *Formation of Political Parties*, 21–88.

8. Mehlinger and Thompson, *Count Witte*, 313–29.

9. It did not help that the physical giant Witte happened to be Alexander III's spitting image and that the latter's portrait—looking uncannily like Witte—hung in Nicholas II's study as an intimate, constant rebuke of the tsar's inadequacy relative to his father. Nicholas II would later ascribe a "truly Easter-like peace" in his heart at news

of Witte's death (among other factors). Witte would observe, "I was born a monarchist and I hope to die one, but I hope there will never again be such a tsar as Nicholas II." Anan'ich and Ganelin, "Opyt kritiki memuarov S. Iu. Vitte," 298–374 (at 299); Vitte, *Vospominaniia* [1960], III: 336. 10. Borodin, *Gosudarstvennyi sovet Rossii*, 49; Aldanov, "Durnovó," 39. 11. The intrigues associated with Stolypin's assumption of the premiership remain murky. *Russkie vedomosti*, July 1, 1906: 2 (Miliukov); Kokovtsov, *Out of My Past*, 146–56; Shipov, *Vospominaniia i dumy o perezhitom*, 445–8, 457; Miliukov, *Vtoraia Duma*, 226; Miliukov, *Vospominaniia* [2000] I: 380; Ascher, *P. A. Stolypin*, 110–14. 12. Various concerns failed to fix the deformity. Ascher, *P. A. Stolypin*, 15. 13. Ascher, *P. A. Stolypin*, 44–6, 88–90, 94–6; Fallows, "Governor Stolypin," 160–90; Waldron, *Between Two Revolutions*, 189, n30 (RGIA, f. 1276, op. 3, d. 959, l. 75).

14. Sidorovnin, *Stolypin, zhizn' i smert'*, 197; Daly, *Watchful State*, 34. 15. Kryzhanovskii, *Vospominaniia*, 209–21.

16. Robinson, *Rural Russia*, 130; Hindus, *Russian Peasant*, 91–2. 17. Mehlinger and Thompson, *Count Witte*, 288–41.

18. Shchëgolëv, *Padenie*, V: 406, 411, 415 (Kryzhanovsky); Lauchlan, *Russian*

*Hide-and-Seek*, 115–23; Ruud and Stepanov, *Fontanka 16*, 111–6. 19. Waldron, *Between Two Revolutions*, 106–14.

20. The tsar was obliged to summon the Duma for only two months every year. In addition, there is good indication that Prime Minister Goremykin, Witte's immediate replacement, and Nicholas II conspired to allow the Duma to remain in session only so long as to discredit itself in the eyes of the public. The Duma was dismissed—and so was Goremykin. Verner, *Crisis of Russian Autocracy*, 332–4. Even after the advent of the Duma, Nicholas II, speaking to the German ambassador, remarked of the autocracy, "there can be no other system with half developed nations: a crowd wants a firm and rough hand over it...I am the master here." Rogger, *Russia in the Age of Modernization*, 19 (citing Seraphim, *Russische Porträts*, I: 250). 21. Ascher, *P. A. Stolypin*, 205–7. According to the new electoral law, two thirds of the electors (in the electoral college) were from gentry and propertied merchants, leaving one third for peasants as well as urbanites and workers. Entire regions of the empire, such as Turkestan, received no representation. Harper, *New Electoral Law*; Doctorow, "The Russian Gentry." Nicholas II appears to have viewed the new electoral law of June 3,

1907, as the first step back to unbridled autocracy. Wortman, *Scenarios of Power*, II: 527.

22. Stockdale, "Politics, Morality and Violence."

23. "Memorandum by Professor Pares respecting his Conversations with M. Stolypin," in Lieven, *British Documents on Foreign Affairs*, VI: 180-4 (at 183). See also Waldron, *Between Two Revolutions*, 58-62.

24. Quoted in Klemm, *Was sagt Bismarck dazu?*, II: 126.

25. Steimetz, *Regulating the Social*; Beck, *Origins of the Authoritarian Welfare State*; Hennock, *Origin of the Welfare State*.

26. Kotsonis, *Making Peasants Backward*.

27. See the suggestive, idiosyncratic interpretation of George Yaney in *Systematization*.

28. Vitte, *Vospominaniia* [2000], I: 724 (letter to the tsar). See also Macey, *Government and Peasant*.

29. Gagliardo, *From Pariah to Patriot*, 238-42.

30. Karpov, *Krest'ianskoe dvizhenie*, 94-7; Frierson, *Aleksandr Nikolaevich Engelgardt's Letters*; Leroy-Beaulieu, *Empire of the Tsars*, II: 45-6; Kofod, *Russkoe zemleustroistvo*, 23.

31. Pallot, *Land Reform in Russia*, 31.

32. Thus, to speak of a general "high modernist" governance style is profoundly mistaken. Scott, *Seeing Like a State*.

33. Ascher, *P. A. Stolypin*, 11 (quoting S. E. Kryzhanovsky).

34. Yaney, "The Concept of the Stolypin Land Reform."

35. On the economic flexibility of the commune, widely noted by contemporaries, see Grant, "The Peasant Commune," esp. 334-6; Nafziger, "Communal Institutions"; and Gregory, *Before Command*, 48-50. About 80 percent of communes were "repartitional"; the rest, mostly in the Polish-Lithuanian borderlands, were hereditary, where usage rights were better and some transfer rights existed. There were no communes in the Baltic provinces or Siberia.

36. Atkinson, *End of the Russian Land Commune*, 71-100; Pallot, *Land Reform in Russia*; Dubrovskii, *Stolypinskaia zemel'naia reforma*. But also see Blobaum, "To Market! To Market!"

37. Davydov, *Vserossiiskii rynok v kontse XIX-nachale XX vv. i zheleznodorozhnaia statistika*. See also Tarasiuk, *Pozemel'naia sobstvennost' poreformennoi Rossii*. In addition, peasants had few horses: an estimate for 1912 indicates 36.5 percent of peasant households had no horses, 40.4 percent had one or two, and 1.9 percent had four or more. Jasny, *Socialized Agriculture*, 147-9.

38. Chernina et al., "Property Rights." Sometimes, conversely, the communes themselves suddenly eliminated their divisions into strips to consolidate contiguous farms. Yaney, *Urge to Mobilize*.

39. Dower and Markevich, "Do property rights in Russia matter?"

40. The November 1906 agrarian reform, supplemented by other measures, would formally pass in the Duma and State Council, and be approved by the tsar, in June 1910. *Polnoe sobranie zakonov Rossiiskoi imperii*, XXX/i, no. 33743: 746-53. The tsar approved a worker insurance bill only after Stolypin was dead.

41. The 1907 electoral shift away from nobles in the professions (Cadets) to landed nobles in the provincial *zemstvos* enabled the latter to fight against Stolypin's attempts to extend and open up local self-government. Wcislo, *Reforming Rural Russia*. See also Weissman, *Reform in Tsarist Russia*.

42. Diakin, "Stolypin i dvoriantsvo"; Waldron, *Between Two Revolutions*, 115-77, 182-3; Borodin, *Gusdarstvennyi sovet Rossii*.

43. Elwood, *Russian Social Democracy*.

44. Lane, *Roots of Russian Communism*, 11-155, 21-8; Zimmerman, *Politics of Nationality*. In November 1901, the Tiflis Committee had officially become the Georgian branch of the Russian Social Democratic Workers' Party, essentially uniting with the Russian party though never losing its self-standing quality. The Duma representatives of the Social Democrats were predominantly from the Caucasus—the orators Tsereteli, Zurabov, Makharadze, and Ramishvili. Jones, *Socialism*, 223; Kazemzadeh, *Struggle for Transcaucasia*, 187.

45. Emmons, *Formation of Political Parties*, 146-7.

46. Perrie, *Agrarian Policy*, 186. The SRs claimed to have 350,000 people "under constant party influence." Radkey, *Agrarian Foes*, 61-3.

47. Rawson, *Russian Rightists*, 59, 62; Spirin, *Krushenie pomeschchik'ikh i burzhuaznykh partii*, 167; Stepanov, *Chernaia sotnia*, 107-8.

48. Rogger, "Formation of the Russian Right: 1900-1906," 66-94.

49. Löwe, "Political Symbols." See also Bohon, "Reactionary Politics in Russia"; Brock, "Theory and Practice."

50. Brunn and Mamatey, *World in the Twentieth Century*, 891. The only contemporary equivalent was the late nineteenth-century/early twentieth-century right-wing street-and-ballot-box mobilization of workers and lower middle classes in Habsburg Vienna, the capital of another polyglot empire, also with a dynasty and large Jewish population. Schorske, *Fin-de-Siècle Vienna*, 116-80.

51. Liubosh, *Russkii fashist*.

52. After its publication in the St. Petersburg periodical, an expanded version of the protocols was issued in book form in 1905 by Sergei Nilus, who complained that no one paid them serious mind. Nilus stayed in Russia after the Bolshevik revolution and finally attained fame for being the publisher of the protocols. Despite multiple arrests, he was always released. He died in 1929. Cohn, *Warrant for Genocide*, 90-8.

53. De Michelis, *Non-Existent Manuscript*. This finding supersedes the earlier hypotheses that the scurrilous "document" was compiled from French anti-Semitic tracts spurred by the 1890s Dreyfus affair and the first international Zionist Congress (Basel, 1897) and midwifed by the *okhranka*. Rollin, *L'apocalypse de notre temps*.

54. Rawson, *Russian Rightists*, 75-106, 172-224.

55. In Kiev, a Polish-speaking and Jewish city surrounded by an Eastern Orthodox, Ukrainian-speaking hinterland, rightists had shown the way, employing street agitation and the ballot box to take hold of the Municipal Duma in 1906. Ukrainian-speaking peasants in the southwest overwhelmingly sent Russian (Eastern Orthodox) nationalists as their representatives to the State Duma. Hillis, "Between Empire and Nation"; Meir, *Kiev. On conservative efforts to organize in 1912-13, see Diakin, *Burzhuaziia*, 54-55, 169-70.

56. Kryzhanovskii, *Vospominaniia*, 153-4.

57. Lauchlan, *Russian Hide-and-Seek*, 278-80.

58. *Krasnyi arkhiv*, 1929, no. 32: 180.

59. Ascher, *P. A. Stolypin*, 121-7, 173-4; Ascher, "Prime Minister P. A. Stolypin"; Geifman, *Thou Shalt Kill*, 99-100.

60. Rogger, *Jewish Policies*, 232; Löwe, *Antisemitismus und reaktionäre Utopie*.

61. Rogger, "Russia," 443-500.

62. Kuzmin, *Pod gnetom svobod*, I: 170.

63. Loukianov, "Conservatives and 'Renewed Russia'"; Newstad, "Components of Pessimism."

64. Kokovtsov, *Out of My Past*, 164-5; Gurko, *Features and Figures*, 497-8; Ascher, *P. A. Stolypin*, 138-42; Lauchlan, "The Accidental Terrorist."

65. The last chief of the tsarist *okhranka* denied complicity in the pogroms while referring to Jewish profiteers "who could simply not be accustomed to earning its livelihood by any means other than business or trade." Vasilyev, *Ochrana*, 101.

66. Rawson, *Russian Rightists*.

67. There were 112 voting delegates—62 Menshevik-leaning, 42 Bolshevik-leaning, and the rest representatives of

the Bund and Social Democrats of Poland and Lithuania, Latvia, Ukraine, and Finland. Georgians comprised a quarter of all Menshevik delegates but were wary of what they saw as the fickleness of the Russian Mensheviks. Jones, *Socialism*, 213.

68. A leading scholar called Georgia "the most successful Social Democratic movement in the Russian empire before 1917." Jones, *Socialism*, xi. Jordania would claim that Social Democracy in the Caucasus, more than in any other part of the empire, was a multicultural movement, but this was not true. Zhordaniia, *Moia zhizn'*, 38–9.

69. This position was also advanced by the Bolshevik delegate S. A. Suvorin. *Chetvertyi (ob'edinitel'nyi) s'ezd RSDRP*, 339; Zhordaniia, *Moia zhizn'*, 34; Arsenidze, Nicolaevsky Collection, box 667, folders 4–5 (interviews with Arsenidze, July 1961); Jones, *Socialism*, 63–4, 69, 95–6, 124. Arsenidze was arrested the same month as the 4th Congress, April 1906.

70. Later, after Jughashvili became Stalin and dictator, his Russian-Bolshevik roommate at the Stockholm hotel, Klim Voroshilov, would recall not the substance of any policy proposals by the Georgian but his ability, in private, to declaim Pushkin as well as Shakespeare, Goethe, and Whitman in Russian translation. Voroshilov would also recall the future Stalin in Stockholm as "stocky, not tall, around my age, with a dark-complexioned face, on which there were scarcely noticeable pockmarks—the vestiges, perhaps, of childhood smallpox." Inevitably, Voroshilov also found the Stockholm Stalin to have "remarkably radiant eyes," and to be "completely suffused with energy, cheerful and full of life." Voroshilov, *Rasskazy o zhizni*, 247. Voroshilov first composed unpublished memoirs about these early events in the 1920s. RGASPI, f. 74, op. 2, d. 130; op. 1, d. 240. See also Trotskii, *Stalin*, I: 112. Stalin also stood out as not being from the noble caste of the west Georgia countryside, unlike Jordania, or Orjonikidze. Ostrovskii, *Kto stoial*, 568–72.

71. Smith, *Young Stalin*, 197; Geifman, *Thou Shalt Kill*, 222–5.

72. Weissman, "Regular Police." Imperial Russia had also introduced so-called land captains (*zemskie nachal'niki*) into villages in 1889; they, too, were roundly despised. Beer, *Kommentarii*.

73. Altogether, political terror claimed at least 17,000 people killed and wounded in the last decades of the tsarist regime. Geifman, *Thou Shalt Kill*, 21, 264, n. 57, 58, 59; Hoover Institution Archives, Boris I. Nicolaevsky Collection, box 205, folder "Lopukhin," protocol 37: 59–66.

74. Spiridovich, *Istoriia bol'shevizma v Rossii*, 120.

75. Geifman, *Thou Shalt Kill*, 249.

76. Lauchlan, *Russian Hide-and-Seek*, 245 (citing GARF, f. 102, op. 295, d. 127, and Hoover Institution Archives, Nicolaevsky Collection, box 205, folder "Lopukhin," protocol 37: 59–66). Fewer than 200 people had been executed for political crimes between 1825 and 1905. For peasant resettlers traveling eastward, the government provided special boxcars to transport accompanying livestock and farm equipment. (During the Soviet era, these "Stolypin wagons" would be outfitted with iron bars to carry prisoners.)

77. V. I. Lenin, "Stolypin i revoliutsiia," *Sotsial-Demokrat*, October 18, 1911, in *Sochineniia*, 2nd and 3rd eds., XVII: 217–25.

78. The *okhranka* foreign department in Paris had been established in 1884; a Berlin agency existed from 1900 to 1905. Lauchlan, *Russian Hide-and-Seek*, 103; Agafonov, *Zagranichnaia okhranka*; Patenaude, *Wealth of Ideas*. Russia had had a mere 3,900 internal exiles as of 1901. Back home, the police lists of persons under investigation, which in 1889 had had 221 names, by 1910 would number 13,000. Lauchlan, *Russian Hide-and-Seek*, 153 (citing Hoover Institution Archives, Okhrana Collection, box 157, folders 2–6).

79. "Sovremennyi moment i ob''edinitel'nyi s''zed rabochei partii," *Sochineniia*, I: 250–76, 410 n74 (at 250–1).

80. GF IML, f. 8, op. 2, ch. 1, d. 43, l. 154 (Aleksandra Svanidze-Monoselidze).

81. Back in September 1905, he hid with the Svanidze family in Tiflis, but he may have been hidden by them before. Kun, *Unknown Portrait*, 341 (citing RGASPI, f. 558, op. 4, d. 651: Elisabedashvili). Svanidze père made a living as a railway worker, but he was a landowner and Kato's mother (Sepora) was descended from Georgian nobility; they sent Alyosha abroad to study in Germany, indicating some means.

82. Ostrovskii, *Kto stoial*, 235–5 (citing Gori, d. 287/1, l. 8-9: M. M. Monoselidze); Dawrichewy, *Ah: ce qu'on*, 228; Tucker, *Stalin as Revolutionary*, 107; Alliluev, *Khronika odnoi sem'i*, 108.

83. According to Stalin's later teenage girlfriend in Vologda exile, Pelageya Onufireva, "He told me how much he had loved her and how hard it was for him to lose her. 'I was so overcome with grief,' he told me, 'that my comrades took my gun away from me.'" Kun, *Unknown Portrait*, 117 (citing RGASPI, f. 558, op. 4, d. 547). Also, Stalin is said to have told his daughter from his second marriage, Svetlana, of Kato, "She was very sweet and beautiful: she melted my heart." Montefiore,

*Young Stalin*, 159 (citing Svetlana interview tapes in the posession of Rosamund Richardson).

84. Ostrovskii, *Kto stoial*, 253 (citing Gori, d. 287/1, l. 14: M. Monoselidze, d. 39/2, l. 49–50: Berdzenoshvili, d. 146/op. 2, d. 39, l. 36–7); GF IML, f. 8, op. 5, d. 213, l. 43–4; RGASPI, f. 71, op. 1, d. 275, l. 31; GF IML, f. 8, op. 2, ch. 1, d. 43, l. 155: A. Svanidze-Monoselidze; Montefiore, *Young Stalin*, 160 (citing GF IML, f. 8, op. 2, ch. 1, d. 34, l. 317–54: Monoselidze).

85. Gegeshidze, *Georgii Teliia*, 34–9.

86. "Among the workers," Lenin wrote in 1899, "a striving for knowledge and for socialism is growing, real heroes are emerging who despite the disgraceful condition of their lives and their forced-labor-like factory regimes, find within themselves such character and strength of will to study, study, and study, making of themselves conscious social democrats, 'a worker intelligentsia.'" Lenin, *Sochineniia*, 2nd and 3rd eds., IV: 258.

87. "Pamiati tov. G. Teliia," *Sochineniia*, II: 27–31 (Dro, March 22, 1907). Mikho Tskhakaya delivered a graveside speech, too, not long before he was forced into emigration and left for Geneva. Gegeshidze, *Georgii Teliia*, 41–2.

88. We shall never know how much of Teliya's work Stalin borrowed, or how much he may have sharpened it. "They were written in parts, right there, at the printing press, hastily, on her knees, given over to the printer," Stalin would later claim. Ilizarov, *Tainaia zhizn'*, 240–1. The first four appeared in *Akhali Tskhovreba* (*New Life*) in June and July 1906. That newspaper was closed, and the four articles were republished, in "generally accessible language" at the request of the editors, in *Akhali Droeba* (*New Times*) in December 1906 and January 1907. Four more articles appeared in February 1907 in *Chveni Tskhovreba* (*Our Life*), which was also soon closed, and another four in *Dro* (*Time*) in April 1907. *Sochineniia*, I: 294–372; the original versions of the first four, are given in an appendix (373–92). Stalin also "corrected" the articles before including them in his *Collected Works*, claiming they were not polished. See Vasily Mochalov notes, December 28, 1945, *Sochineniia*, XVII: 625–6. Mochalov was the chief of the Stalin Desk in the IMEL, and clashed with the IMEL director V. S. Kruzhkov. The Georgian affiliate of IMEL was also involved in finding the originals and in the translations into Russian. The galleys of the first volume of his *Collected Works*, with Stalin's colored pencil markings on "Anarchism and Socialism?," was discovered at the

Kunstevo dacha after his death. Stalin had removed two prefaces, that of the *Collected Works* editor as well as his own. Ilizarov, *Tainaia zhizn'*, 228 (citing RGASPI, f. 558, op. 11, d. 911, l. 15; d. 910, l. 5ob).

89. Also around this time, Plekhanov's 1894 sarcastic brochure *Anarchism and Socialism* appeared in a second, enlarged edition. Plekhanov's pamphlet was originally written in French, and translated into German, English, and Russian (2nd ed. Moscow: V. O. Karchagin, 1906). Jughashvili's essays did not invoke Plekhanov. Privately, in an ingratiating letter abroad to Lenin, after Plekhanov criticized *What Is to Be Done?*, Jughashvili wrote: "Either the man has gone off his nut or is showing hate and hostility." *Sochineniia*, I: 56-7. Stalin had Plekhanov's *K voprosu o razvitii monisticheskogo vzgliada na istoriiu* republished in 1938; a copy with the dictator's markings has been preserved.

90. *Sochineniia*, I: 297 [modified], 375 [original].

91. *Sochineniia*, I: 314-6.

92. *Sochineniia*, I: 331, 344-5, 348, 368.

93. Souvarine, *Stalin*, 109. Trotsky claimed he learned of Stalin's presence in London in 1935 only from Souvarine's biography (French ed.). Trotsky, *Stalin*, 90.

94. Zhordania, *Moia zhizn'*, 53; Service, *Stalin*, 66.

95. On French initiative, between 1865 and 1871, plans were discussed for a single European central bank and a single currency, called "the Europe," but the British and Germans resisted. Instead, in the 1870s the Germans joined the British on the gold standard, which others joined (Japan in 1897), assuring convertibility and stable exchange rates. Einaudi, *Money and Politics*.

96. Jablonowski, "Die Stellungnahme der russischen Parteien," 5: 60-93.

97. From the British side, reconciliation with Russia was facilitated by a displacement of the "Victorians" (those born in the 1830s-40s), vexed over Russian penetration of Central Asia, in favor of the "Edwardians" (those born in the 1850s-60s), who came of age in the aftermath of Bismarck's unification and Wilhelmine Germany's rise. Neilson, *Britain and the Last Tsar*, 48-50, 267-88.

98. McDonald, *United Government*, 103-11.

99. Some issues that could not be settled, such as Tibet, were tabled. Churchill, *Anglo-Russian Convention*; Williams, "Great Britain and Russia," 133-47; Ostal'tseva, *Anglo-russkoe soglashenie 1907 goda*.

100. Bernstein, *Willy-Nicky Correspondence*, 107-8.

101. McDonald, *United Government*, 77-81. *Izvestiia* (December 29, 1917)

later published the dead-letter treaty. See also Nekliudov, "Souvenirs diplomatiques"; Bompard, "Le traité de Bjoerkoe"; Fay, "The Kaiser's Secret Negotiations"; Feigina, *B'orkskoe soglashenie*; Vitte, *Vospominaniia* [1922], II: 476-81; Iswolsky, *Recollections of a Foreign Minister*, 40-3; and Astaf'ev, *Russko-germanskie diplomaticheskie otnosheniia*.

102. Bogdanovich, *Tri poslednikh samoderzhavtsa* [1924], 461.

103. Pashukanis, "K istorii anglo-russkogo soglasheniia," 32; de Taube, *La politique russe*, 118. Perhaps the only other prominent rightist who fully shared Stolypin's foreign policy circumspection was his high-profile conservative critic on domestic issues, Durnovó. But the latter did not fully appreciate that Stolypin—who was not even responsible for foreign or military affairs (prerogatives of the tsar)—had skillfully kept Russia out of repeating a foreign misadventure in 1908. McDonald, *United Government*, 151.

104. Nash, *The Anglo-Japanese Alliance*; O'Brien, *The Anglo-Japanese Alliance*; Daniels et al., "Studies in the Anglo-Japanese Alliance."

105. Coox, *Nomonhan*, 1-16.

106. "Londonskii s"ezd Rossiiskoi sotsial-demokraticheskoi rabochei partii (Zapiski delegata)," in *Sochineniia*, II: 46-77 (at 50-1), from *Bakinskii proletarii*, June 20 and July 10, 1907.

107. Getzler, *Martov*, 124.

108. For Jughashvili, this was neither his first such exercise nor his last, according to Soso Dawrichewy, the former Tiflis seminarian and priest's son from Gori (whom the *okhrana* long confused with Kamo). Dawrichewy, *Ah: ce qu'on*, 174-5, 177, 181, 213, 237-8.

109. Gerasimov, *Na lezvii s terroristami*, 92.

110. The Caucasus military governor also reported that locally, in 1905 and 1906, banditry and assassinations claimed 1,239 lives and an equal number of seriously wounded. Geifman, *Revoliutsionnyi terror*, 21, 34-5, 228.

111. Miklós Kun unearthed the internal party disciplinary file on Litvinov, which proved Stalin's involvement. Kun, *Unknown Portrait*, 74-80. See also Montefiore, *Young Stalin*, 3-16 (citing, among many sources, the unpublished memoirs of Sashiko Svanidze, Stalin's sister-in-law), 178-91. The surviving *okhranka* files on the Yerevan holdup have been purged. Bordiugov, *Neizvestnyi Bogdanov*, II: 120-42. Kamo had obtained mail coach insider information from another postal clerk, Gigo Kasradze.

112. GF IML, f. 8, op. 2, ch. 1, d. 7, l. 64-84 (G. F. Vardoyan); *Perspektivy*, 1991, no. 6: 51-7; Geifman, *Revoliutsionnyi terror*, 163-4; Ostrovskii, *Kto stoial*, 257; Avtorkhanov, *Proiskhozhdenie*, I:

183-6; RGASPI, f. 332, op. 1, d. 53. Kamo had three years of schooling. His adoration of Stalin is related in the subsequent recollections of Kamo's younger sister, Javariya Khutulushvili: Kun, *Unknown Portrait*, 75; *Perspektivy*, 1991, no. 6: 51-7; Ostrovskii, *Kto stoial*, 257; Avtorkhanov, *Proiskhozhdenie*, I: 183-6; RGASPI, f. 332, op. 1, d. 53. See also Uratadze, *Vospominaniia*, 130-2, 163-7; Smith, *Young Stalin*, 193-211; van Ree, "The Stalinist Self," 275-6; van Ree, "Reluctant Terrorists?"; and Montefiore, *Young Stalin*, 7 (citing Candide Charkviani, "Memoirs," manuscript, 15).

113. As the folklore has it, for a moment, amid the bodies and chaos, the robbery seemed to have gone awry—until Kamo, dressed as an army officer, rode his own phaeton through the smoke, scooped up most of the sacks of banknotes, then misdirected an arriving policeman. Medvedeva Ter-Petrosyan, "Tovarishch Kamo," 130. Twenty thousand rubles had been left behind in the stagecoach; one of its drivers tried to pocket another 9,500 rubles but was caught.

114. Wolfe, *Three Who Made a Revolution*, 393-4; Geifman, *Revoliutsionnyi terror*, 164; Krupskaya, *Reminiscences of Lenin*, 155.

115. Trotsky, *Stalin*, 109.

116. Martov, *Spasiteli ili uprazdniteli?*, 22-3.

117. Bibineishvili, *Kamo*, 30-1, 371. The daring Kamo would end up in and out of psychiatric prisons; in 1922, he would be run over by a Soviet official's car while riding a bicycle in Tiflis. He had a damaged left eye (from one of his own bombs in May 1907), and this may have contributed to his accident.

118. Jughashvili may have gone abroad to see Lenin in August 1907 (Stuttgart) and January 1908 (Switzerland).

119. Reiss, *The Orientalist*, 11-3; Hone and Dickinson, *Persia in Revolution*, 158-68.

120. Ordzhonikidze, "Bor'ba s men'shevikami," 42. Many of the Muslim workers were seasonal Azeri migrants, both legal and illegal, from the northern provinces of Iran. Alstadt, "Muslim Workers," 83-91; and Chaqueri, *Soviet Socialist Republic of Iran*, 24-25, who estimates that from 20 to 50 percent of males in northern Iran between the ages of twenty and forty ended up working for some period of time across the border, mainly in the Russian Caucasus.

121. Vereshchak, "Stalin v tiur'me," 1306; Vereshchak, "Okonchanie," 1308.

122. The tsarist regime had turned the Dashnaks against Russian power, too, partly by confiscating Armenian Church properties in 1903 (which Nicholas II had to rescind in 1905).

Suny, *Transcaucasia*, 166-7; Suny, *Looking Toward Ararat*, 48-9, 92.

123. "Otvet na privetstviia rabochikh glavnykh zheleznodorozhnykh masterskikh v Tiflise," in *Sochineniia*, VIII: 174-5. Suny, "Journeyman for the Revolution."

124. Trotskii, *Stalin* [1985], I: 158, 163.

125. Montefiore, *Young Stalin*, 190-3 (citing Svanidze family memoirs and an inerview with a Svanidze cousin).

126. Dawrichewy, *Ah: ce qu'on*, 35; GDMS, f. 87, d. 1955-46, l. 51-6 (Elisabedashvili). The main source on the marriage has long been the émigré Menshevik Iremashvili, who claimed to have attended Kato's funeral, and who pinpointed her death as the break that left Stalin "bereft of any moral restraint." Joseph Iremashvili, *Stalin und die Tragödie*, 30-40.

127. RGASPI, f. 558, op. 4, d. 655, l. 18.

128. Arsenidze, "Iz vospominaniia o Staline," 224; Deutscher, *Stalin*, 110.

129. RGASPI, f. 558, op. 4, d. 647 (Sukhova).

130. Dubinskii-Mukhadaze, *Ordzhonikidze*, 92.

131. RGASPI, f. 71, op. 1, d, 275, l. 23; Smith, *Young Stalin*, 28-9; McNeal, *Stalin*, 336, n15; Kun, *Unknown Portrait*, 18. Svetlana said that he died from a stabbing in a barroom brawl, but without any evidence to that effect. Alliluyeva, *Twenty Letters*, 153n. In 1939, Stalin ordered the Tiflis party organization not to collect historical information about Beso.

132. Among Social Democrats—his supposed comrades—Stalin was dismissed as "Lenin's left foot." Arsenidze, "Iz vospominaniia o Staline," 223.

133. On the frailty of the revolutionary parties, despite working-class radicalism, see McKean, *St. Petersburg*.

134. Daly, *Autocracy Under Siege*, 117-23.

135. Azef had become chief of the Socialist Revolutionary Combat Organization. By some accounts, while in the pay of the *okhranka*, he oversaw twenty-eight successful terrorist attacks on government officials; the *okhranka* never divined his motives and loyalties. In 1909, he fled to Germany, leaving the SR party in disarray and feeling defeated. "Azef" became a metaphor for the entire tsarist system. Nicolaevsky, *Aseff*; Schleifman, *Undercover Agents*; Geifman, *Entangled in Terror*; Daly, *Watchful State*, 81-109.

136. Biggart, "Kirov Before the Revolution"; Mostiev, *Revoliutsionnaia publitsistika Kirova*; Kirilina, *Neizvestnyi Kirov*.

137. Daly, *Watchful State*, 110-1.

138. Shukman, *Lenin and the Russian Revolution*, 126.

139. Shchëgolëv, *Padenie*, VI: 176-7 (N. E. Markov).

140. Vitte, *Vospominaniia* [1960], III: 274-5; Hosking, *Russia*, 479.

141. Jones, "Non-Russian Nationalities," 35-63; Thaden, *Russification in the Baltic Provinces*; Weeks, *Nation and State*; Woodworth, "Civil Society"; Staliunas, *Making Russians*; Kryzhanovskii, *Vospominaniia*, 128. On the incompatibility between Russian nationalism and the tsarist state, see Kappeler, *Russian Empire*, 238-42. Something very similar took place in Hungary's deleterious Magyarization in its diverse half of the Habsburg empire after the 1867 "compromise" forming the Dual Monarchy of Austria-Hungary.

142. Steinberg, *Bismarck*, 3 (citing Karl Heinz Börner, *Wilhelm I, deutscher Kaiser und König von Preussen: eine Biographie* [Berlin: Akadamie, 1984], 221).

143. Kokovtsov, *Iz moego proshlogo*, I: 282-3.

144. McDonald, *United Government*, 10, 209, 213.

145. Rieber, *Politics of Autocracy*.

146. Gurko, *Features and Figures*, 30. For similar remarks, thirty years earlier, see Stead, *Truth About Russia*, 199-200.

147. "K. Kuzakov—syn I. V. Stalina," *Argumenty i fakty*, 1995, no. 39: 12. The story of the peasant Matryona and the bastard son reached the Alliluyevs, who passed it on to Svetlana. Alliluyeva, *Only One Year*, 330.

148. Gromov, *Stalin*, 34-9.

149. A photograph of Pelegeya Onufrieva and Pyotr Chizikov was kept in Stalin's personal papers: *Izvestiia TsK KPSS*, 1998, no. 10: 190. Chizikov died not long after returning to his parents in 1912. He was in his early twenties. Pelegeya died in 1955; her husband, Fomin, was arrested.

150. Hugh O'Beirne, a longstanding British embassy official in St. Petersburg, reported to London in June 1911 that Stolypin was "depressed" and his position "insecure." Neilson, *Britain and the Last Tsar*, 74. See also Chmielski, "Stolypin's Last Crisis."

151. Pipes, *Russian Revolution*, 183-91; Hosking, *Russian Constitutional Experiment*, 136; Shchëgolëv, *Padenie*, VI: 252 (Guchkov). Nicholas II, in January 1913, ended the trial of the police officials linked to the assassination, including A. I. Spiridovich.

152. Ostrovskii, *Kto stoial*, 321-47.

153. *VI (Parizhskaia) Vserossiiskaia konferentsiia RSDRP*. On whether Prague in 1912 inaugurated a self-standing Bolshevik party, see Lars Lih, "1912."

154. Those elected to the Central Committee at Prague included Lenin, Zinoviev, Malinowski (an *okhranka* spy), Filipp Goloshchyokin, D. Schwarzman,

and Stalin's two Caucasus colleagues, the Georgian Orjonikidze and Armenian Suren Spandaryan; those co-opted were Stalin and Ivan Belostotsky, and a bit later Grigory Petrovsky and Yakov Sverdlov.

155. Uratadze, *Vospominaniia*, 234.

156. This point, with many references, is developed by Pipes, *Russia Under the Bolshevik Regime*, 248-9.

157. De Felice, *Mussolini*, 35n; de Begnac, *Palazzo Venezia*, 360; Balabanoff, *My Life as a Rebel*, 44-52.

158. Gregor, *Fascist Persuasion*, 49.

159. Gregor, *Young Mussolini*, 35; Falasca-Zamponi, *Fascist Spectacle*, 42-3.

160. PSS, XXI: 409. In November 1914, after war had broken out, Mussolini would reverse himself and declare support for the Italian government's participation in war, leading to his expulsion from the Socialist Party. Nation, he argued, could not be ignored.

161. Stalin was paid honoraria for the occasional publication and received aid from the Political Red Cross, in addition to his allowance, from 1912, from Bolshevik party coffers. Still, he wrote to seemingly everyone he knew requesting parcels of food and clothing. "I have no choice but to mention this," he wrote to his lover Tatyana Slovatinskaya in 1913. "I have no money and have even run out of food." She sent a parcel, for which he wrote, "I don't know how I can repay you, my darling sweetheart!" Soon, he was begging her again. RGASPI, f. 558, op. 4, d. 5392. In the 1920s, Stalin repaid her with a position in the secret department of the Central Committee—his innermost fief. In 1937, her daughter was imprisoned, her son-in-law executed, and she herself (along with two grandchildren) evicted from the elite residential compound House on the Embankment. Khlevniuk, *Stalinskoe politburo*, 307.

162. Kun, *Unknown Portrait*, 127-8; Trotskii, *Stalin* [1990], I: 192-3.

163. *Pis'ma P. B. Akselroda-Iu. O. Martovu*, I: 292-3.

164. Jones, *Socialism*, 221.

165. Melancon, *The Lena Goldfields Massacre*; Haimson, "Workers' Movement After Lena."

166. Montefiore, *Young Stalin*, 246 (from *Zvezda*, no citation).

167. Melancon, *The Lena Goldfields Massacre*, 155.

168. Mintslov, *Petersburg*, 111, 231; Rogger, *Jewish Policies*, 225; Bogdanovich, *Tri poslednikh samoderzhtsa* [1990], 493; Podbolotov, "Monarchists Against Their Monarch." Back in 1903, officers of the Belgrade garrison had stormed the Serbian royal palace and assassinated their king—a fact noted by

Russian right-wingers. "Let you in on a secret?" B. V. Nikolsky, the Russian Black Hundreds leader and confidant of Nicholas II, confided to his diary in 1905. "I think that it is naturally impossible to bring the Tsar to his senses. He is worse than inept! He is—God forgive me—a total nobody! . . . We need something Serbian." Nikol'skii, "Iz dnevnikov," 77. "I have no hope for the monarchist parties," a rightist professor in Kiev wrote to a colleague in Moscow. "To have power they need a genuine Monarch, but we have instead a kind of miserable *blancmange*." Y. A. Kulakovskii, in Shevtsov, *Izdatel'skaia deiatel'nost' russkikh nesotsialisticheskikh partii*, 26.
169. Nazanskii, *Krushenie velikoi Rossii*, 76–7.
170. Suvorov, *Trekhsotletie doma Romanovykh*; *Moskovskie vedomosti*, February 23, 1913: 1; Wortman, *Scenarios of Power*, II: 439–80.
171. Syrtsov, *Skazanie o Fedorovskoi Chudotvornoi*. The St. Theodore (Fyodor) icon, also known as the Black Virgin, was taken over by the renovationist (*obnovlentsy*) sect, which had it restored in Moscow in 1928. In 1944, when the sect was dissolved, the Orthodox Church repossessed the icon; it remains in Kostroma, even though the Bolsheviks blew up its

original home (Kostroma's Assumption Cathedral).
172. Semevslkii, *Monarkhiia pered krusheniem*; Shchëgolëv, *Padenie*, IV: 195–6.
173. Rossiiskaia Gosudarstvennia Biblioteka, otdel rukopisi (RGB OR), f. 126 (Kireevskii-Novikovikh), k. 13 (Dnevnik A. A. Kireeva, 1900–1904), l. 131. As the years passed, Kireev would continue this refrain: "The sovereign . . . is unstable to such a degree that it is impossible to depend on him." RGB OR, f. 126, k. 14, l. 343ob (December 22, 1908). See also Elpatevskii, *Vospominaniia*, 264.
174. Wortman, *Scenarios of Power*, II: 464, 466 (Ivan Tolstoy).
175. Anan'ich and Ganelin, "Nikolai II"; Lieven, *Nicholas II*; Mark D. Steinberg in Steinberg and Khrustalëv, *Fall of the Romanovs*, 1–37; Warth, *Nicholas II*.
176. Rogger, *Russia in the Age of Modernization*, 22–3.
177. Remnev, *Samoderzhavnoe pravitel'stvo*, 6, 471.
178. Witte's champions would later claim, rightly, that he had anticipated Stolypin by proposing the emancipation of the peasants from the commune and their receiving private property and civil rights, but the champions often fail to note that after

Stolypin introduced the legislation, Witte opposed it in the State Council. For a comparison of the two men, see Struve, "Witte und Stolypin," III: 263–73.
179. As communicated in December 1911 to British professor Bernard Pares: "Papers Communicated by Professor Pares, December 23, 1911," in Lieven, *British Documents on Foreign Affairs*, VI: 185–8 (at 187).
180. Goriachkin, *Pervyi russkii fashist*.
181. McDonald, "A Lever Without a Fulcrum," 268–314.
182. Fascism would flourish in the Russian emigration. See, among a wide literature, Markov, *Voiny temnykh sil*. An ardent anti-Semite, Markov (the younger of two Duma brothers) became a Nazi.
183. Rogger, *Jewish Policies*, 190.
184. Daly, *Watchful State*, xi (citing I. Blok, "Poslednie dni starogo rezhima," in Gessen, *Arkhiv russkoi revoliutsii*, IV: 13).
185. The regime "was in a precarious position," explained one former deputy interior minister. "In normal times no government should use methods employed by revolutionists, for in its hands such methods become double-edged weapons." Gurko, *Features and Figures*, 437.

## PART II: DURNOVÓ'S REVOLUTIONARY WAR

1. It had taken rule-of-law Britain from 1832 until 1912 to effect a transition from greatly limited suffrage (propertied men) to universal manhood suffrage.
2. John Channon, "The Peasantry in the Revolutions of 1917," in Frankel, *Revolution in Russia*, at 117.
3. Kurzman, *Democracy Denied*.
4. Zinaida Gippius's diary entry in August/September 1915: "The right—they understand nothing, they are going nowhere, and they refuse to let anyone else go anywhere. The center—they understand, but they are going nowhere, and wait (for what?). The left—they understand nothing but are going like the blind without knowing whither or to what ultimate aim." *Siniaia kniga*, 32.
5. "Nashi tseli" [unsigned], *Pravda*, April 22, 1912, in *Sochineniia*, II: 248–9.
6. Souvarine, *Stalin*, 133.
7. *PSS*, XLVIII: 162.
8. Medvedev, *Let History Judge*, 820–1.
9. It was issued as a separate pamphlet the next year (St. Petersburg: Priboy, 1914); a much revised version appeared in *Sochineniia*, II: 290–367. See also Fel'shtinskii, *Razgovory s Bukharinym*, 10.
10. There were some fifty-five revolutionaries just on the Moscow *okhranka* payroll as of April 1912.

Smirnov, *Repressirovanoe pravosudie*, 101–3.
11. Wolfe, "Lenin and the Agent"; Lauchlan, *Russian Hide-and-Seek*, 254; Vladimir Ilyich Lenin, "Deposition in the Case of R. V. Malinovsky: Protocols of 26 May 1917, N. A.," in Pipes, *Unknown Lenin*, 35; Elwood, *Roman Malinovsky*.
12. Luchinskaia, *Velikii provokator Evno Azef*; Geifman, *Entangled in Terror*. After being exposed as an *okhranka* agent in 1909, Azev escaped to Germany, where he was imprisoned until 1917 and died the next year, apparently of kidney disease.
13. "Vystuplenie N. I. Bukharina," 78. In the British novelist G. K. Chesterton's *The Man Who Was Thursday* (1908), seven anarchists, code-named for the days of the week, plot to blow up the Brighton Pier, but every one turns out to be a police agent.
14. Lauchlan, *Russian Hide-and-Seek*, 194.
15. Smith, "Monarchy Versus the Nation."
16. Russian foreign ministry personnel were far removed from the roiling social hatreds Durnovó feared. Gurko, *Features and Figures*, 481–562 (commenting, inter alia, on A. P. Izvolsky and S. D. Sazonov).

17. Durnovó to Plehve, in D. N. Liubimov, "Sobytiia i liudi (1902–1906 gg.)" (RGALI, f. 1447, op. 1, d. 39, l. 461).
18. *Novoe vremia*, April 26, 1912; Aldanov, "Durnovó" 39–40; Lieven, "Bureaucratic Authoritarianism." Durnovó's civil service record (RGIA, f. 1162, op. 6, d. 190, l. 82–109) can be found in *Al'manakh: Iz glubiny vremen*, 1995, no. 4: 151–65. See also Borodin, "P. N. Durnovó"; Shikman, *Deiateli otechestvennoi istorii*; and Glinka, *Odinnadtsat' let v Gosudarstvennoi Dumy*. Stolypin and Durnovó became enemies nearly from the moment of their acquaintance in 1904. Ascher, *P. A. Stolypin*, 48–9.
19. "Durnovó stood out among the statesmen of that epoch, including Witte, for his great fund of information, his independent ideas, his courage in expressing his opinion, and his statesmanlike understanding of events," according to his deputy, Vladimir Gurko. Gurko, *Features and Figures*, 413–5.
20. McDonald, "The Durnovó Memorandum."
21. Lieven, *Russia and the Origins*, 5.
22. Durnovó also understood that the war would not be quick, and he foresaw which camps Italy, Turkey, and the Balkan states would join, and how

even Japan and the United States would play a role. Durnovó's memorandum was found among the papers of Nicholas II by the Bolsheviks, and Evgeny Tarle published a version of it in 1922: "Zapiska P. N. Durnovó Nikolaiu II." See also Tarle, "Germanskaia orientatsiia i P. N. Durnovó." In full in English translation: Golder, *Documents of Russian History*, 3–23. Witte had allowed himself to communicate with Nicholas II in brusque terms about the military defeat during the Russo-Japanese War. Dillon, *Eclipse of Russia*, 294–5 (purporting to quote directly from a copy of a letter Witte gave him).

23. Lenin, *Detskaia bolezn' "levizny" v kommunizme* (Petrograd, 1920), reprinted in *PSS*, XLI: 3–90 (at 10).

24. Even before the outbreak of the war, in 1913, widespread fear gripped elites that "the specter of 1905 would once again become a reality," reported M. F. von Kotten. Korbut, "Uchet departamentom politsii opyta 1905 goda," 219. In April 1914, Count V. V. Musin-Pushkin summed up the mood at court, writing to his father-in-law that "the most bourgeois circles are becoming revolutionary, and it is worse in the provinces than in the capital. Absolutely everyone is discontented." The count added that "what is most stupid and annoying is that there are no basic reasons for discontent." Cherniavsky, *Prologue to Revolution*, 12–3.

25. M. O. Gershenzon, in Shagrin and Todd, *Landmarks*, 81; Paléologue, *An Ambassador's Memoirs*, III: 349–50.

26. In fact, neither the British nor the French were confident in the endurance of a Russo-German antagonism, because no essential interests divided St. Petersburg and Berlin. But in Russia, the leading Germanophiles—Witte

and Durnovó—were no longer in positions of power sufficient to influence Nicholas II. A decline in pro-German sentiment in St. Petersburg served as the background for Durnovó's February 1914 memorandum. Lieven, "Pro-Germans"; Bestuzhev, *Bor'ba*, 44–6.

27. Fischer, *War of Illusions*, 334–6.

28. Durnovó's former deputy noted that his boss "could not fathom the psychological depths of the people." Gurko, *Features and Figures*, 415.

29. "Governing a state is a harsh business," Durnovó had explained in late 1910. "Justice itself yields to the demands of higher state interests . . . The tsar has to be terrible [awesome] but gracious, terrible first and foremost and gracious afterwards." *Gosudarstvennyi Sovet: stenograficheskii otchet*, sixth session, December 17, 1910, col. 595; Lieven, "Bureaucratic Authoritarianism," 395, n25.

30. Lieven, *Russia's Rulers*, 277–308.

31. "The heir's illness, the empress's irritability, the sovereign's indecisiveness, the appearance of Rasputin, the unsystematic character of general government politics," recalled Alexander Naumov, another rightist in the State Council, "all this forced honest and serious public officials to ponder the current state of affairs and to look warily upon an indeterminate future." Naumov, *Iz utselevshikh vospominanii*, II: 214–5 (includes the Durnovó quote).

32. Years later, in the emigration, the story would be told that the tsar had invited Durnovó to take up the reins of government as prime minister. "Your Highness," Durnovó is supposed to have demurred, "my system as head of the Government or minister of internal affairs cannot provide quick results, it can only show itself after a number of

years, and these years will be a time of utter rumpus: dissolution of Dumas, assassinations, executions, perhaps armed uprisings. You, Your Highness, will not be able to take these years and you will remove me; under such conditions my being in power would bring nothing good, only harm." The idea that Durnovó would try one more time to win over Nicholas II and then *decline* an invitation to take charge is beyond fanciful. Still, the fanciful quote attributed to him does reflect how he and others had, essentially, lost heart. Vasil'chikov, *Vospominaniia*, 225; Lieven, *Russia's Rulers*, 229–30.

33. Mal'kov, *Pervaia mirovaia voina*, 99.

34. Mendel, "Peasant and Worker." Mendel was commenting on Leopold Haimson, whose influential article argued that revolution in Russia was inevitable, because of a dual social polarization: between workers and the rest of society, and between educated society and the autocracy. Haimson, "Problem of Social Stability."

35. Dan, *Origins of Bolshevism*, 399. Originally published in Russian (1946), on the eve of the émigré Dan's death in New York.

36. Hosking, *Russian Constitutional Experiment*. For an update, see McKean, "Constitutional Russia," and the response by Peter Gatrell (82–94). A civil society is impossible in an illiberal political order, but scholars continue to imagine a civil society in tsarist Russia, focusing on the existence of associations, which enjoyed few civil protections and little influence on the state. Walkin, *Rise of Democracy*; Bradley, *Voluntary Association*; Ely, "Question of Civil," 225–42.

37. Shelokhaev, *Politicheskie partii Rossii*.

38. Holquist, "Violent Russia," 651–2.

## CHAPTER 5: STUPIDITY OR TREASON?

1. *Rech'*, December 13, 1916, translated and reprinted in Golder, *Documents of Russian History*, 154–166 (at 164).

2. Tikhomirov, "Nuzhny li printsipy?," 69.

3. Morris, *Colonel Roosevelt*, 56.

4. "The Kaiser sent me packing like a lackey," the embittered ex-chancellor wrote. Later, Bismarck exacted a form of revenge, choosing as his epitaph, "a loyal German servant of Kaiser Wilhelm I." Steinberg, *Bismarck*, 454–5, 463, 480. The kaiser's dismissal of Bismarck was reminiscent of Nicholas II's handling of Witte.

5. Kennan, *Fateful Alliance*.

6. Offer, *The First World War*, 324–30. The United States was third in international trade at 11 percent: Kennedy, *Over Here*, 298.

7. Steinberg, *Yesterday's Deterrent*.

8. Quoted in Paul Kennedy, "The Kaiser and Weltpolitik: Reflexions on Wilhelm II's Place in the Making of German Foreign Policy," in Röhl and Sombart, *Kaiser Wilhelm II*, 143–68 (at 155). See also J. G. Röhl, "Introduction" and "The Emperor's New Clothes: A Character Sketch of Kaiser Wilhelm II," in the same volume (1–62); Hull, *Entourage of Kaiser Wilhelm II*; and Hewitson, "The Kaiserreich in Question."

9. Neilson, *Britain and the Last Tsar*.

10. McClelland, *German Historians and England*; Sontag, *Germany and England*; and Conrad, *Globalisation and Nation*.

11. Quoted in Ronaldshay, *Life of Lord Curzon*, III: 117.

12. Kennedy, *Rise of the Anglo-German Antagonism*, 360.

13. The literature on the general causes of war has in many ways developed out of the Great War example. Blainey, *The Causes of War*; Howard, *The Causes of Wars*. Alas, the political science literature on the causes of war entered a cul-de-sac some time ago, from which it has not fully emerged: Fearon, "Rationalist Explanations for War." More helpfully there is Jervis, *Perception and Misperception*.

14. Gatrell, *The Tsarist Economy*, 31–2.

15. Stone, *The Eastern Front*, 42; Knox, *With the Russian Army*, I: xix.

16. Fischer, *War of Illusions*, 400; Berghahn, *Germany and the Approach of War*, 181. "Russia grows and grows," noted Germany's civilian chancellor Theobald von Bethmann Hollweg. "She lies on us like a nightmare." See also Pollock, *Creating the Russian*

*Peril*; and Mombauer, *Helmuth von Moltke*. Britain's shipbuilding industry built warships at twice the speed and half the cost of Russia's, but Britain bore the self-assigned burden of dominating the world's sea lanes. Gatrell, *Government, Industry, and Rearmament*.

17. Wohlforth, "The Perception of Power"; John C. G. Röhl, "Germany," in Wilson, *Decisions for War*, at 33–8.

18. Halévy, *The World Crisis*, 24–5; see also Crampton, "The Balkans," 66–79.

19. Fay, *The Origins of the World War*, II: 335; Albertini, *Origins of the War of 1914*, II: 74–88; Dedijer, *The Road to Sarajevo*; Vucinich, "Mlada Bosna and the First World War," 45–70; Zeman, *The Break-Up*, 24–34; Remak, *Sarajevo*; MacKenzie, *Apis*, 123ff. Back on June 3, 1910, Bogdan Žerajić (a twenty-two-year-old Serb) had tried to kill Kaiser Franz Jozef; twelve days later, Žerajić had attempted to kill the then governor of Bosnia-Herzegovina General Marijan Verešanin. Having failed, Žerajić killed himself.

20. Mark Cornwall, "Serbia," in Wilson, *Decisions for War*, 55–96.

21. Trotskii, *Sochineniia*, XVII/1: 190.

22. Franz Josef's aggressive stance, to some, recalled British behavior in the Boer War fifteen years earlier when London, fearing loss of its grip across southern Africa, invented concentration camps and sought to annihilate the "uppity" Afrikaner population on the Cape. Lieven, "Dilemmas of Empire," 187.

23. Wandruszka, *House of Habsburg*, 178.

24. Austria's decision making has been judged severely (Taylor, *The Struggle for Mastery*, 521; Williamson, *Austria-Hungary*, 211). But for a shrewd defense of Austria-Hungary's gamble, see Schroeder, "Stealing Horses," 17–42. When Britain declared war on August 3, 1914, within four minutes British commanders in the Far East knew, via telegraph.

25. Newton, *Lord Lansdowne*, 199.

26. Lieven, *Russia and the Origins*, 77–80. Nicholas may have been influenced not only by Durnovó and the ill-starred Russo-Japanese War but also by the widely discussed book of the Russian-Polish banker Iwan Bloch, *Budushchaia voina*, 6 vols. (St. Petersburg: Efron, 1898). The concluding sixth volume was translated into English as *The Future of War in Its Technical, Economic, and Political Relations: Is War Now Impossible?* (New York: Doubleday & McClure, 1899).

27. Ropponen, *Die Kraft Russlands*; Fuller, "The Russian Empire," 110–20.

28. Immediately after the war began, the Russian foreign minister pressured Serbia to cede the territory of Macedonia (to Bulgaria). Paléologue, *An Ambassador's Memoirs*, I: 22–23 (entry for July 23, 1914).

29. Albertini, *Origins of the War of 1914*, II: 352–62; Lieven, *Russia and the Origins*, 139–51; Spring, "Russia and the Coming of War," 57–86. Albertini, among the general accounts, stands out for having thorough knowledge of Russian sources.

30. Turner, "The Russian Mobilization in 1914," 252–66; Geyer, *Russian Imperialism*, 312–3; Sazonov, *Vospominaniia*, 248–9 (Sazonov was foreign minister). For the relevant documents, see "Nachalo voiny 1914 g.: podennaia zapis'."

31. Hans Rogger, "Russia in 1914." Alexandra, in a letter to Nicholas, fantasized that the war had "lifted spirits, cleansed the stagnant minds, brought unity in feelings," and called the war a "healthy war in the moral sense." Pares, *Letters of the Tsaritsa*, 9 (September 24, 1914). On Nicholas II's public announcement of the war from a balcony of the Winter Palace, see Vasilyev, *Ochrana*, 36.

32. The paper added: "Here begins the second Great Patriotic War." Gatrell, *Russia's First World War*, 18. On the press drumbeat for war in 1914 in both Germany and Russia, see Fischer, *War of Illusions*, 370–88. "Why is it that in general, war is evil but this war alone is somehow good?" wrote Zinaida Gippius, the St. Petersburg poetess, in her diary in August 1914. Gippius, *Siniaia kniga*, 12.

33. As John LeDonne observed, "These were not the goals of a political establishment that had lost its nerve and was mesmerized by the German danger." To be sure, as Boris Nolde rightly observed, Russia's imperialist war aims had not driven the decision for war, but emerged after the war had begun. That emergence, however, did not occur out of the blue. Retrospectively, one of the chief culprits, former Russian foreign minister Aleksandr P. Izvolsky, attempted an exculpation of Russia, arguing that only fears of German hegemony in Europe had motivated Russia's actions. LeDonne, *Russian Empire and the World*, 366–7; Boris Nol'de, "Tseli i real'nost' v velikoi voine," 81–6; Izvolsky, *Memoirs*, 83.

34. "Having so long resisted war for fear of social repercussions," one scholar writes, "the Russian government now entered it for the same reasons." McDonald, *United Government*, 207.

35. Zuber, *Inventing the Schlieffen Plan*. See also Snyder, *Ideology of the Offensive*, chapters 4–5; and Sagan, "1914 Revisited."

36. Förster, "Dreams and Nightmares: German Military Leadership and the Images of Future War," 343–76 (esp. 360, 365, 372); Herwig, "Germany and the 'Short War' Illusion," 688; Snyder, *Ideology of the Offensive*, 112, 122–24; Howard, *The First World War*, 28–9; Offer, "Going to War in 1914."

37. Lambert, *Planning Armageddon*. One of Schlieffen's arguments for the necessity of a lightning victory had been the supposed impossibility of sustaining a war of attrition given the new economic constraints of war. Albertini, *Origins of the War of 1914*, III: 369ff.

38. Clark, *Kaiser Wilhelm II*, 214–18.

39. Ambassador Prince Karl Max Lichnowsky to Berlin, August 1, 1914, in *Die deutschen Dokumente zum Kriegsausbruch*, 2nd ed., 4 vols. (Berlin: Deutsche Verlagsgesellschaft für Politik und Geschichte, 1922), III: 66; Albertini, *Origins of the War of 1914*, III: 171–8, 380–6; Berghahn, *Imperial Germany*, 282–3. On the kaiser's worry and restraint, see Stevenson, *Cataclysm*, 21–35.

40. Tuchman, *Guns of August*, 99 (quoting von Moltke's memoirs).

41. Nicolson, *King George V*, 328–9 (citing Grey's note, from the Royal Archives); Young, "The Misunderstanding of August 1, 1914."

42. Von Moltke, *Erinnerungen*, 21; von Zwehl, *Erich von Falkenhayn*, 58–9.

43. Following an agreement of October 1907, effective January 26, 1910, international law required a declaration of war before commencing hostilities.

44. "The [German] government," the naval cabinet chief approvingly wrote in his diary, "has succeeded very well in making us appear as the attacked." Berghahn, *Germany and the Approach of War*, 213ff.

45. A. J. P. Taylor famously called it the "war by timetable," wrongly blaming mobilization, and even asserting that none of the great powers had sought war. Taylor, *War by Timetable*.

46. The British government had the assets to enforce the blockade but not the ability to coordinate the many British agencies involved. Economic warfare went from being the cornerstone to the afterthought of British grand strategy. Lambert, *Planning Armageddon*, quote at 189 (Robert Brand). See also Ferguson, *Pity of War*, 189–97; and Ferguson, "Political Risk."

47. Whereas Taylor argued that "peace would have brought Germany mastery of Europe within a few years," Ferguson countered that British neutrality would have been followed at worst by a temperate German peace imposed on France and the future integrity of Belgium. Taylor, *The Struggle for Mastery*, 528; Ferguson, *Pity of War*, 168–73, 442–62.

48. Lieven, *Russia and the Origins*, 142–3.

49. This is not meant to absolve von Moltke: In June 1915, after he was replaced by Erich von Falkenhayn, the

megalomaniacal von Moltke complained privately to a friend that "it is dreadful to be condemned to inactivity in this war which I prepared and initiated." He died one year later. Mombauer, "A Reluctant Military Leader?," 419.

50. Stevenson, *Armaments*; Van Evera, "The Cult of the Offensive." See also Dickinson, *International Anarchy*.

51. Lieven, *Russia and the Origins*, 139–40. On honor, see Offer, "Going to War in 1914."

52. For a basic overview of decision making, see Hamilton and Herwig, *Decisions for War*.

53. A focus on statesmen, using memoirs (not then closed archives), characterized the phenomenally influential Tuchman, *Guns of August*. See Strachan, *The First World War* [2004], 68; Strachan, *The First World War* [2003], I: 4–162; Stevenson, *Cataclysm*; and Van Evera, "Why Cooperation Failed."

54. Christensen and Snyder, "Chain Gangs," 66.

55. Horne, *A Companion to World War I*, 249. "All the nations of Europe to-day, in my humble estimation, if I may say so, have gone mad," remarked the prime minister of Canada (Wilfrid Laurier) already a few years before the war (1911). Quoted in Offer, *The First World War*, 268.

56. French, *British Strategy*, xii, 200–1.

57. Pearce, *Comrades in Conscience*, 169; Keegan, *The First World War*, 278–99; Ferro, *The Great War*, 91–2. See also Prior and Wilson, *The Somme*.

58. Edgerton, *The Shock of the Old*, 142–6.

59. Ellis, *Social History of the Machine Gun*.

60. Haber, *The Poisonous Cloud*, 243.

61. Gumz, *Resurrection and Collapse*.

62. Russell, *Justice in War Time*, 13–4.

63. Harding, *Leninism*, 8–11, 113–41.

64. *Bol'shevik*, 1949, no. 1, reprinted in *PSS*, XLIX: 377–9 (at 378); Lih, *Lenin*, 13. Lih, whose corpus of works brims with original insights, unfortunately makes Lenin out to be a mainstream European social democrat, kind of the way that Nietzsche's English-language translator, Walter Kaufmann, made the German radical thinker into an American liberal.

65. "Patriotism was on display only sporadically and disappeared almost completely in 1915 . . . Russians had a pretty good idea against whom they were fighting in the war, but not for whom and for what." Jahn, *Patriotic Culture*, 134, 173. War patriotism was an upper-class sentiment: Gurko, *Features and Figures*, 538.

66. Lieven, *Empire*, 46.

67. Hull, *Absolute Destruction*, 5–90.

68. Hochschild, *King Leopold's Ghost*.

69. Prior and Wilson, *The Somme*, 222; de Groot, *Douglas Haig*, 242 (citing

Haig, "Memorandum on Policy for the Press," May 26, 1916).

70. Kramer, *Dynamic of Destruction*. One historian observed that "The Allies, and particularly the British, managed to give the impression that they acted brutally or unscrupulously with regret; the Germans always looked as though they were enjoying it." In fact, the early unprovoked atrocities in Belgium, although exaggerated, were real. Taylor, *The First World War*, 57.

71. Omissi, *The Sepoy and the Raj*, 117–8.

72. *PSS*, XLIX: 101, 161.

73. Thatcher, *Leon Trotsky*, 212. See also Martynov, "Ot abstraktsii k konkretnoi deiatel'nosti"; and Thatcher, "Trotskii, Lenin, and the Bolsheviks."

74. *Biulleten' oppozitsii*, August 1930, no. 14: 8; Trotsky, *Stalin School of Falsification*, 184–5. The last entry in volume II of Stalin's *Collected Works* dates to January–February 1913, and the first entry in volume III dates to March 1917. Medvedev, *Let History Judge*, 37.

75. Van Ree, "Stalin and the National Question," at 224, 237, n64 (citing RGASPI, f. 30, op. 1, d. 20; f. 558, op. 1, d. 57); Shveitzer, *Stalin v turukhanskoi ssylke*. Even when Stalin was preparing his collective works the unpublished article, which was said to have filled two exercise books in longhand, could not be found. RGASPI, f. 558, op. 4, d. 62, l. 308ff, 424.

76. Van Ree, "Stalin and the National Question," 225 (citing RGASPI, f. 558, op. 1, d. 54, d. 56).

77. Sverdlov, *Izbrannye proizvedennye*, I: 386–90.

78. *Krasnoiarskii rabochii*, July 25, 2003 (citing Gosudarstvennyi arkhiv Krasnoiarskogo kraia): http://www .krasrab.com/archive/2003/07/25/16/ view_article; Pechat' i revoliutsiia, 1924, kn. 2: 66; Sverdlov, *Izbrannye proizvedennye*, I: 276–7. Volkogonov, *Stalin: Politicheskii portret*, I: 51. See also Sverdlova, *Iakov Mikhailovich Sverdlov* [1985], 171–208.

79. This is a quote from October 1938: *Istoricheskii arkhiv* (1994), no. 5: 13; RGASPI, f. 558, op. 11, d. 1122, l. 55. On his marriage vow, see *Istochnik*, 2002, no. 4: 74.

80. The library had belonged to Dubrovinsky. In 1929, when the gendarme Mikhail Merzlyakov faced expulsion from his *kolkhoz* because of his tsarist police past, he wrote to Stalin, who wrote to the village soviet: "Mikh Merzlyakov carried out the task he was given by the chief of police according to the book, but without the usual police zeal. He was not spying on me. He did not make my life a misery. He did not bully me. He tolerated my frequent disappearances. He criticized

his superiors on several occasions for their many orders and prescriptions. I regard it as my duty to confirm this to you." RGASPI, f. 558, op. 4, d. 662.

81. Kvashonkin, *Bol'shevistskoe rukovodstvo*, 21 (RGASPI, f. 558, op. 1, d. 53, l. 1–3: Feb. 27, 1915); Alliluyeva, *Vospominaniia*, 118. Anna was another of Sergei Alliluyev's daughters. RGASPI, f. 558, op. 4, d. 662. Stalin was in Kureika (1914–16), and later told the local children: "I was capricious, sometimes cried, hard, a tough existence." TsKhIDNI Krasnoiarskogo Kraia, f. 42, op. 1, d. 356, l. 22.

82. Ostrovskii, *Kto stoial*, 414–8. Sverdlov escaped the war, too, because he was a Jew.

83. Best, "The Militarization of European Society," 13–29.

84. Russia's army went to battle mostly on foot, with horse-drawn and ox-drawn carts, even though Russia's soldiers were scattered across some 8 million square miles of territory. Each Russian conscript in 1914 had to travel three times as far, on average, as each German, Austro-Hungarian, or French conscript to reach the arena of mobilization. Knox, *With the Russian Army*, I: xxxiii; Dobrorolski, *Die Mobilmachung der russischen Armee*, 28; Golovin, *Voennye usiliia Rossii*, I: 51, 61, II: 69–71; Brusilov, *Moi vospominaniia*, 76; Danilov, *Rossiia v mirovoi voine*, 191–2; Rostunov, *Russkii front*, 100–1.

85. Many of them perished en route to far-off hospitals in the rear, having been "piled up on the floors of freight cars, without any medical care." Of the 5 million Russian soldiers hospitalized, around half had war wounds; the rest suffered disease—typhus, typhoid, cholera, dysentery—or frostbite, which frequently required amputations. Viroubova, *Memories of the Russian Court*, 109. See also Miliukov, *Vospominaniia*, II: 199; Rodzianko, *Reign of Rasputin*, 115–7.

86. In 1916, the belated introduction in tsarist Turkestan of conscription—on top of a forced supply of horses and livestock to the army at below-market prices—provoked full-scale rebellion. In the violence, which killed perhaps 2,500 Russians, at least 300,000 steppe nomads were displaced, many fleeing across the border to China. Piaskovskii, *Vosstanie 1916 goda*; Kendirbai, "The Alash Movement," V: at 855; Pipes, *Formation of the Soviet Union*, 84. The British also faced wartime revolts in India, Egypt, Ireland, and elsewhere in their empire.

87. Stone, *The Eastern Front*, 215.

88. Showalter, *Tannenberg*.

89. Golovine, *The Russian Army*, 220–1. See also Polivanov, *Iz dnevnikov i vospominanii*, 186.

90. Stone, *The Eastern Front*, 12, 93.

Russia's air force, established in 1912, had perhaps owned 360 aircraft and 16 airships in 1914—the largest air force in the world—but most were grounded for want of spare parts, allowing the Germans to move about unobserved.

91. Ol'denburg, *Gosudar' Imperator Nikolai II Aleksandrovich*; later expanded into Ol'denburg, *Istoriia tsarstvovanie Imperatora Nikolaia II*; and translated as Ol'denburg, *Last Tsar*. It was not just the Duma. "The antagonism between the imperial authority and the civilian society is the greatest scourge of our political life," lamented Agricultural Minister Alexander Krivoshein during the war. "The future of Russia will remain precarious so long as Government and society insist upon regarding each other as two hostile camps." Quoted in Paléologue, *La Russie*, I: 289. In February 1914, Krivoshein had declined, citing health reasons, to become prime minister.

92. Gurko, *Features and Figures*, 19; Mamontov, *Na Gosudarevoi sluzhbe*, 144–5, 151–3; Masolov, *Pri dvore imperatora* , 11–12; Lieven, *Nicholas II*, 117; Figes, *A People's Tragedy*, 15–24.

93. The Duma also met July–August 1915, on the war's first anniversary; February–May 1916; and November 1916–February 1917.

94. Gurko, *Features and Figures*, 576. "We need to fight, for the Government consists of scoundrels," explained Vasily Shulgin, of the Nationalist Party. "But since we do not intend to move to the barricades, we cannot egg others on." Lapin, "Progessivnyi blok v 1915–1917 gg.," 114.

95. Shchëgolëv, *Padenie*, VII: 116–75 (Rodzianko, on Maklakov) at 124. See also Gurko, *Features and Figures*, 521–2. The Shchëgolëv volumes were the work of the "Extraordinary Commission of Inquiry for the Investigation of Illegal Acts by Ministers and Other Responsible Persons of the Tsarist Regime," formed by the Provisional Government and discontinued by the Bolsheviks, who nonetheless partly published the materials (which were transcribed by the poet Alexander Blok).

96. The state paid 4,000 rubles for Durnovó's funeral.

97. Kir'ianov, *Pravye partii*.

98. See the table in Eroshkin, *Ocherki istorii*, 310.

99. Gal 'perina, *Sovet ministrov Rossiiskoiimperii*; Cherniavsky, *Prologue to Revolution*. In the western districts close to the front, Russia's high command did push aside the civilian government (such as it was), but administratively, the military men did not do much better. Graf, "Military Rule Behind the Russian Front."

100. Jones, "Nicholas II"; Ol'denburg, *Last Tsar*, IV: 38–42; Brusilov, *Soldier's*

Note-book, 267–8; Gurko, *Features and Figures*, 567–71; Golder, *Documents of Russian History*, 210–1. As Witte remarked of Nicholas II, "a soft haze of mysticism refracts everything he beholds and magnifies his own functions and person." Dillon, *Eclipse of Russia*, 327 (quoting a purported interview with Witte).

101. Gourko, *War and Revolution*, 10–1; Mikhail Lemke, *250 dnei*, 149; Fuller, *Civil-Military Conflict*, 41.

102. Jones, "Nicholas II."

103. The words of Maurice Paléologue, quoted in V. Kantorovich, *Byloe*, 1923, no. 22: 208–9.

104. *Letters of the Tsaritsa*, 114, 116 (August 22, 1915).

105. Fuller, *Foe Within*; Shatsillo, "Delo polkovnika Miasoedova"; Knox, "General V. A. Sukhomlinov."

106. Fülöp-Miller, *Rasputin*, 215; Radzinsky, *Rasputin File*, 40.

107. Court denied his sexual licentiousness. Viroubova, *Souvenirs de ma vie*, 115. The Sarajevo murder occurred on June 28 by the Western calendar, and on June 15 by the Russian calendar; the attempt on Rasputin's life occurred on June 29 by the Western calendar, on June 16 by the Russian. The assassin was Khionia Guseva, from Tsaritsyn.

108. Kokovtsov, *Iz moego proshlogo*, II: 40; Beletskii, *Grigorii Rasputin*, 32–6.

109. Kilcoyne, "The Political Influence of Rasputin."

110. Massie, *Nicholas and Alexandra*, 199–202; Fuhrmann, *Rasputin*, 93–8; Radzinsky, *Rasputin File*, 187. The nerves in Alexei's left leg had atrophied, causing excruciating pain right through the summer of 1913, but the grave danger of 1912 had passed. Gilliard, *Thirteen Years*, 28–30. Gilliard, Alexei's tutor, was not told the cause of Alexei's illness.

111. Crawford and Crawford, *Michael and Natasha*, 122–46.

112. Figes and Kolonitskii, *Interpreting the Russian Revolution*; RGIA, f. 1278, op. 10, d. 11, l. 332; Maylunas and Mironenko, *A Lifelong Passion*, 529.

113. Grave, *Burzhuaziia nakanune fevral'skoi revoliutsii*, 78. See also Wildman, *End of the Russian Imperial Army*, I: 156.

114. On what he calls the "parastatal complex" of social organizations in wartime Russia, see Holquist, *Making War*, 4. Lewis Siegelbaum has pointed out that relative to other powers, cooperation with "social interests and groups previously outside, or even hostile to the state machinery" was "least developed in Russia during the war." But this was probably not true of 1916. Siegelbaum, *Politics of Industrial Mobilization*, xi.

115. Lincoln, *Passage Through Armageddon*, 61.

116. Zagorsky, *State Control of Industry*, 46; Paléologue, *La Russie*, I: 231–2 .

117. Stone, *The Eastern Front*, 227; Pogrebinskii, "Voenno-promyshlennye komitety"; Gronsky and Astrov, *The War and the Russian Government*.

118. Alexeyev objected to Brusilov's "wide-front" approach, urging him instead to attack on a narrow twelve-mile front, but Brusilov stuck with his plan and, as he foresaw, this meant the enemy could not figure out where to commit reserves. Brusilov, *Soldier's Note-book*, 204–75; Brusilov, *Moi vospominaniia*, 237; Hart, *The Real War*, 224–7; Knox, *With the Russian Army*, II: 432–82; Rostunov, *Russkii front*, 321–3; Rostunov, *General Brusilov*, 154–5; Dowling, *The Brusilov Offensive*.

119. Stone, *The Eastern Front*, 243.

120. He also noted, however, that "sometimes in our battles with the Russians we had to remove the mounds of enemy corpses from before our trenches in order to get a clear field of fire against fresh assaulting waves." Von Hindenburg, *Out of My Life*, I: 193; II: 69. See also Asprey, *German High Command*.

121. Quoted in McReynolds, "Mobilising Petrograd's Lower Classes," 171.

122. Knox, *With the Russian Army*, II: 462–9; Lyons, *Diary*, 103–10.

123. Daly, *Watchful State*, 180 (I. G. Shcheglovitov).

124. Fleer, *Rabochee dvizhenie*, 309.

125. Rezanov, *Shturmovoi signal P. N. Miliukova*, 43–61; Ol'denburg, *The Last Tsar*, IV: 99–104; Bohn, "'Dummheit oder Verrat'?"; Lyandres, "Progressive Bloc Politics." Miliukov later tried to rationalize his promotion of falsehoods: Miliukov, *Vospominaniia*, II: 276–7; Diakin, *Russkaia burzhuaziia*, 243. See also Riha, *A Russian European*; and Stockdale, *Paul Miliukov*.

126. Pipes, *Russian Revolution*, 261–6; Golder, *Documents of Russian History*, 166–75. Purishkevich had already been publicly accused of wanting to remove Nicholas II. "Sovremennoe pravosudie," *Dym otechestva*, 1914, no. 22: 1–2. British ambassador George Buchanan had bought into the rumors of German agents at the Russian court, and an operative of Britain's secret intelligence service seems to have been a co-conspirator, fearful of a possible separate Russian peace with Germany: Lieutenant Oswald Rayner, whom Yusupov knew from a stint at Oxford, evidently was present at the murder and dined with Yusupov the day after. An exchange between Rayner's superiors in St. Petersburg indicates his possible involvement. Cook, *To Kill Rasputin*.

127. Voeikov, *S tsarem*, 178; Pipes,

*Russian Revolution*, 266–7. The assassins were never brought to trial.

128. V. Mikhailovich, *Kniga vospominanii*, 186; A. Mikhailovich, *Once a Grand Duke*, 184. Alexander Mikhailovich was the son of a brother (Grand Duke Mikhail Nikolaevich) of Nicholas II's grandfather Tsar Alexander II. Prince Yusupov, one of Rasputin's murderers, was the son-in-law of Grand Duke Alexander Mikhailovich.

129. Lincoln, *Passage Through Armageddon*, 312 (citing "Télégramme secret de M. Paléologue au Ministère des Affaires Etrangères," AdAE, Guerre 1914–1918, Russie, Dossier Générale no. 646: 78–9).

130. Buchanan, *My Mission to Russia*, II: 41.

131. Martynov, okhranka chief in Moscow, noted that the masses were not radicalized because of outside agitators, but because of government errors and a falloff in the tsar's prestige, as well as court scandals. "Tsarskaia okhrana o politicheskom polozhenii v strane i kontse 1916 g.," *Istoricheskii arkhiv*, 1960, no. 1: 204–9; Pokrovskii and Gelis, "Politcheskoe polozhenie Rossii nakanune fevral'skoi revoliutsii v zhandarmskom osveshchenii," excerpted in Daniels, *Russian Revolution*, 9–12.

132. "Fevral'skaia revoliutsiia i okhrannoe otdelenie." "There were no authoritative leaders on the spot in any of the parties. They were all in exile, prison, or abroad." Sukhanov, *Russian Revolution*, I: 21.

133. Burdzhalov, *Vtoraia russkaia revoliutsiia*, 90–1, 107–8.

134. David Longley, "Iakovlev's Question, or the Historiography of the Problem of Spontaneity and Leadership in the Russian Revolution of February 1917," in Frankel, *Revolution in Russia*, 365–87.

135. Manikovskii, *Boevoe snabzhenie russkoi armii* [1923].

136. Matsuzato, "Sōryokusensōto chihōtōchi."

137. Anstiferov, *Russian Agriculture*.

138. Kitanina, *Voina, khleb i revoliutsiia*, 70–2.

139. Kondrat'ev, *Rynok khlebov*, 137–8; Holquist, *Making War*, 31–2.

140. Lih, *Bread and Authority*; Holquist, *Making War*, 44–6. Before the war, only one third of Russian cereal production reached market, and half of that went for export.

141. Kondrat'ev, *Rynok khlebov*, 127; Struve, *Food Supply in Russia*, 128; Zhitkov, "Prodfurazhnoe snabzhenie russkikh armii"; Pavel Volobuev, *Ekonomicheskaia politika Vremmenogo Pravitel'stva*, 384–7; Yaney, *Urge to Mobilize*, 408–19; Kitanina, *Voina, khleb i revoliutsiia*, 217–8.

142. Lih, *Bread and Authority*, 12; "Gibel' tsarskogo Petrograda," 7–72.

"We have grain at flour mills that have no fuel," commented Moscow's mayor, "flour where there aren't any freight cars to move it, and freight cars where there is no freight for them to carry." Quoted in Diakin, *Russkaia burzhuaziia*, 314.

143. The agent warned that "Mothers, exhausted from standing endlessly at the tail of queues, and ... watching their half-starved and sick children, are perhaps much closer to a revolution than Misters Miliukov and Co.— that is, the Duma's Progressive Bloc." But that reckoning underestimated Miliukov. Hasegawa, *February Revolution*, 201 (citing GARF, f. POO, op. 5, d. 669 [1917], l. 25–33); Shchëgolëv, *Padenie*, I: 184 (Khabalov).

144. Gatrell, *Russia's First World War*, 170.

145. Mil'chik, "Fevral'skie dni."

146. Kolonitskii, *Symvoly vlasti i bor'ba za vlast'*, 14–37. Richard Wortman argues that "the symbolic abdication of Nicholas II took place long before he actually left the throne in February 1917." Wortman, "Nicholas II," 127. See also Steinberg, "Revolution," 39–65; and Figes, *A People's Tragedy*, 307–53.

147. Gurko, *Features and Figures*, 546. See also Kir'ianov, *Pravye partii*, II: 604–46; and Sadikov, "K istorii poslednikh dnei tsarskogo rezhima," 241–2.

148. Diakin, "Leadership Crisis"; Diakin, *Russkaia burzhuaziia*, 300–2; Golder, *Documents of Russian History*, 116; *Sovremennye zapiski*, 1928, no. 34: 279 (Maklakov); "Aleksandr Ivanovich Guchkov rasskazyvaet," *Voprosy istorii*, 1991, nos. 7–8: at 205; Rodzyanko, *Reign of Rasputin*, 244–5, 253–4; Gleason, "Alexander Guchkov"; Pares, *Fall of the Russian Monarch*, 427–9; Katkov, *Russia, 1917*, 215; Hasegawa, *February Revolution*, 187. Pipes dismisses the plots as idle chatter. Pipes, *Russian Revolution*, 269–70.

149. Steinberg and Khrustalëv, *Fall of the Romanovs*, 72; Hynes, *Letters of the Tsar*, 315 (February 24, 1917); *Journal intime de Nicholas II*, 93.

150. Steinberg and Khrustalëv, *Fall of the Romanovs*, 73 (Letter from Alexandra to Nicholas, September 25, 1917); *Journal intime de Nicholas II*, 92. Khabalov's first telegram to staff headquarters about the Petrograd disturbances was received on the twenty-fifth at 6:08 p.m., but Alexeyev may only have reported it to the tsar on the twenty-sixth. Sergeev, "Fevral'skaia revoliutsiia 1917 goda," 4–5; Martynov, *Tsarskaia armiia*, 80–1.

151. "What revolution?" scoffed the leading Bolshevik figure in the capital, Alexander Shlyapnikov, a Central Committee member (since 1915) who was also close to the workers' moods,

on February 25, 1917. "Give the workers a loaf of bread and the movement would be gone!" Hasegawa, *February Revolution*, 258 (citing Sveshnikov, "Vyborgskii raionnyi komitet," 83–4). See also "Gibel' tsarskogo Petrograda," 39–41; Shchëgolëv, *Padenie*, I: 191–4 (Khabalov); II: 231–3 (Beliaev).

152. Voeikov, *S tsarem*, 195–200.

153. Chermenskii, *IV Gosudarstvennaia Duma*, 196, n4, 201; Daly, *Watchful State*, 189–92; Pares, *Fall of the Russian Monarchy*, 378–81, 393–96, 416–19.

154. Fuhrmann, *Complete Wartime Correspondence*, 6. There was also War Minister Mikhail Belyaev, known as "dead head," a functionary whom Nicholas II characterized as "an extremely weak man who always gives way in everything." Hasegawa, *February Revolution*, 160–3.

155. Balk led the way in later damning Khabalov, as well as Belyaev, as indecisive. *Poslednie novosti*, March 12, 1921.

156. "Gibel' tsarskogo Petrograda," 32; Burdzhalov, *Vtoraia Russkaia revoliutsiia*, 96; Wildman, *End of the Russian Imperial Army*, I: 121.

157. Ascher, *Revolution of 1905*, I: 225.

158. Burdzhalov, *Russia's Second Revolution*, 91–3. The contingency plan for suppressing street protests in the capital did not entail possibly summoning troops from the front—a consequence, perhaps, of having formed a separate Petrograd military district. Hasegawa, *February Revolution*, 163.

159. Nicholas II's telegram to General Khabalov has not survived. We have only Khabalov's testimony: Shchëgolëv, *Padenie*, I: 190–1. Compare Martynov, *Tsarskaia armiia*, 81.

160. "Gibel' tsarskogo Petrograda," 38.

161. "Gibel' tsarskogo Petrograda," 39–41; Shchëgolëv, *Padenie*, I: 191–4 (Khabalov); II: 231–3 (Beliaev).

162. *Kak russkii narod zavoeval svobodu*, 8.

163. Only hours after inclining to compromise with the Duma, the government ministers now took the initiative to use the tsar's authority to prorogue the Duma! Katkov surmised that Nikolai Golitsyn, head of government, had an undated decree signed by the tsar to prorogue the Duma and acted on his own by filling in the date. Katkov, *Russia, 1917*, 287. See also Vasilyev, *Ochrana*, 201.

164. Sukhanov, *Zapiski*, I: 53, 59. See also the police-perspective account in Daly, *Watchful State*, 201–6.

165. Burdzhalov, *Russia's Second Russian Revolution*, 161; Burdzhalov, *Vtoraia russkaia revoliutsiia*, 182. When the okhranka sought to monitor the political reliability of the armed forces, top military men, their sense of honor offended, resisted. Surveillance on the

military would have made no difference. Lauchlan, *Russian Hide-and-Seek*, 333–6.

166. Some members of the Pavlovsky Guards were imprisoned. "A terrible breach in the stronghold of tsarism," recorded Sukhanov. Sukhanov, *Russian Revolution*, I: 29. Of the encounter on February 26, Balk recalled that his office was visited by large numbers of police and state officials concerned about the situation. "Conversing with them about events, a state coup did not come up. Disorder, yes, but Russia had experienced many disorders over the last years and we, staff of the interior ministry, were far from hysterical: we were accustomed to the fact that avoiding victims on each side was not possible, yet the idea that the troops in the end would not put down the rebellion was unthinkable." "Gibel' tsarskogo Petrograda," 42–3.

167. The words of General K. I. Globachev: Ganelin, "The Day Before the Downfall," 245–55; Ganelin et al., "Vospominaniia T. Kirpichnikova," 178–95. On a December 1916 Cossack refusal to fire on the Don region to fire on women whose husbands were at the front, see Engel, "Not by Bread Alone," 712–6.

168. "Fevral'skaia revoliutsiia i okhrannoe otdelenie," *Byloe*, January 29, 1918: 175–6.

169. Hasegawa, *February Revolution*, 233–8. "I don't know how many collisions I saw during those days," recalled one armored vehicle driver, Viktor Shklovsky. Shklovsky, *Sentimental Journey*, 16.

170. Sergeev, "Fevral'skaia revoliutsiia 1917 goda," 8 (telegram from Khabalov to Nicholas II, February 27, sent 12:10 p.m., received 12:20 p.m.), 15–6 (telegram from Khabalov to Alexeyev, February 27, sent 8:00 p.m., received at 12:55 a.m.).

171. On the evening of February 27, Balk evidently asked the interior minister for permission to retreat with troops to Tsarskoe Selo. "What, you, the City Chief, think you will withdraw from Petrograd? What is that?" Shchëgolëv, *Padenie*, II: 149–50 (Protopopov). Protopopov confused the date.

172. Vasilyev, the last tsarist Department of Police head, was correct when he wrote that "there was no possibility of suppressing the revolt." But like many after him, he wrongly attributes this impossibility to a lack of reliable military units in the capital, arguing that "with a few reliable regiments, order in Petersburg could have been quite easily maintained." Vasilyev, *Ochrana*, 221.

173. Shchëgolëv, *Padenie*, V: 32–49 (at 38) (Frederiks).

174. Bublikov, *Russkaia revoliutsiia,*

17; Kantorovich and Zaslavskii, *Khronika fevral'skoi revoliutsii*, 28–9; Skobelev, "Gibel' tsarizma"; Browder and Kerensky, *Russian Provisional Government*, I: 41–7; Abraham, *Kerensky*, 131–2; Chermenskii, "Nachalo vtoroi rossiiskoi revoliutsii," at 99. See also Lyandres, "On the Problem of 'Indecisiveness.'"

175. *Izvestiia*, February 28, 1917, in Golder, *Documents of Russian History*, 287–8; Avdeev, *Revoliutsiia 1917 goda*, I: 41; A. Blok, "Poslednie dni tsarizma," *Byloe*, 1919, no. 15: 28. A "central worker group" had been formed in November 1915 as a liaison between the military-industrial committee and the workers. Another source of the soviet was an all-socialist-party leadership group in Petrograd that had begun to coalesce in November 1916, and met frequently right before and during the February days. Melancon, *Socialist Revolutionaries*, 256–64.

176. Shul'gin, *Dni*, 127. Prince Nikolai Golitsyn, the last prime minister (appointed in December 1916), had claimed illness and implored Nicholas II not to appoint him. Shchëgolëv, *Padenie*, I: 331 (Golitsyn). See also Gippius, *Siniaia kniga*, 75–6 (diary entry for February 25, 1917).

177. Voeikov, *S tsarem*, 175.

178. Browder and Kerensky, *Russian Provisional Government*, I: 86; Lyandres, "'O Dvortsovom perevorote ia pervyi raz uslyshal posle revoliutsii . . . ,'" 252.

179. Nicholas II noted "frightened expressions" but also that Alexeyev wanted "a very energetic man" named to assume responsibility for restoring order. Steinberg and Khrustalëv, *Fall of the Romanovs*, 83. See also Beckendroff, *Last Days*, 2–3.

180. Martynov, *Tsarskaia armiia*, 114–5; Spiridovich, *Velikaia voina i fevral'skaia revoliutsiia*, III: 240ff; Shchëgolëv, *Padenie*, V: 317–8 (Ivanov); Katkov, *Russia, 1917*, 315–6; Hasegawa, *February Revolution*, 461–4.

181. Hasegawa, *February Revolution*, 473–92.

182. Martynov, *Tsarskaia armiia*, 145; Sergeev, "Fevral'skaia revoliutsiia 1917 goda," 31; S. N. Vil'chkovskii, "Prebyvanie Gosudaria Imperatora v Pskove 1 i 2 marta 1917 goda, po razskazu general-ad' iutanta N. V. Ruzskogo," *Russkaia letopis'*, 1922, no. 3: 169. Alexeev had on his own already ordered Ivanov to desist. Sergeev, "Fevral'skaia revoliutsiia 1917 goda," at 31.

183. Back in February 1916, rather than summon the Duma deputies to the Winter Palace, as per custom on the rare occasions that Nicholas II deigned to meet them, the tsar had gone to the Duma's Tauride Palace himself. Following the Te Deum, Nicholas spoke (his words were

inaudible to many), after which there was a spontaneous singing of Russia's anthem, "God Save the Tsar." But the good feelings of Nicholas II's gesture quickly dissipated. Rodzyanko asked him, again, for a "responsible government." "I shall give it some thought," Nicholas replied, upon exiting. Rodzianko, *Krushenie imperii*, 149–50; Dubenskii, *Ego Imperatorskoe Velichestvo Gosudar' Imperator Nikolai Aleksandrovich*, IV: 221. See also Paléologue, *La Russie*, II: 196; and Miliukov, *Vospominaniia*, II: 226.

184. Steinberg and Khrustalëv, *Fall of the Romanovs*, 103–5; Sergeev, "Fevral'skaia revoliutsiia 1917 goda," 55–9.

185. Sergeev, "Fevral'skaia revoliutsiia 1917 goda," 72–3.

186. Steinberg and Khrustalëv, *Fall of the Romanovs*, 93. Nicholas initially did not mention the abdication to Alexandra, who was given to understand only that the tsar had made "concessions" (which in her view could be withdrawn). Fuhrmann, *Complete Wartime Correspondence*, 699–701. "Never forget that you are and must remain [an] autocratic emperor," she would exhort him. Hynes, *The Letters of the Tsar*, 105.

187. Steinberg and Khrustalëv, *Fall of the Romanovs*, 107; *Journal intime de Nicholas II*, 93. Katkov has argued, plausibly, that Nicholas II was already broken by having conceded a parliamentary government, thereby violating the autocratic principle, so that the abdication itself, counterintuitively, entailed a lesser step. Katkov, *Russia, 1917*, 323.

188. Ol'denburg, *Gosudar' Imperator Nikolai II Aleksandrovich*, 29–31; Ol'denburg, *Last Tsar*, IV: 152–61; Voeikov, *S tsarem*, 207–19; Russky, "An Account of the Tsar's Abdication"; Danilov, "Moi vospominaniia," 223–4; Danilov, "How the Tsar Abdicated"; Bark, "Last Days of the Russian Monarchy." As one scholar summarized, "the army did, in fact, destroy the old regime simply by not defending it." Mayzel, *Generals and Revolutionaries*, 49.

189. By the fall of 1917, Russia had at least 1 million total deserters. Frenkin, *Russkaia armiia*, 197.

190. Danilov, "Moi vospominaniia," 221; Sergeev, "Fevral'skaia revoliutsiia 1917 goda," 37 40; Wildman, *End of the Russian Imperial Army*, I: 120.

191. Airapetov, "Revolution and Revolt," 94–118 (at 114).

192. For an argument that Alexeyev's move against Nicholas II amounted to a de facto coup d'état, see Lohr, "War and Revolution," II: 658, 664–5. On military seizures of power, see Trimberger, *Revolution from Above*.

193. Fuller, *Civil-Military Conflict*, 228, 262.

194. Mayzel, *Generals and Revolutionaries*, 78–9; Shulgin, *Days*, 180–3; Fuller, *Civil-Military Conflict*, 259–63. See also Steinberg, *All the Tsar's Men*.

195. Shchëgolëv, *Padenie*, VI: 263–6 (Guchkov); de Basily, *Memoirs*, 127–31. "Who would stand with him?" Shulgin had despaired of Nicholas II. "He has no one, no one." Shul'gin, *Gody*, 459.

196. Steinberg and Khrustalëv, *Fall of the Romanovs*, 96–100 (at 98).

197. Chamberlin, *Russian Revolution*, I: 85; Ostrovskii, *Kto stoial*, 418–23; Shveitzer, "V achinskoi ssylke"; Shveitzer, *Stalin v Turukhanskoi ssylke*; RGASPI, f. 558, op. 4, d. 662, l. 275 (Shveitzer); Baikalov, "Moi vstrechi s Osipom Dzhugashvili," 118; Baikaloff, *I Knew Stalin*, 27–30; Tutaev, *Alliluyev Memoirs*, 189–90; Shliapnikov, *Kanun semnadtsatogo goda*, II: 444–6; Montefiore, *Young Stalin*, 304.

## CHAPTER 6: KALMYK SAVIOR

1. *VI s"ezd*, 111–2, 114.

2. Trotsky, *History of the Russian Revolution*, II: 150 (quoting Duma representative Fyodor I. Rodichev, member of the Cadet Central Committee).

3. Karpinskii, "Vladimir Il'ich za granitsei," II: 105–6; Figes, *A People's Tragedy*, 385. The month before, the impatient Lenin had complained in a speech to young Swiss socialists, "We, the old people, won't survive to see the decisive battles of the forthcoming revolution." *PSS*, XXX: 328; Tucker, *Lenin Anthology*, 292.

4. Kornakov, "Znamena Fevral'skoi revoliutsii," 12–26; and Kornakov, "Opyt privlecheniia veksilologicheskikh pamiatnikov dlia resheniia geral' dicheskikh problem."

5. Keep, *Russian Revolution*, ix. Only one in nine villages had a soviet before October 1917.

6. White, "1917 in the Rear Garrisons," 152–68 (at 152–3).

7. Steinberg, *Moral Communities*; Steinberg, "Workers and the Cross."

8. Rosenberg, "Representing Workers."

9. Kolonitskii, "Anti-Bourgeois Propaganda."

10. Kizevetter, "Moda na sotsializm."

11. Sukhanov, *Zapiski*, II: 265–6. Sukhanov, wanted by the police, lived illegally in the capital, hiding under his real name (Himmer), which he used to obtain a position in the agricultural ministry as a specialist for irrigation in Turkestan.

12. De Lon, "Stalin and Social Democracy," 198.

13. *Pravda*, April 18, 1917 (May Day on the Russian calendar), in *Sochineniia*, II: 37–8.

14. In all of Lenin's voluminous writings from July to October 1917 (volume XXXIV of *PSS*), Stalin's name is mentioned just once. McNeal, *Stalin's Works*, 51–7. Stalin also took part in the Bolshevik commission preparing elections for the Constituent Assembly, and appeared on the candidate list. (One of his nominal constituencies—Stavropol—had to write to ask his real name, age, address, and occupation, to comply with candidate registration laws.) McNeal, *Stalin* 35–6 (citing *Perepiska Sekretariata TsK RSDRP (b)*, I: 378).

15. The name of the party organ changed several times in 1917 in response to efforts to close it down: *Rabochii i soldat* (July 23–August 9), *Proletarii* (August 13–24), *Rabochii* (August 25–September 2), and *Rabochii put'* (September 3–October 26).

16. "The early version (of authoritarianism) was rule by the few in the name of the few; modern authoritarianism is rule by the few in the name of the many." Perlmutter, *Modern Authoritarianism*, 2.

17. *Sobranie uzakonenii i rasporiazhenii pravitel'stva*, March 6, 1917, no. 54: 344; Golder, *Documents of Russian History*, 297–8; Shchëgolëv, *Otrechenie Nikolaia II*; Martynov, *Tsarskaia armiia*, 160; *Last Days at Tsarskoe Selo*, 46–7. "I cannot part with him," Nicholas remarked of Alexei to Shulgin and Guchkov. Mel'gunov, *Martovskie dni*, 192 (citing the stenogram of the meeting in Pskov); Steinberg and Khrustalëv, *Fall of the Romanovs*, 96–100.

18. De Basily, *Memoirs*, 119–20.

19. Mel'gunov, *Martovskie dni*, 226–7; Miliukov, "From Nicholas II to Stalin." Kerensky would imprison the grand duke four months later on trumped-up charges of treason; the grand duke was executed on June 12, 1918.

20. Rodzyanko in Gessen, *Arkhiv russkoi revoliutsii*, VI: 62; Shul'gin, *Dni*, 295–307; Martynov, *Tsarskaia armiia*, 181; Miliukov, *Istoriia vtoroi*, I: 53–5; Miliukov, *Vospominaniia*, II: 316–8.

21. Vladimir Nabokov and Boris Nolde were the two jurists. Nabokov, "Vremennoe pravitel'stvo," 17–22; Boris Nol'de, "V. D. Nabokov v 1917 g.," in Gessen, *Arkhiv russkoi revoliutsii*, VII: 5–14 (at 6–8); Medlin and Powers, *V. D. Nabokov*, 17–28, 49–55; Mel'gunov, *Martovskie dni*, 356–7; Katkov, *Russia, 1917*, 409–15; Holquist, "Dilemmas." Nor could the Duma legally transfer supreme power to the Provisional Government: the Fundamental Laws of 1906 did not even grant the Duma full legislative authority, and anyway Nicholas II had prorogued the legislature.

22. Miliukov, *Vospominaniia*, II: 299; Shul'gin, *Dni*, 182; Nabokov, *Vremennoe pravitel'stvo*, 67–8. Miliukov appears to have decided, on his own, not to root the Provisional Government in the Duma partly in order to exclude Duma president Mikhail Rodzyanko. This was also the Duma of Stolypin's 1907 electoral "coup," which the Cadets had denounced. In 1920, Miliukov would come to regret his decision to sideline Rodzyanko in favor of the non-entity Prince Lvov. In 1920, Rodzyanko emigrated to the new Kingdom of Serbs, Croats, and Slovenes, where four years later he died penurious at age sixty-four.

23. Kakurin, *Razlozhenie armii*, 25–7; Burdzhalov, *Russia's Second Revolution*, 179.

24. Storozhev, "Fevral'skaia revoliutsiia 1917 g."; Nabokov, *Vremennoe pravitelstvo*, 39–40; Startsev, *Vnutrenniaia politika*, 114–6. In the event, the Provisional Government retained all tsarist laws not expressly overturned or amended until such time as a Constituent Assembly might be convoked.

25. The state subsidized publication of Duma "resolutions" in hundreds of thousands of copies. A June 1917 Congress of Soviets voted to "abolish" the Duma; in fact, the Provisional Government formally abolished the Duma on October 7, as announced in the newspapers. Vladimirova, *Kontrrevoliutsiia*, 72; Drezen, *Burzhuaziia i pomeshchiki 1917 goda*, 4–5; Gal'perina, "Chastnye soveshchanii gosudarstvennoi dumy," 111–7.

26. Miliukov, *Istoriia vtoroi*, I/i: 51; *The Russian Revolution*, I: 36.

27. Browder and Kerensky, *Russian Provisional Government*, I: 135–6.

28. Kochan, "Kadet Policy in 1917." See also Miliukov, *Istoriia vtoroi*, I/i: 51; Miliukov, *The Russian Revolution*, I: 36.

29. Gaida, *Liberal'naia oppozitsiia*. An earlier portrait of the wartime liberals portrayed them as not power-hungry and cowardly: Pearson, *The Russian Moderates*.

30. Hoover Institution Archives, Aleksandr F. Kerensky papers, box 1, folder 19: "The February Revolution reconsidered," March 12, 1957, with Leonard Schapiro (typescript with crossouts); Schapiro is admiring of Kerensky. See also Rogger, *Russia in the Age of Modernization*, 25. The last *okhranka* chief admitted that his agency had had Kerensky under surveillance, but "unfortunately" their target "was protected by his immunity as a member of the Duma"; Vasilyev wrote to the tsarist justice minister asking to revoke

Kerensky's immunity—but before the answer came, Kerensky was himself justice minister and read Vasilyev's request. "In his [new] capacity," added Vasilyev, Kerensky "took cognizance of the proposal that I had made to restrict his liberty." Vasilyev, Ochrana, 213–4. Vasilyev died in Paris in 1928.

31. Zviagintseva, "Organizatsiia i deiatel'nost' militsii Vremmenogo pravitel'stva Rossii"; Hasegawa, "Crime, Police and Mob Justice," 241–71. At least one great okhranka cryptographer-analyst escaped to Britain and helped London break Soviet codes through the 1920s.

32. Avdeev, Revoliutsiia 1917 goda, I: 73; Medlin and Powers, V. D. Nabokov, 62–3, 83–4; Dubentsov and Kulikov, "Sotsial'naia evoliutsiia vysshei tsarskoi biurokratii," 75–84; Orlovsky, "Reform During Revolution," 100–25; Rosenberg, Liberals, 59. On the February revolution in the provinces, see Ferro, La révolution de 1917, 126–31. For Moscow, see Burdzhalov, "Revolution in Moscow." For Turkestan, Khalid, "Tashkent 1917."

33. Kulikov, "Vremennoe pravitel'stvo," 81–3; Wildman, End of the Russian Imperial Army, I: 3. On armies in political crises and revolution, see Finer, Man on Horseback.

34. Melancon, "From the Head of Zeus."

35. Chernov, Great Russian Revolution, 103. The Soviet poorly mapped onto party affiliations, frustrating not only Chernov.

36. Boyd, "Origins of Order Number 1"; Shlyapnikov, Semnatsadtyi god, I: 170; Wildman, End of the Russian Imperial Army, I: 189.

37. Hasegawa, February Revolution, 396.

38. Izvestiia, March 2, 1917; Golder, Documents of Russian History, 386–7; Browder and Kerensky, Russian Provisional Government, II: 848–9; Shliapnikov, Semnatsadtyi god, I: 212–3; Zlokazov, Petrogradskii Sovet rabochikh, 58–62; Miller, Soldatskie komitety russkoi arm, 25–30. See also the slightly different version in Pravda, March 9, 1917.

39. Medlin and Powers, V. D. Nabokov, 88; Shliapnikov, Semnadtsatyi god, II: 236; Gapoenko, Revoliutsionnoe dvizhenie, 429–30. Guchkov himself would go in May.

40. Golder, Documents of Russian History, 386–90; Browder and Kerensky, Russian Provisional Government, II: 851–4. Order No. 2 was not published in the main Soviet organ. Order No. 3, which was published, reiterated the ban on officers' elections. Izvestiia, March 8, 1917.

41. Prince E. N. Trubetskoi, a member of the Cadets, captured elite hopes, too, writing that "everyone has

participated in the revolution, everyone has made it: the proletariat, the military, the bourgeoisie, and even the nobility." Rech', March 5, 1917. On elite fears, see Pipes, Russian Revolution, 289.

42. Purishkevich, Bez zabrala, 3–4. It was also printed in Moscow and Mogilyov, and circulated in typescript to the army and fleet.

43. Purishkevich, Vpered!; Moskovskie vedmoosti, July 23, 1917: 1–3. See also P. Sh. Chkhartishvili, "Chernosotentsy v 1917 godu," Voprosy istorii, 1997, no. 8: 133–43.

44. Rendle, Defenders of the Motherland.

45. Novaia zhizn', June 29, 1917. Gorky had worked on a barge.

46. Daulet, "The First All-Muslim Congress of Russia"; Davletshin, Sovetskii Tatarstan, 64–5; Rorlich, Volga Tatars, 127–9; Dimanshtein, Revoliutsiia i natsional'nyi vopros, III: 294–5.

47. "The great task is accomplished!" the Provisional Government declared on March 6, 1917. "A new, free Russia is born." Vestnik vremmenogo pravitel'stva, March 7, 1917, in Browder and Kerensky, Russian Provisional Government, I: 158; Rech', March 8, 1917: 5; Stepun, Byvshee i nebyvsheesia, II: 48–9.

48. Leonard Schapiro, "The Political Thought of the First Provisional Government," in Pipes, Revolutionary Russia, 97–113; White, "Civil Rights," 287–312.

49. Rechi A. F. Kerenskogo (Kiev, 1917), 8. In April 1917 Kerensky said to frontline soldiers, "We can play a colossal role in world history if we manage to cause other nations to traverse our path." A. F. Kerenskii ob armii i voine (Odessa, 1917), 10, 32; Rech' A. F. Kerenskogo, voennogo i morskogo ministra, tovarishcha predsedatelia Petrogradskogo Soveta rabochikh i sol- datskikh deputatov, proiznesennaia im 29 aprelia, v soveshchanii delegatov fronta (Moscow, 1917), 3; Pitcher, Witnesses, 61. Irakli Tsereteli, Soviet leader, envisioned "the final victory of democracy inside the country and beyond its borders." Tsereteli, Vospominaniia, I: 147.

50. "At present," observed the eminent scholar and Cadet politician Vladimir Vernadsky in May 1917, "we have democracy without the organization of society." Holquist, Making War, 49 (citing Rech', May 3, 1917).

51. Classical liberals, too, quickly rediscovered the importance of "state consciousness" (gosudarstvennost'). Rosenberg, Liberals, 134–69; Holquist, Making War, 49–51.

52. Anton Denikin, who fought side by side with Kornilov in Habsburg Galicia, remarked that "he was extremely

resolute in conducting the most difficult and even apparently doomed operations. He had uncommon personal bravery, which inordinately impressed his soldiers and made him extremely popular with them." Denikin, Ocherki russkoi smuty, 145–6. See also Kerensky, The Catastrophe, 297.

53. Kerensky, "Lenin's Youth—and My Own," 69. Later, Kerensky would go so far as to claim that "after old Ulianoff's death, my father, by virtue of his close association with the Ulianoff family, had become the family's guardian." Kerensky, The Catastrophe, 79.

54. Chernov, Great Russian Revolution, 174.

55. Kolonitskii, "Kerensky," 138–49; Kolonitskii, "'Democracy' in the Consciousness of the February Revolution"; Stankevich, Vospominaniia, 65.

56. Lauchlan, Russian Hide-and-Seek, 48; White, "Civil Rights," 295.

57. "To him came the honest and the dishonest, the sincere and the intriguing, political leaders, and military leaders, and adventurers," wrote General Denikin, "and all with one voice cried: Save us!" Trotsky, History of the Russian Revolution [1961], 463.

58. Fitzpatrick, "The Civil War," 57–76 (at 74).

59. Daniels, Red October, 12–3.

60. Sigler, "Kshesinskaia's Mansion"; Hall, Imperial Dancer; Trotsky, History of the Russian Revolution, III; 58–61. Armed bands seized the property in March 1917. Krzesińska's lawyer appealed to the Provisional Government for redress, to no avail, but she did win a favorable ruling from the courts (the order for eviction of the Bolsheviks did not come until June and it was not immediately enforced).

61. Kshesinskaia, Vospominaniia, 191.

62. Reacting to rumors that the villa had become a nest of orgies, witches' Sabbaths, and gun stockpiling, the police, with agreement of the Petrograd Soviet, evicted the occupants. "Numbering in all about a hundred, they were the lowest dregs of humanity from the slums of Petrograd, clad in tatters and with evil-looking faces bearing every sign of debauchery and vice," recalled Boris Nikitin, the head of the Counter-Intelligence Bureau, which was itself subject to scurrilous rumor. He added: "Most of them had obviously not used soap and water for years. . . . Among the prisoners were about thirty who might, from their clothing, have been women." Nikitin, Fatal Year, 82–98; Sukhanov, Russian Revolution, II: 386–8.

63. Vestnik istorii, 1957, no. 4: 826.

64. Bennigsen and Wimbush, Muslim National Communism, 16.

65. Wade, "Why October?"

66. The Provisional Government, in

March, had discussed whether, if Lenin were to return, to allow him in the country. Medlin and Powers, *V. D. Nabokov*, 143.

67. Lenin's trip across the front lines was arranged by Jacob Fürstenberg, alias Ganetsky, an Austrian-Polish socialist with a smuggling business who worked for Alexander Helphand, known as Parvus, a Minsk-born Jew, German Social Democrat, holder of a doctorate, and a war profiteer. Yevgeniya Sumenson, who was arrested in July 1917 by the Provisional Government counterintelligence, confirmed she handled money, including receiving more than 2 million rubles all told from Ganetsky. After February 1917, Lenin's correspondence with Ganetsky is said to have been exceeded only by letters with Inessa Armand. Shub, *Lenin*, 182; Mel'gunov, "Zolotoi nemetskii klyuchik," 157; Hahlweg, *Lenins Rückkehr nach Russland*, 15–6; *PSS*, XLIX: 406; Krupskaya, *Memories of Lenin*, II: 200–12. Ganetsky continued to run financial errands for Lenin once the Bolsheviks were in power, but in 1937 he was arrested, tortured, and executed as a Polish-German spy and Trotskyite; in fact, Stalin had sent Ganetsky to Poland in September 1933 to retrieve a Lenin archive. Volkogonov, *Lenin: Life and Legacy*, 127–8. The idea of approaching the Germans may originally have been Martov's.

68. Scheidemann, *Memoiren enies Sozialdemokraten*, 427–8; Freund, *Unholy Alliance*, 1.

69. At the German border, the passengers switched to a two-carriage train (one for the Russians, one for their German escorts), for a trip to a Baltic port, boarded a Swedish steamer for Sweden, whence by train they headed for Finland, traveled across the Finnish border in sledges, and boarded a final train for twenty miles to Petrograd. Platten, *Die Reise Lenins*, 56; Zinov'ev, *God revoliutsii*, 503; Hahlweg, *Lenins Rückkehr nach Russland*, 99–100; Shliapnikov, *Kanun semnadtsatogo goda*, II: 77–8; Karl Radek, *Living Age*, February 25, 1922: 451; Senn, *Russian Revolution in Switzerland*, 224–8. Radek remained in Stockholm through October.

70. Martov and his Menshevik comrades waited for official Russian foreign ministry permission and landed back in Russia around a month after Lenin, May 9, 1917, leaving other Mensheviks already in Russia to respond to the challenge of Lenin's April theses. Getzler, *Martov*, 147–50.

71. Katkov, "German Foreign Office Documents."

72. G. Ia. Sokol'nikov, "Avtobiografiia," in Sokol'nikov, *Novaia finansovaia politika*, 39–50 (at 42).

73. Paléologue, *La Russie*, III: 305, 307–8. Much later, Miliukov would write in his memoirs that at the time, he had no knowledge of Lenin's "new" stance. Miliukov, *Vospominaniia*, I: 337.

74. Andreev, *Vospominaniia*, 52–5.

75. Pallot, *Land Reform in Russia*; Pozhigailo, *P. A. Stolypin*. Those who argue that on the eve of the war the land question in Russia was being ameliorated have a point. Frank, "The Land Question."

76. Less than half of the gentry (perhaps one or two of every five) lived on the land in 1914. Becker, *Nobility and Privilege*, 28.

77. One scholar observed that "the generals seemed to be talking and acting like revolutionaries." Yaney, *Urge to Mobilize*, 418.

78. Kotel'nikov and Mueller, *Krest'ianskoe dvizhenie*; Lohr, *Nationalizing the Russian Empire*; Ivan Sobolev, *Bor'ba s "nemetskim zasiliem."* The Orthodox Church and the crown (imperial household) also owned considerable land.

79. Shanin, *Awkward Class*, 145–61.

80. Keller and Romanenko, *Pervye itogi agrarnoi reformy*, 105.

81. "The Peasants' Revolution," in Daniels, *Russian Revolution*, 87–91. Perhaps the most intriguing rendering of the peasant revolution can be found in the fictional Zamyatin, "Comrade Churygin Has the Floor," 193–203.

82. Antsiferov, *Russian Agriculture*, 290–6; Keep, *Russian Revolution*, 211–2.

83. Figes writes of a localized and locally oriented response to an urban-based, largely unsympathetic government. He also notes that the peasants drove out the gentry via land seizures but did not overturn the traditional institutions of local governance. Figes, *Peasant Russia*, 42, 66–7.

84. Channon, "Tsarist Landowners." By late 1927, upward of 10,750 former gentry still lived on their estates in the RSFSR, but more than 4,000 were evicted, placing more land in peasant hands. Danilov, *Rural Russia*, 98.

85. Pipes, *Russian Revolution*, 717–8; Kim, *Istoriia Sovetskogo krest'ianstva*, 16; Danilov, *Pereraspredelenie zemel'nogo fonda Rossii*, 283–7; Atkinson, *End of the Russian Land Commune*, 178–80; Maliavskii, *Krest'ianskoe dvizhenie*.

86. Harding, *Leninism*, 92–5.

87. "Protokoly i rezoliutsii Biuro TsK RSDRP (b) (mart 1917 g.)," *Vestnik istorii KPSS*, 1962, no. 3: 143; Tucker, *Stalin as Revolutionary*, 163; Ulam, *Stalin*, 132–4.

88. *Pravda*, March 15, 1917. Molotov would recall that Kamenev and Stalin "expelled me because they had more authority and were ten years older." Chuev, *Molotov Remembers*, 91.

89. Shliapnikov, *Semnadtsatyi god*, I: 219–20; Slusser, *Stalin in October*, 46–8. Stalin later apologized for his "mistaken stance" upon arriving back in the capital in March 1917. *Sochineniia*, VI: 333.

90. Raskol'nikov, *Kronshtadt i piter*, 54.

91. Lih, "The Ironic Triumph of 'Old Bolshevism.'"

92. Kamenev, *Mezhdu dvumia revoliutsiiami*.

93. Burdzhalov, *Vestnik istorii*, 1956, no. 4: 51; Poletaev, *Revoliutsionnoe dvizhenie*, 15–6; Tucker, *Stalin as Revolutionary*, 168.

94. *PSS*, XXXI: 72–8; Slusser, *Stalin in October*, 60; Trotsky, *History of the Russian Revolution* [1961], 312–3. The day after publication, April 8, a meeting of the Bolshevik Petersburg City Committee voted 13 to 2 to reject Lenin's position. (The Bolshevik committee in the capital did not change its name to Petrograd.)

95. Tsapenko, *Vserossiiskoe soveshchanie soveta rabochikh*; *Revoliutsiia 1917 goda*, I: 114, 162–3. "It's simply shit!" Lenin shouted, while in exile reading a speech by Chkheidze, head of the Petrograd Soviet. "Vladimir, what language!" Krupskaya supposedly interjected. Lenin: "I repeat: shit!" Futrell, *Northern Underground*, 154.

96. Sukhanov, *Zapiski*, III: 26–7, VII: 44.

97. "Russia *at the moment*," Lenin stated, "is the freest of all the belligerent countries in the world," and the revolutionaries had to use this liberty to their advantage. *PSS*, XXXI: 113–6; Daniels, *Red October*, 4; Service, *Lenin*, II: 157.

98. *Leninskii sbornik*, VII: 307–8. No transcript of either the speech or discussion survives, but we have Lenin's notes for the speech: *Leninskii sbornik*, XXI: 33. See also Raskol'nikov, *Na boevykh postakh*, 67.

99. Abramovitch, *Soviet Revolution*, 30.

100. Sukhanov, *Russian Revolution*, I: 287.

101. Uglanov, "O Vladimire Iliche Lenine." Back in 1905, Martov had allowed that in the coming bourgeois revolution, the socialists could take power, but only if the revolution were in danger. In 1917, Martov twisted himself in knots trying to distinguish between a struggle for power (*vlast'*) and for government (*pravitel'stvo*). Getzler, *Martov*, 167 (citing *Iskra*, March 17, 1905, and *Rabochaia gazeta*, August 22, 1917).

102. Service, *Bolshevik Party in Revolution*, 53–7. Many provincials were not in the least Leninist and had to be browbeaten to set aside their desire to reunite with Mensheviks.

103. Ulricks, "The 'Crowd' in the Russian Revolution"; Trotsky, *History of*

the Russian Revolution [1961], 124–66 (esp. 130–1).
104. No *contemporary* source places Stalin there. Trotsky, who was not yet a Bolshevik, also was absent. Slusser, *Stalin in October*, 49–52; Trotsky, *Stalin*, 194. Only later was Stalin inserted, either in the group who had boarded Lenin's train on the Russian side of the Finnish-Russian border (Beloostrov), or as head of the welcoming party at the Finland Station. On Stalin's later insertion, see Zinoviev, "O puteshestvii," *Pravda*, April 16, 1924; Yaroslavsky, *Landmarks*, 94; and Chuev, *Molotov Remembers*, 93. Molotov, late in life, was perhaps "remembering" the Soviet painting of Lenin alighting on the platform with Stalin behind him.
105. "This was a profound mistake, for it implanted pacifist illusions, added grist to the mill of defensism and hindered the revolutionary propagandizing of the masses." *Sochineniia*, VI: 333.
106. Reprinted in Volin, *Sed'maia*, ix–x.
107. Stalin, "Zemliu krest'ianam," *Pravda*, April 14, 1917, reprinted in *Sochineniia*, III: 34–6.
108. Service, *Stalin*, 128; Service, *Lenin*, II: 223–8.
109. *VII aprel'skaia vserossiiskaia konferentsiia*, 225–8, 323.
110. Chuev, *Molotov*, 216–7, 297. This is a slightly enlarged version of Chuev, *Sto sorok*. Chuev, *Molotov Remembers*, 93.
111. Allilueva, *Vospominaniia*, 185–90.
112. Alliluyeva, *Twenty Letters*, 90–4; Tutaev, *Alliluyev Memoirs*, 131–45, 168–75, 211–15.
113. Vasileva, *Kremlin Wives*, 56–8; Allilueva, *Vospominaniia*, 183–91; Kun, *Unknown Portrait*, 211–5; Montefiore, *Young Stalin*, ch. 40.
114. Trotsky, *Stalin*, 207–9. Elsewhere Trotsky called Stalin "a strong, but theoretically and politically primitive, organizer." Trotsky, *History of the Russian Revolution*, I: 288.
115. *VII aprel'skaia vserossiiskaia konferentsiia; Petrogradskaia obshchegorodskaia konferentsiia RSDRP (bol'shevikov)*, 324; *Pravda*, April 24–May 2, 1917. Word of the figure of Sverdlov had reached Lenin in exile, and the Bolshevik leader tried to correspond with him and bring him to party gatherings outside tsarist Russia, but the two did not meet until 1917. Duvall, "The Bolshevik Secretariat," 47 (citing L. D. Trotsky, *Selected Works*, II: 292).
116. "Iz perepiski Sverdlova," *Pechat' i revoliutsiia*, 1924, no. 2: 64; Trotsky, *Stalin*; Wolfe, *Three Who Made a Revolution*, 623; *Iakov Mikhailovich Sverdlov* (1926).
117. *Perepiska sekretariata TsK RSDRP*

*(b)*, I: v–ix; S. Pestkovskii, "Vospominaniia o rabote v Narkomnatse," 126; Trotskii, *Sochineniia*, VIII: 251, XXI: 336; N. Bukharin, "Tovarishch Sverdlov," *Pravda*, March 18, 1919: 1.
118. White, *Socialist Alternative to Bolshevik Russia*, 15.
119. Oskar Anweiler, "The Political Ideology of the Leaders of the Petrograd Soviet in the Spring of 1917," in Pipes, *Revolutionary Russia*, 114–28; Anin, "The February Revolution." On coalition government, see Tsereteli, *Vospominaniia*, II: 401–17.
120. Broido, *Lenin and the Mensheviks*, 14–5. Leonard Schapiro saw the moderate socialist weakness in terms of having scruples: *Origin of the Communist Autocracy* [1956]. Orlando Figes sees the clinging to a bourgeois revolution strategy as destructive of a lost democratic socialist outcome, rather than as tilting at the wrong windmill: *A People's Tragedy*, 331.
121. Miliukov, *Istoriia vtoroi*, I/iii: 3–6; Miliukov, *The Russian Revolution*, III: 1–4. On May 22, Kerensky told the Petrograd Soviet, "parties do not exist for me at the present moment because I am a Russian minister; for me only the people exist and one sacred law—to obey the majority will." Radkey, *Agrarian Foes*, 225. In the provinces, "coalition" worked only briefly: local committees of public organizations arose under liberal auspices and recognized the place, and sometimes the supremacy, of organizations representing workers, soldiers, and peasants, but soon the committees succumbed to governance and economic chaos. Class-based suspicions assumed free rein. Rosenberg, *Liberals*, 59–66; White, "Civil Rights," 290–3 (citing GARF, f. 1788, op. 2, d. 64).
122. Figes and Kolonitskii, *Interpreting the Russian Revolution*, 102.
123. Mel'gunov, *Martovskie dni*, 105–13; Anin, "The February Revolution," 441.
124. Kerensky would recall the "spirit of unity, fraternity, mutual confidence and self-sacrifice" in the Tauride during the early days, lamenting that "afterwards . . . more and more among us turned out to be men with personal ambitions, men with an eye to the main chance, or mere adventurers." In fact, while Karlo Chkheidze followed the Soviet's policy and refused to be considered for a Provisional Government portfolio, Kerensky, after the central executive committee denied his request to serve in the Provisional Government, burst into the Soviet meeting on March 2 and exclaimed, "Comrades! Do you trust me?" He pretended to faint and elicited an ovation, which appeared to bless his acceptance of the post of justice minister. Thus did Kerensky become the only person in both the Soviet and the Provisional

Government. The leadership of the Petrograd Soviet never forgave Kerensky for his manipulation bordering on blackmail. *Izvestiia revoliutsionnoi nedeli*, March 3, 1917; Sverchkov, *Kerenskii*, 21; Kerensky, *The Catastrophe*, 21, 52–61.
125. Keep, "1917."
126. Browder and Kerensky, *Russian Provisional Government*, III: 1305. Majorities at the June Congress of Soviets voted for the Soviet's policy of support for the Provisional Government and for the war. Irakli Tsereteli, by then Minister of Posts and Telegraph, observed that there was no party prepared to assume the responsibilities of governing by itself. "There is!" Lenin rebutted him. The hall erupted in laughter. *PSS*, XXXI: 267; Service, *Lenin*, II: 181.
127. Chamberlin, *Russian Revolution*, I: 159; Keep, *Russian Revolution*, 131–2.
128. The fact that the socialists were pro-peace helped make peace unpalatable to Russia's liberals. It would be "absurd and criminal to renounce the biggest prize of the war . . . in the name of some humanitarian and cosmopolitan idea of international socialism," Miliukov remarked. Richard Stites, "Miliukov and the Russian Revolution," foreword to Miliukov and Stites, *The Russian Revolution*, xii. As Clausewitz observed, war and classical liberalism did not mix well. Von Clausewitz, *On War*, 85.
129. Miliukov behaved as his usual self-defeatingly stubborn self, but Kerensky admitted his own role in bringing "the whole matter to a head." Kerensky, *The Kerensky Memoirs*, 246. Prime Minister Prince Lvov formed a "coalition," that is, he took some leaders of the Soviet (besides Kerensky) into the Provisional Government, prompting Guchkov to resign in protest, and fatefully allowing Kerensky to assume the war portfolio. Browder and Kerensky, *Russian Provisional Government*, III: 1045 (*Rech'*, March 28, 1917: 2), III: 1098 (*Rech'*, April 20, 1917: 4); Sukhanov, *Zapiski*, III: 254–443 (esp. 304–7); Miliukov, *Istoriia vtoroi*, I/i: 91–117; Wade, *Russian Search for Peace*, 38–48. Prince L'vov, *Rech'*, March 28, 1917: 2, in Browder and Kerensky, *Russian Provisional Government*, III: 1045. *Russkie vedomosti*, May 2, 1917: 5, in Browder and Kerensky, III: 1267. "There was no end of disputes between Kerensky and myself at the Cabinet sessions, as to the line to be taken in foreign policy and in general policies," Miliukov wrote of his two months as foreign minister. Miliukov, "From Nicholas II to Stalin."
130. Heenan, *Russian Democracy's Fatal Blunder*, 11–21. See also Rutherford, *The Tsar's War*.

131. Pedroncini, *Les mutineries de 1917*; Smith, *Between Mutiny and Obedience*. Those who blame the Allies for Bolshevism, because of their insistence on Russia mounting an offensive, are partly correct. Wheeler-Bennet, *Forgotten Peace*, 51-2, 292.
132. In mid-April, General Alexeyev had returned from the front to brief the Provisional Government (the meeting took place in War Minister Guchkov's private apartment, because he was ill), and told a story of the anarchic mood of the army and the collapse of discipline. Medlin and Powers, *V. D. Nabokov*, 135, 140.
133. Shliapnikov, *Semnadtsatyi god*, III: 291-3 (March 30, 1917, to Guchkov).
134. Brusilov, *Soldier's Note-book*. See also "The Diary of General Boldyrev," in Vulliamy, *From the Red Archives*, 189-26.
135. Heenan, *Russian Democracy's Fatal Blunder*, 51-2.
136. In one version of his memoirs, Kerensky conceded that when he visited the front in 1917, he sensed that "after three years of bitter suffering, millions of war-weary soldiers were asking themselves: 'Why should I have to die now when at home a new, freer life is only just beginning?'" He also claimed to have found "a healthy patriotism" among some, which he wanted to encourage. Kerensky, *The Kerensky Memoirs*, 276-7. For Kerensky's efforts to balance inevitable concessions to "democracy" in the army with maintaining fighting capacity, see Browder and Kerensky, *Russian Provisional Government*, II: 882.
137. Stankevich, *Vospominaniia*, 246. See also Heenan, *Russian Democracy's Fatal Blunder*, 54; and Wilcox, *Russia's Ruin*, 196-7.
138. Pethybridge, *Spread of the Russian Revolution*, 154-70 (esp. 161).
139. Wildman, *End of the Russian Imperial Army*, II: 53 (Radko-Dmitriev, Commander of the Twelfth Army).
140. Lewis, *Eyewitness World War I*, 279.
141. Viktor Shklovsky, a commissar to the army for the Provisional Government, wrote of an escape from reality into "trench Bolshevism." Shklovsky, *Sentimental Journey*, 60. "The magnitude of the Bolshevik achievement at the front," one historian has written, "was truly spectacular." Wildman, *End of the Russian Imperial Army*, II: 264. See also Ferro, "The Russian Soldier in 1917."
142. Tsereteli, *Vospominaniia*, I: 364-681. On March 14, 1917, the Petrograd Soviet had passed "An appeal to all peoples of the world" denouncing the imperialist war and annexationist aims. *Izvestiia*, March 15, 1917: 1, in

Browder and Kerensky, *Russian Provisional Government*, III: 1077.
143. Fainsod, *International Socialism*; Forster, *Failures of the Peace*, 113-25; Wade, *Russian Search for Peace*, 17-25; Wade, "Argonauts of Peace"; Kirby, *War, Peace, and Revolution*; Sukhanov, *Zapiski*, II: 336-42. Sukhanov gives a portrait of Tsereteli (*Zapiski*, III: 131-8).
144. *Pravda*, April 29, 1917. See also Wildman, *End of the Russian Imperial Army*, I: 38.
145. The Soviet had compelled the Provisional Government to promise not to remove troops from the capital and send them to the front (so as to dampen the revolution). Brusilov, *A Soldier's Note-book*, 291.
146. Wade, "Why October?," 42-3.
147. Browder and Kerensky, *Russian Provisional Government*, II: 1120-1; Getzler, *Martov*, 149-52. It remains unclear how sincerely the Provisional Government intended its June 3, 1917, public profession of a desire to organize an inter-Allied conference to review the war treaties.
148. Ignat'ev, *Russko-angliiskie otnosheniia nakanune*), 42, 48, 50-1; *Berner Tagwacht* [Bern], October 11, 13, 14, 1916. See also Heenan, *Russian Democracy's Fatal Blunder*, 8-9. The German side had indicated a willingness to cede Habsburg Galicia and Bukovina and the Turkish Straits, provided the Russian army managed to occupy them, but in return Germany sought Courland (Latvia) and a protectorate over predominantly Polish-speaking territories. By contrast, Allied victory over Germany promised Russia all that and more—Bukovina, Turkish Armenia, parts of Persia—for nothing in exchange.
149. Browder and Kerensky, *Russian Provisional Government*, II: 967; Feldman, "The Russian General Staff." As in 1916, Brusilov, now supreme commander, used "shock troops" to spearhead the assault, trailed by conscript peasant infantry.
150. Fuller, *Foe Within*, 237-8; Knox, *With the Russian Army*, II: 462.
151. Sir Alfred Knox wrote of the July offensive that Russia's army was "irretrievably lost as a fighting organization." Knox, *With the Russian Army*, II: 648.
152. "The worst thing about the committees was that in no time at all they lost contact with those who elected them," wrote the Provisional Government front commissar Viktor Shklovsky. He added that "the [frontline] delegates to the Soviet did not show up in their units for months at a time. The soldiers were left completely ignorant of what was happening in the Soviets." Shklovsky, *Sentimental Journey*, 18.

153. Figes, *A People's Tragedy*, 380. British media tycoon Lord Beaverbrook asked Kerensky in June 1931, "Would you have mastered the Bolsheviks if you had made a separate peace?" Kerensky replied, "Of course, we should be in Moscow right now." Beaverbrook posed the logical follow-up: "Then why didn't you do it?" "We were too naive," Kerensky answered. Lockhart, *British Agent*, 177.
154. David Bronstein would be expropriated during revolution; Trotsky had set him up as the manager of a requisitioned flour mill near Moscow, but in 1922 he would die of typhus.
155. Ziv, *Trotskii*, 12. See also Carr, *Socialism in One Country*, I: 163; and Volkogonov, *Trotsky*, 5.
156. "Terrorizim i kommunizm," reprinted in Trotskii, *Sochineniia*, XII: at 59.
157. Buchanan, *My Mission to Russia*, II: 120-1.
158. Reed, *Ten Days* [1919], 21. "Trotsky entered the history of our party somewhat unexpectedly and with instant brilliance," Anatoly Lunacharsky would write. *Revolutionary Silhouettes*, 59.
159. Trotsky, *My Life*, 295-6.
160. Moisei Uritsky, quoted in Lunacharskii, *Revoliutsionnye siluety*, 24.
161. *Leninskii sbornik*, IV: 303; Balabanoff, *Impressions of Lenin*, 127-8; Sukhanov, *Zapiski*, VII: 44; Raskol'nikov, "V tiur'me Kerenskogo," 150-2; Slusser, *Stalin in October*, 108-14; Liberman, *Building Lenin's Russia*, 76.
162. Frenkin, *Zakhvat vlasti bol'shevikami*; Stankevich, *Vospominaniia*, 147-8; Denikin, *Ocherki russkoi smuty*, II: 127ff; Pipes, *Formation of the Soviet Union*, 52-6; Shankowsky, "Disintegration of the Imperial Russian Army," esp. 321-2.
163. The crowd bundled Chernov into a vehicle and declared him "arrested." Trotsky rushed outside and got Chernov released. Miliukov, *Istoriia vtoroi*, I/i: 243-4; Sukhanov, *Zapiski*, IV: 444-7; Vladimirovna, "Iiul'skie dni," 34-5; Raskol'nikov, "V iiul'skie dni," 69-71; Rabinowitch, *Prelude*, 188. The regiment from nearby Tsarskoe Selo, sent to arrest the Soviet leadership, is said to have instead decided to guard the Tauride. Sukhanov, *Zapiski*, IV: 448-9.
164. Sukhanov, *Zapiski*, IV: 511-2; Nikitin, *Rokovye gody*, 148; Zinoviev, *Proletarskaia revoliutsiia*, 1927, no. 8-9: 62; *Pravda*, July 17, 1927: 3 (F. F. Raskol'nilov); *Krasnaia gazeta*, July 16, 1920: 2 (Mikhail Kalinin); *Petrogradskaia Pravda*, July 17, 1921: 3 (G. Veinberg); *VI s"ezed RSDRP*, 17 (Stalin); Trotsky, *History of the Russian Revolution*, II: 13; *PSS*, XXXII: 408-9; Drachkovitch and Lazitch, *Lenin and*

the Comintern, I: 95 (citing Trotsky, Bulletin Communiste, May 20, 1920: 6); Buchanan, Petrograd, 131–46 (Buchanan was the daughter of the British ambassador). See also Rabinowitch, Prelude, 174–5.

165. Between July 7 and July 24, the Bolsheviks could not publish their daily newspaper in Petrograd. Budnikov, Bol'shevistskaia partiinaia; Volkogonov, Trotsky, 197; Kolonitskii, "Anti-Bourgeois Propaganda," 184. Lenin is said to have had the Provisional Government dossier on Bolshevik high treason destroyed. Be that as it may, surviving German documents prove German financing beyond a shadow of a doubt. Zeman, Germany and the Revolution in Russia, 94; Latyshev, Rassekrechennyi Lenin; Volkogonov, Lenin: politicheskii portret, I: 220–2; Hahlweg, Lenins Rückkehr nach Russland. That said, the sixty-six telegrams between Petrograd and Stockholm gathered by the Provisional Government's justice ministry for the trial in July 1917 have been debunked as forgeries (by former okhranka operatives). Semyon Lyandres, "The Bolsheviks' 'German Gold' Revisited: An Inquiry into the 1917 Accusations," Carl Beck Papers, 1995; Kennan, "The Sisson Documents"; Stone, "Another Look"; Hill, Go Spy the Land, 200–1.

166. Trotskii, O Lenine, 58; Trotsky, History of the Russian Revolution, III: 127. The Provisional Government supposedly saved the most sensational documents for a public trial.

167. Nikitin, Rokovye gody, 115–6, 122-3; Vaksberg, Stalin's Prosecutor, 13–27. For the specific charges, see Rech', July 22, 1917, translated in Browder and Kerensky, Russian Provisional Government, III: 1370–7.

168. Allilueva, Vospominaniia, 181–90; Volkogonov, Stalin: Triumph and Tragedy, 24–6; Slusser, Stalin in October, 162–78, 139–50; Service, Lenin, 283–91; Kerensky, The Catastrophe, 229–44. Many Mensheviks pressed for Bolshevik release, with the reasoning that today it would be the Bolsheviks, tomorrow the whole Soviet.

169. Polan, Lenin and the End of Politics.

170. After the public accusations of taking German money, which Lenin denied as lies, he did become more careful. Volkogonov, Lenin: Life and Legacy, 116–21. The case against Lenin in the Provisional Government was managed by Pavel A. Aleksandrov, who would be arrested in April 1939 (and held in Butyrka). He supposedly testified that he had worked closely with Kerensky on the Lenin case of "state treason" and "espionage." NKVD investigators deemed Aleksandrov's investigative work against Bolshevism "a fabrication," and it is said Beria had

his men retrieve archival documents of the Provisional Government to incriminate Aleksandrov for his work. Hoover Institution Archives, Volkogonov papers, container 3, Postanovlenie from Kobulov, April 16, 1939.

171. Novaia zhizn', August 5, 1917 (A. S. Zarudnyi); Zhivoe slovo, July 6, 1917: 1; Avdeev, Revoliutsiia 1917 goda, III: 167; Polovtsoff, Glory and Downfall, 256–8.

172. Pol'ner, Zhiznennyi put' kniazia Georgiia Evgenevicha L'vova, 258. That same day, Kerensky ordered Nicholas II and the royal family transferred to detention in Siberia (the actual move would be carried out July 31). On July 15, the Provisional Government asserted authority over the "political commissars" that the Soviet sent to frontline units would be parallel to those of the government.

173. Sanborn, "Genesis of Russian Warlordism," 205–6.

174. The general staff conference called for reintroducing the death penalty in the rear, limiting the soldiers' committees to economic and educational functions, and restricting the powers of political commissars in the military. Browder and Kerensky, Russian Provisional Government, II: 989–1010.

175. Denikin, Ocherki russkoi smuti, 446–7; Trotsky, History of the Russian Revolution, II 570; Sukhanov, Zapiski, IV: 469–70.

176. Russkoe slovo, July 21, 1917: 2.

177. Kerensky finally gave approval for the draft decrees to be submitted for cabinet action on August 17. Martynov, Kornilov, 74–5, 100; Kerensky, Prelude to Bolshevism, 27. Kornilov was in the capital twice, on August 3 and August 10. On August 3, he held discussions with Kerensky and the Provisional Government (one newspaper reported that "Kerensky took a deep bow before General Kornilov"), but evidently, when Kornilov began to discuss war plans, Kerensky and Savinkov, sotto voce, told him to be careful. The implication was that Russia's secret war plans would be leaked by some government ministers, as if by enemy agents. Savinkov, K delu, 12–3; Lukomskii, Vospominaniia, I: 227; Loukomsky, Memoirs of the Russian Revolution, 99; Russkoe slovo, August 4, 1917: 2. The Soviet denounced Kornilov and his visit to the capital. Izvestiia, August 4, 1917.

178. Voprosy istorii, 1966, no. 2: at 12–3 (quoting I. G. Korolev).

179. VI s"ezd RSDRP, 250.

180. VI s"ezd RSDRP, 28, 30–6; Sochineniia, III: 17.

181. During the Bolshevik Party Congress, on July 27, the Georgian Bolshevik Grigol "Sergo" Orjonikidze, who was conducting negotiations on Lenin's

possible appearance to stand trial, asked representatives of the St. Petersburg Soviet how they stood vis-à-vis the Provisional Government's arrest order for Lenin as a German spy. The Mensheviks could have exacted sweet revenge, tricking Bolshevik negotiators by claiming they would defend Lenin to the death, then betraying him. But the head of the Soviet's presidium, the Georgian Menshevik Karlo Chkheidze—whom Lenin had demonstratively insulted in April upon returning to Russia—was a man of principle. "If today they arrest Lenin, tomorrow they will arrest me," he said. "The leaders of the Mensheviks and SRs do not believe in the guilt of Lenin.... They should have energetically demanded investigation of the case of Lenin and Zinoviev, but they did not do that.... We should not turn in comrade Lenin under any circumstances ... we should ... safeguard our comrades out of harm's way until they are guaranteed a fair trial." VI s"ezd RSDRP, 310–1.

182. Tyrkova-Williams, From Liberty to Brest Litovsk, 167; Orlovsky, "Corporatism or Democracy," 67–90. A Conference of Public Figures, also in Moscow, held between August 8 and August 10 at the initiative of the industrialist Ryabushinsky and chaired by Rodzyanko, was said to be a venue for discussing a putsch. Some 400 people attended, and many side private meetings took place. Moskovskie vedomosti, August 11, 1917; Sevost'ianova, Delo Generala Kornilova, II: 223–4 (Lvov's testimony); Katkov, The Kornilov Affair, 142–3 (quoting Maklakov).

183. Izvestiia, August 13, 1917. By contrast, see Russkoe slovo, August 12, 13, 14, 15, and 17, 1917.

184. Pokrovskii and Iakovlev, Gosudarstvennoe soveshchanie, 335.

185. Izvestiia, August 13, 1917.

186. Kornilov also spoke with Kerensky by telephone that night. Russkoe slovo, August 15, 1917: 3–4. Kornilov is said to have believed Kerensky did not want him to attend the Conference. Browder and Kerensky, Russian Provisional Government, III: 1546–54 (Lukomsky). Kerensky evidently summoned Kornilov on August 14 before the session. Miliukov, Istoriia vtoroi, I/ii: 134–5; Miliukov, Russian Revolution, II: 108.

187. Holquist, Making War, 90–1 (citing N. M. Mel'nikov, "A. M. Kaledin," Donskaia letopis', 3 vols. [Vienna; Donskaia istoricheskaia komissiia, 1923–4], I: 24–5).

188. Kornilov concluded: "I believe in the genius of the Russian people, I believe in the reason of the Russian people, and I believe in the salvation of the country. I believe in the bright future of our native land, and I believe

that the fighting efficiency of our army and her former glory will be restored. But I declare that there is no time to lose.... Resolve is necessary and the firm, steadfast execution of the measures outlined. (Applause)." Pokrovskii and Iakovlev, *Gosudarstvennoe soveshchanie*, 60–6; Browder and Kerensky, *Russian Provisional Government*, III: 1474–8; Avdeev, *Revoliutsiia 1917 goda*, IV: 54–5.

189. Stalin, "Protiv moskovskogo soveshchaniia," *Rabochii i soldat*, August 8, 1917, in *Sochineniia*, III: 193–5.

190. Stalin, "Kuda vedet moskovskoe soveshchane?" *Proletarii*, August 13, 1917, in *Sochineniia*, III: 200–5 (at 201)

191. "Will the State Conference be able to insist on the implementation of the Supreme Commander's demands or not?" the rightist paper *New Times* had worried at the outset. "Will everything remain as before?" *Novoe vremia*, August 13, 1917: 5. See also *Rech'*, August 12–17, 1917. For all the immediate reactions in the press to Kornilov's speech, see Browder and Kerensky, *Russian Provisional Government*, III: 1515–22. A second conference of public figures would take place in October 12–14, with Rodzyanko again as chairman, remarking "the political horizon of our country has become darker still.... We are called reactionaries, we are called Kornilovists." *Russkie vedomosti*, October 13, 1917: 5; Browder and Kerensky, *Russian Provisional Government*, III: 1745–7.

192. Miliukov, *Russian Revolution*, II: 100; Savich, *Vospominaniia*, 247, 250–1.

193. Kerensky, *Delo Kornilova*, 81. "General Korniloff came to the Moscow Conference in great pomp," Kerensky later wrote. "At the station he was met by the entire elite of the capital.... On the streets of Moscow pamphlets were being distributed, entitled, 'Korniloff, the National hero.'" Kerensky, *The Catastrophe*, 315. See also Miliukov, *Istoriia vtoroi*, II: 133; Miliukov, *Russian Revolution*, II: 107.

194. Dumova, "Maloizvestnye materialy po istorii kornilovshchiny," 78; Savich, *Vospominaniia*, 246–50. See also Rosenberg, *Liberals*, 196–233, who shows Cadet party complicity in as well as division over a possible Kornilov dictatorship. After Kornilov's imprisonment, Miliukov, on the pretext of taking a holiday, would quietly depart the capital. The newspaper he edited, *Rech'*, was now subjected to Provisional Government censorship. *Novoe vremia*, further to the right, was shut down altogether.

195. George Katkov adduced persuasive evidence that Kerensky engaged in a provocation, but Katkov allowed that "we may presume that Kornilov had certain plans in mind in the event of

the government's not taking the desired action." General Lukomsky, a confidant of Kornilov, had admitted just such plans on the part of Kornilov. Katkov, *Russia, 1917*. Katkov, *The Kornilov Affair*, 65; Lukomskii, *Vospominaniia*, I: 228–9; Loukomsky, *Memoirs of the Russian Revolution*, 100–1.

196. That is why some members of the general staff, disgusted as they were, saw no other way to prosecute the war than by cooperating with the distasteful "democratic" forces (soldiers' committees). Wildman, "Officers of the General Staff and the Kornilov Movement."

197. Lukomskii, *Vospominaniia*, I: 228, 232. "Gentlemen," the Savage Division commander Chavachadze had told his men in June 1917, "I am sorry indeed that the young officers who joined our colors recently will have to start their fighting career by doing a rather repulsive sort of police work." Kournakoff, *Savage Squadrons*, 321.

198. Lih, *Lenin*, 140.

199. *Rabochii*, August 25, 1917, in *Sochineniia*, III: 251–5.

200. For an overview, see Munck, *Kornilov Revolt*. Kerensky and his minions shaped most of the historical record on the Kornilov affair. But R. R. Raupakh, a member of the investigatory commission, collected depositions from witnesses in a way to protect Kornilov. Allan K. Wildman, "Officers of the General Staff and the Kornilov Movement," in Frankel, *Revolution in Russia*, 76–101 (at 101, n36). Kornilov was practically the only participant who did not write an account (he died the next year); for Kornilov's September 1917 deposition, see Katkov, *Russia, 1917*, appendix.

201. "The Kornilov affair represented, on the one hand, a reaction against the disintegration of the old army and, on the other, a juncture of two intrigues, which weren't exactly the same but closely interwoven and headed in the same direction"—i.e. Kerensky's and Kornilov's. Shklovsky, *Sentimental Journey*, 63. There is a third view that the affair involved misunderstanding on both sides; misunderstanding there was aplenty, but matters were darker than that.

202. *Russkoe slovo*, August 31, 1917 (N. V. Nekrasov); Martynov, *Kornilov*, 101. Amid the relentless rumors of a Bolshevik coup, August 27 stood out for being the six-month anniversary of the February Revolution, and may have been part of Kornilov's calculations of dates.

203. Avdeev, *Revoliutsiia 1917 goda*, IV: 98. See also Ukraintsev, "A Document on the Kornilov Affair" (Ukraintsev was a member of the Investigatory Commission established by Kerensky

and he punctures Kerensky's account). See also Pipes, *Russian Revolution*, 448–64; and Rabinowitch, *Bolsheviks Come to Power*, 117–27.

204. Lukomskii, *Vospominaniia*, I: 242; Avdeev, *Revoliutsiia 1917 goda*, IV: 100–1; *Novaia zhizn'*, August 31, 1917; Kerenskii, *Delo Kornilova*, 104–5; Abraham, *Kerensky*, 277; Pipes, *Russian Revolution*, 457–9.

205. Chugaev, *Revoliutsionoe dvizhenie*, 446; Golovin, *Rossiiskaia kontrrevoliutsiia*, I/ii: 37; Pipes, *Russian Revolution*, 460.

206. Trotsky, *My Life*, 331.

207. Rabinowitch, *Bolsheviks Come to Power*, 148–9.

208. Krymov is said to have stated that "The last card for saving the motherland has been beaten—living is no longer worthwhile," and to have left a suicide note for Kornilov, but no text survives. Martynov, *Kornilov*, 135–42, 14–51; Avdeev, *Revoliutsiia 1917 goda*, IV: 143, 343–50; Kerenskii, *Delo Kornilova*, 75–6; Browder and Kerensky, *Russian Provisional Government*, III: 1586–9.

209. Stalin, "Protiv soglasheniia s burzhuaziei," *Rabochii*, August 31, 1917, in *Sochineniia*, 236–7. See also Stalin, "My trebuem," *Rabochii*, August 28, 1917, in *Sochineniia*, 256–60.

210. Gilliard, *Thirteen Years*, 243; Steinberg and Khrustalëv, *Fall of the Romanovs*, 198 (for Nicholas II's own diary entry).

211. Officers in the capital had been alerted to prepare to respond. (Rendle, *Defenders of the Motherland*, 182–3.) The officers took little or no action, but then again, there was no action to be taken: the episode had ended even before Krymov had set foot in Petrograd. Therefore, it is not correct that "hard-core support" was "exceedingly slight." (Allan K. Wildman, "Officers of the General Staff and the Kornilov Movement," in Frankel, *Revolution in Russia*, 98.) Also—it must be kept in mind—Kerensky spread lies and deliberately sowed confusion about what was going on, sowing uncertainty and inaction among potential supporters of Kornilov. (Pipes, *Russian Revolution*, 460-1.) For uncertainty among elites about Kornilov, see Rendle, *Defenders of the Motherland*, 234. That said, Wildman is right that Kornilov enjoyed his strongest support among the most senior officers at headquarters, linked as alumni of the general staff academy.

212. "How was it that Kornilov *sent* his troops while he himself sat quietly at headquarters?" Zinaida Gippius observed in her diary during those days. She perceived, in real time, a provocation by Kerensky instead of a Kornilov coup. Gippius, *Siniaia kniga*, 180–1 (August 31, 1917).

213. Kerensky's obvious betrayal of Kornilov was noted at the time by one contemporary correspondent, Harold Williams, a New Zealander. Zohrab, "The Socialist Revolutionary Party," 153–4.

214. Kolonitskii, "Pravoekstremistskie sily," pt. 1: 111–24. Kornilov's supporters among industrialists and financiers in Petrograd and Moscow, meanwhile, may have damaged him by their mutual animosities. White, "The Kornilov Affair."

215. Most of the high command despised the soldiers' committees (soviets), unable to comprehend that the army's disintegration had been partly contained by the committees' advent. Wildman, *End of the Russian Imperial Army*, I: 246.

216. See the analysis of the sympathetic fellow-lawyer, Vladas Stanka [V. B. Stankevich], Kerensky's political commissar-in-chief to the military, who argued that Kerensky's actions, though ultimately ineffective, were the only ones compatible with upholding democratic values. Stankevich, *Vospominaniia*, 215–22. See also Keep, *Soviet Studies*.

217. Nielsen and Weil, *Russkaia revoliutsiia glazami Petrogradskogo chinovnika*, 9 (September 19, 1917).

218. Golovin, *Rossiiskaia kontrrevoliutsiia*, I/ii: 71, 101. Pipes cites, as final verdict on Kornilov's motives, the observations of the British eyewitness. Wilcox, *Russia's Ruin*, 276; Pipes, *Russian Revolution*, 464.

219. Alexeyev apparently had accepted in order to try to protect Kornilov and other arrested traitors. Ivanov, *Kornilovshcina i ee razgrom*, 207.

220. "The prestige of Kerensky and the Provisional Government," wrote Kerensky's wife, "was completely destroyed by the Kornilov Affair; and he was left with almost no supporters." Figes, *A People's Tragedy*, 455 (quoting O. L. Kerenskaia, "Otryvki vospominanii," 8, in House of Lords Record Office). The Directory endured until September 25, when it was replaced by the so-called third coalition (and final incarnation) of the Provisional Government. Browder and Kerensky, *Russian Provisional Government*, II: 1659–61.

221. At the Third All-Russia Congress of trade unions in Petrograd on June 20–28, 1917, the Bolsheviks claimed 73 delegates out of 211; the Mensheviks, SRs, and other moderate socialists had a majority that defeated Bolshevik motions against cooperation with the "bourgeoisie." *Tret'ia Vserossiiskaia konferentsiia professional'nykh soiuzov* (Moscow: VTsSPS, 1917). In the June 1917 municipal elections in Moscow, the SRs had triumphed (58 percent); the Bolsheviks came in fourth, after

the Cadets and Mensheviks. Colton, *Moscow*, 83.

222. Duvall, "The Bolshevik Secretariat," 57; Steklov, *Bortsy za sotsializm*, II: 397–8; Ia. S. Sheynkman, "Sverdlov," *Puti revoliutsii* [Kazan], 1922, no. 1: 7; Podvoiskii, *Krasnaia gvardiia*, 23; Sverdlova, *Iakov Mikhailovich Sverdlov* [1957], 301, 336; Sverdlov, *Izbrannye proizvedennye*, II: 38, 48–9, 277; Schapiro, *Communist Party*, 173. Sukhanov's wife Galina worked in Sverdlov's secretariat.

223. Sukhanov, *Zapiski*, I: 201.

224. Lih, "The Ironic Triumph of 'Old Bolshevism,'" (citing *Listovki Moskovskoi organizatsii bol'shevikov, 1914–1925 gg.* [Moscow: Politcheskaia literatura, 1954]).

225. Mel'gunov, *Bolshevik Seizure of Power*, 4.

226. Kerensky, *The Catastrophe*, 321; Trotskii, *Istoriia russkoi revoliutsii*, II: 136–40; Chamberlin, *Russian Revolution*, I: 277; Wildman, *End of the Russian Imperial Army*, II: 185; Kolonitskii, "Kerensky," 146.

227. Stalin, "Svoim putem," *Rabochii put'*, September 6, 1917, in *Sochineniia*, III: 272–4.

228. Stalin, "Dve linii," *Rabochii put'*, September 16, 1917, in *Sochineniia*, III: 293–5.

229. V. I. Lenin, "Letter to the Bolshevik Central Committee, the Moscow and Petrograd Committees and the Bolsheviks Members of the Moscow and Petrograd Soviets," in *Selected Works*, II: 390. See also Volkogonov, *Lenin: Life and Legacy*, xxxi (RGASPI, f. 2, op. 1, d. 4269, l. 1); and *PSS*, XXXIV: 435–6.

230. Browder and Kerensky, *Russian Provisional Government*, III: 1641–2.

231. "Every discussion in a public place in Russia now concerns food," wrote one foreigner after having traveled the Volga valley. Price and Rose, *Dispatches from the Revolution*, 65. As of October 15, there were perhaps three to four days' worth of food reserves in the capital. *Ekonomicheskoe polozhenie*, II: 351–2. In early October, the Putilov factory director reported that he had run completely out of coal and that thirteen of the factory's shops were shutting down. *Ekonomicheskoe polozhenie*, II: 163–4.

232. Kitanina, *Voina, khleb i revoliutsiia* (Leningrad, 1985), 332–3 (October 13, 1917); Golovine, *Russian Army*, 175–6.

233. Abraham, *Kerensky*, 244.

234. Daniels, *Red October*, 61.

235. Stalin, "Kontrrevoliutsiia mobilizuetsia—gotovtes' k otporu," *Rabochii put'*, October 10, 1917, in *Sochineniia*, III: 361–3.

236. Trotskii, *O Lenine*, 70–3; Trotsky,

*History of the Russian Revolution* [1961], 148–9; Slusser, *Stalin in October*, 226–36; *Protokoly Tsentral'nogo komiteta RSDRP (b*, 55; Kudelli, *Pervyi legal'nyi Peterburgskii komitet bol'shevikov*, 316 (Kalinin); Abrosimova, *Peterburgskii komitet RSDRP (b)*, 508; Rabinowitch, *Bolsheviks Come to Power*, 209–16.

237. *Novaia zhizn'*, October 18, 1917: 3. Kamenev worried about the supposedly well-organized and loyal government troops, Cossacks and junkers (cadets), and warned that a failed uprising would possibly destroy the party for good. Raskolnikov claims he argued with Kamenev but neither could convince the other. F. F. Raskolnikov, "Nakanune Oktiabr'skoi revoliutsii" [written 1921–2], RGVA, f. 33 987, op. 2, d. 141, l. 463–500, Volkogonov papers, container 17.

238. *PSS*, XXXIV: 419–27; *Protokoly Tsentral'nogo komiteta RSDRP (b)*, 106–7. In forcing the party to a coup, Lenin had threatened to resign from the Central Committee and publicly oppose it, carrying on from the lower ranks, a right he accorded no one else (*Protokoly Tsentral'nogo komiteta RSDRP (b)*, 74).

239. *Novaia zhizn'*, October 18, 1917; *Protokoly tsentral'nogo komiteta RSDRP*, 106–18; Slusser, *Stalin in October*, 234–37.

240. M. V. Fofanova, "Poslednoe pod-pol'e V. I. Lenina."

241. *Izvestiia*, October 14, 1917: 5; Avdeev, *Revoliutsiia 1917 goda*, V: 70–1. See also Sukhanov, *Zapiski*, VII: 40–1; Gronsky, *The War and the Russian Government*, 112. Trotsky had addressed the Petrograd Soviet about MRC, saying, "They say we are setting up a headquarters for the seizure of power. We make no secret of it." Trotskii, *Sochineniia*, III: 15.

242. When the Provisional Government finally announced elections for the Constituent Assembly for November 12, many in the Soviet wanted to cancel the Second Congress of Soviets, but the Bolsheviks helped keep it on course by having the agenda be drafting legislative proposals for the Constituent Assembly.

243. Avdeev, *Revoliutsiia 1917 goda*, V: 109; *Novaia zhizn'*, October 18, 1917: 3.

244. The MRC elected a five-member leadership (three Bolsheviks and two Left SRs), and asserted authority over the garrison. Chugaev, *Petrogradskii voenno-revoliutsionnyi komitet*, I: 63.

245. Sukhanov, *Zapiski*, VII: 91; Volkogonov, *Trotsky*, 88.

246. Chugaev, *Petrogradskii voenno-revoliutsionnyi komitet*, I: 84, 86; Ditetrich Geyer, "The Bolshevik Insurrection in Petrograd," in Pipes, *Revolutionary Russia*, 164–79.

247. Trotsky spoke to the same group and confirmed Stalin's presentation, noting that a consolidation or defensive posture would enable the congress to open. Presumably, the votes were at hand for approving a transfer of "all power to the soviets." Rabinowitch, *Bolsheviks Come to Power*, 252–4; Alexander Rabinowitch, "The Petrograd Garrison and the Bolshevik Seizure of Power," in Pipes, *Revolutionary Russia*, 172–91. Later both Trotsky and Stalin claimed this "defensive" posture had been camouflage. Trotskii, *O Lenine*, 69; Mints, *Dokumenty velikoi proletarskoi revoliutsii*, I: 3 (Stalin).

248. "The existing government of landlords and capitalists must be replaced by a new government, a government of workers and peasants," Stalin's confiscated editorial stated. "If all of you act solidly and staunchly, no one will dare to resist the will of the people." *Sochineniia*, III: 390. See also *Rech'*, October 25, 1917: 2; Kerensky, *The Catastrophe*, 325–6; *Izvestiia*, October 25, 1917: 7.

249. Trotsky, *History of the Russian Revolution*, III: 121. See also Stankevich, *Vospominaniia*, 258. On October 17, the interior minister had reported that he commanded sufficient reliable troops to beat back any insurrection, although not enough to crush the left preemptively. On the night of October 21–22 Kerensky assured Supreme Commander General Dukhonin that he would still come out to meet him at Mogilyov, undeterred "by fear of some kind of unrest, rebellions, and the like." Browder and Kerensky, *Russian Provisional Government*, III: 1744. But nerves were on edge. "I only wish that [the Bolsheviks] would come out and I will put them down," Kerensky told British ambassador Buchanan. Buchanan, *My Mission to Russia*, II: 201. During mass meetings on October 22, proclaimed a "Day of the Petrograd Soviet," Sukhanov recorded "a mood bordering on ecstasy." Sukhanov, *Russian Revolution*, II: 584.

250. "The government of M. Kerensky fell before the Bolshevik insurgents," the *Manchester Guardian* correspondent correctly reported, "because it had no supporters in the country." M. Philips Price, *Manchester Guardian*, November 20, 1917, reprinted in Price and Rose, *Dispatches from the Revolution*, 88. "The ease with which Lenin and Trotsky overthrew the last coalition Government of Kerensky revealed its inward impotence. The degree of this impotence was an amazement at the time even to well-informed people." Trotsky, *History of the Russian Revolution*, III: 870 (quoting Nabokov, without citation).

251. Reed, *Ten Days* [1919], 73; Wade, *Red Guards and Workers' Militias*, 196–207.

252. Daniels, *Red October*, 166; "Stavka 25-26 oktiabria 1917 g."

253. Garrison troops numbered about 160,000 in the city proper, and another 85,000 in the outskirts. Sukhanov estimates that in the city one-tenth took part at most, "very likely fewer." Sukhanov, *Zapiski*, VII: 161; Solov'ev, "Samoderzhavie i dvorianskii vopros," 77; Erykalov, *Oktiabr'skoe vooruzhennoe vosstanie*, 435.

254. Mel'gunov, *Kak bol'sheviki zakhvatili vlast'*, 87–9. About thirty shells were fired from Peter and Paul Fortress and two made contact (one hit a cornice). No one was wounded, let alone killed in the shelling. Avdeev, *Revoliutsiia 1917*, V: 189.

255. Miliukov, *Istoriia*, III: 256.

256. Lutovinov, *Likvidatisiia miatezha Kerenskogo-Krasnogo*, 7.

257. Erykalov, *Oktiabr'skoe vooruzhennoe vosstanie*, 435; Rabinowitch, *Bolsheviks Come to Power*, 305. General Cheremisov on October 14 had issued an order implying that units of the Petrograd garrison would be deployed to the front.

258. Rakh'ia, "Poslednoe podpol'e Vladimira Il'icha," 89–90; Rakh'ia, "Moi predoktiabr'skie i posleoktiabr'skie vstrechi s Leninym," 35–6; Daniels, *Red October*, 158–61; Rabinowitch, *Bolsheviks Come to Power*, 266.

259. Kotel'nikov, *Vtoroi vserossiiskii s"ezd sovetov*, 144–53.

260. Kotel'nikov, *Vtoroi vserossiiskii s"ezd sovetov*, 4, 34–5; Sukhanov, *Zapiski*, VII: 198–9; Mstislavskii, *Piat' dnei*, 72; Mstislavskii, *Five Days*, 125.

261. Sukhanov, *Zapiski*, VII: 203; Trotsky, *History of the Russian Revolution*, III: 311 (quoting Sukhanov).

262. Nikolaevskii, "Stranitsy proshlogo," *Sotsialisticheskii vestnik*, July-August 1958: 150. The Bolshevik who confronted Martov was Ivan Akulov.

263. Park, *Bolshevism in Turkestan*, 12–3; Khalid, "Tashkent 1917," 279; Stalin, "Vsia vlast' sovetam!" *Rabochii put'*, September 17, 1917, in *Sochineniia*, III: 297–99; Blank, "Contested Terrain."

264. Daniels, *Red October*, 226; Wade, *Russian Revolution*, 302–3.

265. "We left not knowing where or why," Sukhanov wrote a few years later, "cutting ourselves off from the Soviet, getting mixed up with elements of the counterrevolution, discrediting and debasing ourselves in the eyes of the masses. . . . Moreover, in departing, we left the Bolsheviks a totally free hand and complete masters of the situation." Sukhanov, *Zapiski*, VII: 219–20. See also Schapiro, *Origins of the Communist Autocracy* [1965], 66–8.

The congress walkouts set up a "Committee for Salvation of the Fatherland and the Revolution," but it lacked the magical resonance of the Soviet. On October 29, military school cadets (junkers) under their command seized the telephone station, the state bank, and the Astoria Hotel, then set their sights on Smolny, but the Military Revolutionary Committee retook all these points and easily dispersed the junkers. *Novaia zhizn'*, October 30, 1917: 3.

266. History has nowhere recorded precisely how many delegates had left the hall. Kotel'nikov, *Vtoroi vserossiiskii s"ezd sovetov*, 53–4; Browder and Kerensky, *Russian Provisional Government*, III: 1797–8; *Dekrety Sovetskoi vlasti*, I: 1–2. On the eve, Lunacharsky had come out against the insurrection, in print, alongside Kamenev and Zinoviev.

267. Kotel'nikov, *Vtoroi vserossiiskii s"ezd sovetov*, 164–5; *Izvestiia*, October 26, 1917: 5–6, October 27: 4, October 28: 4; Rabinowitch, *Bolsheviks Come to Power*, 273–304; Daniels, *Red October*, 187–96. Even though most textbooks place the arrests in the cabinet room (Malachite Hall, on the river side), the government ministers had moved to Tsar Nicholas II's private dining room, facing the inner courtyard. M. Levin, "Poslednie chasy vremennogo pravitel'stva v 1917 g.," *Krasnyi arkhiv*, 1933, no. 156: 136–8 (P. I. Palchinsky notes).

268. Rabinowitch, *Bolsheviks Come to Power*, 269–92; Figes, *A People's Tragedy*, 485–95. John Reed, his wife Louise Bryant, and Albert Rhys Williams just walked into the Winter Palace, hoping to interview Kerensky, strolled around, and left, while Red Guards stood outside; the Red Guards finally entered through windows and unlocked doors. See *Delo naroda*, October 29, 1917: 1–2 (S. L. Maslov).

269. Trotsky, *Stalin*, 228–34; Radzinsky, *Stalin*, 115–19.

270. Lenin had arrived at the Finland Station in April 1917 wearing a dressy hat (it appears in the photograph of him en route in Stockholm). Nikolai I. Podvoiskii, "V. I. Lenin v 1917," *Istoricheskii arkhiv*, 1956, no. 6: 111–32 (at 115).

271. Reed, *Ten Days* [1919], 125–7; Kotel'nikov, *Vtoroi vserossiiskii s"ezd sovetov*, 59, 165–6; Avdeev, *Revoliutsiia 1917 goda*, V: 179–80; *Izvestiia*, October 26, 1917: 7. Lenin had also appeared (after Trotsky) at the parallel session of the Petrograd Soviet held on October 25 around 2:35 a.m.

272. Volkogonov, *Lenin: Life and Legacy*, xxxvi (citing *Obshchee delo* [Paris], February 21, 1921).

273. Volkogonov, *Lenin: Life and Legacy*, xxxvi, (citing *Velikii Lenin* [Moscow, 1982]), 16–7.

274. Kotel'nikov, *Vtoroi vserossiiskii s"ezd sovetov*, 15–21, 59–68.

275. Kotel'nikov, *Vtoroi vserossiiskii s"ezd sovetov*, 22.

276. Sukhanov, *Zapiski*, III: 361.

277. Kotel'nikov, *Vtoroi vserossiiskii s"ezd sovetov*, 25–30, 82–7.

278. McCauley, *Russian Revolution*, 282–3, translation of K. G. Idman, *Maame itsenäistymisen vuosilta* (Porvoo-Helsinki, 1953), 216.

279. Fülöp-Miller, *Mind and Face of Bolshevism* [1927], 29. Robert Service observed that Lenin had "not been a nonentity [in Russia] in 1917; but his celebrity had grown inside the confines of Russia's clandestine political groups." Service, *Lenin*, I: 1.

280. Pavel Malyantovich (a Menshevik), just recently named justice minister, cabled a signed decree to all provincial prosecutors that the arrest order for Lenin was still in effect in September 1917. He was executed by firing squad on January 21, 1940, the anniversary of Lenin's death.

281. On Lenin as a "revolutionary of genius," see Schapiro, "Lenin After Fifty Years," 8.

282. "Had I not been present in 1917 in Petersburg, the October Revolution would still have taken place—on the condition that Lenin was present and in command," Trotsky confided in his diary in late March 1935. "If neither Lenin nor I had been present in Petersburg, there would have been no

October Revolution." *Trotsky's Diary in Exile* [1963], 53–4.

283. *Bolshevik Propaganda: Hearings Before a Subcommittee on the Judiciary, United States Senate*, 790; Hard, *Raymond Robins' Own Story*, 52.

284. Waters, *Rosa Luxemburg Speaks*, 367.

285. Brinton, *Anatomy of Revolution*. Brinton's radicalization process—through three stages (rosy, polarization, radicalization)—ended in counterrevolution (Thermidor), however.

286. Lyttelton, *Seizure of Power*, 86.

287. Wildman, *End of the Russian Imperial Army*, II: xv. During the eight months of the Provisional Government's tortured existence, Russia experienced more than a thousand strikes—far more strike activity than before the monarchy's fall: 41,000 workers in March 1917; 384,000 in July; 965,000 in September; and 441,000 in October. Orlovsky, "Russia in War and Revolution," 244. But strikes did not overturn the Provisional Government any more than they had cashiered the monarchy.

288. Maklakov, "The Agrarian Problem."

289. "Okruzhili mia tel'tsy mnozi tuchny," *Rabochii put'*, October 20, 1917, reprinted in *Sochineniia*, III: 383–6.

290. *Protokoly Tsentral'nogo komiteta RSDRP (b)*, 107 (October 20, 1917).

291. Trotsky, *History of the Russian Revolution*, III: 211. "I spent the decisive night of October 25–26 together

with Kamenev in the offices of the Military Revolutionary Committee, answering inquiries on the telephone and sending out instructions." Trotsky added: "I simply cannot answer the question of what precisely was Stalin's role in those decisive days." Trotskii, *Stalinskaia shkola fal'sifakatsii*, 26. Even Stalin's relations undersold him. "In those days," wrote Fyodor Alliluyev, who witnessed Stalin's catnaps in his family's apartment, "comrade Stalin was genuinely known only to the small circle of people who had come across him in work in the political underground." RGASPI, f. 558, op. 4, d, 668, l. 30 (F. S. Alliluev, "V Moskve [Vstrecha s t. Stalinym]," undated typescript). All the key Bolshevik men on the frontlines in October—Raskol'nikov, Dybenko, Podvoisky, Krylenko—would be murdered by Stalin's regime.

292. The notion, stated by Tucker, that "Stalin was not really in his element in the turbulent mass politics of 1917," is belied by Stalin's Chiatura experience back in 1905. Tucker, *Stalin as Revolutionary*, 178.

293. De Lon, "Stalin and Social Democracy," 204. After the Constituent Assembly was dispersed in January 1918, Sagirashvili dejectedly left Petrograd for Tiflis.

294. Kotel'nikov, *Vtoroi vserossiiskii s"ezd sovetov*, 90, 174–5. The list was likely submitted by Kamenev.

## CHAPTER 7: 1918: DADA AND LENIN

1. Motherwell, *Dada Painters and Poets*, 78–9, 81.

2. Malkov, *Reminiscences*, 178.

3. Miliukov added that "experience showed that this light-minded self-assurance was a profound error." Miliukov, *Istoriia vtoroi*, I/iii: 179. John Reed wrote that it "never occurred to anybody—except perhaps to Lenin, Trotzky, the Petersburg workers and the simpler soldiers"—that "the Bolsheviki would remain in power longer than three days." Reed, *Ten Days* [1919], 117.

4. "I prefer Lenin, an open enemy, to Kerensky, that wolf in sheep's clothing," one official wrote on October 31, 1917. Nielsen and Weil, *Russkaia revoliutsiia glazami Petrogradskogo chinovnika*, 21. Kerensky bitterly denounced such types as "Bolsheviks of the Right."

5. Trotsky, *On Lenin*, 114; Miliutin, *O Lenine*, 4–5; Rigby, *Lenin's Government*, 23.

6. Figes, "Failure of February's Men." See also the bitter remarks of Chernov, *Great Russian Revolution*, 256–7.

7. In 1918, the Julian calendar was thirteen days behind the Gregorian;

Wednesday, January 31, 1918, in Russia was followed by Thursday, February 14. Thereafter, the "February Revolution" would be celebrated on March 13 (at least through 1927, after which official commemoration of February ceased), while the "October Revolution" would be celebrated on November 7. Orthodox Christmas became January 7.

8. Larin, "Ukolybeli," 16–7; Pestkovskii, "Ob oktiabr'skikh dniakh v Pitere," 99–100; Mal'kov, *Zapiski* [1967], 42–7; Chugaev, *Petrogradskii voenno-revoliutsionnyi komitet*, I: 485.

9. Gil', *Shest' let s V. I. Leninym*, 10–3. Lenin also had a luxurious Delaunay-Belleville 70, a six-cylinder ahead of its time, that had been purchased for Nicholas II.

10. Krupskaia, "Lenin v 1917 godu," *Izvestiia*, January 20, 1960, reprinted in *O Lenine*, 54. She made the remarks in 1934.

11. Iroshnikov, *Sozdanie*, 156–61. The best contemporary accounts are M. Latsis, *Proletarskaia revoliutsiia*, 1925, no. 2: esp. 144.

12. The Petrograd Soviet had set up a commission on June 11, 1917, to

manage affairs with the Ukrainian Rada (which was demanding autonomy).

13. The original plan for nationalities may have been for a mere "commission," rather than a full-fledged commissariat. Gorodetskii, *Rozhdenie*, 158.

14. "Lenin," Pestkowski ingratiatingly wrote, "could not get along without Stalin for even a single day." Pestkovskii, "Vospominaniia o rabote v narkomnaste," 128.

15. Trotskii, *Moia zhizn'*, II; 62–4; Sukhanov, *Zapiski*, VII: 266; Zalkind, "N.K.I.D. v semnadtsatom godu." See also Deutscher, *Prophet Armed*, 325.

16. *Izvestiia TsK KPSS*, 1989, no. 5: 155 (August 26, 1918, letter to Vologda party committee). Sagirashvili speculated that Stalin coveted Sverdlov's position, relating hearsay from Stalin's close comrade Orjonikidze. De Lon, "Stalin and Social Democracy," 199. Sverdlov was often out at meetings on behalf of the party's secretariat and seldom on the premises at Smolny.

17. In 1918 Lenin was paid 24,683.33 rubles: 9,683.33 in salary as chair of Sovnarkom and 15,000 as an honorarium

for publications; the payments were made via Bonch Bruevich, who handled party money. RGASPI, f. 2, op. 1, d. 11186, l. 2 (September 20, 1919).

18. Bunyan and Fisher, *Bolshevik Revolution*, 185–7; *Sobranie uzakonenii i rasporiazhenii rabochego i krest'ianskogo pravitel'stva*, 1917, no. 1: 10–1; Goikhbarg [Hoichberg], *Sotsial'noe zakonodatel'stvo sovetskoi respubliki*; Goikhbarg, *A Year in Soviet Russia*; Trotsky, *My Life*, 342.

19. Magerovsky, "The People's Commissariat," I: 29–31.

20. Pestkovskii, "Ob Oktiabr'skikh dniakh v Pitere," 104; Trotsky, *Stalin*, 245.

21. *Izvestiia*, November 27, 1917: 6. Pestkowski was named to the bank job through Wieczysław Mężyński, yet another high-placed Pole.

22. Codrescu, *Posthuman Dada Guide*, 11.

23. Sandqvist, *Dada East*; Dickerman, *Dada*.

24. Nielson and Boris, *Russkaia revoliutsiia glazami Petrogradskogo chinovnika*, 13 (October 22, 1917).

25. Jan Gross correctly surmised that "the architects of the Soviet state discovered early that one accumulates power simply by denying it to others." Gross, "War as Social Revolution," 32.

26. Marx and Engels, *Selected Correspondence* [1965], 331, 338; Marx and Engels, *Selected Works*. See Gouldner, *The Two Marxisms*, 350–1. Louis Auguste Blanqui, the original Leninist, had spent the commune's entire existence in prison.

27. McLellan, *Karl Marx: Selected Writings*, 592–4; Marx and Engels, *The Civil War in France*, in *Selected Works*, I: 473–545; and Marx and Engels, *Selected Correspondence* [1965], 318–20 (letters to Kugelmann, April 12 and 17, 1871).

28. *Zagranichnaia gazeta*, March 23, 1908.

29. Lenin, *Collected Works*, XXIV: 170, n24.

30. Lenin, *Collected Works*, XXVII: 135.

31. Sakwa, "The Commune State in Moscow."

32. Warth, *The Allies*, 159. The head of the Provisional Government chancellery, when asked if he could provide a car for Kerensky's flight from Russia, thought it a ruse by a thief to steal one! Startsev, "Begstvo Kerenskogo"; Medlin and Powers, *V. D. Nabokov*, 157–8. Kerensky reached Tsarskoe Selo (and its crucial radio transmitter), but had to retreat farther, to Pskov (Northern Front Headquarters), where Nicholas II had abdicated. Brief fighting broke out in the Pulkovo Heights near Petrograd on October 30, but anti-Bolshevik forces were easily

turned back. Kerensky never returned to Petrograd.

33. P. N. Krasnov, "Na vnutrennom fronte," in Gessen, *Arkhiv Russkoi revoliutsii*, I: 148–51; Kerensky, *The Catastrophe*, 340–3; Daniels, *Red October*, 205–6.

34. *Novaia zhizn'*, October 30, 1917: 3.

35. *Izvestiia*, November 3, 1917: 5; Kerensky, *Russia and History's Turning Point*, 443–6.

36. *Novaia zhizn'*, October 30, 1917: 3; *Delo naroda*, Ocotber 30, 1917: 2; *Izvestiia*, October 30, 1917: 2; Williams, *Through the Russian Revolution*, 119–49. See also Reed, *Ten Days* [1919], 193–207; and Gindin, *Kak bol'sheviki ovladeli gosudarstvennym bankom*.

37. Malyshev, *Oborona Petrograda*.

38. De Lon, "Stalin and Social Democracy," 257–8.

39. *Novaia zhizn'*, October 30, 1917: 2; Keep, *Debate on Soviet Power*, 44–5; Vompe, *Dni oktiabrskoi revoliutsii i zheleznodorozhniki*, 10.

40. *Izvestiia*, October 31, 1917: 7–8; Avdeev, *Revoliutsiia 1917 goda*, VI: 23, 45.

41. *Protokoly Tsentral'nogo komiteta RSDRP (b)* 1958, 122–3. *The Bolsheviks and the October Revolution: Central Committee Minutes*, 127–8.

42. Avdeev, *Revoliutsiia 1917 goda*, IV: 22–3; *Protokoly Tsentral'nogo komiteta RSDRP (b)*, 271–2, n156; Vompe, *Dni oktiabr'skoi revoliutsii i zheleznodorozhniki*. See also Abramovitch, *Soviet Revolution*.

43. *Rabochii i soldat*, November 1, 1917. See also *Delo naroda*, October 31, 1917: 2.

44. The minutes published in 1927 omit the passage praising Trotsky: *Pervyi legal'nyi Peterburgskii komitet bol'shevikov*. Trotsky reproduced a photograph of the minutes of the Petersburg Committee of Bolsheviks, November 1, 1917. *Biulleten' oppozitsii*, 1929, no. 7: 30–2.

45. *Peterburgskii komitet RSDRP (b) v 1917 godu*, 546. The young Molotov also backed the hard line (544).

46. "Zasedanie TsK 1 noiabria 1917 g.," *Protokoly tsentral'nogo komiteta RSDRP (b)*, 124–30. Stalin is not listed as in attendance.

47. *Protokoly Tsentral'nogo komiteta RSDRP (b)*, 272, n162; *Protokoly zasedanii VTsIK*.

48. *Oktiabr'skoe vosstanie v Moskve: Sbornik dokumentov* (Moscow: Gosizdat moskovskoe otdelenie, 1922), 97–8, reprinted in Bunyan and Fisher, *The Bolshevik Revolution*, 179; Pipes, *Russian Revolution*, 501–3; Koenker, *Moscow Workers*, 332–4; Pethybridge, *Spread of the Russian Revolution*, 198. See also *Sovety v Oktiabre*, 31–86; Mel'gunov, *Kak bol'sheviki zakhvatili vlast'*, 277–382; Nikolai N.

Ovsiannikov (ed.); Ignat'ev, *Oktiabr' 1917 goda*; Grunt, *Moskva 1917-i*, ch. 6.

49. *Protokoly Tsentral'nogo komiteta RSDRP (b)*, 133–4; *The Bolsheviks and the October Revolution: Central Committee Minutes*, 138–40; *Lenin v pervye mesiatsy sovetskoi vlasti*, 46.

50. *Perepiska sekretariata TsK RSDRP (b)*, II: 27.

51. *Izvestiia*, November 4, 1917; Avdeev, *Revoliutsiia 1917 goda*, VI: 423–4; *Protokoly Tsentral'nogo komiteta RSDRP (b)*, 133–7; *Proletarskaia revoliutsiia*, 1927, no. 8–9: 321–51, no. 10: 246–98, no. 11: 202–14; 1928, no. 2: 132–69.

52. *Dekrety Sovetskoi vlasti*, I: 20.

53. Keep, *Debate on Soviet Power*, 86; Rabinowitch, *Bolsheviks in Power*, 48–9. A slightly different accounting of the votes is in Pipes, *Russian Revolution*, 524–5.

54. *Protokoly Tsentral'nogo komiteta RSDRP (b)*, 146; *The Bolsheviks and the October Revolution: Central Committee Minutes*, 151–2; Bonch-Bruevich, *Na boevykh postakh*, 164; *Novaia zhizn'*, November 9, 1917.

55. Steklov, *Bortsy za sotsializm*, II: 400–1; Paustovsky, *Story of a Life*, 529; Trotskii, *Sochineniia*, VIII: 254. Sverdlov had the authority to make decisions on his own, yet he consulted Lenin assiduously. Iroshnikov, *Predsedatel soveta narodnykh komissarov V. I. Ul'ianov (Lenin)*, 57 (citing the unpublished memoirs of Paniushkin).

56. On the rumors to install Grigory Pyatakov as head of a new government, see *Pravda*, December 15, 1923, December 16, 1923, and January 3, 1924; and *Biulleten' oppozitsii*, April 1938, no. 65: 13–4.

57. Raleigh, *Revolution on the Volga*, 319.

58. *VII ekstrennyi s"ezd RKP (b), mart 1918 goda*, 6. The Soviet editors inserted a note deeming Sverdlov's accurate statement "not exact" (359).

59. Fel'shtinskii, *Bol'sheviki i levye esery*.

60. Berlin and Jahanbegloo, *Conversations*, 4. See also Sorokin, *Leaves from a Russian Diary*, 105–6.

62. *Delo naroda*, November 25, 1917: 4.

63. *Izvestiia*, October 28, 1917: 2; Bunyan and Fisher, *Bolshevik Revolution*, 220.

64. Trotskii, *O Lenine*, 102.

65. Holquist, *Making War*, 130–1.

66. Colton, *Moscow*, 103 (Tikhomirov in *Izvestiia*, April 30, 1918).

67. McLellan, *Karl Marx: Selected Writings*, 592–4. See also V. I. Lenin, "Lessons of the Commune," *Zagranichnaia gazeta*, March 23, 1908.

68. "With the functionaries of our body," one finance official recorded, "the Bolsheviks in Smolny were unfailingly polite and only upon

achieving nothing did they turn to threats that, if we do not hand over 15 million in cash, they will seize the State Bank and take as much as they need," breaking open the vaults. Finance ministry personnel (on the Moika) went on strike. Nielsen and Weil, *Russkaia revoliutsiia glazami Petrogradskogo chinovnika*, 14–5 (October 25, 1917), 23 (November 6, 1917).

69. Bunyan and Fisher, *Bolshevik Revolution*, 225–31; *Vlast' sovetov*, 1919, no. 11: 5; Trotskii, "Vospominaniia ob oktiabr'skom perevorote"; Trotsky, *My Life*, 293.

70. *Denezhnoe obrashchenie i kreditnaia sistema Soiuza SSR za 20 let*, 1–2; Morozov, *Sozdanie i ukreplenie sovietskogo gosudarstsvennogo apparata*, 52; *Novaia zhizn'*, November 16, 1917; *Ekonomicheskaia zhizn'*, November 6, 1918: 2–3 (V. Obolensky-Osinsky). Mężyński is sometimes also given the title "temporary" or "acting" people's commissar for the finance ministry. The commissar was, nominally, Skortsov-Stepanov. The Bolsheviks did manage to elicit the cooperation of the finance ministry officials and the director of the treasury (P. M. Trokhimovsky). *Proletarskaia revoliutsiia*, 1922, no. 10: 62–3; Iroshnikov, *Sozdanie*, 195.

71. Larsons, *Im Sowjet-Labyrinth*, 61–6.

72. Nielsen and Weil, *Russkaia revoliutsiia glazami Petrogradskogo chinovnika*, 40 (December 29 and 31, 1917). The Council of People's Commissars issued a decree ordering discontinuance of such payments on January 11, 1918. *Obzor finansogo zakonodatel'stva, 1917–1921, gg.* (Petrograd, 1921), 15.

73. Schwittau, *Revoliutsiia i narodnoe khoziaisto*, 337; D'iachenko, *Istoriia finansov SSSR*, 24–7; *Svoboda Rossii*, April 19, 1918: 5; Katzenellenbaum, *Russian Currency and Banking*, 55–60; Bunyan and Fisher, *Bolshevik Revolution*, 607–9; *Papers Relating to the Foreign Relations of the United States: Russia*, III: 32–3.

74. Debt service had amounted to a hefty 345 million rubles per annum from 1909 to 1913, but by 1918 it had exploded because of vast new wartime debt. Dohan, "Foreign Trade," 218.

75. The Russian State Bank had a monopoly on the issuance of currency (in 1891). The total gold stock in November 1917 amounted to 1.26 billion rubles. Atlas, *Ocherki po istorii denezhnogo obrashcheniia*, 16–8; Carr, *Bolshevik Revolution*, II: 133–7.

76. Lenin, *Collected Works*, XLII: 64. As of February 1918, Lenin estimated state expense obligations at 28 billion rubles, and revenues at 8 billion,

because of nonpayment of taxes. *PSS*, XXXV: 326–7, 331. Very soon, the Bolsheviks began to worry that easily available paper money could finance counterrevolution. *Pravda*, April 19, 1918. Mężyński's stint at finance was shortlived: by April 1918 he was in the Cheka.

77. Owen, *Russian Peasant Movement*.

78. Brutzkus, "Die russische Agrarrevolution." In Ukraine, a critical breadbasket feeding tens of millions, the peasant revolution has been likened to a cyclone. Arthur Adams, "The Great Ukrainian Jacquerie," in Hunczak, *The Ukraine*, 247–70.

79. Pipes, *Russian Revolution*, 718–9. See also Channon, "The Bolsheviks and the Peasantry."

80. Conversely, inflation soon obliterated any savings they had in the state savings bank or buried in the ground near their huts. Pipes, *Russian Revolution*, 719–21.

81. Atkinson, *End of the Russian Land Commune*, 185.

82. *Novaia zhizn'*, December 31, 1917: 2 (Kolegaev). Liberals in the Provisional Government viewed Victor Chernov, leader of the Socialist Revolutionary party and agricultural minister in the Provisional Government, as the inspiration and embodiment of the chaos caused by land seizures, but in the countryside Chernov and the SR party were seen as traitors for opposing immediate land redistribution. Local SRs broke with the central party hierarchs, but the party as a whole got no credit for it. Chernov called the peasantry "the sphinx in the political history of Russia," but the characterization applied to himself. Chernov, *Rozhednie revoliutsionnoi Rossii*, 75. The Bolsheviks borrowed more than the SR land program. "We got a copy of the SR municipal program (they developed it, I believe, in 1905) and began to study it and put together our municipal program in a form much like it," recalled one Moscow Bolshevik of spring 1917. Volin, "Vokrug Moskovskoi Dumy," 98.

83. "No law was more widely published than the land law," recalled Bonch-Bruevich, *Na boevikh postakh*, 115. The anecdote on the calendars does not appear in the first edition from the previous year of the Bonch-Buevich memoir (Federatsiia, 1930), 125–7. See also Pethybridge, *Spread of the Russian Revolution*, 154.

84. Keep, *Russian Revolution*, 178.

85. Siegelbaum, "The Workers Group," at 155.

86. Gatrell, *A Whole Empire Walking*.

87. Chugaev, *Petrogradskii voennorevoliutsionnyi komitet*, II: 111.

88. "The drowned were carried out of the cellars and stacked in rows on

Palace Square." Antonov-Ovseenko, *Zapiski o grazhdanskoi voine*, I: 19–20.

89. *Izvestiia*, December 6, 1917; Bonch-Bruevich, *Na boevykh postakh*, 191. Bonch-Bruevich also collected rumors of enemies in disguise who were stockpiling weapons and counterfeiting documents, to which he responded with peremptory arrests. Zubov, *F. E. Dzerzhinskii*, 161.

90. Iroshnikov, *Sozdanie*, 96, 201, 214–5; Z. Serebrianskii, "Sabotazh i sozdanie novogo gosudarstvennogo apparata," 8–11.

91. GARF, f. 130, op. 1, d. 1, l. 29–30, 30 ob; *Izvestiia*, December 10, 1917; Tsvigun, *V. I. Lenin i VChK* [1975], 34, n1; Belov, *Iz istorii Vserossiiskoi Chrezvychainoi komissii*, 72–9; *Krasnyi arkhiv*, 1924, no. 5: xiv–xv; *PSS*, XXXV: 156–8; *Pogranichnye voiska SSSR 1918–1928*, 67; Chugaev, *Petrogradskii voennorevoliutsionnyi komitet*, III: 663–4; Latsis, *Chrezvychainye komissii*, 7–8; Vladimir Bonch-Bruevich, "Kak organizavovalas VChK," *Ogonek*, 1927, no. 3, reprinted in *Vospominaniia o Lenine*, 134–9 (at 137) and expanded in *Na boevykh postakh*, 193–203 (at 198–9); Carr, "Origins and Status." The Council of People's Commissars' discussion of Dzierżyński's report was presented as a "decree" (and altered) when later published: Belov, *Iz istorii Vserossiiskoi Chrezvychainoi komissii*, 78–9. See also *Proletarskaia revoliutsiia*, 1924, no. 10 (33): 5–6 (Peters) and 1926, no. 9 (58): 82–3 (Vācietis); and *Pravda*, December 18, 1927: 2. For Lenin's note to Dzierżyński, see *PSS*, XXXV: 156–8; Tsvigun, *V. I. Lenin i VChK* [1975], 37, and [1987], 19, 22. The phrase "proletarian Jacobin" appears in Zubov, *F. E. Dzerzhinskii*, 162, and appears as "revolutionary Jacobin" in an earlier edition: *Feliks Edmundovich Dzerzhinskii: kratkaia biografiia*, 2nd ed. (Moscow: OGIZ, 1942), 53. The Cheka technically replaced the MRC, whose power was real and demise sudden on December 5, 1917. Rigby, "The First Proletarian Government"; Pietsch, *Revolution und Staat*, 44–66. The assertion that Lenin hurriedly founded the Cheka because he worried the Left SRs who had agreed to enter the government would insist on moderation is contradicted by the fact that he allowed the Left SRs into the Cheka's governing collegium. Latsis, *Otchet VChK za chetyre goda ee deiatel'nosti, 20 dekabria 1917–20 dekabria 1921 g.* Moscow: VChK, 1922, 8. I: 8; Rabinowitch, *Bolsheviks in Power*, 81–7, 103. But cf. Pipes, *Russian Revolution*, 536–7.

92. RGASPI, f. 76, op. 2, d. 270, l. 32–33.

93. A key instrument in breaking the strike was the closure of the Petrograd

City Duma, which had survived the coup and served as a rallying point. *Dekrety Sovetskoi vlasti*, I: 91.
94. Peters, "Vospominaniia o rabote VChK," 10. One of the Provisional Government's few successes had been the formation of an agency engaged in systematic, sensational leaking of secret files about the *okhranka*'s dirty tricks. Osorgin, *Okhrannoe otdelenie i ego sekrety*; Avrekh, "Chrezvychainaia sledstvennaia komissiia vremennogo pravitel'stva"; Peregudova, "Deitel'nost komissii Vremennogo pravitel'stva i sovetskikh arkhivov"; Ruud and Stepanov, *Fontanka 16*, 315–21. Police archives had been ransacked and burned by rioters; some top *okhranka* officials removed their files when they left office, erasing their failures as well as much else. Still, the work of the commission—chaired by Muravyov (formerly known to the *okhranka* as "The Fly")—would be published in seven volumes [1927], based on GARF, f. 1647 (Avrekh, "Chrezvychainia sledstvennaia komissiia"); Zhilinskii, *Organizatsiia i zhizn' okhrannago otdeleniia*, 4–6. The archive of the Paris branch was thought to have been destroyed by the tsarist ambassador to France, but turned up in 1957 (and is now at the Hoover Institution Archives).
95. "The enemies of Soviet power," Dzierżyński explained, "are both our political opponents and all bandits, thieves, speculators, and all other criminals." *Novaia zhizn'*, June 9, 1918: 4.
96. Klement'ev, *V Bol'shevitskoi Moskve*, 53. Klement'ev, an artillery officer in the Russian imperial army, may have owed his presence in Moscow to General Kornilov; those claiming to be connected to Kornilov had ordered Klement'ev and a colonel (Perkhurov) to prepare anti-Bolshevik forces in Moscow, but Klement'ev claims they met indifference.
97. Bunyan, *Intervention*, 229 (a translation of *Ezhedel'nik chrezvychainoi komissii*, 1918, no. 4: 29–30).
98. Leggett, *The Cheka*, 56.
99. Motives in "nationalizations" (plundering, not assumption of state control) could range from professional ambition—a confiscator hoped to stand out as a better manager of the properties—to greed ("sometimes a competing factory owner would pay a special visit to the provincial council of the national economy bringing the necessary presents"). Gessen, *Arkhiv russkoi revoliutsii*, VI: 310–1 (Gurovich).
100. On January 1, 1918, Lenin had gotten in his car for the drive back to Smolny from Petrograd's Archangel Michael Riding Academy, where he had spoken to a motley "socialist army" heading for the front. "They had

gone only a few yards when their vehicle was strafed from behind," *Pravda* would later report. Inside the car, the Swiss socialist Fritz Platten—an intermediary in the funneling of German money to the Bolsheviks and organizer of Lenin's sealed-train return to Russia—pushed Lenin's head down; one of Platten's hands was said to have been grazed by a bullet. *Pravda*, January 3, 1918, January 14, 1925 (because of the new calendar, the anniversary of the event became January 14, thirteen days later), January 21, 1926; Zinoviev, "Piat' let," manuscript, RGASPI, f. 324, op. 1, d. 267, l. 1–7, in Hoover Institution Archives, Volkogonov papers, container 14; Bonch-Bruevich, *Tri pokusheniie na V. I. Lenina*, 3–77; *Sovetskaia Rossiia*, January 3, 1963; Volkogonov, *Lenin: Life and Legacy*, 229. Lenin's speech that day was published only many years later (*Pravda*, January 17, 1929). Who was behind the attempted assassination remains uncertain. The (Right) Socialist Revolutionary Party newspaper first revealed the incident, while hinting that the Bolsheviks had staged it to discredit the SRs, but the Right SRs may have set the assassination in motion, which others clumsily carried out.
101. *Iz istorii VChK*, 95–6.
102. Rabinowitch, *Bolsheviks in Power*, 97 (citing GARF, f. 130, op. 2, d. 1098, l. 8), 97 (citing TsA FSB RF, f. 1, op. 2, d. 25, l. 1: report of Ivan Polukarov).
103. Just after the October 25 coup, Lenin's fixer Vladimir Bonch-Bruevich went over to the Mariinsk Palace to meet the defunct Provisional Government's head of chancellery, Vladimir Nabokov (father of the future novelist), who had helped write the Provisional Government's dubious founding document—Mikhail Alexandrovich's "abdication" manifesto. "He greeted me like an old friend, was ostentatiously polite," Nabokov wrote, and "tried to convince me that the basis of Bolshevik authority was just as lawful, if not more so than the Provisional Government's." Medlin and Powers, *V. D. Nabokov*, 170–2. See also *Izvestiia*, Ocober 28, 1917: 2.
104. Initially, Lenin had contemplated "postponing" the ballot. Trotsky, *Lenin*, 110. For the October 27, 1917, decree affirming the vote would go forward as scheduled from November 12 to 14, see *Dekrety Sovetskoi vlasti*, I: 25–6.
105. There were no returns for Kaluga and Bessarabia regions, three Far Eastern districts of Kamchatka, Yakutsk, and the Chinese Eastern Railroad, even though voting took place there. The Kuban-Black Sea district of the North Caucasus province had elections only in the capital of Yekaterinodar.

106. *Izvestiia*, December 10, 1917: 3; *Dekrety Sovetskoi vlasti*, I: 165–6; Belov, *Iz istorii Vserossiiskoi Chrezvychainoi komissii*, 66–8; *PSS*, XXVI: 315; Tsvigun, *V. I. Lenin i VChK*, 15–7.
107. GARF, f. 130, op. 1, d. 1, l. 19–20; Volkogonov, *Trotsky*, 91.
108. *Protokoly Tsentral'nogo Komiteta RSDRP (b)*, 157 (November 29, 1917); *The Bolsheviks and the October Revolution: Central Committee Minutes*, 164; Trotsky, *Stalin*, 240–1.
109. Radkey, *Russia Goes to the Polls*.
110. Holquist, *Making War*.
111. Lenin, *Sochineniia* 2nd and 3rd eds., XXIV: 631–49 (at 638).
112. Radkey, *Russia Goes to the Polls*, 16, 34–5; Znamenskii, *Vserossiiskoe Uchreditel'noe Sobranie*, 275, 338, 358, tables 1 and 2. Voting took place according to electoral lists, with proportional representation; a candidate was permitted to stand simultaneously in no more than five districts; those elected in more than one district had to choose.
113. Radkey, *Russia Goes to the Polls*, 14–23.
114. Volkogonov, *Lenin: Life and Legacy*, 252. Sukhanov had taken over the editorship from Maxim Gorky. *New Life (Novaya zhizn')* would be closed by Bolsheviks in 1918 after the assassination of the German ambassador Count Mirbach.
115. As it happened, a revolver was stolen from Lenin's overcoat, hanging on a hook, during a Bolshevik meeting on the Constituent Assembly; the culprit was found to be a sailor supposed to be guarding the assembly. He was promptly taken out back and shot. Iurii Fel'shtinskii, *Brestskii mir, oktiabr' 1917 goda—noiabr' 1918 g.* (Moscow, 1992), 219.
116. *Pravda*, April 20, 1924: 3 (Trotsky).
117. Sviatitskii, *Kogo russkii narod izbral*, 10–1.
118. Znamenskii, *Vserossiiskoe*, 339; Protasov, *Vserossiiskoe Uchreditol'noe Sobranie*.
119. To undercut Bolshevik moderates who had been taking the Constituent Assembly seriously as a people's parliament, he and Sverdlov had manipulated meeting agendas and attendance for the Bolshevik caucus. Bunyan and Fisher, *Bolshevik Revolution*, 363; Rabinowitch, *Bolsheviks in Power*, 88–92.
120. Reed, *Ten Days* [1919], 248.
121. Mal'chevskii, *Vserossiiskoe*, 217; Golikov, *Vladimir Il'ich Lenin*, V: 180–1.
122. Mal'chevskii, *Vserossiiskoe Uchreditol'noe*, 110.
123. Some scholars have argued that the Provisional Government was ultimately responsible for the Constituent Assembly's failure: had elections been held earlier "a parliamentary regime in

Russia would surely have had a fighting chance." Gill, *Peasants and Government*, 98. See also Jonathan Frankel, "The Problem of Alternatives," in Frankel, *Revolution in Russia*, 3–13. Kerensky may have tried to attend the Constituent Assembly, but he had not been elected a delegate and was rebuffed by the Central Committee of the SR party. Vishniak, *Vserossiiskoe uchreditel'noe sobranie*, 106; Vishniak, *Dan' proshlomu*, 365. Vishniak (b. 1883) served as secretary of the Constituent Assembly and bravely recorded its proceedings; he tried to fight Bolshevism, ended up in prison in Kiev, and emigrated to Paris in April 1919.

124. Volkogonov, *Lenin: Life and Legacy*, 177–8 (citing Arkhiv INO OGPU, 17 458, vol. II: 215).

125. "Shall we convene the Constituent Assembly?" asked Moisei Uritsky, put in charge of overseeing it. "Yes. Shall we disperse it? Perhaps; it depends on circumstances." Chamberlin, *Russian Revolution*, I: 368.

126. Volkogonov, *Trotsky*, 121 (citing Trotskii, *Sochineniia*, XVII/i: 201). On December 19, 1917, Trotsky had summoned "the iron steamroller of the proletarian revolution to crush the spinal column of Menshevism." These were fellow Social Democrats, not to mention Trotsky's former party. Volkogonov, *Trotsky*, 78.

127. Radkey speculated that given SR weaknesses, the Constituent Assembly "would have fallen of its own weight." Radkey, *Sickle Under the Hammer*, 466.

128. Several Guards regiments, totaling perhaps 10,000 troops, pledged to turn out with their weapons if requested, but the Socialist Revolutionary leadership wanted no armed defense. The SR Central Committee went so far as to set up a commission to investigate efforts to defend the Constituent Assembly by force. B. F. Sokolov, "Zashchita vserossiiskogo uchreditel'nogo sobraniia," in Gessen, *Arkhiv russkoi revoliutsii* XIII: 5–70 (at 41–4), 50, 60–1; Bunyan and Fisher, *Bolshevik Revolution*, 380–4; *Istochnik*, 1995, 1: 25–40; Rabinowitch, *Bolsheviks in Power*, 95 (citing Sokolov and Bakhmeteff Archive, Zenzinov Collection, SR Central Committee protocols, pp. 18–9). Later, however, one Socialist Revolutionary claimed "there was no attempt at force on January 5, not because we did not wish it, but because we had no strength." *Pravda*, June 15, 1922 (Likhach). The Mensheviks did not have much of an answer to Bolshevik assertiveness either. Just a short time before the opening of the Constituent Assembly, at a Congress of the Russian Social Democratic Workers' Party-Mensheviks attended by some 100 delegates, Yuly Martov had put forth a resolution (which won majority support) accurately labeling Bolshevism a "regime of permanent anarchy." But Martov's own position was scarcely tenable: he urged the Mensheviks to pursue an all-socialist coalition—with Bolsheviks, too—even though the Bolsheviks had no desire to share power and even though, in Martov's own mind, genuine socialism in Russia remained impossible at this historical stage. He embraced the ongoing expropriations of the bourgeoisie, and thought the workers would somehow help carry through the bourgeois-revolution phase of history. Burbank, *Intelligentsia and Revolution*, 13–6 (citing *Novyi luch*, December 3, 1917: 4); Haimson, "The Mensheviks."

129. Figes, *Peasant Russia, Civil War*, 40–69.

130. In Moscow, up to 2,000 demonstrators marched on January 9, 1918; at least 30 were trampled to death or shot. *Pravda*, January 22, 1918: 3 and January 24, 1918: 3; Yarkovsky, *It Happened in Moscow*, 267–75; Colton, *Moscow*, 87 (citing Tsentral'nyi arkhiv obshchestvenno-politicheskoi istorii Moskvy [TsAOPIM], f. 3, op. 1, d. 46, l. 296).

131. Vishniak, *Dan' proshlomu*, 289; Gorkii, *Nesvoevremennye mysli i rassuzhdenii*, 110–1; Mal'chevskii, *Vserossiiskoe uchreditel'noe sobranie*; Radkey, *Sickle Under the Hammer*, 386–416; Novitskaia, *Uchreditel'noe sobranie*; Rabinowitch, *Bolsheviks in Power*, 123–5; Bailey, "The Russian Constituent Assembly of 1918"; Avrich, *Anarchist Portraits*, 107–9. Zhelznyakov is said to have taken part in the "storming" of the winter palace. He was killed in the civil war in 1919, age twenty-four, by a shell from White artillery.

132. Lenin wrote two sets of theses on the Constituent Assembly, one before and one after its dispersal. GARF, f. 130, op. 1, d. 7, l. 15–6, Hoover Institution Archives, Volkogonov papers, container 21; *Pravda*, January 12, 1917, republished in *PSS*, XXXV: 162–6. Just as Lenin and Sverdlov had calculated, the Left Socialist Revolutionaries, after taking some lesser portfolios in the Council of People's Commissars, became significantly less steadfast in defense of the Constituent Assembly.

133. Keep, *Debate on Soviet Power*, 247. From December 24 to 27, 1917, Lenin had briefly gone to a resort in nearby Finland (Stalin signed a December 27 decree on the nationalization of the Putilov Works "for the chairman of the Council of People's Commissars": Hoover Institution Archives, Volkogonov papers, container 14). Instead of resting, however, Lenin was busy writing. In any case, Bolshevik deputies of the Constituent Assembly showed up unannounced in Finland and retrieved Lenin.

134. Simultaneously, two congresses were taking place: one of peasant deputies and one of workers and soldiers' deputies, which merged on January 13, 1918. The Congress of Soviets also reaffirmed "the right of all peoples to self-determination up to complete secession from Russia." *Tret'ii vserossiiskii s"ezd sovetov rabochikh, soldatskikh i krest'ianskikh deputatov* (Petrograd, 1918), 73.

135. Oldenbourg, *Le coup d'état bolchéviste*, 169–70, 173–4. When the congress, the next day, approved the "Decree on Peace," Lenin had repeated his caveat that "wars cannot end by a refusal to fight, they cannot be ended by one side alone." Kotel'nikov, *Vtoroi vserossiiskii s"ezd sovetov*, 62.

136. Avdeev, *Revoliutsiia 1917 goda*, IV: 285–6; Kennan, *Russia Leaves the War*, 75–6.

137. Bunyan and Fisher, *Bolshevik Revolution*, 268–75.

138. *Izvestiia*, November 10, 1917, translated in Bunyan and Fisher, *Bolshevik Revolution*, 242–4; Iroshnikov, *Sozdanie*, 166–7; *DVP SSSR*, I: 11–4

139. Warth, *The Allies*, 168.

140. The surreal quality of the new authority's relation to the military was captured by Alexander Ilin (b. 1894), known as the "Genevan" (from his pre-revolutionary exile days), who was appointed the secretary to the new war commissariat and got a glimpse of the luxurious offices of the tsarist war ministry on St. Petersburg's Moika Canal: "silken furniture, silken wallpaper, curtains over the doors and windows, mirrors, carved chandeliers and thick carpets into which one's feet literally sank." Ilin and his Bolshevik co-administrators insisted on eating "the same cabbage soup that the soldiers lived on," to convey the "democratic character" of their authority. At the same time, Ilin recalled how Krylenko took offense when his authority went unacknowledged ("his entire small figure gave forth a real aura of power"). This imperiousness, however, did not bother Ilin, despite the "democratic" cabbage soup diet. "In circumstances in which we were subjected to lying, slander and, in part, refusal to recognize our authority [*vlast'*]," Ilin noted, "it was very important to maintain a firm line. After all, authority can only be recognized as such if it is convinced of its own competence and by its behavior inspires others with that conviction." Il'in-Zhenevskii, *Bol'sheviki u vlasti*; Il'in-Zhenevskii, *Bolsheviks in Power*.

141. Bunyan and Fisher, *Bolshevik Revolution*, 232–42, 264–8; Spiridovich, *Istoriia bol'shevizma v Rossii*, 406–7;

Wildman, *End of the Russian Imperial Army*, II: 380–401.

142. *Novaia zhizn'*, December 13, 1917; *Russkoe slovo*, December 6, 1917; Bunyan and Fisher, *Bolshevik Revolution*, 267–8; Masaryk, *Making of a State*, 163–4. Dukhonin took over as acting supreme commander only on November 3, 1917, seventeen days before his murder.

143. Fischer, *Germany's Aims*, 477; Wildman, *End of the Russian Imperial Army*, II: 400–1; *Sovetsko-Germanskie otnosheniia*, I: 108; Niessel, *Le triomphe des bolschéviks*, 187–8.

144. *Pravda*, November 15, 1917: 1; Bunyan and Fisher, *Bolshevik Revolution*, 258–9. See also *Izvestiia*, December 2, December 3, December 4, December 5, December 6, and December 9, 1917; and Kamenev, *Bor'ba za mir*. In the event of a "general peace," the Germans pledged to quit Belgium, northern France, Serbia, Romania, Poland, Lithuania, and Courland, thereby seeking to undercut the Allies' contention that they needed to continue fighting to liberate these territories. But the pledge was insincere. Wheeler-Bennett, *Forgotten Peace*, 136.

145. RGASPI, f. 17, op. 109, d. 9, l. 23.

146. Buchan, *History of the Great War*, IV: 135. These divisions had just been brought from the western front to Riga in late 1917. Ludendorff, *My War Memoires*, II: 34.

147. Freund, *Unholy Alliance*, 3. Radek retained his Austrian passport until 1918.

148. Ottokar, *In the World War* [1920], 246; Wheeler-Bennett, *Forgotten Peace*, 113.

149. Trotsky made the point slightly differently: *History of the Russian Revolution to Brest-Litovsk*, 5.

150. *Sovetsko-germanskie otnosheniia*, I: 194–6.

151. Michael Geyer has persuasively argued that societies that mobilized *intensively* (the Russian empire, Germany) rather than *extensively* (France and Britain, which relied on their colonies as well as loans from the United States) suffered the greatest dislocation and social upheaval. Geyer, "The Militarization of Europe," 65–102.

152. *Izvestiia*, March 2, 1922 (Ioffe).

153. *Proceedings of the Brest-Litovsk Peace Conference*, 82; Trotsky, *My Life*, 311, 319–20; Trotsky, *Lenin*, 128.

154. Pavliuckenkov, *Krest'ianskii Brest*, 22 (citing GARF, f. 130, op. 2, d. 11, l. 20: report by Mikhail Bonch-Bruevich, a former tsarist officer who now headed the Red general staff, to the Council of People's Commissars).

155. *Pravda*, February 24, 1918: 2–3 (Lenin's theses, delivered January 7);

Bunyan and Fisher, *Bolshevik Revolution*, 500–5; *PSS*, XXXV: 243–51; Wheeler-Bennett, *Forgotten Peace*, 139. Bolshevik party officials from around the country were in town for an upcoming Congress of Soviets, and Lenin included nearly fifty provincial party chiefs at the Central Committee meeting, hoping to use them as a pressure group. Debo, *Revolution and Survival*, 72–90.

156. *Protokoly Tsentral'nogo Komiteta RSDRP (b)*, 171; *The Bolsheviks and the October Revolution: Central Committee Minutes*, 177.

157. *Protokoly Tsentral'nogo Komiteta RSDRP (b)*, 173. See also *VII ekstrennyi s"ezd RKP (b), mart 1918 goda*, xxvi–xxvii; and Krupskaya, *Reminiscences*, 448.

158. *PSS*, XXXV: 253–4.

159. *Pravda*, January 17 and 18, 1918; *Sochineniia*, IV: 36–7.

160. Price, *My Reminiscences*, 224–5.

161. *Protokoly Tsentral'nogo Komiteta RSDRP (b)*, 174–80; *The Bolsheviks and the October Revolution: Central Committee Minutes*, 185. On January 13, the Central Committees of both the Bolsheviks and the Left SRs had met together, and a majority favored Trotsky's formula of "end the war, don't sign a peace" (283).

162. Wargelin, "A High Price for Bread."

163. Von Kühlmann, *Erinnerungen*, 531.

164. As Hoffmann explained, "the difficulties were transitory; at any time we could support the [Rada] with arms and establish it again." Hoffmann, *War Diaries*, II: 216.

165. Fedyshyn, *Germany's Drive to the East*, 65–86.

166. Fischer, *Germany's Aims*.

167. Ioffe, *Mirnye peregovory v Brest-Litovske*, I: 207–8; *Proceedings of the Brest-Litovsk Peace Conference*, 172–3; Hoffmann, *War Diaries*, II: 218–9; D. G. Fokke, "Na tsene i za kulisami," 207; Wheeler Bennett, *Forgotten Peace*, 227–9; Freund, *Unholy Alliance*, 6; *PSS*, XXII: 555–8.

168. Trotsky, *My Life*, 386. "Versatile, cultivated, and elegant, he could be charming in his occasions of good-humor," one scholar observed of Trotsky. "But in his more usual attitude of contemptuous anger, he was freezing fire." Wheeler-Bennett, *Forgotten Peace*, 152.

169. Il'in-Zhenevskii, *Bolsheviks in Power*, 21–2.

170. Ottokar, *In the World War* [1919], 328; Hoffmann, *War Diaries*, II: 219. Austria-Hungary did not even have a border any longer with Russia, given the separate treaty with Ukraine. (Poles left Austrian military ranks and marched into Ukraine to retake "Polish" territory.)

171. Fischer, *Germany's Aims*, 501–5; *Sovetsko-germanskie otnoshniia*, I: 328.

172. Magnes, *Russia and Germany*, 109–123.

173. Nowak, *Die Aufzeichnungen*, I: 187 (entry of February 22, 1918).

174. Khalid, "Tashkent 1917," 279.

175. Chokaev, "Turkestan and the Soviet Regime," 406.

176. Gordienko, *Obrazovanie Turkestanskoi ASSR*, 309–10.

177. Khalid, *Politics of Cultural Reform*, 273–4. Using contemporary Turkic-language newspapers, this corrects the version set down by Safarov, *Kolonial'naia revoliutsiia*, 64.

178. *Pobeda oktiabr'skoi revoliutsii*, II: 27.

179. Park, *Bolshevism in Turkestan*, 15–22.

180. Khalid, *Politics of Cultural Reform*, 277.

181. Chokaev, "Turkestan and the Soviet Regime," 408.

182. Chaikan, *K istorii Rossiikoi revoliutsii*, 133.

183. Alekseenkov, *Kokandskaia avtonomiia*, 58.

184. Etherton, *In the Heart of Asia*, 154.

185. *PSS*, XXXV: 245–54; Wheeler-Bennett, *Forgotten Peace*, 217–39.

186. *The Bolsheviks and the October Revolution: Central Committee Minutes*, 206; *Protokoly Tsentral'nogo komiteta RSDRP (b)* [1958], 171–2, 199, 202–4, 212–3, 215–7; "Deiatel'nost' Tsentral'nogo komiteta partii v dokumentakh (sobytiia i fakty)," *Izvestiia TsK KPSS*, 1989, no. 4: 142–4.

187. Trotsky, *My Life*, 382–4; Trotsky, *Lenin*, 106–10. To the 7th Party Congress in March 1918, Lenin divulged of his dealings with Trotsky, "it was agreed between us that we would hold out until the Germans presented an ultimatum, and then we would yield." *PSS*, XXXVI: 30; Debo, *Revolution and Survival*, 80.

188. *Protokoly Tsentral'nogo komiteta RSDRP (b)*, 204; *The Bolsheviks and the October Revolution: Central Committee Minutes*, 210–1; *VII ekstrennyi s"ezd RKP (b), mart 1918 goda*, 197–201; *PSS*, XXXV: 486–7; Deutscher, *Prophet Armed*, 383, 390. In favor were Lenin, Stalin, Sverdlov, Zinoviev, Sokolnikov, Smilga, and Trotsky; opposed were Joffe, Lomov, Bukharin, Krestinsky, and Dzierżyński.

189. *Pravda*, February 20, 1918.

190. Upton, *Finnish Revolution*, 62–144.

191. *PSS*, XXXVI: 10.

192. Wheeler-Bennett, *Forgotten Peace*, 254.

193. Trotsky, *My Life*, 333.

194. Trotsky, *My Life* [1930], 388–9.

195. *Protokoly Tsentral'ngo komiteta RSDRP (b)*, 211–8; *Pravda*, February 24, 1918; *Proceedings of the*

*Brest-Litovsk Peace Conference*, 176–7; Wheeler-Bennett, *Forgotten Peace*, 255–7; Debo, *Revolution and Survival*, 142.

196. *Protokoly Tsentral'nogo komiteta RSDRP (b)*, 215; *The Bolsheviks and the October Revolution: Central Committee Minutes*, 223; *Pravda*, February 24, 1918; *PSS*, XXXV: 369–70, 490; Volkogonov, *Stalin: Politicheskii portret*, I: 86; Volkogonov, *Stalin: Triumph and Tragedy*, 36. The other abstentions were Krestinsky, Dzierżyński, and Joffe. Bukharin voted no.

197. *Pravda*, February 26, 1918: 3.

198. *PSS*, XXXV: 381; Rabinowitch, *Bolsheviks in Power*, 172–8.

199. Sokolnikov pronounced "this triumph of the imperialist and the militarist over the international Proletarian Revolution . . . only a temporary and passing one." *Proceedings of the Brest-Litovsk Peace Conference*, 180.

200. Bunyan and Fisher, *Bolshevik Revolution*, 521–3; Wheeler-Bennett, *Forgotten Peace*, 308.

201. Wheeler-Bennett, *Forgotten Peace*, 275–6. Lenin's refusal to discuss the consequences of a revolution before the Bolsheviks had seized power is analyzed in Kingston-Mann, "Lenin and the Beginnings of Marxist Peasant Revolution."

202. Hahlweg, *Diktatfrieden*, 51; *Novaia zhizn'*, April 30, 1918: 2 (S. Zagorsky).

203. Pipes, *Russian Revolution*, 595–7.

204. Dohan, "Soviet Foreign Trade in the NEP Economy," 218.

205. It has been argued that Lenin's German orientation, by cleaving off Bolshevik allies on the left such as the Left SRs, proved conducive to dictatorship, but first, the German orientation almost destroyed the Bolsheviks. Wheeler-Bennett, *Forgotten Peace*, 345–8; Mawdsley, *Russian Civil War*, 39–44.

206. *VII ekstrennyi s"ezd RKP (b), mart 1918 goda*, 11–3, 127–9, 133, 176–7; *PSS*, XXXVI: 1-77. Kin and Sorin, *Sed'moi s'ezd*.

207. Petrograd industries would also be evacuated to the interior. Avdeev, *Revoliutsiia 1917 goda*, V: 23, 30–1; *Rabochii put'*, October 6, 1916; Pethybridge, *Spread of the Russian Revolution*, 188; Colton, *Moscow*, 96. In Kerensky's plan, the Petrograd Soviet and its central executive committee and soviet would have had to fend for themselves being, technically, "private" and not governmental entities. Miliukov, "From Nicholas II to Stalin."

208. On October 9, when the Provisional Government announced it would deploy up to half the immense capital garrison (nearly 200,000) at the city's approaches, to defend it, this provoked additional charges of wanting to snuff out the revolution by dispatching the (radicalized) garrison troops to the front. Avdeev, *Revoliutsiia 1917 goda*, V: 52.

209. "Iz perepiski E. D. Stasovoi."

210. Bonch-Bruevich later claimed that the ruminations over relocating to Nizhny Novgorod on the Volga had been an elaborate charade played out with the SR-dominated railway union (Vikzhel). Bonch-Bruevich, *Pereezd Sovetskogo pravitel'stva*. See also Malinovskii, "K pereezdu TsK RKP (b)." Ryazanov made an analogy to the Communards of Paris in 1871, who went down with the city.

211. Trotskii, *Kak vooruzhalas' revoliutsiia*, I: 105.

212. Sidorov, *Revoliutsionnoe dvizheniie*; Krastin'š, *Istoriia Latyshskikh strelko*; Ģērmanis, *Oberst Vācietis*; "Iz vospominanii glavkoma I. I. Vatsetis."

213. Rabinowitch, *Bolsheviks in Power*, 201 (citing TsA VMF, f. r-342, op. 1, d. 116, l. 34–56ob.).

214. Mal'kov, *Zapiski komendanta [1967]*, 133–5.

215. *Izvestiia*, March 17, 1918: 2. The Soviet had post facto approved the capital's "temporary" relocation. Zinoviev had opposed the move to Moscow; he favored Nizhny Novgorod, precisely because the latter would be temporary.

216. The "Muscovite tsardom" would not be formally dissolved until June 9, 1918, for the sake of "economizing." Lenin, *Leninskie dekrety o Moskve*, 62–3; Ignat'ev, *Moskva*, 85–7. Lenin managed to abolish the province (*oblast*) council in August 1918, and placed Kamenev in charge of Moscow as chairman of the Moscow soviet.

217. *Istoriia Moskvy*, II: 127.

218. The Metropole Hotel became House of Soviets No. 2; the Theological Seminary, on Moscow's innermost ring, House of Soviets No. 3, a residence with offices. The building housing the party's Central Committee apparatus on Vozdvizhenka was designated House of Soviets No. 4. House of Soviets No. 5 was a residential complex on Sheremetev Street (renamed Granovskaya Street). The Central Committee apparatus had also gotten part of Moscow's Hotel Dresden.

219. *Krasnaia Moskva*, 347; *Izvestiia*, January 25, 1921: 4; *Narodnoe khoziaistvo*, 1918, no. 11: 11–14 (V. Obolensky-Osinsky).

220. In December 1920, the Cheka moved its headquarters to the Russia Insurance Co. building on the Lyubyanka Square, 2. Leggett, *The Cheka*, 217–20 (*Spravochnik uchrezdeniia RSFSR*, January 22, 1920, 215–28). Within weeks of the March 1918 move to Moscow, the Cheka launched massive raids on more than two dozen "anarchist" compounds, including at the famous Ryabushinsky mansion designed by the architect Fyodor Shekhtel in art moderne, where the police made no attempt to dispel the large crowd of onlookers—let the masses see the Cheka! *MChK*, 20; Klement'ev, *V Bol'shevistkoi Moskve*, 139.

221. Solomon [Isetskii], *Sredi krasnykh vozhdei*, I: 192–4. Georgy Isetskii (1868–1934), aka Solomon, from a noble family, was close to Lenin. Isetskii claims he started living at the colossal structure of his commissariat (Narkomvneshtorg) on Miliutin Lane.

222. Germany's postwar government, known as the Weimar Republic (where it was founded), had left the 1,200-room Hohenzollern Palace in Berlin empty, seeking to avoid association with the monarchy and militarist old regime. Hitler and the Nazi regime would also steer clear of the Hohenzollern Palace and its connotations of Prussian monarchy.

223. One person who attended Council of People's Commissars meetings in 1918 found the first two floors below Lenin's wing in the enormous structure lifeless. Bortnevskii and Varustina, "A. A. Borman," I: 115–49 (at 129).

224. Mal'kov, *Zapiski [1967]*, 116–20; Malkov, *Reminiscences*, 123–4. In Petrograd, officials of the new regime had commandeered tram cars. Mal'kov, *Zapiski [1967]*, 43.

225. Mal'kov, *Zapiski [1967]*, 133–5.

226. Trotsky, *My Life*, 351–2; Trotskii, *Portrety revoliutsionerov*, 54–5.

227. Stanisław Pestkovskii, "Vospominaniia o rabote v narkomnaste (1917–1919 gg.)," *Proletarskaia revoliutsiia*, 1930, no. 6: 124–31 (at 130).

228. Golikov, *Vladimir Il'ich Lenin*, V: 307–8. Official sources do not record the precise date of Stalin's marriage, and it was left out of his chronology for 1918: *Sochineniia*, IV: 445–56. Stalin would return to Petrograd on only three more occasions for the rest of his life: 1919, when the city fell under threat from anti-Bolshevik forces; 1926, to mark the destruction of the Zinoviev machine; and 1934 when Kirov was murdered. McNeal, *Stalin*, 342, n1.

229. Alliluyeva, *Twenty Letters*, 104 (to Alisa Radchenko).

230. Alliluev, *Khronika odnoi sem'i*, 27.

231. RGASPI, f. 558, op. 4, d, 668, l. 18 (F. S. Alliluev, "V Moskve [Vstrecha s t. Stalinym]," undated typescript); Alliluyeva, *Vospominaniia*, 187.

232. *Moskovskii Kreml'—tsitadel' Rossii* (Moscow, 2008), 185.

233. Trotskii, *Portrety revoliutsionerov*, 54–5.

234. Astrov, *Illustrated History*, II: 509.

235. V. I. Lenin, "Doklad o ratifikatsii mirnogo dogovora 14 marta." *Pravda*,

March 16/17, 1918, in *PSS*, XXXVI: 92–111.

236. The congress also formally approved, belatedly, the relocation of the capital to Moscow on March 16, 1918. Delegate numbers conflict: *Izvestiia*, March 17, 1918: 2.

237. *Chetvertyi Vserossiikii s"ezd sovetov rabochikh*, 30–3; Bunyan and Fisher, *Bolshevik Revolution*, 532.

238. Warth, *The Allies*, 199–205, 235–41.

239. George, *War Memoirs*, II: 1542–3, 1550–1, 1891–2, 1901; Kettle, *Allies and the Russian Collapse*, 172–3. British intervention in Russia recalled the ill-fated Dardanelles campaign of the Great War, an attempt to reap large gains at seemingly low cost.

240. Not coincidentally, many of the British intelligence agents on the ground in Russia had previous India experience. Occleshaw, *Dances in Deep Shadows*.

241. GARF, f. r-130, op. 2, d. 1 (Sovnarkom meeting, April 2, 1918).

242. *Protokoly zasedanii Vserossiiskogo*, 263–70 (Lenin speech of May 14, 1918).

243. *Pravda*, March 26, March 27, 1918.

244. *Pravda*, April 3, April 4, 1918.

245. A. Goldenweiser, "Iz Kievskikh vospominanii (1917–1921 gg.)," in Gessen, *Arkhiv russkoi revoliutsii*, VI: 209–16; N. Mogilianskii, "Tragediia Ukrainy," in Gessen, *Arkhiv russkoi revoliutsii*, IX: 84–90; Bunyan, *Intervention*, 6–17.

246. Bunyan, *Intervention*, 4; Collin Ross, "Doklad … o polozhenii del na ukraine," in Gessen, *Arkhiv russkoi revoliutsii*, I: 288–92; Fedyshyn, *Germanys' Drive to the East*, 133–83.

247. Martov, "Artilleriskaia podgotovka," *Vpered!*, March 18, 1918.

248. *Pravda*, April 1, 1918; *Zaria Rossii*, April 17, 1918.

249. RGASPI, f. 558, op. 2, d. 3, l. 1–63; op. 2, d. 42. Stalin's chief defender at the trial, Sosnovky, editor of *Pravda*, would be murdered in the purges.

250. Hoover Institution Archives, Nicolaevsky Collection, no. 6, box 2, folder 27; Grigorii Aronson, "Stalinskii protsess protiv Martova," *Sotsialisticheskii vestnik*, 19/7–8 (April 28, 1930): 84–9; *Vpered!*, April 14 and April 26, 1918; Wolfe, *Three Who Made a Revolution*, 470–1 (citing oral interviews with Nicolaevsky, Rafael Abramowich, and Samuel Levitas); Chavichvili, *Révolutionnaires russes à Genève*, 74–91; Trotsky, *Stalin*, 101–10; "Delo Iu. Martova v revoliutsionnyi tribunale," *Obozrenie*, 1985, no. 15: 45–6, no. 16: 43–6; Kun, *Unknown Portrait*, 81–4. Later, the Menshevik Nicolaevsky, overreacting to Menshevik memoirs, wrongly argued that "the role played by Stalin in the activities of the Kamo group was subsequently exaggerated." Nikolaevskii, *Tainye stranitsy istorii*, 88. The fate of the affidavits Nicolaevsky gathered from the Georgians remains mysterious.

251. Okorokov, *Oktiabr' i krakh russkoi burzuazhnoi pressy*, 275–7.

252. This episode has often been garbled: Antonov-Ovseenko, *The Time of Stalin*, 3–7.

253. N. Rutych (ed.), "Dnevniki, zapisi, pis'ma generala Alekseeva i vospominaniia ob otse V. M. Alekseevoi-Borel," in *Grani*, no. 125, 1982: 175–85.

254. Lincoln, *Red Victory*, 48 (citing K. N. Nikolaev, "Moi zhiznennyi put'," 150–1, in Bakhmeteff Archive, Columbia University, K. N. Nikoaev Collection).

255. S. M. Paul, "S Kornilovym," in *Beloe delo*, 7 vols. (Berlin: Miednyi vsadnik, 1926–1933), III: 67, 69.

256. Lincoln, *Red Victory*, 88 (citing A. Bogaevskii, "Pervyi kubanskii pokhhod [Ledianoi pokhod]," 82, in Bakhmeteff Archive, Columbia University); Khadziev, *Velikii boiar*, 369, 396.

257. Denikin, *Ocherki russkoi smuti*, II: 301.

258. "Rech' v Moskokskom sovete … 23 aprelia 1918 g.," *Pravda*, April 24, 1919; *Izvestiia*, April 24, 1919, in *PSS*, XXXVI: 232–7.

259. Jászi, *Dissolution*.

260. *Rossiia v mirovoi voine 1914–1918*, 41,

261. Klante, *Von der Wolga zum Amur*, 318; Bradley, *Allied Intervention*, 65–105.

262. Fić, *The Bolsheviks and the Czechoslovak Legion*, 206, 242, 262, 307–8, 313. The Legionnaires were mostly stationed in Ukraine, and in February 1918, when the German and Austrian army entered Ukraine in force, the Czechoslovak Legion had retreated into Soviet Russia.

263. In March 1918, the Omsk Soviet indicated it did not want to receive the Czechoslovak Legion, deeming it a counterrevolutionary force: Stalin telegrammed on March 26, 1918, to inform them it was by decision of the Council of People's Commissars. Bunyan, *Intervention*, 81–2.

264. Maksakov and Turunov, *Khronika grazhdanskoi voiny*, 168. Trotsky had received a Cheka telegram (May 20–21, 1918) concerning a Serbian officer, Georgy Vukmanović, among the Czechoslovak Legion: "I am convinced that the organization of these troops has a counterrevolutionary character, they are being specially formed for dispatch to France but at the same time … they intend to concentrate their troops along the rail stations of Siberia and in the event of a Japanese attack they will take all rail lines into their hands." It was countersigned by Dzierżyński, with a handwritten note, indicating he was skeptical about the Serb ["aforist"] and his alleged Bolshevism but not entirely dismissive. RGASPI, f. 17, op. 109, d. 13, l. 1.

265. Bunyan, *Intervention*, 86–92.

266. Bullock, *Russian Civil War*, 46.

267. Bunyan, *Intervention*, 277, n1.

268. Pestkovskii, "Vospominaniia o rabote v narkomnaste," 130.

269. Stalin, "O iuge Rossii," *Pravda*, October 30, 1918. "Of all the difficulties which confront us," Trotsky remarked in a speech on June 9, "the most pressing … is that of food," citing countless telegrams of hunger and typhus. Bunyan, *Intervention*, 468; Trotskii, *Kak vooruzhalas' revoliutsiia*, I: 74–86 (at 74).

270. Israelin, "Neopravdavshiisia prognoz graf Mirbakha."

271. *Pravda*, April 27, 1918. Radek wrote of "the hate with which every working man in Moscow today greets the representative of German capital." *Izvestiia*, April 28, 1918.

272. RGASPI, f. 17, op. 109, d. 4, l. 10.

273. *Izvestiia TsK KPSS*,1989, no. 4: 143–4.

274. *Nashe slovo*, May 15, 1918: 2.

275. Drabkina, "Dokumenty germanskogo polsa v Moskve Mirbakha," 124; Pipes, *Russian Revolution*, 617 (citing Winfried Baumgart, *Vierteljahreshefte für Zietgeschichte*, 16/1 [1968]: 80).

276. Sverdlov followed up with additional circulars that month to all party organizations to reinforce the point. *Pravda*, May 19, May 22, and May 29, 1918; *Perepiska sekretariata TsK RKP (b)*, III: 64, 72–4, 81–3; Sakwa, "The Commune State in Moscow," 443–7; and Hegelsen, "The Origins of the Party-State Monolith."

277. *PSS*, L: 88.

278. Nicolaevskii, *Tainy stanitsy istorii*, 384–6 (the words of Kurt Riezler).

279. Ludendorff, *My War Memories*, II: 658; Bunyan, *Intervention*, 177–9; Denikin, *Ocherki russkoi smuty*, III: 82–3. Ludendorff forwarded a long memorandum to the imperial chancellor on June 9, 1918.

280. In less than six months, it would be Wilhelm II who was *kaput*. Zeman, *Germany and the Revolution in Russia*, 126–7, 137–9. "Please use larger sums," wrote Germany's state secretary to the German minister (ambassador) Count Mirbach in Moscow on May 18, 1918, "as it is generally in our interests that the Bolsheviks should survive." He added: "If further money required, please telegraph how much. It is very difficult to say from here which trend to support if Bolsheviks fall." Zeman, *Germany and the Revolution in Russia*, 128–9.

281. Wheeler-Bennet, *Forgotten Peace*, 348–55.

282. Baumgart, *Deutsche Ostpolitik 1918*, 84.

283. Even as Germany, despite having signed the Brest-Litovsk Treaty, continued to seize former tsarist territory (Ukraine), Lenin turned to the Reichswehr to intercede against uncontrollable Red units (!). I. I. Vatsetis, *Pamiat'*, 1979, no. 2: 44.

284. N. Rozhkov, "Iskliuchenie oppozitsii iz TsIK," *Novaia zhizn'*, June 18, 1918; Drabkina, "Moskva 1918."

285. Häfner, *Die Partei der linken Sozialrevolutionäre*; Leont'ev, *Partiia levykh sotsialistov-revoliutsionerov*. The Left SRs existed as a standalone party only since November 1917.

286. Makintsian, *Krasnaia kniga VChK*, II: 129–30; Gusev, *Krakh partii levykh eserov*, 193–4. The Cheka volume was soon withdrawn from circulation; during perestroika, it was reissued (Moscow: Politizdat, 1989).

287. Litvin, *Levye esery i VChK*, 69–73 (TsA FSB, d. N-2, t. 2, l. 10). This collection of documents amplifies Makintsian, *Krasnaia kniga VChK*.

288. *V Vserossiiskii s"ezd sovietov*, 5–37; Rabinowitch, "Maria Spiridonova's 'Last Testament,'" 426; Rabinowitch, *Bolsheviks in Power*, 288 (citing TsA SPb, f. 143, op. 1, d. 224, l. 75).

289. Bunyan, *Intervention*, 198, n57.

290. *V vserossiiskii s"ezd sovetov*, 22–3; Bunyan, *Intervention*, 200.

291. *V. vserossiiskii s"ezd sovetov*, 50–61; *Izvestiia*, July 5, 1918: 5; Bunyan, *Intervention*, 207–9. The reintroduction of the death penalty also angered the Left SRs, especially in an instance involving apparent heroism. The Baltic Fleet, still intact, was stationed at its main base Helsingfors (Helsinki), but the landing of German troops on the southwest of Finland in March 1918 jeopardized the fleet as well as Petrograd. The British, wary of German seizure of the Baltic Fleet, were conspiring with Trotsky to scuttle the ships. In March–April 1918, Alexei Schastny, the commander, worked a miracle to bring the fleet to safety at Kronstadt, his path cleared by icebreakers. But Trotsky wrongly suspected Schastny of hesitating to implement his orders to prepare the fleet for destruction. Schastny resigned in May. Unsatisfied, Trotsky himself organized a trial and had him executed on the fabricated charge of attempting to overthrow the Petrograd government. Trotsky was the sole witness allowed to testify. Rabinowitch, "Dos'e Shchastnogo."

292. *V vserossiiskii s"ezd sovetov*, Bunyan, *Intervention*, 210.

293. *V vserossiiskii s"ezd sovetov*, 63, 69; Gogolevskii, *Dekrety Sovetskoi vlasti o Petrograde*, 171.

294. Makintsian, *Krasnaia kniga VChK*, I: 185.

295. Makintsian, *Krasnaia kniga VChK*, I; 201–6 (Blyumin), II: 224–33. See also *Neizvestnaia Rossiia: XX vek* (Moscow, 1992), II: 55.

296. Latsis, *Proletarskaia revoliutsiia*, 1926, no. 9: 90.

297. Sadoul, *Notes sur la révolution bolchevique*, 305; Lockhart, *British Agent*, 295. Both Sadoul and Lockhart were eyewitnesses.

298. RGASPI, f. 4, op. 2, d. 527, l. 13 (recollections of Danishevsky).

299. Strauss, "Kurt Riezler, 1882–1955"; Thompson, *Eye of the Storm*.

300. Erdmann, *Kurt Riezler*, 713–4 (a deposition given in 1952); von Bothmer, *Mit Graf Mirbach in Moskau*, 72, 78; Makintsian, *Krasnaia kniga VChK*, I: 196–7; Hilger and Meyer, *Incompatible Allies*, 5–6, 8–9; Jarausch, "Cooperation or Intervention?" Andreyev would die of typhus in 1919. Their credentials also carried the signature of Ksenofontov, the Cheka secretary.

301. The German military attaché, Bothmer, had raced to the Metropole Hotel to the commissariat of foreign affairs, whence Lev Karakhan, deputy commissar, phoned Lenin. Golikov, *Vladimir Il'ich Lenin*, V: 606.

302. Erdmann, *Kurt Riezler*, 715; Baumgart, *Deutsche Ostpolitik 1918*, 228, n71; Chicherin, *Two Years of Soviet Foreign Policy*; Sadoul, *Notes sur la révolution bolchevique*, 405. Some testimony indicates Lenin signed the condolence book.

303. *Pravda*, July 8, 1918, reprinted in Dzierżyński, *Izbrannye proizvedeniia*, 111–6 (at 114). The quotation was retained in subsequent editions (Moscow, 1967), I: 265; (Moscow, 1977), I: 176–9.

304. "He considers that Lenin is doing secretly what Kamenev and Zinoviev did in October," a Bolshevik party meeting recorded Dzierżyński as having said. "We are a party of the proletariat and we should see clearly that if we sign this peace the proletariat will not follow us." *VII ekstrennyi s"ezd RKP (b): mart 1918 goda*, 245.

305. Bonch-Bruevich, *Ubiistvo germanskogo posla Mirbakha i vosstanie levykh eserov*, 27. See also Spirin, *Krakh odnoi aventiury*, 38. Abram Belenky was also taken hostage with Dzierżyński.

306. Makintsian, *Krasnaia kniga VChK*, II: 194.

307. Litvin, *Levye esery i VChK*, 97 (Lācis: TsA FSB, d. N-8, t. 9, l. 8); Vladimirova, "Levye esery," 121.

308. Steinberg, "The Events of July 1918," 122.

309. Paustovskii, *Povest' o zhizni*, I: 422–24; Lockhart, *British Agent*, 294–300.

310. Litvin, *Levye esery i VChK*, 211–33 (Shliapnikov: *Za zemliu i voliu*, July 16–19, 1918).

311. Steinberg, "The Events of July 1918," 20.

312. *PSS*, L: 114.

313. "Pis'mo V. I. Leninu," *Sochineniia*, IV: 118–9; *Pravda*, December 21, 1929; Voroshilov, *Lenin, Stalin, i krasnaia armiia*, 43; *Bolshevik*, 1936, no. 2: 74.

314. Vatsetis, "Grazhdanskaia voina: 1918 god," 26–7.

315. Muravyov had begun his career as the head of security in Petrograd in 1917. He went on to crush the Rada in Ukraine in February 1918, then was sent to Bessarabia. In April, Dzierżyński had Muravyov arrested for looting, summary executions, discrediting Soviet power, and plotting with anarchists in Moscow. On June 13, 1918, however, the high command had appointed the fearless, no-holes-barred Muravyov as supreme commander of pro-Bolshevik forces on the key Volga front. The German embassy official in Moscow, Kurt Riezler, meanwhile, was funneling bribes to Muravyov to take on the Czechoslovak Legion rebels, a fact that became known to the Cheka. After the Left SR rebellion in Moscow was put down, on July 10, Muravyov declared he was switching sides to make war against Germany, "the vanguard of world imperialism," and invited his enemies of the days before, the Czechoslovaks, to join. He commanded the largest single intact Red force at the time, and his betrayal threatened to detach from the Bolsheviks the entire strategic Volga valley and its food supply—a potential turning point. A young Lithuanian worker Bolshevik in the town of Simbirsk, Jonava Vareikis, saved the day, luring Muravyov to a trap, where on July 11 he was shot and bayonetted to death. (Vācietis would be sent eastward to sort matters out.) Rabinowitch, *Bolsheviks in Power*, 25 (citing *Izvestiia*, November 2, 1917); Savchenko, *Avantiuristy grazhdanskoi voiny*, 44–64 (at 56); Baumgart, *Deutsche Ostpolitik 1918*, 227; Erdmann, *Kurt Riezler*, 474, 711; Alfons Paquet, in Baumgart, *Von Brest-Litovsk*, 76; Pipes, *Russian Revolution*, 631; *Dekrety sovetskoi vlasti*, III: 9–10; Vladimirova, "Levye esery," 120, 131; Lappo, *Iosif Vareikis*, 13–4; Spirin, *Klassy i partii*, 193–194; Mawdsley, *Russian Civil War*, 56–7.

316. Vatsetis, "Grazhdanskaia voina: 1918 god," 16. Many Latvian units had been sent to the Volga valley.

317. Rabinowitch, *Bolsheviks in Power*, 294 (citing GARF, f. 130, op. 2, d. 1098, l. 2).

318. Vatsetis, "Grazhdanskaia voina: 1918 god," 40–1. He claimed the fighting lasted seven hours, from 5:00 a.m. until noon, but this is highly improbable. See also Makintsian, *Krasnaia kniga VChK*, I: 201–4 (Sablin).

319. Valdis Berzins, "Pervyi glavkom i

ego rukopis," *Daugava*, 1980, no. 2–5 (Vācietis memoirs from 1919); V. D. Bonch-Bruevich—I. V. Stalinu," *Izvestiia TsK KPSS*, 1989, no. 4: 199–201.

320. Leggett, *The Cheka*, 70–83; Steinberg, "The Events of July 1918," 21–2 (citing Lacis); Steinberg, *Spiridonova*, 216.

321. *Izvestiia*, July 8, 1918. Even now, one on-site Latvian commander reported that many of his compatriots thought the Bolsheviks' days were numbered. Swain, "Vācietis," 77 (citing Latvian State Archives, f. 45, op. 3, d. 11, l. 3).

322. Chudaev, "Bor'ba Komunisticheskoi partii za uprochnenie Sovetskoi vlasti," 177–226. Dzierżyński had resigned as head of the Cheka the day he was freed (July 7). Unusually, the resignation was announced in all the newspapers and posted throughout the capital. He was replaced, at least formally, by Jēkabs Peterss, an ethnic Latvian, a founding member of the Cheka, and the man who had retaken the Lubyanka headquarters from the Left SR–controlled Combat Detachment. (Peterss soon bragged to a newspaper, "I am not at all as bloodthirsty as people think.") Dzierżyński remained in Moscow over the summer, however, and the extent to which he ceded authority remains unclear. On August 22, he would be formally reinstated as Cheka head. Tsvigun, *V. I. Lenin i VChK*, 69, 83; Bonch-Bruevich, *Vospominaniia o Lenine* [1969], 316; *Utro Moskvy*, November 4, 1918. See also Peters, "Vospominaniia o rabote v VChK." *MChK*, 77–79; Leggett, *The Cheka*, 251. The episode of Dzierżyński's resignation was described, murkily, in Makintsian, *Krasnaia kniga VChK*. As late as June 1919, almost a year after the Left SR party's debacle, the Moscow City Cheka confirmed two former Left SRs to its collegium, the highest decision-making body. *MChK*, 154.

323. Blium, *Za kulisami "ministerstva pravdy,"* 34.

324. Erdmann, *Kurt Riezler*, 715; *Izvestiia*, July 14, 1918: 4. Popov was sentenced to death in absentia; he was captured only in 1921. Litvin, *Levye esery i VChK*, 145–56 (Popov: TsA FSB, d. N-963, l. 50–5).

325. *V Verossiiskii s"ezd sovetov*, 108–28; Trotskii, *Sochineniia*, XVII/i: 451–76; Trotskii, *Kak vooruzhalas' revoliutsiia*, I: 266–74. See also Zinoviev and Trotskii, *O miatezhe levykh s.r.*; and Erde, "Azef i Azefshchina," *Izvestiia*, July 9, 1918. Vācietis, too, would maintain that the Left SRs had attempted a coup but simply failed to act decisively: "Grazhdanskaia voina: 1918 god," 19.

326. Litvin, *Levye esery i VChK*, 99

(Efretov: TsA FSB, D. n-8, t. 1, l. 177); Rabinowitch, *Bolsheviks in Power*, 294, 443, n48 (citing TsA FSB, no. N-8, vol. Ia: 58, and RGALI SPb, f. 63, op. 1, d. 4, l. 155 [Proshyan]); Vladimirova, "Levye esery," 122–3; *PSS*, XXIII: 554–6; Makintsian, *Krasnaia kniga VChK*, II: 148–55. Proshyan eluded capture but soon died of typhus in a provincial hospital under a false passport. Lenin wrote him an obituary! Litvin, *Levye esery i VChK*, 14; *PSS*, XXXVII: 385.

327. Makintsian, *Krasnaia kniga VChK*, II: 129–30, 186; Häfner, "The Assassination of Count Mirbach," *Piatyi vserossiiskii s"ezd sovetov*, 132, 208; *Pravda*, July 9, 1918: 1, 3; *Izvestiia*, July 10, 1918: 5. Pyotr Smidovich understood it was not a coup in real time: *Izvestiia*, July 8, 1918: 5. The Left SRs would also assassinate the German commander in chief in Ukraine (on July 30, 1918).

328. *V Vserossiiskii s"ezd sovetov*, 109.

329. Schapiro, *Origin of the Communist Autocracy* (1977), x.

330. Trotsky, *History of the Russian Revolution*, III: 305. Spiridonova blamed herself for the debacle. Rabinowitch, *Bolsheviks in Power*, 308 (citing TsA FSB, no. N-685, vol. 6, l. 35ob) (letter of Spiridonova from prison to the Left SR 4th Party Congress); Makintsian, *Krasnaia kniga VChK*, 200–1.

331. Paquet, *Im kommunistischen Russland*, 26. See also Erdmann, *Kurt Riezler*, 467.

332. *Znamia truda*, April 19, 1918. "We are against war, and we do not encourage the nation to resume war," Spiridonova had said at the 3rd Left SR Party Congress in June 1918. "We demand that the Peace Treaty be torn to pieces." Quoted in Vladimirova, "Levye esery," 113.

333. During the confused Left SR melee, Kurt Riezler telegrammed Berlin predicting that "Through immediate ruthless action and good organization, the Bolsheviks will maintain the upper hand, and, unless their own troops fail, be once again successful." Jarausch, "Cooperation or Intervention?," 388. Under Stalin, Spiridonova would be re-arrested in Ufa in 1937, while in exile, along with a dozen other Left SRs. The NKVD shot her and a large group in a forest outside Oryol Prison in September 1941 as the Wehrmacht approached.

334. The Bolshevik and former Bundist S. M. Nakhimson wrote to the party secretariat in June 1918 (one month before he was killed in the Left SR uprising in Yaroslavl), that "All soviet and other institutions are only auxiliary organs for the party." Nakhimson had presided over a "trial" against the Mensheviks and SRs in Yaroslavl already in April 1918. D. B.

Pavlov, *Bol'shevistskaia diktatura*, 3 (citing RGASPI, f. 17, op. 4, d. 91, l. 24); I. Rybal'skii, "Iaroslavskii proletaroiat na slam'e podsudimykh," *Vpered!*, April 25, 1918; G. B. Rabinovich, "Kto sudit iaroslavskikh rabochikh (otkrytoe pis'mo)," *Vpered!*, April 27, 1918.

335. Bykov, *Poslednie dni Romanovykh*, 121; Sokolov, *Ubiistvo tsarskoi sem'i*, 266; Smirnoff, *Autour de l'Assassinat des Grand-Ducs*; Crawford and Crawford, *Michael and Natasha*, 356–61; Ioffe, *Revoliutsiia i sud'ba Romanovykh*, ch. 8. The murder was spearheaded by Gavriil Myasnikov, who would be expelled from the Communist party in 1921 and arrested in 1923 for belonging to the party's Workers opposition. Mikhail Romanov's son Georgy (Count Brasov) had been smuggled out of Russia; he died in 1931, on the eve of his twenty-first birthday, in a car crash. Mikhail's wife Natalia Brasova died a pauper in a Parisian charity hospital in 1952.

336. George V worried that the deposed autocrat's presence in Britain would render the house of Windsor unpopular. Rose, *King George V*, 211–5.

337. Pipes, *Russian Revolution*, 745–88; Steinberg and Khrustalëv, *Fall of the Romanovs*, 169–376.

338. Steinberg, *Spiridonova*, 195; *Vechernii chas*, January 12, 1918; *Nashe slovo*, April 13, 1918; *Sovetskaia Rossiia*, July 12, 1987, 4 (G. Ioffe).

339. Pipes, *Russian Revolution*, 763 (citing Trotsky's diary [April 9, 1935], Trotsky archive, Houghton Library, Harvard University, bMS/Russ 13, T-3731, p. 110).

340. Pipes, *Russia Under the Bolshevik Regime*, 257n (citing *Chicago Daily News*, June 23, 1920: 2 [quoting the diary of Empress Alexandra]). The book was found among the possessions of Alexandra in Yekaterinburg: Sokolov, *Ubiistvo tsarskoi sem'i*, 281.

341. The key original documents, with analysis, can be found in Steinberg and Khrustalëv, *Fall of the Romanovs*, 287–93, 310–5, 351–66.

342. No order to kill from Lenin or Sverdlov has come to light. Secondhand reports, the strongest being Trotsky's diary entry, indicate that Lenin and Sverdlov ordered the murders. Pipes, *Russian Revolution*, 770 (citing Trotsky's diary [April 9, 1935], Trotsky archive, Houghton Library, Harvard University, bMS/Russ 13, T-3731, p. iii). The local order to murder Nicholas II was issued the very day Sverdlov reported on the deed at the Council of People's Commissars. GARF, f. R-130, op. 2, d. 2 (Sovnarkom meeting, July 17, 1918). After the European press prematurely reported on the execution of the ex-tsar, Lenin wrote a cable in English: "Rumor not true

ex-Tsar safe all rumors are only lie of capitalist press Lenin." A few hours later, Nicholas was killed. Pipes, *Unknown Lenin*, 47.

343. *Izvestiia*, July 19, 1918; *Pravda*, July 19, 1918; *Dekrety*, III: 22.

344. Kokovtsov, *Out of My Past*, 522. "Order would be re-established and these fantastic socialist ideas would be done away with," the former tsarist prime minister Kokovtsov, who found himself in Kislovodsk, recalled. "The Volunteer Army was being formed, and rumors persisted that the country was to be saved from Bolshevik oppression. . . . Nothing certain was known, and everybody made the most incredible conjectures, such that the Germans were advancing to save Kisolovodsk. The Grand Duchess Maria Pavlovna"— wife of the third son of Alexander II—"told me in all seriousness that she expected a train to come and take her to Petrograd, where everything was ready for a restoration of the old order." Kokovtsov, *Out of My Past*, 496.

345. Pipes, *Russian Revolution*, 654-5.

346. Chicherin, *Two Years of Soviet Foreign Policy*, 15-17.

347. Baumgart, *Deutsche Ostpolitik 1918*, 244; Freund, *Unholy Alliance*, 252-3; Mawdsley, *Russian Civil War*, 42-3.

348. *Pamiat'*, 1979, no. 2: 43-4; Erdmann, *Kurt Riezler*, 112-3.

349. Some six months later, an investigation began in earnest: the Whites captured one of the former guards and dug up a great number of royal family artifacts. Their chief investigator, Nikolai Sokolov, with the help of cryptographers, established the fact and the uncommon brutality of the entire royal family's demise. Sokolov, *Ubiistvo tsarskoi sem'i*, 247-53. See also Bulygin, *Murder of the Romanovs*; Mel'gunov, *Sud'ba Imperatora Nikolaia II*; Bruce Lockhart, *British Agent*, 303-4; Radzinsky, *Ubiistvo tsarskoi sem'i*; and Rappaport, *Last Days of the Romanovs*.

350. "Nonetheless," Lenin assured Zetkin, "we firmly believe that we will avoid the 'usual' course of revolution (as happened in 1794 and 1849) and triumph over the bourgeoisie." *Leninskii sbornik*, XXI: 249 (July 26, 1918).

351. Mawdsley, *Russian Civil War*, 49-52. See also Fischer, *Soviets in World Affairs*, I: 128 (citing conversations with Chicherin).

352. Viktor Bortnevski, "White Intelligence and Counter-intelligence," 16-7; Makintsian, *Krasnaia kniga VChK*, II: 120; Bortnevskii and Varustina, "A. A. Borman," I: 115-49 (at 139).

353. Baumgart, *Deutsche Ostpolitik 1918*, 237-8; Pipes, *Russian Revolution*, 656.

354. Paquet, *Im kommunistischen Russland*, 54.

355. Hoover Institution Archives, Nicolaevsky Collection, no. 128, box 1, file 9: Karl Helfferich, "Moia Moskovskaia missiia," 17; Jarausch, "Cooperation or Intervention?," 392-4; Brovkin, *Mensheviks After October*, 272. Helfferich spent all of nine days in Moscow before being recalled by the foreign ministry.

356. Pipes, *Russian Revolution*, 660-1; Helfferich, *Der Weltkrieg*, III: 653; *PSS*, L: 134-5; Baumgart, *Deutsche Ostpolitik 1918*, 108-10; Erdmann, *Kurt Riezler*, 472n; G. Chicherin, "Lenin i vneshniaia politika," *Mirovaia politika v 1924 godu* (Moscow, 1925), 5; Freund, *Unholy Alliance*, 23-4.

357. Chicherin, *Vneshniaia politika Sovetskoi Rossii za dva goda*, 5; Pearce, *How Haig Saved Lenin*, 71; Wheeler-Bennett, *Forgotten Peace*, 436.

358. *Dokumenty vneshnei politiki*, I: 467; "Geheimzusatze zum Brest-Litowsker Vertrag," *Europäische Gespräche*, 4 (1926): 148-53; Pipes, *Russian Revolution*, 664-5.

359. In the letter, dated August 21, 1918, to Vatslav Vorovsky in Sweden, Lenin added, falsely, that "No one asked the Germans for help, but there were negotiations on *when* and *how* they, the Germans, could carry out their plan to attack Murmansk and General Alexeev." Volkogonov, *Lenin: Life and Legacy*, xxxiii; RGASPI, f. 2, op. 2, d. 122, l. 1.

360. Jarausch, "Cooperation or Intervention?," 394.

361. Meijer, *Trotsky Papers*, I: 117. The Reds recaptured Kazan in early September 1918.

362. Savel'ev, *V pervyi god velikogo oktiabria*, 109.

363. Service, *Spies and Commissars*, ch. 9 (citing a memorandum by Stephen Alley given to the author by Andrew Cook). Alley, a British agent in Russia, returned to England in March 1918, where he was eventually transferred to MI5. He has also been suspected of conspiring in the murder of Rasputin. He had a Caucasus connection: before the 1917 revolutions, he had helped build the Black Sea oil pipeline.

364. Zubov, *F. E. Dzerzhinskii*, 187.

365. *PSS*, XXXVII: 83-5 (*Izvestiia*, September 1, 1918); Bonch-Bruevich, *Pokushenie na Lenina*.

366. Kostin, *Vystrel v serdtse revoliutsii*, 84. The substitute speaker for Lenin was the leftist V. Osinsky [Obolensky], an opponent of the Brest-Litovsk Treaty.

367. Bonch-Bruevich, *Izbrannye sochinenii*, III: 275-90.

368. RGASPI, f. 4, op. 1, d. 91, l. 1-3 (receipts included).

369. McNeal, *Bride of the Revolution*, 209.

370. Bonch-Bruevich, *Tri pokusheniie na V. I. Lenina*, 79-80.

371. Gil', *Shest' let s V. I. Leninym*, 23-4.

372. Golinkov, *Krushenie antisovetskogo podpol'ia v SSSR*, I: 188-90.

373. Orlov, "Mif o Fanni Kaplan," 70-1; *Fanni Kaplan*; Leskov, *Okhota na vozhdei*, 75. Kaplan confessed under interrogation by Peterss. Konopleva was not implicated and joined the Communist party in 1921; she was shot in 1937.

374. *Izvestiia*, August 31, 1918: 1.

375. RGASPI, f. 17, op. 109, d. 18, l. 3-5 (and to frontline commanders: l. 6-13).

376. Trotskii, "O ranenom," in *O Lenine*, 151-6.

377. *Izvestiia*, September 4, 1918; Malkov, *Reminiscences*, 177-80; Mal'kov, *Zapiski* [1959], 160; Fischer, *Life of Lenin*, 282. The 1959 edition of *Zapiski komendanta Moskovskog Kremlia* is the only one to contain the detail of Kaplan's incineration. *Istochnik*, 1993, no. 2: 73.

378. Because of their experiences in Soviet Russia, the Latvian Rifles, upon being repatriated, refrained from defending the Latvian Soviet Socialist Republic, formed in January 1919 and overthrown in May. Swain, "The Disillusioning."

379. Baumgart, *Deutsche Ostpolitik 1918*, 315-6; Pipes, *Russian Revolution*, 661-2.

380. Bonch-Bruevich, *Vospominaniia o Lenine* [1965], 376-81.

381. *PSS*, L: 182; Tumarkin, *Lenin Lives!*, 67. The first stone monument to Karl Marx was erected only on May 1, 1920. *Krasnaia Moskva*, 568-9 (plate between pages).

382. By 1922, more than 200 streets would be renamed. Pegov, *Imena moskovskikh ulits*.

383. Lev Nikulin, in Beliaev, *Mikhail Kol'tsov*, 162; Dimitriev, *Sovetskii tsirk*, 29; Von Geldern, *Bolshevik Festivals*, 114; *Tsirk*. In 1920, Staniewski returned to his native Poland (then an independent country). Raduński soon followed him, but in 1925 he returned to the Soviet Union and reestablished Bim-Bom with a new Bim.

384. Zinov'ev, *N. Lenin*, 64.

385. Gil', *Shest' let s V. I. Leninym*, 27-8; Tumarkin, *Lenin Lives!*, 90.

386. *Dekrety Sovetskoi vlasti*, III: 291-2 (September 5, 1918); Bunyan, *Intervention*, 239.

387. *Izvestiia*, September 7, 1918: 3.

388. Berberova, *Zheleznaia zhenshchina*, 93. "The least opposition, least movement among White Guards, should be met with wholesale executions," wrote the interior affairs commissar (Petrovsky) in a directive. "Local provincial executive committees should take the initiative and set

the example." *Ezhenedel'nik chrezvy-chainykh komissii po bor'be s kontr-revoliutsiei i spekulatsiei*, September 22, 1918: 11.

389. *Izvestiia*, September 3, 1918: 1. See also *Krasnaia gazeta*, September 1, 1918.

390. Vatlin, "Panika," 78–81.

391. Chamberlin, *Russian Revolution*, II: 453; Daniels, "The Bolshevik Gamble," 334, 339.

## CHAPTER 8: CLASS WAR AND A PARTY-STATE

1. Petr Struve, "Razmyshleniia o russkoi revoliutsii," *Russkaia mysl'*, 1921, no. 1–2: 6 (November 1919).

2. *Protokoly zasedanii Vserossiiskogo*, 80. See also Trotskii, "O voennykh kommissarakh" [fall 1918], in *Kak vooruzhalas' revoliutsiia*, I: 183–4.

3. Goulder, "Stalinism." State-building has long been recognized as a principal outcome of the Russian civil war, but the specificity of that state has not been as sharply recognized. Moshe Lewin, "The Civil War: Dynamics and Legacy," in Koenker, *Party, State, and Society*, 399–423; Moshe Lewin, "The Social Background of Stalinism," in Tucker, *Stalinism*, 111–36 (at 116).

4. The Bolsheviks complained about their own propaganda's ineffectiveness and confinement to the towns. Kenez, *Birth of the Propaganda State* 44–9, 53–6.

5. Tilly, *Coercion, Capital, and European States*; Tilly, "War Making and State Making as Organized Crime," 169–91.

6. One scholar correctly wrote that "the civil war gave the new regime a baptism by fire. But it was a baptism the Bolsheviks and Lenin seemed to want." Fitzpatrick, "The Civil War," 57–76 (at 74).

7. Fitzpatrick, "The Civil War," 57–76.

8. *PSS*, XXXVIII: 137–8.

9. As one scholar correctly observed, the Petrograd coup "became a nation-wide revolution only through years of civil war." Pethybridge, *Spread of the Russian Revolution*, 176–180. Another scholar has argued that the "specific forms and methods of exercising power [during revolutions] differ greatly from those practiced during 'normal' times," which is true, but in the Russian revolution emergency rule was permanently institutionalized. Kolonitskii, "Anti-Bourgeois Propaganda."

10. Holquist, *Making War*. Elsewhere, in the best short treatment of the war, revolution, and civil war, Holquist advances the suggestive thesis that Russia's staus as a domestic colonial empire led it to develop counterinsurgency governing techniques, which were brought out by the violent episode of 1905–7 and then by the world war conjuncture. Moreover, he adds a sophisticated statement of the critical role of Marxist ideas. Holquist, "Violent Russia."

11. Reginald E. Zelnik, "Commentary: Circumstance and Political Will in the Russia Civil War," in Koenker, *Party, State, and Society*, 374–81 (at 379).

12. For example, Trotsky's decree, in the name of the Soviet central executive committee, dated October 29, 1917: RGASPI, f. 17, op. 109, d. 1, l. 3.

13. He added that "every day there are 20–35 cases of typhus." Nielsen and Weil, *Russkaia revoliutsiia glazami Petrogradskogo chinovnika*, 46 (March 12, 1918).

14. Gerson, *The Secret Police*, 147–8 (citing *Ezhedel'nik VCheka*, October 13, 1918: 25).

15. Raleigh, *Experiencing Russia's Civil War*, 262ff.

16. See the case of Dmitry Oskin (b. 1892), a peasant from near Tula, a factory town just south of Moscow, who had volunteered for the tsarist army in 1913, earned four St. George's crosses for bravery at the front, and rose up through the army as his superiors—syphilitics and cowards—fell to death or crippling wounds. Oskin himself lost a leg to amputation. Throughout 1917, he tacked ever leftward, like the masses generally, and by 1918 had become "commissar" at Tula. He defended "the revolution" against "counter-revolution" at all costs. When anti-Bolshevik forces closed in on the city, Oskin eagerly imposed martial law, forced the populace to dig trenches, and conducted himself like a despot. Figes, *A People's Tragedy*, 264–5; Os'kin, *Zapiski soldata*. Oskin would rise to become a high military official.

17. *Pravda*, October 18, 1918: 1 (Dukhovskii, an official in the interior ministry or NKVD, separate from the Cheka).

18. Gerson, *The Secret Police*, 195.

19. Quoted in Stites, *Revolutionary Dreams*, 39. In a book Isaac Steinberg completed in Bolshevik prison in 1919, he called the revolution "a great tragedy in which both the hero and the victim often appear to be the people." *Ot fevralia po oktiabr' 1917 g.*, 128–9.

20. McAuley, *Bread and Justice*, 3–6, 427–8.

21. One writer, in his diary, observed that "even the best and cleverest people, scholars included, are beginning to behave as if there were a mad dog in the courtyard outside." Prishvin, *Dnevniki*, II: 169 (September 1918).

22. Holquist, "'Information Is the Alpha and Omega"; Brovkin, *Behind*

the Front Lines, 5–8, 104–5, 149–55. See also the document collection of Voronovich, *Zelenaia kniga*. Specialists in the Soviet state knew about requisition practices during the Great War among both Entente and Central Powers. Viz. Vishnevskii, *Printsipy*, 65.

23. *Novaia zhizn'*, November 2, 1917, reprinted in Lelevich, *Oktiabr' v stavke*, 147–8.

24. Lenin, in the *Immediate Tasks of the Soviet Government* (presented April 7 and published three weeks later), proposed "utilization of bourgeois specialists" in every field. *PSS*, XXXVI: 178. In 1920, Trotsky sought to introduce "political departments" in place of party cells on the railways to make the trains run, but his proposal failed. Soon enough, however, party cells came to resemble the appointed political departments.

25. *Otchet VChK za chetyre gody ee deiatel'nosti*, 82, 274.

26. Iu. M. Shashkov, "Model' chislennosti levykh eserov v tsentral'nom apparate VChk v 1918 g.," *Aktual'nye problem politicheskoi istorii Rossii: tezisy dokladovi soobshchenii* (Briansk, 1992), II: 70.

27. *Iz istorii VChK*, 174.

28. He also made note of how the Cheka "disposed of a reserve of vodka, which enabled it, as occasion arose, to loosen tongues." Agabekov, *OGPU*, 3, 6–7, 10.

29. On July 25, 1918, the chairman (Vetoshkin) of the "extraordinary revolutionary headquarters" in Vologda complained to Lenin that "comrades come through often with written mandates from the Extraordinary Commission [Cheka] giving them unusually broad powers that disorganize the work of the local Cheka and evince a tendency to make the Cheka the lead political organ standing above the executive committee." They engaged in activities said to compromise Soviet power, such as financial machinations and arresting anyone who got in their way. He concluded: "God save us from such archrevolutionary friends and we will handle our enemies ourselves." RGASPI, f. 17, op. 109, d. 13, l. 24–5.

30. "The only temperaments that devote themselves willingly and tenaciously to this task of 'internal defense' were those characterized by suspicion, embitterment, harshness and sadism,"

wrote Victor Khibalchich, known as Victor Serge, who was born in Belgium to Russian émigrés, psychologizing the secret police operatives he observed in Petrograd in 1919. "Long-standing inferiority complexes and memories of humiliation and sufferings in the Tsar's jails rendered them intractable, and since professional degeneration has rapid effects, the Chekas inevitably consisted of perverted men tending to see conspiracy everywhere and to live in the midst of perpetual conspiracy themselves." Serge, *Memoirs of a Revolutionary*, 80; Leggett, *The Cheka*, 189.

31. Trotsky, *Stalin*, [1968], 385.

32. Brinkley, *Volunteer Army*; Kenez, *Civil War in South Russia*; Lehovich, *White Against Red*.

33. Drujina, "History of the North-West Army," 133.

34. Guins, *Sibir'*, II: 368

35. Kvakin, *Okrest Kolchaka*, 124, 167–8. See also Berk, "The Coup d'État of Admiral Kolchak." "*Izvestiya* wrote an obscene article saying: 'Tell us, you reptile, how much did they pay you for that?'" Ivan Bunin, the writer, recorded in his diary. "I crossed myself with tears of joy." Bunin, *Cursed Days*, 177 (June 17, 1919).

36. Restoration remained impossible as a matter of practical poltics. Some monarchist attitudes were found among some White-movement officers. Ward, *With the "Die-Hards" in Siberia*, 160.

37. Kavtaradze, *Voennye spetsialisty*, 21–4.

38. Kavtaradze, *Voennye spetsialisty*, 176–7.

39. Golovine, *Russian Army*, 278; Kenez, "Changes in the Social Composition of the Officer Corps"; Bushnell, "Tsarist Officer Corps." In 1917, almost the only educated privates in the Russian army were Jews, who rose to the fore when soldiers formed soviets because of their education. Shklovsky, *Sentimental Journey*, 66–7.

40. Shklovsky, *Sentimental Journey*, 8.

41. John Erickson, "The Origins of the Red Army," in Pipes, *Revolutionary Russia*, 224–58. The official date for the founding of the Red Army would become February 23, 1918, which in fact had been a failed attempt.

42. Gorodetskii, *Rozhdenie*, 399–401; *Dekrety Sovetskoi vlasti*, II: 334–5.

43. Trotskii, "Krasnaia armiia," in *Kak vooruzhalas' revoliutsiia*, I: 101–22 (April 22, 1918: at 117–8). The French socialist Jean Jaurès had asserted, back in 1911, that a democratic army would be fully compatible with combat effectiveness. Jaurès, *L'Organisation socialiste*.

44. *Dekrety Sovetskoi vlasti*, II: 63–70.

45. Trotsky, *History of the Russian Revolution*, I: 289.

46. Golub, "Kogda zhe byl uchrezhden institut voennykh kommissarov Krasnoi Armi?," 157.

47. *Rabochaia i Krest'ianskaia krasnaia armiia i flot*, March 27, 1918; *Pravda*, March 28, 1918. Benvenuti (*Bolsheviks and the Red Army*, 29–30) points out that Trotsky omitted this interview from his comprehensive compendium *Kak vooruzhalas' revoliutsiia*.

48. Trotskii, "Vnutrennie i vneshnie zadachi Sovetskoi vlasti," in *Kak vooruzhalas' revoliutsiia*, I: 46–67 (April 21, 1918: at 63–4).

49. V. I. Lenin, "Uderzhat li bol'sheviki gosudarstvennuiu vlast'?," in *PSS*, XXXIV: 289–39 (at 303–11); Rigby, "Birth of the Central Soviet Bureaucracy." Even during Lenin's prerevolutionary lyricism about smashing the state, such as *State and Revolution* [1903] in which he had denounced as "opportunist" the view that the "bourgeois" state could be taken over and put to use by the proletariat, he had made clear the Bolsheviks should seek to retain valuable "bourgeois" expertise.

50. "The Soviet Government," Denikin would bitterly complain, "may be proud of the artfulness with which it has enslaved the will and the brains of the Russian generals and officers and made of them its unwilling but obedient tool." Denikin, *Ocherki russkoi smuty*, III: 146.

51. *Istoriia grazhdanskoi voiny*, III: 226.

52. Kavtaradze, *Voennye spetsialisty*, 175–8, 183–96. How many of the generals and staff officers deserted to the Whites or quit and emigrated remains unknown. Altogether, some 70 percent of the tsarist officer corps (250,000) served on either the Red side (75,000) or the White side (100,000).

53. Already the 2nd Congress of Soviets in October 1917, at which the seizure of power had been pronounced, called for new commissars. Von Hagen, *Soldiers in the Proletarian Dictatorship*, 27. Bolshevik political commissars would be subordinated to the all-Russia Bureau of Military Commissars in the Council of People's Commissars, not to the party (which as yet had no bureaucracy).

54. Political departments essentially replaced party cells in the army already by January 1919; they were appointed, not elected, and subordinated to the military experts. Benvenuti, *Bolsheviks and the Red Army*, 52–64 (citing *Pravda*, January 10, 1919); Petrov, *Partiinoe stroitel'stvo*, 58–9.

55. *Voenno-revoliutsionnye komitety deistviiushchei armii*, 30–1, 75–6. See also Kolesnichenko and Lunin, "Kogda zhe byl uchrezhden institut voennykh kommissarov Krasnoi Armi?," 123–6.

56. "The commissar is not responsible for purely military, operational, or combat orders," Trotsky wrote (April 6, 1918), in one of the very few central directives (signed by him alone) to clarify the commissar's powers. Only detection of "counter-revolutionary intentions" was to induce a commissar to prevent a commander's military directives. *Izvestiia*, April 6, 1918, reprinted in Savko, *Ocherki po istorii partiinykh organiizatsii*, 73–4.

57. As one scholar has explained, "The potential for confusion and conflict in the army was heightened by the party workers' formal right to interfere in virtually all command matters through their powers of checking and co-signature." Colton, "Military Councils," 37, 56.

58. Argenbright, "Bolsheviks, Baggers and Railroaders."

59. Gill, *Peasants and Government*.

60. Lih, *Bread and Authority*, 95–6, 106–8. Earlier in August, the Provisional Government had averred that it would not raise state prices paid for grain procurements. Pethybridge, *Spread of the Russian Revolution*, 99 (citing *Vestnik vremennogo pravitel'stva*, August 5, 1917).

61. Sergei Prokopovich, quoted in Holquist, *Making War*, 81.

62. Carr, *Bolshevik Revolution*, II: 227–44; Malle, *Economic Organization of War Communism*, 322–6; Perrie, "Food Supply."

63. Holquist, *Making War*, 108–9 (citing Kondrat'ev, *Rynok khlebov*, 222).

64. *Nash vek*, July 10, 1918: 4.

65. Mary McAuley, "Bread Without the Bourgeoisie," in Koenker, *Party, State, and Society*, 158–79

66. *Svoboda Rossii*, April 18, 1918: 5; Bunyan and Fisher, *Bolshevik Revolution*, 666–8.

67. Pavliuchenkov, *Krest'ianskii Brest*, 26–9 (citing RGASPI, f. 158, op. 1, d. 1, l. 10). Tsyrupa outmaneuvered Trotsky, whose Extraordinary Commission lapsed.

68. "O razrabotke V. I. Leninym prodovol'stvennoi politiki 1918 g.," 77.

69. Gulevich and Gassanova, "Iz istorii bor'by prodovol'stvennykh otriadov rabochikh za khleb" at 104; Lih, *Bread and Authority*, 126–37; Malle, *Economic Organization of War Communism*, 359–61.

70. *Protokoly zasedanii VsTsIK*, 47–8.

71. One scholar has argued that "the actual relation between military necessity and ideological radicalism is the reverse of this supposed chain: the outbreak of civil war caused a conscious retreat from ideological ambitiousness," which is true at the level of rhetorical flourish, though less at the level of practices. Lih, "Bolshevik Razvesrtka," 684–5.

72. "There remains only one solution," Lenin concluded in spring 1918: "to meet the violence of grain owners

against the starving poor with the violence against grain owners." Strizhkov, *Prodovol'stvennye otriady*, 56. "We did not hesitate to wrest land away from landlords . . . and by force of arms to tear the crown from the stupid tsar's head," Trotsky thundered. "Why then should we hesitate to take the grain away from the kulaks?" Trotskii, *Kak vooruzhalas' revoliutisiia*, I: 81–2. See also Iziumov, *Khleb i revoliutsiia*.
73. Figes, *Peasant Russia*.
74. Vodolagin, *Krasnyi Tsaritsyn*, 10; Raleigh, "Revolutionary Politics."
75. Kakurin, *Kak srazhalas'*, I: 261.
76. RGASPI, f. 2, op. 1, d. 6157; Iudin, *Lenin pisal v Tsaritsyn*, 3–12; *Pravda*, May 31, 1918; Genkina, *Tsaritsyn v 1918*, 73 (citing GARF, f. 1235, op. 53, d. 1, l. 106), 75; Trotsky, *Stalin*, 283. Stalin's appointment took place just weeks after he had won his April 1918 slander case against the Menshevik leader Yuly Martov.
77. RGASPI, f. 17, op. 109, d. 3, l. 5–10 (devastating May 29, 1918, report by Snesarev and Nosovich), reprinted— without mention of Nosovich—in Goncharov, *Vozvyshenie Stalina*, 361–7 (at 365). The latter is a reissue of Melikov, *Geroicheskaia oborona Tsaritsyna*, with additional documents in an appendix. See also RGASPI, f. 17, op. 109, d. 3, l. 17–20 (June 30, 1918, report by Snesarev); and Dobrynin, *Bor'ba s bol'shevizmom na iuge Rossii*, 111.
78. *Iz istorii grazhdanskoi voiny v SSSR*, I: 563–4 (quoting K. Ia. Zedin).
79. RGASPI, f. 558, op. 4, d. 668, l. 35–9 (F. S. Alliluev, "Vstrechi s Stalinym").
80. *Pravda*, December 21, 1929; Voroshilov, *Lenin, Stalin, i krasnaia armiia*, 43; "Pis'mo V. I. Leninu," *Sochineniia*, IV: 118–9.
81. *Pravda*, June 11, 1918.
82. *Pravda*, January 3, 1935; Genkina, *Tsaritsyn v 1918*, 87–8. In May 1918 the Caucasus Bolshevik Sergo Orjonikidze, who had just fled Rostov, helped put down an anarchic revolt inside Tsaritsyn; he telegrammed Lenin that "the most decisive measures are necessary, but the local comrades are too flaccid, every offer to help is taken as interference in local affairs." By contrast, Stalin imposed his will. GARF, f. 130, op. 2, d. 26, l. 12; *Sergo Ordzhonikidze*; Genkina, *Tsaritsyn v 1918*, 59–64. Sergei Minin, the top Tsaritsyn Bolshevik, had feared Stalin's interference in local affairs, too, but Minin could not overcome Stalin's will and authority. RGASPI, f. 558, op. 4, d. 668, l. 57 (F. S. Alliluev, "Obed u Minina").
83. Gerson, *The Secret Police*, 139–43 (citing Denikin Commission reports, U.S. National Archives, Washington, D.C., RG 59, roll 36, frames 0248–0250).
84. Bullock, *Russian Civil War*, 36.

85. Gerson, *The Secret Police*, 142–3 (citing U.S. National Archives, Washington, D.C., RG59, roll 36, frames 0248–0250).
86. Chervyakov had been expelled under the tsarist regime from the military medical academy in St. Petersburg for political activity, but completed the law faculty (!) at Moscow University and served as an inspector at the School of Trade in his native city of Lugansk, in the Donetsk basin. In 1918, he had evacuated Ukraine eastward ahead of the advancing Reichswehr, ending up in Tsaritsyn, and bringing along a Lugansk crony who became the local Cheka "investigator." http://rakurs.myftp.org/61410 .html; Argenbright, "Red Tsaritsyn," 171. After Alfred Karlovich Borman, head of the Tsaritsyn Cheka, had the Chervyakov crony Ivanov arrested, Chervyakov arrested Borman and released Ivanov. Nevskii, *Doklad ot narodnogo kommissara putei soobshcheniia*, 28.
87. Raskol'nikov, *Rasskazy michmana Il'ina*, 31–3. See also Genkina, "Priezd tov. Stalina v Tsaritsyn," 82.
88. "The enemy consists of remnants of Kornilov's army, Cossack and other counter-revolutionary units and possibly German troops," a July 10 report observed: RGASPI, f. 17, op. 109, d. 3, l. 23–5 (Z. Shostak, a North Caucasus military inspector).
89. "Pis'mo V. I. Leninu," *Sochineniia*, IV: 120–1. Stalin called Snesarev a "flaccid military leader" in a telegram to Trotsky (July 11, 1918) copied to Lenin and asked "don't you have other candidates?" Kvashonkin, *Bol'shevistskoe rukovodstvo*, 42–4 (RGASPI, f. 558, op. 1, d. 1812, l. 1–3). Stalin had noted to Lenin and Trotsky (June 22, 1918) that Snesarev, traveling to the front lines, had barely escaped arrest, as if he were concerned about Snesarev's welfare, but was in fact raising doubts about him. *Bol'shevistskoe rukovodstvo*, 40–41 (RGASPI, f. 558, op. 1, d. 5404, l. 3). See also Kliuev, *Bor'ba za Tsaritsyn*.
90. Trotsky further allowed that command over military operations could be transferred to a new military council. RGASPI, f. 17, op. 109, d. 3, l. 44. On July 18, Stalin sent a telegram to Moscow demanding that Snesarev be dismissed. RGASPI, f. 558, op. 1, d. 258, l. 1; Vodolagin, *Krasnyi Tsaritsyn*, 80 (RGVA, f. 6, op. 3, d. 11, l. 92, July 17, 1918, resolution in Tsaritsyn).
91. Golikov, *Vladimir Il'ich Lenin*, V: 645–6. The original composition was Stalin, Minin, and a "military leader who will be named by the recommendation of People's Commissar Stalin and Military Commissar Minin." That person, initially, was A. N. Kovalevsky, but from August 5 would be

Voroshilov. Kovalevsky was arrested. Golubev, *Direktivy glavnogo komandovaniiai*, 74–5 (RGVA, f. 3, op. 1, d. 90, l. 268–9); RGASPI, f. 17, op. 109, d. 3, l. 14; Goncharov, *Vozvyshenie Stalina*, 391–2 (RGVA, f. 6, op. 4, d. 947, l. 71–71a); Kvashonkin, *Bol'shevistskoe rukovodstvo*, 40–41 (RGASPI, f. 558, op. 1, d. 5404, l. 3: June 22, 1918); Karaeva, *Direktivy komandovaniia frontov*, I: 289–90 (RGVA, f. 6, op. 4, d. 947, l. 71–71a). The decree (by telegram) of the Revolutionary Military Council of the Republic was dated July 24, which appears to have been issued in connection with an on-site investigation by Nikolai Podvoisky, the head of the Red Army Inspectorate.
92. On July 24, over the Hughes apparatus from Moscow, Lenin told Stalin, "I must say that neither in Piter nor Moscow is bread being distributed. The situation is terrible. Let us know if you can undertake extreme measures, because if not from you, we have nowhere else to obtain food." But Stalin was hard-pressed to deliver. The Whites were closing the noose. Stalin personally rode out in an armored train to inspect rail line repairs. RGASPI, f. 558, op. 4, d. 668, l. 90 (F. S. Alliluev, "T. Stalin na bronepoezde"). On July 26, 1918, following a reconnaissance to the Kuban ("Until now we only had unproven information, but now there are facts"), Stalin deemed the situation critical ("the entire Northern Caucasus, the purchased grain and all the customs duties, the army created by inhuman exertions, will be lost irrevocably") and begged for a division to be sent immediately (the one designated for Baku). "I await the answer. Your Stalin." RGASPI, f. 17, op. 109, d. 3, l. 35. Bonch-Bruevich, sending some troops from Voronezh, a division from Moscow, would hold out until then. RGASPI, f. 17, op. 109, d. 3, l. 37–8.
93. RGASPI, f. 17, op. 109, d. 3, l. 47. A second Remington was added to the inventory sheet by hand.
94. Kvashonkin, *Bol'shevistskoe rukovodstvo*, 41, n2; Genkina, *Tsaritsyn v 1918*, 121.
95. K. E. Voroshilov, "Avtobiografiia," in Gambarov, *Entsiklopedicheskii slovar'*, XLI/i: 96.
96. V. Pariiskii and G. Zhavaronkov, "V nemilost' vpavshii," *Sovetskaia kul'tura*, February 23, 1989.
97. *Leninskii sbornik*, XVIII: 197–99; *Sochineniia*, IV: 122–6.
98. Colton, "Military Councils," 41–50.
99. Chernomortsev [Colonel Nosovich], "Krasnyi Tsaritsyn." The date of this telegram is not specified. Khmel'kov, *K. E. Voroshilov na Tsaritsynskom fronte*, 64 (October 3, Stalin and Voroshilov to Lenin, Sverdlov, and Trotsky). Okulov became a member of

the Revolutionary Military Council of the Southern Front in Tsaritsyn (October–December 1918); Lenin recalled him to Moscow "in view of the extremely sharp relations between Voroshilov and Okulov." Volkogonov, *Triumf i tragediia*, I/i: 94 (citing RGASPI, f. 558, op. 1, d. 486).

100. Argenbright, "Red Tsaritsyn"; Golikov, *Vladimir Il'ich Lenin*, V: 630, 640; *Iz istorii grazhdanskoi voiny v SSSR*, I: 290; Iudin, *Lenin pisal v Tsaritsyn*, 61–2; *Sochineniia*, IV: 116–7; *Leninskii sbornik*, XXXVIII: 212.

101. Argenbright, "Red Tsaritsyn," 165.

102. Argenbright, "Red Tsaritsyn," 166 (citing Nevskii, *Doklad ot narodnogo komissara putei soobshcheniia*, 17–18). Appended to a report by the People's Transport Commissar (V. I. Nevskii), Makhrovsky's report was presented to Lenin.

103. On August 27, 1918—the same day the Supplementary Treaty with Germany was signed in Berlin—Lenin ordered the local Cheka head to release Makhrovsky and the non-party specialist Alekseev, but the Cheka replied that the latter had already been shot. On September 4, Sverdlov would repeat the order to release Makhrovsky; he would be freed on September 21 by a former Baku Chekist who worked in the central fuel supply department. Argenbright, "Red Tsaritsyn," 175–6 (citing Sal'ko, "Kratkii otchet o deiatel'nosti Glavnogo Neftianogo Komiteta"). In May 1921, Makhrovsky would be tried for embezzlement in the fuel industry and sentenced to be shot, a sentence commuted to five years. His wife (Burtseva) also received a prison term. *Gudok*, May 20, 1921.

104. The Tsaritsyn Cheka, in its newsletter, claimed to have arrested "around 3,000 Red Army men," but executed only twenty-three leaders: *Izvestiia Tsaritsynskoi gubernskoi chrezvychainoi komissii*, October 1918: 16–22, and November 1918: 36, in Hoover Institution Archives, Nicolaevsky Collection, no. 89, box 143, folder 11.

105. Magidov, "Kak ia stal redaktorom 'Soldat revoliutsii,'" 30.

106. Meijer, *Trotsky Papers*, I: 134–7; Trotsky, *Stalin*, 288–9.

107. If the city fell to the Cossacks, the prisoner barge was to be blown up and sunk—the source, evidently, for the subsequent rumor that Stalin had had it deliberately sunk to drown the prisoners. Chernomortsev [Colonel Nosovich], "Krasnyi Tsaritsyn"; Khrushchev, *Memoirs*, II: 141, n2. *Izvestiia KPSS*, 1989, no. 11: 157, 161–2.

108. *Izvestiia Tsaritsynskoi gubernskoi chrezvychainoi komissii*, November 1918: 16, in Hoover Institution Archives, Nicolaevsky Collection, no. 89,

box 143, folder 11; Genkina, *Tsaritsyn v 1918*, 126, 154.

109. In a newspaper interview at the time, Stalin praised "two happy phenomena: first, the emergence in the rear of administrators from the workers who are able not only to agitate for Soviet power but build a state on new, communist foundations, and secondly the appearance of a new corps of commanders consisting of officers promoted from the ranks who have practical experience in the imperialist war and enjoy the full confidence of Red Army soldiers." *Izvestiia*, September 21, 1918; *Sochineniia*, IV: 131.

110. The appointment (on September 6, 1918) was sparked by a report, dated August 23, 1918, from Alexander Yegorov about the need for unified command. Krasnov and Daines, *Neizvestnyi Trotskii*, 72–5.

111. Deutscher, *Prophet Armed*, 420. Nikolai Krylenko, the former tsarist ensign, had resigned as Red supreme commander over the decision to build a permanent standing army; he went over to the justice commissariat.

112. Trotsky also decreed that White Army captives who signed an oath to the Reds should be sent into battle, as long as their family members were held as hostages. *Izvestiia*, August 11, 1918; Trotskii, "Prikaz" [August 8, 1932], in *Kak vooruzhalas' revoliutsiia*, I: 232–3. That fall of 1918, at the suggestion that barges carrying grain up the Volga fly the Red Cross flag, to make sure they were not sunk, Trotsky exploded. "The charlatans and fools," he telegrammed Lenin, "will think the delivery of grain means that there is a chance of conciliation and that civil war is not a necessity." Volkogonov, *Trotsky*, 125 (citing RGVA, f. 4, op. 14, d. 7, l. 79).

113. Volkogonov, *Stalin: Triumph and Tragedy*, 40.

114. Chernomortsev [Black Sea Man], "Krasny Tsaritsyn," reprinted in Nosovich, *Krasnyi Tsaritsyn*. It was Voroshilov who identified Black Sea Man as "General [sic] Nosovich." Voroshilov, *Lenin, Stalin, i krasnaia armiia*, 45–7. Nosovich asserted that the specialist Alekseev really was plotting with Serbian officers, but that they did not understand each other well. Nosovich falsely claimed he had been a spy in the Red camp, rather than a willing collaborator (the Whites remained suspicious of him). A prevaricator, he nonetheless should go down as having written the first accurate portrait of one of the most important figures in world history. On White suspicions of Nosovich, see Meijer, *Trotsky Papers*, I: 178–9. Soviet works accepted Nosovich's claims at face value: Genkina, *Tsaritsyn v 1918*, 126–7 (citing a Nosovich report to Denikin of December

1918); *Izvestiia TsK KPSS*, 1989, no., 11: 177 no., 20. Nosovich soon emigrated to France, lived a long life, and died in Nice (1968). Nosovich, *Zapiski vakhmistra Nosovicha*.

115. No known record has survived of Stalin's emotions at that moment. He, Minin, and Voroshilov issued a public order in Tsaritsyn "that deserters from the White side who voluntarily surrender their weapons are not to be executed or abused"—this was regime policy, but evidently not Tsaritsyn practice. RGASPI, f. 17, op. 109, d. 3, l. 114; *Soldat revoliutsii* (September 1, 1918).

116. Denikin would later write that in 1917 Sytin had approached him and other generals with a proposal to save Russia by turning over land—be it gentry, state, or church—gratis to the peasants who were fighting. General Kaledin, who shot himself in early 1918, is said to have replied, "Pure demagogy!" Denikin, *Ocherki russkoi smuty*, I: 93.

117. Kvashonkin, *Bol'shevistskoe rukovodstvo*, 51 (RGASPI, f. 558, op. 1, d. 5412, l. 2); Khmel'kov, *Stalin v Tsaritsyne*, 50–1; Lipitskii, *Voennaia deiatel'nost' TsK RKP (b)*, 126–9. Invariably Trotsky's answer to these incessant requests—not just for ammunition but also guns, armored vehicles, airplanes, pilots—was to cite profligacy in the expenditure of matériel, likely true but no solution to immediate needs. Meijer, *Trotsky Papers*, I: 162; Golubev, *Direktivy glavnogo komandovaniia*, 89–90; *Velikii pokhod K. E. Voroshilova*, 175.

118. Volkogonov, *Trotsky*, 262 (citing RGVA, f. 33987, op. 2, d. 19, l. 16–7).

119. Karaeva, *Direktivy komandovaniia frontov*, I: 345–8 (RGVA, f. 10, op. 1, d. 123, l. 29–30); Volkogonov, *Triumf i tragediia*, I/i: 91.

120. Kolesnichenko, "K voprosu o konflikte," 44.

121. Sverdlov, *Izbrannye porizvedennye*, III: 28.

122. RGASPI, f. 17, op. 109, d. 4, l. 60.

123. Kvashonkin, *Bol'shevistskoe rukovodstvo*, 52–3 (RGASPI, f. 558, op. 1, d. 5413, l. 1–2).

124. Knei-Paz, *Social and Political Social Thought*.

125. Meijer, *Trotsky Papers*, I: 134–6; Kvashonkin, *Bol'shevistskoe rukovodstvo*, 54, n2 (RGASPI, f. 5, op. 1, d. 2433, l. 33); Trotsky, *My Life*, 443. Trotsky's frustrations went beyond Stalin ("Send me communists who know how to obey," he telegrammed Lenin from the front in 1918). Schapiro, *Communist Party*, 262.

126. Kenez, *Civil War in South Russia*, I: 176. The Cossack leader Krasnov had founded a "Don republic," which Germany promptly recognized, but Denikin deplored this as separatism. When

Germany capitulated in November 1918, Krasnov's army disintegrated; he was forced to subordinate himself to Denikin but soon quit the South and joined Yudenich's northern forces operating out of Estonia. He emigrated West in 1920, and would later collaborate with the Nazis.

127. RGASPI, f. 17, op. 109, d. 4, l. 64; Volkogonov, *Trotsky*, 132 (citing RGVA, f. 33987, op. 2, d. 40, l. 29); Kvashonkin, *Bol'shevistskoe rukovodstvo*, 54 (RGASPI, f. 558, op. 1, d. 5414, l. 2–4: Oct. 5, 1918); Meijer, *Trotsky Papers*, I: 134–6. See also Trotskii, "Prikaz" [November 4, 1918], in *Kak vooruzhalas' revoliutsiia*, I: 350–1. Trotsky would later write that "the atmosphere of Tsaritsyn, with its administrative anarchy, guerilla disrespect for the Center, . . . and provocative boorishness toward military specialists was naturally not conducive to winning the good-will of the latter and making them loyal servants of the regime." Trotsky, *Stalin*, 273, 280–1, 288–9.

128. RGASPI, f. 17, op. 109, d. 4, l. 68. Trotsky had reported to Sverdlov on October 5, 1918, that "yesterday I spoke on the direct line and laid the responsibility on Voroshilov as the commander of the Tsaritsyn Army. Minin is in the Military rev Soviet of the 10th Tsaritsyn Army. I did not raise the question of Stalin." RGASPI, f. 17, op. 109, d. 4, l. 67.

129. RGASPI, f. 17, op. 109, d. 3, l. 46–7. See also Sverdlov's note to Lenin (October 5, 1918): Sverdlov, *Izbrannye proizvedenniia*, III: 36.

130. Golikov, *Vladimir Il'ich Lenin*, VI: 156; Genkina, *Tsaritsyn v 1918*, 183. Stalin telegrammed Voroshilov and Minin that day (October 8, 1918), suggesting all could be settled "noiselessly." Kolesnichenko, "K voprosu o konflikte," 45–6. Lenin commented that hiding the money from Stalin was improper: "L. A. Fotievoi i L. V. Krasinu," *PSS*, L: 187 (October 9, 1918).

131. Danilevskii, *V. I. Lenin i voprosy voennogo stroitel'stva*, 37–8.

132. *Dekrety Sovetskoi vlasti*, V: 663; Trotsky, *Stalin*, 291–2; A. L. Litvin et al., "Grazhdanskaia voina: lomka starykh dogm i stereotypov," in *Istoriki sporiat* (Moscow, 1969), 63; *Iuzhnyi front*, 19.

133. RGASPI, f. 17, op. 109, d. 1, l. 20 (October 16, 1919).

134. Meijer, *Trotsky Papers*, I: 158–64, 196.

135. RGASPI, f. 17, op. 109, d. 4, l. 71; Golubev, *Direktivy glavnogo komandovaniia*, 84–5.

136. Trotskii, "Prikaz" [October 5, 1918], in *Kak vooruzhalas' revoliutsiia*, I: 347–8. A caravan went to Moscow to try to bring back some supplies, especially ammunition. On October 24, a

Red Army regiment arrived from Moscow consisting of workers from two factories. The next day, in Moscow the Central Committee considered a letter from Stalin demanding a trial of the Southern Front commander (Sytin) and others (Okulov) for sabotaging the supply of the Tenth Army in Tsaritsyn; Sverdlov brushed off the request. RGASPI, f. 17, op. 109, d. 4, l. 71, 79, 82; Volkogonov, *Triumf i tragediia*, I/i: 101. In Moscow, Lenin received Stalin on October 23, and evidently brokered a peace, which Sverdlov, in Lenin's name, telegrammed to Trotsky. Meijer, *Trotsky Papers*, I: 158–60; *Leninskii sbornik*, XXXVII: 106.

137. D. P. Zhloba, "Ot nevinnomyskoi do Tsaritsyna," in Bubnov, *Grazhdanskaia voina*, I: 28–34, 32–4; Azovtsev, *Grazhdanskaia voina v SSSR*, I: 229; V. Shtyrliaev, "Geroi grazhdanskoi voiny Dmitrii Zhloba," *Voenno-istoricheskii zhurnal*, 1965, no. 2: 44–6; Sukhorukhov, *XI Armiia*, 81, 83–95. On the military situation, see Vācietis's report to Lenin (August 13, 1918): RGASPI, f. 17, op. 109, d. 8, l. 51–66.

138. P. N. Krasnov, "Velikoe voisko donskoe," in Gessen, *Arkhiv russkoi revoliutsii*, V: 190–320 (at 244–5).

139. *Izvestiia*, October 30, 1918; *Sochineniia*, IV: 146–7. Zhloba (b. 1887), the kind of peasant autodidact commander Stalin usually favored, proved to be one of the few people unafraid to argue with the Tsaritsyn warlord—a greater sin for Stalin than Zhloba's soon-to-be-revealed limits as a military leader. Nosovich, *Krasnyi Tsaritsyn*, 60–1. Before the end of 1918, Zhloba's Steel Division was dispersed into the cavalry commanded by Boris Dumenko, against whom Zhloba then intrigued, hating his place. (Dumenko was arrested and executed by his own side on apparently false charges of murder.) In 1920, fighting Wrangel in the Crimea, Zhloba's Red cavalry was surrounded. In 1922, he quit the Red Army. Stalin would have Zhloba executed in 1938.

140. Almost simultaneously, Roman Malinowski, the *okhrana* agent in Bolshevik ranks, faced a revolutionary tribunal on charges of treason at the end of October 1918. The prosecution established that he had betrayed eighty-eight revolutionaries to the tsarist authorities, but the defendant voiced contrition only for two, "my best friends, Sverdlov and Koba. These are my two real crimes." The six judges sentenced Malinowski to death and in the wee hours of November 6, one day before the first anniversary of the seizure of power, he was executed by firing squad. He was the original traitor within Bolshevik ranks. Halfin, *Intimate Enemies*, 7–17 (citing *Delo provokatora Malinovskogo* [Moscow:

*Respublika*, 1992], 159, 216, 108). Minin (*Pravda*, January 11, 1919) began the portrayal of the bungled near-fall of Tsaritsyn in 1918 as a surpassing Red victory, a depiction that only gained in strength under Stalin's rule: Voroshilov, *Lenin, Stalin, i krasnaia armiia*, 42–8; Melikov, *Geroicheskaia oborona Tsaritsyna*, 138–9; Genkina, "Bor'ba za Tsaritsyn v 1918 godu."

141. On the German military's inveterate high-risk gambling, see Hull, *Absolute Destruction*, 291ff.

142. Deist and Feuchtwanger, "Military Collapse of the German Empire."

143. Lieven, "Russia, Europe, and World War I," 7–47; Jones, "Imperial Russia's Forces," I; Pearce, *How Haig Saved Lenin*, 7.

144. Koehl, "Prelude to Hitler's Greater Germany," 65. See also Liulevicius, *War Land on the Eastern Front*; Kitchen, *Silent Dictatorship*; Lee, *The Warlords*; and Ludendorff, *My War Memories*. Compare the Russian army occupation of Galicia in 1915: Von Hagen, *War in a European Borderland*.

145. Quoted in Denikin, *Ocherki Russkoi smuty*, I: 48–9. Germany's naval chief of staff, Admiral Georg von Müller, railed at Hindenburg and Ludendorff in his contemporaneous diary: "Mistake after mistake has been made, above all the casual handling of the peace with Russia, whose collapse had been a boon of immeasurable value to us and should have been exploited to release troops for the West. But instead of this we conquered Latvia and Estonia and became involved with Finland—the results of an excess of megalomania." Von Müller, *The Kaiser and His Court*, 398 (September 29, 1918). Similarly, Major-General Hoffmann would complain of the units desperately needed in the West who remained in the East that "our victorious army on the Eastern Front became rotten with Bolshevism." Wheeler-Bennet, *Forgotten Peace*, 352 (citing *Chicago Daily News*, March 13, 1919).

146. Wheeler-Bennet, *Forgotten Peace*, 327; Wheeler-Bennet, "The Meaning of Brest-Litovsk Today."

147. Geyer, "Insurrectionary Warfare."

148. *PSS*, XXXVII: 150, 164. On November 7, 1918, the first anniversary of the October Revolution, Lenin had made a point of visiting the Cheka club (at Lubyanka, 13). His appearance was unexpected, and greeted with wild applause. Lenin returned the next day to answer questions for two hours. *Izvestiia*, November 9, 1918; Vinogradov, *Arkhiv VChK*, 92–3 (citing internal publication); Latsis, *Otchet Vserossiiskoi chrevzyvhanoi kommissi*, 81; *V. I. Lenin v vospominaniiakh chekistov*, 111–2. See also *Pravda*, December 18, 1927; and *PSS*, XXXVII: 174.

149. On November 18, 1918, Max, Prince of Baden, imperial chancellor, announced the kaiser's abdication of nine days before. Wilhelm lived out his life in comfortable Dutch exile and died from natural causes in June 1941, after the Netherlands fell under Nazi German occupation. Hull, *Entourage of Kaiser Wilhelm II*; Clark, *Kaiser Wilhelm II*.

150. Stevenson, *Cataclysm*, 379–406.

151. Wheeler-Bennet, *Forgotten Peace*, 370–1, 450–3.

152. "The period of sharp divergences between our proletarian revolution and the Menshevik and SR democracy was a historical necessity," Lenin wrote, adding that "it would be preposterous to insist solely on tactics of repression and terror toward petty-bourgeois democracy when the course of events is forcing the latter to turn toward us." *Pravda*, November 21, 1918. See also *PSS*, XXXVII: 207–33 (speech of November 27, 1918).

153. Broadberry and Harrison, *Economics of World War I*.

154. Bond, *War and Society in Europe*, 83–4.

155. Knobler, *Threat of Pandemic Influenza*, 60–1. Russia's 15 million, Germany's 13.1 million, France's 8 million (nearly 80 percent of the prewar population aged 15–49), Britain's 5.25 million (almost half the prewar population of men aged 15–49) plus 3.7 million from the empire, Austria-Hungary's 7.8 million, Italy's 5.6 million, the United States' 4.3 million, Ottoman empire's 2.9 million, Romania's 750,000, and Bulgaria's 1.2 million all contribute to these estimates.

156. Perhaps 775,000 were killed in action; another 2.6 million were wounded, of whom up to 970,000 died. 157. Some 182,000 Russian POWs died. Peter Gatrell, *Russia's First World War*, 255, 259; *Rossiia v mirovoi voine 1914–1918 goda*, 4 and 4n; Krivosheev, *Rossiia i SSSR*, 101–96. Britain, France, and Germany suffered 1.3 million taken prisoner—combined; Austria-Hungary, 2.2 million POWs.

158. *PSS*, XXXVII: 260.

159. *PSS*, XXVI: 16 (March 15, 1918).

160. "What you intend is being carried out by us; what you call 'communism' we call 'state control,'" a German economic negotiator in Berlin in 1918 told the Polish Bolshevik Mieczysław Broński, who had an economics doctorate from Zurich (and had accompanied Lenin on the German-supplied sealed train from Switzerland to Russia). *Trudy i Vserossiiskogo S"ezda Sovetov Narodnogo Khoziiastva*, 157. (Broński, born in 1882 in Lodz, was the father of Wolfgang Leonhard.) Ludendorff went on to coin the expression "total war." Honig, "The Idea of Total War," 29–41; Chickering, "Sore Loser," esp. 176–7.

161. "The Germans," recalled one Jewish imperial Russian subject originally from Vilna/Wilno, "treated the local population as if they were animals that were of use to their master but had no rights whatever themselves." This applied not merely to Jews. Under Russian rule, pogroms became more prevalent during the Great War and immediately after. Abramowicz, *Profiles of a Lost World*, 199; Roshwald, *Ethnic Nationalism*, 122–4.

162. Holquist, *Making War*, 205, 285–7.

163. Genkina, *Tsaritsyn v 1918*, 202. The Tenth Army was only one of several Red forces engaged on the southern front. Nadia, *O nekotorykh voprosakh istorii grazhdanskoi voiny* 106–11.

164. RGASPI, f. 17, op. 109, d. 4, l. 93. Trotsky "declared to Voroshilov and me," Minin stated at the 8th Party Congress, "that I will conduct you back to Moscow by convoy." *Izvestiia TsK KPSS*, 1989, no. 9: 153. Minin was soon moved to the interior commissariat (Decemeber 1918). Sytin was transferred to Moscow (mid-November).

165. RGASPI, f. 17, op. 109, d. 4, l. 117 (December 12, 1918).

166. RGASPI, f. 17, op. 109, d. 14, l. 65, and RGVA, f. 33 987, op. 2, d. 96, l. 10, Hoover Institution Archives, Volkogonov papers, container 17 (telegram from Pyatakov in Kursk to Stalin in the Kremlin, copies to Lenin and Sverdlov); Kvashonkin, *Bol'shevistskoe rukovodstvo*, 75 (RGASPI, f. 17, op. 109, d. 12, l. 70: January 4, 1919).

167. For Ukraine, Trotsky recommended anyone else, even Moisei Rukhimovich (whom he also held in low regard). In the event, both Voroshilov and Rukhimovich were appointed in Ukraine. Deutscher alleges that Trotsky would reproach himself for not having dealt more harshly with his intriguing critics, especially Voroshilov, but in fact Trotsky tried to deal harshly with them. Deutscher, *Prophet Armed*, 431–2 (no citation). Fyodor Sergeyev ("Artyom") was named head of government in Ukraine, replacing Pyatakov, who wrote to Trotsky asking about this: RGASPI, f. 17, op. 109, d. 14, l. 78. Fyodor Sergeyev had met Stalin in 1906; he had lived together with Stalin (and Nadya) in the same railcar in Tsaritsyn. Alexander Yegorov took over the Tenth Army in Tsaritsyn.

168. Deutscher, *Prophet Armed*, 425–6.

169. *Pravda*, December 25, 1918.

170. Trotskii, "Po nauke ili koe-kak?" [January 10, 1919], in *Kak vooruzhalas' revoliutsiia*, I: 169–73 (at 170–2).

171. Robert MacNeal understood that Stalin managed to secure some grain, fulfilling his war-hanging-in-the-balance task, that Lenin hesitated to remove Stalin despite Trotsky's insis-

tence, and that Lenin went on to use Stalin in additional critical assignments. MacNeal, *Stalin*, 55–8. Robert Conquest, by contrast, merely condemned Stalin's insubordination and egoism. Conquest, *Stalin*, 81, 85.

172. Benvenuti, *Bolsheviks and the Red Army*, 89–91. The three reports (January 1, January 13, and January 31, 1919) can be found in *Sochineniia*, IV: 197–224; and *Perepiska sekretariata TsK RKP (b)*, V: 182–3.

173. Volkogonov, *Lenin: Life and Legacy*, 230 (citing RGASPI, f. 2, op. 1, d. 26388, l. 1–2); Ul'ianova, *O Lenine i sem'e Ul'ianovykh*, 113–7; Gil', *Shest' let s V. I. Leninym*, 28–34; Malkov, *Reminiscences*, 190–2; "Kak grabili Lenina." A far more inventive version can be found in Radzinsky, *The Last Tsar*, 247 (no citation). The case was cracked when Lenin's Rolls was found crashed into a wall near Moscow's Church of Christ the Savior, and Cheka operatives traced footprints in the snow away from the car, across the frozen Moscow River, to an apartment where the chief bandit, Yashka Koshelkov, barricaded himself. Koshelkov's gang had killed around two dozen regular police and Chekists since the revolution. "He gave desperate resistance," the Kremlin commandant, Pyotr Malkov, would write, "and was taken only after he had emptied his Mauser and had no more bullets." Mal'kov, *Zapiski*, 159. After the assassination attempt on Lenin in August 1918, a seventeen-man rotating bodyguard detail had been assigned to him, but Lenin disliked bodyguards and had only one that day. Abram Belenky, who had taken part in the interrogation process following the assassination attempt, had become Lenin's head bodyguard (from October 1918), but he was not with him that day. Supposedly, according to a November 1919 report of the political department of the Thirteenth Army, twelve spies had been sent to assassinate Lenin: GARF, f.3, op. 22, d. 306, l. 4, Hoover Institution Archives, Volkogonov papers, container 21.

174. The value of 132 billion gold marks in 1919 would be roughly $442 billion (£284) in 2013. Twice, in 1924 and in 1929, the Germans negotiated the amount down. In 1933, Hitler unilaterally suspended the payments. In 2010, Germany finally finished paying off the levy. Overall, taking inflation into account, Germany paid less to Britain and France than France had paid to Germany after losing the Franco-Prussian War (1870–71).

175. MacMillan, *Paris 1919*. Harold Nicolson, in *Peacemaking*, portrayed a bunch of old men out of their depth (his last chapter was entitled "Failure").

176. Steiner, *The Lights That Failed*, 772.
177. In an all too typical passage, the British ambassador to France had written in his diary in April 1916, "Although the Russians perhaps will have to lose two men for every one German, Russia has sufficient numbers of men to endure disproportionate losses." Quoted in Karliner, "Angliia i Petrogradskaia konferentsiia Antanty 1917 goda," 329.
178. Neilson, *Strategy and Supply*.
179. Thompson, *Russia, Bolshevism and the Versailles Peace*, 398.
180. Thompson, *Russia, Bolshevism and the Versailles Peace*, 310, 395.
181. One of John Maynard Keynes's arguments against Versailles had been that a pariah Germany and a pariah Russia might embrace each other; Lenin had taken favorable note. Keynes warned that Germany might go leftist as well. Keynes, *Economic Consequences*, 288–9; PSS, XLII: 67, 69, XLIV: 294–5.
182. Sadoul waxed that "from beginning to end the delegates were in the best of spirits," and singled out "Lenin's never-ending and resonant laughter, which makes his shoulders shake and his belly quiver—the lofty, majestic laugh of a Danton or a Jaurès; Trotsky's piercing irony; Bukharin's mischievous jocularity; Chicherin's mocking humor. Mixed with these nuances of Russian joy was the boisterous gaiety of the beer drinkers—[Fritz] Platten, [Hugo] Eberlein, Gruber [Karl Steinhardt]—and [Krastyo] Rakovski's subtle wit, more Parisian than Romanian" (Rakovski was Bulgarian). Sadoul, "La Fondation de la Troisiéme international," at 180. See also the British journalist Ransome, *Russia in 1919*, 215, 217.
183. Vatlin, *Komintern*, 57 (RGASPI, f. 488, op. 1, d. 13, l. 13–9).
184. "Rozhdenie tret'ego internatsionala," *Pravda*, March 7, 1919 (Osinsky).
185. *Pravda*, March 6, 1919, reprinted in Trotskii, *Piat' let Kominterna*, II: 28–30.
186. Riddell, *Founding the Communist International*, 8.
187. Schurer, "Radek and the German Revolution."
188. The delegates also approved Trotsky's manifesto narrating the degradation of capitalism and march of Communism. *Pervyi kongress Kominterna*, esp. 250–1 (list of delegates); Riddell, *Founding the Communist International*, esp. 18–9; Carr, *Russian Revolution*, 14.
189. Arkadii Vaksberg offers a variant of the blunt trauma thesis, claiming it was motivated by Sverdlov's Jewishness. Vaksberg, *Iz ada* (citing RGASPI, f. 5, op. 1, d. 2159, l. 36–7).
190. Trotsky, March 13, 1925, printed in *Fourth International*, 7/11 (1946):

327–30. Lenin went to Petrograd by train on March 11, returning on March 14, for the funeral of M. T. Yelizarov.
191. *Izvestiia TsK KPSS*, 1989, no. 8: 164.
192. *VIII s"ezd RKP (b), 18–23 marta 1919g. in PSS*, XXXVIII: 127–215 (Lenin made ten interventions at the congress). Two years later, at the 10th Party Congress in March 1921, Krestinsky rose in remembrance of Sverdlov, recalling his importance as all the delegates stood. *X s"ezd* [1921], 267–70; *X s"ezd* [1933], 499–504.
193. Soviet Russia had about 8,000 party committees, organized in around 40 provincial party organizations, with a total membership of 220,495. Party organizations in the Red Army claimed another 29,706 members. Party organizations of Finland, Lithuania, Latvia, Belorussia, and Poland counted for another 63,565 members. *VIII s"ezd RKP (b)* [1959], 274. See also *Istoriia grazhdanskoi voiny*, III: 312–3 (Stasova).
194. In addition, 7 percent were Latvian, 4 percent were Ukrainian, and 3 percent were Polish, *VIII s"ezd RKP (b)* [1959], 451. These numbers would change little at the 9th Party Congress in 1920, except that Russians would reach 70 percent and Jews would fall to 14.5 percent of the 500-plus attendees: *IX s"ezd RKP (b)*, 551. On the Jewish issue, see Pipes, *Russia Under the Bolshevik Regime*, 99–114.
195. *The Times* of London (March 5, 1919) asserted that Jews held 75 percent of top positions. Medvedev, *Let History Judge*, 560; Trotsky, *History of the Russian Revolution*, I: 225–6.
196. A version of the proceedings was published three times (1919, 1933, 1959), but none was complete; all left out the separate military sessions of March 20–21. Lenin's speech to the closed session on March 21, however, was published (*Leninskii sbornik*, XXXVII: 135–40). Fragments of Stalin's speech were published much later (*Sochineniia*, IV: 249–50). See also Benvenuti, *Bolsheviks and the Red Army*, 106. The military discussion was finally published during glasnost: *Izvestiia TsK KPSS*, 1989, no. 9: 134–90, no. 10: 171–89, no. 11: 144–78.
197. *PSS*, XXXVIII: 137–8.
198. Aralov, *Lenin vel nas k pobede*, 96–7. Aralov was a member of the Revolutionary Military Council of the Republic.
199. Trotsky wrote that on the eve of the congress, under the barrage of talk about tsarist officer treason, he had informed Lenin that at least 30,000 former tsarist officers were serving in Red ranks, making the instances of treason minuscule by comparison. Lenin supposedly expressed surprise. (He could feign surprise.) Deutscher,

*Prophet Armed*, 429–30. Lenin, *Sobranie sochinenii* [1920–26], XVI: 73.
200. Trotskii, *Sochineniia*, XVII/i: 362.
201. *Pravda* and *Izvestiia*, February 25, 1919, reprinted in *Izvestiia TsK KPPS*, 1989, no. 9: 175–81. The military opposition included Smirnov, Georgy Safarov (Voldin), Grigory "Yuri" Pyatakov, Andrei Bubnov, Emelyan Yaroslavsky, V. G. Sorin, Voroshilov, Sergei Minin, Filippr Goloshchyoëkin, Alexander Myasnikov, N. G. Tolmachëv, R. S. Samoilova (Zemlyachka), and others.
202. *Izvestiia TsK KPSS*, 1989, no. 8: 171–3.
203. Some noted that the solution would be to train young Red commanders, but Sergei Minin, of Tsaritsyn, objected that "White Guardism"—former tsarist officers in Red service—blocked young proletarian commanders from rising up. By contrast, Semyon Aralov, a member of the Revolutionary Military Council of the Republic in Moscow, argued the opposite: "in whatever area you take, supply, technology, communications, artillery, we need military specialists for it, and we do not have them." *Izvestiia TsK KPSS*, 1989, no. 9: 153, 1989, no. 10: 183–9, 1989, no. 11: 156–9, 159–66; Danilevskii, V. I. *Lenin i voprosy voennogo stroitel'stva*, 76.
204. Pokrovskii and Iakovlev, *Gusdarstvennoe soveshchanie*, 61–6.
205. *Izvestiia TsK KPSS*, 1989, no. 11: 162–4.
206. Trotsky, too, believed the peasantry would betray the revolution as soon as its own inteests had been secured. Meyer, *Leninism*, 142. On the near universal Russian Social Democrat hostility toward peasants, see Deutscher, *Unfinished Revolution*, 17.
207. Aralov, *Lenin vel nas k pobede*, 101–2.
208. In August 1919, Lenin instructed Mikhail Frunze, commander of the Turkestan front, "to exterminate every Cossack to a man if they set fire to the oil." Pipes, *Unknown Lenin*, 69. On Lenin's hardness, see also *Proletarskaia revoliutsiia*, 1924, no. 3: 168–9; also in Pipes, *Unknown Lenin*, 50.
209. *Izvestiia TsK KPSS*, 1989, no. 11: 170; *Leninskii sbornik*, XXX: 138–9.
210. Danilevskii, V. I. *Lenin i voprosy voennogo stroitel'stva*, 88. Some delegates supporting the position of Trotsky/Sokolnikov walked out after Grigory Yevdokimov's speech.
211. *VIII s"ezd RKP (b)*, 273, 339–40, 412–23.
212. *Izvestiia TsK KPSS*, 1989, no. 9: 173.
213. It was Zinoviev, who in his congress speech had attacked Trotsky—a large, inviting target useful for raising his own profile—who now telegrammed him that concessions had

been made to the military opposition and instructed him to treat this as a "warning." In a speech (March 29, 1919) to the Leningrad party organization he oversaw, Zinoviev indicated that Trotsky needed to absorb the message that in the army the party needed to play a bigger role, because "military specialists" could not be trusted. *Izvestiia TsK KPSS*, 1989, no. 8: 185–98 (at 192–5).

214. *Pravda*, March 1, 1919; Benvenuti, *Bolsheviks and the Red Army*, 72–4.

215. *VIII s"ezd RKP (b)* [1959], 177. On food scarcity, see also Brovkin, "Workers' Unrest."

216. On the army's share (25 percent of all flour, 40 percent of fodder), see Osinskii, "Glavnyi nedostatok," 236.

217. *Piat' let vlasti Sovetov*, 377; Malle, *Economic Organization of War Communism*, 407, 425.

218. Scheibert, *Lenin an der Macht*.

219. *Krasnaia Moskva*, 54. Rationing, which had been introduced by the Provisional Government, had become class-based: workers in heavy physical labor comprised the top category, followed by workers not in physical labor (this included officials), and lastly non-laboring elements or exploiters, those who lived off the labor of others (i.e., the bourgeoisie), who were small in number but conspicuous in symbol. Individuals connived to raise their designations. Before the civil war was out, the "class ration" would give way to the "labor ration," or how much labor a recipient had recently performed.

220. Borrero, *Hungry Moscow*. Potatoes would be the sole important crop over which the government did not declare a monopoly (as of late 1919).

221. Emmons, *Time of Troubles*, 237 (January 31, 1919), 392 (December 6, 1920).

222. *VIII s"ezd RKP (b)* [1933], 170.

223. *Istoriia grazhdanskoi voiny*, IV: 46.

224. Francesco Benvenuti established the depth and breadth of animosity to Trotsky early on, writing, "For his contribution to the creation of the Soviet armed forces, Trotsky was rewarded with the distrust and hatred of a great many of his party comrades." Benvenuti, *Bolsheviks and the Red Army*, 216.

225. Schapiro, *Commmunist Party* (citing Lenin, *Sochineniia*, XXV: 112).

226. The political bureau was already functioning by December 1918; the organizational bureau dated from January 1919. Golikov, *Vladimir Il'ich Lenin*, VI: 284, 319, 328, 435, 577, 588.

227. Sverdlov's safe was not opened until 1935, and duly reported to Stalin: "Kuda khotel bezhat' Sverdlov?," *Istochnik*, 1994, no. 1: 3–4. Rumors in 1919 circulated that the Bolsheviks were transferring money and gold abroad, as if readying their possible flight. Stasova, *Stranitsy zhizni i*

bor'by, 103. Boris Bazhanov claimed that during the civil war, confiscated gems were hoarded just in case, and that Klavdiya Novgorodtseva, Sverdlov's widow, was one of those entrusted with the jewels, locked in a desk, including large diamonds evidently taken from the State Diamond Fund. Bazhanov, *Vospominaniia* [1990], 96.

228. Carsten, *Revolution in Central Europe*.

229. Nettl, *Rosa Luxemburg*.

230. Luxemburg, *Die russische Revolution*, 109.

231. Weitz, *Creating German Communism*, 93.

232. *Pravda*, April 22, 1930.

233. Mitchell, *Revolution in Bavaria*; Waite, *Vanguard of Nazism*.

234. Weitz, *Weimar Germany*; Mawdsley, *Russian Civil War*, 15.

235. Hoover Institution Archives, Thomas T. C. Gregory Papers, box 2: Hungarian Political Dossier, vol. 1: Alonzo Taylor to Herbert Hoover, March 26, 1919.

236. Degras, *The Communist International*, I: 52.

237. Kun telegrams of February 2 and April 19, 1919: RGASPI, f. 17, op. 109, d. 46, l. 1–2; Trotsky's message to Kh. G. Rakovski, N. I. Podvoiski, and V. A. Antonov-Ovseenko: RGASPI, f. 325, op. 1, d. 404, l. 86 (April 18, 1919); Lenin's telegram to S. I. Aralov and J. Vācietis: l. 92 (April 21, 1919); telegram of J. Vācietis and S. I. Aralov to V. A. Antonov-Ovseenko, op. 109, d. 46, l. 3–5 (April 23, 1919).

238. Mitchell, *1919: Red Mirage*, 221 (quoting *Manchester Guardian* correspondent, no citation).

239. Tokés, *Béla Kun*; Janos and Slottman, *Revolution in Perspective*.

240. Bortnevskii, "White Intelligence and Counter-Intelligence"; Kenez, *Civil War in South Russia*, I: 65–78; Holquist, "Anti-Soviet *Svodki*."

241. Bortnevskii, "White Administration," 360 (citing N. M. Melnikov, "Pochemu belye na Iuge Rossiin e pobedili krasnykh?," 29, in N. M. Melnikov Collection, Bakhmetev Archives, Columbia University).

242. Mawdsley, *Russian Civil War*, 275–81.

243. Baron, *The Russian Jew*, 219.

244. Quotation and statistics in Budnitskii, *Rossiiskie evrei mezhdu krasnymi*, 275–6. Antisemitism cut both ways, attracting (especially in Ukraine) and repulsing followers. Kenez, "The Ideology of the White Movement," 83.

245. Kenez, *Civil War in South Russia*, I: 281–4; Filat'ev, *Katastrofa Belogo dvizheniia*, 144.

246. Exchanging messages between Denikin and Kolchak could take up to one month. Denikin, *Ocherki russkoi smuty*, V: 85–90.

247. Kenez, *Civil War in South Russia*, II: xiii. Former tsarist diplomats still resident in Allied capitals—Sergei Sazonov (Paris), Boris Bakhmeteff (Washington), Vasily Maklakov (London)—transferred funds from the Provisional Government's old accounts to the White armies, even as the diplomats viewed the anti-Bolsheviks as incompetent.

248. Erickson, *Soviet High Command*, 59–63.

249. Kenez, *Civil War in South Russia*, I: 90.

250. See also Smilga's telegrams to Lenin and Trotsky in October 1919 on saving the Tsaritsyn front: RGASPI, f. 17, op. 109, d. 3, l. 48–50.

251. Lincoln, *Red Victory*, 217 (citing "Rech' generala Denikina v Tsaritsyne, 20 iiunia 1919 g.," Bakhmeteff Archive, Denikin Collection, box 20); Denikin, *Ocherki russkoi smuty*, V: 108–9; Piontkowski, *Grazhdanskaia voina v Rossii*, 515–6. The Whites refused to recognize the Bolshevik-decreed change to the Gregorian calendar and remained thirteen days behind.

252. Suvenirov, *Tragediv, RKKA 1937–1938*, Medvedev, *Oni okruzhali Stalina*, 229–30; Rapoport and Geller, *Izmena rodine*, 385.

253. Trotskii, *Sochineniia*, VIII: 272–81.

254. Trotsky, *My Life*, 359.

255. Argenbright, "Documents from Trotsky's Train," which includes Trotsky's farewell letter to the staff of his train (July 15, 1924).

256. Trotsky, *My Life*, 411–22 (esp. 413); Volkogonov, *Trotsky*, 164 (citing RGVA, f. 33987, op. 1, d. 25, l. 16–44). Many of the crew were Latvians and headed by Rudolf Peterson. Eventually, Trotsky's train had to be divided in two.

257. Tarkhova, "Trotsky's Train," 27–40.

258. Lunacharsky, *Revolutionary Silhouettes*, 68.

259. Argenbright, "Honour Among Communists," 50–1.

260. *Vospominaniia o Vladimire Il'iche Lenine* [1979], III: 446 (K. Danilevsky).

261. Benvenuti, *Bolsheviks and the Red Army*, 123–8. Trotsky had written urgently to Lenin to remove Antonov, Podvoisky, and Bubnov from overseeing military engagements in Ukraine on May 17, 1919. RGASPI, f. 17, op. 109, d. 12, l. 17 (sent via Sklyansky for Lenin).

262. Meijer, *Trotsky Papers*, I: 578–80 (minutes of the July 3 plenum).

263. *Sochineniia*, IV: 273; Kornatovskii, *Stalin—rukovoditel' oborony Petrograda*; Kornatovskii, *Razgrom kontrrevoliutsionnykh zagovorov*. Stalin had wanted the plenum immediately in June. Naida, *O nekotorykh voprosakh*, 183–5. Over Petrograd,

Stalin clashed again with Alexei Okulov, and Lenin recalled Okulov for a second time (the first having been over Tsaritsyn). Volkogonov, *Triumf i tragediia*, I/i: 94–5.

264. Erickson, *Soviet High Command*, 63. See also the memoirs of the errant brief replacement, Samoilo, *Dve zhizni*, 250ff.

265. Trotsky, *Stalin*, 313–4. The pursuit of Kolchak into the Urals would have the unexpected bonus of expanding Red ranks with Urals factory workers.

266. Close Trotsky supporters removed were Ivan Smirnov and Arkady Rosengoltz; another Trotsky man, Fyodor Raskolnikov, had already been removed in May 1919. Others taken off included Konstantin Mekhonoshin, Semyon Aralov, Nikolai Podvoisky, Konstantin Yurenev, Alexei Okulov. Stalin was returned May 18, 1920 (through April 1, 1922). Bonch-Bruevich's account of the expanded session of the Revolutionary Military Council of the Republic is largely fanciful. Bonch-Bruevich, *Vsia vlast' sovetam*, 351–2. Bonch-Bruevich and Vācietis had bad blood (ibid., 334–5).

267. Meijer, *Trotsky Papers*, I: 590–3; Trotsky, *My Life*, 453.

268. Kamenev's command of the eastern front was assumed by Mikhail Frunze.

269. *Izvestiia*, July 8 and 10, 1919; Trotsky, *My Life*, 398, 452.

270. There are indications Trotsky refused to continue in his work as head of the military, and had to be begged to do so. RGASPI, f. 17, op. 3, d. 705 (September 8, 1927, politburo stenogram).

271. The information could hardly have been the surprise Trotsky asserts it was. Trotsky, *My Life*, 448–9.

272. *PSS*, XXXVII: 525–7; Bubnov, *Grazhdanskaia voina*, I: 246–9.

273. Deutscher, *Prophet Armed*, 413.

274. Benvenuti, *Bolsheviks and the Red Army*, I: 61, 216–7.

275. Gorky, *Lénine et la paysan russe*, 95–6. This passage disappeared from Soviet republications of Gorky's work.

276. In the spring of 1919, Lenin had disparaged the tsarist officers ("the old command staff was made up mainly of the spoiled and depraved sons of capitalists") and contemplated making a party official, Mikhail Lashevich, military commander in chief, but gave in to Trotsky's demand for a real military specialist; still, now Lenin supported Sergei Kamenev, with whom Trotsky had clashed. Mawdsley, *Russian Civil War*, 178–9.

277. Stalin would soon cover up his earlier opposition. Stalin, "Novyi pokhod Antanty na Rossiiu," *Pravda*, May 26, 1920, in *Sochineniia*, IV: 275–7. Stalinist historiography would use Trotsky's theory of hospitable versus

inhospitable terrain, without mentioning Trotsky, to mitigate the embarrassment that Tsaritsyn had fallen. Genkina, *Tsaritsyn v 1918*.

278. *Nash vek*, July 10, 1918: 4.

279. Williams, *The Russian Revolution*, 63.

280. He added that "in spite of my special rations as a Government official, I would have died of hunger without the sordid manipulations of the black market, where we traded the petty possessions we had brought in from France." Serge, *Memoirs of a Revolutionary*, 70–1, 79.

281. Deutscher, *Prophet Armed*, 442–3.

282. Pipes, *Russia Under the Bolshevik Regime*, 93–5.

283. Zinov'ev, *Bor'ba za Petrograd*, 52–3. Deutscher, *Prophet Armed*, 445. In 1925 Lashevich became deputy commissar for the army and navy. That year, he would side with Zinoviev and, in 1926, with the United opposition (Zinov'ev and Trotsky); Stalin sent him to Harbin as representative of the Soviet-controlled Chinese Eastern Railroad (1926–8) at the 15th Party Congress in 1927. He was expelled at the 15th Party Congress in 1927. He died the next year in Harbin, China, under mysterious circumstances.

284. Yudenich would die in quiet exile on the French Riviera in 1933. Rutych, *Belyi front generala Iudenicha*.

285. Trotsky, *Sochineniia*, XVII/ii: 196–7.

286. Kakurin, *Kak srazhalas'*, II: 242–5, 306.

287. Trotsky, *My Life*, 432–3; Trotskii, *Sochineniia*, XVII/ii: 310. Trotsky is the only source for the November 1919 Order of the Red Banner episode; his civil war account stands up everywhere it can be confirmed by other documents.

288. Kvakin, *Okrest Kolchaka*, 175–6.

289. *New York Times*, September 30, 1919.

290. Budnitskii, *Den'gi russkoi emigratsii*.

291. Litvin, *Krasnyi i belyi terror*, 55–6; Holquist, "State Violence," 19–45 (at 27, citing Kvashonkin, *Bol'shevistskoe rukovodstvo*, 150).

292. Krivosheev, *Grif sekretnosti sniat*, 54.

293. "We took too long over every battle, every war, every campaign," Trotsky conceded. Trotskii, "Rech'" [November 2, 1921], in *Kak vooruzhalas' revoliutsiia*, III/i: 57–71 (at 60).

294. The Whites read intercepts of Red wireless communications yet still lost; each side maintained spies in the other camp, but each had difficulty identifying which, if any, were not double agents.

295. Already in September 1918, Trotsky had argued that because a new and potentially long war was again on the horizon, the Bolsheviks had to

plan for equipping the army, restoring all existing military factories to production, and mobilizing society for military needs. (RGASPI, f. 17, op. 109, d. 6, l. 10.) Sometimes locals managed to restore some production. Sokolov, *Ot voenproma k VPK*, 8–28.

296. Manikovskii, *Boevoe snabzhenie russkoi armii* [1930], II: 332–5.

297. Mawdsley, *Russian Civil War*, 184–5.

298. Even with tsarist stockpiles, the Reds were hard-pressed to mount operations. Some tsarist stockpiles were said to be still serving the Reds in 1928: A. Volpe, in Bubnov, *Grazhdanskaia voina*, II: 373.

299. Pipes, *Russia Under the Bolshevik Regime*, 89–90.

300. Mel'gunov, *Tragediia Admirala Kolchaka*, III/i: 69–70; Mawdsley, *Russian Civil War*, 214. Pipes deems the White burden "insuperable." Pipes, *Russia Under the Bolshevik Regime*, 10.

301. Kakurin, *Kak srazahals'*, I: 135.

302. Von Hagen, *Soldiers in the Proletarian Dictatorship*, 69–79; Schapiro, "The Birth of the Red Army," 24–32.

303. Gaponenko and Kabuzan, "Materialy sel'sko-khoziastvennykh perepisei 1916–1917 gg," 102-3.

304. The Bolsheviks, for their part, did not send enough troops to win civil wars in the Baltic states or Finland, but the fact that they did send troops damaged the defense of the Red heartland. Mawdsley, *Russian Civil War*, 123.

305. Chamberlin, *Russian Revolution*, II: 268–9; Pipes, *Russia Under the Bolshevik Regime*, 119–21.

306. *Leninskii sbornik*, XXXVII: 167.

307. *Pravda*, September 23, 1919; *Izvestiia*, September 27, October 5, and October 12, 1919. See also Dzerzhinskii, *Izbrannye proizvedennye*, I: 197–8 (speech of September 24, 1919, to Moscow party committee); and Fomin, *Zapiski starogo chekista*, 108.

308. Makintsian, *Krasnaia kniga VChK*, 315–6; *Iz istorii VChK*, 349–54 (internal Cheka report, December 28, 1919).

309. Once, sometime after December 11, 1919, Lenin, unannounced, turned up at the offices of Supreme Commander Sergei Kamenev at 2:00 in the morning, asked some questions, spoke on the direct wire with Kharkov, and returned to the Kremlin.

310. In the hagiography, not one major decision of the civil war was taken without Lenin. Aralov, *Lenin i Krasnaia Armiia*, 32.

311. Volkogonov judged Trotsky a military "dilettante." Volkogonov, *Trotskii*, I: 254. Mikhail Bonch-Bruevich, a former tsarist officer close to Trotsky, judged his boss to be lacking interest in the technical side of military art but an effective

792 | NOTES TO PAGES 334-339

high-profile spokesman for the military. Bonch-Bruevich, *Vsia vlast' sovetam*, 269-71.

312. The contrast between Trotsky and Kolchak could not have been starker. "He is bursting to be with the people, with the troops," one eyewitness remarked of Kolchak, "but when he faces them, has no idea what to say." Guins, *Sibir'*, II: 367.

313. Trotsky, "Hatred of Stalin?," in *Writings of Leon Trotsky*, 67-71; Medvedev, *Let History Judge*, 64-5 (translator's note, 72).

314. Trotsky, *Stalin*, 243, 270 (quoting Leonid Serebryakov).

315. Kenez, *Civil War in South Russia*, II: 61. E. H. Carr's harsh judgment still stands: "It is no longer possible for any sane man to regard the campaigns of Kolchak, Yudenich, Denikin and Wrangel otherwise than as tragic blunders of colossal dimensions. They were monuments of folly in conception and of incompetence in execution; they cost, directly and indirectly, hundreds of thousands of lives; and except in so far as they may have increased the bitterness of the Soviet rulers against the 'White' Russians and the Allies who half-heartedly supported them, they did not deflect the course of history by a single hair's breadth." If Carr had only been as clear-eyed on Bolshevism. Davies, "Carr's Changing Views," 95.

316. Soviet officials who returned from China saw parallels. The Karakhan Declaration (July 25, 1919) characterized Kolchak as a "counterrevolutionary tyrant who depends upon military might and foreign capital for the strengthening of his own position in Russia." Waldron, "The Warlord." See also Sanborn, "Genesis of Russian Warlordism."

317. An embittered Alexeyev had told the British agent Bruce Lockhart in 1918 that he would sooner cooperate with Lenin and Trotsky than with Kerensky. Lockhart, *British Agent*, 288. Throughout the civil war, Kerensky, whose Soviet police code name was "Clown," hid inside Russia or neighboring Finland. He would depart for good in 1922 for Berlin, and then for Paris.

318. Mawdsley, *Russian Civil War*, 99.

319. Pereira, *White Siberia*.

320. Budberg, "Dnevnik," 269; Mawdsley, *Russian Civil War*, 155.

321. Denikin, *Ocherki russkoi smuty*, III: 262-3, IV: 45-8.

322. Mawdsley, *Russian Civil War*, 215 (citing "Final Report of the British Military Mission, South Russia" [March 1920], PRO, WO 33/971: 29).

323. Ushakov, *Belyi iug*; Slashchov-Krymskii, *Belyi Krym*, 185-93. Wrangel's civilian ministers included Pyotr Struve and Alexander Krivoshein, the

head of agriculture and land resettlement who had accompanied Stolypin to Siberia in 1910.

324. Lazarski, "White Propaganda Efforts." Boris Bakhmeteff, the Provisional Government's ambassador to the United States, who was still in the embassy in Washington, wrote to Vasily Maklakov on January 19, 1920, that the anti-Bolshevik movements failed because they lacked a compelling counter-ideology. Bakhmeteff yearned for a "platform of the national-democratic revival of Russia" based upon private property, genuine sovereignty of the people, democracy, patriotism, and a decentralized political system. Such was the classical liberal view of the failure. Budnitskii, "Sovershenno lichno i doveritel'no!," I: 160-5 (at 161).

325. Denikin, *Ocherki russkoi smuty*, V: 118.

326. Pipes, *Russia Under the Bolshevik Regime*, 14 (citing *Russkaia mysl'*, May-July 1921: 214). "The country needed victory at any costs, and every effort had to be exerted to secure it," Kolchak told a Bolshevik inquisition right before his death. "I had absolutely no political objectives." Of course, military victory could only be achieved with successful politics. Varneck, *Testimony of Kolchak*, 187. Similarly, Denikin later wrote that he had tried "to fence off ourselves and the army from the raging, struggling political passsions and to base ideology on simple, incontestable national symbols. This proved extraordinarily difficult. 'Politics' burst into our work." Denikin, *Ocherki russkoi smuty*, III: 129.

327. Notes for a speech to the Tenth Congress of Soviets, scheduled for December 1922: Getzler, "Lenin's Conception"; "Za derev'iami ne vidiat lesa," *PSS*, XXXIV: 79-85 (at 80); "Tretii vserossiiskii s"ezd sovetov rabochikh, soldatskikh i krest'ianskikh deputatov," *PSS*, XXXV: 261-79 (at 268); "I vserossiiskii s"ezd po vneshkol'nomy obrazovaniiu," *PSS*, XXX-VIII: 329-72 (at 339); "Konspekt rechi na X vserossiiskom s"ezde sovetov," *PSS*, XLV: at 440-1 (440). Usually, scholars quote Lenin complaining about the "bureaucratic deformities" and stifling qualities of the apparatus that socialism conjured into being, but such complaints would emerge mostly during his period of illness and incapacitation. During the civil war, Lenin's views on state building were militant. "It was a great and exalting work," he rhapsodized about the civil war administrative machinery. *PSS*, XLIV: 106.

328. Keep, *Russian Revolution*, ix-x, 471.

329. McAuley, *Bread and Justice*.

330. Trotsky, *Terrorism and Communism*, 162.

331. Thomas F. Remington, "The Rationalization of State Kontrol," in Koenker, *Party, State, and Society*, 210-31.

332. *MChK*, 247; Bazhanov, *Bazhanov and the Damnation of Stalin*, 136.

333. *Krasnaia Moskva*, 631.

334. Trotsky, *My Life*, 477.

335. The Menshevik Martov, in a private letter, pointedly used the old-regime social vocabulary, noting that "as far as the 'commissars' estate' [*soslovie*] is concerned, its superior standard of living is almost out in the open." Brovkin, *Dear Comrades*, 210 (Martov to David Schupack, June 20, 1920). Lenin was sensitive to perceptions; in a letter to Molotov (May 4, 1921), Lenin, noting that he had discovered a resort (*dom otdykha*) expressly in the name of the Council of People's Commissars, wrote, "I fear that this may cause complaints." The facility was renamed Recreation Building no. 9, and was supposed to be shared with the agriculture commissariat. RGASPI, f. 2, op. 1, d. 18552, l. 1-2.

336. Similarly, Adolf Joffe wrote confidentially to Trotsky in May 1920, "There is enormous inequality, and one's material position largely depends on one's post in the party; you'll agree that this is a dangerous situation." Joffe added of Communists in power that "the old party spirit has disappeared, the spirit of revolutionary selflessness and comradely devotion!" The Tula Bolshevik and Joffe quoted in Figes, *A People's Tragedy*, 695-6 (citing GARF, f. 5972, op. 1, d. 245, l. 397-8; RGVA, f. 33987, op. 3, d. 46, l. 143).

337. *PSS*, XVL: 14-15; Rykov, *Izbrannye proizvedenniia*, 10; Iroshnikov, "K voprosu o slome burzhuaznoi gosudarstvennoi mashiny v Rossii."

338. Annenkov, *Dnevnik moikh vstrech*, II: 120-8; Fülöp-Miller, *Mind and Face of Bolshevism* [1928], 136. See also Piotrovskii, *Za sovetskii teatr!*; Nikulin, *Zapiski sputnika*; Petrov, *50 i 500*. Sponsored by the Political Administration of the Red Army, the show was choreographed by a non-Bolshevik, Nikolai Yevreinov, who lost his voice screaming instructions, but was awarded a fur coat (fox); others got tobacco or frozen apples. The battleship *Aurora*, brought in specially from Kronstadt, was supposed to give off three shots, after which the orchestra would play the victory music, but even though technicians kept pressing the button to halt the cannonade, it would not stop firing. Yevreinov burst out laughing.

339. Trotsky, *Stalin*, 279.

340. In late 1919, Ivar Smilga, at a meeting of political workers in the army, stated: "We must now consider how to abolish the institution of the

commissar." His proposal did not carry. *Pravda*, December 13, 1919; Benvenuti, *Bolsheviks and the Red Army*, 155–7.

341. Molotov, *Na shestoi god*.

342. Tucker came close to the mark when he wrote that "Whereas Trotsky emerged from the [civil] war with much glory and little power, Stalin emerged with little glory and much power," but Tucker underestimated the negativity toward Trotsky. Tucker also applied a perhaps false standard: "Although Stalin acquired valuable military experience in the civil war, he did not emerge from it with a party reputation for having a first-class military mind." But who did? Lenin? Zinoviev? Kamenev? Even Trotsky? Tucker did, though, underscore that Stalin had "recommended himself by his wartime service as a forceful leader with an ability to size up complex situations quickly and take decisive action." Tucker, *Stalin as Revolutionary*, 206, 209.

343. "Tomorrow," he told the new lower-order commanders in the fall of 1918, "you will be at the head of platoons, companies, battalions, regiments, and you will be recognized as real exemplars of a newly forming army." Trotskii, "Unter-ofitsery" [fall 1918], in *Kak vooruzhalas' revoliutsiia*, I: 176–80.

344. Trotsky, *Stalin*, 279. Other estimates of the continuing weight of military specialists are higher. Bubnov,

*Grazhdanskaia voina*, II: 95; Erickson, *Soviet High Command*, 33.

345. MacNeal understood that Stalin's "contribution to the Red victory was second only to Trotsky's." McNeal, *Stalin*, 50. In the civil war, Moshe Lewin argued, "Stalin learned the secret of victorious politics in the most daunting situations: State coercion as the secret of success; mobilization, propaganda, military might, and terror were the ingredients of power." Of course, nearly every Bolshevik had learned this lesson, some already from the Great War. Moshe Lewin, "Stalin in the Mirror of the Other," in Lewin, *Russia/USSR/Russia*, 214.

346. Valentinov, *Novaia ekonomicheskaia politika*, 88.

347. America's Red Cross chief in Russia supposedly called Trotsky "the greatest Jew since Christ." Lockhart, *Memoirs of a British Agent*, 225.

348. Volkogonov, *Trotsky*, 23 (citing RGVA, f. 33987, op. 1, d. 21, l. 35–41). The ethnic Korean, Nigay, advised "to create a mighty Jewish army and arm it to the teeth."

349. Kartevskii, *Iazyk, voina i revoliutsiia*, 36.

350. RGVA, f. 33987, op. 3, d. 13s, Hoover Institution Archives, Volkogonov papers, container 19 (Otto von Kurfell). The Nazi Alfred Rosenberg wrote in a pamphlet that "from the day of its inception, Bolshevism was a Jewish enterprise," and that "the proletarian dictatorship over the dazed,

ruined, half-starved people was devised in the Jewish lodges of London, New York, and Berlin." Rosenberg, *Der jüdische Bolschewismus*. See also Bazhanov, *Bazhanov and the Damnation of Stalin*, 144.

351. Valentinov, *Novaia ekonomicheskaia politika*, 88.

352. Carr, *Socialism in One Country*, I: 157.

353. The Ulyanov family's Jewish ancestry would be discovered by Lenin's sister Anna Ulyanova (1864–1935), who conveyed it to Stalin in a 1932 letter stressing how beneficial it would be to reveal Lenin's one-quarter Jewish ancestry. Stalin forbid public mention. Volkogonov, *Lenin: Life and Legacy*, 9. In 1972, all extant documents on Lenin's origins were transferred to the "special file."

354. Volkogonov, *Stalin: Triumph and Tragedy*, 44–5.

355. Bortnevskii and Varustina, "A. A. Borman," I: 115–49 at 119. Borman escaped via Finland. (The Chekists, he later boasted, "mostly were involved in arrests of innocent people, but their real enemies traveled in commissar's trains, occupied important positions in people's commissariats and military staffs.") Bortnevskii, "White Intelligence and Counter-intelligence," 16; GARF, f. 5881, op. 1, d. 81 (Borman, "V stane vragov: vospominaniia o Sovetskoi strane v period 1918 goda"), l. 42.

## CHAPTER 9: VOYAGES OF DISCOVERY

1. Gor'kii, "V. I. Lenin" [1924, 1930], in *Sobranie sochinenii*, XVII: 5–46, reprinted in Bialika, *V. I. Lenin i A. M. Gor'kii*, 238–78 (at 262). Gorky lived on Capri from 1907 to 1913; Lenin stayed with him in 1908. Lenin also visited Gorky in 1910.

2. *X s"ezd* [1933], 573–83; *Vsesoiuznaia Kommunisticheskaia Partiia (b) v rezoliutsiiakh* [5th ed.], I: 393.

3. Stolypin had sketched some ideas for a state reorganization, in May 1911, four months before his assassination, according to a financial expert in local self-government with whom he periodically consulted. The sketch has not been found in the state archives and the consultant's notes of the purported conversation have not been preserved; all we have is the consultant's memoir. Stolypin, in this account, envisioned expansion and strengthening of self-government in localities and expansion and reorganization of the central ministerial system, including a number of new ministries: labor, social security, natural resources, religion, and, most unusually, nationalities. On the latter, Stolypin is said to have

envisioned that "all persons, residing in Russia, independent of their nationality and religious beliefs, should be completely equal citizens," and that "the new ministry of nationalities "should create the conditions so that the cultural and religious desires of each nation should, when possible, be fully satisfied." But he also thought some minorities, such as Poles and Ukrainians, with co-ethnics in neighboring states, posed a special threat. Therefore, the new ministry "must not ignore all the external and internal enemies who strive to dismember Russia. Any kind of Government vacillation and hesitation toward those nationalities who fall under the influence of propaganda by Russia's enemies might easily create complications in the State." Aleksandr V. Zen'kovskii, *Pravda o Stolypine* (New York: Vseslovianskoe, 1956), 79–81, translated, inadequately, as *Stolypin, Russia's Last Great Reformer* (Princeton, N.J.: Kingston Press, 1986), 33–4. Zenkovsky worked as the chief financial expert in the Kiev Zemstvo from 1903 through 1919.

4. *PSS*, XXXVII: 153; Debo, *Revolution and Survival*, 408 (quoting Lenin at the 6th All-Russia Congress of Soviets).

5. Carr, *Bolshevik Revolution*, III: 231–7.

6. White, *Siberian Intervention*; Teruyuki, *Shibberia shuppei*; Stephen, *Russian Far East*, 132, 142–5; Coox, *Nomonhan*, 9.

7. "The civil war between the Reds and Whites was always conducted by relatively insignificant minorities, against the astounding passivity of the population," observed Pyotr Struve, an assessment Pipes accepts: *Russia Under the Bolshevik Regime*, 136–8 (citing *Russkaia mysl*, May–June 1921: 211). By contrast, Figes asserts that "as long as the peasants feared the whites, they would go along, feet dragging, with the demands of the Soviet regime . . . Thus the Bolshevik dictatorship climbed up on the back of the peasant revolution." Figes, *Peasant Russia*, 354.

8. Adelman, "Development of the Soviet Party Apparat," 97.

9. Laruelle, *L'idéologie eurasiste russe*; Widerkehr, "Forging a Concept."

10. *Iskhod k vostoku*, vii.

11. Riasanovsky, "The Emergence of Eurasianism," 57. See also Glebov, "The Challenge of the Modern." The politics of the self-proclaimed Eurasianists varied—from national Bolshevism (Petr Savitskii) to Trotskyism (Petr Suvchinskii) to anti-Sovietism (Prince Nikolai Trubetskoi).

12. McNeal, "Stalin's Conception." Stalin on Russianism: Carr, *Bolshevik Revolution*, I: 102.

13. "Soviet power must become as dear and close to the masses of the borderlands of Russia," he wrote in *Pravda* (October 10, 1920). "But in order to make it dear, Soviet power must above all be understandable to them. Therefore it is necessary that soviet organs in the borderlands, the court, administration, organs of the economy, organs of direct rule (and organs of the party) consist when possible of local people, who know the daily life, mores, customs, and language of the local population." "Politika sovetskoi vlasti po natsional'nomu voprosu v Rossii," in *Sochineniia*, IV: 351–63 (at 358–60).

14. Rieber, "Stalin: Man of the Borderlands."

15. Stalin's writings on the colonial and national questions predate Lenin's: Boersner, *The Bolshevik*, 32–58.

16. Gellner, *Encounters with Nationalism*, 12, quoting "Draft of an Article on Friedrich List's Book: *Das nationalische System der politischen Ökonomie*" (1845).

17. Smith, *Bolsheviks and the National Question*, 9.

18. Luxemburg wrote a series of six articles for her Krakow-based journal, *Przeglad socialdemokratyczny*, five of which are available in translation at: http://www.marxists.org/archive/luxemburg/1909/national-question/.

19. Bauer, "The Nationalities Question."

20. Rieber, "Stalin, Man of the Borderlands," n. 113. The Georgian Pilipe Makharadze had advanced a similar critique of the Austrian position on cultural autonomy. Jones, *Socialism*, 228. Stalin's work recalled that of the Dutch social democrat Anton Pannekoek. Van Ree, *Political Thought of Joseph Stalin*, 67.

21. Stalin's article existed in draft before he arrived in Krakow in early January 1913, where he stayed briefly; he also stayed only briefly in Vienna. Van Ree, "Stalin and the National Question," at 220–1. In private letters Lenin described Stalin's 1913 essay as "very good," but did not see fit to mention it in his own. *PSS*, XLVIII: 169 (February 25, 1913), 173 (March 29, 1913). Another of Lenin's writings on the national question one year later also omitted any reference to Stalin or his work: "O prave natsii na samoopredelenii," in Lenin, *Sochineniia*, 2nd

and 3rd eds., XVII: 427–74. Following publication of Stalin's essay, Lenin wrote to Stepan Shaumyan, who had published a long article in 1906 attacking federalism in the South Caucasus: "Do not forget also to seek out Caucasian comrades who can write articles on the national question in the Caucasus.... A popular brochure on the national question is very necessary." It is hard to imagine what Stalin's essay was if not a "popular brochure." Lenin, *Sochineniia*, XVII: 91.

22. V. I. Lenin, "O natsional'noi gordosti Velikorossov," *Sotsial-Demokrat*, December 2, 1924, *PSS*, XXVI: 106–10. See also Smith, *Bolsheviks and the National Question*, 7–28. Over the years, many changes were made to the corpus of Lenin's writings on the nation, especially those of the years 1915–18; sometimes it is necessary to use earlier editions of his works, rather than the *PSS*.

23. Trotskii, *Literatura i revoliutsiia*, 68.

24. *PSS*, XXVI: 109.

25. "Rossiiskaia Sotsial-demokratich-eskaia partiia i ee blizhaishie zadachi," *Sochineniia*, I: 11–31 (at 11, 22).

26. *Sochineniia*, I: 32–55; RGASPI, f. 558, op. 1, d. 7 (drafts).

27. Van Ree, "Stalin and the National Question," 218 (citing RGASPI, f. 71, op. 10, d. 183, l. 106–7).

28. Smith, "Stalin as Commissar for Nationality Affairs," 54. On occasion, Stalin paid lip service to Great Russian chauvinism. But more typically, in a speech to Turkic Communists on January 1, 1921, he called Great Russians the ruling nation for whom nationalism was beside the point. Turkic Communists, however, "sons of oppressed peoples," had to be vigilant against their nationalist sentiments, "which serves as a break against communism's crystallization in the East of our country." *Pravda*, January 12, 1921, in *Sochineniia*, V: 1–3.

29. Because Lenin's many pre-October writings, as well as Lev Karakhan's description of Bolshevik plans to John Reed, had made no mention of a special agency for nationalities, this has been deemed a mystery rather than an obvious reaction to events by people who did not fully understand them. Blank, *Sorcerer as Apprentice*; Tucker, *Stalin as Revolutionary*, 181. See also Rigby, *Lenin's Government*, 5; Reed, *Ten Days* [1960], 73.

30. Blank, *Sorcerer as Apprentice*, 13–6; Pestkovskii, "ob ktiabr'skie dniakh v Pitere," 101–5; Pestkovskii, "Vospominaniia o rabote v Narkomnatse," 124–31; *Istoriia natsional'no-gosudarstvennogo stroitel'stva*, I: 48; Manusevich, "Pol'skie sotsial-demokraticheskie," 131–33.

31. *Pravda*, May 19, 1918; *Sochineniia*, IV: 88 ff.

32. Carr, *Bolshevik Revolution*, I: 135–6.

33. Carr, *Bolshevik Revolution*, I: 137.

34. "Protiv federalizma," *Pravda*, March 28, 1917, in *Sochineniia*, III: 23–8 (at 27).

35. *Sochineniia*, IV: 32–3, IV: 66–73, 79–80; Gurvich, *Istoriia sovetskoi konstitutsii*, 147–8 (Stalin's draft).

36. Gurvich, *Istoriia sovetskoi konstitutsii*, 33, 146–7 (Stalin's theses).

37. Hardy, "The Russian Soviet Federated Socialist Republic"; Chistiakov, "Obrazovanie Rossiiskoi Federatsii, 1917-1920 gg."; Chistiakov, "Formirovanie RSFSR kak federativnoe gosudarstvo."

38. Carr, *Bolshevik Revolution*, I: 124–50, esp. 139.

39. "Odna iz ocherednikh zadach," *Pravda*, April 9, 1918, in *Sochineniia*, IV: 74–8. "See also Organizatsiia Rossiiskoi federativnoi respubliki," *Pravda*, April 3 and April 4, 1918, in *Sochineniia*, IV: 66–73. Stalin, *Works*, IV: 372.

40. This point was made by Isabelle Kreindler, who, wrongly, attributed its discovery and realization to Lenin: Kreindler, "A Neglected Source of Lenin's Nationality Policy."

41. *VIII s"ezd RKP (b)* [1959], 46–48, 77–81. See also Nenarokov, *K edinstvu ravnykh*, 91–2 (Latsis), 92–3 (Joffe); and Slezkine, "USSR as a Communal Apartment," 420–1. Before 1917 many liberals, too, had regarded the idea of a federation as a utopia. See the arguments of Baron B. E. Nolde, the offspring of a Baltic German father and Ukrainian mother who from 1907 to 1917 helped formulate and implement state policy: Holquist, "Dilemmas," 241–73. Stalin sought a middle ground, reiterating his call to have nation serve class, arguing that the slogan of national self-determination "should be subordinated to the principles of socialism." *Sochineniia*, IV: 158.

42. *VIII s"ezd RKP (b)* [1959], 55.

43. *VIII s"ezd RKP (b)* [1919], 343–4.

44. *VIII s"ezd RKP (b)* [1959], 425; *Izvestiia TsK KPSS*, 1989, no. 8: 177.

45. Davies, *White Eagle, Red Star*, 23.

46. De Gaulle, *Lettres*, II: 27–8 (May 23, 1919, to his mother).

47. The Bolshevik "Western Front," created in late 1918, counted fewer than 10,000 soldiers. Kakurin, *Russko-pol'skaia kampaniia 1918-1920*, 14. Around the same time a German general staged a coup in Latvia; Finland declared war with Russia over Karelia.

48. Debo, *Survival and Consolidation*, 191–212 (esp. 202), 191 (citing *DBFP*, I: 694, 696–8, 689–91, 710–5); Davies, *White Eagle, Red Star*, 91; *Dokumenty i materialy po istorii sovetsko-pol'skikh otnoshenii*, II: 339–43.

49. Carley, "The Politics of Anti-Bolshevism."

50. Debo, *Survival and Consolidation*, 191–212 (esp. 202), 404, 406. See also Korbel, *Poland Between East and West*, 79–93.

51. Borzęcki, *Soviet-Polish Treaty of 1921*; Wandycz, *Soviet-Polish Relations*. See also D'Abernon, *The Eighteenth Decisive Battle of the World*. Polish troops fought six concurrent wars between 1918 and 1922: Pogonowski, *Historical Atlas of Poland*.

52. The Baedeker guide to the Russian empire (1914) stated that "the Western Provinces (the former kingdom of Poland), the Baltic Provinces, and Finland have all preserved their national idiosyncrasies," adding that "Russia proper begins at the line drawn from St. Petersburg via Smolensk and Kiev to Bessarabia." This view turned out to be prescient. Baedeker, *Russia, with Teheran*, xv.

53. V. I. Lenin, "Telegramma L. D. Trotskomu," *PSS*, LI: 145–6, February 27, 1919; Davies, *White Eagle, Red Star*, 98. Kostiushko, *Pol'sko-Sovetskaia voina*, I: 40, 43, 47; Blank, "Soviet Nationality Policy." On March 17, 1920, a jumble of Freikorps and other paramilitary ruffians led by the conservative monarchist Wolfgang Kapp attempted a putsch in Germany; Lenin telegrammed Stalin to accelerate the mopping up of the Whites in Crimea, "in order to have our hands entirely free, given that civil war in Germany could oblige us to move west to assist the Communists." Kapp's putsch failed and to Lenin it looked like a replay of the Kornilov Affair, presaging a decisive shift leftward to revolution. Lenin, *V. I. Lenin*, 330–1 (March 17, 1920); Adibekov and Shirinia, *Politbiuro TsK RKP (b)—VKP (b) i Komintern*, 39; *PSS*, XL: 235–6 (speech to 9th Party Congress, March 29, 1920), XL: 332 (April 29, 1920). See also Balabanoff, *Impressions of Lenin*, 109–12; and Buber-Neumann, *Von Potsdam nach Moskau*, 8.

54. Chamberlin, *Russian Revolution*, II: 301; Wandycz, *Soviet-Polish Relations*, 94–100; Borzęcki, *Soviet-Polish Treaty of 1921*, 27–9. See also Dziewanowski, *Joseph Piłsudski*. The Poles were quick to point out in upholding their claims to the borderlands (*kresy wschodnie*, in Polish) that in the summer of 1918, the Bolsheviks repudiated all imperial Russian treaties, which included those that had legalized the partitions of Poland. Horak, *Poland's International Affair*, doc. 223.

55. Reshetar, *The Ukrainian Revolution*, 301–2; Wandycz, *Soviet-Polish Relations*, 191–2; Palij, *The Ukrainian-Polish Defensive Alliance*.

56. *Pravda*, April 23, 1920. At the Moscow gathering one of the speakers,

Mikhail Olminsky [Vitimsky], a long-time worshipper of Lenin, recalled the ill will that Lenin had generated before the revolution. "Lenin was known then (18 years ago) as a person who loved power, strived for dictatorship, rejected the best old leaders of the social democracy movement, criticized everyone and was at war with everyone," Olminsky noted, before adding that Lenin "was right in promoting the organizing principle of non-democracy and the principle of a military organization." Velikanova, *Making of an Idol*, 34 (citing Bukov, *Nedorisovannyi portret, 1920*). See also Tumarkin, *Lenin Lives!*, 103.

57. Velikanova, *Making of an Idol*, 34 (citing *Nedorisovannyi portret, 1920*).

58. RGASPI, f. 44, op. 1, d. 5, l. 11 (Lenin, political report to the 9th Party Conference).

59. Borzęcki, *Soviet-Polish Treaty of 1921*, 63–8.

60. Trotskii, "Smert' pol'skoi burzhuazii" [April 29, 1920], in *Kak vooruzhalas' revoliutsiia*, II: 91. See also Lenin's speech, that same day, to the All-Russian congress of glass workers: *PSS*, XL: 331–2.

61. Trotsky, *Stalin*, 328. But see also *Pravda*, May 6, 1920.

62. Stalin, "Novyi pokhod Antanty na Rossiiu," *Pravda*, May 25 and May 26, 1920; *Sochineniia*, IV: 319. For Stalin on Polish nationalism, see also *Pravda*, March 14, 1923, in *Sochineniia*, IV: 167.

63. Tiander, *Das Erwachen Osteuropas*, 137.

64. Zamoyski, *Warsaw 1920*, 25–6.

65. Budennyi, *Proidennyi put'*, I: 245.

66. Kuz'min, *Krushenie poslednego pokhoda Antanty*, 133–5; Yiulenev, *Sovetskaia kavaleriia v boiakh za Rodinu*, 169–74.

67. Davies, *White Eagle, Red Star*, 120.

68. *Dirketivy glavnogo komandovaniia Krasnoi Armii*, 735.

69. Kantor, *Voina i mir*, 13–36.

70. Rubtsov, *Marshaly Stalina*, 72–3 (recollections of V. N. Postoronkin, who would join the Whites).

71. One of his recommenders was Avel Yenukidze, secretary of the Soviet's central executive committee. V. O. Daines, "Mikhail Tukhachesvkii," *Voprosy istorii*, 1989, no. 10: day 41; Volkov, *Tragediia russkogo ofitserstva*, 314.

72. Easter, *Reconstructing the State*, 98, citing RGASPI, f. 124, op. 1, d. 302, l. 4.

73. Gul', *Krasnye marshaly*, 23. Ivan Smirnov led Kolchak's detstruction in Siberia.

74. *PSS*, LI: 206–8.

75. RGASPI, f. 17, op. 109, d. 74, l. 28.

76. Zamoyski, *Warsaw 1920*, 60.

77. *Sochineniia*, IV: 336–41; Mikhutina, *Pol'sko-Sovetskaia voina*, 182–3.

78. Reproduced in the appendices to Skvortsov-Stepanov, *S Krasnoi Armiei*, 78.

79. Budennyi, *Proidennyi put'*, II: 168–210.

80. L. D. Trotsky to S. S. Kamenev, copied to E. M. Sklyanskii, Lenin and the Central Committee, July 17, 1920: Krasnov and Daines, *Neizvestnyi Trotskii*, 307.

81. Radek, *Voina pol'skikh belogvardeitsev protiv Sovetskoi Rossii*, 17; Karl Radek, "Pol'skii vopros i internatsional," *Kommunisticheskii internatsional*, 1990, no. 12: 2173–88; Zetkin, *Reminiscences of Lenin* (London: Modern Books, 1929), 20 (omitted in subsequent editions); Lerner, *Karl Radek*, 100–1; Carr, *Bolshevik Revolution*, III: 321. Retrospectively, Radek covered over the differences and aligned himself with Lenin: "Session of the Zentrale with the Representative of the Executive Committee for Germany, Friday, January 28, 1921," in Drachkovitch and Lazitch, *The Comintern*, 285. See also Radek, *Vneshniaia politika sovetskoi Rossii*, 62.

82. *Pravda*, July 11, 1920; *Sochineniia*, IV: 324, 333, 336–41. See also Ullman, *Anglo-Soviet Accord*, 166.

83. Hooker, "Lord Curzon and the 'Curzon Line.'" 137.

84. Borzęcki, *Soviet-Polish Treaty of 1921*, 79–82; Wandycz, *Soviet-Polish Relations*.

85. Meijer, *Trotsky Papers*, II: 228–31; Trotsky, *My Life*, 455–7. Lenin sent a phonegram on July 12–13 asking for Stalin's analysis of the Curzon Note, commenting: "I think this is complete theft for the annexation of Crimea, which is insolently mentioned in the Note. We want a victory to snatch the means of thieving promises." *PSS*, LI: 237–8.

86. Babel, *1920 Diary*; Babel, *Konarmiia*.

87. Airapetian, *Legendarnyi Gai*, 51.

88. Pipes, *Unknown Lenin*, 85–8. The treaty was signed July 12, 1920: Gerutis, *Lithuania*, 164–5; Debo, *Survival and Consolidation*, 222–3.

89. Senn, "Lithuania's Fight for Independence."

90. Airapetian, *Legendarnyi Gai*, 124.

91. Mikhutina, *Pol'sko-Sovetskaia voina*, 303–5 (AVP RF, f. 04, op. 32, d. 25, pap. 205, l. 30–1).

92. Meijer, *Trotsky Papers*, II: 228–31; Deutscher, *Prophet Armed*, 463–7.

93. *Izvestiia TsK KPSS*, 1991, no. 2: 117; *Dokumenty vneshnei politiki*, III: 47–53; Mikhutina, *Pol'sko-Sovetskaia voina*, I: 143, n1, 142–3.

94. *PSS*, LI: 240. Lenin had telegrammed Unszlicht in Minsk (July 15, 1920), asking if he considered "a soviet seizure of power in Poland probable?" Unszlicht answered ingratiatingly that he "considered a soviet seizure of power in Poland in connection with our troops' approach to the border utterly probable in the nearest time,"

but admitted that he could not be sure when the uprising in Poland could be expected. Mikhutina, *Pol'sko-Sovetskaia voina*, 173–4; Golikov, *Vladimir Il'ich Lenin*, IX: 102. Bolshevik propaganda insisted this was not an invasion. "To push westward not with the goal of conquering Poland, Germany, France, but to unite with the Polish, German, French workers—that's our main goal," explained the newspaper *Red Army Man* to the invading Soviet troops. "That is why White Poland must be destroyed, to establish a proletarian Poland, and fly the red colors above Warsaw." Quoted in Wyszczelski, *Varshava 1920*, 67.

95. Golubev, *Direktivy glavnogo komandovaniia*, 643–4.

96. *Iz istorii grazhdanskoi voiny v SSSR*, III: 326; Karaeva, *Direktivy komandovaniia frontov*, III: 225–6.

97. Karaeva, *Direktivy komandovaniia frontov*, III: documents 260, 227.

98. Borzęcki, *Soviet-Polish Treaty of 1921*, 87 (citing RGASPI, f. 2, op. 1, d. 14673: Kamenev on July 13). Trotsky's note on Romania: July 17, 1920.

99. Pipes, *Unknown Lenin*, 90–1; Kvashonkin, *Bol'shevistskoe rukovodstvo*, 148. See also Volkogonov, *Lenin: Life and Legacy*, 388 (citing RGASPI, f. 2, op. 1, d. 348); Service, *Lenin*, III: 120.

100. A census in 1921 gave the city's population of Jews as 39,602 out of a total of 79,792, or 51.6 percent, which was thought to be a decrease from previous years. Poles came in at 46.6 percent, Germans 1.9 percent, Russians 1.8 percent, and Belorussians 0.8 percent. Bender, *Jews of Bialystok*, 18.

101. Julian Marchlewski, the head of the imported Revolutionary Committee, could not establish contact with the city's Polish Communist party (which had 80 members). Mikhutina, *Pol'sko-Sovetskaia voina*, 190.

102. Lerner, "Attempting a Revolution"; Kostiushko, *Pol'skoe biuro TsK RKP (b)*; Materialy "Osoboi papki" *Politbiuro TsK RKP (b)*; Ulam, *Expansion and Coexistence*, 109.

103. Skvortsov-Stepanov, *S Krasnoi Armiei*, 92–5. Skvortsov, an eyewitness who recorded his thoughts in real time, noted indigenous anti-Semitism: "During the German occupation the Jews worked on the railroads. Now the Polish railroad workers of Belostok Junction refuse to take them on" (*S Krasnoi Armiei*, 29). He failed to mention the Jewish exodus on the eve (and during) the Red presence, the expropriation and looting of Polish businesses and property, and the Cheka's dissolution of Jewish communal organizations. Bender, *Jews of Bialystok*, 20 (citing Heschel Farbstein, *Invazja Bolszewicka a Zydzi: Zbior dokumentow* [Warsaw, 1921], I: 13–5).

104. Davies, "Izaak Babel's 'Konarmiya' Stories," 847; Golubev, *Direktivy glavnogo komandovaniia*, 643–4, 649.

105. Zamoyski, *Warsaw 1920*, 64, 69. See also Putna, *K Visle i obratno*, 31.

106. Erickson, *Soviet High Command* [1962], 101.

107. *PSS*, LI: 248.

108. *Iz istorii grazhdanskoi voiny v SSSR*, III: 338–9; Karaeva, *Direktivy komandovaniia frontov*, III: 244–5; Naida, *O nekotorykh voprosakh*, 224.

109. Mikhutina, *Pol'sko-Sovetskaia voina*, 196; *Iz istorii grazhdanskoi voiny v SSSR*, III: 336. *Leninskii sbornik*, XXXVI: 115–6.

110. Budennyi, *Proidennyi put'*, II: 281.

111. Redirected to Crimea to fight Wrangel, Yegorov wanted to take Budyonny's cavalry with him. Budyonny, Voroshilov, and Minin tried to make excuses in a telegram to Trotsky (August 10), pleading to reverse the directive to subordinate themselves to the western front (they cited the danger of exacerbating supply problems). In a conversation over the direct line between Kamenev and Tukhachevsky, the latter held firm: he wanted the First Cavalry Army. Kakurin and Melikov, *Voina s belopoliakami*, 504–6; Kuz'min, "Ob odnoi ne vypolnenoi direktive Glavkoma," 62.

112. Golubev, *Direktivy glavnogo komandovaniia*, 707–8.

113. Tukhachevsky and Kamenev, communicating over the direct line around midnight on August 9–10, disagreed over the location of the bulk of Polish forces: north of the Bug (Tukhachevsky) or south (Kamenev). Golubev, *Direktivy glavnogo komandovaniia*, 650–2.

114. Brown, "Lenin, Stalin and the Failure."

115. Golubev, *Direktivy glavnogo komandovaniia*, 709–10; Karaeva, *Direktivy komandovaniia frontov*, III: 258–9 (Yegorov-Kamenev conversation over the direct wire, August 18, just after midnight).

116. Tucker, *Stalin as Revolutionary*, 205.

117. Trotsky, *Stalin*, 329. The literature has picked up on this: Seaton, *Stalin as Military Commander*, 72.

118. Budennyi, *Priodennyi put'*, II: 204, 294.

119. Egorov, *L'vov-Varshava*, 97; Naida, *O nekotorykh voprosakh*, 226. Note that on August 12, Lenin showed he understood, writing to Sklyansky: "Is it not time to direct Smilga that it is necessary to take *every* adult male *without exception* (after the harvest) into the army? It is time. Since Budyonny is in the South, it's necessary to *strengthen* the North." Naida, *O nekotorykh voprosakh*, 228; Golubev, *Direktivy glavnogo komandovaniia*,

615. Eventually, Yegorov yielded to the supreme commander's insistence, but Stalin, the commissar, refused to co-sign Yegorov's order of transfer for the First Cavalry Army, so Budyonny chose to disregard it.

120. Volkogonov, *Triumf i tragediia*, I/i: 103 (citing RGVA, f. 104, op. 4, d. 484, l. 11).

121. Davies, *White Eagle, Red Star*, 217; Budennyi, *Proidennyi put',* II: 191–339; Egorov, *L'vov-Varshava*, 26–7. See Gerasimov painting of 1935, First Cavalry Army, vol. I, between 288–9.

122. Quoted in von Riekhoff, *German-Polish Relations*, 30.

123. Golubev, *Direktivy glavnogo komandovaniia*, 655; RGASPI, f. 5, op. 1, d. 2136 (Victor Kopp to Lenin, August 19, 1920); Borzęcki, *Soviet-Polish Treaty of 1921*, 86; Himmer, "Soviet Policy," 672; Pipes, *Russia Under the Bolshevik Regime*, 189–90.

124. 217 delegates, 36 countries, 169 eligible to vote: Riddell, *Workers of the World*, I: 11.

125. *PSS*, XLI: 219.

126. *Kommunisticheskii trud*, July 29, 1920; Farbman, *Bolshevism in Retreat*, 137. For a romantic view on the 2nd Comintern Congress, see Carr, *Bolshevik Revolution*, III: 196.

127. Pipes, *Russia Under the Bolshevik Regime*, 177; Degras, *Communist International* [London], I: 111–13.

128. F. Isserson, "Sud'ba polkovodtsa," *Druzhba naorodov*, 1988, no. 5: 184, 187.

129. Golubev, *Direktivy glavnogo komandovaniia*, 662.

130. *PSS*, LI: 264.

131. *PSS*, LI: 266–7; Meijer, *Trotsky Papers*, II: 260–1.

132. Debo, *Survival and Consolidation*, 243 (citing Lloyd George Papers, F/203/1/9, F/203/1/10, August 24).

133. Putna, *K Visle i obratno*, 242. The Polish marshal's redemption following his colleagues' refusal of his offer to resign (twice), a Red Army temporary loss of radio contacts at a critical moment of advantage, and Tukhachevsky's dismissal are as absurd as a copy of Piłsudski's battle plan recovered from a Polish POW.

134. Borzęcki, *Soviet-Polish Treaty of 1921*, 95.

135. Brown, "Lenin, Stalin and the Failure," 43; Karaeva, *Direktivy komandovaniia frontov*, IV: 180–2; Meijer, *Trotsky Papers*, II: 240; Melikov, *Srazhenie na Visle*, 125–7. "The catastrophe on the front was prepared long ago," one commander reported to Trotsky. "In this operation [Warsaw] the Polish forces exceeded ours by a factor of more than three, and in places by six times." Simonova, "Mir i schast'e na shtykakh," 63 (quoting N. Muranov).

136. *Kratkaia istoriia grazhdanskoi*

voiny v SSSR, 444. Stalin was replaced as commissar of the Southwestern Front Revolutionary Military Council by Sergei Gusev.

137. Sumbadze, Sotsial'no-ekonomicheskie predposylki pobedy Sovetskoi vlasti, 211 (Mikoyan to Lenin), 212 (local representative to Stalin); Grazhdanskaia voina v SSSR, II: 330.

138. Meijer, Trotsky Papers, II: 147 (Trotsky to Lenin and Chicherin, April 20, 1920).

139. Reissner, Oktober, 163–5. Orjonikidze had participated in the Tabriz revolts of 1906–11 in northern Iran.

140. The Soviets understood Kuchek to be a nationalist, not a Communist. Izvestiia, June 16, 1920 (Vozhnesensky); Krasnaia gazeta, June 20, 1920 (Soltangäliev).

141. Zabih, Communist Movement in Iran, 18; Lenczowski, Russia and the West in Iran, 9–10, 52–9; Komintern i Vostok, 75; Chaquèri, The Soviet Socialist Republic of Iran, 166–213. Soltangäliev wanted a self-standing Comintern of the East and a Muslim Red Army, with Azerbaijan as a springboard, for spreading revolution. Armenian Communists also wanted to Sovietize Iran. Nariman Narimanov, party leader of Azerbaijan, was opposed, viewing Iranian leftists as weak, and advocated for maintaining an anti-imperialist coalition with bourgeois nationalists.

142. Volodarskii, Sovety i ikh iuzhnye sosedi Iran i Afganistan, 67–72.

143. Chaquèri, The Soviet Socialist Republic of Iran, 214–75.

144. Orjonikidze and Stasova had helped organize the congress. Gafurov, Lenin i natsional'no-osvoboditel'noe dvizhenie, 77.

145. Zinoviev admitted, elsewhere, that a majority of attendees were nonparty. Carr, Bolshevik Revolution, III: 261, n1 (citing Kommunisticheskii internatsional, November 6, 1920). See also Fischer, Soviets in World Affairs, I: 283–4.

146. Riddell, To See the Dawn, 45–52, 231–2.

147. Congress of the Peoples of the East. Baku, September 1920: Stenographic Report, 21–3.

148. "Mustafa Kemal's Movement is a national liberation movement," one delegate from Turkey stated at Baku. "We support it, but, as soon as the struggle with imperialism is finished, we believe this movement will pass over to social revolution." Pervyi s"ezd narodov vostoka, 159.

149. Zinoviev's reckless summons to holy war against British imperialism could have backfired, potentially embroiling the Bolsheviks in a major war thanks to Muslim jihadists whom Moscow did not control, while giving free rein to pan-Turkic nationalists

and others whose political agendas were their own. Blank, "Soviet Politics," 187.

150. Smith, "Stalin as Commissar for Nationality Affairs," 58; Smith, Bolsheviks and the National Question, 32–4.

151. Trotsky, Stalin [1968], 255–62.

152. "'Fate' did not permit Stalin once in three and a half years to function either as commissar of control or commissar of nationalities," Lenin would write to another functionary, Adolf Joffe, in 1921. PSS, LII: 99–101. Stephen Blank, although offering no comparisons to the operation of other commissariats with similar-level resources, asserts that Stalin wanted the nationalities' commissariat to fail to avoid investing national minority Communists with a strong instrument to pursue their own agendas. Blank, Sorcerer as Apprentice, 53, 64, 223–4.

153. Filomonov, Obrazovanie i razvitie RSFSR, 163. In July 1919, the commissariat's ruling board even proposed its own abolition, but the Council of People's Commissars rejected self-liquidation. At the same time, some province soviets had already closed down nationalities commissariat branch offices in their territories. Smith, Bolsheviks and the National Question, 33 (citing GARF, f. 1318, op. 1, d. 2, l. 104). See also Makarova, Narodnyi Komissariat. Stalin would continue to lobby Lenin: "I insist on abolition (after the Union of Republics we do not need NKnats)," but Lenin wrote on Stalin's note, "Nknats is necessary for the satisfaction of the nats [national minorities]". APRF, f.3, op. 22, d. 97, l. 136–7, 137ob., Hoover Institution Archives, Volkogonov papers, container 23.

154. Gizzatullin and Sharafutdinov, Mirsaid Sultan-Galiev, 386.

155. Gizzatullin and Sharafutdinov, Mirsaid Sultan-Galiev, 52.

156. Togan, Vospominaniia, 197. Stalin wrote other civil war articles on the national question, often in a pandering tone. In Izvestiya (February 22, 1919), for example, he repeated Lenin's two-camp imagery that divided the world into "the camp of imperialism and the camp of socialism," placing in the first "the United States and Britain, France, and Japan," and in the second "Soviet Russia with the young Soviet republics, and the growing proletariat revolution in the European countries." Stalin claimed to be confident that imperialism was "headed for its inevitable doom," and accorded European revolutions the highest probability for success, but he also noted that the "roar" of the socialist revolutions could be "heard in the countries of the oppressed East." Reprinted, without much context, in Eudin and North, Soviet Russia and the East, 45–6.

157. Togan, Vospominaniia, 199, 229–30, 256.

158. A petition from the Central Bureau of Communist Organizations of the Peoples of the East, which was headed by Soltangäliev, had been sent to Trotsky on January 2, 1920, requesting Stalin's recall from the civil war front so that he could "directly oversee internal national policy and foreign policy of Soviet power in the East," in order to quell dissatisfaction and overcome chaos. Jughashvili, they wrote, had "colossal authority" among easterners as a man of the Caucasus and an expert on the national question. RGASPI, f. 17, op. 109, d. 76, l. 1–1ob.

159. Schafer, "Local Politics," passim. See also Pipes, "First Experiment"; Zenkovsky, "The Tataro-Bashkir Feud"; Zenkovsky, Pan-Turkism, 161–9; and Blank, "Struggle for Soviet Bashkiria."

160. Togan, Vospominaniia, 193.

161. On the Bashkirs, see Steinwedel, "Invisible Threads of Empire."

162. Even if Stalin had not blocked the formation of a Greater Tataria in 1918, it would not have survived the exigencies of the civil war and the need to win Bashkir allegiance. The March 1918 decree calling for a joint Tatar-Bashkir republic was formally annulled only in December 1919. Iuldashbaev, Obrazovanie Bashkirskoi Avtonomnoi Sovetskoi Sotsialisticheskoi Respubliki, 423.

163. Schafer, "Local Politics," 165–90.

164. Schafer, "Local Politics," 176 (citing GARF, f. 1318, op. 1, d. 45, l. 9 , 44; RGASPI, f. 17, op. 65, d. 22, l. 218); Togan, Vospominaniia, 293; Sultan-Galiev, Stat'i, vtystupleniia, dokumenty, 437.

165. Schafer, "Local Politics," 176; Kul'sharipov, Z. Validov, 128–39 (Validi to Stalin, May 3, 1919); Murtazin, Bashkiriia i bashkirskie voiska, 207–11; Togan, Vospominaniia, 292–5.

166. Togan, Vospominaniia, 250–1.

167. Togan, Vospominaniia, 251.

168. Izvestiia, May 20 and May 29, 1920; Pravda, May 29, 1920; Politika Sovetskoi vlasti, 101–2; Batsell, Soviet Rule in Russia, 142.

169. Smith, Bolsheviks and the National Question, 47–8 (citing RGASPI, f. 17, op. 3, d. 68, l. 4).

170. Magerovskii, Soiuz Sovetskikh Sotsialisticheskikh Respublik, 16n; Pipes, Formation of the Soviet Union, 247.

171. Rorlich, Volga Tatars, 137–8, 146–9.

172. TsK RKP (b)—VKP (b) i natsional'nyi vopros, 42–3 (RGASPI, f. 17, op. 112, d. 100, l. 83–83ob, 4).

173. Stalin had supposedly told his deputy Semyon Dimanshtein in 1919, "Soltangäliev had long looked askance at us and has only recently been

somewhat tame." Blank, "Struggle for Soviet Bashkiria."
174. Dakhshleiger, V. I. Lenin, 186–7; Murtazin, Bashkiria i Bashkirskie voiska, 187–8; Proletarskaia Revoliutsiia, 1926, no. 12: 205–7; Zenkovsky, Pan-Turkism, 205–6.
175. Togan, Vospominaniia, 265–7.
176. Togan, Vospominaniia, 267–9. Validi would write a letter requesting amnesty in late 1922; Rudzutaks conferred with Stalin, who agreed to grant it, provided Validi made a public renunciation and agitated among the basmachi to lay down their arms. Supposedly, nothing more was heard from Validi. Tainy natsiona'noi politiki TsK RKP, 93. Validi fought the Soviets for years before emigrating to Iran, then Turkey, where he took the surname Togan.
177. Bailey, Mission to Tashkent, 119–21. The war commissar, Osipov, escaped to Iran.
178. Zhizn' natsional'nostei, March 2, 1919; Sochineniia, IV: 230–1.
179. Marshall, "Turkfront."
180. Frank, Bukhara.
181. Dokumenty vneshnei politiki, II: 657 (RGASPI, f. 2, op. 1, d. 14345, l. 13).
182. Eleuov, Inostrannaia voennaia interventsiia, II: 513 (RGASPI, f. 2, op. 1, d. 14884, l. 1).
183. Litvak and Kuznetzov, "The Last Emir of Noble Bukhara and His Money." See also Becker, Russia's Protectorates, 273–95.
184. Genis, "S Bukharoi nado konchat'," 39–44, 49–56. Frunze: Istochnik, 1994, no. 5: 38–48.
185. Kvashonkin, Bol'shevistskoe rukovodstva, 245, n2 (RGASPI, f. 5, op. 2, d. 315, l. 83: Chicherin to Molotov).
186. Gvardeitsy Oktiabria, 269 (RGASPI, f. 124, op. 1, d. 1474, l. 3–5: 1928 autobiography); Beatty, Red Heart of Russia, 134–5. Peterss had an English wife and spoke the language with a London accent.
187. Peterss wrote to Moscow: "In my opinion an investigation should be launched and those who did not take measures to prevent these outrages should be called to account." Genis, "S Bukharoi nado konchat'," 49.
188. Genis, "S Bukharoi nado konchat'," 39–49 (citing RGASPI, f. 76, op. 3, d. 234, l. 5; d. 357, l. 1). Plekhanov and Plekhanov, F. E. Dzerzhinskii, 596 (RGASPI, f. 76, op. 3, d. 357, l. 1: to Zinovy Katznelson, March 14, 1925).
189. Urazaev, Turkestanskaia ASSR.
190. Schapiro, "General Department."
191. Istoricheskii arkhiv, I (1992): 14–29, translated in Pipes, Unknown Lenin, 94–115 (Pipes gives the wrong date). See also Westad, Global Cold War, 46. Lenin's speech was omitted from the stenographic record of the 9th Party Conference published in 1972.

192. Service, Lenin, III: 140–5.
193. Pravda, September 29, 1920.
194. IX konferentsiia RKP (b), 34–6 (Radek), 60–2 (Stalin), 75–9 (Trotsky), 82 (Stalin), 372–3, n18. See also Trotsky, Stalin, 327–8; Tucker, Stalin as Revolutionary, 203.
195. "Our foolhardy vanguard, certain of victory," Lenin privately told Clara Zetkin, the German Communist, "had no reinforcements in troops or ammunition and could not even get enough dry bread," inducing them to squeeze "Polish peasants and townspeople," who "looked upon the Red Army men as enemies, not brothers and liberators." Zetkin, Vospominaniia o Lenine, 18–9; Zetkin, Reminiscences of Lenin, 20. Zetkin first published these reminiscences in 1924. See also Pravda, October 9 and October 10, 1920. Lenin would soon tell the 10th Party Congress: "In our offensive we moved too fast—almost to Warsaw; this was undoubtedly a mistake. I will not now analyze whether it was a strategic or a political mistake—this would lead me too far from my topic. I think this will have to be the work of future historians." V. I. Lenin, "Otchet o politicheskoi deiatel'nosti TsK RKP (b)" [March 8, 1921], in PSS, XLIII: 11.
196. Davies, White Eagle, Red Star, 208–10.
197. Even if the Poles had not evicted Tukhachevsky from Warsaw, the way Piłsudski had been evicted from Kiev, would Britain and France have stood aside and allowed an attempt to Sovietize Poland?
198. Told by Soviet agitators they were "liberators," Red Army soldiers found themselves greeted with anger by Polish workers. Putna, K Visle i obratno, 137–8; Carr, Bolshevik Revolution, III: 215, n2; Mikhutina, Pol'skaia-Sovetskaia voina, 191–5.
199. "In 1920 and partly in 1921," one anonymous Polish Communist would recall, the party labored "under an illusion concerning the tempo of the development of the revolution." Dziewanowski, Communist Party of Poland, 95 (citing K., "Poland," Communist International, 1924, no. 1).
200. The Bolshevik presence in Białystok/Belostok lasted from July 28 through August 22, 1920. As one enthusiast eyewitness recorded at the time, "the Polish Revolutionary Committee arrived with very few staff [rabotnikov]. Red Poland will in time create them in the process of work." Skvortsov-Stepanov, S Krasnoi Armiei, 47.
201. Lerner, "Poland in 1920," at 410 (Julian Marchlewski). See also the analysis in Suslov, Politicheskoe obespechenie sovetsko-pol'skoi kampanii.
202. In a fall 1920 conversation with Clara Zetkin, the German Communist,

Lenin acknowledged that "what happened in Poland was perhaps bound to happen . . . The peasants and workers, gulled by the followers of Piłsudski and [vice-premier Ignacy] Daszynski, defended their class enemies, allowed our gallant Red Army men to starve to death, enticed them into ambushes and killed them." Zetkin, Vospominaniia o Lenine, 18–9; Zetkin, Reminiscences of Lenin, 20. See also Pravda, October 9 and October 10, 1920.
203. Lerner, "Poland in 1920." Lerner wrongly speculated that Tukhachevsky had no express orders to march on Warsaw. But of course he did: Mel'tiukhov, Sovtesko-pol'skie voiny, 74.
204. Tukhachevskii, Pokhod za Vislu, chapter 3, translated in Piłsudski, Year 1920 (New York: Piłsudski Institute of New York, 1972), at 242–4. The "Revolution from Abroad" chapter would be omitted from subsequent editions.
205. He wrote, obliquely, that "for a whole series of unexpected reasons, the high command's efforts to bring about a regrouping of the great bulk of the Southwestern Front's forces in the Lublin salient were unsuccessful." Tukhachevskii, Izbrannye proizvedenye, I: 154.
206. Shaposhnikov, Na Visle. More broadly, see McCann, "Beyond the Bug."
207. Many biographers have followed the Stalin insubordination line. Tucker, Stalin as Revolutionary, 203–5. An early exception is Ulam, Stalin, 188–9. Lenin's disciples protected his reputation, at Stalin's expense. "Who on earth would go to Warsaw through Lvov!" Lenin supposedly remarked, according to Bonch-Bruevich, in an obviously fabricated quote: Na boevykh postakh, 283.
208. Kantor, Voina i mir, 206, citing Tukhachesvsky's "zapiski o zhizni" (September 9, 1921), in his police file: TsA FSB, ASD no. R-9000.
209. Lewis and Lih, Zinoviev and Martov.
210. Fischer, Stalin and German Communism, 146 (citing Zinoviev, Zwölf Tage, 74).
211. Angress, Stillborn Revolution, 71–2; Carr, Bolshevik Revolution, III: 217–20; Debo, Survival and Consolidation and Survival, 308–9; Weitz, Creating German Communism, 98.
212. Broué, German Revolution, 502.
213. The Soviets would declare Bessarabia Soviet territory under Romanian occupation. The United States and Japan failed to ratify the treaty. In 1924, in response, the USSR would create a Moldovan Autonomous Soviet Socialist Republic on the left bank of the Dniester River in Ukraine.
214. Wyszczelski, Varshava 1920, 256.
215. Mel'tiukhov, Sovtesko-pol'skie voiny, 104–5.

216. Lenin, "Nashe vneshnee i vnutrennee polozhenie i zadachi partii," *PSS*, XLII: 17–38 (at 22: speech to a Moscow province party gathering, November 21, 1920).

217. Piłsudski, *Year 1920*, 222.

218. *Pravda*, November 7.

219. Davatts and L'vov, *Russkaia armiia na chuzhbine*, 7. Wrangel claimed 160,000: Hoover Institution Archives, Maria Dmitrevna Vrangel' Collection, box 145, folder 28.

220. Zarubin, *Bez pobeditelei*; A. L. Litvin, "VChK v sovremennoi istoricheskoi literatury," in Vinogradov, *Arkhiv VChK*, 51–70 (at 59). Yefim Yevdokimov was the chief of a special department of the southern front.

221. Chamberlin, *Russian Revolution*, II: 431.

222. Kalyvas, *Logic of Violence*, 389.

223. Shklovsky, *Sentimental Journey*, 208.

224. Osipova, *Klassovaia bor'ba v derevene*, 315, 317, 321; Abramovitch, *Soviet Revolution*, 143–5; Iarov, "Krest'ianskoe vol'nenie na Severo-Zapade Sovetskoi Rossii," 134–59; Arthur Adams, "The Great Ukrainian Jacquerie," in Hunczak, *The Ukraine*, 247–70; Graziosi, *Bol'shevikii i krest'iane na Ukraine*; Arshinov, *Istoriia makhnovskogo dvizheniia*; Danilov, *Nestor Makhno*; Aleshkin and Vasil'ev, *Krest'ianskie vosstaniia*; Raleigh, *Experiencing Russia's Civil War*.

225. *Novaia zhizn'*, March 26, 1918: 4 and April 19, 1918: 4, in Bunyan and Fisher, *Bolshevik Revolution*, 664; *Pravda*, March 17, 1918.

226. Graziosi, "State and Peasants," 65–117 (at 76–7, 87).

227. Landis, *Bandits and Partisans*; Danilov, *Krest'anskoe vosstanie*. Previous studies include Singleton, "The Tambov Revolt"; Radkey, *Unknown Civil War*; and Delano DuGarm, "Local Politics and the Struggle for Grain in Tambov, 1918–1921," in Raleigh, *Provincial Landscape*, 59–81.

228. Baranov, *Krest'ianskoe vosstanie*, 79.

229. Aptekar', "Krest'ianskaia voina," 50–55 (citing GARF, f. 6, op. 12, d. 194; f. 235, op. 2, d. 56, l. 6: Shikunov).

230. *X s"ezd* [1921], 231.

231. Shishkin, *Sibirskaia Vandeia*, II: 128.

232. Litvin, *Krasnyi i belyi terror*, 379 (February 13, 1921).

233. Landis, *Bandits and Partisans*, 165–6.

234. "We have to cope with the present situation, which has deteriorated both internally and internationally," Lenin told the Moscow party organization on February 24, 1921. "[A formal peace treaty] with Poland has not yet been concluded, and at home we have a growth of banditry and kulak revolts.

As for food and fuel, things have gone from bad to worse." He blamed the influence of the Socialist Revolutionaries. "Their main forces are abroad; every spring they dream of overthrowing Soviet power." Lenin, *Collected Works*, 42: 272–3.

235. Maslov, *Rossiia posle chetyrekh let revoliutsii*, II: 133.

236. *Pravda*, February 12, 1921.

237. Lenin received a copy of the ninepoint resolutions of the Baltic Factory. "1. Down with Communism and Communist power over the Russian Socialist Republic, for not implementing the interests of the majority of the working people of the Russian Socialist Soviet Republic. 2. Long live Soviet power, that is, that power which will realize the interests of the working peoples of the Russian Socialist Soviet Republic." And so on. The workers demanded a state without bloodshed, and closed their resolution with the cry, "Long live truth, freedom of speech and the press in the free Socialist Republic." RGASPI, f. 2, op. 2, d. 561, l. 40.

238. "Doklad nachal'nika 1-go spetsial'nogo otdela VChK Fel'dmana v osobyi otdel VChK" [December 10, 1920], in Avrich, *Kronstadt, 1921*, 19–23. On February 28, the politburo in Moscow took a hard line concerning Kronstadt, and Cheka deputy chairman Kesnofontov ordered that "SRs and Mensheviks, using the natural dissatisfaction of the workers with the difficult conditions of life, are trying to call forth a strike movement against Soviet power and the Russian Communist party, giving it an organized, all-Russia character." Prikaz VChK, "'Ob usilenii bor'by s konterrevoliutsiie," in Avrich, *Kronstadt, 1921*, 36–7

239. *Izvestiya Vremennogo revoliutsionnogo komiteta matrosov, krasnoarmeitsev i rabochikh*, March 3, 1921; Avrich, *Kronstadt, 1921*, 50–1; in *Kronstadskaia tragediia*, 114–5; Getzler, *Kronstadt*, 205–45 (esp. 213–4). More than 300 volumes of archival documents on Kronstadt are said to sit in FSB archives, gathered from many agencies and publications, including from the Cheka itself: *Kronstadtskaia tragediia*, I: 30. Paul Miliukov, in Paris, gave the Kronstadt slogan as "Soviets without Communists," which was Soviet propaganda against the sailors, and oft repeated. *Poslednie novosti*, March 11, 1921.

240. *Pravda*, March 3, 1921; *Kronstadtskaia tragediia*, I: 130–1. Trotsky had complained on March 1 that he was unable to get solid information on events on Kronstadt. The next day Zinoviev, Kalinin, and Lashevich telephoned Trotsky's assistant Grushin: "We are now convinced that the events in Kronstadt constitute the beginning

of an uprising. . . . Your help is needed." They requested armored cars and trustworthy troops (a phrase crossed out on the version of the telegram that was sent). Avrich, *Kronstadt, 1921*, 59. No former tsarist officers served on the fifteen-member Revolutionary Committee, but some were invited to help plan the defense of Kronstadt.

241. Avrich, *Kronstadt, 1921*, 60, 68.

242. *Kronstadtskaia tragediia*, I: 215; Brovkin, *Behind the Front Lines*, 396–7. The hostage taking included anyone with family ties to Kozlovsky (twenty-seven people, including his wife and children) as well as Petrichenko (including people who had no family ties but only the same name as Petrichenko).

243. Trotskii, *Kak vooruzhalas' revoliutsiia*, III/i: 202; Berkman, *Kronstadt*, 31–2. The newspaper editor, A. Lamanov, would be among those executed. At Kronstadt, at least 900 of the 2,680 Communist party members and candidates quit the party, many requesting publication of their resignations in the newspaper.

244. Krasnov and Daines, *Neizvestnyi Trotskii*, 339–41.

245. *Kronstadskaia tragediia*, I: 287.

246. Krasnov and Daines, *Neizvestnyi Trotskii*, 345.

247. Tukhachevsky was shocked to discover that a Siberian infantry division considered as the absolute most reliable, which he had specially chosen for the crackdown, refused to put down the sailors. "If the 27th Division will not do it," one regime official observed on March 14, "no one will." On March 15, a revolutionary tribunal sentenced many of the insubordinate troops to execution, which newspapers broadcast. Avrich, *Kronstadt, 1921*, 188 (V. Nasonov); Minakov, *Sovetskaia voennaia elita*, 269.

248. *X s"ezd*, 750–65.

249. *Sotsialistickeskoe stroitel'stvo SSSR*, 2–3; Gladkov, *Sovetskoe narodnoe khoziaistvo*, 151, 316, 357; Klepikov, *Statisticheskii spravochnik po narodnomu khoziaistvu*, 26 (table 8); S. G. Wheatcroft, "Agriculture," in Davies, *From Tsarism to the New Economic Policy*, at 94.

250. RGASPI, f. 17, op. 109, d. 6, l. 80.

251. Gimpel'son, *Sovetskii rabochii klass*, 80–2; Selunskaia, *Izmeneniia sotsial'noi struktury sovetskogo obshchestva*, 258. Diane Koenker quipped that "when Bolshevik party leaders saw support slipping away, they blamed the physical disappearance of their supporters rather than changed attitudes." Diane Koenker, "Introduction: Social and Demographic Change in the Civil War," in Koenker, *Party, State, and Society*, at 51.

252. Chamberlin, *Russian Revolution*, II: 431–6; Carr, *Bolshevik Revolution*, I: 197–200.

253. *XX s"ezd*, 98 (Rafail); Pavliuchenkov, "*Orden mechenostsev*": 37–48.
254. Lenin, *Collected Works*, 32: 41, 43, 52, 86. "It was a great mistake to put up these disagreements for broad party discussion and the party congress," he asserted, because debate revealed "the party is sick." Harding, "Socialist, Society, and the Organic Labour State," 33.
255. *X s"ezd* [1921], 1; *X s"ezd* [1933], 4. The Workers' opposition advanced their own resolutions for consideration (the last time resolutions would be submitted by anyone other than the apparatus), but they were not submitted to vote.
256. Lenin, *Collected Works*, 32: 206.
257. *X s"ezd* [1921], 207; *X s"ezd* [1933], 380–1. In a passage from that same speech often quoted out of context, Lenin added, referring to Trotsky's labor army mobilizations that, "first of all we must convince, then coerce [*prinudit'*]. We have not been able to convince the broad masses." *X s"ezd* [1921], 208; *X sezd* [1933], 382.
258. As it happened, Lenin himself signed the treaty. Carr, *Bolshevik Revolution*, I: 386; Arthur Adams, "The Great Ukrainian Jacquerie," in Hunczak, *The Ukraine*, 247–70 (at 260).
259. Borys, *Sovietization of the Ukraine*. See also Wolfe, "The Influence of Early Military Decisions."
260. Magerovsky, "The People's Commissariat," I: 179–84.
261. "Ob ocherednykh zadachakh partii v natsional'nom voprose: tezisy k X s"ezdu RKP (b)," *Pravda*, February 10, 1921, in *Sochineniia*, V: 15–29 (at 21–2). Georgy Chicherin, foreign affairs commissar, argued against Stalin's theses, asserting that Stalin's view of setting up a dichotomy between national and multinational states was outdated because now there had appeared a supranational state, a result of imperialism and global financial entities. The struggle, therefore, was not between strong or weak, independent or colonial states, but between the revolutionary working class and the supranational capitalist trusts. Chicherin, "Protiv tezisov Stalina," *Pravda*, March 6, 8, 9, 1921.
262. Borys, *Sovietization of the Ukraine*, 343.
263. *X s"ezd* [1933], 184–91; *Sochineniia*, V: 33–44.
264. *X s"ezd* [1933], 191–2; *X s"ezd* [1963], 187.
265. *X s"ezd* [1933], 192–205; *X s"ezd*, [1921], 189–96. This bold assertion—that the party did not create the revolution in Turkestan, but the other way around—became the basis for a book-length treatment he published the same year. Safarov, *Kolonial'naia revoliutsiia*, first published as a short essay in *Kommunisticheskii*

*Internatsional*, 1920, no. 14: 2759–2768. Safarov had the distinction of having been among those who had returned with Lenin in the sealed train and, in September 1919, of having been among the victims injured in the terrorist bombing of the Moscow party organization on Leontyev Lane. Following a dispute with Tomsky, the head of the Turkestan party bureau, Safarov as well as Tomsky were recalled.
266. *X s"ezd* [1933], 210. "It was necessary . . . to take local circumstances into account and to accommodate oneself to them," Mikoyan told the 10th Party Congress. Massell, *Surrogate Proletariat*, 44.
267. *X s"ezd* [1933], 214.
268. *X s"ezd* [1933], 214–7; *Sochineniia*, V: 45–9.
269. *X s"ezd* [1933], 573–83, 749; *Vsesoiuznaia Kommunisticheskaia Partiia (b) v rezoliutsiiakh* [5th ed.], I: 393.
270. RGASPI, f. 4, op. 2, d. 527, l. 38 (Danishevsky), f. 17, op. 84, d. 200, l. 18; Pavliuchenkov, *Krest'ianskii Brest*, 261.
271. *X s"ezd* [1921], 327; *X s"ezd* [1933], 856–7; *Izvestiia*, March 23, 1921.
272. *X s"ezd* [1921], 222; *X s"ezd* [1933], 406.
273. Malle, *Economic Organization of War Communism*, 446–7 (Osinsky).
274. Sakharov, *Na Rasput'e*, 12–3. At the 10th Party Congress, Trotsky reminded the delegates that he had proposed the measures already, a year earlier, only to have been rebuffed in the Central Committee (*X s"ezd*, 349–50). To halt the "economic degradation," he had proposed that "the expropriation of surpluses be replaced by a fixed percentage deduction, or tax in kind, so that the best tillage or cultivation would still represent a profit." He had further suggested that "the quantity of industrial goods delivered to the peasants should bear a closer relation to the quantity of grain sowed." In other words, peasants should be given incentives, and a better deal, to raise their output. Trotsky's proposal, "Fundamental Questions of Industrial and Agricultural Policy," was published in 1926. Trotskii, *Sochineniia*, XVII/ii: 543–4. Trotsky's self-presentation in emigration of his alleged anticipation of NEP is wildly inaccurate. Trotskii, *Moia zhizn'*, II: 199. See also Pavliuchenkov, *Krest'ianskii Brest*, 158–9. Cf. Danilov, "We Are Starting to Learn About Trotsky."
275. Baranov, *Krest'ianskoe vosstanie*, 14–5. At the Food Procurement Congress in June–July 1920, some officials had pushed the tax in onto the agenda. Lenin set up a government commission to examine a tax in kind, including the consequence that it would require legal private trade of the

surpluses after tax. The matter was debated in *Pravda* (February 17 and February 26, 1921). Genkina, "V. I. Lenin i perekhod k novoi ekonomicheskoi politike," 11.
276. This went beyond the Bolsheviks: the Menshevik Fyodor Dan, in December 1920, had proposed a food-supply tax but repudiated the suggestion that he also desired free trade. Lih, *Bread and Authority*, 220.
277. *X s"ezd* [1921], 223–4; *X s"ezd* [1933], 409.
278. "Why was the food requisitioning allowed to continue during the autumn of 1920 and the spring of 1921, when the civil war had been won and the famine crisis was already widespread?" asked Orlando Figes. His answer: requisitioning officials, locally, were either unquestioning implementers of central policy or themselves fanatics, ready to do whatever seemed necessary to defend the new regime. Figes, *Peasant Russia*, 271–2. See also Chamberlin, *Russian Revolution*, II: 375.
279. *X s"ezd*, 224, 468; *PSS*, XLIII: 69–70. Ryazanov, in November 1917, had helped Kamenev try to form an all-socialist coalition government.
280. *X s"ezd* [1921], 281; *X s"ezd* [1933], 523–4.
281. *X s"ezd* [1933], 736. Only members of the Workers' opposition—who did not like the introduction of free trade either—opposed "on party unity." A key leader of the Workers' opposition, Yuri Lutovinov (b. 1887), a metalworker and trade unionist from Lugansk—the same coal-mining hometown as Voroshilov—would commit suicide in 1924 over the metastasizing of the bureaucracy as well as the New Economic Policy. He was the first person for whom the new Lenin Mausoleum would be used (on May 10, 1924), when the leadership climbed wooden stairs and addressed the crowd from the raised cube. *Izvestiia*, May 11, 1924. Stalin would soon prevent suicides from being commemorated in such fashion.
282. *X s"ezd* [1921], 289; *X s"ezd* [1933], 540; *X s"ezd* [1933], 533–4. According to Barmine, who later defected, Radek in early 1921 told a group of students at the War College in Moscow that the workers were hungry and exhausted and in no mood for further sacrifice, but that rather than yield to (actual) worker wishes, the party would be resolute and press on to victory. The students were armed with rifles in preparation to join the fight against counterrevolution, but that could mean taking on the very workers in whose name the regime existed—a supreme test of faith. Barmine, *One Who Survived*, 94.
283. Zinov'ev, *Sochineniia*, VI: 626.
284. Pavlova, *Stalinizm*, 47–8 (citing

PANO, f. 1, op. 2, d. 12a, l. 14, 18, 20: K. Danishevsky to Ivan Smirnov, then party boss in Siberia).

285. Krasnov and Daines, *Nizvestnyi Trotskii*, 346; Voroshilov, "Iz istorii podavleniia Kronstadtskogo miatezha," 22. The regime disseminated the slander that rather than the "conscious" sailors of 1917, the rebels were lads fresh from the village, including transfers from the Black Sea Fleet who were "Ukrainian" peasants (a national slander). Therefore, no real socialist should have any qualms about slaughtering them. This was a charge the Mensheviks had used to try to explain away worker support for Bolshevism in 1917. Service, *Bolshevik Party in Revolution*, 44. See also Figes, *A People's Tragedy*, 830.

286. Mlechin, *Russkaia armiia mezhdu Trotskim*, 194. En route the Party Congress delegates encountered Zinoviev heading to Moscow to report to the Party Congress, who painted a grim picture of Kronstadt.

287. Only three of the fifteen members of the Revolutionary Committee were captured: Petr Mikhailovich Perepelkin (1890–1921), Sergei Stepanovich Vershinin (1886–1921), and Vladislav Antonovich Val'k (1883–1921). Avrich, *Kronstadt, 1921*, 179. A majority of the political refugees would return under an amnesty.

288. Getzler, "The Communist Leaders' Role," 35–7.

289. Avrich, *Kronstadt, 1921*, 252–6 (APRF, f. 26, op. 1, d. 80, l.26–34).

290. When the Party Congress crackdown squad returned to Moscow, Lenin received them on March 21 for a commemorative group photograph. Medals were handed out. In the 1930s, those who had led the crushing of the rebellion would be executed. Voroshilov, "Iz istorii podavleniia Kronshtadtskego miatezha."

291. Deutscher, *Prophet Unarmed*, 55–6; Trotskii, *Kak vooruzhalas' revoliutsiia*, III/1: 81.

292. *DVP SSSR*, III: 607–14; *Izvestiia*, May 7, 1921 (Krasin); Krasin, *Voprosy vneshnei torgovli*, 286–8. See also Shishkin, *Stanovlenie vneshnei politiki postrevliutsionnoi Rossii i kapitalisticheskii mir*, 101–16.

293. Glenny, "The Anglo-Soviet Trade Agreement." Debo argues that the agreement reached between Litvinov and James O'Grady in 1920 in Copenhagen "opened the way to the more comprehensive negotiations which followed." Debo, "Lloyd George and the Copenhagen Conference."

294. Andrew, *Her Majesty's Secret Service*, 262–73; Andrew and Gordievsky, *KGB*, 76–9.

295. *Documents on British Foreign Policy*, VIII: 886–9.

296. "Where will we get the goods? Free trade requires goods, and peasants are very smart people and they are extremely capable of scoffing." *X s"ezd* [1921], 227; *X s"ezd* [1933], 413.

297. Poland gained control over western Belorussia and western Ukraine, an addition of 52,000 square miles, and became 30 percent minority (5 million Ukrainians, 1.5 million Belorussians, 1 million Germans, as well as 3 million Jews), a potential source of internal instability. The great powers initially refused to recognize Poland's new eastern borders. The Entente reluctantly acceded to Poland's eastern borders in March 1923; Germany continued to refuse to do so. Wandycz, *Soviet-Polish Relations*, 250–90.

298. Thanks to the diplomatic maneuvering between the Soviets and the Poles, Lithuania, too, like Estonia and Latvia, emerged with its independence reconfirmed. Soviet Russia had contemplated trying to award Wilno/ Vilnius, where Polish speakers predominated, to Lithuania as a Machiavellian means of undermining the Lithuanian national state, but in the end agreed not to intervene in the Polish-Lithuanian conflict over the disputed city, effectively ensuring Poland's de facto control. Boręzcki, *Soviet-Polish Treaty of 1921*, 220–1. In 1923, Moscow would halt the agreed repatriation payments; in addition, more than one million Polish refugees would not be allowed to depart the USSR. The two sides fought bitterly over Poland's share (Congress Poland) of tsarist Russia's gold reserves; Moscow never paid the 30 million gold rubles that had been agreed (reduced from an original claim of 300 million). In 1927, after receiving two large payments in gems, the Poles gave up on obtaining the bulk of this money, and instead settled for return of Polish cultural treasures.

299. Gruber, *International Communism*, 316; Angress, *Stillborn Revolution*, 109–10.

300. Angress, *Stillborn Revolution*, 163 (citing *Rote Fahne*, April 4, 1921).

301. On June 25, 1921, Zinoviev would give a summary report to the 3rd Comintern Congress in Moscow, followed by days of discussion during which he, Bukharin, and Radek would defend the "March Action" in Germany; Lenin, Trotsky, and Kamenev would condemn it. Stalin would be away, and one German attendee would later remark that "it was possible in 1921 to spend six months in Moscow without knowing of his existence." He added that "there was nothing striking about Lenin, nothing impressive. . . . But in discussion—in a small group on the platform at a monster meeting—he was wonderfully convincing by the way he argued, by the tone of his voice, by the logical sequence of statements by which he reached his conclusion." Reichenbach, "Moscow 1921," 16–17.

302. Angress, *Stillborn Revolution*, 137–196.

303. *X s"ezd* [1933], 35; *PSS*, XLIII: 24.

304. Markina and Federovna, *Baltiiskie moriaki*, 322–3; Getzler, *Kronstadt*, 219. See also Getzler, "The Communist Leaders' Role."

305. Avrich, *Kronstadt, 1921*, 138–9 (March 5). The absence of evidence for Kozlovsky's role was whitewashed: on March 25, the politburo created a commission to study Kronstadt, headed by Semyon Sorenson, known as Yakov Agranov (b. 1893), a former Socialist Revolutionary and Cheka operative, and his internal report argued that "the rapid liquidation of the rebellion did not afford the opportunity definitely for the appearance of White Guard elements and slogans." *Kronstadtskaia tragediia*, II: 33–43 at 42–3 (TsA FSB RF, d. 114 728, t. 1A); Avrich, *Kronstadt, 1921*, 230–42. The Cheka would also focus on the Russian Red Cross, which had arrived on Kronstadt on March 8 via Finland, and managed to bring one hundred bags of flour and some medical supplies. The mission included the former commander of the *Sevastopol* Baron Pavel Viktorovich Vilken, who had emigrated to Finland. The sailors had hesitated to allow the Red Cross, despite their desperation for the food and medicine. The Red Cross mission departed the day after it arrived; Vilken had stayed behind, but the sailors had refused his offer of up to eight hundred armed men, knowing he was a monarchist.

306. *PSS*, LXIII: 130–43 (speech to transport workers, March 27, 1921). Lenin understood the Kronstadt sailors were not White Guards per se. He assured the 10th Congress delegates (March 15) that any "conscious peasant" had to understand that "any turn backwards signified a return to the tsarist government. The Kronstadt experience shows this. There, they do not want the White Guards, but no other authority exists, they do not want our state power, and they occupy such a position that it becomes the best agitation for us and against a new government." In other words, supposedly no political possibilities existed between Bolshevism and a White Guard restoration. And yet, the Kronstadt sailors were not White Guards. *X s"ezd* [1921], 227–8; *X s"ezd* [1933], 414.

307. Instead, the Cheka issued a sensational publication, "A Communication on the uncovering in Petrograd of a plot against Soviet Power," which named a Petrograd Combat Organization led by Professor V. N. Tagantsev

(who had been arrested in May 1921). *Izvestiia*, August 31, 1921.

308. Dzierżyński seemed obsessed with the Socialist Revolutionary leader Victor Chernov, citing his publications from exile in Revel as evidence of his cooperation with the Whites. Dzerzhinskii, "Doklad o vserossiiskoi chrezvychainoi komissii o raskrytykh i likvidirovannykh na territorii RSFSR zagorovakh protiv sovetskoi vlasti v period maia-iiunia 1921 goda," TsA FSB, f. 1, op. 5, d. 10, l. 1–20, in Vinogradov, *Arkhiv VChK*, 593–612. Chernov had no involvement in Kronstadt: he had sent a note by courier from Estonia to Kronstadt's Revolutionary Committee indicating that, as the chairman of the (dispersed) Constituent Assembly, he would come to the island to lead the struggle for its restoration, but at a meeting on March 12 only one sailor supported the idea, which was shelved. Petrichenko, on March 13, sent a thank-you note but demurred. *Kronstadtskaia tragediia 1921*, I: 403; Avrich, *Kronstadt, 1921*, 124–5.

309. *Sotsialisticheskii vestnik*, March 18, 1921: 6.

310. Martov, "Kronshtadt," *Sotsialisticheskii vestnik*, April 1921, no. 5: 5; Burgin, *Sotsial-demokraticheskaia menshevistskaia literatura*, 297.

311. Getzler, *Martov*, 204–17; Burbank, *Intelligentsia and Revolution*, 59.

312. *PSS*, XLIII: 241–2.

313. Esikov and Kanishev, "Antonovskii NEP," 60–72.

314. "Zapiska E. M. Sklianskogo 26 Aprelia 1921 g.," in Lenin, *V. I. Lenin*, 428–9, 459–60. Lenin met Tukhachevsky no later than December 19, 1920, in Moscow, where they discussed the southern front, and Lenin requested a report (to be sent to Sklyansky). Lenin received him again in late April 1921, when he was assigned to Tambov. Golikov, *Vladimir Il'ich Lenin*, VIII: 130.

315. *Kronstadskaia tragediia*, I: 291 (Zinoviev).

316. Baranov, *Krest'ianskoe vosstanie*, 147–8; Meijer, *Trotsky Papers*, II: 460–2 (Trotsky retrospectively affixed the wrong date of June; Tukhachevsky's appointment was approved by the politburo on April 28, 1921).

317. Landis, *Bandits and Partisans*, 209–41.

318. Aptekar', "Khimchistka po-Tambovskii," 56 (RGVA, f. 190, op. 3, d. 514; l. 73; f. 34228, op. 1, d. 383, l. 172–4; f. 7, op. 2, d. 511, l. 140, 151; 140, f. 235, op. 2, d. 82, l. 38; op. 3, d. 34, l. 1ob.); Baranov, *Krest'ianskoe vosstaniie*, 179. For difficulties ascertaining the extent of chlorine gas use, see Landis, *Bandits and Partisans*, 265–9.

319. "'Sfotografirovannye rechi': govoriat uchastniki likvidatsii antonovshchiny," *Otechestvennye atrkhivy*, 1996, no. 2: at 65 (chief of camps at Tambov, claiming 2,000 inmates); Werth, "A State Against Its People," 110–17. Tukhachevsky soon wrote up the lessons of his counterinsurgency campaign: "If deportation cannot be organized immediately, then one should establish a wide set of concentration camps." Mikhail Tukhachevskii, "Bor'ba s kontrerevolutsionnymi vosstaniiami," *Voina i revoliutsiia*, 1926, no. 6: 6–9, no. 7: 11–13. Some of the incarceration sites were Great War concentration camps.

320. Baranov, *Krest'ianskoe vosstanie*, 223–4, 226–7. In Tambov between March and September 1922, there were 217 voluntary resignations from the party, alongside just 29 new members, almost none of whom came from the working class. Pavliuchenkov, "*Orden Mechenostsev*," 275 (citing RGASPI, f. 17, op. 11, d. 110, l. 163).

321. Zdanovich, *Organy gosudarstvennoi bezopasnosti*, 236–8; Plekhanov, *VChK-OGPU*, 360; Landis, *Bandits and Partisans*, 277–9.

322. Mnatsakanian, *Poslantsy Sovetskoi Rossii*, 56–7.

323. King, *Ghost of Freedom*, 169.

324. Kazemzadeh, *Struggle for Transcaucasia*, 288–9; Iskenderov, *Iz istorii bor'by kommunisticheskoi partii Azerbaidzhana za pobedu sovetskoi vlasti*, 527–9.

325. As Jordania explained in 1918, drawing upon the authority of Kautsky, "the first steps of the victorious proletariat will be not social reforms, but the introduction of democratic institutions, the realization of the party's minimum program, and only afterwards the gradual transition to the socialist maximum program." Suny, *Georgian Nation*, 195.

326. Jordania, "Staline, L'Écho de la lutte"; Vakar, "Stalin"; Kazemzadeh, *Struggle for Transcaucasia*, 184–210; Suny, *Transcaucasia*, 249.

327. "The Free and Independent Social-Democratic State of Georgia," wrote one perceptive eyewitness of the Menshevik republic, "will always remain in my memory as a classic example of an imperialist 'small nation.' Both in territory snatching outside and bureaucratic tyranny inside, its chauvinism was beyond all bounds." Bechhofer, *In Denikin's Russia*, 14.

328. *Pravda*, May 8, 1920; *Mirnyi dogovor mezhdu Gruziei i Rossiei*. Georgia's secret negotiating team included Grigol Uratadze, David Sagirashvili (former chairman of the soviet of Tsaritsyn in 1917, where he had been exiled), and Aristotle Mirsky-Kobakhidze. Mirsky-Kobakhidze, who had been sent to Georgia to undertake subversion, may have initiated the peace mission from his prison cell at Metekhi. En route to Moscow the men were intercepted by Orjonikidze, who declared he would conduct the negotiations. Mirsky-Kobakhidze managed to contact Lenin, who overruled Orjonikidze. Chicherin had his deputy, Lev Karakhan [Karakhanyan], sign; Uratadze signed for the Georgian government. On May 10, 1921, Lenin received Uratadze in his office. Uratadze and Sagirashvili were also received in Stalin's office. A banquet was held with the Georgian colony in Moscow. De Lon, "Stalin and Social Democracy." Uratadze did not see fit to mention Sagirashvili or Mirsky in his account: Uratadze, *Vospominaniia*. Later in 1921 the Cheka arrested Sagirashvili and imprisoned him in Metekhi (again); he was exiled with a large group in November 1922 to Germany.

329. For the secret codicil, see *Rossiiskaia Sotsialisticheskaia Federativnaia Sovcetskaia Respublika*, 16.

330. *Gleb Maksimilianovich Krzhizhanovskii*, 33–4.

331. David Dallin, "Between the World War and the NEP," in Haimson, *The Mensheviks*, 191–239 (at 236). Dallin, a Menshevik, attended the congress.

332. Smith, *Bolsheviks and the National Question*, 4 (citing RGASPI, f. 17, op. 3, d. 74, l. 3; d. 122, l. 2; d. 46, l. 3; d. 55, l. 5).

333. Boersner, *The Bolsheviks*, 63.

334. *Sochineniia*, IV: 408. In *Pravda* (December 4) Stalin called the Dashnaks "agents of the Entente." *Sochineniia*, IV: 413–4.

335. *Sochineniia*, IV: 162, 237, 372. Further impetus may have come from the specter of Karl Kautsky, the bête noire of Bolshevism and hero of Georgian Menshevism, who was visiting the non-Bolshevik socialist republic from late September 1920 through January 1921, and found that independent "Georgia lacks nothing to make her not only one of the most beautiful, but also one of the richest countries in the world." Kautsky, *Georgia*, 14.

336. Jones, "Establishment of Soviet Power," 620–1.

337. Smith, "The Georgian Affair of 1922," 523 (citing RGASPI, f. 17, op. 3, d. 122, l. 1; op. 2, d. 46, l. 3; d. 55, l. 5; d. 56, l. 1); Makharadze, *Pobeda sotsialisticheskoi revoliutsii v Gruzii*, 420–3; Zhordania, *Moia zhizn'*, 109–12. Trotsky, away in the Urals, demanded an investigation. Makharadze complained in late 1921 to Tskhakaya, the Georgian representative in Moscow: "In the Caucasus bureau there are comrades, even now, who do not recognize the formal existence of Transcaucasus republics, but rather see them as provinces of the RSFSR." Smith, "The Georgian Affair of 1922,"

524 (citing RGASPI, f. 157, op. 1/c, d. 14, l. 1–5).

338. *PSS*, XLII: 367. On March 2, Lenin wrote Orjonikidze ordering "a special policy of concessions for the Georgian intelligentsia and small traders. . . . It is hugely important to seek an acceptable compromise with Jordania or Georgian Mensheviks like him. . . . I ask you to understand that both the internal and international aspects of Georgia demand that the Georgian Communists do not apply the Russian pattern, but that they skillfully and flexibly create a particular tactic based on concessions to all kind of petty-bourgeois elements." Lenin, *Collected Works*, 32: 362.

339. Ordzhonikidze, *Stat'i i rechi*, I: 172.

340. Orjonikidze wanted "with red-hot irons," in Stalin's words, "to burn down the remains of nationalism," as he stated in Tiflis in late November 1921. Ordzhonikidze, *Stat'i i rechi*, I: 216.

341. King, *Ghost of Freedom*, 173; Avalov, *Nezavisimosti Gruzii*, 285.

342. King, *Ghost of Freedom*, 171.

343. See Churchill's August 16, 1919, long memorandum, excerpted in Churchill, *World Crisis*, 251–3.

344. Avalov, *Nezavisimosti Gruzii*, 288–9; Avalishvili, *Independence of Georgia*, 266–8. Oliver Wardrop, a scholar of Georgian literature and history, was British commissioner.

345. *Dokumenty vneshnei politiki*, II: 755; Garafov, "Russko-turetskoe sblizhenie," 247.

346. The Georgians could not manage to create a cultural center abroad. Rayfield, *Literature of Georgia*, 234.

347. More than 150,000 Georgians had fought in the tsarist army during the Great War, but after battlefield deaths, captures, and desertions, General Kvinitadze managed to muster a mere 10,000. General Giorgi Kvinitadze [Chikovani] (1874–1970) was born in Daghestan and graduated from the St. Constantine Infantry School in St. Petersburg and later the General Staff Academy. He did not speak Georgian. He did not get along with Jordania, but the latter invited him to become supreme commander. He was put off by the Georgian Mensheviks' abuses of power, amid rhetorical flourishes about socialism and internationalism, and their flirtation with a "people's militia" rather than a real army. They let him go, then turned to him again at crisis time. In 1922 in Paris he wrote memoirs; he would be buried in the same cemetery as Jordania. Kvinitadze, *Moi vospominaniia*.

348. On March 17–18, Jordania had sent emissaries to negotiate with the Bolsheviks located just outside Batum (Stalin's brother-in-law Alyosha

Svanidze, Avel Yenukidze, and Mamiya Orakhelashvili); the Mensheviks agreed to allow the Red Army to enter via the port of Batum to prevent its seizure by the Turks, and to provide wagons for Dmitry Zhloba's cavalry. The Bolsheviks promised amnesty and positions in a Soviet government. The Mensheviks distrusted the offer.

349. Jordania would set up south of Paris; eventually, he would find a patron in Piłsudski.

350. Kuleshov, "Lukollov mir," 72–3 (RGASPI, f. 78, op. 1, d. 46, l. 1, 3).

351. RGASPI, f. 558, op. 4, d. 675, l. 1–23.

352. RGASPI, f. 2, op. 1, d. 24278, l. 1–2.

353. Golikov, *Vladimir Il'ich Lenin*, VI: 390, IX: 348, 618, X: 348, 566, 588, 639, XI: 47, 113, 128; Meijer, Trotsky Papers, II: 26–9, 66–7; McNeal, *Stalin*, 50. Trotsky was given an eight-week holiday at the same time: RGASPI, f. 17, op. 112, d. 149, l. 93.

354. *TsK RKP (b)—VKP (b) i natsional'nyi vopros*, 47–9 (RGASPI, f. 558, op. 1, d. 3530, l. 1–2; *Kommunist* [Baku], July 31, 1921). Amayak Nazaretyan, one of the five members of the Caucasus bureau, in 1922 became Stalin's top assistant in Moscow.

355. De Lon, "Stalin and Social Democracy," 125.

356. Trotsky, *Stalin*, 359–60; Lang, *Modern History*, 238–9 (no citations, evidently relying on Menshevik émigré accounts); Payne, *The Rise and Fall of Stalin*, 275–6 (repeating Lang's account).

357. Iremashvili, *Stalin und die Tragödie*, 57–62.

358. *Pravda Gruzii*, July 1921, 13; Stalin, "Ob ocherednykh zadachakh kommunizma v Gruzii i Zakavka'e," in *Sochineniia*, V: 88–100 (at 95).

359. Belov, *Baron Ungern fon Shternberg*; Palmer, *Bloody White Baron*.

360. Alioshin, *Asian Odyssey*, 167, 183–7. A sensational insider account of the baron, by a Polish professor at Omsk University, became a bestseller: Ossendowski, *Beasts, Men, and Gods*.

361. Tornovskii, "Sobytiiia v Mongolii-Khalkhe," 168–328 (at 208–13); Alioshin, *Asian Odyssey*, 231.

362. Kuz'min, *Istoriia barona Ungerna*, 184–5.

363. Iuzefovich, *Samoderzhets pustyni*, 3, 133–7.

364. Kuz'min, *Istoriia barona Ungerna*, 410–13; Alioshin, *Asian Odyssey*, 229.

365. The Anglophobe Chicherin played a lead role, insisting that the Peoples of the East consisted not only of Muslims but also Buddhists. Mongolia and Tibet were potential thorns in the side of British India. Amur Sanai, "Kloiuchki k vostokou," *Zhizn' natsional'nostei*, May 26, 1919.

366. For a Soviet account of them, see Genkin, *Severnaia Aziia*, 1928, no. 2: 79–81.

367. Baabar, *Twentieth-Century Mongolia*, 202; Roshchin, *Politicheskaia istoriia Mongolii*, 35–6.

368. Murphy, *Soviet Mongolia*, 13–4.

369. Rupen, *Mongols of the Twentieth Century*, I: 139; Sumiatskii, "Na zare osvobozhdeniii Mongolii," *Pravda*, July 26, 1920, in Eudin and North, *Soviet Russia and the East*, 203–4.

370. Baabar, *Twentieth-Century Mongolia*, 216; Rupen, *Mongols of the Twentieth Century*, I: 141, 155. Retrospectively, this conference became the 1st Party Congress.

371. I. I. Lomakina, "Kommentarii," in Pershin, *Baron Ungern*, 189–259 (at 176–7).

372. Lepeshinskii, *Revoliutsiia na Da'lnem vostoke*, 429–32; Kuz'min, *Istoriia barona Ungerna*, 238.

373. The Warsaw-born Red Army commander Konstanty Rokossowski (b. 1896) joined his substantial cavalry to the Mongol forces led by Sükhbaatar, but Rokossowski was wounded and left the field. Roshchin, *Politicheskaia istoriia Mongolii*, 20–1; Kuz'min, *Istoriia barona Ungerna*, 244–5, 263.

374. *Pravda*, July 9, 1921; Eudin and North, *Soviet Russia and the East*, 196–7. The 3rd Congress met in Moscow from June 22 to July 12, 1921. Stalin was not among the five Soviets (Zinoviev, Bukharin, Radek, Lenin, and Trotsky) elected to the Comintern executive committee. During the congress he was recuperating down south.

375. Morozova, *Comintern and Revolution in Mongolia*, 16 (citing RGASPI, f. 495, op. 154, d. 20, l. 1–7).

376. Alioshin, *Asian Odyssey*, 266.

377. Kuz'min, *Istoriia barona Ungerna*, 287–8.

378. Palmer, *Bloody White Baron*, 228 (citing GARF, f. 9427, op. 1, d. 392, l. 36). See also Kuz'min, *Baron Ungern v dokumentakh i memuarakh*, 199–242 (RGVA, f. 16, op. 3, d. 222, l. 123–4ob., 125, 1–19; f. 16, op. 1, d. 37, l. 128, 337, 333, 329; GARF, f. 9427, op. 1, d. 392, l. 7–13, 47–50, 35–46); *Sovetskaia Sibir'*, September 13, 1921 (Ivan Pavlunovsky, Siberian Cheka).

379. Kuz'min, *Baron Ungern v dokumentakh i memuarakh*, 198–9 (RGASPI, f. 17, op. 3, d. 195, l. 1; op. 163, d. 178, l. 5; op. 163, d. 180, l. 3–3ob.). To ensure nothing went wrong, Moscow sent Minei Gubelman, known as Emilyan Yaroslavsky, as prosecutor; he happened to be Jewish, though this appears not to have factored into the decision of who would condemn the rabidly anti-Semitic baron, for Yaroslavsky was from Eastern Siberia (the son of an exile) and had recently been named a Central Committee secretary.

380. *Sovetskaia Sibir'*, September 16,

September 17, September 18, and September 20, 1921; *Da'lnevostochnaia pravda*, September 25, 1921; Kuz'min, *Baron Ungern v dokumentakh i memuarakh*, 242–63; Kuz'min, *Istoriia barona Ungerna*, 294–304.
381. Kuz'min, *Baron Ungern v dokumentakh i memuarakh*, 263 (RGVA, f. 16, op. 1, d. 37, l. 330).
382. Misshima and Tomio, *Japanese View of Outer Mongolia*, 27.
383. Nyamaa, *Compilation of Some Documents*, 7–8.
384. Slavinskii, *Sovetskii Soiuz i Kitai*, 51–3 (AVP RF, f. 08, op. 5, psap. 3, d. 17, l. 1–2; d. 18, l. 4–5); Tsziun, "Sovetskaia Rossiia i Kitai," 54–5.
385. Roshchin, *Politicheskaia istoriia Mongolii*, 37 (citing RGASPI, f. 495, op. 152, d. 9, l. 12–4: Boris Shumyatsky to Chicherin, August 12, 1921); Kuz'min, *Baron Ungern v dokumentakh i memuarakh*, 264 (RGASPI, f. 5, op. 1, d. 145, l. 38: Joffe letter); Kuz'min, *Istoriia barona Ungerna*, 199. See also Murphy, *Soviet Mongolia*; Hammond, "Communist Takeover of Outer Mongolia."
386. RGASPI, f. 495, op. 152, d. 11, l. 19–23.
387. Chicherin favored a meeting, writing to Lenin that Mongolia's "revolutionary government is the ace of spades in our hands. Its creation foils the plans of Japan to set up an anti-revolutionary front stretching from the Pacific to the Caspian. With a friendly Mongolia our border becomes utterly safe." Luzyanin, "Mongolia," 76.
388. Roshchin, *Politicheskaia istoriia Mongolii*, 70 (citing RGASPI, f. 495, op. 152, d. 9, l. 65); Baabar, *Twentieth-Century Mongolia*, 222 (citing central archives of foreign relations, F-117, H/N-01); Morozova, *Comintern and Revolution in Mongolia*, 43, RGASPI, f. 495, op. 152, d, 9, l. 63–4).
389. Only in early January 1922, some two months later, did the Peking government even begin to hear rumors concerning the contents of the Soviet-Mongolian treaty. Elleman, "Secret Sino-Soviet Negotiations."
390. Bolshevik officials were aware

that Mongolia had little class differentiation or upper-class wealth to expropriate (as reported by the scholar Ivan Maisky, who had been part of a Soviet expedition to Outer Mongolia). Maiskii, *Sovremennaia Mongoliia*, 127.
391. Malle, *Economic Organization of War Communism*, 506–11.
392. Lih, *Bread and Authority*; Narskii, *Zhizn' v katastrofe*, 5.
393. *PSS*, XLIII: 18, 24, XLIV: 159.
394. Vaisberg, *Den'gi i tseny'*, 10.
395. NEP decrees continued right through 1923, legalizing private activity in publishing, credit, and savings and loans; leasing factories from the state; and allowing state factories to do business with private traders, scorned as NEPmen.
396. A decree of October 17, 1921, on confiscation and requisition mandated that a protocol be made at the time of any confiscation, with the names of those whose goods were seized, those who enacted the seizure, and those who received the goods for storage at a warehouse, as well as a full inventory of the articles. The protocol had to be signed, including by at least two witnesses (often neighbors). It also established the principle of compensation for requisitions and restrictions on the use of confiscation solely to legitimate punitive contexts. *Izvestiia*, October 26, 1921; Timashev, *Publichno-pravovoe polozhenie lichnosti*, I: 177–8. The instructions for implementation tried to draw a firm line underneath everything, stipulating an end to fruitless efforts to adjudicate prior legal claims for confiscations. Yet another decree on seizures would follow in 1922, in a further attempt to draw a line under the revolutionary dispossession whirlwind of 1917–22 by allowing those who possessed confiscated goods to retain them. *Izvestiia*, March 29, 1922.
397. Smith, "Stalin as Commissar for Nationality Affairs."
398. *VIII s"ezd RKP (b)*, 82.
399. The Treaty of Riga (1921), which ended the Polish-Soviet War, reinforced the path to a federal

structure—Belorussia and Ukraine were signatories. Working with Alexander Myasnikov (Myasnikyan), a Russified Armenian Bolshevik, Stalin played a significant role in the "annexation" of the Soviet Socialist Republic of Belorussia in Minsk in December 1919. The proclamation was issued in Russian, Polish, and Yiddish, but not Belorussian, the language of the peasants. *Izvestiia*, December 18, 1919; Kvashonkin, *Bol'shevistskoe rukovodstvo*, 71–5.
400. In October 1920 Stalin had noted that "the demand for the secession of the border regions from Russia ... must be rejected not only because it runs counter to the very formulation of the question of establishing a union between the center and the border regions, but mainly because it fundamentally runs counter to the interests of the mass in both center and border regions." *Sochineniia*, IV: 352.
401. *PSS*, LIII: 189–90. The two warring officials were Mikhail Tomsky and Georgy Safarov. The matter was taken up at the politburo on September 13, and within a month personnel in Turkestan were changed.
402. It was in this context that Kamenev, in 1922 (with a second edition in 1923), would publish a fat compendium of his various journalistic articles, *Between Two Revolutions*. Belatedly, it looked like Kamenev had won that famous April 1917 debate with Lenin, when the Bolshevik leader had returned from exile to the Finland Station, railing at Kamenev (and Stalin), who were arguing against the seizure of class power, insisting that the "bourgeois democratic" revolution still had a long way to go. Lih, "The Ironic Triumph of 'Old Bolshevism.'"
403. RGASPI, f. 558, op. 3, d. 299, l. 55.
404. RGASPI, f. 558, op. 3, d. 68, l. 47.
405. Tucker, *Stalin in Power*, 45–9.
406. Kvashonkin, *Bol'shevistskoe rukovodstvo*, 223–7 (RGASPI, f. 5, op. 2, d. 315, l. 252–3, 260).
407. *Sochineniia*, V: 117–27 (at 118–19); Carr, *Bolshevik Revolution*, III: 349–50.

## PART III: COLLISION

1. Stalin, "O Lenine," reprinted in *Sochineniia*, VI: 52–64 (at 61).
2. Sering, *Die Umwälzung der osteuropäischen Agrarverfassung*, 5–6; Antsiferov, *Russian Agriculture During the War*, 382–3.
3. For these and many other intolerant Lenin utterances, see Getzler, "Lenin's Conception" (citing *PSS*, XXXV: 268, XXXVIII: 339). To be sure, once famine broke out in mid-1921 and Lenin was appealing for international food aid, he asserted that the civil war "had

been forced upon the workers and peasants by the landowners and capitalists of all countries." Lenin, *Collected Works*, 32: 502.
4. Lenin, "O vremennom revoliutsionom pravitel'stve [May 1905]," *PSS*, X: 227–50; "Sed'maia (aprels'kaia) vesrossiiskaia konferentsiia RSDRP (b)" [April 1917], *PSS*, XXXI: 339–81 (esp. 353–4). Incredibly, Rabinowitch (again) argues that dictatorship was forced upon Lenin and the Bolsheviks, even as Rabinowitch shows, time and

again, that in response to crises, often precipitated by the Bolsheviks themselves, they resorted to arrests and dirty tricks (e.g., voter fraud), which they always sought to justify by invoking "class war" and the battle against "counterrevolution" (e.g., anyone who opposed them). Rabinowitch, *Bolsheviks in Power*.
5. *Pravda*, August 28, 1919; Lenin, *Collected Works*, 29: 559.
6. Polan, *Lenin and the End of Politics*.
7. Marx, too, never developed a theory

of politics. He never explicitly embraced the possibility of rival political platforms competing in open politics; when critics, such as Mikhail Bakunin, spelled out the likely consequences of such a position, Marx went silent. For Marx, the only consideration was representation of the "interests" of the proletariat, for which he (and Engels) were the spokesmen; they denounced other socialists who claimed to express the interests of the proletariat differently. Politics for Marx was never a legitimate pursuit in itself, let alone a necessity.
8. *PSS*, XXXIII: 109; *Pravda*, January 15, 1919 (Osinsky, a Left Communist). In notes to himself (in power), he wrote of the state as "a tool of the proletariat in its class struggle, a special *bludgeon, rien de plus!*" "O diktature proletariat," *Leninskii sbornik*, III (1925), reprinted in *PSS*, XXXIX: 261–9 (at 262). Lenin never completed the pamphlet "On the Dictatorship of the Proletariat" for which he composed these notes.
9. Carr, *Bolshevik Revolution*, I: 155 (citing a justice commissariat official).
10. Polan, *Lenin and the End of Politics*, esp. 91–2.
11. *Voprosy istorii KPSS*, 1988, no. 10: 6. See also *Izvestiia TsK KPSS*, 1991, no. 2: 128.
12. Volkogonov, *Lenin: Life and Legacy*, 410.
13. RGASPI, f. 17, op. 2, d. 21, l. 18; d. 71, l. 2; op. 3, d. 174, l. 5; *Izvestiia TsK KPSS*, 1991, no. 2: 129, 130, 137; Golikov, *Vladimir Il'ich Lenin*, XI: 47.
14. RGASPI, f. 17, op. 3, d. 240, l. 1.
15. *Ogonek*, 1990, no. 4: 6 (Doctor Osipov). See also, *PSS*, LIV: 203 (Lenin to Varga).
16. *Izvestiia, TsK KPSS*, 1991, no. 2: 131–2 (Darkshevich). On March 6, Lenin told the Communist faction at the metal workers trade union congress, "My illness . . . for several months has not permitted me to take part in political affairs"—divulging a state secret. *PSS*, XLV: 6.
17. Sakharov, *Politicheskoe zaveshchanie*, 160 (RGASPI, f. 5, op. 2, d. 263, l. 1; d. 265, l. 1–2), 162–7. Stalin was first assigned responsibility for the agitprop department on August 22, 1921; then, on September 13, 1921, the politburo resolved that he should spend three quarters of his time on party work, one quarter on Rabkrin. RGASPI, f. 17, op. 3, d. 193, l. 2; d. 201, l. 5–6. See also Chuev, *Sto sorok*, 181, 229–30.
18. RGASPI, f. 17, op. 2, d. 78, l. 7; Golikov, *Vladimir Il'ich Lenin*, XII: 267; Sakharov, *Politicheskoe zaveshchanie*, 170–1; Chuev, *Sto sorok*, 181. For fantasies about other supposed candidates for general secretary (Ivan Smirnov, Jānis Rudzutaks, Mikhail

Frunze), see Pavlova, *Stalinizm*, 56. See also Trotskii, *Stalin*, II: 173–4.
19. Sakharov, *Politicheskoe zaveshchanie*, 172–7.
20. Chuev, *Sto sorok*, 181; Sakharov, *Politicheskoe zaveshchanie*, 170–1 (citing RGASPI, f. 48, op. 1, d. 21, l. 1–469); Sakharov, *Na rasput'e*, 95–6 (RGASPI, f. 17, op. 2, d. 78, l. 2, 6–7ob.; and *PSS*, XLV: 139). After the names of Molotov and Kuibyshev Lenin wrote "secretary." Stalin came in tenth place in the voting for the 27, in terms of how many negative votes he received. The votes for the new Central Committee at the 11th Congress were indicative: for Lenin, 477 out of 478; for Trotsky, the same number (the last time that would happen); for Stalin, 463; for Kamenev, 454; and for Zinoviev, 448. Thus, it was not true that Kamenev or Zinoviev had higher standing in the party than Stalin.
21. *XI s"ezd VKP (b)*, 84–5, 143; *PSS*, XLV: 122.
22. RGASPI, f. 17, op. 3, d. 241, l. 2. In February 1922, the Profintern (trade union international) acquired a "general secretary" (Rudzutaks). RGASPI, f. 17, op. 3, d. 361, l. 15. Lenin had rebuffed Zinoviev's request to relocate the Comintern to Petrograd; the appointment of Kuusinen (in Moscow) was a compromise.
23. Someone, evidently Lenin, blocked a suggestion at the April 3 Central Committee plenum to create a permanent Central Committee chairman (*predsedatel'*) above the general secretary. RGASPI, f. 17, op. 2, d. 78, l. 2, 6.
24. Three days after formalizing Stalin's appointment as general secretary, Lenin ordered a full case of German Somnacetin and Veronal from the Kremlin apothecary. Lenin, *V. I. Lenin*, 529 (RGASPI, f. 2, op. 1, d. 23036).
25. Volkogonov, *Lenin: Life and Legacy*, 412–3. Plans to find Lenin a retreat somewhere in the mountains, whether in the Caucasus or the Urals, had come to naught. Lenin, *V. I. Lenin*, 379, 537; *Leninskii sbornik*, XXXVI: 468–9; *PSS*, LIV: 229–30; *Izvestiia TsK KPSS*, 1991, no. 2: 133–4 (RGASPI, f. 16, op. 3, d. 20); *PSS*, LIV: 241–2; Tsvigun, *V. I. Lenin i VChK* [1987], 536. Suddenly, the old Caucasus bandit Kamo (Ter-Petrosyan) popped up, vowing to protect and serve Lenin in the region. *PSS*, LIV: 230–1.
26. Klemperer told the *New York Times* that Lenin "was sick, but not seriously so," without revealing his diagnosis. *New York Times*, April 4, 1922. The commissar of health wrote in the newspaper that the bullets aimed at Lenin had been dipped in curare, a poison in which Native Americans were known to have dipped their arrows—and which, if true, would have killed

him back in 1918. Tumarkin, *Lenin Lives!*, 114 (citing *Bednota*, April 22, 1922: Semashko). Word of Lenin's "poisoning," whether from Klemperer's bogus diagnosis or Semashko's bogus assertions, ricocheted abroad: *Rul'*, March 26, March 29, June 13, June 15, June 18, June 21, July 19, August 1, and August 2, 1922.
27. *Pravda*, April 28, 1922.
28. Lenin's note concerned the need to set up some model sanitoriums within 500 miles of Moscow. Lenin added as if conspiratorially ("P.S. Secret") a directive to attend to food supply and transport for Zubalovo, where Stalin and Kamenev had state dachas and where one for Lenin was under construction. Volkogonov, *Lenin: politicheskii portret*, II: 34 (APRF, f. 45, op. 1, d. 694, l. 2). Kamenev and Dzierżyński were also said to have dachas in Zubalovo.
29. *Vospominaniia o Vladimir Il'iche Lenine* [1956–61], II: 342 (V. Z. Rozanov, "Zapiski vracha").
30. The official account of Lenin's activities lists the stroke as May 25–27: Golikov, *Vladimir Il'ich Lenin*, XII: 349. See also *Vospominaniia o Vladimire Il'iche Lenine* [1979], III: 320; *Molodaia gvardiia*, 1924, no. 2–3: at 113; Fotieva, *Iz zhizni*, 178–9; Ogonek, 1990, no. 4: 6; *PSS*, LIV: 203; *Izvestiia TsK KPSS*, 1989, no. 1: 215; *Izvestiia TsK KPSS*, 1991, no. 2: 130–6; Trotsky, *My Life* [1930], 475.
31. Chuev, *Sto sorok*, 193.
32. For instance, in late 1921 Lenin wrote to Kamenev, "Poor fellow, weak, frightened, intimidated"—and Lenin had a relatively higher opinion of Kamenev and "loved him more" than Zinoviev (as Molotov recalled). Pipes, *Unknown Lenin*, 138 (December 1, 1921); Chuev, *Sto sorok*, 183. See also Volkogonov, *Lenin: politicheskii portret*, II: 61. In a preface to a collection of his writings, Lenin had inserted damning material against Zinoviev; only right before publication did he excise it (Stalin had urged Lenin to keep it in). Sakharov, *Politicheskoe zaveshchanie*, 143–6.
33. Lidiya Fotiyeva took over Lenin's personal secretariat in August 1918; by 1920, it had seven staff total (including her): five aides and two clerks. Fotiyeva's two key underlings were Glasser and Volodicheva. Others included N. S. Krasina and N. S. Lepeshinskaya. Stalin's wife Nadya Alliluyeva, for a time, was responsible for Lenin's archive and the most secret documents. Rigby, *Lenin's Government*, 103–5; Kolesnik, *Khronika zhizni sem'i Stalina*, 28; Rosenfeldt, *The "Special" World*, I: 123. Gorbunov (who had replaced Bonch-Bruevich) would stay on as head of the Council of People's Commissars business directorate and private secretary under Rykov.

34. "I am a bad judge of people, I don't understand them," Lenin supposedly told a member of his staff, who remarked that Lenin "tried to consult with long-time comrades, with Nadezhda Konstantinova and with Maria Ilichina." Yakov Shatunovsky, quoted in Shatunovskaia, *Zhizn' v Kremle*, 36–7. "In a society where personal attachments were an integral part of social organization, Lenin's detachment was culturally revolutionary." Jowitt, *New World Disorder*, 7.

35. Mal'kov, *Zapiski*, 150–2, 154, 181; Bonch-Bruevich, *Tri pokusheniie na V. I. Lenina*, 102; McNeal, *Bride of the Revolution*, 185–6. It was during the fall 1918 respite among the linden trees at Gorki that Lenin wrote his slashing rebuttal to Kautsky.

36. When guests were not expected the family ate in the kitchen. The dining room door opened to Lenin's room, which contained a writing desk in front of the window—which looked out onto Senate Square—a table, and a small bed. Vera Dridzo, Krupskaya's secretary, was one of the few people to take meals at the apartment with the family. Dridzo, *Nadezhda Konstantinova Krupskaia*.

37. Zdesenko, *Gorki Leninskie*, 115, 144 (photo of the Rolls-Royce, with tractor treads for snow).

38. Trotsky, in cahoots with Zinoviev and Kamenev, would later claim that Stalin had schemed to isolate Lenin (an interpretation adopted by many scholars). In fact, the politburo as a whole, Trotsky included, voted for all the arrangements for Lenin's stays at Gorki.

39. Stalin's visits in 1922 occurred on May 30, July 10, July 30, August 5, August 9, August 15, August 19, August 23, August 30, September 12, September 19, and September 26. Ul'ianova, "Ob otnoshenii V. I. Lenina I. V. Stalina," 198; Ul'ianova, "O Vladimire Il'iche," no. 4: 187. Kamenev visited four times: July 14, August 3, August 27, and September 13; Bukharin visited four times: July 16, September 20, September 23, and September 25; and Zinoviev visited twice, August 1 and September 2. *Izvestiia TsK KPSS*, 1989, no. 12: 200–1.

40. Valentinov, *Novaia eknomicheskaia politika*, 46–53.

41. *Izvestiia TsK KPSS*, 1991, no. 3: 183–7; Volkogonov, *Lenin: Life and Legacy*, 411–2 (citing APRF, f. 3, op. 22, d. 307, l. 136–7).

42. *Izvestiia, TsK KPSS*, 1991, no. 3: 185.

43. "You're being sly?" Lenin said, according to Maria's account. "When did you ever know me to be sly?" Stalin retorted, in her account. *Izvestiia TsK KPSS*, 1989, no. 12: 197–8.

44. *Izvestiia TsK KPSS*, 1991, no. 3: 198.

45. Sakharov, *Politicheskoe zaveshchanie*, 132–3; *Izvestiia TsK KPSS*, 1991, no. 3: 121 (politburo collective letter of December 31, 1923); RGASPI, f. 17, op. 2, d. 209, l. 9–11 (January 1, 1926, plenum). "M. I. Ul'ianova ob otnoshenii V. I. Lenina i I. V. Stalina," *Izvestiia TsK KPSS*, 1989, no. 12: 196–9 (at 197); RGASPI, f. 14, op. 1, d. 398, l. 1–8. Emelyan Yaroslavsky, the Stalin loyalist, recalled that Lenin "had become fatally tired" of Trotsky and his relentless public polemics over doctrine and policy. *Izvestiia TsK KPSS*, 1989, no. 4: 189.

46. Pipes, *Unknown Lenin*, 124 (March 13, 1921).

47. On June 16, 1921, the politburo took up the question of Trotsky's transfer to Ukraine as food supply commissar. Trotsky refused to accept the politburo's decision, which accelerated the summoning of a Central Committee plenum to discuss the issue. Trotsky, in the meantime, telephoned Cristian Rakovski, party boss of Ukraine, who supposedly told him that all measures to bring grain into Ukraine were already under way. Documents that Lenin was receiving contradicted this picture, however. Lenin and Trotsky met between July 16 and July 23 for a series of extended discussions. On July 27, 1921, Lenin, again receiving Trotsky, backed down. The two reached some sort of compromise regarding Trotsky's behavior. Trotsky remained in charge of the Soviet military. Sakharov, *Politicheskoe zaveshchanie*, 135–42 (citing *Izvestiia TsK KPSS*, 1990, no. 7: 187; RGASPI, f. 17, op. 3, d. 190, l. 4; *Voprosy istorii*, 1989, no. 8: 138–9; Golikov, *Vladimir Il'ich Lenin*, XI: 105–6; *Leninskii sbornik*, XXXIX: 359; RGASPI, f. 17, op. 2, d. 71, l. 5, 24; f. 2, op. 1, d. 200015, l. 1–1ob, 5, 24–5; and *PSS*, LIV: 148).

48. Chuev, *Sto sorok*, 193. See also Ulam, *Stalin*, 207–9; and Service, *Stalin*, 189–90.

49. Golikov, *Vladimir Il'ich Lenin*, XII: 357; Fotieva, *Iz zhizni*, 183–4. On June 13, 1922, Lenin was evidently well enough to be moved from the compound's auxiliary building (*fligel'*) to the main manor house, but the next day he had a spasm of the blood vessels in his head, and told Kozhevnikov, "So, that's it. It'll be a stroke." Golikov, *Vladimir Il'ich Lenin*, XII: 353–4; Volkogonov, *Lenin*, 414. On June 18, *Pravda* published a bulletin indicating he was feeling fine, albeit chafing under the physicians' restrictive regime.

50. *Izvestiia TsK KPSS*, 1989, no. 2: 198–200; Volkogonov, *Lenin: politicheskii portret*, II: 23–5.

51. *Izvestiia TsK KPSS*, 1989, no. 12: 197–8; Volkogonov, *Trotskii*, II: 23.

52. RGASPI, f. 558, op. 1, d. 2397, l. 1.

53. *PSS*, LIV, 273; Golikov, *Vladimir Il'ich Lenin*, XII: 359. The July 18 letter to Stalin has an enigmatic opening: "I thought through your answer very thoroughly and I do not agree with you." What this concerns remains unclear.

54. Lenin, *V. I. Lenin*, 547; Volkogonov, *Lenin: Life and Legacy*, 257 (citing RGASPI. f. 2, op. 1, d. 25996, l. 1).

55. Volkogonov, *Lenin: Life and Legacy*, 416 (citing APRF, f. 3, op. 22, d. 307, l. 23). Those in attendance were Kamenev, Trotsky, Stalin, Tomsky, Molotov, Zinoviev, Rykov, Radek, Buhkharin, and Chubar.

56. Mikoyan, "Na Severnom Kavkaze," 202. See also *Pravda*, August 6, 1922.

57. Fotieva, *Iz zhizni*, 285–6.

58. Lenin, *V. I. Lenin* 548–9 (RGASPI, f. 2, op. 1, d. 26002); RGASPI, f. 5, op. 2, d. 275, l. 4–6; *XII s"ezd RKP (b)*, 198; RGASPI, f. 558, op. 11, d. 816, l. 37–43, 49. Kamenev, head of the Moscow soviet and of the Moscow party organization, was already, informally, the principal substitute for Lenin in the government. Rigby, *Lenin's Government*, 201.

59. RGASPI, f. 5, op. 2, d. 275, l. 4–6; Fel'shtinskii, *Kommunisticheskaia oppozitsiia v SSSR*, I: 11.

60. Volkogonov surmises that Lenin expected and hoped Trotsky would decline, especially given that Lenin chose not to get a politburo decision and enforce party discipline on Trotsky after his refusal (in this instance). Volkogonov, *Trotskii*, II: 23–4. Sakharov, otherwise a careful scholar, also speculates that Lenin wanted Trotsky to refuse, which is not documented. Sakharov, *Na rasput'e*, 98; Sakharov, *Politicheskoe zaveshchanie*, 190–1.

61. Lenin, *V. I. Lenin, 548–9*; Pipes, *Unknown Lenin*, 171, 174 (Lenin letter to Stalin with markings, a facsimile, 172–3); Pipes, *Russia Under the Bolshevik Regime*, 464, 466–7.

62. Deutscher, *Prophet Unarmed*, 30–1.

63. RGASPI, f. 17, op. 3, d. 312, l. 4; f. 5, op. 2, d. 275, l. 4–6.

64. Stalin would soon make Trotsky's refusal public at the 12th Congress: *XII s"ezd RKP (b)*, 198.

65. *Sochineniia*, V: 134–6.

66. Karaganov, *Lenin*, I: 382; Golikov, *Vladimir Il'ich Lenin*, XII: 371.

67. Lenin indulged requests to allow a photographer (P. A. Otsup) to record the event with a group picture for posterity, albeit only after the agenda had been completed. Karaganov, *Lenin*, I: 400–2; *Vospominaniia o Vladimire Il'iche Lenine*, IV: 446; *Pravda*, October 4, 1922.

68. Naumov, "1923 god," 36; Volkogonov, *Lenin: Life and Legacy*, 257 (citing RGASPI, f. 2, op. 2, d. 1239, l. 1);

Volkogonov, *Lenin: politicheskii portret*, II: 24. Lenin's response is undated; Naumov speculates it was produced after October 2, 1922, when Lenin returned to Moscow.
69. PSS, XLV: 245–51; *Izvestiia*, November 1, 1922; Fotieva, *Iz zhizni*, 231–2. On November 1, 1922, Lenin held a meeting in his Kremlin office with a triumvirate: Stalin (party apparatus), Kamenev (government), and Zinoviev (Comintern). *Leninskii sbornik*, XXXIX: 435; Golikov, *Vladimir Il'ich Lenin*, XII: 454.
70. PSS, XLV: 270. At the official anniversary celebration in the Bolshoi, an aluminum likeness of Marx and Engels made by a Moscow factory was presented as a gift for Lenin. *Izvestiia*,

November 9, 1922; Golikov, *Vladimir Il'ich Lenin*, XII: 466–7.
71. PSS, XLV: 278–94; *Leninskii sbornik*, XXXIX: 440; *Vospominaniia o Vladimire Il'iche Lenine* [1979], V: 452, 459–61, 462–3, 468–9, 472–3; *Voprosy istorii KPSS*, no. 9: 41–3.
72. Pavliuchenkov, "*Orden mechenostsev*," 195–6 (citing RGASPI, f. 4, op. 2, d. 1197, l. 1); PSS, XLV: 30–9; *Leninskii sbornik*, XXXIX: 440; *Vospominaniia o Vladimire Il'iche Lenine* [1979], IV: 452–3; Kvashonkin, *Bol'shevistskoe rukovodstvo*, 268–9 (RGASPI, f. 85, op. 1/S, d. 13, l. 8–9: Nazaretyan to Orjonikidze, Nov. 27, 1922).
73. Chervinskaia, *Lenin, u rulia strany Sovetov*, II: 240–1 (B. M. Bolin).
74. Rosmer, *Moscou sous Lenine*, 231.

See also Lewin, *Lenin's Last Struggle*, 33–4.
75. *Pravda*, November 21, 1922; PSS, XLV: 300–1; Lenin, *V. I. Lenin*, 566–73 (full transcript).
76. PSS, XLV: 457.
77. *Pravda*, January 21, 1927; Golikov, *Vladimir Il'ich Lenin*, XII: 509; PSS, XLV: 463; Bessonova, *Biblioteka V. I. Lenina*, 56; Fotieva, *Iz zhizni*, 240; *Izvestiia*, December 1, 1922.
78. Boffa, *The Stalin Phenomenon*.
79. Chuev, *Sto sorok*, 381.
80. Sering, *Die Umwälzung der osteuropäischen Agrarverfassung*, 5–6 (italics mine).

## CHAPTER 10: DICTATOR

1. Chuev, *Tak govoril Kaganovich*, 190–1; Chuev, *Kaganovich*, 263.
2. He went on to note that "this year's harvest is patchy and, as a whole, well below expectations: it is probable that even the estimates of a couple of months ago will prove too high. Prospects for next year are not brilliant." Bourne and Watt, *British Documents on Foreign Affairs*, VII: 376 (undated, date deduced from content).
3. L. D. Trotskii, "Kak moglo eto sluchit'sia?" in Trotskii, *Chto i kak proizoshlo*, 25–36 (at 25); Trotsky, *Stalin*, 393. See also Trotsky, *My Life*, 512. Eugene Lyons, the sympathetic left-leaning American correspondent, would grant Stalin possession only of "the tawdry talents of the ward-politician raised to the dimension of near-genius," not understanding that this was a very high compliment. Lyons, *Stalin*, 159.
4. E. O Preobrazhenskii, "Stranitsa iz ego zhizni," *Pravda*, March 18, 1919: 2. See also Duval, "The Bolshevik Secretariat"; Duval, "Yakov M. Sverdlov."
5. On the various demands from regional party committees to the center, see Service, *Bolshevik Party in Revolution*, 277–95.
6. On March 18, 1919, the day of the interment of Sverdlov's ashes in the Kremlin Wall, Lenin said at a meeting in the Metropole Hotel, "The work which he performed alone in the sphere of organization, the selection of people, their appointment to responsible posts according to all varied specializations—that work will now be possible only if each of the large-scale branches that comrade Sverdlov oversaw by himself will be handled by whole groups of people, proceeding in his footsteps, coming near to doing what this one man did alone." PSS, XXXVIII: 79. See also Lenin's obituary for Sverdlov: *Pravda*, March 20, 1919.

7. Trotsky claimed credit for Kalinin's nomination. Trotskii, *Portrety revoliutsionerov*, 182 (Trotsky letter to Lunacharsky, April 14, 1926). The Congress of Soviets, which convened once a year, possessed even less authority than had the tsarist Duma. The best analysis of the real structure of the new authority can be found in Vishniak, *Le regime sovietiste*. In theory, the Council of People's Commissars answered to the central executive committee of the Soviet, which, formally, possessed the right to form the Council of People's Commissars and its commissariats (July 1918 constitution, article 35). The Council of People's Commissars was tasked with issuing decrees and regulations (articles 37, 38), but the central executive committee was supposed to approve such decrees; the Council of People's Commissars was also supposed to report, weekly, on its activities to the CEC (Avdeev, *Revoliutsiia 1917 goda*, VI: 167). In practice, the Council of People's Commmissars behaved as a sovereign entity. Sverdlov, indiscreetly but accurately, had once revealed at a meeting of the central executive committee that the Council of People's Commissars was "not only an executive body as has been claimed; it is legislative, executive and administrative." *Zasedanie vserossiiskogo tsentral'nogo ispolnitel'nogo komiteta 4-go sozyva*, 66–77. Mikhail Vladimirsky was acting chairman of the CEC March 16–30, 1919.
8. Stasova, *Vospominaniia*, 161. See also Isbakh, *Tovarishch Absoliut*.
9. Nikolai Osinsky had written to Lenin (October 16, 1919) suggesting the "formation of an organizational dictatorship consisting of three members of the Central Committee, the best known organizers," naming Stalin, Krestinsky, and Leonid

Serebryakov (while allowing that Dzierżyński could be appropriate, too). RGPASI, f. 5, op. 1, d. 1253, l. 6. Osinsky on Sverdlov at the 8th Party Congress: *VIII s"ezd RKP (b)*, 165. Lenin kept Osinsky away from high posts after his opposition to Brest-Litovsk.
10. Schapiro, *Origin of the Communist Autocracy* [1977], 266.
11. Daniels, "The Secretariat," 33. Krestinsky admitted the defects: *IX s"ezd RKP (b)*, 41.
12. See, for example, Zinoviev's comments at the 11th Party Congress: *Pravda*, April 2, 1921.
13. Even though Lenin blocked Krestinsky's inclusion on the electoral list, 161 of the 479 voting delegates wrote in his name, a unique event in party annals. *X s"ezd* [1963], 402. Krestinsky also lost his seat on the politburo (March 16, 1921) and was sent to Germany as a Soviet envoy. Lenin was not sentimental: Krestinsky's wife had been the first doctor to treat Lenin when he was shot in 1918.
14. Nikonov, *Molotov*, 517–8; Zelenov, "Rozhdeniie partiinoi nomenklatury," 4. See also Ali, "Aspects of the RKP (b) Secretariat."
15. This was up from 82,859 passes to its offices in 1920: *Izvestiia TsK*, no. 3 (39), March 1922: at 55.
16. Harris, "Stalin as General Secretary: The Appointment Process and the Nature of Stalin's Power," 69 (citing RGASPI, f. 17, op. 2, d. 78, l. 2); *Pravda*, April 2, 1922 [Zinoviev]; *Izvestiia TsK KPSS*, 1990, no. 4: at 176.
17. PSS, XLIV: 393–4. Molotov would recall that when he became head of the party secretariat, in 1921, Lenin told him, "as Central Committee secretary you should take up politics [policy], and delegate all the technical work to deputies and aides." Chuev, *Sto sorok*, 181.

18. Daniels, "Stalin's Rise to Dictatorship"; Rosenfeldt, *Knowledge and Power*. See also Daniels, "The Secretariat"; Rigby, "Early Provincial Cliques"; Rosenfeldt, *Stalin's Special Departments*; and the wrongly dismissive reviews by Gábor Rittersporn, *Russian History/Histoire Russe*, 17/4 (1990), 468, and J. Arch Getty, *Russian Review*, 50/3 (1991) 372–74.

19. "Iosif Stalin: opyt kharakteristiki (September 22, 1939)," in Trotskii, *Portrety revoliutsionerov*, 46–60 (at 59), 351, n35 (note by Fel'shtinskii, citing Trotsky's 1930s notebooks). Elsewhere Trotsky wrote that "Stalin took possession of power, not with the aid of personal qualities, but with the aid of an impersonal machine. And it was not he who created the machine, but the machine that created him." Trotsky, *Stalin*, xv.

20. Avtorkhanov, *Tekhnologiia vlasti*, 5; McNeal, *Stalin*, 82.

21. "There was nothing 'automatic' about the process of Stalin's elevation during the twenties," Tucker rightly noted in 1973. "It took an uncommonly gifted man to navigate the treacherous waters of Bolshevik politics with the skill that he showed in those years." Tucker, *Stalin as Revolutionary*, 392.

22. Lenin's personal secretariat overlapped with that of the Council of People's Commissars. It gathered every political mood report from 1918 through 1922, and every cockamamie policy proposal.

23. On March 31, 1920, Dzierżyński had proposed creating two lists of functionaries, one alphabetical, one regional, a suggestion immediately taken up. RGASPI, f. 17, op. 112, d. 14, l. 183.

24. RGASPI, f. 17, op. 11, d. 114, l. 14.

25. *XII s"ezd RKP (b)*, 62–3, 180 (Viktor Nogin, a member of the Revision Commission of the 12th Party Congress). Nogin died in May 1924.

26. Kvashonkin, *Bol'shevistskoe rukovodstvo*, 262–3 (RGASPI, f. 85, op. 1/S, d. 13, l. 10).

27. This chapter makes use of *Vsia Moskva* (Moscow: Moskovskii rabochii, 1923) and *Vsia Moskva v karmane* (Moscow-Leningrad: Gosizdat, 1926), among other sources.

28. Stalin had implored Lenin to be relieved of this or that task, complaining of overwork—not without basis, although Stalin's presence at the workers and peasants inspectorate or nationalities commissariat was minimal. Stalin relinquished both these government posts to concentrate full-time on the party apparatus, though he retained a government office in the Kremlin's Imperial Senate.

29. Sharapov, *Razreshenie agrarnogo voprosa*, 174.

30. This would be the peak rural *proportion* of party members in the regime's entire history. Rigby, *Communist Party Membership*, 135.

31. Pethybridge, *One Step Backwards*. In 1924, Smolensk, a rural province, had 16 Communists for every 10,000 rural working-age inhabitants. Fainsod, *Smolensk Under Soviet Rule*, 44. Zinoviev, at the Party Congress in 1923, flatly stated that the Communists were an urban party. *XII s"ezd RKP (b)*, 39.

32. Pirani, *Russian Revolution in Retreat*, 155.

33. Pirani, *Russian Revolution in Retreat*, 101.

34. "'Menia vstretil chelovek srednego rosta . . .' ."

35. Barmine, *Vingt ans au service de l'U.R.S.S.*, 256–60.

36. Lenin understood that "policy is conducted through people." *PSS*, XLV: 122–3. An early version of Stalin's 1935 slogan "cadres decide everything."

37. Shefov, *Moskva, kreml'*, Lenin; Volkogonov, *Lenin: Life and Legacy*, 230; Duranty, "Artist Finds Lenin at Work and Fit."

38. The rooming house proved to be something of a catch basin: Kalinin, head of the Soviet central executive committee, also set up offices here on the second floor, as did Alexei Rykov, deputy head of the Council of People's Commissars, though they would have their main offices in the Imperial Senate, on the same floor as Lenin. Vozdvizhenka, 3, had held tsarist foreign affairs ministry archives and it became the Soviet state archive (the building that would be torn down for an expansion of the Lenin Library), while Vozdvizhenka, 6, a private clinic, became the Kremlin hospital. Barmin, *Sokoly Trotskogo*, 155. The rooming house, known as Petergof, was built in 1877 and added a fourth story in 1902. It was designated the House of Soviets no. 4. The Central Committee publishing arm was located at Vozdvizhenka, 9, while no. 10, built by the Economic Society of the Officers of the Moscow Military District, would become the military store (*Voentorg*); it also housed the Communist Youth League Central Committee offices, Young Guard publishing association, and a dormitory. Béla Kun lived here, 1923–37, and not in the Hotel Lux. Down Vozdvizhenka stood the Morozov mansion as well as the Sheremetyev family's Moscow compound, known as the Corner House. Vozdvizhenka ran perpendicular to the Kremlin; Mokhovaya, parallel. Vozdvizhenka would be renamed Comintern Street in 1935; Mokhovaya became Karl Marx Prospect. Sytin, *Iz istorii Moskovskikh ulits* [1948].

39. *IX s"ezd RKP (b)*, 357, 610, n118;

Pavliuchenkov, *Rossiia Nepovskaia*, 61; Pavliuchenkov, "Orden mechenostsev," 213–27. Later, Vozdvizhenka, 5, became the State Museum of Architecture, which it remains today.

40. Berkman, *Bolshevik Myth*, 46, 36–7. The headquarters of the Zhenotdel—derisively known as Tsentro-Baba—was also at Vozdvizhenka, 5.

41. Kazakov's building had gained its third story in 1898. Stalin's initial secretariat office, when he was assigned to party work nearly full-time, before he became general secretary, had been set up on September 26, 1921, at Trubnikovskiii pereulok, no. 19, second floor, at least for correspondence. RGASPI, f. 558, op. 1, d. 4505, l. 1, 3; d. 1860, l. 1–4.

42. "We [the party] have become the state," one delegate stated at the 8th Party Congress in 1919. *VIII s"ezd* [1959], 178 (Varlam Avanesov). "Everyone knows, it's a secret for no one, that in fact the leader of Soviet power in Russia is the Central Committee," Zinoviev stated in his report on the 8th Congress to the Leningrad party machine. *Izvestiia TsK KPSS*, 1989, no. 8: 187.

43. Lenin's government was effectively a cabinet, not a cabinet system rooted in parliamentary majority (as in the British case). Rigby, *Lenin's Government*, 230.

44. Rigby, *Lenin's Government*, 176–86. Of course, there were local soviets, but these grassroots bodies mostly recruited new political elites, many of whom moved up and out of the soviets. Abrams, "Political Recruitment and Local Government." The commissariat for local self-government had been formally folded into the commissariat of internal affairs on March 20, 1918; meanwhile, the regime had facilitated elimination of *zemstvo* local government bodies (which dated to Russia's 1860s Great Reforms, and which the Provisional Government had democratized and, on paper, greatly expanded). Gronsky, "The Zemstvo System."

45. Yevgeny Preobrazhensky, at the 9th Party Congress (March 1920), had observed that some delegates had "gone so far as to suggest that the party can be abolished, because we have soviets, in which the Communists are a majority." But Krestinsky, then party secretary, suggested, instead, eliminating the soviets in the provinces. *IX s"ezd RKP (b)*, 68; *Izvestiia TsK KPSS*, 1990, no. 7: 160.

46. *Izvestiia TsK KPSS*, 1921, no. 28 (March 5): 23–4; no. 29: at 7; 1922, no. 3 (39): 54. See also Schapiro, *Communist Party*, 250.

47. Sakwa, *Soviet Communists*, 49–53, 191–3; Figes, *A People's Tragedy*, 688.

48. Rosenfeldt, The *"Special" World*. By 1924, the central party apparatus ballooned to nearly 700.

49. Sytin, *Iz istorii moskovskikh ulits* [2000], 70. "Kitai," in Russian, can signify China, but this is clearly not the meaning of Moscow's Kitaigorod, which no one has definitely established. Kolodnyi, *Kitai-gorod*, 5–16. Vozdvizhenka, no. 5, went to the state planning commission. The separate Moscow party organization apparatus in the capital was all set: following the September 25, 1919, bombing of its headquarters at Leontyev Lane, 18, it had moved to Bolshaya Dmitrovka, 15a, once a wealthy club before the revolution—with a restaurant, exhibit and concert halls, billiard rooms, and card-playing rooms—which had been renowned for artistic salons. The Moscow organization stayed at Bolshaya Dmitrovka until after Lazar Kaganovich, a Central Committee secretary, concurrently became Moscow party boss (1930) and grabbed Old Square, no. 6, from the commissariat of labor in order to remain proximate to the central apparatus and Stalin (at no. 4).

50. Balashov and Markhashov, "Staraia ploshchad', 4 (20-e gody)," no. 5: 192.

51. Bazhanov, *Bazhanov and the Damnation of Stalin*, 38–9.

52. Loginov, *Teni Stalina*, 95. Vlasik dictated his recollections to his wife Mariia; their adopted daughter Nadezhda passed them to Georgii Egnatashivili. Egnatashivili's father, Aleksandr, had worked under Vlasik, as head of bodyguard detail for politburo member Nikolai Shvernik.

53. The politburo generally met on Tuesdays and Thursdays; the Council of People's Commissars, on Wednesdays.

54. Lieven, "Russian Senior Officialdom"; Armstrong, "Tsarist and Soviet Elite Administrators." Some functions of the tsar's secretariat were taken by the Ministry of the Imperial Household, which supervised the emperor's property (known as Cabinet Lands, the largest landowner in Russia).

55. Remnev, *Samoderzhavnoe pravitel'stvo*, 83 (citing unpublished memoirs of A. N. Kulomzin). The imperial chancellery did more than merely summarize; its functionaries rewrote and recast proceedings, going so far as to eliminate arguments to compose smooth narratives of policy formation, creating paperwork designed to be accessible to the tsar. The chancellery often "spared" the tsar reports from the provinces. The heads of imperial chancellery sections conducted the final editing of laws, while the overall chancellery head oversaw appointments and attended virtually all special commissions. Remnev, *Samoderzhavnoe pravitel'stvo*, 68–110; Shepelev,

*Chinovny mir Rossii XVIII–nachalo XX v.*, 47–55.

56. Alexander III had tried to have his chancellery become something of a personal watchdog over the bureaucracy, but he failed. The ministers denounced and obstructed the change, and the autocrat could not gain operational control over the state. Lieven, *Russia's Rulers*, 286–7.

57. E. H. Carr, in his fourteen-volume history of the first twelve years of the revolution, explored the relationship of political contingency (Stalin's dictatorship) and what he saw as the primary structural determinant (Russian backwardness). As a reader progresses through the volumes, the Russian past impresses itself more and more on the reader, as it did on many of the Bolshevik revolutionaries. But in the final volume, which appeared in 1978, Carr would reconsider, writing that the emphasis on tsarism, "though not wrong, now seems to me somewhat overstated." Carr, *Foundations of a Planned Economy*, III/iii: viii.

58. Ilin-Zhenevskii, "Nakanune oktiabria," 15–6; Rabinowitch, *Bolsheviks Come to Power*, 57–9.

59. Balashov and Markhashov, "Staraia ploshchad', 4 (20-e gody)," no. 5: 191–2.

60. *PSS*, XLV: 123. With all members said to be "strictly subordinate to party discipline," as the 8th Party Congress in 1919 emphasized, "the whole matter of assignment of party functionaries is in the hands of the Central Committee of the party. . . . Its decision is binding for everyone. The Central Committee is entrusted with the carrying out of the most determined struggle against any localism or separatism in these questions." The Central Committee seized the right to "systematically rotate functionaries from one sphere to another, from one region to another, with the aim of their most productive use." *VIII s"ezd RKP (b)* [1959], 426–8; *Kommunisticheskaia partiia Sovetskogo Soiuza*, I: 444.

61. From the summer of 1922 through the fall of 1923, 97 of 191 local party secretaries were elected; Moscow "recommended" or outright appointed the rest. Tsakunov, *V labirinte*, 93 (citing RGASPI, f. 17, op. 68, d. 484, l. 170–85); Rigby, "Early Provincial Cliques," 15–19.

62. "The Central Committee," declared a policy statement in 1922, "considered as its duty the constant observation of the internal affairs of local party organizations, trying in every way to eliminate from the localities those frictions and dissensions known under the name of 'skloki.'" *Izvestiia TsK*, March 1922: at 13. In April 1920, for example, the entire membership of the Central Committee of the Communist party of

Ukraine had been transferred to Russia. Ravich-Cherkasskii, *Istoriia kommunisticheskoi partii*, appendix 12. See also Service, *Bolshevik Party in Revolution*.

63. RGASPI, f. 17, op. 84, d. 147, l. 150; *Spravochnik partiinogo rabotnika*, vyp. 3: 108, 118. On the centralizing process in Petrograd, see McAuley, *Bread and Justice*, 145.

64. Daniels, "The Secretariat"; Moore, *Soviet Politics*, 290. After a fall 1921 party purge, the third one in three years, which targeted careerists and "disguised" class enemies and resulted in just under one fourth of the 659,000 members being expelled (many quit of their own volition), a re-registration of the remaining half million Communists followed in 1922; it constituted a party "census," during which the central apparatus collected questionnaires from nearly every member and candidate. *Spravochnik partiinogo rabotnika*, vyp. 3, 128–30; Service, *Bolshevik Party in Revolution*, 164; Gimpel'son, *NEP*, 329 (citing RGASPI, f. 17, op. 34, d. 1, l. 19); *Izvestiia TsK RKP (b)*, March 5, 1921. In 1921, many party commissions invited the non-party mass to voice their opinions about individual Communists. In one military unit of the Moscow garrison, 400 non-party soldiers threw the 36 party members out of the meeting and themselves decided who should be purged, an outcome later nullified. *Izvestiia MK RKP (b)*, 1922, no. 1: 6. The apparatus evidently failed to index all party members by the start of the 11th Congress in spring 1922. *Pravda*, September 10, 1921; *Protokoly XI*, 52; Leonard Schapiro, *Origin of the Communist Autocracy*, 1977, 337–8; Gimpel'son, *NEP*, 329 (citing RGASPI, f. 17, op. 34, d. 1, l. 19); *Izvestiia TsK RKP (b)*, March 5, 1921.

65. Molotov had told the 11th Party Congress (1921) that a three-person commission sent to Samara province had uncovered a "complete lack of discipline" and a membership dropoff from 13,000 to 4,500 (leaving out the fact that a terrible famine raged), compelling Moscow to replace the entire Samara leadership with appointees. *XI s"ezd RKP (b)*, 57–8; *Izvestiia TsK*, March 1922: at 35. Umpteen secret circulars, including one dated November 30, 1922, referred to the "immensely widespread bribe-taking" among functionaries that was threatening "the degeneration and destruction of the workers state apparatus," and called for a person or commission in every region to be responsible for fighting the scourge. Bribe-taking was blamed on "the general lack of culture and economic backwardness of the country." RGASPI, f. 17, op. 11, d. 100, l. 234; op. 84, d. 291a, l. 282.

66. *Izvestiia TsK*, no. 42, June 1922, no. 43, July 1922, no. 9 (45), September 1922, no. 11–12.

67. Harris, "Stalin as General Secretary." Partly because of vast expansion, partly because of turnover, only between 20 and 40 percent of Party Congress delegates carried over from one yearly gathering to the next. Of the 106 voting and non-voting delegates to the 7th Congress, 38 percent appeared at the 8th; of the 442 at the 8th, 23 percent carried over to the 9th; of the 593 at the 9th, 22 percent made it to the 10th; of the 1,135 at the 10th, only 15 percent were at the 11th; only 36 percent were at the 12th. Carryover on the Central Committee, however, was substantial, even as that body, too, expanded (from 23 full and candidate members in 1918 to 46 in 1922). Gill, *Origins*, 58, 61.

68. RGASPI, f. 17, op. 112, d. 370, l. 2; Pavliuchenkov, *Rossiia Nepovskaia*, 70 (citing RGASPI, f. 17, op. 11, d. 142, l. 4).

69. Merridale, *Moscow Politics*, 29.

70. *Izvestiia TsK VKP (b)*, January 1924, no. 1 (59): 64–7; April 1924, no. 4 (62): 41; January 18, 1926, no. 1 (122): 22–4; Balashov and Markhashov, "Staraia ploshchad', 4 (20-e gody)," no. 4: 186; RGASPI, f. 17, op. 68, d. 139, l. 74; Rigby, "Origins of the Nomenklatura System," 241–54; Rigby, "Staffing USSR Incorporated"; Korzhikhina and Figatner, "Sovetskaia nomenklatura."

71. *XII s"ezd RKP (b)*, 704–5; RGASPI, f. 17, op. 69, d. 259, l. 101. Nonetheless, the Central Committee apparatus also seized the initiative to register non-party state bureaucrats, beating an attempt by the Soviet central executive committee to take charge of this function. Pavliuchenkov, *Rossiia Nepovskaia*, 69; Pavliuchenkov, "*Orden mechenostsev*," 227–53. Soon, the nomenklatura system would be required practice in all republics of the Union. Daniels, "The Secretariat," 37–8; Rigby, "Staffing USSR Incorporated," 529–30. By 1924, the list was divided in two, with 3,500 included on list no. 1, and another 1,500 on list no. 2. Those on no. 1 were to be named by the politburo and approved by the Central Committee and encompassed. RGASPI, f, 80, op. 19, d. 1, l. 6–14.

72. *XII s"ezd RKP (b)*, 63.

73. Local party committees had circumscribed authority on paper. A November 1922 Central Committee circular dispatched to all party organizations stipulated that locals had no authority to alter the essence of any party circulars. As if in acknowledgment that this was happening, however, the circular noted that any proposed additions to them had to be agreed with the Central Committee. It was signed by Molotov and Kaganovich. Pavlova, *Stalinizm*, 73 (citing PANO, f. 1, op. 2, d. 238, l. 32).

74. Nikolaev, *Chekisty*, article by Velidov with Ksenofontov bio; Parrish, *Soviet Security*, 219–20. In late 1924 or early 1925, Ksenofontov ordered workers to repair Stalin's office after midnight; Balashov, who happened to have night duty, had not been informed, and he refused to allow the workers into Stalin's office. Ksenofontov called and screamed on the phone; the next day Balashov informed Stalin, who sided with him. Ksenofontov resigned; Stalin did not want to accept his resignation, but Ksenofontov insisted. He moved over to RSFSR social welfare. Balashov and Markhashov, "Staraia ploshchad', 4 (20-e gody)," no. 5: 191. Ksenofontov died March 23, 1926, of stomach cancer, aged forty-two, in agony. His obituary (*Poletarskaia revoliutsiia*, 1926, no. 4: 232–4) credited him as "one of the creators and organizers of the Cheka," even though he had been transferred to CC apparatus for three years.

75. Psurtsev, *Razvitie sviazi v SSSR*. Lenin made extensive use of the telephone; his draft directives for introducing the NEP, for example, had been transmitted by telephone to the politburo. P. I. Makrushenko, "Voploshchenie mechty," *Promyshlenno-ekonomicheskaia gazeta*, April 20, 1958: 3. Underinvestment ensured that phones did not spread much beyond functionaries, but also that commissariats and other official bodies constructed their own telephone networks, which were therefore closed systems (and which was why Soviet officials had so many phones on their desks). Solnick, "Revolution, Reform, and the Soviet Telephone Network," 172–3; Lewis, "Communications Output in the USSR," at 413.

76. Boris Bazhanov claimed he once came upon Stalin listening in on a telephone network, using a special device attached to a wire into the drawer of his desk. Bazhanov, *Bazhanov and the Damnation of Stalin*, 39–41. This incident does not appear in Bazhanov's earlier work: *Avec Stalin dans le Kremlin*.

77. In the 1920s, travelers to the Soviet Union were convinced everything was easvesdropped on—"It was said that in Moscow if one spoke through a telephone one might as well talk directly with the GPU"—but of course all telephones worldwide went through switchboard operators. Lawton, *The Russian Revolution*, 282. See also Hullinger, *Reforging of Russia*, 114.

78. There was a switchboard (*kommutator*) in a small room between Stalin's reception and his office, where two female telephone operators worked in shifts through mid-1925, when they would be replaced by male bodyguards who doubled as telephone operators. The number of regular telephones at Old Square quickly leapt from around 250 to 500. Balashov and Markhashov, "Staraia ploshchad', 4 (20-e gody)," no. 5: 192.

79. *Izvestiia TsK RKP (b)*, September 18, 1920; Pavlova, *Stalinizm*, 46–7 (citing RGASPI, f. 17, op. 84, d. 171, l. 2); G. A. Kurnenkov, "Organizatsiia zashchity informatsii v strulturakh RKP (b)—VKP (b), 1918–1941 gg.: avtoref at kandidatskoi dissertatsii," RGGU, 2010; Anin, *Radioelektronnyi shpionazh*, 24–32. Boki remained in charge of the cipher department from January 1921 through mid-May 1937.

80. Boki's dacha commune was located in the village of Kuchino, east of Moscow, and charged members 10 percent of their monthly paychecks. "The drinking bouts as a rule were accompanied by wild hooliganism and mutual humiliations: drunks spread paint and mustard on their private parts," recalled Yevdokia Kartseva, a Soviet foreign intelligence agent. "Those who were forced to drink were buried as if they had died. . . . All this was done with priestly accoutrements, which had been imported from the Solovki monastery-labor camp (which Boki had helped establish). Usually two or three people wore priestly garb and conducted a drunken liturgy. They drank laboratory spirits from a chemical laboratory obtained under the pretext of technical needs." http://www.solovki.ca/camp_20/butcher_bokii.php; Shambarov, *Gosudarstvo i revoliutsiia*, 592.

81. Rosenfeldt, The *"Special" World*, I: 141–4.

82. *XII s"ezd RKP (b)*: 70, 71, 74.

83. Pavlova, *Stalinizm*, 90 (citing PANO, f. 5, op. 6, d. 142, l. 11).

84. Pavlova, "Mekhanizm politicheskoi vlasti," 63. On November 8, 1919, a politburo minute records Stalin's complaint that "certain information about sessions of the Central Committee, admittedly in corrupt form, somehow reaches our enemies." He suggested a procedure "that would allow only a few of the comrades to get to know the protocols." This prompted institution of rules on who received excerpts from politburo meetings, which were meant to serve as directives or instructions. RGASPI, f. 17, op. 3, d. 37; *Archives of the Soviet Communist Party and Soviet State: Catalog of Finding Aids and Documents* (Hoover Institution Archives, 1995). On June 14, 1923, the politburo resolved to make stenographic records of the principal reports and summary remarks on key agenda items, for the edification of those not present. Adibekov, *Politbiuro TsK RKP (b)—VKP (b):*

*povestki dnia zasedanii*, I: 223. Stenographic records were made rarely, however, evidently because such work was labor intensive: sessions tended to be long and the recorded remarks had to be distributed to each individual for editing and approval. The resultant typeset "red books," so named for their pink binding, could differ substantially from the original hand-recorded oral remarks. On December 8, 1923, the politburo resolved that in its protocols, "nothing other than decisions of the politburo ought to be recorded." *Istochnik*, 1993, no. 5–6: 88–95 (at 91).

85. Dmitrievskii, *Sovetskie portrety*, 108–9. Dmitriesvky, an employee of the Soviet embassy in Sweden, defected in 1930.

86. "'Menia vstretil chelovek srednego rosta . . .' ."

87. Kerzhentsev, *Printsipy organizatsii*. Kerzhentsev was also a playwright and proponent of the mass theater who in 1923–25 worked in the Workers and Peasants Inspectorate and wrote pamphlets about the scientific organization of work (Taylorism) and time management and how to conduct meetings: *Nauchnaia organizatsiia truda (NOT) i zadacha partii* (St. Petersburg, 1923); *Bor'ba za vremia* (Moscow, 1923); *Organizui samogo sebia* (Moscow, 1923); *Kak vesti sobaranie*, 5th ed. (Moscow, 1923).

88. After the success of the coup, one Moscow Bolshevik remarked, "some comrades could not get used to the idea that the underground was finally dead." In fact, the attempt to retain power, within a hostile country and hostile world, made the pseudonyms and coded messages seem no less essential. Smidovich, "Vykhod iz podpol'ia v Moskve," 177. Smidovich chaired the Moscow Military Revolutionary Committee.

89. In 1922, Lenin insisted that the three Central Committee secretaries post office hours—which were to be published in *Pravda*—indicating precisely when the secretariat would be open to receive officials, workers, peasants, or whoever showed up. This was the origin of the logbooks for Stalin's office (which originated not for his Kremlin office, but for his Vozdvizhenka and then Old Square office). Later, Stalin ceased having such open office hours and received officials and others when he summoned them.

90. Pipes, *Unknown Lenin*, 74.

91. In 1918, Znamenka was renamed Red Banner Street—Krasno-Znamënnaya—but colloquially retained its original name. Znamenka no. 23 would be renumbered no. 19 by 1926.

92. RGASPI, f. 17, op. 11, d. 186, l. 129, 108; d. 171, l. 232, 167; op. 112, d. 474, l. 11; op. 11, d. 171, l. 198; op. 68, d. 49, l. 116.

93. On August 5, 1921, Trotsky ordered the political administration of the Red Army to ramp up its work following the civil war victory. He visited Khodynsk camp (*lager'*) and a school for young commanders. He called for publishing better newspapers and organizing collective readings: "Among the Red Army men of the 36th division there are many Ukrainians. Among them are a significant number who spent a long time as POWs of the Polish bourgeoisie. They were treated horribly in POW captivity. The former POWs perk up when the topic of their captivity arises. It is necessary to devote one-two-three days of newspaper material to this question." He suggested finding a journalist who could quote them and select the better stories. He warned them not to forget about uniforms, boots, and rifles either, and to pay attention to their needs, not bathe them in phraseology and clichés. Trotsky wanted to ensure that the oath of service was done properly, not perfunctorily. Trotsky also showed he was guided by Lenin's instructions, asking Lenin on November 23, 1921, for his writings on military doctrine as the discussions were under way (l. 173). The day before, Trotsky asked to be supplied with the new post–Great War Military Regulations (*ustav*) of other countries, "above all the French ones" (l. 182). He wanted two popular-style books written, one on Poland and one on Romania, to be factually based, in order to be used as course material and agitprop for Red Army men—and they had to be accessible. He directed that the *Journal of Military Science and Revolution* be renamed *War and Revolution*. RGVA, f. 33 987, op. 1, d. 448, l. 84–6, Hoover Institution Archives, Volkogonov papers, container 17.

94. *XII s"ezd RKP (b)*, 59.

95. Shanin, *Awkward Class*, 190–2.

96. Zibert, "O bol'shevistskom vospitanii."

97. Shpilrein, *Iazyk krasnoarmeitsa*. For political reasons, the regime distrusted the rural instructors who were supposed to educate the peasants, just as the tsarist regime had not, albeit from a different political vantage point. Pethybridge, *One Step Backwards*, 79.

98. Von Hagen, *Soldiers in the Proletarian Dictatorship*, 271–9, 288.

99. "At the current time," noted a special commission in January 1924, "the Red Army, as an organized, trained, politically educated and mobilizational resource-supplied force, does not exist. In its current form the Red Army is not combat ready." Berkhin, *Voennaia reforma*, 60.

100. Von Hagen, *Soldiers in the Proletarian Dictatorship*, 183.

101. Berkhin, *Voennaia reforma*, 60.

102. Harrison, *Marooned in Moscow*, 227; Leggett, *The Cheka*, 34, 165.

103. On Stalin's early "keen interest" in the secret police, see Gerson, *The Secret Police*, 28.

104. Its staffing poses a bit of a puzzle, partly because of the way personnel were enumerated. Early on, the Cheka managed few records—"everything was done in combat mode, on the fly, they wrote things down when they could," one history-memoir recounted. Latsis, *Otcheta VChK za chetyre goda ee deiatel'nosti (20 dekabria 1917 g.—20 dekabria 1921 g.* [Internal use], 13 (cited in V. K. Vinogradov, "Istoriia formirovaniia arkhiva VChK," in Vinogradov, *Arkhiv VChK*, 5–50 [at 5]).

105. Vinogradov, *Genrikh Iagoda*, 295–305 (TsA FSB, f. 2, op. 1, d. 138, l. 176–9). Soon enough, endless memoranda demanded the elimination of red tape and expenditures. "We need to do away with the superfluous run of paper and reduce the ranks," Dzierżyński wrote to one of his deputies (July 4, 1921). V. K. Vinogradov, "Istoriia formirovaniia arkhiva VChK," in Vinogradov, *Arkhiv VChK*, 9 (citing TsA FSB, f. 66, op. 1, d. 55, l. 108–108ob). There are more than three hundred volumes of archival documents in FSB archives on Kronstadt, gathered from many agencies and publications, including from the Cheka itself: *Kronstadtskaia tragediia*, I: 30.

106. Leonov, *Rozhdenii sovetskoi imperii*, 298–300; Baiguzin, *Gosudarstvennaia bezopasnost' Rossii*, 436.

107. *Pravda*, February 22, 1919 (Vladimir Cheka); *Sotsialistickesii vestnik*, September 21, 1922 (Stavropol Cheka).

108. As the exile Maxim Gorky poetically wrote, Chekists "made their way into power like foxes, used it like wolves, and when caught, perished like dogs." Gorky, *Untimely Thoughts*, 211.

109. Also in 1920, Stalin displaced Bukharin as the politburo representative on the Cheka's governing board (*collegium*). Leggett, *The Cheka*, 132–45, 159, 165. Up until November 1918, in the opinion of Nikolai Krylenko, the Cheka "existed without any statutes or law," let alone supervision. Krylenko, *Sudoustroitstvo RSFSR*, 97.

110. Rayfield, *Stalin and His Hangmen*, 67–8.

111. Popoff, *The Tcheka*; Dmitrievskii, *Sud'ba Rossii*, 214. Members of the tsarist police were mostly refused employment in the Cheka, which few of them sought. Three known *okhranka* operatives worked in the Cheka: one who worked in internal passports, one who helped recruit agents in Paris, and the old regime's top cipher specialist, Ivan A. Zybin, the former head of the tsarist

cryptology department. Soboleva, *Istoriia shifroval'nogo dela*, 417–9. By contrast, an estimated 90 percent of the Bolshevik regime's state control commission members were former staff of the tsarist procuracy. Remington, "Institution Building in Bolshevik Russia." The 1923–24 summary report for the top leadership on the activities of the GPU noted some success in incorporating foreign agents from tsarist times. *Istochnik*, 1995, no. 4: 72–80. In 1925, the OGPU moved the central *okhranka* central archives to Moscow (the foreign archives, in Paris, were said to be lost, but in fact they were spirited away and deposited in the Hoover Institution at Stanford). The OGPU soon published a list of names in the secret agent/informer card index of the *okhranka*, amounting to almost 10,000 people. *Spisok sekretnykh sotrudnikov, osvedomiteli, vspomogatel'nykh agentov byv. Okhrannykh otdelenii i zhandarmskykh upravlenii*, 2 vols. (Moscow, 1926–9).

112. Leggett, *The Cheka*, 190. Latsis, *Chrezvychainye komissii*, 11.

113. Kapchinskii, *Gosbezopasnosti iznutri*, 256–7.

114. When a heckler shouted that he had been imprisoned despite having proof of his innocence, Kamenev promised "the [Moscow] soviet will deal with such injustices," provoking catcalls. Pirani, *Russian Revolution in Retreat*, 39 (citing TsGAMO, f. 180, op. 1, d. 236, l. 9, 11, 21, 28, 46–7).

115. "Comrade Kamenev!" Lenin wrote (November 29, 1921). "I am closer to you than to comrade Dzierżyński. I advise you not to retreat and to bring the matter to the politburo." *PSS*, LIV: 39.

116. Yet another special commission (established December 1, 1921) comprised of Dzierżyński, Kamenev, and Dmitry Kursky, the justice commissar (1918–28) and procurator general, became stalemated. While Dzierżyński worked on Kursky, proposing to introduce more precise procedures for arrests, searches, and detainment, he directed his new first deputy, Józef Unszlicht, to find a way to get what the Cheka wanted without alienating Lenin. Plekhanov and Plekhanov, *F. E. Dzerzhinskii*, 339–40; D. B. Pavlov, *Bol'shevistskaia diktatura*, 54–5 (citing RGASPI, f. 5, op. 1, d. 2558, l. 50); Zhordaniia, *Bol'shevizm*, 71. Kursky (b. 1874) would become Soviet envoy to Italy (1928–32) and commit suicide in December 1932. Voloshin, "Dmitrii Ivanovich Kurskii"; "Dmitrii Ivanovich Kurskii: k 100-letiiu so dnia rozhdeniia," *Sotsialisticheskaia zakonnost'*, 1974, no. 11: 48–9.

117. To carry out the changes, yet another commission was formed, consisting of Stalin, Kamenev, and

Kursky—but this time, also Unszlicht, who conducted a rearguard action on behalf of Dzierżyński. Plekhanov, *VChK-OGPU*, 108–11. Dzierżyński certainly desired greater adherence to legality, so as not to discredit the GPU. See his letter (April 2, 1923) to Unszlicht's former secretary (Andreeva) on not jailing suspects for more than two weeks without charges: RGASPI f. 76, op. 3, d. 49, l. 117. The politburo decree abolishing the Cheka had stated that the new agency should "concentrate on institutionalization of informing and [collecting] internal information and elucidation of all counterrevolutionary and anti-Soviet acts in all spheres." The precise wording of this directive came from the commission on SRs and Mensheviks that had been formed by the politburo in late 1921. D. B. Pavlov, *Bol'shevistskaia diktatura*, 53 (citing APRF, f. 3, op. 59, d. 16, l. 1–2, 4).

118. *Vysylka vmesto rasstrela*, 11. Already by early 1921, more than 2,000 Mensheviks were in Soviet prisons and camps. Plekhanov, *VChK-OGPU*, 400 (TsA FSB, f. 1, op. 6, d. 138, l. 100). The Cheka in the South Caucasus became the GPU in 1926. Confusingly, the plenipotentiary office of the central Cheka based in Tiflis did become the GPU plenipotentiary in 1922, and the head of the South Caucasus Cheka was also the South Caucasus GPU plenipotentiary. Waxmonsky, "Police and Politics in Soviet Society," 126; *Organy VChK-GPU-OGPU na Severnom Kavkaze i v Zakavkaz'e, 1918–1934 gg.* https://www.kavkaz-uzel.ru/system/attachments/0000/3107/%D0%9E%D1%80%D0%B3%D0%B0%D0%BD%D1%8B_%D0%92%D0%A7%D0%9A-%D0%93%D0%9F%D0%A3_%D0%9E%D0%93%D0%9F%D0%A3_%D0%BD%D0%B0_%D0%A1%D0%B5%D0%B2%D0%B5%D1%80%D0%BD%D0%BE%D0%BC_%D0%9A%D0%B0%D0%B2%D0%BA%D0%B0%D0%B7%D0%B5_i_v_Zakavkaz'e_1918–1934_%D0%B3%D0%B3.pdf.

119. *PSS*, XLIV: 396–400 (*pis'mo D. I. Kurskomu*). See also Pavliuchenkov, "*Orden mechenostsev*," 131 (citing RGASPI, f. 5, op. 2, d. 50, l. 64). Stalin had Lenin's letter printed in *Bol'shevik*, January 15, 1937. Already on December 28, 1921, the politburo had accepted Dzierżyński's recommendation to stage a public trial of the SRs, although it took time to manufacture the case. Tsvigun, *V. I. Lenin i VChK* [1987], 518.

120. Argenbright, "Marking NEP's Slippery Path"; Kuromiya, *Freedom and Terror*, 143. No more than a few weeks after the concession of

legalization of private trade, in April 1921, Ivar T. Smilga proposed a mass trial of engineers in the petroleum industry. In the winter of 1921–22, Lenin urged the justice commissariat to mount show trials of economic managers. RGASPI, f. 17, op. 3, d. 155, l. 4; Rees, *State Control in Soviet Russia*, 35.

121. Volkogonov, *Lenin: Life and Legacy*, 359.

122. Pethybridge, *One Step Backwards*, 206.

123. Citing not merely political expediency but principle, Gorky had written to Rykov (July 1, 1922) that "if the trial of the SRs ends in murder—it will be a premeditated murder, a criminal murder! I ask that you convey my opinion to Lev Trotsky and others." He denounced the "senseless and criminal murder of the intellectual forces of our illiterate and uncultured country." It is telling he mentioned Trotsky and not Stalin. *Shpion*, 1993, no. 1: 36 (RTSKH-IDK, f. 7, op. 2, d. 2600, l. 11). Back in 1919, Lenin had written in response to criticism from Gorky that "the lackeys of capital consider themselves the brains of the nation. In fact they are not its brains but its shit." Koenker, *Revelations*, 229–30 (RGASPI, f. 2, op. 1, d. 11164, l.1–6: Lenin letter, September 15, 1919).

124. Vinogradov et al., *Pravoeserovskii politicheskii protsess*; Jansen, *Show Trial*; Morozov, *Sudebnyi protsess sotsialistov-revoliutsionerov*; Shub, "The Trial of the SRs."

125. The death sentences were only formally commuted in January 1924. Trotsky claimed credit for Kamenev's proposal: *Moia zhizn'*, II: 211–2. On March 1, 1922, Mężyński of the GPU had ordered "all forces of informants directed at preventing the unification of SR groupings" and "the smashing of their unification strivings." *Sbornik tsirkuliarnykh pisem VChK-OGPU*, III/i: 301. The GPU engaged specialists on socialist parties as consultants (*referenty*), who helped with public slander campaigns. Such work was led by the large Secret-Operative Department, but fully six of the ten GPU departments were involved in repression against socialists as well as anarchists.

126. *Sbornik zakonodatel'nykh i normativnykh aktov o repressiiiakh*, 12.

127. Gerson, *The Secret Police*, 222. At the fifth anniversary of the Soviet secret police in December 1922 at the Bolshoi Theater, Zinoviev remarked that abroad proletarians "salivated" at hearing the initials "VChK"—All-Russia Cheka—while the bourgeoisie "trembled upon hearing those three awesome letters." The crowd laughed. *Pravda*, December 19, 1922: 3.

128. At the wharf, GPU convoys were said to have doffed their caps. Chamberlain, *Lenin's Private War*, 139

(citing Vera Ugrimova, 204). Ironically, many of these deportees would outlive those who deported them.

129. Robson, *Solovki*; Ascher, "The Solovki Prisoners"; Beliakov, *Lagernaia sistema*, 385–91. There were three camps of special designation: Arkhangelsk, Kholmogorsky, and Pertominsky.

130. Dzierżyński proposed that "a case file [*delo*] should be opened on every intellectual"—guilty by definition. But he subdivided the intelligentsia for surveillance purposes into "roughly, 1) novelists, 2) pundits and politicians, 3) economists (here we need subgroups: experts on finance, fuel, transport, trade, cooperatives and so on), 4) technicians (here also subgroups: engineers, agronomists, doctors, general staff personnel and so on), 5) professors and teachers and so on and so on." He continued: "Every group and subgroup should be illuminated from all sides by qualified comrades, among whom these groups should be divided by our department. The information should be verified from various sides so that our conclusions can be errorless and irreversible, which has not been the case till now owing to the hurriedness and one-sidedness of the illumination." Platova, *Zhizn' studenchestva Rossii*, 134. In one of his last acts as first deputy chairman of the GPU, Unszlicht wrote to the party secretariat (March 17, 1923) about the need "to strengthen the tendency toward schisms and disagreements in the ranks of parties that are our enemies"—meaning non-Bolshevik socialists. D. B. Pavlov, *Bol'shevistskaia diktatura*, 3 (citing APRF, f. 3, op. 59, d. 14, l. 38). On Unszlicht, see also Weiner, "Dzerzhinskii and the Gerd Case."

131. Izmozik, *Glaza*, 115 (RGASPI, f. 76, op. 3, d. 306, l. 156).

132. S. A. Krasil'nikov, "Politbiuro, GPU, ii intelligentsia v 1922–1923 gg.," in *Intelligentsiia, obshchestvo, vlast'*, 53. The party, too, established an "information department," which from 1924 (as part of the battle against Trotsky) would undergo strengthening, but it gathered information not only on party cells, but also workers, peasants, industry, agriculture, nationalities, and regions. *KPSS v rezoliutsiiakh* [1984], III: 159. In fact, almost all organizations, from the Red Army to the Communist Youth League, engaged in surveillance and mood-summaries. *Svodki* had been kept by the Provisional Government, for army and navy, and resumed by the Petrograd Bolsheviks to track the mood of soldiers and of workers. Indeed, within days of the coup, Petrograd Bolsheviks sent a questionnaire to regional party groups on the masses' feelings toward "the seizure of power." Izmozik, *Glaza*, 50. During the Great War, Britain and Germany had engaged in mail perlustration, as well as censorship and propaganda. By 1918, the British employed the same per capita proportion of censors as would the Soviet Union in the 1920s. Holquist, "'Information is the Alpha and Omega,'" 422, 440. The British also sought not just to record but also to shape the mood in the trenches. Englander, "Military Intelligence." The French and German armies were no different. Becker, *The Great War*, 217–9.

134. RGASPI, f. 17, op. 84, d. 176, 196; Sakharov, *Politicheskoe zaveshchanie*, 131, 142–3.

135. The building was also numbered 5/21. The square in front of the commissariat would be renamed for Wacław Worowski, a polyglot literary critic and Soviet diplomat who was assassinated in May 1923 in Switzerland by an anti-Soviet émigré evacuated from Crimea with the White forces of Baron Wrangel. A Swiss court acquitted the assassin, judging the murder a legitimate act of retribution against the Soviet regime for its atrocities. Chistiakov, *Ubit' za Rossiiu!* The famous central Kiev artery Kreshchatik also bore Worowski's name from 1923 until 1937.

136. Liadov, *Istoriia Rossiiskogo protokola*, appendix document 2.

137. Besedovskii, *Revelations of a Soviet Diplomat*, 78–9.

138. Magerovsky, "The People's Commissariat," I: 246–53. A Soviet source gave a total of 1,066 personnel as of January 1924: *Desiat' let sovetskoi diplomatii*

139. Uldricks, *Diplomacy and Ideology*, 97–115.

140. Non-Russian Comintern representatives, known in the jargon as the "best representatives of the working class," were referred to in private as "the best friends of the Russian party." Jacobson, *When the Soviet Union Entered*, 39 (citing Kuusinen to Herbert Droz, February 5, 1923: archives de Jules Humbert Droz, I: 143).

141. Von Mayenburg, *Hotel Lux* [1978]. Baronness Ruth von Mayenburg worked for Soviet military intelligence. See also Vaksberg, *Hôtel Lux*; Von Mayenburg, *Hotel Lux* [1991]. In 1933, the original four stories would be expanded to six, bringing the hotel to 300 rooms, filled with officials and refugees from countries that outlawed Communism. (Originally Tverskaya, 36, became Gorky, 10.)

142. Soviets had to leave an identification card and fill out two questionnaires to enter the Lux; at midnight, all were supposed to be out. Kennel, "The New Innocents Abroad," 15.

143. Kuusinen, *Rings of Destiny*, 44. Besides Kuusinen, the top Comintern staff included Osip Tarshis, known as Pyatnitsky (b. 1882), a Lithuanian Jew and former carpenter; and, eventually, Dmitry Manuilsky (b. 1883), the son of an Orthodox priest from a Ukrainian village and the first secretary of the Communist party in Ukraine and a Stalin loyalist.

144. See Heimo and Tivel, *10 let Kominterna*. (The old Berg mansion went to the Italian embassy in February 1924, when diplomatic relations were restored.) The Comintern library and archives were kept in the basement, where the meetings were also held, in the so-called club room. "It was no joke sitting on narrow benches for hours on end, especially after an eight-hour workday when everyone was tired," Kuusinen's wife Aino noted. "Foreigners who did not understand Russian suffered particularly and had difficulty hiding their yawns. But no one dared to protest, or even to mention the fact that members of the Executive Committee were never to be seen at them." Kuusinen, *Rings of Destiny*, 55. The library was overseen by Allan Wallenius, a Finn who had taken a librarian's course at the New York Public Library; the archivist was Boris Reinstein.

145. Krivitsky, *In Stalin's Secret Service*, 47.

146. Kuusinen, *Rings of Destiny*, 39, 41, 59–60. Besides Pyatnitsky, Meyer Trilliser worked in the International Relations Department before moving to foreign intelligence.

147. "Posledniaia sluzhebnaia zapiska Chicherina," *Istochnik*, 1995, no. 6: 108–10; Kennan, *Russia and the West*, 177.

148. Adibekov and Shirinia, *Politbiuro TsK RKP (b)—VKP (b) i Komintern*, 76 (RGASPI, f. 17, op. 3 d. 164, l. 2). The violation of the ban on illegal activity by embassy personnel was demonstrated when, two years later, the politburo forbid Soviet diplomats from spreading revolutionary literature—unless expressly permitted (by Chicherin) to do so. RGASPI, f. 2, op. 1, d. 24 539; f. 17, op. 3, d. 158, l. 2 and d. 173, l. 2; Drachkovitch and Lazitch, *Lenin and the Comintern*, 534. The Comintern did take over funding foreign Communist parties from the foreign affairs commissariat, and began to develop its own separate set of international couriers, to the delight of Zinoviev. Adibekov and Shirinia, *Politbiuro TsK RKP (b)—VKP (b) i Komintern*, 25–6; Carr, *Bolshevik Revolution*, III: 67.

149. "In Moscow's view," Kennan continued, "non-Communist statesmen were regarded as incapable of doing good intentionally." Kennan, *Russia and the West*, 181–5.

150. Carr, *Bolshevik Revolution*, III: 67–8; Jacobson, *When the Soviet Union Entered*.

151. Stalin in *Pravda*, December 18, 1921, in *Sochineniia*, V: 118–20.

152. The Soviets, in negotiations, understood that their purchases would benefit the economies and important constituencies in those capitalist countries to whom they could appeal. Kennan, *Russia and the West*, 189–95.

153. *Pravda*, October 29, 1921.

154. Orde, *British Policy*; Maier, *Recasting Bourgeois Europe*. On Soviet participation: *Genuezskaia konferentsiia: Materialy i dokumenty* (Moscow: NKID, 1922); Ioffe, *Genuezskaia Konferentsiia*; Liubimov and Erlikh, *Genuezskaia konferentsiia*.

155. Degras, *Soviet Documents on Foreign Policy*, I: 270–2, 287–8. When Russia unilaterally announced that it could represent all six Soviet Socialist Republics at the Genoa Conference, Ukrainian leaders erupted in full fury (the new Union treaty would be signed only later that year).

156. APRF, f. 3, op. 22, d. 306, l. 8–9, Hoover Institution Archives, Volkogonov papers, container 23: Cheka note to Molotov, January 23, 1922. None of the top Bolsheviks went. The Cheka report also mentioned as a target Georgy Chicherin, who would lead the Soviet delegation, which included Maxim Litvinov, Adolf Joffe, Cristian Rakovski, Leonid Krasin, Wacław Worowski, Jānis Rudzutaks (then thirty-two years old), and Alexander Beksadyan (foreign affairs commissar of Armenia).

157. Lenin, "V. M. Molotovu dlia chlenov politbiuro TsK RKP (b)," *PSS*, LIV: 136–7.

158. Lenin added, characteristically, "Of course this must not be mentioned even in secret documents." Pipes, *Unknown Lenin*, 144–5. Chicherin was also under Lenin's strict instructions to remain silent about the inevitability of another imperialist war, the overthrow of capitalism, and so on. Carr and Davies, *Foundations of a Planned Economy*, III/i: 120.

159. White, *Origins of Détente*; Fink, *The Genoa Conference*.

160. In Britain, Lord Curzon and Winston Churchill were the anti-Bolshevik intransigents, opposed to Lloyd George's initiative, but Lenin judged Lloyd George to be the tip of the British imperialist spear. *DBFP*, VIII: 280–306. See also O'Connor, *Engineer of Revolution*; and Khromov, *Leonid Krasin*, 64–82.

161. On Genoa, see Ernest Hemingway, "Russian Girls at Genoa," *Toronto Daily Star*, April 13, 1922, reprinted in *Hemingway By-Line: 75 Articles and Dispacthes of Four Decades* (London: Penguin, 1968), 46–7. See also

Eastman, *Love and Revolution*, 285–90; Degras, *Soviet Documents on Foreign Policy*, I: 298–301 (Chicherin speech). Soviet-German bilateral negotiations had actually commenced over repatriation of Russian POWs. Williams, "Russian War Prisoners"; Shapiro, *Soviet Treaty Series*, I: 40–1. Gustav Hilger, who had been educated in Russian as well as German schools and returned to Soviet Russia in 1919, aged twenty-four, as a machine-construction engineer, oversaw the repatriations: Hilger and Meyer, *Incompatible Allies*, 25. Far from everyone was repatriated; émigrés numbered about 500,000 in Europe by 1921.

162. Peter Krüger, "A Rainy Day, April 16, 1922: The Rapallo Treaty and the Cloudy Perspective for German Foreign Policy," in Fink, *Genoa, Rapallo, and European Reconstruction*, 49–64.

163. Kennan, *Russia and the West*, 198–21; Fink, *Genoa Conference*. See also White, *Origins of Détente*.

164. *Dokumenty vneshnei politiki*, V: 226 (Litvinov).

165. *Izvestiia*, May 10, 1922; *Sbornik deistvuiushchikh dogovorv soglashenii*, III: 36–8. Lenin had also made sure to negotiate a separate treaty with Italy as well, to sow discord among the great powers, but after that treaty was signed (May 1922), he failed to ratify it.

166. Lenin had told Moscow party activists on December 6, 1920, that "although she is herself imperialist, Germany is obliged to seek for an ally against world imperialism, because she has been crushed. That is the situation we must turn to our advantage." "Doklad o kontsessiiakh," *PSS*, 55–78 (at 68).

167. Sandomirskii, *Materialy Genuezskoi konferentsii*, 327–8; Eudin and Fisher, *Soviet Russia and the West*, 202 (Chicherin to Barthou, April 29, 1922).

168. Gorlov, *Sovershenno sekretno, Moskva-Berlin, 1920–1933*; Müller, *Das Tor zur Weltmacht*; Zeidler, *Reichswehr und Rote Armee* [1993]; Erickson, *Soviet High Command* [1962], 247–82. On August 19, 1922, Krestinsky, the newly named Soviet envoy to Berlin, wrote to Trotsky, with a copy to Stalin, requesting they send a military figure to Berlin, like Frunze or Tukhachevsky. RGASPI, f. 558, op. 11, d. 755, l. 1. Bukharin gave a general speech at the Comintern Congress in November 1922, explaining that a worker state could sign military alliances with bourgeois great powers, just as it could accept loans. *IV Vsemirnyi kongress*, 195–6; Eudin and Fisher, *Soviet Union and the West*, 209–10.

169. White, *Origins of Détente*, 181.

170. Jacobson, *When the Soviet Union Entered*, 90–98 (quote at 98).

171. Germany spent a small fortune

beginning in April 1922 to blame Poincaré and France for the Great War (a supposed revenge for the loss of Alsace-Lorraine in 1870), a propaganda blitz in which the Soviets eagerly participated, seeking to further discredit Nicholas II by portraying the war as a Franco-tsarist Russian aggression. Keiger, *Raymond Poincaré*, 288–91; Mombauer, *Origins of the First World War*, 200.

172. Fisher, *Famine*, 300; *Golod 1921–1922*; Lubny-Gertsyk, *Dvizhenie naseleniia na territorii SSSR*; and Adamets, *Guerre civile et famine en Russie*. *Pravda* (June 30, 1921) warned of the catastrophe early. The food supply commissariat foresaw a catastrophic procurement of less than 4.3 million tons (5.4 million had been procured in 1920); the actual amount from the tax would be around 2.7 million. Piat' let vlasti Sovetov, 373; Genkina, *Perekhod*, 302. In 1928, an outside expert estimated that between 1916 and 1924, 8 to 10 million people had died from epidemics. Grant, *Medical Review of Soviet Russia*, 15.

173. Fisher, *Famine*, 96. See also Pethybridge, *One Step Backwards*, 91–119. Fridtjof Nansen, the Norwegian relief coordinator, vacillated in his estimates of population subjected to intense hunger, either 20 to 30 million (September 1921) or 50 million (1922). League of Nations, *Records of the ... Assembly*, II: 545, III: 59. See also Graziosi, "State and Peasants," 65–117 (at 100).

174. Wehner and Petrov, "Golod 1921–1922 gg.," 223 (citing GARF, f. 1065, op. 1, d. 86, l. 12). Some people profited from the crisis: while passengers clamoring for seats on trains were turned away, a guard on a rail express train route in 1922 used an entire compartment, as well as the toilet, to stock salt, the currency of trade, and had his wife conduct transactions at station stops—"so many pounds of salt for a goose, so many for a suckling pig"—which could be resold at astronomical markups in blighted areas the train traveled through. Mackenzie, *Russia Before Dawn*, 229.

175. Logachev, "'V khlebnom raoine Zapadnoi Sibiri': ot prodraverstka k golodu," 36–43.

176. Beisembaev, *Lenin i Kazakhstan*, 325–6.

177. Dzerzhinskii, *Feliks Dzerzhinskii: dnevnik zakliuchennogo*, 229–30; Tishkov, *Dzerzhinskii* [1976], 335–8; Bartashevich, "Moskva zhdet ... khleba," 34–7; Plekhanov and Plekhanov, *F. E. Dzerzhinskii*, 368–9.

178. Berelowich and Danilov; *Sovetskaia derevnia glazami*, I: 572–4 (TsA FSB, 1, op. 6, d. 461, l. 69–76).

179. Edmondson, "The Politics of Hunger." "Instead of the peasantry

relieving the cities," one historian aptly summarized, "millions of peasants themselves became objects of relief." Siegelbaum, *Soviet State and Society*, 89.

180. Patenaude, *Big Show in Bololand*; *Itogi posledgol s 15/X-1922 g. 1/VIII-1923 g.* (Moscow: Tsentral'naia komissiia pomoshchi golodayushchim, 1923), 65. The ARA delivered 784,000 tons of food aid. Total food imports would exceed 2 million tons, including the foreign purchases. Fisher, *Famine*, 298n, 554.

181. As cited in H. Johnson, *Strana i mir*, 1992, no. 2: 21. The ARA benefitted from the Bolsheviks' ruthlessness in clampdowns on railroad workers and others. The regime used Red Army soldiers to guard the trainloads of relief grain being shipped to stricken areas (the soldiers were allotted rations, but if the delivery trains ended up taking longer than expected, many soldiers would arrive at their destination nearly dead themselves). Fisher, *Famine*, 181, 191.

182. *PSS*, XLV: 122, 127, L: 187, 388–9; Golikov, *Vladimir Il'ich Lenin*, VIII: 366, XI: 509; McNeal, *Stalin*, 48; Hoover Institution Archives, Volkogonov papers, container 23.

183. The Bolsheviks assumed the ARA would prioritize feeding "class enemies" of the regime. In fact, Hoover ordered relief workers not even to discuss politics, let alone organize politically, believing that the ARA's example of efficiency would inspire the Russian people to overthrow Bolshevism. Some observers wondered if such a process had perhaps begun. On May 28, 1923, Boris Bakhmeteff, the Provisional Government's ambassador to the United States, wrote to a confidant (Yekaterina Kuskova) about a conversation with Hoover. "Not long ago he very persuasively related to me that in his opinion the formation of surpluses among the peasants will lead to a confrontation with the existing system of Bolshevik rule," wrote Bakhmeteff. "Agents [of the ARA] have correctly apprised Hoover of the pressure on prices of these surpluses and of the natural growth among peasants of the idea that they should bring this grain to market to sell at the highest possible price. As a result of the expansion of this phenomenon, that is, the growth of grain surpluses, landholders will naturally want to sell these surpluses at the maximal highest prices, and a maximal price signifies the conditions of free world trade. I think that Hoover is right and that the antagonism of this natural and insurmountable instinct to receive for one's grain the highest price will become one of the strongest and unconquerable enemies of the Bolshevik system." Pavel Nikolaevich

Miliukov Papers, ca. 1879–1970, Columbia Unviersity, box 1. See also Budnitskii, "Boris Bakhmeteff's Intellectual Legacy"; and Engerman, *Modernization*, 116.

184. It took some time for the NEP to take hold. The term "NEP" was not even used until two months after the policy had been introduced. In Ukraine the NEP's introduction was delayed; in Siberia, only a few districts were initially shifted to the tax in kind from mandatory delivery quotas. *Izvestiia*, March 23, 1921; *PSS*, XLIII: 62; *Pravda*, March 21, 1921; Chamberlin, *Russian Revolution*, II: 502–3; A. M. Bol'shakov, "The Countryside 1917–1924," in Smith, *Russian Peasant*, 48. One provincial party official argued that tax collection "proceed as in war, in the full sense of the word." Quoted in Radkey, *Unknown Civil War*, 366–7. The NEP-era tax collectors often were the previous gunpoint-requisitioners. Gimpel'son, *Sovetskie upravlentsy*.

185. Carr, *Bolshevik Revolution*, II: 289, 295–6.

186. Atkinson, *End of the Russian Land Commune*, 235.

187. In 1928, Alexei Shchusev designed a colossal new headquarters for the agriculture commissariat at Orlikov Lane, no. 1, in constructivist style. That same year, Smirnov was sacked. The next year, a USSR agriculture commissariat was established. Shchusev's masterpiece would be completed in 1933.

188. Heinzen, *Inventing a Soviet Countryside*, 104–35.

189. By 1927, the agriculture commissariat would employ one in five Soviet commissariat personnel. Heinzen, *Inventing a Soviet Countryside*, 93–4; *Gosudarstvennyi apparat SSSR*, 16, 104–5. The statistics commissariat was the fourth largest.

190. Even then, no commissariat received the full amount of funding it sought: the war commissariat received just 37 percent of requests in 1919. Malle, *Economic Organization of War Communism*, 172–82. The dyes for printing money had to be purchased abroad for gold.

191. As of early 1918, £1 sterling could be purchased for R45; one year later, the number was 400, and by the middle of 1920 £1 cost R10,000, an increase of 222 times; the German mark against the ruble, during the same period, rose from 1 to 1 to around 100 to 1. By fall 1921, following the introduction of the NEP, black currency markets had become fully open, even though such exchange would not be formally legalized until April 1922. Feitelberg, *Das Papiergeldwesen*, 50.

192. Aliamkin and Baranov, *Istoriia denezhnogo obrashcheniia*, 194–5.

193. Katsenellenbaum, *Russian Currency*, 10.

194. Preobrazhenskii, *Bumazhnye den'gi*, 4. See also Arnold, *Banks, Credit, and Money*, 95–6; Feldman, *The Great Disorder*; Fergusson, *When Money Dies*.

195. G. Ia. Sokol'nikov, "Avtobiografiia," in Gambarov, *Entsiklopedicheskii slovar'*, XLI/iii: 73–88, republished in Anfert'ev, *Smerch*, 190–205, and in Sokol'nikov, *Novaia finansovaia politika*, 39–50; Oppenheim, "Between Right and Left"; Carr, *Bolshevik Revolution*, II: 351. Krestinsky was made envoy to Berlin.

196. *Pravda*, February 14, 1919 (Stalin); Genis, "G. Ia. Sokolnikov." On the sealed train see Sokolnikov, in Anfert'ev, *Smerch*, 193. It may have been Sokolnikov, rather than Trotsky, who originally suggested coordinating the October 1917 coup with the opening of the 2nd Congress of Soviets. Rubtsov, "Voenno-politcheskaia deiatel'nost' G. Ia. Sokol'nikova," 47.

197. *Pravda*, December 10, 1917; Sokol'nikov, *K voprosu o natsionalizatsii bankov*; Sokolov, *Finansovaia politika Sovetskoi vlasti*, esp. 22–27.

198. Zinoviev refused to go, which is how the task fell to Sokolnikov. Ivan A. Anfert'ev, "Vozvrashchenie Sokol'nikova," in Anfert'ev, *Smerch*, 158–89, and "Neizvestnyi Sokol'nikov," *Vozvrashchenye imena* (Moscow: Novosti, 1989), II: 223–42 (at 224–5); Sokol'nikov, *Brestskii mir*.

199. In 1919 at the 8th Party Congress Lenin entrusted him with presenting the case against the "military opposition" of Voroshilov and others and their partisan-warfare tactics. Back at the front, Sokolnikov wrote a denunciation of the First Cavalry Army's undisciplined, drunken pillaging of the Don Valley civilian population after a victory, thereby eliciting Semyon Budyonny's everlasting hatred. In July 1920, Trotsky asked Sokolnikov to deliver a course of lectures at the General Staff Academy so that, "in addition to the lectures, socialist literature would be enriched by a good book on military matters." *VIII s"ezd RKP (b)* [1959], 144–52, 273 (for the vote on Sokolnikov's theses); Sokol'nikov, "Avtobiografiia," in Anfert'ev, *Smerch*, 190–205 (at 200); Budennyi, *Proidennyi put'*, I: 374–406. Chigir, "Grigorii Iakovlevich Sokol'nikov," 63 (citing RGASPI, f. 760, op. 1, d. 71, l. 124).

200. Golikov, *Vladimir Il'ich Lenin*, IX: 108, 159.

201. G. Ia. Sokol'nikov, "Liquidatsiia Turkestanskogo rublia," *Pravda*, December 30, 1920.

202. Arnold, *Banks, Credit and Money*, 126; Iurovskii, "Arkhitektor denezhnoi reform," at 141; Katzenellenbaum, *Russian Currency and Banking*, 149–52; Nikolaev, "Na puti k denezhnoi

reforme 1922–1924 godov," 89. Katzenellenbaum worked under Sokolnikov. Efforts at private bank restoration had actually begun in the fall of 1919 but did not bear fruit until 1921, when the regime sought to reestablish normal trade relations, which also required determining a value for tsarist-era debts. On Sokolnikov's health problems, see V. Rozanov, "Vladimir Il'ich Lenin," *Krasnaia nov'*, 1924, no. 6: at 153. The State Bank was located at Neglinka, 12, in a solid two-story structure, with allegorical figures on the façade; it had been the Moscow branch of the imperial Russian State Bank built in 1894 on the site of the Vorontsov clan gardens. The vaults (Gokhran) were at Nastasinsky Lane, in the former Moscow Treasury building, built in 1913–16 in the style of the seventeenth century (called Moscow Baroque or neo-Byzantine).
203. Al'tman, "Lichnost' reformatora," 159. Details on the monetary reforms can be found in *Finansovaia politika Sovetsko*; and Sokolov, *Finansovaia politika Sovetskogo gosudarstva*; *Denezhnaia reforma*; Atlas, *Ocherki po istorii denezhnogo obrashcheniia*. Atlas (b. 1903) presents the story of monetary reform without mentioning Sokolnikov's name, an oddity related to the date of his book's publication (1940). He was the top person (professor) in the department of monetary circulation and credit in capitalist countries and the USSR at the economics institute of the USSR Academy of Sciences.
204. Atlas, *Ocherki po istorii denezhnogo obrashcheniia*, 196 (who, again, fails to mention Sokolnikov's name); Goland, "Currency Regulation"; David Woodruff, "The Politburo on Gold, Industrialization, and the International Economy, 1925–1926," in Gregory and Naimark, *Lost Politburo Transcripts*, 199–223. Herbert Hoover, when he learned in 1923 of renewed Soviet exports of food—which, unbeknownst to him, went to pay for imports of rifles and machine guns—suspended ARA operations. Pipes, *Russia Under the Bolshevik Regime*, 418–9.
205. Katzenellenbaum, *Russian Currency and Banking*, 84–8, 105, 145. The ruble went from 10,000 to 1 (January 1, 1922), 100 to 1 (January 1, 1923), and 50,000 to 1 (March 7, 1924). Lawton, *Economic History of Soviet Russia*, I: 151.
206. Goland, *Diskusii ob ekonomicheskoi politike*. 1924 would be the last such surplus of the NEP.
207. In 1924–5, vodka would deliver 500 million rubles to the budget—a spectacular, embarrassing revival of the "drunken budget" of the old regime. Carr, *Interregnum*, 43, n5.
208. Kvashonkin, *Bol'shevistskoe*

*rukovodstvo*, 278 (RGASPI, f. 76, op. 3, d. 231, l. 2).
209. Galina Serebriakova, "Iz vospominanii," in Anfert'ev, *Smerch*, 230–49 (at 234).
210. Mau, *Reformy i dogmy*, 137–51.
211. *XI s"ezd RKP (b)*, 360–1. Larin, in the mid-1920s, recanted utterly: "I think it's safe to say that, first, this is the most intelligent of our commissariats, and secondly, it is the only commissariat with a clear economic line at any time." Quoted in Genis, "Upriamyi narkom s Il'inki," in Sokol'nikov, *Novaia finansovaia politika*, 5–38 (at 19).
212. Carr, *Socialism in One Country*, I: 490. The Workers and Peasants Inspectorate fought for its prerogatives against the finance commissariat.
213. Mikhail Koltsov, the talented young journalist, dubbed Sokolnikov "the stubborn commissar from Ilinka," who imposed all manner of taxes and restrictions—which, however, had conjured into being a real currency and economic stabilization. Kol'tsov, *Izbrannoe*, 39.
214. The society began with sixty-four members, who participated in commemorative evenings and published memoirs. Inside the regime, in parallel, tensions arose over the notion of Old Bolsheviks and whether comparative length of party membership should be treated as a kind of seniority. By 1925, when the party would nearly double in size to 1.1 million members and candidates, just 8,500 of them (0.8 percent) had joined before 1917, and a mere 2,000 (0.2 percent) before 1905 (the earliest date in order to be eligible members of the society). *XIV s"ezd VKP (b)*, 460; Korzhikhina, "Obshchestvo starykh Bol'shevikov," 50–65. *Ustav obshchestva starykh bol'shevikov*; *Rezoliutsii i postanovleniia pervoi Vsesoiuznoi konferentsii Obshchestva starykh bol'shevikov*; *Spisok chlenov Vsesoiuznogo obshchestvo starykh bol'shevikov*.
215. Rigby, "The Soviet Political Elite," 419–20. Rigby points out that only 13 percent of the delegates to the 9th Congress had attended party congresses before the October Revolution: at the 10th Congress, the proportion fell to 5 percent. *IX s"ezd RKP (b)*, 483; *X s"ezd RKP (b)*, 762.
216. Lenin, characteristically, fretted about dilution of the party from admitting too many workers, because many had only recently arrived from a "petty-bourgeois" village milieu, complaining to Molotov that "the proletarian policy of the party is determined not by its composition, but by the immense, indivisible authority of its narrowest stratum, which could be called the old party guard." But most other high officials were embarrassed about the glaring dearth of worker

members in a worker party. *PSS*, XLV: 17–20; Kvashonkin, *Bol'shevistskoe rukovodstvo*, 239–41 (RGASPI, f. 5, op. 2, d. 27, l. 9–10).
217. In the factories, most party members as of 1921 were managers and administrators, not proletarians. The 10th Party Congress reprioritized recruitment of workers, a goal reaffirmed at the 11th Party Congress. Chase, *Workers, Society, and the Soviet State*, 50–1; *X s"ezd*, 236–41, 284, 564; Rigby, *Communist Party Membership*, 93–5.
218. Rigby, "The Soviet Political Elite." See also Raleigh, *Experiencing Russia's Civil War*, 132.
219. "The obvious prominence of the lower-middle strata necessitates rethinking many problems of the revolution," one scholar has correctly noted. "It has been like a missing puzzle piece whose placement permits many new connections." Daniel T. Orlovsky, "State Building in the Civil War Era: The Role of the Lower Middle Strata," in Koenker, *Party, State, and Society*, 180–209 (at 203, n3). See also Buldakov, *Bor'ba za massy*, 164–256; and Hunt, *Politics, Culture, and Class*.
220. "Moi ded, Viacheslav Molotov, ne platil Leninu gonorarov," *Rodnaia gazeta*, May 20, 2005 (interview with Viacheslav Nikonov).
221. Nikonov, *Molotov*, 88, 91–2, 109–13.
222. Watson, *Molotov and Soviet Government*, 43.
223. Bazhanov, *Vospominaniia* [1990], 179.
224. Kuibyshev, *Epizody iz moei zhizni*; Elena Kuibysheva, *Valerian Vladimirovich Kuibyshev*; Berezov, *Valerian Vladimirovich Kuybyshev*; G. V. Kuibysheva, *Valerian Vladimirovich Kuibyshev*; Khromov and Kuibysheva, *Valerian Vladimirovich Kuibyshev*; Flerov, V. V. Kuibyshev; Buzurbaev, *Kuibyshev v Sibiri*; Erofeev, *Valerian Kuibyshev v Samare*.
225. Schapiro, *Communist Party of the Soviet Union*, 260–2; Schapiro, *Origin of the Communist Autocracy* 1977 ed., 288–9. Kuibyshev had replaced Mikhailov in the party secretariat.
226. Trotsky, *Stalin School of Falsification*, 126.
227. Kuibyshev appeared in a compendium of top regime figures, which mostly included politburo members and candidates (Molotov was not included). Volin, *12 biografii*. The twelve, alphabetical in Russian, were Bukharin, Dzierżyński, Zinoviev, Kalinin, Kamenev, Kuibyshev, Rykov, Smirnov, Stalin, Tomsky, Trotsky, and Frunze.
228. Rees, "Iron Lazar," 1–59.
229. "I always laughed at that. I told Makhover, for example, in the presence of everyone, 'You'll never resemble Stalin, you have a different brain

and anyway the main thing is you lack a mustache.'" Balashov and Markhashov, "Staraia ploshchad', 4 (20-e gody)," no. 5: 195. Balashov was short, 153 cm (about five feet).

230. In 1923, Kaganovich noted that entire branches of industry were concentrated in the hands of unverified non-party people, sometimes even not the best non-party specialists but "slick careerists" (lovkikh proidokh). The upshot, he insisted, was that the party had to get involved and insert its people. Pavliuchenko, Rossiia Nepovskaia "Orden mechenostsev," 68 (citing f. 17, op. 68, d. 49, l. 28–31).

231. Bazhanov, Avec Staline dans le Kremlin, 58.

232. On April 7, 1925, Stalin would name Kaganovich party boss in Ukraine, one of the three strategic party organizations, alongside Moscow and Leningrad. Rees, "Iron Lazar," 17. Kaganovich would not obtain an entry in Granat's 1925 bibliography of the top 240 leading personages of the Soviet Union, but he belonged to the innermost core of Stalin's machine. Gambarov, Entsiklopedicheskii slovar'.

233. "Kalinin is a good fellow and for us an irreplaceable person," Voroshilov wrote to Orjonikidze after a spring 1923 trip across the North Caucasus (Dagestan, Chechnya, Vladikavkaz, Nalchik). "In order to judge him properly, one needs to travel with him to villages and hear his conversations with peasants; here, he is utterly in his all peculiar beauty and, I should say straight out, force. One cannot find another like him in our party. Very few can like him set out our theory and practice to the peasants. . . . I had thought he was a bit of a lummox, but now I repent and beg forgiveness from Allah for my sins. I suggested to Kalinin that he visit you in Tiflis, but he clearly explained to me that without permission from the Central Committee he could not do such things." Kvashonkin, Bol'shevistskoe rukovodstvo, 274 (RGASPI, f. 85, op. 24, d. 150, l. 1–2).

234. Sergei Minin, the top Tsaritsyn Bolshevik, would side with the anti-Stalin opposition at the 14th Party Congress in 1925. He appears to have fallen mentally ill by 1927. Minin would survive the terror and live until 1962. Pravda, June 29, 1962. Alexander Chervyakov, the Donbass miner who served as head of the Cheka in Tsaritsyn, returned to his native Ukraine in 1919 after the reestablishment of a Bolshevik regime there, and served as deputy chairman of the Ukraine Cheka. In 1921, he was demoted to a party position in Zhitomir; for a time, he served on the commission for the struggle against famine in Zaporozhe. In 1922, he was transferred over to the Soviet executive committee of Ukraine. He would also survive the terror. With the war's approach to Moscow, he would volunteer for the front but survive by being mostly in the rear. After the war he would teach and write; he would die in 1966. This Chervyakov (Alexander Ivanovich) is not to be confused with Alexander Grigoryevich Chervyakov (1892–1937), who helped found the Belorussian SSR, served in the USSR central executive committee, and committed suicide on June 16, 1937, during an intermission of a Belorussian party conference.

235. Nazarov, Stalin i bor'ba za liderstvo, 93.

236. Nazaretyan was the courier Stalin entrusted with delivering his private letters to Lenin (or Trotsky), and the person Stalin assigned to draft many Central Committee circulars. Bazhanov, Vospominaniia [1983], 53. Kun, Unknown Portrait, 286–8.

237. Rusanova, "I. P. Tovstukha." From 1924 to 1926, Stalin would send him over to the Lenin Institute, as an aide to the director, responsible for Lenin's archive and Collected Works. In 1930–1, Stalin sent Tovstukha back to the Institute of Marx-Engels-Lenin as deputy director and head of the archives. He would die in August 1935, and his ashes would be interred in the Kremlin Wall.

238. Nazaretyan, complaining of overwork, after a stint at Pravda on Stalin's behalf, was returned to Georgia. Proletarskaia revoliutsiia, 1935, no. 6: 129–31.

239. Rubtsov, Iz-za spiny vozhdia, 33.

240. Balashov and Markhashov, "Staraia ploshchad', 4 (20-e gody)," no. 6: 184–5.

241. Demidov, Politicheskaia bor'ba i oppozitsiia, 61–72; Medvedev, On Stalin and Stalinism, 25. Malenkov entered a technical university in Moscow in 1921, where he became the party secretary; his wife, Valeria Golubtsova (whose aunt knew Lenin), got hired in the orgburo and obtained an apartment among the trading rows near the Kremlin at the former Loskutnaya Hotel (House of Soviets no. 5), where many young apparatchiks lived. Malenkov received an invitation to join the central apparatus in 1924, becoming a protégé of Poskryobyshev, responsible for record-keeping on personnel. Nikolai Yezhov (b. 1895) would enter Stalin's apparatus in 1927, as Poskryobyshev was gaining ever greater responsibility, and become Malenkov's new patron. Danilov, Tragediia Sovetskoi derevni, III: 850; Petrov, Kto rukovodil NKVD, 184–6; Rosenfeldt, Knowledge and Power, 131–2. The Loskutnaya Hotel would become the headquarters of Moscow metro construction in the early 1930s; in 1938, it was torn down as the site was opened for a larger square as part of Moscow's reconstruction.

242. Rees, "Iron Lazar," 33–5.

243. "One of the most talented and brilliant Bolshevik leaders," wrote Bazhanov (who worked in both Stalin's secretariat, under Kaganovich, and in the finance commissariat, under Sokolnikov). "Whatever assignments he was given, he handled them." Bazhanov, Vospominaniia [1990], 122.

244. "Our dear, talented, and most valuable in practical matters Sokolnikov does not understand anything in trade. And he will bury us, if given the chance," Lenin complained to Kamenev in a letter. At the same time, Lenin called Sokolnikov's book State Capitalism and the New Financial Policy "very successful." Lenin, PSS, XLIV: 428, LIV: 90. Lenin's Collected Works (vol. LIV) contain considerable correspondence with Sokolnikov in 1921–22.

245. In 1908, Chicherin had a falling out with Lenin and went over to the Mensheviks. In 1917, the British jailed him for preaching peace and socialism (which they deemed to be pro-German, anti-Entente sentiments). Trotsky obtained Chicherin's release in exchange for resuming the granting of visas and diplomatic couriers for the British. He became Trotsky's deputy at foreign affairs, then, quickly, his replacement. Debo, Revolution and Survival, 34–41. See also Debo, "The Making of a Bolshevik"; O'Connor, Diplomacy and Revolution. Chicherin was a leftist. In January 1922, for example, he expressed alarm that, from abroad, "people are sending newspapers by mail to private persons. To allow this means to restore the possibility of press agitation against us. Glaring examples of the White Guard press will circulate in Moscow." Goriaeva, Istoriia sovetskoi politicheskoi tsenzury, 427–8.

246. When Litvinov instead joined the army, despite poor eyesight, he mastered Russian and became familiar with underground revolutionary literature. Stationed in Baku, in 1898, he refused to fire upon a crowd of striking workers and was discharged. Georgii Cherniavskii, "Fenomenon Litvinova," XX Vek: istoriia Rossii i SSSR, January 22, 1924.

247. In the U.K. still, Litvinov was arrested on September 8, 1918, and charged with encouraging Bolshevik propaganda; released after ten days, he was exchanged for the incarcerated British spy Bruce Lockhart. Pope, Maksim Litvinoff, 129–30.

248. Sheinis, "Pervye shagi diplomaticheskoi deiatel'nosti M. M. Litvinov," 153; Hilger and Meyer, Incompatible Allies, 110–2.

249. Voroshilov detested Litvinov. Dullin, *Men of Influence*, 13 (citing *Zvezda* [Odessa], September 21, 1928).

250. Bazhanov, *Bazhanov and the Damnation of Stalin*, 88–9.

251. "Posledniaia sluzhebnaia zapiska Chicherina," *Istochnik*, 1995, no. 6: 100.

252. Georgii Cherniavskii, "Fenomenon Litvinova," *XX Vek: istoriia Rossii i SSSR*, February 4, 1924. An especially unsympathetic portrait of Litvinov can be found in the defector Dmitrievskii [Dmitriev], *Sovetskie portrety*, 240–52, translated as *Dans les coulisses du Kremlin* (Paris: Plon, 1933), 182–207.

253. Ivanov, *Neizvestnyi Dzerzhinskii*; Plekhanov, *Dzerzhinskii*; Plekhanov and Plekhanov, *Zheleznyi Feliks*.

254. Sinyavsky, *Soviet Civilization*, 126 (no citation). The arrested Christian philosopher Nikolai Berdyaev, after an interrogation in the Lubyanka inner prison, wrote that "Dzierżyński gave the impression of a person who was completely convinced and sincere. He was a fanatic.... In the past he had wanted to become a Catholic monk, and he transferred his fanatical faith to Communism." Berdiaev, *Samopoznanie*, 215.

255. *Dvadtsat' let VChK-OGPU-NKVD*, 20–3; Blobaum, *Feliks Dzierżyński*.

256. Tishkov, *Dzherzhinskii* [1976], 75, 78. Once, despite being himself in a weakened state, he is said to have carried an ailing cellmate on his back when they were allowed out to the prison courtyard. Dmitriev, *Pervyi chekist*, 53–62.

257. Sheridan, *From Mayfair to Moscow*, 95.

258. Plekhanov, *VChK-OGPU*, 227 (no citation); Shteinberg, *Ekab Peters*, 119; Viktor Baklanov, "Slovo Dzherzhinskomu," *Gazeta "Dos'e*," November 3, 2002. Victor Chernov called Dzierżyński "a genuine monk-ascetic. And really a good person." D. A. Lutokhin, "Zarubezhnye pastyri," *Minuvshee*, 1997: 71.

259. Ostensibly to prevent operational data from being revealed, Mężyński instructed OGPU officials not to turn over to the procuracy any documents concerning political crimes—thereby thwarting the provision of procuracy supervision of arrests. Kvashonkin, *Bol'shevistskoe rukovodstvo*, 305; Zdanovich, *Organy gosudarstvennoi bezopasnosti*, 142–3, citing TsA FSB, f. 2, op. 3, d. 60, l. 40; Fomin, *Zapiski starogo chekista*, 214. Fomin headed the border guards in the North Caucasus, so he saw a lot of Cheka visitors to the Kislovodsk spa. The daughter of a Soviet diplomat in Berlin recalled Mężyński "as taciturn, gloomy, and extremely polite—he even addressed

me [she was then twelve] with the formal 'You.'" Ioffe, *Vremia nazad*, ch. 2.

260. Deacon, *History of the Russian Secret Service*, 286–7 (unfootnoted).

261. Fomin, *Zapiski starogo chekista*, 220–1; Mozokhin and Gladkov, *Menzhinskii*, 166–74.

262. Vinogradov, *Genrikh Iagoda*, 17.

263. Plekhanov, *VChK-OGPU*, 278–9. Yagoda would rebuild the Lubyanka building, erect the NKVD club and the Dynamo Stadium for police-sponsored sports teams, and oversee a plethora of monumental forced labor construction projects.

264. Vinogradov, *Genrikh Iagoda*, 273–5.

265. Gladkov, *Nagrada za vernost'—kazn'*; Kuvarzin, *Dorogami neskonchaemykh bitv*, 53; Tumshis and Papchinskii, *1937, bol'shaia chistka*, 295.

266. Frunze remarked that "I have data that secret information from the staff of the Red Army is leaking abroad. I, for example, receive information about directives earlier from Poland than from Moscow." Mikhaleva, *Revvoensovet Respubliki*, 335.

267. Vinogradov, *Genrikh Yagoda*, 312–7 (TsA FSB, f. 1, op. 6, d. 37, l. 102–3). See also Plekhanov, *VChK-OGPU*, 228; and *Istochnik*, 1995, no. 6: 154–5 (APRF f. 32, op. 1, d. 1, l. 27–27ob: Unszlicht, April 21, 1922).

268. The operative Jan Berzin was briefly imprisoned. Dzierżyński admitted the latter's fondness for trinkets such as gold rings and watches, but had him released. Gerson, *The Secret Police*, 69–70 (citing *Pravda*, December 25 and December 26, 1918).

269. Ward, *Stalin's Russia*, 36–7.

270. RGASPI, f. 558, op. 1, d. 1594, l. 3; Gromov, *Stalin*, 72.

271. *Leninskii sbornik*, XXXVI: 122; *Biulleten' oppozitsii*, 1933, no. 36–7: 10.

272. Trotsky, *My Life*, 477.

273. Trotsky, *Stalin*, 389 (quoting Serebryakov, who claimed to have heard it from Yenukidze).

274. Trotskii, *Portrety revoliutsionerov*, 54–5.

275. Ilizarov, "Stalin"; Gromov, *Stalin*, 57–9; Volkogonov, *Triumf i tragediia*, I/ii: 118.

276. Bazhanov, *Bazhanov and the Damnation of Stalin*, 105–6.

277. "Stalin Closely Observed," in Urban, *Stalinism*, 6–30 (at 8).

278. Ul'ianov, "Ob otnoshenii V. I. Lenina I. V. Stalina," 197.

279. *Izvestiia*, April 5, 1923.

280. *Sochineniia*, VIII: 66–8; Trotsky, *History of the Russian Revolution*, III: 1156. See also Sukhanov, *Zapiski*, IV: 32–4.

281. Getzler, *Martov*, 218 (citing *Poslednye novosti*, April 11, 1923, and *Sovremennye zapiski*, 1923, vol. 15: 368–70).

282. Budennyi, *Proidennyi put'* I: 339.

283. Trotsky, *Portraits*, 217.

284. Mikhail S. Gorbachev, "Slovo o Lenine," *Pravda*, April 21, 1990 (quoting Alexei Svidersky). Gorbachev was interested in this vignette as an example of supposed apparatus sabotage. Svidersky, under Stalin, worked in the workers and peasants inspectorate and the agriculture commissariat; he had his ashes buried in the Kremlin Wall, after dying a natural death in 1933. See also *PSS, spravochnyi tom, chast'* II: 471.

285. Kvashonkin, *Bol'shevistskoe rukovodstvo*, 256–7 (RGASPI, f. 85, op. 1/S, d. 13, l. 6). Nazaretyan also reported that he had received an apartment, from Avel Yenukidze, the Kremlin commandant. "The apartment is excellent" (Povarskaya Street, no. 11). After August 9, 1922, to Orjonikidze: "Koba is training me big time. I am undergoing a comprehensive but extremely boring education. For the time being they are trying to turn me into the consummate functionary, the most perfect controller of implementation of resolutions of the politburo, orgburo and secretariat." Nazaretyan lobbied Stalin to be moved out of the heavy paperwork position. Kvashonkin, *Bol'shevistskoe rukovodstvo*, 262–3 (RGASPI, f. 85, op 1/S, d. 13, l. 10).

286. Kvashonkin, *Bol'shevistskoe rukovodstvo*, 262–3. See also Chevychelov, *Amaiak Nazaretian*.

287. "We saw Stalin often," recalled Maria Joffe, the wife of Adolf Joffe (b. 1883), who was among the closest people to Trotsky. "We would run into him at the Bolshoi Theater premieres, in the box held by the theater management. Stalin usually showed up in the company of his close associates, among whom were Voroshilov and Kaganovich.... Very sociable, on friendly speaking terms with everyone, but there was not a truthful gesture in any of this... Stalin was an actor of rare ability, capable of changing his mask to suit any circumstance. And one of his favorite masks was precisely this one: simple, ordinary good fellow wearing his heart on his sleeve." Mariia Ioffe, "Nachalo," *Vremia i my*, 1977, no. 20: 163–92 (at 178). Maria emigrated to Israel in 1975.

288. This was established, in a major revision to the literature, by Rigby, "Was Stalin a Disloyal Patron?"

289. RGASPI, f. 558, op. 11, d. 1279, d. 1482.

290. RGASPI, f. 558, op. 11, d. 1289, l. 22

291. Mikoian, *Tak bylo*, 357.

292. Mikoian, *Tak bylo*, 351–2.

293. In 1930, some of the land would go to the construction of an elite sanitorium named Barvikha.

294. Alliluev, *Khronika odnoi sem'i*, 29; *Iosif Stalin v ob"iatiiakh sem'i*, 177.

295. Sergeev and Glushik, *Besedy o Staline.*

296. Stalin's dacha settlement was designated Zubalovo-4. Dzierżyński's was in Gorky-2, where he established a GPU state farm to feed the elite. Molotov was also in Gorky-2 (from the late 1920s).

297. http://protown.ru/information/hide/6965.html (Alexander Bek interview of Fotiyeva).

298. "K istorii polsednikh Leninskikh dokumentov: Iz arkhiva pisatelia Aleksandra Beka, besedovavsheo v 1967 godu s lichnyi sekretariami Lenina," *Moskovskie novosti,* April 23, 1989: 8–9.

299. McNeal, *Stalin,* 46–7.

300. Kvashonkin, *Bol'shevistskoe rukovodstvo,* 262–3. See also Chevychelov, *Amaiak Nazaretian.*

301. Balashov and Markhashov, "Staraia ploshchad', 4 (20-e gody)," no. 5: 193–5. Stalin let Balashov enter the Institute of Red Professors in the fall of 1926.

302. Bazhanov, *Bazhanov and the Damnation of Stalin,* 93.

303. Balashov and Markhashov, "Staraia ploshchad', 4 (20-e gody)," no. 5: 194. One scholar has written that "the foundation of Stalin's power in the party was not fear: it was charm . . . when he set his mind to charming a man, he was irresistible." Charm there was aplenty, but fear as well. Montefiore, *Stalin,* 41–2.

304. Balashov added that "Stalin should see with his own eyes how the people lived, himself spend time with the masses, listen to people, but all we did was send instructions and directives to these people. The main misfortune of Stalin and of other leaders, I think, was that they spent time in the struggle over theoretical issues, all energy went to that, and concerned themselves little with living people. Is it possible to build socialism in one country, is it impossible, that's the cud they chewed from morning to night." After Balashov brought up the idea of what they would say if suddenly confronted with a live peasant, they jokingly began to call him a "kulak." Balashov and Markhashov, "Staraia ploshchad', 4 (20-e gody)," no. 5: 194-5.

305. Dan, "Bukharin o Staline," 182.

306. Balashov and Markhashov, "Staraia ploshchad', 4 (20-e gody)," no. 4: 182. Balashov, as it happened, did see Trotsky often: he shared living quarters with Vera Inber and her father, who was Trotsky's uncle. "Trotsky and his children (Sedov and his two daughters) often came to see him, other comrades, whole assemblies took place" (no. 5: 193). Balashov had met Kaganovich in Turkestan but did not follow him right away to Moscow in March 1922. Balashov had contracted malaria in Samarkand, which prompted him to ask for a transfer to Russia; once he had been transferred, Kaganovich took him in, from June 1, 1922. When Stalin named Kaganovich party boss of Ukraine, Balashov was transferred from Kaganovich's Organization and Instruction Department and became Tovstukha's assistant. Then Balashov became the politburo recording secretary, replacing Maria Burakova.

307. RGASPI, f. 558, op. 3, d. 131, l. 270–1. Van Ree, *Political Thought of Joseph Stalin,* 148.

308. On the the Soviet system as "a vast collection of personal followings," see Armstrong, *Soviet Bureaucratic Elite,* 146. One eminent scholar has suggested that the concept of patronage was the defining characteristic of the imperial Russian, Soviet, and post-Soviet polities, without, however, providing the comparisons to other systems that look remarkably similar. Hosking, "Patronage and the Russian State," which is essentially a gloss on M. N. Afanas'ev, *Klientelizm i Rossiiskaia gosudarstvennost'* (Moscow: Tsentr konstitutsionnykh issledovanii, 1997). See also Orlovsky, "Political Clientelism in Russia," 174–99; and Ransel, "Character and Style of Patron-Client Relations in Russia," among others.

309. Pipes, *Russia Under the Bolshevik Regime,* 368–9.

310. Iu. A. Shchetinov, "Rezhim lichnoi vlasti Stalina," in Kukushkin, *Rezhim lichnoi vlasti Stalina,* 19 (citing GARF. F. 5865, op. 1, d. 41: letter to Yekaterina Kuskova).

311. *PSS,* XLV: 302.

## CHAPTER 11: "REMOVE STALIN"

1. *PSS,* XLV: 345.

2. *PSS,* XLV: 346.

3. Sakharov, *Politicheskoe zaveshchanie.*

4. There were 217 strikes between August and December 1923, including 51 in Moscow. Mozokhin, *VChK-OGPU,* 26 (citing TsA FSB, f. 2, op. 1, por. 794, l. 141).

5. Important exceptions are Smith, *Bolsheviks and the National Question,* 172–212, and van Ree, "Stalin and the National Question."

6. RGASPI, f. 558, op. 1, d. 2479, l. 159–60, 272–4.

7. *Izvestiia TsK KPSS,* 1989, no. 9: 199.

8. Sakharov, *Politicheskoe zaveshchanie,* 646–7 (RGASPI, f. 5, op. 2, d. 278, l. 2; f. 558, op. 1, d. 2479, l. 262–5). The orgburo commission members included Stalin, Kuibyshev, Rakovski, Orjonikidze, and Sokolnikov, as well as representatives of the republics: Alexander Chervyakov (Belorussia), Grigory Petrovsky (Ukraine), Alexander Myasnikyan (Armenia), S. A. Aga-Maly-Ogly (Azerbaijan), and Polikarp "Budu" Mdivani (Georgia), among others.

9. *Izvestiia TsK KPSS,* 1989, no. 9: 192–3, 196. For Stalin's handwritten formal proposal, see Sakharov, *Politicheskoe zaveshchanie,* 647–8 (RGASPI, f. 558, op. 1, d. 2479, l. 241).

10. *PSS,* XLV: 556–8, n136.

11. *Izvestiia TsK KPSS,* 1989, no. 9: 198–9 (RGASPI, f. 5, op. 2, d. 28, l. 23–4: September 22, 1922); *TsK RKP (b)—VKP (b) i natsional'nyi vopros,* 78–9; Smith, *Bolsheviks and the National Question,* 181–4 (citing RGASPI, f. 5, op. 2, d. 28, l. 19–21).

12. Fotieva, *Iz zhizni,* 220.

13. *Leninskii sbornik,* XXXVI; *PSS,* XLV: 211–3. On Lenin's self-congratulation, see Lewin, *Lenin's Last Struggle,* 60.

14. Lenin, *PSS,* XLV: 211–3.

15. As one Soviet scholar tamely put it, "The head of the government of the RSFSR, V. I. Lenin, more than once indicated in his speeches, that the RSFSR in its domestic and foreign policy expressed the interests also of the Soviet republics federated with it." Filimonov, *Vozniknovenie i razvitie RSFSR kak federativnogo gosudarstva,* 22.

16. One estimate has 2 percent of writings by Marx devoted to nationalism, 25 percent by Lenin, and 50 percent by Stalin. Munck, *Difficult Dialogue,* 76.

17. Kun, *Bukharin,* 130–1.

18. Mdvani told Lenin that the Georgians would agree to "a union" of equals in a USSR but not incorporation into the RSFSR—a point Stalin had already conceded, as a politburo note to Lenin had confirmed. Kharmandanian, *Lenin i stanovlenie Zakavkazskoi federatsii,* 344; *Izvestiia TsK KPSS,* 1989, no. 9: 208.

19. Pospelov et al., *Vladimir Il'ich Lenin.* Lenin had accused Stalin of "hurriedness" in an earlier letter. At the politburo on September 28, Stalin and Kamenev exchanged notes. Kamenev: "Ilich has decided on war in defense of independence. He proposes that I meet with the Georgians." Stalin: "We need firmness against Ilich." Kamenev: "I think that given that Ilich insists, it will be worst to resist." Stalin: "I don't know. Do as you see fit." *Izvestiia TsK KPSS,* 1989, no. 9: 206, 208–9; *PSS,*

XLV: 214. Trotsky had been granted holiday from September 13, 1922, but he remained in Moscow; Kamenev was also technically on holiday.

20. Reshetar, "Lenin on the Ukraine"; Szporluk, "Lenin, 'Great Russia,' and Ukraine."

21. *Izvestiia TsK KPSS*, 1989, no. 9: 205. Lenin wrote a note to Kamenev on October 6, 1922, stating, "I have declared a fight to the death against Great Russian chauvinism," and demanding that the chairmanship of the USSR Soviet central executive committee be rotated among the member republics, and not be controlled by the RSFSR. Lenin also carried this point (Stalin wrote on Lenin's note "correct"). PSS, XLV: 214, 559, n136; Lenin, *Sochineniia*, XXXIII: 335.

22. Borys, *Sovietization of the Ukraine*.

23. PSS, XLI: 161–8 (at 164); Lenin, *Sochineniia*, XXV: 624; "Iz istorii obrazovanii SSSR," in *Izvestiia TsK KPSS*, 1989, no. 9: 191–218; 1991, no. 3: 169–82; no. 4: 158–76; no. 5: 154–76. Stalin's letter was drastically abbreviated in later editions of Lenin's works. See also van Ree, *Political Thought of Joseph Stalin*, 209.

24. Smith, "Stalin as Commissar for Nationality Affairs, 1918–1922," in Davies and Harris, *Stalin*, 51–2.

25. *Izvestiia TsK KPSS*, 1991, no. 4: 171. As Jeremy Smith almost uniquely points out, the truth about Lenin as the arch-centralizer runs exactly contrary to what is put forward in the scholarly literature (Pipes, Lewin, Carrère d'Encausse). Smith, *Bolsheviks and the National Question*, 179.

26. Orakhelashvili, *Sergo Ordzhonikidze*; Kirillov and Sverdlov, *Grigorii Konstantinovich Ordzhonikidze*; Ordzhonokidze, *Put' Bol'shevika*; Dubinskii-Mukhadze, *Ordzhonikidze*.

27. Khlevniuk, *In Stalin's Shadow*, 14, 19–20.

28. The Caucasus bureau formally resolved to form a federation on November 2–3, 1921; on November 8, Orjonikidze telegrammed Stalin, informing him that the process had been launched, and asking for the Moscow Central Committee's reaction. Smith, *Bolsheviks and the National Question*, 198–9 (citing Ordzhonikidze, *Stat'i i rechi*, I: 208; RGASPI, f. 17, op. 2, d. 231, l. 2; op. 3, d. 237, l. 2; f. 64, op. 1, d. 61, l. 16; PSS, XLIV: 255; and Kharmandarian, *Lenin i stanovleniie*, 96–8, 202–3).

29. Smith, "The Georgian Affair of 1922," 528 (citing RGASPI, f. 5, op. 2, d. 32, l. 61). Right after the Bolshevik takeover of Menshevik Georgia, a Bolshevik plenipotentiary in Azerbaijan (Behbud aga Shakhtakhtinsky) had proposed a South Caucasus federation in order to manage a host of volatile territorial disputes.

30. Gornyi, *Natsional'nyi vopros*, 144–5. Orjonikidze had taken unilateral steps to unify the South Caucasus railroad system and economy even before forcing the political union. Jones, "Establishment of Soviet Power," 622, citing *Comunisti*, the party organ in Georgia (September 1921).

31. Smith, "The Georgian Affair of 1922," 529–30 (citing Ordzhonikidze, *Stat'i i rechi*, I: 208); RGASPI, f. 17, op. 2, d. 231, l. 2. The politburo, with Lenin's approval, decreed: "Recognize as absolutely correct the federation of South Caucasus republics in principle and as unconditionally to be realized." PSS, XLIV: 255. On September 27, 1922, the day Lenin received Mdivani in Gorki, Kamenev had sent the Bolshevik leader a diagram of the USSR structure with the South Caucasus Federation. Under Stalin's original RSFSR autonomization plan, Georgia was to enter as a self-standing unit granted autonomy, like Ukraine. Smith, *Bolsheviks and the National Question*, 186 (RGASPI, f. 5, op. 2, d. 28, l. 13–4).

32. Kharmandarian, *Lenin i stanovleniie*, 218. Pilipe Makharadze, an elder statesmen of Georgian Bolsheviks, and a person heretofore known for his internationalism, complained to the Central Committee in Moscow on December 6, 1921, that the Red Army's arrival had "had the outward appearance of a foreign occupation . . . We must realize that the Georgian masses had become accustomed to the idea of an independent Georgia," meaning that Georgia should not be forced into a South Caucasus Federation. Lang, *Modern History*, 240 (no citation). Stalin sent Svanidze to Berlin. Tucker, *Stalin as Revolutionary*, 257.

33. Smith, "The Georgian Affair of 1922."

34. Suny, *Georgian Nation*, 214–5; Ordzhonikidze, *Stat'i i rechi*, I: 226ff.

35. *Sochineniia*, IV: 162, 237, 372.

36. The imperial Russian army had opposed separate national units, even insisting that three quarters of all units be eastern Slav. Trotsky welcomed the "national" units in the Red forces in 1918–1919. Ukraine's experience, however, whereby national units wanted to pursue exclusively nationally defined aims, changed his mind. But the desire for a single, integrated Red Army with a single command structure proved elusive in the borderlands of the new state. A Georgian Red Army was set up in August 1922, to blunt political dissatisfaction. Kudriashev, *Krasnaia armiia*, 17 (APRF, f. 3, op. 50, d. 251, l. 158). Some 97 percent of the officer corps in 1922 were former Mensheviks. In 1923 they instituted a draft of the "toiling classes"; one stated aim was to

spread the influence of the party on the non-party mass, especially villagers. By 1925 they had 40,000 soldiers in Georgian units. Kacharava, *Bor'ba za uprochenie sovetskoi vlasti v Gruzii*, 51–3; RGASPI, f. 5, op. 2, d. 32, l. 7–17.

37. Sakharov, *Politicheskoe zaveshchanie*, 244–7 (citing RGASPI, f. 5, op. 2, d. 26, l. 10–12).

38. PSS, XLIV: 299–300; XLV: 595, n210; Pipes, *Formation of the Soviet Union*, 274. Lenin sent a copy of his rebuke of the Georgians to Orjonikidze. On October 21, 1922, Stalin called Orjonikidze as well as Mamia Orakhelashvili, secretary of the Georgian party committee, reporting that Lenin was livid and noting that the Georgian Central Committee members had failed to code their communications, allowing interception by foreigners. Heads would roll. RGASPI, f. 558, op. 1, d. 2441, l. 1–2; d. 2491, l. 1–1ob. Other Georgians, including Makharadze, had sent private communications to Lenin, through Kamenev and Bukharin to obviate Stalin, also seeking once more to secure Georgia's entry into the Union with the same status as Ukraine or Belorussia. Kamenev and Bukharin now sent their own wires to Makharadze and others in Tiflis instructing them to desist. *Sotsialisticheskii vestnik*, January 17, 1923.

39. Kharmandarian, *Lenin i stanovleniie*, 351–4.

40. Smith, *Bolsheviks and the National Question*, 201 (citing RGASPI, f. 5, op. 2, d. 32, l. 49–50: Mikhail Okujava).

41. The other members now chosen were the Lithuanian Communist Vincas Mickevičius-Kapsukas (head of the short-lived Lithuanian Soviet Socialist Republic of 1918) and the Trotsky supporter Lev Sosnovsky, a journalist, but Mdivani objected to Sosnovsky and Stalin seized this moment to substitute his own loyalist, the Ukrainian centralizer Dmitry Manuilsky. Kharmandarian, *Lenin i stanovleniie*, 369–70; *XII s"ezd RKP (b)*, 541, 551. There is a photograph from this time of Dzierżyński, Rykov, and Yagoda with Lakoba at the Zugdid Botanical Garden in Sukhum. A similar commission, headed by Frunze, had been appointed back in May 1922 to investigate a formal protest by the Ukrainian SSR that Soviet Russia had infringed upon its sovereignty. That commission upheld both Ukraine's existence and the Central Committee's prerogatives. *TsK RKP (b)–VKP (b) i natsional'nyi vopros*, 64–6 (RGASPI, f. 17, op. 112, d. 338, l. 122–3), 67–9 (RGASPI, f. 17, op. 84, d. 326, l. 1). See also Pentkovskaia, "Rol' V. I. Lenina," 14–5; Iakubovskaia, *Stroitel'stvo soiuznogo sovetskogo sotsialisticheskogo gosudarstva*, 139–40; and Gililov, *V. I. Lenin*, 145–6.

42. Mikoyan, *Dorogoi bor'by*, 433;

Kharmandarian, *Lenin i stanovleniie*, 370.

43. Sakharov, *Politicheskoe zaveshchanie*, 250–1 (RGASPI, f. 5, op. 2, d. 32, l. 43–43ob.); Kirillov and Sverdlov, *Grigory Konstantinovich Ordzhonikidze*, 174–7.

44. Sakharov, *Na rasput'e*, 41 (citing RGASPI, f. 325, op. 2, d. 50, l. 35–8); *Pravda*, March 17, 1922 (Zinoviev's theses); *XI s"ezd RKP (b)*, 680–7. Lenin acknowledged that Trotsky had a point: Lenin was incapable of functioning at the same level as before, and Stalin was overloaded. Lenin, *PSS*, XLV: 103–4, 113–4, 122.

45. *V. I. Lenin: neizvestnye dokumenty*, 513–5. Rigby's influential account of Lenin's supposed attempt, after he had taken ill, to fight off party domination is contradicted by too many inside sources. Rigby, *Lenin's Government*, 207–22.

46. Fel'shtinskii, *Kommunisticheskaia oppozitsiia v SSSR*, I: 16–7; RGASPI, f. 325, op. 1, d. 88, l. 1, 2, 5. The state planning commission, essentially a continuation of the State Electrification Commission (GOELRO), with about forty staff, had been established almost simultaneously with the NEP. *Piat' let vlasti Sovetov*, 150–2. Krzyżanowski headed the state planning commission from August 1921; Tsyryupa took over in December 1923, lasting about two years (when Krzyżanowski returned), by which time it had a staff of several hundred. Pyatakov was a deputy chairman (from 1923). Trotsky had denounced the state planning commission's impotence almost from its inception; Lenin commented to Zinoviev that "Trotsky is in a doubly aggressive mood." Deutscher, *Prophet Unarmed*, 42; *Leninskii sbornik*, XX: 208–9. Other than Trotsky, no one in the inner circle wanted to invest the state planning commission with extraordinary, dictatorial powers. Stalin had mocked him, writing to Lenin in March 1921 that Trotsky's calls for planning resembled "a medieval artisan who imagines himself an Ibsenite hero summoned to 'save' Russia by means of an old saga." Kalinin, *Stalin: sbornik statei*, reprinted in *Sochineniia*, V: 50–1.

47. *Izvestiia*, March 28 and March 29, 1922; *PSS*, XLV: 69–116 (at 77, 81–2).

48. Therefore, by Lenin's reasoning, should socialist revolution succeed in Western Europe, the Bolsheviks could proceed to override the desires of the vast majority of Soviet Russia's population. *XI s"ezd RKP (b)*, 130.

49. Sakharov, *Na rasput'e*, 43–4.

50. *V Vserossiiskii s"ezd RKSM, 11–19 oktiabria 1922 g.*, 31–2.

51. Lenin added: "Allow me to conclude with an expression of confidence that just as this task is not difficult, it is

not new. . . . All of us, not tomorrow, not in a few years, all of us together will solve this task no matter what it takes, so that from NEP Russia will emerge socialist Russia." *PSS*, XLV: 309; Sakharov, *Na rasput'e*, 33–4.

52. Sakharov, *Na rasput'e*, 30–1.

53. All told, between his return to Moscow on October 2 and December 16, 1922, Lenin wrote 224 letters and memoranda, received 171 recorded visitors, and chaired 32 meetings. Golikov, *Vladimir Il'ich Lenin*, XII: xviii; *Voprosy istorii KPSS*, 1957, no. 4: at 149 (Fotieva).

54. *PSS*, XLV: 469. The substance of the conversation between Lenin and Rykov remains undocumented but likely touched at least partly on the events in Georgia. Fotiyeva's memoir omitted the meeting with Rykov: Fotieva, *Iz zhizni*, 249.

55. Golikov, *Vladimir Il'ich Lenin*, XII: 534; Fotieva, *Iz zhizni*, 250–1; *PSS*, XLV: 596.

56. Volkogonov, *Lenin: Life and Legacy*, 416.

57. Fotieva, *Iz zhizni*, 261.

58. *PSS*, LIV: 331–2.

59. The state's foreign trade monopoly had been introduced in 1918, but with the changeover to the NEP most top Bolsheviks, including Stalin, viewed the monopoly as unsustainable and a relic, but Lenin viewed it as a defense ("otherwise foreigners will buy up and export everything of value") and a critical source of revenue. *PSS*, XLIV: 427, 548, LIV: 325–6, 338.

60. *PSS*, XLV: 596, n210.

61. *PSS*, XLV: 338–9.

62. Trotskii, *Stalinskaia shkola fal'sifikatsii*, 74–5; Trotskii, *Portrety revoliutsionerov*, 279. In fact, Lenin relied on several people for retention of the trade monopoly. Sakharov, *Politicheskoe zaveshchanie*, 203–22; Lenin, *PSS*, XLV: 471.

63. Sakharov, *Politicheskoe zaveshchanie*, 207–22.

64. RGASPI, f. 16, op. 2, d. 13, l. 180–90.

65. *PSS*, XLV: 472; LIV: 325–6.

66. *PSS*, XLV: 327.

67. This letter of Lenin's does not appear in the *PSS*. See Volkogonov, *Lenin: politicheskii portret*, II: 329 (APRF, f. 3, op. 22, d. 307, l. 19); and Sakharov, *Politicheskoe zaveshchanie*, 201 (who dates the letter). According to Maria Ulyanova, Lenin "summoned Stalin and turned to him with the most intimate tasks." *Izvestiia TsK KPSS*, 1898, no. 12: 196.

68. The last face-to-face encounter between Stalin and Lenin may have been December 13, 1922. Golikov, *Vladimir Il'ich Lenin*, XII: 537–43.

69. "O zhizni i deiatel'nosti V. I. Lenina (vospominaniia, pis'ma, dokumenty)," *Izvestiia TsK KPSS*, 1989, no. 12: 189–201 (at 191).

70. Lenin had established the rule that a politburo member's health fell under the jurisdiction of the party. Ulam, *The Bolsheviks*, 560.

71. *Voprosy istorii KPSS*, 1991, no. 9: 44–5.

72. *PSS*, LIV: 327–8, 672. Trotsky mentioned the letter to Kamenev, who, as Trotsky requested, informed Stalin. On December 20, 1922, Doctor Otfried Förster arrived from Germany and saw Lenin that day, but there is no record of him seeing Lenin on December 21 (or 22) and there is nothing in the physician's journal about any changes to Lenin's personal regimen allowing dictation. *Izvestiia TsK KPSS*, 1989, no. 12: 191–2; Fotieva, *Iz zhizni*, 274.

73. Suspiciously, the Lenin letter to Trotsky was published abroad, in the Menshevik *Sotsialisticheski vestnik*, in 1923. Additionally, it was signed "N. Lenin," a signature that Lenin had long ago abandoned, and recorded by "N. K. Ulyanova," a name Krupskaya never used. The copy in Lenin's archive has a handwritten note from Krupskaya to Trotsky to answer Lenin by phone, but when that was written in remains unknown (it may have been added to explain why there was no written answer from Trotsky). Sakharov, *Politicheskoe zaveshchanie*, 387; Trotsky archive, Houghton Library, Harvard University, T 770; Fel'shtinskii, *Kommunisticheskaia oppozitsiia v SSSR*, I: 72; *PSS*, XLIV: 327–8, 672; Golikov, *Vladimir Il'ich Lenin*, XII: 545.

74. The document is signed by Stalin, Zinoviev, and Kamenev. It is likely Stalin showed Lenin the text before the plenum. Sakhahrov, *Politicheskoe zaveshchanie*, 215–6 (citing RGASPI, f. 17, op. 2, d. 86, l. 7–7ob). Scholars have perpetuated Trotsky's falsehood concerning retention of the foreign trade monopoly that only he had won the day at the plenum on Lenin's behalf. Viz. Kumanev and Kulikova, *Protivostoianie*, 14–5. In fact, Krupskaya, on behalf of Lenin, had also written to Yaroslavsky (a Trotsky foe), asking that he find someone to substitute for Lenin at the December 18, 1922, plenum discussion, given Lenin's turn for the worse on December 16. It is noteworthy that Trotsky was not given, nor did he request, a written-out copy of the meeting protocols on the trade monopoly. The monopoly on foreign trade—which supposedly launched Lenin's alienation from Stalin—does not recur in the late documents. Sakharov, *Politicheskoe zaveshchanie*, 203–22.

75. RGASPI, f. 17, op. 2, d. 87, l. 1–2. Trotsky, in his memoirs, invented a conversation with Lenin about attacking the bureaucratism in the state but also in the party, specifically targeting

the orgburo, Stalin's source of power. Lenin, according to Trotsky, concluded "then I offer you a bloc against bureaucracy in general and against the organizational bureau in particular." Trotsky claims he reported this conversation with Lenin to his followers: "Rakovski, I. N. Smirnov, Sosnovsky, Preobrazhensky, and others"—repetition that supposedly helped him remember it. Trotskii, *Moia zhizn'*, II: 215-7; Trotsky, *My Life*, 78-9.

76. Krupskaya sought to record the Stalin rudeness incident by writing to Kamenev that "in connection with the very short letter that Lenin dictated, with the permission of the doctors, Stalin yesterday allowed himself the rudest attack on me.... The interests of the party and Ilich are no dearer to me than they are to Stalin." This letter to Kamenev exists but has no date; a date was inserted—December 23, 1922. *PSS*, LIV: 674-5 (RGASPI, f. 12, op. 2, d. 250); *Izvestiia TsK KPSS*, 1989, no. 1: 192; Lewin, *Lenin's Last Struggle*, 152-3. In turn, Kamenev's note to Stalin conveying that Trotsky had told him he had received a letter from Lenin is undated; retroactively dated "no later than December 22" by archivists, but it refers to "the congress," not the plenum, and the congress took place in March-April 1923. Stalin answered Kamenev: "how could the Old Man conduct a correspondence with Trotsky given Förster's absolute prohibition." Stalin's answer is usually dated December 22—not clear if that is correct. Stalin did not phone Krupskaya on December 22 and curse her out. The Central Committee prohibition against political discussions did not mention contacts with members of the leadership; the politburo imposed that prohibition only on December 24. *Izvestiia TsK KPSS*, 1991, no. 6: 193.

77. *Voprosy istorii KPSS*, 1991, no. 9: 43-5; *PSS*, XLV: 474; Volkogonov, *Lenin: politicheskii portret*, II: 337-8; *Izvestiia TsK KPSS*, 1991, no. 6: 191; 1989, no. 12: 196; Sakharov, *Politicheskoe zaveshchanie*, 202.

78. Golikov, *Vladimir Il'ich Lenin*, XII: 542-6.

79. *Voprosy istorii KPSS*, 1991, no. 9: 45.

80. Sakharov, among other documents, reproduces a facsimile of the handwritten text, which he attributes to Alliluyeva: *Politicheskoe zaveshchanie*, 352-53 (plates). The letter exists in two forms, handwritten and typed. The handwritten version carries the title "Letter to the Congress," evidently added later (since it was demonstrably not such a letter). Tellingly, the typed version lacks that designation. The texts do not match. Fotiyeva wrote to Kamenev on

December 29 that Volodicheva had been present. Volodicheva later said she gave the letter to Stalin, but it is not clear if that is true, even though this is what Fotiyeva wrote to Kamenev (December 29). Nadya might have conveyed it to Stalin. For Volodicheva's stories, see *Izvestiia TsK KPSS*,1989, no. 12: 191-2, 198; Genrikh Volkov, "Stenografistka Il'icha," *Sovetskaia kul'tura*, January 21, 1989 (a manuscript dated October 18, 1963, citing conversations with Volodicheva); and *PSS*, XLV: 343; "K istorii poslednikh Leninskikh dokumentov: Iz arkhiva pisatelia Aleksandra Beka, besedovavshee v 1967 godu s lichnymi sekretariami Lenina," *Moskovskie novosti*, April 23, 1989: 8-9. See also *PSS*, XLV: 474. When Volodicheva (or someone on her behalf) imagined this fanciful scene about giving the letter to Stalin unknowingly, everyone in the scene was dead, besides herself. Note also that publication in the bulletin of the 15th Party Congress did *not* include the December 23 dictation as part of Lenin's so-called Letter to the Congress or Testament. The text was also not numbered as it would be later. Fel'shtinskii, *Kommunisticheskaia oppozitsiia v SSSR*, I: 73-8.

81. Fotiyeva wrote that from December 23, 1922, other than herself and Volodicheva, Glasser (once), the physicians and orderlies, and Krupskaya, no one had any contact with Lenin. But this is wrong. Fotieva, *Iz zhizni*, 275.

82. Sakharov, *Politicheskoe zaveshchanie*, 278-89 (esp. 282-3); *Otechestvennaia istoriia*, 2005, no. 2: 162-74.

83. *Voprosy istorii KPSS*, 1963, no. 2: 68; Ulam, *The Bolsheviks*, 560.

84. *Izvestiia TsK KPSS*, 1990. no. 1: 57.

85. Sakharov, *Politicheskoe zaveshchanie*, 653-8 (RGASPI, f. 5, op. 2, d. 305, l. 1-5; d. 301, l. 1-2).

86. Sakharov, *Politicheskoe zaveshchanie*, 459.

87. *PSS*, XLV: 349-53; Sakharov, *Politicheskoe zaveshchanie*, 375 (RGASPI, f. 5, op. 4, d. 10, l. 13ob).

88. Sakharov, *Na rasput'e*, 58-9, n33 (citing RGASPI, f. 5, op. 4, d. 98, l. 114-45); *XIV s"ezd VKP (b)*, 453-4).

89. Sakharov, *Politicheskoe zaveshchanie*, 557-60 (citing RGASPI, f. 5, op. 1, d. 274, l. 1-2); Fel'shtinskii, *Kommunisticheskaia oppozitsiia v SSSR*, I: 9-11.

90. Sakharov, *Politicheskoe zaveshchanie*, 660-2 (citing RGASPI, f. 5, op. 1, d. 275, l. 2-3); Fel'shtinskii, *Kommunisticheskaia oppozitsiia v SSSR*, I: 9-11.

91. *Izvestiia TsK KPSS*, 1990, no. 10: 178-9 (letter of Trotsky to Central Control Commission, October 1923).

92. On January 20, in another letter,

Trotsky complained of having been absorbed in the recent Comintern Congress. Sakharov, *Politicheskoe zaveshchanie*, 660-72 (RGASPI, f. 5, op. 1, d. 275, l. 2-3; d. 307, l. 5; d. 308, l. 1-5); Fel'shtinskii, *Kommunisticheskaia oppozitsiia v SSSR*, I: 12-5.

93. The Dzierżyński commission report's conclusions were discussed and approved at the orgburo on December 21, 1922. A final draft of the Dzierżyński commission's report, which confirmed that Orjonikidze had struck a fellow Georgian Communist, called for no disciplinary action, and instead recommended that the (former) Georgian Central Committee members be reassigned to Soviet Russia. It was approved at the orgburo on January 13, 1923, and sent to the politburo; a copy of the conclusions went to Lenin. The politburo confirmed the orgburo decision as well as the new composition of the Georgian Central Committee. On January 18 the politburo resolved to delay the discussion for one week, to allow Mdivani and others to acquaint themselves with the materials. RGASPI, f. 17, op. 3, d. 330, l. 3.

94. RGASPI, f. 17, op. 3, d. 331, l. 1. The Dzierżyński commission report: RGASPI, f. 5, op. 2, d. 32, l. 69-73.

95. *PSS*, XVL: 476; Fotieva, *Iz zhizni*, 300; Golikov, *Vladimir Il'ich Lenin*, XII: 568-9.

96. Fotieva, *Iz zhizni*, 301. Sakharov, *Politicheskoe zaveshchanie*, 276-7 (citing RGASPI, f. 5, op. 4, d. 10, l. 23-23ob). It may be noteworthy that Fotiyeva admitted she first asked Dzierżyński, who told her that Stalin had the materials.

97. Molotov provided another possibility: "Stalin introduced a secretariat decision not to allow Zinoviev and Kamenev to visit Lenin, since the doctors forbid such contacts. They complained to Krupskaya. She became outraged, spoke to Stalin, and Stalin answered her, 'the Central Committee decided and the doctors believe that visiting Lenin cannot be done.' 'But Lenin himself wants it!' 'If the Central Committee so decides, we could even forbid you from seeing him.'" Chuev, *Sto sorok*, 212.

98. Chuev, *Sto sorok*, 212-3; Chuev, *Molotov Remembers*, 132.

99. Recollections dating to 1926: Ul'ianova, "Ob otnoshenii V. I. Lenina k I. V. Stalina," 198, 196.

100. *PSS*, LIV: 329; RGASPI, f. 17, op. 3, d. 332, l. 5.

101. *Kentavr*, October-December 1991, 100-1; Sakharov, *Politicheskoe zaveshchanie*, 392.

102. "In the last analysis the working class can maintain and strengthen its guiding position not through the apparatus of government, not through

the army, but through industry, which reproduces the proletariat itself," Trotsky wrote in theses on industry. "The party, the trade unions, the youth league, our schools, and so on, have their tasks in educating and preparing new generations of the working class. But all this work would prove to be built on sand if it did not have a growing industrial base under it." State finances, he urged, should be spent on state industry. Daniels, *Documentary History of Communism* [1960], I: 234–6 (citing Trotsky archives, Houghton Library, Harvard University: March 6, 1923).

103. Stalin won the fight, and the reorganization took place according to his proposals, as confirmed at the Central Committee plenum in summer 1923. Sakharov, *Politicheskoe zaveshchanie*, 663–71; RGASPI, f. 17, op. 3, d. 363, l. 2; d. 364, l. 5; d. 369, l. 5.

104. Naumov and Kurin, "Leninskoe zaveshchanie," 36.

105. Volkogonov, *Lenin: Life and Legacy*, 421 (citing APRF, f. 3, op. 22, d. 307, l. 138–9).

106. *Izvestiia TsK KPSS*,1989, no. 12: 198. The women in the Council of People's Commissars secretariat were evidently ill disposed toward Stalin. Later, they would visit Stalin's apartment at the invitation of their former coworker, Nadya Alliluyeva, for example, on the birth of little Svetlana (February 28, 1926). When Stalin opened the door, and Nadya told him to close it or the baby would get a cold from the draft, he supposedly replied, in his bizarre sense of humor, "If it catches a cold it will die more quickly." Genrikh Volkov, "Stenografistka Il'icha," *Sovetskaia kul'tura*, January 21, 1989: 3 (manuscript dated October 18, 1963).

107. "Dnevnik dezhurnykh sekretarei V. I. Lenina," *PSS*, XLV: 607. See also Lewin, *Lenin's Last Struggle*, 96. This is perhaps the first persuasively documented instance on the Georgia affair with Lenin expressing doubts not just about Orjonikidze and Dzierżyński but Stalin, too.

108. The doctors added that "Vladimir Ilich got angry at this refusal, stated that he had already read the protocols and just needed them for one question." Sakharov, *Politicheskoe zaveshchanie*, 276. Glasser refused to turn over to Lenin a copy of the "Short Letter of the CC to provincial party committees about the conflict in the Communist party of Georgia." *Izvestiia TsK KPSS*, 1990, no. 9: 153 n1, 162–63.

109. Golikov, *Vladimir Il'ich Lenin*, XII: 589 (RGASPI, f. 5, op. 2, d. 32, l. 53–73); Fotieva, *Iz zhizni*, 315. The dossier materials are at: RGASPI, f. 5, op. 2, d. 32, 33, 34. Glasser related to Bukharin that Lenin "had an already

preconceived opinion of our work and literally directed and was terribly worried that we will not be able to prove in our report what he needs and he does not have time to prepare his Congress speech." *Izvestiia TsK KPSS*, 1990, no. 9: 163.

110. Sakharov, *Politicheskoe zaveshchanie*, 501 (citing RGASPI, f. 5, op. 2, d. 31, l. 1, 3, 4).

111. Sakharov, *Politicheskoe zaveshchanie*, 345–62.

112. RGASPI, f. 5, op. 2, d. 34, l. 15; Trotsky, *My Life*, 482–8.

113. Smith, "The Georgian Affair of 1922," 538 (citing RGASPI, f. 5, op. 2, d. 34, l. 3); Smith, *Bolsheviks and the National Question*, 208. Trotsky and Lenin (as well as Rykov) shared a German doctor, F. A. Guetier, so Trotsky could get firsthand information on Lenin's actual condition as well as use this extra channel to communicate with the Bolshevik leader.

114. *PSS*, XLV: 329–30.

115. *Izvestiia TsK KPSS*, 1989, no. 12: 192–3 (RGASPI, f. 2, op. 1, d. 26004, l. 3); Volkogonov, *Stalin: politicheskii portret*, II: 384–5; Volkogonov, *Lenin: Life and Legacy*, 274 (citing APRF, f. 3, op. 22, d. 307, l. 27–9). Note: "about 5 weeks ago"—meaning late January, not December 23. In 1989, Vera Dridzo, Krupskaya's personal secretary (from 1919–1939), suddenly remembered how Stalin had called to apologize to Krupskaya in March 1923; Dridzo did not mention this in her Brezhnev-era memoir. V. Dridzo, 105; cf. Dridzo, *Nadezhda Konstantinovna*.

116. Trotsky, *Between Red and White*, 81.

117. *Kentavr*, 1991, Oktiabr'—dekabr': 109–12. Lenin was also credited with dictating "Better Fewer but Better" (dated March 2–9), a searing condemnation of state administration and of the Workers and Peasants Inspectorate, which was supposed to improve state administration. Trotsky claimed that he forced a meeting to get this dictation published in *Pravda*. Trotsky, *Stalin School of Falsification*, 72.

118. Trotskii, "Zaveshchanie Lenina [*Portrety*]," 280.

119. *Izvestiia TsK KPSS*, 1990, no. 9: 151. Stalin that same day telegrammed Orjonikidze with word of Lenin's letters. Trotsky claimed he informed Kamenev of the letter for Mdivani and Makharadze, but it was addressed "copy to" Kamenev as well as Trotsky. It is not clear if a Kamenev-Trotsky meeting took place on the night of March 6–7 as Trotsky claimed; no such letter from Trotsky to Kamenev was registered in Kamenev's secretariat, while Kamenev said the meeting with Trotsky took place later, after Lenin's hopeless condition had become definitive.

120. *PSS*, LIV: 329–30 (RGASPI, f. 2, op. 1, d. 26004, l. 1–3 [including Stalin's response]); *Izvestiia TsK KPSS*, 1989, no. 12: 192–3. There is one extant copy of the Stalin letter, not signed by him, written in Volodicheva's hand; a second copy, evidently written by Stalin, has his signature—but it looks like a facsimile version. The archives contain a cover note, in Stalin's hand: "Comrade Lenin for Stalin Only personally." It is not clear if this note was written for this letter, however. Sakharov, *Politicheskoe zaveshchanie*, 395–7.

121. *Voprosy istorii KPSS*, 1963, no. 2, reprinted in *PSS*, XLV: 455–86 ("journal" of Lenin's secretaries, November 21, 1922, to March 6, 1923).

122. Volkogonov, *Lenin: politicheskii portret*, II: 343.

123. On March 17: "After a short time he wanted to express either an idea or a wish, but neither the nurse, nor Maria Ilichna, nor Nadezhda Konstantinova could understand him." Sakharov, *Politicheskoe zaveshchanie*, 497. The duty physician journal noted that Lenin was "given dried bread chips, but for a long time he could not put his hand straight onto the plate and kept putting it around it." Volkogonov, *Lenin: Life and Legacy*, 430 (citing RGASPI, f. 16, op. 2, d. 13). See also Volkogonov, *Lenin: politicheskii portret*, II: 343.

124. *Pravda*, March 12 and March 14, 1923; *Izvestiia*, March 14, 1923.

125. Valentinov, *Novaia ekonomicheskaia politika*, 33–40.

126. Velikanova, *Popular Perceptions*, 27 (citing RGASPI, f. 9, d. 287, l. 6–7, 13); Izmozik, *Glaza*, 84.

127. Trotskii, "O bol'nom" (April 5, 1923) in *O Lenine*, 159–61.

128. Karl Radek, "Trotskii, organizator pobedy," *Pravda*, March 14, 1923, reprinted in his *Portrety i pamflety* (Moscow and Leningrad: Gosizdat, 1927), but suppressed from subsequent editions (1930, 1933–34).

129. Valentinov, *Novaia ekonomicheskaia politika*, 54; Valentinov, *Nasledniki Lenina*, 13–4.

130. Sevost'ianov, "Sovershenno sekretno": *Lubianka—Stalinu*, I/i: 51–2 (TsA FSB, f. 2, op. 1, d. 42: March 24, 1923). The editors do not reproduce the full document, only a few excerpts, and do not remark upon the absence of Stalin's name.

131. Lenin had asked Stalin for poison on May 30, 1922, and on December 22, 1922.

132. *Sochineniia*, XVI: 25. The recipients of Stalin's letter were Tomsky, Zinoviev, Molotov, Bukharin, Trotsky, and Kamenev; Rykov and Kalinin were absent. Volkogonov, *Lenin: politicheskii portret*, II: 347–50 (APRF, f. 3, op. 22, d. 307, l. 1–2). After Stalin's death, Fotieva did not repudiate the

poison request, and she explained its absence in the notebook by claiming she had "forgotten" to record it. *Izvestiia TsK KPSS*, 1991, no. 6, 217; Fotieva, *Iz zhizni*; "K istorii poslednikh leninskikh dokumentov," *Moskovskie novosti*, April 23, 1989: 8–9 (1960s interviews by Aleksandr Bek with Fotieva and Volodicheva, published after Bek's death: in Bek's telling, Stalin was miraculously saved by Lenin's stroke); Ulyanova, "O zhizni i deiatel'nosti V. I. Lenina (vospominaniia, pis'ma, dokumenty)," *Izvestiia TsK KPSS*, 1989, no. 12: 189–201 (at 199). Lenin's earlier request for poison (December 22, 1922) was not recorded in the duty journal. *Izvestiia TsK KPSS*, 1991, no. 6: 217.

133. Sakharov, *Politicheskoe zaveshchanie*, 273n.

134. Stalin tried to reassure Orjonikidze in a March 16 telegram: "I think that matters at the [Georgian] congress will go well and just like the 12th Congress of the Russian Communist party will support the policy of the South Caucasus party Committee." RGASPI, f. 558, op. 1, d, 2518, l. 1.

135. Sakharov, *Politicheskoe zaveshchanie*, 505 (citing RGASPI, f. 5, op. 2, d. 33, l. 50).

136. A telegram from Orjonikidze in Tiflis to Voroshilov and Mikoyan in Rostov, conveying that Zinoviev was en route, said of the latter: "He inclines somewhat, it seems, toward the [national] deviationists, but more than him Kamenev, who offers diverse advice to the deviationists. I spoke with Zinoviev. And you both will speak to him. All kinds of attempts at the current moment on their part will give them nothing, and will orient our comrades against Kamenev and create a schism in the South Caucasus delegation to the congress." RGASPI, f. 85, op. 24, d. 2479, l. 1–1ob.

137. *TsK RKP (b)—VKP i natsional'nyi vopros*, 106 (RGASPI, f. 558, op. 1, d. 2522, l. 1). On March 22 at the politburo, Stalin's theses on the national question for the upcoming Party Congress were approved. *XII s"ezd RKP (b)*, 816–9.

138. Trotsky charged that the formation of the USSR had been decided in the secretariat, not the politburo. A March 29 collective letter of the politburo to Trotsky repudiated this lie. The next two days, at the Central Committee plenum Trotsky again tried to get Orjonikidze sacked and again got only a single vote besides his own. Smith, *Bolsheviks and the National Question*, 210. Kaganovich recalled that Trotsky supported the Georgian "national deviationists" fully. Kaganovich, *Pamiatnye zapiski*, 282.

139. Kun, *Bukharin*, 130–1.

140. After the call, Fotieva wrote Stalin a note detailing the date that the article had been "written" [sic!] and how "Vladimir Ilich proposed to publish it," but "I do not have a formal directive of Vladimir Ilich." Fotiyeva did not send Stalin her cover letter: "*Not sent*, since comrade Stalin said he is not getting involved." Fotiyeva did send a letter to Kamenev, with a copy to Trotsky, for the politburo, noting that "not long before his last illness he told me he wanted to publish this article, but later. After that he took sick without giving final directions"—a formula that went beyond what she had conveyed to Stalin. She also noted that Trotsky had already been sent the article. Kamenev responded that Trotsky had showed him the article more than a month ago, and that, as proper procedure, he was forwarding the correspondence to the party secretariat (that is, to Stalin). *Izvestiia TsK KPSS*, 1990, no. 9: 155–6, 161.

141. Everything else in the late dictation materials attributed to Lenin—the correctness of the October path, the need to strengthen party authority and improve apparatus functioning, the dangers of petty-bourgeois corruption of the revolution, the promise of cooperatives as a way peasants could overcome the market toward socialism—comported with his views. Lih, "Political Testament."

142. *Kommunist*, 1956, no. 9, reprinted in *PSS*, XLV: 356–62.

143. Fotieva, *Iz zhizni*, 286.

144. Sakharov, *Politicheskoe zaveshchanie*, 514–8; Sakharov, *Na rasput'e*, 136–44; *Izvestiia TsK KPSS*, 1990, no. 9: 151, 158; *Tainy natsional'noi politiki TsK RKP*, 97.

145. Sakharov, *Politicheskoe zaveshchanie*, 329–30, 335–6.

146. Valentinov, *Nasledniki Lenina*, 17.

147. Stalin got the organizational report, Bukharin substituted for Zinoviev in the report on the Comintern, and Trotsky was assigned to report on industry (but only after the politburo imposed revisions to his theses on the economic role of the state). Kamenev was assigned to substitute for the ill Sokolnikov and report on tax policy. RGASPI, f. 17. op. 3, d. 329, l. 203; op. 2, d. 96, l. 1; op. 3, d. 346, l. 5. More colorfully, Bazhanov has Stalin proposing Trotsky for the main political report, Trotsky refusing and proposing Stalin, and Kamenev brokering the selection of Zinoviev, who was dying for the role. Bazhanov, *Bazhanov and the Damnation of Stalin*, 30.

148. *XII s"ezd RKP (b)*, 8–9. Zinoviev, in his political report, stated: "a division of labor, yes, a division of power, no," in the relations between the party and the state. This was evidently directed at Trotsky. *XII s"ezd RKP (b)*, 41–2. Of Zinoviev, Carr wrote uncharitably, "His ambition to assume the mantle of Lenin was so naively displayed as to make his vanity ridiculous." Carr, *Socialism in One Country*, I: 170. By contrast, Kamenev would hit upon the appropriate stance, remarking of Lenin, "His teaching has been our touchstone every time this or that problem, this or that difficult question, has confronted us. Mentally, each of us has asked himself, 'And how would Vladimir Ilich have answered this?'" *XII s"ezd RKP (b)*, 523.

149. *XII s"ezd RKP (b)*, 199.

150. *Pravda*, December 7, 1923.

151. Valentinov, *Novaia ekonomicheskaia politika*, 54 [1991], 99.

152. Daniels, *Conscience of the Revolution*, 205; *Izvestiia*, April 7, 1923 (Petrovsky). See also Barmine, *One Who Survived*, 212; and Deutscher, *Prophet Unarmed*, 94.

153. *XII s"ezd RKP (b)*, 393. Maurice Dobb printed a different version of the graph, taken from Strumilin: Dobb, *Russian Economic Development*, 222.

154. *XII s"ezd RKP (b)*, 306–22 (at 321).

155. Carr, *Interregnum*, 32–4.

156. Barmine, *One Who Survived*, 93–4.

157. Avel Yenukidze, who had close contact with Stalin, put forth a less innocent explanation. "Comrade Lenin was made a victim of one-sided incorrect information," Yenukidze speculated. "When they come to a person, who out of sickness lacks the possibility to follow daily affairs, and they say that such and such comrades were insulted, beaten, kicked out, displaced and so on, he, of course, can be expected to write such a sharp letter." *XII s"ezd RKP (b)*, 541. On April 18, the presidium of the Party Congress had decided to show the "Notes on the Question of Nationalities" to a council of elders.

158. *Izvestiia TsK KPSS*, 1991, no. 4: 171–2.

159. *Sochineniia*, V: 257.

160. *XII s"ezd RKP (b)*, 449.

161. *XII s"ezd VKP (b)*, 31.

162. *Izvestiia TsK KPSS*, 1991, no. 4: 171.

163. *XII s"ezd RKP (b)*, 571, 650–2.

164. *XII s"ezd RKP (b)*, 561–4; Sakharov, *Politicheskoe zaveshchanie*, 521–34. Some 100 people took part in a special "national section" of the congress on April 25 for the discussion; this included twenty-four people not delegates to the congress but invited especially for this sectional discussion. Stalin reported on the results of the discussion to the congress. *XII s"ezd RKP (b)*, 649–61.

165. *XII s"ezd RKP (b)*, 564. Bukharin nonetheless underscored the problem of Great Russian chauvinism, adding, "I understand that our dear friend comrade Koba does not criticize

Russian chauvinism severely but as a Georgian criticizes Georgian chauvinism." *XII s"ezd RKP (b)*, 614. Bitterness among the Georgians: Orjonikidze and Stalin had stacked the deck, delegate-wise: there were nine voting delegates from Georgia among whom only Makharadze defended the Georgian national line; Mdivani and Cote Tsintsadze (the first commissar of the Georgian Cheka) held the same views but were non-voting attendees. Makharadze declared the Georgian Central Committee, stacked with Orjonikidze supporters, "sick." Orjonikidze charged Mdivani and Pilipe Makharadze with collaborating with the Mensheviks during the latter's government in Georgia (1918–20), harboring class enemies (landowners) in the Georgian party, "leftism" and "adventurism." Radek complained that "a majority of the party does not understand the significance of the [national] question." *XII s"ezd RKP (b)*, 615.

166. *XII s"ezd RKP (b)*, 113. Zinoviev crowed that "the theses of comrade Stalin and the Central Committee are superlative, exhaustive, thoughtthrough to the end, complete, and no one can say there is a mistake in them." *XII s"ezd RKP (b)*, 557, 607.

167. Volkogonov, *Stalin: politicheskii portret*, I: 160.

168. Shvetsov, *Diskussiia v RKP (b)*, 10.

169. Stalin likened the NEP to participating in Duma elections after 1905, rather than pressing on to the revolutionary struggle. *Sochineniia*, V: 215, 238–40, 244–5, 248–9; Himmer, "The Transition from War Communism."

170. Nazarov, *Stalin i bor'ba za liderstvo*, 85 (citing RGASPI, f. 50, op. 1, d. 58, l. 17). Fewer votes were received only by Rakovski, Orjonikidze, Ukhanov, Zalutsky, and Kharitonov, who got the fewest votes of those elected (264).

171. "He has recovered from the sensory aphasia and begun to learn to speak," Doctor Kozhevnikov noted hopefully. Volkogonov, *Lenin: Life and Legacy*, 429, (citing APRF, f. 3, op. 22, d. 307, l. 140).

172. Volkogonov, *Lenin: Life and Legacy*, 430.

173. Angelica Balabanoff had visited Lenin at Gorki in fall 1918, after the assassination attempt, and already then noted of Krupskaya: "I thought how much older and more haggard she looked since I had last seen her. The strain of the past few months had told more heavily upon her than upon her husband." Balabanoff, *My Life as a Rebel*, 186–7.

174. Krupskaya was fond of his second wife, Zlata Lilina Bernstein; the Lenins and Zinovievs had visited each other as couples in the emigration.

175. *PSS*, XLV: 343–8, 593–4, n208; Fotieva, *Iz zhizni*, 279–82. The typescripts of the alleged dictation contain curiosities or odd mistakes: "as I said above," when there is no above; remarks about both Zinoviev and Kamenev that use the pronoun he ("to him [*emu*]"). *PSS*, XLV: 474–6, 482. In connection with dictation for which a shorthand record is extant, they show that Fotieva tended to leave the original jumble of words, while Volodicheva introduced grammatical corrections.

176. Entries in the secretaries' journal for many days are missing: December 17, December 19–22 (the day Stalin supposedly called Krupskaya); for the entire period from December 25 to January 16, there are just two entries, one noting that Lenin was reading Sukhanov. This was supposedly when Lenin was dictating these monumentally significant documents. "Dnevnik dezhurnykh sekretarei Lenina," *PSS*, XLV: 457–86; 608, n297. At age eighty, in 1967, Fotieva told Alexander Bek, "We did not write everything in the diary." "K istorii polsednikh Leninskikh dokumentov: Iz arkhiva pisatelia Aleksandra Beka, besedovavsheo v 1967 godu s lichnyi sekretariami Lenina," *Moskovskie novosti*, April 23, 1989: 8–9. Volodicheva, in 1929, would claim that she first wrote down the dictation, then rewrote it in five copies, then retyped a clean copy that she sent to *Pravda*. Therefore, there should be at least three versions. *PSS*, XLV: 592. But today, there is no such first handwritten version (stenography) and no rewritten versions either. In dictation, one would expect to see multiple copies, corrections, insertions, after, for example, Lenin had gone over the transcribed drafts. Dictation rarely occurs in one clean swoop.

177. Fel'shtinskii, *Kommunisticheskaia oppozitsiia v SSSR*, I: 73. Fotieva wrote that the staff at the Council of People's Commissars secretariat waited with anxiety for her or Volodicheva to return following a summons by Lenin to find out how he looked and felt. "Sometimes after our return from Vladimir Ilich Nadezhda Konstantinova [Krupskaya] or Maria Ilinichna [Ulyanova] would read what he had dictated and share their thoughts about his condition." Fotieva, *Iz zhizni*, 281. Vladimir Naumov concluded that Stalin and the rest all knew about the so-called Testament right away. *Pravda*, February 26, 1988. But all Stalin learned about—as the Fotiyeva letter to Kamenev (December 29) attests—was the December 23 dictation, which in fact was a letter to Stalin; no one learned of the dictation of December 24 or December 25 right away—because it likely did not happen then.

178. Kuromiya, *Stalin*, 64 (citing Trotsky letter to Max Eastman, June 7, 1933: Trotsky manuscripts, Lily Library, Indiana University, Bloomington). See also Bazhanov, *Vospominaniia* [1990], 107.

179. Sakharov, *Politicheskoe zaveschanie*, 311–3.

180. In mid-1922, when Dzierżyński was railways commissar, the politburo created a commission to inquire about purchases made abroad, which effectively constituted a judgment about Trotsky's previous work as the commissar. Stalin, Rykov, Tomsky, and Kamenev voted in favor; Trotsky voted against. Lenin was absent; when apprised, he did not seek to overturn the politburo decision. RGASPI, f. 17, op. 3, d. 298, l. 1, 6; *Izvestiia TsK KPSS*, 1991, no. 3: 189–90; Sakharov, *Politicheskoe zaveshchanie*, 368–9.

181. *PSS*, XLV: 345. Volkogonov speculates that Trotsky, as a man of the utmost self-regard, may have taken the "Letter to the Congress" to mean that Lenin had anointed him as successor—"probably the most able man in the current Central Committee"—and perhaps imagined that Lenin had added some criticisms about him only to soften the blow of his elevation for the others. Volkogonov, *Trotsky*, 264–5.

182. *XII s"ezd RKP (b)*, 122, 136, 139; Valentinov, *Novaia ekoniomicheskaia politika*, 57–8; Tucker, *Stalin as Revolutionary*, 335. At the congress itself, the triumvirate had its people initiate a whispering campaign about Trotsky's supposed Bonapartism. Deutscher, *Prophet Unarmed*, 94–5; Deutscher, *Stalin*, 273. Far from all of this was underground: on April 19, 1923 (the second day of the 12th Party Congress), *Economic Newspaper* had republished Lenin's 1921 attack on Trotsky's proposals for the state planning commission. Sakharov, *Politicheskoe zaveshchanie*, 543–4.

183. *XII s"ezd RKP (b)*, 47, 92–95, 121, 122, 136, 137, 139, 151; Sakharov, *Politicheskoe zaveshchanie*, 418–27. Vladimir Kosior—the younger brother of Stanisław Kosior, party boss of Siberia and one of Stalin's men—would be expelled from the party as a Trotskyite in 1928.

184. Sakharov, *Politicheskoe zaveshchanie*, 423.

185. Sakharov, *Politicheskoe zaveshchanie*, 427. Volkogonov correctly noted that "it is remarkable that Lenin was capable of dictating these lengthy works in such a short time, especially taking into account the sharp deterioration that took place in his condition during the nights of 16 and 22 December," a worsening noted by all the physicians—Kramer, Kozhenikov, Förster, Strumpfell, Hentschell,

Nonne, Bumke, and Yelistratov. But Volkogonov failed to connect the dots: Lenin indeed could not have dictated all that work. Volkogonov, *Lenin: Life and Legacy*, 419.

186. Fel'shtinskii, *Kommunisticheskaia oppozitsiia v SSSR*, I: 56 (Zinoviev cover letter to Stalin dated June 2, 1923). Moshe Lewin correctly grasped that the *message* of the alleged Lenin Testament, essentially, was to fight nationalism in favor of internationalism, to fight bureaucracy, especially the party leadership, and to remove Stalin, but Lewin did not question the legitimacy of the documents, which, after all, were published in Lenin's *Complete Collected Works* by the Institute of Marxism-Leninism. Lewin, *Lenin's Last Struggle*, 132–3.

187. Later, Trotsky himself would give reason to suspect his involvement in the dictation, which, according to him, "rounds out and clarifies the proposal that Lenin made me in our last conversation." According to Trotsky, Lenin "was systematically preparing to deliver at the 12th congress a crushing blow at Stalin as personifying bureaucracy, the mutual shielding among officials, arbitrary rule and general rudeness." Trotsky hilariously added that "The idea of a 'bloc of Lenin and Trotsky' against the apparatus-men and bureaucrats was at that time fully known only to Lenin and me." The reason it was not "known" to anyone else is that Trotsky imagined it. Trotsky, *My Life*, 479–81. Trotsky does not date this alleged conversation with Lenin.

188. In November 1921, for example, Stalin wrote an exasperated letter to Lenin about how Krupskaya had "again" gotten ahead of herself. RGASPI, f. 558, op. 1, d. 2176, l. 1–5ob. On the Krupskaya-Stalin hostility, see also Bazhanov, *Bazhanov and the Damnation of Stalin*, 31 (which follows Trotsky).

189. McNeal, *Bride of the Revolution*, 117.

190. Trotsky, who disliked Maria Ulyanova, calling her "an old maid," surmised that Krupskaya had shunted her aside and pushed her into Stalin's camp, and scholars have tended to follow this line, viewing Ulyanova as on Stalin's side, and Krupskaya on Trotsky's. Trotsky, *Diary in Exile* [1963], 33; Trotskii, *Dnevniki i pis'ma* [1986], 76; Trotskii, *Stalin*, II: 254–5.

191. "It was extremely difficult to maintain equilibrium between Trotsky and the other members of the politburo, especially between Trotsky and Stalin," Ulyanova wrote. "Both of them are people of extreme self-regard and impatience. For them, the personal trumps the interests of the cause." Ul'ianova, "Ob otnoshenii V. I. Lenina k I. V. Stalina," 197.

192. Blank, *Sorcerer as Apprentice*, 157–8 (citing K. A. Khasanov, "Tatariia v bor'be za Leninskuiu natsional'nomu politiku," *Revoliutsiia i natsional'nosti*, 1933, no. 11: 30).

193. Bennigsen and Wimbush, *Muslim National Communism*, 51–7.

194. Tagirov, *Neizvestnyi Sultan-Galiev* 44–5 (TsGA IPD RT, f. 8237, op. 1, d. 2, l. 112). Antonov-Ovseenko asserted the letter resulted from a Stalin provocation, to entrap Soltangäliev, an assertion followed by others. Antonov-Ovseenko, *Stalin bez maski*, 40–3; Landa, "Mirsaid Sultan-Galiev,"

195. Bulat Sultanbekov, "Vvedenie," in *Tainy natsiona'noi politiki TsK RKP*, 4–11. See also Sultanbekov, *Pervaia zhertva Genseka*. There were also secret informant reports to the effect that Soltangäliev was organizing an underground congress of eastern Communists from across the USSR. Tagirov, *Neizvestnyi Sultan-Galiev*, 32–4 (TsGA IPD RT, f. 8237, op. 1, d. 5, l. 22–3). Dzierżyński, complaining of overwork, had assigned Mężyński to the case. Tagirov, *Neizvestnyi Sultan-Galiev*, 71 (TsA IPD RT, f. 8237, op. 1, d. 2, l. 117).

196. *Tainy natsiona'noi politiki TsK RKP*, 15–23. The interrogation protocols do not mention a request to be executed: Tagirov, *Neizvestnyi Sultan-Galiev*, 74–5 (TsGA IPD RT, f. 8237, op. 1, d. 20, l. 103–4; d. 2, l. 121).

197. Skrypnyk added that a Muslim nationalist was being demonstratively called to account, but not one of the many Russian-chauvinist Communists. Trotsky spoke at length, deeming Soltangäliev not a matter of nationalism but of treason, and not treason by Turkish embassy recruitment, but by political evolution from nationalism, which "did not meet the necessary resistance from those who worked closely with him"—even now Tatar comrades were trying to protect him, citing a poor translation of his letters. *Tainy natsiona'noi politiki TsK RKP*, 54–7 (Orjonikidze), 61 (Skrypnyk, Trotsky), 74 (Trotsky).

198. Rakovski and Skrypnyk presented their own draft constitution and pushed for republic commissariats on foreign affairs and foreign trade. Davletshin, "The Federal Principle in the Soviet State," at 24; Sullivant, *Soviet Politics and the Ukraine*, 65–76; TsK *RKP (b)–VKP (b) i natsional'nyi vopros*, 120–9 (RGASPI, f. 558, op. 1, d. 3478, l. 20–25, 30–7: commission meeting of June 14, 1923). Before the Moscow national Communist gathering was brought to a close, Rakovski and Skrypnyk called Stalin to account for using the terms "united" and "indivisible" to describe the USSR; he called their complaints and demands, in a sharp exchange, tantamount to

confederation, in place of the agreed federation. *Tainy natsiona'noi politiki TsK RKP*, 270–2 (Rakovski and Stalin).

199. Hearsay exists (from Kamenev's secretary in 1926) about how only Kamenev and Zinoviev saved Soltangäliev from execution. More persuasively, there is a note from Mężyński expressing doubts about an informant's allegation of secret Soltangäliev contacts with Turkish, Persian, and Afghan diplomats in Moscow—the kind of material needed for such a treason trial. (Stalin mentioned such contacts as a fact during the party gathering.) *Tainy natsiona'noi politiki TsK RKP*, 64.

200. *Tainy natsiona'noi politiki TsK RKP*, 85. (The version of the transcript published in Stalin's *Works* differs slightly: *Sochineniia*, V: 301–12.) On June 6, 1923, the GPU's Mężyński had also recommended release. Tagirov, *Neizvestnyi Sultan-Galiev*, 76–80 (at 80: TsGA IPD RT, f. 8327, op. 1, d. 5, l. 91–5). In his main report on the June 10 evening, Stalin went through a long discussion of how the Russian Communist party had been forged, under tsarism, first in the battle against Menshevism, bourgeois tendencies, rightists, and later in a struggle against left Communists, and that something analogous was going on with the party in national-minority regions. But, he added, the party in the borderlands could not combat rightism and leftism sequentially, with the help of one against the other, as the Russian party had done, but had to struggle against both simultaneously. *Tainy natsiona'noi politiki TsK RKP*, 99–106.

201. *Tainy natsiona'noi politiki TsK RKP*, 270–2 (Kamenev), 273–4. At some point during the four-day proceedings, Zinoviev handed Stalin a note suggesting that "a permanent commission for national affairs in the Central Committee is absolutely necessary." Stalin wrote back: "The matter is complex: we would need to have people from every or the main nationalities. . . . [T]he national Central Committees and national province party committees will be unhappy if issues were decided without them in Moscow . . . More than that they have few people and will not give their best ones to such a commission (they'll give their worst, if they give at all)." Stalin proposed they ask the national minority Communists themselves whether they wanted such a commission. Stalin, in his concluding remarks, rejected the commission idea ("two or three people from Ukraine would not be able to substitute for the Central Committee of the Ukrainian Communist party"). TsK *RKP (b)–VKP (b) i natsional'nyi vopros*, 119 (RGASPI, f. 558, op. 11, d. 734, l. 15–6); *Sochineniia*, V: 338–9.

202. In 1928, he would be arrested again for nationalism and anti-Soviet activity and, in July 1930, sentenced to be shot, but in January 1931 his sentence would be commuted to ten years. In 1934 he would be released and allowed to reside in Saratov province. In 1937 would come yet another arrest, the final one; he would be executed in Moscow on January 28, 1940.

203. Tagirov, *Neizvestnyi Sultan-Galiev*, 81–184 (TsGA IPD RT, f. 15, op. 1, d. 857, l. 1–249). The GPU chief in Tataria was Sergei Shwartz.

204. On July 3, the politburo approved six weeks of holiday for Zinoviev and two months for Bukharin. RGASPI, f. 17, op. 3, d. 362, l. 5. The Harvard historian of Russia Richard Pipes happened to be born in Poland the day after the cave meeting (July 11).

205. Fotieva, *Iz zhizni*, 295.

206. This section closely follows Sakharov, *Politicheskoe zaveshchenie*, 547–66, but differs from him on a crucial point: there was no plot in the summer of 1923 to remove Stalin, only to contain him. See also Chuev, *Sto sorok*, 183.

207. *PSS*, XLV: 343–8. The alleged December 1922 dictation presented as a letter to the congress was meant for the wide party public; the January 4 "postscript" appears to have been for a narrower group: just the conspirators against Stalin. Sakharov, *Politicheskoe zaveshchenie*, 563–5. The alleged postscript can be found in *PSS*, XLV: 346.

208. *Voprosy istorii KPSS*, 1991, no. 9: 45, 47.

209. Sakharov, *Politicheskoe zaveshchanie*, 538–9.

210. Molotov recalled the intrigue as Zinoviev's initiative. Chuev, *Sto sorok*, 183.

211. Voroshilov explained at the 14th Party Congress: "In Rostov I received a telegram from comrade Zinoviev to travel to Kislovodsk. At that time comrades Zinoviev, Bukharin, Yevdokimov, Lashevich and other comrades were there [at the spa]. I arrived in Kislovodsk and at one of the private meetings together with comrades Zinoviev, Bukharin, Yevdokimov, and Lashevich we discussed the issue of collective leadership." *XIV s"ezd VKP (b)*, 398–9. Subsequently, in a letter to the congress, Voroshilov clarified the cave meeting: "at the aforementioned meeting in the 'cave' there were only five people: namely: comrades Zinoviev, Bukharin, Yevdokimov, Lashevich, and I." *XIV s"ezd VKP (b)*, 950.

212. By then, Voroshilov had left. *XIV s"ezd VKP (b)*, 950.

213. *Izvestiia TsK KPSS*, 1991, no. 4: 196. Trotsky had been afforded a vacation from June 15 through September 7, 1923, owing to illness. Molotov also went to Kislovodsk on holiday.

214. Eastman, *Leon Trotsky*. Kislovodsk was buzzing that summer: the July 1926 plenum). American dancer Isadora Duncan was there, too, with her adopted daughter; Eastman ran into them at the train station. Stalin may have had some knowledge of such comings and goings: Yefim Yevdokimov, a top official in the Moscow secret police, had just become the GPU plenipotentiary for the North Caucasus (on June 22, 1923) and Yevdokimov, in Rostov, might have had some role in looking after the security of politburo members and other important personages on holiday in Kislovodsk, although whether he supplied Stalin with information about the clandestine "cave meeting" is unknown.

215. *XIV s"ezd VKP (b)*, 455–7. Perhaps Zinoviev imagined that, given the infamous enmity between Trotsky and Stalin, Zinoviev conveniently could serve as the arbiter.

216. *XIV s"ezd VKP (b)*, 953 (Orjonikidze).

217. *Izvestiia TsK KPSS*, 1991, no. 4: 192–5, 198; Sakharov, *Politicheskoe zaveshchanie*, 557.

218. "Il'ich byl tysiachu raz prav," *Izvestiia TsK KPSS*, 1991, no. 4: 192–208 (at 197–9).

219. Oleg Khlevniuk noted that Orjonikidze allowed himself to get entangled in the intrigue. Khlevniuk, *In Stalin's Shadow*, 18–9. Molotov, later in life, would recall that once Orjonikidze was voicing praise for Zinoviev as a true Leninist and that when Molotov disagreed the two nearly came to blows (Kirov interceded to separate them; later, Bukharin served as peacemaker). Chuev, *Sto sorok*, 190–1.

220. Mikoyan, a member of the Central Committee and party boss in the North Caucasus, where the cave meeting took place, found out about it via a letter from Voroshilov, and noted that he and others in the Central Committee roundly rejected Zinoviev's effort to weaken Stalin's position. Mikoian, *Tak bylo*, 110.

221. *Izvestiia TsK KPSS*, 1991, no. 4: 196–7; Sakharov, *Politicheskoe zaveshchanie*, 554–5.

222. *Izvestiia TsK KPSS*, 1991, no. 4: 199–200.

223. *Izvestiia TsK KPSS*, 1991, no. 4: 201–2.

224. Stalin's letter was marked "copy to Voroshilov." *Izvestiia TsK KPSS, 1991*, no. 4: 203–4. "If the comrades were to persist in their plan, I was prepared to clear out without any fuss and without any discussion, be it open or secret," Stalin would later explain. *XIV s"ezd RKP (b)*, 506.

225. *Izvestiia TsK KPSS*, 1991, no. 4: 205–6.

226. Sakharov, *Politicheskoe zaveshchanie*, 561 (citing RGASPI, f. 17, op. 2,

d. 246, IV vyps. 104: Bukharin at the July 1926 plenum).

227. RGASPI, f. 17, op. 3, d. 370, l. 7 (August 9 politburo approval for a 1.5-month holiday commencing on August 15).

228. Sakharov, *Politicheskoe zaveshchanie*, 565 (RGASPI, f. 17, op. 3, d. 374, l. 1; d. 375, l. 6).

229. Fischer, *The Ruhr Crisis*. Édouard Herriot, mayor of Lyon and leader of France's Radical Party, along with his deputy, Édouard Daladier, had visited the USSR back in September–October 1922 on a trip that, although unofficial, was meant to explore restoration of commercial and diplomatic relations, despite the obstacle of unpaid tsarist debts. "[France] was too magnanimous to its enemy," Herriot told Chicherin and Leonid Krasin (foreign trade commissar) in Moscow. "The price of this magnanimity is that we are hated by everyone and Germany does not pay us. The reparations question will be resolved very quickly. It will have two stages. First stage: Germany is too weak and cannot pay; second phase: Germany is too strong and will not pay. I am absolutely persuaded that in fifteen years Germany will fall upon us again." Carley, "Episodes from the Early Cold War," 1277 (citing AVPRF, f. 04, o. 42, d. 53619, l. 259, 11, 23–25: Bronsky report to Veinshtein, September 22, 1922, and l. 45: Chicherin to Trotsky, October 9, 1922). See also Williams, *Trading with the Bolsheviks*, 111–2; and Namier, "After Vienna and Versailles," 19–33.

230. Feldman, *The Great Disorder*.

231. "The Polish imperialists do not attempt to conceal their plans to seize Russian as well as German soil," noted a Soviet newspaper editorial. "They are endeavoring to break up the united federation of soviet socialist republics into states at odds with one another, and to place some of these states, such as Belorussia and the Ukraine, under their direct influence." *Izvestiia*, January 21, 1923, translated in Eudin and Fisher, *Soviet Russia and the West*, 200–1; Ruge, *Die Stellungnahme*, 32–59; Eichwede, *Revolution und Internationale Politik*, 154–75.

232. Adibekov and Shirinia, *Politbiuro TsK RKP (b)–VKP (b) i Komintern*, 155–6, n2 (RGASPI, f. 495, op. 2, d. 28, l. 45–6), 157–8; Babichenko, "Politbiuro TsK RKP (b)," 126–7. Litvinov, reporting on a conversation with Brockdorff-Rantzau, had warned Zinoviev against the ill effects of Communist subversion in Germany. Sevost'ianov, *Moskva-Berlin*, I: 165–7 (RGASPI, f. 359, op. 1, d. 7, l. 95: June 5, 1923). Back in late 1918, Radek had boasted to Lenin of a revolutionary wave enveloping Germany, and been proved wrong. Drabkin, *Komintern i*

*ideia mirovoi revoliuitsii*, 90-8 (RGASPI, f. 2, op. 2, d. 143, l. 22-6: January 24, 1919). Radek was arrested in Germany on February 12, 1919.

233. Orlova, *Revoliutsionnyi krizis*, 264; Gintsberg, *Rabochee i kommunisticheskoe dvizhenie Germanii*, 117.

234. Adibekov and Shirinia, *Politbiuro TsK RKP (b)—VKP (b) i Komintern*, 159-60, 162-4; Babichenko, "Politbiuro TsK RKP (b)," 129-30 (RGASPI, f. 17, op. 2, d. 317, l. 22). Trotsky reproduced Stalin's letter to Zinoviev: *Stalin*, 368-9. See also Deutscher, *Stalin*, 393-5.

235. *Istochnik*, 1995, no. 5: 116.

236. "'Naznachit' revoliutsiii v Germaniiu na 9 noiabria'," *Istochnik*, 1995, no. 5: 115-39 (at 115-7). In Kislovodsk Zinoviev drafted radical Comintern theses on the revolutionary situation in Germany in the first weeks of August, as he prepared to return to the Soviet capital in mid-August. On his mood, see Kuusinen, *Neudavsheesia izobrazhenie "nemetskogo Oktiabria"*: 10. Radek on August 13 advised Brandler in a letter to be sober and cautious. Adibekov and Shirinia, *Politbiuro TsK RKP (b)—VKP (b) i Komintern*, 165, n1 (RGASPI, f. 495, op. 18, d. 175a, l. 275ob).

237. Adibekov and Shirinia, *Politbiuro TsK RKP (b)—VKP (b) i Komintern*, 166.

238. *Istochnik*, 1995, no. 5: 120-7 (RGASPI, f. 17, op. 3, d. 375, l. 1-6). Bazhanov compiled these discussion notes. See also Bazhanov, *Bazhanov and the Damnation of Stalin*, 46-50.

239. *Kommunisticheskii internatsional*, 196.

240. Adibekov and Shirinia, *Politbiuro TsK RKP (b)—VKP (b) i Komintern*, 168-9 (RGASPI, f. 325, op. 1, d. 518, l. 90).

241. *Istochnik*, 1995, no. 5: 115-39 (at 128). The politburo also adopted Trotsky's suggestion to have the Comintern invite representatives of the Communist parties of France, Poland, Czechoslovakia, and Belgium, along with Germany, for secret joint discussions in Moscow. Adibekov and Shirinia, *Politbiuro TsK RKP (b)—VKP (b) i Komintern*, 168, n1 (RGASPI, f. 495, op. 2, d. 17, l. 163); Babichenko, "Politbiuro TsK RKP (b)," 131 (RGASPI, f. 495, op. 2, d. 19, l. 161-162ob).

242. *Izvestiia TsK KPSS*, 1991, no. 4: 201.

243. *Proletarskaia revoliutsiia*, 1923, no. 9: 227-32.

244. On December 11, 1923, Lenin would request that the staff bring him the September issue of the journal; evidently he had been told about it by someone. Golikov, *Vladimir Il'ich Lenin*, XII: 650.

245. *XIV s"ezd VKP (b)*, 456. Trotsky congratulated himself and Bukharin

for having had "the foresight and imagination to stay away" from org-buro meetings. Trotsky, *Stalin*, 368.

246. Sakharov, *Politicheskoe zaveshchanie*, 550 (citing RGASPI, f. 17, op. 2, d. 246, IV vyp, s. 104: the joint plenum of the Central Committee and Central Control Commission of July 1926).

247. Bukharin, either deputized by Zinoviev or on his own initiative, seems to have written to Kamenev seeking to recruit him to as yet unspecified changes in "org[aniza-tional] methods" even before the July 29 joint letter to Stalin and Kamenev. Certainly Bukharin took a sharper, more direct stance than Zinoviev in the joint letter dated July 29. *Izvestiia TsK KPSS*, 1991, no. 4: 206-7. Sakharov explains how the published letters (in *Izvestiia TsK KPSS*) are out of order: *Politicheskoe zaveschanie*, 553-4.

248. Orjonikidze, in his August 3 letter to Voroshilov, wrote that he had spoken to Kamenev—an indication, perhaps, of Orjonikidze's political vacillation concerning Stalin—and that Kamenev had deemed the complaints of Zinoviev and Bukharin exaggerated. *Izvestiia TsK KPSS*, 1991, no. 4: 201.

249. Hirsch, *Empire of Nations*. A declaration on July 13 stipulated that "all Soviet Socialist Republics which may be founded in the future" would have the option of "voluntarily joining the Union"—evocation of world revolution. That same day Stalin removed the Trotsky supporter Cristian Rakovski as head of the government of Ukraine, planning to exile him into diplomatic work abroad.

250. Chuev, *Sto sorok*, 182-3.

251. Krupskaia, "Poslednie polgoda zhizni Vladimira Il'icha." When Yevgeny Preobrazhensky went out to Gorki and recoiled from shock, Lenin's head of security, Abram Belenky, gestured "over there, they're carrying him." Preobrazhensky, writing privately to Bukharin on July 29, 1923, explained that "I went, not exactly knowing how to behave, or even, really, whom I would see. . . . He pressed my hand firmly, I instinctively embraced him. But his face! It cost me a great effort to keep my mask and not cry like a baby." *Izvestiia TsK KPSS*, 1989, no. 4: 186-7.

252. On August 31, 1923, in Kislovodsk, he received word that the British had consented to receiving Rakovski as Soviet negotiator in talks on diplomatic recognition; Stalin had just removed Rakovski from Ukraine in July, aiming to reduce one of Trotsky's bases of support. RGASPI, f. 558, op. 11, d. 67, l. 1. In Ukraine Vlas Chibar replaced Rakovski.

253. Fischer, *Stalin and German Communism*, 312.

254. The main Bulgarian Communist

leaders of the uprising escaped, including Georgi Dimitrov, who went first to Yugoslavia, then to the Soviet Union, where he moved into the Hotel Lux.

255. RGASPI, f. 558, op. 11, d. 139, l. 11 (Stalin to August Thalheimer). *Rote Fahne* published Stalin's letter of October 10, 1923; Chicherin heard about it over the radio, and wrote to Molotov: "is this radio report a complete fabrication or is something real hidden behind it?" Molotov passed the letter to Stalin. Adibekov and Shirinia, *Politbiuro TsK RKP (b)—VKP (b) i Komintern*, 169-70 (RGASPI, f. 558, op. 11, d. 139, l. 31).

256. Simultaneously, a conference of Russian, German, Polish, Czechoslovak, and French Communists opened under Comintern auspices in Moscow, where speaker after speaker preached to the choir, urging a revolutionary course for Germany. Adibekov and Shirinia, *Politbiuro TsK RKP (b)—VKP (b) i Komintern*, 172-85 (RGASPI, f. 495, op. 19, d. 68, passim).

257. Firsov, "K voprosu o taktike edinogo fronta v 1921-1924 gg.," 118. The politburo unanimously approved Zinoviev's revised Comintern theses, which stipulated that a German revolution was imminent and that hostile actions had to be expected from world imperialism, "but all the same the German Communist party will hold power," because of "an alliance between a Soviet Germany and the USSR." There were intimations that successful revolution in Germany would enable the USSR to repeal the dreaded NEP. Pavlova, *Stalinizm*, 208 (no citation).

258. Luppol, "Iz istorii sovetskogo gosudarstvennogo gerba."

259. *Istochnik*, 1995, no. 5: 130-5. By contrast, *Pravda* (September 22, 1923) observed of Germany that "we consider . . . the seizure of power not difficult and an utterly realizable task. Much more complex and difficult is the question of holding power."

260. *Internatsionale Presse Korrespondenz*, October 6, 1923: 957-9.

261. Kamenev had the general staff academy assess how many divisions the Entente had available for an occupation of Germany. Babichenko, "Politbiuro TsK RKP (b)," 131 (RGASPI, f. 325, op. 1, d. 41, l. 47-50), 135 (f. 17, op. 2, d. 109, l. 15, 18. 19).

262. Babichenko, "Politbiuro TsK RKP (b)," 132, n32; Iwański, *II Zjazd Komunistycznej Partii Robotniczej Polski*, I: 156, 162-3.

263. RGASPI, f. 17, op. 2, d. 101, l. 15-15ob.

264. RGASPI, f. 17, op. 2, d. 103. The plenum's second and third days were given over to reports on cooperatives, wages, appointments versus elections

to party posts (by Dzierżyński), and the scissors crisis. The content of Dzierżyński's report went unspecified in the protocols. RGASPI, f. 17, op. 2, d. 102.

265. According to Deutscher, Zinoviev instead suggested he would go to Germany, as head of the Comintern, but Stalin lightheartedly interjected that the politburo could not yield either of its two most beloved members, and furthermore that there would be no thought of accepting Trotsky's resignations. In this version, Stalin also volunteered not to join the Revolutionary Military Council, as a way of keeping harmony. Deutscher, *Prophet Unarmed*, 111–2 (no citation). It is hard to imagine Trotsky, at this moment, knowing about the "Ilich letter about the [general] secretary" and keeping silent about it.

266. Bazhanov, *Bazhanov and the Damnation of Stalin*, 50–1; Bazhanov, *Vospominaniia* [1980], 67–8; *Izvestiia TsK KPSS*, 1991, no. 3: 216.

267. "The Central Committee constitutes that comrade Trotsky, leaving the meeting hall in connection with the speech by comrade Komarov, in which the Central Committee sees nothing offensive against comrade Trotsky, put the Central Committee in a difficult position. The Central Committee considers that comrade Trotsky behaved incorrectly by refusing to fulfill the request of the Central Committee to return to the meeting and made the Central Committee discuss the question of the composition of the Revolutionary Military Council in his absence." RGASPI, f. 17, op. 2, d. 102.

268. The resolution was for two Trotsky supporters (Pyatakov, Nikolai Muralov), one Zinovievite (Mikhail Lashevich), and three Stalin men (Orjonikidze, Voroshilov, and Stalin). RGASPI, f. 17, op. 2, d. 103, l. 2–3. Ultimately, Pyatakov, Muralov, and Stalin did not become members, but Voroshilov, Orjonikidze, and Lashevich did, along with two others whose appointments took effect in February 1924 (Andrei Bubnov and Ali Heydar-Karaev). Nenarokov, *Revvoensovet Respubliki*. They joined Sklyansky (Trotsky's right hand), Antonov-Oveseyenko (a Trotsky zealot), as well as Kamenev and Frunze; the council had recently added a number of non-Russians (Shalva Eliava, Vatslav Bogutsky, Heydar Vezirov, Inagadan Hydyr-Aliev, and Unszlicht) as well as Semyon Budyonny.

269. Volkogonov, *Trotsky*, 241 (citing Balashov); Volkogonov, *Trotskii*, II: 8–9. Balashov gives no date for this incident.

270. Chase, *Workers, Society, and the Soviet State*, 231–2.

271. *XI s"ezd VKP (b)*, 279 (Tomsky).

See also Chase, *Workers, Society, and the Soviet State*, 231–2.

272. Brovkin, *Russia After Lenin*, 176–7 (citing *Golos rabochego* [Sormovo], September 1923 [an underground periodical]).

273. *Pravda*, December 13 and December 21, 1923.

274. Velikanova, *Popular Perceptions*, 34–5.

275. Brovkin, *Russia After Lenin*, 175 (citing RGASPI, f. 17, op. 87, d. 177, l. 5).

276. Zinov'ev, *Istoriia Rossiiskoi kommunisticheskoi partii*, lecture 1; Pethybridge, *One Step Backwards*, 270 (citing Zinoviev, *History of the Bolshevik Party: A Popular Outline* [London: New Park, 1973], 10).

277. Trotsky and Shachtman, *The New Course*, 154.

278. Gimpel'son, *NEP*, 347–8 (citing RGASPI, f. 17, op. 84, d. 467, l. 128–9); Brovkin, *Russia After Lenin*, 38 (citing RGASPI, f. 17, op. 84, d. 467, l. 2). Already on October 14, Trotsky's October 8 letter was denounced at a meeting of the inner bureau of the Moscow party (Trotsky's primary party organization), which prompted Molotov in the secretariat to accuse Trotsky of distributing his letter more widely than the politburo had permitted; Trotsky, for his part, accused the secretariat of spreading the document. The next day, at a special session of the Central Control Commission presidium, Trotsky's letter was censured as an act of party factionalism. Trotsky sent his blistering theses only to internal party bodies (they were, nonetheless, soon published abroad). RGASPI, f. 17, op. 2, d. 685, l. 53–68; *Izvstiia TsK KPSS*, 1990, no. 5: 165–73; *Izvestiia TsK KPSS*, 1990, no. 10: 184. Excerpts appeared in *Sotsialisticheskii vetsnik*, May 24, 1924. See also Eastman, *Since Lenin Died*, 142–3. Vil'kova, *RKP (b), vnutripartiinaia bor'ba*, 174–5 (RGASPI, f. 17, op. 2, d. 685, l. 93–5), 176–7 (l. 91–2), 178–80 (l. 96–7), 222. 279. Brovkin, *Russia After Lenin*, 44–5. See also RGASPI, f. 17, op. 87, d. 177, l. 5 (Yagoda on the Donbas); Kvashonkin, *Bol'shevistskoe rukovodstvo*, 282–6 (at 284: RGASPI, f. 558, op. 1, d. 2565, l. 2–7: Magidov on the Donbass); and Vil'kova, *RKP (b), vnutripartiinaia bor'ba*, 55–61 (RGASPI, f. 17, op. 87, d. 177, l. 93–94, d. 178, l. 15, 18–19, 22–9), 61–2 (op. 84, d. 531, l. 97–97ob.), 63 (l. 63).

280. Vil'kova, *RKP (b), vnutripartinaia bor'ba*, 409–14 (RGASPI, f. 76, op. 3, d. 318, l. 60–9); *Pravda*, November 7, 1923 (Zinoviev). In November 1923, Anastas Mikoyan came up from the North Caucasus to Moscow and was directed to attend party meetings at universities to gain a sense of the atmosphere; he claimed to have been shocked at the passion among students

on behalf of the opposition. Mikoian, *Tak bylo*, 111. See also Daniels, "The Left Opposition."

281. *Izvestiia TsK KPSS*, 1990, no. 6: 189–93; Fel'shtinskii, *Kommunisticheskaia oppozitsiia v SSSR*, I: 83–8; Carr, *Interregnum*, 367–73; Fel'shtinskii, *Kommunisticheskaia oppozitsiia v SSSR*, I: 83–8.

282. Ivanov and Shmelev, *Leninizm i ideino-politicheskii razgrom trotskizma*, 343. There is no clear evidence that Trotsky wrote the Declaration of the 46. Vil'kova, *RKP (b), vnutripartiinaia bor'ba*. See also Carr, *Interregnum*, 303–7, 374–80.

283. Balashov and Markhashov, "Staraia ploshchad', 4 (20-e gody)," no. 6: 181. See also Bazhanov, *Bazhanov and the Damnation of Stalin*, 57–8. In parallel, Trotsky, Radek, and Pyatakov also formally protested Nazaretyan's "note-taking" at meetings and "deliberate and malicious alteration of the text of official documents." RGASPI, f. 323 [Kamenev]: op. 2, d. 64. See also Graziosi, "New Archival Sources," 40.

284. Trotsky himself may not have been above contemplating unusual means in the fight: see the contacts between E. A. Berens, a former tsarist captain who served under Trotsky in the Military Revolutionary Council and often received special assignments, and the Paris émigré Alexander Guchkov, who had been the initial war minister in the Provisional Government and had supported the Whites. Whether Berens acted on his own or at Trotsky's suggestion remains unclear, but the fact that Stalin did not seek to use the contacts to discredit Trotsky indicates Berens was not conducting a provocation on assignment from the GPU. Volkogonov, *Trotsky*, 329 (citing RGVA, f. 33987, op. 3, d. 1049, l. 96; GARF, f. 5868, op. 1, d. 15: Guchkov to N. N. Chebyshev, whom he called "Admiral B").

285. *XIII s"ezd RKP (b)* [1924], 371–3 (Boris Souvarine); Deutscher, *Prophet Unarmed*, 140–1.

286. Souvarine, *Staline*. When the Polish Communist party, which was in exile in Moscow, sent the Soviet Central Committee letters decrying the hounding of Trotsky, Stalin had the entire Polish Central Committee replaced, with no pretense of holding a Polish party congress. Dziewanowski, *Communist Party of Poland*, 103–10. See also *Bol'shevik*, September 20, 1924; *Sochineniia*, VI: 264–72.

287. Liberman, *Building Lenin's Russia*, 79; Lunacharsky, *Revolutiuonary Silhouettes*, 43, 62; Lunacharskii, *Revoliutsionnye siluety*, 27; Eastman, *Heroes*, 258–9. As Carr observed, Trotsky just "could not establish his authority among colleagues by the

modest arts of persuasion or by sympathetic attention to the views of men of lesser intellectual caliber than himself." Carr, *Socialism in One Country*, I: 166. Deutscher wrongly deemed the reaction to Trotsky's grating personality "a sense of inferiority," rather than indignation. Deutscher, *Prophet Unarmed*, 34.
288. Trotsky, *My Life*, 504. Although he addressed his letters to "Dear Vladimir Ilich," while Stalin wrote "Comrade Lenin," Trotsky, unlike Stalin or Bukharin, did not visit Lenin at home. Volkogonov, *Lenin: Life and Legacy*, 256.
289. Trostky, *My Life*, 481; Eastman, *Since Lenin Died*, 17; Daniels, *Conscience of the Revolution*, 206–7.
290. Trotsky, *My Life*, 498.
291. Trotsky, *My Life*, 500.
292. V. Doroshenko and I. Pavlova, "Posledniaia poezdka," *Altai*, 1989, no. 4: 3–18. Details of Lenin's surprise trip come from his nurse attendant (Zinovy Zorko-Rimsha), his sister Maria, his wife Krupskaya, and witness reports recorded at the time.
293. Volkogonov, *Lenin: Life and Legacy*, 431–2 (citing RGASPI, f. 4, op. 1, d. 142, l. 406–7); "Zapis' Z. I. Zor'ko Rishmi," *Izvestiia TsK KPSS*, 1991, no. 8 (RGASPI, f. 16, op. 2, d. 17, l. 857–76: October 18, 1923; l. 877–88: October 19, 1923); "Poslednii priezd Vladimira Il'icha v Moskvu: vospominaniia M. I. Ul'ianovoi," RGASPI, f. 16, op. 3, d. 37, l. 1–3 (1930s); Krupskaia, "Poslednie polgoda zhizni Vladimira Il'icha (3 fevralia 1924 goda)," *Izvestiia TsK KPSS*, 1990, no. 4: 169–78 (at 174). See also *Kul'tura i zhizn'*, 1975, no. 1: at 11 (G. P. Koblov); *Gudok*, April 23, 1924; Golikov, *Vladimir Il'ich lenin*, XIII: 638–9.
294. *Izvestiia TsK KPSS*, 1991, no. 8: 177 (RGASPI, f. 4, op. 2, d. 1744, l. 7–8: V. I. Ryabov, August 16, 1940).
295. "Poslednii priezd Vladimira Il'icha v Moskvu: vospominaniia M. I. Ul'ianovoi," RGASPI, f. 16, op, 3, d. 37, l. 1–3 (1930s). Also later, a *Pravda* journalist referred to a section of the memoirs of another of Lenin's nurse attendants from that day about Lenin being disappointed not to encounter members of the leadership, but no such passage is in the extant archival record of the referenced memoirs. *Kul'tura i zhizn'*, 1975, no. 1: at 11 (D. I. Novopolianskii, citing V. A. Rukavishnikov).
296. "Voot, voot, voot, voot!" in Russian, according to the attendant V. A. Rukavishnikov (RGASPI, f. 16, op. 2, d. 91, l. 37–8: October 19, 1923).
297. RGASPI, f. 558, op. 11, d. 25, l. 110; RGASPI, f. 17, op. 162, d. 1. l. 21–2.
298. *Izvestiia TsK KPSS*, 1990, no. 7: 176–89; Vil'kova, *RKP (b), vnutripartiinaia bor'ba*, 197–220 (RGASPI, f. 51, op. 1, d. 21, l. 51–4). The

respondents, listed alphabetically (in Russian), were Bukharin, Zinoviev, Kalinin, Kamenev, Molotov, Rykov, Stalin, and Tomsky; Lenin and Rudzutaks did not sign. Bukharin, in Leningrad at the time, sent a telegram insisting on textual changes, which Stalin ignored while affixing Bukharin's name. *Izvestiia TsK KPSS*, 1990, no. 7: 190.
299. Vil'kova, *RKP (b), vnutripartinaia bor'ba*, 266–271. Those from the 46 invited to appear on October 26 included Kosior, Lobanov, Muralov, Osinsky, Preobrazhensky, Serebryakov, and Smirnov. Those who took part in the discussion included Preobrazhensky, Osinsky, Kamenev, Rykov, Yaroslavsky, Bumazhny, and Dzierżyński.
300. Sakharov, *Politicheskoe zaveshchanie*, 478. Fel'shtinskii, *Kommunisticheskaia oppozitsiia v SSSR*, I: 9, 18–19; RGASPI, f. 5, op. 2, d. 305, l. 2–4. Prior to January 1924, there was no practice of making stenographic records of politburo meetings.
301. See also Carr, *Socialism in One Country*, I: 157.
302. Vil'kova, *RKP (b), vnutripartinaia bor'ba*, 255–65 (RGASPI, f. 17, op. 2, d. 685, l. 39–49); Ivanov and Shmelev, *Leninizm i ideinopoliticheskii razgrom trotskizma*, 344 (citing RGASPI, f. 17, op. 2, d. 104, l. 46). A less detailed version of Trotsky's speech by Bazhanov is at: RGASPI, f. 17, op. 2, d. 104, l. 31–8. They were also published in *Izvestiia TsK KPSS*, 1990, no. 10: 183–7; and in *Voprosy istorii* KPSS, 1990, no. 5: 33–9.
303. Vil'kova, *RKP (b), vnutripartinaia bor'ba*, 250–5 (RGASPI, f. 17, op. 2, d. 104, l. 31–8).
304. Vil'kova, *RKP (b), vnutripartinaia bor'ba*, 266–8 (RGASPI, f. 17, op. 2, d. 104, l. 1–4); Koloskov, *XIII konferentsiia RKP (b)*, 14.
305. *Izvestiia TsK KPSS*, 1989, no. 2: 201–2.
306. Babichenko, "Politbiuro TsK RKP (b)," 136 (RGASPI, f. 495, op. 19, d. 362, l. 117). Chicherin attended politburo meetings even though he was not a member.
307. Ruth Fischer, Brandler's leftist rival, wrote that he and Zinoviev detested each other, and asserted that Brandler had become close to Trotsky. Fischer, *Stalin and German Communism*, 318, 323. See also *Lessons of the German Events*, 36–7; *XIII konferentsiia RKP (b)*, 158–78.
308. The Soviet journalist Grigory N. Kaminsky (b. 1895), unlike his colleagues who wrote pie-in-the-sky blather about the strength of the German proletariat, reported the truth on October 15 from Dresden (in Saxony): the German Communists were poorly prepared for battle, reaching only

those workers already affiliated. Babichenko, "Politbiuro TsK RKP (b)," 135 (RGASPI, f. 495, op. 293, d. 673, l. 58; op. 18, d. 182, l. 10–1).
309. Babichenko, "Politbiuro TsK RKP (b)," 134–5 (RGASPI, f. 495, op. 293, d. 14, l. 177).
310. Even in the coalition government in Saxony, the Communists had expended their efforts not building a movement but denouncing and intriguing against the Social Democrats, revealing the limits of even a sincere "united front" strategy ordered from above. Babichenko, "Politbiuro TsK RKP (b)," 143 (RGASPI, f. 17, op. 2, d. 109, l. 22: Pyatakov, January 15, 1924). Adding insult to injury, the Left Communists in Berlin spent more effort battling others in their own party than preparing an insurrection. Babichenko, "Politbiuro TsK RKP (b)," 151 (RGASPI, f. 558, op. 2-e, d. 6968, l. 3: Vasily Shmidt to Stalin and Zinoviev).
311. Kuusinen, *Rings of Destiny*, 63–5.
312. Voss, *Von hamburger Aufstand zur politische Isolierung*, 13; Babichenko, "Politbiuro TsK RKP (b)," 139–40 (RGASPI, f. 495, op. 293, d. 14, l. 37).
313. On November 3, the politburo resolved to summon back to Moscow the team sent to Germany. Adibekov and Shirinia, *Politbiuro TsK RKP (b)— VKP (b) i Komintern*, 216.
314. Out of Berlin, Stalin had been getting regular reports from Pyatakov, mostly complaints about the difficulties in staging the revolution, mixed with worries about the divisive politics at home (Pyatakov was close to Trotsky): "P.S. I am concerned about our internal party conflict in the USSR . . . For God's sake, do not start a fight, or we will abandon our work here." RGASPI, f. 558, op. 11, d. 785, l. 1–8ob.
315. RGASPI, f. 558, op. 11, d. 785, l. 23–6.
316. RGASPI, f. 558, op. 11, d. 785, l. 28. Radek wrote to Moscow that revolution had been "premature." Adibekov and Shirinia, *Politbiuro TsK RKP (b)— VKP (b) i Komintern*, 209–13; *Komintern i ideia mirovoi revoliutsii: dokumenty*, 428–35. Pyatakov was trying to get Stalin to focus on the German Communists, writing to him on November 14 that "All of you, obviously, do not notice that such a party in its present form cannot attract the working class to an armed uprising." The politburo resolved to issue an open letter about German events but failed to come to agreement on the text. Babichenko, "Politbiuro TsK RKP (b)," 145 (RGASPI, f. 495, op. 293, d. 638, l. 20–2). Adibekov and Shirinia, *Politbiuro TsK RKP (b)—VKP (b) i Komintern*, 218–20. It was in November 1923 that the leadership of the

Germans of the Volga Valley proposed setting up an "Autonomous Soviet Socialist Republic of Volga Germans," just after having celebrated the fifth anniversary of the First National Autonomy (*oblast*). GARF, f. 58s, op.1, d. 9, l. 14–10, Hoover Institution Archives, Volkogonov papers, container 21.

317. Gordon, *Hitler and the Beer Hall Putsch.*
318. Sakharov, *Politicheskoe zaveshchanie*, 311.
319. Chuev, *Molotov Remembers*, 135.
320. "M. I. Ul'ianova ob otnoshenii V. I. Lenina k I. V. Stalinu," *Izvestiia TsK KPSS*, 1989, no. 12: 196–201 (at 198–9: RGASPI, f. 14, op. 1, d. 398, l.

1–8). Ulyanova was referring to her statement of July 26, 1926, to the plenum: see chapter 13.
321. Chuev, *Molotov Remembers*, 212.
322. Chuev, *Tak govoril Kaganovich*, 190–1; Chuev, *Kaganovich*, 263.

## CHAPTER 12: FAITHFUL PUPIL

1. "Po povodu smerti Lenina," *Pravda*, January 30, 1924, reprinted in *Sochineniia*, VI: 46–51.
2. Trotsky's best biographer commented that "hardly any Menshevik writer attacked Lenin with so much personal venom." Deutscher, *Prophet Armed*, 93.
3. V. I. Lenin, "Letter to Yelena Stasova and Others," in Lenin, *Collected Works*, 42: 129.
4. V. I. Lenin, "Letter to Grigory Zinoviev," in Lenin, *Collected Works*, 34: 399–400.
5. *Kommunist*, 1988, no. 6: 3–5 (to Goldenberg, October 28, 1909).
6. V. I. Lenin, "Judas Trotsky's Blush of Shame," *Collected Works*, 18: 45. "What a swine that Trotsky is!" Lenin, *Collected Works*, 39: 290.
7. *PSS*, XLIX: 390.
8. Trotskii, *Trotskii o Lenine i Leninizme*; *Lenin o Trotskom i trotskizme.*
9. On Stalin's understanding of his role as Lenin's deputy, see the revealing typescript in the nationalities commissariat, dated 1923, and headed "Biographical Details on Stalin," in Volkogonov, *Stalin: Triumph and Tragedy*, 512 (RGASPI, f. 1318, op. 3, d. 8, l. 85).
10. Carr, *Socialism in One Country*, I: 151–202 (portraits of Trotsky, Zinoviev, Kamenev, Bukharin, and Stalin).
11. Balabanoff, *My Life as a Rebel*, 243–4. Carr, however, mischaracterized Zinoviev, both selling him short ("an intellectual void" and "weakness of conviction") and overselling him (wrongly "the leading figure in the party" during the triumvirate). *Socialism in One Country*, I: 165, 169. By contrast, see Lih, "Zinoviev."
12. Even Walter Duranty understood this, writing: "Yet it had occurred to me that Trotsky, who was essentially an intellectual aristocrat, not to say an intellectual snob, was somewhat out of place in the Bolshevik milieu." Duranty, *I Write as I Please*, 199.
13. Yuri Annenkov, commissioned to paint Trotsky's portrait for the Red Army's fifth anniversary in 1923, discovered him to be not only "a healthy height, thickset, full shouldered and wonderfully muscular," but also familiar with Annenkov's recent portrait

book and conversant about Matisse and Picasso. Annenkov, *Dnevnik moikh vstrech*, II: 286–7. See also Annenkov, *Semnadtsat' portretov*, II: 295–6. This Annenkov book, which contained drawn portraits of Trotsky, Zinoviev, and Kamenev, among others, would be ordered removed from all Soviet libraries, shops, and private collections in 1928. Annenkov also wrote a devastating portrait of Lenin as anti-intellectual: *Dnevnik moikh vstrech*, II: 268–70. Annenkov's 1921 portrait of Lenin was used on Soviet postage stamps and featured at the Soviet Pavilion at the 1925 Paris exhibition.
14. Lawrence Freedman invites us to consider "strategy as a story about power told in the future tense from the perspective of a leading character," which was precisely Stalin's achievement, within the rigid Marxist framework. Freedman, *Strategy*.
15. Stalin's book based on public lectures, *O Lenine*, appeared with his speech to Kremlin military cadets. Zinoviev also published it at his own Leningrad publishing house (Priboi). It also came out in Ukrainian (Kharkov: Derzhavne vyd-vo Ukraïny), German (Vienna: Verlag für Literatur und Politik), French (Paris: Bureau d'éditions), and other languages.
16. Vil'kova, *RKP (b), vnutripartiinaia bor'ba*, 409–14 (RGASPI, f. 76, op. 3, d. 318, l. 60–9).
17. *Pravda*, January 8, 1924.
18. On January 12, the party newspaper reported that of the 72 party cells in Moscow's higher education institutions, 32 (with a combined 2,790 members) had voted for the Central Committee, while 40 (with 6,594 members) had voted for the Left opposition: here is where the impatient program of industry *now*, socialism *now*, appealed. *Moskovskie bol'sheviki*, 83 (citing MPA, f. 3, op. 5, d. 2, l. 200); Abramovich, *Vospominaniia i vzgliadi*, I: 22, 36.
19. Lively polemics ensued as Grigory Sokolnikov (Mr. Fiscal Discipline) went up against Yevgeny Preobrazhensky (Mr. Print Money to Finance Industry), with thuggish rebuttals of the latter by the likes of Bukharin and Nikolai Uglanov, and a stacked voting

majority to back them up. Fel'shtinskii, *Kommunisticheskaia oppozitsiia v SSSR*, II: 34, 101; *XIII konferentsiia RKP (b)*; Vil'kova, *RKP (b): vnutripartiinaia bor'ba*, 390–406.
20. Vil'kova, *RKP (b), vnutripartiinaia bor'ba*, 385–93 (RGASPI, f. 17, op. 2, d. 109, l. 6ob–7ob); RGASPI, f. 17, op. 2, d. 107, l. 14–7 (stenographic records of Central Committee plenums began at this January 14–15, 1924, gathering); *XIII konferentsiia RKP (b)*, 95. Provincial affiliates of the party control commission were activated against oppositionists: Olekh, *Povorot, kotorogo ne bylo*, 146 (citing *Dni*, December 19, 1923).
21. RGASPI, f. 17, op. 2, d. 107, l. 100–1; *X s"ezd*, 524; *Sochineniia*, VI: 15. Schapiro, *Origin of the Communist Autocracy* [1977], 317–8. Radek correctly objected that no Party Congress had lifted the veil of secrecy over this punishment clause, but no body could hold Stalin to account. Daniels, *Conscience of the Revolution*, 230; Vil'kova, *RKP (b), vnutripartiinaia bor'ba*, 403–8 (RGASPI, f. 17, op. 2, d. 109, l. 13ob–14).
22. When Radek charged that Trotsky was "being baited," Stalin seized the moment, in his closing speech on January 18, 1924, to rehearse the September 1923 incident when "Trotsky jumped up and left the meeting. You will recall that the Central Committee plenum sent a 'delegation' to Trotsky to *request* that he return to the meeting. You will recall that Trotsky refused to comply with this request." "Zakliuchitel'noe slovo (18 ianvaria [1924 g.]," *Sochineniia*, VI: 27–45 (at 38–39). But the mauling had become so relentless that Stalin felt compelled to answer criticisms that he had failed to preemptively ban Trotsky's December 11 article on *The New Course*: "that would have been a very dangerous step on the part of the Central Committee. Just try to ban an article of Trotsky's that has already been read aloud in Moscow districts!" (33).
23. *Pravda*, January 26, 1924. See also Halfin, *Intimate Enemies*; Robert Service, "How They Talked: The Discourse of Politics in the Soviet Party Politburo in the 1920s," in Gregory and Naimark, *Lost Politburo*

*Transcripts*, 121–34. Stalin also had the 13th party conference name a military reform commission, headed by Sergei Gusev, a member of the party's Central Control Commission, the battering ram Stalin's men controlled. The conference confirmed a December 5 decision to enroll 100,000 new worker party members.

24. Sakharov, *Politicheskoe zaveshchanie*, 576 (citing RGASPI, f. 16, op. 1, d. 98, l. 107).

25. Stalin was the lead but not the sole pummeler of the absent Trotsky. Alexander Shlyapnikov, the trade unionist and one-time coleader of the outlawed Workers' opposition, shredded Trotsky and the Left opposition for their complicity in repressing the Workers opposition back in 1921. Shliapnikov, "Nashi raznoglasiia," *Pravda*, January 18, 1924.

26. Trotsky, *My Life*, 515.

27. Only belatedly, in late August 1923, after his condition had modestly improved, had the regime revealed the gravity of his illness, but even after this disclosure official reports had continued to contain unwarranted doses of optimism ("substantial improvement . . . great strides"). *Pravda*, August 30, 1923; *Pravda*, October 21, 1923 (Health Commissar Semashko). See also Volkogonov, *Lenin: Life and Legacy*, 414 (citing RGASPI, f. 16, op. 3, d. 6, l. 7), 430 (citing APRF, f. 3, op. 22, d, 307, l. 410); Golikov, *Vladimir Il'ich Lenin*, XII: 646, 650; and Tumarkin, *Lenin Lives!*, 115–7. Kamenev instructed the artist Yuri Annenkov to drive out to Gorki for what was thought to be a final portrait. Krupskaya "said there was no question of a portrait," Annenkov recalled. "And, indeed, Lenin could serve solely as an illustration of his illness, reclining on a chaise-lounge, wrapped in a blanket and looking past us with the helpless, twisted, babyish smile of a man in his second infancy." Annenkov, *Dnevnykh moikh vstrech*, II: 271; Annenkov, "Vospominania o Lenine," 141–9.

28. Golikov, *Vladimir Il'ich Lenin*, XII: 658–9; Krupskaia, "Chto nravilos' Il'ichu iz khudozhestvennoi literatury," *Narodnyi uchitel'*, 1927, no. 1: 4–6. On January 19, at the 11th All-Russia Congress of Soviets, Mikhail Kalinin told the delegates that "rays of hope are already visible" in Lenin's battle to overcome his illness and return to work. "Hurrah," shouted the congress, an episode carried in the newspaper: *Izvestiia*, January 20, 1924.

29. Bukharin showed up nearly every Saturday. *Izvestiia TsK KPSS*, 1989, no. 4: 174–5.

30. Volkogonov, *Lenin: Life and Legacy*, 299–301; Kun, *Bukharin*, 135. Later, Bukharin's presence at Lenin's

death bed would be erased by Stalin's henchmen: Mikoian, *Mysli i vospominaniia*, 235–6. Krupskaya, too, even in her unpublished memoirs, insisted Bukharin had not been allowed in. Volkogonov, *Lenin: Life and Legacy*, 433 (citing APRF, f. 3, op. 22, d. 307, l. 175).

31. Volkogonov, *Lenin: politicheskii portret*, II: 361 (citing APRF, f. 3, op. 33, d. 307, l. 175–6); Volkogonov, *Lenin: Life and Legacy*, 435.

32. Golikov, *Vladimir Il'ich Lenin*, XII: 662, 664; Prof. V. Osipov, "Bolezn' i smert' V. I. Lenina," *Ogonek*, 1990, no. 4; Ul'ianova, "O Vladimire Iliche," no. 3; N. Petrenk [B. Ravdin], "Lenin v Gorkakh: bolezn' i smert'," *Minuvshee: Istoricheski almanakh*, 1986, no. 2: 189–91.

33. Mikoyan wrote that on the afternoon of January 21, he went to Stalin's apartment to discuss strategy, and that "some 30 or 40 minutes into our conversation an excited Bukharin burst in and did not say but shrieked that Maria had called from Gorki and said that 'Lenin has just died at 6:50 p.m.'" This was a lie, designed to undermine the fact that Bukharin was in Gorki with the dying Lenin; the call about Lenin's death came through not to Stalin's apartment but to the Congress of Soviets in session. Mikoian, *Tak bylo*, 113.

34. Ioffe, *Vremia nazad*, ch. 4.

35. Vladimir Bonch-Bruevich also organized a special two-car train for the health commissar and the team of doctors who would perform the autopsy and embalming, as well as family members not already at Gorki (Lenin's sister Anna and brother Dmitry). Bonch-Bruevich, "Smert' i pokhorony Vladimira Il'icha"; *Pravda*, January 21, 1925; *Otchet Komissii TsIK SSSR*, 5.

36. Bonch-Bruevich, "Smert' i pokhorony Vladimira Il'icha," 189–90. Note that Bonch-Bruevich does not mention Bukharin going to Gorki on the sled-tracked vehicles or train, but has him in the room saying good-bye with the others.

37. *Izvestiia*, January 24, 1922.

38. Sakharov, *Politicheskoe zaveshchanie*, 576 (citing RGASPI, f. 16, op. 1, d. 44, l. 1).

39. *Izvestiia*, January 25, 1924; *Pravda*, January 26, 1924. Nikolai Semashko, Soviet health commissar, observed of Lenin's cranial blood vessels that "when struck with a tweezer they sounded like stone." *Pravda*, January 24, 1924; Semashko, *Otchego bolel*, 35. See also Fischer, *Life of Lenin*, 672. The published reports, citing "an incurable disease of the blood vessels," seemed to be saying that Lenin was beyond the doctors' help; they could not have saved him and should not be blamed. But whereas Semashko stressed Lenin's

"superhuman mental activity, life of constant agitation and ceaseless anxiety," Doctor Abrikosov emphasized the hereditary factors in Lenin's arteriosclerosis. *Izvestiia*, January 25, 1924; Tumarkin, *Lenin Lives!*, 172, n34.

40. Valentinov, *Novaia ekonomicheskaia politika*, 87.

41. Volkogonov, *Lenin: Life and Legacy*, 409 (citing APRF, f. 3, op. 22, d. 307, l. 135: doctor's notes discovered in December 1935 by the head of the Kremlin medical administration—Khodorovsky—and placed in secret archive).

42. Service, *Lenin*, III: 255–62. Lenin had consulted specialists in nervous disorders at least as early as 1900, while in Germany. RGASPI, f. 2, op. 1, d. 385, l. 1.

43. Duranty, "Lenin Dies of Cerebral Hemorrhage"; *Pravda*, January 24, 1924. The congress did resume, then closed on January 29, after approving the new constitution of the USSR. *XI Vserossiiskii s"ezd Sovetov*.

44. Maksimov, "U tovarishcha Stalina (po vospominaniiam byvshego detkora)," *Raboche-Krest'ianskii korrespondent*, 1934, no. 10: RGASPI, f. 558, op. 4, d. 649, l. 208 (Viktor Maksimov).

45. Ia. G. Zimin, "Sklianskii Efraim Markovich," in Nenarokov, *Revvoensovet Respubliki*, 56–70 (at 68); Zetkin, *We Have Met Lenin*, 73–5; Gil', *Shest' let s V. I. Leninym*, 100–1; Golikov, *Vladimir Il'ich Lenin*, XII: 664–79.

46. Izmozik, *Glaza*, 84.

47. Sevost'ianov, "Sovershenno sekretno," I/i: 52–3 (TsA FSB, f. 2, op, 2, d. 1, l. 1).

48. Izmozik, *Glaza*, 160–1. Izmozik maintains that unlike party and Soviet officials, Chekists did not dress up the situation in their domains, although he argues their reports became "less objective" by the end of the 1920s.

49. RGASPI, f. 76, op. 3, d. 325, l. 4–6.

50. Von Hagen, *Soldiers in the Proletarian Dictatorship*, 291–2.

51. Bazhanov, *Bazhanov and the Damnation of Stalin*, 63.

52. Valentinov, *Novaia ekonomicheskaia politika*, 88–9.

53. Volkogonov, *Trotsky*, 266 (citing RGVA, f, 33987, op. 3, d. 80, l. 587; RGASPI, f. 2, op. 1, d. 27088, l. 1; RGASPI, f. 558, op. 11, d. 816, l. 75–6).

54. Trotsky, *My Life*, 508; Deutscher, *Prophet Unarmed*, 131–4.

55. *Izvestiia*, January 25 and January 26, 1924.

56. *New York Times*, January 28, 1924 (Walter Duranty). Later, Duranty recreated a conversation with a French journalist of *Le Temps* in Moscow. "My God, what an opportunity to miss! Achilles sulking in his tent. Quel idiot. As if he couldn't understand that the whole strength of his position was his reputation with the masses as Lenin's

chief aide and supporter . . . If he had come to Moscow. . . he would have stolen the whole show, as you say in America." Duranty, *I Write as I Please*, 225–6. This was Henri Louis-Victor-Mars Rollin, who, Duranty omits to mention (or did not know), was perceived as a Bolshevik agent by the Quai d'Orsay. Rollin wrote what for decades was the major historical work (*L'apocalypse de notre temps*, 1939) on the *Protocols of the Elders of Zion*.

57. "One could feel in his letter," Natalya Sedova's mother observed of mail they received from Lev in Moscow, "bitter bewilderment and diffident reproach." Trotsky, *My Life*, 511. See also Patenaude, *Stalin's Nemesis*, 170–3.

58. RGAKFD, ed. khr. 1-14097 (year 1924).

59. Trotsky, *Stalin*, 381.

60. "Lenin is No More" was wired to Moscow for publication in *Pravda* and *Izvestiia*: *Pravda*, January 24, 1924; *Izvestiia*, January 24, 1924; Volkogonov, *Trotsky*, 266 (citing RGASPI, f. 2, op. 1, d. 27088, l. 1).

61. "Po povodu smerti Lenina," *Pravda*, January 30, 1924; *Sochineniia*, VI: 46–51. Stalin's name was absent from the original list of speakers decided at the politburo; on a subsequent list, he was added as "conditional" (*uslovno*). What to make of this remains unclear. Krupskaya's name appeared on none of the speaker lists, but obviously there could never have been any doubt she would speak (as she did). RGASPI, f. 16, op. 2s, d. 47, l. 1–4. Stalin gave another speech to the Kremlin military school cadets on January 28, 1924.

62. "Zavëty Lenina" was the title of the front-page essay in *Izvestiya* on January 24, 1924.

63. *Izvestiia*, January 27, 1924. Ulam, normally a shrewd analyst, misjudged the speech as out of place. Ulam, *Stalin*, 235.

64. *Pravda*, January 30 and January 31, 1924.

65. Golikov, *Vladimir Il'ich Lenin*, XII: 678. In July 1929, the politburo would decide to build a permanent mausoleum, a granite copy of the wooden one; it would be completed in 1933.

66. Adolf Joffe, who was very close to Trotsky, wrote to Zinoviev proposing that no one replace Lenin as chairman of the Council of People's Commissars, suggesting instead a presidium consisting of Trotsky, Zinoviev, and Kamenev; if, however, they did decide on a single government head, Joffe suggested it be Trotsky. Whether Joffe acted on his own or had cleared his letter with Trotsky remains unknown. Vasetskii, *Trotskii*, 193.

67. *Pravda*, February 12, 1924, in *Sochineniia*, VI: 52–64.

68. *Izvestiia TsK KPSS*, 1990, no. 6: 200 (RGASPI, f. 16, op. 2, d. 48, l. 41).

69. A three-day Central Committee plenum concluded on January 31 by rechristening the plan for 100,000 workers to join the party—the "Lenin Enrollment." Golikov, *Vladimir Il'ich Lenin*, XI: 679. The Lenin Enrollment would claim 240,000 new party members.

70. Shelestov, *Vremia Alekseia Rykova*, 222–3. There was a second executive position, which Lenin had also held—chairman of the Council of Labor and Defense—and Kamenev got that. Lenin's sister and wife remained in the Kremlin apartment (until 1939), and preserved Lenin's room as it had been. Stalin evicted Krupskaya and Maria Ulyanova from Lenin's Gorki dacha and initially considered taking it for himself, but then it became a museum. In April 1955, Khrushchev would open Lenin's Kremlin suite to the public (more than 2 million people would visit); in 1994, all the contents of Lenin's Kremlin apartment-museum were removed to his former Gorki dacha, and the senate was again sealed off from the public. From 1994 through 1998, a major renovation took place of the interior of the Imperial Senate, transforming it beyond recognition.

71. Artamonov, *Spetsob"ekty Stalina*, 33–4; Korotyshevskii, "Garazh osobogo znacheniia." The Special Purpose Garage had been overseen by Lenin's principal driver, Stepan Gil', but even before Lenin's death, Stalin's main driver, Pavel Udalov, had replaced him. Nikolai Solovyov, another of Stalin's drivers, had been one of General Brusilov's drivers. The Soviet regime had bought seventy-three Silver Ghosts in England between 1922 and 1925 (when the model was discontinued) for Lenin and others in the elite. Despite the USSR's icy temperatures and snowfalls, they preferred the open-top models.

72. The villa was built in 1922–3, but the property had belonged to Nikolai Smetskoi (sometimes written as Smetskii), and the facility was registered as Resort No. 3 of the central executive committee. No. 1 was in Kursk province (Ivanov-Lgovsky county) and No. 2 in Crimea (Gurzuf). Artamonov, *Spetsob"ekty Stalina*, 128.

73. Trotsky, *My Life*, 509.

74. Rikhter, *Kavkaz nashikh dnei*.

75. Hoover Institution Archives, N. A. Lakoba papers, 1–23. See also Lakoba, "Ia Koba, ty Lakoba," 50–4. Trotsky came with bodyguards, again for his "safety." On January 6, 1924, Abram Belenky, the head of Lenin's bodyguard detail, wrote a letter to Lakoba, marked "Completely Secret," without letterhead: "The doctors have forbidden com. Trotsky from working and [ordered] that he depart immediately

on a two month vacation for recuperation in the south. It seems to me we could not pick a better spot than by you in Sukhum, especially since the doctors insist on Sukhum. I think the best place to put him up would be the Smitskovo dacha, that is, where in the past you put up comrades Dzierżyński and Zinoviev." Belenky noted that the doctors were prescribing complete tranquility, and "I ask you dear Comrade Lakoba to use your accurate eye and solicitude and to take him under your wing, so that we here will be utterly relaxed." Kauzov will be responsible for Trotsky's food and security. "I am certain that you have understood me in everything. It's clear that there should be no meetings and parades. . . . Comrade Kauzov will give you photographs which I took in Zubalovo. Heartfelt and warm greetings to you from comrades Dzierżyński and Yagoda." Lakoba Papers, 1–28.

76. While the couple was still en route to Sukhum, Trotsky's wife Natalya Sedova had noted how "the uncertainty tried one's patience: what sort of life would there be at Sukhum? Would we have enemies or friends about us there?" Trotsky, *My Life*, 508.

77. Vinogradov, *Genrikh Iagoda*, 307–8 (TsA FSB, f. 3, op. 2, d. 9, l. 247).

78. Volkogonov, *Trotsky*, 267 (citing Trotsky archive, Houghton Library, Harvard University, bMS/Russ. 13.1, 8967–86, folder 1/2, 1–2); Fel'shtinskii, *Kommunisticheskaia oppozitsiia v SSSR*, I: 89; Trotsky, *My Life*, 511.

79. *Pravda*, January 3, 1924. Krupskaya had also delivered a speech, published in *Pravda* (January 11, 1924), at Moscow's Bauman ward party organization, in connection with elections to the party conference, on behalf of the ruling triumvirate (she praised only Zinoviev by name). McNeal, *Bride of the Revolution*, 233–4.

80. "It is well known among Trotsky's friends," Max Eastman would write, "that he received a letter from Lenin's wife some days after Lenin died, reminding him of their early friendship." Eastman, *Since Lenin Died*, 13.

81. Kudriashov, *Krasnaia armiia*, 96–102 (APRF, f. 3, op. 50, d. 254, l. 77, 83–84ob., 99–99ob., 103–7). The replacement was formalized on March 11, 1924. RGASPI, f. 17, op. 3, d. 424, l. 8. Dzierżyński, at the Supreme Council of the Economy, took Sklyansky in, naming him head of a Moscow textile trust. RGASPI, f. 17, op. 3, d. 424, l. 8.

82. Lakoba, "'Ia Koba, a ty Lakoba,'" 55.

83. Velikanova, *Making of an Idol*, 52–3 (citing RGASPI, f. 16, op. 2s, d. 49, l. 2–4; d. 48, l. 12; op. 3, d. 412, l. 1; op. 2s, d. 49, l. 37); Bonch-Bruevich, *Vospominaniia o Lenine* [1965], 435; *Izvestiia*, January 26, 1924. Krupskaya

vehemently objected to the Lenin mummification plan and the religious-like veneration. *Pravda*, January 30, 1924. One scholar has pointed out that when Egyptian king Tut's mummy had been discovered at an unplundered site at Luxor in 1922, to worldwide fascination, it received ample coverage in the Soviet press. Tumarkin, *Lenin Lives!*, 179–80. Soviet Russia in 1924 happened to have no crematoria.

84. Religious imagery had already made its appearance when Lenin had been shot in 1918 and Lev Sosnovsky, then editor of the newspaper for peasant activists (*Bednota*), had described Lenin as a Christ figure, asserting that "Lenin cannot be killed... because Lenin is the rising of the oppressed." Tumarkin, *Lenin Lives!* 83–4 (citing L. Sosnovskii, "K pokousheniiu na tov. Lenina," *Petrogradskaia Pravda*, September 1, 1918).

85. Kotyrev, *Mavzolei V. I. Lenina*.

86. Nikolai Gorbunov, the head of the government's business directorate, had pinned his own Order of the Red Banner to the dead Lenin's jacket on January 22. Lenin was awarded his own such medal the next day. But Gorbunov's seems to have stayed on Lenin until perhaps 1943. It is likely Gorbunov received the one awarded to Lenin.

87. Krasin, "Arkhitekturnye uvekovechenie Lenina," *Izvestiia*, February 3, 1924; Ennker, *Die Anfänge des Leninkults*, 234. See also Ennker, "The Origins and Intentions of the Lenin Cult," 118–28.

88. *Izvestiia*, August 2, 1924.

89. *New York Times*, August 4, 1924.

90. "So long as he is there, so long as he does not change, Communism is safe and the new Russia will prosper," noted the visiting American writer Theodore Dreiser. "But—whisper—if he fades or is destroyed, ah, then comes the great, sad change—the end of his kindly dream." Dreiser, *Dreiser Looks at Russia*, 31.

91. *Pravda*, July 8, 1923. The Lenin Museum would attract 37,000 visitors during the first seven months of 1925, most on organized tours. Arosev, "Institut V. I. Lenina"; Tumarkin, *Lenin Lives!*, 125; Holmes and Burgess, "Scholarly Voice or Political Echo?," 387.

92. Annenkov, "Vospominaniia o Lenine," 144. The museum had received Lenin's brain, as well as his heart, on January 25, 1924.

93. The professor tried to explain the Lenin "cult" by its function of inspiring the party's "active element to greater activity," for whom "Lenin is the guide—to be studied and followed, his precepts to be carried out faithfully." For the broad masses, Lenin is portrayed with a suggestion of the supernatural, a "sun breaking through clouds with a bright ray of light." Harper, *Civic Training*, 39–40.

94. *Izvestiia*, August 22, 1923, and September 28, 1927; *Pravda*, October 27, 1923.

95. Kamenev would be removed as director in January 1927.

96. *Izvestiia*, January 21, 1927; *Vestnik Kommunisticheskoi akademii*, 1928, no. 27: at 298; *Zapiski Instituta Lenina*, 1927, no. 1: 176; "IML k 100-letiiu so dnia rozhdeniia V. I. Lenina." *Kommunist*, 1968, no. 17. There were other initiatives: one was the formation of a project to write the history of the party (known in Russian as *Istpart*), which derived from Lenin's conviction that the October coup had vindicated his theory of party organization; another was the conversion of the Marx cabinet, dedicated to the collection and study of documents about and by Marx and Engels, into the Marx-Engels Institute. Both initiatives eventually merged in the Lenin Institute. *PSS*, XLI: 176 (Mikhail Pokrovsky and Vladimir Adoratsky); Komarov, "Sozdanie i deietel'nost' Istparta 1920–1928 gg."; Volin, "Istpart i Sovetskaia istoricheskaia nauka," 189–206; Burgess, "The Istpart Commission"; Komarov, "K istorii instituta Lenina," 181–91; Ivanova, "Institut Marksa-Engelsa-Lenina," IV: 214–23.

97. Lenin, *Sobranie sochinenii*; Lenin, *Sobranie sochinenii*, 2nd and 3rd eds. In 1925, 6,296 publications of Leniniana would be catalogued. Karpovich, "Russian Revolution of 1917," 258.

98. *Otchet 15 s"ezdu partii*, 71.

99. Velikanova, *Making of an Idol*, 110–1 (citing RGASPI, f. 12, op. 2, d. 41, l. 1–1ob). On February 19, 1925, the politburo asked Krupskaya to write Lenin's biography. RGASPI, f. 17, op. 3, d. 489, l. 4.

100. *Pravda*, February 12, 1924.

101. Gor'kii, *Vladimir Ilich Lenin*, 10. Victor Chernov, the émigré former Socialist Revolutionary Party head, in a shrewd portrait that appeared in the American journal *Foreign Affairs*, concluded that Lenin had been a "lifelong schismatic" yet lived in mortal fear of a schism in the party. "Lenin's intellect was energetic but cold... an ironic, sarcastic and cynical intellect," he added. "Nothing to him was worse than sentimentality, a name he was ready to apply to all moral and ethical considerations in politics." Chernov, "Lenin." Bertrand Russell, who had gone to Russia as a Communist but developed doubts, noted of Lenin, "I think if I had met him without knowing who he was, I should not have guessed that he was a great man; he struck me as too opinionated and narrowly orthodox." Russell, *Practice and Theory of Bolshevism*, 42.

102. Chuev, *Sto sorok*, 184.

103. *Soldatskaia pravda*, May 1917, reprinted in *Zapiski instituta lenina*, 1927, no. 2: 24–33; *Pravda*, April 16, 1927, reprinted in *PSS*, XXXII: 21; Savitskaia, "Razrabotka nauchnoi biografii V. I. Lenina," 4. By the summer of 1924, the combination Marxism-Leninism was appearing in many documents. Shcherbakov, "A kratkii kurs blagoslovil," *Pravda*, September 13, 1990. See also Nikolai Babakhan [Sisak Babakhanyan], "Marksizm i leninizm," *Pravda*, April 6, 1923.

104. The Sverdlovka, as it was known, at Miusskaya Square, no. 6, in the former Shanyavsky Moscow City People's University, was best equipped of all institutions of higher education in Soviet Russia. Reznik, *Trotzkizm i Levaia oppozitsiia*, 38; *Desiat' let Kommunisticheskogo universiteta*; Ovsiannikov, *Miusskaia ploshchad'*, 6; Harper, *Civic Training*, 285. Originally, the Communist University had managed to get hold of the premises of the former Moscow merchant association club at Malaya Dmitrovka, 6, executed in the art moderne style (down to the lights, furniture, and drapes), but in 1923 it opened a cinema and a jazz hall.

105. *Sochineniia*, VI: 52–64, 69–188. Sverdlov Communist University eventually gave way to the Higher Party School (established in 1939).

106. Mikoian, *Tak bylo*, 370. Back at the 7th Party Congress in 1918, when Stalin was nominated to serve on the commission to write a new party program, some people objected that he had no theoretical writings, but the session chairman pointed to Stalin's work on the national question and that quieted the objection. *VII ekstrennyi s"ezd RKP (b), mart 1918 goda*, 163.

107. On December 30, 1926, in another private letter, Stalin refused to allow Ksenofontov to cite the 1924 letter. *Sochineniia*, IX: 152.

108. *Uchenie Lenina o revoliutsii*. Medvedev, *Let History Judge*, 821–2.

109. Ksenofontov, *Lenin i imperialisticheskaia voina 1914–1918 gg.*, 16. Filipp Ksenofontov would become editor of the newspaper *Volga commune* in 1929, but was soon removed as a rightist; in the fall of 1930 he left for Moscow's Institute of Red Professoriate. He would be arrested on March 16, 1937, in Samara, and accused of Trotskyism. The Kuibyshev province GB Lieutenant Detkin wrote: "In 1929, serving as editor of the regional newspaper, he grouped around himself a group of Trotskyites from among the workers of the newspaper." Ksenofontov refused to confess, was sent to Moscow, but in Lefortovo still refused to confess. Officially, he died January 1, 1938, during interrogation.

110. Stalin, *O Lenine*; *Sochineniia*, VI: 69–71.
111. Trotskii, *O Lenine*. See also Tucker, *Stalin as Revolutionary*, 356.
112. *Kransaia nov'*, 1924, no. 4: 341–3.
113. *Za leninizm*, 186.
114. *Leningradskaia Pravda*, June 13, 1924; Carr, *Socialism in One Country*, II: 14.
115. Zinoviev, "O zhizni i deiatel'nosti V. I. Lenina," *Izvestiia TsK KPSS*, 1989, no. 7: at 178. Ivan Maisky, who was then working in the former capital, wrote to Molotov (March 10, 1924), that "Comrade Zinoviev does not spend a lot of time in Leningrad." But Zinoviev was there on April 16, 1924, the anniversary (under the new calendar) of Lenin's arrival at the Finland Station, laying of the foundation stone for a Lenin monument. *Pravda*, April 18, 1924; *U Velikoi mogily*, 517–9.
116. Zinoviev also wrote: "Lenin is the Genius of Leninism." Volkogonov, *Lenin: Life and Legacy*, 281 (citing RGASPI, f. 324, d. 246, l. 2; d. 267, l. 4–7), 285 (citing RGASPI, f. 324, op. 1, d. 490, l. 2). Zinoviev's principal Lenin work was his report to the 13th Party Congress, which he published as a book: *Po puti Il'icha* (Leningrad: Priboi, 1924). See also Zinov'ev, *Leninizm*.
117. Rosenfeldt, *Knowledge and Power*, 170–1.
118. The Institute of Red Professors had been founded in 1921, and by 1924 would produce its first graduating class, 51 of the 105 who had started (that year the original three-year course of study was extended to four); more than two thirds were white collar, only a tiny handful were workers. It suffered from a shortage of teachers. Initially it was located inside a former nunnery, the Passion (*Strastnoi*), which had been seized by the war commissariat in 1919 but retaken by the nuns in 1921–2 (who lived alongside the students); soon the institute moved to Ostozhenka, 51, the former Katkov Lycée. By 1929, 19 of the 236 graduates were workers. In April 1928 the nunnery would be given over to the Central Archives; the structure would be torn down in 1937 and replaced by a Pushkin statue and later a cinema. The Red Professors at Ostozhenka, meanwhile, would acquire dormitories in 1932.
119. Slepkov questioned Stalin's presentation of Lenin's conception of NEP (in the chapter "The Peasant Question"), arguing that the worker-peasant "alliance" had not been an afterthought, for in 1917 "the peasantry was compelled, if it wanted land, to support the proletariat in its struggle against capital." *Bol'shevik*, 1924, no. 9 (August 5): 102–5. The next month, Slepkov became a co-editor of *Bolshevik*, under the patronage of

editor in chief Bukharin. Slepkov was also named to *Pravda*'s editorial board, under Bukharin as well, in 1924. In 1925, he would concurrently become editor of *Komsolskaya pravda*.
120. Carr, *Socialism in One Country*, II: 332–3.
121. *XIII s"ezd VKP (b), mai 1924 g.*, 749–66.
122. Vera Dridzo, Krupskaya's longtime, faithful secretary, recalled that negotiations between Krupskaya and the triumvirate "lasted three and a half months, and only on the eve of the congress itself, May 18," did she "turn over the Testament, agreeing to its being read to the delegations of the congress." Dridzo, "O Krupskoi," 105. Evidently unable to win over the ruling triumvirate, she tried to force their hand: on May 18, the very eve of the congress, she sent a handwritten letter to the Central Committee. Sakharov points out that the note indicates Krupskaya had already handed the documents to Zinoviev a year before, and that this document, known as a "protocol of handing over," did not resemble a typical such Central Committee document of that time, and instead concerned publication or distribution, not handing over. Sakharov, *Politicheskoe zaveshchanie*, 535; *PSS*, XLV: 594.
123. Trotsky later asserted that Stalin opened the package in the presence of his aides, Lev Mekhlis and Sergei Syrtsov, and cursed Lenin, but it is not clear how Trotsky could have learned this, if it happened. Trotsky, *Stalin*, 37.
124. Tomsky, Bukharin, Molotov, and Kuibyshev (Central Control Commission presidium) concurred. Trotsky's summary labeled it a meeting of the politburo and Central Control Commission presidium, but did not indicate when the discussion took place. Fel'shtinskii, *Kommunisticheskaia oppozitsiia v SSSR*, I: 56.
125. RGASPI, f. 17, op. 2, d. 129, l. 1–3. Stalin had the secretariat direct the package from Krupskaya to a special "Central Committee commission" consisting of himself, Zinoviev, Kamenev, Bukharin, Kalinin, and Alexander Smirnov (agriculture commissar), which resolved "to bring the documents to the attention of the Central Committee plenum with the suggestion to bring them to the attention of the party congress." Sakharov, *Politicheskoe zaveshchanie*, 579 (citing RGASPI, f. 17, op. 2, d. 246 IV vyp., s. 65).
126. The German writer Emil Ludwig, citing a conversation with Radek, falsely asserted that Stalin read aloud the Testament, an assertion that Trotsky repudiated. Trotsky falsely claimed that the opposition first learned of the Testament now, on May

22, at the council of elders of the congress delegations. Trotsky, "On the Testament of Lenin [December 31, 1932]," in Trotsky, *Suppressed Testament*, 11–3; Sakharov, *Politicheskoe zaveshchanie*, 577–8; Trotskii, "Zaveshchanie Lenina," 267–8.
127. Trotskii, "Zaveshchanie Lenina" [*Gorizont*], 38–41.
128. *XIV s"ezd VKP (b)*, 398–9, 455–7, 506; *Izvestiia TsK KPSS*, 1991, no. 4: 192–207; Chuev, *Sto sorok*, 183.
129. Bazhanov has Zinoviev proposing that Stalin be reelected general secretary, and Trotsky failing to object, and some voting against and a few abstaining (Bazhanov claims he was charged with counting the hands), but this seems garbled: no outgoing Central Committee before a Party Congress had the right to vote on the reelection of the general secretary; this would only be done after the Party Congress by the Central Committee newly elected at the congress. It is possible that Bazhanov has merged the post-congress and pre-congress Central Committee meetings. Bazhanov, *Bazhanov and the Damnation of Stalin*, 75–6; Bazhanov, *Vospominaniia* [1980], 106–7; Bazhanov, *Avec Staline dans le Kremlin*, 43–5; Bazhanov, *Stalin*, 32–4. Other accounts include Eastman, *Since Lenin Died*, 28–31; Wolfe, *Khrushchev and Stalin's Ghost*, 258–9; McNeal, *Stalin*, 110; and Stalin, "Trotskistkaia oppozitsiia prezhde i teper': rech' na zasedanii ob"edinennogo plenuma TsK I TsKKK VKP (b) 23 oktiabria 1927 g.," in *Sochineniia*, X: 172–205. The Stalin loyalist Yaroslavsky recalled that "when these few pages written by Lenin were read to the members of the Central Committee the reaction was one of incomprehension and alarm."
130. The Young Pioneers, formed in 1922, had just 161,000 members Union-wide; on Red Square that day, they recited a new, modified oath "to unswervingly observe the laws and customs of the young pioneers and the commandments of Ilich." *XIII s"ezd RKP (b)* [1924], 629–33. See also Balashov and Nelepin, *VLKSM za 10 let v tsifrakh*, 34–7.
131. *XIII s"ezd RKP (b)*, 106–7. He had it published as a pamphlet: Zinov'vev, *Po puti Il'icha: politicheskii otchet TsK XIII-mu s"ezdu RKP (b)* (Leningrad: Priboi, 1924). Stalin, having allowed Zinoviev to serve as the attack dog, followed with a report on organizational work and appeared reasonable. (Later in the proceedings, Stalin would let loose on Trotsky.) *Sochineniia*, VI: 220–23; *XIII s"ezd RKP (b)*, 259–67.
132. *XIII s"ezd RKP (b)* 153–68 (at 158, 165–6); *XIII s"ezd RKP (b)* [1924], 372; *XIII s"ezd RKP (b)* [1963], 167.
133. *Sochineniia*, VI: 227; Medvedev, *Let History Judge*, 127–8.

134. *Sotsialisticheskii vestnik*, July 24, 1924: 13. Stalin's people attacked, with Nikolai Uglanov stating that at the Sormovo Engineering Works, the workers had voted for "the Central Committee," while the engineers—holdovers of the old regime—had voted for Trotsky, thereby indicating an alien class basis to the opposition; Molotov repeated this assertion that the opposition was rooted in class aliens. *XIII s"ezd RKP (b)*, 169, 523.

135. Sakharov, *Politicheskoe zaveshchanie*, 584–5 (citing RGASPI, f. 17, op. 2, d. 246 IV vyp., 62, 64: a letter from Stalin to the politburo, July 17, 1925, demanding that Trotsky repudiate the Max Eastman book of 1925, which Trotsky would do).

136. *Komsomol'skaia Pravda*, June 11, 1988. Milchakov, who spent sixteen years in Norilsk and Magadan camps, died in 1973.

137. Sakharov, *Politicheskoe zaveshchanie*, 582–3 (citing RGASPI, f. 17, op.1, d. 57, l. 184–6). Khrushchev, in his secret speech to the 20th Congress of the CPSU in February 1956, confirmed that Lenin's "Testament" "was made known to the delegates at the 13th Party Congress who discussed the question of transferring Stalin from the position of Secretary General." Khrushchev, "Secret Speech," 7.

138. RGASPI, f. 17, op. 2, d. 130.

139. The unemployed had jumped from 160,000 as of January 1922 to 1.24 million by January 1924, according to registrations at the labor exchanges run by the labor commissariat. Rogachevskaia, *Likvidatsiia bezrabotitsy*, 76–7.

140. APRF, f. 3, op. 27, d. 13, l. 53–4, in *Istochnik*, 1995, no. 3: 132–3.

141. RGASPI, f. 17, op. 16, d. 175, l. 165; Rozhkov, "Internatsional durakov," 61–6.

142. Half the members of the Italian fascist party in 1922 did not even renew their membership. Bosworth, *Mussolini's Italy*, 152.

143. Italy's government resigned in protest, instead of forming a broad anti-fascist coalition, which would have had to include reformist Socialists, instead of including the fascists in government, on the condition that they renounce their illegal, extra-parliamentary behavior. The latter, however, could only have been achieved by splitting the fascist movement and co-opting its more politically responsible elements, which had not been done. Lyttelton, *Seizure of Power*, 79.

144. "All authority depends on confidence," the great historian of Italian fascism Adrian Lyttelton explained, "and the King, rational to a fault and with a low opinion of man in general,

had none. He gave way . . . the only man who could do anything was convinced of his impotence." Lyttelton, *Seizure of Power*, 93. The king additionally was worried about palace intrigues that placed hopes in his more imposing cousin.

145. Lyttelton, *Seizure of Power*, 85 (Michele Bianchi).

146. Berezin, *Making the Fascist Self*, 81.

147. Kvashonkin, *Bol'shevistskoe rukovodstvo*, 263–5 (RGASPI, f. 5, op. 2, d. 326, l. 20–2). Bukharin, in commentary that went little remarked, also marveled at Italian fascism. "It is characteristic of fascist methods of combat that they, more than any other party, have adopted and applied in practice the experiences of the Russian revolution," he told the delegates to the 12th Party Congress. "If one regards them from the formal point of view, that is, from the point of view of the technique of their political methods, then one discovers in them a complete application of Bolshevik tactics, and especially those of Russian Bolshevism, in the sense of rapid concentration of forces, energetic action of a tightly structured military organization, in the sense of a particular system of committing one's forces, personnel-assignment-organs, mobilization, etc., and the pitiless destruction of the enemy, whenever this is necessary and demanded by the circumstances." *XII s"ezd RKP (b)*, 273–4.

148. *Pravda*, October 31, November 1, 1922.

149. Pipes, *Russia Under the Bolshevik Regime*, 253.

150. *V semirnyi kongress*, I: 156–7, 175–92; *Diskussiia 1923 goda*, 262 (Rykov-sponsored Comintern resolution, June 27, 1924).

151. Deutscher, *Prophet Unarmed*, 141–51.

152. Boersner, *The Bolsheviks*, 152 (citing *Protokoll des Fuenften Kongresses der Kommunistischen International*, 2 vols. [Hamburg: Carl Hoym, 1924], I: 237).

153. *Izvestiia*, June 19, 1924; *New York Times*, June 20, 1924; Tumarkin, *Lenin Lives!*, 193–4. Delegates to the 13th Party Congress back in May 1924 had also been given a glimpse of Lenin's body in a pre-completion mausoleum preview. *Pravda*, June 13, 1924; Zbarskii, *Mavzolei Lenina*, 41.

154. Firsov, "Nekotorye voprosy istorii Kominterna," 89; Claudin, *Communist Movement*, 152–3. Stalin also wrote an enigmatic note: "The defeat of the revolution in Germany is a step towards war with Russia." RGASPI, f. 558, op. 11, d. 25, l. 101 (no date). Stalin, along with Zinoviev, went further, meeting secretly with the German ultraleftists Arkadi Maslow and Ruth Fischer,

whose destructive actions had helped sabotage the coup effort. They were soon promoted, however, being the enemies of the Soviet triumvirate's Left opposition enemies (Radek and Pyatakov).

155. Matteotti, *Un anno di dominazione fascista*.

156. Canali, *Il delitto Matteotti*, 218.

157. Bosworth, *Mussolini's Italy*, 197.

158. De Felice, *Mussolini il fascista*, I: 632–6.

159. Lyttelton, *The Seizure of Power*, 242–3.

160. Bosworth, *Mussolini's Italy*, 212–3.

161. In dialogue with Frunze about a document that labeled Trotsky "the Leader [*vozhd'*] of the Red Army," Stalin advised, "I think that it would be better if we spoke about a *vozhd* only in terms of the party," meaning himself. Kvashonkin, *Bol'shevistskoe rukovodstvo*, 298–9 (RGASPI, f. 558, op. 1, d. 5254, l. 1: Dec. 10, 1924).

162. *Sotsialisticheskii vestnik*, July 24, 1924: 11–2.

163. With Lenin sidelined, Chicherin perhaps imagined he would enjoy greater freedom of action, but soon enough, he would be complaining of Stalin's "interference" in foreign affairs. Debo, "G. V. Chicherin," 27–8; Kvashonkin, *Bol'shevistskoe rukovodstvo*, 295.

164. By 1924, Albania, Austria, Denmark, Greece, Norway, Sweden, Afghanistan, Iran, China, Mexico, and Turkey had also recognized the USSR, as well as the former tsarist territories Estonia, Latvia, Lithuania, and Finland.

165. Anin, *Radioelektronnyi shpionazh*, 24.

166. On Stalin's and Lenin's views of foreign trade missions as spying operations, see *Sochineniia*, V: 117–20; and Carr, *Bolshevik Revolution*, III: 349–50.

167. *Izvestiia*, January 26, 1924.

168. Chicherin had Soviet diplomats duplicitously vow to China that the USSR "recognizes that Outer Mongolia is an integral part of the Republic of China and respects China's sovereignty therein," and promise to withdraw Soviet troops once a timetable had been agreed upon at an upcoming Sino-Soviet conference. Elleman, *Diplomacy and Deception*.

169. Ballis, "The Political Evolution of a Soviet Satellite"; Thomas T. Hammond, "The Communist Takeover of Outer Mongolia: Model for Eastern Europe," in Hammond and Farrell, *Anatomy of Communist Takeovers*; Barany, "Soviet Takeover."

170. The German warned that "the Russians will take up the old tsarist imperial policy against China." Quoted in Elleman, "Secret Sino-Soviet

Negotiations," 546. See also Tang, *Russian and Soviet Policy*, 388–9; and Rupen, *How Mongolia Is Really Ruled*, 44.

171. Murphy, *Soviet Mongolia*, 89–90.

172. The action was known in an extremely narrow circle: most officials in Stalin's apparatus were kept in the dark. Balashov and Markhashov, "Staraia ploshchad', 4 (20-e gody)," no. 6: 187.

173. Zinoviev had evidently concluded from the earlier failures that strikes and mass public protests had only served to put the authorities on alert, and so this time, the Comintern plotted a lightning coup, which would presumably inspire a workers' revolt of support for an Estonian Soviet Socialist Republic. Fischer, *Stalin and German Communism*, 463; Krivitsky, *I Was Stalin's Agent*, 64–5; Leonard, *Secret Soldiers*, 34–7.

174. Saar, *Le 1-er décembre 1924*; Kuusinen, *Rings of Destiny*, 66.

175. "The Reval Uprising," in Neuberg [false name], *Armed Insurrection*, 61–80.

176. Pil'skii, "Pervoe dekabrai," I: 218–9.

177. Rei, *Drama of the Baltic Peoples*, 180–6; Sunila, *Vosstanie 1 dekabria 1924 goda*. See also Krivitsky, *In Stalin's Secret Service*, 48.

178. Stalin, *Na piutiakh k Oktiabriu*; *Sochineniia*, VI: 348–401. Marx and Engels had categorically denied that revolution could succeed in just one country, but their European Social Democrat followers had revised this view. "The final victory of socialism in any one single state or several states" was possible, a Bavarian democratic socialist had allowed in 1878: von Vollmar, *Der isolierte sozialistische Staat*, 4. Kautsky's Erfurt Program of the German Social Democrats in 1891 had adopted a similar position: Kautsky, *Das Erfurter Programm*, 115–6.

179. *PSS*, XLV: 309; van Ree, "Socialism in One Country," which supersedes Carr, *Socialism in One Country*, II: 49–50; and Tucker, *Stalin as Revolutionary*, 368–94. Stalin, in a private letter, dated January 25, 1925, responding to a critical note sent to him about his "Socialism in One Country" article, asserted the rootedness of his views in Lenin's writings, though the *explicit* case was weak. *Sochineniia*, VII: 16–8.

180. Tsakunov, *V labirinte*, 143–4 (citing RGASPI, f. 325, op. 1, d. 108, l.44–5).

181. McNeal, *Stalin's Works*, 110–1; *Sochineniia*, VI: 61–2.

182. Stalin's "socialism in one country" would become institutionalized in the Comintern. Claudin, *Communist Movement*, 76–7.

183. Kamenev, in his article against Trotskyism in November 1924, had cut to the nub, noting that Trotsky's permanent revolution "put the workers' government in Russia in exclusive and complete dependence on an immediate proletarian revolution in the West." Kamenev, "Leninizm ili Trotkizm (Uroki partiinoi istorii)," *Pravda*, November 26, 1924, reprinted in Kamenev, *Stat'i i rechi*, 188–243 (at 229); Carr, *Socialism in One Country*, II: 57.

184. *Sotsialisticheskii vestnik*, June 20, 1925: 21.

185. *Sochineniia*, VI: 358–9.

186. Le Donne, *Russian Empire and the World*, 222.

187. On March 10, 1921, Maxim Litvinov, then Soviet ambassador to Estonia, had sent a note to the Estonian foreign minister protesting the formation of units on Estonian territory from the former Northwest Army for the defense of Kronstadt ("Thus criminal elements are intending to transform Estonia into a base for enemy actions against the Russian Republic"). The Estonian minister categorically denied their presence. *Kronstadtskaia tragediia*, I: 348–9, 371. Soviet counterintelligence evidently detained more than one hundred Estonian agents and their collaborators in the five years from 1922, of whom thirty-five were executed or killed by Chekists in attempted capture. Tumshis and Papchinskii, *1937, bol'shaia chistka*, 307–8.

188. Litvinov and Sidunov, *Shpiony i diversanty*, 39.

189. "A ring formed around the great USSR of small countries, where the bourgeois has held on thanks to the support of the predator nations of Western Europe," Anatoly Lunacharsky, the enlightenment commissar, wrote of Estonia and other former tsarist territories, which he called "mere patches of land." A. V. Lunacharskii, "Okrovavlennaia Estoniia" [1925], in Lunacharskii, *Sobranie sochenii*, II: 308.

190. In early 1925, Stalin had sent a ciphered telegram to Emanuel Kviring, whom he had appointed party boss of Ukraine, noting of Trotsky, "It's necessary to dismiss him from the Revolutionary Military Council," but Stalin added, so far the majority considers it "not expedient to put Trotsky out of the politburo, but to issue a warning," so that in the event of repeat violations of Central Committee policies, the politburo could "immediately remove him from the politburo or from work in the Central Committee." "A minority," according to Stalin, stood for "immediately driving him out of the politburo but retaining him in the Central Committee." Stalin put himself in the ranks of this minority. *Izvestiia TsK KPSS*, 1991, no. 7: 183.

191. *Pravda*, January 20, 1925. Officially, Trotsky was removed by resolution of the Soviet central executive committee on January 26, 1925. A translation of Trotsky's long resignation letter appears in Eastman, *Since Lenin Died*, 155–8. Mikhail Lakoba, Nestor's stepbrother, and the Abkhazia deputy interior minister, was put in Trotsky's bodyguard detail. So was Shalva Tsereteli of the Georgian Cheka. Hoover Institution Archives, Lakoba papers, 1–47, 1–37.

192. *XIV s"ezd VKP (b)*, 484.

193. Józef Unszlicht, who had been moved from the Cheka to head war commissariat supply, became Frunze's first deputy. *Pravda*, February 7, 1925.

194. RGASPI, f. 17, op. 2, d. 162, l. 62; *Sochineniia*, VII: 11–4.

195. "Literatura po leninizmu," *Sputnik politrabotnika*, 1925, no. 8–9: 24–40. See also "Pomoshch' samoobrazovaniiu: kratkaia programma po izucheniiu leninizma po skheme Stalina," *Krasnyi boets*, 1924, no. 13: 58. Stalin also wrote that day to the editorial board of *Worker Newspaper* calling Lenin "teacher" and summoning Soviet inhabitants to love and extol the departed "leader" [*vozhd*]. *Rabochaia gazeta*, January 21, 1921, in *Sochineniia*, VII: 15.

196. *Pravda*, January 30, 1925, in *Sochineniia*, VII: 25–33 (at 27).

197. Some observers believe Chicherin evinced a strong pro-German bias, coupled with a forward policy against the British empire, meaning support for national independence struggles and Communist parties in the East, while Maxim Litvinov, Chicherin's first deputy, plumped for a British-French orientation. Haslam, *Soviet Union and the Threat from the East*, 17.

198. See the wrangling in 1923: *DBFP*, VIII: 280–306.

199. *Izvestiia*, August 10, 1924; *Dokumenty vneshnei politiki*, VII: 609–36; Adibekov, *Politbiuro TsK RKP (b)—VKP (b) i Evropa*, 48–9.

200. *DVP SSSR*, VII: 556–60, 560–1; Jacobson, *When the Soviet Union Entered*, 136–9.

201. A Belorussian group objected, sending an article to *Pravda* ("On the English Treaty"), dated August 18, 1924, citing Rakovski to the effect that "we are paying the old debts" just in order for Britain to offer a new loan. "And so, we have to liquidate almost all the effects of the October Revolution on the foreign bourgeoisie," they wrote. "No one asked us about signing the treaty." They called the treaty "a defeat of the revolution without a fight," and called for a discussion by the whole party. Khromov, *Po stranitsam*, 216–7 (RGASPI, f. 558, op. 11, d. 290, l. 5–7). The article was signed by N. Makarov, P. Leblev, and A. Vasilev,

from a settlement in Minsk province. *Pravda* sent the draft article to Stalin. On August 25, 1924, Stalin sent it to the Belorussian Central Committee (party boss Asatkin): "It is necessary to verify whether the named people are Communists, whether they signed the article, and if yes, what spurred its contents. No repressive measures should be taken against the authors" (l. 3). In other words, the positions of the British conservative Tories and the Belroussian leftist Communists coincided.

202. In fact the Soviets attached a high value to relations with Britain, as reflected in the envoys sent: Krasin, Rakovski, Dovgalevsky, and Maisky.

203. Hilger and Meyer, *Incompatible Allies*, 124.

204. Pro-Western Germans admitted that "the Rapallo agreement gave us a lot and afforded a certain weight in international politics, but the Bolsheviks used it more," and they railed against Comintern agents. D'iakov and Bushueva, *Fashistskii mech kovalsia v SSSR*, 60–4 (RGVA, f. 33987, op. 3, d. 98, l. 153–7: February 5, 1925).

205. The count had been instrumental in getting Karl Radek released from a German prison in 1919. Debo, *Survival and Consolidation*, 67–70.

206. Ulrich Brockdorff-Rantzau, *Dokumente*, 146ff.

207. Rosenbaum, *Community of Fate*; O'Connor, *Diplomacy and Revolution*, 95–6.

208. Volkogonov, *Lenin: Life and Legacy*, xxxiii (RGASPI, f. 2, op. 2, d. 515, l. 1).

209. Akhmatzian, "Voennoe sotrudnichestvo SSSR," Zeidler, *Reichswehr und Rote Armee* [1994].

210. Dyck, "German-Soviet Relations," 68 (citing Archives of the German Foreign Ministry, L337/L1oo564–68: Rantzau to Stresemann, March 9, 1925).

211. Dyck, "German-Soviet Relations," 69 (citing Archives of the German Foreign Ministry, 5265/E317849–52: Rantzau to the Foreign Ministry, Dec. 1, 1924).

212. Carr, *Socialism in One Country*, III: 257.

213. Jacobson, *When the Soviet Union Entered*, 156–8.

214. "K mezhdunarodnomy polozheniiu i zadacham kompartii," *Pravda*, March 22, 1925, in *Sochineniia*, VII: 52–9 (53).

215. By 1933, 450 German Luftwaffe pilots trained at Liptesk.

216. Gorlov, *Sovershenno sekretno: al'ians Moskva-Berlin*, 146.

217. Schroeder, "The Lights That Failed." Beck, *Dernier rapport*. See also Salzmann, *Great Britain, Germany and the Soviet Union*; Johnson, *Locarno Revisited*; Wright, "Locarno: A Democratic Peace?"

218. Jacobson, *When the Soviet Union Entered*, 174. As Jacobson summarized elsewhere, "The security of France was Germany's insecurity; the security of Germany was Poland's insecurity." Jacobson, "Is There a New International History of the 1920s?," 620.

219. *Pravda*, October 20, 1925; *Izvestiia*, November 24, 1925 (Litvinov).

220. A top analyst for the Soviets, the Hungarian economist Jenő Varga (b. 1879), the finance minister in the shortlived Béla Kun Hungarian Soviet government, had been delivering long reports at Comintern congresses on the "crisis of capitalism," but with Locarno, Varga, along with others, began to write of a "stabilization of capitalism." In 1926 Varga would side with Stalin against the united opposition of Trotsky and Zinoviev; Varga would soon become one of Stalin's top foreign policy aides, heading the Institute of World Economy and World Politics, which had been created in 1925. He took over for Fyodor A. Rothstein, who had been born in tsarist Lithuania, and spent thirty years in Great Britain, but published Trotsky in the institute's journal. Eran, *The Mezhdunarodniki*, 32; Duda, *Jenő Varga*, 37, 85, 97–8; Mommen, *Stalin's Economist*.

221. RGASPI, f. 558, op. 11, d. 23, l. 126–7: notes for the main political report to the 14th Party Congress, December 1925. For the report he delivered: *Sochineniia*, VII: 273–4.

222. *Sochineniia*, VII: 12–13, 28, 280.

223. White, "Early Soviet Historical Interpretations." Sergei Kirov, reporting to the Baku party organization he headed in February 1925 on Trotsky's *Lessons of October*, stated that "Here the matter is not some simple theoretical fistfight, rather here the matter in the literal sense, is the fate of our party and our revolution"—an admission, perhaps, of the exhaustion induced by the all-consuming polemics. *Bakinskii rabochii*, February 5, 1925.

224. Lenoe, "Agitation, Propaganda, and the 'Stalinization' of the Soviet Press," 6.

225. Volkogonov, *Trotsky*, 207. An exhibition for the fifth anniversary of the Red Army in 1923 had devoted an entire room to Trotsky's fabled civil war train, but the train, which made its last trip in 1922, was officially decommissioned in July 1924. *Iubileinaia vystavka Krasnykh*; Argenbright, "Documents from Trotsky's Train."

226. Medvedev, *Let History Judge*, 145. Isaac Zelensky had only just been appointed as one of the CC secretaries in June 1924; in August he was shipped out to Tashkent.

227. Uglanov would later remark that Zinoviev and Kamenev "carried on conversations with me from which I understood that they were trying in a roundabout way to fasten on me their disagreements with Stalin," but he "declined their invitation." *XIV s"ezd VKP (b)*, 193. Back in Leningrad, when Uglanov and a number of young party officials clashed with Zinoviev, Lenin, along with Stalin and Molotov, had supported the youngsters. Merridale, *Moscow Politics*, 29 (citing *Moskovskaia Pravda*, February 12, 1989). See also Bazhanov, *Bazhanov and the Damnation of Stalin*, 142; and Carr, *Socialism in One Country*, II: 62.

228. Nadtocheev, "'Triumvirat' ili 'semerka'?," 61–82. The group was also known as the "leading collective." Trotsky certainly suspected people were gathering behind his back. In 1926, Zinoviev, after Stalin had run roughshod over him, too, confessed the existence of the septet to Trotsky. But Trotsky did not speak out against the septet until 1927. Fel'shtinskii, *Kommunisticheskaia oppozitsiia v SSSR*, III: 87; Lars Lih, "Introduction," in Lih, *Stalin's Letters to Molotov*, 5.

229. The Stalin-Bukharin alliance appears to have begun, at Stalin's initiative, in late 1924: *XIV s"ezd VKP (b)*, 136, 397–8, 459–60, 501; Cohen, *Bukharin*, 429, n1. On the breakdown of the triumvirate, see Daniels, *Conscience of the Revolution*, 235–7; Carr, *Socialism in One Country*, II: ch. 13.

230. Trotskii, *Sochineniia*, III/i: xi–lxvii; *Uroki Oktiabria*; "Lessons of October," in Trotsky, *The Essential Trotsky*, 125, 157, 172, 175. See also Deutscher, *Prophet Unarmed*, 151ff; and Pavliuchenkov, *Rossia nepovskaia*, 97 (citing RGASPI, f. 325, op. 1, d. 361, l. 3). Already on October 16, 1924, Stalin, Zinoviev, and Kamenev had convened at Kamenev's apartment to plot how they would go after Trotsky, using *Pravda* and other forums, to put him on the back foot—but he ambushed them. Trotsky wrote "Lessons" as a long introduction to volume III of his *Collected Works*, which dealt with 1917 and was published out of chronological order. Twenty-one volumes would be published by 1927: more than for any other top leader, including Lenin. Trotskii, *Sochineniia*. See also *Ekonomicheskaia zhizn'*, December 10, 1924. Like Trotsky, Zinoviev had aides record his speeches for subsequent publication. Six volumes of Zinoviev's "works" were published in 1924 (the preface to the first volume bore the date October 1923): Zinov'ev, *Sobranie sochinenii*, I, II, III, V, XV, XVI. Kamenev, who edited Lenin's *Collected Works*, did not publish his own; he had tried to issue a three-volume edition in 1907 (a contract was signed but nothing came of it), but in 1924 issued three volumes (I, X, XII) of his *Speeches*. Publication was soon discontinued.

231. *Pravda*, November 2, 1924 (Bukharin), reprinted in *Za leninizm*, 9–25; *Trotskizm i molodezh'*, 41–7 (Zinoviev); *Bol'shevik*, 1925, no. 14 (November 5): 105–13 (Sokolnikov); *Za leninizm*, 28–30, 60–2 (Kamenev).

232. *Pravda*, November 26, 1924. See also Kamenev, *Stat'i i rechi*, I: 188–243; *Za leninizm*, 87–90, 94–5; and Stalin, *Sochineniia*, VI: 324–57. See also Zinoviev, *Bol'shevizm ili trotzkizm?*

233. *Pravda*, December 16, 1924, in Krupskaia, *Izbrannye proizvedeniia*, 142–3; McNeal, *Bride of the Revolution*, 249. It is unclear who might have inserted these pointed words into Krupskaya's bland text.

234. "Yenukidze" [January 8, 1938], in Trotskii, *Portrety revoliutsionerov* [1991], 233–44 (at 241), [1984], 251–72 (at 264–6). On March 22, 1925, Alexander Myasnikyan, known as Myasnikov, the deputy chairman of the South Caucasus Council of People's Commissars, and Solomon Mogilevsky, the head of the South Caucasus Cheka, were killed in the crash of a Junkers plane after takeoff near the Tiflis aerodrome. Two days later, a different plane arrived with friends of Trotsky's, members of the central executive committee: the Soviet ambassador to France Rakovski and the people's commissar of the post Smirnov, who claimed that Avel Yenukidze, a close Stalin associate and the secretary of the central executive committee, had provided them with the airplane. The plane that crashed had caught fire while still in the air; the cause of the fire was never established. Both pilots also died. Beria headed the first, inconclusive investigatory commission; a second and then a third commission headed by Karl Pauker from Moscow never got to the bottom of the incident. Trotsky, who suspected Georgian Mensheviks, went to Tiflis from Sukhum for the funeral. *Trudovaia Abkhazia*, March 25, 1925; *Proletarskaia revoliutsiia*, 1925, no. 6: 234–6; *Biulleten' oppozitsii*, January 1939: 2–15.

235. Nazarov, *Stalin i bor'ba za liderstvo*, 108–9 (citing RGASPI, f. 17, op. 2, d. 179, l. 105).

236. Anfert'ev, *Smerch*, 233. Sokolnikov had met Galina (b. 1905) when she was seventeen—they shared an entrance to their living quarters at the Metropole (she lived one floor above him)—just before she went on to study at Moscow University's medical faculty; he would come by in the evenings to play chess with her first husband, Leonid Serebryakov, whom she married in 1923 but left in 1925 to marry Sokolnikov. Galina Serebriakova, "Iz vospominanii," in Anfert'ev, *Smerch*, 235.

237. Anfert'ev, *Smerch*, 233–4.

238. Woodruff, *Money Unmade*, 27; Sokol'nikov, *Novaia finansovaia politika*, 200–1.

239. Johnson and Temin, "The Macroeconomics of NEP," 753. On the skepticism, see Barmine, *One Who Survived*, 125; and Serge, *Ot revoliutsii k totalitarizmu*, 177.

240. Bourne and Watt, *British Documents on Foreign Affairs*, VII: 376 (undated, date deduced from content).

241. *Vestnik Kommunisticheskoi Akademii*, 1924, no. 8: 47–116, reprinted in *Novaia ekonomika* (1926), 52–126. A rejoinder, from Bukharin, was entitled "How to Wreck the Worker-Peasant Alliance" (*Pravda*, December 12, 1924). See also Carr, *Socialism in One Country*, I: 219–26.

242. L. A. Neretina, "Reorganizatsiia gosudarstvennoi promyshlennosti v 1921–25 godakh: prontsipy i tendentsii razvitiia," in Davies, *NEP*, 75–87; Brovkin, *Russia After Lenin*, 179–81. Private trade was far more substantial than private industry, but was being harassed. Davies, *Soviet Economy in Turmoil*, 76–9.

243. Sokol'nikov, *Gosudarstvennyi kapitalizm*; *Leninskii sbornik*, XXIII: 192–3.

244. Zinoviev made a bid to seize agricultural policy with a call for the party to "turn its face to the countryside," part of a gambit to enhance his stature as Lenin's heir. Zinoviev's cluelessness, however, was evident: as late as July 3, 1924, *Leningrad pravda*, his newspaper, had foreseen major grain exports. *Pravda*, July 30, 1924; *Leningradskaia pravda*, July 30, 1924; Zinov'ev, *Litsom k derevne*.

245. *Izvestiia*, September 3, 1924 (Rykov); Reswick, *I Dreamt Revolution*, 84–96. (Reswick was an American citizen, born in Russia, who was willing to be used by the Soviet regime in exchange for nonpareil access.)

246. Andrei Andreyev, a Central Committee secretary, traveled around Siberia, the Urals, and the North Caucasus and got to the heart of the matter. "A bureaucratic [*chinovnich'e*] introduction of laws magnifies to the scary red-tape of our institutions—here is the main evil," he stated. "Our soviet and party functionaries devote little attention to small concrete matters that the peasant raises, but spend most of their time spewing general answers. The peasant tiller asks a concrete question and he is subjected to verbiage about major state and international issues." Gimpel'son, *NEP*, 384 (citing RGASPI, f. 17, op. 112, d. 733, l. 170).

247. At a January 3, 1925, politburo session Stalin instructed those present to read the feuilleton of David Dallin, serialized in several issues of the émigré Menshevik newspaper, because "it has wonderful data on how the *muzhik*

thinks about agricultural cooperatives and why he prefers them." Stalin disagreed with Sokolnikov's assertion that "consumer cooperatives were a leap into the unknown," but he accepted his emphasis on the need to focus attention on agricultural cooperatives. Stalin argued that kulaks should be allowed to become members: "This would have a gigantic significance, because it would act as a stimulus for whole villages to join the cooperatives." At the same time, he disagreed with the suggestion of Alexander Smirnov, the RSFSR agriculture commissar, to allow kulaks not only to join but also to run them. "In the management of society even one kulak would be dangerous," Stalin stated. "The kulak is a smart person, experienced. In a management capacity, he can win over ten non-kulaks." He recalled Lenin's instruction about how after the end of the civil war kulaks could be allowed to stand for elections to soviets, but, five years after the Whites had been defeated on the battlefield, Stalin stated that "We have a long way to go to full liquidation of the civil war, and we shall not get there soon." Vatlin, *Stenogrammy zasedanii Politburo*, I: 305–7, 314–5; *Sotsialisticheskii vestnik*, 1925, no. 20, 21, 23, 24. See also Plekhanov, *VChK-OGPU*, 91 (citing *Nashe otechestvo* [Moscow: Terra, 1991], II: 197).

248. Male, *Russian Peasant Organization*.

249. *Bol'shevik*, 1924, no. 3–4: 23, 25 (Slepkov).

250. Gladkov, *Sovetskoe narodnoe khoziaistvo*, 73, 343.

251. *Pravda*, December 19, 1924; Carr, *Socialism in One Country*, 208–11.

252. *Sochineniia*, VI: 135, 243–4.

253. *Pravda*, June 4, 1930, in *Sochineniia*, VI: 321.

254. *Pravda*, January 30, 1925, in *Sochineniia*, VII: 25–33 (at 28).

255. *XIV konferentsiia VKP (b)*.

256. See Stalin's glowing remarks on NEP's success, delivered in a report on the 14th party conference at the Moscow party organization: *Pravda*, May 12 and May 13, 1925, reprinted in *Sochineniia*, VII: 90–132 (at 128–9). See also Graziosi, "'Building the First System.'"

257. RGASPI, f. 558, op. 11, d. 23, l. 45. As it happened, when the commissariats were united (in 1926), Stalin would name Mikoyan as trade commissar.

258. Eichengreen, *Golden Fetters*, 4–5; Pittaluga, "The Genoa Conference." It has been argued that the gold standard, and its effect of requiring price deflation, furnished an additional impetus to ideological proclivities for authoritarian interventionism in the economy to administer prices. Polanyi, *The Great Transformation*, 233–4.

259. Vatlin, *Stenogrammy zasedanii Politbiuro*, I: 379 (November 2, 1925), I: 533 (December 12, 1925), II: 507 (January 3, 1927). Thanks to Professor Paul Gregory for pointing me toward Stalin's demonstrations of insight on political economy at party forums.
260. Bukharin, "O novoi ekonomichheskoi politike i nashikh zadachakh," 3–15.
261. Bukharin, to reinforce the message, wrote a pamphlet, *Can We Build Socialism in One Country in the Absence of the Victory of the West-European Proletariat?* (April 1925). In connection with the 14th party conference (April 27–29, 1925), Stalin edited Zinoviev's draft theses, crossing out some passages, inserting others, producing the following: "Leninism teaches that the final victory of socialism in the sense of a full guarantee against the restoration of bourgeois relations is possible only on a world scale (or in several decisive countries)." Further, Stalin added: "In general, the victory of socialism (not in the sense of final victory) is absolutely possible in one country." RGASPI, f. 558, op. 1, d. 3359, l. 11, 6, 15. Zinoviev would launch a critique of the Stalin view in September 1925, with his book on Leninism, but his criticisms were incoherent (at one point he wrote that "if one asks us whether we can and must establish socialism in one country, we will reply that we can and must"). Van Ree, "Socialism in One Country," 107. In September 1925, Jonava Vareikis, head of the press section in the party secretariat, published a pamphlet, *Vozmozhna li pobeda sotsializma v odnoi strane?* (Moscow: Molodaia gvardiia, 1925), praising Stalin's December 1924 article as the only serious contribution to Leninism since the leader's death!
262. Lih, "Zinoviev." Lih is right that Carr was wrong when he wrote that after January 1924 (the 13th party conference) "it could be clearly seen that personalities rather than principles were at stake." Carr, *Interregnum*, 340.
263. Black, "Zinoviev Re-Examined."
264. Brovkin, *Russia After Lenin*, 160 (citing RGASPI, f. 17, op. 16, d. 766, l. 253).
265. *Sochineniia*, VII: 153. The episode is handled in Carr, *Socialism in One Country*, I: 260, 284.
266. *PSS*, XLIII: 330, 333, 357, XLIV: 325, XLV: 372.
267. Carr, *Socialism in One Country*, II: 79.
268. *Pravda*, May 13, 1925; *Sochineniia*, VII: 132.
269. *Sochineniia*, VII: 111, 123–4.
270. "So much anger and frustration can be felt in these letters that one is truly overwhelmed," the editor of the journal *New Village* reported. "Never before have we had letters with so

much resentment, hatred, and envy of the growing new agricultural households as now. A hungry and poor peasant is beginning to hate the prosperous toiling agriculturalists so much that he wants to bring ruin upon them." Brovkin, *Russia After Lenin*, 159 (citing RGASPI, f. 17, op. 87, svodka 45), 160.
271. Ehrenburg, *Memoirs*, 68.
272. Sutton, *Western Technology and Soviet Economic Development*, I: 256 (citing U.S. State Department Decimal File, 316-164-205).
273. One American journalist, who called the NEP "an armed truce, at best," wrote of the NEPmen as "a class existing by sufferance, despised, and insulted by the population and oppressed by the government. It became a curious burlesque on capitalism, self-conscious, shifty, intimidated, and ludicrous." Lyons, *Assignment in Utopia*, 84–5. In 1925, just the official taxes on NEPmen exceeded those on prewar traders. But officals levied additional "punitive" taxation for "luxury goods," whose definition was conveniently inflatable. Trifonov, *Ocherki istorii klassovoi bor'by*, 84.
274. Bribe taking and other forms of corruption began early and persisted: Epikhin and Mozokhin, *VChK-OGPU v borb'e s korruptsiei*, 312 (TsA FSB, f. 66, op. 1, por. 36, l. 324), 315–17 (TSA FSB, f. 66, op. 1, po. 106, l. 64–64ob.), 334–35 (TSA FSB, f. 66, op. 1, d. 108, l. 83), 339 (APRF, f. 3, op. 58, op. 187, l. 16), 482–4 (TsA FSB, 2, op. 4, por. 32, l. 5–6); Plekhanov and Plekhanov, *F. E. Dzerzhinskii*, 442–3 (TsA FSB, f. 66, op. 1-T.D. 100v., l. 6).
275. Deutscher, *Prophet Unarmed*, 202, n1.
276. Lih, *Stalin's Letters to Molotov*, 69–84; Kosheleva, *Pis'ma I. V. Stalina V. M. Molotovu*, 13–26.
277. *Bol'shevik*, 1925, no. 16 [September]: 67–70. See also Carr, *Socialism in One Country*, II: 74–7; Deutscher, *Prophet Unarmed*, 169–70, 247–8; Eastman, *Love and Revolution*, 442–55, 510–16.
278. Stalin would quote Trotsky: "all talk about [Lenin's] 'testament,' allegedly suppressed or violated, is a malicious invention and is directed wholly against Lenin's real will and the interests of the party he founded." *Sochineniia*, X: 175.
279. *Bol'shevik*, 1925, no. 16 [September]: 67–70. *Bolshevik* claimed a print run of 40,000. Kamenev, Bukharin, and Yaroslavsky were three of the five members of the editorial board.
280. Valentinov, *Novaia ekonomicheskaia politika* [1991], 295.
281. Later, Trotsky would claim that his statement had been "forced on me by a majority of the politburo." *Biulleten' oppozitsii*, March 19, 1931 (letter of September 11, 1928).

282. Her repudiatión raised the question of whether she had been involved in the Eastman incident, and was perhaps linked to Trotsky. Shvetsov, "Lev Trotskii i Maks Istmen," 141–63.
283. *Bol'shevik*, 1925, no. 16: 71–3 (Krupskaya letter dated July 7, 1925).
284. Some have speculated that Rakovski had been the intermediary, while others have fingered Krupskaya, who is said to have given it to a member of the opposition who was going abroad in connection with a conference on international debts, and who handed it to the French leftist Boris Souvarine in Paris. McNeal, *Bride of the Revolution*, 258; Trotsky, *The Real Situation in Russia*, 320–3.
285. Frunze also exempted numerous categories of people from conscription, and blessed the Great War experience of national units. Berkhin, *Voennaia reforma*, 116–45; Erickson, *Soviet High Command* [2001], 164–213; Von Hagen, *Soldiers in the Proletarian Dictatorship*; Von Hagen, "The levée en masse," 159–88. Much of the debate behind the reforms had been launched at a closed session at the 10th Party Congress in March 1921. Sergei Gusev and Mikhail Frunze had called for reorganizing the Red Army in line with a new strategy of "a national defensive war," while Trotsky had argued for a Red Army in line with a strategy of "exporting revolution." Simonov, *Voenno-promyshlennyi kompleks SSSR*, 22.
286. Sokolov, *Ot voenproma k VPK*, 39–42 (citing RGAE, f. 2097, op. 1, d. 64, l. 8–24: report of March 2, 1924).
287. Kavtaradze, *Voennye spetsialisty*, 174. As of January 1, 1921, tsarist officers had made up 34 percent of the Red Army commanders at all levels, some 12,000 officers overall. In 1921, the Special Department initiated a Red Army census, gathering some 400,000 responses to a fifteen-question form, looking for those who had served in any of the White or national armies during the civil war. Zdanovich, *Organy gosudarstvennoi bezopasnosti*, 337 (citing TsA FSB, f. 1, op. 6, d. 670, 216–216ob.)
288. Kavtaradze, *Voennye spetsialisty*, 174; Zdanovich, *Organy gosudarstvennoi bezopasnosti*, 342 (citing Arkhiv UFSB po Omskoi oblasti, f. 39, op. 3, d. 4, l. 77); Zdanovich, *Organy gosudarstvennoi bezopasnosti*, 269 (citing TsA FSB, f. 2, op. 3, d. 674, l. 5); Antonov-Ovseenko, *Stroitel'stvo Krasnoi armii*, 31.
289. Trotskii, *Kak vooruzhalas' revoliutsiia*, II: 92–3.
290. Zdanovich, *Organy gosudarstvennoi bezopasnosti*, 102, citing TsA FSB, f. 2, op. 3, d. 773, l. 2 (A. Snesarev). Soviet foreign intelligence managed to recruit agents or representatives in

twenty-seven countries. Plekhanov, *VChK-OGPU*, 283; Kapchinskii, *Gosbezopasnosti iznutri*, 115 (citing GARF, f. 130, op. 5, d. 89, l. 565–6), 117 (citing RGASPI, f. 17, op. 84, d. 227, l. 57). Up to 2 million people had left Russia during the revolution and civil war, and perhaps 1.2 million were still abroad. A very large number of people who did not leave acquired relatives "abroad," often in former pieces of the empire, with whom they corresponded, becoming a target of systematic perlustration. *V zhernovakh revoliutsii*; RGASPI, f. 76, op. 3, d. 331, l. 1–2: March 30, 1924).

291. There are two stories on the origins of the Trust that are not incompatible. By some accounts, the formation of an underground brotherhood of anti-Soviets was originally the work of Polish intelligence: in the spring of 1920, Wiktor Kijakowski-Steckiewicz (b. 1889), a secret member of the underground Polish Military Organization, was supposedly tasked with crossing over into the Soviet Union to organize an intelligence network in Petrograd, but he was arrested and, by some accounts, agreed to collaborate. (Later, after his wife left him, in despair he attempted suicide and ceased to work in counterintelligence. In 1932 he was transferred to foreign intelligence and posted to Mongolia, where he died during an uprising.) The other story centers on Alexander Yakushev, a transport commissariat official and staunch monarchist, whose name evidently emerged in intercepted mail. Instead of rolling up his handful of associates, the GPU persuaded him to cooperate and created the Monarchist Organization of Central Russia, code named "the Trust" (as in the corporation). See Voitsekhovskii, *Trest*.

292. Fleishman, *V tiskakh provokatsii*; Gilensen, "V poednike s pol'skoi 'dvuikoi' pobedili sovetskie 'monarkhisty,'" 75; Gaspar'ian, *Operatsii Trest*; Seregin, "Vyshii monarkhicheskii sovet i operatsiia 'Trest,'" 67–72; and Pares, *My Russian Memoirs*, 595.

293. Minakov, *Sovetskaia voennaia elita*, 58 (citing GARF, f. 5853, op. 1, d. 1–24: a secret analysis from the Berlin emigration, February 15, 1922). A "revolutionary Bonaparte," Wrangel's representative in Berlin, General von Lampe, noted in his private diary of Tukhachevsky. Zdanovich, *Organy gosudarstvennoi bezopasnosti*, 280–1 (citing GARF, f. 5853, op. 1, d. 2, l. 422)".

294. "Glavkoverkh Tukhachevskii," *Rul'*, October 1922 (written by Prince F. Kasatkin-Rostovsky, under the pseudonym Antar); Minakov, *Sovetskaia voennaia elita*, 60–2.

295. Behind the journal stood B. Bortnovsky and G. Teodori, although the editor was M. I. Tmonov (then A. K.

Kelchevsky, then V. Kolossovsky). Teodori worked to explain away Tukhachevsky's defeat at Warsaw by pointing out that his flank had been exposed by the failure of the other Soviet army force to show (an implicit criticism of Stalin); Teodori made the same points in the Soviet press. See also the note by the pundit N. Korzhenevsky in the former Prague archive: Ioffe, "'Trest': legendy i fakty."

296. During maneuvers in the Western Military District, the Special Department became suspicious that Tukhachevsky so desired revenge against Poland he might launch his own war: all his orders and actions were suddenly subject to meticulous investigation in the summer of 1923. After maneuvers had finished, on September 29, 1923, Dzierżyński, who was obsessed with any matters relating to Poland, had ordered that the central OGPU Special Department conduct a still more thorough investigation of Tukhachevsky. After familiarizing himself with the results, Dzierżyński in January 1924 wrote to Wiaczesław Mężyński ordering immediate action. "It is impossible to wait passively while 'Smolensk [Western headquarters]' dictates its will to the Kremlin.'" Zdanovich, *Organy gosudarstvennoi bezopasnosti*, 285–7 (citing TsA FSB, f. 2, op. 1, d. 882, l. 829; op. 2, d. 27, l. 1; d. R-9000, t. 24, l. 165). At the 7th Belorussia Congress of Soviets in Minsk in 1925, Tukhachevsky stated that the Belorussian government "place the issue of war [with Poland] on the agenda." *VII Vsebelorusskii s"ezd sovetov*, 231.

297. On October 8 (Thursday), the doctors decided he had to undergo an operation; the internal bleeding frightened Frunze, but he held back. Stalin sent Mikoyan to urge Frunze to undergo the operation, then went to Frunze himself. Frunze wrote to his wife Sofia in Yalta that "I remain in the hospital still. On Saturday [October 10, 1925] there will be a new consultation. I'm afraid surgery might somehow be refused [*kak by ne otkazali v operatsii*]." Kanonenko, "Kto ubil Mikhail Frunze" (citing RGVA, f. 32392, d. 142, l. 3–5).

298. Volkogonov garbled this letter: Volkogonov, *Triumf i tragediia*, I/i: 127–8. The full text appears in Kanonenko, "Kto ubil Mikhaila Frunze."

299. *Pravda*, October 29 and October 31, 1925; *Pravda*, November 1, 1925 (for the autopsy, conducted by A. I. Abrikosov, and signed by the entire medical team).

300. Bazhanov, *Bazhanov and the Damnation of Stalin*, 100–2; Bazhanov, *Vospominaniia* [1990], 141; Gamburg, *Tak eto bylo*, 181–2.

301. *Pravda*, November 3, 1925.

302. A version of Frunze's murder told by a Trotsky supporter to the writer Boris Pilnyak was soon fixed in a novella, "Tale of the Unextinguished Moon," published in the journal *Novyi mir*; censors would confiscate the entire run. Ulam, *Stalin*, 260–1; Carr, *Socialism in One Country*, II: 123–4. Frunze's comrades demanded a special investigation, under the auspices of the Society of Old Bolsheviks. Health commissar Nikolai Semashko testified that the Central Committee medical commission had had no experts in ulcers and that before the commission had ruled Professor Rozanov had spoken with Stalin and Zinoviev. That may have been as far as the investigation went. Medvedev, *Let History Judge*, 156–8. Later, Stalin would also be accused of organizing the murder of Yefraim Sklyansky, Trotsky's former first deputy at the war commissariat, who died in August 1925 in a boating accident on a lake in upstate New York, 350 miles north of Manhattan, on a visit to Isaiah Hoorgin, head of the Soviet-American Trading Co. (Amtorg). The two were waiting for their train to return to New York City and killing time in a canoe when a sudden strong wind overturned their small vessel. Neither was a champion rower and accompanying staff, in rowboats, proved too far off (or perhaps too inebriated) to rescue the pair. Hoorgin was thirty-eight, Sklyansky thirty-three. L. Trotskii, "Sklianskii pogib," *Pravda*, August 29, 1925; *New York Times*, August 30, 1925; *Time*, September 14, 1925; *Pravda*, Seepetember 22, 1925. Bazhanov leveled the accusations of murder; the death took place after he had left Stalin's employ: Bazhanov, *Bazhanov and the Damnation of Stalin*, 65–6. The loss of Hoorgin was significant. Litvinov wrote to Stalin in late 1925, urging the appointment of "an authoritative comrade, who could immediately take up leadership of the political work, meet with official representatives of the American government for unofficial negotiations, make overtures, respond to similar overtures from the other side, and so on." Gaiduk, "Sovetsko-Amerikanskie otnosheniia" (citing RGAE, f. 413, op. 2. d. 2040, l. 144–5). Pyotr Ziv, Hoorgin's deputy, took over temporarily. Amtorg was soon given to Saul Bron.

303. Zal'kind, "O zabolevaniiakh partaktiva." In November 1925, Leonid Krasin fell deathly ill; blood tests revealed acute anemia. Alexander Bogdanov, who had been experimenting with blood transfusions, recommended one and Krasin looked over the research himself, agreed, and seemed rejuvenated—word spread of a miracle cure, and Stalin supposedly

summoned Bogdanov. Bogdanov's visit to Stalin (late December 1925) was recorded in Bogdanov's diary but not in Stalin's office logbook; what they discussed remains unknown. Bogdanov would die in 1928 in an experiment gone awry: for yet another transfusion, he used the blood of a student suffering from malaria and tuberculosis; it may have been an incompatible type. Krementsov, *A Martian Stranded*, 61 (citing GARF, f. A-482, op. 42, d. 590). Zalkind would die of a heart attack on the way home in 1936 at the age of forty-eight.

304. RGASPI, f. 17, op. 84, d. 704, l. 27.

305. See Adibekov, *Politbiuro TsK RKP (b)–VKP (b): povestki dnia zasedanii*, I: 421; RGASPI, f. 17, op. 3, d. 533, l. 10; Krementsov, *A Martian Stranded*, 66 (citing RGASPI, f. 17, op. 84, d. 701, l. 73–95); *Izvestiia*, February 28, 1926: 5. The Germans were Friedrich Krause and Otfried Förster.

306. Teplianikov, "Vnikaia vo vse," 169–70. Orjonikidze was made a member of the Revolutionary Military Council of the Republic.

307. *Voennye arkhivy Rossii*, vyp. 1: 406.

308. *Pravda*, November 7, 1925.

309. Tukhachevsky wrote (January 31, 1926), "I already reported to you orally that the Red Army general staff works in abnormal conditions, which make productive work impossible, and prevents the staff from bearing the responsibility laid upon it." Minakov, *Stalin i ego marshal*, 356–7.

310. Samuelson, *Soviet Defense Industry Planning*, 41.

311. Merridale, *Moscow Politics*, 260. Kamenev was making proposals for a 20 percent increase in worker pay, even though, as head of the Council of Labor and Defense (the executive body parallel to the government), he knew no such funds were available. He also proposed that workers share in factory profits (almost all factories were unprofitable). *Moskovskie bol'sheviki*, 128–9 (citing MPA, f. 3, op. 6, d. 28, l. 45; *XIV Moskovskaia gubpartkonferentsiia: biulleten' no. 1*, 133).

312. Carr, *Socialism in One Country*, II: 66. The intrigues escalated into several "private sessions" of the members: Dmitrenko, *Bor'ba KPSS za edinstvo svoikh riadov*, 211.

313. *Politicheskii dnevnik*, 238–41; Kvashonkin, *Bol'shevistskoe rukovodstvo*, 309–12 (RGASPI, f. 76, op. 2, d. 28, l. 1–8); Kun, *Bukharin*, 159–61.

314. Blobaum, *Feliks Dzierżyński*, 231. On Dzierżyński's defense of the OGPU, especially against Bukharin, see Koenker, *Revelations*, 18–9 (RGASPI, f. 76, op. 3, d. 345, l. 1–1ob, 2–2ob); and Kvashonkin, *Bol'shevistskoe rukovodstvo*, 297–98, 302–6. Economic functionaries viewed Dzierżyński as a "rightist" Bolshevik. Valentinov, *Novaia*

*ekonomicheskaia partiia*, 23, 102–6; Izmozik, *Glaza1*, 131.

315. Khelemskii, "Soveshchanie v Sovnarkome o gosapparate [1923 g.]," 113–4, 118: RGAE, f. 3429, op. 6, d. 86, l. 12–31: 1923.

316. There were at least 1.85 million white-collar functionaries as of 1925. Gimpel'son, *NEP*, 386 (citing GARF, f. 374, op. 171, delo omitted, l. 14–15). If before the revolution there had been 600 specific titles for positions in the state, there were now more than 2,000. *Tekhnika upravleniia*, 1925, no. 1: 23–4.

317. "Even on Sundays, at the dacha outside the city," recalled his wife Zofia Muszkat, "instead of relaxing he would sit with his papers, verify what was presented to him by the departments of the Supreme Council of the Economy, all the tables of data, go through whole mountains of figures." Mozokhin and Gladkov, *Menzhinskii*, 174.

318. On January 9, 1924, Dzierżyński wrote to Stalin: "Personally. To comrade Stalin. The party discussion established that the situation, in terms of the party-political aspect, in the agencies entrusted to me by the Central Committee is unhealthy to the highest degree—in the GPU and in the commissariat of railways. That worries me, especially because I am so busy with Soviet work, that personally cannot devote sufficient time to party work to overcome the evil and even to expose it in timely manner." Dzierżyński requested two secretaries (a line Stalin underscored in his text), one for the GPU and one for the railways, who would look after party affairs there, as well as other helpmates. Stalin agreed to these requests: he could implant his own people. RGASPI, f. 558, op. 11, d. 726, l. 28–9.

319. RGASPI, f. 3, op. 1, d. 527, l. 1.

320. Khromov, *Po stranitsam*, 92 (no citation); Plekhanov, *VChK-OGPU*, 277.

321. RGASPI, f. 558, op. 11, d. 35, l. 43, in Liubianka, *Stalin i VChK*, 108.

322. *Pravda*, December 10, 1925 (Bukharin's speech); *Rabochaia Moskva*, December 13, 1925 (Kamenev's speech); *Pravda*, December 20, 1925 (Moscow party committee answer to the Leningraders); *Novaia oppozitsiia* (Leningrad, 1926) (Leningraders' pamphlet refuting the charges point by point). The Moscow party committee published an answer to the Leningraders, defending the NEP and socialism in one country, in *Pravda* on December 20, 1925. Carr, *Socialism in One Country*, II: 133–43; Merridale, *Moscow Politics*. Carr was wrongly dismissive of the New opposition as being merely personal and careerist.

323. *Sotsialisticheskii vestnik*, 1926, no. 17–18: 5.

324. Brovkin, *Russia After Lenin*, 156 (citing RGASPI, f. 17, op. 16, d. 533, l. 199).

325. *Kommunist*, 1989, no. 8: 82–4. He had written an earlier note for Stalin, dated December 6, 1925, about the initiative-crushing state apparatus, which he did not send. Plekhanov, *VChK-OGPU*, 278.

326. Plekhanov, *VChK-OGPU*, 278. In the immediate aftermath of Lenin's death there had been rumors that Dzierżyński would take over the government (rumors generated, it seems, by fear: he was thought to be a heartless type). Velikanova, "Lenina v massovom soznanii," 182.

327. *XIV s"ezd VKP (b)*, 99–130.

328. *XIV s"ezd VKP (b)*, 130–53. Like Bukharin, Stalin employed the now clichéd dismissal of Zinoviev: "Hysteria, not a policy." *Sochineniia*, VII: 378. "When there is a majority for Zinoviev, he is for iron discipline, for subordination," Mikoyan observed. "When he has no majority . . . he is against [iron discipline]." *XIV s"ezd VKP (b)*, 186.

329. *XIV s"ezd VKP (b)*, 158–66. Stalin rejected Krupskaya's characterization of NEP as capitalism, adding, politely, "and may she pardon me." At a later moment, however, he became more barbed: "and what precisely distinguishes comrade Krupskaya from any other responsible comrade?" *Sochineniia*, VII: 364–5, 383–4. Krupskaya did not officially quit the opposition until the 15th Congress in December 1927. She was never forced to recant publicly, and was not arrested. In 1927 she just delivered a speech to the effect that in 1925 it had been necessary to "verify there was enough socialism in our structure," which she now said had proved to be the case, so she was no longer in the opposition. In fact she had ceased to identify with the opposition a year earlier. *Pravda*, November 5, 1927.

330. Molotov, at the congress, remarked upon Kamenev's penchant for addressing issues always "by way of discussion," as if he were getting ready to back away even as he was just beginning. *XIV s"zed VKP (b)*, 484–5. On impressions of Kamenev's "soft" character, see also Sukhanov, *Zapiski*, II: 243–5.

331. *XIV s"ezd VKP (b)*, 96, 246. *Leninskii sbornik*, V: 8–11.

332. *XIV s"ezd VKP (b)*, 18-31 dekabria 1925 g., 273–5; Daniels, *Documentary History of Communism* [1984], I: 183–6.

333. *XIV s"ezd VKP (b)*, 289–92.

334. Genis, "G. Ia. Sokolnikov," 80 (citing the then-unpublished autobiography of G. I. Serebriakova); Galina Serebriakova, "Iz vospominanii," in Anfert'ev, *Smerch*, 230–49 (at 241).

335. *XIV s"ezd VKP (b)*, 327–35.

336. Chigir, "Grigorii Iakovlevich Sokol'nikov," 119–32 (citing RGASPI, f. 54, op. 1, d. 13, l. 76–117, esp. 111–2, 114–5). The official stenogram removed all sentences perceived to undermine Stalin's authority and edited Sokolnikov's text to enlarge the distance between him and Stalin; words and sometimes whole phrases were inserted in Sokolnikov's mouth. Rykov taunted the opposition over its divisions: Krupskaya supported Zinoviev from the vantage point of the poor, while Sokolnikov supported them "from the Right" (advocacy for deeper market relations). Carr, *Socialism in One Country*, II: 156.

337. *XIV s"ezd VKP (b)*, 397.

338. *XIV s"ezd VKP (b)*, 455–6.

339. *XIV s"ezd VKP (b)*, 508.

340. *XIV s"ezd VKP (b)*, 601.

341. *XIV s"ezd VKP (b)*, 570, 600–1.

342. *Sochineniia*, VII: 262; Carr, *Socialism in One Country*, III: 491; Carr and Davies, *Foundations of a Planned Economy*, III/i: 3–5.

343. David Woodruff, "The Politburo on Gold, Industrialization, and the International Economy, 1925–1926," in Gregory and Naimark, *Lost Politburo Transcripts*, 214–5.

344. Kuz'min, *Istoricheskii opyt sovestkoi industrializatsii*, 28–9. Stalin dismissed Sokolnikov's designation of "state capitalism," pointing to the state-owned railroads, foreign trade, and banking system. "Perhaps our Soviet apparatus also represents capitalism and not a proletarian type of state as Lenin constituted?" Stalin said mockingly. RGASPI, f. 54, op. 1, d. 13, l. 82; f. 558, op. 3, d. 33; *XIV s"ezd*, 14.

345. *Resolutions and Decisions of the Communist Party*, II: 258–60.

346. *Pravda*, December 29, 1925; *XIV s"ezd VKP (b)*, 504–5. Much of Stalin's speech was rendered far sharper in the published stenogram: RGASPI, f. 54, op. 1, d. 13, l. 60; f. 558, op. 3, d. 33; *XIV s"ezd*, 8. The passage on Bukharin's blood was excised when the speech was reprinted. *Sochineniia*, VII: 363–91 (at 379–80).

347. *XIV s"ezd VKP (b)*, 710–1.

348. Harris, "Stalin as General Secretary: The Appointment Process and the Nature of Stalin's Power."

349. Mawdsley and White, *Soviet Elite*, 36–9.

350. Trotsky, *My Life*, 521–2. Serebryakov told the 14th Congress that "Zinoviev proposed an alliance with comrade Trotsky," who "categorically rejected a bloc, however." Trotsky—who was present—made no effort to repudiate this statement. *XIV s"ezd VKP (b)*, 455–6.

351. Stalin is said to have personally approached Leonid Serebryakov. When Serebryakov replied that they had no faction—factions being illegal—Stalin is said to have remarked, "Leonid, I summoned you for a serious conversation. Pass on my proposal to your 'old man' [*starik*]" (meaning Trotsky). Tsakunov, *V labirinte*, 169 (citing a conversation with I. Vrachev, who lived in the same building as Leonid Serebryakov).

352. Dewey, *The Case of Leon Trotsky*, 322–3; Trotskii, *Moia zhizn'*, II: 273; Deutscher, *Prophet Unarmed*, 248–9.

353. V. L. Genis, "Upriamyi narkom s Il'inki," in Sokol'nikov, *Novaia finansovaia politika*, 5–38 (at 23); Genis, "G. Ia. Sokolnikov," 80 (citing the then-unpublished autobiography of G. I. Serebriakova); Galina Serebriakova, "Iz vospominanii," in Anfert'ev, *Smerch*, 230–49 (at 241).

354. RGASPI, f. 17, op. 3, d. 680. See also *XIV s"ezd*, 323–36 (esp. 335–6).

355. Stalin may have also contemplated naming Kamenev agriculture commissar. During the politburo meeting, Zinoviev passed Kamenev a note: "You need to state (among everything else) that if Sokolnikov cannot be the finance commissar, that I [Kamenev] cannot be the agriculture commissar." Zinoviev's note also contained a hint about their need to bring Trotsky onto their side. But Zinoviev remained pessimistic based on the fact that Trotsky had remained silent over Moscow's forced replacement of the editor of *Leningrad pravda*. Nazarov, *Stalin i bor'ba za liderstvo*, 138 (citing RGASPI, f. 17, op. 2, d. 210, l. 101–229; f. 323, op. 2, d. 29, l. 59–60, 73).

356. Kvashonkin, *Bol'shevistkoe rukovodstvo*, 318 (RGASPI, f. 85, op. 25, d. 118, l. 2–3).

357. Nazarov, *Stalin i bor'ba za liderstvo*, 143–4 (citing RGASPI, f. 324, op. 1, d. 540, l. 37–38ob). On Molotov at these meetings, see also Grigorov, *Povoroty sud'by i proizvol*, 413–9; and *Leningradskaia pravda*, January 22, 1926.

358. Kvashonkin, *Bol'shevistkoe rukovodstvo*, 319 (RGASPI, f. 558, op. 1, d. 2756, l. 1), 323–4. (RGASPI, f. 85, op. 25, d. 120, l. 1–2).

359. Grigorov, *Povoroty sud'by i proizvol*, 420. Kirov was officially confirmed as the new party boss at a Leningrad province conference, also attended by Dzierżyński, in February 1926. *Leningradskaia pravda*, February 12, 1926. The Leningrad second secretary, Nikolai Shvernik (b. 1888), a former telephone-factory worker, lacked comparable abilities. Stalin soon returned Shvernik to the central party apparatus.

360. Nazarov, *Stalin i bor'ba za liderstvo*, 150 (no citation).

361. Leonid Serebryakov wrote to Stalin on March 27, 1926, indicating a desire to cooperate with his proposal to afford more normal working conditions in the Central Committee, but wondering why the smearing of the 1923 opposition continued unabated in the press. "No one can believe that this is done without the authorization of the secretariat," Serebryakov wrote. "I spoke with Trotsky, Pyatakov, and Radek. They expressed complete readiness to continue the conversations that Trotsky had both with Bukharin and with you and that you and I had." Kvashonkin, *Bol'shevistkoe rukovodstvo*, 324–5 (RGASPI, f. 85, op. 1/s, d. 171, l. 1). Trotsky wrote to Serebryakov (April 2, 1926 ) that he found it odd that Stalin would use "a circuitous path" (through Serebryakov) to further discussions after having spoken directly to Trotsky already. Fel'shtinskii, *Kommunisticheskaia oppozitsiia v SSSR*, I: 188.

362. Trotsky, *Stalin*, 417; Trotskii, *Moia zhizn'*, II: 265–6. See also Fischer, *Stalin and German Communism*, 547–8 (citing a conversation with Zinoviev).

363. Serge, *Memoirs of a Revolutionary*, 212; Deutscher, *Prophet Armed*, 267.

364. Trotsky's ailments remain unclear, but on the advice of one doctor, his tonsils were extracted. Trotskii, *Moia zhizn'*, II: 266–8. Trotsky stayed at a private clinic, until the German police passed word of a possible assassination attempt by White émigrés, and Trotsky relocated to the Soviet embassy (his supporter Krestinsky was in exile as ambassador). Deutscher, *Prophet Unarmed*, 265–6.

365. *Biulleten' oppozitsii*, March 1937, no. 54–5: 11 (quoting Sergei Mrachkovsky).

366. Although Chagin is our only source for this anecdote, it has plausibility. Chagin added: "The unexpectedness of this declaration surprised me so that I have preserved it almost literally in my memory." APRF, f. 3, op. 24, d. 493, l. 1–2 (Chagin letter to Khrushchev, March 14, 1956), Hoover Institution Archives, Volkogonov papers, container 23. Also there in Kirov's apartment: N. P. Komarov, N. K. Antipov, and I. P. Zhukov. Chagin (1898–1967) had served as second secretary to Kirov in Azerbaijan.

367. Zakharov, *Voennye aspekty* (RGVA, f. 33988, op. 3, d. 78, l. 67–76); Akhtamzian, "Soviet-German Military Cooperation," 100.

368. Akhtamzian, "Voennoe sotrudnichestvo," 12.

369. Quoted in Dyck, *Weimar Germany and Soviet Russia*, 76.

370. Korbel, *Poland Between East and West*; Dyck, "German-Soviet Relations," 81 (citing Archives of the German Foreign Ministry, K281/K097454–60: memorandum by Dirksen, Sept. 19, 1927).

371. Dyck, *Weimar Germany and Soviet Russia*, 13, 68–72; Kennan,

Russia and the West, 208–23; Carr, Socialism in One Country, III: 438–9.
372. "I have continually striven since taking up my post here to create, through a close relationship with Soviet Russia, a counterweight against the West, in order not to be at the mercy—the very expression is repugnant to me—of the favor or disfavor of the Entente Powers," German ambassador von Brockdorff-Rantzau wrote to President von Hindenburg after the April treaty. "Our relation to Soviet Russia . . . will always rest to a certain extent on bluff, i.e. it will be useful to create vis-à-vis our so-called former enemies the impression of greater intimacy with Russia than in fact exists." Carr and Davies, Foundations of a Planned Economy, III/i: 36 (citing Brockdorff-Rantzau Nachlass, 9101/24038-224046).
373. Moggridge, The Return to Gold, 45–6.
374. McIlroy, Industrial Politics; Robertson, "A Narrative of the General Strike of 1926."
375. That same day, Stalin passed word of the British coal miners' strike to Rykov and Bukharin, requesting their views. RGASPI, f. 558, op. 11, d. 34, l. 68.
376. Adibekov, Politbiuro TsK RKP (b)—VKP (b) i Evropa, 117–20, 123–7.
377. G. Zinov'ev, "Velikie sobytiia v Anglii," Pravda, May 5, 1926; Carr, Socialism in One Country, III: 494. Zinoviev had already publicly elevated Britain in place of Germany as top candidate for proletarian revolution in advanced Europe.
378. Rothschild, Piłsudski's Coup d'Etat, 20–1; Rothschild, East Central Europe Between the World Wars, 46, 54–5.
379. Kvashonkin, Bol'shevistkoe rukovodstvo, 329–30 (RGASPI, f. 76, op. 3, d. 390, l. 3–4). Dzierżyński had written to Yagoda that Poland was likely to launch a war to seize Ukraine and Belorussia. RGASPI, f. 76, op. 3, d. 364, l. 55.
380. Rothschild, Piłsudski's Coup d'Etat, 47–64, 360–1 (citing Kurjer Poranny, May 27, 1926).
381. Wandycz, Twilight of French Eastern Alliances, 48. At the same time, British officials encouraged Germany to recover Danzig and the Polish Corridor, proposing that Poland be compensated with part, or even all, of independent Lithuania. Von Riekhoff, German-Polish Relations, 248–55.
382. Karl Radek published close analyses in Pravda of the divisions in Poland's army and society, mocking Piłsudski ("the last Mohican of Polish nationalism"), but proved unable to deny his triumph. Pravda, May 15, May 18, May 22, and June 1, 1926.
383. Pravda, May 16, 1926; Korbel, Poland Between East and West, 205.
384. Wandycz, August Zaleski, 35.
385. Livezeanu, Cultural Politics in Greater Romania.
386. Dokumenty vneshnei politiki, VIII: 72–6; Lensen, Japanese Recognition of the USSR.
387. Anosov, Koreitsy v ussuriiskom krae, 7–8; Brianskii, Vsesoiuznaia perepis' naseleniia 1926 goda, VII: 8.
388. Gelb, "The Far-Eastern Koreans"; Martin, "The Origins of Soviet Ethnic Cleansing," 835 (citing GARF, f. 1235, op. 140, d. 141, l. 144).
389. Iazhborovskaia and Papsadanova, Rossiia i Pol'sha, 83.
390. "The most potent source of the dominant ethnic suspicion of the mobilized diaspora is the existence of its 'homeland' outside the dominant elite's territorial control," one scholar has noted, adding that "the dominant ethnic elite's suspicions tend to be self-fulfilling." Armstrong, "Mobilized and Proletarian Diasporas," 400–2.
391. Medvedev, Let History Judge, 111–2.
392. Trotsky, Stalin, 215; Trotskii, Predannaia revoliutsiia [1937], 25–7.
393. Medvedev, Let History Judge, 90–1 (Igor Sats, Lunacharsky's top aide).
394. One scholar put it, "one of the factors in Stalin's eventual success was his ability to evoke an image of his relationship with Lenin that was more appealing to the rank-and-file members than were those of his opponents." Gill, "Political Myth and Stalin's Quest for Authority in the Party," 99.
395. "Dve besedy s L. M. Kaganovichem," 114. See also Bazhanov, Bazhanov and the Damnation of Stalin, 114–7, 122.

## CHAPTER 13: TRIUMPHANT DEBACLE

1. Cherniavskii, "Samootvod," 68–69 (RGASPI, f. 17, op. 2, d. 335, l. 4–8: Rykov's copy of the stenogram for correction). See also Murin, "Eshche raz ob otstavkakh I. Stalina," 72–3.
2. This is where she would kill herself, in 1932. The structure still stands: Nadya's former room is visible, from the theater ticket booth of the Kremlin Palace of Congresses, looking right.
3. On Stalin's early Kremlin apartments: Mikoian, Tak bylo, 351.
4. Lenin wrote to Kremlin officials three times between November 1921 and February 1922 to force the issue of a new apartment for Stalin. PSS, LIV: 44; Golikov, Vladimir Il'ich Lenin, V: 622–3; Shturman, Mertvye khvataiut zhivykh, 23; Alliluyeva, Twenty Letters, 108. Belenky had been arrested along with Dzierżyński by left SRs in 1918. From 1919 to 1924, he was chief of Lenin's bodyguard detail, and from 1921 until January 1928, also in charge of all bodyguards for leadership. Stalin had Belenky arrested in 1938 and shot in 1940.
5. "Comrade Stalin is a living person, not a museum rarity and himself does not want to live in a museum, refusing the residence suggested to him, just as last year Zinoviev declined that same residence," Sedova wrote to Lenin. "Comrade Stalin would like to take over the apartment where Flakserman and Malkov currently reside." Sakharov, Politicheskoe zaveshchanie, 150 (citing RGASPI, f. 5, op. 1, d. 1417, l. 1–1ob.); PSS, XLIV: 162. Trotsky imagined that Leonid Serebryakov, an apparatchik in the party secretariat (who was close to Trotsky), had ended the row by offering Stalin his own apartment. Trotskii, Portrety revoliutsionerov [1991], 54–5. The outbuilding where Stalin had originally lived was eventually demolished for the post-WWII Palace of Congresses.
6. RGASPI, f. 558, op. 11, d. 753, l. 3 (June 12, 1925).
7. Iosif Stalin v ob"iatiakh sem'i, 14 (letter written sometime after September 9, 1927). Artyom would return to live with his mother, Elizaveta, who had a room at Moscow's National Hotel.
8. Shatunovskaia, Zhizn' v Kremle, 188; Bazhanov, Vospominaniia [1983], 154.
9. Iosif Stalin v ob"iatiakh sem'i, 154 (APRF, f. 44, op. 1, d. 1, l. 417–9).
10. Alliluyeva, Dvadtsat' pisem, 98; Alliluyeva, Twenty Letters, 103.
11. Iosif Stalin v ob"iatiiakh sem'i, 177.
12. Sergeev and Glushik, Besedy o Staline, 19–20.
13. Iosif Stalin v ob"iatiakh sem'i, 22 (APRF, f. 45, op. 1, d. 155, l. 5, now RGASPI f. 558, op. 11: Stalin to Nadya, April 9, 1928). See also Alliluev, Khronika odnoi sem'i, 179; and Alliluyeva, Dvadtsat' pisem, 124.
14. The baby (Galina) was born February 7, 1929. After the baby's death at eight months of age, the couple broke up; Zoya, still technically married to Yakov, moved in with Timon Kozyrev, an employee of the regular police (militsia). Yakov took some technical training and got an assembly job as an electrician. Komsomol'skaia Pravda, December 20, 2005.
15. RGASPI, f. 558, op. 11, d. 34, l. 21.
16. Lih, Stalin's Letters to Molotov, 103;

*Pis'ma Stalina Molotovu*, 55. In 1926, Sochi-Matsesta became a special "state resort." At that time it had six general state sanitoriums with 465 beds, but another twenty-one with 1,175 beds owned by individual state agencies exclusively for their personnel.

17. Mikoian, *Tak bylo*, 351–2.

18. Khromov, *Po stranitsam*, 10 (citing RGASPI, f. 558, op. 11, d. 69, l. 23–24ob.).

19. RGASPI, f. 558, op. 11, d. 69, l. 5 (M. Gorbachev).

20. "Neopublikovannye materialy iz biografii tov. Stalina," *Antireligioznik*.

21. Medvedev, *Let History Judge*, 590–1 (citing unpublished memoirs of K. K. Orjonikidze).

22. Trotsky, *Where Is Britain Going?*

23. Lih, *Stalin's Letters to Molotov*, 108 (RGASPI, f. 558, op. 1, d. 3266, l. 1–2).

24. Carr and Davies, *Foundations of a Planned Economy*, III/i: 18 (citing DBRFP, series I A, ii [1968], 724–9).

25. Gorodetsky, "The Soviet Union and Britain's General Strike of May 1926."

26. Vatlin, *Stenogrammy zasedanii Politburo*, I: 743–827 (at 743, 780: RGASPI, f. 17, op. 163, d. 686, l. 146–51, 152–6); Nazarov, *Stalin i bor'ba za liderstvo*, 152 (citing RGASPI, f. 323, op. 2, d. 22, l. 47). See also Stalin's instructions: *Pis'ma Stalina Molotovu*, 55–69.

27. *Zaria vostoka*, June 10, 1926; *Sochineniia*, VIII: 173–5.

28. *Sochineniia*, VIII: 168–72.

29. Vatlin, *Stenogrammy zasedanii Politburo*, II: 109.

30. Adibekova and Latsis, "V predchuvstvii pereloma," 85–6; Plekhanov and Plekhanov, *F. E. Dzerzhinskii*, 654–5 (RGASPI, f. 76, op. 2, d. 257, l. 46–8); Gimpel'son, *NEP*, 382, 384.

31. RGASPI, f. 76, op. 2, d. 270. Back when Dzierżyński had written him on April 5, 1926, asking for a replacement first deputy to help him run the economy, complaining of his ever-widening differences with Pyatakov, Rykov responded that Pyatakov and Trotsky were conspiring with Kamenev and Zinoviev, and that if Pyatakov were freed of the burdens of administration he would have more time to conspire politically. It is unclear if Rykov was trying to avoid finding a replacement or if he was driven by precisely these calculations. Kvashonkin, *Bol'shevistskoe rukovodstvo*, 326 (RGASPI, f. 76, op. 2, d. 168, l. 11).

32. Dzierżyński concluded: "I too am exhausted from these contradictions." *Kommunist*, 1989, no. 8: 87–8; Plekhanov and Plekhanov, *F. E. Dzerzhinskii*, 659–60 (RGASPI, f. 76, op. 2, d. 270, l. 29–30: July 3, 1926). A red-brown transformation was an old song for him: on July 9, 1924, Dzierżyński had written to Stalin and other politburo members warning that if the situation

did not improve, a dictator would appear who would bury the revolution "no matter what red feathers were affixed to his clothing." Plekhanov, *VChK-OGPU*, 277 (citing TsA FSB, f. 2, op. 2, d. 746, l. 14, 17).

33. http://kremlin-9.rosvesty.ru/news/111/.

34. RGASPI, f. 558, op. 11, d. 1289, l. 6, 6ob.

35. Ilizarov, *Tainaia zhizn'*, 113.

36. Valedinskii, "Organizm Stalina vpolne zdorovyi," 68.

37. Merridale, *Moscow Politics*, 38. The meeting in question occurred on June 6, 1926, although there may have been more than one.

38. Serge, *Memoirs of a Revolutionary*, 220.

39. *Moskovskie bol'sheviki*, 189–90 (citing MPA, f. 69, op. 1, d. 374, l. 107).

40. Zdanovich, *Organy gosudarstvennoi bezopasnosti*, 316–7 (citing TsA FSB, f. 2, op. 4, d. 145, l. 15: V. Vasilev).

41. Lih, *Stalin's Letters to Molotov*, 100 (citing RGASPI, f. 613, op. 1, d. 46, l. 21–2).

42. Lih, *Stalin's Letters to Molotov*, 115–7; *Pis'ma Stalina Molotovu*, 72–5. Stalin also predicted that "Trotsky will once again become loyal," and advised he be treated leniently. Trotsky joined a written protest to the July 1926 plenum with Zinoviev, Kamenev, Krupskaya, and others (thirteen in all), but the statement was not included in the record. Lih, *Stalin's Letters to Molotov*, 116, n1.

43. Kvashonkin, *Bol'shevistskoe rukovodstvo*, Khromov, *po stranitsam*, 1—1 (RGASPI, f. 558, op. 11, d. 69, l. 53).

44. Carr and Davies, *Foundations of a Planned Economy*, III/i: 76–80.

45. *F. E. Dzerzhinskii—predsedatel'*, 663–4 (RGASPI, f. 76, op. 3, d. 364, l. 57–8, 70); Khromov, *Po stranitsam*, 326 (citing RGASPI, f. 558, op. 11, delo unspecified, l. 56–56ob). On July 18, Dzierżyński wrote to Yagoda asking what had been done to strengthen counterintelligence against Poland, Belorussia, Ukraine, and Romania: *F. E. Dzerzhinskii—predsedatel'*, 668 (RGASPI, f. 76, op. 3, d. 364, l. 62).

46. Plekhanov and Plekhanov, *F. E. Dzerzhinskii*, 665 (RGASPI, f. 76, op. 3, d. 88, l. 37).

47. Shishkin, *Vlast', politika, ekonomika*, 296.

48. *F. E. Dzerzhinskii—predsedatel'*, 670 (RGASPI, f. 76, op. 4, d. 30, l. 50–1); *Pravda*, August 1, 1926; Dzerzhinskii, *Izbrannye proizvedennia*, II: 381–92; Dzerzhinskaia, *V gody velikikh boev*, 400–3.

49. *Pravda*, July 22, 1926, in *Sochineniia*, VIII: 192–3. See also *Torgovo-promyshlennaia gazeta*, August 1, 1926.

50. Trotskii, *Stalin*, II: 184. According to Trotsky, Stalin conveyed the impression that it was the letter of an

ill person—the illness was speaking—and that Lenin was unduly influenced by women (*baby*), meaning Krupskaya and perhaps Fotieva and Volodicheva. Trotskii, *Stalin*, II: 253.

51. RGASPI, f. 17, op.2, d. 246, IV vyp., s. 62, 66–7 (*Steongraficheskii otchet Ob"edinennogo plenuma TsK i TsKK VKP (b)*, 14–23 iuinia 1926 g.).

52. RGASPI, f. 17, op. 2, d. 246, IV vyp., s. 105.

53. Medvedev, *Let History Judge*, 85–6.

54. RGASPI, f. 17, op.2, d. 246, IV vyp., s. 66.

55. Sakharov, *Politicheskoe zaveshchanie*, 599–601.

56. RGASPI, f. 17, op.2, d. 246, IV vyp., s. 66.

57. *Pravda*, July 25, 1926; *KPSS v rezoliutsiiakh* [1970], III: 332–54.

58. RGASPI, f. 558, op. 11, d. 69, l. 89, 102, 105.

59. Orjonikidze refused: "I am no good for that kind of work, for I'm improbably explosive and rude, illiterate—in a word, I cannot write.... Don't forget that I was given a reprimand that was published in the press for a physical altercation [*mordoba*]," the infamous slap back in early 1923. He recommended instead Rudzutaks, Kaganovich, or Andreyev. Kvashonkin, *Bol'shevistskoe rukovodstvo*, 39, 323–4 (RGASPI, f. 85, op. 25, d. 120, l. 1–2: March 17, 1926); Khlevniuk, *In Stalin's Shadow*, 23–4; RGASPI, f. 558, op. 1, d. 34, l. 84, 87; *Pis'ma Stalina Molotovu*, 82–6.

60. Khlevniuk, *In Stalin's Shadow*, 23–4. Stalin wrote to Molotov on August 30, 1926, instructing that the decree be reworded post facto; Molotov took responsibility, in a letter to "Dear Sergo" of September 9, 1926, and observed, "From my side, I hope that you will not remain in the North Caucasus for long and that you'll transfer to Moscow in the not distant future." *Pis'ma Stalina Molotovu*, 82–6; Kvashonkin, *Bol'shevistskoe rukovodstvo*, 336–7 (RGASPI, f. 85, op. 25, d. 151, l. 1–3: Sept. 9, 1926).

61. Sinyavsky, *Soviet Civilization*, 128 (no citation); Polikarenko, *O Felikse Edmundoviche Dzerzhinskom*; "Nad grobom Dzerzhinskogo," *Pravda*, July 23, 1926: 1. See also Pavlov, *Chekisty*, 12. The archives got a boost from Dzierżyński's death, which induced the regime to compile his "personal files," on the example of the Lenin archives. Dzierżyński's personal file in the party archives (RGASPI, f. 76) contains more than 5,000 folders. Newly minted foreign intelligence operatives would swear their duty oaths on his birthday (September 11). Later, all Chekist salaries would be paid on the eleventh of every month. Leonov, *Likholet'e*, 354; Andrew and Mitrokhin, *Mitrokhin Archive*, 30.

62. Andrew and Gordievsky, *KGB*, 42 (citing interview with defector Peter Deriabin, former member of the guards). On the religious aspects to the Dzierżyński cult, see Sinyavsky, *Soviet Civilization*, 125–34.

63. Fedor, *Russia and the Cult of State Security*, 11–29; Hingley, *The Russian Secret Police*, 130. See also Mikoian, *Feliks Dzerzhinskii*.

64. Mozokhin and Gladkov, *Menzhinskii*, 353 (no citation). Sobol became a writer under the pen name Irina Guro. There was about Mężyński an interesting secret fact. Back in June–July 1915, behind a pseudonym, he had savaged Lenin in a Russian-language newspaper based in Paris (*Our Echo*). "Lenin considers himself not only the sole successor to the Russian throne, once it opens up, but the sole successor of the International," Mężyński perspicaciously wrote, adding that "Lenin . . . is a political Jesuit, twisting Marxism over many years to his aims of the moment, ending up irredeemably confused. . . . The Leninists are not even a faction, but a clan of party gypsies, with stentorian voices and love of brandishing whips, they imagined an unchallengeable right to be the drivers of the working class." Quite possibly Stalin, through denunciations, learned Mężyński had written this pseudonymous tirade, and kept a copy, to hold over Mężyński. S. D., "Lenin," *Nashe ekho*, June 19, 1915: 6–7, July 15: 6–7. *Our Echo* was published from April to August 1915. Scholars have often misquoted and misdated the article: see, for example, Rayfield, *Stalin and His Hangmen*, 110. Mężyński would become a member of the Central Committee in December 1927; he was never elevated to the politburo.

65. RGASPI, f. 17, op. 2, d. 246, IV vyp., s. 32.

66. RGASPI, f. 17, op. 2, d. 246, IV vyp., s. 105.

67. *Izvestiia TsK KPSS*, 1989, no. 12: 194–6. *Izvestiia TsK KPSS*, 1991, no. 4: 78. For Trotsky's letter and notebook on her, whom he labeled "an old spinster," see Trotskii, *Dnevniki i pis'ma* [1990], 76–7.

68. Ul'ianova, "Ob otnoshenii V. I. Lenina k I. V. Stalinu," 198–9 (RGASPI, f. 14, op. 1, d. 398, l. 1–8).

69. Trotsky has Krupskaya privately remarking among friends in 1926, "If Volodya were alive today, he would now be in prison." Trotskii, *Moia zhizn'*, II: 219; Trotskii, *Portrety revoliutsionerov* [1984], 56.

70. RGASPI, f. 17, op. 2, d. 246, IV vyp., s. 64. The Testament would be published in a special bulletin of the 15th Party Congress and, after Stalin's death, in a new edition of the regular proceedings. *XV s"ezd VKP (b)*, II;

1477–8. Thousands would be arrested for trying to spread the Testament, including, in 1929, twenty-two-year-old Moscow student Varlam Shalamov.

71. *Moskovskie bol'sheviki*, 174–5.

72. Kuusinen, *Rings of Destiny*, 78. Stalin, however, could be an impatient taskmaster. Upon receiving Kuusinen's draft of Comintern text on the autonomy of Alsace-Lorraine, a territory France had seized back from Germany in the Treaty of Versailles, Stalin wrote sternly on August 14, 1926, "You need to insert a paragraph . . . about how the struggle for autonomy does not signify the weakening of ties of the Alsace-Lorraine proletariat with the proletariat of France but, on the contrary, significantly strengthens those ties." Stalin also objected to the tone of the text, which he found condescending, and suggested it be pared down to eliminate repetitions. RGASPI, f. 558, op. 11, d. 755, l. 114, 118–20.

73. Pogerelskin, "Kamenev in Rome," 102 (citing ACDS, Busta, 15 Fasciola: Kameneff, Mussolini: colloquio con Kameneff, February 3, 1927), 103.

74. *Na prieme*, 765. Davis carried letters of introduction from the U.S. Senate foreign affairs committee chairman William Borah. He also had Osinsky, who had visited the United States in 1924–25, write a letter to Stalin indicating that Davis would publish a report of the American delegation's trip to the USSR, to be used in gaining U.S. recognition for the Soviet state. RGASPI, f. 558, op. 11, d. 726, l. 95–95ob, 96. Davis prepared written questions in advance (l. 89–90).

75. Davis, "Stalin, New Leader." Russian translation: RGASPI, f., 558, op. 11, d. 726, l. 119–32. Davis claimed he understood Stalin's Russian; the session was translated by Tivel. The conversation was transcribed by the Soviet side. Stalin forbid publication of the Russian translation, claiming nine tenths of it departed from what he had said, disingenuously adding that it had not been recorded by anyone. RGASPI, f. 558, op. 11, d. 726, l. 139. Davis does not appear in Stalin's Kremlin logbook; the interview took place at Old Square office. Davis tried to see Stalin again the next year in Moscow but was rebuffed. See also Harper and Harper, *The Russia I Believe In*, 234–5; Hollander, *Political Pilgrims*, 162, 165.

76. RGASPI, f. 558, op. 11, d. 726, l. 148.

77. RGASPI, f. 558, op. 11, d. 726, l. 97–105; Khromov, *Po stranitsam*, 249–57.

78. On peasants: "We hope that the peasant will ultimately join with us. . . . We are creating such material conditions as will push them over to our side. The peasant is a practical man. What does he need? He must be supplied with manufactured goods at

reasonable prices, he needs credits, he wants to feel that the Government considers his interests, helps him in time of famine, and is anxious to work with him and for him. . . . The peasants realize that we have protected them from the former landlords who would take back their land. We are giving them a cultural life they never had before." Davis also claimed to have met Stalin's mother in Tiflis in 1927.

79. Nolan, *Visions of Modernity*.

80. Henry Ford, "Mass Production," *Encyclopedia Britannica* (13th ed.), XV: 38–41.

81. *Na prieme*, 759–66. Ivan Ksenofontov, the former head of the party business affairs department, died of stomach cancer, age forty-two, on March 23, 1926.

82. Lih, *Stalin's Letters to Molotov*, 119–20; RGASPI, f. 558, op. 11, d. 34, l. 98–101.

83. RGASPI, f. 558, op. 11, d. 70, l. 20.

84. "Ob edeintsve partii," in Fel'shtinskii, *Kommunisticheskaia oppozitsiia v SSSR*, II: 77–82 (at 79–80).

85. Trotsky, *Stalin School of Falsification*, 89–90 (a letter of Trotsky's to the Central Committee, dated November 22, 1927).

86. On October 9, 1926, thirteen members of the joint opposition "active" gathered at the apartment of one of them, Ivan Bakayev, in Moscow's Sokolniki ward, to hammer out a Trotsky-Zinoviev text about desisting from opposition activity. *Moskovskie bol'sheviki*, 205 (citing MPA, f. 85, op. 1, d. 318, l. 228).

87. *Pravda*, October 17, 1926.

88. Eastman wrote to Isaac Deutscher in 1956 that he had obtained the full Testament in a copy from Krupskaya via an emissary who had brought it to Boris Souvarine in Paris. Carr and Davies, *Foundations of a Planned Economy*, II: 16, n2.

89. Murin, "Eshche raz ob otstavkakh I. Stalina," 72–3 (APRF, f. 45, op. 1, d. 126, l. 69–9: misdated as 1924).

90. *Sochineniia*, VII: 233.

91. *Pravda*, October 24, 1926; *KPSS v rezoliutsiiakh*, III: 360–1.

92. *XV konferentsiia VKP (b)*, 531–3. See also Trotskii, *Kommunistichekii internatsional posle Lenina*, 109–10.

93. *XV konferentsiia VKP (b)*, 564, 566.

94. "O sotsial-demokraticheskom uklone v nashei partii," *Pravda*, November 5–6, 1926, in *Sochineniia*, VIII: 234–97 (at 276).

95. Serge, *La vie et la mort*, 180–1 (citing the recollections of Trotsky's wife Natalya Sedova, who misdates the incident to 1927); Deutscher, *Prophet Unarmed*, 296–7; Carr and Davies, *Foundations of a Planned Economy*, II: 16–17. See also RGASPI, f. 323, op. 2, d. 98, l. 304.

96. *XV konferentsiia VKP (b)*, 535.
97. *XV konferentsiia VKP (b)*, 578.
98. *XV konferentsiia vsesoiuznoi kommunisticheskoi partii (b)*, 599, 601. See also Deutscher, *Prophet Unarmed*, 305; and Cohen, *Bukharin*, 240.
99. *Pravda*, November 12, 1926, in *Sochineniia*, VIII: 298–356.
100. Simonov, "'Strengthen the Defense of the Land of Soviets,'" 1357.
101. Golubev, *Esli mir obrushitsia na nashu Respubliku*, 98–104; Samuelson, *Soviet Defence Industry Planning*, 40–4.
102. O'Connor, *Diplomacy and Revolution*, 131–2.
103. Golubev, *Esli mir obrushitsia na nashu Respubliku*, 98–104.
104. Ken and Rupasov, *Politbiuro TsK VKP (b)*, 484–5, 491, 497.
105. Wandycz, *Twilight of French Eastern Alliances*, 50.
106. Plekhanov, *VChK-OGPU*, 305: Zakovsky to Mężyński, January 31, 1927.
107. Plekhanov, *VChK-OGPU*, 318 (citing TsA FSB, f. 2, op. 5, d. 32, l. 16. 19).
108. Neilson, *Britain, Soviet Russia and the Collapse*, 52–3.
109. Melville, *Russian Face of Germany*.
110. *Pravda*, December 16, 1926, in Eudin and Fisher, *Soviet Union and the West*, 208–9; Fischer, *Stalin and German Communism*, 529–36.
111. Neilson, *Britain, Soviet Russia and the Collapse*, 53 (citing FO 371/11787/ N5670/387/38: J. D. Gregory memorandum).
112. Samuelson, *Plans for Stalin's War Machine*, 36 (citing RGVA, f. 33987, op. 3, d. 128, l. 24: January 29, 1927).
113. D'iakov and Bushueva, *Fashistskii mech kovalsia v SSSR*, 80 (RGVA, f. 33987, op. 3, d. 128, l. 26: Jan Berzin to Voroshilov, January 29, 1927); Duraczyński and Sakharov, *Sovetsko-Pol'skie otnosheniia*, 63.
114. Davies, review of David Stone (citing *Vestnik finansov*, 1927, no. 8: 140–1).
115. Erickson, *Soviet High Command* [2001], 301–4.
116. Stone, *Hammer and Rifle*, 22.
117. Erickson, *Soviet High Command* [2001], 288.
118. Kudriashov, *Krasnaia armiia*, 139–41 (APRF, f. 3, op. 50, d. 257, l. 30–31); Sokolov, *Ot voenproma k VPK*, 62–3 (citing GARF, f. 8418, op. 16, d. 3, l. 355); Ken, *Mobilizatsionnoe planirovanie*, 21.
119. Murin, "Eshche raz ob otstavkakh I. Stalina," 73 (APRF, f. 45, op. 1, d. 131, l. 64–5).
120. Lih, *Stalin's Letters to Molotov*, 131–2.
121. *Pravda*, January 9, 1927.
122. *Pravda*, January 9, January 13, January 14, and January 20, 1927.
123. The myth-manipulation interpretation takes a superficial view: L. N.

Nezhinskii, "Byla li voennaia ugroza SSSR v kontse 20-x—nachale 30-x godov?" *Istoriia SSSR*, 1990, no. 6: 14–30; Velikanova, "The Myth of the Besieged Fortress."
124. Samuelson, *Plans for Stalin's War Machine*, 35 (citing PRO, Foreign Office, N530/190/38: January 26, 1927). Some scholars properly surmised that the war scare was genuine: Schapiro, *Communist Party*, 303–4.
125. Prokofiev, *Soviet Diary 1927*, 43–4, 59, 66, 106, 156. In the early 1930s Prokofiev would return for good to Stalin's USSR, and work alongside Shostakovich, who had never left.
126. Loginov, *Teni Stalina*, 95.
127. *Na prieme*, 766–73.
128. Von Riekhoff, *German-Polish Relations*, 248–55.
129. D'iakov and Bushueva, *Fashistskii mech kovalsia v SSSR*, 71–6 (RGVA, f. 33987, op. 3, d. 151, l. 18–23).
130. Akhtamzian, "Voennoe sotrudnichestvo," 14–5; Akhtamzian, "Soviet-German Military Cooperation," 105. See also Dyck, *Weimar Germany and Soviet Russia*, 96–7; and Jacobson, *When the Soviet Union Entered*, 227–9.
131. Samuelson, *Plan's for Stalin's War Machine*, 32–3 (citing RGASPI, f. 17, op. 3, d. 611, l. 18: January 13, 1927).
132. Plekhanov, *VChK-OGPU*, 53–4 (TsA FSB, f. 2, op. 6, d. 110, l. 114–5).
133. APRF, f. 3, op. 63, d. 137, l. 23–47 (courtesy of Sergei Kudryashov). The informant's report might have been written and/or supplied by Mieczysław Loganowski (b. 1895), a functionary in the foreign affairs commissariat—someone using red pencil wrote his name in block letters on the typescript. Loganowski was a veteran of Red Army intelligence and had previously served under diplomatic cover as concurrent civilian (GPU) and military intelligence (GRU) station chief in Warsaw, where he organized armed sabotage brigades and plotted an assassination of Piłsudski. A protégé of Dzierżyński and especially Unszlicht, fellow Poles, Loganowski then played a similar role in Austria, before being posted to the foreign affairs commissariat in Moscow. One Soviet diplomat in Warsaw recalled him as "a person of strong will, iron stamina, and animal savagery." Besedovskii, *Na putiakh k terimodoru*, 92–3; Sever and Kolpakidi, *Spetsnaz GRU*. Stalin knew Loganowski as a result of his own close involvement in the Unszlicht-coordinated sabotage-coup squads in multiple countries. Loganowski's name on the document could refer to his authorship, or it could have been a reminder to contact him for follow-up.
134. Samuelson, *Plans for Stalin's War Machine*, 39 (citing RGASPI, f. 74, op. 2, d. 39, l. 6).

135. *Anglo-Sovetskie otnosheniia*, 100–4; *DVP SSSR*, X: 6–62.
136. Chernykh, *Stanovlenie Rossii sovetskoi*, 13. Word got to Moscow in 1927 of a group of a few dozen people in Yakutia agitating against Soviet power and predicting its downfall. The spring rains and mud prohibited sending in a police team until September to apprehend the conspirators before they could launch their "uprising." Plekhanov, *VChK-OGPU*, 386 (TsA FSB, f. 2, op. 4, d. 204, l. 19).
137. *Pravda*, March 3, 1927, in *Sochineniia*, IX: 170.
138. *Izvestiia TsK KPSS*, 1989, no. 8: 199–201 (A. G. Gorbunov: April 16, 1927). Some reports from the countryside deemed the political allegiance of peasants firm. "We don't want war—we haven't recovered from the last one yet—but we won't give up Soviet power for anything," one report from Ulyanovsk summarized. In the event of a war, these peasants pledged "every last one of us will fight." Penner, "Stalin and the Ital'ianka," 53 (citing RGASPI, f. 17, op. 32, d. 110, l. 10: July 20, 1927).
139. Lenin, *Collected Works*, 30: 93–104 (September–October 1919).
140. Van Ree, *Political Thought of Joseph Stalin*, 222 (citing RGASPI, f. 558, op. 4, d. 598, l. 5–8).
141. Smith, *A Road Is Made*.
142. Smith, *A Road Is Made*, 28.
143. Wilbur and How, *Documents on Communism*, 733.
144. Smith, *A Road Is Made*, 168.
145. Smith, *A Road Is Made*, 171.
146. Stalin put great store in the Guomindang army. In November 1926, he likened the Chinese revolutionary movement to that of Russia in 1905, but added that "In China it is not an unarmed people that faces the troops of an old government but an armed people in the person of its revolutionary army. In China an armed revolution is fighting against an armed counterrevolution." *Sochineniia*, VII: 357–8, 363.
147. *VKP (b), Komintern i natsional'no-revoliutsionnoe dvizhenie v Kitae*, I: 64.
148. *VKP (b), Komintern i natsional'no-revoliutsionnoe dvizhenie v Kitae*, I: 494.
149. Michael Weiner, "Comintern in East Asia, 1919–39," in McDermott and Agnew, *Comintern*, 158–190 (at 164, no citation).
150. Wilbur and How, *Missionaries of Revolution*, 248–50. CU East Asian DS740.5.S65 W55 1989.
151. Liu, *Military History of Modern China*, ch. 2.
152. Karl, *Staging the World*, 195 (quoting Chen Duxiu, writing in 1904).
153. Evans and Block, *Leon Trotsky on China*, 113–5.

154. *Pravda*, May 22, 1925; RGASPI, f. 558, op. 1, d. 2714, l. 17, reprinted in *Sochineniia*, VII: 133–52 (but without the clause "after the model of the Guomindang"). Stalin, in China, was leftist even when he appeared not to be. Pantsov, *Bolsheviks and the Chinese Revolution*, 86–9, 129; Kara-Murz, *Strategiia i taktika Kominterna v natsional'no-kolonial'noi revoliutsii*, 112.
155. Brandt, *Stalin's Failure in China*, 44–5.
156. Kartunova, "Kitaiskii vopros," Kartunova, "Novyi vzgliad na razryv s Chan Kaishi. . ."; Peskova, "Stanovleniie diplomaticheskikh otnoshenii mezhdu Sovetskoi Rossiiei i Kitaem"; Peskova, "Diplomaticheskie otnosheniia mezhdu SSSR."
157. *VKP (b), Komintern, i natsional'no-revolutsionnoe dvizhenie v Kitae*, I: 549–53; Pantsov, *Tainaia istoriia*, 126; Pantsov, *Bolsheviks and the Chinese Revolution*, 84–5.
158. Slavinskii, *Sovetskii soiuz i Kitai*, 101, citing Tszian Chzhun-chzhen [Chiang Kai-shek], *Sovetskii Soiuz v Kitae*, 26 (March 14, 1924).
159. RGASPI, f. 17, op. 3, d. 561, l. 1.
160. RGASPI, f. 17, op. 162, d. 3, l. 55 (April 29, 1926).
161. Brandt, *Stalin's Failure in China*, 155–60; Pantsov, *Bolsheviks and the Chinese Revolution*, 101–23.
162. Brandt, *Stalin's Failure in China*, 73 (citing Trotsky archives: "Voprosy nashei politiki v otnoshenii Kitaia i Iaponii"). Voroshilov was on the same committee.
163. *VKP (b), Komintern i natsional'no-revoliutsionnoe dvizhenie v Kitae*, II: 36–40; Pantsov, *Tainaia istoriia*, 163 (citing RGASPI, f. 495, op. 1, d. 73, l. 15: Zinoviev to Hu, February 8, 1926, and f. 514, op. 1, d. 233, l. 33); Pantsov, *Bolsheviks and the Chinese Revolution*, 111–2.
164. Isaacs, *Tragedy of the Chinese Revolution*, 162, 351–2, n12.
165. *Izvestiia*, April 8, 1927; Wilbur and How, *Documents on Communism*, 8–9.
166. Slavinskii, *Sovetskii soiuz i Kitai*, 131–3; Kapitsa, *Sovetsko-kitaiskie otnosheniia*, 177–81; Schwartz, *Chinese Communism*, 42–60.
167. Wilbur, *Nationalist Revolution in China*, 108.
168. Paul R. Gregory, Hsiao-ting Lin, Lisa Nguyen, "Chiang Chooses His Enemies," *Hoover Digest*, 2010, no. 2; RGASPI, f. 17, op. 2, d. 279, l. 1–7, 10, 12, d. 280, l. 2–17, d.281, l. 1–17, d. 282, l. 94–154 (Zinoviev's theses), d. 283, l. 259–60, d. 284 (the edited, shortened published plenum, with April 15 cut), l. 22–30 (protocols with Zinoviev's theses appended); Golubev, '*Esli mir obrushitsia na nashu Respubliku*,' 49 (citing TsDOOSO, f. 4, op. 5, d. 448, l. 20).

169. Brandt, *Stalin's Failure in China*, 115 (citing Trotsky archives, letter of April 18, 1927).
170. Slavinskii, *Sovetskii soiuz i Kitai*, 155–6.
171. Deutscher, *Prophet Unarmed*, 327. "Our first disagreements with the leading core of the present politburo in regard to the Chinese question already refer to the beginning of 1926," Zinoviev and Trotsky would write in late May 1927. The Trotsky-Zinoviev proposal that the Chinese Communists break with the Guomindang was confirmed by Bukharin and Stalin at the July 1926 plenum. Pantsov, *Tainaia istoriia*, 162 (RGASPI, f. 495, op. 166, d. 189, l. 2; *Ob"edeninennyi plenum TsK i TsKK VKP (b), 14–23 iiulia 1926 g.* Vyp. 1, l. 15, 75).
172. Brandt, *Stalin's Failure in China*, 90.
173. Vygodskii, *Vneshniaia politika SSSR*, 292, 145 (citing *Izvestiia*, December 4, 1962).
174. *Lubianka: Stalin i VChk-OGPU-NKVD*, 133–4 (RGASPI, f. 17, op. 162, d. 5, l. 35). Gorodetsky, *Precarious Truce*, 221–31; Fischer, *Soviets in World Affairs*, 500–10; Fischer, *Russia's Road from Peace to War*, 169.
175. Khinchuk, *K istorii anglo-sovietskikh otnoshenii*, 46; *Izvestiia*, May 18, 1927 (Mikoian).
176. *Lubianka: Stalin i VChK-OGPU-NKVD*, 131.
177. It would do so again in March 1928. Slavinsky, *Japanese-Soviet Neutrality Pact*.
178. Fel'shtinskii, *Kommunisticheskaia oppozitsiia v SSSR*, III: 57–9; Volkogonov, *Trotsky*, 287.
179. *VKP (b), Komintern i natsional'no-revoliutsionnoe dvizhenie v Kitae*, II/ii: 763–4.
180. *Bol'shevik*, May 31, 1927, in *Sochineniia*, IX: 311–2.
181. Deutscher, *Prophet Unarmed*, 336–7.
182. Trotsky and Zinoviev, along with more than four score supporters, signed a long document known as the Declaration of the 84 for the initial signatories (a number that would grow above 300) to the Central Committee requesting a confidential Central Committee session to discuss the blowup of the revolutionary movement in China. It also enumerated Stalin's domestic failures in peasant policy and industrialization, employment, wages, housing—in short, it was a full-throated anti-NEP, pro-revolution leftist manifesto. "Declaration of the 84," in Trotsky, *Challenge of the Left Opposition*, II: 224–39.
183. Gorodetsky, *Precarious Truce*; Jacobson, *When the Soviet Union Entered*, 222. Henderson and Dovgalevsky, "Anglo-Soviet Relations." Relations would not be restored until 1929.
184. Since trade relations had resumed

in 1921, Moscow had sold London goods worth £70 million, while purchasing £24.3 million—cotton, wools, machinery, rubber, and tools. Velikanova, *Popular Perceptions*, 54 (citing Foreign Office 371, 1927, vol. 12595: 191, 193; vol. 12593: 161).
185. Werth, "Rumeurs défaitistes et apocalyptiques"; Viola, "The Peasant Nightmare." See also Simonov, "'Strengthen the Defense of the Land of Soviets,'" 1355–6; *Lubianka: Stalin i VChK-OGPU-NKVD*, 117. Leonard Schapiro speculated that the Soviet leadership may have been genuinely worried—which was true. Schapiro, *Communist Party*, 303–4. See also Sontag, "Soviet War Scare"; Meyer, "The Soviet War Scare of 1927"; and Romano, "Permanent War Scare," 103–20.
186. Rykov, *Angliia i SSSR*, 4–5, 21–31, 36.
187. Von Riekhoff, *German-Polish Relations*, 248–55.
188. Eudin and North, *Soviet Russia and the East*, 303–4; *Sochineniia*, X: 31–3; Brandt, *Stalin's Failure in China*, 133.
189. Wu, "A Review of the Wuhan Débâcle."
190. Valedinskii, "Organizm Stalina vpolne zdorovyi," 69.
191. Criminal codes were issued at republic level, not all-Union, and in the 1926 RSFSR criminal code a person could be sentenced as "dangerous" even without having committed a crime, merely for "connection to a criminal environment" or "past activity" (article 7). The criminal code also contained a special section (article 58) devoted to crimes against the Soviet political order, which were deemed "the most dangerous" and carried the death penalty. Goliakov, *Sbornik dokumentov po istorii ugolovnogo zakonodatel'stva SSSR*, 220–3, 267–9, 293–7; Berman, *Soviet Criminal Law*, 23–4; *Lubianka: Stalin i VChK-OGPU-NKVD*, 796–8, n61. "There is no step, thought, action, or lack of action under the heavens," Alexander Solzhenitsyn would write, "which could not be punished by the heavy hand of Article 58." Solzhenitsyn, *The Gulag Archipelago*, I: 60.
192. "Sovetskii Azef," *Segodnya* [Riga], May 9, 1927. The OGPU had decided to unwind its grand operation targeting Russian émigrés known as the Trust. Polish intelligence had already figured it out: the information from the Trust did not match what the Poles were getting from other intelligence channels. The Trust also kept putting off the planned uprising against the Soviet regime, saying the time was not ripe, furthering suspicions. The game had essentially been played. Many people had been caught in the web, but the secret police had failed to lure back

General Kutepov, who headed the All-Russia Military Union, the main émigré organization for officers and the principal target of Soviet foreign intelligence. But the double agent Alexander Upeninysh (Upelints), a Latvian, who used the names Alexander Opperput and Eduard Staunitz, among others, crossed from the USSR into Finland without permission on the night of April 12–13, 1927, and gave himself up, exposing the Trust in a Russian-language émigré publication. His exposé conveyed the impression that the GPU was ubiquitous, omniscient, had penetrated everything and everyone. But for the GPU, the exposure was stinging. Kutepov went to Finland and insisted that Opperput-Staunitz, as well as Maria Zakharchenko-Shultz, Kutepov's niece, prove the sincerity of their break with the GPU by sneaking back into the USSR and carrying out a terrorist act. The operatives felt they had no choice but to implement Kutepov's directives, to demonstrate their bona fides, but in their attempt in flight, near Smolensk, Opperput-Staunitz would be killed; Zakharchenko-Shultz would die later on, either in a shootout or by her own hand. Andrew and Gordievsky, *KGB*, 150.
193. Plekhanov, *VChK-OGPU*, 323–4. On January 26, 1930, OGPU agents would manage to kidnap Kutepov in Paris. He had a heart attack and died, either while still in Paris or on the Soviet ship *Spartak* sailing from Marseilles to Novorossiyka. Sudoplatov, *Special Tasks*, 91; *Nedelia*, 1989, no. 49.
194. Arsen'ev, *Podzhigateli voiny*, 21–2; *Dokumenty i materialy po istorii sovetsko-pol'skikh otnoshenii*, V: 151–2; Zhukovskii, *Polnomochnyi predstavitel' SSSR*, 202–5; Shishkin, *Stanovlenie vneshnei politiki postrevliutsionnoi Rossii i kapitalisticheskii mir*, 283–91; Blackstock, *Secret Road to World War Two*, 136–61; Korbel, *Poland Between East and West*, 217–20. The Polish courts sentenced the assassin Boris Koverda to life imprisonment, but on June 15, 1937, the Polish government amnestied him.
195. Shishkin, *Stanovlenie vneshnei politiki postrevliutsionnoi Rossii i kapitalisticheskii mir*, 289–90. Soviet protest: Degras, *Soviet Documents on Foreign Policy*, II: 220–1, 228–31.
196. *Lubianka: Stalin i VChK-OGPU-NKVD*, 133 (RGASPI, f. 558, op. 11, d. 71, l. 2–3); *Pravda*, June 8, 1927. See also Shishkin, *Stanovlenie vneshnei politiki postrevliutsionnoi Rossii i kapitalisticheskii mir*, 283–91; Degras, *Soviet Documents on Foreign Policy*, II: 220–1, 228–31; *Dokumenty i materialy po istorii sovetsko-pol'skikh otnoshenii*, V: 151–2; Zhukovskii, *Polnomochnyi predstavitel' SSSR*, 202–5; Blackstock, *Secret Road to World War Two*,

136–61; Korbel, *Poland Between East and West*, 217–20.
197. *Lubianka: Stalin i VChK-OGPU-NKVD*, 137–8 (APRF, f. 3, op. 58, d. 3, l. 113–113ob.), 796, n60.
198. RGASPI, f. 558, op. 11, d. 767, l. 35–6.
199. *Pravda*, June 10, 1927. As per Stalin's directives, the OGPU also reinforced its agent networks with new recruits among so-called former people (members of the tsarist upper-class and priests). Plekhanov, *VChK-OGPU*, 313.
200. Plekhanov, *VChK-OGPU* 130 (citing TsA FSB, f. 2, op. 5, d. 136, l. 10; d. 36, l. 3). On June 19, Mężyński limited "the quantity of [summary] executions by a relatively small number." Danilov, *Tragediia sovetskoi derevni*, I: 24. Mężyński admitted (July 19, 1927) that "few active monarchist groups were unearthed in Belorussia, Smolensk, Moscow, Leningrad, and so on." Vinogradov, "Zelenaia lampa," 5.
201. *Lubianka: Stalin i VChK-OGPU-NKVD*, 135 (RGASPI, f. 558, op. 11, d. 71, l. 29). As if on cue, Stalin received a secret report on the smashing of a British spy ring in Leningrad, with agents in Finland, which supposedly aimed to ascertain the combat level of the Red Army and fleet, including chemical weapons capabilities; some two dozen people were arrested. Plekhanov, *VChK-OGPU, 1921–1928*, 285 (citing TsA FSB, f. 2, op. 5, d. 136, l. 26–9).
202. *Pravda*, July 10, 1927.
203. Tepliakov, "Nepronizaemye nedra," 194.
204. Zdanovich, *Organy gosudarstvennoi bezopasnosti*, 299 (citing TsA FSB, f. 2, op. 5, d. 394, l. 9).
205. Velikanova, *Popular Perceptions*, 74–5. See also Simonov, "Krepit' oboronu stranam sovetov," 157; and Solomon, *Soviet Criminal Justice*, 66–7.
206. Sevost'ianov, "Sovershenno sekretno," V: 362–78, 401–8, 411–83, 484–584, 855–906 (TsA FSB, f. 2, op. 5, d. 385, l. 256–361, 422–81; op. 4, d. 386, l. 45–84; op. 5, d. 394, l. 99–108; op. 6, d. 394, l. 109–12). Werth, "Rumeurs défaitistes et apocalyptiques"; Viola, "The Peasant Nightmare."
207. Fischer spent several days with Chicherin in Wiesbaden, Germany, in August 1929. Fischer, *Russia's Road from Peace to War*, 172; on the war scare episode as a whole, see 165–79. Chicherin's deputy Litvinov felt out of his depth against the politburo. Sheinis, *Maxim Litvinov*, 194. "They say that we, the opposition, are exploiting the threat of war," Trotsky remarked at the Central Committee in June 1927. "It is you who are exploiting the threat of war to persecute the opposition and to prepare to destroy it." Fel'shtinskii, *Kommunisticheskaia oppozitsiia v SSSR*, III: 96.

208. Velikanova, *Popular Perceptions*, 47, 76–7; M. M. Kudiukhina, "Krasnaia armiia i 'voennye trevogi' vtoroi poloviny 1920-kh godov," and A. V. Baranov, "'Voennaia trevoga' 1927 g. kak factor politischeskikh nastroenii v neposvskom obshchvestve (po material iuga Rossii)," *Rossiia i mir glazami druga druga: iz istorii vzaimovospriiatiia* (Moscow: IRI RAN, 2007), 153–74, 175–93.
209. Danilov, *Tragediia sovetskoi derevni*, I: 25.
210. Lih, *Stalin's Letters to Molotov*, 135. On June 24, Stalin had Trotsky before the central control commission presidium (Aaron Solts); they debated the French Revolution!
211. Fel'shtinskii, *Kommunisticheskaia oppozitsiia v SSSR*, III: 126–7.
212. Deutscher, *Prophet Unarmed*, 388–9.
213. RGASPI, f. 558, op. 11, d. 767, l. 35–9, 45–8, 56–60; Gorlizki and Khlevniuk, "Stalin and his Circle," III: 243–67; *Pravda*, June 26, 1927.
214. Trotsky archives, T 965 (June 28, 1927).
215. *Sochineniia*, IX: 315–21. Pokrovsky (b. 1905) would be arrested on January 16, 1934, for counterrevolutionary agitation. He would be sentenced to three years' exile in Ufa. He would survive the Great Terror.
216. Deutscher, *Prophet Unarmed*, 339.
217. Lih, *Stalin's Letters to Molotov*, 136–7.
218. Khlevniuk, *Master of the House*, 3–4. RGASPI, f. 558, op. 4, d. 767, l. 56–60.
219. Rigby, *Communist Party Membership*, 113.
220. Lih, *Stalin's Letters to Molotov*, 138, 139, 141–2, 143.
221. Samuelson, *Plans for Stalin's War Machine*, 40–1 (citing RGVA, f. 33987, op. 3, d. 250, l. 60). Voroshilov, in top secret memoranda, was positive about the achievements of the military reforms and the condition of the army in 1927, but not when it came to the defense industry. Kudriashov, *Krasnaia armiia*, 161–71 (APRF, f. 3, op. 50, d. 257, l. 98–119).
222. Ken, *Mobilizatsionnoe planirovanie*, 21.
223. Velikanova, *Popular Perceptions*, 93.
224. Dyck, "German-Soviet Relations," 80 (citing Archives of the German Foreign Ministry, L337/L100554–60: memorandum by von Brockdorff-Rantzau, July 24, 1927).
225. Dyck, *Weimar Germany and Soviet Russia*, 96–7; Dyck, "German-Soviet Relations," 67 (citing Dirksen memorandum, September 19, 1927), 83. See also Dyck, *Weimar Germany and Soviet Russia*, 66–107; and Erickson, *Soviet High Command* [1962], 144–63, 247–82.

226. The OGPU reported to him that the Mensheviks in exile believed the Communist party would fall because of him. In fact, the Mensheviks in exile correctly surmised that Trotsky and the opposition would be crushed. Volkogonov, *Trotsky*, 293–4 (Arkhiv INO OGPU, d. 672, tom 1, l. 196); *Sotsialisticheskii vestnik*, August 1, 1927.

227. "Zametki na sovremennye tenmy," *Pravda*, July 28, 1929, in *Sochineniia*, IX: 322–61 (at 322, 327–30).

228. Nazarov, *Stalin i bor'ba za liderstvo*, 162 (citing RGASPI, f. 17, op. 2, d. 317, vyp. 1, l. 76, 50, 81).

229. Nazarov, *Stalin i bor'ba za liderstvo*, 163 (no citation).

230. *Pravda*, July 25, 1927.

231. *Sochineniia*, X: 3–59 (at 51).

232. Boersner, *The Bolsheviks*, 244–6.

233. RGASPI, f. 17, op. 162, d. 5, l. 74–9, 86–8 (August 17, 1927). The Comintern agent Borodin had told a foreigner upon leaving China that "When the next Chinese general comes to Moscow and shouts, 'Hail to the revolution,' better send at once for the GPU. All that any of them want is rifles." Strong, *China's Millions*, 242. Borodin also told the Society of Old Bolsheviks that he had regretted his irresoluteness regarding Chiang Kai-shek: "a fateful error. The moment to liquidate Chiang Kai-shek after the capture of Nanjing was missed by our fault." *VKP (b), Komintern i natsional'no-revoliutsionnoe dvizhenie v Kitae*, II/ii: 926.

234. Plekhanov, *VChK-OGPU*, 90.

235. Vatlin, *Stenogrammy zasedanii Politbiuro*, I: 579–80.

236. Vatlin, *Stenogrammy zasedanii Politbiuro*, II: 566, 573–4, 582. On September 12, Trotsky asked his supporter Yeltsin to look into Yenukidze's party affiliation during the period April–October 1917: Fel'shtinskii, *Kommunisticheskaia oppozitsiia v SSSR*, IV: 176–7

237. Vatlin, *Stenogrammy zasedanii Politbiuro*, II: 586.

238. Vatlin, *Stenogrammy zasedanii Politburo*, II: 593–6.

239. Vatlin, *Stenogrammy zasedanii Politbiuro*, II: 597 (RGASPI, f. 17, op. 3, d. 705).

240. RGASPI, f. 17, op. 3, d. 650, l. 1–2.

241. Vatlin, *Stenogrammy zasedanii Politbiuro*, I: 579–80, 595.

242. When they were done, Stalin put his own questions: why did only 3.5 million of America's 18–19 million industrial workers belong to trade unions, and why did the AFL-CIO not support recognition of the USSR? "The working class of America," one replied, "is not interested in international affairs." *Pravda*, September 15, 1927; *Sochineniia*, X: 92–148; *Na prieme*, 25.

243. Serge and Trotsky, *Life and Death*, 148; *Pravda*, September 29 and October 1, 1927; Carr and Davies, *Foundations of a Planned Economy*, II: 35–6. Mrachkovsky, chairman of the State Sewing Machine Trust, along with Preobrazhensky and Leonid Serebryakov, who collectively took responsibility, were immediately expelled from the party.

244. Zdanovich, *Organy gosudasrtvennoi bezopasnosti*, 289–93, 382–3.

245. Fel'shtinskii, *Kommunisticheskaia oppozitsiia v SSSR*, IV: 189; Zdanovich, *Organy gosudarstvennoi bezopasnosti*, 320 (citing TsA FSB, delo R-8209, l. 69; f. 2, op. 5, d. 98, l. 43, 98). Trotsky had admitted at the joint Central Committee–Central Control Commission plenum back in August 1927 that "some military workers, under the influence of the possible war threat, exchanged opinions recently on the situation in our armed forces . . . among those comrades I would name comrade Muralov (inspector of land-naval forces), comrades Putna and Primakov (commanders of corps), removed for opposition views, comrades Mrachkovsky and Bakayev." They produced a document on necessary measures for the country's defense, to raise the revolutionary and fighting mood in the army; Trotsky had intended to convey the document to Rykov, head of the government, for discussion at the politburo. This was a basis for accusations that Trotsky was preparing a military coup—an accusation Trotsky predicted. Fel'shtinskii, *Kommunisticheskaia oppozitsiia v SSSR*, IV: 44.

246. Mężyński spoke to the October 1927 plenum; he told them that the OGPU had arrested five participants in the military coup preparations in late September: two were middle-range commanders, the others had been recently demobilized. He claimed they had been discovered in the course of the underground printing press operation. In fact, they had been first discovered before the printing press, but attention turned to them only after the printing press idea came to light. Central Control Commission member Yaroslavsky, a Stalin surrogate, instructed Mężyński not to interrogate all those in detention; the military coup idea was enough, no need for details or complications. Zdanovich, *Organy gosudarstvennoi bezopasnosti*, 321 (citing TsA FSB, f. 2, op. 5, d. 54, l. 88, 93–4).

247. Deutscher, *Prophet Unarmed*, 357–8; *Sochineniia*, X: 187.

248. Volkogonov, *Trotsky*, 291–3 (citing RGASPI, f. 505, op. 1, d. 65, l. 1–35). The motion to expel Trotsky from the Comintern was made by John Murphy, who soon quit the party himself: Murphy, *New Horizons*, 274–7.

249. *Pravda*, September 23 and October 25, 1927.

250. V. Ia. Bliukher v Kitae.

251. Pantsov, *Bolsheviks and the Chinese Revolution*, 156.

252. By 1914, Russia had accounted for 11 percent of global cross-border borrowing, second only to the United States in absolute terms. Because the United States engaged in significant lending as well, Russia was the single largest *net* borrower globally. Cameron and Bovykin, *International Banking*, 13.

253. Dallin, *Soviet Espionage*, 32–41 (quote at 36, citing *New York Times*, April 11, 1927).

254. Rakovskii, *Kniaz' Metternikh*. Rakovski published a succinct survey of Soviet foreign policy practice for the U.S. audience: "The Foreign Policy of Soviet Russia," *Foreign Affairs*, 4/4 (July 1926): 574–84.

255. *Izvestiia*, August 11, 1927. Kamenev, ambassador to Italy, also signed the manifesto, but Mussolini and the Italian government paid it no mind.

256. Jacobson, *When the Soviet Union Entered*, 273–80.

257. *Le Matin*, September 13, 1927.

258. *Pravda*, September 16, 1927 (Litvinov); *Izvestiia*, September 16, 1927; "Novaia ugroza franko-sovetskomu soglasheniiu," *Kommunisticheskii internatsional*, October 7, 1927: 7–8; Senn, "The Rakovski Affair"; Carley, "Episodes from the Early Cold War." The failure occurred despite the fact that the Soviets had added sweeteners and reduced the size of the loan requested. Degras, *Soviet Documents on Foreign Policy*, II: 248–54.

259. Conte, *Christian Rakovski*, 196–204.

260. Naville, *Trotsky Vivant*.

261. Fel'shtinskii, *Kommunisticheskaia oppozitsiia v SSSR*, IV: 219–24.

262. Nazarov, *Stalin i bor'ba za liderstvo*, 164–5 (RGASPI, f. 17, op. 2, d. 321, l. 4–5).

263. Fel'shtinskii, *Kommunisticheskaia oppozitsiia v SSSR*, IV: 223, 230–1; Miliukov, *Vospominaniia*, II: 19–20.

264. "Trotskistskaia oppozitsiia prezhde i teper'," *Pravda*, November 2, 1927, in *Sochineniia*, X: 172–205 (at 172–6).

265. *Pravda*, November 2, 1927, in "Trotskistskaia oppozitsiia prezhde i teper'," *Sochineniia*, X: 172–205; Stalin, *Ob oppozitsii*, 723. Stalin's later *Collected Works* leave out the direct quotation from the Testament. Carr, *Interregnum*, 267.

266. Fel'shtinskii, *Kommunisticheskaia oppozitsiia v SSSR*, IV: 230–1; Kun, *Bukharin*, 208–9 (no citation).

267. *KPSS v rezoliutsiiakh* [1984], IV: 210–49.

268. *Voprosy torgovli*, 1927, no. 1: 63.

269. Carr and Davies, *Foundations of a Planned Economy*, II: 41.

270. Stalin, *Beseda s inostrannymi rabochimi delegatsiaiami*, 44–8; *Pravda*, November 13 and November 15, 1927, reprinted in *Sochineniia*, X: 206–38 (at 237). The meeting was not recorded in Stalin's office logbooks, evidently because the group was too large to be received in his office.
271. Daniels, *Conscience of the Revolution*, 314 (citing *Inprecor*, November 3, 1927).
272. Fel'shtinskii, *Kommunisticheskaia oppozitsiia v SSSR*, IV: 254–6 (Trotsky letter to politburo and CC, November 9, 1927); Carr and Davies, *Foundations of a Planned Economy*, II: 42–3.
273. "Big cloud, little rain," noted a dismissive pro-regime foreign correspondent, using the peasant proverb. Reswick, *I Dreamt Revolution*, 205. Reswick understood that the quixotic actions gave Stalin a pretext for intensified crackdown (207–8). In the cleverest of opposition actions, Smilga, Preobrazhensky, and others were able to call out to marchers heading to Red Square from a balcony at the well-placed former Grand Hotel Paris, where, in the three-story structure on the corner of Hunter's Row and Tver St. across from the Kremlin, Smilga had an apartment. Smilga had led the Baltic fleet into the Neva River to support the October coup in 1917, and he and his helpmates unfurled portraits of Lenin, Trotsky, and Zinoviev, as well as a slogan, "Fulfill Lenin's Testament." Evidently, some marchers cheered. But the party boss for the Krasnaya Presnya ward drove up in his car along with Red squads, who began to shout "Beat the Jew-opposition," while hurling bricks up toward the balcony. In parallel, from the six-story National Hotel across the way, pro-regime personnel began throwing potatoes and blocks of ice at Smilga's balcony. Soon, fifteen to twenty military academy and police academy cadets broke down the door, removed the banner, and smashed the place up. Fel'shtinskii, *Kommunisticheskaia oppozitsiia v SSSR*, IV: 250–2 (note by Muralov, Smilga, and Kamenev, November 7, 1927), 258–60 (Smilga letter, November 10, 1927). The National was returned to its function as a hotel in the late 1920s; the Paris was torn down in 1935 when Tver St. was widened, and near its old site a new Council of People's Commissars building arose. One historian has opposition figures speaking from the balcony of a building on the corner of Vozdvizhenka and Mokhovaya, which could have been Comintern headquarters or former party headquarters that housed offices of the central executive committee of the Soviet. Medvedev, *Let History Judge*, 173.
274. Volkogonov, *Trotsky*, 300–1. See

also Fel'shtinskii, *Kommunisticheskaia oppozitsiia v SSSR*, IV: 256–7 (Nikolayev letter to the CC and Central Control Commission, November 10, 1927). A similar scene unfolded in Leningrad near the Winter Palace, where Zinoviev gave a brief speech from a window opposite and other members of the Leningrad opposition tried to disrupt the flow of official marchers on Palace Square. Mounted soldiers and sailors arrived and dispersed the counter-demonstrators. Lashevich, the former second in command of the Military Revolutionary Committee, and Bakayev, the former head of the Leningrad GPU, wearing their soldiers' greatcoats shorn of insignia, shouted that policemen should be ashamed of themselves. At least eighty-one arrests were made. There were further disorders and arrests the next day. Velikanova, *Popular Perceptions*, 183 (citing TsGAIPD SPb, f. 16, op. 1, d. 8485, l. 258–9); Trotskii, *Moia zhizn'*, II: 280; Serge, *Memoirs of a Revolutionary*, 226–7. Marches by unemployed workers were to be blocked from joining up with the opposition marches by making sure all columns were pre-approved and supervised. Velikanova, *Popular Perceptions*, 181–2 (citing TsGAIPD SPb, f. 24, op. 5, d. 75, l. 69). Rykov had been sent to Leningrad for the anniversary celebrations, and in the old Tauride Palace, he delivered a speech at a jubilee session of the central executive committee of the Soviet, unfurling a colossal chart showing a V-shaped economic recovery, with the nadir in 1921 and 1927 well surpassing 1913 levels. *Izvestiia*, October 19, 1927; Rykov, *Ten Years of Soviet Rule*. The Institute of School Work Methods carried out a large-scale sociological study of 120,000 people and collected 1.5 million statements in connection with the tenth anniversary of the revolution. Kozlov and Semenova, "Sotsiaologiia detstva," 47–8.
275. Chertok, *Stop-Kadr*, 54. At a tenth anniversary exhibition of the Council of People's Commissars, portraits of oppositionists were discovered and quickly removed. Matvei Shkiryatov, of the party Control Commission, managed to get the portraits removed, but he was still fighting to remove a sculpture of Lenin's casket being carried not by Stalin and the comrades but by symbolic figures, so he wrote to Stalin apologetically asking for his intervention (the matter was placed on the politburo agenda). *Voprosy istorii*, 2004, no. 11: 16–7 (RGASPI, op. 11, d. 826, l. 1–2), reprinted in Pikhoia and Zelenov, *I. V. Stalin: istoricheskaia ideologiia*, I: 44–7.
276. *Pravda*, November 16, 1927.
277. Fel'shtinskii, *Kommunisticheskaia oppozitsiia v SSSR*, IV: 264.

278. In the summer of 1925, all residents of the Kremlin not related to state functions had had to relocate within a week; tourism had been reduced. More broadly, on Bolshevik colonization of the Kremlin, see Rolf, *Sovetskie massovy prazdniki*, 149.
279. "Mariia Ioffe, Nachalo," *Vremia i my*, 1977, no. 20: 163–92 (at 178–82). Ioffe, *One Long Night*. See also Ioffe, *Back in Time*.
280. Trotskii, *Portety revoliutsionerov*, 396–8; Deutscher, *Prophet Unarmed*, 381–2; Volkogonov, *Trotsky*, 303.
281. Medvedev, *Let History Judge*, 174 (Mikhail Yakubovich, who spent twenty-four years in prisons and camps, and lived out his life in a home for invalids in Karaganda, Kazakhstan). Medvedev's source, Yakubovich, claims to have seen Stalin's wife, Nadya Alliluyeva, walking inconspicuously behind the coffin in the crowd, but this is not corroborated. Medvedev, *Let History Judge*, 174 (citing unpublished recollections of Mikhail Yakubovich). Yagoda and Yenukidze were on the scene. Of the 143 oppositionists who were expelled from the Moscow party organization in 1927, 82 were students and 41 were white-collar employees; 16 were workers. Merridale, *Moscow Politics*, 44. "The opposition consists mostly of intellectuals, who in their intellectual level stand above the rest of the mass of party members and that causes a certain distrust toward them," noted I. Girs, head of a Czechoslovak diplomatic mission. "The strength of the Stalinist position consists in the fact that they represent the numerically dominant part of the party, that is, the intellectually middling people." Shishkin, *Vlast', politika, ekonomika*, 149.
282. Fischer, *Men and Politics*, 94; Deutscher, *Prophet Unarmed*, 383–4; Shishkin, *Stanovlenie vneshnei politiki postrevliutsionnoi Rossii i kapitalisticheskii mir*, 282. N. P. Ryutin and A. M. Lezhava were there on behalf of the Moscow party committee.
283. Volkogonov, *Trotsky*, 279, 303 (GARF, f. 5446, op. 2, d. 33, l. 19).
284. *Pravda*, November 25, 1927.
285. *Moskovskie bol'sheviki*, 106 (citing MPA, f. 63, op. 1, d. 153, l. 75; f. 3, op. 5, d. 2, l. 200: *Pravda*, December 2, 1927).
286. *XV s"ezd VKP (b)*, I: 43–74.
287. *XV s"ezd VKP (b)*, II: 1596–8.
288. *XV s"ezd VKP (b)*, I: 89–90; *Sochineniia*, X: 351.
289. *XV s"ezd VKP (b)*, I: 291. Medvedev, *Let History Judge*, 175.
290. *XV s"ezd VKP (b)*, I: 279–85.
291. *XV s"ezd VKP (b)*, I: 411–21; *Sochineniia*, X: 354–71 (at 371).
292. *XV s"ezd VKP (b)*, I: 623; Medvedev, *Let History Judge*, 86.
293. *XV s"ezd VKP (b)*.

294. Bulletin no. 30, supplement no. 1: 35–7. Medvedev, *Let History Judge.* The Testament was published in a post-Stalin edition of the proceedings: *XV s"ezd VKP (b),* II: 1477–8.

295. Danilov, *Tragediia sovetskoi derevni,* I: 119–35 (TsA FSB, f. 2, op. 5, d. 386, l. 1–3, 15–45). A grim joke made the rounds: "They're saying that they abolished the letter 'M'—there's no meat (*miaso*), no butter (*maslo*), no material to make clothing (*manufaktura*), no soap (*mylo*), and no reason to retain the 'M' just for the single surname Mikoyan" (the head of Soviet trade). Another pun was equally bitter: "The revolution gave workers a report (*doklad*), functionaries a salary (*oklad*) and their wives a treasure chest (*klad*), and the peasants hell (*ad*)." Ivanova, *Gulag v sisteme totalitarnogo gosudarstva,* 30.

296. Sevost'ianov, *"Sovershenno sekretno,"* V: 675.

297. Mif, "Kitaiskaia Kommunisticheskaia partiiia v kriticheskie dni," 106.

298. "Iz istorii kollektivizatsii 1928 god: poezdka Stalina v Sibir'," *Izvestiia TsK KPSS,* 1991, no. 7: 182–6.

299. *XV s"ezd VKP (b),* II: 1599. See also Deutscher, *Prophet Unarmed,* 385–9.

300. *XV s"ezd VKP (b),* II: 1599–1600.

301. *XV s"ezd VKP (b),* II: 1398–1400.

302. A congress resolution formally submitted by Orjonikidze as chair of the Central Control Commission called for the expulsion of seventy-five prominent oppositionists; it passed without debate. *XV s"ezd VKP (b),* II:

1468–70. The oppositionists were formally accused of creating "an ideological orientation" of defeatism that "has transformed the Trotskyite opposition into an instrument of petit bourgeois democracy within the USSR and into an auxiliary detachment of international social democracy outside its borders." *Pravda,* December 20 and December 21, 1927; *KPSS v rezoliutsiakh,* IV: 13–74. In the aftermath of the congress, some 1,500 party members would be expelled, while around 2,500 would sign written recantations. Popov, *Outline History of the C.P.S.U.,* II: 327; Conquest, *The Great Terror,* 11 (no citation).

303. Trotsky, *My Life,* 521.

304. Of Central Committee members only 49 percent were Great Russian between 1917 and 1923; that number would reach 54 percent in 1934, but become heavily Great Russian by 1939. Evan Mawsday, "An Elite Within an Elite: Politburo/Presidium Membership Under Stalin, 1927–1953," 74.

305. Grigorov, *Povoroty sud'by i proizvol,* 507. Trotsky [Bronstein] believed his, Zinoviev's, and Kamenev's Jewishness played a significant role in their defeat. Trotskii, *Stalin,* II: 224–5.

306. *Pravda,* December 18, 1927.

307. Mozokhin, *VChK—OGPU,* 24 (TsA FSB, f. 2, op. 5, por. 1, l. 31).

308. Gerson, *The Secret Police,* 269.

309. Shreider, *NKVD iznutri,* 22.

310. Cherniavskii, "Samootvod," 67–70 (RGASPI, f. 17, op. 2, d. 335, l. 4–8: Rykov's copy of the stenogram for

correction). See also Murin, "Eshche raz ob otstavkakh I. Stalina," 72–3.

311. RGASPI, f. 17, op. 2, d. 335, l. 3–7. See also Cherniavskii, "Samootvod."

312. *KPSS v rezoliutsiiakh* [1970], III: 247; Carr and Davies, *Foundations of a Planned Economy,* I/i: 710.

313. Kvashonkin, *Bol'shevistskoe rukovodstvo,* 357–61 (GARF, f. R-5446, op. 55, d. 1338, l. 1–4).

314. *XV s"ezd VKP (b),* II: 1132.

315. *XV s"ezd VKP (b),* II: 1454–68; *Pravda,* December 20, 1927.

316. *XV s"ezd VKP (b), dekabr' 1927 goda,* I: 66–7, II: 1419. One scholar asserted that not even close observers of the 15th Party Congress could have surmised that the country stood on the cusp of a revolutionary remaking. Pethybridge, *One Step Backwards,* 230.

317. *XV s"ezd VKP (b),* I: 63, 66–7, II: 1419–22.

318. Stalin held meetings in his office on his birthday: *Na prieme,* 773.

319. *Pravda,* December 18, 1927; Reswick, *I Dreamt Revolution,* 210–9. On November 6, 1926, Stalin had written to *Leningrad Pravda* refusing permission to publish a Russian version of his conversation with Davis.

320. Ivan P. Tovstukha, "Stalin," in Gambarov, *Entsiklopedicheskii slovar',* XLI/iii: 107–10; Tovstukha, *Iosif Vissarionovich Stalin.* It was slightly expanded and published in *Pravda* in 1929 on the occasion of Stalin's birthday. See *Proletarskaia revoliutsiia,* 1935, no. 6: 130; and Tucker, *Stalin as Revolutionary,* 428.

## CHAPTER 14: A TRIP TO SIBERIA

1. *Sochineniia,* XI: 170 (first published 1952); Viola, *War Against the Peasantry,* 101.

2. Chuev, *Tak govoril Kaganovich,* 1.

3. *Sochineniia,* XI: 369–70. The office logbooks have Stalin receiving visitors in his office on January 17—Antipov and Goto of Japan—but they were likely received by someone else in Stalin's office, since he was gone. Stetsky is listed as being received on January 28, 1928, when Stalin was still in Siberia. *Na prieme,* 26, 768, 774, 781.

4. Paul R. Gregory, "National Income," in Davies, *From Tsarism to the New Economic Polic* [1990], at 247.

5. Kindleberger, *World in Depression,* 46.

6. Carr and Davies, *Foundations of a Planned Economy,* I/ii:943 (table 7).

7. Koniukhov, *KPSS v bor'be,* 66 (citing RGASPI, f. 17 op. [unnumbered], d. 95, l. 29–30).

8. Jasny, *Socialist Agriculture,* 223–7; Dohan, "The Economic Origins of Soviet Autarky," 605; Davies, *Socialist Offensive,* 419 (table 1); Carr and

Davies, *Foundations of a Planned Economy,* I/ii: 698, 916–9, 1,027 (table 38). The postrevolutionary record harvest of the NEP occurred in 1925–26: 76.8 million tons.

9. Davies, *Socialist Offensive,* 1–18.

10. *Itogi vypolneniia pervogo piatiletnego plana,* 135.

11. Davies and Wheatcroft, *Years of Hunger,* 446; Davies, *Socialist Offensive,* 4, 13. Harvest data for the Soviet Union in the 1920s were estimates: statisticians asked a sample of peasants to estimate their harvests before the gathering had commenced, on a scale of one to five, then derived a percentage of a projected average, then multiplied by a prerevolutionary average. Finally, they would raise their guesstimates, believing peasants were lowballing anticipated harvests to evade taxes. The official results likely overestimated the harvest size. In 1929, statisticians would invalidate the use of the prerevolutionary average, thereby invalidating all their estimates of the 1920s harvests. Tauger,

"Statistical Falsification in the Soviet Union." Collectivization made possible accurate assessments of the Soviet harvest, although that did not mean accurate results were reported.

12. Both the regime policies and the understandings of economics in support of industrialization—in circles far wider than the Stalin faction—were incompatible with the NEP before Stalin went to Siberia. Davies and Wheatcroft, "Further Thoughts," 798. One scholar colorfully wrote that "NEP was a house built on sand." But only because of the regime's anti-market behavior. Pethybridge, *One Step Backwards,* 250.

13. L. A. Neretina, "Reorganizatsiia gosudarstvennoi promyshlennosti v 1921–25 godakh: prontsipy i tendentsii razvitiia," in Davies, *NEP,* 75–87 (at 84).

14. Davies and Wheatcroft, "Further Thoughts," 798; Dmitrenko, "Chto takoe NEP?," 46. Designed to aid farmers, the harassment of private traders and imposition of price controls actually turned the terms of trade against

farmers, while damaging the monetary stabilization, in a dynamic the Bolsheviks did not understand. Allowing the market to determine prices would have been better for farmers and for the overall macroeconomy. Johnson and Temin, "The Macroeconomics of NEP"; Gregory and Mokhtari, "State Grain Purchases."
15. "V. V. Kuibyshev i sotsialisticheskaia industrializatsiia SSSR," *Istoricheskii arkhiv*, 1958, no. 3: at 56.
16. Quoted in Bogushevskii, "Kanun piatiletki," 478. See also Kuromiya, *Stalin's Industrial Revolution*, 7.
17. Carr, *Interregnum*, 20–2; Barsov, *Balans stoimostnykh obmenov mezhdu gorodom*, 23; Millar and Nove, "A Debate on Collectivization," 57; S. G. Wheatcroft, "Agriculture," in Davies, *From Tsarism to the New Economic Policy* [1990], 79–103; Gregory, *Russian National Income*, 102–21, 194. For the results of a survey of peasants on *their* reasons for not selling grain, see *Statistika i narodnoe khoziaistvo*, 1928, no. 2: at 146.
18. Dohan, "Soviet Foreign Trade in the NEP Economy," 343–5. During an earlier crisis of grain procurements, in 1925, the authorities had raised the price paid for grain. Davies, *Socialist Offensive*, 37–41. See also Woodruff, "The Politburo on Gold, Industrialization, and the International Economy, 1925–1926," 206–8.
19. Harrison, "Prices in the Politburo, 1927," 224–46. Rykov, during the 15th Party Congress, met with officials of grain regions and forbid them from even mentioning price rises for grain, a stance formulated in a politburo resolution on December 24, 1927: Danilov, *Tragediia sovetskoi derevni*, I: 112.
20. Carr and Davies, *Foundations of a Planned Economy*, I/i: 46, I/ii: 724–30. The issue of summertime productivity is confounding. One study of textile workers in 1927, for example, claimed that *average* worker productivity rose during the months of May, June, and July, the time when workers who owned land generally returned to their village on holiday. Antropov, "Sviaz' tekstil'nykh rabochikh," 4–7. Even as averages went up, however, absolute production declined.
21. Sevost'ianov, "Sovershenno sekretno," VI: 58–60 (TsA FSB, f. 2, op. 6, d. 575, l. 1–58).
22. Contemporary analysts attributed the goods shortage to difficulties in paying for imports of raw materials for light industry (cotton, cloth, wool, leather). Dohan, "Foreign Trade," 223. The regime sought to cut costs and raise efficiency in the trade bureaucracy via mergers and staff reductions. Koniukhov, *KPSS v bor'be*, 95 (citing *Molot*, February 1, 1928), 131–2 (citing *Izvestiia Sibkraikoma*, 1928, no. 4: 4–5).

23. Danilov, *Tragediia sovetskoi derevnia*, I: 27, 108. See also *XVI s"ezd VKP (b)*, 762–3, 975–7; Velikanova, *Popular Perceptions*, 86–8.
24. Cleinow, *Neue Sibirien*, 408. Mikoyan, perhaps the principal official at the top keeping track, in early December 1927 stated: "we believe that the drop in grain procurements is temporary and in the near term will be replaced by a rising tendency." *Ekonomicheskaia zhizn'*, December 3, 1927. A week later, Rykov deemed the situation a "crisis," but optimistically noted it could be overcome by supplying more manufactured goods. *XV s"ezd VKP (b)*, II: 859–60.
25. Danilov, *Kak lomali NEP*, I: 9 (RGASPI, f. 17, op. 3, d. 662, l. 3).
26. Danilov, *Tragediia sovetskoi derevni*, I: 136 (TsA FSB, f. 2, op. 6, d. 982, l. 99). The use of article 107 against private traders had been especially concerted from 1927. On October 29, 1927, Yagoda had written to the head of the government, Alexei Rykov, warning "we need to implement quick repressive measures, in order to spur an immediate improvement on the markets," and submitted a draft decree regarding "speculators" (private traders) to be issued in the government's name. Danilov, *Tragediia sovetskoi derevni*, I: 100–1 (TsA FSB, f. 2, op. 6, d. 567, l. 1–5). The OGPU already had the prerogative of extrajudicial investigation and sentencing (up to execution) for certain crimes, such as those committed by OGPU personnel in the line of duty, as well as counterfeiters and bandits; additionally, the OGPU could request such a prerogative for specific cases, but not usually for economic crimes. See also Nove, *Economic History of the USSR*, 137.
27. Mozokhin and Gladkov, *Menzhinskii*, 257 (no citation).
28. "Iz istorii kollektivizatsii 1928 god," no. 5: 193–5; Viola, *War Against the Peasantry*, 32–4, 45–7.
29. Egorova, "Khlebozagotovitel'naia kampaniia 1927–1928," 262 (PANO, f. 2, op. 1, d. 2571, l.310–1), 264–5.
30. Carr and Davies, *Foundations of a Planned Economy*, I/i: 44–6. On Bolshevik understandings of peasant market behavior, see Larin, *Sovetskaia derevnia*, 217.
31. Danilov, *Tragediia sovetskoi derevni*, I: 105–8 (at 107: TsA FSB, f. 2, op. 6, d. 53, l. 32–49).
32. *Ugolovnyi Kodeks RSFSR* [1926], 31; *Ugolovnyi Kodeks RSFSR* [1927], 178; *Ugolovnyi kodeks RSFSR* [1929], 64–5. On the turn to coercive measures, see Manning, "The Rise and Fall of 'the Extraordinary Measures.'"
33. *Pravda*, January 8, 1928.
34. Andreev, *Vospominaniia*, 168–9 (letter dating to January 27, 1928). *Pravda* (December 24, 1927) had

announced that central officials would descend upon the key grain regions— Andrei Zhdanov to the Volga valley, Nikolai Shvernik to the Urals, and Anastas Mikoyan to the North Caucasus.
35. *Izvestiia TsK KPSS*, 1991, no. 5: 193. One historian has asserted that the report of Orjonikidze's illness was mere pretext for Stalin to go himself. But of course, Stalin could have assigned himself to go without inventing a pretext. Shishkin, "Poezdka I. V. Stalina v Sibir'," 44.
36. *Izvestiia TsK KPSS*, 1991, no. 5: 193-5; *Na prieme*, 779.
37. Pavlova, "Poezdka Stalina v Sibir'," 133–55; Kosachev, "Nanakune kollektivizatsii," 101–5; Chuev, *Sto sorok*, 377. Two plenipotentiaries, Alexander Dogadov, a functionary in the central orgburo apparatus, and Pankratov, were already in Novosibirsk, and met with the Siberian leadership on January 6 and January 9, 1928; on January 10, Siberian officialdom established a special "troika," with a military-style HQ in Novosibirsk, to direct grain procurement operations; it consisted of Syrtsov, Robert Eihe, an ethnic Latvian and the head of the Siberian Soviet Executive Committee, and the trade chief in Siberia, A. N. Zlobin (GANO, f. 47, op. 5, d. 68, l. 197–9). Copycat troikas to expedite grain procurements would be established lower down in all counties by the end of January. Danilov, *Tragediia sovetskoi derevni*, I: 780, n55; Shishkin, "Poezdka I. V. Stalina v Sibir'," 196–9; Gushchin, *Sibirskaia derevnia*, 185; Egorova, "Khlebozagotovitel'naiakampaniia 1927–1928," 262 (citing PANO, f. 2, op. 1, d. 217, l. 229); Gushchin and Il'inykh, *Klassovaia bor'ba*, 172. On January 12, 1928, seven hundred railway officials and workers in Novosibirsk met to discuss labor discipline and expediting grain shipments; a few bosses were fired, to make examples. Hughes, *Stalin, Siberia*, 136. Dogadov soon joined the so-called Right (1928–29), and in 1931 would be demoted to Transcaucasia.
38. Bazhanov had joined the orgburo staff in 1922 and served briefly as technical secretary for the politburo (August 1923–May 1924) in place of Maria Glyasser. On November 28, 1927, he was named head of the business directorate (*upravdelami*) in the Turkmenistan party secretariat. RGAE, f. 7733, op. 18, d. 527, l. 1–25 (Bazhanov's personnel file). Balashov claims that Bazhanov begged the British consulate in Askhabad to organize his escape across the border, and that his married lover arrived from Moscow to join him in flight but that she was caught trying to cross the border.
39. Agabekov, *OGPU*, 132–8, 234;

Bazhanov, *Bazhanov and the Damnation of Stalin*, 191. See also Bortnevskii, "Oprichnina." Agabekov defected June 13, 1930, while stationed in Istanbul; in the summer of 1937 he was hunted down and killed near the French-Spanish border.
40. Brook-Shepherd, *Storm Petrels*, 19–84, 107–8 (no footnotes). On January 12, 1937, Bazhanov gave a briefing to Polish intelligence—a document that fell into Soviet hands during the 1939 capture of Eastern Poland (Western Belorussia). Duraczyński and Sakharov, *Sovetsko-Pol'skie otnoshenii*, 65–6 (RGANI, f. 453, op. 1, d. 54, l. 25–33).
41. *Stalin, der rote Diktatur* (Berlin: Aretz, 1931), 21.
42. Bazhanov, *Bazhanov and the Damnation of Stalin*, 105–6.
43. Kindleberger, *World in Depression*, 73–4; Malenbaum, *World Wheat Economy*.
44. This also meant selling goods abroad that were in deficit at home, such as cotton cloth. Dohan, "Soviet Foreign Trade in the NEP Economy," 482–3; Dohan, "Foreign Trade," 223.
45. Rieber, "Stalin as Foreign Policy Maker: Avoiding War, 1927–1953," 141–2.
46. Cited in Danilov, "Vvedenie," in Danilov, *Tragediia sovetskoi derevni*, I: 25 (June 1927). See also Ken and Rupasov, *Politbiuro TsK VKP (b)*, 484–5, 491, 497.
47. Zdanovich, *Organy gosudarstvennoi bezopasnosti*, 382 (citing TsA FSB, d. PF 10289, t. 2, l. 393, 395). Pnevsky (b. 1874) died a natural death in 1928, unlike most other former tsarist officers in Red Army service.
48. RGASPI, f. 17, op. 163, d. 103 (January 3, 1927).
49. Nazarov, *Missiia Russkoi emigratsii*, I: 43–4.
50. Based on hearsay, one Soviet émigré characterized Syrtsov's efforts as setting up Potemkin villages, as if that were possible given Stalin's reliance on the OGPU. Avtorkhanov, *Stalin and the Communist Party*, 11–2.
51. Zakovsky had been posted to Novosibirsk at the same time as Syrtsov. He replaced Ivan Pavlunovsky, who had the misfortune of being transferred to the South Caucasus, where a young political climber named Lavrenti Beria ate him for lunch.
52. RGASPI, f. 558, op. 11, d. 119, l. 1–2.
53. Soviet measurements were in poods (units equal to about 36 pounds). Stalin called for 60 million poods, out of 82 million, for the center.
54. On January 9, 1928, A. N. Zlobin, the third member of the Siberian grain procurement troika, had reported to Dogadov that the Siberian harvest was average. According to M. Basovich of the Siberian party organization, per capita harvest data came to 6.9 poods in Siberia, 7.5 in the Urals, 12 in the Middle Volga, 13.3 in the Lower Volga, 13.9 in Ukraine, and 14 in the North Caucasus. Pavlova, "Poezdka Stalina v Sibir'," 134 (no citation). There had been almost no exports of Siberian grain from 1913 to 1925; it went to the Moscow and Leningrad industrial regions as well as the Russian Far East. In 1926–27, 345,000 tons of Siberian wheat were exported, but in 1927–28 just 5,700 tons would be exported. Gushchin, *Siberiskaia dervenia*, 108; *Vneshniaia torgovlia SSSR*, 94, 110.
55. *Izvestiia TsK KPSS*, 1991, no. 5: 196–9; Danilov, *Tragediia sovetskoi derveni*, I: 152–4 (GANO, f. 2, op. 4. d. 24, l. 26–28ob); Viola, *War Against the Peasantry*, 69–71; *Za chetkuiu klassovuiu liniiu*, 76 (Syrtsov report at March 1928 Siberian party plenum); Gushchin and Il'inykh, *Klassovaia bor'ba*, 172–3.
56. RGASPI, f. 558, op. 11, d. 121, l. 6–7, 47–9.
57. RGASPI, f. 558, op. 11, d. 121, l. 2. Konstantin Sergeyev (b. 1893), the traveling aide who made the record of Stalin's trip (including his remarks), listed the following brochures: *Rodinskii raion Slavgorodskogo okruga: materialy obsledovaniia sibirskoi derevni* (Novosibirsk, 1927); *Men'shikovskii raion Barabinskogo okruga: materialy obsledovaniia sibirskoi derevni* (Novosibirsk, 1927); *Abakinskii raion Minusinskogo okruga: materialy obsledovaniia sibirskoi derevni* (Novosibirsk, 1927). Sergeyev, originally from Tula, served as an aide to Stalin from January 1925 through June 1928.
58. Sevost'ianov, "Sovershenno sekretno," VI: 58–60 (TsA FSB, f. 2, op. 6, d. 575, l. 1–58).
59. RGASPI, f. 558, op. 11, d. 121, l. 4–4o, 9.
60. "At our own risk we issued a directive about repressions against kulaks in every grain procurement region," Syrtsov later bragged. "We issued the directive of the Regional Committee thinking we could not delay it although we already knew that comrade Stalin was en route." Demidov, "Khlebozagotovitel'naia akampaniia 1927/28 g. v sibirskoi derevne," at 126. In a telegram to Syrtsov in early January 1928, Stalin had belittled "as a road to panic" party officials' calls for bartering grain for manufacturing goods in Siberia. *Za chetkuiu klassovuiu liniiu*, 75–6.
61. *Izvestiia TsK KPSS*, 1991, no. 5: 201–2; Viola, *War Against the Peasantry*, 74–5. In the same January 19 (morning) telegram, Stalin also ordered that Molotov be sent to the Central Black Earth Region. Later that same day (5:35 p.m.), Stalin sent another telegram, this time to Molotov as well as Kosior, indicating the challenges were perhaps even greater, but reiterating that he anticipated success. It should be noted that Siberia's procurement campaigns usually only began in September (the harvest took place a little later in Siberia, from August through early September). Also, in 1928, only four undersized grain elevators were in operation in all Siberia, thanks to underinvestment dating back to before the revolution, but belatedly several new ones were under construction. Lebedev, "Sostoianie i perspektivy razvitiia elevatornogo khoziaistva," 34.
62. RGASPI, f. 558, op. 11, d. 121, l. 11.
63. *Izvestiia TsK KPSS*, 1991, no. 5: 193–204 (199–201); Danilov, *Tragediia sovetskoi derevni*, 154–6; Viola, *War Against the Peasantry*, 71–4. In 1930, Zagumyonny (b. 1897) would be deemed an invalid and granted a pension, but he would be elected a collective farm chairman and continue working, eventually becoming head of a state farm in his native Saratov province, where, on August 5, 1937, he would be arrested. He would stand trial publicly in May 1938 and be executed on November 28, 1938. Gusakova, "Veril v luchshuiu zhizn' naroda."
64. "Iz istorii kollektivizatsii 1928 god," no. 6: at 212. See also *Sochineniia*, XI: 3. From January through March 1928, 3,424 people were convicted in the North Caucasus, including more than 2,000 middle and poor peasants (by the regime's statistics). Osklokov, *Pobeda kolkhoznogo stroia*, 134.
65. The decision was taken at a meeting of the "grain troika" on January 26, 1928, in which Stalin participated. Papkov, *Obyknovenyi terror*, 33 (citing GANO, f. P-20, op. 2, d. 176, l. 92–3); *Sovetskaia sibir'*, January 29, 1928; *Sochineniia*, XI: 4.
66. RGASPI, f. 558, op. 11, d. 118, l. 1–74 (stenogramma zasedaniia Sibkraikoma ot 20 ianvaria 1928 g.).
67. In 1928 all Siberia counted perhaps 700 agronomists, most of whom lacked higher education. *Sibir'skaia Sovetskaia entsiklopediia*, I: 17-8.
68. *Izvestiia TsK KPSS*, 1991, no. 6: 203–5; RGASPI, f. 558, op. 11, d. 118, l. 23–6.
69. *Sochineniia*, VII: 122–29 (April 1926), 286–7 (November 1926).
70. *XVI partiinaia konferentsiia VKP (b), aprel' 1929 g.*, 293. Bukharin had told the 14th party conference in April 1925, "The collective farm is a powerful thing, but not the royal road to socialism." *XIV konferetnisia RKP (b)*, 188.

71. "Partiia i oppozitsiia," *Pravda*, November 24, 1927, reprinted in *Sochineniia*, X: 252-68 (at 259).

72. *XVI Moskovskaia gubernskaia konferentsiia VKP (b)*, bulletin no. 10: 88. *Stenograficheskii otchet*, 492-520, 544-7. Stalin moved Bauman into the party secretariat in April 1928. He would be promoted to first secretary in Moscow in 1929, taking over for Molotov, then yield to Kaganovich in 1930. Bauman would get the Central Asian bureau from 1931 to 1934.

73. *Izvestiia TsK KPSS*, 1991, no. 5: 194-6.

74. Danilov, *Tragediia sovetskoi derevni*, I: 172-92 (RGASPI, f. 82, op. 2, d. 137, l. 1-55).

75. Word of the general secretary's presence spread, of course. One party secretary in Krasnoyarsk wrote to Stalin to convey a workers' request that he speak at their factory, to which Stalin answered that he "has arrived *unofficially* for the instruction of comrades on an *internal* basis. To speak at a mass open meeting would be to exceed my mandate and deceive the Central Committee of the party." RGASPI, f. 558, op. 11, d. 119, l. 1045.

76. Donald Treadgold, *Great Siberian Migration*, 155-83.

77. Ascher, *P. A. Stolypin*, 323.

78. After Stolypin returned from Siberia, he wrote privately to Nicholas II (September 26, 1910) that "my general impression is more than comforting," but warned that "we are establishing the commune in a land that was accustomed to private property, in the form of squatter's rights.... All this and much else are urgent and immediate questions. Otherwise, in an unconscious and formless manner will be created an enormous, rudely democratic country, which will soon throttle European Russia." "Iz perepiski P. A. Stolypina s Nikolaem Romanovym," *Krasnyi arkhiv*, 1928, no. 5: 82-3. See also Syromatnikov, "Reminiscences of Stolypin," 86; and Pokrovsky, *Brief History of Russia*, II: 291. In Siberia, "free" land tenure developed whereby peasants just showed up and plowed and planted, but as arable land in any one place began to be fully occupied, a transition to "equalized" land tenure, with assignment and redistribution— that is, the appearance of the commune—began to be observed. Such a transition was usually not sudden or in a single leap. And it occurred only in the thickly settled areas (mostly in Tobolsk province, closer to European Russia), but this was an ominous sign for Stolypin, who was thinking about the long-term, when still more settlement would occur. Soldatov, "Izmeneniia form obshchinnogo zemlepol'zovaniiia," 36; Kocharovsky,

"Aleksandr Arkadievich Kaufman," VIII: 550. Stolypin traveled to Siberia accompanied by minister of land and settlement Krivoshein, and sought to counter assertions that all arable land had already been settled. A 1910 crop failure did induce large numbers of settlers to retreat back to European Russia. Robinson, *Rural Russia*, 250-1; Pavlovsky, *Agricultural Russia*, 177-8; Treadgold, *Great Siberian Migration*, 84.

79. Ascher, *P. A. Stolypin*, 325; Treadgold, *Great Siberian Migration*, 182-3.

80. *Poezdka v Sibir' i povol'zhe*, 114, 117; Antsiferov, *Russian Agriculture*, 340-3; "Zemel'nye poriadki za uralom," I: 537. In Siberia, land was owned by the state, the imperial household, or the Cossacks, but peasants viewed the land they had registered under right of usufruct (*zemlepol'zovanie*) as equivalent to property. Peasants already felt the land was theirs, de facto, but they needed to have it surveyed and registered in order to legalize the right of resale, especially where original migrants had made large claims but the plots were too big for them to farm and they were trying to rent them to later migrants. Treadgold, *Great Siberian Migration*, 182-3; *Poezdka v Sibir' i povol'zhe*, 55-6, 64-5. In 1917 the Provisional Government transferred the Cabinet Lands (owned by the royal household) to the treasury; local officials issued land grants from them. Brike, "Ekonomicheskie protsessy," 13-4; Zhidkov, "Krest'iane Altaia ot fevralia k Oktiabriu," vyp. 2: 92-110.

81. Voshchinin, *Na sibirskom prostore*, 47-8.

82. As of January 1927 in the RSFSR, 95 percent of arable land, some 630 million acres (233 million *desiatinas*), was held communally; 3.4 percent was held as individual private property. Carr, *Socialism in One Country*, I: 214; Thorniley, *Rise and Fall of the Soviet Rural Communist Party* [Basingstoke], 10. By contrast, the Belorussian SSSR had a high percentage of consolidated farms persisting from before 1917. Pershin, *Uchastkovoe zemlepol'zovanie Rossii*, 46-7.

83. Danilov, *Rural Russia*, 160; Atkinson, *End of the Russian Land Commune*, 246.

84. Danilov, *Rural Russia*, 169.

85. The notion that Stalin may have visited a village derives from the line, in the amalgamated and edited stenogram of his Siberia speeches, that "I traveled around the districts of your territory" (*Sochineniia*, XI: 2). But this does not demonstrate he visited any villages. Avtorkhanov, relying on hearsay (Sorokin), has Stalin conversing with peasants. Avtorkhanov, *Stalin and the Communist Party*, 12.

86. For example, Moshe Lewin asserted that Stalin searched for a solution to crises he had brought about, and did not impose a premeditated, ideological plan to collectivize: Lewin, *Russian Peasants*, 107-16, 296-302. Similarly, Carr and Davies wrote that "The pronouncements of Stalin and Molotov at this time were the utterances, not of men who had made a calculated move to the Left, and still less of men who believed that mass collectivization of the peasantry was a practicable policy for the near future, but of men hesitant and bewildered in the face of an intractable problem, and still hoping somehow to muddle through." Carr and Davies, *Foundations of a Planned Economy*, I/i: 85. Lewin, Carr, and Davies were working under restricted access to many key documents; it is unclear whether the additional documentation would have induced them to alter their argument, and if so, in what direction.

87. Pavliuchenkov, *Krest'ianskii Brest*, 158 (citing RGASPI, f. 325, op. 1, d. 67, l. 5: March 1920).

88. Danilov, *Sovetskoe krest'ianstvo*, 233.

89. Fewer than one peasant household in 140 could claim a party member. *Izvestiia Tsk RKP (b)*, 1928, no. 23 (255): at 9; Rigby, *Communist Party Membership*, 418. As one scholar wrote, "Whether the party sought to control or to woo, its manpower and points of contact were hopelessly inadequate for the task." Carr and Davies, *Foundations of a Planned Economy*, II: 188. On the rural party numbers, see also Thorniley, *Rise and Fall of the Soviet Rural Communist Party* [New York], 11-7, 200-4.

90. *Izvestiia Sibkraikoma VKP (b)*, 1928, no. 7-8: 1-2.

91. Pethybridge, *One Step Backwards*, 306-7.

92. Carr, for example, wrongly called Stalin's Marxism merely "skin deep." Carr, *Russian Revolution*, 163.

93. *Pravda* marked the occasion (January 15) by publishing letters that the OGPU had intercepted, under the rubric "Trotskyite subversion against the Comintern."

94. Fel'shtinskii, *Razgovory s Bukharinym*, 14 (citing a letter of Natalya Sedova, February 29, 1960: Institute of International History, Amsterdam, papers of Sara Jacobs-Weber).

95. Scheffer, *Sieben Jahre Sowjetunion*, 158-61.

96. Serge, *Le tournant obscur*, 155. Also present were the widow of Adolf Joffe and a sister (Bertha) of Abram Belenky. On Belenky, see the note from Beria to Stalin, September 6, 1940: http://stalin.memo.ru/spravki/13-038.HTM.

97. Trotsky, *My Life*, 539-50; Deutscher, *Prophet Unarmed*, 391-4.

98. Trotsky, *My Life*, 539–42; Serge and Trotsky, *Life and Death*, 155–7; Patenaude, *Stalin's Nemesis*, 88–9; Volkogonov, *Trotsky*, II: 92–5.

99. *Izvestiia TsK KPSS*, 1991, no. 5: 201, n2.

100. The politburo had discussed Trotsky's exile on numerous occasions, with Nikolai Bukharin and Alexei Rykov opposed, Stalin and Voroshilov as the most vocal in favor, and the rest acceding. Volkogonov, *Trotsky*, 308 (citing APRF, f. 45, op. 1, d. 19, 20).

101. *Izvestiia TsK KPSS*, 1991, no. 5: 201. When Ivars Smilga, who was being sent to work in the planning department of the Far East in Khabarovsk, arrived at the Yaroslavl Station on June 9, 1927, his farewell turned into something of an opposition public demonstration; Trotsky and Zinoviev delivered speeches. Stalin moved quickly to have their actions condemned as a violation of their October 16, 1926, promise to desist from factionalism. Trotsky, *My Life*, 530–1.

102. Reswick, *I Dreamt Revolution*, 226–9. Reswick was afforded a Soviet-arranged exclusive on Trotsky's deportation; his was the only journalist eyewitness account and won the AP's award for outstanding story of the year.

103. Deutscher, *Prophet Unarmed*, 394.

104. After continuously protesting, the Trotsky family was soon moved to a four-room residence.

105. On the phrase, see Baumont, *La faillite de la paix*, I: 370.

106. Lerner, *Karl Radek*, 150. Radek was soon relocated to Tomsk.

107. Volkogonov, *Trotsky*, 280 (citing RGASPI, f. 326, op. 1, d, 113, l. 72: February 27, 1928). Radek, despairing over life in long-term exile, soon began to write criticisms of Trotsky in his letters, a way of ingratiating himself with Stalin, and a step toward his begging for rehabilitation.

108. *Pravda*, January 31, 1928; Koniukhov, *KPSS v bor'be*, 146–7.

109. Bezrukov, "Za chem Stalin priezhal na Altai?"; Bezrukov, *Priezd I. V. Stalina na Altai*; Dmitrieva, *Barnaul v vospominaniiakh starozhilov*, 97 (P. I. Zakharov). The sled driver was Ivan Sergovantsev.

110. "Iz istorii kollektivizatsii 1928 god," no. 6: 212–4; RGASPI, f. 558, op. 11, d. 118, l. 78–84.

111. Kavraiskii and Nusinov, *Klassy i klassovaia bor'ba*, 78 (citing PAAK, f. 4, op. 2, d. 27, l. 48).

112. RGASPI, f. 558, op. 11, d. 119, l. 35.

113. "Stalin v Rubtsovske," *Khleborod Altaia*, December 28, 1991 (recollections of L. A. Nechunaev); Popov, *Rubtsovsk 1892-2000*, 107–8.

114. *Bol'shevik*, 1927, no. 15-16: 90–9, 100–16. The author, Georgy Safarov [Voldin], had returned to Russia in 1917 with Lenin on the sealed train and become a leader in the Communist Youth League. Hughes, *Stalin, Siberia*, 88–96.

115. Sosnovskii, "Chetyre pis'ma iz ssylki," 27. Sosnovsky wrote three letters that year to Trotsky in Kazakhstan. (A fourth, dated May 30, 1928, was addressed to Vardin.) Subsequently, Sosnovsky was arrested and imprisoned in the Chelyabinsk isolator.

116. Hughes, *Stalin, Siberia*, 58.

117. See the Left opposition analysis for their defeat by Christian Rakovski, in Trotskii, *Predannaia revoliutsiia segodnia* [1990], 61 (letter from Astrakhan to Trotsky in Alma-Ata, August 6, 1928).

118. Isaev and Ugrovatov, *Pravokhranitel'nye organy Sibiri*, 150–1; Tepliakov, "Nepronitsaemye nedra," 262–4 (citing GANO, f. 1204, op. 1, d. 4, l. 57–8); Tumshis and Papchinskii, *1937, bol'shaia chistka*, 7–78 (at 23–4).

119. *Sochineniia*, XI: 3–4.

120. *Sochineniia*, XI: 4. See also *Pravda*, July 3, 1928, reprinted in *Sochineniia*, XI: at 105. Later that year he denounced such officials as people who "do not understand the basis of our class policy and who are striving to conduct affairs in such a way that no one in the countryside is offended." *Sochineniia*, XI: 235 (speech to the Moscow party committee and Control Commission, October 19, 1928).

121. *Za chetkuiu klassovuiu liniiu*, 56 (Syrtsov speech to the party active on February 17, 1928). "Stalin is right in saying that the party is ready for the slogan of dekulakization," O. Barabashev, a leftist and former Zinovievite exiled to Siberia, concluded in the local newspaper. "Pressure on the kulaks implants in the power party ranks a mood for dekulakization in the old way." *Sovetskaia Sibir'*, January 28, 1928.

122. *Sovetskaia Sibir'*, January 25, 1928. On January 22, the Siberia procurator general (I. D. Kunov) published an article in the local press, twisting himself into knots trying to explain the legal justification for how article 107 could be applied not just to private traders dealing in manufactures but also to peasants who refused to sell grain. *Sovetskaia Sibir'*, January 22, 1928.

123. *Stepnoi pakhar'*, February 8, 1928; Kavraiskii and Nusinov, *Klassy i klassovaia bor'ba*, 82; Koniukhov, *KPSS v bor'be*, 101.

124. *Soverskaia Sibir'*, January 27 and January 29, 1928 (report of a trial of fourteen kulaks in Biysk county accused of buying up grain in neighboring provinces for resale).

125. The authorities also seized 78 flour mills and 68 barns, and shuttered 1,500 leather workshops. *Pravda*, February 14 and February 29, 1928 (Syrtsov); *Za chetkuiu klassovuiu liniiu*, 251; Gushchin, *Sibirskaia derevnia*, 186, 190. The number of those arrested reached 1,748 by the end of May, of whom 92 percent were convicted. Many "middle" peasants and poor peasants were also convicted under article 107 in Siberia. Egorova, "Khlebozagotovitel'naia kampaniia 1927-1928," 269 (citing PANO, f. 2, op. 2, d. 217, l. 744). By May 1928, around 8,000 households in Siberia had been "dekulakized." *Istochnik*, 2001, no. 1: 64.

126. As of 1928, the GPU in Siberia had 36,674 names on watch lists. Ugrovatov, *Krasnyi banditizm v Sibiri*, 187. By February 29, 1928, the Siberian GPU had arrested 123 people under article 58 (counterrevolution), 64 of whom had been forwarded as required to the procuracy for verification (only 20 were approved). Tepliakov, "Nepronitsaemye nedra": 222–3.

127. Leonidov and Reikhsbaum, "Revoliutsonnaia zakonnost' i khlebozagotovtoski," 36–40. See also Hughes, *Stalin, Siberia*, 211.

128. *Na Leninskom puti*, January 31, 1928: 3.

129. *Izvestiia Sibkraikoma VKP (b)*, 1928, no. 13: 10.

130. Another delegate was quoted demanding reduced prices paid for peasant grain in the spring. *Pravda*, March 2, 1928.

131. *Altaiskaia pravda*, December 8, 1988.

132. Gushchin, *Sibir'skaia derevnia*, 188 (RGASPI, f. 17, op. 67, d. 365, l. 9). On Syrtsov, see Hughes, "Patrimonialism and the Stalinist System"; Hughes, *Stalin, Siberia*, 200–4. Policy-wise, Syrtsov would identify with the Right, but he would support Stalin in the struggle against the Right.

133. Moletotov, *Sibkraikom*, 24.

134. *III Sibir'skaia partiinaia kraevaia konfeterentsiia VKP (b)*, 33.

135. *III Sibir'skaia partiinaia kraevaia konfeterentsiia VKP (b)*, 30–1, 43–4, 197; Hughes, *Stalin, Siberia*, 62.

136. In April 1932, Zakovsky would be transferred to Minsk as head of the GPU for Belorussia, where he brought a large team of those he had assembled in Siberia.

137. "Iz istorii kollektivizatsii 1928 god," no. 6: 214–5.

138. RGASPI, f. 558, op. 11, d. 119, l. 97, 112.

139. "Iz istorii kollektivizatsii 1928 god," no. 7: 178–92.

140. Papkov, *Obyknovenyi terror*, 34–5 (citing Tsentr khraneniia i izucheniia

dokumentov noveishei istorii Krasnoiarskgo kraia, f. 42, op. 1, d. 435, l. 2–2ob; d. 438, l. 1–8 [recollections of eyewitnesses, interviewed and recorded in 1953–4]), 36 (citing *Krasnoiarskii rabochii*, February 2, 1928).

141. Il'inykh, *Khroniki khlebnogo fronta*, 143 (citing GANO, f. P-2, op. 2, d. 217, l. 151), 158 (citing GANO, f. P-2, op. 2, d. 217, l. 472).

142. "Iz istorii kollektivizatsii 1928 god," no. 7: 179–82. See also *Pravda*, February 10, 1928 (Mikoyan).

143. *Sochineniia*, XI: 10–19. An unsigned article in *Pravda* (February 15) repeated many of the lines in the secret circular ("The rural economy has increased and prospered. Above all, the kulak has increased and prospered"). Between February and May, 1928, 1,434 Communist officials were disciplined (278 of them expelled)—a small taste of what was to come. Ikonnikova and Ugrovatov, "Stalinskaia repetitsiia nastupleniia na krest'ianstvo," 74–7.

144. Shanin, *Awkward Class*, 1–2, 46–74; Fainsod, *Smolensk Under Soviet Rule*, 239.

145. *Izvestiia TsK VKP (b)*, 1928, no. 12–13: 1; *Istoriia kommunisticheskoi partii Sovetskogo Soiuza*, 544–5. As many as 10,000 were sent just for Ukraine alone. Koniukhov, *KPSS v bor'be*, 118 (citing *Visti*, March 28, 1928).

146. *Sovetskaia Sibir'*, January 28, 1928. Barabashev, "Isil'kul'skie zheleznodorzhniki o klhebe," 47–8; Carr, *Socialism in One Country*, II: 118, 177. Barabashev went on to work in Irkutsk, then Crimea, where he would be arrested and executed in 1937. "Kak skladyvalas' zhizn' O. V. Rissa": www.oleg-riss.ru/files/Riss_part01.doc.

147. Senin, *A. I. Rykov.*

148. Trotsky archive, Houghton Library, Harvard University, T 1106; *Sotsialisticheskii vestnik*, July 23, 1928: 15; *XVII s"ezd VKP (b)* [1934], 210; Carr and Davies, *Foundations of a Planned Economy*, I/i: 61; "Materialy fevral'sko-martovskogo plenuma TsK VKP (b) 1937 goda," 19 (Bukharin/Pyatakov). See also Medvedev, *Let History Judge*, 194–5; Lewin, *Russian Peasants*, 218–20; Cohen, *Bukharin*, 278, 444, n31.

149. Only Molotov and Kuibyshev had backed Stalin without reservation. Rykov would admit that he had underestimated the extent of the crisis; Molotov, its duration. Lewin, *Russian Peasants*, 217–9.

150. Kvashonkin, *Sovetskoe rukovodstvo*, 22–4.

151. Danilov, *Kak lomali NEP*, I: 29–30.

152. Khlevniuk, *Stalinskoe politburo*, 113 (editor's note). See also the sagacious essay by E. A. Rees, "Stalin, the Politburo, and Rail Transport Policy," 104–33.

153. Mikoian, *Tak bylo*, 292.

154. Rosenfeldt, *Knowledge and Power*, 34.

155. Rosenfeldt, *The "Special" World*, I: 468–74.

156. *Pravda*, March 10, 1928: 1. At a March 16 meeting of the North Caucasus party secretariat, Andreyev directed Yevdokimov to compose a local editorial "in the spirit of the *Pravda* editorial and the formulation of the question in Moscow." Kislitsyn, *Shakhtinskoe delo*, 30–1. The politburo formed an investigatory commission, consisting of Molotov (sent to Stalino), Tomsky (sent to Shakhty), and Yaroslavsky (sent to Artemovsk), whose speeches were so rabid even Stalin had to send a telegram to rein him in, so as not to discredit the trial that had yet to take place. Kukushkin, *Rezhim lichnoi vlasti Stalina*, 96.

157. The settlement had originally been known as Grushevka (for the local river), but, in memory of the assassinated Tsar Alexander II, had been renamed Alexandrovsk-Grushevsky, a name it held until February 1920. In November 1923, 10,000 workers at Shakhty, nearly the entire workforce, had struck, disarmed the mine guards, and marched on the local GPU building, demanding higher wages and adherence to safety norms. Soldiers fired on the crowd, killing several protesters and dispersing the others. The GPU locked the miners out and arrested all presumed activists. Nikolai Krylenko arrived on November 4. When he demanded that workers beaten with whips identify themselves, no one did so, either afraid or distrusting. *Sotsialisticheskii vestnik*, 1924, no. 1: 7.

158. *Z arkhiviv VUChK-GPU-NKVD-KGB*, 1997, no. 1–2: at 321.

159. Yevdokimov's circle of loyalists included Mikhail Frinovsky, Fomin, Elza Grundman, Nikolai Nikolayev-Zhuid, V. Kursky, and others.

160. Plekhanov, *VChK-OGPU*, 382–5; *Istochnik*, 1995, no. 5, 140–51 (APRF, f. 3, op. 61, d. 648, l. 9–14).

161. *Voprosy istorii*, 1995, no. 2: 3–7. Yevdokimov's proximity to Stalin was well known inside the secret police. Orlov, *Secret History*, 28.

162. Plekhanov, *VChK-OGPU*, 130 (citing TsA FSB RF f. 2, op. 5, d. 29, l. 1). See also Wheatcroft, "Agency and Terror," 30.

163. Yevdokimov got credit at the 16th Party Congress in 1930: *XVI s"ezd VKP (b)*, 538ff; Ordzhonikidze, *Stat'i i rechi*, II: 230. The first arrests, evidently following denunciations by workers, had taken place on June 14, 1927, and initially the case involved six people. The GPU evidently had trouble getting the case in gear and continually had to request formal extensions

of the deadlines for either bringing a case or releasing those under investigation. As of January 16, 1928, the disposition of the case remained unclear. But on February 9, 1928, the OGPU informed Rykov of the case. By then, the "investigation" was nearly six months old. Krasil'nikov, *Shakhtinskii protsess*, 822, n1 (TsA FSB, f. r-49447, t. 26, ch. 1, l. 213–4, 608–9), n2. See also Avtorkhanov, *Stalin and the Communist Party*, 26–30 (citing conversations with Rezhnikov); Bailes, *Technology and Society*, 69–94; Solzhenitsyn, *The Gulag Archipelago*, 44–5; and Carr and Davies, *Foundations of a Planned Economy*, I/ii: 584–90.

164. Andrei Andreyev, newly appointed to the North Caucasus, had inherited the Shakhty hot potato, and he wrote to Stalin (on February 27, 1928) that Yevdokimov would come in person for a direct report. Andreev, *Vospominaniia*, 209; Krasil'nikov, *Shakhtinskii protsess*, t: 72.

165. Danilov, *Kak lomali NEP*, I: 348–400 (RGASPI. f. 558, op. 11, d. 132, l. 3–18); *Na prieme*, 27. Yevdokimov had brought along to Moscow Konstantin I. Zonov, the head of the North Caucasus OGPU economic department and the progenitor of the Shakhty case from the trenches: GARF, f. 3316, op. 2, d. 628, l. 20. See also Starkov, "Perekhod k 'politike razgroma,'" vyp. 2: 260–1; Iu. A. Shchetinov, "Rezhim lichnoi vlasti Stalina," in Kukushkin, *Rezhim lichnoi vlasti Stalina*, 9–97 (at 68, citing GARF without specifics).

166. Krasil'nikov, *Shakhtinskii protsess*, 163–4, 177–81.

167. Krylenko attended a March 30 plenum of the North Caucasus party committee, at which Yevdokimov delivered the main report. Krylenko stated "that the issue of specialists should be clear for all, that without them we could not manage." Andreyev echoed him: "With our hands alone we cannot build socialism, we need to use specialists. . . . I think that among us, among the managers, there is internal distrust of our GPU organs, that the latter busy themselves with finding crimes, that they overdo it, and so on. Such distrust exists. I think we need to extirpate this distrust." Mozokhin and Gladkov, *Menzhinskii*, 267–93.

168. Kislitsyn, *Shakhtinskoe delo*, 51–2.

169. Mikhhutina, "SSSR glazami pol'skikh diplomatov," 58; Rosenbaum, *Community of Fate*, 248.

170. In January 1928, a clarification had been issued regarding the criminal statute on wrecking (article 58.7) to the effect that proof of "counterrevolutionary intent" was not required for prosecution. Solomon, *Soviet Criminal Justice*, 139–40. Already, a 1927 OGPU circular had equated negligence (*khalatnost'*) with sabotage, if

it resulted in industrial fires, cave-ins, or explosions, with or without criminal intent. The circular granted the OGPU the power to impose sentences outside the courts. Viktorov, *Bez grifa "sekretno,"* 147.
171. Kuromiya, "The Shakhty Affair," 46–7 (citing GARF, f. 1652, d. 49, l. 1–9 [no opis']).
172. Mężyński's leg pain subsided, but his hearing deteriorated sharply, said to be from arteriosclerosis; doctors noted a small enlargement of his heart and aorta as well. Mozokhin and Gladkov, *Menzhinskii,* 345–6 (no citation).
173. When Yagoda was being destroyed, Yevdokimov had this to say in 1937: "I ask, you, Yagoda, you were then my boss, what help did you provide from your side? (Yagoda: 'In the Shakhty Case? You yourself did not believe in it.') Don't give me that rubbish." *Voprosy istorii,* 1995, no. 2: 6–7.
174. *Lubianka: Stalin i VChK-GPU-OGPU-NKVD,* 148–52 (APRF, f. 3, op. 58, d. 328, l. 20–5).
175. *Lubianka: Stalin i VChK-GPU-OGPU-NKVD,* 148–61; Krylenko, *Ekonomicheskaia kontr-revoliutsiia.* Yevdokimov is said to have possessed "intercepted letters" between the engineer and people abroad, claiming their innocuous content was actually a code, but the documents would not be introduced at trial. Avtorkhanov, *Stalin and the Communist Party,* 28–29. Back in 1927, the cynical Radek—perhaps sensing the political winds, perhaps out of conviction—had condemned bourgeois specialists, naming names, while criticizing corrupt, "rightist" bureaucrats and worker alienation from the regime's industrialization drive. Graziosi, "Stalin's Antiworker Workerism," 252.
176. Rosenbaum, "The German Involvement in the Shakhty Trial." Litvinov had suggested forming an authoritative commission solely for determining the guilt of the Germans, and guaranteeing the presence of a representative of the German foreign ministry at their interrogations. No such special commission was formed; Voroshilov, who oversaw Soviet-German military relations, was added to the Shakhty politburo commission on March 13.
177. Krasil'nikov, *Shakhtinskii protsess,* I: 164–5; ADAP, Serie B, VIII: 300–1; Dyck, *Weimar Germany and Soviet Russia,* 129–30 (citing Archives of the German Foreign Ministry, 2860/D559468–70: Rantzau to Stresemann, March 6, 1928, and 2860/D559755-6: Rantzau to Stresemann, March 16, 1928); Hilger and Meyer, *Incompatible Allies,* 217–8.
178. Akhtamzian, "Sovetsko-Germanskie ekonomicheskie otnosheniia," 53; Dyck, *Weimar Germany and Soviet Russia,* 119–29.

179. Krasil'nikov, *Shakhtinskii protsess,* I: 163–4.
180. *Torgovaia promyshlennaia gazeta,* March 17, 1928: 1; Dyck, *Weimar Germany and Soviet Russia,* 131 (citing 5265/E319203–5: Stresemann to Rantzau regarding a conversation with Litvinov).
181. RGASPI, f. 558, op. 11, d. 824, l. 54–64.
182. Kislitsyn, *Shakhtinskoe delo,* I: 218–9 (March 19, 1928).
183. Kislitsyn, *Shakhtinskoe delo,* I: 231–3, 239–41; Rosenbaum, *Community of Fate,* 254–5. The disorganization and mismanagement in the Soviet coal industry is well detailed in "Report of Stuart, James & Cooke, Inc. to V.S.N.H.," ch. 1, p. 2, Hoover Institution Archives, Charles E. Stuart papers, box 1. In the late 1980s, the USSR procuracy invalidated the charges of deliberate wrecking or working on behalf of émigré former mine owners or foreign intelligence, citing insufficient evidence. Mozokhin, *VChK-OGPU, karaiushchii mech diktatury proletariat,* 315.
184. Kislitsyn, *Shakhtinskoe delo,* I: 839, n48. On March 21, the politburo resolved that the GPU verify "an exact list" of those arrested and being held. *Lubianka: Stalin i VChK-GPU-OGPU-NKVD,* 153–4 (APRF, f. 3, op. 58, d. 328, l. 195); Kislitsyn, *Shakhtinskoe delo,* I: 222–3.
185. Chicherin wrote to Stalin (March 12, 1928) about the strong foreign reaction, not just in Germany, and recommended the formation of a commission headed on the German citizens who were accused, but Stalin refused. Krestinsky, the Soviet envoy in Berlin, wrote a long, plaintive letter to Stalin (March 16–17, 1928) about the consequences for Soviet-German relations ("we are heading for a difficult, prolonged conflict with German industry and, it happens, with the government, and with public opinion"). Krasil'nikov, *Shakhtinskii protsess,* I: 203–4, 210–1, II: 856–61.
186. Rosenbaum, *Community of Fate,* 258–63.
187. Terpigorev, *Vospominaniia gornogo inzhenera,* 183; Starkov, "Perekhod k 'politike razgroma,'" 255–6 (March 15, 1928, police mood summary).
188. The letter went on: "Could it be that the cause of Lenin will die?" Mozokhin and Gladkov, *Menzhinskii,* 291–2 (Boris Sysoev, June 9, 1928). Vlas Chubar, the head of the government in Ukraine, had sent the suicide note to Stalin, who distributed it to the politburo.
189. Bailes, *Technology and Society,* 79.
190. *Sovetskoe rukovodstvo: perepiska,* 28 (Voroshilov to Tomsky, March 29, 1928); Kuromiya, *Stalin's Industrial*

*Revolution,* 30–1. Voroshilov knew Yevdokimov from his time as commissar on the southern front during the civil war and as head of the North Caucasus military district (1921–24). On Rykov and Shakhty, see *Pravda,* March 11, 1928; and Reswick, *I Dreamt Revolution,* 246–51.
191. *Pravda,* March 28, 1928. The politburo already had a standing commission for political cases, but it had formed a special Shakhty commission consisting of Rykov, Orjonikidze, Molotov, Kuibyshev, and Stalin; Voroshilov, responsible for German-Soviet military cooperation, was soon added.
192. *Torgovo-promyshlennaia gazeta,* March 6, 1928. The announcement of the Shakhty case in the newspaper of Kuibyshev's agency had been muted. *Torgovo-promyshlennaia gazeta,* March 10 and March 11, 1928; Khavin, *U rulia industrii,* 79–81.
193. *Torgovo-promyshlennaia gazeta,* March 29, 1928.
194. Trotskii, *Portrety revoliutsionerov,* 228.
195. *Stenograficheskii otchet pervoi Leningradskoi oblastnoi konferenetsii VKP (b),* 19.
196. Kvashonkin, *Sovetskoe rukovodstvo,* 28 (RGASPI, f. 74, op. 2, d. 45, l. 4–4ob, 6–60b).
197. *Pravda,* April 19, 1928; Danilov, *Kak lomali NEP,* I: 417–37. See also Bukharin, *Izbrannye proizvedenie,* 376.
198. *Trud v SSSR,* 61; Schwarz, *Labor in the Soviet Union,* 6–7. See also Krzhizhanovskii, *Desiat' let khoziiastvennogo stroitel'stva.*
199. Merridale, *Moscow Politics,* 18, calculating from *Statisticheskii spravochnik goroda Moskvy i Moskovskoi gubernii* (Moscow: Mosgorkomstat, 1927); Davies, *Economic Transformation of the Soviet Union,* 84.
200. Duranty, *I Write as I Please,* 145–7.
201. Kuromiya, *Freedom and Terror,* 104–5 (citing GARF, f. 9474, op. 7, d. 259, l. 110), 141.
202. Chase, *Workers, Society, and the Soviet State,* 278–82; Chase, "Workers' Control and Socialist Democracy," 235–6.
203. Graziosi, "Stalin's Antiworker Workerism," 228.
204. Kislitsyn, *Shakhtinskoe delo,* II: 943–6.
205. Storella, *Voice of the People,* 244–5 (RGAE, f. 396, op. 6, d. 114, l. 748–50).
206. Kuromiya, "The Shakhty Affair," 51 (citing GARF, f. 5459, op. 9, d. 354, l. 5); Lyons, *Assignment in Utopia,* 116.
207. Kislitsyn, *Shakhtinskoe delo,* II: 940–2.
208. Sanukov, "Stalinist Terror in the Mari Republic."
209. Kuromiya, "Crisis of Proletarian Identity."

210. *Izvestiia TsK KPSS*, 1991, no. 5: 195–6.

211. Just 452 of the 1,017 arrests in Ukraine in the first several months of 1928 were of kulaks; 1,087 of the 2,661 arrests in the North Caucasus over the same period; and 272 of 903 arrests in the Urals. Even in Siberia, where initially "kulaks" predominated in the arrest statistics, arrests of those officially classified as middle peasants began to rise. Manning, "The Rise and Fall of 'the Extraordinary Measures,'" 15 (citing TsA FSB, f. 2, op. 6, d. 567, l. 498–504).

212. Manning, "The Rise and Fall of 'the Extraordinary Measures,'" 15 (citing GARF, f. 353s, op. 16s, d. 6, 16–17: February 23, 1928). Mikoyan, in *Pravda* back on February 12, had admitted "irregularities" and called for arrests to be limited to actual kulaks, defined as peasants possessing at least 36 tons of grain (2,000 poods), and the politburo the next day had urged officials to follow these guidelines strictly.

213. Shemelev, *Bor'ba KPSS*. See also Brower, "The Smolensk Scandal and the End of NEP."

214. Danilov, *Kak lomali NEP*, I: 156–68. See also Lutchenko, "Rukovodstvo KPSS formirovaniem kadrov tekhnicheskoi intelligentsia," 29–42 (at 33, citing RGASPI, f. 17, op. 2, d. 354, l. 790); and Gimpel'son, *NEP*, 254 (citing *Pravda*, October 3, 1988).

215. Danilov, *Kak lomali NEP*, I: 203, 214–24.

216. Danilov, *Kak lomali NEP*, I: 233–5.

217. *KPSS v rezoliutsiiakh* [8th ed.], IV: 84.

218. *Lubianka: Stalin i VChK-GPU-OGPU-NKVD*, 158–61 (APRF, f. 3, op. 58, d. 329, l. 32–7: April 25, 1928).

219. *Lubianka: Stalin i VChK-GPU-OGPU-NKVD*, 156–8 (APRF, f. 3, op. 58, d. 329, l. 28–31).

220. Carr and Davíes have argued of April 1928 that "It would be premature to assume that at this time a majority of the leaders, or Stalin in particular, was committed to coercion, or had decided to abandon the methods of the market for a policy of direct action." But the full scope of Stalin's actions indicates otherwise. Carr and Davies, *Foundations of a Planned Economy*, I: 65–6.

221. *KPSS v rezoliutsiiakh* [1984], IV: 315–6; Manning, "The Rise and Fall of 'the Extraordinary Measures,'" 13.

222. As Bukharin would point out in a report on the plenum to the Leningrad party organization: Bukharin, *Put' k sotsializmu*, 284.

223. Danilov, *Kak lomali NEP*, II: 6 (RGASPI, f. 74, op. 2, d. 38, l. 30).

224. Campbell, who was in high demand globally, was brought to the Soviet Union twice, the first time in

January 1929, when he met Stalin, then in June 1930. He was shown large mechanized farms in the North Caucasus. Campbell, *Russia: Market or Menace*.

225. Danilov, *Kak lomali NEP*, II: 462–5.

226. *Pravda*, April 18, 1928, reprinted in *Sochineniia*, XI: 54 (at 46, 48). See also Fitzpatrick, "The Foreign Threat During the First Five Year Plan."

227. Zima, *Chelovek i vlast' v SSSR*, 77–8 (citing GARF, f. 5446, op. 89, d. 11, l. 94–5: F. Cherepanov).

228. Manning, "The Rise and Fall of 'the Extraordinary Measures,'" 22 (citing RGASPI, f. 17, op. 165, d. 13, l. 5).

229. RGASPI, f. 17, op. 3, d. 683, l. 89.

230. *Moskovskie b'olsheviki*, 251 (citing *Ob"edinennyi plenum MK i MKK VKP (b), 23–25 aprelia 1928 g.: doklady i rezoliutsii*. Moscow, 1928, 34–5).

231. Danilov, *Tragediia sovetskoi derevni*, I: 236 (RGASPI, f. 17, op. 3, d. 683, l. 1–2), 261–2 (d. 684, l. 18–20), 255–62. On April 21, the regime had replaced the poll tax with a progressive tax on farm income that included an "individual" tax on high incomes and a wealth surtax on the absolute top stratum or kulak elites, in line with the sentiment to press the kulak by economic means. Atkinson, *End of the Russian Land Commune*, 329. Pyotr Wrangel, the former White Guard officer, died suddenly on April 25, 1928, aged forty-nine, in Brussels, of a severe form of tuberculosis, which by most accounts he had not contracted before. Family members believed he had been poisoned by a suspected Soviet agent, either in the household or in the guise of a former orderly who visited him ten days before his death. *Bolezn', smert' i pogrebenie general-leitenanta barona Petra Nikolaevicha Vrangelia*.

232. Ugrovatov, *Informatsionnaia deiatel'nost' organov bezopasnosti*, 82–4; *Sovetskaia derevnia glazami VChK-OGPU-NKVD*, II: 7–8, 21, 38, 46; Krasil'nikov, *Shakhtinskii protsess*, I: 242–83.

233. Plekhanov, *VChK-OGPU, 1921–1928*, 420–1 (citing TsA FSB, f. 66, op. 1, d. 187, l. 227ob). That same day, Stalin told a Communist Youth League congress, "No, comrades, our class enemies exist. And they not only exist but are gaining strength and trying to act against Soviet power." He urged them to "organize mass criticism from below." *Pravda*, May 17, 1928, in *Sochineniia*, XI: 66–77 (at 69).

234. *Izvestiia*, May 19, 1928. There had been some trials in the interim: in 1925, some engineers and former employees of once foreign-owned metallurgical plants had been tried and convicted of espionage. *Pravda*, June 4–16, 1925. In 1926, perhaps 50

percent of the technical staff in the Donbass coal basin were put on trial as a result of industrial accidents. Kuromiya, *Freedom and Terror*, 143 (citing GARF, f. 5459, op. 7, d. 2, l. 139, 150), 144–5.

235. Ivanovich, "Finliandskie shpiony," 193–7; *Vozrozhdenie*, January 6, 1928; *Pravda*, January 1, 1928.

236. Markova, "Litso vraga," 79–99 (at 80–1).

237. Lyons, *Assignment in Utopia*, 42.

238. Bailes, *Technology and Society*, 90.

239. One scholar speculated that Stalin aimed to undermine their technocratic ethos and possible political solidarity. Bailes, "Politics of Technology," 464.

240. Bailes, *Technology and Society*, 91–2.

241. Reswick, *I Dreamt Revolution*, 247.

242. Hilger and Meyer, *Incompatible Allies*, 219–20. Hilger attended the trial. Bashkin had been educated in Germany.

243. Mozokhin, *VChk—OGPU*, 274–75 (TsA FSB, f. ugolovnoe delo N-3738). The Soviets also discovered that the German technical director of the Junkers concession was listed in tsar-era archives as the former head of intelligence for the German eastern army during the Great War. This prior history, akin to unchangeable physical attributes, was taken as prima facie evidence of ongoing espionage activity on his part.

244. Lyons, *Assignment in Utopia*, 125–6.

245. *Torgovaia promyshlennaia gazeta*, July 4, 1928.

246. Kuromiya,"The Shakhty Affair," 48–9 (citing GARF, f. 9474, op. 7, d. 253, l. 106–16).

247. Walter Duranty, *New York Times*, May 19, 1928.

248. Kvashonkin, *Sovetskoe rukovodstvo*, 29–31 (RGASPI, f. 78, op. 7, d. 120, l. 1–3; f. 17, op. 162, d. 6, l. 100, 113).

249. Carr and Davies, *Foundations of a Planned Economy*, I/ii: 702–4.

250. Zima, *Chelovek i vlast' v SSSR*, 78 (citing GARF, f. 5446, op. 89, d. 11, l. 110: A. Lesnikov).

251. Plekhanov, *VChK-OGPU, 1921–1928*, 420 (citing TsA FSB, f. 66, op. 1, d. 187, l. 8, 15, 280).

252. Papkov, *Obyknovennyi terror*, 39 (citing GANO, f. P-2, op. 2, d. 289A, l. 69ob). Nikolai Zimin, the head of Irkutsk regional party committee, under Syrtsov in Novosibirsk, had denounced Syrtsov to Moscow in March 1928 for failing to implement regime policy, sparking what would be called the Irkutsk Affair: Moletotov, *Sibkraikom*, 44; Hughes, "The Irkutsk Affair."

253. Gushchin, *Sibirskaia derevnia*, 187 (citing PANO, f. 2, op. 2, d. 279, l. 6); Il'inykh, *Khroniki khlebnogo*

*fronta*, 165–6 (citing GANO, f. P-2, op. 2, d. 217, l. 738); Rosenfeldt, *The "Special" World*, I: 164.

254. The harvest of 1927–28 came in at least 5 million tons below that of 1926–27, but by June 30, 1928, state procurements of wheat and rye equaled those of 1926–27. Carr, "Revolution from Above," 321.

255. Bordiugov and Kozlov, "The Turning Point of 1929."

256. The journal passed the letter to Rykov, head of the government. Zima, *Chelovek i vlast' v SSSR*, 75 (citing GARF, f. 5446, op. 89, l. 12–15, 25, 56–64; V. Repin).

257. Carr and Davies, *Foundations of a Planned Economy*, I: 67. Grain delivery quotas risked provoking what one scholar has rightly called "the two traditional replies of the peasant: the short-term reply of concealment of stocks and the long-term reply of refusal to sow more land than was necessary to feed his own family." Carr, *Bolshevik Revolution*, II: 154.

258. Avtorkhanov, *Tekhnologiia vlasti*, 7–11.

259. Avorkhanov, *Tekhnologiia vlasti*, 11–2.

260. *Pravda*, June 2, 1928, in *Sochineniia*, XI: 81–97.

261. Carr, *Socialism in One Country*, II: 106–7 (citing Shokhin, *Kratkaia istoriia VLKSM*, 115–6); Kenez, *Birth of the Propaganda State*, 168–9; Balashov and Nelepin, *VLKSM za 10 let v tsifrakh*, 21–2.

262. Manning, "The Rise and Fall of 'the Extraordinary Measures,'" 30 (citing TsA FSB, f. 2, op. 6, d. 599, l. 385–7).

263. Zima, *Chelovek i vlast' v SSSR*, 81–2 (citing GARF, f. 5446, op. 89, d. 9, l. 9–10).

264. Zdanovich, *Organy gosudarstvennoi bezopasnosti*, 306 (citing TsA FSB, f. 2, op. 6, d. 48, l. 15–6).

265. Kun, *Bukharin*, 229–34, citing a copy of Frumkin's letter in the Trotsky archive, Houghton Library, Harvard University; *Sochineniia*, XI: 116–23.

266. In a published document collection, Bukharin's letter is dated August 1928, but in April 1929, when Bukharin would read this letter aloud at a plenum, he would date it to June 1–2, 1928. Kvashonkin, *Sovetskoe rukovodstvo*, 38–40 (RGASPI, f. 329, op. 2, d. 6, l. 58–60); Bukharin, *Problemy teorii i praktiki sotsializma*, 298–99.

267. Stalin did respond to a letter (June 15, 1928) from Moisei "Mikhail" Frumkin, the deputy agriculture commissar, inveighing against Stalin's coercive agrarian line, which he said was playing into the hands of the international bourgeoisie. Party rules specified that such a letter was to receive a

collective answer from the politburo within a week. Stalin, in his fury, responded in his own name without waiting. *Sochineniia*, XI: 116–26.

268. On June 27, 1928, Rykov received a letter from a well-known acquaintance from a village in Ukraine's Chernihiv province. "Alexei! Having received from Lenin such wealth in terms of experiments, you with your false apparatus are leading the country to ruin. . . . You know, us old revolutionaries need to go into the forest and start another revolution." Zima, *Chelovek i vlast' v SSSR*, 79 (citing GARF, f. 5446, op. 89, d. 9, l. 5–6: T. S. Tregubov).

269. Danilov, *Kak lomali NEP*, IV: 558–63 (RGASPI, f. 84, op. 2, d. 40, l. 2–11); Larina, *This I Cannot Forget*, 117.

270. Storella, *Voice of the People*, 235–6 (RGAE, f. 396, op. 6, d. 114, l. 747–8).

271. Danilov, *Kak lomali NEP*, II: 184–7, 448. See also "Foreign Trade," 225–6.

272. Aaron Solts, a member of the Central Control Commission presidium, wrote to Orjonikidze on July 1 regarding the launching of emergency measures at the beginning of the year that "the trips of Molotov and Stalin, whether they desired this or not, were a comprehensive summons to arbitrariness and spitting on the law." Kvashonkin, *Sovetskoe rukovodstvo*, 31–4 (RGASPI, f. 85, op. 1/s, d. 156, l. 2–15: July 1, 1928).

273. Scheffer, *Sieben Jahre Sowjetunion*, 323. Brockdorff-Rantzau died in Berlin on September 8, 1928.

274. Unpublished transcripts in GARF, f. 9474sch, op. 7s, d. 181–261.

275. Krumin, *Shakhtinskii protsess*. Krumin (1894–1943), shortened from Kruminsh, a graduate of the Petrograd University history department (1916), edited the newspaper *Ekonomicheskaia zhizn'* and, in 1928, joined the editorial board of *Pravda*.

276. *Sochineniia*, XI: 47. For evidence of working-class enthusiasm for the Shakhty trial and the 1928–31 terror against "class enemies" see Kuromiya, "The Shakhty Affair," 51, 56.

277. Danilov, *Kak lomali NEP*, I: 361; *Sochineniia*, XI: 158–87. On the transcript given to him for editing his remarks, Stalin inserted: "Is it not a fact that the grain collection crisis was the first attack of capitalist elements in the village against Soviet policy." He then invoked Lenin, using a rhetorical question: "Should not Lenin's slogan about reliance on the poor peasant, alliance with the middle peasant, and battle with the kulak be the basis for our work in the countryside?" (I: 360).

278. Danilov, *Kak lomali NEP*, II: 354, 513.

279. *Sochineniia*, XI: 159, 188–9 (first published in 1949).

280. Danilov, *Kak lomali NEP*, 354–5. Later in the discussion, Stalin stated that an increase in the grain price of 40 percent, to induce peasant grain sales, would cost 300 million rubles annually, and "in order to get this money it would be necessary to take something from either industry or trade" (II: 519, the uncorrected typescript).

281. Danilov, *Kak lomali NEP*, II: 360–1; *Sochineniia*, XI: 170–1.

282. In notes for a pamphlet on the dictatorship of the proletariat that he jotted down September–October 1919, Lenin wrote of a "special (higher) ferocity of class struggle and new forms of resistance in connection with capitalism and its highest stage (conspiracies + sabotage + influence on the petty-bourgeoisie, etc. etc.) . . . The resistance of the exploiters begins *before* their overthrow and *sharpens* afterwards from *two* sides." "O diktature proletariata," *PSS*, XXXIX: 261–3. Similarly, a joint circular by Dzierżyński and Molotov (February 1921), for example, asserted that "having lost the battle on the external front, the counter-revolution is focusing its efforts on overthrowing Soviet power from within. It will use any means to attain this goal, drawing on all of its experience, all of its techniques of betrayal." Lauchlan, "Young Felix Dzerzhinsky," 1–19 (citing RGASPI, f. 17, op. 84, d. 228, l. 52).

283. Van Ree, *Political Thought of Joseph Stalin*, 114–5.

284. *Sochineniia*, XI: 45; Kuromiya, *Stalin's Industrial Revolution*, 6 (citing Trotsky archive, Houghton Library, Harvard University, T-1835).

285. Kun, *Bukharin*, 233–4.

286. Danilov, *Kak lomali NEP*, II: 380.

287. On April 19, two thousand unemployed people smashed the Leningrad labor exchange; on May 3, ten thousand revolted at the Moscow labor exchange, bloodying the regular police (*militia*) and attacking trading stalls; and on May 15 in Semipalatinsk (Kazakhstan), three thousand people forced their way into the town hall and looted stores. Danilov, *Kak lomali NEP*, II: 5–6 (RGASPI, f. 17, op. 85, d. 307, l. 28–31, 41–5).

288. Danilov, *Kak lomali NEP*, II: 382–7.

289. Danilov, *Kak lomali NEP*, II: 460–1.

290. Fel'shtinskii, *Razgovory s Bukharinym*, 43. See also Lewin, *Russian Peasants*, 306.

291. Danilov, *Kak lomali NEP*, II: 516–7.

292. *KPSS v rezoliutsiiakh* [1984], IV: 351; *KPSS v rezoliutsiiakh* [1984], II: 516–7.

293. *Pravda*, August 5, 1928 (Molotov).
294. At the same time, procurator general Krylenko instructed the judicial machinery to be ready for mass application of article 107 against speculators and those trying to corner the grain market. *Pravda*, July 20, 1928; Danilov, *Kak lomali NEP*, III: 6. Fainblitt's amnesty for arrested peasants was belatedly passed and on August 7, justice commissar Yanson ordered all poor and middle peasants sentenced under article 107 to be released from prison. Manning, "The Rise and Fall of 'the Extraordinary Measures,'" 41 (citing TsA FSB, f. 66, op. 1, d. 243, l. 243). Fainblitt, *Amnistiia i sudebnyi prigovor*.
295. Stalin told the Leningrad party organization, in a summary report on the plenum, that "all the same, the grain had to be got." *Pravda*, July 15, 1928, in *Sochineniia*, XI: 204–18.
296. Kumanev and Kulikova, *Protivostoianie*, 142–4.
297. "In early 1927," Trotsky would write, "Zinoviev had been ready to capitulate," until events in China rescued him from his fecklessness, but only temporarily, for whereas Trotsky and his supporters had refused to recant at the 15th Party Congress, Trotsky pointed out that Zinoviev and Kamenev had gone begging back to Stalin. Trotskii, *Moia zhizn'* [1991], 502.
298. Nazarov, *Stalin i bor'ba za liderstvo*, 119–20 (citing RGASPI, f. 326, op. 1, d. 99, l. 12). In January 1928, Zinoviev stated that there had been a "struggle" inside his bloc with Trotsky. Nazarov, *Stalin i bor'ba za liderstvo*, 119 (citing RGASPI, f. 324, op. 1, d. 363, l. 7).
299. Medvedev, *Let History Judge*, 196–8.
300. Danilov, *Kak lomali NEP*, IV: 558–63 (RGASPI, f. 84, op. 2, d. 40, l. 2–11). See also Daniels, *Documentary History of Communism* [1960], I: 308–9 (from the Trotsky archive, Houghton Library, Harvard University, T-1897); and Kun, *Bukharin*, 251–61.
301. Larina, "Nezabyvaemoe," 120; Larina, *This I Cannot Forget*, 118.
302. Danilov, *Kak lomali NEP*, IV: 561.
303. "He's lost his mind," Bukharin is said to have remarked of Stalin, in the presence of Trotsky, before the latter's exile to Kazakhstan. "He thinks that he can do it all, that he alone can shoulder everything, that all others are only a hindrance." Trotsky, "Iz chernovikov nezakonchennoi Trotskim biografii Stalina" [1939?], in Trotskii, *Portrety revoliutionerov* [1991], 180–1 (at 181); [1988], 141.
304. Kamenev was evidently frustrated by Trotsky's continued scolding of him and Zinoviev for "capitulation," and in September 1928 would tell a few Trotsky supporters outside the Bolshoi

Theater that Trotsky was a "stubborn person," adding that Trotsky would never ask to be summoned back to work in Moscow, like Kamenev and Zinoviev, "and will sit in Alma-Ata until they send a special train for him, but they'll send that train only when the situation in the country is such that Kerensky will be standing on the threshold." "Vstrecha i razgovor tt. K. i P. s Kamenevym 22 sentiabria 1928 goda," in Fel'shtinskii, *Razgovory s Bukharinym*, 51–4 (at 53).
305. Stalin's alleged remarks circulated in many forms: *Trotsky's Diary in Exile* [1958], 64; Ioffe, *Odna noch'*, 33–4; Serebriakova, "Oni delali v chest' idee," 3.
306. Kamenev would be forced to insist that he and Zinoviev were upholding the conditions of their reinstatement to the party. RGASPI, f. 84, op. 2, d. 40, l. 12–3.
307. Bukharin added that "as a whole, the document is not reliable and false." Danilov, *Kak lomali NEP*, III: 572–6 (RGASPI, f. 84, op. 2, d. 40, l. 25–31: letter to Orjonikidze, January 30, 1929).
308. Sokolnikov added that Bukharin had not sought a bloc with Kamenev and Zinoviev, but their neutrality in the struggle against Stalin. Danilov, *Kak lomali NEP*, IV: 564–5 (RGASPI, f. 84, op. 2, d. 40, l. 14–5: letter to Orjonikidze, January 28, 1929).
309. Larina, *This I Cannot Forget*, 115–7. Larina was fifteen years old at the time of the incident.
310. Danilov, *Kak lomali, NEP*, II: 531, 535.
311. McDermott and Agnew, *Comintern*, 70.
312. Budnitskii, *"Sovershenno lichno i doveritel'no!,"* III: 404–10 (August 16, 1928).
313. Vatkin, "Goriachaia osen' dvadtsat vos'mogo," 103.
314. Trotsky sent a critique of the draft program to the congress from Alma-Ata supported by nearly two hundred oppositionists in exile. Degras, *The Communist International* [London], II: 446–55.
315. Adibekov and Shirinia, *Politbiuro TsK RKP (b)—VKP (b) i Komintern*, 541–3 (RGASPI, f. 17, op. 3, d. 700, l. 1–2), 551–2 (RGASPI, f. 495, op. 19, d. 228, l. 129); McDermott and Agnew, *Comintern*, 68–90.
316. According to Bukharin's third wife, Anna Larina, Stalin once said to Bukharin's father, "How did you make your son? I want to adopt your method. Oh, what a son, what a son!" Larina, *This I Cannot Forget*, 221–3.
317. Alliluyeva, *Twenty Letters*, 31; and Gregory, *Politics, Murder, and Love*, 16–8; Young, "Bolshevik Wives."
318. The draft program had not been discussed by any party other than the Soviet one; no less tellingly, the theses

that would be voted up had not even been available when the congress opened. Eudin and Slusser, *Soviet Foreign Policy*, I: 106–20; Carr and Davies, *Foundations of a Planned Economy*, III/i: 193–222.
319. Firsov, "N. I. Bukharin v Kominterne," 189–90; *International Press Correspondence*, August 23, 1928: 941.
320. *International Press Correspondence*, September 4, 1928: 1,039.
321. The British delegation issued a declaration (August 22, 1928) against the so-called right-wing deviation: "We wish to express our emphatic protest against the time and method of polemics introduced by Comrade Kuusinen and certain other comrades," especially "the method of hurrying to tie labels on comrades who hold different opinions." *International Press Correspondence*, December 27, 1928: 1,743–4; McDermott and Agnew, *Comintern*, 233–4.
322. Molotov turned over no letters from Stalin for that year. Lih, *Stalin's Letters to Molotov*, xiv. Stalin's last recorded meeting in Moscow was August 1 (Jay Lovestone, the American Communist); his first recorded meeting back in Moscow was October 5, 1928 (Fadeyev, the writer). *Na prieme*, 28, 774, 780–1.
323. Valedinskii, "Organizm Stalina vpolne zdorovyi," 68–73.
324. Danilov, *Kak lomali NEP*, IV: 689; Trotskii, *Moia zhizn'*, II: 111.
325. Khlevniuk, *Politbiuro*, 22 (no citation or date given).
326. Dohan, "Foreign Trade," 223.
327. Danilov, *Kak lomali NEP*, III: 591–3 (at 592: RGASPI, f. 558, op. 11, d. 765, l. 48–49ob).
328. Vernadskii, *Dnevniki*, 76, 87. V. G. Yakovenko, chairman of the land and election commission under Kalinin at the Soviet executive committee, following a trip to actual Siberian villages in June–August 1928, wrote to Stalin on October 3, 1928, that "farmers are decidedly of the opinion that Soviet power does not want them to live decently." *Izvestiia TsK KPSS*, 1991, no. 7: 186–90.
329. Pribytkov, *Apparat*, 87–90 (with facsimile from Mikoyan's archive). Stalin edited the letter by inquiring about Orjonikidze's health.
330. Pribytkov, *Apparat*, 100 (with facsimile: 98–9).
331. Kvashonkin, *Sovetskoe rukovidstvo*, 44–8 (RGASPI, f. 669, op. 1, d. 30, l. 124–9).
332. Danilov, *Kak lomali NEP*, III: 591–3 (at 592–3: RGASPI, f. 558, op. 11, d. 765, l. 48–49ob).
333. Tauger, "Grain Crisis or Famine?," 167 (citing *Visty*, September 27, 1928: 2).
334. *International Press Correspondence*, October 19, 1928: 1337–8, October 26, 1928: 1383, in Daniels,

*Documentary History of Communism* [1993], I: 164–6.

335. Daniels, *Documentary History of Communism* [1993], I: 166–9. See also Cohen, *Bukharin*, 295–6.

336. Danilov, *Kak lomali NEP*, III: 12.

337. Vaganov, *Pravyi uklon v VKP (b)*, 161–3, 174–5.

338. Pribytkov, *Apparat*, 108.

339. Danilov, "Vvedenie," in Danilov, *Tragediia sovetskoi derevni*, I: 59. See also Carr and Davies, *Foundations of a Planned Economy*, I/i: 237.

340. *Izvestiia*, February 7, February 19, and February 22, 1929.

341. Bukharin, *Problemy teorii i praktiki sotsializma*, 306–7 (April 18, 1929).

342. Kvashonkin, *Sovetskoe rukovodstvo*, 58–9 (RGASPI, f. 669, op. 1, d. 30, l. 133–42).

343. Danilov, *Kak lomali NEP*, III: 16 (RGASPI, f. 17, op. 2, d. 417, l. 125).

## CODA: IF STALIN HAD DIED

1. Viola, *Peasant Rebels*, 238; Danilov, *Tragediia sovetskoi derevni*, II: 787–808 (TsA FSB, f. 2, op. 8, d. 679, l. 36–72: March 15, 1931).

2. Nove, *The Soviet Economy*, 186. Courtois, *Black Book of Communism*, 167–8.

3. Kravchenko, *I Chose Freedom*, 67.

4. Alec Nove, "Was Stalin Really Necessary?" 86–92, reprinted in Nove, *Was Stalin Really Necessary?*, 17–39, and review of Nove's book by Gregory Grossman, *Europe-Asia Studies*, 17/2 (1965): 256–60; von Laue, *Why Lenin?*; Hobsbawm, *Age of Extremes*. See also Kotkin, "Left Behind."

5. Nove, "The Peasants, Collectivization, and Mr. Carr"; Lih, "Bukharin's 'Illusion.'"

6. Davis, *Economic Transformation*, 11–13.

7. Cohen, "The 1927 Revaluation of the Lira."

8. Sloin and Sanchez-Sibony, "Economy and Power in the Soviet Union." This is based upon a reading of Dohan, "Soviet Foreign Trade in the NEP Economy"; Dohan, "The Economic Origins of Soviet Autarky."

9. Analyses of Soviet debates are cogent, except on the issue of ideological narrowness: Ehrlich, *The Soviet Industrialization Debate*; Lewin, *Political Undercurrents*.

10. Ustrialov, *Pod zankom revoliutsii*; Bukharin, *Tsezarizm pod maskoi revoliutsii*.

11. Sakharov, *Politcheskoe zaveshchanie*, 645.

12. Bukharin, *Izbrannye proizvedeniia*, 146–230 (at 196–7). See also Siegelbaum, *Soviet State and Society*, 228.

13. Bukharin, "O novoi ekonomichheskoi politike," 3–15.

14. Manning, "The Rise and Fall of 'the Extraordinary Measures,'" 15 (citing GARF, f. 374, op. 217, d. 1556, l. 22–8).

15. Brovkin, *Russia After Lenin*, 168. On Bukharin's downplaying of the kulaks, see Cohen, *Bukharin*, 187–92.

16. Davies, *Socialist Offensive*, 27.

17. Liberman, *Building Lenin's Russia*, 65–8.

18. Carr and Davies, *Foundations of a Planned Economy*, I/ii: 733–5. R. W. Davies, who wrote the best analysis of the New Economic Policy and its dilemmas, maintained that the NEP

was doomed by the Soviet industrialization program. That may or may not be true. But what drove the industrialization program, and indeed everything pushed by Bolshevism, was the commitment to socialism (anticapitalism). It was ideology. Davies, *Socialist Offensive*, 36–7. See also Carr, *Socialism in One Country*, I: 520.

19. Johnson and Temin, "The Macroeconomics of NEP"; Chaudhry, "The Myths of the Market."

20. Sokol'nikov, *Finansovaia politika revoliutsii*, II: 479–90.

21. *Pravda*, May 8, 1927. Others found the Soviet delegation disappointing: Runciman, "The World Economic Conference at Geneva."

22. *Pravda*, August 3, 1927.

23. In 1926, partially to discredit Sokolnikov, Stalin railroaded through a conviction and execution of a finance commissariat official for allegedly disorganizing the foreign exchange markets; in fact, publicity about the arrest and execution essentially froze foreign exchange markets, which, however, Rykov applauded. "The black market in foreign exchange is Sokolnikov's creature, he gave birth to it, nourished it, cared for it the whole time," Rykov told the July 1926 party plenum. "And we annihilated this creature of Sokolnikov. . . . And we do not have to spend more money" (supporting the exchange rate of the convertible chervonets). Mozokhin, *VChK-OGPU*, 208–10 (citing APRF, f. 3, op. 57, d. 91, l. 58; TsA FSB, f. 2, op. 5, pro. 581, l. 121–2); RGASPI, f. 17, op. 2, d. 246, l. 53.

24. Stephen F. Cohen, *Bukharin*, 329.

25. *Khrushchev Remembers*, 222.

26. *Pravda*, August 10, 1928.

27. Sutton, *Western Technology and Soviet Economic Development*, vol. II. There is cause for doubt about whether the USSR could have managed without massive Western technical assistance, a circumstance not peculiar to the USSR, except for the politics involved. Keller, *Ost minus West = Null*.

28. Sanchez-Sibony, "Depression Stalinism."

29. Soon, the OGPU would create prison research institutes (*sharashki*) for "bourgeois" specialists. Viktorov, *Bez grifa "sekretno,"* 108, 146–7.

30. Avtorkhanov, *Tekhnologiia vlasti*, 26.

31. Moshe Lewin posed the question of what would have happened had Stalin died, but did not answer it fully: *Journal of Modern History*, 47/2 (1975): 364–72 (review of Tucker, *Stalin as Revolutionary*).

32. Lenin wrote to his secretary Fotiyeva (December 28, 1921), "I ought to meet with Stalin and before that connect me by telephone with [Doctor V. A.] Obukh to talk about Stalin." PSS, LIV: 99; Golikov, *Vladimir Il'ich Lenin*, IX: 565, 572. On Stalin's appendix, see one of the first extant documents on his health: RGASPI, f. 558, op. 4, d. 675, l. 1–23 (March 25, 1921).

33. Nikolai Nad, "Kto ubil Mikhaila Frunze," *Izvestiia*, October 26, 2010.

34. Golikov, *Vladimir Il'ich Lenin*, VI: 390, IX: 348, 618, X: 348, 566, 588, 639, XI: 47, 113, 128; Meijer, *Trotsky Papers*, II: 26–9, 66–7; McNeal, *Stalin*, 50.

35. Golikov, *Vladimir Il'ich Lenin*, IX: 565, 572.

36. RGASPI, f. 558, d. 1279, d. 1482.

37. Plekhanov and Plekhanov, *F. E. Dzerzhinskii*, 583 (TsA FSB, f. 2, op. 3, d. 4, l. 2: February 8, 1925).

38. Bosworth, *Mussolini's Italy*, 240.

39. Tumshis and Papchinskii, *1937, bol'shaia chistka*, 52. Mikhail Frinovsky (b. 1898), then the head of the OGPU Special Department for the Moscow military district, caught the terrorists some fifteen miles out on the Serpukhov Highway. The captured perpetrators were Georgy Radkovich and Dmitri Monomakhov. In November 1928, Frinovsky would be promoted by Yagoda to head of the Kremlin garrison.

40. Loginov, *Teni vozhdin*.

41. Fel'shtinskii, *Razgovory s Bukharinym*, 43. See also Deutscher, *Prophet Unarmed*, 442.

42. "Samoubiistvo ne opravdanie," 93. Tomsky would never mention the incident again (except in his suicide note to Stalin of August 22, 1936), but Tomsky's aides (A. Slepkov, D. Maretsky, and L. Ginzburg) retold the story of Tomsky's threat in the fall of 1929.

43. "Few great men," Carr also wrote, "have been so conspicuously as Stalin the product of the time and place in which they lived." Carr, *Socialism in One Country*, I: 151, 192.

# BIBLIOGRAPHY

Over many years of research and teaching, I have spent some time in most of the archives listed below (with the key exception of the former KGB archive, which is closed to almost all researchers). I have worked comprehensively in the former Communist party archive and the Hoover Institution Archive (which has immense duplicate holdings of Soviet-era archival files as well as bounteous original material). Since the advent of scanning and digitization, many archival files can be consulted without visits in person (particularly if Russian colleagues with good access share). But given the scope of this undertaking, the most efficient research strategy appeared to be to work in archives as much as possible while also conducting exhaustive research in published document collections and the works of scholars who use unpublished sources extensively and reliably. Document collections, as well as the tiny handful of researchers with privileged access to restricted archives, are especially crucial for secret police and military matters. I also made sure to comb the rich periodical literature of the time, and not to neglect scholarship that may have been produced a long time ago. Readers are advised that the research has been conducted in different times in different places, and some repositories happen to have one edition of, say, a party congress or a published memoir, others have another edition, which is reflected in the endnotes. Readers will also notice names are given in different variants—"Trotsky" in the text and the bibliography when referring to books of his in English, "Trotskii" (per Library of Congress) for his Russian-language works. Such are the frustrations of transliteration. Names of non-Russians, meanwhile, are rendered in the original in the text—thus Dzierżyński, an ethnic Pole, is Russified (Dzerzhinskii) only in the notes and bibliography.

APRF: Russian Presidential Archive (former politburo archive)

AVP RF: Foreign Policy Archive of the Russian Federation

GANO: State Archive of Novosibirsk

GARF: State Archive of the Russian Federation

GF IML: Georgian Affiliate of the Communist Party Archive

GIAG: Georgia State Historical Archive

Hoover Institution Archive, Stanford University

RGAE: Russian State Economic Archive

RGAKFD: Russian State Archive of Photographs and Film

RGALI: Russian State Archive of Literature and Art

RGASPI: Russian State Archive of Social and Political History (former central party archive)

RGIA: Russian State Historical Archive

RGVA: Russian Military Archive

TsA FSB: Central Archive of the Federal Security Service (former KGB)

TsGAKFFD SPb: Central State Archive of Photographs, Film, and Phonographic Documents, St. Petersburg

Abraham, Richard. *Alexander Kerensky: The First Love of the Revolution*. New York: Columbia University Press, 1987.

Abramovich, Isai L. *Vospominaniia i vzgliadi*, 2 vols. Moscow: KRUK-Prestizh, 2004.

Abramovitch, Raphael R. *The Soviet Revolution, 1917–1939*. New York: International Universities Press, 1962.

Abramowicz, Hirsz. *Profiles of a Lost World: Memoirs of East European Jewish Life before World War II.* Detroit: Wayne State University Press, 1999.

Abrams, R. "Political Recruitment and Local Government: The Local Soviets of the RSFSR, 1918–1921," *Soviet Studies*, 19/4 (1968): 573–80.

Abrosimova, T. A., et al., eds. *Peterburgskii komitet RSDRP (b) v 1917 godu: protokoly imaterialy zasedanii.* St. Petersburg: Bel'veder, 2003.

Adamets, Serguei. *Guerre civile et famine en Russie: le pouvoir bolchevique et la population face à la catastrophe démographique, 1917–1923.* Paris: Institut d'études slaves, 2003.

Adelman, Jonathan R. "The Development of the Soviet Party Apparat in the Civil War: Center, Localities, and Nationality Areas," *Russian History* 9/1 (1982): 86–110.

Adibekov, G. M., and Shirinia, K. K., eds. *Politbiuro TsK RKP(b)—VKP(b) i Komintern, 1919–1943: dokumenty.* Moscow: Rosspen, 2004.

Adibekov, G. M., et al., eds. *Politbiuro TsK RKP (b)—VKP (b) i Evropa: resheniia 'osoboi papki', 1923–1939.* Moscow: Rosspen, 2001.

———. *Politbiuro TsK RKP (b)—VKP (b): povestki dnia zasedanii 1919–1952*, 3 vols. Moscow: Rossen, 2000–1.

Adibekova, Zh., and Latsis, O. "V predchuvstvii pereloma: poslednye pis'ma i zapiski F. E. Dzerzhinskogo," *Kommunist*, 1989, no. 8: 79–88.

Agabekov, Georges. *OGPU: The Russian Secret Terror*. New York: Brentano's, 1931.

Agafonov, V. K. *Zagranichnaia okhranka*. Petrograd: Kniga, 1918.

Agursky, Mikhail. "Stalin's Ecclesiastical Background," *Survey* 28/4 (1984): 1–14.

Airapetian, G. A. *Legendarnyi Gai.* Moscow: Voenizdat, 1965.

Airapetov, Oleg. "Revolution and Revolt in the Manchurian Armies, as Perceived by a Future Leader of the White Movement," in *The Russian Revolution of 1905: Centenary Perspectives*, edited by Jonathan D. Smele and Anthony Heywood. London and New York: Routledge, 2005.

Akhtamzian, Abdulkahn. "Voennoe sotrudnichestvo SSSR i Germanii v 1920–1933 gg.," *Novaia i noveishaia istoriia*, 1990, no. 5: 3–24.

———. "Soviet-German Military Cooperation, 1920–1933," *International Affairs* [Moscow] (1990), no. 7: 95–113

———. "Sovetsko-Germanskie ekonomicheskie otnosheniia v 1922–1932 gg.," *Novaia i noveishaia istoriia*, 1990, no. 5: 42–56.

Albertini, Luigi. *The Origins of the War of 1914*, 3 vols. New York: Oxford University Press, 1952–57.

Aldanov, Mark. "Durnovó: Prophet of War and Revolution," *Russian Review*, 2/1 (1942): 31–45.

Aleksandrov, G. F. *Iosif Vissarionovich Stalin: kratkaia biografiia*, 2nd ed. Moscow: OGIZ, 1947.

Alekseenkov, P. *Kokandskaia avtonomiia*. Tashkent: Uzgiz, 1931.

Aleshkin, P. F., and Vasil'ev, Iu. A., eds. *Krest'ianskie vosstaniia v Rossii v 1918-1922 gg.: ot makhnovshchiny do antonovshchiny.* Moscow: Veche, 2012.

Alfred Rosenberg, *Der jüdische Bolschewismus*. N.p., 1921.

Ali, J. "Aspects of the RKP(b) Secretariat, March 1919–April 1922," *Soviet Studies*, 26/3 (1974): 396–416.

Aliamkin, Andrei V., and Baranov, Aleksandr G. *Istoriia denezhnogo obrashcheniia v 1914–1924 gg.: po materialam Zaural'ia*. Ekaterinburg: Ural'skii gos. universitet, 2005.

Alioshin, Dmitri. *Asian Odyssey*. New York: Henry Holt, 1940.

Allen, W.E.D. "The Caucasian Borderland," *Geographical Journal*, 99/5–6 (1942): 225–37.

———. *A History of the Georgian People from the Beginning Down to the Russian Conquest in the Nineteenth Century*. London: K. Paul, Trench, Trubner, 1932.

Alliluev, Sergei. "Moi vospominaniia," *Krasnaia letopis'*, 1923, no. 5: 169–81.

———. "Vstrechi s tovarishchem Stalinym," *Proletarskaia revoliutsiia*, 1937, no. 2.

———. *Proidennyi put'*. Moscow: OGIZ, 1946.

Alliluev, Vladimir. *Khronika odnoi sem'i: Alliluevy-Stalin*. Moscow: Molodaia gvardiia, 1995.

Allilueva, Anna S. *Vospominaniia*. Moscow: Soevtskii pisatel', 1946.

Allilueva, Svetlana. *Dvadtsat' pisem k drugu*. New York: Harper and Row, 1967.

Alliluyeva, Svetlana. *Only One Year*. New York: Harper and Row, 1969.

———. *Twenty Letters to a Friend*. New York: Harper and Row, 1967.

Alstadt, Audrey. "Muslim Workers and the Labor Movement in Pre-War Baku," in *Turkic Culture: Continuity and Change*, edited by S. M. Akural. Bloomington: Indiana University Press, 1987.

Al'tman, M. M. "Lichnost' reformatora: narkom finansov G. Ia. Sokol'nikova 1888–1939," in *Denezhnaia reforma v Rossii, istoriia i sovremennost': sbornik statei*. Moscow: Drevlekhranilishche, 2004.

Amelung, Heinz. *Bismarck-Worte*. Berlin: Deutsches Verlagshaus Bong, 1918.

Anan'ich, Boris V., and Ganelin, R. Sh. "Nikolai II," *Voprosy istorii*, 1993, no. 2: 58–76.

———. "Opyt kritiki memuarov S. Iu. Vitte," *Voprosy istoriografii i istochnikovedeniia istorii SSSR: sbornik statei*. Moscow-Leningrad: Akademiia nauk SSSR, 1963.

Anchabadze, I. D., and Volkova, N. Ia. *Stary Tblisi: Gorod i gorozhane v XIX veka*. Moscow: Nauka, 1990.

Anderson, K. M., ed. *Stenogrammy zasedanii politbiuro Tsk RKP (b)—VKP (b) 1923–1938 gg.*, 3 vols. Moscow: Rosspen, 2007.

Andreev, A. A. *Vospominaniia, pis'ma*. Moscow: Politicheskaia literatura, 1985.

Andrew, Christopher M. *Her Majesty's Secret Service: The Making of the British Intelligence Community*. New York: Viking, 1986.

———, and Gordievsky, Oleg. *KGB: The Inside Story of its Foreign Operations from Lenin to Gorbachev*. New York: HarperCollins, 1990.

———, and Mitrokhin, V. M. *The Mitrokhin Archive*. London: Allen Lane, 1999.

Anfert'ev. I. A., ed. *Smerch*. Moscow: DOSAAF SSSR, 1988.

*Anglo-sovetskie otnosheniia so dnia podpisaniia torgovogo soglasheniia do razryva (1921–1927 gg.): noty i dokumenty*. Moscow: Litizdat narkomindela, 1927.

Angress, Werner T. *Stillborn Revolution: The Communist Bid for Power in Germany, 1921–1923*. Princeton, NJ: Princeton University Press, 1963.

Anin, Boris Iu. *Radioelektronnyi shpionazh*. Moscow: Tsentropoligraf, 2000.

Anin, David S. "The February Revolution: Was the Collapse Inevitable?" *Soviet Studies*, 18/4 (1967): 435–57.

Anisimov, Evgeny. *The Reforms of Peter the Great: Progress through Coercion*. Armonk, NY: M. E. Sharpe, 1994.

Annenkov, Iurii. "Vospominania o Lenine," *Novyi zhurnal*, no. 65, 1961.

———. *Dnevnikh moikh vstrech: tsikl tragedii*, 2 vols. New York: Inter-Language Literary Associates, 1966.

———. *Semnadtsat' portretov*, 2 vols. Leningrad: Gosizdat, 1926.

Anosov, S. D. *Koreitsy v ussuriiskom krae*. Khabarovsk-Vladivostok: Knizhnoe delo, 1928.

Anstiferov, Alexis, et al. *Russian Agriculture During the War*. New Haven, CT: Yale University Press, 1930.

Antonov-Ovseenko, Anton. *Stalin bez maski*. Moscow: Vsia Moskva, 1990.

———. *The Time of Stalin: Portrait of a Tyranny*. New York: Harper and Row, 1981.

———. *Stroitel'stvo Krasnoi armii v revoliutsii*. Moscow: Krasnaia nov', 1923.

Antonov-Ovseenko, Vladimir. *Zapiski o grazhdanskoi voine*, 4 vols. Moscow: Gosizdat/Otdel voennoi literatury, 1924–33.

Antropov, S. V. "Sviaz' tekstil'nykh rabochikh s zemleiu i iiul'skie otpuska," *Izvestiia tekstil'noi promyshlennosti i torgovli*, 1927, no. 23–24.

Antsiferov, Alexis N., et al. *Russian Agriculture During the War: Rural Economy*. New Haven, CT: Yale University Press, 1930.

Aptekar', Pavel A. "Khimchistka po-Tambovskii," *Rodina*, 1994, no. 5: 56–7.

———. "Krest'ianskaia voina," *Voenno-istoricheskii zhurnal*, 1993, no. 1: 50–55.

Aralov, Semen I. *Lenin i Krasnaia armiia: vospominania*. Moscow: Znanie, 1958.

———. *Lenin vel nas k pobede: vospominaniia*. Moscow: Gospolitizdat, 1962.

Arenshtein, A. "Tipografiia Leninskoi 'Iskry' v Baku," *Voprosy istorii*, 1956, no. 11: 105–12.

Argenbright, Robert. "Bolsheviks, Baggers and Railroaders: Political Power and Social Space, 1917–1921," *Russian Review*, 52/4 (1993): 506–27.

———. "Documents from Trotsky's Train in the Russian State Military Archive: A Comment," *Journal of Trotsky Studies*, 4/1 (1996): 1–12.

———. "Honour among Communists: 'The Glorious Name of Trotsky's Train,'" *Revolutionary Russia*, 11/1 (1998): 45–66.

———. "Marking NEP's Slippery Path: The Krasnoshchekov Show Trial," *Russian Review*, 61/2 (2002): 249–75.

———. "Red Tsaritsyn: Precursor of Stalinist Terror," *Revolutionary Russia*, 4/2 (1991): 157–83.

Arkomed, S. T. *Rabochee dvizhenie i sotsial-demokratiia na Kavkaze: s 80-kh godov po 1903 g.*, 2nd ed. Moscow-Leningrad: Gosizdat, 1923.

Armstrong, John. "Mobilized and Proletarian Diasporas," *American Political Science Review* 70/2 (1976): 393–408.

Armstrong, John A. "Tsarist and Soviet Elite Administrators," *Slavic Review*, 31 (1972): 1–28.

———. *The Soviet Bureaucratic Elite: A Case Study of the Ukrainian Apparatus*. New York: Praeger, 1959.

Arnold, Arthur Z. *Banks, Credit and Money in Soviet Russia*. New York: Columbia University Press, 1937.

Arosev, A. "Institut' V. I. Lenina," *Proletarskaia revoliutsiia*, 1923, no. 11: 269–74.

Arsen'ev, E. *Podzhigateli voiny*. Moscow: Moskovskii rabochii, 1931.

Arsenidze, Razhden. "Iz vospominaniia o Staline," *Novyi zhurnal*, no. 72 (1963): 218–36.

Arshinov, Petr. *Istoriia makhnovskogo dvizheniia, 1918–1921 gg*. Berlin: Izd. Gruppy russkikh anarkhistov v Germanii, 1923.

Artamonov, Andrei. *Spetsob'ekty Stalina: ekskursiia pod grifom "sekretno."* Moscow: Algoritm, 2013.

Ascher, Abraham. "Prime Minister P. A. Stolypin and his 'Jewish' Adviser," *Journal of Contemporary History*, 30/3 (1995): 515–32.

———. "The Coming Storm: The Austro-Hungarian Embassy on

Russia's Internal Crisis, 1902–1906," *Survey*, 53 (1964): 148–64.

———. "The Solovki Prisoners, the Mensheviks and the Socialist International," *Slavonic and East European Review*, 47 (1969): 423–35.

———. *P. A. Stolypin: The Search for Stability in Imperial Russia.* Stanford, CA: Stanford University Press, 2001.

———. *The Revolution of 1905*, 2 vols. Stanford, CA: Stanford University Press, 1988–1992.

Askew, William C. "An American View of Bloody Sunday," *Russian Review*, 11/1 (1952): 35–43.

Asprey, Robert B. *The German High Command at War: Hindenburg and Ludendorff Conduct World War.* New York: W. Morrow, 1991.

Astaf'ev, I. I. *Russko-germanskie diplomaticheskie otnosheniia, 1905–1911 gg.: ot Portsmutskogo mira do Potsdamskogo soglasheniia.* Moscow: Moskovskii Universitet, 1972.

Astrov, W., et al., eds. *An Illustrated History of the Russian Revolution*, 2 vols. New York: International Publishers, 1928.

Atkin, Muriel. "Russian Expansion in the Caucasus to 1813," *Russian Colonial Expansion to 1917*, edited by Michael Rywkin. London: Mansell, 1988.

Atkinson, Dorothy. *The End of the Russian Land Commune, 1905–1930.* Stanford, CA: Stanford University Press, 1983.

Atlas, Zakharii V. *Ocherki po istorii denezhnogo obrashcheniia v SSSR 1917–1925 gg.* Moscow: Gos. finansovoe izdatel'stvo, 1940.

Avalov, Z. D. *The Independence of Georgia in International Politics, 1918–1921.* London: Headley Brothers, 1940.

———. *Prisoedinenie Gruzii k Rossii.* St. Petersburg: A. S. Suvorin, 1901.

———. *Nezavisimost' Gruzii v mezhdunarodnoi politike 1918–1921 gg : vospominaniia, ocherki.* Paris: Imprimerie de Navarre, 1924.

Avdeev, N., et al. *Revoliutsiia 1917 goda: khronika sobytii* , 6 vols. Moscow: Gosizdat, 1923–30.

Avrekh, A. Ia. "Chrezvychainaia sledstvennaia komissiia Vremennogo pravitel'stva: zamysl' i ispolnenie," *Istoricheskie zapiski*, 118 (1990): 72–101.

Avrich, Paul. *Anarchist Portraits.* Princeton, NJ: Princeton University Press, 1988.

———. *Kronstadt, 1921.* New York: W. W. Norton, 1974.

Avtorkhanov, Abdurakhman. *Proiskhozhdenie partokratii*, 2 vols. Frankfurt-am-Main: Posev, 1973.

———. *Stalin and the Communist Party: A Study in the Technology of Power.* New York: Praeger, 1959.

———. *Tekhnologiia vlasti.* Munich: Tsentral'noe ob'edinenie politicheskikh emigrantov iz SSSR, 1959.

Aydin, Cemil. *The Politics of Anti-Westernism in Asia: Visions of World Order in Pan-Islamic and Pan-Asian Thought.* New York: Columbia University Press, 2007.

Azhavakov, A. "Gorod Gori," in *Sbornik materialov dlia opisaniia mestnosti i plemen Kavkaza.* Tiflis: Upravlenie Kavkazskogo uchebnogo okruga, 1883.

Azovtsev, N. K. *Grazhdanskaia voina v SSSR*, 2 vols. Moscow: Voenizdat, 1980–5.

Baabar, C. *Twentieth-Century Mongolia.* Cambridge: White Horse, 1999.

Babel, I. *1920 Diary.* New Haven, CT: Yale University Press, 1995.

———. *Konarmiia.* Moscow: OGIZ, 1926.

Babichenko, Leonid G. "Politbiuro TsK RKP (b), Komintern i sobytiia v Germanii v 1923 g.: novye arkhivnye materialy," *Novaia i noveishaia istoriia*, 1994, no. 2: 125–57.

Babkov, Andrew. "National Finances and the Economic Evolution of Russia," *Russian Review*, 1/3 (1912): 170–91.

Baddeley, John F. *The Russian Conquest of the Caucasus.* London: Longmans, Green, 1908.

Badriashvili, N. I. *Tiflis.* Tiflis: Tifsovet, 1934.

Baedeker, Karl. *Russia: A Handbook for Travelers.* New York: C. Scribner's Sons, 1914. New York: Arno Press, 1971.

Bagilev, K. N. *Putevoditel' po Tiflisu.* Tiflis: K. N. Begichev, 1896.

Baiguzin, R. N. *Gosudarstvennaia bezopasnost' Rossii: istoriia i sovremennost'.* Moscow: Rosspen, 2004.

Baikaloff, A. *I Knew Stalin.* London: Burns Oates, 1940.

———. "Moi vstrechi s Osipom Dzhugashvili," *Vozrozhdenie*, 1950, no. 3–4.

Bailes, Kendall E. "The Politics of Technology: Stalin and Technocratic Thinking among Soviet Engineers," *American Historical Review*, 79/2 (1974): 445–69.

———. *Technology and Society Under Lenin and Stalin: Origins of the Soviet Technical Intelligentsia, 1917–1941.* Princeton, NJ: Princeton University Press, 1978.

Bailey, F. M. *Mission to Tashkent.* London: J. Cape, 1946.

Bailey, Sydney D. "The Russian Constituent Assembly of 1918," *Parliamentary Affairs*, VII/3 (1953): 336–44.

Balabanoff, Angelica. *Impressions of Lenin.* Ann Arbor: University of Michigan Press, 1964.

———. *My Life as a Rebel.* New York: Greenwood Press, 1938.

Balashov, A.P. and Markhashov, Iu. S., "Staraia ploshchad', 4 (20-e gody)," *Polis*, 1991, no. 1: 180–7, no. 2: 166–74, no. 4: 182–8, no. 5: 189–96, no. 6: 180–7.

Balashov, A. P. and Nelepin. *VLKSM za 10 let v tsifrakh.* Moscow: Molodaia gvardiia, 1928.

Ballis, William B. "The Political Evolution of a Soviet Satellite: The Mongolian People's Republic," *Western Political Quarterly*, 9/2 (1956): 293–329.

Barabashev, O. "Isil'kul'skie zheleznodorzhniki o klhebe," *Na leninskom puti*, 1928, no. 1 (January 31).

Baranov, A. V. "'Voennaia trevoga' 1927 g. kak faktor politischeskikh nastroenii v neposvskom obshchvestve (po material iuga Rossii)," *Rossiia i mir glazami druga druga: iz istorii vzaimovspriiatiia.* Moscow: IRI RAN, 2007, 175–93.

Baranov, Valentin. *Krest'ianskoe vosstanie v Tambovskoi gubernii: 1920–1921 gg.* Tambov: n.p., 1991.

Barany, Zoltan. "Soviet Takeover: The Role of Advisers in Mongolia and in Eastern Europe after World War II," *East European Quarterly*, 28/4 (1994): 409–33.

Bark, Sir Peter. "The Last Days of the Russian Monarchy: Nicholas II at Army Headquarters," *Russian Review*, 16/3 (1957): 35–44.

Barmin, A. G. *Sokoly Trotskogo.* Moscow: Sovremennik, 1997.

Barmine, Alexandre. *Vingt ans au service de l'U.R.S.S.: souvenirs d'un diplomate soviétique.* Paris: Albin Michel, 1939. Translated as *One Who Survived: The Life Story of a Russian Under the Soviets.* New York: G. P. Putnam's Sons, 1945.

Baron, Salo W. *The Russian Jew under Tsars and Soviets.* New York: Macmillan, 1964.

Baron, Samuel H. "Between Marx and Lenin: G. V. Plekhanov," *Soviet Survey*, 32 (1960): 94–101.

———. *Plekhanov: Father of Russian Marxism.* Stanford, CA: Stanford University Press, 1963.

Barraclough, Geoffrey. *An Introduction to Contemporary History.* New York: Basic Books, 1964.

Barrett, Thomas M. *At the Edge of Empire: The Terek Cossacks and the North Caucasus Frontier, 1700–1860.* Boulder, CO: Westview, 1999.

Barsov, A. A. *Balans stoimostnykh obmenov mezhdu gorodom i derevnei.* Moscow: Nauka, 1969.

Bartashevich, K. M. "Moskva zhdet . . . khleba," *Pogranichnik*, 1967, no. 16: 34–37.

Batenina, E. S. *Kavkaz.* Moscow: Transpechat' NKPS, 1927.

Batsell, Walter Russell. *Soviet Rule in Russia.* New York: Macmillan, 1929.

Batumskaia demonstratsiia 1902 goda. Moscow: Partizdat, 1937.

Bauer, Otto. "The Nationalities Question and Social Democracy" [1907], in The Nationalism Reader, edited by Omar Dahbour and Micheline R. Ishay. Atlantic Highlands, NJ: Humanities Press, 1995.

Baumgart, Winfried, ed. Von Brest-Litovsk zur deutschen Novemberrevolution. Göttingen: Vandenhoeck & Ruprecht, 1971.

———. Deutsche Ostpolitik 1918: Von Brest-Litowsk bis zum Ende des Ersten Weltkrieges. Vienna and Munich: Oldenbourg, 1966.

———. The Crimean War 1853–1856. New York: Oxford University Press, 2000.

Baumont, Maurice. La faillite de la paix, 1918–1939, 2 vols. Paris: Presses universitaires de France, 1951.

Bazhanov, Boris. Avec Staline dans le Kremlin. Paris: Les Éditions de France, 1930.

———. Bazhanov and the Damnation of Stalin, edited by David W. Doyle. Columbus: Ohio State University Press, 1990.

———. Bajanov révèle Staline: souvenirs d'un ancien secrétaire de Staline. Paris: Gallimard, 1979.

———. Stalin: der Rote Diktatur. Berlin: P. Aretz, 1931.

———. Vospominaniia byvshego sekretaria Stalina. Paris: Tret'ia vol'na, 1980. 2nd ed. Paris and New York: Tret'ia vol'na, 1983. Moscow: SP Sofinta, 1990.

Beatty, Bessie. The Red Heart of Russia. New York: Century Co., 1918.

Bechhofer, Carl Eric. In Denikin's Russia and the Caucasus, 1919–1920. London: W. Collins Sons, 1921.

Beck, Hermann. The Origins of the Authoritarian Welfare State in Prussia: Conservatives, Bureaucracy, and the Social Question, 1815–70. Ann Arbor: University of Michigan Press, 1995.

Beck, Józef. Dernier rapport: Politique polonaise 1926–1939. Neuchâtel: Éditions de la Baconnière, 1951.

Beckendorff, Paul. Last Days at Tsarskoe Selo: An Inside Account. Found at http://www.alexanderpalace.org/lastdays/intro.html.

———. Last Days at Tsarskoe Selo. London: W. Heinemann, 1927.

Becker, Jean-Jacques. The Great War and the French People. Dover, NH: Berg, 1985.

Becker, Seymour. Nobility and Privilege in Late Imperial Russia. Dekalb: Northern Illinois University Press, 1985.

———. Russia's Protectorates in Central Asia: Bukhara and Khiva, 1865–1924. Cambridge, MA: Harvard University Press, 1968.

Beer, V. A. Kommentarii novykh provintsial'nykh uchrezhdenii 12 iulia 1889 goda. Moscow: Tip. A. I. Mamontova, 1894.

Beisembaev, S. Lenin i Kazakhstan, 2nd ed. Alma-Ata: Kazakhstan, 1987.

Beletskii, Stepan P. "Grigorii Rasputin: Iz vospominanii," Byloe, no. 20 (1922), no. 21, 22 (1923).

Beletskii, S. P. Grigorii Rasputin: iz zapisok. Petrograd: Byloe, 1923.

Beliaev, N. Z., et al. Mikhail Kol'tsov, kakim on byl. Moscow: Sovetskii pistael', 1989.

Beliakov, L. P. Lagernaia sistema i politicheskie represii, 1918–1953. Moscow-St. Petersburg: VSEGEI, 1999.

Belov, Evgenii. Baron Ungern fon Shternberg: biografiia, ideologiia, voennye pokhody, 1920–1921 gg. Moscow: Agraf IV RAN, 2003.

Belov, G. A., ed. Iz istorii Vserossiiskoi Chrezvychainoi komissii, 1917–1922 gg.: sbornik dokumentov. Politicheskaia literatura, 1958.

Bender, Sara. The Jews of Bialystok during World War II and the Holocaust. Hanover, MA: University Press of New England, 2008.

Bennigsen, Alexandre S., and Wimbush, S. Enders. Muslim National Communism in the Soviet Union: A Revolutionary Strategy for the Colonial World. Chicago: University of Chicago Press, 1979.

Benvenuti, Francesco. The Bolsheviks and the Red Army, 1918–1922. New York: Cambridge University Press, 1988.

Berberova, Nina. Zheleznaia zhenshchina. Moscow: Knizhnaia palata, 1991.

Berdiaev, Nikolai. Samopoznanie. Moscow: Mysl', 1991.

Berdzenishvili, V. "Iz vospominanii," Zaria vostoka, February 28, 1938.

Berelowich, A., and Danilov, V. P., eds. Sovetskaia derevnia glazami VChK-OGPU-NKVD: dokumenty i materialy, 1918–1939, 4 vols. Moscow: Rosspen, 1998.

Berezin, Mabel. Making the Fascist Self: The Political Culture of Interwar Italy. Ithaca, NY: Cornell University Press, 1997.

Berezov, Pavel I. Valerian Vladimirovich Kuibyshev, 1888–1935. Moscow: Molodaia gvardiia, 1958.

Berghahn, Volker R. Germany and the Approach of War in 1914, 2nd ed. New York: St. Martin's Press, 1993.

———. Imperial Germany, 1871–1914: Economy, Society, Culture, and Politics. Providence, RI: Berghahn Books, 2005.

Beria, Sergo. Beria My Father: Inside Stalin's Kremlin. London: Duckworth, 2001.

Beriia, L. P., and Broido, G., eds. Lado Ketskhoveli: sbornik. Moscow: Partizdat, 1938.

Berk, Stephen M. "The Coup d'État of Admiral Kolchak: The Counter-Revolution in Siberia and Eastern Russia, 1917–1918." Phd diss., Columbia University, 1971.

Berkhin, I. B. Voennaia reforma v SSSR 1924–1925. Moscow: Voenizddat, 1958.

Berkman, Alexander. Kronstadt. Berlin: Der Syndikalist, 1922.

———. The Bolshevik Myth: Diary 1920–1922. London: Hutchinson, 1925, 1925.

Berlin, Isaiah, and Jahanbegloo, Ramin. Conversations with Isaiah Berlin. New York: Scribner's, 1991.

Berman, Harold J. Soviet Criminal Law and Procedure: The RSFSR Codes, rev. ed. Cambridge, MA: Harvard University Press, 1972.

Bernstein, Herman. The Willy-Nicky Correspondence. New York: Knopf, 1918.

———. Na putiakh k terimodoru. Paris: Mishen, 1931,

Besedovskii, Grigorii. Revelations of a Soviet Diplomat. London: Williams and Norgate, 1931.

Bessonova, A. M., et al. Biblioteka V. I. Lenina v Kremle. Moscow: Vsesoiuznaia knizhnaia palata, 1961.

Best, Geoffrey. "The Militarization of European Society, 1870–1914," in The Militarization of the Western World, edited by John Gillis. New Brunswick, NJ: Rutgers University Press, 1989.

Bestuzhev, I. V. Bor'ba v Rossii po voprosam vneshnei politiki 1906–1910. Moscow: Akadaemiiia nauk SSSR, 1961.

Bezobrazov, Vladimir Mikhailovich. Diary of the Commander of the Russian Imperial Guard, 1914–1917. Edited by Marvin Lyons. Boynton Beach, FL: Dramco, 1994.

Bezrukov, Grigorii N. "Za chem Stalin priezhal na Altai?" Altaiskaia pravda, December 8, 1988.

———. Priezd I. V. Stalina na Altai: ianvar' 1928 g.: materialy k seminarskim zaniatiiam po politistorii dlia studentov. Barnaul: BGPU, 1997.

Bialika, B. A., et al., eds. V. I. Lenin i A. M. Gor'kii: pis'ma vospominaniia, dokumenty, 2nd ed. Moscow: Akademiia Nauk, 1961.

Bibineishvili, B. Kamo. Moscow: Staryi bol'shevik, 1934.

Biggart, John. "Kirov before the Revolution," Soviet Studies, 23/3 (1972): 345–72.

Black, Clayton. "Zinoviev Re-Examined: Comments on Lars Lih's 'Populist Leninist,'" in The NEP Era: Soviet Russia, 1921–1928, 2 (2007): 25–38.

Blackstock, Paul W. *The Secret Road to World War Two: Soviet Versus Western Intelligence, 1921–1939.* Chicago: Quadrangle Books, 1969.

Blainey, Geoffrey. *The Causes of War.* New York: Free Press, 1973.

Blank, Stephen. "Soviet Nationality Policy and Soviet Foreign Policy: the Polish Case, 1917–1921," *International History Review,* 7/1 (1985): 103–28.

———. "Soviet Politics and the Iranian Revolution 1919–1921," *Cahiers du monde russe et soviétique,* 21/2 (1980): 173–94.

———. "The Contested Terrain: Muslim Political Participation in Soviet Turkestan, 1917–19," *Central Asian Survey,* 6/4 (1987): 47–73.

———. "The Struggle for Soviet Bashkiria, 1917–1923," *Nationalities Papers,* 11/1 (1983): 1–26.

———. *The Sorcerer as Apprentice: Stalin as Commissar of Nationalities, 1917–1924.* Westport, CT: Greenwood, 1994.

Blium, Arlen V. *Za kulisami "ministerstva pravdy": tainaia istoriia sovetskoi tsenzury 1917–1929.* St. Petersburg: Akademicheski proekt, 1994.

Blobaum, Robert E. "To Market! To Market! The Polish Peasantry in the Era of the Stolypin Reforms," *Slavic Review,* 59/2 (2000): 406–26.

———. *Feliks Dzierżyński and the SDKPiL: A Study of the Origins of Polish Communism.* Boulder, CO: East European Monographs, 1984.

Blum, Jerome. *Lord and Peasant in Russia from the Ninth to the Nineteenth Century.* Princeton: Princeton University Press, 1961.

Boersner, Demetrio. *The Bolsheviks and the National and Colonial Question 1917–1928.* Genève: Librairie E. Droz, 1957.

Boffa, Giuseppe. *The Stalin Phenomenon.* Ithaca, NY: Cornell University Press, 1992.

Bogdanovich, A. V. *Tri poslednikh samoderzhavtsa: dnevnik.* Moscow and Leningrad, L. D. Frenkel', 1924, Novosti, 1990.

Bogushevskii, V. "Kanun piatiletki," in *God vosemnadtsatyi: al'manakh vos'moi,* edited by M. Gor'kii. Moscow: Khudozhestvennaia literatura, 1935.

Bohn, T. M. "'Dummheit oder Verrat'—Gab Miljukov am 1. November 1916 das 'Sturmsignal' zur Februarrevolution?" *Jahrbücher für Geschichte Osteuropas,* 41/3 (1993): 361–93.

Bohon, J. W. "Reactionary Politics in Russia: 1905–1909." Phd diss., University of North Carolina at Chapel Hill, 1967.

*Bolezn', smert' i pogrebenie general-leitenanta barona Petra Nikolaevi-cha Vrangelia.* Brussels: Soiuz gallipoliitsev v Belgii, 1928.

*Bolsheviks and the October Revolution: Central Committee Minutes of the Russian Social-Democratic Labour Party (bolsheviks), August 1917–February 1918.* London: Pluto, 1974.

*Bolshevik Propaganda: Hearings before a Subcommittee on the Judiciary, United States Senate, Sixty-fifth Congress, third session and thereafter, pursuant to S. Res. 439 and 469 : February 11, 1919, to March 10, 1919.* Washington, D.C.: Government Printing Office, 1919.

Boltinov, S. "Iz zapisnoi knizhki arkhivista: novye dannye ob ubiistve Lado Ketskhoveli," *Krasnyi arkhiv,* 91 (1938): 271–75.

Bompard, M. "Le traité de Bjoerkoe," *Revue de Paris,* 25 (1918): 423–48.

Bonch-Bruevich, Mikhail D. *Vsia vlast' sovetam: vospominaniia.* Moscow: Voenizdat, 1957, 1958, 1964.

Bonch-Bruevich, Vladimir D. "Smert' i pokhorony Vladimira Il'icha (po lichnym vospominaniiam)," *Krasnaia nov',* 1925, no. 1: 186–91.

———. *Izbrannye sochinenii,* 3 vols. Moscow: Akademiia nauk SSSR, 1959–63.

———. *Na boevykh postakh fevral'skoi i oktiab'rskoi revoliutsii,* 2nd ed. Moscow: Federatisia, 1931.

———. *Pereezd Sovetskogo pravitel'stva iz Petrograda v Moskvu (po lichnym vospominaniam).* Moscow: Zhizn' i znanie, 1926.

———. *Pokushenie na Lenina 30 Avgusta 1918 g.: po lichnym vospominaniiam.* Moscow: Zhizn' i znanie, 1924.

———. *Tri pokusheniii na V. I. Lenina.* Moscow: Federatisia, 1930.

———. *Ubiistvo germanskogo posla Mirbakha i vosstanie levykh eserov (po lichnym vospominaniiam).* Moscow: Gudok, 1927.

———. *Vospominaniia o Lenine.* Moscow: Akademiia nauk, 1963. Nauka, 1965. Nauka, 1969.

Bond, Brian. *War and Society in Europe, 1870–1970.* New York: St. Martin's Press, 1984.

Bordiugov, G. A., ed., *Neizvestnyi Bogdanov,* 3 vols. Moscow: Airo-XX, 1995.

Bordiugov, G. A., and Kozlov, V. A. "The Turning Point of 1929 and the Bukharin Alternative," *Soviet Studies in History,* 28 (1990): 8–39.

Borges, E. "The New Czar and What We May Expect from Him," *Harper's,* June, 1895: 129–38.

Borodin, A. P. "P. N. Durnovó: Portret tsarskogo sanovnika," *Otechestvennaia istoriia,* 2000, no. 3: 48–69.

———. *Gosudarstvennyi sovet Rossii, 1906–1917.* Kirov: Viatka, 1999.

Borrero, Mauricio. *Hungry Moscow: Scarcity and Urban Society in the Russian Civil War, 1917–1921.* New York and Oxford: Peter Lang, 2003.

Bortnevski, V. G. "White Administration and White Terror: the Denikin Period," *Russian Review,* 52/3 (1993): 354–66.

———. "Oprichnina: nevozvrashchenets Grigorii Agabekov i sekretnaia sluzhba Stalina," *Sobesednik,* 1989, no. 34 (August): 12–3.

———. "White Intelligence and Counter-Intelligence During the Russian Civil War," Carl Beck Papers, no. 1108, 1995.

———, and Varustina, E. L., eds. "A. A. Borman: Moskva 1918 (iz zapisok sekretnogo agenta v Kremle)," in *Russkoe proshloe.* Leningrad: Svelen, 1991.

Borys, Jurij. *The Sovietization of the Ukraine, 1917–1923: The Communist Doctrine and Practice of National Self-Determination.* Edmonton: Canadian Institute of Ukrainian Studies, 1960, 1980.

Borzęcki, Jerzy. *The Soviet-Polish Treaty of 1921 and the Creation of Interwar Europe.* New Haven, CT: Yale University Press, 2008.

Borzunov, V. F. "Istoriia sozdaniia transsibirskoi zhelezno-dorozhnoi magistrali—nachala XX. vv," 3 vols, PhD diss., Tomsk, 1972.

Bosworth, R. J. B. *Mussolini's Italy: Life under the Fascist Dictatorship, 1915–1945.* New York: Penguin, 2006.

Bourne, Kenneth, and Watt, D. Cameron, eds. *British Documents on Foreign Affairs: Reports and Papers from the Foreign Office Confidential Print,* Part II, From the First to the Second World War. Series A, the Soviet Union, 1917–1939, 17 vols. Bethesda, MD: University Publications of America, 1984–92.

Boyd, John. "The Origins of Order Number 1," *Soviet Studies,* 19/3 (1967): 359–72.

Brackman, Roman B. *The Secret File of Joseph Stalin: A Hidden Life.* London and Portland, OR: Frank Cass, 2001.

Bradley, James F. N. *Allied Intervention in Russia.* New York: Basic, 1968.

Bradley, Joseph. *Voluntary Associations in Tsarist Russia: Science, Patriotism, and Civil Society.* Cambridge, MA: Harvard University Press, 2009.

Brandt, Conrad. *Stalin's Failure in China, 1924–1927.* Cambridge, MA: Harvard University Press, 1958.

Brewer, John. *Sinews of Power: War, Money, and the English State, 1688–1783.* Cambridge, MA: Harvard University Press, 1988.

Breyfogle, Nicholas. *Heretics and Colonizers: Forging Russia's Empire in* the South Caucasus. Ithaca, NY: Cornell University Press, 2005.

Brianskii, A. M., et al. *Vsesoiuznaia perepis' naseleniia 1926 goda.* Moscow: TsSU SSSR, 1928.

Bridge, F. R. *Great Britain and Austria-Hungary 1906–1914: A Diplomatic History.* London: London School of Economics and Political Science; Weidenfeld and Nicolson, 1972.

Brike, S. "Ekonomicheskie protsessy v sibirskoi derevne," *Zhizn' sibiri,* 1927, no. 1.

Brinkley, George A. *The Volunteer Army and the Allied Intervention in South Russia, 1917–1921.* South Bend, IN: University of Notre Dame Press, 1966.

Brinton, Crane. *Anatomy of Revolution.* New York: W. W. Norton, 1938.

Broadberry, Stephen, and Harrison, Mark, eds. *The Economics of World War.* New York: Cambridge University Press, 2005.

Brock, J. "The Theory and Practice of the Union of the Russian People, 1905–1907." Phd diss., University of Michigan, 1972.

Broido, Vera. *Lenin and the Mensheviks: The Persecution of Socialists under Bolshevism.* Aldershot, England: Gower/M. Temple Smith, 1987.

Brook-Shepherd, Gordon. *Storm Petrels: The First Soviet Defectors, 1928–1938.* London: Collins, 1977.

Broué, Pierre. *The German Revolution, 1917–1923.* Leiden, Netherlands: Brill, 2005.

Brovkin, Vladimir N. *The Mensheviks After October: Socialist Opposition and the Rise of the Bolshevik Dictatorship.* Ithaca, NY: Cornell University Press, 1987.

———. "Workers' Unrest and the Bolsheviks' Response in 1919," *Slavic Review* 49/3 (1990): 350–73.

———. *Behind the Front Lines of the Civil War: Political Parties and Social Movements in Russia, 1918–1922.* Princeton, NJ: Princeton University Press, 1994.

———, ed. *Dear Comrades: Menshevik Reports on the Bolshevik Revolution and the Civil War.* Stanford, CA: Hoover Institution Press, 1991.

———. *Russia after Lenin: Politics, Culture, and Society, 1921–1929.* London and New York: Routledge, 1998.

Browder, Robert Paul, and Kerensky, Alexander F., eds. *The Russian Provisional Government: Documents,* 3 vols. Stanford, CA: Hoover Institution Press, 1961.

Brower, Daniel R. "The Smolensk Scandal and the End of NEP," *Slavic Review,* 45/4 (1986): 689–706.

Brown, Stephen. "Lenin, Stalin and the Failure of the Red Army in the Soviet-Polish War of 1920," *War and Society,* 14/2 (1996): 35–47.

Brunck, Helma. *Bismarck und das preussische Staatsministerium, 1862–89.* Berlin: Duncker and Humboldt, 2004.

Brunn, Geoffrey, and Mamatey, Victor S. *The World in the Twentieth Century,* 4th ed. Boston: Heath, 1962.

Brusilov, A. A. *A Soldier's Note-book, 1914–1918.* London: Macmillan, 1930.

———. *Moi vospominaniia.* Moscow: Voenizdat, 1963.

Brutzkus, B. D. "Die russische Agrarrevolution," *Zeitschrift für die gesamte Staatswissenschaft,* 78 (1924): 301–45.

Buber-Neumann, Margarete. *Von Potsdam nach Moskau: Stationen eines Irrweges.* Stuttgart: Deutsche Verlags-Anstalt, 1957.

Bublikov, A. A. *Russkaia revoliutsiia.* New York: [s.n.] , 1918.

Bubnov, Andrei, et al., eds. *Grazhdanskaia voina 1918–21,* 3 vols. Moscow: Voennyi vestnik, 1928–30.

Buchan, John. *A History of the Great War,* 4 vols. Boston: Houghton Mifflin, 1922.

Buchanan, Sir George. *My Mission to Russia and Other Diplomatic Memories,* 2 vols. Boston: Little, Brown, 1923.

Buchanan, Meriel. *Petrograd: The City of Trouble, 1914–1918.* London: Collins, 1918.

Budberg, Aleksei. "Dnevik," in *Arkhiv russkoi revoliutsii,* ed. Gessen. XV (1924): 254–345.

Budennyi, S. M. *Proidennyi put',* 3 vols. Moscow: Voenizdat, 1958–1973.

Budnikov, V. P. *Bol'shevistskaia partiinaia pechat' v 1917 g.* Kharkov: Kharkovskii universitet, 1959.

Budnitskii, O. V. *Rossiiskie evrei mezhdu krasnymi i belymi (1917–1920).* Moscow: Rosspen, 2006.

Budnitskii, Oleg, ed. *Sovershenno lichno i doveritel'no!' B. A. Bakhmetev–V. A. Maklakov: perepiska 1919–1951,* 3 vols. Moscow and Stanford: Rosspen and the Hoover Institution Press, 2001–2.

———. "Boris Bakhmeteff's Intellectual Legacy in American and Russian Collections," *Slavic and East European Information Resources,* 4/4 (2003): 5–12.

———. *Den'gi russkoi emigratsii: kolchakovskoe zoloto 1918–1957.* Moscow: Novoe literaturnoe obozrenie, 2008.

Bukharin, N. K. "O novoi ekonomicheskoi politiki i nashikh zadachakh," *Bol'shevik,* 1925, no. 9–10 (June 1): 3-15.

———. *Izbrannye proizvedeniia.* Moscow: Politicheskaia literatura, 1988.

———. *Problemy teorii i praktiki sotsializma.* Moscow: Politizdat, 1989.

———. *Put' k sotsializmu v Rossii:*

*izbrannye proizvedeniia.* Novosibirsk: Nauka, Sibirskoe otdelenie, 1990.

———. *Tsezarizm pod maskoi revoliutsii: po povodu knigi prof. N. Ustrialova Pod znakom revoliutsii.* Moscow: Pravda, 1925.

Bukhnikashvili, G. *Gori: Istoricheskii ocherk.* Tblisi: Zaria vostoka, 1947.

Bukov, K. I., et al., eds. *Nedorisovannyi portret, 1920: 50-letie V. I. Lenina v rechakh stat'iakh, privetstviiakh.* Moscow: Moskovskii rabochii, 1990.

Buldakov, V. P., et al. *Bor'ba za massy v trekh revoliutsiiakh v Rossii: proletariat i srednie gorodskie sloi.* Moscow: Mysl', 1981.

Bullock, David. *The Russian Civil War, 1918–1921.* Oxford: Osprey, 2008.

Bulygin, Paul. *The Murder of the Romanovs.* London: Hutchinson, 1935.

Bunin, Ivan. *Cursed Days: A Diary of Revolution.* Chicago, Ivan R. Dee, 1998.

Bunyan, James. *Intervention, Civil War, and Communism in Russia, April–December 1918: Documents and Materials.* Baltimore: Johns Hopkins University, 1936.

———, and Fisher, Harold H., eds. *The Bolshevik Revolution, 1917–1918: Documents and Materials.* Stanford, CA: Stanford University Press, 1934.

Burbank, Jane. *Intelligentsia and Revolution: Russian Views of Bolshevism, 1917–1922.* New York: Oxford University Press, 1986.

Burdzhalov, E. N. "Revolution in Moscow," *Soviet Studies in History,* 26/1 (1987–8): 10–100.

———. *Vtoraia russkaia revoliutsiia: vosstanie v Petrograde.* Moscow: Nauka, 1967. Translated as *Russia's Second Revolution: The February 1917 Uprising in Petrograd.* Bloomington: Indiana University Press, 1987.

Burgess, William Francis. "The Istpart Commission: The Historical Department of the Russian Communist Party Central Committee, 1920–1928." Phd diss., Yale University, 1981.

Burgina, Anna. *Sotsial-demokraticheskaia menshevistskaia literatura.* Stanford, CA: Hoover Institution Press, 1967.

Bushkovitch, Paul. "Princes Cherkasskii or Circassian Murzas: The Kabardinians in the Russian Boyar Elite, 1560–1700," *Cahiers du monde russe,* 45/1–2 (2004): 9–30.

———. *Peter the Great: The Struggle for Power, 1671–1725.* New York: Cambridge University Press, 2001.

Bushnell, John. "The Tsarist Officer Corps 1881–1914: Customs, Duties, Inefficiencies," *American Historical Review,* 86/4 (1981): 753–80.

———. *Mutiny amid Repression: Russian Soldiers in the Revolution of 1905-1906.* Bloomington: Indiana University Press, 1985.

Buzurbaev, G. U. *Kuibyshev v Sibiri.* Novosibirsk: Novosibirskoe obl. gosizdat, 1939.

Bykov, P. M. *Poslednie dni Romanovykh.* Sverdlovsk: Ural-kniga, 1926.

Cameron, G. Poulet. *Personal Adventures and Excursions in Georgia, Circassia, and Russia,* 2 vols. London: Henry Colburn, 1845.

Cameron, Rondo, and Bovykin, V. I., eds. *International Banking, 1870-1914.* New York: Oxford University Press, 1991.

Campbell, T. D. *Russia: Market or Menace.* London: Longman, 1932.

Canali, M. *Il delitto Matteotti: affarismo e politica nel primo governo Mussolini.* Bologna: Il Mulino, 1997.

Carley, Michael Jabara. "Episodes from the Early Cold War: Franco-Soviet Relations 1917-1927," *Europe-Asia Studies,* 52/7 (2000): 1275-1305.

———. "The Politics of Anti-Bolshevism: The French Government and the Russo-Polish War, December 1919 to May 1920," *Historical Journal,* 19/1 (1976): 163-89.

———. *Silent Conflict: A Hidden History of Early Soviet-Western Relations.* Lanham, Md.: Rowman & Littlefield, 2014.

Carr, Edward Hallett. "Revolution from Above: Some Notes on the Decision to Collectivize Soviet Agriculture," in *The Critical Spirit: Essays in Honor of Herbert Marcuse,* edited by K. H. Wolff and Barrington Moore, Jr. Boston: Beacon (1967): 313-27.

———. "The Origins and Status of the Cheka," *Soviet Studies,* 10/1 (1958): 1-11.

———. *Socialism in One Country 1924-1926,* 3 vols. New York: Macmillan, 1958.

———. *The Bolshevik Revolution, 1917-1923,* 3 vols. New York: Macmillan, 1953.

———. *The Interregnum, 1923-1924.* New York: Macmillan, 1954.

———. *The Russian Revolution from Lenin to Stalin, 1917-1929.* New York: Macmillan, 1979.

———, and Davies, R. W. *Foundations of a Planned Economy, 1926-1929,* 3 vols. London and Basingstroke: Macmillan, 1969-1978.

Carsten, Frederick L. *Revolution in Central Europe, 1918-1919.* Berkeley: University of California Press, 1972.

Chaikan, Vadim A. *K istorii Rossiikoi revoliutsii,* vyp. 1. Moscow: Grzhebin, 1922.

Chakhvashvili, I. A. *Rabochee dvizhenie Gruzii, 1870-1904.* Tbilisi: Sabchota Sakartvelo, 1958

Chamberlain, Lesley. *Lenin's Private War: The Voyage of the Philosophy Steamer and the Exile of the Intelligentsia.* New York: St. Martin's Press, 2006.

Chamberlin, William Henry. *The Russian Revolution,* 2 vols. New York: Macmillan, 1935.

Channon, John. "The Bolsheviks and the Peasantry: The Land Question during the First Eight Months of Soviet Rule," *Slavonic and East European Review,* 66/4 (1988): 593-624.

———. "Tsarist Landowners After the Revolution: Former Pomeshchiki in Rural Russia during the NEP," *Soviet Studies,* 34/4 (1987): 575-98.

Chaquèri, Cosroe. *The Soviet Socialist Republic of Iran, 1920-1921: Birth of the Trauma.* Pittsburgh: University of Pittsburgh Press, 1995.

Chase, William J. *Workers, Society, and the Soviet State: Labor and Life in Moscow, 1918-1929.* Urbana: University of Illinois Press, 1987.

———. "Workers' Control and Socialist Democracy," *Science and Society,* 50/2 (1986): 226-38.

Chaudhry, Kiren Aziz. "The Myths of the Market and the Common History of Late Developers," *Politics and Society,* 21 (1993): 245-74.

Chavchavadze, David. *The Grand Dukes.* New York: Atlantic International Publications, 1990.

Chavichvili, Khariton A. *Patrie, prisons, exil—Stalin et nous.* Paris: Defense de la France, 1946.

———. *Révolutionnaires russes à Genève en 1908.* Geneva: Poésie vivante, 1974.

Chelidze, Karlo S. *Iz revoliutsionnogo proshlogo Tbilisskoi dukhovnoi seminarii.* Tbilisi: Tbilisskoi universitet, 1988.

Chermenskii, E. D. "Nachalo vtoroi rossiiskoi revoliutsii," *Istoriia SSSR,* 1987, no. 1.

———. *IV Gosudarstvennaia Duma i sverzhenie tsarizma v Rossii.* Moscow: Mysl', 1976.

Cherniavskii, Georgii. "Samootvod: kak Stalin sam sebia s genseka snimal," *Rodina,* 1994, no. 1: 67-69.

Cherniavsky, Michael, ed. *Prologue to Revolution: Notes of A. N. Iakhontov on the Secret Meetings of the Council of Ministers, 1915.* Englewood Cliffs, NJ: Prentice-Hall, 1967.

———. *Tsar and People: Studies in Russian Myths.* New Haven, CT: Yale University Press, 1969.

Chernina, Eugenia, Dower, Paul Casteñeda, and Markevich, Andrei. "Property Rights, Land Liquidity, and Internal Migration," working paper.

Chernomortsev A. "Krasnyi Tsaritsyn," *Donskaia volna (ezhede'lnik istorii, literatury i satiri),* February 3, 1919: 6-10.

Chernov, Victor M. "Lenin: A Contemporary Portrait," *Foreign Affairs* (March 1924): 366-372.

———. *The Great Russian Revolution.* New Haven, CT: Yale University Press, 1936.

Chernov, V. M. *Rozhdenie revoliutsionnoi Rossii (fevral'skaia revoliutsiia).* Paris, Prague, New York: Iubeleiyni komitet po izdaniiu trudov V. M. Chernova, 1934.

Chernykh, Alla I. *Stanovlenie Rossii sovetskoi: 20-e gody v zerkale sotsiaologii.* Moscow: Pamiatniki istoricheskoi mysli, 1998.

Chertok, Semen. *Stop-Kadr.* London: OPI, 1988.

Chervinskaia, N. S. *Lenin, u rulia strany Sovetov: po vospominaniiam sovremennikov i dokumentam, 1920-1924,* 2 vols. Moscow: Politcheskaia literatura, 1980.

Chevychelov, Viacheslav Ia. *Amaiak Nazaretian.* Tblisi: Sabchota Sakartvelo, 1979.

Chicherin, G. *Two Years of Soviet Foreign Policy: The Relations of the Russian Socialist Federal Soviet Republic with Foreign Nations, from November 7, 1917, to November 7, 1919.* New York: The Russian Soviet Government Bureau, 1920.

Chicherin, G. V. *Vneshniaia politika Sovetskoi Rossii za dva goda: ocherk, sostavlennyi k dvukhletnei godovshchine raboche-krest'ianskoi revoliutsii.* Moscow: Gosizdat, 1920.

Chickering, Roger. "Sore Loser: Ludendorff's Total War," in *The Shadows of Total War: Europe, East Asia, and the United States, 1919-1939,* edited by Roger Chickering and Stig Förster. New York: Cambridge University Press, 2003.

Chigir, Olesia Ia. "Grigorii Iakovlevich Sokol'nikov: lichnost' i deiatel'nost'." Phd diss., Ryazan, 2009.

Chistiakov, K. *Ubit' za Rossiiu! Iz istorii Russkogo emigrantskogo "aktivizma," 1918-1939 gg.* Moscow: Ippolitov, 2000.

Chistiakov, O. I. "Formirovanie RSFSR kak federativnoe gosudarstvo," *Voprosy istorii,* 1968, no. 8: 3-17.

———. "Obrazovanie Rossiiskoi Federatsii, 1917-1920 gg.," *Sovetskoe gosudarstvo i pravo,* 1957, no. 10: 3-12.

Chkhetia, Shalva K. *Tblisi v XIX stoletii* (1865-1869). Tblisi, 1942.

Chmielski, E. "Stolypin's Last Crisis," *California Slavonic Papers,* 3 (1964): 95-126.

Chokaev, Mustapha. "Turkestan and the Soviet Regime," *Journal of the Royal Central Asian Society,* 18 (1931): 403-20.

Christensen, Thomas J., and Snyder,

Jack. "Chain Gangs and Passed Bucks: Predicting Alliance Patterns in Multipolarity," *International Organization*, 44/2 (1990): 137–68.

Chudaev, D. A. "Bor'ba Komunisticheskoi partii za uprochnenie Sovetskoi vlasti: razgrom levykh eserov," *Uchenye zapiski Moskovskogo oblastnogo pedagogicheskogo instituta*, XXVII/ii (Moscow, 1953), 177–226.

Chuev, Feliks. *Kaganovich, Shepilov.* Moscow: Olma, 2001.

——. *Molotov: poluderzhavnyi vlastelin.* Moscow: Olma, 1999.

——. *Molotov Remembers: Inside Kremlin Politics.* Chicgao: I. R. Dee, 1993.

——. *Sto sorok besed s Molotovym.* Moscow: Terra, 1991.

——. *Tak govoril Kaganovich: ispoved' stalinskogo apostola.* Moscow: Otechestvo, 1992.

Chugaev, D. A. *Revoliutsionne dvizhenie v Rossii v avguste 19–17 g.: razgrom kornilovskogo miatezha.* Moscow: Akademiia nauk SSSR, 1959.

——, et al., eds. *Petrogradskii voenno-revoliutsionnyi komitet: dokumenty i materialy,* 3 vols. Moscow: Nauka, 1966–67.

Chulok, I. S. *Ocherki istorii batumskoi kommunisticheskoi organizatsii 1890–1921 gody.* Batum: Sabtsota Adzara, 1970.

Churchill, Rogers Platt. *The Anglo-Russian Convention of 1907.* Cedar Rapids, IA: The Torch, 1939.

Churchill, Winston. *The World Crisis: The Aftermath.* London: T. Butterworth, 1929.

Clark, Christopher. *Kaiser Wilhelm II.* Harlow: Longman, 2000.

——. *The Sleepwalkers: How Europe Went to War in 1914.* New York: Penguin, 2012.

Claudin, Fernando. *The Communist Movement: from Conmintern to Cominform.* New York: Monthly Review Press, 1975.

Cleinow, Georg. *Neue Sibirien (Sibkrai): eine Studie zum Aufmarsch der Sowjetmacht in Asien.* Berlin: R. Hobbing, 1928.

Codrescu, Andrei. *The Posthuman Dada Guide: Tzara and Lenin Play Chess.* Princeton, NJ: Princeton University Press, 2009.

Cohen, Jon S. "The 1927 Revaluation of the Lira: A Study in Political Economy," *Economic History Review,* 25/4 (1972): 642–54.

Cohn, Norman. *Warrant for Genocide: The Myth of the Jewish World-Conspiracy and the Protocols of the Elders of Zion.* London: Eyre & Spottiswoode, 1967.

Colton, Timothy J. "Military Councils and Military Politics in the Russian Civil War," *Canadian Slavonic Papers,* 18/1 (1976): 36–57.

——. *Moscow: Governing the Socialist Metropolis.* Cambridge, MA: Belknap Press of Harvard University, 1995.

Conant, Charles A. *Wall Street and the Country: A Study of Recent Financial Tendencies.* New York and London: G. P. Putnam's Sons, 1904.

Conquest, Robert. *Stalin: Breaker of Nations.* New York: Viking, 1991.

——. *The Great Terror: A Reassessment.* New York: Oxford University, 1990.

Conrad, Sebastian. *Globalisation and Nation in Imperial Germany.* New York: Cambridge University Press, 2010.

Conte, Francis. *Christian Rakovski, 1873–1941: A Political Biography.* Boulder, CO: East European Monographs, 1989.

Cook, Andrew, *To Kill Rasputin: The Life and Death of Gregori Rasputin.* London: Tempus, 2006.

Coox, Alvin D. *Nomonhan, Japan against Russia, 1939.* Stanford, CA: Stanford University Press, 1985, 1990.

Cotton, Sir Henry. *New India, or India in Transition.* London: Kegan Paul, Trench, Trübner, 1907.

Courtois, Stéphane, et al. *The Black Book of Communism.* Cambridge, MA: Harvard University Press, 1999.

Crampton, R. J. "The Balkans, 1914–1918," in *The Oxford Illustrated History of the First World War,* edited by Hew Strachan. New York: Oxford University Press, 1998.

Crawford, Rosemary A., and Crawford, Donald. *Michael and Natasha: The Life and Love of Michael II, the Last of the Romanov Tsars.* London: Weidenfeld & Nicolson, 1997.

Crisp, Olga. "The State Peasants under Nicholas I," *Slavonic and East European Review,* 37, no. 89 (1959): 387–412.

——. *Studies in the Russian Economy Before 1914.* New York: Barnes and Noble, 1976.

D'Abernon, Edgar V. *The Eighteenth Decisive Battle of the World: Warsaw 1920.* London: Hodder & Stoughton, 1931.

Dakhshleiger, G. F. *V. I. Lenin i problem kazakhstanskoi istoriografii.* Alam-Ata: Nauka KSSR, 1973.

Dallin, David J. *Soviet Espionage.* New Haven, CT: Yale University Press, 1955.

Daly, Jonathan W. *Autocracy Under Siege: Security Police and Opposition in Russia, 1866–1905.* DeKalb: Northern Illinois University Press, 1998.

——. *The Watchful State: Security Police and Opposition in Russia, 1906–1917.* DeKalb: Northern Illinois University Press, 2004.

Dan, Lidiia. "Bukharin o Staline," *Novyi zhurnal,* 1964, no. 75: 181-2.

Dan, Theodore. *The Origins of Bolshevism.* New York: Harper and Row, 1964.

Daniels, Gordon, et al. "Studies in the Anglo-Japanese Alliance (1902–1923)," London School of Economics, Suntory and Toyota International Centres for Economics and Related Disciplines, Paper No. IS/2003/443, January 1903. Found at http://sticerd.lse.ac.uk/dps/is/is443.pdf.

Daniels, Robert V. "Stalin's Rise to Dictatorship," in *Politics in the Soviet Union,* edited by Alexander Dallin and Alan F. Westin. New York: Harcourt, Brace and World, 1966.

——. "The Bolshevik Gamble," *Russian Review,* 26/4 (1967): 331–40.

——. "The Left Opposition as an Alternative to Stalinism," *Slavic Review,* 50/2 (1991): 277–85.

——. "The Secretariat and Local Organizations in the Russian Communist Party, 1921–1923," *American Slavic and East European Review,* 16/1 (1957): 32–49.

——. *Conscience of the Revolution: Communist Opposition in Soviet Russia.* Cambridge, MA: Harvard University Press, 1960.

——. *Red October: The Bolshevik Revolution of 1917.* New York: Scribner's, 1967.

——. *The Nature of Communism.* New York: Random House, 1962.

——, ed. *The Russian Revolution.* Englewood Cliffs, NJ: Prentice Hall, 1972.

——, ed., *A Documentary History of Communism,* 2 vols. New York: Random House, 1960. rev. ed., 2 vols. Hanover, NH: University Press of New England for University of Vermont, 1984, 3rd ed. Hanover, NH: University Press of New England for University of Vermont, 1993.

Danilevskii, A. F. *V. I. Lenin i voprosy voennogo stroitel'stva na VIII s"ezde RKP (b).* Moscow: Voenizdat, 1964.

Danilov, G. "How the Tsar Abdicated," *Living Age,* no. 336 (April 1929): 99–104.

Danilov, Iu. N. *Rossiia v mirovoi voine, 1914–1915 gg.* Berlin: Slovo, 1924.

——. "Moi vospominaniiu ob imperatore Nikolae II-om i vel. kniaze Mikhaile Aleksandroviche," in *Arkhiv russkoi revoliutsii,* edited by Gessen. XIX, 1928.

Danilov, V. P. "We Are Starting to Learn about Trotsky," *History Workshop,* 29 (1990): 136–46.

——. "Pereraspredelenie zemel'nogo fonda Rossii v rezul'tate Velikoi Oktiabr'skoi revoliutsii," in I. I.

Mints, ed., *Leninskii dekret "o zemle" v deistvii; sbornik statei.* Moscow: Nauka, 1979, 261–310.

——. *Rural Russia under the New Regime.* Bloomington: Indiana University Press, 1988.

——, and Khlevniuk, Oleg, eds. *Kak lomali NEP: stenogrammy plenumov TsK VKP(b) 1928–1929 gg.,* 5 vols. Moscow: Demokratiia, 2000.

——, ed. *Nestor Makhno, krest'ianskoe dvizhenie na Ukraine, 1918–1921: dokumenty i materialy.* Moscow: Rosspen, 2006.

——, et al., eds. *Krest'ianskoe vosstanie v Tambovskoi gubernii v 1919–1921 gg., "Antonovshchina": dokumenty i materialy.* Tambov: MINTS, 1994.

——. *Sovetskoe krest'ianstvo: kratkii ocherk istorii, 1917–1970,* 2nd ed. Moscow: Politizdat, 1973.

——. *Tragediia sovetskoi derevni: kollektivizatsiia i raskulachivaniie, dokumenty i materialy, 1927–1939,* 5 vols. Moscow; Rosspen, 2000.

Darlington, Thomas. *Education in Russia.* London: Wyman and Sons, 1909.

Daulet, Shafiga. "The First All-Muslim Congress of Russia, Moscow, 1–11 May 1917," *Central Asian Survey,* 8/1 (1989): 21–47.

Davatts, V. Kj., and L'vov, N. N. *Russkaia armiia na chuzhbine.* Belgrad: Russkoe izdate'stvo, 1923.

Davies, Norman. "Izaak Babel's 'Konarmiya' Stories, and the Polish-Soviet War," *Modern Language Review,* 67/4 (1972): 845–57.

——. *White Eagle, Red Star: The Polish-Soviet War, 1919–1920.* London: Macdonald, 1972.

Davies, R. W. "Carr's Changing Views of the Soviet Union," in *E. H. Carr A Critical Appraisal,* edited by Michael Cox. London: Palgrave, 2000.

Davies, Robert W. *From Tsarism to the New Economic Policy: Continuity and Change in the Economy of the USSR.* Basingstroke: Macmillan, 1990.

——. *From Tsarism to the New Economic Policy: Continuity and Change in the Economy of the USSR.* Ithaca, NY: Cornell University Press, 1991.

——. Review of David Stone, *International History Review,* 23/3 (2001): 699–701.

——. *The Socialist Offensive: The Collectivization of Soviet Agriculture, 1929–1930.* Cambridge, MA: Harvard University Press, 1980.

——. *The Soviet Economy in Turmoil, 1929–1930.* Cambridge, MA: Harvard University Press, 1989.

——, and Wheatcroft, Stephen G. "Further Thoughts on the First Soviet Five-Year Plan," *Slavic Review,* 34/4 (1975).

——. *The Years of Hunger: Soviet Agriculture, 1931–1933.* New York: Palgrave Macmillan, 1994.

Davies, Robert W., et al. *The Economic Transformation of the Soviet Union, 1913–1945.* New York: Cambridge University Press, 1994.

——, eds. *NEP: priobreteniia i poteri.* Moscow: Nauka, 1994.

Davies, Sarah, and Harris, James, eds. *Stalin: a New History.* New York: Cambridge University Press, 2005.

Davis, Jerome. "Stalin, New Leader, Explains Aims and Policies of Soviets," *New York American,* October 3, 1926: 1–2.

——. *Behind Soviet Power: Stalin and the Russians.* West Haven, CT: Reader's Press, 1949.

Davis, Mike. *Late Victorian Holocausts: El Niño, Famines, and the Making of the Third World.* London and New York: Verso, 2001.

Davletshin, Tamurbek. "The Federal Principle in the Soviet State," *Studies on the Soviet Union,* 6/3 (1967).

——. *Sovetskii Tatarstan: teoriia i praktika Leninskoi natsional'noi politiki.* London: Our World, 1974.

Davydov, Mikhail A. *Vserossiiskii rynok v kontse XIX-nachale XX vv. i zheleznodorozhnaia statistika.* St. Petersburg: Aleteiia, 2010.

Dawrichewy, Joseph. *Ah: ce qu'on rigolait bien avec mon ami Staline!* Paris: Jean-Claude Simoen, 1979.

de Basily, Nicolas. *Diplomat of Imperial Russia, 1903–1917: Memoirs.* Stanford, CA: Hoover Institution Press, 1973.

de Begnac, Yvon. *Palazzo Venezia: storio di un Regime.* Rome: La Rocca, 1950.

de Felice, Renzo. *Mussolini il fascista.* Turin: G. Einaudi, 1966–68.

——. *Mussolini il rivoluzionario, 1883–1920.* Turin: G. Einaudi, 1966.

de Gaulle, Charles. *Lettres, notes et carnets,* 12 vols. Paris: Plon, 1980–88.

de Groot, Gerard J. *Douglas Haig, 1861–1928.* London: Unwin Hyman, 1988.

De Lon, Roy Stanley. "Stalin and Social Democracy: The Political Memoirs of David A. Sagirashvili." Phd diss., Georgetown University, 1974.

de Madariaga, Isabel. *Russia in the Age of Catherine the Great.* New Haven, CT: Yale University Press, 1981.

De Michelis, Cesare G. *The Non-Existent Manuscript: A Study of the Protocols of the Sages of Zion.* Lincoln, NB: University of Nebraska Press, 2004.

de Taube, Michel. *La politique russe d'avant-guerre et la fin de l'empire des tsars (1904–1917): mémoires.* Paris: E. Leroux, 1928.

Deacon, Richard. *A History of the Russian Secret Service.* New York: Taplinger, 1972.

Deal, Zack. *Serf and Peasant Agriculture: Khar'kov Province, 1842–1861.* New York: Arno, 1981.

Debo, Richard K. "G. V. Chicherin: A Historical Perspective," in *Soviet Foreign Policy, 1917–1991: A Retrospective.* London: Frank Cass, 1994, ed. by Gabriel Gorodetsky.

——. "Lloyd George and the Copenhagen Conference of 1919–1920: The Initiation of Anglo-Soviet Negotiations," *The Historical Journal* 24/2 (1981): 429–41.

——. "The Making of a Bolshevik: Georgii Chicherin in England, 1914–1918," *Slavic Review,* 25/4 (1966): 651–62.

——. *Revolution and Survival: The Foreign Policy of Soviet Russia, 1917–18.* Toronto: University of Toronto Press, 1979.

——. *Survival and Consolidation: The Foreign Policy of Soviet Russia, 1918–21.* Montreal and Buffalo: McGill-Queen's University Press, 1992.

Dedijer, Vladimir. *The Road to Sarajevo.* New York: Simon & Schuster, 1966.

Degoev, Vladimir V. *Kavkaz i velikie derzhavy, 1829–1864 gg.: Politika, voina, diplomatiia.* Moscow: Rubezhi XXI, 2009.

Degras, Jane, ed. *Soviet Documents on Foreign Policy,* 3 vols. London and New York: Oxford University Press, 1951–53.

——. *The Communist International, 1919–1943: Documents,* 3 vols. New York: Oxford University Press, 1956–65.

——. *The Communist International, 1919–1943: Documents,* 2 vols. London: Frank Cass, 1971.

Deist, Wilhelm, and Feuchtwanger, E. J. "The Military Collapse of the German Empire: The Reality behind the Stab in the Back Myth," *War in History,* 3/2 (1996): 186–207.

*Dekrety Sovetskoi vlasti,* 16 vols. Moscow: Gosizdat/Rosspen, 1957.

Demidov, V. V. "Khlebozagotovitel'naia kampaniia 1927/28 g. v sibirskoi derevne," in *Aktual'nye problemy istorii sovetskoi Sibiri,* edited by V. I. Shishkin. Novosibirsk: Nauka, sibirskoe otdelenie, 1990.

——. *Politicheskaia bor'ba i oppozitsiia v Sibiri, 1922–1929 gg.* Novosibirsk: Sibirskii kadrovyi tsentr, 1994.

*Denezhnaia reforma 1921–1924 gg., sozdanie tverdoi valiuty: dokumenty i materialy.* Moscow: Rosspen, 2008.

*Denezhnoe obrashchenie i kreditnaia sistema Soiuza SSR za 20 let: sbornik vazhneishikh zakonodatel'nykh materialov za 1917–1937 gg.* Moscow: Gosfinizdat, 1937.

Denikin, A. I. *Ocherki russkoi smuty: Krushenie vlasti i armii,* 5 vols.

Paris and Berlin: J. Povolozky & cie, 1921–26.

Desiat' let Kommunisticheskogo universiteta im. Ia. M. Sverdlova: 1918–1928 gg. Moscow: Kommunisticheskii universitet, 1928.

Desiat' let sovetskoi diplomatii: akty i dokumenty. Moscow: Litizdat narkomindela, 1927.

Deutscher, Isaac. Stalin: A Political Biography, 2nd ed. New York: Oxford University Press, 1967.

———. The Prophet Armed: Trotsky, 1879–1921. New York: Oxford University Press, 1954.

———. The Prophet Unarmed: Trotsky, 1921–1929. New York: Oxford University Press, 1959.

———. The Unfinished Revolution: Russia, 1917–1967. New York: Oxford University Press, 1967.

Dewey, John, et al. The Case of Leon Trotsky: Report of Hearings on the Charges Made Against Him in the Moscow Trials, by the Preliminary Commission of Inquiry. New York: Harper and Row, 1937.

D'iachenko, V. P. Istoriia finansov SSSR 1917–1950 gg. Moscow: Nauka, 1978.

Diakin, V. S. "Stolypin i dvoriantsvo (Proval mestnoi reformy)," in Problemy krest'ianskogo zemlevladeniia i vnutrennei politiki Rossii: dooktiabr'skii period. Leningrad: Nauka, 1972, 231–74.

———. "The Leadership Crisis in Russia on the Eve of the February Revolution," Soviet Studies in History, 23/1 (1984): 10–38.

———. Burzhuaziia, dvorianstvo i tsarizm v 1911–1914 gg. Leningrad: Nauka, 1988.

———. Russkaia burzhuaziia i tsarizm: v gody pervoi mirovoi voiny (1914–1917). Leningrad: Nauka, 1967.

D'iakov, Iu. L., and Bushueva, T. S., eds. Fashistskii mech kovalsia v SSSR, Krasnaia Armiia i Reikhsver, tainoe sotrudnichestvo 1922–1933: neizvestnye dokumenty. Moscow: Sovetskaia Rossiia, 1992.

Dickerman, Leah, ed. Dada. Washington, D.C.: National Gallery of Art, 2006.

Dickinson, G. Lowes. The International Anarchy, 1904–1914. New York: The Century Co., 1926.

Dickson, P. G. M. Finance and Government under Maria Theresa 1740–1780. Oxford: Clarendon, 1987.

Dillon, Emile Joseph. The Eclipse of Russia. London and Toronto: J. M. Dent & Sons, 1918.

Dimanshtein, S. M., ed. Revoliutsiia i natsional'nyi vopros. Moscow: Kommunisticheskaia akademiia, 1930.

Dimitriev, Iu. A. Sovetskii tsirk: ocherki istorii, 1917–1941. Moscow: Iskusstvo, 1963.

Dirketivy glavnogo komandovaniia

Krasnoi Armii (1917–1920). Moscow: Voenizdat, 1969.

Diskussiia 1923 goda: materialy i dokumenty. Moscow: Gosizdat, 1927.

Dmitrenko, Sergei L. Bor'ba KPSS za edinstvo svoikh riadov, oktiabr' 1917–1937 gg. Moscow: Politizdat, 1976.

Dmitrenko, V. P. "Chto takoe NEP?" Voprosy istorii, 1988, no. 9: 44-7.

Dmitriev, Iurii. Pervyi chekist. Moscow: Molodaia gvardiia, 1968.

Dmitriev, V. K. Kriticheskie issledovaniia o potreblenii alkogoliia v Rossii. Moscow: V. P. Riabushinskii, 1911.

Dmitrieva, L. M., ed. Barnaul v vospominaniiakh starozhilov: XX vek. Barnaul: Altaiskii gos. universitet, 2007.

Dmitrievskii, Sergei V. Sovetskie portrety. Berlin: Strela, 1932.

———. Sud'ba Rossii: pis'ma k druz'iam. Stockholm: Strela, 1930.

Dnevnik imperatora Nikolaia II, 1890–1906 gg. Berlin: Slovo, 1923. Moscow: Polistar, 1991.

Dobb, Maurice. Russian Economic Development since the Revolution, 2nd ed. London: Routledge, 1929.

Dobrorolski, S. K. Die Mobilmachung der russischen Armee 1914. Berlin: Deutsche Verlagsgesellschat für Politik und Geschichte m.b.h, 1922.

Dobrynin, V. V. Bor'ba s bol'shevizmom na iuge Rossii: uchastie v bor'be donskogo kazacehstva. Prague: Slvianskoe izdatel'stvo, 1921.

Doctorow, Gilbert S. "The Russian Gentry and the Coup D'État of 3 June 1907," Cahiers du monde russe et soviétique, 17/1 (1976): 43–51.

Doctorow, G. S. "The Fundamental State Law of 23 April 1906," Russian Review, 35/1 (1976): 33–52.

———. "The Introduction of Parliamentary Institutions in Russia during the Revolution of 1905–1907." Phd diss., Columbia University, 1975.

Documents on British Foreign Policy, 1919–1939, 62 vols. London: H. M. Stationery Office, 1946–. Cited as DBFP.

Dohan, Michael R. "Soviet Foreign Trade in the NEP Economy and Soviet Industrialization Strategy." Phd diss., Massachusetts Institute of Technology, 1969.

———. "Foreign Trade," in From Tsarism to the New Economic Policy: Continuity and Change in the Economy of the USSR, ed. by R. W. Davies. Ithaca, NY: Cornell University, 1991, 212–34.

———. "The Economic Origins of Soviet Autarky, 1927/8–1934," Slavic Review, 35/4 (1976): 603–35.

"Dokladnaia zapiska Vitte Nikolaiu II," Istorik-Marksist, 1935, no. 2-3: 130-39.

Dokumenty i materialy po istorii

sovetsko-pol'skikh otnoshenii, 12 vols. Moscow: Akademiia nauk SSSR, 1963–1986.

Dokumenty vneshnei politiki SSSR, 21 vols. Moscow: Politcheskaia literatura, 1957-77. Cited as DVP SSSR

Dolbilov, Mikhail. "Rozhdenie imperatorskikh reshenii: monarkh, sovetnik i 'vysochaishaia volia' v Rossii XIX v.," Istoricheskie zapiski, 9 (2006), 5–48.

Dower, Paul Casteñeda, and Markevich, Andrei. "Do Property Rights in Russia Matter? The Stolpyin Titling Reform and Agricultural Productivity," working paper, New Economic School, Moscow, Russia (2012).

Dowling, Timothy C. The Brusilov Offensive. Bloomington: Indiana University Press, 2008.

Drabkin, Iakov S., et al., eds. Komintern i ideia mirovoi revoliuitsii: dokumenty. Moscow: Nauka, 1998.

Drabkina, E. "Moskva 1918," Novyi mir, 1958, no. 9: 156–57.

Drabkina, S. M. "Dokumenty germanskogo polsa v Moskve Mirbakha," Voprosy istorii, 1971, no. 9: 120–30.

Drachkovitch, Milorad M., and Lazitch, Branko, eds. The Comintern: Historical Highlights, Recollections, Documents. New York: Praeger, 1966.

———. Lenin and the Comintern. Stanford, CA: Hoover Institution Press, 1971.

Dreiser, Theodore. Dreiser Looks at Russia. New York: H Liveright, 1928.

Drezen, A. K. Burzhuaziia i pomeshchiki 1917 goda: chastnye soveshehaniia chlenov Gosudarstvennoi Dumy. Moscow-Leningrad: Partizdat, 1932.

Dridzo, Vera. Nadezhda Konstantinovna. Moscow: Politicheskaia literatura, 1958.

———. "O Krupskoi: pis'mo v redakstiiu," Kommunist, 1989, no. 5: 105–6.

Drujina, Gleb. "The History of the North-West Army of General Iudenich." Phd diss., Stanford University, 1950.

Dubenskii, D., ed. Ego Imperatorskoe Velichestvo Gosudar' Imperator Nikolai Aleksandrovich v desitvuiushchei armii, 4 vols. Petrograd: Ministerstvo Imp. Dvora, 1915–16.

Dubentsov, B., and Kulikov, A. "Sotsial'naia evoliutsiia vysshei tsarskoi biurokratii vo votroi polovine XIX-nachale XX v.," in Problemy sotsial'no-ekonomicheskoi i politicheskoi istorii Rossii XIX-XX vekov: sbornik statei, edited by Boris Ananich et al. St. Petersburg: Aleteiia, 1999.

Dubinskii-Mukhadaze, Ilya Moiseevich. Ordzhonikidze. Moscow: Molodaia gvardiia, 1963, 1967.

Dubrovskii, Sergei M. Stolypinskaia zemel'naia reforma: iz istorii sel'skogo khoziaistva i krest'ianstva

*Rossii v nachale XX veka.* Moscow: Akademiia nauk, 1963.

Duda, Gerhard. *Jenő Varga und die Geschichte des Instituts für Weltwirtschaft und Weltpolitik in Moskau 1921–1970: zu den Möglichkeiten und Grenzen wissenschaftlicher Auslandsanalyse in der Sowjetunion.* Berlin: Akademie, 1994.

Dullin, Sabine. *Men of Influence: Stalin's Diplomats in Europe, 1930–1939.* Edinburgh: Edinburgh University Press, 2010.

Dumova, N. "Maloizvestnye materialy po istorii kornilovshchiny," *Voprosy istorii,* 1968, no. 2: 69–93.

Duraczyński, E., and Sakharov, A. N., eds. *Sovetsko-Pol'skie otnosheniia v politicheskikh usloviakh Evropy 30-x godov XX stoletiia: sbornik statei.* Moscow: Nauka, 2001.

Duranty, Walter. "Artist Finds Lenin at Work and Fit," *New York Times,* October 15, 1922.

———. "Lenin Dies of Cerebral Hemorrhage; Moscow Throngs Overcome With Grief; Trotsky Departs Ill, Radek in Disfavor," *New York Times,* January 23, 1924.

———. *I Write as I Please.* New York: Simon & Schuster, 1935.

Durnovo, Nikolai. *Sud'ba gruzinskoi tserkvi.* Moscow: Russkii stiag, 1907.

Duval, Jr., Charles. "The Bolshevik Secretariat and Yakov Sverdlov: February to October 1917," *Slavonic and East European Review,* 51, no. 122 (1973): 47–57.

———. "Yakov M. Sverdlov and the All-Russian Central Executive Committee of Soviets (VTsIK): A Study in Bolshevik Consolidation of Power, October 1917–July 1918," *Soviet Studies,* 31/1 (1979): 3–22.

*Dvadtsat' let VChK-OGPU-NKVD.* Moscow: OGIZ, 1938.

"Dve besedy s L. M. Kaganovichem," *Novaia i noveishaia istoriia,* 1999, no. 2: 101–22.

Dyck, Harvey L. "German-Soviet Relations and the Anglo-Soviet Break 1927," *Slavic Review,* 25/1 (1966): 67–83.

———. *Weimar Germany and Soviet Russia, 1896–1933: A Study in Diplomatic Instability.* New York: Columbia University Press, 1966.

Dzerzhinskaia, S. *V gody velikikh boev.* Moscow: Mysl', 1964.

———. *Izbrannye proizvedeniia.* Moscow: OGIZ, 1947.

Dzerzhinskii, F. E. *Feliks Dzerzhinskii: dnevnik zakliuchennogo, pis'ma.* Minsk: Belarus, 1977.

Dziewanowski, M. K. *Communist Party of Poland: An Outline of History.* Cambridge, MA: Harvard University Press, 1959.

———. *Joseph Piłsudski: A European Federalist, 1918–1922.* Stanford: Hoover Institution Press, 1969.

Easter, Gerald M. *Reconstructing the State: Personal Networks and Elite Identity in Soviet Russia.* New York: Cambridge University Press, 2000.

Eastman, Max. *Heroes I Have Known: Twelve Who Lived Great Lives.* New York: Simon & Schuster, 1942.

———. *Leon Trotsky: The Portrait of a Youth.* New York: Greenberg, 1925.

———. *Love and Revolution: My Journey through an Epoch.* New York: Random House, 1964.

———. *Since Lenin Died.* New York: Boni & Liveright, 1925.

Edgerton, David. *The Shock of the Old: Technology and Global History since 1900.* New York: Oxford University Press, 2006.

Edmondson, Charles M. "The Politics of Hunger: The Soviet Response to the Famine of 1921," *Soviet Studies,* 29/4 (1977): 506–18.

Egorov, Aleksandr. *L'vov-Varshava, 1920 god: vzaimodeistvie frontov.* Moscow-Leningrad: Gosizdat otdel voennoi literatury, 1929.

Egorova, L. P. "Khlebozagotovitel'naia kampaniia 1927–1928 gg. i bor'ba s kulachestvom v zapadnosibir'skoi derevne," *Voprosy istorii Sibiri,* Tomsk: Tomskii gosudarstvenyi universitet, 1967, vyp. 3: 255-70.

Ehrenburg, Ilya. *Memoirs: 1921–1941.* Cleveland, OH: World Pub., 1968.

Ehrlich, Alexander. *The Soviet Industrialization Debate, 1924–1928.* Cambridge, MA: Harvard University Press, 1960, 1967.

Eichengreen, Barry J. *Golden Fetters: The Gold Standard and the Great Depression, 1919–1939.* New York: Oxford University Press, 1992.

Eichwede, Wolfgang. *Revolution und Internationale Politik: zur kommunistischen Interpretation der kapitalistischen Wetlt, 1921–1925.* Cologne: Böhlau, 1971.

Einaudi, Luca. *Money and Politics: European Monetary Unification and the Gold Standard, 1865–1873.* New York: Oxford University Press, 2001.

*Ekonomicheskoe polozhenie Rossii nakanune Velikoi Oktiabr'skoi sotsialisticheskoi revoliutsii: dokumenty i materialy,* 3 vols. Moscow: Akademiia nauk, 1957; Leningrad: Nauka, 1967.

Eleuov, T. E. *Inostrannaia voennaia interventsiia i grazhdanskaia voina v Srednei Azii i Kazakhstane: dokumenty i materialy.* Alma-Ata: Akademiia nauk Kazakhskogo SSR, 1964.

Elleman, Bruce A. "Secret Sino-Soviet Negotiations on Outer Mongolia, 1918–1925," *Pacific Affairs,* 66/4 (1993–4): 539–63.

———. *Diplomacy and Deception: The Secret History of Sino-Soviet Diplomatic Relations, 1917–1927.* Armonk, NY: M. E. Sharpe, 1997.

Ellis, John. *Social History of the Machine Gun.* Baltimore: Johns Hopkins University Press, 1976, 1986.

Elpatevskii, S. Ia. *Vospominaniia.* Leningrad: Priboi, 1929.

Elwood, Ralph Carter. *Roman Malinovsky: A Life without a Cause.* Newtonville, MA: Oriental Research Partners, 1977.

———. *Russian Social Democracy in the Underground: A Study of the RSDRP in the Ukraine, 1907–1914.* Assen: Van Gorcum, 1974.

Ely, Christopher. "The Question of Civil Society in Late Imperial Russia," in *A Companion Volume to Russian History,* edited by Abbott Gleason. Oxford: Blackwell, 2009.

Emmons, Terence, ed. *Time of Troubles: The Diary of Iurii Vladimirovich Got'e.* Princeton, NJ: Princeton University Press, 1988.

———. *The Formation of Political Parties and the First National Elections in Russia.* Cambridge, MA: Harvard University Press, 1983.

Engel, Barbara. "Not By Bread Alone: Subsistence Riots in Russia During World War I," *Journal of Modern History,* 69/3 (1997): 696–721.

Engelstein, Laura. *Moscow 1905: Working Class Organization and Political Conflict.* Stanford, CA: Stanford University Press, 1982.

Engerman, David C. *Modernization from the Other Shore: American Intellectuals and the Romance of Russian Development.* Cambridge, MA: Harvard University Press, 2003.

Englander, David. "Military Intelligence and the Defence of the Realm," *Bulletin of the Society for the Study of Labour History,* 52/1 (1987): 24–32.

Ennker, Benno. "The Origins and Intentions of the Lenin Cult," in *Regime and Society in Twentieth Century Russia,* edited by Ian Thatcher. London: Macmillan Press, 1999, 118-28.

———. *Die Anfänge des Leninkults in der Sowjetunion.* Cologne: Böhlau, 1997.

Enukidze, A. *Nashi podpol'nye tipografii na Kavkaze.* Moscow: Novaia Moskva, 1925.

Epikhin, A. Iu., and Mozokhin, O. B. *VChK-OGPU v borb'e s korruptsiei v gody novoi ekonomicheskoi politiki, 1921–1928.* Moscow: Kuchkovo pole, 2007.

Erdmann, Karl Dietrich, ed. *Kurt Riezler: Tagebücher, Aufsätze, Dokumente.* Göttingen: Vandenhoeck & Ruprecht, 1972.

Erickson, John. *The Soviet High Command: A Military-Political History, 1918–1941.* New York: St. Martin's, 1962. 3rd ed. London and Portland, OR: Frank Cass, 2001.

Erikson, Erik H. *Young Man Luther: A Study in Psychoanalysis and History.* New York: W. W. Norton, 1958.

Erofeev, Valerii. *Valerian Kuibyshev v Samare: mif stalinskoi epokhi.* Samara: Samarskoe otdelenie Litfonda, 2004.

Eroshkin, N. P. *Ocherki istorii gosudarstvennykh uchrezdenii dorevoliutsionnoi Rossii.* Moscow: Gos. Uchebno-pedagogicheskoe izdatel'stvo, 1960.

Erykalov, E. F. *Oktiabr'skoe vooruzhennoe vosstanie v Petrograde.* Leningrad: Lenizdat, 1966.

Esadze, Semen. *Istoricheskaia zapiska ob upravlenii Kavkazom,* 2 vols. Tblisi: Guttenberg, 1907.

Esikov, S. A., and Kanishev, V. V. "Antonovskii NEP," *Otechestvennaia istoriia,* 1993, no. 4: 60–71.

Esthus, Raymond A. "Nicholas II and the Russo-Japanese War," *Russian Review,* 40/4 (1981): 396–411.

Etherton, P. T. *In the Heart of Asia.* London: Constable and Co., 1925.

Eudin, Xenia, and Fisher, Harold T., eds. *Soviet Russia and the West, 1920–1927: A Documentary Survey.* Stanford, CA: Hoover Institution Press, 1957.

———, and Slusser, Robert, eds. *Soviet Foreign Policy, 1928–1934: Documents and Materials.* University Park, PA: Pennsylvania State University Press, 1967.

Eudin, Xenia Joukoff, and North, Robert C., eds. *Soviet Russia and the East, 1920–1927: A Documentary Survey.* Stanford, CA: Stanford University Press, 1957.

Evans, Les, and Block, Russell, eds. *Leon Trotsky on China.* New York: Monad, 1976.

Evreinoff, N. *Histoire du Théâtre Russe.* Paris: du Chène, 1947.

Faerman, E. "Transportirovka 'Iskry' iz-za granitsy i rasprostranenie ee v Rossii v 1901–1903 gg.," *Muzei revoliutsiii SSSR: pervyi sbornik.* Moscow, 1947.

Fainblitt, S. *Amnistiia i sudebnyi prigovor: s prilozheniem vazhneishikh aktov ob amnistii za 10 let.* Moscow: Gosizdat, 1928.

Fainsod, Merle. *International Socialism and the World War.* Cambridge, MA: Harvard University Press, 1935.

———. *Smolensk Under Soviet Rule.* Cambridge, MA: Harvard University Press, 1958.

Falasca-Zamponi, Simonetta. *Fascist Spectacle: The Aesthetics of Power in Mussolini's Italy.* Berkeley: University of California Press, 1997.

Fallows, T. "Governor Stolypin and the Revolution of 1905 in Saratov," in *Politics and Society in Provincial Russia: Saratov, 1590–1917,* edited by Rex A. Wade and Scott J. Seregny.

Columbus: Ohio University Press, 1990.

Farbman, M. *Bolshevism in Retreat.* London: Collins, 1923.

Fay, Sidney B. "The Kaiser's Secret Negotiations with the Tsar, 1904–1905," *American Historical Review,* 2/1 (1918): 48–72.

———. *The Origins of the World War,* 2 vols. New York: Macmillan, 1929.

Fearon, James D. "Rationalist Explanations for War," *International Organization,* 49/3 (1995): 379–414.

Fedor, Julie. *Russia and the Cult of State Security: The Chekist Tradition, from Lenin to Putin,* Abingdon, Oxon, and New York: Routledge, 2011.

Fedyshyn, Oleh S. *Germany's Drive to the East and the Ukrainian Revolution, 1917–1918.* New Brunswick, NJ: Rutgers University Press, 1971.

Feigina, L. A. *B'orskkoe soglashenie.* Moscow: Izd. M. i S. Sabashnikovykh, 1928.

Feis, Herbert. *Europe: The World's Banker 1870–1914: An Account of European Foreign Investment and the Connection of World Finance with Diplomacy before the War.* New Haven, CT: Yale University Press, 1930.

Feitelberg, M. *Das Papiergeldwesen in Räte-Russland.* Berlin: Praeger, 1920.

Feldman, Gerald D. *The Great Disorder: Politics, Economics, and Society in the German Inflation, 1914–1924.* New York: Oxford University Press, 1993.

Feldman, Robert. "The Russian General Staff and the June 1917 Offensive," *Soviet Studies,* 19/4 (1968): 526–42.

Fel'shtinskii, Iurii, ed. *Kommunisticheskaia oppozitsiia v SSSR, 1923–1927: iz arkhiva L'va Trotskogo,* 4 vols. Benson, VT: Chalidze, 1988.

Fel'shtinskii, Iurii. *Bol'sheviki i levye esery: oktiabr' 1917–iun' 1918: na puti k odnoi partiinoi diktatury.* Paris: YMCA, 1985.

———. *Brestskii mir, oktiabr' 1917 goda–noiabr' 1918 g.* Moscow: Terra, 1992.

———. *Razgovory s Bukharinym.* New York: Telex: 1991.

Ferguson, Niall. "Political Risk and the International Bond Market between the 1848 Revolution and the Outbreak of the First World War," *Economic History Review,* 59/1 (2006): 70–112.

———. *The Pity of War.* New York: Basic Books, 1999.

Fergusson, Adam. *When Money Dies: The Nightmare of Deficit Spending, Devaluation, and Hyperinflation in Weimar Germany.* New York: Public Affairs, 2010.

Ferris, John. "Turning Japanese: British Observations of the Russo-Japanese War," in *Rethinking the Russo-Japanese War, 1904–05,* 2 vols., edited by Rotem Kowner. Folkstone: Global Oriental, 2007.

Ferro, Marc. "The Russian Soldier in 1917: Undisciplined, Patriotic, and Revolutionary," *Slavic Review,* 30/2 (1971): 483–512.

———. *La révolution de 1917: la chute du tsarisme et les origines d'Octobre.* Paris: Aubier, 1967.

———. *The Great War.* London: Routledge and Keegan Paul, 1973.

"Fevral'skaia revoliutsiia i okhrannoe otdelenie," *Byloe,* 1918, no. 1: 158–76.

Fić, Victor M. *The Bolsheviks and the Czechoslovak Legion: The Origins of Their Armed Conflict.* New Delhi: Abinav, 1978.

Field, Daniel, trans. "Petition Prepared for Presentation to Nicholas II," Documents in Russian History. Found at: http://academic.shu.edu/russianhistory/index.php/Workers'_Petition,_January_9th,_1905_(Bloody_Sunday).

Figes, Orlando, and Kolonitskii, Boris. *Interpreting the Russian Revolution: The Language and Symbols of 1917.* New Haven, CT: Yale University Press, 1999.

Figes, Orlando. "The Failure of February's Men," *The Historical Journal,* 31/2 (1988): 493–9.

———. *A People's Tragedy: The Russian Revolution, 1891–1924.* London: Jonathan Cape, 1996.

———. *Peasant Russia, Civil War: The Volga Countryside in Revolution, 1917–1921.* Oxford: Clarendon Press, 1989.

Filat'ev, D. F. *Katastrofa Belogo dvizheniia v Sibiri, 1918–1922 gg.: vpechatleniia ochevidtsa.* Paris: YMCA-Press, 1985.

Filimonov, V. G. *Vozniknovenie i razvitie RSFSR kak federativnogo gosudarstva: material i pomoshch' lektoru.* Moscow: Obshchestvo po rasprostraneniiu politicheskogo i nauchnogo znanii, 1958.

———. *Obrazovanie i razvitie RSFSR.* Moscow: Iuridicheskaia literatura, 1963.

*Finansovaia politika Sovetskoi vlasti za 10 let: sbornik statei.* Moscow: Moskovskii rabochii, 1928.

Finer, Samuel E. *The Man on Horseback: The Role of the Military in Politics,* 2nd ed. New York: Penguin, 1976.

Fink, Carole. *The Genoa Conference: European Diplomacy, 1921–1922.* Chapel Hill: University of North Carolina Press, 1984.

———, et al., eds. *Genoa, Rapallo, and European Reconstruction in 1922.* New York: Cambridge University Press, 1991.

Firsov, F. I. "K voprosu o taktike edinogo fronta v 1921–1924 gg.," *Voprosy istorii KPSS*, 1987, no. 10: 113–27.

———. "N. I. Bukharin v Kominterne," in *Bukharin: chelovek, politik, uchenyi*, edited by V. V. Zhuravlev and A. N. Solopov. Moscow: Politicheskaia literatura, 1990.

Firsov, Fridrikh I. "Nekotorye voprosy istorii Kominterna," *Novaia i noveishaia istoriia*, 1989, no. 2: 75–107.

Fischer, Conan. *The Ruhr Crisis, 1923–1924*. New York: Oxford University Press, 2003.

Fischer, Fritz. *Germany's Aims in the First World War*. New York: W. W. Norton, 1967, 1976.

———. *War of Illusions: German Policies from 1911 to 1914*. London: Chatto & Windus, 1975.

Fischer, George. *Russian Liberalism: From Gentry to Intelligentsia*. Cambridge, MA: Harvard, 1958.

Fischer, Louis. *Men and Politics: Europe Between the Two World Wars*. New York: Harper & Row, 1946.

———. *Russia's Road from Peace to War: Soviet Foreign Relations 1917–1941*. New York: Harper & Row, 1969.

———. *The Life of Lenin*. New York: Harper & Row, 1964.

———. *The Soviets in World Affairs: A History of Relations between the Soviet Union and the Rest of the World, 1917–1929*, 2 vols. Princeton, NJ: Princeton University Press, 1951.

Fischer, Ruth. *Stalin and German Communism: A Study in the Origins of the State Party*. Cambridge, MA: Harvard University Press, 1948.

Fisher, Harold H. *The Famine in Soviet Russia, 1919–1923: The Operations of the American Relief Administration*. New York: Macmillan, 1927.

Fitzpatrick, Sheila. "The Civil War as Formative Experience," in *Bolshevik Culture: Experience and Order in the Russian Revolution*, edited by Abbott Gleason et al. Bloomington: Indiana University Press, 1985.

———. "The Foreign Threat during the First Five Year Plan," *Soviet Union/ Union soviétique*, 5/1 (1978): 26–35.

Fleer, M. G., ed. *Rabochee dvizhenie v gody voiny*. Moscow: Voprosy truda, 1925.

Fleischhauer, Ingeborg. *Die Deutschen im Zarenreich: Zwei Jahrhunderte deutsch-russiche Kulturgemeinschaft*. Stutgart: Deutsche verlags-Anstalt, 1986.

Fleishman, L. *V tiskakh provokatsii: operatisiia "Trest" i russkaia zrubezhnaia pechat'*. Moscow: Novoe literaturnoe obozrenie, 2003.

Flerov, Vasilii S. *V. V. Kuibyshev— vydaiushchiisia proletarskii revoliutsioner i myslitel': stat'i, vospominaniia, dokumenty*. Tomsk:

Tomskii gosudarstvennyi universitet imeni V. V. Kuibysheva, 1963.

Fofanova, M. V. "Poslednoe podpol'e V. I. Lenina," *Istoricheskii arkhiv*, 1956, no. 4: 166–72.

Fokke, D. G. "Na tsene i za kulisami Brestskoi tragikomedii tmemuary uchastnika," ed. by Gesseu, *Arkhiv russkoi revoliutsii*, 1930, no. 20, 5–207.

Fomin, Fedor T. *Zapiski starogo chekista*, 2nd ed. Moscow: Politicheskaia literatura, 1964.

Forster, Kent. *The Failures of the Peace: The Search for a Negotiated Peace During the First World War*. Washington, D.C.: American Council on Public Affairs, 1942.

Förster, Stig. "Dreams and Nightmares: German Military Leadership and the Images of Future War," in Manfred F. Boemke, et al., eds. *Anticipating Total War: The German and American Experiences, 1871–1914*. Washington, D.C.: German Historical Institute, 1999, 343–76.

Fotieva, L. A. *Iz zhizni V. I. Lenina*. Moscow: Politcheskaia literatura, 1967.

Frank, Allen J. *Bukhara and the Muslims of Russia: Sufism, Education, and the Paradox of Prestige*. Leiden and Boston: Brill, 2013.

Frank, V. S. "The Land Question and the 1917 Revolution," *Russian Review*, 1/1 (1945): 22–35.

Frankel, Edith Rogovin, et al., eds. *Revolution in Russia: Reassessments of 1917*. New York: Cambridge University Press, 1992.

Freedman, Lawrence. *Strategy: A History*. New York: Oxford University Press, 2013.

Freeze, Gregory L. "Reform and Counter-Reform 1855–1890," in *Russia: A History*, edited by Gregory L. Freeze. New York: Oxford University Press, 1997.

French, David. *British Strategy and War Aims, 1914–1916*. London: Allen & Unwin, 1986.

Frenkin, Mikhail. *Zakhvat vlasti bol'shevikami v Rossii i rol' tylovykh garnizonov armii: podgotovka i provedenie Oktiabr'skogo miatezha, 1917–1918 gg.* Jerusalem: Stav, 1982.

Frenkin, Mikhail S. *Russkaia armiia i revoliutsiia, 1917–1918*. Munich: Logos, 1978.

Freund, Gerald. *Unholy Alliance: Russian-German Relations from the Treaty of Brest-Litovsk to the Treaty of Berlin*. New York: Harcourt, Brace, 1957.

Fridenson, Patrick. "The Coming of the Assembly Line to Europe," in *The Dynamics of Science and Technology*, edited by Wolfgang Krohn et al. Dordrecht, Holland, and Boston: D. Reidel Publishing Company, 1978.

Frierson, Cathy A., ed. *Aleksandr*

Nikolaevich Englehardt's Letters from the Country, 1872–1887. New York: Oxford University Press, 1993.

Fuhrmann, Joseph T. *Rasputin: A Life*. New York: Prager, 1990.

———, ed. *The Complete Wartime Correspondence of Tsar Nicholas II and the Empress Alexandra: April 1914–March 1917*. Westport, CT: Greenwood, 1999.

Fuller, Jr., William C. "The Russian Empire," in *Knowing One's Enemies: Intelligence Assessments before the Two World Wars*, edited by Ernest F. May. Princeton: Princeton University Press, 1985.

———. *Civil-Military Conflict in Imperial Russia, 1881–1914*. Princeton, NJ: Princeton University Press, 1985.

———. *Strategy and Power in Russia 1600–1914*. New York: Free Press, 1992.

———. *The Foe Within: Fantasies of Treason and the End of Imperial Russia*. Ithaca, NY: Cornell University Press, 2006.

Fülöp-Miller, Réné. *Rasputin: The Holy Devil*. New York: Viking Press, 1928.

———. *The Mind and Face of Bolshevism: An Examination of Cultural Life in Soviet Russia*. London and New York: G. P. Putnam's Sons, 1927.

———. *The Mind and Face of Bolshevism: An Examination of Cultural Life in Soviet Russia*. New York: Knopf, 1928.

Futrell, Michael. *Northern Underground: Episodes of Russian Revolutionary Transport and Communication through Scandinavia and Finland*. New York: Praeger, 1963.

Gafurov, B. G. *Lenin i natsional'no-osvoboditel'noe dvizhenie v stranakh vostoka*. Moscow: Vostochnaia literatura, 1970.

Gagliardo, J. *From Pariah to Patriot: The Changing Image of the German Peasant, 1770–1840*. Lexington: University Press of Kentucky, 1975.

Gaida, Fedor A. *Liberal'naia oppozitsiia na putiakh k vlasti (1914—vesna 1917 g.)*. Moscow: Rosspen, 2003.

Gaiduk, Il'ia "Sovetsko-Amerikanskie otnosheniia v pervoi polovine 20-x godov i sozdanie 'Amtorga,'" *Russkii vopros*, 2002, no. 2.

Galai, Shmuel. *The Liberation Movement in Russia, 1900–1905*. New York: Cambridge University Press, 1973.

Galoian, G. A. *Rabochee dvizhenie i natsional'nyi vopros v Zakavkaz'e, 1900–1922*. Erevan: Aiastan, 1969.

Gal'perina, B. D., et al., eds. *Sovet ministrov Rossiiskoi imperii v gody Pervoi mirovoi voiny: Bumagi A. N. Iakhontova*. St. Petersburg: Bulanin, 1999.

———. "Chastnye soveshchanii gosudarstvennoi dumy—tsentr splocheniia burzhuaznykh partii Rossii," in *Neproletarskie partii Rossii v trekh revoliutsiakh: sbornik statei*, edited by K. V. Gusev. Moscow: Nauka, 1989.

Gambarov, Iu. S., et al., eds. *Entsiklopedicheskii slovar' russkogo bibliograficheskogo instituta Granat*, 58 vols. Moscow: Russkii biograficheskii institut Granata, 1922–48.

Gamburg, Iosif K. *Tak eto bylo: vospominaniia*. Moscow: Politcheskaia literatura, 1965.

Gammer, Moshe. *Muslim Resistance to the Tsar: Shamil and the Conquest of Chechnia and Daghestan*. London and Portland, OR: F. Cass, 1994.

Ganelin, Rafail. "The Day Before the Downfall of the Old Regime: 26 February 1917 in Petrograd," in *Extending the Borderlands of Russian History: Essays in Honor of Alfred J. Rieber*, edited by Marsha Siefert. New York: Central European University Press, 2003.

Ganelin, Rafail, et al. "Vospominaniia T. Kirpichnikova kak istochnik po istorii fevral'skikh revoliutsionnykh dnei 1917 g. v Petrograde," *Rabochii klass Rossii, ego soiuzniki i politicheskie protivniki v 1917 godu.* Leningrad: Nauka, 1989.

Gann, Lewis H. "Western and Japanese Colonialism: Some preliminary Comparisons," in *The Japanese Colonial Empire, 1895–1945*, edited by Ramon Meyers et al. Princeton, NJ: Princeton University Press, 1984.

Gapon, George. *The Story of My Life*. London: Chapman and Hall, Ltd., 1905

Gaponenko, L. S., ed. *Revoliutsionnoe dvizhenie v Rossii posle sverzheniia samoderzhaviia*. Moscow: Akaademiia nauk SSSR, 1958.

———, and V. M. Kabuzan. "Materialy sel'sko-khoziastvennykh perepisei 1916–1917 gg.," *Voprosy istorii*, 1961, no. 6: 97–115.

Garafov, Vasif. "Russko-turetskoe sblizhenie i nezavisimost' Azerbaijana 1919–1921 gg.," *Kavkaz i globalizatsiia*, 4/1–2 (2010): 240–48.

Gaspar'ian, Armen. *Operatsiia Trest: Sovetskaia razvedka protiv russkoi emigratsii, 1921–1937 gg.* Moscow: Veche, 2008.

Gatrell, Peter. *Government, Industry, and Rearmament in Russia, 1900–1914: The Last Argument of Tsarism*. New York: Cambridge University Press, 1994.

———. *Russia's First World War: A Social and Economic History*. Harlow, England: Pearson-Longman, 2005.

———. *The Tsarist Economy, 1857–1914*. New York, 1986.

———. *A Whole Empire Walking: Refugees in the Russian Empire during the First World War*. Bloomington: Indiana University Press, 1999.

Gegeshidze, Zinaida T. *Georgii Teliia: biograficheskii ocherk*. Tblisi: Sabchota Sakartvelo, 1958.

Geifman, Anna. *Entangled in Terror: The Azef Affair and the Russian Revolution*. Wilmington, DE: Scholarly Resources, 2000.

———. *Revoliutsionnyi terror v Rossii, 1894–1917*. Moscow: Kron Press, 1997.

———. *Thou Shalt Kill: Revolutionary Terrorism in Russia, 1894–1917*. Princeton, NJ: Princeton University Press, 1993.

Gelb, Michael. "The Far-Eastern Koreans," *Russian Review* 54/3 (1995): 389–412.

Gellner, Ernest. *Encounters with Nationalism*. Oxford: Blackwell, 1994.

Genis, Vladimir L. "G. Ia. Sokolnikov," *Voprosy istorii*, 1988, no.12: 59–86.

———. "S Bukharoi nado konchat'": k istorii butaforskikh revoliutsii, dokumental'naia khronika. Moscow: MNPI, 2001.

Genkina, Esfir' B. "Bor'ba za Tsaritsyn v 1918 godu," *Proletarskaia revoliutsiia*, 1939, no. 1: 75–110.

———. "Priezd tov. Stalina v Tsaritsyn," *Proletarskaia revoliutsiia*, 1936, no. 7: 61–92

———. "V. I. Lenin i perekhod k novoi ekonomicheskoi politike," *Voprosy istorii*, 1964, no. 5: 3-27.

———. *Perekhod sovetskogo gosudarstva k novoi ekonomicheskoi politike, 1921–1922*. Moscow: Politicheskaia literatura, 1954.

———. *Tsaritsyn v 1918 godu*. Moscow: Politizdat pri TsK VKP(b), 1940.

George, David Lloyd. *War Memoirs*, 2 vols. London: Odhams Pm, 1942.

Gerasimov, Aleksandr V. "Na lezvii s terroristami," in *Okhranka: vospominaniia rukovoditelia politicheskogo syska*, 2 vols, edited by Z. I. Peregudovaia. Moscow: NLO, 2004.

———. *Na lezvii s terroristami*. Paris: YMCA, 1985.

Gerassimoff, Alexander. *Der Kampf gegen die erste russische Revolution: Erinnerungen*. Frauenfeld: Leipzig, 1934.

Ģērmanis, Uldis. *Oberst Vācietis und die lettischen Schützen im Weltkrieg und in der Oktoberrevolution*. Stockholm: Almqvist & Wiksell, 1974.

Gershchenkron, Alexander. "Agrarian Policies and Industrialization in Russia 1861–1917," in *The Cambridge Economic History of Europe*, edited by H. J. Habakkuk and M. Postan. New York: Cambridge University Press, VI/ii: 706–800.

Gerson, Lennard D. *The Secret Police in Lenin's Russia*. Philadelphia: Temple University, 1976.

Gerutis, Albertis, ed. *Lithuania: 700 Years*. New York: Manyland Books, 1969.

Gessen, I. V., ed. *Arkhiv russkoi revoliutsii*, 22 vols. Berlin: Slowo, 1921–37.

Getzler, Israel. "Lenin's Conception of Revolution As Civil War," *Slavonic and East European Review*, 74/3 (1996): 464–72.

———. "The Communist Leaders' Role in the Kronstadt Tragedy of 1921 in the Light of Recently Published Archival Documents," *Revolutionary Russia*, 15/1 (2002): 24–44.

———. *Kronstadt, 1917–1921: The Fate of a Soviet Democracy*. New York: Cambridge University Press, 2002.

———. *Martov: A Political Biography of a Russian Social Democrat*. New York: Cambridge University Press, 1967.

Geyer, Dietrich. *Russian Imperialism: The Interaction of Domestic and Foreign Policy 1860–1914*. New Haven, CT: Yale University Press, 1987.

Geyer, Michael. "Insurrectionary Warfare: The German Debate about a *Levée en masse* in October 1918," *Journal of Modern History*, 73/3 (2001): 459–527.

———. "The Militarization of Europe," in *The Militarization of the Western World*, edited by John Gillis. New Brunswick, NJ: Rutgers University Press, 1989.

"Gibel'" tsarskogo Petrograda: fevral'skaia revoliutsiia glazami gradonachal'nika A. P. Balka," *Russkoe proshloe: Istoriko-dokumental'nyialm al'manakh*, 1991, no. 1: 7–72.

Gil', Stepan K. *Shest' let s V. I. Leninym: vospominaniia lichnogo Shofera Vladimira Il'icha Lenina*, 2nd ed. Moscow: Molodaia gvardiia, 1957.

Gilensen, V. M. "Neizvestnoe iz zhizni spetsshluzb: 'dvuikoi' pobedili sovetskie 'monarkhisty,'" *Voenno-istoricheskii zhurnal*, 2001, no. 6: 71–76.

Gililov, Solomon S. *V.I. Lenin, organizator Sovetskogo mnogonatsional'noe gosudarstvo*. Moscow: Politicheskaia literatura, 1960.

Gill, Graeme J. *Peasants and Government in the Russian Revolution*. New York: Barnes and Noble, 1979.

———. "Political Myth and Stalin's Quest for Authority in the Party," in *Authority, Power, and Policy*, ed. by T. H. Rigby. New York: St. Martin's, 1980, 98–117.

———. *The Origins of the Stalinist Political System*. New York: Cambridge University Press, 1990.

Gilliard, Pierre. *Thirteen Years at the Russian Court*. London: Hutchinson, 1921.

Gimpel'son, Efim G. *NEP i Sovetskaia politicheskaia sistema 20-e gody*.

Moscow: Institut Rossiiskoi istorii RAN, 2000.

——. *Sovetskie upravlentsy, 1917–1920 gg.* Moscow: Institut Rossiiskoi istorii RAN, 1998.

——. *Sovetskii rabochii klass, 1918–1920 gg.* Moscow: Nauka, 1974.

Gindin, Aron M., ed. *Kak bol'sheviki ovladeli gosudarstvennym bankom: fakty i dokumenty oktiabr'skikh dnei v Petrograde.* Moscow: Gosfinizdat, 1961.

Gintsberg, L. I. *Rabochee i kommunisticheskoe dvizhenie Germanii v bor'be protiv fashizma, 1929–1933.* Moscow: Nauka, 1978.

Gippius, Zinaida. *Siniaia kniga: Peterburgskii dnevnik, 1914–1918.* Belgrade: Radenkovich, 1929.

Gizzatullin, I. G., and Sharafutdinov, D. R., eds. *Mirsaid Sultan-Galiev: stati, vystupleniia, dokumenty.* Kazan: Tatarskoe knizhnoe izd-vo, 1992.

Gladkov, I. A. *Sovetskoe narodnoe khoziaistvo 1921–25 gg.* Moscow: Akademiia nauk SSSR, 1960.

Gladkov, Teodor. *Nagrada za vernost'—kazn'.* Moscow: Tsentrpoligraf, 2000.

Gleason, William. "Alexander Guchkov and the End of the Russian Empire," *Transactions of the American Philosophical Society,* New Series, 73/3 (1983): 1–90.

*Gleb Maksimilianovich Krzhizhanovskii: zhizn' i deiatel'nost'.* Moscow: Nauka, 1974.

Glebov, Serguei. "The Challenge of the Modern: The Eurasianist Ideology and Movement, 1920–1929." Phd diss., Rutgers University, 2004.

Glenny, M. V. "The Anglo-Soviet Trade Agreement, March 1921," *Journal of Contemporary History,* 5/2 (1970): 63–82.

Glinka, Ia. V. *Odinnadtsat' let v Gosudarstvennoi Dumy, 1906–1917: dnevnik i vospominaniia* (Moscow: NLO, 2001

Glurdzhidze, G. "Pamiatnye gody," *Rasskazy starykh rabochikh Zakavkaz'ia o velikom Staline.* Tblisi: Molodaia gvardiia, 1937: 17–21.

Gogokhiia, D. "Na vsiu zhizn' zapomnilis' eti dni," *Rasskazy starykh rabochikh Zakavkaz'ia o velikom Staline,* 2nd ed. Tblisi: Molodaia gvardiia, 1937: 7-16.

Gogolevskii, A. V., et al., eds. *Dekrety Sovetskoi vlast o Petrograde, 25 oktiabria (7 noiabria) 1917 g.—29 dekabria 1918 g.* Leningrad: Lenizdat, 1986.

Goikhbarg, A. G. *A Year in Soviet Russia: A Brief Account of the Legislative Work of 1917–1918.* London: People's Information Bureau, 1929.

——. *Sotsial'noe zakonodatel'stvo sovetskoi respubliki.* Moscow:

Narodnyi kommissariat iustitsii, 1919.

Goland, Iurii. "Currency Regulation in the NEP period," *Europe-Asia Studies,* 46/8 (1994): 1251–96.

——. *Diskusii ob ekonomicheskoi politike v gody denezhnoi reformy, 1921–1924.* Moscow: Ekonomika, 2006.

Golder, Frank A., ed. *Documents of Russian History, 1914–1917.* New York and London: The Century Co., 1927.

Goliakov, Ivan T. *Sbornik dokumentov po istorii ugolovnogo zakonodatel'stva SSSR i RSFSR, 1917–1952 gg.* Moscow: Iuridicheskaia literatura, 1953.

Golikov, Georgii N., ed. *Vladimir Il'ich Lenin: biograficheskaia khronika,* 12 vols. Moscow: Politicheskaia literatura, 1970–82.

Golinkov, D. L. *Krushenie antisovetskogo podpol'ia v SSSR,* 2 vols. Moscow: Politizdat, 1978.

*Golod 1921–1922: sbornik.* New York: Predstavitel'stvo Rossiskogo obshchestva Krasnogo kresta v Amerike, 1923.

Golovin, N. N. *Rossiiskaia kontrrevoliutsiia v 1917–1918 gg.,* 5 vols. Paris: Illustrirovaniia Rossiia, 1937.

——. *The Russian Army in the World War.* New Haven, CT: Yale University Press, 1931.

——. *Voennye usiliia Rossii v mirovoi voine,* 2 vols. Paris: Tovarishchestvo ob'edinennykh izdatelei, 1939.

Golub, P. A. "Kogda zhe byl uchrezhden institute voennykh kommissarov Krasnoi Armii?" *Voprosy istorii KPSS,* 1962, no. 4: 155–60.

Golubev, A. V. *Esli mir obrushitsia na nashu Respubliku': sovetskoe obshchestvo i vneshniaia ugroza.* Moscow: Kuchkovo pole, 2008.

——, et al., eds. *Direktivy glavnogo komandovaniia Krasnoi Armii, 1917–1920: sbornik dokumentov.* Moscow: Voenizdat, 1969.

Goncharov, V. L., ed. *Vozvyshenie Stalina: oborona Tsaritsyna.* Moscow: Veche, 2010.

Goodwin, Barry K., and Grennes, Thomas. "Tsarist Russia and the World Wheat Market," *Explorations in Economic History* 35 (1998): 405–30.

——. *Vladimir Ilich Lenin.* Leningrad: Gosizdat, 1924.

Gordienko, A. A. *Obrazovanie Turkestanskoi ASSR.* Moscow: Iuridicheskaia literatura, 1968.

Gordon, Jr., Harold J. *Hitler and the Beer Hall Putsch.* Princeton, NJ: Princeton University Press, 1972.

Gorgiladze, "Rasprostranenie marksizma v Gruzii," in *Ocherkii istorii Gruzii,* V (1990), ch, 15, edited by M. M. Gaprindashvili, and O. K. Zhordaniia. Tblisi: Metsniereba.

Goriachkin, F. T. *Pervyi russkii fashist: Petr Arkadievich Stolypin.* Kharbin: Merkurii, 1928.

Goriaeva, T. M. *Istoriia sovetskoi politicheskoi tsenzury: dokumenty i kommentarii.* Moscow: Rosspen, 1997.

Gor'kii, A. M. "Prazdnik shiitov," *Nizhegorodskii listok.* June 28, 1898.

——. *Nesvoevremennye mysli i rassuzhdenii o revoliutsii i kul'ture 1917–1918 gg.* Moscow: Interkontakt, 1990.

Gor'kii, Maksim. *Sobranie sochinenii,* 2nd ed., 25 vols. Moscow-Leningrad: Khudozhestvennaia literatura, 1933.

Gorky, Maxime. *Lénine et la paysan russe.* Paris: Editions du Sagittaire chez Simon Kra, 1925.

——. *Untimely Thoughts: Essays on Revolution, Culture, and the Bolsheviks, 1917–1918.* New York: P. S. Eriksson, 1968.

Gorlizki, Yoram, and Khlevniuk, Oleg. "Stalin and His Circle," in *The Cambridge History of Russia,* edited by Ronald Grigor Suny. New York: Cambridge University Press, 2006.

Gorlov, S. A. *Sovershenno sekretno: al'ians Moskva-Berlin, 1920–1933.* Moscow: Olma, 2001.

Gorlov, Seregi A. *Sovershenno sekretno, Moskva-Berlin 1920–1933: (Voenno-politicheskiie otnosheniia mezhdu SSSR i Germaniei).* Moscow: IVI RAN, 1999.

Gornyi, V. A., ed. *Natsional'nyi vopros v perekrestke mnenii, 20-e gody: dokumenty i materialy.* Moscow: Nauka, 1992.

Gorodetskii, E. N. *Rozhdenie Sovetskogo gosudarstva (1917–1918 gg.).* Moscow: Nauka, 1965.

Gorodetsky, Gabriel. "The Soviet Union and Britain's General Strike of May 1926," *Cahiers du monde russe et soviétique,* 17/2–3 (1976): 287–310.

——. *Precarious Truce: Anglo-Soviet Relations, 1924–1927.* New York: Cambridge University Press, 1977.

*Gosudarstvennyi apparat SSSR, 1924–1928 gg.* Moscow: Tsentral'noe statisticheskoe upravlenie SSSR, 1929.

*Gosudarstvennyi Sovet: stenograficheskie otchety,* thirteen sessions. St. Petersburg: Gosudarstvennaia tip., 1906–17.

Goulder, Alvin. "Stalinism: A Study of Internal Colonialism," *Telos,* no. 34 (1977–8): 5–48.

——. *The Two Marxisms: Contradictions and Anomalies in the Development of Theory.* London: Macmillan, 1980.

Gourko, Basil. *War and Revolution in Russia.* New York, Macmillan, 1919.

Graf, D. W. "Military Rule behind the Russian Front, 1914–1917: The Political Ramifications," *Jahrbücher für Geschichte Osteuropas,* 22/3 (1974): 390–411.

Grant, S. "The Peasant Commune in Russian Thought, 1861–1905." Phd diss., Harvard University, 1973.

Grant, W. Horsley. *A Medical Review of Soviet Russia*. London: British Medical Association, 1928.

Grave, Berta, ed. *Burzhuaziia nakanune fevral'skoi revoliutsii*. Moscow: Gosizdat, 1927.

*Grazhdanskaia voina v SSSR*. Moscow: Voenizdat, 1986.

Graziosi, Andrea. "'Building the First System of State Industry in History': Piatakov's VSNKh and the Crisis of the NEP, 1923–1926," *Cahiers du monde russe et soviétique*, 32/4 (1991): 539–80.

———. "Stalin's Antiworker Workerism, 1924–1931," *International Review of Social History*, 40/2 (1995): 223–58.

———. "State and Peasants in the Reports of the Political Police, 1918–1922," in *A New, Peculiar State: Explorations in Soviet History, 1917–1937*, edited by Andrea Graziosi. Westport, CT: Praeger, 2000.

———. "The New Archival Sources: Hypotheses for a Critical Assessment," *Cahiers du monde russe*, 40/1–2 (1999): 13–64.

———. *Bol'sheviki i krest'iane na Ukraine, 1918–1919 gg.* Moscow: Airo-XX, 1997.

Gregor, A. James. *The Fascist Persuasion in Politics*. Princeton, NJ: Princeton University Press, 1974.

———. *Young Mussolini and the Intellectual Origins of Fascism*. Berkeley: University of California Press, 1979.

Gregory, Paul R. "Grain Marketings and Peasant Consumption, Russia, 1885–1913," *Explorations in Economic History* 17/2 (1980): 135–64.

———. *Before Command: An Economic History of Russia from Emancipation to the First Five-Year Plan*. Princeton, NJ: Princeton University Press, 1994.

———. *Politics, Murder, and Love in Stalin's Kremlin: The Story of Nikolai Bukharin and Anna Larina*. Stanford, CA: Hoover Institution Press, 2010.

———. *Russian National Income, 1885–1913*. New York: Cambridge University Press, 1983.

———, and Naimark, Norman. *The Lost Politburo Transcripts: From Collective Rule to Stalin's Dictatorship*. New Haven, CT: Yale University Press, 2008.

Gregory, Paul, and Mokhtari, Manouchehr. "State Grain Purchases, Relative Prices, and the Soviet Grain Procurement Crisis," *Explorations in Economic History*, 30/2 (1993): 182–94.

Grigorov, Grigorii I. *Povoroty sud'by i proizvol: vospominaniia, 1905–1927 gody*. Moscow: OGI, 2005.

Grinevetskii, V. I. *Poslevoennye perspektivy Russkoi promyshlennosti*, 2nd ed. Moscow: Vserossiiskii tsentral'nyi soiuz potrebitel'skikh obshchestv, 1922.

Gromov, Evgenii S. *Stalin: iskusstvo i vlast'*. Moscow: EKSMO Algoritm, 2003.

Gronsky, Paul P. "The Zemstvo System and Local Government in Soviet Russia, 1917–1922," *Political Science Quarterly*, 38/4 (1923): 552–68.

———, and Astrov, Nicholas J. *The War and the Russian Government*. New Haven, CT: Yale University Press, 1920.

Gross, Jan. "War as Social Revolution," in *The Establishment of Communist Regimes in Eastern Europe, 1944–1949*, edited by Norman Naimark and Leonid Gibianskii. Boulder, CO: Westview Press, 1997.

Gruber, Helmut. *International Communism in the Era of Lenin: A Documentary History*. Ithaca, NY: Cornell University Press, 1967.

Grunt, A. Ia. *Moskva 1917–i: Revoliutsiia i kontrrevoliutsiia*. Moscow: Nauka, 1976.

"Gruzinskii ekzarkhat," *Pravoslavnaia bogoslovskaia entsiklopediia*, ed. by A. P. Lopukhin. St. Petersburg: Milshtein, Nevskaia, Rossiia, 1900–11.

Guins, George Constantine. *Sibir', soiuzniki i Kolchak, povorotnyi moment russkoi istorii, 1918–1920: vpechatleniia i mysli chlena Omskogo pravitel'stva*, 2 vols. Pekin: Russkaia dukhovnaia missiia, 1921.

Gul', Roman B. *Krasnye marshaly: Tukhachevskii, Voroshilov, Bliukher, Kotovskii*. Moscow: Molodaia gvardiia, 1990.

Gulevich, K., and Gassanova, R. "Iz istorii bor'by prodovol'stvennykh otriadov rabochikh za khleb i ukreplenie sovetskoi vlasti (1918–1920 gg.)," *Krasnyi arkhiv*, 89–90 (1938): 103–54.

Guliev, A. *Muzhestvennyi borets za kommunizm: Lado Ketskhoveli*. Baku: Arzernesir, 1953.

Gumz, Jonathan E. *The Resurrection and Collapse of Empire in Habsburg Serbia, 1914–1918*. New York: Cambridge University Press, 2009.

Gurko, Vladimir Iosifovich. *Features and Figures of the Past: Government and Opinion in the Reign of Nicholas II*. Stanford, CA: Stanford University Press, 1939.

Gurvich, Georgy S. *Istoriia sovetskoi konstitutsii*. Moscow: Sotsialisticheskaia akademiia, 1923.

Gusakova, Z. "Veril v luchshuiu zhizn' naroda," *Gazeta nedeli* [Saratov], November 20, 2012.

Gusev, K. V. *Krakh partii levykh eserov*. Moscow: Sotsial'no-ekonomicheskaia literatura, 1963.

Gushchin, N. Ia. *Sibirskaia derevnia na puti k sotsializmu: sotsial'no-ekonomicheskoe razvitie sibirskoi derevni v gody sotsialisticheskoi rekonstruktsii narodnogo khoziaistva 1926–1937 gg.* Novosibirsk: Nauka, sibirskoe otdelenie, 1973.

———, and Il'inykh, V. A. *Klassovaia bor'ba v sibir'skoi derevne, 1920-e-seredina 1930-x gg.* Novosibirsk: Nauka, 1987.

*Gvardeitsy Oktiabria: rol' korennykh narodov stran Baltii v ustanovlenii i ukreplenii bol'shevistskogo stroia*. Moscow: Indrik, 2009.

Gvosdev, Nikolas K. *Imperial Policies and Perspectives towards Georgia, 1760–1819*. New York: St. Martin's Press, 2000.

Haber, Ludwig F. *The Poisonous Cloud: Chemical Warfare in the First World War*. Oxford: Clarendon, 1986.

Häfner, Lutz. "The Assassination of Count Mirbach and the 'July Uprising' of the Left Socialist Revolutionaries in Moscow, 1918," *Russian Review* 50/3 (1991): 324–44.

———. *Die Partei der linken Sozialrevolutionäre in der russischen Revolution von 1917/18*. Cologne: Böhlau Verlag, 1994.

———. *Gesellschaft als lokale Veranstaltung: Die Wolgastädte Kazan und Saratov (1870–1914)*. Cologne: Böhlau Verlag, 2004.

Hahlweg, Werner. *Der Diktatfrieden von Brest-Litowsk 1918 und die bolschewistische Weltrevolution*. Münster: Aschendorff, 1960.

———. *Lenins Rückkehr nach Russland, 1917: die deutschen Akten*. Leiden: E. J. Brill, 1957.

Haimson, Leopold H. "The Mensheviks after the October Revolution, Part II: The Extraordinary Party Congress," *Russian Review*, 39/2 (1980): 181–207.

———. "The Problem of Social Stability in Urban Russia, 1905–17," *Slavic Review*, 23/4 (1964): 619–42, and 24/1 (1965): 1–22.

———. "The Workers' Movement After Lena: The dynamics of labor unrest in the wake of the Lena goldfield massacre (April 1912–July 1914)," in *Russia's Revolutionary Experience, 1905–1917: Two Essays*. New York: Columbia University Press, 2005.

———, ed. *The Mensheviks: From the Revolution of 1917 to the Second World War*. Chicago: University of Chicago Press, 1974.

Halévy, Élie. *The World Crisis of 1914–1918: An Interpretation*. Oxford: Clarendon, 1930.

Halfin, Igal. *Intimate Enemies: Demonizing the Opposition, 1918–1928*.

Pittsburgh: University of Pittsburgh Press, 2007.

Hall, Coryne. *Imperial Dancer: Mathilde Kschessinskaya and the Romanovs.* Thrupp, Stroud, Gloucestershire: Sutton, 2005.

Hamilton, Richard F., and Herwig, Holger H. *Decisions for War, 1914–1917.* New York: Cambridge University Press, 2004.

Hammond, Thomas T. "The Communist Takeover of Outer Mongolia: Model for Eastern Europe?," *Studies on the Soviet Union,* 11/4 (1971): 107–44.

———, and Farrell, Robert, eds. *The Anatomy of Communist Takeovers.* Munich: Institute for the Study of the USSR, 1971.

Harcave, Sidney. *Count Sergei Witte and the Twilight of Imperial Russia: A Biography.* Armonk, NY: M. E. Sharpe, 2004.

Hard, William. *Raymond Robins' Own Story.* New York and London: Harper & Bros., 1920.

Harding, Neil. *Leninism.* Durham, NC: Duke University Press, 1996.

Hardy, Eugene. "The Russian Soviet Federated Socialist Republic: The Role of Nationality in its Creation." Phd diss., University of California, Berkeley, 1955.

Harper, Samuel N. *Civic Training in Soviet Russia.* Chicago: University of Chicago Press, 1929.

———. *The New Electoral Law for the Russian Duma.* Chicago: University of Chicago Press, 1908.

———, and Harper, Paul V. *The Russia I Believe In.* Chicago: University of Chicago Press, 1945.

Harris, James. "Stalin as General Secretary: The Appointment Process and the Nature of Stalin's Power," in *Stalin: A New History,* ed. by Davies and Harris, 63–82.

Harrison, Margeurite. *Marooned in Moscow: The Story of an American Woman Imprisoned in Russia.* New York: Doran, 1921.

Harrison, Mark. "Prices in the Politburo, 1927: Market Equilibrium Versus the Use of Force," in *Lost Politburo Transcripts,* ed. by Gregory and Naimark, 224–46.

Hart, B. H. Liddell. *The Real War: 1914–18.* Boston: Little, Brown and Co., 1930.

Hasegawa, Tsuyoshi, "Crime, Police and Mob Justice in Petrograd During the Russian Revolution of 1917," in *Religious and Secular Forces in Late Tsarist Russia: Essays in Honor of Donald W. Treadgold,* edited by Charles E. Timberlake. Seattle: University of Washington Press, 1992.

———. *The February Revolution: Petrograd, 1917.* Seattle: University of Washington Press, 1981.

Haslam, Jonathan. *The Soviet Union and the Threat from the East, 1933–41: Moscow, Tokyo, and the Prelude of the Pacific War.* Houndmills, Basingstoke: Macmillan, 1992.

Headrick, Daniel R. *The Tools of Empire: Technology and European Imperialism in the Nineteenth Century.* New York: Oxford University Press, 1981.

Heenan, Louise Erwin. *Russian Democracy's Fatal Blunder: the Summer Offensive of 1917.* New York: Praeger of Greenwood, 1987.

Hegelsen, M. M. "The Origins of the Party-State Monolith in Soviet Russia: Relations between the Soviets and the Party Committees in the Central Provinces, October 1917–March 1921." Phd diss., University of New York at Stony Brook, 1980.

Heimo, M., and Tivel, A. *10 let Kominterna v resheniiakh i tsifrakh.* Moscow: Gosizdat, 1929.

Heinzen, James W. *Inventing a Soviet Countryside: State Power and the Transformation of Rural Russia, 1917–1929.* Pittsburgh: University of Pittsburgh Press, 2004.

Helfferich, Karl. *Der Weltkrieg,* 3 vols. Berlin: Ullstein & Co, 1919.

Hellie, Richard. "The Structure of Russian Imperial History," *History and Theory,* 44/4 (2005): 88–112.

Henderson, Arthur, and Dovgalevsky, V. "Anglo-Soviet Relations, 1918–1929," *Bulletin of International News,* 6/7 (October 10, 1929): 3–12.

Hennock, E. P. *The Origin of the Welfare State in England and Germany, 1850–1914: Social Policies Compared.* New York: Cambridge University Press, 2007.

Herwig, Holger H. "Germany and the 'Short War' Illusion: Toward a New Interpretation," *Journal of Modern History,* 66/3 (2002): 681–93.

Hewitson, Mark. "The Kaiserreich in Question: Constitutional Crisis in Germany before the First World War," *Journal of Modern History,* 73/4 (2001): 725–80.

———. *Germany and the Causes of the First World War.* New York: Berg, 2004.

Hickey, Paul C. "Fee-Taking, Salary Reform, and the Structure of State Power in Late Qing China, 1909–1911," *Modern China,* 17/3 (1991): 389–417.

Hilger, Gustav, and Meyer, A. G. *The Incompatible Allies: A Memoir-History of German-Soviet Relations, 1918–1941.* New York: Macmillan, 1953.

Hill, George. *Go Spy the Land.* London: Cassell, 1932.

Hillis, Faith. "Between Empire and Nation: Urban Politics, Violence, and Community in Kiev, 1863–1907." Phd diss., Yale University, 2009.

Himmer, Robert. "First Impressions Matter: Stalin's Brief Initial Encounter with Lenin, Tammerfors 1905," *Revolutionary Russia,* 14/2 (2001): 73–84.

———. "Soviet Policy toward Germany during the Russo-Polish War, 1920," *Slavic Review,* 35/4 (1976): 665–82.

———. "The Transition from War Communism to the New Economic Policy: An Analysis of Stalin's Views," *Russian Review,* 53/4 (1994): 515–29.

Hindus, Maurice. *The Russian Peasant and the Revolution.* New York: Holt, 1920.

Hingley, Ronald. *The Russian Secret Police: Muscovite, Imperial Russian, and Soviet Political Security Operations.* New York; Simon & Schuster, 1971.

Hirsch, Francine. *Empire of Nations: Ethnographic Knowledge and the Making of the Soviet Union.* Ithaca, NY: Cornell University, 2005.

*Hitler Trial Before the People's Court in Munich, The.* Arlington, VA: University Publications of America, 1976.

Hoare, S. *The Fourth Seal: The End of a Russian Chapter.* London: W. Heinemann Ltd, 1930.

Hobsbawm, Eric. *Age of Extremes: A History of the World, 1914–1991.* New York: Pantheon Books, 1994.

Hoch, Steven L. *Serfdom and Social Control in Russia: Petrovskoje, a Village in Tambov.* Chicago: University of Chicago, 1986.

Hochschild, Adam. *King Leopold's Ghost: A Story of Greed, Terror, and Heroism in Colonial Africa.* New York: Houghton Mifflin, 1998.

Hoetzsch, Otto. *Russland.* Berlin: G. Reimer, 1915.

Hoffmann, Max. *War Diaries and other Papers,* 2 vols. London: M. Secker, 1929.

Hollander, Paul. *Political Pilgrims: Western Intellectuals in Search of the Good Society.* New Brunswick, NJ: Transaction, 2004.

Holmes Larry E., and Burgess, William. "Scholarly Voice or Political Echo? Soviet Party History in the 1920s," *Russian History/Histoire Russe,* 9/1–2 (1982): 378–98.

Holquist, Peter. "'Information Is the Alpha and Omega of Our Work': Bolshevik Surveillance in Its Pan-European Context," *Journal of Modern History,* 69/3 (1997): 415–50.

———. "Anti-Soviet *Svodki* from the Civil War: Surveillance as a Shared Feature of Russian Political

Culture," *Russian Review*, 56/3 (1997): 445–50.

———. "Dilemmas of a Progressive Administrator: Baron Boris Nolde," *Kritika*, 7/2 (2006): 241–73.

———. "State Violence as Technique: The Logic of Violence in Soviet Totalitarianism," in *Modernity and Population Management*, edited by Amir Weiner. Stanford, CA: Stanford University Press, 2003.

———. "Violent Russia, Deadly Marxism? Russia in the Epoch of Violence, 1905–21," *Kritika*, 4/3 (2003): 627–52.

———. *Making War, Forging Revolution: Russia's Continuum of Crisis, 1914–1921*. Cambridge, MA: Harvard University Press, 2002.

Hone, Joseph N., and Dickinson, Page L. *Persia in Revolution: With Notes of Travel in the Caucasus*. London: T. Fisher Unwin, 1910.

Honig, Jan Willem. "The Idea of Total War: from Clausewitz to Ludendorff," in *The Pacific War as Total War*. Tokyo: NIDS International Forum on War History, National Institute for Defence Studies, 2012.

Hooker, James R. "Lord Curzon and the 'Curzon Line,'" *Journal of Modern History*, 30/2 (1958).

Horak, Stephen, ed. *Poland's International Affairs, 1919–1960: A Calendar of Treaties, Conventions, and Other International Acts, with Annotations, References, and Selections from Documents and Texts of Treaties*. Bloomington: Indiana University Press, 1964.

Horne, John, ed. *A Companion to World War I*. Chichester, U.K., and Malden, MA: Wiley-Blackwell, 2010.

Horney, Karen. *Neurosis and Human Growth: The Struggle toward Self-Realization*. New York: W. W. Norton, 1950.

———. *The Neurotic Personality of our Time*. New York: W. W. Norton, 1937.

Hosking, Geoffrey A. *The Russian Constitutional Experiment: Government and Duma, 1907–1914*. New York: Cambridge University Press, 1973.

———. "Patronage and the Russian State," *Slavonic and East European Review*, 78 (2000): 306–13.

———. *Russia: People and Empire, 1552–1917*. Cambridge, MA: Harvard University Press, 1997.

Hounshell, David. *From the American System to Mass Production, 1800–1932*. Baltimore, MD: John Hopkins University Press, 1984.

Howard, Michael. *The Causes of Wars*. Cambridge, MA: Harvard University Press, 1983.

———. *The First World War*. New York: Oxford University Press, 2002.

Hughes, J. R. "The Irkutsk Affair: Stalin, Siberian Politics and the End of NEP," *Soviet Studies*, vol. 41/2 (1989): 228–53.

———. *Stalin, Siberia, and the Crisis of the New Economic Policy*. New York: Cambridge University Press, 1991.

———. "Patrimonialism and the Stalinist System: the Case of S. I. Syrtsov," *Europe-Asia Studies*, 48/4 (1996): 551–68.

Hughes, Lindsey. *Peter the Great: A Biography*. New Haven, CT: Yale University Press, 2002.

Hull, Isabel V. *Absolute Destruction: Military Culture and the Practices of War in Imperial Germany*. Ithaca, NY: Cornell University Press, 2005.

———. *The Entourage of Kaiser Wilhelm II, 1888–1918*. New York: Cambridge University Press, 1982.

Hullinger, Edward Hale. *The Reforging of Russia*. New York: E. P. Dutton, 1925.

Hunczak, Taras, ed. *The Ukraine, 1917–1921: A Study in Revolution*. Cambridge, MA: Harvard Ukrainian Research Institute, 1977.

Hunt, Lynn. *Politics, Culture, and Class in the French Revolution*. Berkeley: University of California Press, 1984.

Hynes, A. L., et al., eds. *Letters of the Tsar to the Tsaritsa, 1914–1917*. New York: Dodd, Mead, 1929.

*Iakov Mikhailovich Sverdlov: sbornik vospominanii i statei*. Leningrad: Gosizdat, 1926.

Iakubovskaia, S. I. *Stroitel'stvo soiuznogo sovetskogo sotsialisticheskogo gosudarstva, 1922–1925 gg*. Moscow: Akademiia nauk SSSR, 1960.

Iaroslavsky, E. *O Tovarishche Staline*. Moscow: OGIZ, 1939.

Iarov, S. V. "Krest'ianskoe vol'nenie na Severo-Zapade Sovetskoi Rossii v 1918–1919 gg.," in *Krest'ianovedenie, teoriia, istoriia, sovremennost': ezhegodnik*, edited by P. Danilov and T. Shanin. Moscow: Aspekt, 1996.

Iazhborovskaia, I. S., and Papsadanova, V. C. *Rossiia i Pol'sha: sindrom voiny 1920 g*. Moscow: Academia, 2005.

Ignat'ev, Anatolii V. *Russko-angliiskie otnosheniia nakanune Oktiabr'skoi revoliutsii, fevral'-oktiabr' 1917 g*. Moscow: Nauka, 1966.

Ignat'ev, Gennadii S. *Moskva v pervyi god proletarskoi diktatury*. Moscow: Nauaka, 1975.

———. *Oktiabr' 1917 goda v Moskve*. Moscow: Nauka, 1964.

*III Sibir'skaia partiinaia kraevaia konferentsiia VKP (b): stenograficheskii otchet*. Novosibirsk: Sibkraikom VKP (b) , 1927.

Ikonnikova, I. P., and Ugrovatov, A. P. "Stalinskaia repetitsiia nastupleniia

na krest'ianstvo," *Voprosy istorii KPSS*, 1991, no. 1: 68–81.

Il'inykh, Vladimir A. *Khroniki khlebnogo fronta: zagotovitel'nye kampanii kontsa 1920-kh gg. v Sibiri*. Moscow: Rosspen, 2010.

Il'in-Zhenevskii, Aleksandr F. "Nakanune oktiabria," *Krasnaia letopis'*, 1926, no. 4 (19): 5–26.

———. *The Bolsheviks in Power: Reminiscences of the Year 1918*. London: New Park, 1984.

Ilizarov, B. S. *Tainaia zhizn' Stalina*. Moscow: Veche, 2002.

Ilizarov, S. "Stalin, Strikhi k portretu na fone ego biblioteki i arkhiva," *Novaia i noveishaia istoriia*, 2000, no. 3: 182–205, and no. 4: 152–66.

Ioffe, A. A. (V. Krymskii). *Genuezskaia Konferentsiia*. Moscow: Krasnaia nov', 1922.

———. *Mirnye peregovory v Brest-Litovske s 22/9 dekabria 1917 g. po 3 marta (18 fevralia) 1918 g*. Moscow: NKID, 1922.

Ioffe, Genrikh. "Trest': legendy i fakty," *Novyi zhurnal*, 2007, no. 2047.

———. *Revoliutsiia i sud'ba Romanovykh*. Moscow: Respublika, 1992.

Ioffe, Mariia. *Odna noch': povest' o pravde*. New York: Khronika, 1978.

Ioffe, Nadezhda. *Vremia nazad: moia zhizn', maia sud'ba, moia epokha*. Moscow: Biologicheskie nauki, 1992.

*Iosif Stalin v ob'iatiakh sem'i: iz lichnogo arkhiva*. Moscow: Edition q, 1993.

Iremashvili, Joseph. *Stalin und die Tragödie Georgiens*. Berlin: Verfasser, 1932.

Iroshnikov, M. P. "K voprosu o slome burzzhuaznoi gosudarstvennoi mashiny v Rossii," in *Problemy gosudarstvennogo stroitel'stva v pervye gody Sovetskoi vlasti: sbornik statei*. Leningrad: Nauka, 1973, 46-66.

———. *Predsedatel' soveta narodnykh komissarov V. I. Ul'ianov (Lenin): ocherki gosudarstvennoi deiatel'nosti v 1917–1918 gg*. Leningrad: Nauka, 1974.

———. *Sozdanie sovetskogo tsentral'nogo gosudarstvenogo apparata*. Moscow: Nauka, 1966.

Isaacs, Harold R. *The Tragedy of the Chinese Revolution*, rev. ed. Stanford, CA: Stanford University Press, 1951.

Isaev, V. I., and Ugrovatov, A. P. *Pravokhanitel'nye organy Sibiri v sisteme upravleniia regionom, 1920-e gg*. Novosibirsk: Nuaka-Tsentr, 2006.

Isbakh, Aleksandr A. *Tovarishch Absoliut*. Moscow: Znanie, 1963, 1973.

Iskenderov, M. S. *Iz istorii bor'by kommunisticheskoi partii Azerbaidzhana za pobedu sovetskoi vlasti*.

Baku: Azerbaidzhanskii gosizdat, 1958.

Iskhod k vostoku. Sofia: Rossiisko-Bolgarsko knigo, 1921.

Iskrov, M. V. "O razrabotke V. I. Leninym prodovol'stvennoi politiki 1918 g.," *Voprosy istorii KPSS*, 1963, no.7: 74–86.

Israelin, V. L. "Neopravdavshiisia prognoz graf Mirbakha: Iz istorii antisovetskoi politki germanskogo imperializma v 1917–1918 gg.," *Novaia i noveishaia istoriia*, 1967, no. 6: 56–65.

*Istoricheskie mesta Tblisi: putevoditel' po mestam sviazannym s zhizn'iu i deiatel'nost'iu I. V. Stalina.* 2nd ed. Tblisi: GF IML, 1944.

*Istoricheskii ocherk razvitiia tserkovnykh shkol za istekshee dvadtsatipiatiletie, 1884–1909.* St. Petersburg: Uchilishchnyi sovet pri Sviateishem synode, 1909.

*Istoriia grazhdanskoi voiny v SSSR*, 5 vols. Moscow: Gosizdat, 1935–60.

*Istoriia kommunisticheskoi partii Sovetskogo Soiuza.* Moscow: Politizdat, 1970.

*Istoriia Moskvy*, 6 vols. Moscow: Akademiia nauk, 1952–59.

*Istoriia natsional'no-gosudarstvennogo stroitel'stva v SSSR 1917–1972*, 2 vols. Moscow: Mysl', 1972.

Iswolsky, A. P. *Recollections of a Foreign Minister.* New York: Doubleday, 1921.

*Itogi vypolneniia pervogo piatiletnego plana razvitiia narodnogo khoziaistva Soiuza SSR.* Moscow: Gosplan SSSR, 1933.

*Iubileinaia vystavka Krasnykh Armii i Flota, 1918–1923: kratkii putevoditel'.* Moscow: Muzei Krasnykh Armii i Flota, 1923.

Iudin, V. N. *Lenin pisal v Tsaritsyn: Dokumental'no-publitsistkie ocherki.* Volgograd: Nizhne-Volskoe knizhnoe izdatel'stvo, 1985.

Iuldashbaev, B. Kh., ed. *Obrazovanie Bashkirskoi Avtonomnoi Sovetskoi Sotsialisticheskoi Respubliki: Sbomik dokumentov i materialov.* Ufa: Bashkirskoe knizhnoe izdatel'stvo, 1959.

Iurovskii, V. E. "Arkhitektor denezhnoi reform 1922–1924," *Voprosy istorii*, 1995, no. 2: 138–43.

Iurtaeva, E. *Gosudarstvennyi sovet v Rossii (1906–1917 gg.).* Moscow: Editorial URSS, 2001.

Iuzefovich, L. *Samoderzhets pustyni: fenomenon sud'by barona R. F. Ungern-Shternberga.* Moscow: Ellis-Bak, 1993.

*Iuzhnyi front (mai 1918–mart 1919), bor'ba sovetskogo naroda s interventami i belogvardeitsami na iuge Rossii: sbornik dokumentov.* Rostov-na-Donu: Rostovskoe knizhnoe izd-vo, 1962.

Ivanov, Anatolii. *Neizvestnyi Dzer-zhinskii: fakty i vymysly.* Minsk: Valev, 1994.

Ivanov, I. E. *Podpol'nye tipografii Leninskoi "Iskry" v Rossii: 1901–1903 gody.* Kishinev: Shtintsa, 1962.

Ivanov, N. Ia. *Kornilovshcina i ee razgrom.* Leningrad: Leingradskii universitet, 1965.

Ivanov, Vsevolod M., and Shmelev, A. N. *Leninizm i ideino-politicheskii razgrom trotskizma.* Leningrad: Lenizdat, 1970.

Ivanova, Galina M. *Gulag v sisteme totalitarnogo gosudarstva.* Moscow: Moskovskii obshchestvennyi nauchnyi fond, 1997.

Ivanova, L. V. "Institut Marksa-Engelsa-Lenina: Komissiia po istorii oktiabr'skoi revliutsii i istorii kommunisticheskoi partii (Istpart)," in *Ocherki istorii istoricheskoi nauki v SSSR*, edited by M. V. Nechkina. Moscow: Nauka, 1966.

Ivanovich, P. "Finliandskie shpioni: delo Pauku i drugie v Voennom tribunale Leningradskogo voenogo okruga," *Sud idet* [Leningrad], 1928, no. 4.

Iwański, Gereon, et al., eds. *II Zjazd Komunistycznej Partii Rabotniczej Polski, 19.IX–2.X.1923: Protokoły, Obrad, i Uchwały.* Warsaw: Książka i Wiedza, 1968.

*I Leningradskaia oblastnaia konferentsiia VKP (b), 15–19 noiabria 1927 goda: stenografinlcheskii otchet.* Leningrad: VKP (b), 1929.

*III vserossiiskii s'ezd sovetov rabochikh, soldatskikh i krest'ianskikh deputatov.* Petrograd: TsIK, 1918.*IV Vsemirnyi kongress Kommunisticheskogo Internatsionala, 5 noiabria-3 dekabria 1922 g.: izbrannye doklady, rechi i rezoliutsii.* Petrograd: Gosizdat, 1923.

*IV Vserossiikii s'ezd sovetov rabochikh, soldatskikh, krestianskikh, i kazach'ikh deputatov: Stenografischeskii otchet.* Moscow: Gosizdat, 1919.

*IX s'ezd RKP (b), mart-aprel' 1920: Protokoly.* Moscow: Politicheskaia literatura, 1960.

*IX konferentsiia RKP (b), sentiabr' 1920 goda: protokoly.* Moscow: Politcheskaia literatura, 1972.

"Iz besedy tovarishcha Stalina s nemetskim pisatelem Emilem Liudvigom, 13 Dekabria 1931 g.," *Bol'shevik*, 1932, no. 8: 33–42.

*Iz istorii grazhdanskoi voiny v SSSR: sbornik dokumentov i materialov*, 3 vols. Moscow: Sovetskaia Rossiia, 1960–1.

"Iz istorii kollektivizatsii 1928 god: poezdka Stalina v Sibir'," *Izvestiia TsK KPSS*, 1991, no. 5: 193–204, no. 6: 202–16, no. 7: 179–86.

*Iz istorii VChK: sbornik dokumentov, 1917–1921 gg.* Moscow: Politizdat, 1958.

Iziumov, Aleksei S., ed. *Khleb i revoliutsiia: prodovol'stvennaia politika kommunisticheskoi partii i sovetskogo pravitel'stva v 1917–1922 gg.* Moscow: Sovetskaia Rossiia, 1972.

Izmozik, Vladlen S. *Glaza i ushi rezhima: gosudarstvennyi politicheskii kontrol' za naseleniem sovetskoi Rossii v 1918–1928 godakh.* St. Petersburg: Sankt-Peterburgskii universitet ekonomiki i finansov, 1995.

"Iz perepiski E. D. Stasovoi i K. T. Novgorodtsevoi (Sverdlovoi), mart-dekaibr' 1918 g.," *Voprosy istorii*, 1956, no.10: 91–2.

Izvolsky, Alexander. *The Memoirs of Alexander Izwolsky.* London: Hutchinson, 1920.

"Iz vospominaniia I. I. Vatsetisa," *Voenno-istoricheskii zhurnal*, 1962, no. 4.

"Iz zaiavleniia uchashchiksia tifliskoi dukhovnoi seminarii ekzarkhu Gruzii, 1 dekabria 1893," in *Lado Ketsokhevli: sbornik dokumentov i materialov.* Tblisi: Sabchota sakartvelo, 1969.

Jablonowski, Horst. "Die Stellungnahme der russischen Parteien zur Aussenpolitik der Regierung von der russisch-englischen Verständigung bis zum ersten Weltkrieg," in *Forschungen zur osteuropäischen Geschichte*, 5, (1957): 60-92.

Jacobson, Jon. "Is There a New International History of the 1920s?" *American Historical Review*, 88/3 (1983): 617–45.

———. *When the Soviet Union Entered World Politics.* Berkeley: University of California Press, 1994.

Jahn, Hubertus F. *Patriotic Culture in Russia during World War I.* Ithaca, NY: Cornell University Press, 1995.

Janos, Andrew C., and Slottman, William, eds. *Revolution in Perspective: Essays on the Hungarian Soviet Republic of 1919.* Berkeley: University of California Press, 1971.

Jansen, Marc. *A Show Trial Under Lenin: The Trial of the Socialist Revolutionaries, Moscow, 1922.* The Hague and Boston: M. Nijhoff and Kluwer, 1982.

Jarausch, Konrad H. "Cooperation or Intervention? Kurt Riezler and the Failure of German Ostpolitik, 1918," *Slavic Review*, 31/2 (1972): 381–98.

———. *The Enigmatic Chancellor: Bethmann Hollweg and the Hubris of Imperial Germany.* New Haven, CT: Yale University Press, 1972.

Jasny, Naum. *The Socialized Agriculture of the USSR: Plans and Performance.* Stanford, CA: Stanford University Press, 1949.

Jászi, Oscar. *The Dissolution of the Habsburg Monarchy.* Chicago: University of Chicago Press, 1929.

Jaurès, Jean. *L'Organisation socialiste de la France: l'armée nouvelle*. Paris: L'Humanité, 1911.

Jersild, Austin. *Orientalism and Empire: North Caucasus Mountain Peoples and the Georgian Frontier, 1845–1917*. Montreal: McGill-Queen's University Press, 2002.

Jervis, Robert. *Perception and Misperception in International Relations*. Princeton, NJ: Princeton University Press, 1976.

Joffe, Maria. *One Long Night: A Tale of Truth*. London: Clapham, 1978.

Joffe, Nadezhda. *Back in Time: My Life, My Fate, My Epoch*. Oak Park, MI: Labor Publications, 1995.

Johnson, Gaynor, ed. *Locarno Revisited: European Diplomacy 1920–1929*. London: Routledge, 2004.

Johnson, Simon, and Temin, Peter. "The Macroeconomics of NEP," *Economic History Review*, 46/4 (1993): 750–67.

Jones, David R. "Imperial Russia's Armed Forces at War, 1914–1917: An Analysis of Combat Effectiveness" (1986), in *Military Effectiveness*, ed. by Millet, A. R. and Murray, W., 3 vols. Boston: Allen and Unwin, 1988, I: 249–328.

———. "Nicholas II and the Supreme Command: An Investigation of Motives," *Study Group on the Russian Revolution: Sbornik*, no. 11 (1985): 47–83.

Jones, Stephen F. "Russian Imperial Administration and the Georgian Nobility: The Georgian Conspiracy of 1832," *Slavonic and East European Review*, 65/1 (1987): 55–76.

———. "The Non-Russian Nationalities," in *Society and Politics in the Russian Revolution*, edited by Robert Service. New York: St. Martin's Press, 1992.

———. *Socialism in Georgian Colors: The European Road to Social Democracy, 1883–1917*. Cambridge, MA: Harvard University Press, 2005.

———. "The Establishment of Soviet Power in Trascaucasia: The Case of Georgia, 1921–1928," *Soviet Studies*, 40/4: 616–639.

Jordania, N. N. "Staline, L'Écho de la lutte" [October 1936], unpublished manuscript in Hoover Institution Archives, Boris Nicolaevsky Collection, box 144, folder 3, 1–2.

*Journal intime de Nicholas II (juillet 1914–juillet 1918)*. Paris: Payot, 1934.

Jowitt, Ken. *New World Disorder: The Leninist Extinction*. Berkeley: University of California Press, 1992.

Kabuzan, Vladimir M. *Russkie v mire: dinamika chislennosti i rasseleniia (1719–1989): formirovanie etnicheskikh i politicheskikh granits russkogo naroda*. St. Petersburg: BLITS, 1996.

———. *Izmenenie v razmeshchenii naseleniia Rossii v XVIII-pervoi polovine XIX vv.* Moscow: Nauka, 1971.

Kacharava, Iu. M., ed. *Bor'ba za uprochenie sovetskoi vlasti v Gruzii: sbornik dokumentov i materialov (1921–1925 gg.)* Tblisi: Sabchota Sakartvelo, 1959.

Kaganovich, L. M. *Pamiatnye zapiski rabochego, kommunista-bol'shevika, profsoiuznogo, partinogo i sovetsko-gosudarstvennogo rabotnika*. Moscow: Vagrius, 1996.

Kahan, Arcadius. *The Plow, The Hammer and the Knout: An Economic History of Eighteenth-Century Russia*. Chicago: University of Chicago Press, 1985.

Kahn, David. *The Codebreakers: The Story of Secret Writing*. New York: Macmillan, 1967.

*Kak russkii narod zavoeval svobodu: Obzor revoliutsionnykh sobytii*. Petrograd: S. Samoilov, 1917.

Kakurin, N. E. *Kak srazhalas' revoliutsiia*, 2 vols. Moscow-Leningrad: Gosizdat, 1925-6.

———. *Russko-pol'skaia kampaniia 1918–1920: politiko-strategicheskii ocherk*. Moscow: Vysshii voenno-redaktsionnyi sovet, 1922.

———. *Razlozhenie armii v 1917 godu*. Moscow-Leningrad: Gosizdat, 1925.

———, and Melikov, V. A. *Voina s belopoliakami 1920 goda*. Moscow: Voenizdat, 1925.

Kalinin, M. I. *Stalin: sbornik statei k piatidesitiletiu so dnia rozhdeniia*. Moscow-Leningrad: Gosizdat, 1929.

Kalyvas, Stathis N. *The Logic of Violence in Civil War*. New York: Cambridge University Press, 2006.

Kamenev, Lev B. *Bor'ba za mir: otchet o mirnykh peregovorakh v Breste*. Petrograd: Zhizn' i znanie, 1918

———. *Stat'i i rechi*. Leningrad: Gosizdat, 1925.

Kamenev, Lev. *Mezhdu dvumia revoliutsiiami: sbornik statei*, 2nd ed. Moscow: Novaia Moskva, 1923.

Kaminskii, V. and Vereshchagin, I. "Detstvo i iunost' vozhdia." *Molodaia Gvardiia*, no 12. 1939.

Kann, S. K. "Opyt zheleznodorozhnogo stroitel'stva v Amerike i proektirovanie Transsiba," in *Zarubezhnye ekonomicheskie i kul'turnye sviazi Sibiri (XVIII-XX vv.)*, edited by L. M. Goriushkin. Novosibirsk: RAN, Sibirskoe otdelenie, 1995.

Kanonenko, Veronika. "Kto ubil Mikhail Frunze," *Shpion*, 1994, no. 1 (3): 78–81.

Kantor, Iulia. *Voina i mir Mikhaila Tukhachevskogo*. Moscow: Ogonek, 2005.

Kantor, R. "K istorii chernykh kabinetov," *Katorga i ssylka*, XXXVII (1927).

Kantorovich, V., and Zaslavskii, D. *Khronika fevral'skoi revoliutsii: fevral'–mai 1917*. Moscow: Byloe, 1924.

Kapchinskii, Oleg. *Gosbezopasnosti iznutri: Natsional'nyi i sotsial'nyi sostav*. Moscow: Iauza-Eksmo, 2005.

Kapitsa, Mikhail S. *Sovetsko-kitaiskie otnosheniia*. Moscow: Politicheskaia literatura, 1958.

Kappeler, Andreas. *The Russian Empire: A Multiethnic History*. Harlow, U.K.: Longman, 2001.

Karaeva, T. F., ed. *Direktivy komandovaniia frontov krasnoi armii, 1917–1922 gg.: sbornik dokumentov*, 4 vols. Moscow: Voenizdat, 1971–8.

Karaganov, A. V. *Lenin: sobranie fotografii i kinokadrov*, 2nd ed., 2 vols. Moscow: Iskusstvo, 1980.

Kara-Murz, G. S., et al. eds. *Strategiia i taktika Kominterna v natsional'no-kolonial'noi revoliutsii na primere Kitaia: sbornik dokumentov*. Institut MKh i MP, 1934.

Karl, Rebecca. *Staging the World: Chinese Nationalism at the Turn of the Twentieth Century*. Durham, NC: Duke University Press, 2002.

Karliner, M. M. "Angliia i Petrogradskaia konferentsiia Antanty 1917 goda," in *Mezhdunarodnye otnosheniia, politika, diplomatiia XVI-XX veka: Sbornik statei k 80-letiiu akademika I. M. Maiskogo*, edited by V. V. Al'tman. Moscow: Nauka, 1964.

Karpinskii, V. A. "Vladimir Il'ich za granitsei v 1914–1917 gg.," in *Zapiski instituta Lenina*, 3 vols. Moscow: Institute Lenina pri TsK VKP (b), 1927–8.

Karpov, Nikolai. *Krest'ianskoe dvizhenie v revoliutsii 1905 goda v dokumentakh*. Moscow: Gosizdat, 1926.

Karpovich, Michael. "The Russian Revolution of 1917," *Journal of Modern History*, 2/2 (1930): 258–80.

———. "Two Types of Russian Liberalism: Maklakov and Miliukov," in *Continuity and Change in Russian and Soviet Thought*, edited by Ernest J. Simmons. Cambridge, MA: Harvard University Press, 1955.

Kartevskii, S. I. *Iazyk, voina i revoliutsiia*. Berlin: Russkoe universal'noe izdatel'stvo, 1923.

Kartunova, A. I. "Kitaiskii vopros v perepiske G. V. Chicherin i L. M. Karakhana," *Novaia i noveishaia istoriia*, 1998, no. 6: 3–18.

———. "Novyi vzgliad na razryv s Chan Kaishi," *Vostok*, 1997, no. 1.

*Katalog Tiflisskoi deshevoi biblioteki*, chast' 1. Tiflis, 1896.

Katkov, George. "German Foreign

Office Documents on Financial Support to the Bolsheviks in 1917," *International Affairs*, 32/3 (1956): 181–9.

———. *Russia, 1917: The February Revolution*. New York: Harper & Row, 1967.

———. *The Kornilov Affair: Kerensky and the Breakup of the Russian Army*. New York: Longman, 1980.

Katsenellenbaum, S. S. *Russian Currency and Banking, 1914–1924*. London: P. S. King, 1925.

Kaufman, A. E. "Cherty iz zhizni gr. S. Iu. Vitte," *Istoricheskii vestnik*, no. 140 (April 1915).

Kautsky, Karl. *Das Erfurter Programm in seinem grundsätzlichen Teil erläutert*. Berlin-Bad-Godesberg: Verlag J.H.W. Dietz Nachf., 1974.

———. *Georgia, A Social-Democratic Peasant Republic: Impressions and Observations*. London: International Bookshops, 1921.

*Kavkaz: Opisanie kraia i kratkii istoricheskii ocherk ego prisoedineniia k Rossii*, 3rd ed. Moscow: I. V. Leont'eva, 1911.

*Kavkaz: spravochnaia kniga storozhila*, 2nd ed., chast' 1. Tiflis: E. G. Meskhi, 1889.

Kavraiskii, V., and Nusinov, I. *Klassy i klassovaia bor'ba v sovremennoi derevne*. Novosibirsk: Sibkraiizdat, 1929.

Kavtaradze, A. G. *Voennye spetsialisty na sluzhbe Respubliki sovetov, 1917–1920 g*. Moscow: Nauka, 1988.

Kazemzadeh, Firuz. *The Struggle for Transcaucasia, 1917–1921*. New York: Philosophical Library, 1951.

Keegan, John. *The First World War*. New York: Knopf, 1999.

Keep, John L. H. *The Russian Revolution: A Study in Mass Mobilization*. New York: W. W. Norton, 1976.

———. *The Rise of Social Democracy in Russia*. Oxford: Clarendon, 1963.

———. "1917: The Tyranny of Paris over Petrograd," *Soviet Studies*, 20/1 (1968–9): 22–35.

———. "Light and Shade in the History of the Russian Administration," *Canadian-American Slavic Studies*, 6/1 (1972): 1–9.

———. *Soviet Studies*, 18/3 (1967): 376–80.

———, ed. and trans. *The Debate on Soviet Power: Minutes of the All-Russian Central Executive Committee, Second Convocation*. Oxford, 1979.

Keiger, John F. V. *Raymond Poincaré*. New York: Cambridge University Press, 2002.

Keller, V., and Romanenko, I. *Pervye itogi agrarnoi reformy*. Voronezh: Gosizdat, Voronezhskoe otdelenie, 1922.

Keller, Werner. *Ost minus West = Null: der Aufbau Russlands durch den Western*. Munich-Zurich: Drömersche Verlagsanstalt Th. Knauer Nach folger, 1960. Translated as *East minus West = Zero: Russia's Debt to the Western World, 1862–1962*. New York: Putnam, 1962.

Ken, O. H. *Mobilizatsionnoe planirovanie i politicheskie resheniia, konets 1920-seredina 1930-kh godov*. St. Petresburg: Evropeiskii universitet, 2002.

Ken, O. N., and Rupasov, A. I. *Politbiuro TsK VKP (b) i otnosheniia SSSR s zapadnymi sosednimi gosudarstvami (konets 20-30-kh gg.): problemy, dokumenty, opyt kommentariia*. St. Petersburg: Evropeiskii dom, 2000.

Kendirbai, Gulnar. "The Alash Movement," in *The Turks*, edited by Hasan Celal Guzel et al. Ankara: Yeni Turkiye, 2002.

Kenez, Peter. "Changes in the Social Composition of the Officer Corps during World War I," *Russian Review*, 31/4 (1972): 369–75.

———. "The Ideology of the White Movement," *Soviet Studies*, 32/1 (1980): 58–83.

———. *Civil War in South Russia*, 2 vols. Berkeley: University of California Press, 1971, 1977.

———. *The Birth of the Propaganda State: Social Methods of Mass Mobilization, 1917–1929*. New York: Cambridge University Press, 1985.

Kennan, George F. "The Sisson Documents," *Journal of Modern History*, 37/2 (1956): 130–54.

———. *Russia and the West Under Lenin and Stalin*. Boston: Little, Brown, 1961.

———. *Russia Leaves the War*. Princeton, NJ: Princeton University Press, 1956.

———. "The Breakdown of the Tsarist Autocracy," in *Revolutionary Russia*, Richard Pipes ed., 1–15.

———. *The Fateful Alliance: France, Russia and the Coming of the First World War*. New York: Pantheon, 1984.

Kennedy, David. *Over Here: The First World War and American Society*. New York: Oxford University Press, 1980.

Kennedy, Paul M. *The Rise of the Anglo-German Antagonism, 1860–1914*. Boston: George Allen and Unwin, 1980.

Kennel, Ruth. "The New Innocents Abroad," *American Mercury*, XVII (May 1929).

Kerenskii, A. F. *Delo Kornilova*. Ekaterinoslav, 1918. Translated as *The Prelude to Bolshevism: The Kornilov Rising*. New York: Dodd, Mead, and Company, 1919.

Kerensky, Alexander F. "Lenin's Youth—and My Own," *Asia*, 34/2 (1934): 69-74.

———. *The Catastrophe: Kerensky's Own Story of the Russian Revolution*. New York: D. Appleton, 1927.

———. *The Kerensky Memoirs: Russia and History's Turning Point*. New York, Duell, 1965.

Kern, Stephen. *The Culture of Time and Space, 1880–1918*. Cambridge, MA: Harvard University Press, 1983.

Kerzhentsev, P. M. *Printsipy organizatsii*, 3rd ed. Moscow-Petrograd: Gosizdat, 1924.

Ketskhoveli, Vano. "Druz'ia i soratniki tovarishcha Stalina," *Rasskazy o Velikom Staline*, kn. 2. Tblisi: Zaria vostoka, 1941.

———. "Iz vospominanii o Lado Ketskhoveli," *Zaria vostoka*, August 17, 1939.

———. "Na zare sozdania partii rabochego klassa," *Zaria vostoka*, July 17, 1939.

Keyes, Ralph. *The Quote Verifier: Who Said What, Where, and When*. New York: Macmillan, 2006.

Keynes, J. M. *The Economic Consequences of the Peace*. London: Macmillan, 1919.

Khachapuridze, G. "Gruziia vo vtoroi polovine XIX veka," *Istorik Marksist*, 1940, no. 8: 46-66.

Khadziev, Khan. *Velikii boiar*. Belgrade: M. A. Suvorin, 1929.

Khalid, Adeeb. "Tashkent 1917: Muslim Politics in Revolutionary Turkestan," *Slavic Review*, 55/2 (1996): 270–96.

———. *The Politics of Cultural Reform: Jadidism in Central Asia*. Berkeley: University of California Press, 1998.

Kharmandanian, Segvard V. *Lenin i stanovlenie Zakavkazskoi federatsii, 1921–1923 gg*. Yerevan: Aiasgan, 1969.

Khaustov, V.N., et al., eds. *Lubianka: Stalin i VChK-GPU-OGPU-NKVD, ianvar' 1922-dekabr' 1936*. Moscow: Mezhdunaordnyi fond demokratiia, 2003.

Khavin, A. F. *U rulia industrii*. Moscow: Politizdat, 1968.

Khelemskii, Iu. S.. "Soveshchanie v Sovnarkome o gosapparate [1923 g.]," *Sovetskoe gosudarstvo i pravo*, 1990, no. 9: 111–12.

Khinchuk, L. M. *K istorii anglo-sovietskikh otnoshenii*. Moscow: Gosizdat, 1928.

Khlevniuk, Oleg V. *In Stalin's Shadow: The Career of "Sergo" Ordzhinikidze*. Armonk, NY: M. E. Sharpe, 1995.

———. *Master of the House: Stalin and His Inner Circle*. New Haven, CT: Yale University Press, 2009.

———. *Politburo: mekhanizmy politcheskoi vlasti v 30-e gody*. Moscow: Rosspen, 1996.

———, et al., eds. *Stalinskoe politburo v 30-e gody: Sbornik dokumentov*. Moscow: AIRO-XX, 1995.

Khmel'kov, Andrei I., ed. *K. E. Voroshilov na Tsaritsynskom fronte: sbornik dokumentov.* Stalingrad: Stalingradskoe oblastnoe knizhnoe izdatel'stvo, 1941.

——, ed. *Stalin v Tsaritsyne: sbornik statei i dokumentov.* Stalingrad: Stalingradskoe oblastnoe knizhnoe izdatel'stvo, 1939.

Khoshtaria-Brose, Edisher V. *Ocherki sotsial'no-ekonomicheskoi istorii Gruzii: promyshlennost', goroda, rabochii klass (XIX v.-nachalo XX v.).* Tblisi: Metsniereba, 1974.

Khromov, S. S. *Po stranitsam lichnogo arkhiva Stalina.* Moscow: Moskovskii gos. universitet, 2009.

Khromov, S. S., and Kuibysheva, G. V. *Valerian Vladimirovich Kuibyshev: biografiia.* Moscow: Politicheskaia literatura, 1988.

Khromov, Semen S. *Leonid Krasin: neizvestnye stranitsy biografii, 1920-1926 gg.* Moscow: Insitut Rossiiskoi istorii RAN, 2001.

Khrushchev, Nikita. *Khrushchev Remembers.* Boston: Little, Brown, 1970.

——. *Memoirs,* 4 vols. University Park, PA: Pennsylvania State University Press, 2004-7.

——. "Secret Speech to 20th Congress CPSU," in *The Anti-Stalin Campaign and International Communism: A Selection of Documents.* New York: Columbia University, Russian Institute, 1956.

Kilcoyne, Martin. "The Political Influence of Rasputin." Phd diss., University of Washington, 1961.

Kim, M. P., ed. *Istoriia Sovetskogo krest'ianstva i kolkhoznogo stroitel'stva v SSSR: materialy nauchnoi sessii, sostoiavsheisia 18-21 aprelia 1961 g. v Moskve.* Moscow: Akademiia nauk SSSR, 1963.

Kimitaka, Matsuzato. "Sōryokusensōto chihōtōchi: daiichiji sekaitaisenki roshsia no shokuryōjigyō to nōjishidō." Phd diss., Tokyo University, 1995.

Kin, D., and Sorin, V., eds. *Sed'moi s'ezd: mart 1918 goda.* Moscow: Gosizdat, 1928.

Kindleberger, Charles P. *The World in Depression, 1929-1939.* Berkeley: University of California Press, 1986.

King, Charles. *The Ghost of Freedom: A History of the Caucasus.* New York: Oxford University Press, 2008.

Kingston-Mann, Esther. "Deconstructing the Romance of the Bourgeoisie: A Russian Marxist Path Not Taken," *Review of International Political Economy,* 10/1 (2003): 93-117.

——. "Lenin and the Beginnings of Marxist Peasant Revolution: The Burden of Political Opportunity July-October, 1917," *Slavonic and East European Review,* 50 (1972): 578-88.

Kirby, D. G. *War, Peace, and Revolution: International Socialism at the Crossroads, 1914-1918.* Aldershot, UK: Glower, 1986.

Kir'ianov, Iu. I. *Pravye partii v Rossii, 1911-1917.* Moscow: Rosspen, 2001.

——, ed. *Pravye partii: dokumenty i materialy, 1905-1917,* 2 vols. Moscow: Rosspen, 1998.

Kirilina, Alla. *Neizvestnyi Kirov: mify i real'nost'.* Moscow: Olma, 2001.

Kirillov, V. S., and Sverdlov, A. Ia. *Grigorii Konstantinovich Ordzhonikidze (Sergo): biografiia.* Moscow: Politicheskaia literatura, 1962.

Kirion, Episkop. *Kratkii ocherk istorii Gruzinskoi tserkvi i ekzarkhata.* Tiflis: K. P. Kozlovskii, 1901.

Kislitsyn, S. A. *Shakhtinskoe delo: nachalo stalinskikh represii protiv nauchno-tekhnicheskoi intelligentsia v SSSR.* Roston-na-Donu: NMTs Logos, 1993.

Kitanina, T. M. *Voina, khleb i revoliutsiia: Prodovol'stvennyi vopros v Rossii 1914-oktiabr' 1917 g.* Leningrad: Nauka, 1985.

Kitchen, Martin. *The Silent Dictatorship: The Politics of the German High Command under Hindenburg and Ludendorff, 1916-1918.* New York: Holmes & Meier, 1976.

Kizevetter, A. A. "Moda na sotsializm," *Russkie vedomosti,* June 25, 1917.

Klante, Margarete. *Von der Wolga zum Amur: Die tschechische Legion und der russische Bürgerkrieg.* Berlin: Ost-Europa Verlag, 1931.

Klement'ev, Vasilii F. *V Bol'shevitskoi Moskve (1918-1920).* Moscow: Russkii put', 1998.

Klemm, Max, ed. *Was sagt Bismarck dazu?,* 2 vols. Berlin: A Scherl, 1924.

Klepikov, S. A. *Statisticheskii spravochnik po narodnomu khoziaistvu, vyp. 2.* Moscow: Gosudarstvennoe izdatel'stvo, 1923.

Klier, John Doyle. *Russia Gathers Her Jews: The Origins of the "Jewish Question" in Russia, 1772-1825.* Dekalb: Northern Illinois University Press, 1986

Kliuev, Leonid. *Bor'ba za Tsaritsyn 1918-1919 gg.* Moscow-Leningrad: Gosizdat, otdel voennoi literatury, 1928.

Klyuchevsky, Vasily. *Peter the Great.* Boston: Beacon, 1958.

Knei-Paz, Baruch. *The Social and Political Social Thought of Leon Trotsky.* Oxford: Clarendon, 1978.

Knobler, S., et al., eds. *The Threat of Pandemic Influenza: Are We Ready? Workshop Summary.* Washington, D.C.: The National Academies Press, 2005.

Knox, Alfred. "General V. A.

Sukhomlinov," *Slavonic Review,* 5/ 13 (1926): 148-52.

——. *With the Russian Army, 1914-1917; being chiefly extracts from the diary of a military attaché,* 2 vols. New York, Dutton, 1921.

Kochan, Lionel. "Kadet Policy in 1917 and the Constituent Assembly," *Slavonic and East European Review,* 45 (1967): 183-92.

Kocharovsky, K. "Aleksandr Arkadievich Kaufman," in *Encyclopedia of the Social Sciences,* edited by Edwin Seligman and Alvin Johnson. New York: Macmillan, 1948.

Koda, Yoji. "The Russo-Japanese War: Primary Causes of Japanese Success," *Naval War College Review,* 58/2 (2005): 10-44.

Koehl, Robert Lewis. "A Prelude to Hitler's Greater Germany," *American Historical Review,* 59/1 (1953): 43-65.

Koenker, Diane. *Moscow Workers and the 1917 Revolution.* Princeton, NJ: Princeton University Press, 1981.

——, et al., eds. *Party, State, and Society in the Russian Civil War: Explorations in Social History.* Bloomington: Indiana University Press, 1990.

——, ed. *Revelations from the Russian Archives: Documents in English Translation.* Washington, D.C.: Library of Congress, 1997.

Kofod, A. A. *Russkoe zemleustroistvo,* 2nd ed. St. Petersburg: Sel'skii vestnik, 1914.

Kokovtsov, Vladimir N. *Iz moego proshlogo: vospominaniia, 1903-1919,* 2 vols. Paris: Privately published, 1933.

——. *Out of My Past.* Stanford, CA: Hoover Institution Press, 1935.

Kol'tsov, M. E. *Izbrannoe.* Moscow: Moskovskii rabochi, 1985.

Kolesnichenko, I. "K voprosu o konflikte v Revvoensovete Iuzhnogo fronta (sentiabr'-oktiabr' 1918 goda)," *Voenno-istoricheskii zhurnal,* 1962, no. 2.

——, and Lunin, V. "Kogda zhe byl uchrezhden institut voennykh kommissarov Krasnoi Armi?" *Voenno-istoricheskii zhurnal,* 1961, no. 9.

Kolesnik, Aleksandr. *Khronika zhizni sem'i Stalina.* Moscow: IKRA, 1990.

Kolodnyi, Lev. *Kitai-gorod: avtorskii putevoditel'.* Moscow: Golos-Press, 2004.

Kolonitskii, Boris I. "'Democracy' in the Consciousness of the February Revolution," *Slavic Review,* 57/1 (1998): 95-106.

——. "Anti-Bourgeois Propaganda and anti-'Burzhui' Consciousness in 1917," *Russian Review,* 53/2 (1994): 183-96.

——. "Kerensky," in *Critical Companion to the Russian Revolution*

*1914–1921*, ed. by Edward Acton, et al. Bloomington: Indiana University Press, 1997.

———. "Pravoekstremistskie sily v marte-oktiabre 1917 g. (na materialakh petrogradskoi pechati)," *Natsional'naia pravaia prezhde i teper':  istoriko-sotsiologicheskie ocherki*, edited by O. T. Vite. 3 vols. in 7. St. Petersburg: Institut sotsiologii Rossiiskoi Akademii nauk, Sankt-Peterburgskii filial, 1992.

———. *Symvoly vlasti i bor'ba za vlast': K izucheniiu politicheskoi kul'tury Rossiiskoi revoliutsii 1917 goda*. St. Petersburg: Dmitrii Bulanin, 2001.

Koloskov, V. V. *XIII konferentsiia RKP (b)*. Moscow: Vysshaia shkola, 1975.

Komarov, N. S. "K istorii instituta Lenina i tsentral'nogo partiinogo arkhiva 1919–1931 gg.," *Voprosy istorii*, 1956, no. 10: 181-91.

———. "Sozdanie i deietel'nost' Istparta 1920–1928 gg.," *Voprosy istorii KPSS*, 1958, no. 5: 153–65.

*Komintern i Vostok: bor'ba za leninskuiu strategiiu i taktiki v natsional'no osvoboditel'nom dvizhenii*. Moscow: Vostochnaia literatura, 1969.

*Kommunisticheskaia partiia Sovetskogo Soiuza v rezoiliutsiiakh i resheniiakh s'ezdov, konferentsii i plenumov TsK, 1898–1986*, 15 vols., 9th ed. Moscow: Politicheskaia literatura, 1983–.

*Kommunisticheshkaia partiia Sovetskogo Soiuza v rezoliutsiiakh i resheniiakh s'ezdov, konferentsii i plenumov TsK*, 8th ed., 13 vols. Moscow: Politicheskaia literatura, 1970.

*Kommunisticheskii internatsional: kratkii istoricheskii ocherk*. Moscow: Politizdat, 1969.

Kondratenko, E. *Kratkii ocherk ekonomicheskogo polozheniia Kavkaza po noveishim ofitsial'nym i drugim otchetam: prilozhenie k Kavkazskomu kalendariu (na 1888 g.)*. Tiflis: [s.n.], 1888.

Kondrat'ev, Nikolai. *Rynok khlebov i ego regulilirovanie vo vremia voiny i revoliutsii*. Moscow: Novaia derevnia, 1922.

Koniukhov, Grigorii A. *KPSS v bor'be s khlebnymi zatrudneniami v strane 1928–1929 gg*. Moscow: Sotsial'no-ekonomicheskaia literatura 1960.

Korbel, Josef. *Poland Between East and West: Soviet and German Diplomacy toward Poland, 1919–1933*. Princeton, NJ: Princeton University Press, 1963.

Korbut, M. "Uchet departamentom politsii opyta 1905 goda," *Krasnyi arkhiv*, 18 (1926): 219–27.

Korkunov, N. M. *Russkoe gosudarstvennoe pravo*. St. Petersburg: M. M. Stasiulevich, 1901.

Kornakov, P. K. "Opyt privlecheniia veksilologicheskikh pamiatnikov dlia resheniia geral'dicheskikh problem," *Novye numizmaticheskie issledovaniia*, no. 4, Trudy Gosudarstvennogo Istoricheskogo muzeia, 1986, vyp. 61: 134–48.

———. "Znamena Fevral'skoi revoliutsii," *Geral'dika: materialy i issledovaniia: sbornik nauchnykh trudov*, edited by G. V. Vilinbakhov Leningrad: Gos. Ermitazh, 1983.

Kornatovskii, Nikolai A. *Razgrom kontrrevoliutsionnykh zagovorov v Petrograde v 1918–1919 gg*. Leningrad, Lenizdat, 1972.

———. *Stalin—rukovoditel' oborony Petrograda, vesna-leto 1919 goda*. Leningrad: Gazetno-zhurnal'noe i knizhnoe izd-vo Leningradskogo soveta RK i KD, 1939.

Koroleva, V. V. "Deiatel'nost' V. I. Lenina po organizatsii dostavki 'Iskry' v Rossiiu (dekabr' 1900 g.–noiabr' 1903 g.)," *Trudy Kazanskogo aviatsionnogo instituta*, vyp. 54 (1962): 17–30.

Korotyshevskii, Viktor. "Garazh osobogo znacheniia," *Proza*, May 27, 2009. Found at http://www.proza.ru/2009/05/27/581.

Korros, Alexandra. *A Reluctant Parliament: Stolypin, Nationalism, and the Politics of the Russian Imperial State Council, 1906–1911*. Lanham, MD: Rowman and Littlefield, 2002.

Korzhikhina, T. P., and Figatner, Iu. "Sovetskaia nomenklatura: stanovlenie, mekhanizmy, deistviia," *Voprosy istorii*, 1993, no. 7: 25-38.

Korzhikhina, T. Z. "Obshchestvo starykh Bol'shevikov (1922–1935)," *Voprosy istorii KPSS*, 1989, no. 11: 50–65.

Kosachev, V. G. "Nanakune kollektivizatsii: poezdka I. V. Stalina v Sibir'," *Voprosy istorii*, 1998, no. 5.

Kosheleva, L., et al. *Pis'ma I. V. Stalina V.M. Molotovu, 1925–1936 gg. : sbornik dokumentov*. Moscow, Rossiia molodaia, 1995.

Kostin, N.D. *Vystrel v serdtse revoliutsii*. Moscow: Politizdat, 1989.

Kostiushko, I. I. *Pol'skoe biuro TsK RKP (b) 1920–1921 gg*. Moscow: RAN Institut slavianovedeniia, 2005.

Kostiushko, Ivan, ed. *Pol'sko-Sovetskaia voina 1919–1920 gg : ranee neopublikovanye dokumenty i materialy*, 2 vols. Moscow: Institut slavianovedeniia i balkanistiki RAN, 1994.

Kostrikova, A. M., and Kostrikova, E. M. *Eto bylo v Urzhume*. Kirov, 1962.

Kotel'nikov, K. G., ed. *Vtoroi vserossiiskii s'ezd sovetov R. i S.D.* Moscow-Leningrad: Gosizdat, 1928.

Kotel'nikov, K. G., and Mueller, V. L., eds. *Krest'ianskoe dvizhenie v 1917 godu*. Moscow-Leningrad: Gosizdat, 1927.

Kotkin, Stephen. "Left Behind: Is Eric Hobsbawm History?" *New Yorker*, September 29, 2003.

———. "Modern Times: the Soviet Union and the Interwar Conjuncture," *Kritika*, 2/1 (2001): 111–64.

———. *Magnetic Mountain: Stalinism as a Civilization*. Berkeley: University of California, 1995.

Kotsonis, Yanni. *Making Peasants Backward: Managing Populations in Russian Agricultural Cooperatives, 1861–1914*. New York: St. Martin's Press, 1990.

Kotyrev, Andrei N. *Mavzolei V. I. Lenina: proektirovanie i stroitel'stvo*. Moscow: Sovetskii khudozhnik, 1971.

Kournakoff, Sergei. *Savage Squadrons*. Boston and New York: Hale, Cushman, and Flint: 1935.

Kozhevnikova, V. "Gody staroi *Iskry: 1901–1902 gg.*," *Proletarskaia revoliutsiia*, 1924, no. 3 (26): 133–41.

Kozlov, V. A., and Semenova, E. A. "Sotsiaologiiia detstva: obzor sotsial'no-pedagogicheskikh obsledovanii 20-x godov," *Shkola i mir kul'tury etnosov*. Moscow, 1993, vyp. 1.

Kramer, Alan. *Dynamic of Destruction: Culture and Mass Killing in the First World War*. New York: Oxford University Press, 2007.

Krasil'nikov, S. A., ed. *Shakhtinskii protsess 1928 g.: podgotovka, provedenie, itogi*, 2 vols. Moscow: Rosspen, 2011.

———, et al., eds. *Intelligentsiia, obshchestvo, vlast': opyt vzaimootnosheni, 1917-konets 1930 gg*. Novosibirsk: RAN, Sibirskoe otdelenie, 1995.

Krasin, Leonid. *Voprosy vneshnei torgovli*. Moscow: Gosizdat, 1928.

*Krasnaia Moskva, 1917–1920 gg*. Moscow: Moskovskii sovet, 1920.

Krasnov, Valerii G., and Daines, V., eds. *Neizvestnyi Trotskii: krasnyi Bonapart: dokumenty, mneniia, razmyshleniia*. Moscow: Olma, 2000.

Krastiņš, Jānis, ed. *Istoriia Latyshskikh strelkov, 1915–20*. Riga: Zinatne, 1972.

*Kratkaia istoriia grazhdanskoi voiny v SSSR*. Moscow: Politicheskaia literatura, 1962.

Kravchenko, Victor. *I Chose Freedom: The Personal and Political Life of a Soviet Official*. New York: Scribner's, 1947.

Kreindler, Isabelle. "A Neglected Source of Lenin's Nationality Policy," *Slavic Review*, 36/1 (1977): 86–100.

Krementsov, Nikolai. *A Martian Stranded on Earth*. Chicago: University of Chicago Press, 2011.

Krivitsky, Walter G. *In Stalin's Secret Service*. New York: Harper & Bros., 1939.

———. *I Was Stalin's Agent*. London: H. Hamilton, 1939.

Krivosheev, G. F., ed. *Grif sekretnosti sniat*. Moscow: Voennoeizdat, 1993.

———. *Rossiia i SSSR v voinakh XX veka: Poteri vooruzhenykh sil, statisticheskoe issledovanie*. Moscow: Olma, 2001.

*Kronstadskaia tragediia 1921 g.: dokumenty*, 2 vols. Moscow: Rosspen, 1999.

Krumin, Garal'd I. *Shakhtinskii prostess*. Moscow-Leningrad: Moskovskii rabochii, 1928.

Krupskaia, N. K. *Izbrannye proizvedeniia*. Moscow: Politicheskaia literatura, 1988.

———. *O Lenine: sbornik stat'ei i vystuplenii*. Moscow: Politicheskaia literatura, 1965.

———. "Poslednie polgoda zhizni Vladimira Il'icha (3 fevralia 1924 goda)," *Izvestiia TsK KPSS*, 1989, no. 4: 169–78.

Krupskaya, N. K. *Memories of Lenin*. New York: International Publishers, n.d. [1930].

———. *Reminiscences of Lenin*. Moscow: Progress, 1959.

Krylenko, Nikolai V. *Sudoustroitstvo RSFSR: lektsii po teorii i istorii sudoustroitstva*. Moscow: Iuridicheskoe izdatel'stvo NKIu, 1924.

———, ed. *Ekonomicheskaia kontrrevoliutsiia v Donbasse: itogi shakhtinskogo dela, stat'i i dokumenty*. Moscow: Iuridicheskoe izsatel'stvo NKIu RSFSR, 1928.

Kryzhanovskii, Sergei E. *Vospominaniia iz bumag S. E. Kryzhanovskago, poslIedniogo gosudarstvennago sekretaria Rossiiskoi imperii*. Berlin: Petropolis, 1938.

Krzhizhanovskii, G. M. *Desiat' let khoziaistvennogo stroitel'stva v SSSR, 1917–1927*, 2nd ed. Moscow: Gosplan, 1927.

Ksenofontov, F. A. *Lenin i imperialisticheskaia voina 1914–1918 gg.: k desiatiletiiu imperialisticheskoi voiny*. Tashkent: Sredne-aziatskoe biuro, 1924.

Kshesinskaia, M. *Vospominaniia*. Moscow: ART, 1992.

Kudelli, Praskov'ia. F., ed. *Pervyi legal'nyi Peterburgskii komitet bol'shevikov v 1917 godu: sbornik materialov i protokolov zasedanii*. Moscow and Leningrad: Gosizdat, 1927.

Kudiukhina, M. M. "Krasnaia armiia i 'voennye trevogi' vtoroi poloviny 1920-kh godov," *Rossiia i mir glazami druga druga: iz istorii vzaimovospriiatiia*. Moscow: IRI RAN, 2007, 153–74.

Kudriashov, Sergei, ed. *Krasnaia armiia v 1920-e gody*. Moscow: Vetsnik arkhiva prezidenta Rossiiskoi Federatsii, 2007.

Kuibyshev, V. V. *Epizody iz moei zhizni*. Moscow: Staryi bol'shevik, 1935.

Kuibysheva, Elena. *Valerian Vladimirovich Kuibyshev, 1888–1935: iz vospominanii sestry*. Moscow: Politicheskaia literatura, 1938.

Kuibysheva, G. V. *Valerian Vladimirovich Kuibyshev: biografiia*. Moscow: Politicheskaia literatura, 1966.

Kukushkin, Iu. S. *Rezhim lichnoi vlasti Stalina: k istorii formirovanii*. Moscow: Moskovskii universitet, 1989.

Kuleshov, Sergei. "Lukollov mir." *Rodina*, 1991, no. 9–10: 72–5.

Kulikov, S. "Vremennoe pravitel'stvo i vysshaia tsarskaia biurokratiia," *The Soviet and Post-Soviet Review*, 24/1–2 (1997): 67–83.

Kul'sharipov, M. M. *Z. Validov i obrazovanie Bashkirskoi Avtonomnoi Sovetskoi Respubliki (1917–1920 gg.)* Ufa: Bashkirskoe knizhnoe izdatel'stvo, 1992.

Kumanev, V. A., and Kulikova, I. S. *Protivostoianie: Krupskaia-Stalin*. Moscow: Nauka, 1994.

Kun, Miklos. *Bukharin: ego druz'ia i vragi*. Moscow: Respublika, 1992.

———. *Stalin: An Unknown Portrait*. Budapest: Central European University Press, 2003.

Kuromiya, Hiroaki. "The Crisis of Proletarian Identity in the Soviet Factory, 1928–1929," *Slavic Review*, 44/2 (1985): 280–97.

———. "The Shakhty Affair," *South East European Monitor*, 4/2 (1997): 41–64.

———. *Freedom and Terror in the Donbas: A Ukrainian-Russian Borderland, 1870–1990s*. New york: Cambridge University Press, 1998.

———. *Stalin*. New York: Pearson/Longman, 2005.

———. *Stalin's Industrial Revolution: Politics and Workers, 1928–1932*. New York: Cambridge University Press, 1988.

Kuropatkin, A. N. *The Russian Army and the Japanese War*, 2 vols. London: J. Murray, 1909.

Kurzman, Charles. *Democracy Denied, 1905–1915: Intellectuals and the Fate of Democracy*. Cambridge, MA: Harvard University Press, 2008.

Kuusinen, Aino. *Rings of Destiny: Inside Soviet Russia from Lenin to Brezhnev*. New York: Morrow, 1974.

Kuusinen, Otto. *Neudavsheesia izobrazhenie "nemetskogo Oktiabria": po povodu "Uroki Oktiabria" Trotskogo*. Leningrad: Gosizdat, 1924.

Kuvarzin, A. I. *Dorogami neskonchaemykh bitv*. Kiev: Politicheskaia literatura Ukrainy, 1982.

Kuz'min, N. F. *Krushenie poslednego pokhoda Antanty*. Moscow: Politicheskaia literatura, 1958.

———. "Ob odnoi ne vypolnennoi dikertive glavkoma," *Voenno-istoricheskii zhurnal*, 1962, no. 9: 49–66.

Kuz'min, S. *Pod gnetom svobod (Zapiski natsionalista)*. St. Petersburg: M. Aleneva, 1910.

Kuz'min, Sergei L., ed. *Baron Ungern v dokumentakh i memuarakh*. Moscow: KMK, 2004.

———. *Istoriia barona Ungerna: opyt rekonstruktskii*. Moscow: KMK, 2011.

Kuz'min, V. I. *Istoricheskii opyt sovestkoi industrializatsii*. Moscow: Mysl', 1969.

Kvakin, A. V., ed. *Okrest Kolchaka: dokumenty i materialy*. Moscow: AGRAF, 2007.

Kvashonkin, A. V., ed. *Bol'shevistskoe rukovodstvo: perepiska, 1912–1927*. Moscow: Rosspen, 1996.

Kvinitadze, G. I. *Moi vospominaniia v gody nezavisimosti Gruzii 1917–1921*. Paris: YMCA, 1985.

*Lado Ketskhoveli: Sbornik dokumentov i materialov*. Tblisi: Sabchota Sakartvelo, 1969.

LaFeber, Walter. *The Clash: A History of U.S.-Japanese Relations*. New York: W. W. Norton, 1997.

Lakoba, Stanislav. "'Ia Koba, a ty Lakoba,'" in *Moe serdtse v gorakh: ocherki o sovremennoi Abkhazii*, edited by Fasil Iskander. Ypshkar Ola, 2001: 50–78.

Lambert, Nicholas A. *Planning Armageddon: British Economic Warfare and the First World War*. Cambridge, MA: Harvard University Press, 2012.

Lamzdorf, V. N. *Dnevnik, 1891–1892*. Moscow: Akademiia, 1934.

Landa, R. G. "Mirsaid Sultan-Galiev," *Voprosy Istorii KPSS*, 1999, no. 8: 53-70.

Landis, Erik C. *Bandits and Partisans: The Antonov Movement in the Russian Civil War*. Pittsburgh: University of Pittsburgh Press, 2008.

Lane, D. *Roots of Russian Communism: A Social and Historical Study of Russian Social-Democracy, 1898–1907*. Assen: Van Gorcum, 1969.

Lang, David Marshall. *A Modern History of Soviet Georgia*. New York: Grove Press, 1962.

———. *The Last Years of the Georgian Monarchy, 1658–1832*. New York: Columbia University Press, 1957.

Lapin, N., ed. "Progessivnyi blok v 1915–1917 gg.," *Krasnyi arkhiv*, 56 (1933): 80–135.

Laporte, Maurice. *Histoire de l'Okhrana, la police secrète des tsars, 1880–1917*. Paris: Payot, 1935.

Lappo, D. *Iosif Vareikis*. Moscow: Politicheskaia literatura, 1966.

Larin, Iurii. "Ukolybeli," *Narodnoe khoziaistvo*, 1918, no. 11.

———. *Sovetskaia derevnia*. Moscow: Ekonomicheskaia zhizn', 1925.

Larina, Anna. "Nezabyvaemoe," *Znamia*, 1988, no. 11.

———. *This I Cannot Forget: The Memoirs of Nikolai Bukharin's Widow*. New York: W. W. Norton, 1993.

Larsons, M. J. *Im Sowjet-Labyrinth*. Berlin: Transmare Verlag, 1931.

Laruelle, Marlène. *L'idéologie eurasiste russe, ou Comment penser l'empire*. Paris: L'Harmattan, 1999.

Latsis, M. *Chrezvychainye komissii po bor'be s kontr-revoliutsiei*. Moscow: Gosizdat, 1921.

———. *Otchet VChK za chetyre goda ee deiatel'nosti, 20 dekabria 1917–20 dekabria 1921 g.* Moscow: VChK, 1922.

———. "Vozniknoveniie Narodnogo kommissariata vnutrennikh del i organizatsiia vlasti na mestakh," *Proletarskaia revoliutsiia*, 1925, no. 2 (37): 136–59.

Latyshev, A. G. *Rassekrechennyi Lenin*. Moscow: Izd-vo Mart, 1996.

Lauchlan, Iain. "The Accidental Terrorist: Okhrana Connections to the Extreme-Right and the Attempt to Assassinate Sergei Witte in 1907," *Revolutionary Russia*, 14/2 (2001): 1–32.

———. "Young Felix Dzerzhinsky and the Origins of Stalinism." http://www.ed.ac.uk/polopoly_fs/1.124547!/fileManager/wp-iain-lauchlan-YoungFelix.pdf

———. *Russian Hide-and-Seek: The Tsarist Secret Police in St. Petersburg, 1906–1914*. Helsinki: Suomalaisen Kirjiallisuuden Seura/Finnish Literature Society, 2002.

Lawton, Lancelot. *An Economic History of Soviet Russia*, 2 vols. London: Macmillan, 1932.

———. *The Russian Revolution, 1917–1926*. London: Macmillan, 1927.

Lazarski, Christopher. "White Propaganda Efforts in the South during the Russian Civil War, 1918–19: The Alekseev-Denikin Period," *Slavonic and East European Review*, 70/4 (1992): 688–707.

League of Nations, *Records of the … Assembly, Plenary Meetings*, 26 vols. Geneva: Publications Department of the League of Nations, 1920–46.

Lebedev, M. "Sostoianie i perspektivy razvitiia elevatornogo khoziaistva v sibkrae," *Zhizn' sibiri*, 1928, no. 2.

Le Donne, John P. *The Russian Empire and the World 1700–1917: The Geography of Expansion and Containment*. New York: Oxford University Press, 1997.

———. *Absolutism and Ruling Class: The Formation of the Russian Political Order, 1700–1825*. New York: Oxford University Press, 1991.

———. *The Russian Empire and the World, 1700–1917: The Geopolitics of Expansion and Containment*. New York: Oxford University Press, 1997.

Lee, Hermione. *Virginia Woolf's Nose: Essays on Biography*. Princeton, NJ: Princeton University Press, 2005.

Lee, John. *The Warlords: Hindenburg and Ludendorff*. London: Weidenfeld & Nicolson, 2005.

Leggett, George. *The Cheka: Lenin's Political Police*. Oxford: Clarendon, 1981.

Lehovich, Dimitry V. *White Against Red: The Life of General Anton Denikin*. New York: W. W. Norton, 1974.

Lelashvili, G. "Lado Ketskhoveli, besstrashnyi revoliutsioner," *Rasskazy o Velikom Staline*, kn. 2. Tblisi: Zaria vostoka, 1941.

Lelevich, G. (L. G. Kal'manson.) *Oktiabr' v stavke*. Gomel: Istpart, 1922.

Lemke, Mikhail. *250 dnei v tsarskoi stavke (25 sentabria 1915–2 iiulia 1916)*. Petersburg: Gosudarstvennoe izdatel'stvo, 1920.

Lenczowski, George. *Russia and the West in Iran, 1918–1948*. Ithaca, NY: Cornell University Press, 1949.

*Lenin v pervye mesiatsy sovetskoi vlasti: sbornik statei i vospominanii*. Moscow: Partizdat, 1933.

*Lenin v vospominaniiakh chekistov*. Moscow: Pogranichnik 1969.

Lenin, V. I. *Collected Works*, 45 vols. Moscow: Foreign Languages Pub. House, 1960–70.

———. *Lenin o Trotskom i trotskizme*. Moscow: Novaia Moskva, 1925.

———. *Leninskie dekrety o Moskve*. Moscow: Moskovskii rabochii, 1978.

———. *Pol'noe sobranie sochinenii [PSS]*, 5th ed., 55 vols. Moscow: Politicheskaia literatura, 1958–65. Cited as *PSS* (author understood).

———. *Sobranie sochinenii*, 20 vols. Moscow-Leningrad: Gosizdat, 1920–6.

———. *Sobranie sochinenii*, 2nd and 3rd eds., 30 vols. Moscow-Leningrad: Gosizdat, 1925–32.

———. *Sobranie sochinenii*, 4th ed, 45 vols. Moscow: Politicheskaia literatura, 1941–67.

———. *V. I. Lenin: neizvestnye dokumenty: 1891–1922*. Moscow: Rosspen, 1999.

———. *Selected Works*, 3 vols. Moscow: Progress, 1975.

*Leninskii sbornik*, 40 vols. Moscow: Gosizdat, 1924–85.

Lenoe, Matthew E. "Agitation, Propaganda, and the 'Stalinization' of the Soviet Press, 1922–1930," *Carl Beck Papers*, no. 1305, 1998.

Lensen, George A. "Japan and Tsarist Russia: The Changing Relationship," *Jahrbücher für geschichte Osteuropas*, 10/3 (1962): 337–49.

Lensen, George Alexander. *Japanese Recognition of the USSR: Japanese-Soviet Relations, 1921–1930*. Tallahassee, FL: Diplomatic Press, 1970.

Leonard, Raymond W. *Secret Soldiers of the Revolution: Soviet Military Intelligence, 1918–1933*. Westport, CT: Greenwood Press, 1999.

Leonidov, I., and Reikhsbaum, A. "Revoliutsonnaia zakonnost' i khlebozagotovski," *Na leninskom puti*, 1928, no. 1–2 (January 31).

Leonov, Nikolai S. *Likholet'e*. Moscow: Mezzhdunarodnye otnosheniia, 1994.

Leonov, S. V. *Rozhdenie sovetskoi imperii: gosudarstvo i ideologiia, 1917–1922 gg.* Moscow: Dialog-MGU, 1997.

Leont'ev, Iaroslav V., ed. *Partiia levykh sotsialistov-revoliutsionerov: dokumenty i materialy, 1917–1925 gg.*, 3 vols. Moscow: Rosspen, 2000.

Leontovitsch, Victor. *Geschichte des Liberalismus in Russland*. Frankfurt am Main: Vittorio Klostermann, 1957.

Lepeshinskii, I. *Revoliutsiia na Da'lnem vostoke*. Moscow: Gosizdat, 1923.

Lerner, Warren. "Attempting a Revolution from Without: Poland in 1920," *Studies on the Soviet Union*, 11/4 (1971): 94–106.

———. "Poland in 1920: A Case Study in Foreign-Policy Decision Making under Lenin," *South Atlantic Quarterly*, 72/3 (1973):406–14.

———. *Karl Radek: The Last Internationalist*. Stanford, CA: Stanford University Press, 1970.

Leroy-Beaulieu, Anatole. *The Empire of the Tsars and Russians*, 3 vols. New York and London: G. P. Putnam's Sons, 1898.

Leskov, Valentin. *Okhota na vozhdei: ot Lenina do Trotskogo*. Moscow: Veche, 2005.

*Lessons of the German Events*. London: London Caledonian Press, 1924.

Levine, Isaac Don. *Stalin's Great Secret*. New York: Coward-McCann, 1956.

Lewin, Moshe. *Lenin's Last Struggle*. New York: Panetheon, 1968.

———. *Political Undercurrents in Soviet Economic Debates: From Bukharin to the Modern Reformers*. Princeton, NJ: Princeton University Press, 1974.

———. *Russia/USSR/Russia: The Drive and Drift of a Superstate*. New York: New Press, 1995.

———. *Russian Peasants and Soviet Power: A Study of Collectivization*. New York: W. W. Norton, 1968.

Lewis, Ben, and Lih, Lars, eds. *Zinoviev and Martov: Head to Head in Halle*. London: November Publications, 2011.

Lewis, J. Patrick "Communications Output in the USSR: A Study of the

Soviet Telephone Systems," *Soviet Studies*, 28/3 (1976): 406–17.

Lewis, Jon E. *The Mammoth Book of Eyewitness World War I: Over 280 First-Hand Accounts of the War to End All Wars*. Philadelphia: Running Press, 2003.

Liadov, M. "Zarozhdenie legal'nogo i revoliutsionnogo marksizma v Rossii," *Front nauki i tekhniki*, 1933, no. 2.

Liadov, P. F. *Istoriia Rossiiskogo protokola*. Moscow: Mezhdunarodnye otnosheniia, 2004.

Liberman, Simon. *Building Lenin's Russia*. Chicago: University of Chicago Press, 1945.

Liebich, André. "Menshevik Origins: The Letters of Fedor Dan," *Slavic Review*, 45/4 (1986): 724–8.

Lieven, Dominic C. B. "Bureaucratic Authoritarianism in Late Imperial Russia: The Personality, Career, and Opinions of P. N. Durnovó," *Historical Journal*, 26/2 (1983): 391–402.

———. "Dilemmas of Empire 1850–1918: Power, Territory, Identity," *Journal of Contemporary History*, 34/2 (1999): 163–200.

———. "Pro-Germans and Russian Foreign Policy 1890–1914," *International History Review*, 2/1 (1980): 34–54.

———. "Russia, Europe, and World War I," in *Critical Companion to the Russian Revolution, 1914–1921*, edited by Edward Acton et al. Bloomington: Indiana University Press, 1997.

———. "Russian Senior Officialdom under Nicholas II: Careers and Mentalities," *Jahrbücher für Geschichte Osteuropas*, 32/2 (1984): 199–223.

———. *Empire: The Russian Empire and its Rivals*. New Haven, CT: Yale University Press, 2002.

———. *Nicholas II: Twilight of the Empire*. New York: St. Martin's Press, 1994.

———. *Russia and the Origins of the First World War*. New York: St. Martin's Press, 1983.

———. *Russia's Rulers under the Old Regime*. New Haven, CT: Yale University Press, 1989.

———. *The Aristocracy in Europe, 1815–1914*. New York: Columbia University Press, 1992.

———, ed. *British Documents on Foreign Affairs: Reports and Papers from the Foreign Office Confidential Print*. Part I, Series A, Russia, 1859–1914, 6 vols. Frederick, MD: University Publications of America, 1983.

Lih, Lars. "The Ironic Triumph of 'Old Bolshevism'," *Weekly Worker*, November 25, 1010. Found at http://www.cpgb.org.uk/home/weekly-worker/843/the-ironic-triumph-of-old-bolshevism.

Lih, Lars T. *Lenin Rediscovered: What is to be Done? in Context*. Leiden: Brill, 2006.

———. "1912: 'A faction is not a party'," *Weekly Worker* 912, May 3, 2012.

———. "Bolshevik *Razverstka* and War Communism," *Slavic Review*, 45/4 (1986): 673–88.

———. "Bukharin's 'Illusion': War Communism and the NEP," *Russian History/Histoire Russe*, 27/4 (2000): 417–59.

———. "Political Testament of Lenin and Bukharin and the Meaning of NEP," *Slavic Review*, 50/2 (1991): 240–52.

———. "Zinoviev: Populist Leninist," *The NEP Era: Soviet Russia, 1921–1928*, 2 (2007): 1–23.

———. *Bread and Authority in Russia, 1914–1921*. Berkeley: University of California Press, 1990.

———. *Lenin*. London: Reaktion Books, 2011.

———, et al., eds. *Stalin's Letters to Molotov*. New Haven, CT: Yale University Press, 1995.

Lincoln, W. Bruce. *Passage Through Armageddon: The Russians in War and Revolution, 1914–1918*. New York: Simon & Schuster, 1986.

———. *Red Victory: A History of the Russian Civil War*. New York: Simon & Schuster, 1989.

Lipatnikov, Iu. "Byl li agentom okhranki Sverdlov?" *Situatsii*, 1991, no. 1.

Lipitskii, S. V. *Voennaia deiatel'nost' TsK RKP (b), 1917–1920*. Moscow: Politizdat, 1973.

Litvak, Dmitriy, and Kuznetzov, Alexander. "The Last Emir of Noble Bukhara and His Money," *International Bank Note Society journal*, 50/3 (2011).

Litvin, Al'ter, ed. *Levye esery i VChK: sbornik dokumentov*. Kazan: NKT, 1996.

———. *Krasnyi i belyi terror v Rossii, 1918–1922 gg*. Kazan: Tatarskoe gazetno-zhurnalnoe izd-vo, 1995.

Litvinov, M. Iu., and Sidunov, A. V. *Shpiony i diversanty: bor'ba s pribaltiiskim spionazhem i natsionalisticheskim bandformirovaniiami na Severo-Zapade Rossii*. Pskov: Pskovskaia oblastnaia tipografiia, 2005.

Liu, F. F. *A Military History of Modern China, 1924–1929*. Princeton, NJ: Princeton University Press, 1956.

Liubimov, Nikolai Nikolaevich, and Erlikh, Aleksandr Nikolaevich. *Genuezskaia konferentsiia: vospominaniia uchastnikov*. Moscow: Institut mezhdunarodnykh otnoshenii, 1963.

Liubosh, S. *Russkii fashist: Vladimir Purishkevich*. Leningrad: Byloe, 1925.

Liulevicius, Vejas Gabriel. *War Land on the Eastern Front: Culture, National Identity, and German Occupation in World War I*. New York: Cambridge University Press, 2000.

Livezeanu, Irina. *Cultural Politics in Greater Romania: Regionalism, Nation Building, and Ethnic Struggle, 1918–1930*. Ithaca, NY: Cornell University Press, 1995.

Lobanov, M. P. *Stalin v vospominaniiakh sovremennikov i dokumentakh epokhi*. Moscow: Eksmo-Algoritm, 2002.

Lockhart, R. H. Bruce. *British Agent*. New York: G. P. Putnam's Sons, 1933.

———. *Memoirs of a British Agent: Being an Account of the Author's Early Life in Many Lands and of His Official Mission to Moscow in 1918*. New York: G. P. Putnam's Sons, 1932.

Loewe, Heinz-Dietrich. *Antisemitismus under reaktionaere Utopie: Russischer Konservatismus um Kampf gegen Wandel von Staat under Gesellschaft, 1890–1917*. Hamburg: Hoffmann und Campe, 1978.

Logachev, Vladimir A. "'V khlebnom raoine Zapadnoi Sibiri': ot prodraverstka k golodu," *Vestnik Tomskogo gusudarstvennogo universiteta: Istoriia*, 2012, no. 3.

Loginov, V. T. *Leninskaia "Pravda" 1912–1914 gg*. Moscow, 1962.

Loginov, Vladimir. *Teni Stalina: General Vlasik i ego soratniki*. Moscow: Sovremennik, 2000.

Lohr, Eric. "War and Revolution, 1914–1917," in *The Cambridge History of Russia*, edited by Dominic Lieven. New York: Cambridge University Press, 2006.

———. *Nationalizing the Russian Empire: The Campaign Against Enemy Aliens During World War I*. Cambridge, MA: Harvard University Press, 2003.

Loukianov, Mikhail. "Conservatives and 'Renewed Russia,' 1907–1914," *Slavic Review*, 61/4 (2002): 762–86.

Loukomsky, A. S. *Memoirs of the Russian Revolution*. London: Fisher, Unwin, 1922.

Löwe, Heinz-Dietrich. "Political Symbols and Rituals of the Russian Radical Right, 1900–1914," *Slavonic and East European Review*, 76/3 (1998): 441–66.

Lubny-Gertsyk, I. L. *Dvizhenie naseleniia na territorii SSSR za vremia mirovoi voiny i revoliutsii*. Moscow: Planovoe khoziaistvo, 1926.

Luchinskaia, A. V. *Velikii provokator Evno Azef*. Petrograd: Raduga, 1923.

Ludendorff, Erich. *My War Memories, 1914–1918*, 2 vols. London: Hutchinson, 1919.

Lukomskii, A. S. *Vospominaniia*. Berlin: Otto Kirchner, 1922.

Lunacharskii, A. V. *Sobranie*

*sochinenii*, 8 vols. Moscow: Khudozhestvennaia literatura, 1963–67.

——. *Revoliutsionnye siluety*. Moscow: Deviatoe ianvaria, 1923.

Lunacharsky, Anatoly. *Revolutionary Silhouettes*. New York: Hill and Wang, 1967.

Luppol, A. P. "Iz istorii sovetskogo gosudarstvennogo gerba," in *Ezhegodnik Gosudarstvennogo istoricheskogo muzeia*. Moscow: Sovetskaia Rossiia, 1960.

Lutchenko, A. I. "Rukovodstvo KPSS formirovaniem kadrov tekhnicheskoi intelligentsia, 1926–1933 g.," *Voprosy istorii KPSS*, 1966, no. 2: 29–42.

Lutovinov, I. S. *Likvidatsiia miatezha Kerenskogo-Krasnogo*. Moscow and Leningrad: Voenizdat, 1965.

Luxemburg, Rosa. *Die russische Revolution: eine kritische Würdigung*. Berlin: Gesellschaft und Erziehung, 1920.

Luzyanin, S. G. "Mongolia: Between China and Soviet Russia (1920–1924)," *Problems of the Far East*, 1995, no. 2.

Lyandres, Semyon. "On the Problem of 'Indecisiveness' among the Duma leaders during the February Revolution: The Imperial Decree of Prorogation and the decision to Convene the private meeting of February 27, 1917," *The Soviet and Post-Soviet Review*, 24/1–2 (1997): 115–27.

——. "Progressive Bloc Politics on the Eve of the Revolution: Revisiting P. N. Miliukov's 'Stupidity or Treason' Speech of November 1, 1916," *Russian History*, 31/4 (2004): 447–64.

——, ed. "'O Dvortsovom perevorote ia pervyi raz uslyshal posle revoliutsii . . .': Stenogramma besedy N. Z. Bazili s A. S. Lukomskim (parizh, 24 fevralia 1933 g.)," *Russian History*, 32/3-4 (2005): 215-58.

Lyons, Eugene. *Assignment in Utopia*. New York: Harcourt, Brace, 1937.

——. *Stalin: Czar of All the Russias*. Philadelphia: J. B. Lippincott, 1940.

Lyttelton, Adrian. *The Seizure of Power: Fascism in Italy 1919–1929*, 2nd ed. Princeton, NJ: Princeton University Press, 1987.

Macey, David A. J. *Government and Peasant in Russia, 1861–1906: The Prehistory of the Stolypin Reforms*. DeKalb: Northern Illinois University Press, 1987.

Machiavelli, Niccolo, *Gosudar'*, edited by N. Kurochkin. St. Petersburg, 1869.

MacKenzie, David. *Apis: The Congenial Conspirator. The Life of Colonel Dragutin T. Dimitrijević*. Boulder, CO: East European Monographs, 1989.

Mackenzie, F. A. *Russia Before Dawn*. London: T. F. Unwin, 1923.

MacMillan, Margaret. *Paris 1919: Six Months that Changed the World*. New York: Random House, 2002.

Magerovskii, D. A. *Soiuz Sovetskikh Sotsialisticheskikh Respublik: obzor i materialy*. Moscow: NKID, 1923.

Magerovsky, E. L. "The People's Commissariat for Foreign Affairs, 1917–1946." Phd diss., Columbia University, 1975.

Magidov, B. "Kak ia stal redaktorom 'Soldat revoliutsii'," *Bol'shevistskaia pechat'*, 1936, no. 11: 30–3.

Magnes, Judah L. *Russia and Germany at Brest-Litovsk*. New York: Rand School of Social Science, 1919.

Maier, Charles S. *Recasting Bourgeois Europe: Stabilization in France, Germany, and Italy in the Decade after World War I*. Princeton, NJ: Princeton University Press, 1975.

Maiskii, Ivan. *Sovremennaia Mongoliia*. Irkutsk: Irkutskoe otdelenie, 1921.

Makarov, S. V. *Sovet ministrov Rossiiskoi Imperii 1857–1917*. St. Petersburg: St. Petersburg University Press, 2000.

Makarova, G. P. *Narodnyi Komissariat po delam natsional'nostei RSFSR 1917–23 gg*. Moscow: Nauka, 1987.

Makeev, N. Ia. "Bakinskaia podpol'naia tipografiia 'Nina' (1901–1905)," *Trudy Azerbaidzhanskogo filiala IML pri TsK KPSS*. Baku, 1952.

Makharadze, F. K tridsatiletiiu sushchestvovaniia Tiflisskoi organizatsii: podgotovitel'nyi period, 1870–1890. *Materialy*. Tiflis: Sovetskii Kavkaz, 1925.

Makharadze, F. E., and Khachapuridze, G. E. *Ocherki po istorii rabochego i krest'ianskogo dvizheniia v Gruzii*. Moscow: Zhurnal'nogazetnoe obidenenie, 1932.

Makharadze, Filipp. *Ocherki revoliutsionnogo dvizheniia v Zakavkaz'e*. Tblisi: Gosizdat Gruzii, 1927.

Makharadze, N. B. *Pobeda sotsialisticheskoi revoliutsii v Gruzii*. Tblisi: Sabchota Sakartvelo, 1965.

Makintsian, P., ed. *Krasnaia kniga VChK*, 2 vols. Moscow: Gosizdat, 1920.

Maklakov, V. A. "The Agrarian Problem in Russia before the Revolution," *Russian Review*, 9/1 (1950): 3–15.

——. *Pervaia Gosudarstvennaia Duma: vospominaniia sovremennika*. Paris: L. Beresniak, 1939.

Maksakov, B., ed. "Iz arkhiva S. Iu. Vitte" and "Doklady S. Iu. Vitte Nikolaiu II," *Krasnyi arkhiv*, 11–12 (1925): 107–43, 144–58.

Maksakov, V., and Turunov, A. *Khronika grazhdanskoi voiny v Sibiri 1917–1918*. Moscow and Leningrad: Gosizdat, 1926.

Mal'chevskii, I. S., ed. *Vserossiiskoe Uchreditel'noe Sobranie*. Moscow-Leningrad: Gosizdat, 1930.

Male, Donald J. *Russian Peasant Organization Before Collectivization: A Study of Communes and Gathering, 1925–1930*. New York: Cambridge University Press, 1971.

Malenbaum, Wilfred. *The World Wheat Economy, 1885–1939*. Cambridge, MA: Harvard University Press, 1953.

Malia, Martin. *Alexander Herzen and the Birth of Russian Socialism, 1812–1855*. Cambridge, MA: Harvard, 1961.

Maliavskii, A. D. *Krest'ianskoe dvizhenie v Rossii v 1917 g. (mart-oktiabr')*. Moscow: Nauka, 1981.

Malinovskii, Iu. P. "K pereezdu TsK RKP (b) i Sovetskogo pravitel'stva iz Petrograd v Moskvu (mart 1918 g.)," *Voprosy istorii*, 1968, no. 11: 99–103.

Mal'kov, Pavel D. *Zapiski komendanta Moskovskogo Kremlia*, 3rd ed. Moscow: Molodaia gvardiia, 1959, 1967.

Mal'kov, V. L., ed. *Pervaia mirovaia voina: prolog XX veka*. Moscow: Nauka, 1998.

Malkov, Pavel D. *Reminiscences of a Kremlin Commandant*. Moscow: Progress, 1960.

Malle, Silvana. *The Economic Organization of War Communism, 1918–1921*. New York: Cambridge University Press, 1985.

Malozemoff, Andrew. *Russian Far Eastern Policy, 1881–1904, with Special Emphasis on the Causes of the Russo-Japanese War*. Berkeley: University of California Press, 1958.

Malyshev, M. O. *Oborona Petrograda i izgnanie nemetskikh okkupantov s severeozapada v 1918 godu*. Leningrad: Leningradskii universitet, 1974.

Mamontov, V. I. *Na Gosudarevoi sluzhbe: vospominaniia*. Tallinn: Tallinna Eesti Kirjastus-Ühisuse trükikoda, 1926.

Manchester, Laurie. *Holy Fathers, Secular Sons: Clergy, Intelligentsia, and the Modern Self in Revolutionary Russia*. DeKalb: Northern Illinois University Press, 2008.

Manikovskii, A. A. *Boevoe snabzhenie russkoi armii, 1914–1918 gg*. Moscow: Voennyi Redaktsion, 1923.

Manikovskii, Aleksei A. *Boevoe snabzhenie russkoi armii v mirovoiu voinu*, 2 vols. Moscow: Voennaia literatura, 1930.

Manning, Roberta T. "The Rise and Fall of 'the Extraordinary Measures', January–June 1928: Towards a Reexamination of the Onset of the Stalin Revolution," *Carl Beck Papers*, no. 1504, 2001.

Manuil (Lemeshevskii), Metropolitan. *Die Russischen orthodoxen Bischöfe von 1893 bis 1965: Bio Bibliographie,* 6 vols. Erlangen: Lehrstuhl für Geschichte und Theologie des Christlichen Ostens, 1979–89.

Manusevich, A. Ia. "Pol'skie sotsialdemkoraticheskie i drugie revoliutsionnye grupy v Rossii za pobedu v uprochenie sovetskoi vlasti (oktiabr' 1917–ianvar" 1918 gg.)," in *Iz istorii pol'skogo rabochego dvizheniia.* Moscow: Sotsial'no-ekonomicheskaia literatura, 1962.

March, G. Patrick. *Eastern Destiny: Russia in Asia and the North Pacific.* Westport, CT: Praeger, 1996.

Markina, N. A., and Federovna, T. S., eds. *Baltiiskie moriaki v bor'be za vlast' Sovetov v 1919 godu: dokumenty i materialy.* Leningrad: Nauka, 1974.

Markov, Evgenii. *Ocherki Kavkaza: Kartiny kavkazskoi zhizni, prirody i istorii,* 2nd ed. St. Petersburg and Moscow: M. F. Vol'f, 1904.

Markov, Nikolai E. *Voiny temnykh sil.* Paris: Doloi zlo, 1928–30.

Markova, Liliana. "Litso vraga," in *Kino: politika i liudi, 30-e gody.* Moscow: Materik, 1995.

Marks, Steven. *Road to Power: The Trans-Siberian Railroad and the Colonization of Asian Russia, 1850–1917.* Ithaca, NY: Cornell University Press, 1991.

Marshall, Alexander. "Turkfront: Frunze and the Development of Soviet Counter-insurgency in Central Asia," in *Central Asia: Aspects of Transition,* edited by Tom Everett-Heath. London: Routledge-Curzon, 2003.

Martin, Terry. "The Origins of Soviet Ethnic Cleansing," *Journal of Modern History,* 70/4 (1998): 813–61.

Martov, L. *Spasiteli ili uprazdniteli? Kto i kak razrushal R.S.D.R.P.* Paris: Golos Sotsialemokrata, 1911.

Martynov, A. "Ot abstraktsii k konkretnoi deiatel'nosti," *Nashe slovo,* Setpember 16, 1915.

Martynov, A. P. *Moia sluzhba otdel'nom korpuse zhandarmov: Vospominaniia.* Stanford, CA: Hoover Institution Press, Stanford University, 1972.

Martynov, Evgenii I. *Kornilov: popytka voennogo pervorota.* Leningrad-Moscow: Izdatel'stvo voennoi tip. upr. delami Nkvm. i RVS SSSR, 1927.

———. *Tsarskaia armiia v fevral'skom perevote.* Leningrad: Izd. Voennoi Tip. upr. delami narkomvoenmor i RVC SSSR, 1927.

Marx, Karl, and Engels, Friedrich. *Selected Correspondence of Karl Marx and Friedrich Engels: A Selection with Commentary and Notes.* London: M. Lawrence, 1944.

———. *Selected Correspondence.* Moscow: Progress, 1965.

———. *Collected Works,* 50 vols. New York: International Publishers, 1975-2004.

———. *Selected Works.* London: Lawrence and Wishart, 1968.

———. *The Communist Manifesto,* with a new afterword by Stephen Kotkin. New York: Signet, 2010.

Masaryk, T. G. *The Making of a State.* London: Allen and Unwin, 1927.

Maslov, P. *Agrarnyi vopros v Rossii,* 2 vols. St. Petersburg, 1905–8.

Maslov, S. S. *Rossiia posle chetyrekh let revoliutsii.* Paris: Russkaia pechat', 1922

Masolov, Aleksandr. *Pri dvore imperatora.* Riga: Fillin, n.d.

Massell, Gregory J. *The Surrogate Proletariat: Moslem Women and Revolutionary Strategies in Soviet Central Asia, 1919–1929.* Princeton, NJ: Princeton University Press, 1974.

Massie, Robert K. *Nicholas and Alexandra.* New York: Atheneum, 1967.

"Materialy fevral'sko-martovskogo plenuma TsK VKP (b) 1937 goda," *Voprosy istorii,* 1992, no. 2–3.

*Materialy "Osoboi papki" Politbiuro TsK RKP (b)–VKP (b) po voprosu sovetsko-pol'skikh otnosheniii 1923–1944 gg.* Moscow: RAN Institut slavianovedeniia, 1997.

Matteotti, Giacomo. *Un anno di dominazione fascista.* Rome: Uffacio stampa del Partito Socialista Unitario, 1924.

Mau, Vladimir. *Reformy i dogmy, 1914–1929: ocherki istorii stanovleniia khoziastvennoi sistemy sovetskogo totalitarizma.* Moscow: Delo, 1993.

Mawdsley, Evan, and White, Stephen, eds. *The Soviet Elite from Lenin to Gorbachev: The Central Committee and Its Members, 1917–1991.* New York: Oxford University Press, 2000.

———. *The Russian Civil War.* Boston: Allen & Unwin, 1987.

———. "An Elite Within an Elite: Politburo/Presidium Membership under Stalin, 1927–1953," in *The Nature of Stalin's Dictatorship: The Politbburo, 1924–1953,* E. A. Rees, ed. New York: Palgrave Macmillan, 2004, 59–78.

Maylunas, Andrei, and Mironenko, Sergei, eds. *A Lifelong Passion: Nicholas and Alexandra, Their Own Story.* New York: Doubleday, 1997.

Mayzel, Matitiahu. *Generals and Revolutionaries: The Russian General Staff During the Revolution. A Study in the Transformation of Military Elites.* Osnabrück: Biblio, 1979.

McAuley, Mary. *Bread and Justice: State and Society in Petrograd, 1917–1922.* Oxford: Clarendon, 1991.

McCann, James M. "Beyond the Bug: Soviet Historiography of the Soviet Polish War of 1920," *Soviet Studies,* 36/4 (1984): 475–93.

McCauley, Martin, ed. *The Russian Revolution and the Soviet State 1917–1921: Documents.* London and Basingstoke: Macmillan, 1975.

McClelland, Charles E. *The German Historians and England: A Study in Nineteenth-Century Views.* New York: Cambridge University Press, 1971.

McCullough, David. *The Path Between the Seas: The Creation of the Panama Canal, 1870–91.* New York: Simon & Schuster, 1977.

McDermott, Kevin, and Agnew, Jeremy. *The Comintern: A History of International Communism from Lenin to Stalin.* Houndmills, Basingstoke: Macmillan, 1996.

McDonald, David MacLaren. "A Lever without a Fulcrum: Domestic Factors and Russian Foreign Policy, 1905–1914," in *Imperial Russian Foreign Policy,* edited by Hugh Ragsdale. Washington, D.C., and New York: Woodrow Wilson Center and Cambridge University Press, 1993.

———. "The Durnovo Memorandum in Context: Official Conservatism and the Crisis of Autocracy," *Jahrbücher für Geschichte Osteuropas,* 44/4 (1996): 481–502.

———. "United Government and the Crisis of Autocracy, 1905–1914," in *Reform in Modern Russian History,* edited by Theodore Taranovski. Washington, D.C., and New York: Woodrow Wilson Center and Cambridge University Press, 1995.

———. *United Government and Foreign Policy in Russia, 1900–1914.* Cambridge, MA: Harvard University Press, 1992.

*MChK: iz istorii Moskovskoi chrezvychainoi komissii (1918–1921).* Moskva: Moskovskii Rabochii, 1978.

McIlroy, John, et al., eds. *Industrial Politics and the 1926 Mining Lockout,* 2nd ed. Cardiff: University of Wales Press, 2009.

McKean, Robert. *The Russian Constitutional Monarchy, 1907–1917.* New York: St. Martin's Press, 1977.

McKean, Robert B. "Constitutional Russia," *Revolutionary Russia,* 9/1 (1996): 33–42.

———. *St. Petersburg Between the Revolutions: Workers and Revolutionaries, June 1907–February 1917.* New Haven, CT: Yale University Press, 1990.

McLellan, David, ed. *Karl Marx: Selected Writings.* Oxford: Oxford University Press, 2000.

McNeal, Robert H. "Stalin's Conception of Soviet Federalism," *Annals of the Ukrainian Academy of Arts and Sciences in the United States,* 9/1–2 (1961): 12–25.

——. *Bride of the Revolution: Krupskaya and Lenin.* Ann Arbor: University of Michigan Press, 1972.

——. *Stalin: Man and Ruler.* New York: New York University Press, 1988.

——. *Stalin's Works: An Annotated Bibliography.* Stanford, CA: Hoover Institution Press, 1967.

McReynolds, Louise. "Mobilising Petrograd's Lower Classes to Fight the Great War," *Radical History Review,* 57 (1993): 160–80.

Medish, Vadim. "The First Party Congress and its Place in History," *Russian Review,* 22/2 (1963): 168–80.

Medlin, Vergil D., and Powers, Steven L., eds. *V. D. Nabokov and the Russian Provisional Government 1917.* New Haven, CT: Yale University Press, 1976.

Medvedev, Roy. "New Pages from the Political Biography of Stalin," in *Stalinism: Essays in Historical Interpretation,* edited by Robert C. Tucker. New York: W. W. Norton, 1977.

——. *Let History Judge: The Origins and Consequences of Stalinism.* New York: Columbia University Press, 1989.

——. *On Stalin and Stalinism.* Oxford and New York: Oxford University Press, 1979.

Medvedeva Ter-Petrosyan, S. F. "Tovarishch Kamo," *Proletarskaia revoliutsiia,* 1924, no. 8–9 (31–32): 117–48.

Mehlinger, Howard D., and Thompson, John M. *Count Witte and the Tsarist Government in the 1905 Revolution.* Bloomington: Indiana University Press, 1972.

Meijer, Jan M., ed. *The Trotsky Papers, 1917–1922,* 2 vols. The Hague: Mouton, 1971.

Meir, Natan. *Kiev, Jewish Metropolis: A History, 1859–1914.* Bloomington: Indiana University Press, 2010.

Mel'tiukhov, Mikhail. *Sovetsko-pol'skie voiny: voenno-politicheskoe protivostoianie 1918–1939 gg.* Moscow: Veche, 2001.

Melancon, Michael S. *The Lena Goldfields Massacre and the Crisis of the Late Tsarist State.* College Station: Texas A&M University Press, 2006.

——. *The Socialist Revolutionaries and the Russian Anti-War Movement.* Columbus: Ohio State University Press, 1990.

——. "From the Head of Zeus: The Petrograd Soviet's Rise and First Days, 27 February–2 March 1917," Carl Beck Papers, no. 2004, 2009.

Mel'gunov, Sergei P. "Zolotoi nemetskii kliuch" k bol'shevitskoi revoliutsii. Paris: Dom knigi, 1940.

——. *Kak bol'sheviki zakhvatili vlast': oktiabr'skii perevorot 1917 goda.* Paris: La Renaissance, 1953.

——. *Martovskie dni 1917 goda.* Paris: Editeurs reunis, 1961.

——. *Sud'ba Imperatora Nikolaia II posle otrecheniia.* Paris: La Renaissance, 1951.

——. *Tragediia Admirala Kolchaka: iz istorii grazhdanskoi voiny na Volge, Urale i v Sibiri,* 3 vols. Belgrade: Russkaia tipografiia, 1930–1.

Melgunov, Sergei P. *The Bolshevik Seizure of Power.* Santa Barbara, CA: ABC-Clio, 1972.

Melikov, V. A. *Geroicheskaia oborona Tsaritsyna v 1918 godu.* Moscow: Voenizdat, 1940.

——. *Srazhenie na Visle v svete opyta maisko-avgustskoi kampanii 1920 goda: politiko-strategicheskii i operativnyi ocherk.* Moscow: Krasnoznamennaia voennaia akademiia R.K.K.A. im. M. V. Frunze, 1931.

Melville, Cecil F. *The Russian Face of Germany: An Account of the Secret Military Relations Between the German and Soviet-Russian Governments.* London: Wishardt and Co., 1932.

Mendel, Arthur. "Peasant and Worker on the Eve of the First World War," *Slavic Review,* 24/1 (1965): 23–33.

"'Menia vstretil chelovek srednego rosta . . .' Iz vospominaniia skul'ptura M. D. Ryndiuksoi o rabote nad biustom I. V. Stalina v 1926 g.," *Golosa istorii: muzei revoliutsii. Sbornik nauchnykh trudov,* vyp. 23 kn. 2 (Moscow, 1992): 111–8.

Menning, Bruce W. *Bayonets Before Bullets: The Imperial Russian Army, 1861–1914.* Bloomington: Indiana University Press, 1992.

Merridale, Catherine. *Moscow Politics and the Rise of Stalin: The Communist Party in the Capital, 1925–32.* New York: St. Martin's Press, 1990.

Meyer, Alfred G. "The Soviet War Scare of 1927," *Soviet Union,* 5/1 (1978): 1–25.

Meyer, Alfred. *Leninism.* Cambridge, MA: Harvard University Press, 1957.

Mgaloblishvili, Sofron. *Vospominaniia o moei zhizni: Nezabyvaemye vstrechi.* Tblisi: Merani, 1974.

Mgeladze, Akaki. *Stalin, kakim ia ego znal: stranitsy nedavnogo proshlogo.* Tblisi, 2001.

Michel Kettle, *The Allies and the Russian Collapse, March 1917–March 1918.* Minneapolis: University of Minnesota Press, 1981.

Mif, Pavel. "Kitaiskaia kommunisticheskaia partiia v kriticheskie dni," *Bol'shevik,* 1927, no. 21, 23–24.

Mikhailovich, Alexander. *Once a Grand Duke.* New York: Farrar and Rinehart, 1932.

Mikhailovich, Velikii kniaz' Aleksandr. *Kniga vospominanii,* 2 vols. Paris: Biblioteka illiustrirovanoi Rossoi, 1933.

Mikhaleva, V. M., ed. *Revvoensovet Respubliki: protokoly 1920–1923 gg.* Moscow: Editorial URSS, 2000.

Mikhutina, I. B. "SSSR glazami pol'skikh diplomatov (1926–1931 gg.)," *Voprosy istorii,* 1993, no. 9: 45-58.

Mikhutina, I. V. *Pol'sko-Sovetskaia voina, 1919–1920 gg.* Moscow, Institut slavianovedeniia i blakanistiki, 1994.

Mikoian, A. I. "Na Severnom Kavkaze," *Novyi mir,* 1972, no. 12.

——. *Dorogoi bor'by: kniga pervaia.* Moscow: Politizdat, 1971.

——. *Feliks Dzerzhinskii.* Moscow: Partizdat, 1937.

——. *Mysli i vospominaniia o Lenine.* Moscow: Politizdat, 1970.

——. *Tak bylo.* Moscow: Vargrius, 1999.

Mil'chik, I. I. "Fevral'skie dni," *Leningradskaia pravda,* February 28, 1917.

Miliukov, P. N. "From Nicholas II to Stalin: Half a Century of Foreign Politics," typescript (n.d.), Hoover Institution Archives (the manuscript appears to date from 1942).

——. *Istoriia vtoroi russkoi revoliutsii,* 3 vols. in 1. Sofiia: Rossiisko-Bolgarskoe izd-vo, 1921–4.

——. *Ocherki po istorii Russkoi kul'tury.* St. Petersburg: I. N. Skorokhodov, 1904.

——. *Vospominaniia, 1859–1917,* 2 vols. New York: Izd-vo im. Chekhova, 1955.

——. *Vtoraia Duma: publitsitskaia khronika 1907.* St. Petersburg: Obshchestvenaia polza, 1908.

——, and Stites, Richard. *The Russian Revolution.* Gulf Breeze, FL: Academic International Press, 1978.

Miliukov, Paul, et al. *Histoire de Russie,* 3 vols. Paris: E. Leroux, 1932–3.

Miliutin, Vladimir. *O Lenine.* Leningrad: Gosizdat, 1924.

Millar, James R., and Nove, Alec. "A Debate on Collectivization: Was Stalin Really Necessary?" *Problems of Communism,* 25/4 (1976): 49–62.

Miller, Viktor I. *Soldatskie komitety russkoi army v 1917 g.: vozniknovenie i nachal'nyi period deiatel'nosti.* Moscow: Nauka, 1974.

Minakin, S. T. *Sovetskaia voennaia elita.* Orel: Orelizdat, 2000.

——. *Stalin i ego marshal.* Moscow: Yauza Eksmo, 2004.

Minczeles, Henri. *Histoire générale du Bund: un mouvement révolutionnaire juif.* Paris: Editions Austral, 1995.

*Ministerstvo finansov, 1802–1902,* 2 vols. St. Petersburg: Ekspeditsiia zagotovleniia gosudarstvennykh bumag, 1902.

*Ministerstvo vnutrennykh del: istoricheskii ocherk,* 2 vols. St. Petersburg, 1902.

Mints, I. I. *Dokumenty velikoi proletarskoi revoliutsii*, 2 vols. Moscow: Gosizdat, 1938, 1948.

Mintslov, S. R. *Peterburg v 1903–1910 godakh*. Riga: Kniga dlia vsekh, 1931.

*Mirnyi dogovor mezhdu Gruziei i Rossiei*. Moscow: Prodput', 1920.

Mironov, Georgii E. *Gosudari i gosudarevy liudi: gosudari i gosudarevy liudi, rossiiskie reformatory i kontrreformatory XIX-nachala XX veka*. Moscow: Mart, 1999.

Misshima, Yasuo, and Tomio, Goto. *A Japanese View of Outer Mongolia*. New York: Institute of Pacific Relations, 1942.

Mitchell, Allan. *Revolution in Bavaria, 1918–1919: The Eisner Regime and the Soviet Republic*. Princeton, NJ: Princeton University Press, 1966.

Mitchell, David J. *1919: Red Mirage*. New York: Macmillan, 1970.

Mitchell, Mairin. *The Maritime History of Russia, 848–1948*. London: Sidgwick and Jackson, 1949.

Mlechin, L. M. *Russkaia armiia mezhdu Trotskim i Stalinym*. Moscow: Tsenrtopoligraf, 2002.

Mnatsakanian, A. *Poslantsy Sovetskoi Rossii v Armenii*. Erevan: Aipetrat, 1959.

Moggridge, D. E. *The Return to Gold, 1925: The Formulation of Economic Policy and Its Critics*. Cambridge, U.K.: Cambridge University Press, 1969.

Moletotov, I. A. *Sibkraikom: partiinoe stroitel'stvo v Sibiri 1924–1930 gg.* Novosibirsk: Nauka, 1978.

Molotov, V. M. *Na shestoi god*. Moscow: Gosizdat, 1923.

Mombauer, Annika. "A Reluctant Military Leader? Helmuth von Moltke and the July Crisis of 1914," *War in History*, 6/4 (1999): 417–46.

———. *Helmuth von Moltke and the Origins of the First World War*. New York: Cambridge University Press, 2001.

———. *The Origins of the First World War*. London: Longman, 2002.

Mommen, André. *Stalin's Economist: The Economic Contributions of Jenő Varga*. London and New York: Routledge, 2011.

Monas, Sidney. "The Political Police: The Dream of a Beautiful Autocracy," in *The Transformation of Russian Society*, edited by Cyril Black. Cambridge, MA: Harvard University Press, 1967.

———. *The Third Section: Police and Society in Russia under Nicholas I*. Cambridge, MA: Harvard University Press, 1961.

Montefiore, Simon Sebag. *Young Stalin*. New York: Knopf, 2007.

———. *Stalin: Court of the Red Tsar*. London: Weidenfeld, 2003.

Moore, Barrington. *Soviet Politics: The Dilemma of Power*. Cambridge, MA: Harvard University Press, 1950.

Morozov, K. N. *Sudebnyi protsess sotsialistov-revoliutsionerov i tiuremnoe protivostoianie (1922–1926): etika i taktika protivoborstva*. Moscow: Rosspen, 2005.

Morozov, V. M. *Sozdanie i ukreplenie sovetskogo gosudarstsvennogo apparata, noiabr' 1917 g.—mart 1919 g.* Moscow: Politicheskaia literatura, 1957.

Morozova, Irina Y. *The Comintern and Revolution in Mongolia*. Cambridge: White Horse, 2002.

Morris, Edmund. *Colonel Roosevelt*. New York: Random House, 2010.

Moskalev, M. A. *bol'shevistskie organizatsii Zakavkaz'ia pervoi russkoi revoliutsii i v gody stolypinskoi reaktsii*. Moscow, 1940.

*Moskovskie Bol'sheviki v bor'be s pravym i "levym" opportunizmom, 1921–1929 gg.* Moscow: Moskovskii rabochii, 1969.

Moskvich, Grigorii. *Putevoditel' po Kavkazu*, 20th ed. St. Petersburg: Putivoditeli, 1913.

Mostashari, Firouzeh. *On the Religious Frontier: Tsairst Russia and Islam in the Caucasus*. London and New York: I. B. Tauris, 2006.

Mostiev, B. M., ed. *Revoliutsionnaia publitsistika Kirova, 1909–1917 gg.* Ordzhonokidze: Ir, 1971.

Motherwell, Robert. *Dada Painters and Poets: An Anthology*. New York: Wittenborn, Shultz, 1951.

Motojirō, Akashi. *Rakka ryūsui: Colonel Akashi's Report on His Secret Cooperation with the Russian Revolutionary Parties during the Russo-Japanese War*. Translated [abridged] by Inaba Chiharu. Helsinki: Suomen Historiallinen Seura, 1988.

Mozokhin, O. *VChK-OGPU, karaiushchii mech diktatury proletariat: na zashchite ekonoimicheskoi ezopasnosti gosudarstva i v bor'be s terrorizmom*. Moscow: Iauza-Eksmo, 2004.

Mozokhin, Oleg, and Gladkov, Teodor. *Menzhinskii: intelligent s Lubianki*. Moscow: Iauza, 2005.

Mstislavskii, Sergei D. *Five Days Which Transformed Russia*. Bloomington, Indiana University Press, 1988.

———. *Piat' dnei: nachalo i konets Fevral'skoi revoliutsii*, 2nd ed. Berlin: Z. I. Grzhebin, 1922.

Müller, Rolf-Dieter. *Das Tor zur Weltmacht: Die Bedeutung der Sowjetunion für die deutsche Wirtschafts-und Rüstungspolitik zwischen den Weltkriegen*. Boppard am Rhein: Harald Boldt, 1984.

Munck, J. L. *The Kornilov Revolt: A Critical Examination of the Sources*

*and Research*. Aarhus, Denmark: Aarhus University Press, 1987.

Munck, Ronaldo. *The Difficult Dialogue: Marxism and Nationalism*. London: Zed, 1986.

Murin, Iurii. "Eshche raz ob otstavkakh I. Stalina," *Rodina*, 1994, no. 7: 72–3.

Murphy, George G. S. *Soviet Mongolia: A Study of the Oldest Political Satellite*. Berkeley: University of California Press, 1966.

Murphy, J. T. *New Horizons*. London: J. Lane, 1941.

Murtazin, M. L. *Bashkiriia i bashkirskie voiska v grazhdanskuiu voinu*. Moscow: Voennaia tipografiia upr. delami Narkomvoenmor i RVS, 1927.

Nabokov, V. D. *Vremennoe pravitelstvo: vospominaniia*. Moscow: Mir, 1924.

———. "Vremennoe pravitel'stvo," in *Arkhiv russkoi revoliutsii*, ed. by Gessen, I: 9–96.

"Nachalo voiny 1914 g: podennaia zapis' b. ministerstva innostrannykh del," *Krasnyi arkhiv*, 1923, no. 4: 3–62.

Nad, Nikolai. "Kto ubil Mikhaila Frunze," *Izvestiia*, October 26, 2010.

Nadezhdin, P. P. *Kavkazskii krai: priroda i liudi*, 2nd ed. Tula: E. I. Druzhinina, 1895.

Nadtocheev, Valerii. "'Triumvirat' ili 'semerka'? Iz istorii vnutripartiinoi bor'by v 1924–1925 godakh," in *Trudnye voprosy istorii: poiski, razmyshleniia, novyi vzgliad na sobytiia i fakty*, edited by V. V. Zuravlev. Moscow: Politicheskaia literatura, 1991.

Nafziger, Steven. "Communal Institutions, Resource Allocations, and Russian Economic Development, 1861–1905." Phd diss., Yale University, 2006.

Naida, S. F. *O nekotorykh voprosakh istorii grazhdanskoivoiny v SSSR*. Moscow: Voenizdat, 1958.

Nalbandian, E. N. "'Iskra' i tipografiia 'Nina' v Baku," *Trudy Azerbaizhanskogo filiala IML pri TsK KPSS*. Baku, 1960.

Namier, Lewis. "After Vienna and Versailles," in *Conflicts: Studies in Contemporary History*, edited by Lewis Namier. London: Macmillan, 1942.

*Na prieme u Stalina: tetradi (zhurnaly) zapiseĭ lits, priniatykh I.V. Stalinym: 1924–1953 gg.* Moscow: Novyi khronograf, 2008.

Narskii, I. V. *Zhizn' v katastrofe: budni naseleniia Urala v 1917–1922 gg.* Moscow: Rosspen, 2001.

Nash, Ian Hill. *The Anglo-Japanese Alliance: The Diplomacy of Two Island Empires 1894–1907*. London: Athlone, 1966; Curzon reprint, 2004.

Naumov, A. N. *Iz utselevshikh vospominanii, 1868–1917*, 2 vols. New York:

A. K. Naumova and O. A. Kusevits-kaia, 1954–5.

Naumov, V. and Kurin. L. "Leninskoe zaveshchanie," in *Urok daet istoriia*, edited by V. Afanas'ev and G. Smirnov. Moscow: Politizdat, 1989.

Naumov, Vladimir. "1923 god: sud'ba leninskoi al'ternativy," *Kommunist*, 1991, no. 5: 30–42.

Naville, Pierre. *Trotsky vivant*. París: Juillard, 1962.

Nazanskii, V. I. *Krushenie velikoi Rossii i doma Romanovykh*. Paris, 1930.

Nazarov, Mikhail. *Missiia Russkoi emigratsii*. Stavropol: Kavkazskii krai, 1992.

Nazarov, O. G. *Stalin i bor'ba za liderstvo v bol'shevistkoi partii v usloviakh NEPa*. Moscow: IVI RAN, 2002.

Neilson, Keith. *Britain and the Last Tsar: British Policy and Russia, 1894–1917*. Oxford: Clarendon Press, 1995.

———. *Britain, Soviet Russia and the Collapse of the Versailles Order, 1919–1939*. New York: Cambridge University Press, 2006.

———. *Strategy and Supply: The Anglo-Russian Alliance, 1914–1917*. London: George Allen & Unwin, 1984.

Nekliudov, M. A. "Souvenirs diplomatiques: l'Entrevue de Bjoerkoe," *Revue des deux mondes*, 44 (1918): 423–48.

Nenarokov, A. P. *K edinstvu ravnykh: kul'turnye faktory ob"edinitel'nogo dvizheniia sovetskikh narodov, 1917–1924*. Moscow: Nauka, 1991.

Nenarokov, Al'bert P., ed. *Revvoensovet Respubliki, 6 sentiabria 1918 g.–28 avgusta 1923 g*. Moscow: Politizdat, 1991.

"Neopublikovannye materialy iz biografii tov. Stalina," *Antireligioznik*, 1939, no. 12: 17–21.

Nettl, J. P. *Rosa Luxemburg*. New York: Oxford University Press, 1966.

Neuberg, A. *Armed Insurrection*. London: NLB, 1970.

Nevskii, V. I. *Doklad ot narodnogo kommissara putei soobshcheniia predesedateliu soveta narodnykh komissarov tov. Leninu*. Moscow: Narkomput, 1919.

Newstad, E. R. W. "Components of Pessimism in Russian Conservative Thought, 1881–1905." Phd diss., University of Oklahoma, 1991.

Newton, Lord Thomas. *Lord Lansdowne: A Biography*. London: Macmillan, 1929.

Nicolaevsky, Boris. *Aseff: The Russian Judas*. London: Hurst and Blackett, 1934.

Nicolson, Harold. *King George V: His Life and Reign*. London: Constable, 1952.

———. *Peacemaking 1919: Being Reminiscences of the Paris Peace Conference*. New York: Houghton Mifflin, 1933.

Nielsen, Jes Peter, and Weil, Boris, eds. *Russkaia revoliutsiia glazami Petrogradskogo chinovnika: dnevnik 1917–1918 g*. Oslo: Represtentralen Universitetet i Oslo Slavisk-Baltisk Institut, 1986.

Niessel, Henri A. *Le triomphe des bolchéviks et la paix de Brest-Litovsk: Souvenirs, 1917–1918*. Paris: Plon, 1940.

Nikoalevskii, Boris. *Tainye stranitsy istorii*, ed. by Iu. Fel'shtinskii. Moscow: Gumanitarnaia literatura, 1995.

Nikolaev, A. N. *Chekisty: sbornik*. Moscow: Molodaia gvardiia, 198.

Nikolaev, M. G. "Na puti k denezhnoi reforme 1922–1924 godov: chetyre arestov N. N. Kutlera," *Otechestvennaia istoriia*, 2001, no. 1.

"Nikolai II—imperatritse Marii Fedeorovne, 12 ianvaria 1906," *Krasnaia nov'*, 1927, tom 3 (22).

Nikolai-on [Danielson]. *Ocherki nashego poreformennogo obshchestvennogo khoziaistva*. St. Petersburg: A. Benke, 1893.

Nikol'skii, B. V. "Iz dnevnikov 1905 g.," in *Nikolai II. Vospominaniia. Dnevniki*, edited by B. V. Anan'ich and R. Sh. Ganelin. St. Petersburg: D. Bulanin, 1994.

Nikonov, V. A. *Molotov: molodost'*. Moscow: Vagrius, 2005.

Nikulin, Lev. *Zapiski sputnika*. Leningrad: Izd. Pisatelei, 1932.

Nish, Ian. "The Clash of Two Continental Empires: the Land War Reconsidered," in *Rethinking the Russo-Japanese War, 1904–05*, 2 vols, edited by Rotem Kowner. Folkstone: Global Oriental, 2007.

———. *The Origins of the Russo-Japanese War*. London: Longman, 1985.

Nolan, Mary. *Visions of Modernity: American Business and the Modernization of Germany*. New York: Oxford University Press, 1994.

Nol'de, Boris. "Tseli i real'nost' v velikoi voine," in *Dalekoe i blizkoe: istoricheskie ocherki*. Paris: Sovremennye zapiski, 1930.

Nosovich, A. L. *Krasnyi Tsaritsyn, vzgliad iznutri: zapiski belogo razvedchika*. Moscow: AIRO-XXI, 2010.

———. *Zapiski vakhmistra Nosovicha*. Paris: self-published, 1967.

Nove, Alec. "The Peasants, Collectivization, and Mr. Carr," *Soviet Studies*, 10/4 (1958–9): 384–9.

———. *An Economic History of the USSR*. London: Allen Lane, 1969.

———. *The Soviet Economy: An Introduction*, 2nd ed. New York: Praeger, 1969.

———. "Was Stalin Really Necessary?" *Encounter*, April 1962: 86–92.

———. *Was Stalin Really Necessary? Some Problems of Soviet Political Economy*. New York: Praeger, 1964.

Novitskaia, T. E. *Uchreditel'noe sobra-nie, Rossiia, 1918: stenogrammy i drugie dokumenty*. Moscow: Nedar, 1991.

Nowak K. F., ed. *Die Aufzeichnungen des Generalmajors Max Hoffmann*, 2 vols. Berlin: Kulturpolitik, 1929.

Nyamaa, D., ed. *A Compilation of Some Documents Relating to the Foreign Relations of the Mongolian People's Republic*. Ulaanbaatar: State Publishing House, 1964.

O'Brien, Phillips Payson. *The Anglo-Japanese Alliance, 1902–1922*. London: RoutledgeCurzon, 2004.

Occleshaw, Michael. *Dances in Deep Shadows: The Clandestine War in Russia, 1917–20*. New York: Carroll and Graf, 2006.

O'Connor, Timothy. *The Engineer of Revolution: L. B. Krasin and the Bolsheviks, 1870–1926*. Boulder, CO: Westview Press, 1992.

———. *Diplomacy and Revolution: G. V. Chicherin and Soviet Foreign Affairs, 1918–1930*. Ames: Iowa State University Press, 1988.

Odet Eran, *The Mezhdunarodniki*. Ramat Gan: Turtledove Publishers, 1979.

Offer, Avner. "Going to War in 1914: a Matter of Honour?" *Politics and Society*, 23/2 (1995): 213–41.

———. *The First World War: An Agrarian Interpretation*. Oxford: Clarendon, 1989.

Okorokov, A. Z. *Oktiabr' i krakh russkoi burzuazhnoi pressy*. Moscow: Mysl', 1970.

Oldenbourg, Serge, ed. *Le coup d'état bolchéviste, 20 octobre–3 decembre 1917*. Paris: Payot, 1929.

Ol'denburg, Sergei S. *Gosudar' Imperator Nikolai II Aleksandrovich*. Berlin: Stiag i fond po izdaniiu tsarskikh portretov, 1922.

———. *Istoriia tsarstvovaniia Imperatora Nikolaia II 1894–1917*, 2 vols. Belgrad: Obshchestvo rasprostraneniia russkoi natsional'noi i patrioticheskoi literatury, 1938.

———. *Last Tsar: Nicholas II, His Reign, and His Russia*, 4 vols. Gulf Breeze, FL: Academic International Press, 1975–8.

Olekh, G. L. *Povorot, kotorogo ne bylo*. Novosibirsk: Novosibirsk universiteta, 1992.

Omissi, David. *The Sepoy and the Raj: The Indian Army, 1860–1940*. Basingstoke: Macmillan, 1994.

Oppenheim, Samuel A. "Between Right and Left: Grigorii Yakovlevich Sokolnikov and the Development of the Soviet State, 1921–1929," *Slavic Review*, 48/4 (1989): 592–613.

Orakhelashvili, Mamia. *Sergo Ordzhonikidze: biograficheskii ocherk*. Leningrad: Partizdat, 1936.

Orde, Anne. *British Policy and European Reconstruction after the First World War*. New York: Cambridge University Press, 1990.

Ordzhonikidze, G. K. *Stat'i i rechi*, 2 vols. Mosow: Politicheskaia literatura, 1956–7.

———. "Bor'ba s men'shevikami," in *Dvadtsat' piat' let bakinskoi organizatsii bol'shevikov*. Baku: 1924.

Ordzhonokidze, Zinaida G. *Put' Bol'shevika: stranitsy iz zhizni G.k. Ordzhonikidze*. Moscow: Politcheskaia literatura, 1956, 1967.

Orlov, Alexander. *Secret History of Stalin's Crimes*. New York, Random House, 1953.

Orlov, Boris, "Mif o Fanni Kaplan," *Istochnik*, 1993, no. 2: 70–1.

Orlova, M. I. *Revoliutsionnyi krizis 1923 g. v Germanii i politika kommunistitcheskoi partii*. Moscow: Moskovskii universitet, 1973.

Orlovsky, Daniel. "Corporatism or Democracy: The Russian Provisional Government of 1917," in *Landscaping the Human Garden: Twentieth Century Population Management in a Comparative Framework*, edited by Amir Weiner. Stanford, CA: Stanford University Press, 2003.

———. "Political Clientelism in Russia: The Historical Perspective," in *Leadership Selection and Patron-Client Relations in the USSR and Yugoslavia*, edited by T. H. Rigby and B. Harasymiw. London and Boston: Allen & Unwin, 1983.

———. "Reform During Revolution: Governing the provinces in 1917," *Reform in Russia and the USSR: Past and Prospects*, edited by in Robert O. Crummey. Urbana: University of Illinois Press, 1989.

———. "Russia in War and Revolution," in *Russia: A History*, edited by Gregory Freeze. New York: Oxford University Press, 1997Osipova, T. V. *Klassovaia bor'ba v derevene v period podgotovki i provedeniia oktiabr'skoi revoliutsii*. Moscow: Nauka, 1974.

O'Rourke, Kevin, and Williamson, Jeffrey. *Globalization and History: The Evolution of a Nineteenth-Century Atlantic Economy*. Cambridge, MA: Massachusetts Institute of Technology Press, 1999.

Osinskii. "Glavnyi nedostatok," in *Prodovol'stvennaia politika v svete obshchego khoziaistvennogo stroitel'stva sovetskoi vlasti: sbornik materialov*. Moscow: Gosizdat, 1920.

Os'kin, D. P. *Zapiski soldata*. Moscow: Federatisia, 1929.Osklokov, E. N. *Pobeda kolkhoznogo stroia v zernoykh raionakh Severnogo Kavkaza*. Rostov-na-Donu: Rostovskii universitet, 1973.

Osorgin, M. A. *Okhrannoe otdelenie i ego sekrety*. Moscow: Griadushchee, 1917.

Ossendowski, Ferdinand. *Beasts, Men, and Gods*. New York: E. P. Dutton, 1922.

Ostal'tseva, Alevtina F. *Anglo-russkoe soglashenie 1907 goda: vliianie russko-iaponskoi voiny i revoliutsii 1905–1907 godov na vneshniuiu politiku tsarizma i na peregruppirovku evropeiskikh derzhav*. Saratov: Saratovskii universitet, 1977.

Ostrovskii, Aleksandr V. "Predki Stalin," *Genealogicheskii vestnik*, no 1. 2001.

———. *Kto stoial za spinoi Stalina?* Moscow: Tsentropoligraf-Mim Delta, 2004. (Earlier edition, Olma 2002.)

*Otchet 15 s"ezdu partii*. Moscow: VKP (b), 1925.

*Otchet Komissii TsIK SSSR po uvekovecheniiu pamiati V. I. Ul'ianova (Lenina)*. Moscow: TsIk SSSR, 1925.

*Otchet po revizii Turkestankogo kraia*. St. Petersburg: Senatskaia tip., 1910.

Ottokar (Theobald Otto Maria) Czernin von und zu Chudenitz, Graf. *In the World War*. New York: Harper & Brothers, 1920.

Ovsiannikov, A. A. *Miusskaia ploshchad'*, 6. Moscow: Moskovskii rabochii, 1987.

Owen, Launcelot A. *The Russian Peasant Movement, 1906–1917*. London: P. S. King & Son, 1937.

Paléologue, Maurice. *An Ambassador's Memoirs*, 3 vols. Paris: Plon, 1921–2.

———. *La Russie des Tsars pendant la grand guerre*, 3 vols. Paris: Plon, 1921–2.

Palij, Michael. *The Ukrainian-Polish Defensive Alliance, 1919–1921: An Aspect of the Ukrainian Revolution*. Edmonton: Canadian Institute of Ukrainian Studies, 1995.

Pallot, Judith. *Land Reform in Russia, 1906–1917: Peasant Responses to Stolypin's Project of Rural Transformation*. New York: Oxford University Press, 1999.

Palmer, James. *Bloody White Baron: The Extraordinary Story of the Russian Nobleman Who Became the Last Khan of Mongolia*. New York: Basic Books, 2009.

Pankratova, A. N., et al., eds. *Revoliutsiia 1905–1907 gg. v Rossii: Dokumenty i materialy*, 5 vols. Moscow: Akademiia nauk, 1955–61.

Pantsov, Alexander. *Tainaia istoriia sovetsko-kitaiskikh otnoshenii: bol'sheviki i kitaiskaia revoliutsiia 1919–1927*. Moscow: Muravei-Gaid, 2001. Translated as *The Bolsheviks and the Chinese Revolution, 1919–1927*. Richmond, Surrey: Curzon, 2000.

*Papers Relating to the Foreign Relations of the United States: Russia, 1918*, 3 vols. Washington, D.C.: Department of State, 1931–2.

Papkov, Sergei. *Obyknovenyi terror: politika Stalinizma v Sibiri*. Moscow: Rosspen, 2012.

Paquet, Alfons. *Im kommunistischen*

*Russland: Briefe aus Moskau*. Jena: E. Diederichs, 1919.

Pares, Bernard, ed. *Letters of the Tsaritsa to the Tsar, 1914–1916*. Westport, CT: Hyperion, 1979.

———. *My Russian Memoirs*. London: J. Cape, 1931.

———. *The Fall of the Russian Monarchy: A Study of Evidence*. New York: Knopf, 1939.

Park, Alexander G. *Bolshevism in Turkestan, 1917–1927*. New York: Columbia University Press, 1957.

Parkadze, G. "Boevye bol'shevistskie druzhiny v Chiature v 1905 gody," *Rasskazy o Velikom Staline*, kn. 2. Tblisi: Zaria vostoka, 1941.

Parrish, Michael. *Soviet Security and Intelligence Organizations, 1917–1990: A Biographical Dictionary and Review of Literature in English*. New York: Greenwood Press, 1992.

Parsons, J. W. R. "The Emergence and Development of the National Question in Georgia, 1801–1921." Phd diss., University of Glasgow, 1987.

Pashukanis, S., ed. "K istorii anglo-russkogo soglasheniia 1907 g.," *Krasnyi arkhiv*, 69–70 (1935): 3–39.

Patenaude, Bertrand. *A Wealth of Ideas: Revelations from the Hoover Institution Archives*. Stanford, CA: Stanford General Books, 2006.

———. *Stalin's Nemesis: The Exile and Murder of Leon Trotsky*. London: Faber and Faber, 2009.

———. *The Big Show in Bololand: The American Relief Expedition to Soviet Russia in the Famine of 1921*. Stanford, CA: Stanford University Press, 2002.

Paustovskii, Konstantin. *Povest' o zhizni*. Moscow: Sovremennyi pisatel', 1993, 1966–7.

Paustovskii, Konstantin. *The Story of a Life*. New York: Pantheon Books, 1967.

Pavel Sudoplatov, *Special Tasks: The Memoirs of an Unwanted Witness, a Soviet Spymaster*. Boston: Little, Brown, 1994.

Pavlovsky, George. *Agricultural Russia on the Eve of the Revolution*. London: G Routledge and Sons, 1930.

Pavliuchenkov, Sergei A. "*Orden mechenostsev": Partiia i vlast posle revoliutsii 1917–1929*. Moscow: Sobranie, 2008.

———. *Krest'ianskii Brest, ili predystoriia bol'shevistskogo NEPa*. Moscow: Russkoe knigoizdatel'skoe t-vo, 1996.

———. *Rossiia Nepovskaia*. Moscow: Novyi khronograf, 2002.

Pavlov, A. A., ed. *Chekisty: sbornik dokumental'nykh rasskazov i povesti*. Gorky: Volgo-Vyatskoe knizhnoe izdatel'stvo, 1968.

Pavlova, Irina V. "Mekhanizm politicheskoi vlasti v SSSR v 20–30-e gody," *Voprosy istorii*, 1998, no. 11–12: 49–66.

———. "Poezdka Stalina v Sibir': pochemu v Sibir'?" *Eko*, 1995, no. 2.

———. *Stalinizm: Stanovlenie mekhanizma vlasti.* Novosibirsk: Sibirskii khronograf, 1993.

Pavlovich, M. "SSSR i vostok," *Revoliutsionnyi vostok.* Moscow-Leningrad, 1927.

Payne, Robert. *The Rise and Fall of Stalin.* New York: Simon & Schuster, 1965.

Pearce, Brian. *How Haig Saved Lenin.* New York: St. Martin's Press, 1987.

Pearce, Cyril. *Comrades in Conscience: The Story of an English Community's Opposition to the Great War.* London: Francis Boutle, 2001.

Pearson, Raymond. *The Russian Moderates and the Crisis of Tsarism, 1914–1917.* New York: Barnes and Noble, 1977.

Pedroncini, Guy. *Les mutineries de 1917,* 2nd ed. Paris: Publications de la Sorbonne, Presse Universitaires de France, 1983.

Pegov, A. M., et al. *Imena moskovskikh ulits.* Moscow: Moskovskii rabochii, 1979.

Penner, D'Ann R. "Stalin and the Ital'ianka of 1932–1933 in the Don Region," *Cahiers du monde russe,* 39/1–2 (1998): 27–67.

Pentkovskaia, V. V. "Rol' V. I. Lenina v obrazovanii SSSR," *Voprosy istorii,* 1956, no. 3: 13–24.

Peregudova, Z. I. "Deitel'nost komissii Vremennogo pravtitel'stva i sovetskikh arkhivov po raskrytiiu sekretnoi agentury tsarskoi okhranki," *Otechestvennye arkhivy,* no. 5 (1998): 10–22.

———. *Politicheskii sysk Rossii, 1880–1917.* Moscow, 2000.

Pereira, Norman G. O. *White Siberia: The Politics of Civil War.* Montreal and Kingston: McGill-Queen's University Press, 1996.

*Perepiska sekretariata TsK RSDRP (b) s mestnymi partiinymi organizatsiiamii: sbornik dokumentov,* 8 vols. Moscow: Politicheskaia literatura, 1957–74.

*Perepiska V. I. Lenina i rukovodimykh im uchrezhdenii s partiinymi organizatsiiami, 1903–1905 gg.* Moscow, 1975.

Perlmutter, Amos. *Modern Authoritarianism: A Comparative Institutional Analysis.* New Haven, CT: Yale University Press, 1981.

Perrie, Maureen. "Food Supply in a Time of Troubles: Grain Procurement and the Russian Revolution," *Peasant Studies,* 17/3 (1990): 217–25.

———. "The Russian Peasant Movement of 1905–1907: Its Social Composition and Revolutionary Significance," *Past and Present,* 57 (1972): 123–55.

———. *The Agrarian Policy of the Russian Socialist-Revolution Party: From its Origins through the Revolution of 1905–1907.* New York: Cambridge University Press, 1976.

Pershin, D. P., ed. *Baron Ungern: Urga i Altan-Bulak.* Samatra: Agni, 1999.

Pershin, P. N. *Uchastkovoe zemlepol'zovanie Rossii: khutora i otruba, ikh rasprostranenie za desiatiletie 1907–1911 gg. i sud'by vo vremia revoliutsii (1917–1920 gg.).* Moscow: Novaia derevnia, 1922.

*Pervaia vseobshchaia perepis' naseleniia Rossiiskoi imperii, 1897 g.,* LXIX (Tiflisskaia guberniia). St. Petersburg: Tsentral'nyi statisticheskii komitet MVD, 1905.

*Pervyi kongress Kominterna mart 1919 g.* Moscow: Partizdat, 1933.

*Pervyi legal'nyi Peterburgskii komitet bol'shevikov v 1917 godu: sbornik materialov i protokolov zasedanii.* Moscow and Leningrad: Gosizdat, 1927.

*Pervyi s"ezd narodov vostoka, Baku, 1–8 sentiabria, 1920 g.: stenograficheskie otchety.* Petrograd: Kommunisticheskii internatsional, 1920.

Peskova, G. N. "Diplomaticheskie otnosheniia mezhdu SSSR i Kitaem, 1924–1929 gg.," *Novaia i noveishaia istoriia,* 1998, no. 1, 2.

———. "Stanovleniie diplomaticheskikh otnoshenii mezhdu Sovetskoi Rossiiei i Kitaem, 1917–1924 gg.," *Novaia i noveishaia istoriia,* 1997, no. 4: 105–34, 1998, no 1: 106–19, no. 2: 66–88.

Pestkovskii, S. S. "Ob oktiabr'skie dniakh v Pitere," *Proletarskaia revoliutsiia,* 1922, no. 10: 94–104.

———. "Vospominaniia o rabote v Narkomnatse," *Proletarskaia revoliutsiia,* 1930, no. 6: 124–31.

Peters, [Ia]. "Vospominaniia o rabote VChK v pervyi gody revoliutsii," *Proletarskaia revoliutsiia,* 1924, no. 10 (33): 5–32.

Peterson, Claes. *Peter the Great's Administrative and Judicial Reforms: Swedish Antecedents and the Process of Reception.* Stockholm: A.-B/ Nordiska Bokhandeln, 1979.

Pethybridge, Roger. *One Step Backwards, Two Steps Forward: Soviet Society and Politics in the New Economic Policy.* Oxford: Clarendon, 1990.

———. *The Spread of the Russian Revolution: Essays on 1917.* New York: St. Martin's Press, 1972.

*Petrogradskaia obshchegorodskaia konferentsiia RSDRP (bol'shevikov), aprel' 1917 goda: protokoly.* Moscow: Politicheskaia literatura, 1958.

Petrov, Iurii P. *Partiinoe stroitel'stvo v Sovetskoi armii i flote: deiatel'nost'*

*KPSS po sozdaniiu i ukrepleniiu politorganov, partiinykh i komsomolskikh organizatsii v vooruzhennykh silakh (1918–1961 gg.).* Moscow: Voenizdat, 1964.

Petrov, Nikolai. *50 i 500.* Moscow: Vserossiiskoe teatral'noe obshchestvo, 1960.

Pflanze, Otto. *Bismarck and the Development of Germany,* 2nd ed., 3 vols. Princeton, NJ: Princeton University Press, 1990.

Piaskovskii, A. B., ed. *Vosstanie 1916 goda v Srednei Azii i Kazakhstane: sbornik dokumentov.* Moscow: Akademiia Nauk, 1960.

*Piat' let vlasti Sovetov.* Moscow: TSIK, 1922.

Pietsch, Walter. *Revolution und Staat: Institutionen als Träger der Macht in Sowjetrussland 1917–1922.* Cologne: Verlag Wissenschaft und Politik, 1969.

Pikhoia, R. G., and Zelenov, M.V., eds. *I. V. Stalin: istoricheskaia ideologiia i SSSR v 1920–1950-e gody: perepiska s istorikami, stat'i i zametki po istorii, stenogrammy vystuplenii. Sbornik dokumentov i materialov.* St. Petersburg: Nauka-Piter, 2006.

Pilenko, Aleksandr, ed. *At the Court of the Last Tsar; Being the Memoirs of A. A. Mossolov, Head of the Court Chancellery, 1900–1916.* London: Methuen, 1935.

Pil'skii, P. M. "Pervoe dekabrai," in *Baltiiskii arkhiv: russkaia kul'tura v Pribal'tike,* edited by Irina Belobrovtseva, et al. Tallinn: Avenarius, 1996.

Piontkowski, S. *Grazhdanskaia voina v Rossii: khrestomatiia.* Moscow: Kommunisticheskii universitet im. Ia. M. Sverdlova, 1925.

Piłsudski, Josef. *Year 1920.* New York: Piłsudski Institute of New York, 1972.

Piotrovskii, Adrian. *Za sovetskii teatr!* Leningrad: Academiia, 1925.

Pipes, Richard. "The First Experiment in Soviet Nationality Policy: the Bashkir Republic, 1917–1920," *Russian Review,* 9/4 (1950): 303–9.

———. *Peter Struve,* 2 vols. Cambridge, MA: Harvard University Press, 1970, 1980.

———. *Russia Under the Bolshevik Regime.* New York: Knopf, 1994.

———. *The Degaev Affair: Terror and Treason in Tsarist Russia.* New Haven, CT, and London: Yale University Press, 2003.

———. *The Formation of the Soviet Union: Communism and Nationalism, 1917–1923.* Cambridge, MA: Harvard University Press, 1953.

———. *The Russian Revolution.* New York: Knopf, 1990.

Pipes, Richard, ed. *The Unknown Lenin: From the Secret Archive.* New

Haven, CT: Yale University Press, 1996.

——. *Revolutionary Russia*. Cambridge, MA: Harvard University Press, 1968.

Pirani, Simon. *The Russian Revolution in Retreat, 1920–24: Soviet Workers and the New Communist Elite*. London: Routledge, 2008.

Pitcher, Harvey J. *Witnesses of the Russian Revolution*. London: John Murray, 1994.

Pittaluga, Giovanni B. "The Genoa Conference: Was it Really a Failure?" Found at http://dev3.cepr.org/meets/wkcn/1/1671/papers/The_Genoa_Conference_finale.pdf.

Platova, E. E. *Zhizn' studenchestva Rossii v perekhodnuiu epokhu, 1921–1927 gg*. St. Petersburg: SPb-GUAP SPbGU, 2001.

Platten, Fritz. *Die Reise Lenins durch Deutschland in plombierten Wagen*. Berlin, 1924.

Plekhanov, A. A., and Plekhanov, A. M. *Zheleznyi Feliks: Belye piatna i biografii chekista*. Moscow: Olma, 2010.

——, eds. *F. E. Dzerzhinskii— predsedatel' VChK-OGPU: sbornik dokumentov, 1917–1926*. Moscow: Mezhdunarodnyi fond Demokratiia, 2007.

Plekhanov, A. M. *VChK-OGPU v gody novoi ekonomicheskoi politiki 1921–1928*. Moscow: Kuchkovo pole, 2006.

——. *VChK-OGPU, 1921–1928*. Moscow: X-History, 2003.

Plekhanov, Aleksandr. *Dzerzhinskii: Pervyi chekist Rossii*. Moscow: Olma, 2007.

*Pobeda oktiabr'skoi revoliutsii v Uzbekistane: sbornik dokumentov*, 2 vols. Tashkent: Fan, 1963–72.

Podbolotov, Sergei. "Monarchists Against their Monarch: The Rightists' Criticism of Tsar Nicholas II," *Russian History*, 31/1–2 (2004): 105–20.

"Podpol'naia titpografiia 'Iskra' v Baku (Materialy Vano Sturua)," in *Iz proshlogo: Stat'i i vospominaniia iz istorii Bakinskoi organizatsii i rabochego dvizheniia v Baku*. Baku: Bakinskii rabochii, 1923.

Podvoiskii, N. I. *Krasnaia gvardiia v oktiabr'skie dni*. Moscow-Leningrad: Gosizdat, 1927.

*Poezdka v Sibir' i povol'zhe: zapiska P. A. Stolypina i A. V. Kriosvehina*. St. Petersburg: A. S. Suvorin, 1911.

Pogerelskin, Alexis. "Kamenev in Rome," *The NEP Era: Soviet Russia, 1921–1928, 1* (2007): 101–81.

Pogrebinskii, A. P. "Voenno-promyshlennye komitety," *Istoricheskie zapiski*, 11 (1941): 160–200.

——. *Ocherki istorii finansov dorevoliutsionnoi Rossii, XIX-XX vv*. Moscow: Gosfinizdat, 1954.

Pokhlebkin, V. V. *Velikii psevdonim*. Moscow: Iudit, 1996.

Pokrovskii, M., and Gelis, I. R., eds. "Politcheskoe polozhenie Rossii nakanune fevral'skoi revoliutsii v zhandarmskom osveshchenii," *Krasnyi arkhiv*, 17 (1926): 3–35.

Pokrovskii, M. N., and Iakovlev, Ia. A., eds. *Gosudarstvennoe soveshchanie*. Moscow-Leningrad: Gosizdat, 1930.

Pokrovsky, M. N. *A Brief History of Russia*, 2 vols. London: Martin Lawrence, 1933.

Polan, A. J. *Lenin and the End of Politics*. Berkeley: University of California Press, 1984.

Polanyi, Karl. *The Great Transformation*. Boston: Beacon, 1957.

Poletaev, V. E. et al. *Revoliutsionnoe dvizhenie v Rossii: aprel'skii krizis*. Moscow: Akademiia nauk, 1958.

Polikarenko, I. E., ed. *O Felikse Edmundoviche Dzerzhinskom: vospominaniia, stat'i, ocherki sovremennikov*. Moscow: Politiizdat, 1977.

*Politicheskii dnevnik, 1964–1970*. Amsterdam: Fond Imeni Gertsena, 1972.

*Politika Sovetskoi vlasti po natsional'nym delam za tri goda. 1917–1920 gg*. Moscow: Gosizdat, 1920.

Polivanov, A. A. *Iz dnevnikov i vospominanii po dolzhnosti voennogo ministra i ego pomoshchnikov, 1907–1916 gg*. Moscow: Vysshii voen. redaktsionnyi sovet, 1924.

Pollock, Troy E. *Creating the Russian Peril: Education, the Public Sphere, and National Identity in Imperial Germany, 1890–1914*. Rochester, NY: Camden House, 2010.

Pol'ner, T. I. *Zhiznennyi put' kniazia Georgiia Evgenevicha L'vova*. Paris: [s.n.], 1932; Moscow: Russkii put', 2001.

*Polnoe sobranie zakonov Rossiiskoi imperii*, series 3. St. Petersburg: Tipografiia II Otdieleniia Sobstvennoi Ego Imperatorskago Velichestva Kantseliarii, 1830–1916.

Polovtsoff, Peter A. *Glory and Downfall: Reminiscences of a Russian General Staff Officer*. London: G. Bell, 1935.

Polovtsov, A. A. *Dvenik gosudarstvennogo sekretaria*, P. A. Zaionchkovskii, ed. 2 vols. Moscow: Nauka, 1966.

Pope, Arthur. *Maksim Litvinoff*. New York: I. B. Fischer, 1943.

Popoff, George. *The Tcheka: The Red Inquisition*. London: A. M. Philpot, 1925.

Popov, M. A. *Rubtsovsk 1892–2000: istoricheskie ocherki*. Rubtsovsk: [s.n.], 2004.

Popov, Nikolai. *Outline History of the C.P.S.U.*, 2 vols. New York, International Publishers, 1934.

Pospelov et al., Petr N. *Vladimir Il'ich Lenin; biografiia*. Moscow: Politicheskaia literatura, 1960, 1963.

Pozhigailo, P. A., ed. *P. A. Stolypin – programma reform: dokumenty i materialy*, 2 vols. Moscow: Rosspen, 2003.

Pravilova, Ekaterina. *Zakonnost' i prava lichnosti: administrativnaia iustitsiia v Rossii, vtoraia polovina 19 veka—oktiabr' 1917*. St. Petersburg: Obrazovanie-Kultura, 2000.

Preobrazhenskii, Evgenii. *Bumazhnye den'gi v epokhu proletarskoi diktatury*. Moscow: Gosizdat, 1920.

Pribytkov, Viktor. *Apparat*. St. Petersburg: VIS, 1995.

Price, M. Philips. *My Reminiscences of the Russian Revolution*. London: G. Allen & Unwin, 1921.

Price, Morgan Philips, and Rose, Tania, eds. *Dispatches from the Revolution: Russia 1916–1918*. London and Chicago: Pluto, 1997.

Prior, Robin, and Wilson, Trevor. *The Somme*. New Haven, CT: Yale University Press, 2005.

Prishvin, Mikhail M. *Dnevniki*, 11 vols. Moscow: Moskovskii rabochii, 1991–2012.

*Proceedings of the Brest-Litovsk Peace Conference [electronic resource]: the peace negotiations between Russia and the Central Powers 21 November, 1917–3 March, 1918*. Washington, D.C.: Government Printing Office, 1918.

Prokofiev, Sergei. *Soviet Diary 1927 and Other Writings*. London: Faber and Faber, 1991.

Protasov, L. G. *Vserossiiskoe Uchreditol'noe Sobranie: istoriia rozhdeniia i gibeli*. Moscow: Rosspen, 1997.

*Protokoly Tsentral'nogo komiteta RSDRP (b), Avgust 1917 g.—fevral' 1918 g*. Moscow-Leningrad: Gosizdat, 1929. Moscow: Poiticheskaia literature, 1958.

*Protokoly zasedanii Vserossiiskogo Tsentral'nogo Ispolnitel'nogo Komiteta V-go sozyva: stenograficheskii otchet*. Moscow: VTsIK, 1919.

*Protokoly zasedaniia VTsIK Sovetov rabochikh, soldatskikh, krest'ianskikh i kazach'ikh deputatov II sozyva*. Moscow: VTsIK, 1918.

Psurtsev, N. D. *Razvitie sviazi v SSSR*. Moscow: Sviaz', 1967.

Purishkevich, V. M. *Bez zabrala: otkrytoe pis'mo bol'shevikam Soveta Petrogradskikh rabochikh deputatov*. Harbin: Bergut, syn i ko., 1917.

——. *Vpered! Pod dvukhtsvetnym flagom (Otkrytoe pis'mo russkomu obshchesvtu)*. Petrograd, 1917.

Putintsev, N. D. "Statisticheskii ocherk Tomskoi gubernii," *Otchet po komandovaniiu predsedatelia ot voennogo ministerstva v ekspeditsiiu dlia izyskaniia Zapadno-Sibirskoi Zheleznoi dorogi*. Samara, 1892.

Putna, Vitovt. *K Visle i obratno*. Moscow: Voennyi vestnik, 1927.

Rabinowitch, Alexander. "Dos'e Shchastnogo: Trotskii i delo geroia Baltiiskogo flota," *Otechestvennaia istoriia*, 2001, no. 1: 61–81.

——. "Maria Spiridonova's 'Last Testament'," *Russian Review*, 54/3 (1995): 424–44.

——. *Prelude to Revolution: The Petrograd Bolsheviks and the July 1917 Uprising*. Bloomington: Indiana University Press, 1968.

——. *The Bolsheviks Come to Power: The Revolution of 1917 in Petrograd*. Bloomington: Indiana University Press, 1976.

——. *The Bolsheviks in Power: The First Year of Soviet Rule in Petrograd*. Bloomington: Indiana University Press, 2007.

Radek, Karl. *Vneshniaia politika sovetskoi Rossii*. Moscow-Petrograd: Gosizdat, 1923.

——. *Voina pol'skikh belogvardeitsev protiv Sovetskoi Rossii (Doklad na sobranii agitatorov Moskovskikh organizatsii komunisticheskoi partii 8 maia 1920 g.)* Moscow: Gosizdat, 1920.

Radkey, Oliver H. *Agrarian Foes of Bolshevism*. New York: Columbia University Press, 1968.

——. *Russia Goes to the Polls: The Election to the Russian Constituent Assembly of 1917*. Ithaca, NY: Cornell University Press, 1989.

——. *The Sickle Under the Hammer: The Russian Socialist Revolutionaries in the Early Months of Soviet Rule*. New York: Columbia University Press, 1963.

——. *Unknown Civil War in Soviet Russia: A Study of the Green Movement in the Tambov Region, 1920–1921*. Stanford, CA: Hoover Institution Press, 1976.

Radzinskii, Edvard. *Ubiistvo tsarskoi sem'i*. Moscow: Novosti, 1991. Translated as *The Last Tsar: The Life and Death of Nicholas II*. New York: Doubleday, 1992.

Radzinsky, Edvard. *Stalin: The First In-depth Biography Based on Explosive New Documents from Russia's Secret Archives*. New York: Doubleday, 1997.

——. *The Rasputin File*. New York: Nan A. Talese/Doubleday, 2006.

Raeff, Marc. *Understanding Imperial Russia*. New York: Columbia University Press, 1984.

——. "Some Reflections on Russian Liberalism," *Russian Review*, 18/3 (1959): 218–30.

——. "The Bureaucratic Phenomenon of Imperial Russia, 1700–1905," *American Historical Review*, 84/2 (1979): 399–411 (esp. 405–6).

——. "The Russian Autocracy and its Officials," *Harvard Slavic Studies*, 4 (1957): 77–91.

Rakh'ia, Eino. "Poslednoe podpol'e Vladmira Il'icha," *Krasnaia letopis'*, 1934, no. 1 (58): 79–90.

——. "Moi predoktiabr'skie i posleoktiabr'skie vstrechi s Leninym," *Novyi mir*, 1934, no. 1:24–39.

Rakovskii, Kh. *Kniaz' Metternikh: ego zhizn' i politicheskaia deiatel'nost'*. St. Petersburg: Iu.N. Erlikh, 1905.

Raleigh, Donald J. "Revolutionary Politics in Provincial Russia: the Tsaritsyn 'Republic' in 1917," *Slavic Review*, 40/2 (1981): 194–209.

——. *Experiencing Russia's Civil War: Politics, Society, and Revolutionary Culture in Saratov, 1917–22*. Princeton, NJ: Princeton University Press, 2002.

——. *Revolution on the Volga: 1917 in Saratov*. Ithaca, NY: Cornell University Press, 1984.

——, ed. *Provincial Landscapes: Local Dimensions of Soviet Power, 1917–1953*. Pittsburgh: University of Pittsburg Press, 2002.

Randolph, John. *The House in the Garden: The Bakunin Family and the Romance of Russian Idealism*. Ithaca: Cornell, 2007.

Rank, Otto. *The Trauma of Birth*. New York: Harcourt, Brace, 1929, 1973.

Ransel, David. "Character and Style of Patron-Client Relations in Russia," in *Klientelsysteme im Europa der Frühen Neuzeit*, edited by Antoni Maczak. Munich: R. Oldenbourg, 1988.

Ransome, Arthur. *Russia in 1919*. New York: B. W. Heutsch, 1919.

Rapoport, V. N., and Geller, Iu. *Izmena rodine*. Moscow: Pik strelets, 1995.

Rappaport, Helen. *The Last Days of the Romanovs: Tragedy at Ekaterinburg*. New York: St. Martin's Press, 2009.

Raskol'nikov, F. F. "V iiul'skie dni," *Proletarskaia revoliutsiia*, 1923, no. 5: 53–101.

——. *Krosnshtadt i piter v 1917 godu*. Moscow and Leningrad: Gosizdat, 1925.

——. *Na boevykh postakh*. Moscow: Voerilzdat, 1964

——. *Rasskazy michmana Il'ina*. Moscow: Sovetskaia literatura, 1934.

——. "V tiur'me Kerenskogo," *Proletarskaia revoliutsiia*, 1923, no. 10 (22): 150–2.

Ravich-Cherkasskii, M. *Istoriia kommunisticheskoi partii (bol'shevikov) Ukrainy*. Kharkov: Gosizdat Ukrainy, 1923.

Rawson, Don C. *Russian Rightists and the Revolution of 1905*. New York: Cambridge University Press, 1995.

Rawson, Donald. "The Death Penalty in Tsarist Russia: An Investigation of Judicial Procedures," *Russian History*, 11/1 (1984): 29–52.

Rayfield, Donald. "Stalin as Poet," *PN Review*, 41 (1984): 44–7.

——. *Stalin and His Hangmen: An Authoritative Portrait of a Tyrant and Those Who Served Him*. New York: Viking, 2004.

——. *The Literature of Georgia: A History*, 3rd ed. London: Gannett, 2010.

——. *The Literature of Georgia: A History*. Oxford: Clarendon, 1994.

Reed, John. *Ten Days That Shook the World*. New York: Boni and Liveright, 1919. New York: Vintage, 1960.

Rees, E. A. *"Iron Lazar": A Political Biography of Lazar Kaganovich*. London and New York: Anthem Press, 2012.

——. "Stalin, the Politburo, and Rail Transport Policy," in *Soviet History 1917–1953: Essays in Honour of R. W. Davies*, edited by Julian Cooper, Maureen Perrie, and E. A. Rees. New York: St. Martin's Press, 1995.

——. *State Control in Soviet Russia: The Rise and Fall of the Workers' and Peasants' Inspectorate, 1920–1934* (1987)

Rei, August. *The Drama of the Baltic Peoples*. Stockholm: Kirjaustus Vaba Eesti, 1970.

Reichenbach, Bernard. "Moscow 1921: Meetings in the Kremlin," *Survey*, 53 (1964): 16–22.

Reiss, Tom. *The Orientalist*. New York: Random House, 2005.

Reissner, Larisa. *Oktober, ausgewählte Schriften*. Berlin: Neuer deutscher Verlag, 1927.

Remak, Joachim. *Sarajevo: The Story of a Political Murder*. New York: Criterion, 1959.

Remington, Thomas. "Institution Building in Bolshevik Russia: The Case of 'State Kontrol'," *Slavic Review*, 41/1 (1982): 91–103.

Remnev, Anatolii V. *Samoderzhavnoe pravitel'stvo: komitet ministrov v sisteme vysshego upravleniia Rossiiskoi imperii (vtoraia polovina XIX–nachalo XX veka)*. Moscow: Rosspen, 2010.

Rendle, Matthew. *Defenders of the Motherland: The Tsarist Elite in Revolutionary Russia*. New York: Oxford University Press, 2010.

Reshetar, John. *The Ukrainian Revolution, 1917–1920*. Princeton, NJ: Princeton University Press, 1952.

——. "Lenin on the Ukraine," *Annals of the Ukrainian Academy of Arts and Sciences in the United States*, 9/1–2 (1961): 3–11.

*Resolutions and Decisions of the Communist Party of the Soviet Union, 5* vols. Toronto and Buffalo, NY: University of Toronto Press, 1974.

Reswick, William. *I Dreamt Revolution*. Chicago: H. Regnery Co., 1952.

Rezanov, A. S. *Shturmovoi signal P. N. Miliukova: s prilozheniem pol'nago teksta rechi, proiznesennoi Miliukovym v zasiedanii Gosudarstvennoi Dumy 1 noiabria 1916 g.* Paris: self-published, 1924.

Reznik, Aleksandr V. *Trotzkizm i levaia oppozitsiia v RKP (b) v 1923–1924 gody.* Moscow: Svobodnoe maksistskoe izdatel'stvo, 2010.

*Rezoliutsii i postanovleniia pervoi Vsesoiuznoi konferentsii obshchestva starykh bol'shevikov (25–28 ianv. 1931).* Moscow, 1931.

Riabushinskii, V. P., ed., *Velikaia Rossiia*, 2 vols. Moscow: P. P. Riabushinkii, 1911

Riasanovsky, Nicholas V. "The Emergence of Eurasianism," *California Slavic Studies* 4 (1967): 39–72.

——. *The Teaching of Charles Fourier.* Berkeley: University of California, 1969.

Riddell, John, ed. and trans. *Workers of the World and Oppressed Peoples, Unite!: Proceedings and Documents of the Second Congress, 1920*, 2 vols. New York: Pathfinder Press, 1991.

——, ed. *Founding the Communist International: Proceedings and Documents of the First Congress, March 1919.* New York: Pathfinder Press, 1987.

——. *To See the Dawn: Baku 1920—First Congress of the Peoples of the East.* New York: Pathfinder Press, 1993.

Rieber, Alfred, ed. *The Politics of Autocracy: Letters of Alexander II to Prince A. I. Bariatinskii, 1857–1864.* Paris: Mouton, 1966.

Rieber, Alfred J. "Stalin: Man of the Borderlands," *American Historical Review*, 106/5 (2001): 1651–91.

——. "Alexander II: A Revisionist View," *Journal of Modern History*, 43/1 (1971), 42–58.

——. "Persistent Factors in Russian Foreign Policy: An Interpretive Essay," in *Imperial Russian Foreign Policy*, edited by Hugh Ragsdale. Washington, D.C.: Wilson Center Press, 1993.

——. "Stalin as Foreign Policy Maker: Avoiding War, 1927–1953," in *Stalin: A New History*, Davies and Harris, eds. New York: Cambridge University Press, 2005, 140–58.

——. "Stalin as Georgian: The Formative Years," in *Stalin: A New History*, Davies and Harris, eds. New York: Cambridge University Press, 2005, 18–44.

Rigby, T. H. "Birth of the Central Soviet Bureaucracy," *Politics* [Sydney], 7/2 (1972): 121–135.

——. "Early Provincial Cliques and the Rise of Stalin," *Soviet Studies*, 33/1 (1981): 3–28.

——. "Staffing USSR Incorporated: The Origins of the Nomenklatura System," *Soviet Studies*, 40/4 (1988): 523–37.

——. "The First Proletarian Government," *British Journal of Political Science*, 4/1 (1974): 37–51.

——. "The Origins of the Nomenklatura System," in *Felder und Vorfelder russischer Geschichte*, edited by Inge Auerbach, et al. Freiburg (im Breisgau): Rombach, 1985.

——. "The Soviet Political Elite, 1917–1922," *British Journal of Political Science*, 1/4 (1971): 415–36.

——. "Was Stalin a Disloyal Patron?" *Soviet Studies*, 38/3 (1986): 311–24.

——. *Communist Party Membership in the U.S.S.R., 1917–1967.* Princeton, NJ: Princeton University Press, 1968.

——. *Lenin's Government: Sovnarkom, 1917–1922.* New York: Cambridge University Press, 1979.

——, et al., eds. *Authority, Power, and Policy in the USSR: Essays Dedicated to Leonard Schapiro.* London: Macmillan, 1980.

Riha, Thomas. *A Russian European: Miliukov.* South Bend, IN: University of Notre Dame Press, 1969.

Rikhter, Zinaida. *Kavkaz nashikh dnei.* Moscow: Zhizn' i znanie, 1924.

Robbins, Jr., Richard G. "Choosing the Russian Governors: The Professionalization of the Gubernatorial Corps," *Slavonic and East European Review*, 58 (1980): 541–60.

——. *The Tsar's Viceroys: Russian Provincial Governors in the Last Years of the Empire.* Ithaca, NY: Cornell University Press, 1987.

Robertson, D. H. "A Narrative of the General Strike of 1926," *Economic Journal*, 36 (1926): 375–93.

Robinson, Geroid T. *Rural Russia under the Old Regime.* New York: Columbia University Press, 1934.

Robson, Roy P. *Solovki: The Story of Russia Told Through its Most Remarkable Islands.* New Haven, CT: Yale University Press, 2004.

Rodzianko, M. V. *Krushenie imperii.* Leningrad: Priboi, 1929.

——. *Reign of Rasputin: An Empire's Collapse.* Gulf Breeze, FL: Academic International Press, 1973.

Rodzyanko, Mikhail V. *The Reign of Rasputin.* London: Philpot, 1927.

Rogachevskaia, L. S. *Likvidatsiia bezrabotitsy v SSSR 1917–1930 gg.* Moscow: Nauka, 1973.

Rogger, Hans. "Russia in 1914," *Journal of Contemporary History*, 1/4 (1966): 95–120.

——. "Russia," in *The European Right: A Historical Profile*, edited by Hans Rogger and Eugen Weber. Berkeley: University of California Press, 1965.

——. "The Formation of the Russian Right: 1900–1906," in *California Slavic Studies*, III, edited by Nicholas Riasanovsky and Gleb Struve. Berkeley and London: University of California Press, 1964.

——. "Was There a Russian Fascism? The Union of Russian People," *Journal of Modern History*, 36/4 (1964): 398–415.

——. *Russia in the Age of Modernization 1881–1917.* London and New York: Longman, 1983.

——. *Jewish Policies and Right-Wing Politics in Imperial Russia.* London: Macmillan, 1986

Röhl, John C. G., and Sombart, Nicolaus, eds. *Kaiser Wilhelm II, New Interpretations: The Corfu Papers.* New York: Cambridge University Press, 1982.

Rolf, Matte. *Sovetskie massovy prazdniki.* Moscow: Rosspen, 2009.

Rollin, Henri. *L'apocalypse de notre temps: les dessous de la propagande allemande d'après des documents inédits.* Paris: Gallimard, 1939.

Romano, Andrea. "Permanent War Scare: Mobilization, Militarization, and Peasant War," in *Russia in the Age of Wars, 1914–1945*, edited by Andrea Romano and Silvio Pons. Milan: Feltrinelli, 2000.

Romanov, B. A. "Rezentsiia: Graf S. Iu. Vitte, Vospominaniia tsarstvovaniia Nikolaia II," *Kniga i revoliutsiia: ezhemesiachnyi kritiko-bibliograficheskii zhurnal*, 1923, no. 2 (25): 54–6:

——. *Rossiia v Man'chzhurii 1892–1906.* Leningrad: Institut Dal'nego vostoka, 1928.

Ronaldshay, Earl of. *The Life of Lord Curzon: Being the Authorized Biography of George Nathtaniel, Marquess Curzon of Kedleston, K. G*, 3 vols. London: Ernest Benn, 1928.

Ropponen, Risto. *Die Kraft Russlands.* Helsinki: Historiallisia tutkimiksia, 1968.

Rorlich, Azade-Ayşe. *The Volga Tatars: a Profile in National Resilience.* Stanford, CA: Hoover Institution Press, 1986.

Rose, Kenneth. *King George V.* New York: Random House, 1984.

Rosenbaum, Kurt. "The German Involvement in the Shakhty Trial," *Russian Review*, 26 (1962): 238–60.

——. *Community of Fate: German-Soviet Diplomatic Relations, 1922–1928.* Syracuse, NY: Syracuse University Press, 1965.

Rosenberg, Alfred. *Der jüdische Bolschewismus.* [s.l.] [s.n.], 1921.

Rosenberg, William G. "Representing Workers and the Liberal Narrative of Modernity," *Slavic Review*, 55/2 (1996): 245–69.

————. *Liberals in the Russian Revolution: The Constitutional Democratic Party, 1917–1921*. Princeton, NJ: Princeton University Press, 1974.

Rosenfeldt, Nils Erik. *Knowledge and Power: The Role of Stalin's Secret Chancellery in the Soviet System of Government*. Copenhagen: Rosenkilde and Bagger, 1978.

————. *Stalin's Special Departments: A Comparative Analysis of Key Sources*. Copenhagen: C. A. Reitzels Forlag, 1989.

————. *The "Special" World: Stalin's Power Apparatus and the Soviet System's Secret Structures of Communication System*, 2 vols. Copenhagen: Museum Tusculanum, 2009.

Roshchin, S. K. *Politicheskaia istoriia Mongolii, 1921–1940 gg.* Moscow: Institut vostokovedeniia RAN, 1999.

Roshwald, Aviel. *Ethnic Nationalism and the Fall of Empires: Central Europe, Russia and the Middle East, 1914–1923*. London and New York: Routledge, 2001.

Rosmer, Alfred. *Moscou sous Lenine*. Paris: Pierre Horay, 1953.

*Rossiia: entsiklopedicheskii slovar'*. St. Petersburg: Brokgauz i Efron, 1898.

*Rossiia v mirovoi voine 1914–1918 (v tsifrakh)*. Moscow: Tip. M.K. Kh. imeni F. Ia. Lavrova, 1925.

*Rossiiskaia Sotsialisticheskaia Federativnaia Sovetskaia Respublika i Gruzinskaia demokraticheskia respublika, ikh vzaimootnoshenii*. Moscow: Gosizdat, 1922.

Rostunov, I. I. *General Brusilov*. Moscow: Voenizdat, 1964.

————. *Russkii front pervoi mirovoi voiny*. Moscow: Nauka, 1976.

Rothschild, Joseph. *East Central Europe Between the World Wars*. Seattle: University of Washington Press, 1974.

————. *Piłsudski's Coup d'Etat*. New York: Colombia University Press, 1966.

Rozhkov, A. "Internatsional durakov," *Rodina*, 1999, no. 12: 61–66.

Rubakin, N. A. *Rossiia v tsifrakh*. St. Petersburg, 1912

Rubtsov, Iurii. *Iz-za spiny vozhdia: politicheskaia i voennaia deiatel'nost' L.Z. Mekhlisa*. Moscow: Ritm Esteit, 2003.

————. *Marshaly Stalina*. Moscow: Feniks, 2002.

Rubtsov, V. I. "Voenno-politcheskaia deiatel'nost' G. Ia. Sokol'nikova, 1917–1920 gg.," kandidatskaia dissertatsiia, Moscow, 1991.

Ruge, Wolfgang. *Die Stellungnahme der Sowjetunion gegen die Besetzung des Ruhrgebiets: zur Geschichte der deutsch-sowjetischen Beziehungen von Januar bis September 1923*. Berlin: Akademie-Verlag, 1962.

Runciman, W. Leslie. "The World Economic Conference at Geneva," *Economic Journal*, 37 (1927): 465–72.

Rupen, Robert. *How Mongolia is Really Ruled—A Political History of the Mongolian People's Republic 1900–1978*. Stanford, CA: Hoover Institution Press, 1979.

————. *Mongols of the Twentieth Century*, 2 vols. Bloomington: Indiana University Press, 1964.

Rusanova, I. B. "I. P. Tovstukha: k 80-letiiu so dnia rozhdeniia," *Voprosy istorii KPSS*, 1969, no. 4: 128–30.

Russell, Bertrand. *Justice in War Time*. Chicago: Open Court, 1916.

————. *The Practice and Theory of Bolshevism*. New York: Harcourt, Brace and Howe, 1920.

Russky, N. S. "An Account of the Tsar's Abdication," *Current History*, 7/2 (1917): 262–4.

Rutherford, Ward. *The Tsar's War, 1914–1917: The Story of the Imperial Russian Army in the First World War*, rev. ed. Cambridge, U.K.: Ian Faulkner, 1992.

Rutych, Nikolai N. *Belyi front generala Iudenicha: biografii chinov Severo-Zapadnoi armii*. Moscow: Russkii put', 2002.

Ruud, Charles A., and Stepanov, Sergei A. *Fontanka 16: The Tsars' Secret Police*. Montreal: McGill-Queen's University, 1999.

Rykov, A. I. *Angliia i SSSR: doklad na plenume Moskovskogo soveta 1 iiunia 1927 g.* Moscow: Gosizdat, 1927

————. *Izbrannye proizvedenniia*. Moscow: Ekonomika, 1990.

————. *Ten Years of Soviet Rule: An Economic, Social and Political Survey of the Soviet Government's Achievements from 1917 to 1927*. London: National Committee of Friends of Soviet Russia by the Labour Research Dept, 1928.

Saar, Juhan (Eduard Laaman). *Le 1-er décembre 1924: l'échec du coup d'état tenté par les communistes à Tallinn (Esthonie)*. Tallinn: Walwur, 1925.

Sadikov, P., ed. "K istorii poslednikh dnei tsarskogo rezhima (1916–1917 gg.)," *Krasnyi arkhiv*, 14 (1926): 227–49.

Sadoul, Jacques. "La Fondation de la Troisiéme international," *La Correspondance international*, 4/17 (March 12, 1924).

————. *Notes sur la révolution bolchevique, octobre 1917–janvier 1919*. Paris: Éditions de la Sirène, 1919.

Safarov, Georgii I. *Kolonial'naia revoliutsiia: opyt Turkestana*. Moscow: Gosizdat, 1921.

Sagan, Scott D. "1914 Revisited: Allies, Offense, and Instability," *International Security*, 11/2 (1986): 151–76.

Sakharov, Valentin A. *Na rasput'e: diskussiia po voprosam perspektiv i putei razvitiia sovetskogo obshchestva, 1921–1929*. Moscow: Akva-Term, 2012.

————. *Politicheskoe zaveshchanie Lenina: real'nost' istorii i mify politiki*. Moscow: Moskovskii universitet, 2003.

Sakwa, Richard. "The Commune State in Moscow in 1918," *Slavic Review*, 46/3–4 (1987): 429–49.

————. *Soviet Communists in Power: A Study of Moscow During the Civil War, 1918–21*. New York: St. Martin's Press, 1988.

Sal'ko, S. V. "Kratkii otchet o deiatel'nosti Glavnogo Neftianogo Komiteta za pervyi god ego sushchestvovaniia," *Izvestiia Glavnogo Neftianogo Komiteta*, no. 213 (1919): 77.

Salzmann, Stephanie C. *Great Britain, Germany and the Soviet Union: Rapallo and After, 1922–1934*. Rochester, NY: Boydell Press, 2003.

Samoilo, A. A. *Dve zhizni*, 2nd ed. Leningrad: Lenizdat, 1963.

Samoilov, F. *Pervyi sovet rabochikh deputatov*. Leningrad: Molodaia gvardiia, 1931.

"Samoubiistvo ne opravdanie: predsmertnoe pis'mo Tomskogo Stalinu," *Rodina*, 1996, n. 2: 90–93.

Samuelson, Lennart. *Plans for Stalin's War Machine: Tukhachevskii and Military Planning, 1925–1941*. New York: St. Martin's Press, 2000.

————. *Soviet Defence Industry Planning: Tulhachevskii and Military-Industrial mobilization*. Stockholm: Stockholm Institute of East European Economies, 1996.

Sanborn, Joshua. "The Genesis of Russian Warlordism: Violence and Governance during the First World War and the Civil War," *Contemporary European History*, 19/3 (2010): 195–213.

Sanchez-Sibony, Oscar. "Depression Stalinism: the Great Break Reconsidered," *Kritika*, 15/1 (2014): 23–39.

Sandomirski, German, ed. *Materialy Genuezskoi konferentsii: podgotovka, otchety zasedanii, raboty komissii, diplomaticheskaia perepiska i pr.* Moscow: Izd. pisatelei, 1922.

Sandqvist, Tom. *Dada East: The Romanians of Cabaret Voltaire*. Cambridge, MA: Massachusetts Institute of Technology Press, 2006.

Santoni, W. "P. N. Durnovo as Minister of the Interior in the Witte Cabinet." Phd diss., University of Kansas, 1968.

Sanukov, Ksenofont. "Stalinist Terror in the Mari Republic: the Attack on 'Finno-Ugrian Bourgeois

Nationalism'," *Slavonic and East European Review*, 74/4 (1996): 658–82.

Sapir, Boris, ed. *Fedor Il'ich Dan: pis'ma (1899–1946)*. Amsterdam: Stichtung Internationaal Instituut voor Sociale Geschiedenis, 1985.

Sarkisov, A. *Bakinskaia tipografiia leninskoi "Iskry."* Baku, 1961.

Savchenko, Viktor A. *Avantiuristy grazhdanskoi voiny: istoriucheskie rassledovaniie*. Kharkov: Folio; Moscow: AST, 2000.

Savel'ev, Iu. S. *V pervyi god velikogo oktiabria*. Moscow: Mysl', 1985.

Savich, G. G., ed. *Novyi gosudarstvennyi stroi Rossii: spravochnaiai kniga*. St. Petersburg: Brokgauz-Efron, 1907.

Savich, N. *Vospominaniia*. St. Petersburg and Dusseldorf: Logos and Gluboĭ vsadnik, 1993.

Savinkov, B. S. *K delu Kornilova*. Paris: Union, 1919.

Savitskaia, R. M. "Razrabotka nauchnoi biografii V. I. Lenina," *Voprosy istorii*, 1971, no. 4: 120-30.

Savko, N. *Ocherki po istorii partiinykh organiizatsii v Krasnoi Armii, 1917–1923 gg.* Moscow and Leningrad: Gosizdat, 1928.

Sazonov, S. D. *Vospominaniia*. Paris: E. Sial'skaia, 1927.

*Sbornik deistvuiushchikh dogovorv soglashenii i konventsii, zakliuchennykh R.S.F.S.R. s inostrannymi gosudarstvami*, 5 vols. St. Petersburg: Gosizdat, 1921–23.

*Sbornik tsirkuliarnykh pisem VChK-OGPU*. Moscow, 1935.

*Sbornik zakonodatel'nykh i normativnykh aktov o repressiiakh i reabilitatsii zhertv politicheskikh repressii*. Moscow: Respublika, 1993.

Schafer, Daniel E. "Local Politics and the Birth of the Republic of Bashkortostan, 1919–1920," in *A State of Nations: Empire and Nation-Making in the Age of Lenin and Stalin*, edited by Ronald Grigor Suny and Terry Martin. New York: Oxford University Press, 2001.

Schapiro, Leonard. "Lenin after Fifty Years," in *Lenin, the Man, the Theorist, the Leader: a Reappraisal*, edited by Leonard Schapiro and Peter Reddaway. New York: Praeger, 1967.

———. "The Birth of the Red Army," in *The Red Army*, edited by Liddel Hart. New York: Harcourt, Brace, 1956.

———. "The General Department of the CC of the CPSU," *Survey*, 21/3 (1975): 52–65.

———. *The Origin of the Communist Autocracy: Political Opposition in the Soviet State, First Phase 1917–1922*. Cambridge, MA: Harvard University, 1955; New York: Praeger, 1965; London: LSE, 1977.

———. *Soviet Treaty Series: A Collection of Bilateral Treaties, Agreements, and Coventions, Etc., Concluded Between the Soviet Union and Foreign Powers*, 2 vols. Washington, D.C.: Georgetown University Press, 1950.

Scheffer, Paul. *Sieben Jahre Sowjetunion*. Leipzig: Bibliographisches Institut Ag., 1930.

Scheibert, Peter. *Lenin an der Macht: Das Russische Volk in der Revolution 1918–1922*. Weinheim: Acta Humaniora, 1984.

Scheidemann, Philipp. *Memoiren enies Sozialdemokraten*. Dresden: Reissner, 1930.

Schimmelpenninck van der Oye, David. *Toward the Rising Sun: Russian Ideologies of Empire and the Path to War with Japan*. DeKalb: Northern Illinois University Press, 2001.

Schleifman, Nurit. *Undercover Agents in the Russian Revolutionary Movement: The SR Party, 1902–14*. Basingstoke, Hampshire: Macmillan, 1988.

Schneiderman, Jeremiah. *Sergei Zubatov and Revolutionary Marxism: The Struggle for the Working Class in Tsarist Russia*. Ithaca, NY: Cornell University Press, 1976.

Schorske, Carl. *Fin-de-Siècle Vienna: Politics and Culture*. New York: Knopf, 1980.

Schroeder, Paul W. "Stealing Horses to Great Applause: Austria-Hungary's Decision in 1914 in Systemic Perspective," in *An Improbable War: The Outbreak of World War I and European Political Culture before 1914*, edited by Holger Afflerbach and David Stevenson. New York: Berghahn Books, 2007.

———. "The Lights that Failed—and Those Never Lit," *International History Review*, 28/1 (2006): 119–26.

Schurer, H. "Radek and the German Revolution," *Survey*, 53 (1964): 59–69, 55, (1965): 126–40.

Schwartz, Benjamin I. *Chinese Communism and the Rise of Mao*. Cambridge, MA: Harvard University Press, 1951.

Schwarz, Solomon. *Labor in the Soviet Union*. New York: Praeger, 1952.

Schwittau, G. G. *Revoliutsiia i narodnoe khoziaistvo v Rossii 1917–1921*. Leipzig: Tsentral'noe t-vo kooperativnogo izdatel'stva, 1922.

Scott, James C. *Seeing like a State: How Certain Schemes to Improve the Human Condition have Failed*. New Haven, CT: Yale University Press, 1998.

Seaton, Albert. *Stalin as Military Commander*. New York: Praeger, 1976.

*VII (aprel'skaia) Vserossiiskaia konfer-*

*entsiia RSDRP (bol'shevikov)*. Moscow: Politicheskaia literatura, 1958.

*VII ekstrennyi s"ezd RKP (b), mart 1918 goda: stenograficheskii otchet*. Moscow: Politicheskaia literatura, 1962.

*Selected Correspondence of Karl Marx and Friedrich Engels: A Selection with Commentary and Notes*. London: Lawrence, 1944.

*Sel'skokhoziaistvennoe vedomstvo za 75 let, 1837-1912*. St. Petersburg: Kantselariia Glavnoupravleniia zemleustroitsom i zemledeliem, 1914.

Selunskaia, V. M. *Izmeneniia sotsial'noi struktury sovetskogo obshchestva: oktiabr" 1917–1920*. Moscow: Mysl', 1974.

Semashko, Nikolai. *Otchego bolel i umer V. I. Lenin*. Leningrad: Gosizdat, 1924.

Semevslkii, V. P. *Monarkhiia pered krusheniem*. Moscow-Leningrad, 1927.

Senin, A. S. *A. I. Rykov: stranitsy zhizni*. Moscow: Rosvuznauka, 1993.

Senn, Alfred Erich. "Lithuania's Fight for Independence: The Polish Evacuation of Vilnius, July 1920," *Baltic Review*, 23 (1961): 32–9.

———. "The Rakovski Affair: A Crisis in Franco-Soviet Relations, 1927," *Études Slaves et Est-Européennes/Slavic and East-European Studies*, 10/3–4 (1965–6): 102–17.

———. *The Russian Revolution in Switzerland, 1914–1917*. Madison: University of Wisconsin Press, 1971.

Seraphim, Ernst. *Russische Porträts: die Zarenmonarchie bis zum Zusammenbruch 1917*, 2nd ed., 2 vols. Zurich-Leipzig-Vienna: Almathea, 1943.

Serebriakova, Galina. "Oni delali v chest' idee, kotoroi sluzhili," *Izvestiia*, January 30, 1989.

Serebrianskii, Z. "Sabotazh i sozdanie novogo gosudarstvennogo apparata," *Proletarskaia revoliutsiia*, 1926, no. 10: 5–17.

Seregin, A. V. "Vyshii monarkhicheskii sovet i operatsiia 'Trest'," *Voprosy istorii*, 2012, no. 11.

Serge, Victor. *La vie et la mort de Léon Trotsky (avec Natalya Sedova)*. Paris: Amiot-Dumont, 1951.

———. *Le tournant obscur*. Paris: Îles d'or, 1951.

———. *Memoirs of a Revolutionary, 1901-1941*. New York: Oxford University Press, 1963.

———. *Ot revoliutsii k totalitarizmu: vospominaniia revoliutsionera*. Orenburg: Praksis, 2001.

Serge, Victor, and Trotsky, Natalya Sedova. *The Life and Death of Leon Trotsky*. New York: Basic Books, 1975.

Sergeev, A. A., ed. "Fevral'skaia

revoliutsiia 1917 goda," *Krasnyi arkhiv*, 21 (1927): 3–78.

Sergeev, A. F., and Glushik, E. F. *Besedy o Staline*. Moscow: Krymskii most, 2001.

Sergeev, Evegeny. *Russian Military Intelligence in the War With Japan, 1904–5: Secret Operations on land and at Sea*. New York: Routledge, 2007.

*Sergo Ordzhonikidze v Tsaritsyne i Stalingrade*. Stalingrad: Obl. kn-vo, 1937.

Sering, Max. *Die Umwälzung der osteuropäischen Agrarverfassung*. Berlin: Deutsche Landbuchhandlung, 1921.

Service, Robert. *Lenin: A Political Life*, 3 vols. Bloomington: Indiana University Press, 1985.

———. *Spies and Commissars: Bolshevik Russia and the West*. London: Macmillan, 2011.

———. *Stalin: A Biography*. Cambridge, MA.: Harvard Belknap, 2005.

———. *The Bolshevik Party in Revolution: A Study in Organisational Change, 1917–1923*. New York: Barnes and Noble, 1979.

Seton-Watson, Hugh. *The Russian Empire, 1801–1917*. Oxford: Clarendon, 1967.

Sever, Aleksandr, and Kolpakidi, Aleksandr. *Spetsnaz GRU: samaia pol'naia entsiklopediia*. Moscow: Eksmo-Iauza, 2012.

Sevost'ianov, G. N., ed. *Moskva-Berlin, politika i diplomatii Kremlia, 1920–1941: sbornik dokumentov*, 3 vols. Moscow: Rosspen, 2011.

———. *"Sovershenno sekretno": Lubianka—Stalinu o polozhenii v strane (1922–1934 gg.)*, 10 vols. Moscow: IRI RAN, 2001–13.

———. *Delo Generala Kornilova, materialy Chrezvychainoi komissii po rassledovaniiu dela o byvshem Verkhovnom glavnokomanduiushchem generale L. G. Kornilove i ego souchastnikakh, avgust 1917–iiun' 1918: dokumenty*, 2 vols. Moscow: Mezhdunarodnyi fond Demokratiia, 2003.

Shagrin, Boris, and Todd, Albert, eds. *Landmarks: A Collection of Essays on the Russian Intelligentsia*. New York: Karz Howard, 1977.

Shambarov, Valerii. *Gosudarstvo i revoliutsiia*. Moscow: Algoritm, 2001.

Shanin, Teodor. *Late Marx and the Russian Road: Marx and the Peripheries of Capitalism*. New York: Monthly Review Press, 1983.

———. *The Awkward Class: Political Sociology of Peasantry in a Developing Society*. Oxford: Clarendon Press, 1972.

———. *The Rots of Otherness: Russia's Turn of the Century*, 2 vols. New Haven, CT, and London: Yale University Press, 1986.

Shankowsky, Lew. "Disintegration of the Imperial Russian Army in 1917," *Ukrainian Quarterly*, 13/4 (1957): 305–28.

Shaposhnikov, B. M. *Na Visle: k istorii kampanii 1920 g.* Moscow: Voenizdat, 1924.

Sharapov, German V. *Razreshenie agrarnogo voprosa v Rossii poske pobedy oktiabr'skoi revoliutsii, 1917–1920 gg.* Moscow: VPSh i AON pri TsK KPSS, 1961.

Shatsillo, K. F. "Delo polkovnika Miasoedova," *Voprosy istorii*, 1967, no. 4: 103–16.

Shatunovskaia, Lidiia. *Zhizn' v Kremle*. New York: Chalidze Publications, 1982.

Shchëgolëv, P. E. *Okhranniki i avantiuristy, sekretnye sotrudniki i provokatory*. Moscow: GPIB, 2004.

———, ed. *Padenie tsarskogo rezhima: stenograficheskie otchety doprosov i pokazanii, dannykh v 1917 g. v Chrezvychainoi sledstvennoi komissii Vremennogo pravitel'stva*, 7 vols. Leningrad: Gosizdat, 1924–7.

———. *Otrechenie Nikolaia II*. Leningrad: Krasnaia gazeta, 1927.

Shefov, A. N. *Moskva, kreml', Lenin*. Moscow: Politizdat, 1969.

Sheinis, Z. "Pervye shagi diplomaticheskoi deiatel'nosti M. M. Litvinov," *Novaia i noveishaia istoriia*, 1988, no. 1: 152–69.

Sheinis, Zinovy. *Maxim Litvinov*. Moscow: Progress Publishers, 1990.

Shelestov, Dmitrii. *Vremia Alekseia Rykova*. Moscow: Progress, 1990.

Shelokhaev, V. V. *Politicheskie partii Rossii, konets XIX–pervaia tret' XX veka: entsiklopediia*. Moscow: Rosspen, 1996.

———, ed. *Russkii liberalizm: istoricheskie sud'by i perspektivy. Materialy mezhdunarodnoi nauchnoi konferentsii, Moskva, 27–29 maia 1998 g.* Moscow: Rosspen, 1999.

Shepelev, L. E. *Chinovny mir Rossii XVIII–nachalo XX v.* St. Petersburg: Iskusstvo-SPB, 1999.

Sheridan, Clare. *From Mayfair to Moscow: Clare Sheridan's Diary*. London: Boni and Liveright, 1921.

Shestakov, Andrei V. *Krest'ianskaia revoliutsiia 1905–1907 gg. v Rossii*. Moscow: Gosizdat, 1926.

Shevtsov, A. V. *Izdatel'skaia deiatel'nost' russkikh nesotsialisticheskikh partii nachala XX veka*. St. Petersburg: Rossiiskaia Natsional'naia Biblioteka, 1997.

Shikman, A. P. *Deiateli otechestvennoi istorii: Biograficheskii spravochnik*. Moscow, 1997.

Shin, Peter Yong-Shik. "The Otsu incident: Japan's Hidden History of the Attempted Assassination of Future Emperor Nicholas II of Russia in the town of Otsu, Japan, May 11, 1891 and its Implication for Historical Analysis." Phd diss., University of Pennsylvania, 1989.

Shipov, D. N. *Vospominaniia i dumy o perezhitom*. Moscow: M. i. S. Sabashnikov, 1918.

Shishkin, V. I. "Poezdka I. V. Stalina v Sibir' (15 ianvaria–6 fevralia 1928 g.)," in *Problemy agrarnogo i demograficheskogo razvitiia Sibiri v XX-nachale XXI vv.: materialy vserossiiskoi nauchnoi konferentsii*, edited by V. A. Il'inykh.Novosibirsk: Institut istorii SO RAN, 2009.

———, ed. *Sibirskaia Vandeia, 1920–1921*, 2 vols. Moscow: Mezhdunarodnyi fond Demokratiia, 2000–01.

Shishkin, Valerii A. *Stanovlenie vneshnei politiki postrevliutsionnoi Rossii i kapitalisticheskii mir 1917–1930 gody: ot revoliutsionnogo "zapadnichestva" k "natsional-bol'shevizmu," ocherk istorii*. St. Petersburg: Dmitrii Bulanin, 2002.

———. *Vlast', politika, ekonomika: Poslerevoliutsionnaia Rossiia (1917–1928 gg.)* St. Petersburg: Dmitrii Bulanin, 1997.

Shklovsky, Viktor. *A Sentimental Journey: Memoirs, 1917–1922*. Ithaca, NY: Cornell University Press, 1984.

Shliapnikov, A. G. *Kanun semnadtsatogo goda: vospominaniia i dokumenty o rabochem dvizhenii i revoliutsionnom podpol'e za 1914–1916 gg.*, 2 vols. Moscow: Gosizdat, 1923.

Shliapnikov, Aleksandr G. Nashi raznoglasiia," *Pravda*, January 18, 1924.

———. *Semnadtsatyi god*, 4 vols. Moscow and Leningrad: Gos. Sotsekon. izd., 1923–31.

Shmelev, N. N. *Bor'ba KPSS za razvitie tiazheloi promyshlennosti na Severnom Kavkaze, 1926–1932 gg.* Rostov-na-Donu: Rostovskii universitet, 1981.

Shokhin, Andrei. *Kratkaia istoriia VLKSM*, 2nd ed. Moscow: Molodaia gvardiia, 1928.

Showalter, Dennis E. *Tannenberg: Clash of Empires*. Hamden, CT: Archon, 1991.

Shpilrein, I. N., et al. *Iazyk krasnoarmeitsa*. Moscow-Leningrad: Gosizdat, 1928.

Shreider, Mikhail. *NKVD iznutri: zapiski chekista*. Moscow: Vozvrashchenie, 1995.

Shteinberg, Valentin. *Ekab Peters*. Moscow: Politicheskaia literatura, 1989.

Shturman, D. *Mertvye khvataiut zhivykh: chitaia Lenina, Bukharina, i Trotskogo*. London: Overseas Publication Interchange, 1982.

Shtyrliaev, V. "Geroi grazhdanskoi voiny Dmitrii Zhloba," *Voenno-istoricheskii zhurnal*, 1965, no. 2: 44–46.

Shub, David. "The Trial of the SRs," *Russian Review*, 23/4 (1964): 362–9.

———. *Lenin: A Biography*. Garden City, NY: Doubleday, 1949.

Shukman, Harold. *Lenin and the Russian Revolution* (New York: Putnam, 1967; 1981).

Shul'gin, V. V. *Chto nam v nikh ne nravitsia: ob antisemitizme v Rossii*. Paris: Russia Minor, 1929.

———. *Dni*. Belgrad: M. A. Suvorin, 1925.

———. *Gody. Dni. 1920*. Moscow: Novosti, 1990.

———. *Days of the Russian Revolution: Memoirs from the Right, 1905–1917*. Gulf Breeze, FL: Academic International Press, 1990.

Shveitzer, V. I. "V achinskoi ssylke," *Izvestiia*, March 12, 1937.

Shveitzer, Vera. *Stalin v turukhanskoi ssylke: vospominaniia starogo podpol'shchika* Moscow: Molodaia gvardiia, 1943.

Shvetsov, V. V. "Lev Trotskii i Maks Istmen: istoriia odnoi politicheskoi druzhby," *Novaia i noveishaia istoriia*, 1990, no. 6: 152–69.

———. *Diskussiia v RKP (b) 1923 goda: k 70-letiu nepa*. Moscow: Znanie, 1991.

*Sibir' i velikaia zheleznaia doroga*. St. Petersburg: I. A. Efron, 1896.

*Sibir'skaia Sovetskaia entsiklopediia, 3 vols*. Novosibirsk: Sibirikoe kraevoe izd, 1929–32.

Sidorov, Arkadii L., ed. *Revoliutsionnoe dvizheniie v armii i na flote v gody pervoi mirovoi voiny, 1914–fevral' 1917*. Moscow: Nauka, 1966.

Sidorov, Vasilii. *Po Rossii. Kavkaz. Putevye zametki i vpechatleniia*. St. Petersburg: M. Akifiev i I. Leontiev, 1897.

Sidorovnin, Gennadii, ed. *Stolypin, zhizn' i smert': sbornik*, 2nd ed. Saratov: Sootchestvennik, 1997.

Siegelbaum, Lewis H. "The Workers Group and the War-Industries Committees: Who Used Whom," *Russian Review*, 39/2 (1980).

———. *Soviet State and Society Between Revolutions, 1918–1929*. New York: Cambridge University Press, 1992.

———. *The Politics of Industrial Mobilization in Russia, 1914–1917*. New York: St. Martin's Press, 1983.

Sigler, Krista Lynn. "Kshesinskaia's Mansion: High Culture and the Politics of Modernity in Revolutionary Russia." Phd diss., University of Cincinnati, 2009.

Simonov, N. S. "'Strengthen the De-

fense of the Land of Soviets': The 1917 'War Alarm' and its Consequences," *Europe-Asia Studies*, 48/8 (1996).

———. "Krepit' oboronu stranam sovetov (voenna trevoga 1927 i ee posledstviia)," *Otechestvennaia istoriia*, 1996, no. 3: 155–61.

———. *Voenno-promyshlennyi kompleks SSSR v 1920–1950-e gody: tempoy ekonomicheskogo rosta, struktura, organizatsiia proizvodstva i upravlenie*. Moscow: Rosspen, 1996.

Simonova, T. "Mir i schast'e na shtykakh," *Rodina*, 2000, n. 10: 60–64.

Sinel'nikov, S. S. *Kirov*. Moscow, 1964. aaa

Singleton, Seth. "The Tambov Revolt," *Slavic Review*, 25/3 (1969): 497–512.

Sinyavsky, Andrei. *Soviet Civilization: A Cultural History*. New York: Arcade, 1990.

Skobelev, M. "Gibel' tsarizma," *Ogonek*, March 13, 1927: 1–2.

Skvortsov-Stepanov, Ivan I. *S Krasnoi Armiei na panskuiu Pol'shu: vpechatleniia i nabliudeniia*. Moscow: Gosizdat, 1920.

Slashchov-Krymskii, Ia. S. *Belyi Krym 1920 g*. Moscow: Nauka, 1990.

Slavinskii, Dmitrii B. *Sovetskii Soiuz i Kitai: istoriia diplomaticheskikh otnoshenii, 1917–1937 gg*. Moscow: Iaponiia segodnia, 2003.

Slavinsky, Boris N. *The Japanese-Soviet Neutrality Pact: A Diplomatic History, 1941–1945*. London and New York: RoutledgeCurzon, 2004.

Sletov, S. *K istorii vozniknoveniia partii sotsialistov revoliutsionerov*. Petrograd: P. P. Soikina, 1917.

Slezkine, Yuri. "The USSR as a Communal Apartment, or How a Socialist State Promoted Ethnic Particularism," *Slavic Review*, 53/2 (1994): 414–52.

Sloin, Andrew, and Sanchez-Sibony, Oscar. "Economy and Power in the Soviet Union, 1917–39," *Kritika*, 15/1 (2014): 7–22.

Slusser, Robert. *Stalin in October: The Man Who Missed the Revolution*. Baltimore, Johns Hopkins University Press, 1987.

Smidovich, P. G. "Vykhod iz podpol'ia v Moskve," *Proletarskaia revoliutsiia*, 1923, no. 1 (13): 171–77.

Smirnoff, Serge. *Autour de l'assassinat des Grand-Ducs*: Ekaterinbourg, Alapaievsk, Perm, Pétrograd. Paris: Payot, 1928.

Smirnov, N. *Repressirovanoe provosudie*. Moscow: Gelios ARV, 2001.

Smith, Edward Ellis. *The Young Stalin: The Early Years of an Elusive Revolutionary*. New York: Farrar, Strauss and Giroux, 1967.

Smith, Jeffrey R. "The Monarchy Versus the Nation: The 'Festive Year' 1913 in Wilhelmine Germany," *German Studies Review*, 23/2 (2000): 257–74.

Smith, Jeremy. *The Bolsheviks and the National Question, 1917–1923*. New York: Macmillan, 1999.

———. "The Georgian Affair of 1922—Policy Failure, Personality Clash or Power Struggle?" *Europe-Asia Studies*, 50/3 (1998): 519–44.

———. "Stalin as Commissar for Nationality Affairs, 1918–1922," in *Stalin: A New History*, Davies and Harris, eds., 45–62.

Smith, Leonard V. *Between Mutiny and Obedience: The Case of the French Fifth Infantry Division during World War I*. Princeton, NJ: Princeton University Press, 1994.

Smith, R. E. F., ed. *The Russian Peasant 1920 and 1984*. London: Cass, 1977.

Smith, Steve A. *A Road is Made: Communism in Shanghai 1920–1927*. Honolulu: University of Hawaii Press, 2000.

Snyder, Jack. *Ideology of the Offensive: Military Decision Making and the Disasters of 1914*. Ithaca, NY: Cornell University Press, 1984.

Sobolev, Ivan. *Bor'ba s "nemetskim zasiliem" v Rossii v gody Pervoi Mirovoi Voiny*. St. Petersburg: Rossiiskaia natsional'naia biblioteka, 2004.

Soboleva, T. A. *Istoriia shifroval'nogo dela v Rossii*. Moscow: OLMA, 2002.

Sokol'nikov, G. Ia. *Brestskii mir*. Moscow: Gosizdat, 1920.

———. *Finansovaia politika revoliutsii*, 2 vols. Moscow: Nauka, 2006.

———. *Gosudarstvennyi kapitalizm i novaia finansovaia politika*. Moscow: NKF, 1922.

———. *K voprosu o natsionalizatsii bankov*. Moscow, 1918.

———. *Novaia finansovaia politika: na puti k tverdoi valiute*. Moscow, 1995.

Sokolov, A. K. *Ot voenproma k VPK: sovetskaia voennaia promyshlennost' 1917–iiun' 1941 gg*. Moscow: Novyi khronograf, 2012.

Sokolov, Aleksandr S. *Finansovaia politika Sovetskogo gosudarstva 1921–1929 gg*. Moscow: Zvedopad, 2005.

Sokolov, E. N. *Finansovaia politika Sovetskoi vlasti (oktiabr' 1917–avgust 1918 gg.)*. Ryazan: Riazanskii gos. universitet im. S. A. Esenina, 2008.

Sokolov, Nikolai A. *Ubiistvo tsarskoi sem'i*. Berlin: Slowo, 1925.

Soldatov, V. V. "Izmeneniia form obshchinnogo zemlepol'zovaniia v Sibiri," *Voprosy kolonizatsii*, 1910, no. 7.

Solnick, Steven L. "Revolution, Reform and the Soviet Telephone System,

1917–1927," *Soviet Studies*, 43/1 (1991): 157–76.

Solomon [Isetskii], Georgii. *Sredi krasnykh vozhdei: lichno perezhitoe i vidennoe na sovetskoi sluzhbe*, 2 vols. Paris: Mishen, 1930.

Solomon, Jr., Peter H. *Soviet Criminal Justice Under Stalin*. New York: Cambridge University Press, 1996.

Solov'ev, E. D., and Chugunov, A. I. *Pogranichnye voiska SSSR, 1918–1928: sbornik dokumentov i materialov*. Moscow: Nauka, 1973.

Solov'ev, Iu. G. "Samoderzhavie i dvorianskii vopros v kontse XIX v." *Istoricheskie zapiski*, 1971, no. 88: 150–209.

Solzhenitsyn, Aleksandr. *The Gulag Archipelago*, 3 vols. New York: Harper & Row, 1973.

Sontag, John P. "The Soviet War Scare of 1926–1927," *Russian Review*, 34/1 (1975): 66–77.

Sontag, Raymond James. *Germany and England: Background of Conflict, 1848–1894*. New York and London: D. Appleton-Century, 1938.

Sorokin, Pitirim A. *Leaves from a Russian Diary*. New York: E. P. Dutton & Co, 1924.

Sosnovskii, L. S. "Chetyre pis'ma iz ssylki," *Biulleten' oppozitsii*, September 1929, 3–4: 15–29.

*Sotsialistickheskoe stroitel'stvo SSSR*. Moscow, 1923.

Souvarine, Boris. *Stalin: A Critical Survey of Bolshevism*. New York: Longman, Green, 1939.

——. *Staline; aperçu historique du bolchévisme*. Paris: Plon, 1935.

*Sovetsko-Germanskie otnosheniia ot peregovorov v Brest-Litovske do podpisaniia Rapall'skogo dogovora: sbornik dokumentv*, 2 vols. Moscow: Politicheskaia literatura, 1968–71.

*Sovety v Oktiabre: sbornik dokumentov*. Moscow: Kommunisticheskaia akademiia, 1928.

"Sovremennoe pravosudie," *Dym otechestva*, 1914, no. 22: 1–2.

Spiridovich, Aleksander I. *Istoriia bol'shevizma v Rossii: ot vozniknoveniia do zakhvata vlasti, 1883–1903–1917*. Paris: Franko-Russkaia pechat', 1922.

——. *Zapiski zhandarma*. Kharkov: Proletarii, 1928.

——. *Raspoutine 1863–1916, d'après les documents russes et les archives privées de l'auteur*. Paris: Payot, 1935.

——. *Velikaia voina i fevral'skaia revoliutsiia 1914–1917 gg.*, 3 vols. New York: Vseslavianskoe izd., 1960–2.

Spirin, L. M. *Klassy i partii v grazhdanskoi voine v Rossii*. Moscow: Mysl', 1968.

——. *Krakh odnoi aventiury, miatezh levykh eserov v Moskve 6–7 iiulia 1918 g.* Moscow: Politicheskaia literatura, 1971.

——. *Krushenie pomeschchik'ikh i burzhuaznykh partii v Rossii nachalo XX v–1920 g.* Moscow: Mysl', 1977.

*Spisok chlenov Vsesoiuznogo obshchestvo starykh bol'shevikov na i ianv. 1933.* Moscow: 1933.

Spring, D. W. "Russia and the Coming of War," in *The Coming of the First World War*, edited by R. J. W. Evans and Hartmut Pogge von Strandmann. Oxford: Clarendon, 1988.

Stalin, I. V. *Beseda s inostrannymi rabochimi delegatsiaiami*. Moscow-Leningrad: Gosizdat, 1927.

——. *Na piutiakh k Oktiabriu*. Moscow: Gosizdat, 1925.

——. *Ob oppozitsii: stat'i i rechi, 1921–1927*. Moscow: Gosizdat, 1928.

——. *Na putiakh k Oktiabriu: stat'i i rechi, mart-oktiabr' 1917*. Moscow: Gosizdat, 1925.

——. *O Lenine i o leninzme*. Moscow: Gosizdat, 1924.

—— *Sochineniia*, 13 vols. Moscow: Politicheskaia literatura, 1946–51. vols. 14–16, Robert H. MacNeal, ed. Stanford, CA: Hoover Institution, 1967. Cited as *Sochineniia* (author understood).

Staliunas, Darius. *Making Russians: Meaning and Practice of Russification in Belarus and Lithuania After 1863*. Amsterdam: Rodopi, 2007.

Stankevich, V. B. *Vospominaniia 1914–1919 gg.* Berlin: J. Ladyschnikow, 1920.

Starkov, Boris A. "Perekhod k 'politike razgroma': shakhtinskoe delo," in *Istoriki otvechaiut na voprosy*, ed. by N. N. Maslov and A. N. Svalov. Moscow: Moskovskii rabochii, 1988.

Starr, S. Frederick. *Decentralization and Self-Government in Russia, 1830–1870*. Princeton: Princeton University Press, 1972.

Startsev, Vitalii I. "Begstvo Kerenskogo," *Voprosy istorii*, 1966, no. 11: 204–5.

——. *Vnutrenniaia politika Vremennogo pravitel'stva: pervogo sostava*. Leningrad: Nauka, 1980.

Stasova, E. D. *Vospominaniia*. Moscow: Mysl', 1969.

Stasova, Elena. *Stranitsy zhizni i bor'by*. Moscow: Politizdat, 1957.

"Stavka 25-26 oktiabria 1917 g.," in *Arkhiv russkoi revoliutsii*, ed. by Gessen, VII: 279–320.

Stead, W. T. *Truth About Russia*. London and New York: Cassell & Company, 1888.

Steimetz, George. *Regulating the Social: The Welfare State and Local Politics in Imperial Germany*.

Princeton, NJ: Princeton University Press, 1993.

Steinberg, Isaac. "The Events of July 1918," undated manuscript, Hoover Institution Archive.

——. *Spiridonova: Revolutionary Terrorist*. London: Methuen, 1935

——. *Ot fevralia po oktiabr' 1917 g.* Berlin-Milan, Skify, 1919.

Steinberg, John W. *All the Tsar's Men: Russia's General Staff and the Fate of Empire, 1898–1914*. Washington, D.C., and Baltimore: Woodrow Wilson Center/Johns Hopkins University, 2010.

Steinberg, Jonathan. *Bismarck: A Life*. New York: Oxford University Press, 2011.

——. *Yesterday's Deterrent: Tirpitz and the Birth of the German Battle Fleet*. London: Macdonald, 1965.

Steinberg, Mark. "Revolution," in *The Fall of the Romanovs: Political Dreams and Personal Struggles in a Time of Revolution*, edited by Mark D. Steinberg and Vladimir M. Khrustalëv. New Haven, CT: Yale University Press, 1995.

——. "Workers and the Cross: Religious Imagery in the Writings of Russian Workers 1910–1924," *Russian Review*, 53/2 (1994): 213–39.

——. *Moral Communities: The Culture and Class Relations in the Russian Printing Industry 1867–1907*. Berkeley: University of California Press, 1992.

——, and Khrustalëv, Vladimir M., eds. *The Fall of the Romanovs: Political Dreams and Personal Struggles in a Time of Revolution*. New Haven, CT: Yale University Press, 1995.

Steiner, Zara S. *The Lights that Failed: European International History 1919–1933*. Oxford: Oxford University Press, 2005.

Steinwedel, Charles Robert. "Invisible Threads of Empire: State, Religion, and Ethnicity in Tsarist Bashkiria, 1773–1917." Phd diss., Columbia University, 1999.

Steklov, Iu. M. *Bortsy za sotsializm*, 2nd ed., 2 vols. Moscow-Leningrad: Gosizdat, 1923–24.

Stephan, John J. "The Crimean War in the Far East," *Modern Asian Studies*, 3/3 (1969), 257–77.

——. *The Russian Far East: A History*. Stanford, CA: Stanford University Press, 1994.

Stepnaov, S. A. *Chernaia sotnia v Rossii 1905–1914 gg.* Moscow: Rosvuznauka, 1992.

Stepun, Fedor. *Byvshee i nesbyvsheesia*, 2 vols. New York: Izd-vo im. Chekhova, 1956.

Stevenson, David. *Armaments and the Coming of War: Europe, 1904–1914*. Oxford: Clarendon, 1996.

———. *Cataclysm: The First World War as Political Tragedy.* New York: Basic Books, 2004.

Stites, Richard. *Revolutionary Dreams: Utopian Vision and Experimental Life in the Russian Revolution.* New York: Oxford University Press, 1989.

Stockdale, Melissa Kirschke. *Paul Miliukov and the Quest for a Liberal Russia.* Ithaca, NY: Cornell University Press, 1996.

———. "Politics, Morality and Violence: Kadet Liberals and the Question of Terror," *Russian History,* 22/1 (1995): 455–80.

Stone, David R. *Hammer and Rifle: The Militarization of the Soviet Union, 1926–1933.* Lawrence: University Press of Kansas, 2000.

Stone, Helena M. "Another Look at the Sisson Forgeries and their Background," *Soviet Studies,* 37/1 (1985): 90–102.

Stone, Norman. *The Eastern Front, 1914–1917.* New York: Scribner's, 1975.

Storella, Carmine J., and Sokolov, A.K., eds., *The Voice of the People: Letters from the Soviet Village, 1918–1932.* New Haven, CT: Yale University Press, 2013.

Storozhev, V. N. "Fevral'skaia revoliutsiia 1917 g.," *Nauchnye izvestiia* (Moscow, 1922), sbornik 1: 142–3.

Strachan, Hew. *The First World War.* New York: Oxford University Press, 2003.

———. *The First World War.* New York: Viking, 2004.

Strauss, Leo. "Kurt Riezler, 1882–1955," *Social Research,* 23/1 (1956): 3–34.

Strizhkov, Iu. K. *Prodovol'stvennye otriady v gody grazhdanskoi voiny I inostrannoi interventsii, 1917–1922.* Moscow: Nauka, 1973.

Strong, Anna Louise. *China's Millions: The Revolutionary Struggles from 1927 to 1935.* New York: Knight Publishing Co., 1935.

Struve, P. V. "Istoricheskii smysl russkoi revoliutsii i natsional'nye zadachi," in *Iz glubiny: sbornik statei o russkoi revoliutsii.* Moscow: Moskovskii universitet, 1990.

———, ed. *Food Supply in Russia During the War.* New Haven, CT: Yale University Press, 1930.

———. "Witte und Stolypin," in *Menschen die Geschichte machten: viertausend Jahre Weltgeschichte in zeit- und lebensbildern,* 3 vols, edited by Peter Richard Rohden and Georg Ostrogorsky. Vienna: L. W. Seiden & Sohn, 1931.

Sukennikov, M. *Krest'ianskaia revoliutsiia na iuge Rossii: s pis'mami L. N. Tol'stogo tsariu.* Berlin: Ioann Réde, 1902.

Sukhanov, Nikolai. *The Russian Revolution, 1917: Eyewitness Account,* 2 vols. New York: Harper and Row, 1962.

———. *Zapiski,* 7 vols. Berlin: Z. I. Grzhebin, 1922–23.

Sukhorukhov, V. T. *XI Armiia v boiakh na Severnom Kavkaze i Nizhnei Volge, 1918–1920 gg.* Moscow: Voenizdat, 1961.

Suliashvili, David. *Uchenicheskie gody.* Tblisi: Zarya vostoka, 1942.

Sullivant, Robert S. *Soviet Politics and the Ukraine, 1917–1957.* New York: Columbia University Press, 1962.

Sultanbekov, Bulat. *Pervaia zhertva Genseka: Mirsaid Sultan-Galiev, sud'ba, liudi, vremia.* Kazan: Tatarskoe knizhnoe izdatel'stvo, 1991.

Sultan-Galiev, Mirsaid. *Stat'i, vtstupleniia, dokumenty.* Kazan: Tatarskoe knizhnoe izdatel'stvo, 1992.

Sumbadze, A. S. *Sotsial'no-ekonomicheskie predposylki pobedy Sovetskoi vlasti v Azerbaidzhane.* Moscow: Nauka, 1972.

Sunila, August A. *Vosstanie 1 dekabria 1924 goda: opyt kommunisticheskoi partii Estonii v podgotovke i provedenii vooruzhennogo vosstaniia estonskogo proletariata 1924 goda i ego istoricheskoe znachenie.* Tallinn, Eesti Raamat, 1982.

Suny, Ronald Grigor, ed. *Transcaucasia, Nationalism, and Social Change: Essays in the History of Armenia,* 2nd ed. Ann Arbor: University of Michigan Press, 1996.

———. "A Journeyman for the Revolution: Stalin and the Labor Movement in Baku, June 1907–May 1908," *Soviet Studies,* 23/3 (1972): 373–94.

———. "Beyond Psychohistory: The Young Stalin in Georgia," *Slavic Review,* 50/1 (1991): 48–58.

———. "Tiflis, Crucible of Ethnic Politics, 1860–1905," in *The City in Late Imperial Russia,* edited by Michael F. Hamm. Bloomington: Indiana University Press, 1986.

———. *Looking Toward Ararat: Armenia in Modern History.* Bloomington: Indiana University Press, 1993.

———. *The Making of the Georgian Nation,* 2nd ed. Bloomington: Indiana University Press, 1994.

Suslov, P. V. *Politicheskoe obespechenie sovetsko-pol'skoi kampanii 1920 g.* Moscow: Gosizdat, 1930.

Sutton, Antony C. *Western Technology and Soviet Economic Development,* 3 vols. Stanford, CA: Hoover Institution on War, Revolution, and Peace, Stanford University, 1968–73.

Suvorin, A. S. *Dnevnik.* Moscow-Petrograd, 1923.

Suvorin, S. A. *Chetvertyi (ob"edinitel'nyi) s"ezd RSDRP: Aprel' (aprel'-mai) 1906 goda: protokoly.* Moscow, Politicheskaia literatura, 1959.

Suvorov, N. I., ed. *Trekhsotletie doma Romanovykh 1613–1913: istoriches-* *kie ocherki.* Moscow: A. I. Mamontov, 1913.

Sverchkov, Dmitrii F. *Kerenskii,* 2nd ed. Leningrad: Priboi, 1927.

Sverdlov, Iakov Mikhailovich. *Izbrannye proizvedennye,* 3 vols. Moscow: Politcheskaia literatura, 1957–60.

Sverdlova, K. T. *Iakov Mikhailovich Sverdlov.* Moscow: Molodaia Gvardiia, 1957, 1960, 1976. 4th ed. Moscow: Molodaia gvardiia, 1985.

Sviatitskii, N. V. *Kogo russkii narod izbral svoimi predstaviteliami.* Moscow: Zemlia i volia, 1918.

*Svod zakonov Rossiiskoi imperii,* 16 vols. St. Petersburg: Obshchestvennaia pol'za, 1897.

Swain, Geoffrey. "The Disillusioning of the Revolution's Praetorian Guard: Latvian Riflemen Summer-Autumn 1918," *Europe-Asia Studies,* 51/4 (1999): 667–86.

———. "Vācietis: The Enigma of the Red Army's First Commander," *Revolutionary Russia,* 16/1 (2003): 68–86.

Syromatnikov, Sergius. "Reminiscences of Stolypin," *Russian Review,* 1/2 (1912): 71–88.

Syrtsov, V. A. *Skazanie o Fedorovskoi Chudotvornoi ikone Bozhei materi, chto v g, Kostrome.* Kostroma, 1908.

Sytin, P. V. *Iz istorii Moskovskikh ulits.* Moscow: Moskovskii rabochii, 1948. Sovremennik, 2000.

Szeftel, Marc. *The Russian Constitution of April 23, 1906: Political Institutions of the Duma Monarchy.* Brussels: Éditions de la Librarie encyclopédique, 1976.

Szporluk, Roman. "Lenin, 'Great Russia,' and Ukraine," *Harvard Ukrainian Studies,* 28/1–4 (2006): 611–26.

Tagantsev, N. A. *Perezhitoe: uchrezhdenie Gosudarstvennoi Dumy v 1905–1906 gg.* Petrograd: Gos. Tip. 1919.

Tagirov, I. R., ed. *Neizvestnyi Sultan-Galiev: rassekrechennye dokumenty i materialy.* Kazan: Tatarskoe knyzhnoe izdatel'stvo, 2002.

*Tainy natsional'noi politiki TsK RKP: chetvertoe soveshchanie TsK RKP (b) s otvestvennymi rabotnikami natsional'nykh respublik i oblastei v Moskve 9–12 iiunia 1923 g.* Moscow: INSAN, 1992.

Talakavadze, Sevastii. *K istorii kommunisticheskoi partii Gruzii.* Tiflis: Glavpolitprosvet, 1926.

Tang, Peter S. H. *Russian and Soviet Policy, in Manchuria and Outer Mongolia, 1911–1931.* Durham, NC: Duke University Press, 1959.

Taranovski, Theodore. "The Politics of Counter-Reform: Autocracy and Bureaucracy in the Reign of Alexander III, 1881–1994." Phd diss., Harvard University, 1976.

Tarasiuk, D. A. *Pozemel'naia*

*sobstvennost' poreformennoi Rossii: istochnikovedchestvennoe issledovanie po perepisi 1877-1878 gg.* Moscow: Nauka, 1981.

Taratuta, V. K. "Kanun revoliutsii 1905 g. na Kavkaze (iz vospominaniia)," *Zaria vostoka*, December 19, 1925.

Tarkhova, N. S. "Trotsky's Train: An Unknown Page in the History of the Civil War," in *The Trotsky Reappraisal*, edited by Terry Brotherstone and Paul Dukes. Edinburgh: Edinburgh University Press, 1992.

Tarle, E. V. "Germanskaia orientatsiia i P. N. Durnovó v 1914 g.," *Byloe*, 1922, no. 19: 161–76.

———. "Zapiska P. N. Durnovó Nikolaiu II: Fevral 1914 g.," *Krasnaia nov'*, 1922, no. 10: 178–99.

Tatishchev, S. S. *Imperator Aleksandr Vtoroi*, 2 vols. St. Petersburg: A. S. Suvorin, 1903.

Tauger, Mark B. "Grain Crisis or Famine? The Ukranian State Commission for Aid to Crop-Failure Victims and the Ukranian Famine of 1928-1929," unpublished paper courtesy of the author.

Tauger, Mark B. "Statistical Falsification in the Soviet Union: A Comparative Case Study of Projections, Biases, and Trust," Donald Treadgold Papers, University of Washington, 2001.

Taylor, A. J. P. *The First World War: An Illustrated History*. London: H. Hamilton, 1963.

———. *The Struggle for Mastery in Europe*. Oxford: Clarendon, 1963.

———. *War by Timetable*. London: Macdonald, 1969.

Tepliakov, Aleksei G. *"Nepronitsaemye nedra": VChK-OGPU v Sibiri 1918-1929 gg.* Moscow: AIRO-XXI, 2007.

Teplianikov, I. A. "Vnikaia vo vse," in *Marshal Tukhachevskii: vospominaniia druzei i soratnikov*, edited by Nikolai Koritskii, et al. Moscow: Voenizdat, 1965.

Terpigorev, Aleksandr M. *Vospominaniia gornogo inzhenera*. Moscow: Akademiia nauk SSSR, 1956.

Teruyuki, Hara. *Shibberia shuppei: kakumei to kanshō, 1917-1922.* Tokyo: Chikuma Shobō, 1989.

Thaden, Edward, ed. *Russification in the Baltic Provinces and Finland, 1855-1914.* Princeton, NJ: Princeton University Press, 1981.

Thatcher, Ian D. "Trotsky, Lenin, and the Bolsheviks, August 1914-February 1917," *Slavonic and East European Review*, 72/1 (1994): 72–114.

———. *Leon Trotsky and World War One: August 1914-February 1917.* New York: St. Martin's Press, 2000.

Thompson, John M. *Russia, Bolshevism and the Versailles Peace.*

Princeton, NJ: Princeton University Press, 1966.

Thompson, Wayne C. *In the Eye of the Storm: Kurt Reizler and the Crisis of Modernity.* Ames: University of Iowa Press, 1980.

Thorniley, Daniel. *The Rise and Fall of the Soviet Rural Communist Party, 1927-1939.* New York: Macmillan, 1988.

Thun, Alphons. *Istoriia revoliutsionnykh dvizhenii v Rossii.* St. Petersburg: Ligi Russk. Revoliuts. Sots.-Dem., 1906.

Tiander, Karl. *Das Erwachen Osteuropas: Die Nationalbewegung in Russland und der Weltkrieg.* Vienna and Leipzig: Wilhelm Braumueller, 1934.

Tikhomirov, L. A. "Nuzhny li printsipy?," in *K reforme obnovlennoi Rossii: Stat'i 1909, 1910, 1911 gg*, edited by Tikhomirov. Moscow: V. M. Sablina, 1912.

Tilly, Charles. "War Making and State Making as Organized Crime," in *Bringing the State Back In*, edited by Peter B. Evans et al. New York: Cambridge University Press, 1985.

———. *Coercion, Capital, and European States, AD 990-1990.* Cambridge, MA: Blackwell, 1990.

Timashev, N. S. *Publichno-pravovoe polozhenie lichnosti. Pravo Sovetskoi Rossii.* Prague: Plamia, 1925.

Tishkov, A. V. *Felix Dzerzhinskii: Commemorating the Centenary of His Birth.* Moscow: Novosti Press Agency Publishing House, 1976.

Togan, Zaki Validi. *Vospominaniia: bor'ba musul'man Turkestana i drugikh vostochnikh tiurok za natsional'noe sushchestvovanie i kul'turu.* Moscow: [s.n.], 1997.

Tokés, Rudolf L. *Béla Kun and the Hungarian Soviet Republic: The Origins and Role of the Communist Party of Hungary in the Revolutions of 1918-1919.* New York: Praeger, 1967.

Tolf, Robert W. *The Russian Rockefellers: The Saga of the Nobel Family and the Russian Oil Industry.* Stanford, CA: Hoover Institution Press, 1976.

Torke, Hans-Joachim. "Das Russische Beamtentum in der ersten Hälfte des 19. Jahrhunderts," *Forschungen zur osteuropäischen Geschichte*, 13 (1967): 7–345.

Tornovskii, M. G. "Sobytiiia v Mongolii-Khalkhe v 1920-1921 godakh: voenn-istoricheskii ocherk (vospominaniia)," in *Legendarnyi baron: neizvestnye stranitsy Grazhdanskoi voiny*, edited by Sergei L. Kuz'min. Moscow: KMK, 2004.

*Tovarishch Kirov: rasskazy rabochikh, inzhenirov, khoziaistvennikov, uchenykh, kolkhoznikov i detei o vstrechakh s S. M. Kirovym.* Moscow: Profizdat, 1935.

Tovstukha, I. P., ed. *Iosif Vissarionovich Stalin: kratkaia biografiia.* Moscow: Gosizdat, 1927.

Treadgold, Donald. *The Great Siberian Migration.* Princeton, NJ: Princeton University Press, 1957.

Trepov, "Vespoddaneishaia zapiska D. F. Trepova (16 oktiabria 1905)," *Byloe*, 1919, no. 14: 109–11.

Trifonov, Ivan Ia. *Ocherki istorii klassovoi bor'by v SSSR, 1921-1937 gg.* Moscow: Politcheskaia literatura, 1960.

Trimberger, Ellen Kay. *Revolution from Above: Military Bureaucrats and Development in Japan, Turkey, Egypt and Peru.* New Brunswick, NJ: Transaction, 1978.

Troitskii, S. M. *Russkii absoliutizm i dvorianstvo v XVIII veke: Formirovanie biurokratii.* Moscow: Nauka, 1974.

Trotskii, L. "Vospominaniia ob oktiabr'skom perevorote," *Proletarskaia revoliustiia*, 1922, no. 10: 59–61.

———. "Zaveshchanie Lenina [December 1932]," in *Portrety revoliutsionerov* [1991], 265–91. Also in *Gorizont*, 1990, no. 6: 38–41.

———. *Chto i kak proizoshlo: shest' statei dlia mirovoi burzhuaznoi pechati.* Paris: Navarre, 1929.

———. *Dnevniki i pis'ma.* Tenafly, NJ: Ermitage, 1986, 1990.

———. *Kak vooruzhalas' revoliutsiia (na voennoi rabote)*, 3 vols. Moscow: Vysshii voennyi redaktsionnyi sovet, 1923–25.

———. *Kommunistichekii internatsional posle Lenina: velikiii organizator porazhenii.* Moscow: Spartakovets-printima, 1993.

———. *Literatura i revoliutsiia.* Moscow: Krasnaia nov', 1923.

———. *Moia zhizn': opyt avtobiografii*, 2 vols. Berlin: Granit, 1930. Moscow: Panorama, 1991. *Note: All endnote citations refer to the 1930 edition unless otherwise indicated.*

———. *O Lenine: materialy dlia biografii.* Moscow: Gosizdat, 1924.

———. *Piat' let Kominterna.* Moscow: Gosizdat, 1924.

———. *Portrety revoliutsionerov*, ed. Iu. Fel'shtinski. Benson, VT: Chalidze, 1984 and 1988. Moskovsky rabochii, 1991.

———. *Predannaia revoliutsiia.* Moscow: NII kul'tury, 1991.

———. *Sochineniia*, 21 vols. Moscow: Gosizdat, 1920–27.

———. *Stalin*, 2 vols. Benson, VT: Chalidze, 1985. Moscow: Politicheskaia literatura, 1990.

———. *Stalinskaia shkola fal'sifakatsii: popravki i dopolneniia k literature epigonov.* Berlin: Granit, 1932.

———, and Safarov, G. I. *Trotskii o Lenine i leninizme: sbornik materialov.* Leningrad: Priboi, 1925.

*Trotskizm i molodezh': sbornik materialov.* Leningrad: Priboi, 1924.

Trotsky, Leon. *1905.* Moscow: Gosizdat, 1922. New York: Random House, 1971.

———. *Between Red and White: a Study of Some Problems of Revolution, with Particular Reference to Georgia.* London: Communist Party of Great Britain, 1922.

———. *Challenge of the Left Opposition, 1926–27,* 2 vols. New York: Pathfinder Press, 1975, 1980.

———. *Lenin.* New York: Garden City Books, 1959.

———. *On Lenin: Notes Toward a Biography.* London: Harrap, 1971.

———. *My Life: An Attempt at an Autobiography.* New York: C. Scribner's Sons, 1930. New York: Pathfinder Press, 1970. *Note: All endnote citations refer to the 1970 edition unless otherwise indicated.*

———. *Stalin: An Appraisal of the Man and His Influence.* New York: Harper and Brothers, 1941. New York: Stein and Day, 1946. London: Macgibbon and Kee, 1968. *Note: All endnote citations refer to the 1941 edition unless otherwise indicated.*

———. *Terrorism and Communism: A Reply to Karl Kautsky.* Ann Arbor: University of Michigan Press, 1961.

———. *The Essential Trotsky.* New York: Barnes & Noble, 1963.

———. *The History of the Russian Revolution to Brest-Litovsk.* London: Socialist Labour Party, 1919.

———. *The History of the Russian Revolution,* 3 vols. New York: Simon & Schuster, 1932.

———. *The History of the Russian Revolution.* Ann Arbor, University of Michigan Press, 1961.

———. *The Real Situation in Russia.* London: Allen & Unwin, 1928.

———. *The Stalin School of Falsification.* New York: Pioneer, 1937.

———. *The Suppressed Testament of Lenin.* New York: Pioneer Publishers, 1935.

———. *Trotsky's Diary in Exile, 1935.* Cambridge, MA: Harvard University, 1958. New York: Atheneum, 1963.

———. *Where Is Britain Going?* London: Communist Party of Great Britain, 1926.

———. *Writings of Leon Trotsky, 1936–1937.* New York: Pathfinder Press, 1978.

———, et al. *Portraits: Political and Personal.* New York: Pathfinder Press, 1977.

———, and Shachtman, Max. *The New Course.* New York: New International, 1943.

*Trud v SSSR: ekonomiko-statisticheskii spravochnik.* Moscow: Ekonomgiz, 1932.

*Trudy i Vserossiiskogo S"ezda Sovetov Narodnogo Khoziiastva, 25 maia–4 iuinia 1918: Stenograficheskii otchet.* Moscow: Vysshii sovet narodnogo khoziaistva, 1918.

Trusova, N. S., ed. *Nachalo pervoi russkoi revoliutsii: ianvar'-mart 1905 goda.* Moscow, 1955.

Tsakunov, S. V. *V labirinte doktriny: iz opyta razrabotki ekonomicheskogo kursa strany v 1920-e gody.* Moscow: Rossiia molodaia, 1994.

Tsapenko, M. N. *Vserossiiskoe soveshchanie soveta rabochikh i soldatskikh deputatov.* Leningrad: Gosizdat, 1927.

"Tsensura," *Bol'shaia sovetskaia entsiklopediia,* 1st ed., LX.

Tsereteli, I. G. *Vospominaniia o fevral'skom revoliutsii,* 2 vols. Paris: Mouton, 1963.

*Tsirk: malenkaia entsiklopediia,* 2nd ed. Moscow: Sovetskaia entsiklopediia, 1979.

*TsK RKP (b)—VKP (b) i natsional'nyi vopros.* Moscow: Rosspen, 2005.

Tsvigun, S. K., et al., eds. *V. I. Lenin i VChK: sbornik dokumentov 1917–1922 gg.* Moscow: Politizdat, 1975.

Tsziun, Lin. "Sovetskaia Rossiia i Kitai v nachale 20-x godov," *Novaia i noveishaia istoriia,* 1997, no. 3: 46–57.

Tuchman, Barbara Wertheim. *Guns of August.* New York: Macmillan, 1962.

Tucker, Robert C. "A Case of Mistaken Identity: DJughashvili-Stalin," *Biography,* 5/1 (1982): 17–24.

———. "A Stalin Biography's Memoir," in *Psychology and Historical Interpretation,* edited by William McKinley Runyan. New York and Oxford: Oxford University Press, 1988.

———. *Stalin as Revolutionary, 1879–1929: A Study in History and Personality.* New York: W. W. Norton, 1973.

———. *Stalin in Power: The Revolution from Above, 1929–1941.* New York: W. W. Norton, 1990.

———, ed. *Stalinism: Essays in Historical Interpretation.* New York: W. W. Norton, 1977.

———. *The Lenin Anthology.* New York: W. W. Norton, 1975.

Tukhachevskii, M. N. *Izbrannye proizvedenniia.* Moscow: Voenizdat, 1964.

———. *Pokhod za Vislu: lektsii, prochitannye na dopolnitel'nom kurse Voennoi Akademii RKKA 7–10 fevralia 1923 goda.* Smolensk: Tipografiia Zapfronta, 1923.

Tumarkin, Nina. *Lenin Lives! The Lenin Cult in Soviet Russia.* Cambridge, MA: Harvard University Press, 1983.

Tumshis, Mikhail, and Papchinskii, Aleksander. *1937, bol'shaia chistka:*

*NKVD protiv ChK.* Moscow: Iauza-EKSMO, 2009.

Turner, L. F. C. "The Russian Mobilization in 1914," in *The War Plans of the Great Powers, 1880–1914,* edited by Paul M. Kennedy. Boston: George Allen and Unwin, 1979.

Tutaev, David, Alliluyev, Sergei, and Alliyueva, Anna. *The Alliluyev Memoirs: Recollections of Svetlana Stalina's Maternal Aunt Anna Alliluyeva and her Grandfather Sergei Alliluyev.* New York: Putnam, 1968.

Tyrkova-Williams, Ariadna. *From Liberty to Brest Litovsk: The First Year of the Russian Revolution.* London: Macmillan, 1919.

*Uchenie Lenina o revoliutsii i diktature roletariat.* Moscow: Gosizdat, 1925.

Uglanov, N. A. "O Vladmire Iliche Lenine (v period 1917–1922 gg.)," *Izvestiia TsK KPSS,* 1989, no. 4: 192.

*Ugolovnyi Kodeks RSFSR.* Moscow: NKIu, 1926, 1927, 1929.

Ugrovatov, A. P. *Krasnyi banditizm v Sibiri, 1921–1929 gg.* Novosibirsk: IUKEA, 1999.

Ukhtomskii, E. E. *Puteshestvie na Vostok ego imperatorskogo vysohchestva gosudaria naslednika tsarevicha, 1890–1891,* 3 vols. St. Petersburg, 1893–97.

Ukraintsev, N. "A Document on the Kornilov Affair," *Soviet Studies,* 25/2 (1973): 283–98.

Ulam, Adam B. *Expansion and Coexistence: The History of Soviet Foreign Policy.* New York: Praeger, 1968.

———. *Stalin: The Man and His Era.* New York: Viking Press, 1973.

———. *The Bolsheviks: The Intellectual and Political History of the Triumph of Communism in Russia.* New York: Macmillan, 1965.

Uldricks, Teddy. *Diplomacy and Ideology: The Origins of Soviet Foreign Relations 1917–30.* London: Sage, 1979.

Ul'ianova, M. I. *O Lenine i sem'e Ul'ianovykh: vospominaniia, ocherki, pis'ma.* Moscow: Politicheskaia literatura, 1978.

———. "O Vladimire Il'iche (poslednie gody zhizni," *Izvestiia TsK KPSS,* 1991, no. 1: 127–38, no. 2: 125–40, no. 3: 183–200, no. 4: 177–91.

———. "Ob otnoshenii V. I. Lenina k I. V. Stalinu," *Izvestiia TsK KPSS,* 1989, no. 12: 196–99.

Ullman, Richard H. *The Anglo-Soviet Accord.* Princeton, NJ: Princeton University Press, 1972.

Ulrich Brockdorff-Rantzau, Graf. *Dokumente.* Charlottenburg: Detusche Verlags, 1920.

Ulricks, T. J. "The 'Crowd' in the Russian Revolution: Towards Reassessing the Nature of Revolutionary Leadership," *Politics and Society,* 4/3 (1974): 397–413.

Upton, Anthony F. *The Finnish Revolution, 1917–1918*. Minneapolis: University of Minnesota Press, 1980.

Uratadze, Grigorii I. *Vospominaniia gruzinskogo sotsial-demokrata*. Stanford, CA: Hoover Institution Press, 1968.

Urazaev, Sh. Z. *Turkestanskaia ASSR—pervoe sotsialisticheskoe gosudarstvo v Srednei Azii*. Moscow: Politicheskaia literatura, 1961.

Urban, G. R. *Stalinism: Its Impact on Russia and the World*. London: Maurice Temple Smith, 1982.

*Uroki Oktiabria*. Berlin: Berlinskoe knigoizd-vo, 1924.

Urusov, S. D. *Zapiski tri goda gosudasrtvennoi sluzhby*. Moscow: NLO, 2009.

Ushakov, A. I. *Belyi iug: noiabr' 1919–noiabr' 1920 gg*. Moscow: AIRO-XX, 1997.

*Ustav obshchestva starykh bol'shevikov: Instruktsiia po organizatsii filial'-nykh otdelenii, Spisok chlenov Obshchestvo i anketa*. Moscow, 1928.

Ustrialov, Nikolai. *Pod zankom revoliutsii*. Harbin: Russkaia zhizn', 1925.

*U Velikoi mogily*. Moscow: Krasnaia zvezda, 1924.

*V Vserossiiskii s"ezd RKSM, 11–19 oktiabria 1922 g.: stenograficheskii otchet*. Moscow-Leningrad: [AU: Please provide publisher], 1922.

*V zhernovakh revoliutsii: russkaia intelligentsia mezhdu belymi i krasnymi v porevoliutsionnye gody, sbornik doumentov i materialov*. Moscow: Russkaia panorama, 2008.

*V. I. Lenin: neizvestnye dokumenty, 1891-1922*. Moscow: Rosspen, 1999.

*V. Ia. Bliukher v Kitae 1924–1927 gg.: novye dokumenty glavnogo voennogo sovetnika*. Moscow: Natalis, 2003.

Vaganov, F. M. *Pravyi uklon v VKP (b) i ego razgrom, 1928-1930*. Moscow: Politicheskaia literatura, 1970.

Vaisberg, Roman E. *Den'gi i tseny: podpol'nyi rynok v period "voennogo kommunizma."* Moscow: Gosplan SSSR, 1925.

Vakar, N. "Stalin: Po vospominaniiam N. N. Zhordaniia," *Poslednie novosti*, December 16, 1936.

Vaksberg, Arkadii. *Hôtel Lux: les partis frères au service de l'Internationale communiste*. Paris: Fayard, 1993.

———. *Iz ada v rai i obratno*. Moscow: Olimp, 2003.

———. *Stalin's Prosecutor: The Life of Andrei Vyshinsky*. New York: Grove Weidenfeld, 1991.

Valedinskii, Ivan Aleksandrovich. "Organizm Stalina vpolne zdorovyi," *Istochnik*, 1998, no. 2: 68–73.

Valentinov, N. *Nasledniki Lenina*. Moscow: Terra, 1991.

———. *Novaia ekonomicheskaia politika i krizis partii posle smerti Lenina*. Stanford, CA: Hoover Institution Press, Stanford University, 1971. Moscow: Sovremennik, 1991. *Note: All endnote citations refer to the 1971 edition unless otherwise indicated*.

Valliant, Robert Britton. "Japan and the Trans-Siberian Railroad, 1885–1905." Phd diss., University of Hawaii, 1974.

Valuev, P. A. *Dnevnik P. A. Valueva*, 2 vols. Moscow: Akademiia nauk SSSR, 1961.

van de Ven, Hans J. "Public Finance and the Rise of Warlordism," *Modern Asian Studies*, 30/4 (1996): 829–68.

Van Evera, Stephen. "The Cult of the Offensive and the Origins of the First World War," *International Security*, 9/1 (1984): 58–107.

———. "Why Cooperation Failed in 1914," *World Politics*, 38 (1985): 80–117.

Van Halen, D. J. *Memoirs of Don Juan Van Halen*, 2 vols. London: Henry Colburn and Richard Bentley, 1830.

van Ree, Erik. "Reluctant Terrorists? Transcaucasian Social-Democrats 1901–9," *Europe-Asia Studies*, 60/1 (2008): 127–54.

———. "Socialism in One Country: a Reassessment," *Studies in East European Thought*, 50/2 (1998): 77–117.

———. "Stalin and the National Question," *Revolutionary Russia*, 7/2 (1994): 214–38.

———. "The Stalinist Self," *Kritika*, 11/2 (2010): 257–82.

———. *The Political Thought of Joseph Stalin: A Study in Twentieth-Century Revolutionary Patriotism*. New York: RoutledgeCurzon, 2002.

Varneck, Elena, ed. *The Testimony of Kolchak and Other Siberian Materials*. Stanford, CA: Stanford University Press, 1935.

Vasetskii, N. A. *Trotskii: opyt politicheskoi biografii*. Moscow: Respublika, 1992.

Vasil'chikov, Boris. *Vospominaniia*. Moscow-Pskov: Nashe nasledie, 2003.

Vasileva, Larisa. *Kremlin Wives*. New York: Arcade, 1994.

Vasilyev, A. T. *The Ochrana: The Russian Secret Police*. Philadelphia: Lippincott, 1930.

Vatkin, Iu. "Goriachaia osen' dvadtsat vos'mogo (k voprosu o stalinizatsii kominterna)" in *Oni ne molchali*, ed. by A. V. Afanas'ev. Moscow: Politizdat, 1991.

Vatlin, A. "Panika: Sovetskaia Rossiia oseni 1918 goda glazami nemtsa," *Rodina*, 2002, n. 9: 78–81.

Vatlin, Aleksandr. *Komitern: idei, resheniia, sud'by*. Moscow: Rosspen, 2009.

———, et al., eds. *Stenogrammy zasedanii politburo TsK RKP (b), 1923–1938*. Moscow: Rosspen, 2007.

Vatsetis, J. "Grazhdanskaia voina: 1918 god," in *Pamiat': istoricheskii sbornik* (Moscow 1977, Paris 1979), no. 2.

Velikanova, O. V. "Lenina v massovom soznanii," *Otechestvennaia istoriia*, 1994, no. 2.

Velikanova, Olga. "The Myth of the Besieged Fortress: Soviet Mass Perception in the 1920s–1930," Stalin-Era Research and Archives Project, University of Toronto Centre for Russian and East European Studies, working paper no. 7 (2002).

———. *Popular Perceptions of Soviet Politics in the 1920s. Disenchantment of the Dreamers*. Basingstoke: Palgrave Macmillan, 2013.

———. *The Making of an Idol: On Uses of Lenin*. Göttingen: Muster-Schmidt, 1996.

*Velikii pokhod K. E. Voroshilova ot Luganska k Tsaritsynu i geroicheskaia oborona Tsaritsyna*. Moscow: Gos. voen. izd-vo Narkomata Oborony Soiuza SSR, 1938.

Vereshchak, Semyon. "Stalin v tiur'me (vospominaniia politicheskogo zakliuchennogo)," *Dni*, January 22, 1928.

Vernadskii, V. I. *Dnevniki, 1926–1934*. Moscow: Nauka, 2001.

Verner, Andrew. *The Crisis of Russian Autocracy: Nicholas II and the 1905 Revolution*. Princeton: Princeton University Press, 1990.

*V Vsemirnyi kongress Kommunisticheskogo Internatsionala 17 iiunia–8 iiulia 1924 g.: stenograficheskii otchet*, 2 vols. Moscow: Gosizdat, 1925.

*V Vserossiiskii s"ezd sovetov rabochikh, krest'ianskikh, soldatskikh i kazach'ikh deputatov, Moskva, 4–10 iiulia'1918 g.: stenograficheskii otchet*. Moscow: VTsIK, 1918.

*VI s"ezd RSDRP (bol'shevikov), avgust 1917 goda: protokoll*. Moscow: Politicheskaia literatura, 1958.

*VI (Parizhskaia) Vserossiiskaia konferentsiia RSDRP, 18–30 (5–17) aprelia 1912 g.: sbornik statei i dokumentov*. Moscow: Politicheskaia literatura, 1952.

*VII Vsebelorusskii s"ezd sovetov: stenograficheskii otchet*. Minsk: TsIK BSSR, 1925.

*VIII s"ezd RKP (b), mart 1919 goda: protokoly*. Moscow: Politicheskaia literatura, 1933. Politizdat, 1959.

*VIII s"ezd RKP (b), 18–28 marta 1919 goda: stenograficheskii otchet*. Moscow: Kommunist, 1919. Partizdat,

1933. Politicheskaia literatura, 1959.

Viktorov, B. V. *Bez grifa "sekretno": zapiski voennogo prokurora.* Moscow: Iuridicheskaia literatura, 1990.

Vil'kova, V. P., ed. *RKP (b), vnutripartiinaia bor'ba v dvadtsatye gody: dokumenty i materialy.* Moscow: Rosspen, 2004.

Vinogradov, V. K. "Zelenaia lampa," *Nezavisimaia gazeta,* April 20, 1994.

———, ed. *Genrikh Iagoda: narkom vnutrennykh del SSSR, general'nyi kommissar gosudarstvennoi bezopasnosti: sbornik dokumentov.* Kazan: [s.n.], 1997.

———. *Arkhiv VChK: sbornik dokumentov.* Moscow: Kuchkovo Pole, 2007.

———, et al. *Fanni Kaplan, ili kto strelial v Lenina: sbornik dokumentov,* 2nd ed. Moscow: X-History, 2003.

Vinogradov, V. K., et al. *Pravoeserovskii politicheskii protsess v Moskve, 8 iiunia–4 avgusta 1922 g.: stenogrammy sudebnykh zasedanii.* Moscow: Rosspen, 2011.

Viola, Lynne. "The Peasant Nightmare: Visions of Apocalypse in the Soviet Countryside," *Journal of Modern History,* 62/4 (1990): 747–70.

———. *Peasant Rebels Under Stalin: Collectivization and the Culture of Peasant Resistance.* New York: Oxford University Press, 1996.

———, ed. *The War Against the Peasantry, 1927–1930: The Tragedy of the Soviet Countryside.* New Haven, CT: Yale University Press, 2005.

Viroubova, Anna. *Memories of the Russian Court.* New York: Macmillan, 1923.

———. *Souvenirs de ma vie.* Paris, 1927.

Vishnevskii, N. M. *Printsipy i metody organizivannogo raspredeleniia produktov prodovol'stviia i predmetov pervoi neobkhodimosti.* Moscow: VSNKh, 1920.

Vishniak, Mark. *Dan' proshlomu.* New York: Chekhov, 1954.

———. *Le regime sovietiste.* Paris: Union, 1920.

———. *Vserossiiskoe uchreditel'noe sobranie.* Paris: Sovremennyia zapiski, 1932.

Vitte, S. Iu. *Samoderzhavie i zemtsvo: konfidential'naia zapiska ministra finansov stats-sekretaria S. Iu. Vitte (1899 g.),* 2nd ed. Stuttgart: J. H. W. Sietz Nachf., 1903.

———. *Vospominaniia: tsarstvovanie Nikolaia II,* 3 vols. Moscow-Leningrad: Gosizdat, 1923–4. Moscow: Izd. sotsial'no-ekonomicheskoi literatury, 1960. Moscow: AST, 2000.

*VKP (b), Komintern i natsional'no-revoliutsionnoe dvizhenie v*

*Kitae: dokumenty,* 4 vols. Moscow: Buklet, 1994–2003.

Vladimirova, Vera. *Kontr-revoliutsiia v 1917 g.: kornilovshchina.* Moscow: Krasnaia nov', 1924.

———. "Levye esery v 1917–1918 gg.," *Proletarskaia revoliutsiia,* 1927, no. 4: 101–40.

———. "Iul'skie dni 1917 goda," *Proletarskaia revoliutsiia,* 1923, no. 5: 3–52.

*Vneshniaia torgovlia SSSR za 1918–1940 gg.: statisticheskii obzor.* Moscow: Vneshtorgizdat, 1960.

Vodolagin, Mikhail A. *Krasnyi Tsaritsyn.* Volgograd: Nizhne-Volzhskoe knizhnoe izd-vo 1967.

Voeikov, Vladimir N. *S tsarem i bez tsaria: vospominaniia poslednego Dvortsovogo Komendanta Gosudaria Imperatora Nikolaia II.* Helsinki: [s.n.], 1936.

Voitsekhovskii, Sergei L. *Trest: vospominaniia i dokumenty.* Ontario, Canada: Zaria: 1974.

Volin, B. M. *12 biografii.* Moscow: Rabochaia Moskva, 1924.

———, ed. *Sed'maia (aprel'skaia) konferentsiia RSDRP (b).* Moscow: Politicheskaia literatura, 1955.

Volin, M. S. "Istpart i Sovetskaia istoricheskaia nauka," in *Velikii oktiabr': istoriia, istoriografiiia, istochnikovendenie: sbornik statei,* edited by Iu. A. Poliakov. Moscow: Nauka, 1978.

Volin, S. Iu. "Vokrug Moskovskoi Dumy," *Proletarskaia revoliutsiia,* 1922, no. 6.

Voline [Vsevolod Mikhailovich Eichenbaum], *The Unknown Revolution, 1917–1921.* New York: Free Life Editions, 1974.

Volkogonov, D. A. *Lenin: politicheskii portret,* 2 vols. Moscow: Novosti, 1994.

———. *Stalin: politicheskii portret,* 4th ed., 2 vols. Moscow: Novosti, 1996.

———. *Stalin: Triumph and Tragedy.* New York: Grove Weidenfeld, 1991.

———. *Triumf i tragediia: politicheskii portret I. V. Stalina,* 2 vols. Moscow, Novosti, 1989,

———. *Trotskii: politcheskii portret,* 2 vols. Moscow: Novosti, 1992.

Volkogonov, Dmitri. *Lenin: Life and Legacy.* London: HarperCollins, 1994.

———. *Trotsky: The Eternal Revolutionary.* New York: The Free Press, 1996.

Volkov, S. V. *Tragediia russkogo ofitserstva.* Moscow: Tsentropoligraf, 2002.

Volobuev, Pavel. *Ekonomicheskaia politika Vremmenogo Pravitel'stva.* Moscow: Nauka, 1962.

Volodarskii, M. I. *Sovety i ikh iuzhnye sosedi Iran i Afganistan 1917–1933.* London: Overseas Publications Interchange, 1985.

Voloshin, F. F. "Dmitrii Ivanovich Kurskii (k 100-letiiu so dnia rozhdeniia)," *Sovetskoe gosudarstvo i pravo,* 1974, no. 12: 98–102.

Vompe, P. *Dni oktiabrskoi revoliutsii i zheleznodorozhniki: Materialy k izucheniiu istorii revoliutsionnogo dvizheniia na zheleznykh dorogakh.* Moscow: TsK zheleznodorozhnikov, 1924.

von Bothmer, Karl Freiherr. *Mit Graf Mirbach in Moskau: Tagebuch-Aufzeichnungen und Aktenstrücke vom 19 April bis 24 August 1918,* 2nd ed. Tübingen: Osiander'sche Buchhandlung, 1922.

von Clausewitz, Carl. *On War.* New York: Knopf, 1993.

Von Geldern, James. *Bolshevik Festivals, 1917–1920.* Berkeley: University of California Press, 1993.

Von Hagen, Mark. "The *levée en masse* from the Russian Army to the Soviet Union, 1874–1938," in *People in Arms: Military Myth and National Mobilization since the French Revolution,* edited by Daniel Moran and Arthur Waldron. New York: Cambridge University Press, 2003.

———. *Soldiers in the Proletarian Dictatorship: The Red Army and the Soviet Socialist State, 1917–1930.* Ithaca, NY: Cornell University Press, 1990.

———. *War in a European Borderland: Occupations and Occupation plans in Galicia and Ukraine, 1914–1918.* Seattle: University of Washington Press, 2007.

von Hindenburg, Paul. *Out of My Life,* 2 vols. New York: Harper and Brothers, 1921.

von Korostowetz, W. K. *Graf Witte, der Steuermann in der Not.* Berlin: Brückenverlag, 1929.

von Kühlmann, Richard. *Erinnerungen.* Heidelberg: L. Schneider, 1948.

von Laue, Theodore H. "A Secret Memorandum of Sergei Witte on the Industrialization of Russia," *Journal of Modern History,* 26/1 (1954): 60–74.

———. "The Fate of Capitalism in Russia: The Narodnik Version," *American Slavic and East European Review,* 13/1 (1954): 11–28.

———. "The High Cost and the Gamble of the Witte System: A Chapter in the Industrialization of Russia," *Journal of Economic History,* 13/4 (1953): 425–48.

———. *Sergei Witte and the Industrialization of Russia.* New York, Columbia University Press, 1963.

———. *Why Lenin? Why Stalin? A Reappraisal of the Russian Revolution, 1900–1930.* Philadelphia, Lippincott: 1964, 1971.

von Mayenburg, Ruth. *Hotel Lux: Das*

*Absteigequartier der Weltrevolution*. Munich: Piper, 1991.

———. *Hotel Lux: Mit Dimitroff, Ernst Fischer, Ho Tschi Minh, Pieck, Rakosi, Slansky, Dr. Sorge, Tito, Togliatti, Tschou En-lai, Ulbricht und Wehner im Moskauer Quartier der Kommunistischen Internationale*. Munich: Bertelsmann, 1978.

von Moltke, Helmuth. *Erinnerungen, Briefe, Dokumente 1877 bis 1916*. Stuttgart: Der kommende Tag Verl., 1922.

von Müller, Georg. *The Kaiser and His Court*. London: MacDonald, 1961.

von Riekhoff, Harald. *German-Polish Relations, 1918–1933*. Baltimore: Johns Hopkins Press, 1971.

von Vollmar, Georg. *Der isolierte sozialistische Staat: eine sozialökonomische Studie*. Zurich: Volksbuchhandlung, 1878.

von Zwehl, Hans. *Erich von Falkenhayn: General der Infanterie: eine biographische Studie*. Berlin: E. S. Mittler, 1926.

Voronin, E. P., et al., eds. *Voennorevoliutsionnye komitety deistviiushchei armii, 25 oktiabria 1917–mart 1918 g*. Moscow: Nauka, 1978.

Voronovich, N., ed. *Zelenaia kniga: istoriia krest'ianskogo dvizheniia v chernomorskoi gubernii*. Prague: Chernomorskaia krest'ianskaia delegatsiia, 1921.

Voroshilov, K. E. "Iz istorii podavleniia Kronshtadtskego miatezha," *Voenno-istoricheskii zhurnal*, 1961, no. 3: 15–35.

———. "Iz istorii podavleniia Kronstadskogo mitaezha," *Voenno-istoricheskii zhurnal*, 1961, no, 3: 15–35.

———. *Lenin, Stalin, i krasnaia armiia: stat'i i rechi*. Moscow: Partizdat, 1934.

———. *Rasskazy o zhizni (vospominaniia)*. Moscow: Politizdat, 1968.

Voshchinin, V. P. *Na sibirskom prostore: kartiny pereselentsev*. St. Petersburg: Nash vek, 1912.

*Vospominaniia o Vladimire Il'iche Lenine*, 3 vols. Moscow: Politcheskaia literatura, 1956–61. 2nd ed, 5 vols. Moscow: Politcheskaia literatura, 1979.

Voss, A., et al. *Von hamburger Aufstand zur politische Isolierung: kommunistische Politik 1923–1933 in Hamburg und in deustchen Reich*. Hamburg: Landeszentrale für politische Bildung, 1983.

*Vsesoiuznaia Kommunisticheskaia Partiia (b) v rezoliutsiiakh s''ezdov, konferetnsii i plenumov TsK, 1898–1935*, 5th ed., 2 vols. Moscow: Partizdat, 1935–6.

*Vsesoiuznaia Kommunisticheskaia Partiia (b) v rezoliutsiiakh s''ezdov, konferetnsii i plenumov TsK,* *1898–1939*, 6th ed., 2 vols. Moscow: Partizdat, 1940–41.

Vucinich, Wayne S. "Mlada Bosna and the First World War," in *The Habsburg Empire in World War I: Essays on the Intellectual, Political, Military and Economics of the Habsburg War Effort*, edited by Robert A. Kann et al. Boulder, CO: East European Quarterly, 1977.

Vulliamy, C. E., ed. *From the Red Archives*. London: Geoffrey Bles, 1929.

Vygodskii, Semen Iu. *Vneshniaia politika SSSR, 1924–1929*. Moscow: Politcheskaia literatura, 1963.

*Vysylka vmesto rasstrela 1921–1923: deportazatsiia intelligentsii v dokumentakh VChK-GPU*. Moscow: Russkii put', 2005.

"Vystuplenie N. I. Bukharina posviashchennoe pamiati Skvortsova-Stepanova," *Voprosy istorii*, 1988, no. 5: 75–84.

Wade, Rex A. "Argonauts of Peace: The Soviet Delegation to Western Europe in the Summer of 1917," *Slavic Review*, 26/3 (1967): 453–67.

———. "Why October? The Search for Peace in 1917," *Soviet Studies*, 20/1 (1968): 36–45.

———. *Red Guards and Workers' Militias in the Russian Revolution*. Stanford, CA: Stanford University Press, 1984.

———. *The Russian Revolution, 1917*. New York: Cambridge University Press, 2000.

———. *The Russian Search for Peace: February–October 1917*. Stanford, CA: Stanford University Press, 1969.

Wagner, Moritz. *Travels in Persia, Georgia and Koordistan*, 3 vols. London: Hurst and Blackett, 1856.

Waite, Robert G. L. *Vanguard of Nazism: The Free Corps Movement in Post-War Germany, 1918–1923*. New York: W. W. Norton, 1952.

Waldron, Arthur. "The Warlord: Twentieth-Century Chinese Understandings of Violence, Militarism, and Imperialism," *American Historical Review*, 96/4 (1991): 1073–1100.

Waldron, Peter. *Between Two Revolutions: Stolypin and the Politics of Renewal in Russia*. London: UCL, 1998.

Walkin, Jacob. *The Rise of Democracy in Pre-Revolutionary Russia: Political and Social Institutions Under the Last Three Czars*. New York: Praeger, 1962.

Waller, Bruce. *Bismarck at the Crossroads: The Reorientation of German Foreign Policy After the Congress of Berlin, 1878–1880*. London: Athlone, 1974.

Wandruszka, Adam. *House of Habsburg: Six Hundred Years of a*

*European Dynasty*. New York: Doubleday, 1964.

Wandycz, Piotr S. *August Zaleski: Minister Spraw Zagranicznych RP 1926–1932 w Świetle Wspomnień i Dokumentów*. Paris: Instytut Literacki, 1980.

———. *Soviet-Polish Relations, 1917–1921*. Cambridge, MA: Harvard University Press, 1969.

———. *Twilight of French Eastern Alliances, 1926–1936: French-Czechoslovak-Polish Relations from Locarno to the Remilitarization of the Rhineland*. Princeton, NJ: Princeton University Press, 1988.

Ward, Chris. *Stalin's Russia*. New York: Routledge, Chapman and Hall, 1993.

Ward, John. *With the "Die-Hards" in Siberia*. London: Cassell, 1920.

Wargelin, Clifford F. "A High Price for Bread: The First Treaty of Brest-Litovsk and the Break-Up of Austria-Hungary, 1917–1918," *International History Review*, 19/4 (1997): 757–88.

Warth, Robert D. *Nicholas II: The Life and Reign of Russia's Last Monarch*. Westport, CT: Praeger, 1997.

———. *The Allies and the Russian Revolution*. Durham, NC: Duke University Press, 1954.

Waters, Brenda Meehan. *Autocracy and Aristocracy: The Russian Service Elite of 1730* New Brunswick, NJ: Rutgers University Press, 1982.

Waters, M. A., ed. *Rosa Luxemburg Speaks*. New York: Pathfinder Press, 1970.

Watson, Derek. *Molotov and Soviet Government: Sovnarkom, 1930–41*. New York: St. Martin's Press, 1996.

Waxmonsky, Gary Richard. "Police and Politics in Soviet Society 1921–1929." Phd diss., Princeton University, 1982.

Wcislo, Francis W. *Reforming Rural Russia: State, Local Society and National Politics, 1855–1914*. Princeton, NJ: Princeton University Press, 1990.

———. *Tales of Imperial Russia: The Life and Times of Sergei Witte, 1849–1915*. New York: Oxford University Press, 2011.

Weeks, Theodore. *Nation and State in Late Imperial Russia and Russification on Russia's Western Frontier, 1861–1914*. De Kalb: Northern Illinois University Press, 1994.

Wehner, Markus, and Petrov, Iu. A. "Golod 1921–1922 gg. v Smarskoi gubernii i reaktsiia sovetskogo pravitel'stva," *Cahiers du monde russe*, 38/1/2 (1997): 223–41.

Weiner, Douglas. "Dzerzhinskii and the Gerd Case: The Politics of Intercession and the Evolution of 'Iron Felix' in NEP Russia," *Kritika*, 7/4 (2006): 759–91.

Weissman, Neil. "Regular Police in

Tsarist Russia, 1900–1914," *Russian Review*, 44/1 (1985): 45–68.

Weissman, Neil B. *Reform in Tsarist Russia: The State Bureaucracy and Local Government, 1900–1914.* New Brunswick, NJ: Rutgers University Press, 1981.

Weitz, Eric D. *Creating German Communism, 1890–1990: From Popular Protests to Socialist State.* Princeton, NJ: Princeton University Press, 1997.

———. *Weimar Germany: Promise and Tragedy.* Princeton, NJ: Princeton University Press, 2007.

Werth, Nicolas. "Rumeurs défaitistes et apocalyptiques dans l'URSS des années 1920 et 1930," *Vingtième siècle, revue d'histoire*, 71 (2001): 25–35.

Westad, Odd Arne. *The Global Cold War: Third World Interventions and the Making of Our Times.* Cambridge: Cambridge University Press, 2005.

Westwood, J. N. *A History of Russian Railways.* London: G. Allen and Unwin, 1964.

———. *The Historical Atlas of World Railroads.* Buffalo, NY: Firefly, 2009.

———. *Russia Against Japan, 1904–5: A New Look at the Russo-Japanese War.* Albany: State University of New York, 1986.

Wheatcroft, Stephen G. "Agency and Terror: Evdokimov and Mass Killing in Stalin's Great Terror," *Australian Journal of Politics and History*, 53/1 (2007): 20–44.

Wheeler-Bennett, John. *The Forgotten Peace: Brest-Litovsk, March 1918.* London: Macmillan, 1938.

———. "The Meaning of Brest-Litovsk Today," *Foreign Affairs*, 17/1 (1938): 137–152.

Wheen, Francis. *Karl Marx.* London: Fourth Estate, 1999.

White, Elizabeth. *The Socialist Alternative to Bolshevik Russia: The Socialist Revolutionary Party, 1921–1939.* London and New York: Routledge, 2011.

White, Howard J. "1917 in the Rear Garrisons," in *Economy and Society in Russia and the Soviet Union, 1860–1930: Essays for Olga Crisp*, edited by Linda Edmondson and Peter Waldron. New York: St. Martin's Press, 1992.

———. "Civil Rights and the Provisional Government," in *Civil Rights in Imperial Russia*, edited by Olga Crisp and Linda Edmondson. Oxford: Clarendon Press, 1989.

White, J. D. "The Kornilov Affair: A Study in Counter Revolution," *Soviet Studies*, 20/2 (1968): 187–205.

White, James D. "Early Soviet Historical Interpretations of the Russian Revolution, 1918–1929," *Soviet Studies*, 37/3 (1985): 330–52.

White, John Albert. *The Diplomacy of the Russo-Japanese War.* Princeton, NJ: Princeton University Press, 1964.

———. *The Siberian Intervention*. Princeton, NJ: Princeton University Press, 1950.

White, Stephen. *The Origins of Détente: The Genoa Conference and Soviet-Western Relations, 1921–1922.* New York: Cambridge University Press, 1985.

Widerkehr, Stefan. "Forging a Concept: 'Eurasia' in Classical Eurasianism," paper presented at the 2007 Annual Soyuz Symposium, Princeton University, April 2007.

Wilbur, C. Martin. *The Nationalist Revolution in China, 1923–1929.* New York: Cambridge University Press, 1984.

———, and How, Julie Lien-ying. *Documents on Communism, Nationalism, and Soviet Advisers in China, 1918–1927: Papers Seized in the 1927 Peking Raid.* New York: Columbia University Press, 1956.

———. *Missionaries of Revolution: Soviet Advisers and Nationalist China, 1920–1927.* Cambridge, MA: Harvard University Press, 1989.

Wilcox, E. H. *Russia's Ruin.* London: Chappell & Hall, 1919.

Wildman, Allan K. *The End of the Russian Imperial Army*, 2 vols. Princeton, NJ: Princeton University Press, 1980, 1988.

———. "Officers of the General Staff and the Kornilov Movement," in *Revolution in Russia*, Frankel, ed., 76–101.

Williams, A. R. *Through the Russian Revolution.* New York: Boni and Liveright, 1921. Williams, Andrew J. *Trading with the Bolsheviks: The Politics of East-West Trade, 1920–1939.* Manchester: Manchester University Press, 1992.

Williams, B. J. "Great Britain and Russia, 1905–1907 Convention," in *British Foreign Policy under Sir Edward Grey*, edited by F. H. Hinsley. New York: Cambridge University Press, 1977.

Williams, Beryl. *The Russian Revolution, 1917–1921.* Oxford: Basil Blackwell, 1987.

Williams, Robert C. "Russian War Prisoners and Soviet-German Relations, 1918–1921," *Canadian Slavonic Papers*, 9/2 (1967): 270–95.

Williamson, Jeffrey G. "Globalization, Factor Prices and Living Standards in Asia before 1940," in *Asia Pacific Dynamism 1550–2000*, edited by A. J. H. Latham et al. London: Routledge, 2000.

Williamson, Jr., Samuel. *Austria-Hungary and the Origins of the First World War.* Houndmills and London: Macmillan, 1991.

Wilson, Keith, ed. *Decisions for War, 1914.* New York: St. Martin's Press, 1995.

Wohlforth, William C. "The Perception of Power: Russia in the Pre-1914 Balance," *World Politics*, 39/3 (1987): 353–81.

Wolfe, Bertram D. "Lenin and the Agent Provocateur Malinovsky," *Russian Review* 5/1 (1945): 49–69.

———. "The Influence of Early Military Decisions upon the National Structure of the Soviet Union," *American Slavonic and East European Review*, 9/3 (1950): 169–79.

———. *Three Who Made a Revolution.* New York: Dial Press, 1948.

———, ed. *Khrushchev and Stalin's Ghost.* New York: Praeger, 1957.

Woodruff, David. *Money Unmade: Barter and the Fate of Russian Capitalism.* Ithaca, NY: Cornell University Press, 1999.

———. "The Politburo on Gold, Industrialization, and the International Economy, 1925–1926," in *Lost Politburo Transcripts*, ed. by Gregory and Naimark, 199–223.

Woodworth, Bradley. "Civil Society and Nationality in the Multiethnic Russian Empire: Tallinn/Reval, 1860–1914." Phd diss., Indiana University, 2003.

Wortman, Richard. "Nicholas II i obraz samoderzhaviia," *Istoriia SSSR*, 1991, no. 2: 119–28.

———. "Russian Monarchy and the Rule of Law: New Considerations of the Court Reform of 1864," *Kritika*, 6/1 (2005): 145–70.

———. *Scenarios of Power: Myth and Ceremony in Russian Monarchy*, 2 vols. Princeton: Princeton University Press, 2000.

———. *The Crisis of Russian Populism.* New York: Cambridge University Press, 1967.

Wright, Jonathan. "Locarno: a Democratic Peace?" *Review of International Studies* 26/2 (2010): 391–411.

Wu, Tien-wei. "A Review of the Wuhan Débâcle: The Kuomintang-Communist Split of 1927," *Journal of Asian Studies*, 29/1 (1969): 125–43.

Wyszczelski, Lech. *Varshava 1920.* Moscow: Astrel', 2004.

*X s'ezd RKP (b), mart 1921 goda: stenograficheskii otchet.* Moscow: Gosizdat, 1921. Moscow: Partizdat, 1933. Moscow: Politicheskaia literatura, 1963.

*XI s'ezd RKP (b): protokoly.* Moscow: Partizdat, 1936. *Stenograficheskii otchet.* Moscow: Politicheskaia literatura, 1961.

*XI Vserossiiskii s'ezd Sovetov: stenograficheskii otchet.* Moscow: VTsIK SSSR, 1924.

*XII s'ezd RKP (b): stenograficheskii otchet.* Moscow: Politizdat, 1968.

*XIII konferentsiia RKP (b): biulleten'.* Moscow: Krasnaia nov', 1924.

*XIII s"ezd VKP (b), mai 1924 g.: stenograficheskii otchet.* Moscow: Politizdat, 1963.

*XIV konferetnisia RKP (b): stenograficheskii otchet.* Moscow-Leningrad: Gosizdat, 1925.

*XIV s"ezd VKP (b): stenograficheskii otchet.* Moscow-Leningrad: Gosizdat, 1926.

*XV konferentsiia VKP (b), 26 oktiabria–3 noiabria 1926 g.: stenograficheskii otchet.* Moscow and Leningrad: Gosizdat, 1927.

*XV s"ezd VKP (b): stenograficheskii otchet,* Moscow, Gosizdat, 1928. 2 vols. Moscow: Politicheskaia literatura, 1961–2.

*XVI Moskovskaia gubernskaia konferentsiia VKP (b).* Moscow: MGK VKP (b), 1927.

*XVI partiinaia konferentsiia VKP (b), aprel' 1929 g.: stenografischekii otchet.* Moscow: Politicheskaia literatura, 1962.

*XVI s"ezd VKP (b): stenograficheskii otchet.* Moscow: Partizdat, 1935.

*XVII s"ezd VKP (b): stenograficheskii otchet, 26 ianvaria—10 fevralia 1934 g.* Moscow: Partizdat, 1934.

Yaney, George L. "Some Aspects of the Imperial Russian Government on the Eve of the First World War," *Slavonic and East European Review,* 43/ (1964): 68–90.

——. "The Concept of the Stolypin Land Reform," *Slavic Review,* 23/2 (1964): 275–93.

——. *The Systematization of Russian Government: Social Evolution in the Domestic Administration of Imperial Russia, 1711–1905.* Urbana: University of Illinois Press, 1973.

——. *Urge to Mobilize: Agrarian Reform in Russia, 1861–1930.* Urbana: University of Illinois Press, 1982.

Yanov, Alexander. *The Origins of Autocracy: Ivan the Terrible in Russian History.* Berkeley: University of California Press, 1981.

Yarkovsky, Jan M. *It Happened in Moscow.* New York: Vantage Press, 1961.

Yaroslavsky, E. *Landmarks in the Life of Stalin.* Moscow: Foreign Publishing House, 1940.

Yevtuhov, Catherine. *Portrait of a Russian Province: Economy, Society, and Civilization in Nineteenth-Century Nizhnii Novgorod.* Pittsburgh: University of Pittsburgh Press, 2012.

Yiulenev, I. V. *Sovetskaia kavaleriia v boiakh za Rodinu.* Moscow: Voenizdat, 1957.

Young, Harry F. "The Misunderstanding of August 1, 1914," *Journal of Modern History,* 48/4 (1976): 644–65.

Young, James. "Bolshevik Wives: A Study of Soviet Elite Society." Phd diss., Sydney University, 2008.

*Za chetkuiu klassovuiu liniiu: sbornik dokumentov kraikoma VKP (b) i vystuplenii rukovodiashchikh rabotnikov kraia.* Novosibirsk: Sibkraikom VKP (b), 1929.

*Za leninizm: sbornik statei.* Moscow and Leningrad: Gosizdat, 1925.

Zabih, S. *The Communist Movement in Iran.* Berkeley and Los Angeles: University of California Press, 1966.

Zagorsky, S. O. *State Control of Industry in Russia During the War.* New Haven, CT: Yale University Press, 1928.

Zaionchkovskii, P. A. *Pravitel'stvennyi apparat samoderzhavnoi Rossii v XIX v.* Moscow: Mysl', 1978.

Zakharov, Vladimir V. *Voennye aspekty vzaimootnosheniia SSSR i Germanii: 1921-iiun' 1941.* Moscow: Gumanitarnaaia Akademiia vooruzhennykh sil, 1992.

Zal'kind, Aron B. "O zabolevaniiakh partaktiva," *Krasnaia nov',* 1925, no. 4: 187–203.

Zalkind, I. A. "N.K.I.D. v semnadtsatom godu," *Mezhdunarodnaia zhizn',* 1921, no. 10.

Zamoyski, Adam. *Warsaw 1920: Lenin's Failed Conquest of Europe.* London: HarperCollins, 2008.

Zamyatin, Yevgeny. "Comrade Churygin Has the Floor," in *The Fatal Eggs and Other Soviet Satire 1918–1963,* edited by Mirra Ginsburg. New York: Grove, 1964.

Zarubin, V. G. *Bez pobeditelei: iz istorii grazhdanskoi voiny v Krymu.* Simfereopol: Tavriia, 1997.

*Zasedanie vserossiiskogo tsentral'nogo ispolnitel'nogo komiteta 4-go sozyva: protokoly.* Moscow: Gosizdat, 1920.

Zashikhin, A. N. "O chisle zhertv krovavogo voskresen'ia," *Vestnik pomorskogo universiteta,* 2008, no. 3: 5–9.

Zbarskii, B. I. *Mavzolei Lenina.* Moscow: Politcheskaia literatura, 1945.

Zdanovich, A. A. *Organy gosudarstvennoi bezopasnosti i Krasnaia armiia: deiatel'nost' organov VChK-OGPU po obespecheniiu bezopasnosti RKKA, 1921–1934.* Moscow: Kuchkovo pole/Iks-Khistori, 2008.

Zdesenko, V. I. *Gorki Leninskie.* Moscow: Moskovskii rabochii, 1985.

Zeidler, Manfred. *Reichswehr und Rote Armee 1920–1933: Wege und Stationen einer ungewöhnlichen Zusammenarbeit,* Munich: R. Oldenbourg, 1993; 2nd ed., 1994.

Zelenov, M. V. "Rozhdeniie partiinoi nomenklatury," *Voprosy istorii,* 2005, no. 2: 3–24.

Zeman, Z. A. B. *The Break-Up of the Habsburg Empire, 1914–1918.* New York: Oxford University Press, 1961.

——, ed. *Germany and the Revolution in Russia 1915–1918: Documents from the Archives of the German Foreign Ministry.* New York: Oxford University Press, 1958.

"Zemel'nye poriadki za uralom," in *Aziatskaia Rossiia,* 3 vols, edited by G. V. Glinka. St. Petersburg: A.F. Marks, 1914.

Zen'kovskii, Aleksandr V. *Pravda o Stolypine.* New York: Vseslovianskoe, 1956.

Zenkovsky, Serge. "The Tataro-Bashkir Feud of 1917–1920," *Indiana Slavic Studies,* 2 (1958): 37–61.

——. *Pan-Turkism and Islam in Russia.* Cambridge, MA: Harvard University Press, 1967.

Zetkin, Klara. *Reminiscences of Lenin.* New York: International, 1934.

——. *Vospominaniia o Lenine.* Moscow: Politicheskaia literatura, 1955.

——, et al. *We Have Met Lenin.* Moscow: Foreign Languages Publishing House, 1939.

Zhidkov, G. P. "Krest'iane Altaia ot fevralia k oktiabriu: k istorii krakha kabinetskogo zemlevladeniia," in *Voprosy istorii sotsial'no-ekonomicheskoi i kul'turnoi zhizni Sibiri i Dal'nego Vostoka.* Novosibirsk: Nauka, Sibirskoe otdelenie, 1968.

Zhilinskii, V. B. *Organizatsiia i zhizn' okhrannago otdeleniia vo vremia tsarskoi vlasti.* Moscow: T-vo Riabushkinskikh, 1918.

Zhitkov, N. "Prodfurazhnoe snabzhenie russkikh armii v mirovuiu voinu," *Voenno-istoricheskii zhurnal,* 1940, no. 12: 65–81.

Zhordaniia, N. *Moia zhizn'.* Stanford, CA: Hoover Institution Press, 1968.

——. *Bol'shevizm.* Berlin: TsK sotsial-demoktraticheskoi rabochei partii, no date.

Zhukov, G. K. *Vospominaniia i razmyshleniia,* 3 vols. Moscow: Novosti, 1995.

Zhukovskii, N. P. *Polnomochnyi predstavitel' SSSR.* Moscow: Politizdat, 1968.

Zhvaniia, G. K. *Bol'shevistkaia pechat' Zakavkaz'ia nakanune i v period pervoi Russkoi revoliutsii.* Tblisi: Tsentral'nyi komitet Kommunisticheskoi partii Gruzii, 1958.

Zibert, V. "O bol'shevistkom vospitanii," *Na strazhe,* 1924, no. 25: 9–10.

Zima, V. F. *Chelovek i vlast' v SSSR v 1920–1930e gody: politiki represii.* Moscow: Sobranie, 2010.

Zimmerman, Joshua D. *Poles, Jews, and the Politics of Nationality: The Bund and the Polish Socialist Party in Late Tsarist Russia, 1892–1914.* Madison: University of Wisconsin Press, 2005.

Zinov'ev, G. *Leninizm: vvedenie v izuchenie Leninizma.* Leningrad: Gosizdat, 1925.

———. *Litsom k derevne!* Leningrad: Gosizdat, 1925.

———. *N. Lenin.* Petrograd: Petrogradskii Sovet, 1918.

———. *God revoliutsii: fevral' 1917—mart 1918.* Leningrad: Gosizdat, 1925.

———. *Istoriia Rossiiskoi kommunisticheskoi partii (bol'shevikov).* Yekaterinburg: Ural-kniga, 1923.

———. *Bol'shevizm ili trotzkizm?* Leningrad: proletarii, 1925.

———. *Bor'ba za Petrograd, 15 oktiabra–6 noiabria 1919.* Petrograd: Gos. sotsial'no-ekonomicheskoe izd., 1920.

———. *Zwölf Tage in Deutschland.* Hamburg: C. Hoym Nachf. L. Cahnbley, 1921.

———. and Trotskii, L. *O miatezhe levykh s. r.* Moscow: Petrogradskii Sovet, 1918.

Zitser, Ernest A. *The Transfigured Kingdom: Sacred Parody and Charismatic Authority at the Court of Peter the Great.* Ithaca, NY: Cornell University Press, 2004.

Ziv, G. A. *Trotskii: kharakteristika (po lichnym vospominaniiam).* New York: Narodopravstvo, 1921.

Zlokazov, G. I. *Petrogradskii Sovet rabochikh i soldatskikh deputatov v period mirnogo razvitiia revoliutsii.* Moscow: Nauka, 1969.

Znamenskii, Oleg N. *Vserossiiskoe Uchreditel'noe Sobranie: istoriia sozyva i politicheskogo krusheniia.* Leningrad: Nauka, 1976.

Zohrab, Irene. "The Socialist Revolutionary Party, Kerensky and the Kornilov Affair: From the Unpublished papers of Harold W. Williams," *New Zealand Slavonic Journal* (1991): 131–61.

Zuber, Terence. *Inventing the Schlieffen Plan: German War Planning, 1871–1914.* New York: Oxford University Press, 2002.

Zubov, Nikolai. *F. E. Dzerzhinskii: biografiia,* 2nd ed. Moscow: Politicheskaia literatura, 1965.

Zubov, Platon. *Kartina Kavkazskogo kraia prinadlezhashchago Rossii, i sopredel'nykh onomu zemel': v istoricheskom, statisticheskom, etnograficheskom, finansovom i torgovom otnosheniiakh,* 4 vols. St. Petersburg: Konrad Vingeber, 1834–5.

Zuckerman, Fredric S. *The Tsarist Secret Police in Russian Society, 1880–1917.* Basingstoke, Hampshire: Macmillan, 1996.

Zviagintseva, A. P. "Organizatsiia i deiatel'nost' militsii Vremmenogo pravitel'stva Rossii v 1917 g.," Phd diss., Moscow State University, 1972.

# ILLUSTRATION CREDITS

AGKM: Altai State Regional Museum
RGAKFD: Russian State Archive of Photographs and Film
RGKFAD SPb: Russian State Archive of Films and Photographs, St. Petersburg
RGASPI: Russian State Archive of Social and Political History (former central party archive)

**INSERT 1**

Page 1: Above: Russian State Archive of Film and Photo Documents (RGAKFD), albom, 1068, no. 80; Below: State Museum of Political History of Russia (GMPIR)

Page 2: Above: RGAKFD, albom 830, no. 20; Below: *Adskaia pochta*, 1906, no. 3

Page 3: Above: RGAKFD, ed. khr. 5-4736; Below: TsGAKFFD, E-6486

Page 4: Above: RGAKFD, albom 1057, foto 2; Below: Getty Images

Page 5: Top Left: Stalin Museum Gori; Top Right: Russian State Archive of Social and Political History (RGASPI), f. 558, op. 11, d.1671, l. 01; Bottom Left: RGAKFD, ed. khr. 4-8936; Bottom Right: Stalin Museum Gori

Page 6: Above: Stalin Museum Gori; Below: Stalin Museum Gori

Page 7: Above: Stalin Museum Gori; Below: Ostrovskii, *Kto stoial za spinoi Stalina*

Page 8: Above: Hoover Institution Archives; Middle: RGAKFD, ed. khr. 0-44748; Below: RGAKFD, ed. khr. 2-19694

Page 9: Above: Georgian Soviet Socialist Republic Archive (II), fond no. 6, I. Stalin's documents; Below: RGAKFD, ed. khr. V-2

Page 10: Above: Sarajevo Historical Archives; Below: National Archive of Bosnia and Herzegovina

Page 11: Above: RGAKFD, ed. khr. 4-8391; Below: RGAKFD, ed. khr. 0-140426

Page 12: Top: *Kornilov* (series: *zhizn' zamechatel'nykh liudei*); Bottom Left: RGAKFD, ed. khr. 2-30761; Bottom Right: The Granger Collection, New York

Page 13: Above: TsGAKFFD Sankt-Peterburga, d. 19316; Below: Jonathan Sanders

Page 14: Above: RGAKFD, ed. khr. V-2410; Below: Hoover Institution Archives

Page 15: Above: RGASPI, f. 393, op. 1, d. 26; Below: RGAKFD, ed. khr. 58898

Page 16: Above: RGASPI, f. 558, op. 11, d. 1651, l. 18, 19; Below: RGAKFD, ed. khr. G-343

**INSERT 2**

Page 1: Above: Vladimir Genis, *S Bukharoi nado konchat': k istorii butaforskikh revoliutsii: dokumental'naia khronika*; Below: S. L. Kuz'min, *Istoriia barona Ungerna : opyt rekonstruktsii*

Page 2: Above: David King Collection, London; Below: Hoover Institution Archives

Page 3: Above: RGASPI, f. 393, op. 1, d. 32, l.3; Below: RGAKFD, ed khr. V-1438

Page 4: Top Left: RGASPI, f. 393, op. 1, d. 39, l. 7; Top Right: RGAKFD, ed. khr. 4-8538; Bottom Left: RGASPI, f. 394, op. 1, d, 30. l. 4; Bottom Right: David King Collection, London

Page 5: Above: Shchusev Museum of Architecture; Right: RGAKFD; Bottom Left: Russian State Library (Leninka), Moscow, postcard; Bottom Right: David King Collection, London

Page 6: Above: David King Collection, London; Below: RGAKFD, ed. khr. V-20

Page 7: Above: Alexander Plekhanov et al., *Feliks Dzerzhinskii: k 130-letiiu so dnia rozhdeniia*; Below: RGAKFD, ed. khr. V-3334

Page 8: Top Left: RGAKFD; Top Right: *Artuzov* (series: *zhizn' zamechatel'nykh liudei*); Bottom Left: *Artuzov* (series: *zhizn' zamechatel'nykh liudei*); Bottom Right: Public domain

Page 9: Above: RGASPI, d. 74, op. 2, d. 168, l. 21; Below: RGAKFD, ed. khr. 5-10767

Page 10: Above: RGASPI, ed. khr. G-21; Left: Shchusev Museum of Architecture, Moscow; Below: Sergei Deviatov et al., *Blizhnaia dacha Stalina*

Page 11: Top Left: Artem Sergeev, *Besedy o*

# INDEX

Abashidze, David, 36–37, 46
*ABC of Communism, The* (Bukharin and Preobrazhensky), 695
Abkhazia, Abkhazians, 15, 496, 541, 557, 564
Abramidze-Tsikhitatrashvili, Masho, 17
Adelkhanov Tannery, 22, 25, 43, 48
Afghanistan, 109, 391
Africa, 65, 71, 316
Agabekov, Georgy (Arutyunov), 667
"Against Federalism" (Stalin), 350
agriculture, Russian, 65, 93, 298–300
  consolidation in, 674
  exports of, 93, 136, 164
  "extraordinary measures" policy for, 697, 705, 709–10, 712, 713, 722
  famine of 1921–22 and, 447–49
  lack of modernization in, 449–50, 663, 671–72
  low yields of, 93, 447, 566, 568, 649, 659, 662–64, 680, 700–701, 721, 722–23
  Stolypin's reforms in, 95, 96–97
  and wartime land confiscation, 189
  *see also* peasants, Russian
agriculture commissariat, 449–50, 470
Alekseev, N. P., 304, 305
Alexander I, tsar, 89
Alexander II, tsar, 59–60, 89
  assassination of, 60, 134
  Great Reforms of, 29, 59–60, 66, 85
Alexander III, tsar, 60, 85, 89, 120, 158, 353
Alexander Mikhailovich, Grand Duke, 163
Alexandra, tsarina, 89–90, 119, 128, 159, 163, 166, 167, 168, 170, 172, 280
  murder of, 281
  Rasputin and, 159–61
Alexei, tsarevich, 90, 126, 128, 158–59, 166, 170, 171
  hemophilia of, 160–61, 178
  murder of, 281

Alexeyev, Mikhail, 159, 163, 166, 170–72, 182, 197, 207, 211, 228, 248, 268, 282, 295
Allies (Great War), *see* Entente (Allies)
Alliluyev, Sergei, 53, 55, 117, 264, 594
Alliluyeva, Anna, 193, 314
Alliluyeva, Nadezhda "Nadya," 264, 301, 314, 398, 593, 633
  headaches and depressions of, 466, 468, 594
  in Lenin's secretariat, 413, 466, 467, 484
  party purge and reinstatement of, 467–68
  Stalin's courtship of, 193
  Stalin's marriage to, 117, 264, 466–67, 594–95, 707, 719
Alliluyeva, Olga, 193, 594
Alliluyeva, Svetlana, 10, 595, 633, 719
Alliluyev family, 155, 193, 466
All-Russia Congress of Muslims, 183
All-Russia Congress of Peasants' Deputies, First, 187
All-Russia Cooperative Society, 631–32
Alma-Ata, 676–79, 719
American Relief Administration (ARA), 448–49
anarchism, anarchists, 39, 334
"Anarchism or Socialism?" (Stalin), 107–8, 544
Andreyev, Andrei, 457, 607, 666, 720
Andreyev, Nikolai, 275
Anglo-Russian Entente (1907), 109, 110, 135, 136, 140
Anna, tsarina, 88
anti-Semitism, 19, 99, 100, 326
  *Protocols of the Elders of Zion* and, 100, 129
  of Stalin, 112
  in White armies, 325–26
Antonov, Alexander, 346, 381, 394
Antonov-Ovseyenko, Vladimir, 346, 381, 394
apparatchiks, 426, 430, 431–32
"April Theses" (Lenin), 191
Arkhangelsk, 269
  British landing at, 282, 283

Armand, Inessa, 151, 188, 285, 413, 531
Armenia, 238, 343, 365, 395, 397, 400, 475, 480
Armenians, 115, 479
  in Georgia, 15, 496
  in Tiflis, 29, 49, 479
  Turkish genocide against, 150
Armenian Soviet Republic, 395
Article 107, 666, 669, 670, 681, 682, 700, 701,
  705, 707, 713
Artuzov, Artur, 461, 635, 657
Asia:
  Japanese imperialism in, 111
  nationalist liberation movements in, 554
  Russian expansion in, 68, 111, 554
  Stalin's views on revolution in, 625
Austria, 316, 347–48
Austria-Hungary, 2, 5, 6, 34–35, 109, 343
  Balkans and, 141
  Bosnia annexed by, 110, 142, 144
  Brest-Litovsk Treaty and, 258
  in Great War, 140, 162, 185, 197, 200,
    248–249, 269; see also Central Powers
  in onset of Great War, 143–44, 148–49
  wartime food shortages in, 251–52
autocratic system, Russian, 3, 10, 57–60, 88, 125
  agriculture in, 65
  bureaucracy of, 57–59, 69, 70–71, 83, 120
  chancellery of, 430
  constitutionalism and, 56, 60, 78, 79, 82, 84,
    85, 90, 92, 93–94, 98, 99, 100, 103, 109, 122,
    127, 128, 132, 137, 157, 171, 173, 223
  Council of Ministers in, 60, 86
  Duma in, see Duma
  Great War and collapse of, 173
  industrialization in, 65
  intransigence of, 54, 66–67, 74, 137, 157–58
  mass politics as distasteful to, 130
  modernity and, 62–63, 65–67
  Peter the Great and, 56–57
  political parties disdained by, 137, 157
  political terrorism and, 101, 102, 103–4
  prime ministership in, 83–85
  uprisings of 1905–6 and, 81
automobiles, 612
  as special interest of Stalin, 540–41
Avilov, Boris, 221, 258
Axelrod, Pavel, 45, 135, 188
Azerbaijan, 343, 365–66, 368, 395, 397, 400,
  475, 480

Babel, Isaac, 359
Baku, 12, 50, 55, 266, 301
  Congress of the Peoples of the East in, 367
  oil industry in, 115, 283

  proletariat in, 366
  Red Army capture of, 366
  Stalin in, 112, 114–16, 117, 121, 123
  strikes in, 144
Baku-Batum pipelines, 51
Bakunin, Mikhail, 41–42, 191
Baku Proletarian, 106, 112
Balabanoff, Angelica, 531–32
Balashov, Alexei, 429, 431, 456–57
  on Stalin, 468–69
Baldwin, Stanley, 559
Balk, Alexander, 167, 168, 169
Balkans, 141, 143
Balkan wars (1912–13), 142, 143
Balkaro-Kabarda, 688
Baltic fleet, as Bolshevik stronghold, 187
Baltic littoral, German occupation of, 243, 283
Balytsky, Vsevolod, 665, 688, 699
Balzac, Honoré de, 36
banks, Bolshevik seizure of holdings of, 238–39
Barabashev, Oleg, 685
Baramyants, Iosif, 15–16
Barbusse, Henri, 1
Barmine, Alexander, on Stalin's
  appearance, 427
Barnaul, 661–62, 668, 679, 681, 682
Bashkir Autonomous Soviet Socialist Republic
  (Bashkiria), 370–72, 447
Bashkir First Cavalry, 370
Bashkir Revolutionary Committee, 370
Bashkirs, 368, 369, 479
"Basmachi," 371–72
Batum, 77, 301
  massacre of workers in, 52, 53
  Stalin in, 51–52
Bauer, Otto, 133, 347–48
Baumanis, Kārlis (Bauman, Karl), 673
Bavarian Soviet Republic, 323–24
Bazhanov, Boris, 454, 455, 456, 458, 463, 523,
  666–67
Beck, Józef, 562
Bedny, Demyan (Pridvorov, Yefim), 260,
  602, 604
Belenky, Abram, 593–94
Belenky, Grigory, 603
Belgium:
  in Great War, 145–46, 147, 152
  in Locarno Pact, 561
Beloborodov, Alexander, 676
Belorussia, Belorussians, 98, 119, 125, 157, 353,
  354, 388, 475, 546
  as independent republic, 343, 368
  Poland and, 352, 616–17
  Soviet Union plan and, 475

Belorussian Soviet Republic, 406
Belostotsky, Ivan "Vladimir," 124
Benes, Edvard, 316
Beria, Lavrenti, 8, 395, 542
Berlin, Treaty of (1926), 587, 588
Bernstein, Eduard, 78–79
Berzin, Jan (Ķuzis, Pēteris), 554, 618
Besser, Lidiya, 154
Bezobrazov, Alexander, 72
Bismarck, Otto von, 4, 70, 72, 83, 94, 95, 109,
    113, 119, 139, 140, 141
    on art of politics, 5–6
    Russia and, 5, 7
    unification of Germany by, 4, 5, 6–7, 18, 732
Björkö, Treaty of, 110, 139
Black Hundreds (Holy Brigades), 77, 86, 99, 182
Black Repartition, 189
Black Sea, 12, 14
Blackshirts (*squadristi*), 549
Blacksmith Bridge, 15 (*Kuznetskii most*), 441
Blanqui, Louis Auguste, 79
Blanquism, 79, 80
Blok, Alexander, 130
Blok, Ivan, 74
Bloody Sunday, 73–74, 126, 164
Blyukher, Vasily, 629, 631, 644
Blyumkin, Yakov, 274–75
Bodoo, 402
Bogrov, Mordekhai "Dmitry," 122
Boki, Gleb, 375, 433
*Bolshevik* (publication), 545
Bolshevik regime (1918–22):
    armed insurrections against, 231
    Brest-Litovsk Treaty and, 257–58, 264–65,
        269, 272–73, 283, 312, 315, 642
    chaotic nature of, 230–33
    civil war and, *see* civil war, Russian
    and collapse of financial system,
        238–39, 242
    counterrevolution as obsession of, 233–34,
        241, 244, 287–88, 290–91, 392–93
    Dadaism compared with, 230, 232
    decline of labor force under, 385
    as dictatorship, 231
    excluded from Versailles peace talks, 317
    federalism and, 343
    food shortages in, 290, 299–302, 307, 321–22
    fuel shortages in, 321
    grain monopoly of, 299
    grain seizures by, 380, 389, 447
    grassroots organizations targeted by, 336–37
    Great War and, 231, 247
    ideological zealotry of, 292–93, 597
    Jews in, 340–41

Kamenev's attempts to include other
    socialists in, 233–36
Mirbach on likely collapse of, 271, 272
national authority lacked by, 254–55
as party-state, 339, 345, 469
in peace talks with Central Powers, 249–50
Petrograd evacuated by, 259–61
police force lacked by, 240
propaganda machine of, 289–90
property seized by, 241–42
Red Terror of 1918 in, 287–88
Romanov property nationalized by, 281
siege mentality in, 338
Stalin as dominant force in, 295
Stalinist faction in, 390
state building by, *see* state building, Soviet
territory ceded by, 258
Trotskyist faction in, 390
tsarist debt repudiated by, 239
universal suffrage under, 243
*see also* Communist Party; Council of
    People's Commissars; Russian Soviet
    Federated Socialist Republic
Bolshevik regime (1918–22), bureaucracy of,
    289–90, 427
    corruption in, 292, 322, 337, 338, 527
    elite perquisites in, 338
    expansion of, 385, 578, 601
    financial burden of, 337–38
    hierarchical nature of, 337
    incompetence in, 292, 424
    internecine competition in, 420
    redundancy in, 428–29
Bolshevik Revolution, 137, 233
    as bourgeois democratic revolution, 407
    Stalin in, 138, 177
    Stalin's view on, 555–56
    *see also* February Revolution; October
        Revolution
Bolsheviks, Bolshevism, 3, 79, 103, 106, 108,
    114, 118, 124, 137, 176
    as alternative world order, 343
    bourgeois historical phase expected by, 190
    in Constituent Assembly election,
        244–45
    as enemies of colonialism, 368–69
    excluded from Moscow State
        Conference, 206
    at First Congress of Soviets, 196
    given new life by Kornilov's coup attempt,
        212–13, 225
    Kerensky's treason charges against, 202–3
    Lenin's zealotry criticized by, 191–92
    loss of confidence of, 213

Bolsheviks, Bolshevism *(cont.)*
 Menshevik split with, 78, 79–81, 103, 108,
  114, 122–23, 124, 137
 October coup of, *see* October Revolution
 peasants ignored by, 237, 426
 Petrograd headquarters of, 186–87, 190,
  191, 203, 215
 Petrograd Soviet controlled by, 212–13,
  218–19
 political polarization welcomed by, 208
 Prague conference of, 122–23
 Provisional Government and, 177–78, 208
 Russia Bureau of, 190, 222
 Russian army agitation by, 198
 Russification of, 348
 7th (Extraordinary) Party Congress of, 259
 6th Party Congress of, 204–5, 212
 Stalin as, 112, 176–77
 Tiflis bank robbery of, 113–14
 Trotsky's joining of, 200, 202
Bonch-Bruevich, Mikhail, 250, 328
Bonch-Bruevich, Vera, 285
Bonch-Bruevich, Vladimir, 240, 250, 260, 275,
 276, 285, 287
Borisov, Sergei, 401–2
Borman, Arkady, 341
Borodin, Mikhail (Grusenberg), 628, 629, 631
Bosnia-Herzegovina, 110, 142, 144
bourgeoisie, 40
 Marxist view of, 190, 292, 293
 in Russia, 66
 serf owners replaced by, 42
bourgeois revolution, 42, 78, 175, 195, 199, 407
Boxer rebellion, 64
Brandler, Heinrich, 509–10, 514–15, 525
*Brdzola (Struggle)*, 50, 55, 348
Brest-Litovsk, 249, 354, 361
Brest-Litovsk, Treaty of, 257–58, 264–65, 269,
 272–73, 315, 389, 451, 459, 642
 addenda to, 283
 Left SR denunciation of, 273, 274
 Russia's repudiation of, 312
Briand, Aristide, 562
British empire, 4, 141, 151, 316
British intelligence, Russian codes cracked by,
 391–92
Brockdorff-Rantzau, Ulrich, Count von, 553,
 559, 638, 691, 693, 704, 709
 Chicherin and, 559–60
Broido, Gersh, 373
Bronstein, Aneta, 200
Bronstein, David, 200
Brusilov, Alexei, 162, 163, 164, 166, 185, 196,
 197, 199, 248

Brutzkus, Boris, 239
Bryant, Louise, 440
Budyonny, Semyon, 345, 355–56, 357, 358, 359,
 362, 363, 365, 456, 464
Bug River, 358
Bukhara, 90, 255, 342
 Red Army sack of, 373–75
Bukharan People's Soviet Republic, 375
Bukharin, Nikolai, 133, 246, 250, 256, 257, 259,
 262, 276, 314, 322, 331, 334, 351, 354, 385,
 389, 392, 414, 464, 469, 493, 497, 512, 535,
 596, 608, 613, 619, 631, 632, 640, 656, 676,
 686, 695, 708, 739
 as alternative Soviet leader, 728–29
 in "cave meeting," 505, 506, 658
 as Comintern head, 719
 on "extraordinary measures" policy, 711–12
 and German Communist coup attempt,
  509–10
 and "Ilich's letter about the secretary,"
  504–9, 512
 on industrialization, 722
 Kamenev and, 727
 and Lenin's death, 534
 as Lenin's possible successor, 492
 Lenin's Testament and, 499
 NEP and, 569–71, 727
 and plot to oust Stalin as general secretary,
  713–17, 720
 in politburo, 596
 Stalin and, 615–16, 707–8, 714–15,
  718–19, 723
 on Stalin's dictatorship, 472, 474, 507–9,
  513, 731
 and succession power struggle, 563, 564, 578,
  580, 584, 641–42, 644
Bulgakov, Mikhail, 620
Bulgaria, 316
 failed Communist coup in, 514–15
Burckhardt, Jacob, 144

Campbell, Thomas, 700
capitalism, 39, 190, 482, 733
 colonialism and, 625
 Lenin on, 151, 291, 403, 444, 446, 625
 Marxist view of, 39–40, 78–79, 151, 190, 288,
  292, 347
 nationalism and, 347
 in Russia, 42, 195
 Sokolnikov on, 565–66
 Stalin on, 107, 444, 561, 562–63, 583, 653,
  698–99
Carr, E. H., 739
Catherine I, tsarina, 88

Catherine II, "the Great," tsarina, 89, 90, 263
Caucasus, 16, 43, 365, 439, 700
   Bolsheviks in, 108, 266
   British army in, 270, 397–98
   Mensheviks in, 112, 124
   political terrorism in, 115
   Russian conquest of, 3, 12–13
   Stalin's 1926 trip through, 598, 600, 601
Central Asia, 372–76
   Muslims in, 373–74
   Russian expansion into, 67–68, 111
Central Committee, 123, 154, 191, 214, 233,
     234, 235, 255, 271, 321, 322, 328, 329, 350,
     385, 390, 426, 430, 434, 476, 488, 502, 577,
     637, 730
   Bolshevik takeover of, 122–23, 124, 133
   Bukharin's triumvirate plan for, 512
   dictatorial powers given to Lenin's inner
     circle by, 243
   economic naïveté of, 569
   elections for, 193, 322, 497, 547, 584
   and German peace talks, 250, 251, 256–57
   grain shortages and, 665–66, 669, 673, 684
   joint plenums of Central Control
     Commission and, 522–25, 608–9, 614, 640,
     646–49, 651, 698–700, 709–10, 711
   Kamenev's resignation from, 235–36
   Lenin's criticisms of, 192
   Lenin's proposed expansion of, 485
   October Revolution and, 214, 216
   plenums of, 123, 328, 362, 411, 430, 477, 484,
     485, 515–16, 522, 533, 546, 557, 586, 604,
     605, 614, 622, 630–31, 648
   as policy-making body, 428–29
   and Polish-Soviet War, 359, 362
   secretariat of, see secretariat
   secret departments of, 434–35
   Soviet Union plan approved by, 477, 484
   Stalin in, 123–24, 132–33, 193
   Stalin loyalists in, 454, 455
   Stalin's expansion of, 497
   Stalin's resignation offers to, 224, 508, 607,
     614, 619, 648, 657–59, 660
   trade monopoly upheld by, 484
   Trotsky as chairman of, 214–15
   Trotskyites excluded from, 390, 411–12, 423,
     584, 651
   Trotsky's economic plan rejected by, 484
   Trotsky's expulsion from, 648
   Zinoviev's expulsion from, 648
Central Committee apparatus, 428–29, 433, 438
   corruption and excess in, 518–19
   Council of People's Commissars functions
     duplicated by, 428–29

   endless reports demanded by, 435
   leaks and security violations in, 434
   Molotov's criticism of, 518–19
   mystique of, 435
   Old Square offices of, 429, 430–31
   Stalin loyalists in, 453–57, 469–70
   Stalin's control of, 478, 486–87
   Stalin's expansion of, 425–26
   Stalin's obsession with fulfilling directives
     of, 433
   Trotsky's denunciation of, 518–19, 522
   see also orgburo; politburo; secretariat
Central Control Commission, 375, 430, 451,
     454, 502–3, 522, 577, 583, 594, 607–8, 614,
     636, 640
   circulation of Lenin's Testament banned
     by, 540
   joint plenums of Central Committee and,
     522–25, 608–9, 614, 640, 646–49, 651,
     698–700, 709–10, 711
   Trotsky investigated by, 520
Central Powers, 140, 157, 196, 197
   Lenin's cease-fire offer to, 247–49
   in peace talks with Bolsheviks, 249–50
Chagin, Pyotr (Boldovkin), 586
Chamberlain, Austen, 559, 561, 562
Charkviani, Kristopore, 16, 20, 21
chauvinism, Great Russian, 348, 407,
     487, 496, 497
Chavchavadze, Ilya, 32, 33, 36, 38, 43, 44
Chechnya, Chechens, 304, 688
Cheka, 237, 262, 264, 273, 291, 374–75, 384, 433
   in assassination of Grand Duke Mikhail, 280
   corruption in, 294
   formation of, 241
   in Georgia, 399, 541–42
   Kronstadt rebellion and, 393
   Latvian assault on, 277–78
   Left SRs arrested by, 278
   local branches of, 293–94
   Lubyanka headquarters and prison of,
     437–38
   in Mirbach assassination plot, 275–76
   in murder of Tsar Nicholas and family, 281
   National Center plot uncovered by, 333
   in Petrograd, 382
   property seized by, 241–42
   proposed curbs on, 439
   replaced by GPU, 439, 448
   sadistic reputation of, 438
   Stalin's control of, 438
   summary executions by, 294
   in Tsaritsyn, see Tsaritsyn Cheka
   widespread hatred of, 241

Chekhov, Anton, 10
Cheremisov, V. A., 217
Chernov, Victor, 135, 164, 185, 198, 202, 228, 234, 279
Cherry Orchard, The (Chekhov), 10
chervonets, 452
Chervyakov, Alexander I., 302, 303, 304
Chiang Kai-shek, 185, 627, 631, 632, 644, 655, 717
  Communists distrusted by, 628
  massacre of Shanghai Communists ordered by, 629–30
  Stalin's support of, 630–31
Chiatura, 86, 301
  Stalin in, 76–77, 81
Chicago, Ill., Haymarket riots in, 49–50
Chicherin, Georgy, 262, 275, 283, 359, 366, 386, 392, 404, 443, 444, 446, 511, 525, 560, 562, 589, 616, 617–18, 622, 631, 635–36, 651, 692, 693
  Brockdorff-Rantzau and, 559–60
  Litvinov's relationship with, 458
  as Stalin appointee, 457
  Stalin's correspondence with, 407–8
  work habits of, 457–58
China, 63, 67, 364
  Comintern and, 626, 627–28, 629–30, 640
  Communists in, see Communist Party, Chinese
  famine in, 63, 64
  Nationalists in, see Guomindang
  Qing dynasty in, 4, 64, 66, 401
  revolution of 1911 in, 131–32, 625–26
  Soviet advisers in, 626–28, 629
  Soviet Russia and, 404–5
  Soviet Union and, 617, 623, 625–33, 651, 655
  Stalin and, 625, 627–33, 640, 655
  Trotsky and, 627, 628–29, 630, 631, 632
  Zinoviev and, 629, 630–31
Chizikov, Pyotr, 121
Chkheidze, Nikoloz "Karlo," 51, 191, 647
Choqai-Beg, Mustafa, 253
Chubar, Vlas, 390
Churchill, Winston, 398
civil war, Russian, 231, 269, 282–83, 298, 325–29, 350, 356–60, 369, 380, 436, 642
  aftermath of, 405–6
  barter economy of, 450
  Bolshevik advantages in, 332–33
  Bolshevik regime strengthened by, 290, 336–37
  casualties in, 332
  as economic war, 406
  grain shortages and, 405

  inflation in, 450
  Lenin in, 334
  mass exodus of professional class during, 405
  nationalism and, 345–46
  1919 offensive in, 335, 370–71
  propaganda campaigns in, 335–36
  Stalin's role in, 295, 297, 302–4, 305–7, 308–10, 314, 320, 327, 328, 332, 334–35, 339, 379
  Trotsky's role in, 284, 285–86, 289, 297, 298, 302–4, 306–10, 313–14, 319–21, 325–31, 334–35, 339–40
  Ungern-Sternberg in, 400–401
  Whites' definitive defeat in, 379
Civil War, U.S., 18–19
Civil War in France (Marx), 232
class warfare:
  as central tenet of Lenin's thought, 291, 443, 444, 737
  as foundation of Soviet state, 291–92
  as justification for mass executions, 293–94
  Marx on, 291–92, 737
  peasant rebellions and, 381
  Soviet foreign policy and, 443–44
  Stalin's fervent belief in, 306–7, 308–9, 345, 444, 681, 688, 698, 710–11, 732, 734
Clemenceau, Georges, 315, 317
collectivization, 103, 420–21, 449, 570, 584, 660, 674–75, 682–83, 695, 722–23, 725, 733, 739
  Bukharin on, 708
  capitalist farming as superior to, 725
  Communist ideology of, 724–27
  dekulakization and, 421
  famine and, 724
  global economy and, 726
  industrialization and, 725
  low yields in, 725
  peasant resistance to, 724
  politburo and, 675–76
  Rykov and, 731
  as Stalin's great gamble, 734–35
  Stalin's speeches on, 671–73, 676, 679, 706–7, 713, 718
  Trotsky on, 675
colonialism, 62, 65, 66, 343, 364, 653
  Bolsheviks as enemies of, 368–69
  capitalism and, 625
  Comintern and, 367–68
  famine and, 63–64
  Great War and, 151–52
  statism and, 96
  Treaty of Versailles and, 316

commissars:
  expanding role of, 339
  in Red Army, 339, 351
communes, 41–42, 65–66, 95, 96–97, 189–90,
  299, 430, 449, 567
Communism, 40, 190, 336, 597
  see also Leninism; Marxism, Marxists
Communist, 259
Communist Academy, 706, 718
Communist International (Comintern), 392,
  412, 510
  First Congress of, 317, 347, 369
  Second Congress of, 41, 318, 363–64
  Third Congress of, 403, 442
  Fourth Congress of, 418, 427
  Fifth Congress of, 550–51
  Sixth Congress of, 718–20
  Baku Congress and, 367
  Bukharin as head of, 719
  China policy of, 626, 627–28, 629–30, 640
  colonialism and, 367–68
  and German Communist coup attempt, 511,
    525, 526, 559
  GPU agents in, 442–43
  inefficiency and corruption in, 442–43
  Kuusinen as head of, 442
  Mongolian-Tibetan department of, 401–2
  Soviet foreign relations and, 558, 559
  Stalin's control of, 506, 609
  Trotsky expelled from, 644
  Zinoviev as head of, 609, 615
Communist Manifesto, The (Marx and Engels),
  39–40, 43, 45, 99, 107, 151
Communist Party, 259, 265, 271–72, 297, 339
  9th conference of, 376–77
  13th conference of, 533, 534
  14th conference of, 569, 571
  15th conference of, 614–15
  6th Congress of, 555
  8th Congress of, 318–22, 329, 369, 370, 396
  10th Congress of, 344, 384–91, 405–6, 410,
    423, 455, 459
  11th Congress of, 411, 431, 465, 481, 482
  12th Congress of, 415–16, 425, 433, 436, 488,
    494–95, 502
  13th Congress of, 546–49, 552, 573, 607, 609
  14th Congress of, 579–84, 586
  15th Congress of, 597, 640, 641, 643–44,
    652–56, 659, 660, 664–65, 673, 730
  Central Committee of, see Central
    Committee
  collective leadership proposed for, 422–23
  growth of, 344
  hierarchical structure of, 289, 432, 469

  local organizations in, 432–33
  Muslims in, 502–3, 527, 716
  nationalism and, 345
  NEP and, 420
  Stalin appointed general secretary of,
    411–12, 424, 481, 486, 530
  Stalin's nationalities report to, 496
  Stalin's organizational report to, 495
  Stalin's triumph over Trotsky at, 501
  Trotsky and Zinoviev expelled from, 651, 656
  Trotsky at, 495–96
  Trotskyites culled from, 495
  Zinoviev and, 495
Communist Party, Chinese, 640
  in alliance with Guomindang, 626–27
  Chiang's distrust of, 628
  Guomindang betrayal of, 637–38, 640, 655
  Shanghai massacre of, 629–30
  Sixth Congress of, 717
  Soviet aid to, 627, 640
  Stalin on tactics of, 627–28
  Stalin's betrayal of, 631
Communist Party, French, 519–20, 645
Communist Party, Georgian:
  Central Committee of, 475, 477, 480, 493
  Dzierżyński's investigation of, 480–81, 487
  insubordination of, 479, 487, 489–90,
    493, 494
  Second Congress of, 493
Communist Party, German, 318, 323, 378, 704
Communist Party, German, coup attempt of,
  392, 473, 550
  Bukharin and, 509–10
  Comintern and, 511, 525, 526, 559
  lack of worker support for, 525, 526
  politburo aid to, 511, 515
  Stalin and, 510–11, 515, 522, 525–26, 557
  Trotsky and, 511
  Zinoviev and, 509–10, 511, 514–15
Communist Party, Hungarian, 324–25
Communist Party, Italian, 550, 551, 609, 720
Communist Party, Polish, 349, 515, 519–20, 600
Communist Party, Ukrainian, Central
  Committee of, 476
Communist Youth International, 644
Communist Youth League, 548, 574, 585, 707
Congress, U.S., Russia famine relief and,
  448–49
Congress of Soviets, 350, 354
  First, 196
  Second, 215, 217, 219, 220, 225, 233, 247,
    258, 396
  Third, 247, 251
  Fourth, 264–65

Congress of Soviets *(cont.)*
Fifth, 273–75, 276, 278, 279–80
Sixth, 311
Tenth (First USSR), 485–86
Eleventh (Second USSR), 534, 535, 539–40
Congress of the Peoples of the East, 367, 372, 395
conservatism, 39
Constituent Assembly, 242–47, 251, 279
Constitutional Democrats (Cadets), Russian, 90, 93–94, 98, 105, 109, 130, 132, 136, 137, 157, 175, 178, 180, 184, 195, 196, 199, 202, 205, 239, 242–43, 244, 343, 464
constitutionalism, 56, 60, 78, 79, 82, 84, 85, 90, 92, 93–94, 98, 99, 100, 103, 109, 122, 127, 128, 131–32, 137, 157, 171, 173, 175–76, 178–80, 207, 223
Cossacks, 13, 254, 268, 270, 296, 304, 305, 310, 326, 356, 401
Council of Five, 211–12
Council of Labor and Defense, 416–17, 476
Council of Ministers, Russian, 60, 86, 179
Council of People's Commissars, 227–29, 233, 234, 236, 241, 242, 263, 266, 270, 278, 280, 350, 412, 416–17, 425, 428, 476, 492, 686
duplicate functions of Central Committee apparatus and, 428–29
Left SRs and, 237, 265, 273
Lenin's control of, 229, 236
Council of People's Commissars, USSR, 540
counterrevolution, 183, 186
Bolshevik obsession with, 233–34, 241, 244, 287–88, 290–91, 392–93
and Kornilov's attempted coup, 207–11, 212, 219
Moscow State Conference and, 207
Soviet laws against, 634
Stalin on, 207, 209, 213, 214
Stalin's use of label as political strategy, 305–7
*Credo* (Stalin), 77
Crimea, 332, 357–59, 362, 365, 374, 379, 447
Crimean War, 59, 66, 67, 91
Curzon, Lord, 358, 359, 360, 397–98
Czechoslovakia, 316, 325, 511, 561–62, 589
Czechoslovak Legion, 269, 280, 282–83, 296, 331
revolt of, 269–70, 277

Dadaism, 230, 232
"Dada Manifesto" (Tzara), 227
Dagestan, 12
Dalai Lama, 401
Dan, Fyodor, 137, 396, 469

Danielson, Nikolai F., 42, 65–66
Danzan, 346, 402, 404
Danzig, 315, 363, 364, 621
Dashnaks (Revolutionary Armenian Federation), 115, 137, 351, 395, 400
Davis, Jerome, 610–11, 660
Davitashvili, Mikheil "Mikho," 37, 38, 47, 48
Davrishevi, Damian, 20
Davrishevi, Iosif "Soso," 25
*Days of the Turbins* (Bulgakov), 620
Declaration of the 46, 519, 522–23, 524
decreeism, 435
de Gaulle, Charles, 352
dekulakization, 421, 685, 707, 724, 727
Denikin, Anton, 297, 300, 329–30, 335, 336, 352, 353, 355, 356, 357, 358, 366, 386
Cossack support for, 296
failed Moscow assault of, 331
Kiev seized by, 330
in 1919 offensive, 326, 328
in retreat to Crimea, 332
as Volunteer Army head, 295, 325–26
Denmark, Prussia's war with, 5, 6
Desart, Lord, 146, 147
Devdariani, Seid, 35, 38, 104
Dgebuadze, Alexander, 399
dialectical materialism, 107
Didi Lilo, 15, 25, 48
Dirksen, Herbert von, 587
Dmitrievsky, Pyotr Alexandrovich, 276, 278
Dogadov, Alexander, 657
Donetsk Coal Trust, 690, 691, 703
Don River, 268, 296, 300, 310, 330
Don Soviet Republic, 238
Dorpat (Yurev) University, 38
Dukhonin, Nikolai, 248
Duma, 82–83, 84, 85, 90–91, 93, 99, 109, 113, 119, 136, 144, 145, 157, 163, 168, 179, 181, 223
Lena goldfields investigation in, 126
Nicholas II and, 74, 82–83, 90–91, 93–94, 101, 127, 128, 158, 163, 166, 169
Provisional Committee of, 170–71, 172, 173
Provisional Government and, 179–80
right wing and, 101, 102
Stalin on, 105
Stolypin and, 94, 97, 101
Duranty, Walter, 543
Durnovó, Pyotr, 85–86, 87, 90, 92, 102, 125, 129, 130, 146, 149, 157, 167, 173, 187, 408, 409, 558
democracy as viewed by, 136
Nicholas II and, 134

political insight and prescience of,
135–37
on probable outcome of war with Germany,
131, 135
resignation of, 91
in State Council, 134
Dzierżyński, Felix, 104, 121, 235, 241, 250,
257, 260, 275–76, 278, 284, 300, 314, 333,
352, 358, 360, 365, 375, 393, 396, 438,
459, 452, 468, 482, 579, 588, 596, 602,
688, 738
background of, 459
as Cheka-GPU head, 459
death of, 605
on expanded bureaucracy, 601
and famine of 1921–22, 447–48
Georgian insubordination investigated by,
480–81, 487, 489
as head of OGPU, 577–78
imprisonment and internal exiles of, 459
Left SR capture of, 276
Lenin's death and, 492–93, 534–35, 536
and Lenin's mummification, 542–43
as Lenin's possible successor, 493
Mężyński and, 460
NEP and, 578
new Polish attack feared by, 604–5
and succession power struggle, 577–78
Supreme Council of the Economy chaired by,
578, 579, 601
and Trotsky's Sukhum stay, 541

Eastern Orthodox Christianity, 10, 12, 13
Eastman, Max, 506, 572–73, 647–48
Lenin's Testament published by, 614
economy, global, 64–65
dichotomy in, 64–65
Soviet collectivization and, 726
Stalin on, 569
economy, Soviet, 408
in civil war, 450
currency in, 450, 452
foreign debt and, 720–21, 733
inflation in, 450, 583, 663
monetary emissions in, 569, 585, 664
monetary reforms in, 376, 451–52, 566, 568,
569, 583, 585
1924 harvest and, 566
Trotsky's quest for dictatorship of, 481, 484,
485, 486–87, 488, 501, 518
unemployment in, 695
see also finance commissariat; New
Economic Policy
Egnatashvili, Mrs., 17

Egnatashvili, Yakov "Koba," 16, 20, 23, 24, 25,
46, 106
Egnatashvili family, 17, 28
Eighteenth Brumaire of Louis Bonaparte, The
(Marx), 107
Eihe, Roberts, 683
Eisenstein, Sergei, 651
Eisner, Kurt, 323–24
Elisabedashvili, Grigory, 7
Elizabeth, tsarina, 88
embassies, Soviet:
Comintern offices in, 443
GPU in, 443
Engels, Friedrich, 8, 39, 151, 232
Enlightenment, Stalin's article in, 133
En Route, 327
Entente (Allies), 140, 147, 221, 247, 256, 258,
273, 364, 561
and Bolshevik takeover of Georgia, 397
continued eastern front operations desired
by, 265
and Lenin's cease-fire offer to Central
Powers, 247–48
military aid to Whites by, 296
in partitioning of Ottoman empire, 367
and Polish-Soviet War, 353, 355, 359
Romania and, 378–79
total German defeat as goal of, 258
Trotsky's secret negotiations and, 265
White army supplied by, 326, 352
Erdman, Nikolai, 620
Eristavi, Rapiel, 34
Estonia, 283, 295, 330, 331, 604
aborted Communist coup in, 554–55,
556–57
as independent nation, 238, 342–43
Ethiopia, 64
Eurasia, 1, 138, 243, 343, 344, 349
civil wars in, 294, 345
diversity of, 56
Muslims in, 349, 366, 367–72
nationalism in, 406
proletariat as minority in, 349
use of term, 345
Europe:
fear of Bolshevism in, 336
Russian expatriates in, 104, 393, 489, 553,
555, 557, 575
Exodus to the East, 345
Extraordinary Commission for Combating
Counter-revolution, Sabotage, and
Speculation, 293
Extraordinary Commission for Food and
Transport, 299

Fabergé, Peter Carl, 127
famine, in nonindustrialized countries,
    63–64
famine of 1921–22, 447–49
    grain requisitioning and, 447–48
    Lenin and, 447–48
    U.S. relief for, 448–49
Farinacci, Roberto, 552
fascism, 123, 549–52, 725
    in Romania, 589–90
    Stalin's misunderstanding of, 550–51
February Revolution, 168–73, 174–75, 176, 182,
    183, 188, 194, 290, 297, 453
    army and, 169, 172, 175
    as bourgeois revolution, 175, 195, 199
    as liberal coup, 180, 223
    navy and, 172, 175
Federal Democratic Russian Republic, 254
federalism, 343
    Stalin's dedication to, 346, 349–51
Federation of Anarchist-Communists, 187
feudalism, 40, 190
Figner, Nikolai, 127
finance commissariat, 450–51, 452, 470, 730
    Sokolnikov as commissar of, 565
Finance Ministry, tsarist:
    Internal Affairs Ministry's rivalry with, 69
    Witte as head of, 69–70
financial industries, 63
Finland, 90, 478, 556–57, 604
    German occupation of, 243
    as independent nation, 238, 342–43
    Kronstadt rebels given asylum by, 391
    Lenin in, 114, 213, 222
    Soviet Union and, 590
Finnish civil war, 256
Finnish Socialist Workers Republic, 256
First Cavalry Army (Red), 259, 355–56, 357,
    359, 362, 456
First International, 317, 347
Fischer, Louis, 635
Foch, Ferdinand, 311, 315, 317
food supply commissariat, 449
Ford, Henry, 612
foreign affairs commissariat, 229, 441–42, 443,
    622, 624
foreign policy, Soviet, 558, 698–99
    class warfare and, 443–44
    as dictated by Lenin, 446–47
    Litvinov's critique of, 622–23
    Stalin and, 553, 583, 623–24
    two-faced nature of, 443, 645, 667
foreign trade commissariat, 451
Forest, The (Ostrovsky), 620

Förster, Otfried, 412
Fotiyeva, Lidiya, 417, 467, 487, 489, 504, 527
    and Lenin's alleged article on nationalities,
        493–94
    Lenin's Testament and, 473
"Foundations of Leninism" (Stalin), 532,
    544–45, 555
Fourier, Charles, 39, 40
France, 83
    anti-Bolshevik policy of, 247, 343
    colonial empire of, 4, 151, 316
    in defensive alliance with Russia, 109, 110
    and German war reparations, 509
    in Great War, 150, 152, 156, 197, 198, 199
    in Locarno Pact, 561–62
    in onset of Great War, 147
    Poland and, 558, 589, 623
    Soviet relations with, 560, 645, 693, 733
    in Triple Entente, 140, 147
    Versailles Treaty and, 315–16, 559
Franz Ferdinand, Archduke, assassination of,
    142–43, 149, 269
Franz Josef, kaiser of Austria-Hungary, 142,
    143, 144
Frederick II, "the Great," king of Prussia, 59
free trade, NEP as concession to, 389,
    406, 416
Freikorps, 323–24
French army, 1917 mutiny in, 197
French Revolution, 95, 186, 196, 233, 349, 650
Frunze, Mikhail, 326, 346, 505, 507, 738
    in Crimea, 374, 379
    illness and death of, 575–76
    in Turkestan, 373–75, 387
    as war commissar, 557
    as war commissariat deputy, 542, 574
"Fundamental Law of Socialist Accumulation,
    The" (Preobrazhensky), 566
Fundamental Laws, 85, 94, 97, 179

Gai Dmitrievich Gai (Bzhishkyan, Haik), 345,
    359, 360, 361, 365, 370
Galicia, 353, 360
Gasprinski, Ismail, 368
Gegen, Bogd, 401–2, 404–5, 553–54
Geladze, Gio, 28
Geladze, Ketevan, see Jughashvili, Ketevan
    "Keke"
Geladze, Sandala, 28
General Staff Academy, 574
Genoa, international conference on Russia and
    Germany in, 444–45, 599
gentry, Russian, 57–58, 69, 84
    land holdings of, 188–89, 190

geopolitics:
  history as driven by, 4–5
  modernity as consequence of, 4–5, 62–65
George I, king of England, 83
George V, king of England, 90, 147, 280
Georgia, 86, 342, 366, 473, 475
  Armenians in, 496
  Bolsheviks in, 106, 267
  Bolshevik takeover of, 396, 397–400
  as independent republic, 238, 343, 395
  Marxism in, 30, 38, 43, 44
  Mensheviks in, 103, 106, 108, 123, 133, 244,
    395–97, 399–400
  Muslims in, 13, 24
  nationalism in, 9–10, 30, 32, 400, 601
  peasant rebellion in, 67
  Red Army invasion of, 397, 398
  religious and ethnic makeup of, 13–14
  Russian language in, 14
  and Soviet Union plan, 475–76, 478, 479–80
  Turkey's invasion of, 398
Georgian language, Stalin's abandonment of,
  112–13
Georgian Literacy Society, 32, 36, 38
Georgian Republic, Soviet, 397
Georgy, Grand Duke, 160
Germany, Imperial:
  anti-Bolsheviks courted by, 272
  Austria-Hungarian POWs and, 269
  Balkans and, 141
  Baltic littoral occupied by, 243, 283
  Brest-Litovsk Treaty and, 257–58, 264–65,
    269, 272–73, 283, 315, 642
  Britain and, 139–40
  bureaucracy of, 58–59
  in Central Powers alliance, 140
  economic growth in, 7
  expansionism in, 145
  in Great War, 150, 152, 156–157, 197, 198,
    206–207, 231, 247–253, 310, 312; see also
    Central Powers
  industrialization of, 18, 65, 70
  Lenin's policies on, 272, 282, 283–84
  nationalism in, 34–35
  naval buildup of, 139–40, 150
  1918 western offensive of, 310–11
  Odessa captured by, 264
  in onset of Great War, 143–49
  Poland occupied by, 243, 283
  in "reinsurance treaty" with Russia, 6
  renewed Russian offensive of, 253, 255–56,
    259, 271
  Schlieffen Plan of, 145, 147
  Sevastopol naval base captured by, 271

  steel production in, 63, 141
  in Triple Alliance, 6
  tsarist Russia and, 109, 139
  Ukraine occupied by, 253, 265, 266–67, 270,
    272, 273, 283, 301, 303
  unification of, 4, 5, 6–7, 18, 732
  wartime shortages and strikes in, 165, 251
Germany, Weimar, 293
  Britain and, 560, 561, 587, 621
  Communist coup attempt in, see Communist
    Party, German, coup attempt of
  general strike in, 323
  hyperinflation in, 450, 509
  in Locarno Pact, 561–62
  mass strikes in, 510
  in military cooperation agreement with Red
    Army, 446, 561, 587, 617–18, 621, 638,
    704–5
  and Polish-Soviet War, 363
  in Rapallo Treaty with Soviet Russia,
    445–46, 473, 509, 560, 561, 599
  rapprochement with West as goal of, 446
  Soviet nonaggression pact with, 587, 588
  Soviet relations with, 558, 559–61, 611, 623,
    638–39, 692, 704
  Versailles Treaty and, 315
  war reparations owed by, 509
Gil, Stepan, 228, 285, 314
Gilliard, Pierre, 210
Gladstone, William, 19
Glasser, Maria, 488–89
Glinka, Mikhail, 127
Goglichidze, Simon, 21
Gogol, Nikolai, 58
Goldstein, Franz, 692–93
Goloshchokin, Isai "Filipp," 548, 653
Gori, 2, 8, 9, 14–15, 20–21, 23–26, 28, 36, 53
Göring, Hermann, 527
Gorki estate:
  Lenin at, 413–14, 416–17, 428, 440,
    476, 482
  Stalin's visits to, 413–14, 416–17, 476
Gorky, Maxim, 133, 183, 329, 448, 544
gosudarstvennost, 343
Gothier, Yuri, 322
GPU (State Political Administration), 439, 448,
  459–62
  corruption in, 461, 462
  deportation and internal exiles ordered
    by, 440
  extra-legal powers of, 440
  show trials and, 440
  see also OGPU
Gramsci, Antonio, 123–24

*Granat Encyclopedia,* Stalin biography
  published in, 660
Great Britain:
  anti-Communist policy of, 247, 343, 344,
    558–59, 624
  Arkhangelsk landing by, 282, 283
  Bismarck seen as threat by, 6
  Caucasus expedition of, 270, 397–98
  in Crimean War, 59, 67
  economy of, 7, 148, 587–88
  in entente with tsarist Russia, 109, 110, 135,
    136, 140
  foreign trade of, 108–9, 139, 146
  general strike in, 588, 598–99, 613
  and German war reparations, 509
  Germany and, 139–40, 560, 561, 587, 621
  as global power, 108–9
  in Great War, 150, 152, 156, 197, 198, 199,
    312, 316–17
  Industrial Revolution in, 40
  Japan and, 111
  liberalism in, 132
  in Locarno Pact, 561
  navy of, 111, 140
  in onset of Great War, 146–49
  Poland and, 616
  police raid on Soviet offices in, 631–32
  Polish-Soviet War and, 355, 358–59
  prime ministership in, 83–84
  Russian policy of, 265–66
  Secret Service Bureau of, 284
  Soviet codes broken by, 553
  Soviet relations with, 617–18, 622, 623, 624,
    632, 638
  Soviet trade with, 391–92, 599, 632
  Soviet Union recognized by, 558
  Stalin's view of, 558
  Stalin's view of, as Soviet Union's primary
    enemy, 623, 624, 631–33, 634–35
  steel production in, 63
  trade unions in, 599
  in Triple Entente, 140, 147
  tsarist Russia and, 108–9
  Versailles Treaty and, 315–16
Great Depression, Soviet Union and, 733–34
Great Reforms, 29, 59–60, 66, 85
Great War, 2, 3, 129, 136–37, 185, 556, 562, 588
  aftermath of, 150–51, 312, 323–24, 343
  Allied strategy in, 197, 198, 199
  Anglo-German rivalry as root of, 141
  armistice in, 311–12
  Austria-Hungary in, 162, 185, 197, 200,
    248–49, 269
  Bolshevik regime and, 247

Britain in, 150, 152, 156, 197, 198, 199, 312,
    316–17
  casualties in, 150, 152, 166, 312
  and collapse of Russian autocracy, 173
  colonialism and, 151–52
  conscription and, 156
  Dadaism and, 230
  February Revolution and, 175
  German-Russian peace talks in, 247–52
  German's renewed Russian offensive in,
    253, 259
  Germany in, 150, 152, 156–57, 197, 198,
    206–7, 231, 247–53, 310, 312
  Germany's renewed Russian offensive in,
    253, 255–56
  nationalism and, 475
  1917 Russian offensive in, 196–200, 204,
    212, 219, 224
  onset of, 141–49
  Poland in, 355
  Provisional Government and, 187, 194–95,
    196–200
  Russia in, 150, 156–57, 162, 166, 206–7, 212,
    219, 224, 231, 247–53, 296, 312, 316–17
  stalemate in, 149–50
  U.S. in, 248, 310–11
  Versailles Treaty in, *see* Versailles, Treaty of
Grey, Edward, 146–47, 149
Grodno, 91, 354, 360
Guchkov, Alexander, 166, 173, 182, 588–89
Guetier, Fyodor, 534
Gunina, Zoya, 595
Guomindang, 640, 651, 717
  in alliance with Communists, 626–27
  army of, 626–27
  Communists attacked by, 655
  Communists betrayed by, 637–38, 640
  left-wing (Wuhan) faction of, 629, 633,
    637–38
  as nationalist movement, 626
  in Northern Expedition, 629, 631
  Soviet military aid to, 626–27, 628, 640
Gurian Republic, 67, 86
Gurko, Vladimir, 87
Gurvich, Esfir, 719
Gurvich, Fyodor, *see* Dan, Fyodor
Gusev, Sergei (Drabkin, Yakov), 328, 583

Haig, Douglas, 152
Harriman, Averell, 611
Haymarket riots, 49–50
Hearst, William Randolph, 610
Hegel, G.W.F., 40
Heimo, Mauno, 442

Helfferich, Karl, 283
Henry, E. R., 61
Herrero, 151–52
Herzen, Alexander, 41–42
Hess, Rudolf, 527
Hilferding, Rudolf, 151, 378, 392
Hindenburg, Paul von, 162, 253, 311
history:
    as driven by geopolitics, 4–5
    Marxist view of, 40, 78
Hitler, Adolf, 23
    in Beer Hall putsch, 527
    nationalism and, 34–35
    rise of, 2–3
Hitler, Alois, 34–35
Hitler, Klara, 23, 35
Hobson, John, 151
Ho Chi-Minh, 550
Hoffmann, Max, 249, 252, 255, 256, 258, 259
Holy Brigades (Black Hundreds), 77, 86, 99, 182
Holy Roman Empire, 18
Hoover, Herbert, Russian famine relief
    organized by, 448
Horthy, Miklós, 325
Hötsendorf, Franz Conrad, Baron von, 148
"How Social Democracy Understands the
    National Question" (Stalin), 77
Hugo, Victor, 36
Hungarian Soviet Socialist Republic, 324–25
Hungary, 316, 324, 325, 336

"Ilich's letter about the secretary," 504–9,
    511–12, 513, 514, 546, 658
    Stalin and, 512, 514
    Trotsky and, 516
    see also Lenin's Testament
Ilin, Alexander ("The Genevan"), 431
Ilinka, 9, 426, 450–52, 470
Imenitov, Solomon, 703, 704
Imperialism: The Highest Stage of Capitalism
    (Lenin), 151, 154
Imperial Senate, 89, 263, 264, 278, 285, 317, 319,
    334, 413, 428, 429, 521, 522, 540
Independent Social Democrat Party, German,
    378, 392
India, 64
indigenization, 496, 504
industrialization, 725
    of Germany, 18, 65, 70
    global dichotomy in, 63–65
    of Japan, 65
    NEP and, 571, 672
    raw materials in, 63
    Sokolnikov on, 659–60

    in Soviet Union, 565–66, 571, 574, 582, 583,
        587, 605, 625, 638, 659, 662, 663, 664, 686,
        694, 695, 698, 710, 722, 725, 733
    in Tiflis, 30
    in tsarist Russia, 65, 67, 69–70, 91, 92, 141, 645
    in U.S., 19
Industrial Revolution, 39–40
industry, state-run, 433
Inspector General (Gogol), 58
Institute of Red Professors, 545–46, 705, 713
intelligentsia, 37, 41
Internal Affairs Ministry, Russian:
    Finance Ministry's rivalry with, 69
    see also okhranka; police, tsarist
"Internationale," 41, 176, 220
International Workingmen's Association,
    40–41
Ipatyev, Nikolai, 280
Iran (Persia), 12, 109, 145, 344
    British in, 366
    constitutional revolution in, 131–32
    Soviet invasion of, 366
    Soviet Russia in treaty with, 391
Iranians, 29, 30, 344
Iremashvili, Iosif (Ioseb) "Soso" 23, 31, 38, 399
Iskra (Spark), 45, 50, 51, 78
Italian Socialist Party Congress (1912), 123
Italy, 110, 336
    aftermath of Great War in, 324
    anti-fascist demonstrations in, 551–52
    Communists in, 550, 551
    fascism in, 549–50, 551–52, 725
    Kamenev as ambassador to, 609–10
    in Locarno Pact, 561
    in Triple Alliance, 6
Ivan IV "the Terrible," tsar, 7, 11, 12, 27
Ivanov, Nikolai, 170–71
Iveria, 33, 38, 44
Izvestiya, 206, 288, 293, 464, 540, 550, 704

Japan:
    anti-Soviet policy of, 621–22
    Britain and, 111
    East Asian trade of, 71–72
    imperialism in, 71, 151
    industrialization in, 65
    Korea annexed by, 617
    Meiji restoration in, 4, 18, 732
    modernization of, 18
    navy of, 72, 111, 140
    Siberia invaded by, 343–44
    Soviet Union and, 590, 617, 621–22, 632
    tsarist Russia and, 72–75, 109, 111–12
    Vladivostok invaded by, 266

Jewish Labor Bund, 37, 44, 80, 98, 103, 137, 351
Jewish Social Democratic Workers' Party (Poale-Zion), 137
Jews, 12, 101, 112, 129, 182–83, 316
  in Bolshevik regime, 340–41
  Trotsky as, 340–41, 523
Jibladze, Silibistro "Silva," 33, 43, 44, 48, 114, 267
Joffe, Adolf, 249, 322, 407, 640
  suicide of, 651–52
Joffe, Maria, 651
Jordania, Noe, 43, 44, 48, 50, 51, 54, 74, 80, 108, 113, 395
Jughashvili, Besarion "Beso," 107
  alcoholism of, 20, 24
  appearance of, 19–20
  back taxes owed by, 48–49
  death of, 116, 117
  fall of, 25, 28
  Keke's marriage to, 16–17, 20
  as shoemaker, 15–16, 20
  Stalin's relationship with, 22, 24
Jughashvili, Giorgy, 738
Jughashvili, Ioseb, see Stalin, Iosif
Jughashvili, Ketevan "Keke," 16, 19, 25, 48–49, 105, 594
  Beso's marriage to, 16–17, 20
  menial jobs of, 21, 26
  rumored promiscuity of, 20
  Stalin's devotion to, 23
  Stalin's education pushed by, 21
  Stalin's return to Gori demanded by, 22–23
Jughashvili, Vano, 15
Jughashvili, Yakov, 106, 114, 116, 466, 593, 595
Jughashvili, Zaza, 15
Jūsis, Ivan, 602, 739

Kabakhidze, Akaki, 481, 487, 489
Kaganovich, Lazar, 321, 376, 422, 529, 613, 641, 647, 656, 661, 666, 697, 699
  background of, 455, 457
  as Central Committee secretary, 455
  as head of Organization and Instruction Department, 455
  as Stalin loyalist, 456, 731
  Trotsky and, 455, 591
Kalinin, Mikhail, 50, 214, 322, 331, 383, 423, 455, 498, 513, 585, 668, 673, 700, 712
  Lenin's death and, 535–36
  and plot to oust Stalin as general secretary, 713, 714, 715
  in politburo, 596
  as Stalin loyalist, 731

Kalmyks, 174
Kaluga, 238
Kamenev, Lev (Rozenfeld), 53, 80, 121, 132, 133, 135, 153, 173, 190, 203, 221, 224, 226, 279, 322, 331, 341, 360, 365, 385, 416, 440, 471, 490, 491, 493, 497, 504, 531, 544, 557, 596, 599, 605, 615, 650, 712, 739
  as ambassador to Italy, 609–10
  in attempts to include other socialists in Bolshevik regime, 233–36
  Bukharin and, 727
  in Council of People's Commissars, 416–17
  as editor of Pravda, 190–91, 193
  ejected from Central Committee, 651
  and failure to force Stalin's removal at 13th Party Congress, 552
  and 15th Party Congress, 653–54
  at 14th Party Congress, 580–81, 586
  imprisonment of, 204, 212
  internal exile of, 713
  as intriguer, 512
  Lenin and, 476–77
  Lenin's death and, 535
  as Lenin's possible successor, 492
  Lenin's Testament and, 499, 606–7, 648
  October Revolution and, 214, 224, 499, 563–64, 606, 641, 648
  and plot to oust Stalin as general secretary, 714–17, 720
  police reform sought by, 439
  in resignation from Central Committee, 235–36
  in resignation from Soviet central executive committee, 236, 423
  Sokolnikov and, 713–14
  on Stalin, 422
  Stalin and, 192, 512–14
  in succession power struggle, 563, 564, 577, 578, 580–81, 582, 584, 586, 605–6, 614–15, 636, 639, 641, 653–54, 655–56, 713, 729, 736
  as trade commissar, 585
  in triumvirate with Stalin and Zinoviev, 517, 563
  Trotsky and, 224–25, 474
Kamenev, Sergei, 328, 329–30, 356, 359, 360, 361, 362, 363, 365, 371, 377, 381, 384, 394, 515
Kanner, Grigory, 468
Kapanadze, Peti "Pyotr," 35, 38, 598
Kapital, Das (Marx), 40, 88
  Russian translation of, 42–43, 65–66
Kaplan, Fanya, 285–86

Karakhan, Lev (Karakhanyan), 366, 458, 623, 628, 651
Kautsky, Karl, 43, 79, 133, 151, 201, 347
Kazakhstan, 677, 700–701
Kazan, 74, 238, 282, 284, 306, 326, 331, 369, 371
Kazan Soviet, 266
Kedrov, Mikhail, 438–39
Kemal, Mustafa, 398, 503
Kennan, George, 443–44
Kerensky, Alexander, 3, 126, 178, 180, 181, 184, 202, 213, 228, 233, 259, 278, 338–39
    as anathema to both left and right, 195, 211
    arrests of Bolshevik leaders ordered by, 216
    background of, 185–86
    Bolsheviks charged with treason by, 202–3
    Council of Five created by, 211–12
    feared return of, 234, 235
    Kornilov and, 204, 205, 208–9, 210, 212, 219
    Lenin and, 195–96, 200, 205
    1917 Russian offensive launched by, 196–200, 212, 219, 224, 269
    in Provisional Government, 185–86
    role of supreme commander assumed by, 211
    Romanovs and, 280
    State Conference convened by, 205–7
Ketskhoveli, Vladimir "Lado," 33, 50
    death of, 55
    as Stalin's mentor, 30–31, 38, 44, 47, 48, 50, 55, 735
Khabalov, Sergei, 167, 168, 169, 170, 203, 382
Khan, Chinggis, 346, 374, 400
Kharkov, 15, 79, 266, 326, 327, 355
Khartishvili, David "Mokheve," 52
Khiva, 90, 342, 373
Khorezm People's Soviet Republic, 373
Khoroshenina, Serafima, 121
Khrushchev, Nikita, 732
Khutsishvili, Vano, 19
Kiev, 15, 252, 258, 330
    Polish capture of, 354, 355, 357, 377
    Red Army recapture of, 357
Kireev, Alexander, 127
Kirov, Sergei, 27–28, 117–18, 304, 390, 455, 467, 585, 586, 607, 731
Kirshon, Vladimir, 699
Kirtava-Sikharulidze, Natasha, 53
Kitiashvili, Maria, 48
Klyuchevsky, Vasili, 121
Knox, Alfred, 223
Kokovtsov, Vladimir, 281
Kolchak, Alexander, 207, 210, 297, 300, 314, 328, 330, 355, 356–57, 358, 369, 559
    dictatorship of, 335
    execution of, 331
    as leader of Siberian Cossacks, 295–96
    1919 offensive of, 326, 335, 370–71
    in Siberia, 372
    tsarist gold seized by, 331–32
Kollontai, Alexandra, 346, 385
Koltsov, Mikhail, 566
Komarov, Nikolai, 516
Konopleva, Lidiya, 285
Korea, Koreans, 111, 364, 590, 617
Kornilov, Lavr, 174, 177, 184–86, 200, 228, 248, 320, 356
    coup attempt of, 207–11, 212, 219
    death of, 268, 295
    Kerensky and, 204, 205, 208–9, 210, 212, 219
    at Moscow State Conference, 206–7
    as Petrograd military commander, 203–4, 211
    as Volunteer Army commander, 268
Korotkov, Ivan, 512
Kosior, Stanisław, 457, 670, 677–78, 705, 712
Kosior, Vladimir, 500
Kosovo, Battle of (1389), 142
Kotlarevsky, S. A., 183
Koverda, Boris, 634
Kozhenikov, A. M., 414
Kozlovsky, Alexander, 346, 392–93
Krakow, 133
Kramer, V. V., 414, 489, 491, 535
Krasin, Leonid, 50, 55, 113, 413, 441, 543
Krasnov, Pyotr, 305
Krasnoyarsk, 173, 661, 684
Kremlin, 262
    Lenin in October, 1923 visit to, 520–22
    as new Bolshevik headquarters, 263
    Stalin's apartments in, 262, 593–94
Krestinsky, Nikolai, 322, 390, 423, 425, 428, 441, 451, 453, 596, 621, 692
Kronstadt naval base, 182, 187, 202, 218
    1921 sailors' rebellion at, 383–84, 387, 390–91, 392–93, 457, 575
Krupskaya, Nadezhda, 114, 188, 192, 228, 314, 413, 483, 489, 498, 504, 520, 534, 608, 615
    anti-Dzierżyński dossier and, 490
    Lenin memoir of, 544
    and Lenin's alleged dictations, 484, 490–91, 494, 501, 512, 513, 514
    and Lenin's death, 534
    and Lenin's request for cyanide, 493
    Lenin's Testament and, 473, 498, 500–501, 527, 528, 609
    *Since Lenin Died* repudiated by, 573–74
    Stalin and, 487–88, 490, 514, 527, 528, 544

Krupskaya, Nadezhda (cont.)
and succession power struggle, 564, 577, 580
Trotsky and, 501, 525, 542, 547, 572,
573–74, 632
Krushevan, Pavel (Cruşeveanu,
Pavalachii), 100
Krylenko, Nikolai, 248, 690, 698, 702, 709
Krylenko, Yelena, 572
Krymov, Alexander, 166, 208–9, 233
Kryukova, Sofia, 121
Kryżanowski, Gleb, 220, 485
Kryzhanovsky, Sergei, 83, 100
Krzesińska, Matylda, 127, 186
Ksenofontov, Filipp, 544–45
Ksenofontov, Ivan, 433
Kuban, 268, 270, 297
Kuchek Khan, Mirza, 346, 366
Kühlmann, Richard, Baron von, 249
Kuibyshev, Valerian, 375, 390, 493, 502–3, 511,
516, 563, 601, 663–64, 686, 694, 698,
720, 722
as Central Control Commission head, 454
as Stalin loyalist, 454–55, 456
as Supreme Council of the Economy
chairman, 607
kulaks (rich peasants), 42, 300, 567, 570, 571,
579, 582, 616, 649, 669, 670–71, 676, 680,
684, 711, 712
arrests and trials of, 669, 670, 671, 680,
681–82, 697, 705
collectivization and, 421
Communist tolerance of, 300, 389, 578, 582,
681, 683, 684–85, 689
forced exile of, 712
grain hoarding by, 568, 669, 670, 671, 680,
682, 695–96
large-scale farms of, 671, 672
NEP and, 727–28
tax-in-kind policy and, 389
Kun, Béla, 324–25, 367
Kuprin, Alexander, 220
Kureika, 154, 194
Kuusinen, Aino, 526
Kuusinen, Otto, 412, 442, 526, 609
Kuzakova, Matryona, 121
Kvali (The Furrow) (Giorgi), 34, 43, 44, 48,
50, 55

Lācis, Mārtiņš (Sudrabs, Jānis), 276, 278, 439
Lakoba, Nestor, 541, 542
Larin, Yuri (Lurye, Mikhail), 452, 615
Larina, Anna, 262
Lashevich, Mikhail, 331, 505, 506, 536, 548,
576, 603–4, 652

Latvia, 98, 249, 509, 556–57, 604
and German Communist coup
attempt, 522
as independent nation, 238, 342–43
Latvian brigades, 261, 276, 281–82
in assault on Cheka, 277–78
Latvian Riflemen, 260–61
Lazard Brothers, 148
League of Nations, 315, 562, 730
Left Communists, 265, 314, 385, 578
Left opposition, 518, 519, 524, 533, 541, 544,
546, 547, 603–4, 672, 678–79, 680, 737
Left Socialist Revolutionaries, 234–35, 242,
244, 257, 265, 273, 649
in Council of People's Commissars, 237
Dzierżyński captured by, 276
mass executions of, 278
in Mirbach assassination plot, 274–75
Third Party Congress of, 273–74
"Left-Wing" Communism: An Infantile Disorder
(Lenin), 363–64
Lena goldfields massacre, 125–26, 135
Lenin, Vladimir, 9, 45, 73, 79, 81, 124, 135, 192,
226, 228, 231, 260, 266, 280, 322, 324, 334,
342, 350, 354, 365, 392, 407, 411, 424, 493,
544, 550
alleged article on nationalities by,
493–94, 501
"April Theses" of, 191
arrest warrant for, 222
assassination attempt against, 231, 285,
307, 413
autopsy of, 535
background of, 185
Bolshevik criticism of, 191–92, 385
and Bolshevik-Menshevik split, 79–80,
108, 124
and Bolshevik takeover of Georgia, 396, 397
Brest-Litovsk Treaty and, 257, 259, 265, 642
capitalism as viewed by, 151, 291, 403, 444,
446, 625
cease-fire offer of, 247–49
charisma of, 221–22
class warfare as central tenet of, 291, 443,
444, 737
and Communist International Second
Congress, 363–64
convalescence of, 307
as Council of People's Commissars
chairman, 229
on counterrevolutionaries, 392, 550
and creation of Soviet Union, 475, 480
cyanide requested by, 414, 483, 493
death of, 3, 534–37

dictations by, 483, 484–85, 489–91, 501, 504, 505, 527, 528, 546–47
as dictator, 238, 245, 419
failing health of, 409, 410–18, 422, 489–94, 498, 501, 505, 535
and famine of 1921–22, 447–48
February Revolution and, 174
foreign policy of, 443–45, 446–47
funeral of, 537–38, 540
Genoa conference sabotaged by, 444–45
and Georgian insubordination, 480, 487, 489–91
and German peace talks, 249–51, 255
German policy of, 272, 282, 283–84
at Gorki estate, 413–14, 416–17, 428, 440, 476, 482
Great Russian chauvinism opposed by, 348, 407, 487
Great War and, 151, 312–13
as head of Bolshevik Party, 186
on impact of civil war, 336
insomnia and headaches of, 410
intelligentsia-centric party advocated by, 51, 79, 107
Iskra editorials written by, 50, 51
isolation of, 487–88
in journey from Zurich to Petrograd, 187–88
Kamenev and, 234, 235, 236, 476–77
Kerensky and, 195–96, 200, 205
Kronstadt revolt and, 392
land seizure decree of, 220–21
Luxemburg's attack on, 323
Martov and, 78, 267, 393
Marxism of, 151
Mirbach assassination and, 275–76
in move to Kremlin, 263
mummification of, 542–43
on nationalism and self-determination, 347–48, 351
nationalization of land proposed by, 103
on need to win over indigenous peoples, 407
NEP and, 344, 388–89, 405–6, 408, 416, 447, 449, 457, 473–74, 481–82, 487, 527, 568, 571, 580
in 1917 flight from Petrograd, 203, 260
in October 1917 return to Petrograd, 214, 222
in October 1923 visit to Kremlin, 520–22
in October Revolution, 220–21, 222, 278
in overhaul of Revolutionary Military Council, 328
party unity and, 389–90
peasants as poorly understood by, 299–300
physical appearance of, 220

police reform undermined by, 440
Polish-Soviet War and, 353, 354, 359–60, 362–63, 376–78
politburo's relationship with, 413, 415, 484, 489
political violence as principle of, 409–10
press censorship by, 237, 245
on primacy of international relations, 343
Provisional Government's treason charges against, 203
Red Army and, 297
rule of law rejected by, 410
rumored death of, 287
at Second Congress of Soviets, 220
self-exiles of, 104, 114, 135, 152–53, 164, 173, 187, 196, 204, 205, 212, 213, 222, 230
in showdown over control of Council of People's Commissars, 236
show trials ordered by, 439–40
Siberian exile of, 45
Sovietization of Europe as goal of, 360–61, 364
Soviet Union plan of, 476–77, 478, 484, 485–86, 496
Stalin and, see Lenin-Stalin relationship
Stalin seen as unlikely successor to, 422–23
Stalin's first exposure to ideas of, 50–51
Stalin's real name forgotten by, 152–53
Stalin-Trotsky relationship and, 415
strokes of, 3, 412, 440, 447, 474, 482–83, 484, 491, 494, 530
support for Provisional Government opposed by, 190
Sverdlov and, 193–94, 234, 318–19
Testament of, see Lenin's Testament
at Third Comintern Congress, 403
Tiflis bank robbery and, 113–14
Trotsky and, 202, 214, 221, 222–23, 234, 256, 341, 357, 385–86, 390, 414–415, 472, 481–82, 523, 531, 647
Trotsky as possible successor to, 416–17
Workers' opposition and, 385
world revolution as goal of, 407
zealotry of, 191–92, 194–95, 200, 213–14, 217, 232, 258, 278–79
Lenin and the Imperialist War 1914–1918 (Ksenofontov), 545
Leningrad, 540, 586
food shortages in, 721
strikes and job actions in, 570, 624
Zinoviev machine in, 577, 578, 584, 585
see also Petrograd
Leningrad Pravda, 580
Lenin Institute, 543–44, 580

Leninism, 190–91, 533, 563, 627
  Stalin's espousal of, 205, 419–20, 544–45,
    591, 615, 699
  Trotsky's conversion to, 202
  see also Marxism, Marxists
Lenin's Doctrine of Revolution
    (Ksenofontov), 544
Lenin-Stalin relationship, 121, 133, 335
  and blame for Polish War defeat, 377
  correspondence of, 155, 301–2, 308–9, 362,
    364, 483, 484–85
  federalism as common agenda of, 346
  and 5th RSDRP Congress, 108
  Lenin's alleged nationalities article and, 494
  Lenin's death and, 534–35, 536
  Lenin's mentoring role in, 81, 419, 471,
    531, 600
  Lenin's perception of, 341, 412
  Lenin's reliance on Stalin in, 229, 465, 608
  and Lenin's request for cyanide, 414, 493
  Lenin's stroke and, 412–15
  Lenin's Testament and, see Lenin's Testament
  mutual loyalty in, 192–93, 226, 234, 250, 255,
    257, 341, 390, 735
  and plan for Soviet Union, 476–77
  Stalin's 1921 illness and, 398–99
  Stalin's Central Committee appointment
    and, 123–24
  and Stalin's expanded role, 411–12, 417
  and Stalin's willingness to criticize Lenin's
    ideas, 192–93
  and Stalin's willingness to take up any
    assignment, 232
  succession issue and, 418
  Tammerfors congress and, 80–81
  Ulyanova on, 527–28, 608–9
Lenin's Testament, 418–19, 472–73, 498–501,
    527–29, 530–31, 581, 582, 608
  Central Committee plenum report on,
    546–47
  Eastman's publication of, 614
  Kamenev and, 499, 606–7, 648
  Krupskaya and, 473, 498, 500–501, 527,
    528, 609
  Stalin and, 547, 552–53, 592, 605–7, 614, 643,
    647–48, 657, 735–36
  Stalin's depiction in, 499–500
  Stalin's restricted publication of, 654
  13th Party Congress reading of, 548
  Trotsky and, 500, 572–73, 605–7, 643, 646,
    647–48
  Trotskyites' circulation of, 540, 573, 605
  uncertain authorship of, 473, 489
  Zinoviev and, 498, 499, 606–7, 648

Leopold, Prince of Bavaria, 249
"Lessons of October" (Trotsky), 563–64
"Letter to the Congress," see Lenin's
    Testament
"Lev Trotsky—Organizer of Victory"
    (Radek), 492
liberals, liberalism, 132, 223
Liberman, Simon, 728
liberty, 131–32
Liebknecht, Karl, 323
Life for the Tsar, A (Glinka), 127
Life of Jesus (Renan), 37
limitrophe, 556, 604, 616, 623, 723, 732
Lincoln, Abraham, 410
Lithuania, 91, 249, 283, 353, 354, 509, 589,
    604, 623
  as independent nation, 232–33, 238
  military coup in, 618
  nationalists in, 359
  Polish invasion of, 352
  Soviet nonaggression treaty with, 617–18
Lithuanian National Union, 618
Little Newspaper, 210–11
Litvinov, Maxim (Finkelstein, Meir; Wallach,
    Max), 108, 114, 458, 583, 621, 622–23,
    651, 692
Lloyd George, David, 315–16, 317, 392, 444–45
Locarno Peace Pact (1925), 561–62
Lominadze, Besarion "Beso," 640
Louis XIV, king of France, 18
Lublin, 362
Lublin-Warsaw salient, 360
Lubyanka, 2, 426, 437–41
Ludendorff, Erich, 172, 248, 272–73, 282, 311,
    313, 352
Ludwig, Emil, 11
Lunacharsky, Anatoly, 225, 227, 300
Lurye, Alexander "Sasha," 462
Luxemburg, Rosa, 80, 223, 318, 578
  assassination of, 323
  Lenin and Bolshevism attacked by, 323
  on nationalism, 347–48
Luxemburgism, 347, 349, 351, 369
Lvov, Prince Georgy, 166, 203, 207
Lwów (Lviv, Lvov), 249, 353, 360, 362, 365
  Red Army's failure to capture, 362–63
Lyttelton, Adrian, 223–24
Lytton, Lord, 64

Machiavelli, Niccolò, 53
Maier, Max, 702–3, 709
Makharadze, Pilipe, 346, 397, 399, 489, 490, 491
Makhrovsky, K. E., 304–5
Maklakov, Vasily, 224, 718

Malenkov, Georgy, 457
Malinowski, Roman, 133, 154
Malkov, Pavel, 227, 263, 285, 286
Mamontov, Savva, 262
*Manchester Guardian,* 617, 621
Manchuria, 71, 72, 73, 111, 400–401, 590,
    628–29
*Mandate, The* (Erdman), 620
Mannerheim, Carl Gustav, 256, 330
Mantashov, Alexander, 51
Manuilsky, Dmitry, 526, 573
Mao Zedong, 626, 640, 655
Markus, Maria, 586
Martov, "Yuly" (Tsederbaum, Julius), 45, 78, 80,
    108, 113, 135, 164, 188, 198, 218, 228, 265,
    267, 273, 279, 378, 385, 393, 463–64, 527
Marx, Karl, 5, 7, 8, 18, 39, 57, 65–66, 88, 99, 107,
    151, 232
    on class war, 291–92, 737
    on nationalism, 346–47
Marx, Wilhelm, 618
Marxism, Marxists, 30, 38, 39–40, 44, 78–79,
    151, 544
    Austrian, 347–48
    bourgeoisie as viewed by, 292, 293
    capitalism as viewed by, 78–79, 292
    history as viewed by, 39, 42, 78, 190
    in Russia, 42–45, 54, 74, 78, 79, 93, 137
    self-determination as viewed by, 347
    Stalin's dedication to, 10, 88, 93, 107, 137,
        307, 676
    theory of state in, 232
    *see also* Communism; Leninism
"Marxism and the National Question" (Stalin),
    133, 153
Masaryk, Tomáš, 316
*Mass Exile, 1906–1916* (Sverdlov), 154
Matteotti, Giacomo, 551, 552
May Day marches, 49–50, 79, 106, 126
Mdivani, Polikarp "Budu," 346, 399, 477–78,
    479–80, 487, 490, 491, 493, 497, 606
Mehklis, Lev, 456–57
Meiji restoration, 4, 18, 732
Mendeleev, Dimitri, 37, 91
Mensheviks, 103, 104, 106, 108, 114, 123, 124,
    133, 137, 188, 195, 196, 198, 201, 212, 221,
    226, 234, 242–43, 244, 257, 265, 273, 279,
    297, 312, 351, 382, 385, 393, 439, 735
    Bolshevik split with, 78, 79–81, 103, 108, 114,
        122–23, 124, 137
    in Caucasus, 112, 124
    in Europe, 393, 489, 553, 555
    in Georgia, 103, 106, 108, 123, 133, 244,
        395–97, 399–400

Jews in, 112
    October Revolution and, 218
    Provisional Government supported by, 195
    in show trials, 464
Merkulov, Sergei, 535
Metekhi Prison, 48, 55
Mexican Revolution, 131–32
Meyerhold, Vesvolod, 620
Mężyński, Wiaczesław, 238–39, 250, 329, 504,
    617, 635, 647, 656, 665, 691, 712
    background of, 459–60
    as GPU deputy head, 459, 461
    as OGPU chairman, 608
Mif, Pavel, 655
Mikhaiklovskaya, Praskovya Georgievna
    "Pasha," 46
Mikhail Aleksandrovich, Grand Duke, 126,
    160, 161, 166, 170, 171
    assassination of, 280, 403
    named as successor by Nicholas II, 178
Mikhailov, Vasily, 424
Mikhelson Machine Factory, 284, 285, 307, 418
Mikoyan, Anastasy "Anastas," 387, 415–16, 455,
    684, 687, 701, 709, 720
    as Stalin loyalist, 455, 465–66, 584, 608, 731
    and Stalin's Caucasus trip and, 598, 600, 601
    Stalin's correspondence with, 684, 721, 722
    as trade commissar, 607–8
Milchakov, Alexander, 548
Military Commissariat of the North Caucasus,
    301, 303
military controversy, 319–21
Military Revolutionary Committee (MRC),
    215–16, 217, 219, 233, 511
Miliukov, Paul, 90, 132, 139, 157, 163, 178–80,
    181, 188, 194–95, 196, 201, 207, 227, 228
Minin, Sergei, 303, 308, 309, 313, 314
Minsk, 354, 358, 360
    RSDRP founded in, 44–45
Mirabeau, Comte de, 185–86
Mirbach, Count Wilhelm, 270–71, 273, 274
    anti-Bolsheviks courted by, 271
    assassination of, 274–75, 442
    on Bolsheviks' likely collapse, 271, 272
modernity, 92, 119, 132, 134
    as geopolitical process, 4–5, 62–65
    in Russia, 65–67, 94, 97, 119, 129
"Modern Nationality" (Kautsky), 347
Mogilyov, 158, 167, 354
Molotov, Vyacheslav (Skryabin), 121, 190, 193,
    339, 375, 390, 413, 420, 423–24, 425, 428,
    429, 488, 499, 513, 527, 564, 666, 673, 692,
    698, 708, 719, 723
    background of, 453–54

Molotov, Vyacheslav (Skryabin) *(cont.)*
Central Committee apparatus criticized
by, 518–19
on Lenin's cruelty, 544
Lenin's death and, 534
on Lenin's Testament, 528
in politburo, 585, 596
retaliatory executions ordered by, 634–35
as Stalin loyalist, 454, 456, 528, 639, 672, 686,
694, 701, 715, 717, 720, 731
Stalin's correspondence with, 578,
596, 599, 604, 613, 619, 622, 634–35,
636, 637
and succession power struggle, 644, 649
Trotsky and, 545, 598, 639
Moltke, Helmuth von (the Elder), 4
Moltke, Helmuth von (the Younger), 141, 145,
147, 148
Mongolia, Mongols, 145, 344, 401, 402,
553–54, 617
Chinese troops driven out of, 403–4
Mongolian People's Party, 402, 405, 554
Mongolian People's Republic, 553–54
Monoselidze, Mikheil, 105
Moscow, 235, 238
Bolshevik evacuation to, 259–61
February Revolution in, 172
food shortages in, 270, 321
fuel scarcity in, 304
Kitaigorod neighborhood of, 450–51
1905 uprising in, 86
renaming of streets in, 286
strikes in, 206
Moscow Center, 560
Moscow Council of People's Commissars,
238, 261
Moscow Soviet, 261–62, 310, 482
Moscow State Conference, 205–7, 218, 320
Mtkvari River, 14, 22
Mukden, Battle of, 73, 75
Munich Beer Hall Putsch, 2, 527
Muralov, Nikolai, 576, 641, 653, 654, 656
Muravyov, Mikhail, 277
Murmansk, British landing at, 265–66, 282
Murmansk Railway, 265
Muslims:
in Central Asia, 373–74
in Communist Party, 502–3, 527, 716
in Eurasia, 349, 366, 367–72
in Georgia, 13, 24
OGPU surveillance of, 502
Qoqand massacre of, 255
in Russia, 12–13, 183–84, 368–69
Stalin's cultivation of, 368

Sunni-Shiite split of, 503
in Turkestan, 253–54, 502–3
Mussolini, Benito, 123–24, 552, 610, 725
assassination attempts on, 738–39
Matteotti's murder and, 551, 552
as prime minister, 549, 551
Mussorgsky, Modest, 134
Muszkat, Zofia, 447

Nani, Agosto, 1
Napoleon I, emperor of France, 2, 4, 185, 186
Napoleon III, emperor of France, 7
Napravnik, Eduard, 127
National Center, 333–34
National Democrats, Polish, 600
nationalism, 119, 342, 345–49, 359, 370, 475, 502
in Eurasia, 406
in Georgia, 400, 601
in Germany, 34–35
indigenization policy and, 496, 504
Lenin on, 347–48, 351
Lenin's alleged article on, 493–94, 501
in Russia, 118–19, 125, 202
Stalin on, 153–54, 347–48, 406, 477, 478,
496, 503
Nationalists, Chinese, *see* Guomindang
nationalities commissariat, 228, 238, 251, 254,
264, 266, 349, 368, 429, 456
"National Question and Social Democracy,
The" (Stalin), 347
Naville, Pierre, 646
Navy, U.S., 140
Nazaretyan, Amayak, 425, 427, 456, 464–65,
468, 519
Nazis, 704
Nechayev, Sergei, 53
NEPmen, *see* private traders
Neuilly, Treaty of (1919), 316
New Economic Policy (NEP), 344, 376, 388–89,
405–6, 408, 416, 420, 446, 447, 449, 457,
470, 473–74, 481–82, 495, 497, 517, 524,
527, 578, 580, 616, 656, 662, 663, 670, 674,
681, 695, 727
as concession to capitalism, 571, 672, 711
industrialization and, 571, 672
kulaks and, 727–28
Rykov and, 685, 728–29
Sokolnikov and, 565, 577, 579
Stalin and, 419, 487, 497, 527, 568–69, 571,
592, 671, 672, 682, 683, 706, 711, 737
Zinoviev's criticisms of, 570–71
*New Times,* 73
*New York American,* 610
*New York Times,* 538, 543, 614

*New York Tribune,* 18
Nicholas, Grand Duke "Nikolasha," 82, 158,
    159, 166
Nicholas I, tsar, 59, 89
Nicholas II, tsar, 60, 62, 65, 70, 71, 72, 75, 82,
    85, 89–90, 91–92, 101, 122, 127, 131, 157,
    160, 161, 163, 186, 197, 209, 223, 441
    abdication of, 3, 171–72, 178, 230, 258
    in aborted return to Petrograd, 170–71
    aristocratic plots against, 166
    constitution promised by, 84, 85
    crackdown on 1917 protests ordered by,
        167–68
    Duma and, 74, 82–83, 90–91, 93–94, 101, 127,
        128, 158, 163, 166, 169, 171
    Durnovó and, 134
    Far East policy of, 72–73
    as frontline commander, 158–59, 167
    Fundamental Laws issued by, 85
    growing disillusion with, 126, 127–28
    house arrest of, 280
    murder of, 281
    October Manifesto issued by, 82, 84, 85,
        90, 92
    and onset of Great War, 144–45
    political intrigues of, 120, 127
    in secret pact with Germany, 109–10, 139
    Stolypin's relationship with, 92, 119–20
    Witte's relationship with, 70, 72, 84, 91
    workers' petition to, 73–74
Nicolaevsky, Boris, 218, 267
Niedermeyer, Oskar von, 560
Nina (underground printing press), 50
Nobel brothers, 51, 115
Nogin, Viktor, 322
"nomenklatura," 432–33, 436
North Caucasus, 447, 666, 688–89, 700
Nosovich, Anatoly, 305, 306–7
"Notes of an Economist" (Bukharin), 722
"Notes on the Question of Nationalities"
    (Lenin), 493–94, 497, 501, 606
    Stalin's refutation of, 496–97
Novgorod, Nizhny, 59
Novogorodtseva, Klavdiya, 154
Novonikolaevsk, 403–4
Novosibirsk, 661, 669–70, 673, 713

*October* (film), 651
Octobrists, 98
October Manifesto, 82, 84, 85, 90, 92
October Revolution, 215–23, 354, 418
    absence of political authority after,
        230–31
    Central Committee and, 214, 216

as coup against Petrograd Soviet, 223
Kamenev and, 214, 224, 499, 563–64, 606,
    641, 648
Lenin in, 220–21, 222, 278
MRC in, 215–16, 217
predicted failure of, 227–28
Red Guards in, 216, 219
Stalin in, 224–25
tenth anniversary of, 650–52, 664–65
Trotsky in, 215, 219, 220, 221–22
Zinoviev and, 214, 224, 499, 515, 563–64,
    606, 641, 648
Odessa, 15, 74, 264
OGPU, 504, 577, 616, 688–89
    Dzierżyński as head of, 577–78
    Eastern Department of, 502
    extrajudicial powers of, 635, 650
    food and goods shortages reports of, 655
    and German Communist coup attempt, 525
    GPU replaced by, 485
    grain requisitions and, 665, 666, 669
    Lenin's death and, 492–93, 536
    Mężyński as chairman of, 608
    NEPmen and, 572
    Red Army and, 574–75
    Stalin's control of, 687
    strikers arrested by, 517
    tenth anniversary celebration of, 656–57
    terrorism and, 634
    and Trotsky's exile, 677–78
    Western attack feared by, 616
*okhranka* (*Okhrannoe otdelenie*; political
    police), 61–62, 67, 69, 71, 75–76, 79, 93,
    104, 114, 115, 126, 130, 160, 439, 441
    February Revolution and, 168–69
    Provisional Government's abolition of, 180
    revolutionary groups infiltrated by, 117, 118,
        133, 164
    right wing and, 100
    Stalin arrested by, 133
    Stalin surveilled by, 117, 121
    Stolypin's assassination and, 122
    *see also* police, tsarist
Okulov, Alexei, 304
"Old Ninika" (Soselo), 34
Old Square, 4, 426, 429, 430
*On Lenin* (Trotsky), 545
*On Lenin and Leninism* (Stalin), 555, 557
"On the Grain Front" (Stalin), 706
*On the Leninist Path,* 682
*On the Path to October* (Stalin), 555
*On the Tax in Kind* (Lenin), 393
Onufrieva, Pelageya, 121
Orakhelashvili, Mamiya, 399

Order No. 1, 181–82, 200, 297
Orenburg, 238
Orenburg Soviet, 266
Organization and Instruction Department, 455
orgburo (organization bureau), 322, 423, 424,
    425, 430, 432, 435, 438, 512, 522, 548
Orjonikidze, Grigol "Sergo," 116, 124, 366, 367,
    395, 399, 425, 464–65, 477, 493, 503, 507,
    513, 541, 576, 577, 585, 598, 600, 601, 654,
    656, 666, 694, 700, 721, 723
  background of, 28, 479
  and Bolshevik takeover of Georgia,
    396–97, 401
  as Central Control Commission head, 607–8,
    636, 640
  Kabakhidze struck by, 481, 487, 489
  Mdivani and, 479–80
  and plot to oust Stalin as general secretary,
    713, 715, 717
  South Caucasus Federation and, 479, 493
  as Stalin loyalist, 390, 455, 456, 467, 506, 731
  Stalin's correspondence with, 415, 493, 596
Orthodox Christianity, 99, 118, 119–20, 125,
    129, 351
Oryol, Battle of, 330, 331, 357
Osinsky, Valerian, 659
Ossetia, Ossetians, 15, 496, 688
Ostrovsky, Alexander, 620
Otto, Ernest, 709
Ottoman empire, 1–2, 49, 59, 66, 82, 110, 258,
    343, 365
  Armenian genocide in, 150
  Balkans and, 141
  in Great War, 150
  partitioning of, 367
  Russian expansion and, 12, 13, 15, 51
  Young Turk Revolution in, 131–32, 172
Our Differences (Plekhanov), 42
Our Lady of Kazan Cathedral, 126, 127, 128
Our Lady of St. Theodore, 127
"Our Tasks in the East" (Stalin), 369
Owen, Robert, 39

Pale of Settlement, 12, 44, 99, 100, 112, 200,
    249, 455
Panchen Lama, 401
Panina, Sofia, 439
pan-Islamism, 386–87, 502
Paole Zion party, 456
Pares, Bernard, 94
Paris Commune (1871), 232, 233, 318
  fiftieth anniversary of, 391
Parliament-2, Operation, 502
Passau, Germany, 35

Path to Socialism and the Worker-Peasant
    Alliance, The (Bukharin), 727
Patricide, The (Qazbegi), 23–24
Paul I, tsar, 89, 90
Pavlovich, Dmitri, Grand Duke, 163
Pavlov, Ivan, 37
Pavlova, Anna, 127
Pavlovsky Guards, 169
peasants, Russian, 11, 37–38, 42, 43, 93,
    100, 409
  Bolsheviks' initial lack of interest in, 237, 426
  collectivization and, see collectivization
  communes of, 41–42, 65–66, 95, 96–97,
    189–90, 299, 430, 449, 567
  Communists as viewed by, 474, 548–49, 570,
    611, 625, 655, 675
  in Constituent Assembly election, 243–44
  food shortages of, 165
  as ignorant about farming best practices,
    449–50
  land seizures by, 189–90, 220–21, 239, 296,
    420–21, 449
  Lenin's poor understanding of, 299–300
  as market for industrial goods, 570, 664, 681
  NEP and, see New Economic Policy
  party membership among, 426
  proletariat supported by, 205
  rebellions by, 67, 75, 84, 132, 135, 224,
    379–80, 388–89, 393–94, 405, 410,
    470, 575
  Stalin and, 103, 320, 568–69; see also
    collectivization
  Stolypin and, 95, 96
  and winter of 1920–21, 379–82
  see also agriculture, Russian; kulaks
peasants, Russian, grain requisitions from, 447,
    662–66, 669–72, 679–80, 682, 684–85,
    686, 698, 700–701, 705, 709–13, 721,
    722, 727
  "extraordinary measures" and, 697, 705,
    709–10, 712, 713, 722
  hoarding by, 649, 659, 664, 665, 666, 668,
    669, 680, 700, 711, 712
  protests, 707, 708–9, 722
  replaced by tax in kind, 376, 380, 382,
    388–89, 393, 405, 449
People's Cause, 237
People's Will, 60
Pereprygin, Alexander, 155
Pereprygina, Lidiya, 155
Perm, 314, 403
Persia, see Iran
Persian empire, 12
Persian language, 12, 344

Persian Soviet Socialist Republic, 366–67
Pestkowski, Stanisław, 264, 270, 349, 368
  as Stalin's assistant, 228–30
Pétain, Philippe, 197
Peter I "the Great," tsar, 56–57, 88
Peter II, tsar, 88
Peter III, tsar, 89
Petersburg Soviet, 81–82, 84, 85–86
Peterss, Jēkabs, 287, 346, 374–75, 502
Petliura, Symon, 353
Petrichenko, Stepan, 383
Petrograd, 159, 173, 214, 235, 298
  "Bloody Sunday" massacre in, 73–74, 126, 164
  Bolshevik evacuation of, 259–61
  Bolshevik headquarters in, 186–87, 190, 191,
    203, 215
  Cheka in, 382
  food shortages in, 270
  German advance on, 259, 271
  soldier-sailor uprising in, 202
  Stalin in, 117, 121–22, 132–33, 186, 190
  "storming" of Winter Palace reenacted in,
    338–39
  strikes and protests in, 81–82, 144, 164, 166,
    167, 382–83, 410
  troops stationed in, 168
  Vyborg district of, 186–87, 204
  White army advance on, 330
  women's bread march in, 165, 167
  see also Leningrad
Petrograd Soviet of Workers' and Soldiers'
    Deputies, 170, 182, 198, 202, 206, 247
  Bolshevik control of, 212–13, 218–19
  central executive committee of, see Soviet
    central executive committee
  Duma replaced by, 181
  Military Revolutionary Committee of, see
    Military Revolutionary Committee
  October Revolution as coup against, 223
  Provisional Government and, 181–82, 191
  Trotsky as chairman of, 212–13
  see also Moscow Soviet
Petrovskaya, Stefania, 121
Petrovsky, Hryhory "Grigory," 390, 579,
    596, 613
Piłsudski, Józef, 333, 345, 352, 377, 379, 562,
    617, 622
  in move to right, 600–601
  in 1926 coup, 589, 600, 622
  in Polish-Soviet War, 353–55, 364–65
Plehve, Vyacheslav von, 100
Plekhanov, Georgi, 42, 43, 45, 78, 80, 711
Pnevsky, Nikolai, 668
Poincaré, Raymond, 445

Pokrovsky, Serafim, 636–37
Poland, Poles, 98, 119, 157, 249, 258, 271, 315,
    344, 349, 377, 406, 478, 522, 556, 557, 560,
    588, 605
  in aftermath of Great War, 352
  Belorussia and, 616–17
  France and, 558, 589, 623
  German occupation of, 243, 283, 352
  in Great War, 355
  as independent nation, 238, 342–43
  in Locarno Pact, 561–62
  and new threat of war with Soviet Union,
    622–23
  Piłsudski's coup in, 589, 600, 604, 622
  Romania and, 590, 616
  Soviet Russia in treaty with, 392
  Soviet Union's relationship with, 589
  Ukraine and, 352, 353–54, 616–17
police, tsarist, 49, 61, 69, 85, 130, 164
  disbanding of, 180, 223
  inadequacy of, 103–4
  Stalin arrested by, 48–49, 52
  Stalin files of, 49, 52, 76
  see also okhranka
Polish Corridor, 315, 363, 364, 509, 621
Polish Revolutionary Committee, 360, 361,
    365, 377
Polish-Soviet War (1919–20), 352–65,
    376–79, 406
  Stalin on, 354–55, 357, 358
  Stalin's role in, 361–63, 365, 377–78
politburo (political bureau), 322, 330, 390, 391,
    423, 424, 426, 428, 430, 582, 585, 607, 615,
    652, 730
  British general strike and, 598–99
  collectivization and, 675–76
  German Communist coup aided by,
    511, 515
  as key to Stalin dictatorship, 596
  and Lenin's impending death, 492–93
  Lenin's relationship with, 413, 415,
    484, 489
  Russian majority in, 656
  special cipher unit of, 433–34
  Stalin dictatorship and, 687, 699–700
  Stalin's resignation offers to, 508, 607, 614
  as top policy-making body under Lenin,
    428–29
  Trotsky and, 414–15, 488, 520, 522, 615
  Zinoviev's expulsion from, 607
Polkovnikov, Georgy, 216
Popov, Dmitri, 277–78
Populists, Populism, 38, 42, 43
Port Arthur (Lushun), China, 71, 73, 111

Portsmouth, Treaty of (1905), 75, 81
Poskryobyshev, Alexander, 375–76, 705
*Potemkin,* workers' seizure of, 74
Potëmkin, Prince, 90
Prague, RSDRP conference in, 122–23, 124,
    132, 154
*Pravda:*
    anti-Trotsky articles in, 564
    Kamenev as editor of, 190–91
    Lenin's "April Theses" published in, 191
    on Lenin's illness, 492
    Provisional Government policy attacked
        by, 199
    Provisional Government's seizure of, 203
    Stalin as editor of, 193
    Stalin's articles in, 177, 266, 267, 555, 564, 639
Preobrazhensky, Yevgeny, 205, 390, 412, 423,
    497, 507, 566, 695
press:
    Lenin's censorship of, 237, 245
    *see also specific publications*
Princip, Gavrilo, 143, 149, 268–69
*Principles of Organization* (Kerzhentsev), 435
private traders (NEPmen), 299–300, 568,
    571–72, 605, 616, 649, 662, 665, 666,
    695, 730
Prokofyev, Sergei, 620, 621, 678
*Proletarian Revolution,* 512
*Proletariat,* Stalin's articles in, 177
proletariat, Russian, 25, 40, 42, 43–44, 54, 115,
    169, 349
    "Bloody Sunday" massacre of, 73–74
    Bolshevik agitation among, 186
    Communists' shaky standing among,
        426–27
    "dictatorship" of, 203, 225, 232, 337
    as increasingly unhappy with Soviet regime,
        695–97
    Lena massacre of, 125–26, 135
    mass arrests of, 164
    1905–6 uprisings of, 73–74, 76, 92, 104, 130,
        132, 167
    peasant support for, 205
    Shakhty affair and, 696
    strikes and protests by, 43–44, 48, 67, 73, 74,
        79, 81–82, 84, 85–86, 125–26, 144, 164,
        166, 167, 382–83, 410, 517–18, 570
    trade unions demanded by, 385
    unemployment among, 548
*Proletariatis Brdzola,* 348
Proshyan, Prosh, 278
*Protocols of the Elders of Zion,* 99–100, 129,
    281, 295
Protopopov, Alexander, 167–68

Proudhon, Pierre-Joseph, 39
Provisional Government, 174, 177–78, 183, 213,
    223, 224, 230, 242, 259, 272, 280, 296, 298,
    338–39, 383, 453
    Bolshevik coup feared by, 208
    Bolsheviks charged with treason by,
        202–3
    as bourgeois institution, 176
    and breakdown of order, 180–81
    Cadet defection from, 202
    collapse of, 216, 217, 218
    constitutionalism and, 175–76, 178–80
    Duma and, 179–80
    grain monopoly of, 298–99
    Great War and, 187, 194–95, 196–200
    land redistribution resisted by, 189
    mass resignation of, 209
    Menshevik support of, 195
    1917 offensive launched by, 196–200
    Order No. 1 of, 181–82, 200, 297
    Order No. 2 of, 182
    Petrograd Soviet and, 19, 181–82
    plenary powers transferred to, 178
    police and *okhranka* abolished by, 180, 223
    in relocation to Winter Palace, 213–14, 216,
        217, 219–20
    right wing and, 182–83
    as socialist, 176
    Stalin and, 190, 205
    *see also* Kerensky, Alexander
Provisional Revolutionary Committee, 383,
    384, 393, 402
Prussia, 5–6, 58, 83–84, 95
Pskov, 173
Purishkevich, Vladimir, 99, 163, 182–83
Pushkin, Alexander, 417
Putilov Works, 164
Putin, Spiridon, 413
Pyatakov, Grigory "Yuri," 237, 351, 440, 605,
    614, 615
    Lenin's Testament and, 499
Pyatnitsky, Osip, 526

Qazbegi, Aleksandre, 23–24
Qing dynasty, 4, 64, 66, 401
Qoqand, 254, 255
Qoqand Autonomy, 254–55, 373

Rabinovich, Isaak, 620
Rabinovich, Lazar, 703, 704
Radchenko, Stepan, 44*n*
Radek, Karl, 188, 249, 250, 258, 275, 315, 318,
    358, 365, 367, 376–77, 390, 407, 464, 492,
    495, 510, 560, 678–79

Raduński, Iwan, 286
*Rails Are Buzzing, The* (Kirshon), 699
Rákosi, Mátyás, 325, 525
Rakovski, Cristian (Stanchev, Kryasto), 476, 478, 496, 497, 503, 572, 645–46, 650, 651, 656, 677, 692
Ramishvili, Isidor, 51, 267, 399
Ramishvili, Noe, 78
Rapallo, Treaty of (1922), 445–46, 473, 509, 560, 561, 599
Raskolnikov, Fyodor (Ilin), 302, 306, 366, 393
Rasputin, Grigory, 159–60, 167, 168
   murder of, 163, 182
Rathenau, Walther, 445–46
Red Army, 266, 268, 277, 286, 289, 293, 343, 366, 451, 642, 688
   Azerbaijan captured by, 395
   Bukhara assault by, 373–74
   in clashes with Romania, 360
   combat unreadiness of, 557, 604, 619, 621, 622, 638
   commissars in, 339, 351
   in Crimea, 379
   demobilization of, 344, 426, 436
   food shortages and, 649, 662
   former tsarist officers in, 297–98, 306, 309, 314, 319–21, 329, 339–40, 351, 356–57, 393, 574–75
   Georgia invaded by, 397, 398
   industrialization and, 574, 587
   in military cooperation agreement with Germany, 446, 561, 587, 617–18, 621, 638, 704–5
   nomenklatura of, 436
   OGPU and, 574–75
   party members in, 344, 574
   peasants in, 297, 344
   Poland invaded by, 361
   political commissars in, 298, 320, 339, 351
   political departments in, 436
   provisioning of, 299
   in reconquest of Ukraine, 386
   reform of, 574
   Stalin in call for strong discipline in, 320
   Stalin's rejection of military experts in, 297
   Stalin's use of, for political education, 436–37
   Tambov rebellion and, 394
   Trotsky's demand for discipline and expertise in, 297
   tsarist arms acquired by, 332–33
   in Tsaritsyn, 302, 305
   in Turkestan, 372–74
   Urga captured by, 403

Red Army Political Administration, 557
*Red Cavalry* (Babel), 359
Redens, Stanisław, 314
Red Guards, 213, 216, 219, 233, 240, 242, 252, 256, 303, 339
Red Guards, Hungarian, 325
Red Hundreds, 77, 81
*Red Moscow,* 337
*Red Star,* 451
Red Terror, 287–88, 373, 405
Reed, John, 201, 220, 246, 367
Reisner, Larissa, 366
Renan, Ernest, 37
*Revolution and Culture,* 468
Revolutionary Military Council of the Republic, 286, 307–9, 328, 335, 436, 557
   Trotsky as head of, 286, 341, 516, 537
Revolutionary Tribunal, 381–82
Reza Khan, 346, 391
Rhineland, demilitarization of, 315
Rhodes, Cecil, 71
Ricardo, David, 40
Riezler, Kurt, 275, 282, 283
Riga, German capture of, 206, 208
Riga, Treaty of (1921), 392
Right Socialist Revolutionaries, 273, 279, 285, 396, 440
Rochau, August von, 6
Rodzyanko, Mikhail, 157, 166, 168, 169, 171, 178, 207
Romania, 316, 343, 344, 352, 556, 604, 605
   Bessarabia annexed by, 378–79
   in clashes with Red Army, 360
   fascism in, 589–90
   in Great War, 162
   Hungarian invasion of, 325
   Poland and, 590, 616
   and threat of war with Soviet Union, 622–23
Romanov, Mikhail Fyodorovich, 127
Romanov family, 88–89, 280, 281
   tercentenary of rule by, 126–28, 129, 132, 134
Roosevelt, Theodore, 75, 139
Rosenberg, Alfred, 340
Rostov, 271
*Rote Fahne, Die,* 515
Rothschild brothers, 51, 115
Roy, Manabendra Nath, 367–68, 625, 633
Rozanov, V. N., 576, 738
Rozengolts, Arkady, 306
Rudzutaks, Jānis, 511, 534, 596, 607, 641–42
Rukhimovich, Moisei, 327
Russell, Bertrand, 151
Russia, revolutionary:
   border provinces of, 183

Russia, revolutionary *(cont.)*
  civil liberties in, 183–84, 186
  food shortages in, 240, 298–99
  lack of central authority in, 238
  language and class in, 175, 187
  Muslims in, 183–84
  nationalist splintering of, 202, 238
  socialism in, 231
  violence and anarchy in, 239–40, 242
  *see also* Bolshevik regime; Bolshevik
    Revolution; February Revolution;
    October Revolution; Provisional
    Government
Russia, tsarist:
  agriculture in, *see* agriculture, Russian
  aristocracy in, 57–58, 69, 84
  autocratic political system of, *see* autocratic
    system, Russian
  Britain and, 108–9, 110, 135, 136, 140
  in Crimean War, 59, 91
  economy of, 141, 161–62
  education system in, 66–67, 74
  expansionist policies of, 1, 3, 12, 66, 67–68,
    71, 111, 127, 140, 145, 556
  February Revolution in, *see* February
    Revolution
  food shortages in, 165, 189
  foreign debt of, 66, 69
  foreign policy of, 6, 71–73, 108–12, 129,
    139, 144
  geographical extent of, 1, 11, 56, 68, 342
  grain exports of, 67, 662, 709
  Great Reforms in, 29, 59–60, 66, 85
  in Great War, 150, 156–57, 162, 166, 206–7,
    212, 219, 224, 231, 296, 312, 316–17
  industrialization in, 65, 67, 69–70, 91, 92,
    141, 645
  Japan and, 72–75, 109, 111–12
  Jews in, 12, 129
  land-owning establishment in, 11, 16, 97,
    188–89
  Marxism in, 42–45, 54, 74, 78, 79, 93, 137
  modernity in, 92, 94, 97, 119, 129
  nationalism in, 118–19, 125
  navy of, 73, 75
  in onset of Great War, 144–45, 146–49
  peasants in, *see* peasants, Russian
  political elite in, 65, 70–71, 92, 93, 95,
    128–29, 136, 223
  political terrorism in, 59–61, 74, 88, 89, 94,
    99, 101, 115, 134
  population of, 175
  proletariat in, *see* proletariat, Russian
  right wing in, 98–102, 118, 122, 126, 157

  Romanov tercentenary celebration in,
    126–28, 129, 132, 134
  socialism in, 41, 176
  State Council of, 82–83, 129, 134, 179
  suffrage in, 82, 94, 97, 109, 113
  in Triple Entente, 140, 147
  universal conscription in, 155–56
  uprisings of 1905–6 in, 3, 81–87, 92
  Westernization of, 56
Russian army, 13, 15–16
  Bolshevik agitators in, 198
  collapse of, 248, 252
  in Constituent Assembly election, 244
  demobilization of, 258
  desertions from, 172, 197
  February Revolution and, 169, 172, 175
  food shortages of, 164, 166
  material shortages of, 156, 162
  mutinies in, 163, 200
  nationalist splintering of, 202
  1917 offensive of, 196–200, 204, 212,
    219, 224
  Order No. 1 and, 181–82, 200
  Order No. 2 and, 182
  Provisional Government's destruction of, 181
  radicalization of, 223–24
  Stalin exempted from, 155
  *see also* Red Army
Russian Association of the Social Science
    Research Institute, 706
*Russian Messenger,* 198
Russian navy, 11, 224
  in Constituent Assembly election, 244
  demobilization of, 258
  February Revolution and, 172, 175
Russian Orthodox Church, 13, 14
  *see also* Eastern Orthodox Christianity
Russian Social Democratic Workers' Party
    (RSDRP), 45, 51, 52, 76, 98, 107, 114, 118,
    130, 259
  1st Congress of (Minsk), 44–45
  2nd Congress of (London), 78, 79, 80, 201
  3rd Congress of (Tammerfors), 80–81
  4th Congress of (Stockholm), 102–3
  5th Congress of (London), 108, 112, 113
  antiterrorism policy adopted by, 113–14
  Bolshevik-Menshevik split in, 78, 79–81, 103,
    108, 114, 122–23, 124, 137
  Central Committee of, *see* Central
    Committee
  Prague conference of, 122–23, 124, 132, 154
  *see also* Social Democrats, Russian
Russian Social Democratic Workers' Party
    (RSDRP), Caucasus branch of, 50–51

bad blood between Stalin and, 52, 53, 78
Menshevik-Bolshevik split in, 78, 80,
    81, 114
Russian Soviet Federated Socialist Republic
    (RSFSR; Soviet Russia):
    Armenia invaded by, 395
    autonomous national republics and, 371
    British trade agreement with, 391–92
    central executive committee of, 476
    China and, 404–5
    and creation of Soviet Union, 475
    diplomatic relations, 391–92
    economy of, *see* economy, Soviet
    famine of 1921–22 in, *see* famine of 1921–22
    founding of, 251, 350
    4th Congress of, 580
    Kronstadt rebellion and, 383–84, 387
    and Mongolian independence, 404–5
    Muslims in, 368–69
    in Polish War, *see* Polish-Soviet War
        (1919–20)
    in Rapallo Treaty with Germany, 445–46,
        473, 509, 560, 561, 599
    Stalin's work on constitution of, 266
    Tambov rebellion and, 380–82
    trade monopoly of, 483, 484
    Turkestan annexed by, 388
    Ukraine and, 386, 475–76
    winter of 1920–21 in, 379–82
    *see also* Bolshevik regime
Russian State Bank, 238–39
    Tiflis robbery of, 113–14
"Russia's New Ruler" (Davis), 610
Russification, 348
Russo-Japanese War (1904–5), 73, 75, 76, 81,
    109, 134, 167, 185
Russo-Ottoman War, 66
Rustaveli, Shota, 10, 16
Ruzsky, General, 171–72
Ryazanov, David, 389
Rykov, Alexei, 236, 328, 394, 464, 480–81, 482,
    483, 498, 513, 516, 534, 538, 563, 566–67,
    596, 613, 619, 633, 652, 654, 676, 685–86,
    707–8, 721, 723
    as alternative Soviet leader, 730–31
    as chairman of USSR Council of People's
        Commissars, 540, 657, 658, 686
    and grain shortages, 721–22
    NEP and, 685, 728–29
    and plot to oust Stalin as general secretary,
        714, 715, 716–17
    Shakhty affair and, 687–88, 698
    Stalin and, 658, 686–87, 699–700
    in succession power struggle, 563, 564

Ryndin, Kuzma, 653
Ryndzyunskaya, Marina, 427, 435

Safarov, Georgy (Voldin), 346, 387
Sagirashvili, David, 177, 225–26, 233
Said-Galiev, Sahib Garei, 345–46, 371
St. Germain, Treaty of (1919), 316
St. Petersburg, *see* Petrograd
St. Petersburg Imperial University, 91
Saint-Simon, Count Henri de, 39, 40
Sakhalin Island, 75, 590
Samara, 291, 326
Sarajevo, 142–43
Saratov, 91–92, 95, 381
Savenko, A. I., 88
Schlieffen, Alfred, Count von, 145
Schlieffen Plan, 145, 147, 310
Schweitzer, Vera, 155, 173
secretariat, 423–5, 430, 434
Sedov, Lev, 538
Sedova, Natalya, 533, 541, 593–94, 677
self-determination, 343, 346–48, 351, 419
Serbia, 141–44, 148–49, 150, 173
Serebryakov, Leonid, 390, 423, 463
Serebryakova, Galina, 565, 581, 585
serfs, serfdom, 8, 11, 15, 16, 57
    emancipation of, 16, 23, 37–38, 41, 42, 59,
        60, 726
Sergei, Grand Duke, 61
Sergeyev, Artyom, 466–67, 593
Sering, Max, 409, 420–21
Sevastopol naval base, 271
Seventeenth Amendment, U.S., 83
    show trial in, 702–4, 709, 711, 734
    Stalin and, 689, 691, 694, 698, 709, 711,
        714–15, 733
Sèvres, Treaty of (1920), 316, 367
Shakhty, alleged sabotage in, 687–96, 699
Shanghai, 629–30
Shaposhnikov, Boris, 378
Shchurovsky, Vladimir, 720
Shchusev, Alexei, 543
Sheridan, Clare, 459
Shklovsky, Viktor, 380
Shlyapnikov, Alexander, 190, 222, 300, 346, 385
Shostokovich, Dmitry, 620
show trials, 464
    Lenin's call for, 439–40
    in Shakhty affair, 702–4, 709, 711, 734
Shulgin, Vasily, 173
Shumyatsky, Boris, 404
Siberia, 15, 41, 68, 97, 132, 244, 270, 372, 381,
    402, 403, 447
    Communist Party in, 680–81, 683, 684

Siberia *(cont.)*
  Japanese invasion of, 343–44
  Lena goldfields massacre in, 125–26, 135
  Stalin's 1928 trip to, 661–66, 668, 674–75,
    676, 679, 684, 739
  Stalin's exiles to, 9, 53, 133, 152–53, 173
Simbirsk, 356
*Since Lenin Died* (Eastman), Stalin's response
    to, 572–73
Sino-Japanese War (1894–95), 72
Sklyansky, Yefraim, 262, 327–28, 394, 511, 542
Skorutto, Nikolai, 703–4
Skrypnyk, Mykola, 346, 387, 497, 503
Slepkov, Alexander, 545–46
*Small Biography of a Big Man, A,* 500
Smetona, Antanas, 618
Smilga, Ivar, 328, 358, 359
Smirnov, Alexander, 449
Smirnov, Ivan, 306, 390, 404
Smirnov, Vladimir, 320
Smith, Adam, 39, 40
Smolensk, 355, 358
Smolny, 216, 226, 228
Smolny Institute, 215
Snesarev, Andrei, 301–4
Sobinov, Leonid, 127
Sobol, Raisa, 608
Sochi, Stalin's holidays in, 596, 598, 601–2, 613,
    633, 636–37, 720
Sochi affair, 698
Social Democrats, 9, 151, 195, 336, 397, 550
Social Democrats, Austrian, 43
Social Democrats, Caucasus, 103, 113
  bad blood between Stalin and, 52, 53, 78
Social Democrats, Georgian, 37, 49, 50, 67,
    77–78, 98, 395, 735
Social Democrats, German, 41, 43, 78–79,
    113, 129, 201, 272, 318, 323, 378, 510, 515,
    525–26, 550, 617–18, 704
Social Democrats, Hungarian, 324
Social Democrats, Latvian, 103
Social Democrats, Polish, 103
Social Democrats, Russian, 50–51, 82, 98, 102,
    125, 129, 135, 242–43, 244, 458, 464
Social Democrats, South Caucasus, 53
socialism, 3, 39, 40, 176, 190
  right-wing embrace of, 210–11
  in Russia, 41, 132, 231
  as Stalin's life mission, 9, 31
  *see also specific parties*
*Socialism and Political Struggle* (Plekhanov), 42
*Socialism in One Country* (Stalin), 532
"Socialism in One Country" (Stalin), 555
*Socialist Herald,* 393, 489, 553, 555

Socialist Party, Polish, 137
Socialist Revolutionaries of Ukraine, 244, 245
Socialist Revolutionary Land Decree, 239–40
Socialist Revolutionary Party (SRs), 79, 98, 103,
    113, 117, 133, 135, 137, 176, 185, 187, 195,
    196, 198, 212, 217–18, 221, 234–35, 239–40,
    242–44, 246, 381, 382, 392, 393, 439
  *see also* Left Socialist Revolutionaries
Society of Old Bolsheviks, 453
Sokolnikov, Grigory (Brilliant, Gersh "Garya"),
    257, 271, 320, 376, 475, 486, 567, 614, 710,
    712, 716, 739
  as alternative Soviet leader, 729–31
  background of, 451, 457
  on capitalism, 565–66
  economic reforms of, 452, 566, 568, 569, 583
  as finance commissar, 451, 452, 565, 729
  at 14th Congress, 581–82
  on industrialization, 659–60
  Kamenev and, 713–14
  market socialism as envisioned by, 729–30
  NEP and, 564, 577, 579
  and plan to oust Stalin as general
    secretary, 714
  possibility of planned economy rejected by,
    729–30
  removed from finance commissariat and
    politburo, 585, 730
  and succession power struggle, 564, 577, 729
  in Turkestan, 451–52
Sokolov, Nikolai, 200
*Soldier,* 216
*Soldier of the Revolution,* 305
Soltangäliev, Mirsäyet, 345–46, 368–69, 371,
    372, 502–4, 716
Solvychegodsk, 116, 121
Somme, Battle of the, 150, 152, 162
Sosnovsky, Lev, 680–81
South Caucasus, *see* Caucasus
South Caucasus Federation, 479, 480, 496, 497
Southern Manchurian Railway, 111
South-West Africa, Herrero rebellion in,
    151–52
Souvarine, Boris, 520
Soviet central executive committee, 200, 215,
    221, 226, 233, 235, 236, 247, 257, 260,
    262–63, 264–65, 268, 273–74, 285–86, 423,
    429, 535
Soviet republics, Stalin's opposition to
    independence of, 386, 388, 390
Soviet Russia, *see* Russian Soviet Federated
    Socialist Republic
Soviet Union:
  border states and, 556, 732

Britain and, 558, 617–18, 622, 623, 624, 631–33, 634–35
British general strike supported by, 588, 598–99, 613
China and, 617, 623, 625–33, 651, 655
Constitution of, 513, 540
economy of, *see* economy, Soviet
food shortages in, 164–65, 189
foreign policy of, 558, 698–99
foreign recognition of, 553, 558
foreign trade of, 599, 632, 709, 720, 733–34
formal inauguration of, 485–86
France and, 560, 645, 646, 693, 733
German nonaggression pact with, 587, 588
German relations with, 558, 559–61, 611, 623, 638–39, 692, 704
goods shortages in, 654–55
grain exports of, 662, 665, 667
grain imports by, 568, 720
grain shortages in, 641, 649, 654–55, 659, 661–66, 669–72, 679–80, 682, 684–85, 686, 698, 700–701, 705, 709–13, 721, 722, 727–28
Great Depression and, 733–34
industrialization in, 517, 565–66, 571, 574, 582, 583, 587, 605, 625, 638, 659, 662, 663, 664, 672, 686, 694, 695, 698, 710, 722, 725, 733
Japan and, 517, 590, 621–22, 632
Lenin's plan for, 476–77, 478, 485–86, 496
Locarno Pact and, 562
1923 strikes in, 517–18
oil exports of, 709
Stalin's role in creation of, 419, 475, 478, 486; of war with Romania, 622–23
tsarist debts repudiated by, 611, 616, 623, 645
U.S. relations with, 611–12
war scares in, 619–20, 621–25, 635–36, 639, 649, 659, 664, 668, 721, 736, 737
Western technology needed by, 558–59, 667–68, 693, 705, 732–33
world revolution and, 555–56
Spandaryan, Suren, 106, 124, 155, 173
*Spark,* 393
Spartacus League, 272, 323
Spiridonova, Maria, 246, 274–76, 278–79
*SR Trial, The* (film), 440
*Stalin* (Barbusse), 1
Stalin, Iosif (Jughashvili):
aggrandizement of, 334, 341, 390, 424, 469, 532
ambition of, 21, 38, 54–55, 463, 469
appointed party general secretary, 411–12, 424, 481, 486, 530

arts as interest of, 620–21
as autodidact, 21, 30, 117, 676
background of, 2, 8, 9–10
Bolshevik takeover of Georgia urged by, 396–97
charm of, 465, 603, 736
childhood of, 17, 20–28, 735
as class-warfare zealot, 306–7, 308–9, 345, 444, 681, 688, 698, 710–11, 732, 734
competitiveness of, 331
cunning of, 4, 424, 427, 465, 502, 532, 537
false humility of, 600, 659
federalist agenda of, 346, 349–51
as food affairs director for South Russia, 270, 300–310
get-things-done style of, 54–55, 124, 307, 335, 341, 462, 465, 468, 597, 739
grudges held by, 9, 591
illnesses of, 17, 20, 398–99, 602, 738
imperiousness of, 9
imprisonments of, 116, 117, 121–22
intellect of, 7
internal exiles of, 9, 53, 116, 121, 122, 133, 152–55, 173
"Koba" as nickname of, 24, 52, 598
Lenin and, *see* Lenin-Stalin relationship
Marxist-Leninist worldview of, 10, 88, 93, 107, 137, 307, 341, 419–20, 427, 462, 470, 622, 676, 699, 731, 737
military ignorance of, 297, 306
military posts resigned by, 365
as nationalities commissar, 228, 238, 251, 254, 264, 266, 349, 368, 429, 456
1928 Siberian trip of, 661–66, 668, 674–75, 676, 679, 684
organizational skills of, 4, 55, 390, 424, 425
Orthodox faith of, 28
paranoia of, 597–98, 723, 736
pessimism of, 407–8
physical ailments of, 20–22, 465–66, 602–3, 633, 661, 720
poetry by, 33–34
on Polish-Soviet War, 354–55, 357, 358
political skills of, 7, 422, 424–25, 739
as propagandist, 48, 115, 177, 187, 193, 225, 259, 305–6, 462
religious disenchantment of, 36–37
schooling of, 21, 25–26, 28
self-centeredness of, 155, 468
self-improvement as goal of, 4, 7, 10, 21, 117
self-pity of, 474, 508, 528, 591, 595, 614, 619, 647, 657, 659, 735–36
as seminary student, 2, 26–27, 30–38, 44–47

Stalin, Iosif (Jughashvili) *(cont.)*
  siege mentality of, 591–92, 597, 659, 736
  socialism as life mission of, 9, 31
  in succession power struggle, 416–17, 522–25,
    532–34, 540, 555, 563–64, 572–73, 577,
    578, 580, 582, 584, 586, 590–91, 597, 604,
    605–6, 614–15, 636–37, 638, 639, 641–44,
    646–48, 653–54, 655–56, 713, 735, 736
  in Tiflis, 8–9, 22, 113–14, 121, 125, 267–68,
    399, 600
  touchiness of, 116, 597
  vanity of, 362
  vengefulness of, 597–98, 615–16, 715–16, 719,
    723, 731, 736
  as voracious reader, 32, 36–37, 45, 47–48,
    116, 117, 153, 155, 463, 536, 669
  womanizing of, 3, 8, 121, 155
Stalin, Iosif, dictatorship of, 419–20, 422–71,
    527, 586, 652
  alternatives to, 727–32
  apparatchiks in, 426, 430, 431–32
  Bukharin's opposition to, 472, 474, 513, 731
  14th Party Congress debate on, 580–84
  general secretary post as key step toward,
    425–26
  informant networks of, 441
  Kamenev's view of, 512–14
  Lenin's death and, 539
  opposition "conspiracies" against, 603–4
  peasants and, *see* collectivization; peasants,
    Russian
  politburo and, 426, 596, 687, 699–700
  Rykov and, 658
  Stalin's ambivalence toward, 595–96
  triumph of, 659–60
  Trotsky and, 472, 486, 487, 532, 613–14
  as unforeseen by party leadership, 422–23
  Zinoviev and, 472, 474, 506–9, 513
Stalin, Vasily "Vasya," 10, 466–67, 593,
    595, 633
Staniewski, Mieczysław, 286–87
Stasova, Yelena, 423, 428, 596
*State and Revolution* (Lenin), 135, 203
state bank, Soviet, Sokolnikov's restoration
    of, 452
state building, Soviet, 289–92, 343
State Council, 99, 129, 134, 136, 179
state planning commission, 483, 501, 523
  Trotsky and, 485, 486
statism, Stalin's dedication to, 346
steel production, 63, 76, 141
Steinberg, Isaac, 292, 293, 294
Sten, Jan, 708
Stockholm, 102–3

stock market crash of 1929, 733
*Stock Market Gazette,* 176
Stolypin, Pyotr, 100, 101, 118, 125, 134, 136, 167,
    179, 239, 343, 726
  assassination attempt on, 102
  assassination of, 122, 674
  autocratic opposition to, 128–29
  Duma and, 94, 97, 101, 119
  elevated to prime ministership, 91, 92
  failed governmental reforms of, 92–93, 120,
    129, 130
  foreign policy of, 108–9, 110, 111–12, 129
  as governor of Saratov, 91–92, 95
  mass arrests and executions by, 104, 106
  modernization as goal of, 92, 94, 97, 119, 129
  Nicholas II's relationship with, 92, 119–20
  Orthodox Christianity and, 118, 119, 129
  social reforms of, 95, 96–97, 673–74
Stravinsky, Igor, 620
Stresemann, Gustav, 510, 561, 562
Struve, Pyotr, 45, 289, 336
Sukhanov, Nikolai, 176, 215
Sükhbaataar, 346, 402, 403, 404–5
Sukhomlinov, Vladimir, 159, 161, 163
Sukhova, Tatyana, 116
Sukhum, 534, 537, 541–42
*Sunday Worker,* 573
Sun Yat-sen, 626–27
Supreme Council of the Economy, 242, 262,
    264, 459, 485, 486, 578, 579, 601, 607,
    663–64, 694
Supreme Revolutionary Tribunal, 433
Suvorin, Aleksei A., 210
Svanidze, Alyosha, 105, 479
Svanidze, Ketevan "Kato," 114, 594
  death of, 115–16, 738
  Stalin's marriage to, 105–6
Svanidze, Maria, 594–95
Svanidze-Monoselidze, Alexandra "Sashiko,"
    105, 106
Sverdlov, Yankel "Yakov," 204, 212–13, 214,
    226, 228, 235, 237, 251, 256, 260, 262,
    263, 271–72, 275, 280, 285, 286, 307, 313,
    398–99, 413, 738
  death of, 318–19, 423
  Lenin and, 193–94, 234, 318–19
  Martov case and, 267–68
  in October Revolution, 224
  organizational skills of, 194, 212, 236,
    319, 423
  Siberian exile of, 154–55, 194
  as Soviet central executive committee
    chairman, 236, 274, 423
  Stalin's relationship with, 154–55, 194

and Stalin-Trotsky conflict, 308–10
Trotsky and, 318–19
Sverdlov Communist University, 544, 545, 555, 705–6
Switzerland, Lenin in, 135, 173, 187
Syrtsov, Sergei, 457, 668–70, 679, 680, 683, 705
Sytin, Pavel, 308, 309, 310

Tambov, peasant rebellion in, 380–82, 389, 393–94, 410, 575
Tammerfors, Finland, 80–81
Tashkent, 254, 372–73
Tashkent Congress of Soviets, 253
Tashkent Soviet, 218, 253, 254–55, 266, 373
Tatar Autonomous Soviet Socialist Republic, 371
Tataria, Tatar Republic, 371, 447, 502
Tatars, 183, 368, 370, 371, 401, 479
Teliya, Giorgi, 106–7, 544
Terek, 118
Ter-Petrosyan, Simon "Kamo," 113–14
Third Cavalry Corps (Red), 359
Third Group (Mesame Dasi), 43, 44, 51
Third (Communist) International (Comintern), 317–18
Three Emperor's League, 109
Tiflis (Tblisi), 15, 20, 29–30, 49, 53, 105–6, 537
    Armenians in, 29, 49, 479
    Bolshevik bank robbery in, 8–9, 113–14, 267
    ethnic diversity of, 29–30
    government of, 29–30
    May Day marches in, 49–50
    Ottoman Bank branch in, 475
    Red Army capture of, 397
    Stalin in, 22, 47–50, 113–14, 121, 125, 267–68, 399, 600
    strikes in, 43–44, 48, 600
Tiflis Theological Seminary, 43
    forbidden books at, 36–37, 45
    Stalin at, 2, 26–27, 30–38, 44–47
Tikhomirov, Lev, 139
Til, Karolina, 595
Times (London), 340
Timoshenko, Semyon, 356
Tirpitz, Alfred von, 148
Tkhinvaleli, Kita, 105
Togliatti, Palmiro, 720
Tolstoy, Lev, 67
Tomsky, Mikhail (Yefremov), 416, 498, 513, 517, 563, 581, 596, 599, 613, 676, 694–95, 698, 712, 719, 739
    and plot to oust Stalin as general secretary, 714, 715, 716–17, 720
    and succession power struggle, 563, 564

Tovstukha, Ivan, 456–57, 463, 544, 598, 604, 660
trade unions, 518
    10th Party Congress debate on, 385, 390, 423, 455, 459
Transcaucasus Railway, 14, 51
Trans-Siberian Railway, 68, 71, 75, 173, 270
Trepov, Dmitry, 82
Trianon, Treaty of (1920), 316
Triple Alliance, 6, 110
Triple Entente, see Entente (Allies)
triumvirate, 512, 517, 519–20, 546, 563
Trotsky, Lev (Bronstein), 9, 62, 80, 81–82, 86, 108, 114, 115, 143, 158, 182, 193, 221, 226, 235, 245, 263, 274, 322, 354, 358, 420, 424, 454, 464, 467, 469, 510, 545, 596, 597, 598, 605, 615, 686, 715, 734, 737
    Alma-Ata exile of, 676–79
    antipathy toward, 322, 340, 341, 390, 500, 505, 512, 516–17, 520, 531, 532, 533
    armor-plated train of, 327–28, 331, 339
    attempted assassination of, 286
    background of, 200–201
    on Bolshevik bureaucrats, 314
    Bolsheviks joined by, 200, 202
    Bolshevik takeover of Georgia urged by, 396–97
    and Brest-Litovsk Treaty, 257
    British general strike and, 598–99
    Central Committee apparatus denounced by, 518–19, 522
    as Central Committee chairman, 214–15
    Central Committee's expulsion of, 648
    Central Control Commission investigation of, 520
    chairmanship of state planning commission rejected by, 486
    chairmanship of Supreme Council rejected by, 486
    China and, 627, 628–29, 630, 631, 632
    on collectivization, 675
    Communist Party's expulsion of, 651, 656
    in Constituent Assembly, 246
    Council of People's Commissars membership rejected by, 416–17
    and creation of Soviet Union, 475
    on dangers of other socialist parties, 396
    and defense of Petrograd, 330–31
    deportation and internal exile justified by, 440–41
    deputy chairmanship of Soviet Union rejected by, 486
    on dictatorship of the proletariat, 337
    expulsion from Comintern of, 644

Trotsky, Lev (Bronstein) *(cont.)*
  as Extraordinary Commission for Food and
    Transport chairman, 299
  flulike fevers of, 520, 522, 533
  as foreign affairs commissar, 229
  and Georgian insubordination crisis,
    489–90, 491, 493
  and German Communist coup attempt, 511
  and German peace talks, 249–51,
    255–56, 258
  as head of Revolutionary Military Council,
    286, 341, 516, 537
  "Ilich's letter about the secretary" and, 516
  imperious manner of, 322, 328, 329
  imprisonment of, 204, 212
  on institution of commissars, 339
  internal exile of, 737
  as a Jew, 340–41, 523
  Joffe and, 651–52
  joint plenums on factionalism of, 522–25,
    646–47
  Kaganovich and, 455
  Kamenev and, 224–25, 584
  Kronstadt rebellion and, 384, 387
  Krupskaya and, 501, 542, 547, 572,
    573–74, 632
  Left opposition and, 518, 529
  Lenin and, 202, 214, 221, 222–23, 234, 238,
    256, 341, 357, 385–86, 390, 414–15, 472,
    481–82, 523, 531, 647
  and Lenin's alleged article on
    nationalities, 494
  Lenin's death and, 534, 537–39
  as Lenin's possible successor, 416–17,
    492, 494
  Lenin's Testament and, 500, 546, 572–73,
    605–7, 643, 646, 647–48
  NEP and, 481–82, 495, 497
  in October Revolution, 215, 219, 220, 221–22
  *On Lenin* published by, 545
  as orator, 215, 221, 250, 251
  as Petrograd Soviet chairman, 212–13
  physical appearance of, 340
  on Polish-Soviet War, 354
  politburo expulsion of, 615
  in quest for economic dictatorship, 481, 484,
    485, 486–87, 488, 501, 518
  in secret negotiations with Entente, 265
  self-imposed exiles of, 152–53, 164, 201
  *Since Lenin Died* repudiated by, 573
  on Stalin, 8, 295, 422, 463
  Stalin biography by, 37
  Stalin's antagonistic relationship with, 224,
    306–10, 313–14, 329, 334, 339–40, 341, 357,

    369, 377, 385, 390, 415, 416, 460, 470–71,
    474, 505, 719
  Stalin's dictatorship opposed by, 472, 486,
    487, 613–14
  and Stalin's role in Tsaritsyn, 302–3, 642
  in succession power struggle, 416–17,
    519–20, 522–25, 532–34, 540, 555, 563–64,
    572–73, 584, 586, 590–91, 605–6, 614–15,
    636–37, 638, 639, 641–44, 646–48, 713,
    735, 736
  Sukhum convalescence of, 534, 537, 541–42
  Sverdlov and, 318–19
  and Tsaritsyn defense, 307–10
  at 12th Party Congress, 495–96
  use of former tsarist officers defended by,
    319–20, 329
  Voroshilov and, 309, 313–14
  as war and naval commissar, 258, 289, 297,
    306–10, 313–14, 319–20, 326, 327–31,
    339–40, 356, 359, 391, 436, 542
  war commissar post resigned by, 557
  Zinoviev and, 474, 525, 545
Trotskyites, 341 390, 411–12, 423, 429, 540, 656
Tsaritsa River, 300
Tsaritsyn, 283, 300, 330, 357, 642
  Red Army in, 302, 305
  Revolutionary Military Council of, 303
  Stalingrad as new name of, 689
  Stalin in, 270, 276, 291, 300–310, 313–14,
    320, 340
  Stalin's recall from, 309–10, 314, 642
  White army siege and capture of, 305–6, 310,
    326–27
Tsaritsyn Cheka, 302, 304
  Makhrovsky food expedition subverted by,
    304–5
Tsarskoe Selo, 74, 86, 92, 167, 170, 171, 172
  White army capture of, 330
Tsereteli, Akaki, 32, 34
Tsereteli, Giorgi, 34, 43
Tsereteli, Irakli, 192, 198–99
Tskhakaya, Mikho, 81, 105
Tsushima Strait, Battle of, 73
Tsyurupa, Alexander, 299, 569
Tuchapsky, Pavel, 44*n*
Tukhachevsky, Mikhail, 345, 357, 360, 561, 576,
  589, 619
  in capture of Baku, 366
  as chief of general staff, 576
  as Great War POW, 356
  Kronstadt rebellion and, 384, 391, 575
  OGPU surveillance of, 575
  in Polish-Soviet War, 361–62, 363–65,
    377–78

in Russian civil war, 356–60
Tambov rebellion and, 394, 575
Voroshilov's rivalry with, 576–77
Turcomans, 372
Turkestan, 58, 145, 243, 253, 254, 266, 371, 372, 387, 407, 451–52
Frunze in, 373–75, 387
Muslims in, 253–54, 502–3
Red Army in, 372–74
Validi's escape to, 371–72
Turkestan Autonomous Socialist Republic, 375, 388
Turkey, 391, 395, 398
Turkic language, 12, 344
Turkic peoples, 29, 183, 184, 344
Turkish Straits, 136, 145
Turukhansk, 454, 614, 621, 686
Stalin's exile in, 152–55, 173
Tzara, Tristan, 227, 230

U-boat warfare, 310
Ufa, 238, 269, 326, 368, 371
Ufa Soviet, 266
Uglanov, Nikolai, 432, 548, 563, 596, 613, 723
in succession power struggle, 563, 641, 715
Ukraine, Ukrainians, 41, 98, 125, 200, 342, 475, 546, 666, 687, 700
anti-Semitism in, 326
food harvests in, 721–22
German occupation of, 253, 265, 266–67, 270, 272, 273, 283, 301, 303
as independent republic, 238, 343, 368
nationalists in, 119, 351, 400
1921–22 famine in, 447
Poland and, 353–54, 616–17
Polish invasion of, 352, 354
Red Army's reconquest of, 386
in separate peace treaty with Germany, 252
Soviet Russia's relations with, 475–76
and Soviet Union plan, 475–76, 478, 479
White army's capture of, 330
Ukrainian Central Rada, 252, 258, 266–67
Ukrainian Soviet Socialist Republic, 386, 406
Ulrich, Vasily, 381–82
Ulyanov, Alexander, 60, 185
Ulyanov, Vladimir, see Lenin, Vladimir
Ulyanova, Maria, 413, 414, 415, 416, 417, 488, 501, 520, 521, 527, 608
Lenin's death and, 534
on Lenin-Stalin relationship, 608–9
Ulyanov family, 185
Ungern-Sternberg, Roman, Baron von, 346, 400–404, 549

Unification, 101
Union of Railroad Employees, 231, 234, 237
Union of Soviet Socialist Republics (USSR), see Soviet Union
Union of the Russian People, 98–99, 100–101, 118, 137, 163, 182
Union of the Toiling Peasantry, 381
United opposition, 613, 614, 652, 655–56, 672, 686, 713, 729
United States:
economic growth in, 18, 19, 612
financial panic of 1914 in, 148
in Great War, 248, 310–11
industrialization in, 19, 662
liberalism in, 132
mass production in, 612
railroad bubble in, 64
Seventeenth Amendment in, 83
slavery in, 19
Soviet relations with, 611–12
steel production in, 63
Versailles Treaty and, 315–16
Unszlicht, Józef, 345, 358, 360, 461, 587, 621, 638
Urals Bolsheviks, Romanov murders blamed on, 281
Urals Soviet, 280
Urga, 401–3
Uritsky, Moisei, 284
Urutadze, Grigol, 123

Vācietis, Jukums, 261, 277, 282, 284, 310, 313, 314, 330
arrest of, 329
as Red Army commander in chief, 286, 306, 328
Valedinsky, Ivan, 602–3, 633, 720
Validi, Akhmetzaki, 346, 368
Stalin's patronage of, 369–71, 372
Vareikis, Jonava "Iosif," 356
Vasilchikov, Boris A., 58
Verdun, Battle of, 150, 162, 310
Verkhovsky, Alexander, 293
Vernadsky, Vladimir, 721
Versailles, Peace of, 150
Versailles, Treaty of (1919), 315–17, 445, 559, 560, 588
German war guilt and, 315, 316, 559
territorial revisionism in, 315–16
Versailles Order, 352–53, 363, 380
Vertov, Dziga, 440
Verzilov, Vasily, 720
Victoria, queen of England, 89, 128
Vilna (Wilno), 354, 359, 378

Vittorio Emanuele III, king of Italy, 549, 551
Vladivostok, 269, 344, 590
    Japanese landing at, 266
Vlasik, Nikolai, 739
Voikov, Pyotr, 442, 634
Voitinsky, Grigory, 628
Volga valley, 270, 300, 326, 447, 566, 568
Volhynian Guards, 169
Volodicheva, Maria, 473, 487, 489, 490, 527
Vologda, 260
    Stalin in, 121, 122, 124
Volunteer Army (Armed Forces of South
    Russia), 268, 270, 295–96, 332
    1919 offensive of, 326–27, 328
    see also Whites
Voroshilov, Klimenty "Klim," 104, 308, 310,
    320, 327, 328, 355, 357, 390, 391, 456, 495,
    507, 582, 585, 596, 602, 619, 622, 656, 657,
    694–95, 700, 704
    in "cave meeting," 505, 506
    in defense of Tsaritsyn, 303–4
    and plot to oust Stalin as general secretary,
    713, 714, 715
    as Stalin's protégé, 303, 306, 313, 320–21, 387,
    627, 731
    Trotsky and, 309, 313–14
    Tukhachevsky's rivalry with, 576–77
    as war commissar, 576, 638, 639
Vozdvizhenka, 4, 428
Vozdvizhenka, 5, 426, 428
Vujović, Voja, 644
Vyshinsky, Andrei, 203, 702–3, 709

War and Peace (Tolstoy), 575
War and the Crisis in Socialism (Zinoviev), 407
Warsaw, 15–16, 355
    Red Army advance on, 361–63, 364
Warsaw, Treaty of (1920), 353
Wealth of Nations (Smith), 39
Weimar Republic, see Germany, Weimar
What Ilich Wrote and Thought About
    Trotsky, 500
What Is to Be Done? (Lenin), 51, 79, 287
White armies, 300, 330, 350, 356, 369, 370
    anti-Semitism in, 325–26
    collapse of, 331–32
    in Crimea, 357, 379
    disorganization in, 335
    Entente's supplying of, 326, 352
    former tsarist officers in, 297–98
    1919 offensive of, 326–27, 328, 335, 370–71
    Tsaritsyn siege and capture by, 305–6, 310,
    326–27
    see also Cossacks; Volunteer Army

White Guards, 604, 635
Whites (anti-Bolsheviks), 282–83, 292, 295–96,
    298, 325, 335, 344, 379, 380
White Terror, in civil war, 405
Wilhelm I, kaiser of Germany, 6, 119
Wilhelm II, kaiser of Germany, 89, 134, 136,
    139, 159, 253
    abdication of, 311
    naval buildup of, 139–40
    and onset of Great War, 143, 144–45,
    146–47
    in secret pact with Russia, 109–10, 139
Wilson, Woodrow, 315, 343
Winter Palace, 70, 73, 90, 102, 126, 127, 186
    Provisional Government relocation to,
    213–14, 216, 217, 219–20
    so-called storming of, 219–20, 338–39
Witte, Sergei, 75, 76, 82, 83, 85, 95, 110, 118–19,
    126, 129
    assassination attempt on, 102
    background of, 68–69
    as finance minister, 69–70, 645
    Nicholas II's relationship with, 70, 72, 84, 91
    October Manifesto and, 84, 92
    as prime minister, 84–85, 86
    resignation of, 90–91
    Trans-Siberian Railway and, 68, 71
Worker and Soldier, 207
workers, see proletariat, Russian
workers' and peasants' inspectorate, 451, 456
Workers' opposition, 385, 389
Workers' Path, 177, 216
    Stalin as editor of, 212, 259
world revolution:
    as primary goal of Lenin, 407
    Soviet Union and, 555–56
    Stalin on, 407–8, 555–56, 557–58, 562–63,
    570, 592, 698–99, 731
World War I, see Great War
World War II, 4
Wrangel, Baron Pyotr, 332, 335, 357, 358,
    361–62, 374, 379
"wrecking," 691, 694, 695, 696, 709, 711, 734

Yagoda, Genrikh (Jehuda, Jenokhom), 441, 461,
    536, 541–42, 566, 588, 605, 656–57, 665,
    689, 701, 717
    background of, 460–61
    as GPU second deputy head, 461–62
    and plot to oust Stalin as general
    secretary, 715
    Shakhty affair and, 691, 693, 699
Yakovlev, Yakov, 579, 729
Yanson, Nikolai, 697

Yaroslavsky, Yemelyan (Gubelman, Minei), 390, 424, 434, 549–50, 698
Yegorov, Alexander, 357, 361, 362, 365, 378, 456, 589
Yekaterinburg, 280–81, 282
Yenukidze, Avel, 50, 55, 463, 480, 515, 535, 641
Yevdokimov, Grigory, 505, 506, 653, 654, 655
Yevdokimov, Yefim, 688–89
Young Bosnia, 142–43
Young Pioneers, 547
Young Turk Revolution, 131–32
Yudenich, Nikolai, 295, 326, 330, 331, 335, 358
Yugoslavia, 511
Yurovsky, Leonid, 452
Yurovsky, Yakov, 281
Yusupov, Prince Felix, 163

Zagorsky, Vladimir, 334
Zagumyonny, Sergei, 670–71
Zakovsky, Leonid, 617, 669, 679, 681, 682, 683
Zasulich, Vera, 45
Zetkin, Clara, 282, 410
Zhdanov, Andrei, 457
Zhloba, Dmitry, 310
Zhukov, Georgy, 356
Zinoviev, Grigory (Radomylsky), 104, 121, 123, 152, 188, 193, 194, 203, 224, 226, 234, 236, 261, 287, 318, 322, 330, 341, 354, 367–68, 378, 382, 385, 387, 392, 407, 412, 471, 490, 491, 495, 497, 501, 512, 517, 518, 531–32, 596, 597, 599, 636, 652, 715
ambition of, 513
in attempts to include other socialists in Bolshevik regime, 235
in "cave meeting," 505, 506, 513, 658
China and, 629, 630–31
as Comintern chairman, 510, 609, 615
and German Communist coup attempt, 509–10, 511, 514–15
and "Ilich's letter about the secretary," 504–9, 512, 513
internal exile of, 713
Lenin memoir of, 545
Lenin's death and, 534–35
Lenin's Testament and, 498, 499, 606–7, 648
NEP criticized by, 570–71
October Revolution and, 214, 224, 499, 515, 563–64, 606, 641, 648
self-exiles of, 204, 205, 212
Stalin's dictatorship and, 472, 474, 506–9, 513
and succession power struggle, 493, 525, 552, 563, 564, 577, 578, 580, 582, 584, 586, 604, 605–6, 607, 614–15, 636, 641–43, 648, 651, 656, 713, 716, 729, 736
in triumvirate with Kamenev and Stalin, 517, 563
Trotsky and, 474, 525, 545
Ziv, G. A., 201
Znamenka, 23, 426, 436–37
*Znamya*, 100
Zubalov, Levon (Zubalashvili), 466
Zubalovo dacha, 466–67, 594
Zurich, 187, 188, 230